NEW TESTAMENT COMMENTARY

New Testament Commentary

Exposition of Thessalonians, the Pastorals, and Hebrews

William Hendriksen
and
Simon J. Kistemaker

BakerBooks
A Division of Baker Book House Co
Grand Rapids, Michigan 49516

Originally published in separate volumes:

I-II Thessalonians © 1955 by William Hendriksen

I-II Timothy and Titus © 1957 by William Hendriksen

Hebrews © 1984 by Simon J. Kistemaker

Thessalonians, Timothy and Titus combination volume issued 1979
Double combination volume issued 1996

First printing, December 1995

Published by Baker Books
a division of Baker Book House Company
P.O Box 6287, Grand Rapids, MI 49516-6287

Second printing, July 2002

12 volume set, first available 2002
ISBN 0-8010-2606-7

Printed in the United States of America

ISBN 0-8010-2079-4

TABLE OF CONTENTS

LIST OF ABBREVIATIONS

The letters in book-abbreviations are followed by periods. Those in periodical-abbreviations omit the periods and are in italics. Thus one can see at a glance whether the abbreviation refers to a book or to a periodical.

A. *Book Abbreviations*

A.R.V.	American Standard Revised Version
A.V.	Authorized Version (King James)
B.D.B.	Brown-Driver-Briggs, *Hebrew and English Lexicon to the Old Testament*
Gram.N.T.	A. T. Robertson, *Grammar of the Greek New Testament in the Light of Historical Research*
H.B.A.	Hurlbut, *Bible Atlas* (most recent edition)
I.S.B.E.	*International Standard Bible Encyclopedia*
L.N.T.	Thayer's *Greek-English Lexicon of the New Testament*
M.M.	*The Vocabulary of the Greek Testament Illustrated from the Papyri and Other Non-Literary Sources,* by James Hope Moulton and George Milligan (edition Grand Rapids, 1952)
N.N.	*Novum Testamentum Graece,* edited by D. Eberhard Nestle and D. Erwin Nestle (most recent edition)
N.T.C.	W. Hendriksen, *New Testament Commentary*
R.S.V.	Revised Standard Version
W.D.B.	*Westminster Dictionary of the Bible*
W.H.A.B.	*Westminster Historical Atlas to the Bible*

B. *Periodical Abbreviations*

BTr	*The Bible Translator*
EQ	*Evangelical Quarterly*
ExT	*Expository Times*
Int	*Interpretation*
JBL	*Journal of Biblical Literature*
RB	*Revue biblique*
RHPR	*Revue d'histoire et de philosophie religieuses*

Please Note

In order to differentiate between the second person singular and the second person plural, without reverting to the archaic "thou" and "ye" except where it is proper to do so, we have indicated the former as follows: "you"; and the latter as follows: "y o u."

Introduction
to
I and II Thessalonians

I. Reasons for Studying These Epistles

We are about to study certain epistles written by a man who, with the aid of his associates, "turned the world upside down." Interest in Paul never lags.[1]

This interest is varied. Some focus their attention particularly upon Paul *the theologian.* They ask such questions as, Was Paul the constructor of a doctrinal system or was he a disciple of Jesus? What were his views with respect to various doctrinal themes? Should the Church of the present day allow itself to be guided by these views or should it regard them as being without normative value?

Others, again, sketch a portrait of Paul *the man.* Their main interest may be called *psychological.* These ask, How can we account for his seemingly boundless energy? Was he normal or abnormal? Can his experience on the way to Damascus be explained psychologically or did something of a supernatural character occur? Was he fearless or fearful? Was he cold or sympathetic?

Finally, there are also those for whom Paul is, above all, *the missionary.* In this group there are some who stress the idea that Paul is the missionary whom we should copy. They argue that however great his advantages may have been, they cannot have been so great as to rob his example of all value for the present day and age. They conclude that *Paul's* methods should be *our* methods. If he believed in the indigenous (self-supporting, self-propagating, self-governing) church, so should we. Others, however, while going along with this view to a considerable extent, are not so sure that Paul's principles and methods are applicable today without extensive

---

[1] Thus, among the important works either newly published or appearing as reprints during the single decade 1940-1950 were the following:

R. M. Hawkins, *The Recovery of the Historical Paul,* Nashville, 1943.
C. W. Quimby, *Paul for Everyone,* New York, 1944.
John Knox, *Chapters in a Life of Paul,* New York and Nashville, 1946.
E. J. Goodspeed, *Paul,* Philadelphia, Toronto, 1947.
R. Machen, *The Origin of Paul's Religion,* reprinted Grand Rapids, 1947.
F. Postma, *Paulus,* Pretoria, 1949.
W. Ramsay, *St. Paul the Traveler and the Roman Citizen,* reprinted Grand Rapids, 1949.
W. Ramsay, *The Cities of St. Paul,* reprinted Grand Rapids, 1949.
W. J. Conybeare and J. S. Howson, *The Life and Epistles of St. Paul,* reprinted Grand Rapids, 1949.
A. Barnes, *Scenes and Incidents in the Life of the Apostle Paul,* reprinted Grand Rapids, 1950.

modification. They call attention to the greatness of *this* missionary, his extraordinary charismatic gifts and qualifications. They also emphasize the fact that times and circumstances have changed, and consequently, that often that which was the right thing to do for Paul is the wrong thing to do for us.

Thus we have the *theological,* the *personal or psychological,* and the *missionary* interest in Paul (to say nothing about the various ways in which these interests blend and combine).

Now it is a fact that these three lines converge beautifully in the two epistles to the Thessalonians. To begin with the *theological* or *doctrinal* interest: to be sure, there are epistles that are more consistently doctrinal, yet nowhere do we find so much source-material for the doctrine *of the last things* ("eschatology") as in these eight chapters. It is a well-known fact that *in I Thessalonians every chapter ends with a reference to the second coming.* See 1:10; 2:19, 20; 3:11-13; 4:13-18; 5:23, 24. Also II Thessalonians abounds in eschatological material; see especially 1:7-10 and 2:1-12. For information on such subjects as "the rapture" (in whatever sense one conceives of it), the time of Christ's return, the great apostasy or "falling away," "the man of sin," "the one who (or: that which) restrains," "the mystery of lawlessness," and "the manifestation of his (Christ's) coming" – we naturally turn first of all to I and/or II Thessalonians.

Again, though it is certainly true that other passages in Paul's epistles and in Acts may be regarded as windows which afford a look into the heart of the great apostle, none are more revealing in this respect than I Thess. 2:1-12; 3:1-10; 5:12-24; and II Thess. 3:7-10. Here truly is a portrait of Paul *the man.* In these two epistles he stands out "in all the charm of his rich and varied personality" (George Milligan, *St. Paul's Epistles to the Thessalonians,* London, 1908, p. xliii).

And as to Paul *the missionary,* his "strategy" – proclaiming the message in the great centers, making use of the synagogue, basing his argumentation upon the prophecies of the Old Testament, etc. – is as clearly evident at Thessalonica as anywhere else. In fact, special studies devoted to this subject refer again and again not only to Acts 17:1-19, which contains a brief report of the work at Thessalonica, but also to I Thess. 1:8-10, which tells us something about the contents and amazing success of Paul's missionary message. Cf. also Phil. 4:16.

I and II Thessalonians may be regarded therefore as an important source for the subsequent formulation of doctrine, as an indispensable guide for the study of the man Paul, and as an important chapter in a handbook for missionaries. What is offered in these two short epistles is all this *and more.* It is above all a part of God's infallible special revelation, which comes *to every believer* with absolute, divine authority, and shows him what he should believe and how he should live.

II. The Founding of the Church

The evangelization of Europe began in earnest when Paul set his foot on what is today the long and narrow stretch of N.E. Greece. Here was Philippi, situated about ten miles inland from the Aegean Sea. It was "a city of Macedonia, the first of the district, a (Roman) colony" (Acts 16:12).

To this city came Paul, Silas – the companion whom he had chosen for this journey (Acts 15:40) –, Timothy as assistant (Acts 16:3), and Luke the beloved physician (Acts 16:10). In Philippi a church was established which Paul afterward called "my joy and crown" (Phil. 4:1). Here Lydia was converted, and she and her household were baptized (Acts 16:14, 15). The masters of a girl who had a spirit of divination became angry when Paul expelled the demon. They reasoned that "the hope of their gain" was gone. As a result Paul and Silas were imprisoned and beaten with rods. About midnight God sent an earthquake which opened the prison-doors. The jailer was converted and "was baptized, together with all his, immediately" (Acts 16:16-34). After an honorable release from prison, Paul and Silas "entered into the house of Lydia: and when they had seen the brothers, they encouraged them and departed," leaving the town (Acts 16:40). Luke stayed behind, as is clear from the fact that in relating further events he no longer says "we" (as in Acts 16:16) but "they" (Acts 17:1). From the fact that Timothy's name is not mentioned again until Acts 17:14 is reached some infer that he also remained for a while in Philippi, and that he did not rejoin the other two (Paul and Silas) until they, having labored for a while in Thessalonica, had reached Berea. Others, however, believe that Timothy too had traveled from Philippi to Thessalonica (either in the company of the others or a little later). They are of the opinion that this may be safely inferred from the fact that his name, together with that of Paul and Silas, is included in the salutation of both of the epistles (I Thess. 1:1; II Thess. 1:1). This view, as I see it, deserves the preference. It is not so strange that the youthful (cf. I Tim. 4:12) assistant Timothy is not always mentioned along with the others. Even today the newspapers in reporting that the president made a trip to California usually omit the names of most of the members of his entourage. But that does not mean that they were absent.

From Philippi a person could travel on one of the most famous of Roman military roads, the Egnatian Way. When completed it extended all the way from Byzantium (=Constantinople=Istanbul) on the Bosporus to Dyrrhachium situated straight west on the Adriatic (in what is now Albania). Thus it formed the connecting link with Rome. It was of sturdy construction, well kept, relatively safe, and marked by milestones (as Strabo informs us). The missionaries took this road, first to Amphipolis, called thus because the river Strymon flowed *around* it, and then to Apollonia. They continued on to Thessalonica. Altogether the distance of actual travel from Philippi to Thessalonica was about a hundred miles, comparable to that from: Detroit to Lansing (Mich.); Detroit to London (Ont.); Grand Rapids to Flint (Mich.); Atlanta to Columbus (Ga.); Los Angeles to San Diego (Cal.); London to Bristol (England); or Amsterdam to the Belgian border near Eindhoven (The Netherlands).

Of all the cities and towns on this great highway, Thessalonica, situated on what is now called the Gulf of Salonica, and built in the form of an amphitheater on the slopes at the head of the bay, was the largest and most influential. The road ran through the heart of the city, just as a remnant of it does even today. In Thessalonica it is still called by the ancient name, The Egnatian.

The city had been founded in 315 B. C. by Cassander, on or near the site of ancient Therma. This Cassander had been an officer under Alexander the Great. Having killed the latter's mother Olympias because she opposed him, and having crushed her army, Cassander subsequently for political reasons married Alexander's half-sister. Her name was Thessalonica. Convenient to bear in mind is the following:

Paul wrote a letter to the church at *Philippi.* That place was founded (about 358 B. C.) by *Philip* II of Macedon. The apostle also wrote two letters to the church at *Thessalonica.* This city was named in honor of *Philip's daughter Thessalonica.*

When the Romans, having conquered Macedonia, divided it into four parts, Thessalonica was made the capital of one of these. Later – about 146 B. C. – it became the capital of the entire province of Macedonia. In the struggle between Pompey and Caesar, Thessalonica became one of the former's chief bases, but soon afterward – 42 B. C. – it sided with Anthony and Octavian. The loyalty of the city was not left unnoticed. The great emperor Augustus rewarded it by making Thessalonica a free city. Thus it obtained a considerable measure of "home rule," self-government in internal affairs. It chose its own magistrates, who were called "politarchs."

Although most of the Thessalonians were Greeks, sothat the culture of the city was basically Hellenic, yet there were also some Romans and many Orientals. It is hardly necessary to add that the commerce of the city also attracted many a Jew. The presence of these Jews and their missionary activity exerted a measure of influence upon pagan religion, causing some of the Gentiles to attend the synagogue and to become "God-fearers."

Under the Romans the city enjoyed great prosperity. In the days of the Byzantine Empire it ranked second only to Byzantium.

In the history of the Church there is especially one event which made Thessalonica famous. A. D. 390 the emperor Theodosius the Great caused the massacre of no less than seven thousand of its citizens on account of a riot which had occurred there. He ordered them to be put to death regardless of rank, sex, or degree of guilt. It was then that the great bishop Ambrose, wishing to vindicate the rights of the moral law – and incidentally the rights of the Church over against the State – refused him communion. It was only after the emperor had submitted to public penance, had begged for pardon, and had made certain definite promises, that absolution was finally granted.

The city figures prominently in the history of the Crusades. It came under more or less stable Ottoman rule in the year 1430. The Turks had held it before but had lost it again. From 1430 until 1912 they kept it. In 1912 it was reconquered by the Greeks. During World War I the Allies began their *Salonica* (as the city got to be called) *Campaigns* here, and during World War II it suffered considerable damage. Having always been a center of trade, the city attracted many Jews.

Today Salonica is next to the largest city in Greece, having a population of about a quarter of a million. It is the heart of a district which produces textiles, leather goods, machine tools, and cigarettes. It is connected by rail with Athens. In fact, owing to its strategic location, it is a center of road, rail, sea, and air-transportation. It trades in such commodities as tobacco, livestock, wheat, cotton, silk, and vegetables. Its university was opened in the year 1926. Among the famous churches which one can find here today are Hagia Sophia, St. George, and Demetrius. One of its most famous ancient relics is the triumphal arch of Emperor Constantine.

Paul's activity in Thessalonica was twofold: a. he earned his living by working with his hands for his daily bread (I Thess. 2:9; II Thess. 5:8), and b. he preached the Gospel (Acts 17:2; I Thess. 1:5; 2:2, 8, 11, 12; 4:1, 2). He did the former in order that he might not burden anyone and in order that it might be clear to everyone that he was not to be classified with traveling philosophers whose aims and interests were often selfish.

Paul remained in Thessalonica at least three weeks. The three week figure is mentioned in Acts 17:2, but it should be noted that it probably merely indicates the duration of his teaching *in the synagogue*. If it be borne in mind that a church of considerable size was established here (implied in I Thess. 5:12), that many of the citizens of Thessalonica turned from the worship of idols to serve the living God (I Thess. 1:9), that this spiritual awakening was so far-reaching that its report spread in every direction, and especially that during the "campaign" in this city Paul twice received a bounty from the church at Philippi (Phil. 4:16), the conclusion lies ready at hand that the *total* period of time which the missionaries spent in founding the new church was somewhat longer than three weeks.[2]

---

[2] Thus also L. Berkhof, *New Testament Introduction*, Grand Rapids, 1915, pp. 222, 223; F. W. Grosheide, *Handelingen* (in *Korte Verklaring*), Kampen, second

The preaching (teaching and exhortation) began in the synagogue. That was in line with Paul's custom. As already suggested, it was probably continued elsewhere. According to some "the house of Jason" was used for this subsequent preaching-activity. Others, however, are of the opinion that this house served as lodging-place for the missionaries and as Paul's workshop (cf. in this connection Acts 18:2, 3).

The inspired sources do not give us a complete and detailed survey of the contents of Paul's message at Thessalonica. A few important matters are mentioned however. Thus we learned that he taught that the Messianic prophecies had attained their fulfilment in Jesus, he being the Christ; that he suffered, died, was raised from the dead, and will come again, all this according to the Scriptures; that by his work he delivered from the wrath to come all those who trust in him; that idol-worship is evil; and that believers, having been called into his glorious kingdom, should live a life of sanctification so as to please the God who saved them, and should be orderly in their daily conduct in the midst of a wicked world ("If any man will not work neither let him eat"). See Acts 17:3; I Thess. 1:9, 10; 2:12; 4:1-3; II Thess. 3:10.

On one point – namely, the Lord's return and the events that will precede it – Paul had given somewhat detailed instruction while he was with the Thessalonians (II Thess. 2:1-5). It is not improbable that the teaching on other doctrinal themes had been just as thorough.

The circumstances under which all this evangelistic activity was carried on were partly discouraging, partly encouraging. Paul had "suffered" and had been "shamefully treated" in Philippi (I Thess. 2:2). Hence, it took courage to enter a new field after such experiences. On the other hand this labor was not in vain. Moreover, as already remarked, there was encouragement from Philippi.

Paul's heart was in his message. He preached "straight from the shoulder." There never was any attempt at flattery. Nevertheless, the truth was spoken in the spirit of tender affection and gentleness. Thus with the warmth of inner conviction, deeply persuaded of the supreme importance of his message, the great missionary, dealing with *each man* as a father with his children, taught, exhorted, and encouraged. See I Thess. 1:1-5; 2:4, 5, 7, 8, 10, 11.

And the Holy Spirit applied the message to the hearts of several of the hearers (I Thess. 1:5). Many were converted. They accepted the message as being the word not of men but of God (I Thess. 2:13). From that moment on they sought, with the help of the Spirit, to please God (I Thess. 4:1). Love ruled the brotherhood (I Thess. 4:9, 10). A church was estab-

---

edition 1950, p. 55; George Milligan, *op. cit.*, p. xxviii; but not R. C. H. Lenski, *The Interpretation of the Acts of the Apostles*, Columbus, Ohio, 1944, p. 693.

lished. Its membership was filled with contagious enthusiasm. In every heart there was a song, on every lip a testimony.

It is clear both from the book of Acts and from the epistles that most of the converts were from the Gentiles: "some" Jews and "a great multitude" of Greek proselytes (who were in the habit of attending the Synagogue) were persuaded, as were also many of the city's women, those of the upper class, wives of leaders (Acts 17:4). Many pagan idol-worshippers, having listened to the Gospel as proclaimed by Paul and his associates, experienced a fundamental change, a transformation of mind and heart (I Thess. 1:9; cf. 2:14 and Acts 20:4).

Paul never forgot the extraordinary response which his message had received in Thessalonica. When a little while later he writes a letter to this church, he makes mention of the joyful and enthusiastic manner in which the word had been taken to heart (I Thess. 1:6), and of the fact that this congregation had become an example to all believers in Macedonia and Achaia (I Thess. 1:7). He even adds that whenever people talk about him they describe him as the man through whose preaching a mighty spiritual change had been brought about in Thessalonica. The great missionary feels very happy about this, for it makes his work easier. Wherever he goes the fame of his message has preceded him. Indeed, the new converts have not kept quiet. See I Thess. 1:6-10.

It is not at all surprising that Paul's "success" made the Jews who were not converted very jealous and angry. With the help of certain street-loafers they hurried to the house of Jason where they expected to find the proclaimers of the new message. Failing to find them there, they dragged Jason and some other converts off to the "politarchs" (city-magistrates [3]) and shouted, "These fellows, who have turned the world upside down have come here also, and Jason has welcomed them. And they are all acting contrary to the decrees of the emperor, saying that there is another king, Jesus" (Acts 17:6, 7). The people and the politarchs were disturbed when they heard this, and "when they had taken security from Jason and the rest, they let them go" (Acts 17:8, 9).

The brothers immediately sent Paul and Silas away by night to Berea. The Jews here were "more noble" than those of Thessalonica, and eagerly welcomed the message, making a daily study of the Scriptures to see whether what Paul proclaimed were true. But when everything was going splendidly, the Jews at Thessalonica, hearing about the success which the missionaries were having, came to Berea in order to stir up a riot against

---

[3] The word "politarch" (Acts 17:6, 8) was at one time considered an error on the part of Luke. However, the discovery of seventeen inscriptions at Salonica containing this very term has proved that Luke was right and that the critics were wrong. See J. P. Free, *Archaeology and Bible History,* Wheaton, Ill., third printing 1952, p. 321.

them. The result was that, while Silas and Timothy were left behind in Berea in order to give spiritual support to the infant church, Paul himself, escorted by some of the brothers, made his way to the coast. Those who conducted Paul brought him as far as Athens. As they were leaving, he told them to ask Silas and Timothy to come to him as soon as possible (Acts 17:10-15).

There followed an interesting ministry at Athens. Read about it in Acts 17:16-34. However, the response here was not nearly as favorable as at Berea. Meanwhile Paul was anxiously awaiting the arrival of Silas and Timothy with tidings from Macedonia. From I Thess. 3:1, 2 it may be safely inferred that Timothy left Berea and found Paul while the latter was still in Athens. It is probable (though not certain) that also Silas rejoined Paul at Athens. One fact, however, is clear: Paul was deeply concerned about the recently won converts whom he had left behind in Thessalonica. Twice (once while at Berea and once while at Athens?) he made a plan to revisit them, but by a method which is not indicated, Satan prevented him from carrying out these plans (I Thess. 2:17, 18). Meanwhile his anxiety persisted. Finally, when he could stand it no longer, he (or he and Silas) decided to be left at Athens alone, and sent Timothy to strengthen and encourage the brothers at Thessalonica (see comments on I Thess. 3:1, 2). If Silas spent any time with Paul at Athens, he must have returned to Macedonia soon (perhaps to Philippi), for it is clear that both he and Timothy "came down from Macedonia" to Corinth after Paul had begun his labors in that city (Acts 18:1, 5; cf. I Thess. 3:6).

III. Paul's Purpose in Writing

A. *I Thessalonians*

Corinth was the commercial and political metropolis of Greece. Its name was a synonym for licentiousness. For a while the great missionary labored alone here. He struck up an acquaintance with Aquilla and Priscilla, driven from Rome by the edict of Emperor Claudius (who ruled from A. D. 41-54), and stayed with them because he was of the same trade, a tentmaker. He first preached in the synagogue, but afterward in the house of a Gentile who lived next to it.

It seems probable that while Paul was alone at Corinth – i.e., before Silas and Timothy had returned from Macedonia – he received some very disquieting news from the churches at Galatia. He heard that the Judaizers had been at work and had succeeded all too well in their attempt to destroy the edifice which he had reared with so much suffering and patience. Accordingly, the apostle wrote his Epistle to the Galatians.

Meanwhile the young church of Thessalonica was also on his mind. He feared lest, as a result of his very brief stay and sudden departure, of his inability to return personally, and of the scoffing and ridicule which the Macedonian church-members would have to endure from their relatives and neighbors, the temptation to drift back into paganism or Judaism might prove to be overpowering (I Thess. 3:5). To be sure, *some* of the Jews had accepted the Gospel, but how would they fare at the hands of those Jews – by far the majority – who had *not* accepted it? The answer to this question was not difficult to surmise. Paul knew all about the assault upon the house of Jason. Moreover, in addition to the hostile Jews there were the Judaizers who, according to the latest reports, were doing such damage in Galatia. Were they going to enter and ruin Macedonia also? Again, a great many of the devout Greeks and not a few of the leading women had been converted; but what about the proselytes who had *not* been converted, and especially . . . what about the *husbands* of the converted women? The very thought of what these husbands might do to their wives in attempting to force them to give up their faith in Christ was disconcerting. True, in the little while which Paul had spent in Thessalonica multitudes of pagans had renounced their idolatry and accepted the new religion; but was this faith firmly-rooted and genuine? Would it be able to endure persecution from the side of the wicked rabble, the same rabble which always stood ready to be bribed into deeds of violence? The Thessalonian believers (only a few of whom are mentioned by name: Jason, Aristarchus, Secundus, Acts 17:5-9; 20:4) were still so immature, so deficient in religious knowledge and experience! Also, on the whole they were poor (II Cor. 8:2, 3). Would Timothy, who at this very moment was working among them, be able to cope with the situation which he found? Would he come back safely, and if so, what news would he bring? In this connection, it is interesting to note that a very similar concern was going to fill the heart of Paul on his *third* missionary journey. *Then* conditions at *Corinth* – the very church where Paul was now laboring – would fill his mind with distress, and *then* the helper whose return was anxiously awaited would be *Titus* instead of Timothy. Read about it in II Cor. 2:12, 13; 7:5-15. Truly, in addition to dangers from without – and these were many! – there was that which oppressed the apostle daily, namely, "anxiety for all the churches" (II Cor. 11:28).

Great was Paul's relief when Timothy returned (Silas also came back from Macedonia, Acts 18:5). The report which he brought from the church at Thessalonica was so encouraging that the heart of the great missionary was filled with joy and thanksgiving. "Now I (really) *live,*" said Paul, as Timothy brought him the wonderful news of the undiminished faith and love of the infant church (cf. I Thess. 3:8). Not only did the arrival of Silas and Timothy and the information which they conveyed add zest to his preaching (Acts 18:5), but he also decided to express his feeling of gratitude in a letter to the Thessalonians. This was to be a letter of encouragement, the tenor of which would be "Y o u're doing fine, continue to do so more and more (cf. I Thess. 4:1). Do not let persecutions get y o u down. These are necessary; also, they are to be expected, just as I told y o u when I was still with y o u (cf. I Thess. 3:2-4)."

Mingled with the good news which predominated in the report which Timothy brought there was some bad news. Base opponents, filled with prejudice and hatred, were casting insinuations at the character and ministry of Paul (I Thess. 2:3-10), and were trying thus to undermine his influence and destroy the comfort which his message had brought. And comfort was badly needed, comfort blended with further instruction. This was true especially with respect to one important matter. Some members of the church had "fallen asleep." Would they share in the glory of Christ's return? See I Thess. 4:13 ff. Moreover, if this return was imminent, why work any longer? Why toil for the things which were soon to perish? (cf. I Thess. 4:11).

It is clear that Paul was filled with deep concern and warm affection for this church, so recently established. He writes his letter in order:

a. to meet head-on the whispering campaign with reference to his "personality" and motives (see chapters 1 and 2),

b. to express his joy and gratitude because of the good news which Timothy had brought (see chapter 3),

c. to shed further light upon the question which had arisen with respect to those who had fallen asleep (see 4:13-18) and the related question of the manner of Christ's return (see 5:1-11), and

d. to give exactly such directions as could be expected from a missionary who is writing to men who have just recently been drawn out of the kingdom of darkness (idolatry, immorality, etc.) into the kingdom of light (see 4:1-12; 5:12-28). Thus he stresses the fact that the new faith demands a complete break with the immoral conduct which characterizes heathendom (I Thess. 4:1-8), and he emphasizes the need of proper respect for the offices, of love and peace among all the brothers, of readiness to help those in distress, and of orderly conduct in the sight of the world (I Thess. 5:12-14).[4]

---

[4] The question with reference to the purpose of I Thessalonians has recently been revised with respect to one particular point, namely, whether the apostle in this epistle is trying to give an answer to a letter from Thessalonica which Timothy presumably had brought with him. One can find something on this topic in the older commentaries, but see especially the recent discussion by Chalmer E. Faw, "On The Writing of First Thessalonians," *JBL* 71 (December 1952), 217-225. Faw presents strong (yet, as I see it, not wholly convincing) arguments for the position that there was such a letter *from* Thessalonica, and that the apostle, in addition to expressing his reaction to an oral report which Timothy had brought him, takes up the various items mentioned in this letter, shedding light on matters with respect to

which the church at Thessalonica (particularly its leaders) desired further instruction. Faw's arguments may be summarized as follows:

a. Expressions such as these: *"Now concerning* love of the brothers" (I Thess. 4:9), *"now concerning* (notice, however, word-transposition in the original) those that have fallen asleep" (4:13), *"now concerning* the times and the seasons" (5:1) reveal a pattern which in Paul's epistles has its parallel *only* in I Corinthians (*"Now concerning* virgins," *"now concerning* the things sacrificed to idols," *"now concerning* spiritual gifts," *"now concerning* the collection for the saints" — see I Cor. 7:25; 8:1; 12:1; 16:1), and which in *that* epistle is introduced by the phrase, "Now concerning *the matters about which you wrote"* (I Cor. 7:1). Hence, if this literary pattern (of introducing several items in a series by using the phrase *now concerning,* with similar variants in both I Thessalonians and I Corinthians) when used in I Corinthians indicates that the apostle is giving a seriatim answer to *a letter,* why should we not reach the same conclusion with respect to its use in I Thessalonians?

b. The abrupt manner in which some of these matters are introduced (here in I Thessalonians) confirms the position that Paul has before him *the letter from the Thessalonians,* on which he is commenting item by item.

c. The fact that Paul seems to be reluctant to write on certain subjects (see I Thess. 4:9; 5:1) but does so anyway, though hesitantly, points in the same direction.

Though, as I see it, Faw's article is well written and conveys much valuable information, and though his theory — that here in I Thessalonians Paul is answering a letter — *may* be true, this article and this theory have failed to convince me that this is the only possible conclusion, and this for the following reasons:

a. The solitary parallel of I Corinthians is too flimsy a ground for such a conclusion. After all, as Faw's article clearly shows, the New Testament contains other instances of the use of the phrase *now concerning,* instances in which it clearly does *not* introduce a reflection on an item in *a letter* (Mark 12:26; 13:32; John 16:11; Acts 21:25).

b. In one respect I Corinthians is not a parallel, for *there* (I Cor. 7:1) Paul specifically informs us that he is taking up the matters *about which they had written. In I Thessalonians he makes no mention of any letter which the Thessalonians had written!* It is even possible that they did not deem it necessary to write such a letter, seeing that Timothy could be trusted to give a full oral report.

c. Faw's second and third arguments do not prove that Paul had before him *a letter* from the Thessalonians. A memorandum carefully prepared by Timothy himself or even a systematic oral report fills all the requirements. As to the third argument it should not be immediately assumed that the manner in which Paul phrases I Thess. 4:9 and 5:1 indicates real *reluctance* on his part. Another explanation is also possible. See comments on these verses.

Anyone who is interested in this subject should read (in addition to Faw's article of recent date) what the following have to say respecting it:

Bacon, B. W., *An Introduction to the New Testament,* New York, 1900, p. 73.

Barnett, Albert E., *The New Testament, Its Making and Meaning,* New York, 1946, p. 37.

Frame, James E., *A Critical and Exegetical Commentary on the Epistles of St. Paul to the Thessalonians* (in The International Critical Commentary), New York, 1912, pp. 9, 157, 178.

Harris, J. Rendel, "A Study in Letter Writing," *The Expositor* Series 5, Vol. 8 (September, 1898), 161-180.

Lenski, R. C. H., *op. cit.,* pp. 318, 319.

Moffatt, James, *An Introduction to the Literature of the New Testament,* New York, 1917, p. 67.

Plummer, Alfred, *A Commentary on St. Paul's First Epistle to the Thessalonians,* London, 1916, p. xviii.

Smith, David, *The Life and Letters of St. Paul,* New York, 1920, pp. 152-166.

Van Leeuwen, J. A. C., *Paulus' Zendbrieven aan Efeze, Colosse, Filemon, en*

B. *II Thessalonians*

We can imagine with what joy I Thessalonians was read by the members of the newly-established congregation. Yet, it soon became apparent that a second letter was necessary. Tidings reached Paul – by means of the very men who had delivered the first letter to its destination and had now returned? – that believers in Thessalonica, while experiencing spiritual growth, were still being persecuted, in fact more than ever. Also with respect to the second coming of Christ, on which the apostle had written such comforting words, there was still some confusion: some were thinking that the Lord's *sudden* coming, of which Paul had written (I Thess. 5:3), implied his *immediate* coming. There was need not only of further instruction on this point but also of an admonition that the church adhere to the teaching which it had received previously. In this connection it seems that someone claimed to have (or to have heard about) a letter, coming or purporting to come from Paul; and this too had had its damaging effect. The notion that the Lord was most certainly going to return "any day now" may have encouraged disorderly conduct (cf. I Thess. 4:11, 12) to continue and increase. This matter had to be dealt with. There was also the question, "What must be done with those who do not obey the instructions which they receive? Just how must the church deal with these disobedient ones?" And finally Paul himself (and those with him in Corinth), experiencing many difficulties, felt the need of asking for the prayers of the Thessalonians.

Accordingly, Paul's purpose in writing II Thessalonians is as follows:

a. To express his gratitude for the spiritual growth (increase in faith and love) which believers in Thessalonica are experiencing even in the midst of persecution, and to encourage them with the assurance that *at Christ's second coming* their enemies would be punished and they themselves would be glorified (see chapter 1),

b. To calm those who had become excited and confused with respect to *the second coming,* and to inform them that certain events must take place before that *second coming* occurs (see 2:1-12),

c. In this connection, to exhort all to keep clinging to the traditions which they had been taught whether by word or epistle, to warn against imaginary or spurious letters that distort the truth regarding *the second coming,* to admonish the disorderly (who seem to have given up their occupations because of fanaticism with respect to *the second coming*), and to give directions with respect to those who do not obey the instructions which they have received (see 2:13-4:18; cf. 2:2).

Interspersed with these thoughts are passages in which the believers at

---

Thessalonika (in *Kommentaar op het Nieuwe Testament*), Amsterdam, 1926, pp. 359, 360.

Thessalonica are asked to remember Paul and his associates in prayer, and in which they are committed to God's loving care, that their hearts might be established, and that they might receive good hope through grace, peace at all times in all ways, the love of God, and the patience of Christ.

From this brief purpose-summary it is evident that this is clearly a *Second Coming* epistle.

IV. The Time and the Place

Of late an attempt has been made to invent an entirely new chronology of the life of Paul.[5] But in view of the fact that this attempt is based on the opinion that the book of Acts is not entirely reliable, it is not necessary to enlarge on it (see, however, the note). Turning, then, to Acts and to the two epistles now under study, we find a very noticeable parallel. *This parallel indicates, without a shadow of a doubt, that I and II Thessalonians were written while Paul was on his second missionary journey. The probable place of writing is Corinth.*

We base this conclusion on the following considerations:

(1) According to Acts 16:11-40 the apostle on his second missionary journey worked in Philippi. From there he went to Thessalonica and Berea, and from there to Athens (Acts 17). From Athens he proceeded to Corinth (18:1). For a while he was at Athens alone, but when he reaches Corinth, Silas and Timothy arrive from Macedonia (18:1, 5). The order of places is therefore: Philippi, Thessalonica, Berea, Athens, Corinth. Now this corresponds with what is found in I Thessalonians. Here too we meet a Paul who had been in Philippi (I Thess. 2:2), and who from there went to Thessalonica, and from there (via Berea, which is not mentioned here) to Athens (I Thess. 3:1). When, in addition, we read that Timothy had now arrived (I Thess. 3:6), the natural inference is that this refers to the same

[5] I refer to the attempt by John Knox; see his *Chapters In A Life Of Paul,* New York and Nashville, 1946. Here the reliability of Acts is attacked (e.g., p. 35). The author has apparently joined the list of those who regard Luke as a more or less biased writer, who overemphasized the role of Jerusalem in the early history of the church. (*Essentially* the position of these authors has been refuted adequately by J. G. Machen, *The Origin of Paul's Religion,* Grand Rapids, Mich., 1947 reprint.) Especially important from the point of view of chronology is Knox's opinion that the letters of Paul reveal not the slightest awareness on his part that he was engaged in great journeys (p. 40). Naturally, if the three missionary journeys described in the book of Acts are not allowed to stand, the entire chronology changes. To see the difference between the old and the new (Knox's) chronology one should consult *Contemporary Thinking About Paul,* edited by Thomas S. Kepler, cf. the tables on pp. 158, 159 with the one on p. 169. But is it true that Paul's epistles fail to indicate any consciousness that he was engaged in great journeys? I do not see how this can be maintained, especially in view of the following passages: Rom. 1:15; 15:24, 28; I Cor. 16:5; II Cor. 1:15, 16, 23; 2:12, 13; 7:5-15; 9:2; 10:16; 12:14; 13:1; Phil. 4:15, 16.

arrival of which Acts speaks, and that Paul, accordingly, is now in Corinth.

(2) From the salutations (I Thess. 1:1; II Thess. 1:1) it appears that *Silas* (also Timothy) was with Paul when he wrote the epistles to the Thessalonians. And according to the book of Acts, Silas accompanied Paul on his *second* missionary journey (after Acts 18:5 Luke does not refer to him again), *not on his first, nor on his third.* Although this is not positive proof, nevertheless it definitely points in the direction of the conclusion that I and II Thessalonians were written on Paul's *second* missionary journey.

Is it possible to fix the date even more precisely? In this connection mention is often made of the fact that in the year 1909 near Delphi a gray limestone inscription was found which perpetuates a letter of the emperor Claudius to the citizens of Delphi, and contains the name of Gallio and an important date. This date clearly indicates that Gallio, before whose tribunal Paul was brought while in Corinth (Acts 18:12-17) was proconsul for either a one-year or a two-year term sometime during the period A. D. 51-53.[6] From the fact that Paul had been in Corinth *alone* before he wrote I Thessalonians, and that when he wrote it Silas and Timothy had joined him, it is clear that we cannot place this epistle at the very beginning of the period 51-53. From the fact that a sufficient period must have intervened before I Thessalonians could be followed by II Thessalonians, it is also clear that the first letter cannot be placed at the end of that period. If, therefore, we accept a date for the two epistles "about the year A. D. 52" (or simply "sometime during the period 51-53"), we cannot be far from the truth.

In the aforegoing we have been assuming that the order in which Paul's two epistles to the Thessalonians follow each other in our Bibles is the correct one, that is, that what we now call I Thessalonians was actually written before what we now call II Thessalonians. A careful and unbiased perusal of the two letters seems to establish the correctness of this view. Reasons:

(1) Although I Thessalonians contains many references to the fact that Paul has had *personal* contact with the church in question, a contact the memory of which is still very vivid (cf. 1:5; 2:1-16; 3:4) and which must have been very recent, this letter does not contain a single reference to an earlier *letter.* But II Thessalonians does contain a clear and definite reference to an earlier letter, for Paul says: "So then, brothers, stand firm and hold to the traditions which you were taught by us, either by word of mouth *or by letter*" (II Thess. 2:15).

(2) In I Thess. 1:6; 2:13 Paul indicates that the Thessalonians have accepted the Gospel by a true and living faith. In II Thess. 1:3 he expresses his gratitude with reference to the fact that this faith *is growing.* Similarly,

---

[6] See: Millar Burrows, *What Mean These Stones,* New Haven, 1941, p. 86.

in the first letter (3:12; 4:10) he exhorts believers to increase in love for one another, and in the second (1:3) he rejoices over the fact that this gradual increase in love has become a fact.

(3) In I Thess. 4:17 the apostle predicts the "rapture" (the being caught up in the clouds to meet the Lord in the air); in II Thess. 2:1 he clearly assumes that the readers have received previous instruction with reference to this subject.

(4) From I Thess. 1:6; 2:14; 3:3 it is evident that from the very beginning believers in Thessalonica suffered persecution. From II Thess. 1:4, 6 it is evident that this grievous trial of their faith has not subsided. If there has been any change at all, it would seem that it has been for the worse.

(5) The first letter contains several injunctions (4:1-12, 5:12-28). In the second some of these injunctions are more sharply expressed (particularly the one with respect to idle and disorderly persons), and the church is given explicit direction how to deal with the disobedient (3:6-15).

(6) In the first letter the sudden and unexpected character of Christ's second coming is set forth (cf. 4:13-18; 5:1-11; note especially the phrase "as a thief in the night"). In the second it is clearly pointed out that this sudden coming does not imply an immediate coming (2:1-12).

(7) In the second letter Paul warns against imaginary or purported, and possibly even against spurious letters (2:2), and in appending the greeting he writes, "This is the mark in *every* letter of mine" (3:17), which is easier to understand if this were a *second* than if it were a *first* letter.

For these reasons we cling to the priority of I Thessalonians. II Thessalonians, as has been shown (see points 1-7 above), presupposes that those addressed are acquainted with I Thessalonians. This also shows that the view according to which I Thessalonians was directed to the "Gentile" community, and II Thessalonians to the "Jewish" community in Thessalonica is uncalled for. Both epistles are directed to the same group of readers, namely, "the church of the Thessalonians" (I Thess. 1:1; II Thess. 1:1).[7]

---

[7] Lyle O. Bristol in an article, "Paul's Thessalonian Correspondence," *ExT* 55 (1944), 223, regards the priority of II Thessalonians probable because: a. it is shorter than I Thessalonians; b. when I Thessalonians was written some members of the Thessalonian church had already died; and c. the organization which it presupposed in I Thess. 5:12, 13 implies a longer time-interval than is possible if I Thessalonians was written first.

But none of these reasons is strong enough to prove anything. Why the first of two letters should necessarily be the shorter one is not clear. It is not at all surprising that in an interval of a few months, with a fierce persecution taking place in Thessalonica, some deaths had occurred. Finally, there had been ample time to organize the church, either during Paul's own ministry or subsequently (for example, after Timothy's arrival in the city; in that case Titus 1:15 would supply an interesting parallel). Paul was a great organizer (Acts 14:23).

Another article is that by Edward Thompson, "The Sequence of the Two Epistles

V. Authorship

A. *Of I Thessalonians*

The authenticity of I Thessalonians is today accepted on nearly every side. Nevertheless, there have always been those who disagree with this well-nigh unanimous opinion, and who consider this epistle to be, either as a whole or in part, the work of a forger.[8]

Their arguments may be summarized as follows:

(1) *This epistle is far less doctrinal than those which are known to have been written by Paul. It is rather insignificant in contents.*

But why must all the writings of the great apostle be equally doctrinal in character? Paul's epistles arose out of certain concrete situations. These situations naturally differed. In one church it was clarification of doctrine that was needed most; in another admonition, exhortation, rebuke, or at

---

to the Thessalonians," *ExT* 56 (1945), 306, 307. This writer defends the priority of I Thessalonians. Among other things he points out that nothing in ancient tradition supports the priority of II Thessalonians, that the more Jewish character of II Thessalonians (discussion of Jewish apocalyptic) does not imply the priority of that epistle, and that it is not true that Paul's allusion to his autograph (II Thess. 3:17) proves that II Thessalonians was written first, for a similar allusion is found in I Cor. 16:21 though a previous letter had been written to the church at Corinth (see I Cor. 5:9).

For the view of A. Harnack and Kirsopp C. Lake (II Thessalonians was directed to a Jewish community, I Thessalonians to a Gentile community) see the latter's chapter in *Contemporary Thinking About Paul* (edited by Thomas S. Kepler), New York, Nashville (no date), pp. 234-238.

[8] For the arguments against the authenticity see especially F. C. Baur, *Paulus,* Stuttgart, 1845, pp. 480 ff. (For an even earlier criticism see Schrader, *Der Apostel Paulus,* V, 1836, pp. 23 ff.) Baur's criticism was the most serious and effective. He convinced some: Noack, Volkmar, Holsten, etc. Cf. also Vander Vies, *De Beide Brieven aan de Thessalonicenzen,* 1865, pp. 128-164. But Baur's denial of the Pauline authorship of I Thessalonians is vitiated by the Hegelian bias upon which it rests. For Baur the question whether an epistle is characterized by the anti-Judaistic line of argumentation seems to settle everything. Thus, all of Paul's thinking and writing is forced into one groove. This is manifestly unfair.

In recent literature a somewhat similar subjectivism is at times apparent. An author starts from the presupposition that whatever is apocalyptic is un-Pauline, and that Paul taught salvation by means of identification through faith with a dying and rising Christ. As a result, certain passages and even entire paragraphs of I Thessalonians are rejected: 1:10; 2:14-16; 4:13-18; 5:1-10; and, for similar reasons the following sections of II Thessalonians are regarded as not genuine: 1:5-10; 2:1-17. Cf. R. M. Hawkins, *The Recovery of the Historical Paul,* Nashville, Tenn., 1943; see especially pp. 234, 241, 292.

However, Paul was a Hebrew of the Hebrews. Now, Hebrew thought has always been characterized by the presence of eschatological and apocalyptic ideas. Paul must have been acquainted with the book of Daniel and with many similar trends of thought in other Old Testament writings (to limit ourselves to canonical scriptures). Moreover, there are similar ideas in the teachings of Jesus (Matt. 24, 25; Mark 13; Luke 21). The total absence of such ideas from Paul's epistles would have been surprising.

times consolation was called for. Besides, it is not true that I Thessalonians is doctrinally insignificant. It sheds needed light on the doctrine of the Second Coming.

(2) *This epistle does not attack the idea that justification is by the works of the law.*

But was Paul a man with one, and *only one,* idea? The situation in Thessalonica was not the same as that in Galatia!

(3) *It is impossible that within a period of a few months the Thessalonian converts could have exerted an influence for good as intensive and extensive as that which is pictured in I Thess. 1:7, 8; 4:10.*

Our answer is: Why not? In fact, it so happens that exactly this bit of information which is furnished by *the letter* is confirmed by that which is supplied by *the narrative in Acts* (17:6). Even the enemies of Paul and of his companions considered the work of the missionaries to be so effective in character that they spoke of "the men who have turned the world upside down." When the Holy Spirit operates in the hearts and lives of consecrated ministers and of converts filled with the enthusiasm of a real, inner conviction, things actually begin to happen!

(4) *The "strong language" which in I Thess. 2:14-16 is used with reference to the Jews could not have been employed by one who in his genuine epistle to the Romans states, "I could wish that I myself were anathema from Christ for the sake of my brothers."*

But why should it be impossible for an inspired author, on the one hand to reveal a terrible reality (namely, the outpouring of God's wrath upon a disobedient people), and yet, on the other hand, in a very touching manner, to express his own genuine sorrow and pain of heart with respect to this reality which concerned his kith and kin? Besides what is taught in I Thess. 2:14-16 does not differ materially from that which is taught in Rom. 9:22; 10:21; and 11:22, 25.

(5) *This epistle is too Pauline! It contains too many passages that resemble those in Paul's genuine epistles (especially I and II Corinthians). Hence, it is clear that a forger is at work.*

But this type of reasoning is the very opposite of that which was followed in arguments (1) and (2) above. *There* I Thessalonians was rejected because it was too un-Pauline. *Here* it is attacked because it is too Pauline! The two arguments cancel each other. Besides, it is not immediately clear why Paul cannot have been the author of an epistle which contains Pauline passages!

On the positive side, there is first of all *the evidence supplied by the epistle itself. This definitely points to Paul as the author* (though two others join him in sending greetings and in confirming whatever he writes). Note the following:

(1) *The epistle presents itself as a letter from Paul* (1:1; 2:18).

(2) *Those who are represented as being with the author as he sends this letter are known (from the book of Acts) to have been with Paul on his second missionary journey.*

They are Silvanus (i.e., Silas) and Timothy (1:1; 3:2, 6); cf. Acts 15:40; 16:1-3, 19; 17:4, 10, 14; 18:5.

(3) *The letter has the typical Pauline form; that is, it has the epistolary structure which characterizes Romans, I Corinthians, II Corinthians, and Galatians, the writings which are ascribed to Paul even by most of those who reject the authenticity of I Thessalonians.*

This letter-plan is as follows (with minor variations): the mention of the writer's name (often: *and* office), the designation of those to whom the letter is addressed (sometimes with brief description), the salutation, the thanksgiving or doxology, the body of the letter (argumentation, admonition, exhortation, consolation, instruction, etc.), the concluding salutation (not always present; when present not always equally circumstantial) and benediction.

(4) *The vocabulary is definitely that of Paul.*

More than 4/5 of the words used in I Thessalonians are found also in the four so-called major Pauline epistles (Romans, I Corinthians, II Corinthians, and Galatians). If we include the prison-epistles (Ephesians, Philippians, Colossians, and Philemon) among those that must be regarded as being genuinely Pauline, we find that almost 9/10 of the words employed by the author of I Thessalonians occur also in these eight letters (the four major and the four prison epistles). And if the pastoral epistles (I Timothy, II Timothy, Titus) are also added, the percentage becomes even a little higher.[9]

(5) *Not only the single words point to Paul as author but so do also many of the characteristic phrases, phrases that are elsewhere found only in Paul.*

a. Phrases[10] found in I Thessalonians (not in II Thessalonians); elsewhere only in the epistles of Paul:

---

[9] In order to reach these percentages I carefully jotted down for myself on cards and in alphabetical order every word found in I Thessalonians (and I did the same for II Thessalonians), and, using *Moulton and Geden's Concordance* to the Greek Testament, I checked the use of these words in Paul's major, prison, and pastoral epistles. It was on that basis that I drew my conclusions. As these conclusions agree, in the main, with those drawn by J. E. Frame, *A Critical and Exegetical Commentary on the Epistles of St. Paul to the Thessalonians* (in The International Critical Commentary) a reference to the pages of that work should suffice (pp. 28-32).

[10] These phrases (in Greek) are found also in Frame (*op. cit.*, pp. 32-34), but he omits the references to the major epistles. I have given a reference also in such cases (for a complete list *Moulton and Geden's Concordance* should be used). Furthermore, I have given the English equivalents, and have re-arranged the phrases according to their chapter and verse sequence.

1:2 in our prayers;	Rom. 1:10
1:3; 3:11, 13 our God and Father	Gal. 1:4
1:5, 6; 2:2, 17 in much (ἐν πολλῇ)	Rom. 9:22
2:4, 15 pleasing God	Rom. 8:8
2:5, 10 God is (my) witness	Rom. 1:9
2:12; 5:24 who is calling you	Gal. 5:8
2:12 in order that you should live lives worthy of God	Col. 1:10
2:18 once and again	Phil. 4:16
3:2 God's fellow-worker	I Cor. 3:9 (pl.)
3:2 the Gospel of Christ	Rom. 15:19
3:5 in vain (εἰς κενόν)	II Cor. 6:1
3:8 you stand firm in the Lord	Phil. 4:1
4:1 in the Lord Jesus	Rom. 14:14
4:11 working with your hands	I Cor. 4:12
4:1 we do not want you to remain ignorant	Rom. 1:13
4:15, 17 we who are alive	II Cor. 4:11
4:17 be with the Lord	Phil. 1:23
5:9 through our Lord Jesus Christ	Rom. 5:1
5:10 live together with him	II Cor. 13:4
5:18 in everything (ἐν παντί)	I Cor. 1:5
5:24 who is calling you	Gal. 5:8
5:26 holy kiss	Rom. 16:16

b. Phrases found in I Thessalonians and II Thessalonians; elsewhere only in the epistles of Paul:

I Thess.	*II Thess.*		
1:5	2:14	our Gospel	II Cor. 4:3
2:9	3:8	in order that not (πρός τὸ μή w. inf.)	II Cor. 3:13
2:9	3:8	labor and toil	II Cor. 11:27
4:1	3:1	for the rest, brothers	II Cor. 13:11
5:6	2:15	So then (ἄρα οὖν)	Rom. 5:18

Besides these there are several phrases which, though found here and there outside of Paul, occur *chiefly* in those epistles which are generally ascribed to the apostle. It is certainly true that there are also many phrases which may be called *unique* (occurring in I Thessalonians and/or II Thessalonians but nowhere else in the New Testament or nowhere else in Paul's epistles). The difference in subject-matter as well as the natural tendency of almost any author (and particularly of a versatile writer like Paul) to vary his expressions when he writes letters to different people under wholly different circumstances cause us to expect this. The very considerable number of phrases which are either exclusively or chiefly Pauline certainly points in the direction of Paul as the author.

(6) *The epistle clearly reflects the character of Paul.*

Here, as elsewhere in the epistles commonly ascribed to Paul, we are brought face to face with a man who is so very deeply interested in those whom he addresses that he is ever thanking God for them and making mention of them in his prayers (1:2 ff; cf. Rom. 1:8, 9); is anxious to see them (2:17, 18; cf. Rom. 1:11; Phil. 2:24), and when he is unable to do so, sends one of his associates (3:2; cf. Phil. 2:19-23). He takes delight in showering praise upon the readers whenever this is possible, and in imparting encouragement (1:3, 6-10; cf. II Cor. 8:7; Phil. 4:15-17). In this connection note close resemblance between 2:19, 20 and Phil. 4:1. Nevertheless, this praise never ends in man. The writer is always quick to ascribe whatever is good in the believer to the sovereign grace of God, viewing it as an evidence of the believer's election and of the presence of the Holy Spirit in his heart (1:4, 5; cf. Rom. 8:28-30; 8:23; Gal. 5:22-25; Phil. 1:6). He does not hesitate to defend his motives in preaching the Gospel, whenever these motives are attacked, and in doing so he likes to review his manner of entrance among the people who now constitute the church (2:1-12; cf. I Cor. 2:1-5; 3:1, 2). He shows great tact in admonishing (4:9, 10; cf. Philemon 8-22), but is never afraid to assert his authority (5:27; cf. I Cor. 16:1). He takes up, one by one, subjects of special interest to the readers, matters on which they need (or have requested) further instruction (4:13; 5:1, 12; cf. I Cor. 7:1, 25; 8:1; 12:1; 16:1).

The more one studies this *intensely personal* side of the epistle, the more one also becomes convinced that only one man could have written it, namely, Paul!

(7) *There is nothing in this epistle which is not in complete harmony with the doctrine proclaimed in Paul's major epistles* (to say nothing about the prison epistles and the pastoral epistles):

Although, barring the exception already noted (see p. 4), this epistle is not pre-eminently doctrinal, nevertheless it everywhere presupposes the Pauline emphasis on important doctrinal points. Thus, the writer of I Thessalonians teaches us that by nature man is headed straight for the revelation of God's wrath (1:10; 5:9; cf. Rom. 1:18; 2:8; 9:22); he is under the rule of darkness (5:5; cf. Rom. 2:19; 13:12; II Cor. 6:14). But out of this fallen mass God, of sovereign mercy, has elected some (1:4; cf. Rom. 9:11; 11:5, 7). This election has as its purpose the believers' sanctification, his assurance, and his final, complete salvation, to God's glory (1:3-5; 3:13; 4:3, 7; 5:23; cf. Rom. 6:1, 22; 11:36; I Cor. 1:30; 10:31). It was the Lord Jesus Christ who died for believers (5:10; cf. Gal. 2:20), that they might live with and for him. While the believer is in this life, he is being tempted by Satan, who tries to lead him astray (3:5; cf. Rom. 16:20; I Cor. 7:5; II

Cor. 2:11; 12:7). But God preserves him until the day of the glorious manifestation of the Lord Jesus Christ from heaven, when forever the believer will be with Christ (1:10; 2:19; 3:13; 3:17; 5:23; cf. Rom. 8:18, 19; I Cor. 15:50-58; 16:22).

The testimony of the early church is in harmony with the conclusion which has been derived from the epistle itself. Thus Eusebius, having made a thorough investigation of the literature at his command, states:

"But clearly evident and plain (πρόδηλοι καὶ σαφεῖς) are the fourteen (letters) of Paul; yet it is not right to ignore that some dispute the (letter) to the Hebrews" (*Ecclesiastical History* III. iii. 4, 5). Obviously Eusebius, writing at the beginning of the fourth century, had never heard of anyone who doubted the authenticity of I and II Thessalonians.

Before him Origen (fl. 210-250) again and again refers to (and quotes from) these epistles and definitely ascribes them to Paul. He is especially fond of quoting from II Thess. 2.

From Origen we can go back still farther, to his teacher, Clement of Alexandria (fl. 190-200). He too is well acquainted with the epistles to the Thessalonians, and ascribes them to Paul. The following are some of the references to (or quotations from) I Thessalonians in the works of Clement:

I Thess.	
2:4	The Stromata (Miscellanies) VII. xii
2:5-7	The Stromata I. i
2:6, 7	The Instructor (Educator, Pedagogue) I. v
4:3-8	The Stromata IV. xii
4:9	The Instructor I. vi
4:17	The Stromata VI. xiii
5:5-8	The Instructor II. ix
5:6-8	The Stromata IV. xxii
5:13-15; 19-22	The Instructor III. xii

About this same time Tertullian, writing *Against Marcion,* and definitely mentioning Paul by name and "all his apostolic writings" (V. i) not only quotes I Thess. 2:15 (V. xv) but also implies that Marcion and other heretics, about the middle of the second century, considered I Thessalonians to be an authentic epistle of the apostle to the Gentiles, a fact which can be gathered also from other sources. Tertullian refers to (and quotes from) I and II Thessalonians (especially II Thess. 2) again and again.

Clement's contemporary was Ireneus. Because of his many travels and intimate acquaintance with almost the entire church of his day, what Ireneus says about the authorship of I and II Thessalonians must be considered of great significance. His voice in a matter as important as this may be considered the voice of the church. Now in his work *Against Heresies* (V. vi. 1) he not only quotes I Thess. 5:23 but also clearly assigns it to Paul. He also refers to (and quotes) other passages from both epistles to the Thessalonians.

The Muratorian Fragment, an incomplete list of New Testament books, written in poor Latin and deriving its name from Cardinal L. A. Muratori (1672-1750) who discovered it in the Ambrosian Library at Milan, may be assigned to the period 180-200. It contains the following:

"Now the epistles of Paul, what they are, whence or for what reason they were sent, they themselves make clear to him who will understand. First of all he wrote at length to the Corinthians to prohibit the schism of heresy, then to the Galatians against circumcision, and to the Romans on the order of the Scriptures, intimating also that Christ is the chief matter in them — each of which it is necessary for us to discuss, seeing that the blessed apostle Paul himself, following the example of his predecessor John, writes to no more than seven churches by name in the following order: to the Corinthians (first), to the Ephesians (second), to the Philippians (third), to the Colossians (fourth), to the Galatians (fifth), to the Thessalonians (sixth), to the Romans (seventh). But . . . he writes twice for the sake of correction to the Corinthians and to the Thessalonians. . . ." Both I and II Thessalonians are also contained in the Old Latin and Old Syriac versions.

It is true that before the time of the witnesses which have thus far been mentioned there are no quotations that are either definitely said to have been derived from Paul's letters to the Thessalonians or can be derived from these letters *with certainty*. This, of course, is not surprising. The writings which can be confidently ascribed to that early period are very few. Moreover, the letters to the Thessalonians are small and (with the exception noted; see p. 4) contain little doctrinal material. They were probably not as well known as, for example, Romans or I Corinthians.

It is possible, nevertheless, that certain expressions in I and II Thessalonians find an echo in the literature of the sub-apostolic age. This can be neither proved nor disproved. Cf. the following:

I Thess. 1:6 "Y o u became imitators of us and of the Lord."	Ignatius, *To The Ephesians* X. iii "Let us be eager to imitate the Lord."
I Thess. 2:4 "not as pleasing men but God who proves our hearts."	Ignatius, *To The Romans* II. i "I would not have y o u be men-pleasers but God-pleasers."
I Thess. 4:9 "Y o u yourselves are taught of God."	Barnabas, Epistle of, XXI. vi (cf. IV. ix) "Be taught of God" (God-instructed).

I Thess. 4:16
"For the Lord himself shall descend from heaven with a shout, with the voice of the archangel, and with the trump of God; and the dead in Christ shall rise first."

The Teaching (Didache) *of the Twelve Apostles* XVI. vi
"And then shall appear the signs of the truth. First the sign spread out in heaven, then the sign of the sound of the trumpet, and thirdly the resurrection of the dead."

I Thess. 5:13
"Be at peace among yourselves."

The Shepherd III. ix. 10
"at peace among themselves."

I Thess. 5:17
"Pray without ceasing."

Ignatius, *To The Ephesians* X. i
"Pray without ceasing."

This evidence does not constitute absolute proof for the position that at the end of the first and beginning of the second century A. D. Paul's letters to the church at Thessalonica were being quoted in writings that have come down to us. The expression "taught of God" (I Thess. 4:9; cf. Barnabas XXI. vi) was a very common one, which may have been derived from the Old Testament as well as from Paul. The following passages immediately occur to the mind: Is. 54:13; 60:2, 3; Jer. 31:33, 34; Joel 2:28; Mic. 4:2; Zeph. 3:9; and Mal. 1:11. Jesus quotes it (see John 6:45) as an expression that is "written in the prophets." Similarly, the passage about the signs (I Thess. 4:16; cf. *The Teaching* XVI. vi) may possibly go back to a saying of Jesus which is also reported by Matthew (24:30, 31). The passage about being at peace (I Thess. 5:13, cf. The Shepherd III. ix. 10) may have been derived from the saying of the Lord reported by Mark (9:50). On the other hand, if in each instance quoted we have before us the genuine text of Ignatius, it would seem that his use of I Thessalonians may be considered as *probable* (though not *certain*).

The important point is this: nowhere in early literature (not even in the writings of the heretics!) is any doubt cast on the Pauline authorship of I Thessalonians! Whenever the epistle is ascribed to anyone, it is always ascribed to the apostle Paul (thus Origen, Tertullian, Clement, Ireneus, etc.). And this external testimony, as has been pointed out, is in perfect agreement with the internal, the evidence supplied by the epistle itself. The only reasonable conclusion is that Paul was, indeed, the author.

B. *Of II Thessalonians*

The arguments of those who reject, either as a whole [11] or in part,[12]

---

[11] See especially Kern, "Ueber II Thess. 2:1-12, Nebst Andeutungen über den Ursprung des zweiten Briefes an die Thessalonicher," *Tübinger Zeitschrift für Theologie* (1839 Zweites Heft), 145-214. Cf. also the conclusion reached by Mayerhof, Baur, Weizsäcker, Wrede. The argumentation varies.

[12] One of the most recent is R. M. Hawkins, *The Recovery of the Historical Paul,*

the Pauline authorship of II Thessalonians are, with individual variations, as follows:

(1) *II Thess. 2:1-12 is an apocalyptic passage. It fixes the attention on Christ's future glory when he shall vanquish his enemies. This representation is in sharp contrast with Paul's emphasis on the necessity of growth in faith, hope, and love, here and now.*

This wholly subjective argument has already been answered. See footnote 8. The passage (2:1-12) is entirely natural, as recent studies in apocalyptic literature have shown. To reject it because it is apocalyptic is arbitrary.

(2) *If Paul wrote I Thess. 4:13-18; 5:1-11, he cannot also have written II Thess. 2:1-12; for while the first views Christ's coming as imminent, the second regards it as non-imminent.*

The fact is that the first epistle represents Christ's second coming as *sudden,* the second as *non-imminent* (preceded by certain events). These two ideas are not mutually exclusive. Certain signs will precede Christ's return. Yet when it occurs, it will take people by surprise. This representation, moreover, is in line with such passages as Dan. 11:1-12:3; Matt. 24:1-44; and Luke 17:20-37.

(3) *The passage 2:1-12 refers to Nero (the man of sin), reportedly dead but here represented as actually hiding and about to return (according to others, as really dead but about to arise), and to Vespasian (the restrainer); or (according to still others) it refers to the days of Trajan and to the advancing tide of gnosticism. This shows that Paul (who was no longer alive during the reigns of Vespasian and of Trajan) cannot have written it.*

Nothing in the context supports this interpretation. See on 2:1-12.

(4) *The rigorous predestinarianism of 2:11, 12, 13 is un-Pauline.*

But why could not he who wrote Rom. 8:28, 39; 9:10-24; Eph. 1:4, 11; 2:10 also have written II Thess. 2:11, 12, 13? In justice to those who urge argument (4) it must be admitted, however, that they would also scrap the predestinarian passages from Romans and Ephesians, viewing also them as being un-Pauline. The objection to this procedure is that the doctrine of predestination harmonizes with the entire course of reasoning in Paul's epistles. Wherever it is not definitely stated, it is presupposed. It is, *in a sense,* the keystone of the theology of the man who taught that "of him and through him and unto him are all things" (Rom. 11:36). To be consistent, the critics should also reject that passage and many others with it. What, if anything, would be left? (And is not also the Gospel of John, which

---

Nashville, Tenn., 1943, pp. 262-269, 292. Earlier interpolation theories (according to which II Thessalonians is partly genuine, partly spurious) were held by J. E. C. Schmidt (1801), who subsequently rejected the entire epistle as un-Pauline, Paul Schmidt (1881), and several others. Some regard 2:1-12 as spurious; others view it as the only genuine part of the letter.

records the teaching of Jesus, predestination from start to finish?[13]) There is, however, nothing *rigorous* with reference to this predestinarianism. Ample provision is always made for the factor of human responsibility. For the rest, see on 2:11, 12, 13.

(5) *To a very large extent II Thessalonians is a repetition of I Thessalonians. Clearly, a forger is at work!*

Actual comparison — let anyone check this! — shows that the new material in II Thessalonians (new as compared with the first letter) comprises about two-thirds of the letter. That there should be a certain amount of overlapping is exactly what one can reasonably expect when it is considered that *the same* author writes to *the same* church during *the same* period of time (only a few months intervening between the two letters) and under *the same* circumstances (by and large).

(6) *II Thessalonians differs in too many respects from the genuine Pauline epistles to be regarded as a product of Paul's "pen." Specifically, it is much "cooler" (less friendly, more "official") and also much more "Jewish" in coloring than I Thessalonians.*

It was especially Wrede who, in *Die Echtheit des zweiten Thessalonicherbriefs,* enlarged on this. But to some extent arguments (5) and (6) cancel each other. For the rest, the close relationship between the two letters has been shown. See pp. 16, 17; and see what is said about the resemblance between II Thessalonians and other Pauline epistles (pp. 21, 28).

(7) *The salutation (3:17) looks suspicious. It is clearly a deliberate attempt by a forger to make the letter look authentic.*

The answer to this is that in view of the item of information which 2:2 conveys — see on that passage — the autographic conclusion of 3:17 is altogether natural.

The same internal evidence that has been adduced to prove the authenticity of I Thessalonians establishes that of II Thessalonians. See pp. 22, 23. Hence, in view of what has been said in connection with the first letter a brief statement will suffice:

This second epistle (as well as the first) represents itself as having been written by Paul (1:1; 3:17), with whom are associated the men who are known to have accompanied him on his second journey (1:1). Here too the usual Pauline epistolary form is present, with interesting variation in detail. The vocabulary is definitely Pauline, the percentage of words which the second letter has in common with other epistles that are ascribed generally to Paul being even slightly higher than the percentage of words common to the first letter and the other epistles.

---

[13] See *New Testament Commentary* (hereafter referred to as N.T.C.), John's Gospel, Vol. I, p. 46.

To the list of phrases which II Thessalonians has in common with other Pauline epistles *and which are also found in I Thessalonians* (see p. 21) may now be added those which are found in the second letter and in others generally ascribed to Paul *but not in I Thessalonians.*

Note the following:

II Thess.		
1:1 God our Father	Rom. 1:7	
1:8 obey the Gospel	Rom. 10:16	
1:10 was believed in (ἐπιστεύθη with impersonal subject)	Rom. 10:10	
2:2 as that (or: as if ὡς ὅτι)	II Cor. 5:19	
2:3 let no one (μή τις with aor. subjunctive)	I Cor. 16:11	
2:7 forward position of the word *only* (μόνον)	Gal. 2:10	
2:10 those that are perishing	I Cor. 1:18	
2:17 comfort y o u r hearts		Col. 2:2
3:4 have confidence in the Lord		Phil. 2:24
3:13 be not weary in well-doing	Gal. 6:9	
3:14 our word	II Cor. 1:13	
3:17 the greeting of Paul, with my own hand	I Cor. 16:21	

Here, just as in the first letter, the personal character of Paul is reflected. (For the passages in the other epistles of Paul which reflect these same traits see p. 22.) In II Thessalonians we are face to face with a person who *is deeply interested in his readers* (1:3, 11, 12) and *displays warm affection* for them. He shares (*has fellowship* with) their experiences, and *is fond of commending* whatever is good in them (1:4; 3:4). Nevertheless, he *ascribes their virtues to the proper source:* God and his sovereign election (2:13). He *shows great tact* in admonishing them (3:4, 6-15), and *takes up matters of special interest to them* (2:1-12; 3:6-15). His *tender fatherly concern* for the readers is evident also in this, that when he describes the day of the revelation of God's wrath, he immediately adds that this wrath is only for the enemies of the church ("to repay with affliction them that afflict y o u"), and that believers (among whom he also counts the readers) will receive nothing but glory when Christ returns (1:3-10; 2:8-14).

The kind of character which is displayed in this letter points unmistakably to Paul. Nevertheless, at this point we must be careful. Some of the traits revealed in these two letters and in those by the same author occur also in the writings of other apostles. It is therefore not so much *the fact* that they do occur here as *the manner in which they are expressed* (the specific style) that points to Paul as the author. This is often overlooked. Take, as an example, *the sense of fellowship* (with the readers) of which we spoke. The apostle makes mention of the fact that the saints at Thessalonica have become imitators of Paul (and of his companions, yea of the

Lord himself!) in their afflictions (I Thess. 1:6); and that they will again be associated with Paul in the blessed rest which awaits them "at the revelation of the Lord Jesus from heaven" (II Thess. 1:7). However, this amiable way of addressing the readers in order to gain their full confidence and to make them feel that the writer is standing on common ground with them is just as Johannine as it is Pauline, as the beautiful expression in Rev. 1:9 shows.[14] It is the mark of the Christian, not just the mark of Paul! But the manner of expressing it differs: Paul's *y o u with* (and *of*) *us* becomes John's *I with y o u*. Paul tells the readers that *they* have become *imitators* (a noun not found anywhere in John's writings). John states that *he* has become a *fellow-partaker*. (Paul in a similar context also uses this term but with characteristic difference, Phil. 1:7: *"y o u* are fellow-partakers *with me."* Same term, but different context: Rom. 11:17; I Cor. 9:23.) Similarly, when Paul commends the virtues of the readers, he is simply doing what according to the book of Revelation, the great Church-Visitor also does (Rev. 2:2, 3, 13, 19, etc.). But here again the manner of expression is entirely different. The solemn and oft-recurring phrase, "I know thy works, etc." characterizes the book of Revelation, not Paul.

As to external evidence, for the testimony of Eusebius, Origen, Tertullian, and the Muratorian Fragment, in favor of Pauline authorship see pp. 23, 24.

Clement of Alexandria (fl. 190-200) in *Stromata* V. iii quotes II Thess. 3:1, 2. Ireneus, his contemporary, quotes from this epistle again and again:

II Thess.	Against Heresies
1:6-8	IV. xxxiii. 11
1:6-10	IV. xxvii. 4
2:4	III. vi. 5
2:8	III. vii. 2 (cf. V. xxv. 3)
2:11	IV. xxix. 1

He, moreover, makes it very clear that "the apostle" whose passages he quotes is Paul. See IV. xxiv. 1; xxxiii. 11. Though some see possible references to II Thessalonians in *The Epistle of Vienne and Lyons* (as quoted in Eusebius, *Ecclesiastical History* V. i) or in Ignatius, The *Teaching (Didache)*, or Barnabas, such conclusions appear to be rather far-fetched. A mere phrase or a very common saying proves nothing. We seem to be on somewhat firmer ground in finding a reference to II Thess. 2:3 in Justin Martyr's *Dialogue with Trypho* (Cx; cf. XXXII): "the man of apostasy who speaks strange things against the Most High." See the entire context

[14] See my *More Than Conquerors* (Interpretation of the book of Revelation), Grand Rapids, Mich., seventh edition 1954, p. 69.

in the Thessalonian passage. Clearest of all is a reference in (the Latin version of) Polycarp's *Epistle to the Philippians* (XI. iii), cf. II Thess. 1:4: "he glories about y o u in all the churches," and another reference immediately following (hence, Polycarp, *Philippians* XI. iv), cf. II Thess. 3:15: "and yet count them not as enemies." Not only does Polycarp quote from II Thessalonians, but he does so in a context in which he definitely mentions "the blessed Paul." Polycarp was very fond of "the blessed and glorious Paul" (see his *Philippians* III. ii).

What has been presented in support of the Pauline authorship of II Thessalonians may be summarized as follows:

(1) II Thessalonians was known in the early Church, the testimony going back from Eusebius and Origen all the way to Polycarp (about 135 A. D.).

(2) Whenever the letter was ascribed to anyone, it was ascribed to the apostle Paul. Ireneus, whose testimony being of a representative character, is especially valuable, nowhere casts any doubt on the position that the great apostle to the Gentiles was the writer of II Thessalonians.

(3) The internal evidence is in complete agreement with the external.

VI. General Contents

A. *Of I Thessalonians*

Many Bible-books, including several epistles, have definite themes. They cover a specific, well-defined subject. A little study reveals the nature of this central theme.[15] This, however, is not true with respect to *every* Bible-book. It is not true either with respect to every communication written today. Letters differ. You have heard that a friend has suffered a grievous loss. So you write him in order to comfort him. Your letter throughout dwells on that *one* theme, for you are aware of the fact that right now it would not be wise to bother him with many other matters. But a year later when time and reflection on God's promises have performed their work of mercy and when circumstances have returned to normal again (as far as this is possible), you write another letter. This is a message filled with news, advice, questions, etc. You communicate with your friend *about various matters.* Now it certainly would be arbitrary for anyone who subsequently examines this your second letter to try to crowd all your thoughts under one central theme (unless you make that theme so very broad in scope and so indefinite that it is a *caption* rather than a definite, specific, material *theme*). Now if attempts to deal thus arbitrarily with uninspired documents are wrong, it is even more wrong to treat Paul's divinely inspired

[15] As I have shown in *Bible Survey,* Grand Rapids, Mich., third edition (fourth printing), 1953, pp. 36, 37.

epistles in that manner. What results is a merely imagined unity. Often, as a consequence of trying to get everything under one central theme, this or that very important matter is omitted completely from the theme and/or from the Outline under it.[16]

It stands to reason that, in view of the various purposes which the apostle (and his associates) has in mind in writing this letter (see the section on *Purpose,* above), he comments on various subjects. Hence, in this case a rather general and comprehensive caption will have to take the place of a definite, unified, material theme. The caption and subjoined division which I have chosen match what has been said about Paul's *purpose* in writing this letter (see p. 12).

Paul[17] *Writes To The Thessalonians*

chapters 1 and 2 or 1:1-3:5	*Reminding Them,* in connection with his *Thanksgiving* for Them, How the Gospel Had Come to Thessalonica, as a Genuine Work of God and Not as a Product of Human Deception;[18]
chapter 3 or 3:6-13	*Informing* Them How He *Rejoices* over Timothy's Report of Their Continued Spiritual Progress Even in the Midst of Persecution;
4:13-5:11	*Instructing* Them How Christ Will Come Again, namely, *with impartiality* toward *all* believers, sothat survivors will have no advantage over those who have fallen asleep; and *with suddenness,* sothat people will be taken by surprise; and accordingly:
4:1-12 and 5:12-28	*Exhorting* Them How They Should Conduct Themselves, living sanctified lives with respect to all classes and at all times.[19]

---

16 It is for that reason that I cannot agree with the theme and the outline that has been suggested by Edward P. Blair in his article "The First Epistle to the Thessalonians," *Int.* Vol. II, Number 2 (April, 1948), 209-217. Where, either in the theme which he suggests or in the outline (see p. 216 of that article), is anything said about the important section on Christ's second coming? Will anyone who looks at the theme or at the outline as given by Blair know that a considerable portion of Paul's letter deals with a specific problem that had arisen with respect to the Lord's Return? — For the rest, I gladly admit that the article itself is splendid in many ways, and on several points contains exactly the advice which everyone who proceeds to study a Bible-book should heed. Because of its excellence it deserves careful study!

17 Or more fully: Paul, Silvanus, and Timothy write, etc. But Paul, at any rate, is mainly responsible.

18 This is the Apostle's *Thanksgiving* and his *Defence* by means of Reminiscence.

19 I realize that this broad caption and subjoined division is too lengthy for

Thus, in general, there are four divisions (Thanksgiving and Defence, Expression of Joy, Instruction, and Exhortation), but these divisions are not rigid or clearcut (see on 4:1). Thoughts already expressed in one section recur in the next. Besides, the fourth division – Exhortation – comprises both 4:1-12 and 5:12-28. Hence, the four divisions really become five:

Thanksgiving and Defence
Expression of Joy
Exhortation
Instruction
Exhortation.[20]

B. *Of II Thessalonians*

This epistle is considerably shorter than the first. Its material is more definitely organized around one central theme, even though the theme is not introduced immediately, as in a formal essay on a definite topic, but rises to the surface gradually. Thus, in the first chapter it becomes clearly evident when we reach verse 5, and stays with us for six entire verses (verses 5 through 10). Though it seems to subside somewhat in the last two verses (11 and 12), it is still presupposed, for the prayer contained in that little closing paragraph is uttered "with a view to" the realization of the expectations mentioned in verses 5-10. The theme mentioned in this chapter is "The Revelation of the Lord Jesus from heaven" (verse 7).

That this theme is continued in chapter 2 requires no argument, for this chapter is immediately introduced by the words, "Now concerning the coming of our Lord Jesus Christ and our gathering (to meet) him."

Not every interpreter is ready to grant that the thought of this second coming also underlies chapter 3. Some deny any connection between disorderliness, treated in that chapter, and ideas with reference to the return of the Lord. Yet, a comparison of several passages in both epistles would seem to indicate that there is this connection. It is true, of course, that I Thessalonians is not II Thessalonians, and that the circumstances underlying the second epistle are *not exactly* the same as those presupposed or described in the first. The evil had become aggravated when the second letter was written. Nevertheless, it is hard to imagine that the disorderly persons mentioned in the first letter were such for an *entirely* different reason than those characterized similarly in the second (cf. I Thess. 5:14

---

memorization, particularly if one is trying to commit to memory the themes or captions or brief outlines of all the Bible-books. Hence, for such practical purposes I have suggested a shorter caption and division; see my *Bible Survey*, pp. 340, 341; cf. p. 37.

[20] Approximately this fivefold division is also given in my *Bible Survey*, pp. 340, 341, where three of these five are grouped together under one larger division, and two under the other.

with II Thess. 3:6). If then we may assume that *in general* the same evils prevailed and for the same reason, we get the following picture (combining references in both epistles):

The Thessalonians were shaken from their normal state of mind (II Thess. 2:1, 2), were not calm (I Thess. 4:11), because of their erroneous views regarding Christ's return. This is plainly stated as the reason in II Thess. 2:2. They thought that the day of the Lord had arrived already. It was this disturbed condition which caused them to leave their daily occupations and to become disorderly (I Thess. 4:11; cf. 5:14; then II Thess. 3:6), even to the extent of depending on others for physical sustenance (II Thess. 3:7, 8).

If this position be correct, then also chapter 3 presupposes the same theme as that which controls chapters 1 and 2. Hence, the following theme and outline are suggested:

The Revelation of the Lord Jesus from Heaven

chapter 1	has a twofold purpose
chapter 2 (or 2:1-12)	will be preceded by the falling away and by the revelation of the lawless one
chapter 3 (or 2:13-3:17)	is a firmly anchored hope whose contemplation should result not in disorderliness but in calm assurance, stedfast endurance, and strength-imparting peace.

As indicated on pp. 14, 15, also in this case there are important interspersions.

Commentary on I Thessalonians

Summary of I Thessalonians 1, 2 (or 1:1-3:5)

Paul Writes to the Thessalonians

Reminding Them, in connection with his Thanksgiving for Them, How the Gospel Had Come to Thessalonica, as a Genuine Work of God and Not as a Product of Human Deception.

This Section Comprises the *Apostle's Thanksgiving and his Defence by means of Reminiscence.*

In Chapter 1 the Thanksgiving Predominates, but there is an Undertone of Defence against the Slander of the Adversaries. In Chapter 2 the Defence Predominates, although the Thanksgiving Continues.

The Section, accordingly, may be summarized as follows:

1:1 Names of Senders and Addressee, Salutation

1:2-10 Thanksgiving with Undertone of Defence

1:2, 3 *Immediate* reason for thanksgiving

the presence of fruits of the Spirit in the lives of the Thessalonian believers, their:

work resulting from faith
exertion prompted by love
endurance inspired by hope

1:4-10 *Ultimate* reason for thanksgiving (in which an undertone of defence can easily be detected)

their election from eternity. Proof:

objectively, the *trustworthiness* of the message and of the messengers

subjectively, the admirable manner in which this message and these messengers had been received and the new faith had been spread, a sign of the Spirit's *operation* in the midst of the church, which, in turn, is proof of divine election

Let not the adversary deny either this trustworthiness or the genuine character of this operation.

2:1-20 (or 2:1-3:5) Defence with Continuing Thanksgiving

2:1-16 *Apologia pro Vita Sua,* that is, Paul's defence of his manner of life in Thessalonica, defence of his message, motive, and method (with note of thanksgiving to God for the way in which the message had been accepted by those who turned to God)

2:17-20 (or 2:17-3:5) *Apologia pro Absentia Sua,* that is, Paul's defence of his sudden departure and continued absence from Thessalonica

CHAPTER I

I THESSALONIANS 1:1

1 1 Paul and Silvanus and Timothy to the church of the Thessalonians in God
the Father and the Lord Jesus Christ; grace to y o u and peace.
2 We give thanks to God always for y o u all, making mention (of y o u) in
our prayers, 3 continually bearing in mind y o u r work resulting from faith and
(y o u r) exertion prompted by love and (y o u r) endurance inspired by hope [21]
in our Lord Jesus Christ in the presence of our God and Father; 4 knowing,
brothers beloved by God, y o u r election, 5 inasmuch as [22] our gospel did not come
to y o u in words only but also in power and in the Holy Spirit and full assurance,
just as y o u (well) know what kind of men we became among y o u for y o u r sake.
6 And y o u became imitators of us and of the Lord, when amid great tribulation
y o u welcomed the word with joy imparted by the Holy Spirit, 7 so that y o u
became an example to all the believers in Macedonia and Achaia. 8 For, from
y o u the word of the Lord has echoed forth not only in Macedonia and Achaia,
but in every place y o u r faith (directed) toward God has gone forth, so that it is
not necessary for *us* to say anything; 9 for they themselves are reporting about us,
what kind of entering in we had among y o u, and how y o u turned to God from
those idols (of y o u r s), to serve God, the living and real One, 10 and to await his
Son out of the heavens, whom he raised from the dead, Jesus, who rescues us from
the wrath to come.

1:1-10

1:1. In our day when you write a letter, you first of all address the person to whom you are sending it; for example, Name of Addressee; then,

"Dear Friend:"

At the conclusion of the letter you write your own name; thus:

"Yours truly,
John Brown"

In Paul's time, however, a letter would begin with the name of the sender. This would be followed by the name of the person(s) addressed, to which, in turn, would be appended the customary greeting. Examples

---

[21] *Literally: y o u r work of faith and exertion* (or: *labor*) *of love and endurance of hope;* but such language conveys little meaning in English.

[22] The sense of this statement is: "for . . . that y o u were chosen (elected) we know *from the fact that* our gospel," etc.

are Acts 15:23 and 23:36. So also this epistle: **Paul and Silvanus and Timothy.**

Since the great apostle was mainly responsible for the present letter, he first of all writes his own name, then the names of those who had been associated with him in bringing the Gospel to the Thessalonians, and who were with him now in Corinth as this letter was being written.

The apostle's Jewish name was Saul. This Hebrew name was very appropriate because its bearer belonged to the tribe of Benjamin from which centuries earlier king Saul had arisen (Phil. 3:5; cf. I Sam. 9:1, 2). Its meaning is *asked of God.* But as the apostle was a Roman citizen by birth (Acts 22:28), it is not strange that at the time of his circumcision (cf. Lk. 1:59) he had been given a Roman (Latin) name (Paulus, cf. our: Paul) in addition to the Jewish name (Saul).

Now the Roman name somewhat resembled the Jewish in sound, though not in meaning.[23] The meaning of the Roman name – Paul-us, also written Paullus, (for paurulus; cf. parvus), whence Greek Paul-os (cf. παῦρος) – is *little.* There are those who see special significance in the meaning of this name, or make certain comments about it. Thus, for example, Augustine, playing on the apostle's Roman cognomen, styles him *paullum modicum quid,* and Chrysostom calls him, "the man three cubits tall." The *Acts of Paul and Thecla* describe him as follows: "baldheaded, bowlegged, strongly built, *a man small in size,* with meeting eyebrows, with a rather large nose, full of grace, for at times he looked like a man and at times he had the face of an angel." Others point out that whatever may have been Paul's physical stature (cf. II Cor. 10:10), spiritually he was destined by God's sovereign grace to regard himself as very *little* or *insignificant:* "less than the least of all saints" (Eph. 3:8). Be that as it may – and neither Paul in any of his epistles nor Luke gives definite indication of attaching any value to the meaning of the name, whether Hebrew or Latin –, *one* fact at least is certain, and it is that fact upon which the emphasis should fall, namely, that although here in I Thess. 1:1 Paul does not immediately add to his name the appositive "an apostle" (as he does when he writes to places where his office was in dispute), he is, nevertheless, writing in that capacity. As has already been pointed out (see p. 22), while he writes, he is conscious of his *authority.*

Associated with him, fully endorsing everything he says, are Silvanus and Timothy. Silvanus is a Roman proper name. Originally it was the name of the god of the woods (cf. our adjective *sylvan* and cf. *Pennsylvania:*

---

[23] The question might be asked, "But why did not the apostle simply keep his Hebrew name with Grecianized ending to be used in a Greek-speaking environment? In other words, why was he not simply called Saul-os (instead of Paul-os)?" This, however, would not have been very pleasant. Who likes to be called *loose, wanton, straddling, waddling* (σαῦλος)?

Penn's woods). The name as such bears no relation to the character or personality of this fellow-soldier nor to the place where he was born. It is merely a matter of sound-transposition. From what was probably originally an Aramaic name (with a meaning the same as Saul) comes the Greek Silas, and (without any similarity in meaning, only in sound) the Latin Silvan-us (though the Greek ending is, of course, -os). While Luke uses the name Silas, Paul very naturally refers to the same person as Silvan-us (-os), just as he calls himself Paul-us (-os). A comparison of the passages in Paul's letters with those in Acts makes it altogether probable that by Silas and Silvanus the same person is meant. He figures prominently in the proceedings of the council of Jerusalem (Acts 15:22, 27, 32), and was sent with Paul to Antioch to communicate the council's decision to that city. It has already been indicated (see pp. 5, 16) that after the argument between Paul and Barnabas with reference to John Mark, whom Paul refused to take with him on his second journey, the apostle chose Silas, that is, Silvanus, to accompany him and to carry out special missions; and that after the second journey the book of Acts contains no further reference to him. Also in the epistles of Paul the references to Silvanus always point to the second journey (II Cor. 1:19; I Thess. 1:1; II Thess. 2:1). The question whether the Silvanus mentioned by Peter (I Peter 5:12) was the same person, and in exactly what relation the former stood to the latter and to his letter need not detain us here.

If the mention of Silas, as associated with Paul in the sending of the letter, is not surprising, the mention of Timothy is even less so. The reason for our belief that he as well as Silas had labored with Paul in Thessalonica has already been stated (p. 5). But in addition to laboring there with Paul, Timothy had been sent back to that field afterward and had just now reported his findings (I Thess. 3:1, 2, 6).

We know much more about Timothy than about Silas. But the information furnished will be summarized in the proper place; see N.T.C. on the Pastorals.

The order in which the three names are mentioned is the one which we would expect: first Paul, because he is, in the fullest sense of the term, the apostle. It is he who writes (i.e. dictates) the letter. Next mentioned is Silvanus, who in all probability was the older of the two companions and who had been with Paul from the very beginning of the journey during which the Thessalonians had received the Gospel. Last of all is Timothy, who seems to have been the youngest and who had been added to the little mission-band while the journey was already in progress (Acts 16:1-3). The three are writing (and in the immediate context are transmitting [24] a salu-

[24] τῇ ἐκκλησίᾳ is sometimes called the dative of transmittance.

tation) **to the church of the Thessalonians.** The term translated *church* [25] is *ecclesia* (cf. the adjective *ecclesiastical*). Originally it indicated *the popular assembly,* as for example in Athens, in which every free citizen could vote. In the LXX (Greek translation of the Old Testament) it refers to *the community of Israel* (whether or not viewed as assembled for any particular purpose). In the New Testament it refers to *the company of those whom God has called out of darkness into his marvelous light* (cf. I Peter 2:9), whether, a. as here, they be viewed as constituting a *local congregation,* b. as in Eph. 1:22, *the whole body of believers,* or c. as in I Cor. 11:18, *a gathering for worship.*

It is not clear just why Paul employs the expression "of the [26] Thessalonians" instead of "at (or in) Thessalonica" (which is the more usual form; cf. Rom. 1:7; I Cor. 1:2; II Cor. 1:1; Phil. 1:1; Col. 1:2). It is certain, however, that the expression *the Thessalonians* indicates all the members of the church which had very recently been established **in** (and was still in existence by virtue of its vital union with) **God the Father and the Lord Jesus Christ.** The combination of both terms (a. God the Father, b. the Lord Jesus Christ) after one preposition (*in;* that is *grounded in*) would seem to indicate that the two are entirely co-ordinate, that is, that the reference is to the first and to the second person of the Holy Trinity.[27] Note also the trinitarian character of verses 3-5. Hence, the third person (Holy Spirit), mentioned in verse 5, is implied already in verse 1. Paul often mentions the three together in series of closely connected passages (II Thess. 2:13, 14; I Cor. 12:4-6; II Cor. 13:14; Eph. 2:18; 3:2-5; 3:14-17; 4:4-6; 5:18-20). In referring to the second person the full name is used here: the Lord Jesus Christ.

In the LXX the name *Lord* (κύριος) translates *Jehovah,* the God of Israel. It is more often the rendering of Jehovah than of anything else. (At times it is the equivalent of Adon, Adonai, Baal, etc.) Now the Jews were strict monotheists. Yet Paul, though himself a Jew, again and again gives to Jesus the title *Lord.* This shows that, in the thinking of the apostle, Jesus is just as fully divine as is God the Father: one and the same essence is

---

[25] Our English word *church* (cf. German *Kirche,* Dutch *kerk*) is also, in all probability related to the Greek κυριακός-ή-όν, and means "that which is the Lord's."

[26] It is probably best not to look for any profound reason why the article is omitted in the original. Some, nevertheless, suggest that the reason might be that not *all* but only *some* of the inhabitants of Thessalonica had been converted. Far more simple is the explanation given by A. T. Robertson and others, namely, that *Thessalonians,* being a proper name, is definite even without the article. In line with A.V., A.R.V., R.S.V., etc., we abide by the usual rendering "of the Thessalonians."

[27] Thus also in II Thess. 1:2. If the idea were: "from the triune God through Jesus Christ" we would have expected two prepositions, namely, ἀπό and διά. I agree with Lenski (*op. cit.,* p. 219) and others that the expression *God the Father* (I Thess. 1:1; II Thess. 1:1, 2) refers here to the first person as such. Cf. A. M. Perry, "Translating The Greek Article," *JBL* 68 (Dec., 1949) 329-334.

possessed by the Father and by the Son (also by the Spirit, II Cor. 13:14). For Paul, Jesus is our Lord because: a. he is the second person in the Holy Trinity (I Cor. 13:3; Phil. 2:11), the highly exalted One, rightful object of worship, b. he has made us (Col. 1:3, 16), and c. he has bought (redeemed) us with his precious blood (Col. 1:3, 14); hence, we belong to him according to body and soul, in life and death and throughout all eternity. We owe him our full allegiance. This description of Jesus as *Lord* was not derived from the pagan world nor necessarily from the Christian communities in such cities as Antioch, Tarsus, and Damascus. No, Paul "received" it from the original disciples. The early church at Jerusalem (the Aramaic-speaking and then also the Greek-speaking believers) already used the title with reference to Jesus (cf. Gal. 1:18, 19; I Cor. 16:22: "Maranatha," meaning "Our Lord, come," or simply "Lord, come"; [28] John 20:28. Acts 6:1 shows that the early Jerusalem church was bilingual).

To the title *Lord* Paul adds the name *Jesus*. Our English word *Jesus* is really Latin from the closely resembling Greek name (Ἰησοῦς). This, in turn, is the hellenized form of the late Hebrew *Jeshua* (see post-exilic historical books; e.g., Ezra 2:2), the contracted form of *Jehoshua* (cf. *Joshua*, Josh. 1:1; Zech. 3:1). This has been interpreted to mean *Help of Jehovah*. By another approach it has been explained as indicating: *he will certainly save* (this agrees with Matt. 1:21). Accordingly, by giving this name to the Mediator, God meant to indicate that a. no one can save himself, b. salvation ever comes from God, c. this salvation is bestowed through the person and work of him who according to his divine nature is the Son of God, and according to his human nature, the son of Mary, d. it is he who saves, and *he alone*. No one else in all the wide world has been appointed to perform this task.

Anyone can arrive at this meaning by carefully reading the following four passages:

Matt. 1:21: "You must call his name Jesus, for *he* will save his people from their sins."

Matt. 11:27-30: ". . . No one knows the Son except the Father, and no one knows the Father except the Son and anyone to whom the Son chooses to reveal him. Come to me, all who labor and are heavily burdened, and I will cause y o u to rest."

John 14:6: "I am the way and the truth and the life; no one comes to the Father but by me."

---

[28] The latter, if the original meaning of the suffix had been obscured, which is possible. On the use, derivation, and meaning of the word κύριος see especially J. Y. Campbell, art. "Lord," in *A Theological Word Book of the Bible* (edited by Alan Richardson), New York, 1952; also J. G. Machen, *The Origin of Paul's Religion*, Grand Rapids, 1947 (reprint), chapter 8; and G. Vos, *The Self-Disclosure of Jesus*, New York, 1926, chapter 9.

Acts 4:12: "And not by anyone else is there this salvation; for neither is there under heaven any other name that has been given among men by which we must be saved."

Finally, to the title *Lord* and the personal name *Jesus* is added the official name *Christ.*[29] This is the Greek equivalent of the Hebrew Messiah. It is clear, therefore, that for Paul the One here indicated was the fulfilment of prophecy, God's *anointed* (*ordained* and *qualified* by God to carry out the task of saving his people).

By combining these three appellatives into one glorious designation, "the Lord Jesus Christ," Paul indicates that the One thus named, together with God the Father, is able to be and actually is the source of the blessings contained in the salutation which is now pronounced: **grace to you and peace.** This form of salutation may have been suggested by the combination of the ordinary Greek and Hebrew greetings. Paul, however, deepens and spiritualizes both.[30] The apostle uses the term *grace* (χάρις) about a hundred times in his thirteen epistles. In the Old Testament it indicates gracefulness, beauty (Prov. 31:30), favor (Gen. 6:8). The various shades of meaning which this word acquires in Paul's epistles should be distinguished, somewhat as follows:

(a) *A quality or attribute of God or of the Lord Jesus Christ: his kindness.* In this connection II Cor. 8:9 is often referred to: "For you know the grace of our Lord Jesus Christ." (However, in connection with this passage, meaning (b) might also be considered.)

(b) The *favor* toward his people which results from this kindness of disposition and which manifests itself a. in their deliverance from the guilt and punishment of sin, b. in the *dynamic,* transforming operation of the Holy Spirit in their hearts, and finally, c. in their entrance into glory. On God's part, this favor is entirely *sovereign and unconditional;* on man's part, it is completely *unmerited.* Cf. Eph. 2:8; "For by grace have you been saved through faith, and that not of yourselves; it is the gift of God." Salvation by grace stands in opposition to salvation by the works of the law.

(c) The state of salvation, the sum-total of the blessings of salvation, or, at times, any particular blessing or endowment, viewed (in each case) as *the free gift of God.* Cf. Rom. 5:2: "this grace wherein we stand." Eph. 4:7: "But to each one of us was this grace given according to the measure of the gift of Christ."

(d) The *gratitude* which is the believer's reaction when, led by the Spirit, he focusses his attention upon his own unworthiness and upon the greatness of God's goodness toward him. Cf. II Cor. 2:14: "Thanks be to God . . ."

In the present passage (I Thess. 1:1) meaning (b) would seem to be the

---

[29] On this name see G. Vos, *op. cit.,* chapter 8.
[30] See M.M., p. 685.

most fitting. Paul takes the "greetings" (χαίρειν) of the ordinary letter in the Greek-speaking world (cf. also Acts 15:23; 23:26; Jas. 1:1), deepens it into "grace" (χάρις): God's love for the undeserving, his unmerited favor in operation in the hearts and lives of his children, and then adds *peace*.

This addition is natural, for when grace is received, there is *peace* (εἰρήνη) in the heart, *the consciousness of having been reconciled with God through Christ.* Grace is the fountain, and peace is the stream which issues from this fountain (cf. Rom. 5:1). It can hardly be doubted that this *peace* is closely related to the Hebrew *shalom* (cf. Judg. 19:20): wholeness, prosperity, welfare; here (I Thess. 1:1), spiritual welfare. It is the peace of which Jesus spoke in John 14:27 (see on that passage). Paul uses the word more than forty times.

This grace and this peace have their origin in God the Father, and have been merited for the believer by the Lord Jesus Christ.

Just what is the character of this salutation? Is it an exclamation, a declaration, a mere wish? Some consider it to be an exclamation. They are of the opinion that no verb is even implied.[31] Many, however, are not able to follow this reasoning. When a man says to his neighbor, "More power to you!" he is uttering an exclamation, and he does not use any verb. Yet, everyone immediately understands that a verb is implied, the sense being: "May you receive more power!" And so also in the present case. Paul, however, never *uses* a verb in his salutations. John employs the future *indicative* (II John 3: "Grace, mercy, peace *shall be* with us"). In a context which closely resembles Paul's style in Ephesians, Peter employs the *optative* (I Peter 1:2). Compare:

Eph. 1:1-3	I Peter 1:1-3
"Paul, an apostle of Christ Jesus . . . to the saints. . . . Grace to you and peace from God our Father and the Lord Jesus Christ. Blessed be the God and Father of our Lord Jesus Christ. . . ."	"Peter, an apostle of Jesus Christ . . . to the elect . . . Grace to you and peace *be multiplied*. Blessed be the God and Father of our Lord Jesus Christ. . . ."

From the similarity in the general structure and context of these salutations it may be safely inferred that Paul's implied verb resembles Peter's expressed verb. See also II Peter 1:2 and Jude 2 where the same form of the verb (optative mood) is used. Accordingly, A.V. is probably not in error when it inserts a verb and translates the salutation:

---

[31] See R. C. H. Lenski, *Interpretation of Galatians, Ephesians, Philippians*, Columbus, Ohio, 1937, p. 27.

"Grace *be* unto you, and peace.[32]

However, exactly at this point a question arises. Is it not true then that those are right who contend that the salutation is *a mere wish?* And must we not, in all honesty, conclude that the traditional position of the church with respect to the salutation, as pronounced at the beginning of the service in public worship, is wrong; and that those authorities in Liturgics who contend that the salutation is an act of God whereby he bestows his grace and peace upon those who are ready to receive it by faith,[33] are also wrong?

We believe, however, that this conclusion by no means follows. The traditional position of the church is entirely correct. It has grammar on its side.[34]

The question, in the final analysis, is not: Does the traditional view with respect to the nature of the salutation (as being an actual declaration that God imparts his favor, and that he places his blessings upon the congregation) harmonize with my notion as to what a service of the Word should be? Does it tally with my opinion of the office of the minister? It is this: What is the real sense of Scripture? Then, if the teaching of the Bible happens to go contrary to my way of thinking, let me try to change not the teaching but the way of thinking. And if I am not willing to do this, I should say very plainly, I do not agree with the Bible.

---

[32] The addition "from God our Father and the Lord Jesus Christ" is not supported by the best texts (but see II Thess. 1:1).

[33] Cf. Andrew W. Blackwood, *The Fine Art of Public Worship,* Nashville, 1939, p. 153. (He is referring to the benediction at the conclusion of the service, but with respect to the point at issue this makes no essential difference.) See also W. Heyns, *Liturgiek,* Holland, Mich., 1903, p. 150: "It (the salutation) is a declaration of God that he dwells in the midst of the congregation in order to bless it with his grace and peace"; and A. Kuyper, *Onze Eeredienst,* Kampen, 1911, p. 196: "It is not the cordial wish of that man in the pulpit, who prays that whatever is good, including grace and peace, may come your way; but it is God Triune, who pronounces his grace and peace upon you, and who for that purpose uses his servant."

[34] To say that an implied optative indicates that the salutation "amounts to the expression of a *mere* wish" is an indication of a superficial and altogether too limited view of the meaning of the optative mood *in certain specific connections* in Biblical (LXX and New Testament) Greek.

A few examples will make this clear. According to Mark 11:14 Jesus said to the fig tree that produced nothing but leaves:

"Forevermore may no one eat fruit from you again." The verb (may eat) is in the optative mood. But this optative did not express "a *mere* wish." On the contrary, the wish was *effective.* It amounted to nothing less than pronouncing an effective curse upon that tree. As they passed by the next morning, the disciples saw the fig tree completely withered, to its very roots (Mark 11:20).

More to the point, we have a similar use of the optative in connection with the Aaronitic benediction (Num. 6:24-26). The *jussive* of the verbal forms in the Old Testament passage ("let it come to pass") very appropriately indicates *effective impartation,* not *mere* wishing but *effective* wishing. Note the optative mood in the LXX translation of this passage. See Gesenius-Kautzsch, *Hebrew Grammar,* Oxford, 1910, p. 321.

Now the fact that the traditional view is correct is clear both from the Old and from the New Testament. Note the following:

Num. 6:24-26:

Immediately after the words of the Aaronitic benediction we read, "So shall they put my name upon the children of Israel; and I will bless them." Hence, the act of pronouncing the benediction was viewed as an effectual *putting* of the name of Jehovah upon Israel, sothat his blessing would actually result.

Luke 10:5, 6:

"And when y o u enter into any house, first say, 'Peace to this house.' And if a son of peace be there, y o u r peace shall rest upon him; but if not, it shall turn back to y o u."

II John 3:

"Grace, mercy, and peace will be with us . . ." As was indicated earlier, the indicative mood is used. It is a declaration of something that will actually happen. This harmonizes completely with the idea of the expressed optative (Peter and Jude) or implied optative (Paul), when the latter is viewed as expressing an *effective* (not a *mere*) wish.

What Paul, writing officially as Christ's apostle, meant here in I Thess. 1:1 may, accordingly, be summed up as follows:

"May grace and peace rest upon y o u all. As God's official representative I (together with my associates Silas and Timothy) declare that this is what will actually happen."

Two objections should be answered:

(a) "But is it not true that God's grace and his peace *always* rest on the church?" True, indeed, but the effective wish or the declaration is that this grace and this peace shall be applied abundantly especially in connection with this particular service of public worship (for example, when this letter or any part of it is read).

(b) "Is not this a mechanical view?" Indeed not! These blessings are bestowed upon those – and *only* upon those – who are ready to receive them by faith. Read Luke 10:5, 6 quoted above.

2, 3. In letters written by men who were Paul's contemporaries the greeting is often followed by a statement which indicates that the person(s) addressed is being remembered in prayer to *the gods.* Hence, it is not surprising that Paul's epistles contain a similar item. (See also Rom. 1:8; I Cor. 1:4; Phil. 1:3; Col. 1:3; II Thess. 1:3; II Tim. 1:3; Philem. 4.) The resemblance, however, is in form but not in essence. The readers, many of whom were recent converts from the pagan world, must have been impressed by the fact that *this* letter is different. Paul and his companions have excluded the idol-gods from their letter as decisively as the Thessalonians had expelled them from their homes. The thanksgiving is here, but it is addressed to the one true God: **We give thanks to God always for you all.**

The verb "we give thanks" (εὐχαριστοῦμεν) is related to the noun "grace" (χάρις; see on 1:1, meaning d.). Paul and his companions thank God for the fruits of grace that were found in the hearts and lives of the church-members. They do this continually, never skipping a single day. They recognize the unity of faith, love, and hope which characterized the membership: "for you *all.*"

The main clause, "We give thanks," has three participial modifiers, as follows:

verse 2b: "making mention (of you) in our prayers"
verse 3: "continually bearing in mind your work. . . ."
verse 4: "knowing . . . your election . . ."

The first and the second of these clauses indicate the accompanying circumstances of the thanksgiving; that is, they show what Paul, Silas, and Timothy did when they gave thanks for the Thessalonians: how they would mention them by name, and would specify the spiritual fruits which adorned their lives (work resulting from faith, exertion prompted by love, endurance inspired by hope). The second clause, however, does more than this. It also begins to indicate *the reason why* the missionaries are so thankful. They express their gratitude because of these fruits! That is the *immediate* reason. But there is also an *ultimate* reason, which is expressed in the third participial modifier: "knowing your election."

Beginning with the first of these modifiers, Paul says: **making mention (of you) in our prayers.** It would seem that the missionaries prayed *unitedly* (in addition, of course, to praying individually). They may have taken turns in leading the devotions. These prayers were not marked by any vagueness. On the contrary, the needs of the various churches were mentioned one by one, as the occasion demanded. The thought is not excluded that individual members may have been mentioned by name.

Now such prayers consisted not only in a series of petitions, but also in thanksgivings, praises, words of adoration. God was given the honor that was due to him in view of the marvelous things he had done. In fact, that is exactly the point which receives the emphasis here, as is indicated in the second participial modifier: **continually bearing in mind your work resulting from faith and (your) exertion prompted by love and (your) endurance inspired by hope in our Lord Jesus Christ in the presence of our God and Father.**

With respect to the meaning of this beautiful passage commentators differ widely.[35] This is the first time the series *faith, hope, and love* occurs in

---

[35] The main theories are best represented by the various renderings which have been suggested, of which we shall mention three:

Paul's epistles. Here hope is mentioned last (faith . . . love . . . hope) in order to link it with "in our Lord Jesus Christ in the presence of our God and Father." In an epistle which deals so extensively with the subject of the confident expectation of (or the "waiting for") Christ's Return, it is

---

"remembering without ceasing" (or a similar clause):

(1) "your work of faith
and labour of love
and patience of hope."

We reject this for the simple reason that it makes little or no sense. What is "patience of hope" anyway?

(2) "your work, namely, faith
and labor, namely, love
and patience, namely, hope."

Aside from doctrinal objections, we reject this because, though it is grammatically possible, it can hardly be said to be true to the Pauline emphasis. Also, the concept, "patience, namely, hope," is difficult.

(3) "your active faith
and industrious love
and tenacious hope."

But this places the emphasis where, according to the original, it does not belong. The words stressed in the original are not faith, love and hope, but work, exertion (or labor), and endurance.

As we see it, the grammatical construction of the clause is as follows:

The nouns *work, exertion,* and *endurance* are object-genitives after the verb *bearing in mind* (being mindful *of*).

The word *your* modifies all three, hence, your work, your exertion, your endurance.

Each of these nouns has a modifier in the genitive. It matters little whether this is called "adjectival" or "descriptive" or "subjective" genitive or genitive "of source." All four terms have been used, but basically the idea is the same (though with a slight variation in emphasis). The idea is that the work is definitely *faith*-work, that is, it is work which springs from, is accomplished by, and reveals *faith.* Were it not for the presence of living faith, this work would not be in evidence. And so with the other modifiers: the exertion is prompted by (and reveals) love; and the endurance is inspired by (and gives evidence of) hope.

We construe *Lord Jesus Christ* to be objective genitive (hence, "in our Lord Jesus Christ") after the noun *hope,* which stands closest to it. That is the most natural construction, yields an excellent meaning, which, moreover, is in harmony with parallel passages (cf. 4:13; 5:8, 9; II Thess. 2:16). The fact that, thus construed, the third element in the series (work . . . exertion . . . *endurance* . . .) is of greater length than the other two does not worry us in the least. Paul is no lover of *"rigid* symmetry." He frequently lengthens (or at least varies) the last of several elements in a series. That makes for progression in thought. Note, for example, how in this very letter when the series "faith, love, hope" is mentioned in 5:8, the apostle enlarges on *hope* ("the hope of salvation, for . . ."). For the opposite view (according to which "our Lord Jesus Christ" belongs to all three items in the series, so that the meaning becomes: work . . . labor . . . hope, all three embracing him, or centering in him) see Lenski's diagram on p. 221 of his Commentary; and see Van Leeuwen (*Kommentaar,* p. 300; *Korte Verklaring,* pp. 15-17).

We do not see any need of linking "in the presence of" (ἔμπροσθεν) with the remote participle "bearing in mind" (μνημονεύοντες). Much more natural is the construction of this preposition with the immediately preceding words, just as in 2:19 and 3:13.

natural that the term *hope* is placed in a climactic position; just as it is natural that in I Cor. 13 *love* is stressed.

Paul thanks God for *the work* accomplished by these recent converts to the Christian religion. He does not immediately reveal what is meant by this *work.* It is probably best not to restrict the meaning too rigidly. Caring for the sick, comforting the dying, instructing the ignorant, all this and much more occurs to the mind. Yet, in view of verses 6-10 of this chapter, it would seem that the apostle (and those with him) is thinking especially of the work of making propaganda for the gospel, and doing this even in the midst of bitter persecution. This, indeed, was work *resulting from faith.* In fact, it was exertion (labor) *prompted by love.* Had there been no love in return for the love of which they were the objects, these Thessalonians would never have been able to accomplish what they did. That they did accomplish the almost unbelievable will be pointed out in connection with verses 6-10.

When we speak of love-labor, we are prone to look only for deeds that can be seen, weighed, and measured. But *suffering* for the name and sake of Christ also falls under the heading of "exertion prompted by love." It implies *endurance.* A person who suffers such persecution is willing, if need be, to *remain under* (cf. the verb ὑπομένω) stress and strain, *confidently expecting* that *in the very presence of the God who will one day judge all men* he will find a safe shelter with his *Lord Jesus Christ* (on this designation see 1:1); in other words, his endurance is "inspired by hope in our Lord Jesus Christ in the presence of our God and Father." (On God the Father – here *our God and Father* – see 1:1.)

4. knowing, brothers beloved by God, y o u r election . . .

In the final analysis, the reason for the joy and gratitude which fill the hearts of the missionaries is the fact that they know that (speaking by and large) the members of the Thessalonian church are God's *chosen* ones. Paul, Silas, and Timothy actually *know* this. They *know* (knowing εἰδότες, is the participle used) it because the facts speak so clearly that the conclusion is inevitable, direct, immediate. This passage is a most forceful repudiation of the position of those who say that one can never really know whether he or whether anybody else is included in God's eternal decree of election. The missionaries had become acquainted with the readers in the recent past. After a very brief stay among them, they had been forced to move on. Nevertheless, they do not hesitate to state, "The ultimate reason why thanksgiving fills our hearts is that *we know* that y o u were chosen (from eternity)." [36]

---

[36] Excellent are the practical remarks with reference to this in the book by H. Veldkamp, *In De Schemering Van Christus' Wederkomst,* Kampen, 1928, pp. 20-25.

The noun *election* also occurs in the following passages of Paul's epistles: Rom. 9:11; 11:5, 7, 28 (cf. II Peter 1:10).

The apostle, who was himself an "elect vessel" (Acts 9:15), dwells on the theme of sovereign election in such passages as the following (in addition to those already mentioned): Rom. 8:33; 11:29; 16:13; I Cor. 1:27, 28; Eph. 1:4-6; Col. 3:12-17; II Tim. 2:10, 19; Titus 1:1. There are several additional passages which, though not containing the word *elect*, are of value for the study of this subject; e.g., Rom. 8:28-30; I Cor. 4:7; Eph. 2:8; Phil. 4:3.[37]

On the basis of all these passages, Paul's teaching on election can be summarized as follows:

(1) It (election) is from eternity (Eph. 1:4, 5).

(2) It becomes evident in life (I Thess. 1:4). This does not mean that anyone has the right to assign his neighbor to hell or to call him a reprobate: *God* sees the heart; *we* do not. Also, *we* are not infallibly inspired, as Paul's teaching was. There may be a death-bed conversion.

(3) It is sovereign and unconditional; that is, it is not conditioned on foreseen works or foreseen faith (I Cor. 1:27, 28; 4:7; Eph. 1:4; 2:8). See also *Canons of Dort*, I, ix, x.

(4) It is just (Rom. 9:14, 15).

(5) It is not limited to Gentiles; in every age a remnant of the Jews is also included (Rom. 11:5).

(6) It is immutable and effectual; the elect actually reach heaven at last. They obtain salvation (Rom. 11:7). God's "chain" cannot be broken (Rom. 8:28-30; cf. 11:29; II Tim. 2:19).

(7) It affects life in all its phases, is not abstract. Although election belongs to God's decree from eternity, it becomes a dynamic force in the hearts and lives of God's children. That is clearly also the meaning here in I Thess. 1:4; see verses 5-10. It produces such fruits as adoption as sons, calling, faith, justification, etc. (Rom. 8:28-30, 33; Eph. 1:4, 5; Titus 1:1). *The proposition: "If a man has been elected, he will be saved regardless of how he lives (e.g., whether or not he believes in Christ, whether or not he gives evidence of possessing the fruits of the Holy Spirit)," is wicked and absurd. No true and sane believer of any denomination, whether he be Methodist, Baptist, Calvinist, Lutheran, or whether he belongs to any other denomination or religious group, will ever subscribe to it. Everyone should read and reread the beautiful description of the truly elect person which is found in Col. 3:12-17.*

---

[37] See also N.T.C. on John 15:19; H. Bavinck, *The Doctrine Of God* (translated by W. Hendriksen), Grand Rapids, Mich., 1951, pp. 337-407; and L. Berkhof, *Systematic Theology*, Grand Rapids, Mich., 1949, pp. 109-125. The term *elect* does not always refer to the divine decree; see Luke 10:42; John 6:70; Acts 1:24; 6:5, cf. Deut. 4:37; 7:6-8; I Sam. 10:24, etc.

(8) It concerns individuals (Rom. 16:13; Phil. 4:3; cf. Acts 9:15).

(9) It comprehends these individuals "in Christ," sothat they are definitely viewed as one body (Eph. 1:4; II Tim. 2:10).

(10) It is an election not only unto salvation but definitely also (as a link in the chain) unto service (Col. 3:12-17; cf. Acts 9:15, 16).

(11) It is taught not only by Paul, but also by Jesus himself. See N.T.C. on John 6:39; 10:11, 14, 28; 17:2, 9, 11, 24.

(12) It has as its final aim God's glory, and it is the work of his delight (Eph. 1:4-6).

The elect are called "brothers beloved by God." Paul loves the designation *brothers,* using it again and again (I Thess. 1:4; 2:1, 9, 14, 17; 3:7; 4:1, 10, 13; 5:1, 4, 12, 14, 25, 26, 27; II Thess. 1:3; 2:1, 13, 15; 3:1, 6, 13; and many times in the other epistles). In the present instance he adds the beautiful description "beloved of God" (cf. II Thess. 2:13; further also Rom. 1:7; 11:28; 12:19; 16:8, 9, 12; I Cor. 4:14, 17, etc.). Because of its combination with the word "of God" it would seem probable that the deepest and fullest sense must be ascribed to the participle (pl. mascul., perfect passive) *beloved.* See N.T.C. on John 21:15-17. This love of God extends backward to eternity, as the preceding context clearly implies. It also extends forward and is still continuing (as is implied in the tense of the participle). No one can ever separate believers from the love of God in Christ. Moreover, as the parallel passages indicate, *God's* beloved ones are also *Paul's* (and Silas' and Timothy's) beloved ones.

5. But how is it to be explained that the missionaries have a right to be so convinced about the fact that these Thessalonians are God's elect? The reason is given in the verses which follow, which should be considered as a unit (verses 5-10); to begin with: **inasmuch as our gospel did not come to you in words only but also in power and in the Holy Spirit and full assurance.**

The meaning is: "that you were chosen (elected) we know from the fact that our gospel did not come to you in words only," etc.

As we see it, the sense of the entire passage (verses 5-10) can be summarized as follows: "Do not be deceived by the enemies of the faith who are trying, by means of an attack on our integrity, to undermine your faith and your assurance of salvation. Our behavior among you was proof of our integrity and of the reliability of our message. Your own joyful acceptance of the gospel which we preached, sothat you began to spread the news everywhere, and turned away from those idols of yours to serve the living God and to await his Son from heaven, clearly indicate that what happened (and is happening) in Thessalonica was (is) wrought by the Holy Spirit and was (is) the fruit of election. Any doubt about the genuine character of y o u r faith was removed by Timothy. (See on 3:5.) So continue stedfastly."

In order to confirm the faith of the Thessalonians Paul, accordingly, does two things: he shows:

a. that the message which they had received and the messengers who brought it could be trusted. See verse 5.

b. that the manner in which they received it was proof of the operation of the Spirit of God. See verses 6-10.

Just as at Corinth (I Cor. 2:4), where Paul was carrying on his missionary activity while he was writing this letter, so also at Thessalonica, he was not interested in mere *words* (I Cor. 2:4) but in a genuine demonstration of the Spirit. To this the people addressed will readily testify. The original has the singular — "in *word,* in a mere *discourse.*" There was spiritual *dynamite* (δύναμις) in the message, enough dynamite to demolish the idol-gods (verse 9). In fact, the dynamite *of the Spirit* was of a different kind than physical dynamite, for whereas the latter is limited to *de*structive operations, this dynamite was also *con*structive ("to serve God, the living and real One," etc.). Notice how the concepts *Spirit* and *power* go together here, as so often (see Rom. 1:4; 15:13, 19; I Cor. 2:4; Gal. 3:5; and cf. Rom. 1:4, II Tim. 1:7, 8). This is in accordance with Christ's promise (Acts 1:8. Cf. also Luke 1:17, 35; 4:14; Acts 10:38). The reason why there was such power in the message was because when *Paul* (and those associated with him) spoke, *God* was speaking. This also accounts for the fact that the missionaries had spoken *with full assurance* (a word — used also in Col. 2:2; Heb. 6:11; 10:22; cf. the verb in Luke 1:1; Rom. 4:21; 14:5; Col. 4:12; II Tim. 4:5, 17 — which without even the addition of an article is linked immediately with *the Holy Spirit,* for the full assurance is an immediate effect of the Spirit's presence and power in the hearts of the ambassadors). Because of the immediately preceding and the immediately following context, it would seem that those commentators are wrong who confine this assurance to *the Thessalonians.* The reference here is (at least primarily) to the full assurance *of the missionaries* as they spoke the word.

Paul appeals to the memory of those addressed when he adds: **just as y o u (well) know what kind of men we became among y o u for y o u r sake.** All kinds of traveling philosophers were roving about in the world of that day. They plied their trade for their own sake, in their own interest. Paul, Silas, and Timothy were different. They carried on their difficult tasks for the sake of the people, that they might be saved. In that spirit and frame of mind they had entered Thessalonica, and the experiences which they had endured there had added to their spiritual vigor (hence, it is not at all necessary to weaken the sense of the verb "became").

The obverse side of the events that had recently transpired at Thessalonica (the side which shows how the good news had affected *the Thessalonians*) is shown in the verses which follow.

6, 7. And you became imitators of us and of the Lord.

The genuine character of the religious experience of the Thessalonians is portrayed here. They had become *imitators* (μιμηταί, our word *mimickers* is from the same root), not merely *talkers*. Cf. I Thess. 2:14; then also I Cor. 4:16; 11:1; Eph. 5:1; Heb. 6:12. Paul is not afraid to say, "You must be imitators *of me*" (I Cor. 4:16). He dares to say this because, by sovereign grace, he is able to add, ". . . as I also am *of Christ*" (I Cor. 11:1). And those who are imitators of Paul and of Christ are also imitators *of God* (Eph. 5:1). Thus the arrow points back from Paul (and his associates), to Christ, to God. That is the logical order. That is also why here in I Thess. 1:6 "of us" precedes "of the Lord." The missionaries had been physically present with them. Even before any conversion had taken place, the earnestness, devotion, enthusiasm, willingness to suffer for Christ, etc., of the missionaries could be seen and watched. These missionaries, in turn, pointed to and spoke about *the Lord* (see on I Thess. 1:1 for the title).

Now it is not possible to imitate Christ in every respect. For example, in his capacity as the Savior of men he cannot be imitated. But *the third of comparison* (the point with reference to which both the missionaries and the Christ who commissioned them can be imitated) is clearly stated in the words: **when amid great tribulation you welcomed the word with joy imparted by the Holy Spirit.** Rejoicing amid *tribulation* (for the meaning of the term see N.T.C. on John 16:33) was something about which Paul and Silas could tell a very touching story! And the story had reference to an event that had occurred just before the missionaries had wended their way toward Thessalonica. At Philippi they had been cast into a dungeon, their feet fastened in the stocks. But about midnight Paul and Silas had been singing hymns to God! And this is only one illustration of their rejoicing amid tribulation. Jesus, too, had rejoiced in the midst of tribulation. See N.T.C. on John 12:20-36 and on 16:33. Hence, when amid similar pressure (see p. 9) those who are here addressed had *welcomed the word* (the gospel of salvation) with Spirit-wrought joy, they had given unmistakable evidence of being imitators of the missionaries and of Christ himself. (In this connection read the beautiful passage: Acts 5:41.) They had proved themselves to be *God's elect.* The connection with I Thess. 1:4 must not be lost sight of.

Now *imitators* become *examples.* There is a kind of *circle* here: first, God performs his works on earth: the Father elects; the Son (and also his special ambassadors) gives an example of rejoicing amid suffering; the Holy Spirit imparts joy. Then the Thessalonians believe, welcome the word, become imitators. They, in turn, carry the good news to others, whose praises (after also *they* have experienced the great change) glorify God in heaven. Thus the circle has been completed. The Thessalonians, as it were, stand in the middle: the word of the Lord came to them, and they, having accepted it by faith, have sounded it forth sothat others also might hear and believe. That this is the right interpretation is shown by what follows immediately: **sothat y o u became an example to all the believers in Macedonia and in Achaia.** One who is not an *imitator* cannot become an *example* (τύπος, derived from τύπτω; hence, the *mark* of a blow, the *figure* made by it; see N.T.C. on John 2:25; further, *image,* Acts 7:43; *mould,* Acts 23:25; and thus *model* or *pattern* for imitation, Acts 7:44; Phil. 3:17). To all believers in the two Roman provinces of *Macedonia* (here, besides Thessalonica itself, was Philippi and Berea) and *Achaia* (here was Athens and Corinth) the Thessalonian converts had become an example. The reason, in exact correspondence with the preceding, is set forth in the following words:

8. For, from y o u the word of the Lord has echoed forth. We repeat what was said in connection with verses 6 and 7: the Thessalonians stood in the middle. They are here compared to a parabolic arch or a sounding-board which re-inforces sounds and causes them to travel in various directions. The arch or the sounding-board does not of itself create the sounds. It occupies a middle-position, receiving them, re-inforcing them, and sending them on. Thus also the word of the Lord, having been received by those people in Thessalonica who are here addressed, had been re-inforced by their own joyful experience in accepting it, and, thus strengthened, had been *echoed* forth (the verb is ἐξήχηται; our word *echo* is related to it), and this **not only in Macedonia and Achaia**[38] **but in every place y o u r faith toward God has gone forth, sothat it is not necessary for us to say anything.** When Paul says, "in every place," he must mean "also in regions outside of Macedonia and Achaia"; hence, probably also *at least* in Palestine, Syria, and Asia Minor. It should be borne in mind that the populous trading-center, Thessalonica, was so located (on the Egnatian Highway, thus linking the East with the West, and at the head of the Thermaic Gulf, thus connecting it with harbors all over the then-known world) that news could spread very quickly to regions far and near. All the believers at Thessalonica had to do was avail themselves of the opportunities which their strategic location afforded. Now the point certainly is not that merely the rumor with reference to the great change at Thessalonica had been spreading, but rather that the believers there, in the enthusiasm of a great discovery, actively propagated their "faith toward God." The preposition *toward* (πρός; see also N.T.C. on John 1:1) prepares us for the prepo-

---

[38] Perhaps here viewed as a unit; we might say: *Greece,* but the correct reading is somewhat uncertain: it cannot be established with certainty whether the definite article here in verse 8 also precedes Achaia.

sition *from* in the next verse: they had turned *from* idols, *toward* God. There had been a complete turn-about in the direction of their lives.

But how did *Paul* know all this? It must be assumed that he had by this time received messages from these various centers. That is not strange at all. Good highways connected the cities of the Roman world, and travel, though slow compared to our own day and age, was not nearly as retarded as some commentators (who reject Thessalonians because of the facts related here in verses 7-10) seem to think. Paul naturally was anxious to relate to all who came to him what great things God had accomplished in Thessalonica. But before he could even get started, the visitors were telling him what they had heard! Well, Paul did not mind that at all. He rather enjoyed it, as is clear from the words:

9. for they themselves are reporting about us, what kind of entering in we had among y o u, and how y o u turned to God from those idols (of y o u r s), to serve God, the living and real One.

Paul and his companions do not need to report. People *are doing* (note present continuative tense) this for them. The missionaries hear the report. Others also hear it. The missionaries hear that others hear it. It is the great news about Paul, Silas, and Timothy ("about *us*") and what God has accomplished through them. The tidings, coming from all the regions which had been penetrated by the faith of the Thessalonians, are spreading far and wide.

Now this report, circulated from mouth to mouth, contains two main topics, the second of which is again divided into two subordinate news-items, as follows:

A. "Paul, Silas, and Timothy entered in among the Thessalonians in such and such a manner." (As a result, through the operation of the Spirit)

B. "The Thessalonians turned to God from *the* idols" (meaning: from those idols of theirs):

1 "to serve a God living and real

and

2 "to await his Son out of the heavens, whom he raised from the dead, Jesus, who rescues us from the wrath to come."

Various corroborative details are undoubtedly added: there is amplification and clarification.

Naturally, Paul in writing *to the Thessalonians* changes the direct to the indirect form of discourse: in the present instance the pronoun "they" becomes "we," "the Thessalonians" (or something similar) becomes "y o u," and there is undoubtedly abbreviation. Hence, we read:

A. ". . . *how* we entered in among *y o u,* and

B. *"how y o u* turned to God from the idols:

1 "to serve a God living and real

and

2 "to await his Son from heaven, whom he raised from the dead, Jesus, who rescues us from the wrath to come."

The "entering in" (εἴσοδος also 2:1; cf. Acts 13:24; Heb. 10:19; II Peter 1:11) of which Paul speaks must not be viewed as a mere "introduction," as is done by some ("how we were introduced to you"). It has reference to whatever pertained to the coming of the missionaries to Thessalonica and to their work in and outside of the synagogue. The commentary is supplied by Paul himself in I Thess. 1:5 and 2:1-12; see on these verses. What Paul means, therefore, is this: "The charges that are being leveled against us by base opponents are vain. Our way of operating when we came to you and worked among you has become a matter of public knowledge. You yourselves remember it, and others far and wide have heard about it."

And how you turned. A very significant verb is used (ἐπεστρέψατε from ἐπιστρέφω): *to turn,* often *to return,* but here obviously not the latter but the former. The readers (many of whom must have been Gentiles, for they had been worshipping idols) had experienced a real, inner change which had become outwardly manifest: their whole active life was now moving in the opposite direction: *away from* (ἀπό) idols, *to* (πρός; see N.T.C. on John 1:1) God.[39]

When God *converts* a man, he changes the entire person, not only *the emotions,* sothat one *regrets* his former manner of life (cf. the idea which predominates in the verb μεταμέλομαι), but also *the mind and will,* with respect to which he experiences a complete change-over (cf. the thought that is placed in the foreground by μετάνοια [40]), and all of this becomes apparent in his *outward conduct* (this being the main import of the verb used here in I Thess. 1:9).

It was from *the* [41] *idols* (both the images themselves and the deities

---

[39] For the various terms used in Scripture to indicate *conversion,* and a discussion of their meaning, see L. Berkhof, *Systematic Theology,* Grand Rapids, Mich., 1949, pp. 480-492; R. C. Trench, *Synonyms of the New Testament,* Grand Rapids, Mich., 1948 (reprint), par. lxix. On the synonym μετάνοια see especially W. D. Chamberlain, *The Meaning of Repentance,* Philadelphia, 1943.

[40] Though mind and will are in the foreground when μετάνοια is used, the emotions are not excluded: complete "transformation" or "conversion" is meant. The word looks forward as well as backward; hence, "repentance," a term which merely looks backward, is not the proper translation, and, of course, "penance" is even worse. An excellent study-passage in this connection is II Cor. 7:8-10, in the original.

[41] Generic use of the article. This comprehends the class as a single whole, definitely present to the mind of the writer (and, of course, to the mind of the reader), especially from the point of view of this or that characteristic: the idols in all their helplessness! In such a case the article should not be omitted in the translation (hence not: "from idols"), for if this is done one loses the flavor of the original. I would suggest that in translating such a generic article, one either simply retain it

whom they represented) that the Thessalonians had turned away. The apostle and his companions had observed this idol-worship, and knew all about it. These idols were merely "vain things" (see the parallel passage, Acts 14:15). They were dead; hence, totally unable to render any assistance to anyone in time of need.

Now it must have been a momentous change, this turning away from the idols. It is not easy to reject and eject gods which one has worshipped from the days of childhood, and which by one's ancestors, from hoary antiquity, have always been considered very real, sothat their names and individual peculiarities have become household-words. It amounts to nothing less than a religious revolution. The enemies were right when they said that the missionaries were men who "turned the world upside down." Idol-worship affected life in all its phases. And we can well imagine that especially to the Thessalonians these deities had seemed very real, for it must be borne in mind that Mt. Olympus, whose celebrated summit was considered the home of the gods, was close by, only about fifty miles to the S.W. And according to tradition, when Zeus shook his ambrosial curls, that mighty mountain trembled!

Nevertheless, as a result of the operation of God's grace whereby the message was applied to the hearts, the eyes of the Thessalonians had been opened, sothat they saw that their idols were vanities. They had turned from them to *a God living and real.* Here the true God is not so much pointed out as described. All the emphasis is on his character, which is the very opposite of the idols. *They* are dead, *he* is living. *They* are unreal, *he* is real, genuine. *They* are unable to help, he is almighty and eager to help. To this God the Thessalonians have turned *to serve* him continually, submitting themselves to him as completely as does a slave to his master, nay *far more completely* and *far more willingly*.[42]

Now, turning to a God living and real implies turning to his only-begotten Son and salvation through him; hence, there follows:

10. and to await his Son out of the heavens. It seems that it was especially the teaching with reference to Christ's return upon the clouds of

---

in English (hence, "the idols") or else — in order to bring out its force even more clearly — choose as its English equivalent the demonstrative (hence *"those idols* which y o u used to serve," or simply "those idols of y o u r s"). Cf. a similar use of the article in Matt. 8:20 ("the foxes"), and with a noun in the sing. Luke 10:7 ("the laborer"); I Tim. 3:2 ("the overseer or bishop"). In the use of the generic article (as well as the article with abstract nouns) German and Dutch usage more nearly approaches the Greek than does English usage. Here in I Thess. 1:9 the German "von den Abgöttern" and the Dutch "van de afgoden" is very normal.

[42] For that reason I do not favor the translation *to be slaves of.* Although that rendering does bring out the idea of complete submission, it clashes with the voluntary and joyful character of the worship that is rendered to God. See also N.T.C. on John 15:15.

heaven that had captivated the minds and hearts of the readers. *As they saw it — and rightly so — a man is not truly converted (or "turned," verse 9) unless he glories in this doctrine and shows its force in his life.* For them true conversion implied (at least) these two things: a. turning away from the idols, and b. turning to God and to his Son who is coming *out of the heavens* (cf. Eph. 4:10 for the plural; and for the idea of the descent see 4:16; II Thess. 1:7; then also Dan. 7:1; Matt. 24:30; 25:31-46; 26:64; Acts 3:21; and Rev. 1:7).

From the heaven of heavens (where in a special sense dwells God surrounded by the redeemed and the angels), and the starry heaven, and the heaven of the clouds, Jesus will descend to take into his embrace his people. This coming they are *awaiting.* The force of the verb *to await* must not be lost sight of. It means *to look forward to with patience and confidence.* This *awaiting* means far more than merely *saying,* "I believe in Jesus Christ, who ascended into heaven, and from thence he shall come to judge the living and the dead." It implies (both in Greek and in English) *being ready* for his return. When you *await* a visitor, you have prepared everything for his coming. You have arranged the guest-room, the program of activities, your time and your other duties, and all this in such a manner that the visitor will feel perfectly at home. So also, awaiting the very *Son of God* (see N.T.C. on John 1:14) who is coming out of the heavens implies the sanctified heart and life.

This Son of God who is coming out of the heavens is none other than the "historical" **Jesus** (see on 1:1), the very One whom God actually and physically raised from the dead (cf. Rom. 4:24, 25; 8:11; I Cor. 15:15; Gal. 1:1; Eph. 1:20; Col. 2:12; II Tim. 2:8; and cf. N.T.C. on John 20:1-10).

The thought of his coming does not spell terror for the believer. Rather, "the lord is at hand . . . in nothing be anxious!" (Phil. 4:5, 6), for it is this Jesus **who rescues** (is rescuing) **us from the wrath to come** (the coming wrath). Jesus, *the Savior* (see on 1:1) is ever true to his name: he *saves, rescues.* He does not rescue everybody but *us* (Paul, Silas, Timothy, believers at Thessalonica, all the elect).

From *the settled indignation* (ὀργή) which by nature rests on the sinner (Eph. 2:3), and which by his idolatry and immorality and especially (in the case of those who have heard the good news) by his rejection of the gospel he daily increases, and which will be revealed most fully in the coming day of judgment, Jesus delivers all those who embrace him by living faith. For the concept *wrath* see also N.T.C. on John 3:36. In II Thess. 1:5-12 (see on that passage) Paul amplifies the thought of 1:10.

The Synthesis is found at the end of chapter 2.

CHAPTER II

I THESSALONIANS **2:1**

2 1 Indeed, you yourselves know, brothers, our entering in among you, that
it was not empty-handed. 2 On the contrary, though we had previously suffered and had been shamefully treated at Philippi as you know, still by the help
of our God we summoned courage to tell you the good news[43] of God with profound solicitude.[44] 3 For our appeal (does) not (spring) from delusion or from
impurity nor (does it come) with deceit. 4 On the contrary, as we have been
approved by God to be entrusted with the good news, so we are accustomed to
tell it, as pleasing not men but God who tests our hearts. 5 Indeed, we never
came with flattering speech, as you (well) know, or with a pretext for greed—God
is witness! — 6 or seeking honor from men, whether from yourselves or from others,
although we were in a position to make ourselves formidable as apostles of Christ.
7 But we were gentle in the midst of you, as when a nurse cherishes her own
children: 8 so, being affectionately desirous of you, we gladly shared with you
not only the gospel of God but also our own souls, because you had become very
dear to us. 9 For you remember, brothers, our toil and hardship: by night and
by day (we were) working at a trade, in order not to be a burden to any of you
while we proclaimed to you the gospel of God. 10 You (are) witness and (so
is) God, how piously[45] and righteously and blamelessly we conducted ourselves in
the estimation of you, believers; 11 just as you know how, like a father (dealing)
with his own children (so we were) admonishing each and all of you, and encouraging and testifying 12 that you should live lives worthy of God, who calls
you into his own kingdom and glory.

2:1-12

2:1. Indeed, you yourselves know, brothers, our entering in among you, that it was not empty-handed.

A careful study of Paul's Defence shows that the slander by means of which his enemies were trying to undermine the influence of his message amounted to this: "Paul and his associates are deluded individuals who for selfish reasons and with trickery are trying to exploit the people." For

---

[43] We generally speak of "proclaiming (or preaching) the gospel" and of "telling good news." As the verb which is used here in the original is *telling* rather than *proclaiming*, I have here given as the English equivalent: to tell you the good news.

[44] Or "with deep anxiety (concern)" or "with strenuous exertion." Not, however, "in spite of heavy opposition."

[45] Or *holily*

the sake of the gospel this charge had to be answered, in order that suspicion might be swept aside. The opponents knew very well what they were doing. They reasoned thus: "If we succeed in awakening distrust with respect to *the messengers, the message* will die a natural death." Accordingly, Paul had no choice: love for the gospel necessitated self-defence.

For the meaning of the expression "our entering in" see on 1:9. It is the apostle's contention that this entering in had not been *empty* (κενή). The question is, "Just what is meant by *empty?*" Does Paul mean, "Our entering in has not been *futile;* there were results"? Thus the term is explained by some. However, no one denied this. Every one knew that the work of the missionaries had borne fruit. Besides, if that should be the meaning here, it is very difficult to establish any connection between this verse and those which immediately follow. But the word used in the original may also mean *empty-handed;* e.g., "And they took him and beat him and sent him away empty-handed" (Mark 12:3; cf. Luke 1:53; 20:10, 11). According to this meaning of the word, what Paul is saying is this: "Far from aiming to take something away from y o u, we *brought* y o u something. When we came to y o u, our hands were not empty." We adopt this interpretation for the following reasons:

(1) It harmonizes beautifully with the preceding context; see 1:5: "our gospel did not come to y o u in words only but also in power and in the Holy Spirit and with full assurance." The message had not been empty: it was filled with divine meaning, being the good news which came from God. It was accompanied by power and the Holy Spirit, and it was presented with firm conviction.

(2) It also matches the following context, in which Paul stresses the fact that he (and his associates) had come to Thessalonica with the good news from God, with courage, and with real, deep-seated concern for the people. Truly, the hands of the missionaries had not been empty! They had something to bring, something to give away.

(3) It is in keeping with the general trend of Paul's defence against the malicious insinuations coming from the camp of the evil one. Throughout the apostle represents himself as one who did *not* come *to take* but *to give* (see especially 2:5, 8, 9). And what was true with respect to himself was true also with respect to Silas and Timothy.

Once this interpretation of verse 1 is adopted, what follows is not difficult:

2. On the contrary, though we had previously suffered and had been shamefully treated at Philippi as y o u know, still by the help of God we summoned courage to tell y o u the good news of God with profound solicitude.

For the treatment which the missionaries (especially Paul and Silas) had received at Philippi read Acts 16:11-40; also see on 1:6, 7. We do not share the view of those who think that when Paul spoke of having been *shamefully treated* (insulted, abused), he was referring only to the fact that he and Silas, uncondemned men, *had been beaten publicly though they were Roman citizens.* That was *part* of the shameful treatment but not all of it: the men – Roman citizens, yes; apostles of Jesus Christ besides! – had been arrested, dragged into the market-place before the rulers, slandered, robbed of their clothing, thrown into a prison with their feet made fast in the stocks, etc. The verb employed in the original (study its use in Acts 14:5; then Matt. 22:6 and Luke 18:32) is comprehensive enough in meaning to include *all* this insolent treatment to which the missionaries had been exposed and which had caused them much suffering.

Nevertheless (i.e., in spite of this suffering and shameful treatment), *by virtue of their union with God* (ἐν τῷ θεῷ), hence, by his help, they had summoned courage [46] to continue the work. They had done what Jesus had enjoined, "When they persecute you in this city, flee into the next" (Matt. 10:23). Thus a journey of a hundred miles had brought them to Thessalonica. Their interest in this city did not spring from any selfish motive. They desired most eagerly to tell, in plain language and in a forthright manner, the good news of God, uttering (note the verb λαλῆσαι) the message which God himself had given them, and doing this with profound solicitude (deep anxiety) for the people involved. The phrase ἐν πολλῷ ἀγῶνι has been interpreted variously, as follows:

a. "in spite of heavy opposition" (cf. A.V. "with much contention"; A.R.V. "in much conflict," which may also be linked with b.)

b. "in great anguish"

c. "with strenuous exertion"

d. "with profound solicitude (deep concern or anxiety)"

The term (ἀγών) refers first to a gathering, especially for games or contests; then the contest itself, and finally the *agony* (cf. the Greek word), anguish, or anxiety that is connected with it, or also any kind of agony, anguish, or anxiety, concern or solicitude. Hence, viewed by itself (apart from the context) it could have any of the four meanings listed above. The context, however, seems to favor c. and d. (there is not much difference between these two). The *affectionate desire* or *yearning* of the missionaries for the people of Thessalonica is mentioned also in verse 8 (and see verse 11). Paul and his companions had exerted themselves to the utmost, as an athlete who is aiming for the prize, in order that they might do the will of God (2:4) and might win these people for whom they yearned so earnestly.

Now this profound solicitude or affectionate desire was, of course, the

---

[46] In this context the ingressive or inceptive aorist seems the most natural.

very opposite of the base selfishness of which their enemies accused them. Hence, Paul continues:

3. For our appeal (does) not (spring) from delusion or from impurity nor (does it come) with deceit.

The noun and the verb *appeal* (παράκλησις, παρακαλέω related to παράκλητος; see N.T.C. on John 14:16), basically a calling to one's side, can have various meanings: appeal or entreat(y), exhort(ation), encourage(ment), comfort. The exact meaning depends on the context in each instance. Here *appeal* or *entreaty* (cf. the use of the verb in II Cor. 5:20), fits as well as any. It was the message by means of which the missionaries, clothed with authority from God and with yearning sympathy, had pleaded with the hearers to forsake their wicked ways and to turn to God in Christ.

Now in connection with this appeal, the slur from the side of the opponents probably amounted to this:

a. "Their appeal springs from error. They are self-deluded imposters."

b. "Their motives are not pure."

Did these opponents ascribe sexual uncleanliness to Paul, Silas, and Timothy? – Pagan religions were characterized by immorality – . Did they perhaps insinuate that it was strange that so many *women* were to be found among the converts? Cf. Acts 17:4. The context, however, does not point in that direction. Desire for *money* and a hankering after *honor,* rather than sexual abberation, seem to have been the vices of which they accused the missionaries.

c. "They use trickery (guile, deceit) to capture their audience." The world of that day was full of roaming "philosophers," jugglers, sorcerers, fakers, swindlers. In order to impress their audiences many tricks were used. See on II Thess. 2:9; then also Matt. 24:24; Rev. 13:14.

Now here in verse 3 Paul denies all three charges. Then he places the truth over against the lie. It is characteristic of Paul to employ this method of argumentation: direct refutation of the charge, followed by a positive assertion (see 1:5; 2:3, 4; 2:5 ff.).

Paul is his own best commentator. Notice:

"Our appeal does not spring from delusion (or *error*)." Commentary: "We have been approved by God to be entrusted with the good news" (verse 4).

". . . or from impurity" (impure motives). Commentary: "We never came with flattery . . . a disguise for greed . . . seeking honor from men" (verses 5, 6). The very opposite is the truth. Our motives were wholly unselfish: "being affectionately desirous of y o u, we gladly shared with y o u not only the gospel of God but also our own selves" (verse 8).

"nor (does it come) with deceit." Commentary: "Y o u (are) witnesses and (so is) God, how piously and righteously and blamelessly we conducted ourselves" (verse 10).

4. On the contrary, as we have been approved by God to be entrusted with the good news, so we are accustomed to tell it, as pleasing not men but God who tests our hearts.

Not error but truth, the good news that comes from God, had been the objective source of Paul's appeal to the Thessalonians. These three official ambassadors *had been approved* by God and therefore *stand approved* (the perfect of abiding result of a verb which in the present tense means *to test;* perfect tense, *to have been tested,* here: with favorable results; hence, *approved;* cf. II Macc. 4:3). For the divine approbation entrusting Paul, Silas, and Timothy with the gospel of salvation, the following passages come into consideration: Acts 9:15; 13:1-4; 15:40; 16:1, 2; I Tim. 1:2, 12, 18; 6:12, 20; II Tim. 1:5, 13, 14.

Now it was in strict accordance with God's directive, that these missionaries were always telling (note present continuative) the good news. Hence, their message was not an error, but truth springing from the highest source. And the motive in bringing it was not selfish — for instance, pleasing men in order to gain favor; cf. Gal. 1:10 — but most commendable: pleasing God (cf. 4:1; II Thess. 2:4), the One before whom nothing is hid, and who tests our hearts (see Jer. 17:10; then 11:20; Ps. 7:9; Ps. 139). The human eye cannot discern the inner motive of his fellowman, whether good or bad; hence, Paul, as it were, appeals to God's omniscience.

5, 6. Indeed, we never came with flattering speech, as you (well) know, or with a pretext for greed — God is witness! — or seeking honor from men, whether from yourselves or from others, although we were in a position to make ourselves formidable as apostles of Christ.

Not any impure but the purest possible motive had been the subjective source of the entreaty. To prove this, Paul permits the facts to speak for themselves. By saying, "as you (well) know," he appeals to the readers' memory of these facts. Had the motive been impure and selfish (see verse 3), the missionaries would have copied the charlatans who roamed the country. Like these quacks they too would have made use of flattery. And their message would have amounted to nothing more than *a pretext to cover up their greed.*[47] But with an appeal to God the writer of this

---

[47] It makes little difference whether "of greed" is viewed as objective genitive: *a pretext for greed* (to cover up greed) or as subjective genitive: *a pretext of greed* (produced by greed, used by greed as a cover-up). The resultant idea is about the same. The rendering *a cloke (cloak) of covetousness* (A.V.; A.R.V.; R.S.V.: *a cloak for greed*) is also excellent, though *pretext* (something that is woven *in front*) or *pretense* (something that is spread *in front*) — hence, *a disguise* — brings out more precisely the meaning of the prefix in the Greek word. Note also that while

epistle solemnly affirms that they have never made use of either flattery or disguise. Their aim, moreover, had never been to seek human fame (see N.T.C. on John 5:41), whether from the Thessalonians or from anybody else; and this in spite of the fact that they were in a position to make *weighty* claims with respect to themselves, being Christ's apostles (used in the broader sense) commissioned to represent him, and therefore invested with authority over life and doctrine. For *apostle* see N.T.C. on John 13:16; 20:21-23.

7. But we were gentle in the midst of y o u.

Over against *formidable* stands *gentle.*[48] The Thessalonians had discovered that these missionaries were affable, easy to speak to. They were mild, kind in their dealings. Paul's own commentary on this word *gentle* is found in verses 8, 9, 11, as well as in the remainder of verse 7: **as when a nurse cherishes her own children.** The sense, in all probability, is not "as when a nurse takes care of the children of her mistress," namely, the children that had been entrusted to the care of this nurse; but "as when a mother-nurse warms, fondles, cherishes the children that are *her very own* (because she gave birth to them)." This interpretation is in line with the more usual sense of the original for *her own,* with Paul's language elsewhere (Gal. 4:19), and with the immediate context (verse 11): the missionaries, far from trying to promote their own interests, had become both father and mother to the Thessalonians! Their love had reached a glorious climax of tenderheartedness, as is clear from the words which follow:

8. so, being affectionately desirous of y o u, we gladly shared with y o u not only the gospel of God but also our own souls.

What a powerful combination: here is the true gospel combined with the most affectionate presentation! And all this in the service of the Holy Spirit! How then can it cause surprise that these missionaries had been so successful?

It is probably impossible (except for the spacing of the letters of the pronoun) to improve on the rendering "being affectionately desirous of you" (thus A.V., taken over by A.R.V., and retained even by R.S.V.). Wy-

---

the older Dutch rendering is *bedeksel* (i.e., cloak or cover), the new translation, Amsterdam, 1951, has *voorwendsel* (pretext).

[48] This is the correct word, not *infants,* though that has considerable textual support. But the change from *gentle* to *infants* (the difference is just one letter in the original: ἤπιοι to νήπιοι) may have arisen from the fact that *gentle* is rare (used in the New Testament only here and in II Tim. 2:24. See also M.M., p. 281). This is better than to say (with those who favor the reading *infants*) that the first letter of νήπιοι was omitted by scribal error because the same letter ends the preceding word. After all, the context very definitely argues for *gentle: gentle* stands over against "in weight" (*formidable, weighty*); it also matches the description which immediately follows: "as when a nurse cherishes her own children."

clif translates: "desirynge you with greet loue." Others: "yearning for (or yearning after) you." The word used in the original occurs only here in the New Testament. Cf. its use in Job 3:21: the bitter in soul "long for" death. In a sepulchral inscription the sorrowing parents are described as "greatly desiring their son." [49]

It is very well possible that there is a bit of irony in this expression, as if Paul wanted to say, "Those who slander us are saying that we were out to get y o u; well, they are right, we were indeed yearning for y o u, but the purpose was not to take something from y o u but to share something with y o u." And that something consisted of nothing less than these two treasures: *the gospel of God and our very souls* (or perhaps *selves* as in John 10:11; see N.T.C. on that passage), our talents, time, energies; see on the next verse; and all this **because y o u had become very dear to us.** Paul, Silas, and Timothy have a vivid recollection of their work in Thessalonica. All those scenes of joyful acceptance of the good news, and this in spite of bitter persecution, pass in review once more. They recall how close had been the fellowship and how the bond between themselves and these people had become more and more strong and enduring. These believers who were God's beloved had also become very dear to God's special envoys. An appeal is made to their own memory:

9. For y o u remember, brothers, our toil and hardship: by night and by day (we were) working at a trade (or "working for a living"), in order not to be a burden to any of y o u while we proclaimed to y o u the gospel of God.

The trend of the connection between this passage and what precedes is: "What we have just now affirmed with respect to the fact that we were not trying to receive anything from y o u (see verse 5 above) but rather to impart something to y o u, who had become very dear to us (see verse 8), is true, *for* our toil and hardship in order not to burden any of y o u while we were with y o u proves it."

The word of endearment *brothers* is very fitting especially in the present connection: Paul, Silas, and Timothy had placed themselves on one level with the laborers of Thessalonica: they all worked for a living! See also on I Thess. 1:4. Yet, *more* is implied: the bond is spiritual! They are brothers *in Christ!* The expression *toil and hardship* — or "toil and moil" (the words used in the original rhyme: κόπος — μόχθος) — refers not so much to the labor and weariness connected with tent-making as to the entire thought expressed in the sentence, namely, that the missionaries had been working by night and by day [50] (part of the night, part of the day; note the geni-

[49] See ὁμείρομαι in M.M., p. 447. Cf. the use of the word in Symm. Ps. 62:2.
[50] Night and day (instead of day and night) is the order also in 3:10; II Thess. 3:8; I Tim. 5:5; II Tim. 1:3; cf. Jer. 14:17; contrast 16:13.

tive), and had been preaching besides! It must have been very hard, indeed, to find time for all this, and not to break down under the load. Yet, for the sake of the gospel of God and out of love for the Thessalonians, most of whom were ordinary laborers, the burden had been gladly borne. Note: "the gospel *of God.*" Had it been *from men,* for example from traveling "philosophers," the Thessalonians would not have been treated with such consideration.

Paul and his companions must have reflected very carefully on the question, "Shall we accept financial remuneration for the work of bringing the gospel; particularly, shall we accept it from the converts themselves?" Paul's stand may be summarized in the following ten propositions:

(1) Titus 1:11: He definitely does not want to give any occasion for being placed in a class with "vain talkers" who are interested in "filthy lucre."

(2) I Cor. 9:6-15: He, nevertheless, emphatically asserts *the right* to receive remuneration from the church for performing spiritual work, and to receive it even from the converts themselves (see especially verse 11).

Nevertheless, as far as the latter group is concerned (the converts), *he has decided not to make use of that right* (see verse 15).

(3) Acts 20:33: He will now be able to say, "I coveted no man's silver, gold, or apparel."

(4) II Cor. 11:8: He does at times "take wages" from already established churches, while he is working in a new field.

(5) Phil. 4:10-20: He accepts gifts from an already established church (Philippi).

(6) Acts 20:34, 35; I Thess. 2:9 and II Thess. 3:8: Most of all, he provides for his own needs (and even for the needs of others) by laboring with his own hands.

(7) Acts 18:3: He is tent-maker by trade.

(8) I Cor. 6:12; 8:9, 13; 9:12; 10:23: The principle on which he insists again and again (applying it to various questions) is this: All things are lawful, but not all things are helpful: there are a good many things which I have a right to do, but that does not mean that I should therefore do them! The real question is always: "What course of action will be most useful in promoting the work of the kingdom and the glory of God?"

(9) II Cor. 11:7: Even so, in spite of this carefully worked out plan with respect to work and wages, he does not escape criticism. If he takes money, or if his enemies suspect that he does, they are ready to charge him with selfishness, greed; if he does not, they accuse him of making a show of his humility.

(10) I Cor. 4:12; Eph. 4:28; I Thess. 2:9; II Thess. 3:8, 10: He (and the Holy Spirit through him!) dignifies labor, and proclaims the great principle: "If any man will not work neither let him eat." Now in his day

and age, laboring with the hands is not always and everywhere being held in honor. Cicero (Roman orator and writer, 106-43 B. C.) states that the "general opinion" was as follows:

"The callings of hired laborers, and of all that are paid for their mere work and not for their skill, are unworthy of a free man and vulgar; for their wages are given for menial service. . . . All mechanics are engaged in vulgar business; for a workshop can have nothing respectable about it. . . . Commerce, if on a small scale, is to be regarded as vulgar; but if large and rich . . . it is not so very discreditable" (*De Officiis* I. xlii).

In sharp contrast with all this stands the gospel of God, the teaching of Paul and his companions!

10. You (are) witnesses and (so is) God, how piously and righteously and blamelessly we conducted ourselves in the estimation of you, believers.

The writers appeal to *the believers* to bear witness that in the latter's own estimation — had some of them openly expressed it on occasion? — Paul and Silas and Timothy had *carried on their work* (ἐργαζόμενοι) among them with devotion to God (*piously, holily,* as men separated unto God and his service), ever striving to do what is *right* according to his law; hence, in an *irreproachable* manner. But inasmuch as man's judgment is, after all, fallible, — for, "Man looks on the outward appearance, but Jehovah looks on the heart" — the statement, "*You* are witnesses," is immediately followed by: "and (so is) *God.*"

The idea here begun is amplified in verses 11, 12:

11, 12. just as you know how, like a father (dealing) with his own children, (so we were) admonishing each and all of you, and encouraging and testifying that you should live lives worthy of God, who calls you into his own kingdom and glory.[51]

---

[51] The attempts at constructing this difficult sentence are legion. The one which looks the best to us is as follows:

(1) Literal translation: "just as you know how each one of you as a father his own children admonishing you and encouraging and testifying for you to walk worthy of God, the One calling you into his own kingdom and glory."

(2) The statement beginning with "just as you know" runs parallel with the one beginning with "you are witness and (so is) God" (verse 10); hence, "how each one of you" is co-ordinate in thought with "how piously," etc. The thought with reference to the holy, righteous, and blameless manner in which these three had carried on their work (verse 10) is elaborated in the statement that they had dealt with the Thessalonians as does a father with his children, admonishing them, encouraging and testifying that they should live lives worthy of God, etc.

(3) The participles *admonishing, encouraging, and testifying* should be combined with the imperfect of the verb *to be* (understood), forming the imperfect periphrastic. The use of the periphrastic has the effect of making the sentence more vivid, as if to say, "We *were doing* so and so; don't you remember?" The omission

Paul, Silas, and Timothy, while in Thessalonica, had loved these people like a mother loves and cherishes her own children (verse 7), and had admonished them as does a father. As Bengal points out, they had *admonished* them so that they would act *freely, encouraged* them, sothat they would act *gladly,* and *testified,* sothat they would act *reverently* (with a proper sense of respect for the will of God as expressed in his Word; hence, with fear). They had dealt with *each one of them,* having done individual pastoral work among them. (The stay in Thessalonica must have lasted more than three weeks.) They had also dealt with *all* of them as a group, addressing them collectively, teaching them, explaining the Word of God to them, and exhorting them to accept it by faith and to live in accordance with it.[52] They had figured with the immaturity of these people, and had loved them dearly. Both of these ideas (immaturity, love) are implied in the term *children.*

Now the object of all this fatherly exhortation was that the readers would *walk* (pass their lives) in a manner *worthy of* (in harmony with) their relation to God, who, by means of preaching and pastoral care, was calling them into that *future realm* (cf. II Thess. 1:5; I Cor. 6:9, 10; Gal. 5:21; Eph. 5:5; II Tim. 4:1, 18) where his kingship is fully recognized and his *glory* (radiant splendor; cf. N.T.C. on John 1:14) is reflected in the hearts and lives of all his subjects.

---

of the copula in such cases is not at all unusual (cf. II Cor. 7:5) and may be due to Aramaic influence.

(4) The words "his own children" are to be considered the object of the main idea in the participles. Had the sentence been more fully expressed, the participles would have been repeated.

(5) The pronoun *y o u* after *admonishing* (see literal translation above, under 1) is resumptive, resuming the idea expressed in *each one of y o u.* This repetition of the pronoun may also be due, in part, to Aramaic influence. However, in Koine Greek (as well as in other languages, even today) such "redundance" is not rare. It should not be viewed as superfluous repetition: the missionaries, while in Thessalonica, had administered to each person *individually,* and had also dealt with the people *collectively.*

(6) More fully expressed, the sentence, accordingly, would run somewhat as follows: (after verse 10: "Y o u are witnesses and so is God, how piously," etc., verse 11 continues) "just as y o u know how, like a father admonishing his own children, and encouraging and testifying, so we were admonishing each and all of y o u, and encouraging and testifying that y o u should live lives worthy of God, who calls y o u into his own kingdom and glory." In slightly abbreviated form this is the rendering which we have adopted in the text.

[52] As Calvin says so strikingly (Commentarius In Epistolam Pauli Ad Thessalonicenses I, *Corpus Reformatorum,* vol. LXXX, Brunsvigae, 1895, p. 150): Et certe nemo unquam bonus erit pastor, nisi qui patrem se ecclesiae sibi creditae praestabit. Nec vero se universo modo corpori talem fuisse asserit, sed etiam singulis. Neque enim satis est, si pastor omnes pro suggestu in commune doceat, nisi particularem quoque adiungat doctrinam, prout vel necessitas postulat, vel occasio se offert.

13 And for this reason we also thank God constantly, that when you had received from us the word which you heard, namely, God's word, you accepted it not as a word of men but as it really is, a word of God, which is also at work in you who believe. 14 For you, brothers, became imitators of the churches of God in Christ Jesus which are in Judea; for you suffered the same things from your own countrymen as they did from the Jews, 15 who killed both the Lord, namely, Jesus, and the prophets, and drove us out, and please not God, and we are contrary to all men 16 in that they try to prevent us from speaking to the Gentiles in order that they may be saved, so as always to fill up the measure of their sins. But upon them the wrath has come to the uttermost! [53]

2:13-16

2:13. And for this reason we also thank God constantly, that when you had received from us the word which you heard, namely, God's word, you accepted it not as a word of men but as it really is, a word of God, which is also at work in you who believe.

That in this section the Defence continues will become clear, the main point being, "The enemy is trying to undermine your faith, but your willingness to suffer persecution for the sake of Christ proves that your faith is genuine, and that the foe will not succeed."

In order to bring home this idea Paul states that not only the Thessalonians are grateful for the spiritual blessings which they have received, but so are the missionaries (hence, "we also," that is, "we as well as you"). Without ceasing they thank God for the manner in which the Thessalonians have accepted the message and for the influence which this word of God has exerted upon their lives. In other words, we have here a further elucidation and amplification of 1:6, just as 2:1-12 is an expatiation of the thought begun in 1:5. For that very reason we do not agree with those who would interpret the present passage as if it meant: "We thank God that when you received our message, you actually obtained the Word of God, and not merely the word of men." The sense is: when you *received* (external reception) from us "the word of hearing" (meaning: the word which you heard), which was nothing less than God's own word, you *accepted* (inward welcoming) it *as such,* that is, as a word of God and not as a word of men. The genuine character of this acceptance was proved by the fact that this divine word was actually bearing fruit in the lives of the people, as the passage 1:6-10 has already shown (they had turned away from idols toward God and toward the coming of his Son, and even amid much affliction they were joyfully proclaiming the new faith); and as verse 14 is going to show. The word, accordingly, was operating; it was "at work," [54] effective in the lives of believers. And the reason why the

---

[53] Or *at last;* or *to the end.*

[54] Paul is fond of this verb *is at work* (ἐνεργέω). He uses it again and again (Rom.

word was at work, and this in a favorable sense, was that it was the word *of God:* by means of that word, God himself was working (cf. Phil. 2:13). To substantiate this fact, namely, that the word was really at work, and that it was *God's* word, Paul continues:

14. For you, brothers, became imitators of the churches of God in Christ Jesus which are in Judea; for you suffered the same things from your own countrymen as they did from the Jews.

Willingness to suffer for Christ is proof of discipleship. It shows that the word of God is at work in the heart. It unites believers, sothat they constitute a true brotherhood (note: "for you, *brothers*"; see on 1:4), to which no one belongs who is not willing thus to suffer.

Now the Thessalonians were not only willing to suffer but had actually experienced persecution. Hence, they had become imitators of other believers. The story is ever the same. It is repeated in every age and in every clime (see on II Tim. 3:12 and N.T.C. on John 15:20; 16:33). For a true believer not to suffer persecution in some form is impossible. The readers had become imitators of the missionaries and of Christ himself (see on 1:6). Now another thought is added, namely, that they had also become imitators of the Judean believers. Now in Judea there were various *assemblies* (see on 1:1), by no means all of them Christian. To indicate clearly that the assemblies here meant are *Christian* assemblies or *churches* (*assembly* or *church* is the same word in the original: ἐκκλησία) there is added: "of God in Christ Jesus" (literally, "imitators of the assemblies of God that are in Judea *in* – in spiritual union with – Christ Jesus," cf. Gal. 1:22). These Judean churches had suffered *from the Jews.* Paul knew all about it, for he himself, while still unconverted, had taken part in it (Gal. 1:13; cf. Acts 9:1, 13) at the behest of the Jewish authorities. Moreover, think of Stephen, of James (the brother of the apostle John), and of Peter (Acts 6 and 7; 12:1-19; note especially 12:3, "it pleased *the Jews*"). Again and again persecution from the side of the Jews had flared up in Judea (Acts 8:1; 11:19). And it was going to flare up again, as Paul himself was going to discover (Acts 21:27-36; 23:12; 24:1-9).

Believers in Thessalonica had been similarly persecuted. However, the persecution which Paul has immediately in mind here in verse 14 is not (at least not primarily) the one recorded in Acts 17:5-8 but the one which just now had been reported by Timothy. This later persecution had

---

7:5; I Cor. 12:6, 11; II Cor. 1:6; 4:12; Gal. 2:8 twice; 3:5; 5:6; Eph. 1:11, 20; 2:2; 3:20; Phil. 2:13 twice; Col. 1:29; I Thess. 2:13; II Thess. 2:7). Of the twenty-one instances in which this verb occurs in the N.T., no less than eighteen are to be found in Paul. In addition to this he alone employs the corresponding nouns (ἐνέργεια, ἐνέργημα; cf. our *energy*). In Paul's way of thinking principles are never dead; they are always doing something; though not always something good (Rom. 7:5; II Cor. 4:12; II Thess. 2:7).

taken place after the departure of the missionaries. That the Gentiles had taken a prominent part in it is clear. On any different interpretation the comparison: "You suffered the same things from your fellow-countrymen as they did from the Jews" would make no sense. Is it not altogether probable that the husbands of those many women who had become Christians (Acts 17:4) – these husbands being themselves leading men – were making life hard for their wives? And is it not logical that these men and their friends would also subject other believers (both men and women) to scorn, ridicule, physical suffering, and even death?

Two important lessons are clearly implied:

(1) Whether the persecution comes from the Jews or from the Gentiles, it is ever *the same* in character, because at bottom it is the age-old warfare of the devil against "the Christ, the woman, and the rest of her seed." See my book *More Than Conquerors* (Interpretation of the book of Revelation), Grand Rapids, Mich., seventh edition, 1954, pp. 162-188. This conflict goes back to Gen. 3:15.

(2) Willingness to suffer such persecution reflects honor on the one who experiences it. It is as if Paul and his companions are saying, "The church in Jerusalem is generally thought of as an example for others. Now you, Thessalonians, by your willingness to suffer as the mother-church suffered, have shown that you are equal to her in honor."

When Paul mentions the Jews and the havoc which they had wrought in *Judea,* he realizes, of course, that they, too, as well as the Gentiles, had tried and were trying to destroy the faith of the *Thessalonian* believers. It was as a result of *their* instigation that the missionaries had been forced to leave the city (Acts 17:5-9). In the beginning the Jews had aroused the Gentiles, including the magistrates, to take a stand against the Gospel and its messengers. There is no good reason to believe that their hostile attitude had ceased since that time (see, e.g., Acts 17:13). It is for this reason that the apostle, having made specific mention of the persecution carried on by the Jews in Judea, and mindful of their sinister plotting in Thessalonica and elsewhere, continues:

15. who killed both the Lord, namely, Jesus, and the prophets,
and drove us out,
and please not God,
and are contrary to all men.

In the original the words *Lord* and *Jesus* are separated (the order of the words being: "who the Lord killing Jesus"), thus stressing the fact that it was no one less than the exalted Lord whom the Jews had killed, the one who as to his earthly manifestation was Jesus, the Savior. For both names see on 1:1. All attempts (also modern attempts) to mitigate the guilt of the Jews in killing Jesus (by saying that not they but the Gentiles – particularly

Pilate – committed this crime) are crushed by this passage: I Thess. 2:15. Just as at Thessalonica the Jews had aroused the Gentile rabble, so also before this in Jerusalem the Jews had used Pilate as their tool in bringing about the crucifixion of the Lord (see N.T.C. on the Gospel of John, chapters 18 and 19). Note how Paul, having mentioned Jesus, reaches back in time to the Old Testament *prophets* and then forward to the New Testament *apostles,* particularly to himself, Silas, and Timothy. Thus it becomes apparent that at bottom the hostility is ever directed against the central figure, namely, the Lord, even Jesus (see on 2:14).

As will be indicated in connection with verse 16, it is probable that the apostle was thinking of the actual words of Jesus with respect to the Jews, for example, such words as those which are recorded in Matt. 23:37-39 (for similar passages see under verse 16). If this is correct, it also becomes evident that "the prophets" are not those of the New Testament but those of the Old (see Matt. 23:34, 35).

For the meaning of "and drove us out" see Acts 17:5-9 (cf. Acts 17:10-15; then 9:29, 30). The clause "and please not God" is, of course, a typical understatement. To glorify God and *to please* him is the purpose of man's existence (see on 4:1; cf. Rom. 8:8; I Cor. 7:32; 10:31). These Jews not only displease *God* but are also "contrary to all *men,*" and this not only in the sense that they are filled with "terrible hatred against all others" (Tacitus, *History* V. v), but in the sense indicated in verse 16:

16. in that they try to prevent us from speaking to the Gentiles in order that they may be saved, . . .

The Jews are constantly interfering, *hindering,* though they cannot *actually prevent* the progress of the Gospel. They are obstructionists, and their constant opposition marks them as the enemies of all men, for the more the Gospel spreads, the more are all men benefited. Right here in Corinth, the place where this epistle was being written, the work of the missionaries was being impeded, as is indicated very vividly in Acts 18:6. And this in spite of the fact that Paul, Silas, and Timothy were trying to be the means in God's hand for bestowing upon the Corinthians the greatest gift of all, namely, salvation full and free.

With respect to the Jews, the old story was being repeated: the story of rebellion against God. Again and again in times past this spirit of obstinacy had revealed itself: e.g., in the wilderness-journey from Egypt to Canaan, during the period of the judges, during the reigns of several kings, just before the Babylonian Captivity. In the ministry of Christ (especially on Golgotha) and in the period immediately following this it had risen to a climax. Hence, Paul is able to write **so as always to fill up the measure of their sins.** Note that adverb *always.* However, God's wrath had overtaken the mass of the Jews. We read: **but upon them the wrath has come.**

We immediately understand that *the* wrath is God's wrath. (It is not necessary nor even advisable to adopt the weakly attested reading which would add these words: "of God").

The explanation offered by several commentators, to the effect that when Paul wrote these words he was in a bad mood because his work at Corinth was being hampered by the Jews, is without any foundation. The theory which finds in events unfavorable to the Jews which had happened during the reign of Caligula and that of Claudius (who at first was kindly disposed to them) a complete commentary of Paul's statement about the arrival of God's wrath, is equally objectionable. Worst of all is the position of those who hold that I Thess. 2:16 must refer to the fall of Jerusalem in the year A. D. 70, and that, accordingly, Paul cannot have written this epistle or at least that he cannot have written this passage, it being an interpolation.

The true explanation is simple: Paul was well acquainted with the words which Jesus had spoken while still on earth. In very emphatic language the Lord had revealed that, as a punishment for the sin of rejecting him, God's displeasure (his *vengeance*) was now resting upon the Jewish people, and that this wrath would manifest itself in woes to be visited upon them (which woes, in turn, would foreshadow those immediately preceding the end of the world). Anyone can see this for himself by reading such passages as the following: Matt. 21:43; 23:38; 24:15-28; 27:25; Mark 11:14, 20 (in its context); Luke 21:5-24; 23:27-31. In this connection it must not be overlooked that the apostle does not say that God's wrath has even now been fully poured out, or that it has become outwardly manifest in punishments. All he says is that *the wrath itself has come!* The woes will follow.

This wrath, moreover, has come **to the uttermost.** While *previously,* whenever Israel sinned grievously it had been *punished, this time* it is not only punished but *rejected.* This time God himself hardens Israel with a hardening which lasts "until the fulness of the Gentiles be come in" (Rom. 11:25). Hence, this time God's wrath has come upon them *to the uttermost.*[55]

What Paul teaches is in full harmony with Rom. 9-11. (See also p. 19.) However, in Romans there is additional revelation. He there shows that though this wrath to the uttermost has reached the Jewish *masses,* there is, nevertheless, in every period of history, "a remnant according to the election of grace." These remnants of all the ages, taken together, constitute

---

[55] Though "to the uttermost" (so also A.V., A.R.V., Lenski, footnote R.S.V., etc., and see N.T.C. on John 13:1) would seem to be the meaning that best suits the context, it is not certain. The phrase εἰς τέλος can also mean *at last* (cf. Luke 18:5; here in I Thess. 2:16 it is so rendered by R.S.V., Berkeley Version, Williams, Robertson, Frame); or *to the end* (study Dan. 9:27; see the use of the phrase in Matt. 10:22; 24:13; Mark 13:13; here in I Thess. 2:16 it is so rendered by the New Dutch Version, by Van Leeuwen in *Korte Verklaring,* etc.).

"all Israel" which "shall be saved" (Rom. 11:26 a).[56] Hence, no one has a right to say, "God is through with the Jews." Anti-Semitism, moreover, is very definitely anti-scriptural! In the present passage (I Thess. 2:16), however, all the emphasis is on the curse which the Jews have called down upon themselves by rejecting the Christ and his ambassadors.

---

17 Now we, brothers, having been torn away from you for a short time – out of sight but not out of heart[57] – endeavored all the more eagerly to see your face with intense longing; 18 for we did wish to come to you, I, Paul, myself once and again, but Satan stopped us. 19 For who is our hope or joy or glory-wreath – or are not also you – in the presence of our Lord Jesus Christ at his coming? 20 Indeed, it is you who are our glory and (our) joy!

2:17-20

2:17. Now we, brothers, having been torn away from you for a short time – out of sight but not out of heart – endeavored all the more eagerly to see your face with intense longing.

The Defence continues. Not inaptly what precedes verse 17 has been called Paul's *apologia pro vita sua;* while 2:17-3:5 (see also on 3:1) has been called *apologia pro absentia sua.* Not only was it true that during their stay in Thessalonica the missionaries had conducted themselves in a most unselfish manner, as has now been shown, but also after the enforced departure from that city their loving concern for the *brothers* (note that word in verse 17; and see on 1:4) whom they had left behind had asserted itself. At this point Paul's style becomes intensely emotional. The very words seem to tremble. The reason for the depth of feeling which comes to expression here is probably that the enemies of the faith were insinuating that the sudden departure of the missionaries proved lack of genuine concern for the people whom they had misled. Over against that charge Paul stresses the fact that by the missionaries the separation which had taken place was felt as being nothing less than a being *torn away from* those whom they loved so dearly. The verb (ἀπορφανισθέντες) occurs only here in the New Testament (see, however, Aeschylus, *Choephori* 249; cf. for the form without prefix Theocritus, *Epigrammata* V. vi). Literally, the meaning is, first, *to be orphaned;* then, *to be bereaved.* However, the meaning of the prefix (ἀπό, *from, away from*) of the composite verb is brought out better in the rendering which we favor, namely, *to be torn away from.*[58]

---

[56] See my booklet *And So All Israel Shall be Saved,* Grand Rapids, Mich. (Baker Book House), 1945.
[57] Literally *in face not in heart.*
[58] For this translation of the verb as used here in I Thess. 2:17 we are indebted to H. G. Liddell and R. Scott, *A Greek-English Lexicon,* Oxford, 1940, Vol. I, p. 216. Words, in the course of their history, often acquire a slightly modified mean-

The clause "having been torn away from you a short time," *may* (but does not necessarily) convey the idea that Paul was convinced that he would soon revisit the Thessalonians. In all probability he actually revisited them on the third missionary journey (Acts 20:1, 2). However, the meaning might also be, "When (or *though*) we had been torn away from you for a short time only, we already endeavored all the more eagerly to return to you." According to this second view the *short time*[59] is wholly antecedant to the action of the main verb. The attempt to revisit those left behind was given an added impetus by the enforced character of the separation. It is as if Paul were saying, "The more Satan tried to effect a separation the harder we tried to effect a reunion." (For this sense of περισσοτέρως see Phil. 1:14.) With this interpretation agrees the final phrase: *with intense longing* (or *desire*).

The parenthetical "in face not in heart"[60] (cf. II Cor. 5:12; Col. 2:5) must probably also be viewed as a refutation of the slander that the missionaries did not really care for those whom they had "duped"; that they would know better than to try to return to them; in short, that for Paul and company "out of sight" meant "out of heart." Thus interpreted, we can also understand what immediately follows, namely,

18. for we did wish[61] to come to you, I, Paul, myself once and again, but Satan stopped us.

"We endeavored" (verse 17), "for we wished" (verse 18): this sequence is logical. Far from being glad that we had an excuse to get away from Thessalonica, we – Paul, Silas, and Timothy – having been driven out, longed to come back. In view of the fact that the sinister attack of the enemy was directed against Paul more than against anyone else, the apostle adds, "I, Paul, *once and again*" (cf. Phil. 4:16), that is, *repeatedly*.

Satan, however, had prevented the missionaries from carrying out their ardent wish to return to Thessalonica. Just how did Satan do this? By influencing the minds of the politarchs at Thessalonica, sothat they would have caused Jason to forfeit his bond (Acts 17:9) in case the missionaries had returned? By bringing about a sufficient amount of trouble elsewhere sothat neither Paul alone nor all three were able to return? We just do

---

ing. Thus the word *orphan* in John 14:18 tends in the direction of *friendless*. Even in English the adjective *orphan* may have the wider meaning *bereaved*. So also here in 2:17 the basic element of the verb has attained a somewhat modified meaning.

59 The expression πρὸς καιρὸν ὥρας combines πρὸς καιρόν (Luke 8:13; I Cor. 7:5) and πρὸς ὥραν (II Cor. 7:8; Gal. 2:5).

60 *We* say "out of sight out of *mind*", but the Greek has *heart;* cf. the Dutch: *uit het oog, uit het hart.*

61 Those who favor the rendering, "We made deliberate plans," fail to show a solid reason why the verb θέλω rather than βούλομαι was used. The enemy denied that Paul and his companions (but *especially* Paul) ever even *wished* to return to Thessalonica!

not know. Moreover, it does not matter. The fact as such that Satan exerts a powerful influence over the affairs of men, especially when they endeavor to promote the interests of the kingdom of God, is sufficiently clear from other passages (Job 1:6-12; Zech. 3:1; cf. Daniel, chapter 10). Nevertheless, God ever reigns supreme, over-ruling evil for good (II Cor. 12:7-9; the book of Job). Even when the devil tries to *chop up* the road that lies ahead, thus apparently blocking our advance, God's hidden plan is never wrecked. Satan may *cut in on* us, preventing us from doing what, for the moment, seems best *to us,* God's ways are always better than ours.

The reason why Paul and his companions were so eager to revisit the Thessalonians is now stated:

19, 20. For who is our hope or joy or glory-wreath – or are not also y o u – in the presence of our Lord Jesus Christ at his coming? Indeed, it is y o u who are our glory and (our) joy!

Paul and his companions love these Thessalonians, and "are proud" of them. It must be borne in mind that amid severe persecution these people had turned away from their idols and had turned to God, the living and true One, and that they are now waiting for the glorious coming of the Lord.

At this *coming* of *the Lord Jesus Christ* (for this full title see on 1:1) for the purpose of blessing his people with his abiding *presence* the missionaries will see the ultimate realization of their *hope,* and will experience supreme *joy* when they behold the fruits of their missionary efforts standing there, with gladness, thanksgiving, and praise, at Christ's right hand. For these missionaries this will be the *glory-wreath,* the prided victor's chaplet.[62]

The term *coming* (in *at his coming*) is Parousia (παρουσία). This word is sometimes used in the non-technical sense of a. *presence;* for the use of the term in that sense the following passages come in for consideration: I Cor. 16:17; II Cor. 10:10; Phil. 1:26 (?); 2:12; or of b. *a coming, advent,* or *arrival:* II Cor. 7:6, 7; Phil. 1:26(?); II Thess. 2:9. In other passages – and I Thess. 2:19 is one of them – it definitely refers to the *Return* or *Advent of the Lord,* his "coming" *in order to bless his people with his presence.* See Zech. 9:9. In addition to I Thess. 2:19 to illustrate this meaning, the following should be studied: I Thess. 3:13; 4:15; 5:23; II Thess. 2:1, 8; Matt. 24:3, 27, 37, 39; I Cor. 15:23; Jas. 5:7, 8; II Peter 1:16; 3:4, 12;

---

[62] We take the genitive καυχήσεως to be adjectival in nature. This is in harmony with similar expressions in other passages: Prov. 16:31; Is. 28:5; Jer. 13:8; Ezek. 16:12; 23:42. Besides, the New Testament has many genitives of this kind, the frequency of their occurrence being due, perhaps, to Aramaic influence (see also on 1:3). Hence, the main concept here is not *boasting* (or glorifying) but *wreath.* The new Dutch translation has *erekrans;* cf. *roemkrans.* That is correct.

and I John 2:28. This meaning may be viewed as a modification of the sense: "the arrival" or "the visit" of the king or emperor.[63]

Paul and his companions, stirred by the slanders of those who insinuate that the missionaries are people who do not care a whit about their converts, express the deepest conviction of their hearts in the form of a question, but that question requires an affirmative answer. It may be paraphrased as follows: "For who is our hope or joy or glory-wreath? Others only? Or are not also y o u (along with others; see, e.g., Phil. 4:1) in the presence of our Lord Jesus Christ at his coming?" And that there may be no doubt about it, Paul himself supplies the answer: "Indeed (this is the meaning of γάρ here) it is y o u (note the emphatic position of ὑμεις) who are our *glory* (that is, our reason for glorying in the Lord) and (our) joy!"

Synthesis of Chapters 1 and 2

See p. 36. *Defence. Paul writes to the Thessalonians, reminding them how the Gospel had come to Thessalonica, as a genuine work of God and not as a product of human deception.*

chapter 1 This chapter contains the names of the senders (Paul and his companions Silvanus and Timothy) and of the addressee (the church of the Thessalonians), the salutation, and the thanksgiving together with its grounds.

The reasons why Silvanus (or Silas) and Timothy are mentioned in one breath with Paul as authors and senders is that they have been associated with the great apostle in bringing the gospel to Thessalonica and are with him now in Corinth where this letter is written.

Upon the readers the missionaries pronounce *grace* (God's unmerited favor in operation) and its result, *peace* (the conviction of reconciliation through the blood of the cross, spiritual prosperity).

They inform the Thessalonians that they never allow a day to go by without giving thanks for them, in view of their "work resulting from faith, exertion prompted by love, and endurance inspired by hope in our Lord Jesus Christ." The ultimate reason for this thanksgiving is the conviction that the readers have been chosen from eternity unto salvation. The writers base this conviction on two facts:

a. the message which the readers had received and the messengers who had brought it are trustworthy.

b. the manner in which the readers had responded is proof positive of the operation of the Spirit of God in their hearts. They had welcomed God's word with Spirit-imparted joy even in the midst of great tribulation.

---

[63] See A. Deissmann, *Light From The Ancient East,* fourth edition, New York, 1922, p. 368; G. Milligan, *St. Paul's Epistles to the Thessalonians,* London, 1908, p. 145 ff.

They had cast away their idols, "to serve God, the living and real One, and to await his Son out of the heavens." From *imitators* they had become *examples.* Their faith was being broadcast and was having its blessed effect everywhere.

Paul (i.e., "Paul, Silvanus and Timothy," but Paul is chiefly responsible) gives evidence of deep concern for his readers. Probably as an answer to malicious slander he declares, "Y o u well know what kind of men we became among y o u for y o u r sake." Thus, even in the first chapter there is an undertone of *defence.* This gains strength in the next chapter.

chapter 2 The apologetic tone continues and becomes predominant. First, the missionaries defend their *manner of life* while still at Thessalonica (verses 1-16); then, their *departure and continued absence* from Thessalonica (2:17-20, or even 2:17-3:5). As the charges were hurled especially against *Paul,* this may be considered *his* defence even more than *theirs.* Accordingly, we have:

Apologia pro vita sua

The key-passage is verse 3, "For our appeal does not spring from delusion or from impurity nor does it come with deceit." It may probably be inferred from this that the slanderers had directed their attack against Paul's *m* essage, *m* otive, and *m* ethod.

Accordingly, in this section Paul points out that his *message* was the good news which had come directly from God; that the *motive* in presenting it was most unselfish, even the motive of self-sacrificing love, the attitude of a father or of a mother toward his (her) own children; and that the *method* was above reproach ("Y o u are witnesses and so is God, how piously and righteously and blamelessly we conducted ourselves in the estimation of y o u, believers"). Paul shows that the willingness of the readers to suffer persecution for the sake of Christ proves that the word is "at work" in them, and that they are equal in honor with the mother-church in Judea. In a passage filled with deep emotion he reveals that upon the Jewish instigators of persecution God's wrath has come to the uttermost.

Apologia pro absentia sua

The enemy seems also to have insinuated that Paul's departure from Thessalonica and his failure to return had not been entirely unplanned, or that, while he complained about "tribulation," he had not been entirely unhappy about finding an excuse to get away. The apostle definitely and with much feeling denies this, ardently and unequivocally avowing his love for the readers, whom he calls "our hope or joy or glory-wreath in the presence of our Lord Jesus Christ at his coming." He states that he and his companions had been "torn away" from the readers, and had repeatedly "endeavored all the more eagerly" to see their face "with intense longing," but had been stopped by Satan.

Summary of I Thessalonians 3 (or 3:6-13)

Paul Writes to the Thessalonians

Informing Them How He Rejoices over Timothy's Report of Their Continued Spiritual Progress Even in the Midst of Persecution.

This section comprises *the Apostle's Expression of Joy over Timothy's Report.*

It may be divided as follows:

3:1-5 What moved Paul to send Timothy

3:6-10 What reason for rejoicing Timothy's report had brought

3:11-13 A fervent wish

CHAPTER III

I THESSALONIANS 3:1-13

3 1 Therefore when we could not stand it any longer, we thought it best to
be left behind in Athens alone; 2 and we sent Timothy, our brother and
God's minister in the gospel of Christ, in order to strengthen y o u and to encourage (y o u) with respect to your faith; 3 to prevent any one of y o u from being
deceived in the midst of these afflictions. For y o u yourselves know that we are
appointed for this; 4 for when we were with y o u, we kept telling y o u in advance
that we were about to be afflicted, just as y o u know that it (actually) happened.
5 For this reason I, too, when I could stand it no longer, sent to learn about y o u r
faith, (fearing) lest by any means the tempter might have tempted y o u, and our
toil might turn out to have been useless.
6 But now that Timothy has just come to us from y o u, and has brought us
the glad tidings of y o u r faith and love, and that y o u cherish an affectionate
recollection of us at all times, longing to see us, just as we also (long to see) y o u,
7 for this reason, brothers, in all our distress and affliction, we were comforted
about y o u, through y o u r faith; 8 for now we (really) live if y o u stand fast in
the Lord. 9 For what thanksgiving can we offer to God concerning y o u in return
for all the joy by means of which we rejoice on account of y o u in the presence
of our God, 10 by night and by day praying with intense earnestness that we may
see y o u r faces and may supply the deficiencies of y o u r faith?
11 Now may he, our God and Father and our Lord Jesus, direct our way to
y o u; 12 and as for y o u, may the Lord cause y o u to abound and overflow in love
toward one another and toward all, just as also we (do) toward y o u, 13 in order
that he may strengthen y o u r hearts so that they may be blameless in holiness in
the presence of our God and Father at the coming of our Lord Jesus with all his
saints!

3:1-13

The transition between Defence and Expression of joy is very gradual. In fact, the information which Paul supplies with respect to the decision to send Timothy is, in a sense, a part of the Defence, for it shows that far from being indifferent to the needs of the Thessalonians (as the enemies charged), the apostle was willing to make a real sacrifice in their interest. Hence, there can be no great objection to extending the first main division sothat it ends at 3:5 (see also on 2:17). The reason why, nevertheless, *this entire chapter* may be considered *as a unit* is that even the first five verses, as well as the rest, concern *Timothy:* what moved Paul (or Paul after consultation with the others) to send him (verses 1-5), and what comfort his report had brought (verses 6-10, closing with a fervent wish which almost amounts to a prayer, verses 11-13).

3:1. Therefore when we could not stand it any longer, we thought it best to be left behind in Athens alone.

The sense of verse 1 is: in view of the fact that our immediate attempt to return to y o u was frustrated by Satan, and that, nevertheless, we could not *stand* or *endure* (cf. I Cor. 9:12; 13:7) the separation any longer, we *decided* (*thought it good;* cf. the noun εὐδοκία, *good pleasure,* Lk. 2:14; Eph. 1:5, 9; Phil. 1:15; 2:13; see on II Thess. 1:11) to deprive ourselves of the valued presence of one of our number, even though that meant that we would be left alone in the very worldly and idolatrous city of Athens.[64]

The position of the clause "to be left behind at Athens alone" shows that the emphasis falls on this decision, which disclosed so beautifully Paul's love for the Thessalonians.

The problem which arises at this point is, "Just what is meant by *alone* (the plural μόνοι is used, but that, demanded by concord, does not decide the issue either way); does this have reference to Paul only or to Paul *and Silas?*" Commentators are sharply divided, as follows:

a. Some conveniently skip the problem, or treat it as if it did not exist;

b. some, while expressing a preference, leave room for the possibility that the truth might be on the other side;

c. some are certain that what Paul meant was that *he* had decided to remain *all alone* at Athens; and finally,

d. some are of the opinion that Paul, Silas, and Timothy had consulted together, sothat the "we" is not a *literary* (or *editorial* or *author's*) plural,[65] but a *real* plural. To this it is sometimes added that while the departure of Timothy left Paul *and Silas* behind in Athens, Silas too must have departed very soon (see Acts 18:5), sothat for a while, at least, Paul must have been *all alone* in Athens.

The information which can be gleaned from the book of Acts and from I Thessalonians does not *definitely* settle the question, so as to leave no inkling of doubt. Surely, if Silas (for any length of time) was with Paul in Athens, the *we* here in I Thess. 3:1 could include him. But *was* he actually with Paul in Athens? A probable view is that *Timothy* had left Berea

---

[64] As we see it, the idea of Lenski, *op. cit.,* p. 281 that Timothy was chosen because he had not been driven out of Thessalonica, finds no support in the text. See also above, p. 5.

[65] See Gram.N.T., p. 407 for a discussion of the *literary* plural. Those who believe that Paul at times makes use of this plural refer to such passages as the following: I Thess. 2:18 (see, however, our explanation); then also Rom. 1:5; I Cor. 9:11, 12, 15; II Cor. 2:14; 10:1-11:6; Col. 4:3. Very interesting is also the article by W. R. Hutton, "Who Are We?" in *BTr,* Vol. 4, Number 2 (April, 1953) 86-90.

and had found Paul while the latter was still in Athens; that Paul, anxious about the affairs of the church at Thessalonica, sent him back to that congregation in order to establish and comfort it, and that *sometime later* both Silas and Timothy rejoined the apostle at Corinth (see I Thess. 3:1, 2, 6; Acts 18:5). However, this still leaves open the question, "Did Silas rejoin Paul *twice,* not only subsequently at Corinth, when also Timothy rejoined the group, but even before this (though for only a very short time), when Paul was still in Athens?" As far as the book of Acts is concerned, the only hint in the direction of a possible answer is found in Acts 17:15, 16 according to which Paul, arriving in Athens, tells the brothers, who had accompanied him to this city and are now departing, that they must tell Silas and Timothy to "come to him with all speed." Paul, accordingly, waited for *them* at Athens, that is, *for both of them.*

As to I Thessalonians, the idea that there was a joint consultation and that here in 3:1 the phrase *at Athens alone* refers to both Paul and Silas would seem to have at least this in its favor, that the reader, perhaps half consciously, has been including Silas and Timothy in all the "we" sections so far. Thus, not only Paul, but Paul, Silvanus, and Timothy pronounce the salutation (1:1). Not only Paul but also Silvanus and Timothy give thanks (1:2). Not only Paul but also Silvanus and (very probably) Timothy had been involved in the "entering in" of which 2:1 speaks. Also, we know that not only Paul had suffered and had been shamefully treated at Philippi (2:2). Not only Paul but also the others had been entrusted with the gospel (2:4). And not only Paul but also Silvanus and Timothy had been torn away from the brothers at Thessalonica (2:17). On that basis when now once more the reader meets a "we" (namely, here in 3:1) he is hardly prepared to think only of Paul. "We . . . alone" accordingly, in the light of the context, *probably* means: Silvanus and I *without the brothers who had accompanied us to Athens and without the valued presence of Timothy.* That this was a sacrifice of love follows not only from the fact that by and by Silvanus too would be sent to Macedonia, but also from the high esteem in which Paul held his young companion Timothy, as is clear from the next verse:

2. and we sent Timothy, our brother and God's minister in the gospel of Christ, in order to strengthen y o u and to encourage (y o u) with respect to y o u r faith.

Timothy is called a *brother* (cf. II Cor. 1:1; Col. 1:1), that is, a fellow-believer (see on 1:4), one who by sovereign grace belongs to the family of God in Christ. He is *our* brother, the word *our* being probably inclusive: brother of the Thessalonian believers as well as of the missionaries. But while he is *our* brother, he is at the same time *God's* minister.[66] The term

[66] The external evidence in favor of the reading *God's co-worker* is not any stronger

minister (διάκονος) indicates a servant, attendant (see N.T.C. on John, vol. I, p. 119). It is the same term as our *deacon,* and is at times employed in that technical sense (Phil. 1:1; I Tim. 3:8, 12). On Timothy see N.T.C. on the Pastoral Epistles. The particular sphere in which Timothy ministers is *the gospel of Christ,* the glad tidings (good news) of salvation through him.

The purpose for which Timothy was sent was *in order to strengthen* (by Paul used also in 3:13; II Thess. 2:17; 3:3; further, in Rom. 1:11; 16:25) and *to encourage* (see on 2:11; then also on 2:3). An additional purpose is stated in verse 5, namely, "to know your faith." In view of fierce persecution and a sinister slander-campaign from without and also in view of the immature intellectual, moral, and spiritual development of the Thessalonian believers, the mission of Timothy was altogether proper, though it meant a real sacrifice for those who were left behind at Athens. Timothy, then, must tell these recent converts to the Christian faith, "You're doing fine. Continue to do so. But do so more and more." That this *encouragement* was proper is shown by the following passages: 1:3, 4, 6-10; 2:13-14; 3:6-8; 4:1, 9, 10; 5:11. That *strengthening* was likewise needed follows from 3:5, 10; 4:1, 3, 4-8, 10; 5:23. It is true, of course, that the two terms overlap: when one is encouraged, he is also strengthened!

3, 4. The hoped for result of Timothy's mission of encouragement and strengthening is now stated: **to prevent anyone of you from being deceived in the midst of these afflictions.**

The enemy of the faith does not always come *only* with the sword. Sometimes he appears "with horns like a lamb" (Rev. 13:11), with soft words and flattery, like a dog *wagging his tail* (which is the primary meaning of the verb "deceived" used in the original). The danger was very real that those who were already being *oppressed* (note "in the midst of these afflictions") might be beguiled (either for the time being, if their faith was genuine, or permanently if it was merely historical or temporal) by language such as this:

"We can fully understand how it was that you were led astray by these enthusiastic foreigners who came from Philippi. You were led to believe that they had your interest at heart. But their sudden departure and failure to return clearly proves that they are not concerned about you at all. Moreover, the things that have happened to you since their coming shows that the gods are not pleased with you. Why exchange that which is tried and tested for something novel? Rejoin our ranks, the ranks of

---

than that in favor of the reading *God's minister.* The assumed scribal substitution of *minister* for *co-worker,* a substitution supposed to have been made because of the *bold* character of the latter designation, is answered by I Cor. 3:9. Frame is among those who favor *God's co-worker, op. cit.,* pp. 126, 127.

those who have always admired and respected y o u, and we'll promise y o u that we'll never mention the subject again." [67]

To prevent such fawning amid the stress of persecution from being successful, Timothy was sent.

For y o u yourselves know that we (inclusive: the missionaries and the believers at Thessalonica; in a sense, all believers) **are appointed for this.** Some of the reasons why believers are "set" for this (tribulation) and/or why they should rejoice in it may be found in passages such as the following: John 16:33; Acts 14:22; Rom. 5:3; 8:35-39; 12:12; II Cor. 1:4; 7:4; II Tim. 3:12. The Thessalonians are reminded of the fact that these afflictions should not take them by surprise. After all, they have been warned: **for when we were with y o u, we kept telling y o u in advance that we were about to be afflicted, just as y o u know that it (actually) happened.** How these words resemble those of the Master himself, spoken on the eve of his most bitter suffering! See N.T.C. on John 16:1, 4. Afflictions that have been *predicted,* and that take place in accordance with this prediction, serve to strengthen faith.

5. For this reason I, too, when I could stand it no longer, sent to learn about y o u r faith. For this reason, then, that is, in view of the fact that Paul had been frustrated once and again by Satan in his ardent desire to return to the believers at Thessalonica (who were his hope, joy, and glory-wreath), in view of the fact that his love for them was genuine, and also in view of the fact that on the basis of what he himself had seen and experienced in the past (Acts 17:5-9, 13) he was convinced that they must be suffering severe persecution and was wondering how they were faring under it, in view therefore of all that is stated and implied in 2:17-3:4, the apostle, no longer able to stand the suspense, sent *to learn* (or *to get to know*) about their faith. It is clear that verse 5 resumes the thought of verses 1, 2, with these differences: a. that another reason is now added to the two stated previously, and b. that the apostle stresses the fact that he himself no less than the others (hence, "also I") was responsible for the sending of Timothy. Since the slander of maligners must have been directed especially against Paul, this additional statement was altogether proper.

The purpose of the mission as now expressed was in order that Paul might get to know their faith, (fearing) **lest by any means the tempter might have tempted y o u, and our toil would turn out to have been useless.**[68]

---

[67] We cannot agree here with those commentators (for example, Van Leeuwen) who are of the opinion that here in 3:3, 4 Paul is thinking only of the tribulations suffered by the missionaries themselves. Passages such as 1:6 and 2:14 (cf. Acts 17:5-10) clearly indicate that the reference is to the afflictions borne alike by Paul, Silas, Timothy, the Thessalonian believers, and, in a sense, by all true believers.

[68] The past (aorist) indicative (ἐπείρασεν after μή πως) is best explained as that

Such fear on the part of Paul was altogether reasonable, and does not contradict 1:4 ("knowing your election") in any way. The sequence was as follows:

a. Paul and his companions carry on their evangelistic activity in Thessalonica but are soon forced to leave. While still there, the Thessalonians (that is, many of them) appear to accept the gospel with enthusiasm. But was this a merely emotional reaction or was it genuine faith?

b. In their absence, the missionaries wonder about this. Meanwhile persecution continues. Will the genuine character of the faith of the Thessalonians be proved by their willingness to endure tribulation for the sake of Christ? Will they understand that this tribulation is not contrary to God's plan but in accordance with it?

c. So Timothy is sent in order to learn about this. He returns with a glowing report, praising the Thessalonians for their work, exertion, and endurance under persecution.

d. Being now thoroughly convinced that the conversion of the Thessalonians had been genuine (that their acceptance of the Gospel "with joy" had been a work of the Spirit) and not merely outward, Paul sits down at once to write I Thessalonians. He now writes about their work *resulting from faith,* their exertion *prompted by love,* and their endurance *inspired by hope,* and he derives all this from their *election* by God.

If we view the order of events in this light, justice is done both to the *fear* expressed here in 3:5 and the *conviction* expressed in 1:3-6. In no sense whatever is it true that 3:5 teaches that God's truly chosen ones can, after all, perish everlastingly.

Here, in close connection with verse 3, the prince of evil is called *the tempter.* His meanness consists especially in this, that he first tempts a man into sin and then accuses him of it! Moreover, he will even continue to accuse the man after the latter's sin has been forgiven. He is, accordingly, the *devil* or *slanderer* (Eph. 4:27; 6:11; II Tim. 2:26); he is *Satan,* the wicked *adversary* (I Cor. 5:5; II Cor. 2:11; II Thess. 2:9). He is, moreover, *the god of this world* (II Cor. 4:3), *the prince of the powers of the air* (Eph. 2:2) and of *the world-rulers of this darkness, spiritual hosts of wickedness in the heavenlies, seducing spirits and demons* (I Tim. 4:1). Indeed, for Paul the devil was real, an actually existing, very powerful and very terrible opponent! Those who deny the real and personal existence of Satan should be honest enough to admit that they do not believe in the Bible!

---

which expresses unfulfilled purpose: the tempter actually failed in his endeavor to lead the Thessalonians astray. Cf. Gal. 2:2: actually Paul had not run in vain. The use of the past indicative in such clauses may be compared to its use in contrary-to-fact conditional sentences. — The subjunctive (γένηται "and in vain would get to be our toil," that is, "and our toil would turn out to have been useless") is regular in such clauses of negative purpose or fear (cf. I Cor. 9:27; II Cor. 9:3; and see Gram.N.T., pp. 987, 988).

The fears of the missionaries were banished by Timothy's return and gladdening report:

6, 7. But now that Timothy has just come to us from you, and has brought us the glad tidings of your faith and love, and that you cherish an affectionate recollection of us at all times, longing to see us, just as we also (long to see) you, for this reason, brothers, in all our distress and affliction, we were comforted about you, through your faith; . . .

Here at least (if not even before; see on 3:1) the emphasis shifts from Defence to Expression of Joy, though consciousness of opposition in Thessalonica is never completely absent. The expression "Timothy has come to us from you" is much more cordial and intimate than the formal "Timothy returned" would have been. It is as if Paul were writing, "Timothy was our representative to you. Now he has become your representative to us, revealing to us your very heart." As disclosed in verses 6 and 7, the report which Timothy brought was twofold. It was somewhat as follows:

"a. The faith and the love of the Thessalonians endure even in the midst of persecution; hence, they are genuine; and

"b. the yearning to see one another is mutual. On the side of the Thessalonians it is an evidence of the loving remembrance in which they constantly retain you (Paul and Silas)."

Note the expression ". . . has *just* come to us." Hence, Paul must have replied immediately. A hint for all those who tend to postpone answering important letters! For the term of endearment *brothers* see on 1:4 and on 2:17. From the side of Paul and Silas (more precisely: and *probably* Silas; see on 3:1) it was not only *absence* but also *distress and affliction* (cf. Job 15:24; Zeph. 1:15) which had made the heart grow fonder. For *affliction* or *tribulation* see on 1:6. The original term which is correctly rendered *distress* (thus A.V., A.R.V.) is related to our *anguish* (see also I Cor. 7:26; II Cor. 6:4; 12:10).

The expression "*all* our affliction and distress" shows that the difficulties which Paul and Silas had been (and, to a certain extent, were still) experiencing were considerable. We can hardly agree that opposition from the side of the Jews here in Corinth – where I Thessalonians was being written – was not included. It is true, of course, that the particular (and probably most vehement) flare-up recorded in Acts 18:5-17 *followed* the return of Silas and Timothy, but it would be strange if the underlying hostile attitude had been wholly dormant before that time. Among other afflictions and distresses which Paul may have had in mind are, perhaps, all or some of the following (and maybe others besides): doubt with respect to the effectiveness of the work in Thessalonica, concern about the safety of Timothy (these distresses were now removed), bad news from Galatia, and the physical strain due to the double load: on the one hand, carrying on an important and time-consuming gospel-ministry here at Corinth, and on the other hand, making good tents! And see also II Cor. 11:28.

But amid all these afflictions and distresses Paul and Silas were immeasurably *comforted* (see on 2:3; 2:11; also N.T.C. on John 14:16) by the report which Timothy brought. It is not at all surprising that Paul, in reply, comments on the *love* and on the *faith* of the Thessalonians (both mentioned by Timothy, *faith,* as the most basic, being repeated and viewed here as the agency that produced comfort), that is, on the work resulting from faith, and the exertion prompted by love, and the endurance inspired by hope (see on 1:3).

8. Paul continues: **for now we (really) live if y o u stand fast in the Lord.**

This is the utterance of profound and overpowering emotion. Paul's heart is on fire for the Lord (see on 1:1), and at the same time is filled with tender affection for the believers at Thessalonica who have made possible Timothy's favorable report. The thoughts crowd each other, sothat verse 8 is actually a combination of two ideas:

a. We live if y o u stand fast in the Lord

and

b. Now we live seeing that y o u are standing fast in the Lord.

Paul is saying, therefore, that whenever the Thessalonians *stand fast* (keep on taking a firm position; cf. II Thess. 2:15; also I Cor. 16:13; Gal. 5:1; Phil. 1:27) *in* (*metaphorical* use of this preposition, derived from the local sense) the Lord, rooted in him, trusting in him, loving him, hoping in him, those who brought them the gospel really live, being filled with joy and gratitude (cf. the use of the word *live* in Deut. 8:3 and Is. 38:16); and that such a climax of blessedness has now arrived. That such *living* does, indeed, include thanksgiving is indicated in the next two verses:

9, 10. For what thanksgiving can we offer to God concerning y o u in return for all the joy by means of which we rejoice on account of y o u in the presence of our God, by night and by day praying with intense earnestness that we may see y o u r faces and may supply the deficiencies of y o u r faith?

This is a rhetorical question. Paul's soul is flooded with gratitude to God, and this to such an extent that the consciousness of his own inability to make *an adequate return* to God grieves him. What has been received by the Thessalonians has also been received, in a different form, and *on account of them,* by him and his companions. The report of Timothy has given Paul and Silas a new lease on life. It has caused them to revive. They are deeply convinced of the fact that anything they can bring to God *in return for*[69] "all the joy by means of which they rejoice" is as nothing. See N.T.C. on John 3:29: the cup of joy is running over; cf. Is. 66:10.

But even though Paul is still struggling with the problem how to make an adequate return for blessings already received, this does not deter him from asking for still more! In fact, the very manner in which previous petitions have been answered makes him all the more earnest (note *over-abundantly* or *with intense earnestness*) in praying for something in addition to what has already been received. Hence, thanksgiving ("rejoicing before our God") is accompanied by prayer. Note how Paul, though working at a trade *by night and by day* (see on 2:9), still finds time to pray, and this also *by night and by day!*

The content of the prayer or petition is stated in *two* infinitive-clauses, but the two really express *one* idea, namely, that God's providence may permit the missionaries to return sothat they may once more see the face(s) of (that is, be present among, and rejoice in the fellowship of) the Thessalonian believers in order to supply *the deficiencies* (see also I Cor. 16:17; Phil. 2:30; Col. 1:24; then II Cor. 8:13, 14; 9:12; 11:9) of their faith. The verb *to supply* has the primary meaning *to knit together, to unite* (I Cor. 1:10). The idea of knitting together (think of the work of an *artisan,* which is related to the Greek verb), by an easy transition, has become *to make whole, to round out* (cf. Gal. 6:1 *to re-instate* or *restore*) or, as here, *to supply* what is still lacking.

Deficiencies have to be supplied or made up. Although the nature of these deficiencies is not pointed out in the present passage, the epistle contains the following hints:

a. The Thessalonians are somewhat confused with respect to the doctrine of Christ's return. Hence, by speaking about deficiencies Paul is already preparing for what he is going to say in 4:13-5:3.

b. Though these recent converts have been blessed with many a spiritual grace, there is room for improvement. The virtues already present must begin to abound *more and more* (4:1, 10).

c. Some of the members of the congregation are disorderly, some faint-hearted, some weak (5:14).

If this exposition of the term *deficiencies* be correct, it is clear that the

---

[69] The verb ἀνταποδίδωμι occurs in a favorable sense in Luke 14:14; Rom. 11:35; I Thess. 3:9; in an unfavorable sense in Rom. 12:19; II Thess. 1:6; and Heb. 10:30. In Luke 14:12-14 it is used in connection with ἀντικαλέω. In that same passage we also find ἀνταπόδομα, which occurs there in the favorable sense; in Rom. 11:9, unfavorable. Note also the slightly different form of the noun in Col. 3:24. The fact that the prefix ἀντί in all these cases must mean *in return* is immediately clear from the vivid passage Luke 14:12-14. No other meaning would give a comprehensible sense to the entire passage. See W. Hendriksen, *The Meaning of the Preposition* ἀντί *in the New Testament,* doctoral dissertation submitted to the Faculty of Princeton Seminary, 1948, Princeton Seminary Library, pp. 78, 79.

word *faith* ("the deficiencies of your faith") is used in a sense which includes both *the subjective* exercise of trust in the Lord and *the objective* revelation of God with respect to the work of redemption.

Having informed the readers about the constant prayer which both Paul and Silas are constantly uttering – a prayer that "we may see your faces" –, the ardent wish is now expressed that this petition may be granted (verse 11), and that additional spiritual blessings may be bestowed upon the Thessalonians (verses 12 and 13):

11. Now may he, our God and Father and our Lord Jesus, direct our way to you.

Although with respect to its solemn tone this statement approaches a prayer, we cannot agree with those commentators who call it a prayer. In a prayer God is addressed, and the second person is *generally* used; here the exalted names or titles are *entirely* in the third person (note the pronoun *he*). This, then, is not quite a prayer but rather the devout utterance of a wish that the petition of verse 10 may be fulfilled. For the names of the exalted persons mentioned here see on 1:1. Nevertheless, there are a few points of difference between the titles of 1:1 and those here in 3:11. Note *our* here in 3:11 (cf. 1:3). Also the official name *Christ* is here omitted. The intensive pronoun *he* precedes. Moreover, the essential unity (hence, unity of work and purpose) of the Father and the Son is stressed, the pronoun *he* referring to the combination, and the singular verb (third person singular aorist optative) being employed. We consider the pronoun αὐτός intensive (hence, *he*), not reflexive (*himself*), as if the thought had ever occurred either to Paul or to Silas that *they* might wish to direct their own way. The context here is very clear: note verse 9: thanksgiving was offered *to God,* the rejoicing was in *his* presence; and verse 10: the accompanying prayer was, of course, also uttered *to God.* Hence, very logically, there follows in verse 11, "Now may *he,* our God and Father and our Lord Jesus," etc. It is comforting to know that the Father and the Son are, indeed *one.* We never need to be afraid that the Father is less loving than the Son or that the two work at cross-purposes.

The wish, so touchingly expressed here, is that *our* (inclusive sense) God and Father and *our* (again inclusive, of course) Lord Jesus *may direct* (*make straight;* then *direct, prosper*) our way to you. It is obvious that the verb is used here in a more literal sense than in II Thess. 3:5 or in Luke 1:79.

The question may be asked, "Did God really grant this petition?" If we bear in mind that the prayer had been offered in complete submission to the divine will, the answer is, "Yes." See N.T.C. on John 14:13; 15:7; 15:16; and 16:23. Besides, there is Acts 20:1, 2, which indicates that Paul, on his third Missionary Journey, "gave much encouragement" to those in Macedonia. See also Acts 20:3, 4. The possibility of a still later visit (between the first and the second Roman imprisonment) must not be excluded (see on I Tim. 1:3). Of course, the time and the manner in which God answers prayer is not determined by us but by him.

12. Paul, however, also realizes that the spiritual progress of the Thessalonians can be considered even apart from any visit which he (or he and his companions) might make. Hence, there follows: **and as for y o u, may the Lord cause y o u to abound and overflow in love toward one another and toward all, just as also we (do) toward y o u.**

"*As for ourselves,* we ardently hope that God may direct our way to y o u; and (or *but*) *as for y o u*, whether or not God permits us to revisit y o u, may *the Lord* (that is, *the Lord Jesus* in closest possible connection with *our God and Father;* see on verse 11) cause y o u to abound and overflow in love." That expresses the sense of the passage in the light of its preceding context. Note the emphatic position of "as for y o u" at the very beginning of the sentence. The verbs *to abound* and *(to)overflow* are close synonyms. Together they express *one* idea, namely, that the Thessalonian believers may not merely *increase* in that most eminent virtue, namely, love – as the outward evidence of their living faith –, but may actually *abound* (also used by Paul in II Thess. 1:3; then Rom. 5:20; 6:1; II Cor. 4:15; 8:15; Phil. 4:17); yes, that they may *abound* in such a manner that this ocean of love, being full, reaches to the top edge of its borders *round about* (περισσεύσαι, a very descriptive verb of which Paul is fond, using it also in 4:1, 10, and frequently elsewhere), and even *over*flows (for the sense of περισσεύω is probably not far removed from that of ὑπερπερισσεύω, as in Rom. 5:20; II Cor. 7:4), sothat it reaches not only fellow-Christians, in fulfilment of Christ's "new commandment" (see N.T.C. on John 13:34), but even outsiders (5:15; cf. Gal. 6:10; cf. Matt. 5:43-48), being a love "toward one another *and toward all.*"

For the meaning of the noun *love* and of the verb *to love* see N.T.C. on John 13:35 and 21:15-17. The addition "just as we also (do) toward y o u" (that is, "just as we also abound and overflow in love toward y o u") finds its commentary in preceding passages (see on 2:7-12; 2:17-3:1; 3:7-11; see also on 1:6).

13. The *purpose* (cf. 3:2) of this abounding and overflowing in love is expressed as follows: **in order that he may strengthen**[70] **y o u r hearts, sothat they may be blameless in holiness in the presence of our God and Father.**

The Lord by means of love *strengthens* (see on 3:2) the inner purposes and desires. Hearts thus strengthened will be less prone to crave the

---

[70] As to form, the verb can be either aorist infinitive active or third person singular aorist optative active, but in harmony with the verbs which precede, the latter is probably intended.

unseparated life, the life of the world. Rather, they will tend in the direction of the wholly *separated* life, sothat, trusting entirely in Christ and in his redemption and having experienced the transforming influences of his Spirit, they will be *blameless* (cf. I Thess. 2:10), in a state and condition of *holiness* (separation from sin, consecration to God), and this in the very presence of *our God and Father,* that is, before his judgment-seat (Rom. 14:10).

This immediately introduces the thought of Christ's second coming unto judgment, as is evident both from the parallel passage (5:23) and from the immediately following phrase **at the coming of our Lord Jesus with all his saints.**

With respect to this compound phrase there is wide disagreement among commentators. There is first of all a difference of opinion with respect to the term *coming* or *Parousia,* which we have defined as being "the return of the Lord in order to bless his people with his presence" (see on 2:19).[71] But the main point of controversy has to do with the modifier *with all his saints.* And here again there are two problems that require solution:

a. What does this phrase modify?

b. What is the meaning of the word *saints?*

As to the first question, many commentators (for example, Van Leeuwen and Lenski) make this phrase dependent upon "in order that he may strengthen," or connect it loosely with the entire first part of verse 13. The sense then would be somewhat on this order (starting with verse 12): "And as for y o u, may the Lord cause y o u to abound and to overflow in love . . . in order that he may strengthen y o u r hearts sothat they *with all his saints* may be blameless in holiness in the presence of our God and Father at the coming of our Lord Jesus."

We doubt, however, whether any reader (either of the Greek original or of the English translation) will mentally so construe the phrase. The translations (A.V., A.R.V., R.S.V., Weymouth, etc., etc.), in strict accordance with the original, place the words *with all his saints* immediately after *at the coming of our Lord Jesus.* In fact, though Lenski says that these two phrases should be separated by a comma, even in his own rendering he does not so separate them! (See R. C. H. Lenski, *op. cit.,* p. 301, then p. 296.) Other versions indicate the right connection by translating: "when our Lord Jesus appears (or *comes back*) with all his people (or *with all his consecrated ones*)." Thus, for example, Goodspeed and Williams.

The reason we agree with the translators and not with some commentators (Van Leeuwen, Lenski) is that we regard the construction favored by the latter to be unnatural (so does also Frame, *op. cit.,* p. 140). Surely, un-

---

[71] We disagree with the view of Lenski, according to which the Parousia is the Lord's presence *and not his coming out of heaven; op. cit.,* p. 301.

less there is a sound reason for an exception, we should not depart from the rule that a phrase should be construed with the words nearest (or at least *near*) to it.

One sometimes wonders whether the difficulty of conceiving the saints as coming *with* the Lord has led to the unnatural construction. Whether or not one happens to belong to the camp of the Premillennialists, in all fairness to them one must admit that when they link *with all his saints* with the immediately preceding words, sothat we get, "at the coming of our Lord Jesus with all his saints," they are entirely correct!

As we see it, they (as well as others who do not share their millennial views) are also correct in interpreting the term *saints* (ἅγιοι) as referring to the redeemed, and not to the angels. This introduces problem b. mentioned above. On this point we are in complete agreement with those commentators (like Van Leeuwen and Lenski) whose view with respect to the construction of the sentence we have just criticized. And, on the other hand, we are in complete disagreement here with Frame, who boldly translates "with all his angels" (*op. cit.,* p. 136). Reasons for our position:

(1) Paul loves this word *saints,* using it again and again in his epistles. Not once does he employ it to indicate the angels, always the redeemed. Why then introduce an exception here in I Thess. 3:13?

(2) Paul in this same passage mentions the terms *holiness* (ἁγιωσύνη) and *saints* (ἅγιοι). In the original the two words are from the same root, just as are our words *consecration* and *consecrated ones.* Hence, those who at Christ's coming will be blameless in holiness most likely resemble the redeemed saints.

(3) In the parallel passage (4:14), these saints are defined as *those who have fallen asleep in Jesus.* See on that verse.

It is certainly true that the angels will accompany Christ at his return (see on II Thess. 1:7; Matt. 25:31), but that is not taught here in I Thess. 3:13. Here the thought is that when the Lord Jesus (see on 1:1) returns, God will *bring with him* (exactly as is stated in 4:14) those who, throughout the ages, have lived the life of Christian separation from the world and of devotion to God. By God they had been "set apart" to his worship and service sothat, through the sanctifying power of the Holy Spirit, they had become saints "in experience as well as position" (to use a phrase employed by K. S. Wuest, *Golden Nuggets,* p. 72), and at death had entered the kingdom above. Not a single one of them will be left behind in heaven: *all* those who at death went to heaven – and therefore are now with him in heaven – will leave their celestial abodes at the very moment when the Lord begins his descent. Very quickly they will reunite with their bodies, which now become *gloriously resurrected* bodies, and will then immediately (together with those children of God who still survive on earth, and who will be changed "in a moment, in the twinkling of an eye") ascend in order to meet the Lord.

This interpretation brings 3:13 into complete harmony with 4:13-18; see on that passage. It also shows that there is no need nor good reason to accept the theory, held by *many* (but not by all of our brothers in Christ, the) Premillennialists, according to which Christ comes first *for* his saints, and seven years later *with* his saints. The coming is *one;* but it is a coming both *with* and *for* his saints.

Synthesis of Chapter 3

See p. 80. *Expression of Joy. Paul writes to the Thessalonians, informing them how he rejoices over Timothy's report with respect to their continued spiritual progress even in the midst of persecution.*

Verses 1-5. *What moved Paul (or Paul after consultation with the others) to send Timothy*

Paul informs the Thessalonians that the continued separation had at length become unbearable. Hence the decision had been reached to be left behind in Athens *alone* (which may mean either *all alone* or, perhaps preferably, *alone with Silas*), and to send Timothy to them, with this threefold purpose:

a. in order to strengthen the Thessalonians

b. in order to encourage them

c. in order to learn (and bring back information) about their faith.

In view of the fact that Thessalonica counted among its members some that were disorderly, some that were faint-hearted, and some that were weak (perhaps, prone to fall back into the immorality of heathendom), *strengthening* was necessary. In view of oppression and the valiant resolution to stand up under it *encouragement* was in order. In view of the constant and sinister attempt of the tempter to "lure away" God's children from the faith, by striving to entice them with words of flattery, *information* about the state of their faith was desired.

In connection with this last point, one of the older commentators points out that the devil is often more dangerous when he fawns than when he roars: David won the victory over Satan in the field of battle (I Sam. 17:49), but in the cool of the evening on the housetop Satan won the victory over David.

Paul reminds the Thessalonians that, while the missionaries were still with them, the tribulation under which they were now suffering had been predicted again and again. "Forewarned is fore-armed." Persecution that has been planned by God in his love and that happens "according to plan" should strengthen faith.

Verses 6-10. *What comfort (or reason for rejoicing) Timothy's report had brought*

Timothy had returned and had brought tidings concerning the readers' faith and love, their deficiencies, and their yearning to see Paul and Silas. *On the whole* (but note "the deficiencies") the report had been very encouraging. It had given Paul and Silas a new lease on life. The great apostle gives expression to his feeling of inadequacy in attempting to bring a proper thank-offering to God. He informs the readers of his constant, intense, and earnest prayer for the privilege of returning to them in order to see them face to face and to supply the deficiencies of their faith.

Verses 11-13. *The fervent wish*

He expresses the fervent wish that his prayer may be heard and that, whether or not it be granted, the Lord may fill them with such an overflowing measure of love that their hearts may be strengthened, sothat there may be fruit for the day of judgment, when Jesus comes with all his saints.

Summary of I Thessalonians 4:1-12

Paul Writes to the Thessalonians

Exhorting Them How They Should Conduct Themselves
This Section Comprises *the Apostle's Exhortation:*

4:1-8 with respect to sex and marriage
sex in general: immorality condemned, sanctification urged
in particular, the taking of a wife "in sanctification and honor"
and
the duty with respect to the brother, namely, not to defraud him "in this matter"

4:9-12 with respect to love of the brotherhood and diligence in daily conduct
commendation of love toward the brotherhood
commendation of diligence in daily conduct: fanatics, busybodies, and loafers are reprimanded

CHAPTER IV

I THESSALONIANS 4:1

4 1 For the rest, brothers, we request y o u and urge y o u in the Lord Jesus,
that as y o u received from us (instructions) as to how y o u ought to conduct
yourselves [72] and to please God — as in fact y o u are conducting yourselves — that
y o u abound the more. 2 For y o u know what instructions we gave y o u through
the Lord Jesus. 3 For this is God's will, y o u r sanctification, that y o u abstain
from immorality, 4 that each one of y o u know how to take a wife [73] for himself in
sanctification and honor, 5 not in the passion of lust like also the heathen who do
not know God; 6 that no one go beyond what is proper and defraud his brother in
this matter, because an Avenger is the Lord in all these things, as previously we told
y o u and solemnly testified. 7 For God did not call us for uncleanness but in sanctification. 8 Therefore, he who rejects (this instruction), rejects not man but God
who even gives his Holy Spirit to y o u.
9 Now concerning love to the brothers y o u have no need to (have anyone)
write to y o u, for y o u yourselves have been taught by God to love each other; 10
and in fact y o u are also doing this to all the brothers in the whole of Macedonia.
But we urge y o u, brothers, to abound the more, 11 and to be ambitious about
living calmly, and to be engaged in y o u r own affairs, and to work with y o u r
hands, just as we charged y o u, 12 in order that y o u may conduct yourselves
properly with respect to outsiders and be dependent on nobody.

4:1-12

4:1. For the rest, brothers, we request y o u and urge y o u in the Lord Jesus, that as y o u received from us (instructions) as to how y o u ought to conduct yourselves and to please God — as in fact y o u are conducting yourselves —, that y o u abound the more.

Both the phrase of introduction ("for the rest") and the subject-matter makes it clear that a new section begins here. This is neither Defence nor Expression of Joy but Exhortation to live sanctified lives with respect to all classes and at all times.

This Exhortation extends from verse 1 through verse 12 of the fourth chapter, and is resumed in chapter 5. The first 11 verses of that chapter form a transition, and may be classified either as Exhortation (see espe-

---

[72] Or: *how y o u ought to live* (literally *walk*); so also in verse 12; cf. 2:12.
[73] Literally *vessel.*

cially verses 6, 8, 11) or (together with 4:13-18) as Instruction with respect to the return of Christ. From 5:12 on the Exhortation has been fully resumed, as is clear from all the "instructions" found in that section.

It is evident then that the section with reference to Christ's return is wedged in between two Exhortation-paragraphs dealing with the affairs of daily life and conduct. This is significant. It indicates that Paul was neither an ascetic nor an ecstatic or dreamer. He wanted his readers to have a healthy outlook upon life, sothat in meditating upon events "on the other side" (of death) they would not forget about their duties "on this side."

Nevertheless, he did not want them to separate these two. On the contrary, he desired that "on this side" they would arrange everything sothat they would be ready for "the other side." Or, stating it differently, *he wanted them to set their house in order with a view to the earnestly awaited coming of the glorious Visitor from "the other side," even the Lord Jesus.* They must ever be ready to receive him.

In a sense there is a difference between the present section (4:1-12) and the resumption of admonitions (5:12-28). The present section emphasizes the duty of living sanctified lives and of giving evidence of this both to fellow-Christians (by loving them, particularly by not trespassing the bounds of propriety in matters pertaining to sex) and to outsiders (by proper conduct). The section at the close of the epistle is far more specific. It contains a good many detailed directions with respect to various matters (see especially 5:12-22, 24-27).

In another sense, however, there is a close resemblance between the two sections, as the following comparison will show:

4:1-12	5:12-28
verses 1, 2, 3, 4, 7: y o u r *sanctification*	verse 23: "Now may he, the God of peace, *sanctify* y o u completely."
verse 3: ". . . that y o u abstain from immorality."	verse 22: "Abstain from every form of evil."
verse 6: "An Avenger is the Lord."	verse 15: "Take care that none of y o u repays evil for evil."
verse 8: ". . . who even gives his Holy Spirit to y o u."	verse 19: "Quench not the Spirit."
verse 9: ". . . love each other."	verse 14: "Admonish the disorderly, encourage the fainthearted, help the weak, have patience with all."
verse 11: ". . . be ambitious about living calmly."	verse 13: "Be at peace among yourselves."

verse 12: ". . . conduct yourselves properly with respect to outsiders."

verse 15: "Always aim at doing good to each other *and to all.*"

Note how here in 4:1 (and also in what follows) Paul is dealing with the Thessalonian believers "as a nurse cherishes (and as a father admonishes) her (his) own children" (2:7, 11). For the meaning of *brothers* see on 1:4. The apostle (supported by his companions, of course) *requests* (the asking is friendly and polite, yet is no begging; see N.T.C. on John 11:22; 14:16) and *admonishes* or *urges* (see on 2:11; 3:2, 7) *"in* the Lord Jesus" (see on 1:1) – that is, by virtue of union with the Lord whom he represents and whose spirit inspires him – that they will *overflow* or *excel* or *abound* (περισσεύω see on 3:12) more and more in the business of conducting themselves properly, thus pleasing God. It is evident that what he desires so ardently is that the Thessalonians, in keeping God's law, shall be prompted by gratitude for their deliverance. With wonderful tact he injects the parenthetical clause: "as in fact y o u are conducting yourselves." What the apostle really desires, therefore, is that the branches that bear fruit shall bear *more* fruit (see N.T.C. on John 15:2). That was necessary not only in view of the immaturity of these recent converts from paganism and of "the deficiencies of faith" which had to be supplied in their particular case (3:10), but also in view of the more general consideration, namely, that the believer never attains to complete spiritual perfection in this life. For the concept *pleasing God* see on 2:15.

2. For y o u know what instructions we gave y o u through the Lord Jesus.

In order to preclude the charge of being guilty of issuing arbitrary orders, hence, in order to add weight to his exhortation, the apostle stresses two matters:

a. That those *instructions* or *directives* (a military term occurring also in Acts 5:28; 16:24; I Tim. 1:5, 18) are *not new.* They are orders given previously, while Paul was with them.

b. That they are given *through* the Lord Jesus; that is, at his command; hence, with his authority. Though commentators differ with respect to the interpretation of the preposition *through* as here used, the explanation which we have just given has the context in its favor (see below on verse 8). The readers must be made aware of the fact that whoever rejects the instructions here given rejects not man but God.

When this interpretation is adopted, the logic of the statement which immediately follows is clear at once. Note the connection: "through the Lord Jesus Christ. For this is God's will." It is not merely *Paul* writing but *God* directing.

3-8. Because of the exegetical problem involved in verses 3-8, and in order to show the relationship of the several parts to each other and to the whole, it was necessary to print these six verses together as one unit, and to print them in such a manner that these relationships are at once apparent.

For this is God's will, y o u r sanctification,

(a) **that y o u abstain from immorality,**

(b) **that each one of y o u know how to take a wife for himself in sanctification and honor, not in the passion of lust like also the heathen who do not know God;**

(c) **that (no one) go beyond what is proper and defraud his brother in this matter,**

because an Avenger is the Lord in all these things, as previously we told y o u, and solemnly testified. For God did not call us for uncleanness but in sanctification. Therefore, he who rejects (this instruction), rejects not man but God who even gives his Holy Spirit to y o u.

Thus, it becomes apparent at once that, according to the most simple construction (also the most logical, it seems to us), the words *This . . . God's will . . . y o u r sanctification* are in apposition. The three co-ordinate clauses (a, b, and c) are added for further elucidation (in other words, they are *epexegetical*) of the concept *y o u r sanctification.* (See also on verse 9.) They are in apposition with it and give it a somewhat restricted application. Also (b) sheds light on (a), (a) on (b), (c) on (b), and (b) on (c). Though (b) and (c) are parallel to each other and in a sense also to (a), yet they may be viewed as presenting a specific exemplification of (a).

The clause "because an Avenger is the Lord in all these things . . ." modifies (a), (b), and (c), as the very words *all these things* indicate. The sense of that clause is: God avenges immorality, and in particular the taking of a wife in the passion of lust, and the evil of going beyond what is proper and defrauding the brother in the matter of marital relationships. God punishes the man who refuses to tread the path of sanctification. This is true, "*for* God did not call us for uncleanness but in sanctification." The final sentence — "Therefore, he who rejects (this instruction) rejects not man but God who even gives his Holy Spirit to y o u" — shows that because it was God himself who called in connection with sanctification, the man who disregards this admonition squarely opposes *him* (see N.T.C. on John 13:20; cf. I Sam. 8:7; Luke 10:16), and that this is all the more reprehensible because the Author of sanctification is God's great *gift* to the Church.

From the preceding it is clear that Paul is discussing *one* matter, not *two.* He is discussing *sanctification,* and here in verses 3-8 in particular the duty of everyone to abstain from *immorality,* such as is practiced, for example, by those who, instead of taking a wife and doing this in a manner that is in keeping with the requirement of sanctification, are motivated by lust; or, disregarding the bounds of decency, enter into illicit, clandestine relationships with their brother's wife or daughter. Though the brother, who has thus been outwitted and defrauded, may never discover the wrong that was done against him, there is, nevertheless, an Avenger, even God (cf. Lev. 25:14, 17; Ps. 94:1), just as Paul had solemnly declared while he was still with them. Let the believers in Thessalonica, so recently converted from a world in which such sinful practices prevail, bear in mind that they have been called out of this world, and this not for the purpose of committing uncleanness, but in connection with the great work of *sanctification*[74] which the Holy Spirit, God's gift to the Church, is performing in their hearts. For the name, character, coming, and work of the Holy Spirit see N.T.C. on John 14:16, 17, 26; 15:26; 16:7, 8, 13-15.

That, in brief, seems to be the plain import of the entire passage (verses 3-8). There are, however, certain translators and commentators who adhere to a view which, in one important respect, differs radically from ours. Their view amounts to this, that Paul in this brief paragraph is condemning *two* heathen vices, namely, *sexual immorality* and *dishonest business practices*. Verse 6 is then translated as follows (or on this order): "that no one go too far and cheat his brother *in business*." We believe, however, that those translators are correct who have: "that no one go beyond what is proper and defraud his brother *in this matter*."[75]

Our reasons for adopting the rendering, "that no one go beyond what is proper and defraud his brother *in this matter*" are as follows:

---

[74] The active verbal noun ἁγιασμός is here used, also in I Thess. 4:7; II Thess. 2:13; then Rom. 6:19, 22; I Cor. 1:30; Heb. 12:14; I Peter 1:2. The verbal idea is probably not entirely absent either in I Thess. 4:4 (in choosing a wife the principle of sanctification should make itself manifest) or in I Tim. 2:15. The resultant state or quality is expressed by the term ἁγιασύνη as the ending suggests.

[75] In favor of the rendering "in this matter" (or something similar) and of interpreting the admonition as a warning against "sins of the flesh," especially the sin of illicit sexual relationships (for example, of a man with his fellow believer's wife or daughter) are the following: A.R.V., R.S.V., Goodspeed, Weymouth, Williams, the new Dutch rendering, the French (Version d'Ostervald); also: Alford, Bengel, Denney (in *The Expositor's Bible*), Ellicott, Erdman, Frame, Fausset (in Jamieson, Fausset, Brown *Commentary*), George Milligan, Moffatt (in *Expositor's Greek Testament*), and Robertson (in *Word Pictures*), these in addition to many other commentators among whom there are some whose works are probably less well known or less easily accessible.

In favor of the rendering "in business" (or something similar) are the following: Wyclif ("in chaffaringe"), Tyndale ("in bargayninge"), Cranmer, Rheims, the Berkeley Version (by Verkuyl), the older German versions, Frisian, South African; also: Auberlen-Riggenbach (in Lange's Commentary), Calvin, Grotius, Lenski, Veldkamp, and several others.

Barnes is among those who accept the position that the injunction is against defrauding in any sense, shape, or manner, whether in business or otherwise. Cf. "in *any* matter" of the Geneva Version and of the A.V.

(1) When a subject is introduced with so much feeling, an abrupt change to something quite different (like "in business") is not to be expected. Paul is speaking about sanctification, and in that connection, about abstaining from immorality and uncleanness. *Sanctification, immorality, uncleanness,* are the key-words of the entire paragraph (verses 3-8).

(2) The injunction, "that each one of you know how *to take* (κτᾶσθαι *present* infinitive; hence, not *to possess,* for which we would rather expect the *perfect* tense) a wife (literally *vessel,* a term used also by the rabbis for *wife*) for himself in sanctification and honor" certainly supports the idea that the πρᾶγμα about which Paul is speaking in verse 6 is that of purity in sex and marital relationships. One should choose a wife for himself, and in this choice the sanctifying power of God, which causes one to hold his wife in honor, should come to expression. The evil of shamefully defrauding a brother (by practicing immorality with his wife or daughter) instead of honorably taking a wife is here condemned.

(3) Our interpretation is also supported by what Paul says in a somewhat parallel passage: I Cor. 7:2, and cf. verse 39: in order not to fall into the temptation of committing immorality a man should have *a wife of his own.* Marriage, moreover, must ever be *in the Lord.*

(4) The verbs a. *go beyond* or *step over* or *over-reach* (ὑπερβαίνω-ειν, occurring only here in the New Testament), whether used intransitively (*to go beyond what is proper*) or transitively (*to over-reach or outwit the brother*), and b. *have more than, take advantage of, defraud* (πλεονέκτω-ειν), are very fitting in connection with immoral practices in sex-relationships. (It is not true that they can apply only to business-transactions.) Such sins are often practised *in secret:* the father or the husband does not know what is going on and his rights are being denied; he is being *defrauded.* But God knows, and he will prove to be the Avenger!

(5) In the New Testament the word πρᾶγμα nowhere else means *business,* but always means *thing, matter* (sometimes *deed, practice*). See footnote 76. Objections to this explanation are answered in the same footnote.[76]

---

[76] The main objections are as follows:

a. *The majority of commentators favor the translation "in business."*
Answer: When so many scholars of high rank are to be found on each side of a question, this argument (which is never strong) has very little value.

b. *The clause, "An Avenger is the Lord in all these things" indicates that at least two different sins must have been mentioned in the preceding.*
Answer: Strictly speaking, even *two* is not enough to account fully for the expression *all these things.* But on our own explanation the three co-ordinate clauses, mentioning the sin of immorality, the taking of a wife in the passion of lust, and the going beyond what is proper and defrauding the brother, are all that is needed, especially if it be borne in mind that this is not a little problem in addition, and that similar sins, though not actually mentioned, are *implied.*

c. *The omission of a subject in connection with "go beyond what is proper and defraud his brother in this matter" shows that a new sin, not yet thought of before, is mentioned here.*

9. A new admonition is now added. Nevertheless, it is not entirely new. Love to the brothers is another illustration of *sanctification,* mentioned in verse 3. Moreover, in verse 6 *defrauding the brother* was prohibited. Hence, it is not surprising that something is now said with reference to *loving the brother*(s):

Now concerning love to the brothers you have no need to (have anyone) write to you, for you yourselves have been taught by God to love each other.

The question whether Paul is here reflecting on a letter from the Thessalonians has been discussed in footnote 4. No such letter is required to explain the present passage. As has already been indicated, the transition from verses 3-8 to verse 9 is not abrupt. And the expression "You have no need to (have anyone) write to you," does not necessarily indicate reluctance on Paul's part. Rather, it is accounted for as follows:

(1) Paul has just said that the Holy Spirit had been given to the Church (in this case specifically to the brothers at Thessalonica); see verse 8. In this very connection he now adds that this indwelling Spirit (in connection with the message from the missionaries) has already taught them to love each other. Hence, writing about this at length is not now considered necessary. The mere mention ought to suffice.

(2) The Thessalonians – see the next verse (10) – are actually showing

---

Answer: The omission of the subject, so that it has to be supplied (perhaps from the preceding clause; hence, "that each one of you . . . not" or "that no one . . .") does not in and by itself settle the question in either direction. In arriving at a conclusion it is the predicate, far more than the subject, that is of importance.

d. *The articular infinitive in verse 6* (τὸ μὴ ὑπερβαίνειν), *by its very contrast with the anarthrous infinitives in the two preceding clauses* (ἀπέχεσθαι *and* εἰδέναι) *proves that a new sin is introduced here, namely, that of dishonesty in business.*
Answer: The use of the article with the infinitive in verse 6 (so that τὸ μὴ ὑπερβαίνειν results) may be explained as an attempt to indicate that this μή is not parallel to the μή at the beginning (and again toward the end) of verse 5, but introduces a new clause. (There are other explanations.) It is not true that the article proves that a new sin is introduced here.

e. Πρᾶγμα *is a regular commercial term, meaning "business." Hence, that must be the meaning here in I Thess. 4:6.*
Answer: The simple fact is that nowhere else in the entire New Testament does the word have that meaning.
Matt. 18:19: "as touching any *thing*"
Luke 1:1: "a narrative concerning those *matters.*"
Acts 5:4: ". . . this *thing* (perhaps *deed*) in thy heart"
Rom. 16:2: "assist her in whatever *matter*"
I Cor. 6:1: ". . . having a *matter* (or *grievance* or *law-suit*) against his neighbor
II Cor. 7:11: ". . . to be pure in the *matter*"
Heb. 6:18: "by two immutable *things*"
Heb. 10:1: "not the very image of the *things*"
Heb. 11:1: "a conviction of *things* not seen"
Jas. 3:16: "and every vile *deed* (or *practice*)"

this love, and this on a very wide scale (cf. 1:3). Why then should Paul write about it at length?

(3) Paul was probably the most tactful missionary who ever walked the earth. He wishes to avoid giving offence, and he desires to give credit where credit is due. By stating that, broadly speaking, it is not even necessary to write about love to the brothers, inasmuch as the readers have been taught by God and are showing the effects of this teaching in their lives, he is the better prepared to point out certain deficiencies. Let it be borne in mind that the man who is writing is the one who told others that their speech should ever be gracious, seasoned with salt (Col. 4:6). He never flatters (see on I Thess. 2:5), but he is gentle as when a nurse cherishes (or as when a father deals with) her (his) own children (see on 2:7, 11).

The term *philadelphia* (φιλαδελφία) or *love to the brother*(s), which in classical Greek means love to the brother *by birth,* in the New Testament always denotes love to the brother *in Christ* (thus also in Rom. 12:10; Heb. 13:1; I Peter 1:22; II Peter 1:7). The Thessalonians had been *taught by God* thus to love one another. The passive verbal adjective θεοδίδακτοι occurs only here in the New Testament, but cf. Is. 54:13; 60:2, 3; Jer. 31:33, 34; Joel 2:28; Mic. 5:2; Zeph. 3:9; Mal. 1:11; and see N.T.C. on John 6:45. For loving one another see N.T.C. on John 13:34; 15:12. On the verb *to love* see N.T.C. on John 21:15-17.

10. The effectiveness of this divine teaching is now indicated:

And in fact you are also doing this to all the brothers in the whole of Macedonia.

To the industrial, political, and social connections between the people of the large city of Thessalonica and those of other places in Macedonia (for example, Philippi, Berea) the faith-in-Christ relationship had now been added. To all the brothers in Christ with whom the Thessalonians came into contact, throughout the whole of Macedonia, genuine "brotherly love" was being revealed. Cf. 1:7, 8. Hence, Paul can only add: **But we urge** (see on 2:11) **you, brothers, to abound the more.** See on 4:1. Perfection had not yet been reached. This admonition is always timely, for in this life no Christian ever reaches the ideal of ethical perfection. Besides, in *this* case there were special reasons why the admonition was necessary, as is clearly intimated in such passages as 3:10; 4:3-8, 11; 5:13-15.

11. A few brief admonitions are added. Also with respect to the matters here mentioned the work of sanctification (see verse 3) must become evident:

a. **and to be ambitious about living calmly**

b. **and to be engaged in your own affairs**

c. **and to work with your hands, just as we charged you,**

Fanatics, busybodies, and *loafers,* nearly every church has them! Often one and the same person is all three. Hence, the three admonitions do not concern three separate classes of people, but in a sense the entire congregation, for the seed of every sin is embedded in every heart.

The attempt to find in the second and the third admonition a reference to two distinct groups – businessmen and laborers – must be rejected. Certain commentators favor this idea, probably in order to add a touch of realism to the "businessmen" whom they have introduced in verse 6 ("in business"?). The admonitions concern the membership in general, though naturally they concern some far more than others. Also, the first admonition was particularly adapted to one person, the second to another, etc.

Although there is nothing here that proves a connection between conditions in the church and excitement about Christ's expected return, such a connection is, nevertheless, probable. See on II Thess. 2:1, 2. Note also that here in I Thess. 4 the three admonitions are immediately followed by instruction with reference to the second coming.

Some people had become restless. Paul now urges that this restlessness be turned into the proper channel. With that admirable ability to express himself paradoxically which again and again becomes evident in his epistles, Paul admonishes the Thessalonians to become all stirred up about being quiet (living calmly)! Let the restless one *be ambitious* about attaining this goal. The original has here the verb φιλοτιμεῖσθαι. The primary meaning is *to love honor,* then *to be ambitious, to aspire, to strive* (perhaps *to take pride in;* see also Rom. 5:20; II Cor. 5:9).[77]

Glorying in the doctrine of Christ's Return is proper. Awaiting this blessed coming is natural for the genuine believer. But being so excited about it that one becomes arrogant, thinking that he – he alone! – has discovered "the light," sothat as a result one begins to meddle in the affairs of other people, particularly with the affairs of the leaders of the church, is all wrong. Hence, to the first admonition a second is added: ". . . to be engaged in *y o u r own affairs* (τὰ ἴδια)." It seems that the busybodies did not take this admonition to heart. Their meddling grew worse instead of better (see on II Thess. 3:11).

The tendency of such people to leave their workshop or other form of manual labor evoked the third admonition: ". . . to work with y o u r own hands, just as we charged y o u." See on 2:9. Manual labor was even more common in those days than it is now. There were slaves, hired laborers, independent artisans (cf. Acts 19:24) each having his own workshop, farmers or helpers on farms. Of course, a harbor-city like Thessalonica also had its ship-owners and its leaders in commercial enterprises. And there were the men who owned or worked in bazaars. It is certainly within the realm

[77] See the article by J. S. M. Hooper "Translation of Biblical Terms: An Illustration," in *BTr,* Vol. 4, Number 3 (July, 1953), 126-129.

of possibility that some of the men in control of business, whether big or small, belonged to the church. In many cases, no doubt, manual labor was combined with business on a small scale. But in the present passage, at any rate, the emphasis is not on doing business but on working with the hands. The bulk of the membership must have consisted of manual laborers, skilled or unskilled. See also p. 11. Paul knew what this meant. Perhaps he himself, just before writing this letter, had been working on a tent! The intent then of the present admonition is that the members of the recently established congregation, instead of seeking to be supported by the church and of interfering with the leaders if they did not get their way, should continue at their daily occupation, earning their own living. The gospel of salvation is intensely practical. It dignifies labor. All these things had been made perfectly plain to the Thessalonians when the missionaries first visited them. Definite orders had been given. Hence, fanatics, busybodies, and loafers could not offer any reasonable excuse for their misconduct.

12. The purpose of these admonitions is stated in the following words: **in order that [78] you may conduct yourselves properly with respect to outsiders and be dependent on nobody.[79]**

To *walk* (same verb as in 2:12; 4:1) or behave "according to good fashion" or "in good form" (εὐσχημόνως from εὖ and σχῆμα; cf. I Cor. 14:40; then Rom. 13:13), becomingly, with respect to *outsiders,* that is, non-Christians (cf. I Cor. 5:12; Col. 4:5), sothat the Gospel would not be brought into discredit; and *to be dependent on* (literally *to have need of*) nobody, is a worthy aim. Thus, one is able even to help support those worthy persons who are really in need (cf. Acts 20:34, 35).

Synthesis of 4:1-12

See p. 96. *Exhortation. Paul writes to the Thessalonians exhorting them how they should conduct themselves*

verses 1-8 *with respect to sex and marriage*

Very tactfully the apostle points out that he is not issuing new commands, that his precepts are given through the Lord Jesus Christ (in harmony with Christ's will and by his authority), and that to a certain extent the readers are already pleasing God by their conduct in harmony with his will. They should, however, abound the more.

[78] The change from infinitives to ἵνα would seem to imply purpose here (perhaps result: *so that;* the difference being very trivial in this case), not an object-clause after "We urge you." It is entirely true, of course, that ἵνα frequently introduces an object-clause, but for the reason stated that is not probable here.

[79] Of course, μηδενός can also mean *on nothing,* but in view of the immediately preceding πρὸς τοὺς ἔξω, the translation *on nobody* is probably better.

Now, the will of God is their *sanctification.*

Applying this to the sphere of sex and marriage, Paul insists that each man, far from clinging to or falling back into heathen vice, for example, defrauding a brother by means of dishonorable conduct with that brother's wife or daughter, should take a wife for himself in sanctification and honor, not in the passion of lust. He points out, moreover:

a. that God is an Avenger,

b. that the readers must bear in mind that they have been called not for uncleanness but in sanctification,

c. that anyone who rejects this instruction rejects not man but God, and

d. that this God, in order to help them in their struggle against sin, even gives his Holy Spirit to them.

verses 9-12 *with respect to love of the brotherhood and diligence in daily conduct*

With respect to love toward brothers in Christ, Paul can be brief, for God's indwelling Spirit has taught the brothers to love each other; besides, they are already doing this on a wide scale. Let them *abound* in this virtue, however.

With respect to diligence, *fanatics* – afflicted probably with Parousia hysteria (cf. II Thess. 2:1, 2) – should become "ambitious to be calm"; *busybodies* (Paul uses the actual term in II Thess. 3:11, but *the idea* is implied here in I Thess. 4:11) should begin to mind their own affairs; and *loafers* should start working with their hands. (In all probability the same persons were all three: fanatics, busybodies, and loafers.) No offence should be given to outsiders. Besides, by working diligently a person develops the art of being "dependent on nobody."

Summary of I Thessalonians 4:13 – 5:11

Paul Writes to the Thessalonians

Instructing Them How Christ Will Come Again

This Section Comprises *the Apostle's Instruction,* showing that the Lord's Return will be

4:13-18 *with impartiality* toward all believers, sothat survivors will have no advantage over those who have fallen asleep

5:1-11 *with suddenness,* taking people by surprise, though believers will be (and ever should exert themselves to be) fully prepared

13 Now we do not wish y o u to be in ignorance, brothers, concerning those
who fall asleep, in order that y o u do not grieve as do the rest, who have no hope.
14 For if we believe that Jesus died and rose again, so also those who fell asleep
through Jesus God will bring with him.[80] 15 For this we say to y o u by the word
of the Lord that we, those who remain alive, who are left until the coming of the
Lord, shall have no advantage at all over those who fell asleep. 16 For with a
shouted command, with a voice of an archangel and with a trumpet of God the
Lord himself will descend from heaven, and the dead in Christ will rise first; 17
then we who are alive, who are left, shall be caught up together with them in
clouds to meet the Lord in the air. 18 And so we shall always be with the Lord.
Therefore encourage one another with these words.

4:13-18

A new section begins here. This is neither Defence nor Expression of Joy nor Exhortation but Instruction, though these four are never entirely separated. Note, for example, the exhortation in verse 18.

This section shows how Christ will come again. It has two subdivisions, showing first, that he will come with impartiality toward all believers, sothat survivors will have no advantage over those who have fallen asleep (4:13-18), and secondly, that his arrival will be sudden, taking people by surprise (5:1-11).

4:13. Now we do not wish y o u to be in ignorance, brothers, concerning those who are falling asleep.

The introductory clause, *Now we do not wish y o u to be in ignorance,* has its analogies in many letters that have come down to us from the ancient world. Paul often uses this formula (Rom. 1:13; 11:25; I Cor. 10:1; 12:1; II Cor. 1:8; cf. Phil. 1:12; Col. 2:1). But in Paul's epistles words are never mere empty forms. They are divinely inspired. There is a special reason for them. So also in the present case. Ignorance concerning spiritual realities is always bad for the believer. It leads to lack of comfort. That was particularly true in this case. The *brothers* (note affectionate form of address; see on 1:4) are worrying about those who *fall* (an inferior reading has *had fallen) asleep.*

The death of believers is often compared to sleep (Matt. 27:52; John 11:11-13; Acts 7:60; I Cor. 7:39; 15:6, 18; cf. "rest from their labors," Rev. 14:13). The expression is based on Old Testament terminology with reference to death (Gen. 47:30; II Sam. 7:12). The comparison of death to sleep is particularly appropriate in implying not only rest from labor but also the glorious awakening which believers expect on the other side. This falling asleep does not indicate an intermediate state of unconscious re-

---

[80] We have tried to retain in the translation the amphibolous position of the phrase διὰ τοῦ Ἰησοῦ. See on verse 14.

pose (soul-sleep). Though the soul is asleep to the world which it has left (Job 7:9, 10; Is. 63:16; Eccl. 9:6), it is awake with respect to its own world (Luke 16:19-31; 23:43; II Cor. 5:8; Phil. 1:21-23; Rev. 7:15-17; 20:4). For other beautiful and comforting words and phrases describing the death of believers see N.T.C. on John 11:11-13.

A fair inference from the present passage is that during the short period which had elapsed since the Thessalonians first heard the Gospel some believers had passed from this earthly scene. It was with reference to them that friends and relatives were deeply disturbed. In fact, they were so alarmed that Paul adds: **in order that y o u do not grieve as do the rest, who have no hope.**

The reason for this perturbation is not stated in so many words, though a safe but very general inference can be drawn from the following verses. That these friends and relatives actually thought that the departed ones "were lost" [81] does not necessarily follow from anything in the present paragraph. It is possible, especially in view of the immediately following context, that they had given up all hope for the future glory of *the bodies* of the deceased. See on verse 15. However, verse 13 does not even state in so many words that believers were *actually* grieving "as the rest who have no hope." It may simply mean that there was that definite danger, that tendency. If so, then in order to prevent wrong beliefs and wrong reasons for sadness from deteriorating into *pagan* grief Paul writes as he does.

The Greek and Roman world of Paul's day was, indeed, a *hopeless* world (Eph. 2:12). According to the Greek (and afterward also the Roman) conception, there was no future for *the body,* which came to be regarded as the soul's "prison-house." As for *the soul* of man, it reluctantly departs from the body with the dying breath or by means of open wounds. This soul, in its separate existence, is not entirely immaterial. Its texture, however, is very thin. It retains many of the characteristics of its former body and is therefore immediately recognized when it appears in the other world. It enters Hades, a very dismal realm of "shades." Compared to its former life on the sunny earth, sunless Hades where the dead bemoan their existence, failed to inspire any comfort. The modification of this pagan myth of the Hereafter, sothat Elysian fields were introduced as the special abode for a few favorites of the gods, the creation of Tartarus (for the condemned) and of Erebus (for the unsentenced), all this did not furnish any reliable ground for confidence. The pagan world was without real hope. The Iliad ends with funeral-rites! Philosophers, at least by implication, rejected the highly colored descriptions transmitted from generation to generation by illustrious poets, and began to interpret them

[81] As Lenski seems to think, *op. cit.,* p. 325.

allegorically. They taught the immaterial nature of *the soul* and based arguments upon it in favor of its indestructibility and immortality. For *the body* they held out no hope whatsoever. In public plays the fancies accepted by the more unsophisticated were at times subjected to open ridicule. The Stoics expressed grave doubts with respect to man's future state. Conditional survival was the best they could offer, but even this was temporary. At length the soul is swallowed up in the fiery substance which is identical with deity. The Epicurians adopted a position which amounted to this: "The punishments of Tartarus are not to be feared, for *the soul,* being material, will share the fate of *the body.* As long as we are alive, *death* does not exist for us, and when death appears, *we* no longer exist." The Mystery religions (even assuming that our main sources are trustworthy and not too late), with their weird stories of resurrections which are hardly deserving of the name – hair that begins to grow, a little finger that begins to move, sections of a dead body that are reunited and become alive –, and with, at best, a promise to make one *happy* but not to make one *holy,* could not give lasting satisfaction.

Indeed, apart from Christianity there was no solid basis for hope in connection with the after-life. In the second century A. D. a certain Irene, an Egyptian, writes a letter to a family in mourning. She writes that she is sorry and that she weeps over her friend's departed one just as she had previously wept over the loss of her own dear one. She concludes her letter by saying:

> "But, nevertheless, against such things one can do nothing.
> Therefore, comfort one another. Farewell."

It is clear that such an expression "Comfort one another," when every ground for comfort was lacking, is, to put it mildly, very insufficient! [82]

14. For (i.e., such ignorance and hopelessness is inexcusable, *for*) **if we believe that Jesus died and rose again, so also those who fell asleep through Jesus God will bring with him.**

Over against pagan hopelessness Paul now proceeds to lay a solid foundation for Christian hope with reference to believers who have departed from this life.

Verse 14 has been interpreted in various ways. It is necessary to say

---

[82] For thoughts regarding the after-life in Greek and Roman literature see The Loeb Classical Library, especially such Latin-English volumes as Vergil (Aeneid, the sixth book), *The Letters* of Pliny the Younger, Lucretius, Horace; also: Greek-English: Homer (*Iliad* and *Odyssey*), Aeschylus, Diogenes Laertius, Epictetus, Euripedes, and Plato (Apology, Crito, Cheaedo). W. R. Alger, *A Critical History of the Doctrine of a Future Life,* New York, 1866, contains much worthwhile material. For the letter of "Irene" see A. Deissmann, *Light from the Ancient East,* English translation, New York, 1927, pp. 176-178.

something with reference to its grammatical structure, its logic, and its meaning.

With respect to a. *grammatical structure,* the main question for controversy is, "Just where does the phrase *through Jesus* belong?" Should we place a comma before or after this phrase? Either is possible, and *the difference is really rather unimportant.* Those who maintain that the sense is, "For if we believe that Jesus died and rose again, so also *through Jesus God will bring with him* those who are fallen asleep" [83] are willing to admit that it is also through the mediation of Christ that believers are able *to fall asleep* in him. In other words, they (with few exceptions) have no real objection to the expression "those who fall asleep through Jesus," but they do not believe that in the text as we have it Paul says this. They often assert that if the apostle had meant to write anything of the kind, he would have written "those who fall asleep *in* Jesus" (cf. I Cor. 15:18), not *"through* Jesus."

On the other hand, those who favor the rendering ". . . even so *them also which sleep in Jesus* (or: *who fell asleep through Jesus*) will God bring with him" [84] – gladly confess that not only the falling asleep is *in* (or *through*) Jesus, but so is also the act whereby God brings with Jesus those believers who have already departed from this life. Cf. I Cor. 15:21. In favor of reading "fell asleep through Jesus" are the following arguments: (1) thus we get a logical and sharply expressed grouping: on the one hand, *Jesus;* on the other, those who fell asleep through *Jesus;* cf. I Cor. 15:23: *Christ,* the firstfruits, then they that are *Christ's;* and (2) the expression "God will bring" already has a modifier, namely, *with him* (that is, with Jesus). It is doubtful whether in such a case it must be loaded down with still another modifier, especially with one which also makes excellent sense if construed with "fell asleep." But either construction is possible and makes good sense.

With respect to b. *logic,* it is immediately evident that something must be mentally inserted if the statement is to be made intelligible. As it stands, the conclusion does not fit the condition. The implied words, however, are readily supplied. Were the thought fully expressed, the sentence would read somewhat as follows:

"For if we believe that Jesus died and rose again, *we should also believe that* God will bring with him those who fell asleep through Jesus" (or: ". . . that through Jesus God will bring with him those who are fallen asleep"). If we are right in believing *this,* we must also believe *that.*

---

[83] So, for example, the following: A.R.V. (margin), R.S.V., Dutch (the new version), Bavinck, Denney, De Wette, Goodspeed, Lenski, Lünemann, Moffatt, Van Leeuwen, and Williams.

[84] So, for example, the following: A.V., A.R.V. (text), Auberlen-Riggenback, Barnes, Bengel, Berkeley (Verkuyl), Calvin, Chrysostom, Frame, Grotius, Hilgenfeld, Luther, and Robertson (though he leaves room for either construction).

Finally, with respect to c. *meaning,* the main question which divides commentators is, "Just what is meant by the clause *God will bring with him?*" Some maintain that the meaning is sufficiently clear from verses 15-17, and that the logic of the entire passage is as follows:

"For if we believe that Jesus died and rose again, we should also believe that the same God who raised Jesus will raise believers who have fallen asleep, and will cause them, together with such believers as are still left on earth, to be caught up in the clouds, to meet the Lord in the air, and to remain always with him." This *raising, catching up* in the clouds *to meet the Lord* in the air, *and remaining ever with him,* is what Paul meant by saying, "God *will bring* them with Jesus." As proof for this position they usually state that the conjunction *for,* at the beginning of verse 15, shows that *all* that which is stated in verses 15-17 is simply the expanded form of the clause, "God will bring them with Jesus."

Others, however, while by no means denying that there is a considerable element of truth in the above representation, have felt that it is not entirely adequate:

(1) The clause "God will bring with him" (verse 14) refers directly only to the departed ones; but the passage 15-17 refers clearly to two groups: the already departed and the survivors. Hence, it will not do to carry *all* that is said in these verses into the final clause of verse 14.

(2) This interpretation hardly does full justice to the meaning of the expression *bring with.* It will hardly do to say that the clause "God *will bring them with* Jesus" means simply this: by raising their bodies and causing them to ascend, God will *bring them up to Jesus,* sothat they meet him in the air.

It is for this reason that several commentators, without in any way doing injustice to the very clear connection between verse 14 and the following verses, have felt, nevertheless, that the expression "God will bring them with him (Jesus)" has a meaning which in a sense is more restricted and in another sense broader than what is stated in verses 15-17. It is more restricted, for it refers only to those who have already departed, not to the others. It is broader, for it refers to these departed ones not only *after* but even *before* they have been raised.

To Paul and his companions (as well as to the readers, of course) the departed ones are very real. *They are persons!* They are definitely alive and active! They are persons, moreover, whom Jesus will bring with him from heaven at his coming. However, Paul does not say that *Jesus* will bring them (though this is implied in the phrase *with him*), but that *God* will bring them. The characteristically Pauline (cf. Rom. 8:11) reasoning seems to be this: "The same *God* who raised Jesus from the dead will also raise from the dead those who belong to Jesus." He will cause them to come along with Jesus, from heaven, that is, *he will bring their souls along from heaven, sothat these may be reunited quickly (in a flash) with their bodies, in which they go forth to meet the Lord in the air, to remain with him forever.* The *bringing with him,* then, includes everything that happens to these departed ones, from the moment of their departure from heaven until in their raised and glorified bodies they meet the Lord in the air, nevermore to be separated from him in any sense whatever.[85] It is in that full sense that 3:13 mentions "the coming of our Lord Jesus *with all his saints.*" See also on that passage.

15. Verse 14 has made clear that Christ, at his coming, will think of the departed ones, and not only of the survivors. Verse 15 carries this thought a little farther, and shows that in no sense whatever will those who are still on earth at the return have any advantage over those who have fallen asleep in Jesus. The inspired writer expresses it this way: **For this we say to you by the word of the Lord that we, those who remain alive, who are left until the coming of the Lord, shall have no advantage at all over those who fell asleep.**

This passage comes closer than any other in suggesting the nature of the difficulty in Thessalonica regarding the doctrine of the second coming. But even this states the problem only in a general way. So much is clear, namely, that the readers wondered whether, in some way or other, at the Parousia, the believers who had departed from this life would be at a disadvantage in comparison with those still living on earth. Did they believe that for those that had been previously translated to heaven there would be no rapture in any sense? Did they suppose (at least, were they in danger of supposing) that though *the souls* of these departed ones would be in glory, yet their *bodies* would remain buried, and is that why Paul in verse 13 compares their attitude (or their fear) to that of the heathen (who also had no hope with respect to the body)? Did they suppose that while both as to soul and body *all* believers (departed and survivors) would share in the glory of Christ's Return, yet in the rapture the already departed saints would receive a lesser degree of glory or would have to follow the others in going forth to meet the Lord in the air? Or were they thinking of some other disadvantage for those who had fallen asleep? Scripture does not reveal the answer.

It is enough to know that Paul, *by a word of the Lord* (whether directly to Paul or through oral tradition, but not by means of any passage recorded in the Gospels), assures the readers that they can dismiss their fears. At

[85] This interpretation is in line with a remark by A. Kuyper, *Dictaten Dogmatiek,* second edition, Grand Rapids, Mich., 1910, Locus de Consummatione, p. 244 ("alle zielen moeten naar de aarde terug") and also meets an objection which he raises. See also B. B. Warfield, *Biblical and Theological Studies,* Philadelphia, 1952, p. 467: "The rising of Christ's dead is secured before he reaches the earth." That is correct.

Christ's coming the most absolute impartiality will be shown. One group of believers will have no advantage over another. This thought receives further elaboration in verses 16, 17.

16, 17. For [86] with a shouted command, with a voice of an archangel and with a trumpet of God, the Lord himself [87] will descend from heaven, and the dead in Christ will rise first; then we who are alive, who are left, shall be caught up together with them in clouds to meet the Lord in the air.

By separating these two verses — 16 and 17 — many readers have failed to see the true meaning. By printing and reading them together we see at once that here are the same two groups of believers whom we met in verse 15.[88] One might present this graphically as follows:

Verse 15	Verses 16, 17
"we, those who remain alive, who are left until the coming of the Lord"	"we who are alive, who are left"
"those who fell asleep"	"the dead in Christ"

It is clear also that both groups — the survivors and the dead (or those fallen asleep) — are *believers.* Anyone can see at once that the apostle is not drawing a contrast between believers and unbelievers, as if, for example, believers would rise first, and unbelievers a thousand years later. He states:

"And *the dead* in Christ will rise first; then *we who are alive, who are left* shall be caught up together with them in clouds . . ."

Both groups ascend to meet the Lord. *Both* consist of nothing but believers.

The various elements in this vivid description of Christ's descent and the rapture of the saints are as follows:

a. *With a shouted command.*

This is the first of *three* phrases showing the *two* circumstances that will attend the Lord's glorious return. He returns as Conqueror.[89] The *shouted*

---

[86] Not *that.* Had this been the meaning ὅτι would have been replaced or preceded by καί.

[87] Or *he, the Lord.*

[88] Note, however, that verse 15 is negation, verses 16 and 17 affirmation. This too is characteristically Pauline. Also, note the chiastic order: verse 15: survivors, sleepers; verses 16, 17: sleepers, survivors (the latter, however, *together with* the former).

[89] The idea of the Conquering Christ is as a thread running through the book of Revelation. Christ has conquered, is conquering, is going to return as Conqueror. See my *More Than Conquerors* (Interpretation of the book of Revelation), Grand Rapids, Mich., seventh edition, 1954, p. 116. Paul's presentation is in complete harmony with this.

command (κέλευσμα, in the New Testament occurring only here, but see Prov. 30:27 in the LXX) is originally the order which an officer shouts to his troops, a hunter to his dogs, a charioteer to his horses, or a ship-master to his rowers. In the present connection it is clearly the command of the Lord, as he leaves heaven, for the dead to arise. Note the context: those who have fallen asleep shall not be at a disadvantage (verse 15), *for* with a *shout* . . . the Lord himself will descend from heaven, *and the dead in Christ will rise* . . . (verse 16). Just as even here and now the voice of the Son of God is life-giving, causing those who are spiritually dead to be quickened (see N.T.C. on John 5:25), so also when he comes back "all who are in the tombs will hear his voice and will come out" (see N.T.C. on John 5:28). The command, therefore, is definitely *his own,* proceeding from *his* lips. It is not a command issued *to* him, but an order given *by* him. Leaving heaven in his human nature, he utters his voice, and immediately the souls of the redeemed also leave, and are quickly reunited with their bodies, which, thus restored to life, arise gloriously.

b. *With a voice of an archangel and with a trumpet of God.*

These two phrases, united by the conjunction *and,* probably belong together, sothat the archangel is represented as sounding God's trumpet. The term *archangel* or chief angel occurs only here and in Jude 9. In the latter passage Michael is the archangel. On Michael see also Rev. 12:7; then Dan. 10:13, 21; 12:1. He is represented as leader of good angels and as defender of God's people.[90] With respect to the question whether Michael is the only archangel Dr. A. Kuyper expressed himself as follows:

"This question cannot be answered, because Scripture says nothing about it. It is possible that Michael is *the* archangel, that is, the *only* archangel, but it is also possible that he is *one of* the archangels (one of the seven angels that stand before God's throne), as in Daniel 10:13 he is called *one of the chief princes,* sothat Gabriel as well as Michael might be an archangel." [91] With that opinion we are in hearty agreement. The fact that the article (*the*) is not used here — sothat we have translated *"an* archangel" — does not definitely decide the matter. It may indicate that he is one of several, but it is also possible that the term *archangel* was felt to be definite (a proper name, as it were) even without a preceding article. However that may be, one fact at least is well-nigh certain: "a shouted command" and "an archangel's voice" are two different things. The former proceeds from the Christ, the latter from his archangel. Nevertheless, the two sounds have this in common, that they are the signal for the dead to be raised (I Cor. 15:52). (Note that also in Josh. 6:5 and Judg. 7:21, 22 the shout and the trumpet-blast go together.) At the sound of the trumpet the surviving be-

---

[90] See *More Than Conquerors,* p. 170.

[91] A. Kuyper, *De Engelen Gods,* Kampen, 1923, p. 189.

lievers are changed, in a moment, in the twinkling of an eye (again I Cor. 15:52).

The trumpet-blast, in this connection, is certainly very fitting. In the old dispensation, when God "came down," as it were, to meet with his people, this meeting was announced by a trumpet-blast (e.g., Ex. 19:16, 17: "and the sound of a trumpet exceeding loud . . . and Moses brought the people out of the camp to meet God"; cf. Ex. 19:19). Hence, when the marriage of the Lamb with his bride reaches its culmination (cf. Rev. 19:7), this trumpet-blast is most appropriate. Also, the trumpet was used as a signal of Jehovah's coming to rescue his people from hostile oppression (Zeph. 1:16; Zech. 9:14). It was the signal for their deliverance. So also this final trumpet-blast, the signal for the dead to arise, for the living to be changed, and for all the elect to be gathered from the four winds (Matt. 24:31) to meet the Lord, may well be interpreted as being also the fulfilment of the trumpet-ordinance found in Lev. 25, and, accordingly, as proclaiming liberty throughout the universe for all the children of God, their everlasting jubilee!

From all this it becomes abundantly clear that the Lord's coming will be open, public, not only visible but also audible. There are, indeed, interpreters, who, in view of the fact that the Bible at times employs figurative language, take the position that we can know nothing about these eschatological events. To them these precious paragraphs in which the Holy Spirit reveals the future convey no meaning at all. But this is absurd. Scripture was written to be understood, and when it tells us that the Lord will descend from heaven with a shout, with a voice of an archangel and a trumpet of God, it certainly must mean at least this: that in addition to the shouted command of our Lord (which might be compared with John 11:43; see N.T.C. on that passage), a reverberating sound will actually pervade the universe.[92] What forces of nature will be employed to produce this sound has not been revealed. One fact has now become evident: for believers this sound will be full of cheer. This is *God's* trumpet! It is *his* signal, for the archangel is *his* angel. It is sounded to proclaim *his* deliverance for *his* people. Cf. Rev. 15:2 ("harps *of God*"). It announces the coming of *his* Son (as "Lord of lords and King of kings," Rev. 19:16) for the deliverance of *his* people!

c. *The Lord himself* (or *he, the Lord*) *will descend from heaven.*

This descent is visible (Rev. 1:7), audible (as has just been shown), majestic (see on II Thess. 1:7), unto judgment and deliverance (Matt. 25:31-46). If the words, "He shall so come in like manner as you beheld him going into heaven" may be interpreted somewhat broadly, it would seem

---

[92] Cf. J. J. Knap, *The Resurrection and Life Eternal,* Grand Rapids, Mich., 1928, p. 48. Also my *Lectures on the Last Things,* Grand Rapids, 1951, p. 34.

that the actual *descent* (as distinguished now from the suddenness and unexpectedness of Christ's appearance, and from the suddenness and finality that characterizes the entire return) will be characterized by a kind of majestic leisureliness. Note the description of the ascension in Acts 1:9, 10. At any rate, it will not be an *instantaneous* change of location from heaven to earth. There will be time (Rev. 10:6, correctly interpreted, is not in conflict with this [93]) for the souls of those who had fallen asleep to leave their heavenly abodes, to be reunited with their bodies, and then in these gloriously raised bodies to ascend to meet the Lord in the air!

d. *And the dead in Christ will rise first.*

See what has been said about this in the preceding. The meaning here is very clearly that those who departed from this life in Christ, and are here viewed as having remained in Christ, shall not be at a disadvantage. They will rise before the believers who survive on earth will ascend to meet the Lord. The survivors will have to wait a moment, as it were.

e. *Then we who are alive, who are left, shall be caught up together with them in clouds to meet the Lord in the air.*

In addition to what has already been said, note the following: the fact that Paul says *we* does not necessarily mean that he expected to be among those who would still be living at Christ's return. He says *we* because right now he, Silas, Timothy, the readers, are among those believers still living on earth. He immediately modifies this by interpreting it to mean: "those who are left (when the Lord comes)," in order to indicate that only God knows who they may be. Paul knows that the second coming will not take place immediately (see on II Thess. 2:2); and while he was in Thessalonica, this element in his teaching regarding the last things was not neglected (II Thess. 2:5). Moreover, the saying of Jesus recorded in Matt. 24:36 was certainly not unknown to Paul (see also on I Thess. 5:1). Of course, it is also true that Paul never taught that the Lord would definitely not come during this apostle's life-time. He probably hoped that he might live to see it. He wanted everyone to conduct himself in such a manner as to be always ready. But he does not set any date.

Note: *we, together with them.* There is complete impartiality: survivors have no advantage. The predicate is *shall be caught up* (cf. for the verb also Acts 8:39 – Philip the evangelist was caught away by the Spirit of the Lord; II Cor. 12:2-4 – a man in Christ was caught up to the third heaven; and Rev. 12:5 – the Christ-child is caught up, snatched away, from the power of the dragon).

The suddenness, the swiftness, and the divine character of the power which is operative in this *being snatched up* are here emphasized. The survivors have been changed "in a moment, in the twinkling of an eye"

---

[93] See *More Than Conquerors,* p. 150.

(I Cor. 15:52). The heavens and the earth, in their present form, are *put to flight* (Rev. 20:11; cf. 6:14). Now while figurative language abounds in this vivid description, one fact remains: the dramatic suddenness and swiftness of the series of events is stressed. Once the Lord appears upon the clouds of heaven and begins to descend, there will be no opportunity for conversion. His coming is absolutely decisive. He comes not to convert but to judge. See also on II Thess. 2:8; cf. Matt. 25:31 ff; II Cor. 6:2; and II Peter 3:9. *Now* is the acceptable time; *now* is the day of salvation.

The raised and the changed are caught up together *in clouds to meet the Lord in the air.* Although these clouds may well be taken literally, nevertheless, they also have a symbolical meaning. They are associated with the coming of the Lord in majesty, for the punishment of the enemies of his saints, hence for the salvation of his people (cf. Dan. 7:13; then Matt. 26:64; finally, Ex. 19:16, 20; Ps. 97:2; Nah. 1:3).

According to M.M. (p. 53) the expression *to meet* (εἰς ἀπάντησιν) was used in connection with an official welcome accorded to a newly arrived dignitary. No doubt the *welcoming* idea is also included in the expression as used here in I Thess. 4:17. That all believers, the raised as well as (and together with) the changed, shall ascend to meet the Lord *in the air* is clearly taught here. Whether such passages as Job 19:25; Acts 1:11 actually teach that *the judgment* is going to take place *on earth* is debatable. At any rate, nothing with respect to this is taught in the present passage. However, the main thrust of I Thess. 4:17 is not that we shall meet the Lord *in the air,* but that all believers together shall *meet the Lord, never to be separated from him:*

18. And so shall we always be with the Lord. Therefore encourage one another with these words. In these words is stated the conclusion of the entire paragraph. Since it has become clear that those who fell asleep in Christ are not at a disadvantage as compared with those who survive, there is solid ground for encouragement. For the verb here used (*encourage*) see on 2:11. See also on 5:14. Naturally such encouragement is meant not only for the close relatives of bereaved ones, but for all. It must be borne in mind that the members of this very young church were closely united by the bond of love. Hence, when *one* sorrowed, *all* sorrowed; when *one* rejoiced, *all* rejoiced. The encouragement, then, is for all. The members must encourage *one another.*

The Synthesis is found after the explanation of 5:11.

CHAPTER V

5 1 Now concerning the duration-periods and the appropriate seasons,
brothers, y o u have no need that anything be written to y o u. 2 For y o u
yourselves know very well that the day of the Lord comes like a thief in the night.
3 When they are saying, "Peace and Safety," then a sudden (thing) comes upon
them, namely, destruction,[94] like a birth-pang upon the pregnant woman, and by
no means will they escape.
4 But y o u, brothers, are not in darkness, so that that day should seize y o u
as a thief. 5 For y o u are all sons of light and sons of day. We belong neither to
night nor to darkness. 6 Accordingly, let us not sleep as do the rest, but let us
remain watchful and sober. 7 For it is at night that sleepers sleep, and at night
that drunkards are drunk. 8 But since we belong to the day, let us be sober, putting
on a breastplate of faith and love, and for a helmet (the) hope of salvation; 9 for
God did not appoint us for wrath but for the obtaining of salvation through our
Lord Jesus Christ, 10 who died for us, in order that [95] whether we wake or whether
we sleep we may live in fellowship with him. 11 Therefore encourage one another, and build up one the other, as in fact y o u are doing.

5:1-11

5:1. Now concerning the duration-periods and the appropriate seasons,[96] brothers, y o u have no need that anything be written to y o u.

The relation of this paragraph to the rest has been shown (see on 4:13). The question whether Paul is here replying to a *written* question has been discussed (see footnote 4 above).

It would seem that in addition to worry with respect to a possible disadvantage which departed believers might suffer at Christ's return (4:13-18), there was also curiosity with respect to the exact time when this great event would take place. "How long" do the readers still have to wait? "Just when" is the Lord going to arrive? It was for them a question of *times* or *duration-periods* (χρόνοι) and *appropriate seasons* (καιροί). See also N.T.C. on John 7:6, and see on Titus 1:2, 3.

---

[94] Or "then suddenly there comes upon them destruction." That is the correct rendering if the adjective *sudden* is here used for the adverb *suddenly*.
[95] Or *so that*.
[96] A trifle less exact but, perhaps, more understandable would be the rendering, "Now concerning the *How long?* and the *When?* . . ."

With an obvious reference to:

a. a saying of the Lord spoken when he was about to ascend to heaven ("It is not for you to know duration-periods and appropriate seasons," Acts 1:7);

b. the truth, also clearly revealed by the Lord, that no man knows the day and the hour of the coming of the Son of man (Matt. 24:36), which, accordingly, will be as a thief in the night (cf. Matt. 24:43); and

c. the fact that these facts had previously been made clear to the readers,

Paul informs them – affectionately addressing them as "brothers" (see on 1:4) –

"You have no need that anything be written to you." Cf. 4:9.

2. For, says Paul, **you yourselves know very well that the day of the Lord comes**[97] **like a thief in the night.**

The thief takes the owner of the house by surprise. He does not send a warning letter to this effect, "Tomorrow, at such and such a time, I'll pay you a visit. Be sure to hide all your valuables." He comes *suddenly* and *unexpectedly.* So also will be the coming of the day of the Lord (that is, the day of his arrival unto judgment). Hence, it is foolish to inquire about the *how long* and the *when.*

However, the comparison holds also in another, closely related, respect: the thief generally finds people *unprepared.* But here the comparison is true only with respect to unbelievers, not with respect to believers (see on verse 4). Several passages immediately occur to the mind: Matt. 24:43 (= Luke 12:39); II Peter 3:10; Rev. 3:3; 16:15.

These matters had been so clearly presented to the Thessalonians while the missionaries were still with them that, if they will only reflect on them, they will realize that the things about which they are wondering are really *very well* (ἀκριβῶς accurately, cf. Luke 1:3) known to them. Sometimes men wonder about facts which, deep down in their hearts, they really know accurately!

3. Turning now to the second application with respect to the figure of the thief at night (namely, that he not only arrives suddenly, but that his victim is totally unprepared), Paul continues:

When they are saying *Peace and Safety,* then a sudden (thing) comes upon them, namely, destruction, like a birth-pang upon the pregnant woman, and by no means will they escape.

Note the combination of *suddenness* and *unpreparedness.* Note also the striking sentence-order, retained in our translation, making both the adjective *sudden* and the noun *destruction* very emphatic. The world in

[97] Gnomic – not prophetic – present. Yet the reference is here to the coming day, as the context shows.

general will be eating and drinking, buying and selling, building and planting, marrying and giving into marriage, when Jesus comes again. Of course, in themselves not any of these things is wicked. What could be wrong with receiving physical nourishment, carrying on commerce and industry, being engaged in agriculture, or planning a wedding? By means of these things God can even be glorified (I Cor. 10:31). But when the soul becomes entirely wrapped up in them, sothat they become ends in themselves, and sothat the higher, spiritual needs are neglected, they are a curse and no longer a blessing. "All for the body and its enjoyments, nothing for the soul," was the slogan of the wicked contemporaries of Noah and of Lot; and that too will be the outstanding characteristic of the human race in the evil days to come. Cf. Ezek. 13:10; Amos 6:1; Matt. 24:37-44; Luke 17:26-30. Meanwhile, like the artist on top of the ocean-rock, painting the beauty of the village upon the shore, and so completely absorbed in his painting that he sees no danger and pays no attention to the returning tide, though the waves lash higher and higher against the pedestal of his very temporary throne, so also these foolish and wicked people, fascinated with earthly charms, will not realize that judgment is creeping in upon them, coming closer and closer, until very suddenly it overtakes them, catching them wholly *unprepared.* They will be saying "Peace and Safety." Some will even ridicule the very idea of Christ's return (cf. II Peter 3:1-10). However, they will by no means escape, no more than the pregnant woman who is seized by a very sharp and sudden birth-pang while she is helpless. Cf. Ex. 15:14; Is. 13:8; Jer. 4:31; 6:24; 13:21; 22:23; 49:24; 50:43; Hos. 13:13; Mic. 4:9, 10; see also Matt. 24:8; Mark 13:8. (The figure and the third of comparison is, however, not always exactly the same. Sometimes the point of resemblance is entirely different; cf. N.T.C. on John 16:21, 22.) The desperate attempt of the wicked to escape is also vividly portrayed in Rev. 6:12-17. No one escapes.

4. A contrast is now drawn: **But you, brothers, are not in darkness, sothat that day should seize you as a thief.**

What Paul desires is that the readers, instead of being filled with vain curiosity or getting all excited, shall be *prepared.* He again uses the term of affectionate address, *brothers* (see on 1:4). These brothers form a sharp antithesis with the people of the world. The latter are *in darkness,* surrounded by it and embedded in it. The darkness has penetrated their hearts and minds, their whole being. This is the darkness of sin and unbelief. It is on account of this darkness that unbelievers are not sober and watchful (hence, not prepared). It is because of this that they lack faith, love, and hope. As has been stated repeatedly in the present series of Commentaries, *in order to grasp the meaning of a word one must read on and on.* In the present instance the meaning of *darkness* becomes plain by reading verses 5-8. See also N.T.C. on John 1:5 for the concepts *darkness* (which in that passage is personal) and *seize* (καταλαμβάνω).

The day is, of course, the day of Christ's return unto judgment, as is clear from the entire preceding context, beginning at 4:13. That day, here personified, will *seize* unbelievers, catching them *unprepared,* just as a thief *seizes* [98] the owner of the house. Believers, however, are not in darkness. They are not seized, for they are *prepared.*

5. For you are all sons of light and sons of day. We belong neither to night nor to darkness. By means of this truly striking Hebraism, Paul stresses the fact that *all* the brothers at Thessalonica (for "you . . . all" refers back to "brothers" in the preceding verse), that is, all those who by sovereign grace have been adopted into the family of Jesus Christ, are *lights.* See N.T.C. on John 12:36. Cf. Rom. 13:11, 12. The idea is *one:* the light of day has already arisen in their hearts, and they are destined for the realm of everlasting light. They belong to it, for it has taken possession of them. They have faith, love, hope, etc. They are "light in the Lord" (Eph. 5:9). And because *he* is the light of the world (see N.T.C. on John 8:12), *they too* are the light of the world (Matt. 5:14). As "sons of light and of day" (lights shining in the day) they form a sharp contrast with the "sons of this age" (Luke 16:8). They belong neither to night nor to darkness, that is, sin no longer has dominion over them. Wrath is not in store for them. A great change has taken place. Cf. Eph. 5:8; 2:1-10.

Note the tactful transition from *you* to *we: "You* are all sons of light . . . *we* (the readers, Paul, Silas, Timothy, all other believers) belong neither to night nor to darkness." The reason for this transition is that Paul is about to convey a solemn warning. By including himself (hence, not *you* but *we*) he makes the following exhortation more palatable and effective:

6-8a. Accordingly, let us not sleep as do the rest, but let us remain watchful and sober. For it is at night that sleepers sleep, and at night that drunkards (or that those who get drunk) **are drunk. But since we belong to the day, let us be sober.**

In view of the fact, then, that the writers and the readers (together with all Christians everywhere) are sons of light and not of darkness, belonging to the day and not to the night (see on verse 5), they are exhorted not to sleep but to remain watchful and sober.

---

[98] We disagree here with Frame, *op. cit.,* p. 179. The illustration of *the thief in the night,* both here and elsewhere, is that the thief surprises (or at least tries to surprise) the owner of the house, not that the thief is himself taken by surprise. The meaning is not: "so that the day should seize (or *surprise*) you as a thief (or *as thieves*) is (*are*) seized (or *surprised*)," but "so that the day should seize you as a thief seizes" the owner of the house, in order to rob him of his goods. Cf. Matt. 12:29.

It is clear that the terms *to sleep, to be watchful,* and *to be sober* are used metaphorically here. *Thus used,* their meaning is as follows:

To sleep (cf. Mark 13:36; Eph. 5:14) means to live as if there will never be a judgment-day. Spiritual and moral laxity is indicated. Luke 12:45 pictures this condition vividly. So does the description of the foolish virgins, who had taken no oil in their vessels with their lamps (Matt. 25:3, 8). It means *not* to be *prepared.*

To be watchful means to live a sanctified life, in the consciousness of the coming judgment-day. Spiritual and moral alertness is indicated. The watchful individual has his lamps burning and his loins "girded," and it is in that condition that he looks forward to the return of the Bridegroom. On this read Luke 12:35-40. The watchful person is *prepared.*

A study of this verb *to be watchful* (γρηγορέω, whence the proper name *Gregory*), as used elsewhere, is rewarding. In addition to I Thess. 5:6 the passages in which the verb indisputably has a figurative sense are the following: Matt. 24:42; 25:13; Mark 13:35, 37; Acts 20:31; I Cor. 16:13; Col. 4:2; I Peter 5:8; Rev. 3:2, 3; 16:15.[99]

These passages lead to the following conclusions:

a. The uncertainty (on our part) of the day and the hour of Christ's return is a reason for watchfulness (Matt. 24:42; 25:13; Mark 13:35, 37).

b. Another reason for constant vigilance is the presence of enemies, seen and unseen, who threaten the flock (Acts 20:31; I Peter 5:8).

c. To be watchful means to be spiritually awake (Rev. 3:2, 3; 16:15).

d. It implies the habit of regular prayer, including thanksgiving (Col. 4:2).

e. What is probably the fullest description of watchfulness is given in I Cor. 16:13, 14: "Be watchful, stand fast in the faith, acquit yourselves like men, be strong. Let all that y o u do be done in love."

To be sober means to be filled with spiritual and moral earnestness, being neither overly excited on the one hand, nor indifferent on the other, but calm, steady, and sane (cf. I Peter 4:7), doing one's duty and fulfilling one's ministry (II Tim. 4:5). The *sober* person lives deeply. His pleasures are not primarily those of the senses, like the pleasures of the drunkard for instance, but those of the soul. He is by no means a Stoic. On the contrary, with a full measure of joyful anticipation he looks forward to the return of the Lord (I Peter 1:13). But he does not run away from his task! Note how both here and also in I Peter 5:8 the two verbs *to be watchful* and *to be sober* are used as synonyms.

The apostle's exhortation, then, amounts to this: "Let us not be lax and unprepared, but let us be prepared, being spiritually alert, firm in the

---

[99] This is not the proper place to discuss the question whether or not this verb is used in its literal or in its metaphorical sense (or perhaps a combination of the two) in Matt. 26:41 and Mark 14:38.

faith, courageous, strong, calmly but with glad anticipation looking forward to the future day. Let us, moreover, do all this because we belong to the day and not to the night." The opposite course of action, namely, to be asleep spiritually and morally (instead of being on guard), and to be drunk spiritually and morally (instead of being sober), befits people who belong to the night (the realm of darkness and sin), just as even in the natural realm it is generally at night that sleepers sleep and that drunkards are drunk. (It is clear, of course, that here in verse 7 the words *sleepers, sleep, drunkards,* and *are drunk* are used in their primary, literal sense.)

8b. It befits the man who is of the day to be watchful and sober: **putting on a breastplate of faith and love, and for a helmet (the) hope of salvation.**

The question may be asked, "How is it that Paul suddenly and somewhat unexpectedly comes up with these articles of defensive armor: breastplate and helmet?" The answer given by A. T. Robertson (*Word Pictures,* Vol. IV, p. 35) may well be correct: "The idea of *watchfulness* brings the figure of a sentry, on guard and armed, to Paul's mind. . . ."

By the exercise of calm and stedfast faith in and love for God in Christ — which in the midst of a wicked world becomes *an aggressive testimony* — the watchful and sober person wards off the poisonous arrows of temptation. He puts on *faith* ("a *certain* knowledge of God and of his promises . . . and a hearty confidence that all his sins are forgiven him for Christ's sake") and *love* (the yielding of the self to God, the object of his delight, in the spirit of joy and gratitude) just like a warrior would put on his breastplate.

Faith and love (genitives of apposition) constitute the Christian's coat of mail. The readers understood this illustration. The *breastplate* protected the sentry's breast, shoulders, and back. It was made of various materials, for instance, leather, quilted cloth, linen (Herodotus III. xlvii), brass, iron (I Sam. 17:5; Rev. 9:9) or at times even gold (I Macc. 6:2). The warrior Goliath wore a scale-armor coat (I Sam. 17:5). The soldiers of Antiochus Eupator had chain coats (I Macc. 6:35). Compare today's "bullet-proof vest."

What is important to note, in this connection (yet, is generally overlooked) is that Paul calls *active* faith and love a piece of *defensive* armor, a breastplate! How perfectly true is this comparison, for in matters of religion (and often also in so-called secular matters) the best defence is an offense; the most positive protection is an attack. The believer's spontaneous and aggressive testimony of faith in and love for God in Christ keeps him from the dissolute habits of the world. The *work* resulting from faith and the *exertion* prompted by love — the "walking by faith" — keep one from "fulfilling the lust of the flesh" (Gal. 5:16).

To *faith* and *love,* Paul adds *hope,* just as he did in 1:3. Here too, just like in 1:3, he expands the third element in the series; hence, "and for a helmet the hope *of salvation* (objective genitive)," etc. To be sure, *in principle* believers in Thessalonica were already in possession of salvation. But this is *full* salvation, the salvation which was going to be theirs at the coming of the Lord Jesus Christ.

Paul is fond of this word *salvation* (σωτηρία). He uses it again and again (in addition to its use in the present passage see also 5:9; II Thess. 2:13; II Tim. 2:10; 3:15; then Rom. 1:16; 10:1, 10; 11:11; 13:11; II Cor. 1:6; 6:2 twice; 7:10; Eph. 1:13; Phil. 1:19, 28; 2:12). This salvation is a. *negatively:* rescue from the guilt, pollution, and punishment of sin (specifically, it is often represented as a deliverance from the wrath of God which rests upon sin and which will one day be revealed; cf. 1:10; II Thess. 1:8, 9; Eph. 2:3, 5; Phil. 1:28) this rescue being a result of Christ's objective substitutionary atonement; and b. *positively:* that sum-total of every spiritual endowment which God grants to his people on the basis of the redemptive work of his Son. Both the negative aspect of this salvation (deliverance from wrath) and the positive aspect (for instance, "living together with him") are mentioned here in the immediately following context (see on verses 9 and 10). Since salvation is here an eschatological concept, it is understandable that the apostle speaks about *"the hope* of salvation," for *hope* ever looks to the future. It is the confident and firmly anchored assurance that the full inheritance will one day be ours.

This hope is the Christian's *helmet.* The helmet of iron and brass (I Sam. 17:5, 38; II Chron. 26:14; cf. I Macc. 6:35) afforded a measure of protection for the head, as did the breastplate for the heart. Much more did hope – and the endurance inspired by hope, cf. 1:3 – preserve the believer in safety over against the seduction of the world. Here too the assault upon the fortress of darkness by those Christians who endured to the very end, ever ready to testify, was their best defence. On the entire armor of the Christian read Eph. 6:10-20.

9, 10. As already remarked, Paul expands the concept *salvation* (or, if one prefers, "hope of salvation") in the following two verses: **For God did not appoint us for wrath but for the obtaining of salvation through our Lord Jesus Christ, who died for us, in order that whether we wake or whether we sleep we may live in fellowship with him.**

This passage indicates the reasonable character of the aforementioned hope. This hope is not visionary. It will be fulfilled, as is clear from the fact that God did not *appoint* (this verb combines duty and destination) us for *wrath* (to be revealed at Christ's return, 1:10; cf. II Thess. 1:8-10), but for *the obtaining*[100] of *salvation* (see on verse 8 above) through our *Lord Jesus Christ* (see on 1:1).

---

[100] As this noun (περιποίησις, which at times means *possession,* Eph. 1:14; I Peter 2:9) is clearly used in the active sense in II Thess. 2:14 (cf. Heb. 10:39) and as both

While the expression *the obtaining* places the emphasis on that which, according to God's purpose, is *our* duty, the immediately added phrase "through our Lord Jesus Christ" indicates that it is only through *him* (his death for us, his power operating in us) that we are able to carry this out. Paul is fond of this juxtaposition of the divine and the human element in the acquisition of salvation (cf. Eph. 2:8; 2:10; Phil. 2:12, 13).

When the apostle mentions the Lord Jesus Christ as the cause of our salvation, he immediately thinks of the Savior's *death* for us, inasmuch as that is basic. This death *concerns* us. Literally we read, ". . . who died *with reference to* (περί) us (though there is also some textual support for another preposition, ὑπέρ, for the meaning of which see N.T.C. on John 10:11. The Good Shepherd gave his life *for the benefit of* the sheep). Paul says "for *us*." In this *us* he includes all believers, whether they be readers or writers or anyone else who can lay claim to the name *believer*. Specifically, he is thinking here of the same two groups which he has mentioned before (see on 4:13-18): the survivors and the departed ones. The purpose (or the result, it makes little difference in this connection) of Christ's death for his own is that whether at his coming we be *waking* or *sleeping* the sleep of death (καθεύδωμεν cf. Mark 5:39), we may together live in fellowship with him. Compare and see on 4:17.

This is the simplest explanation. Those who are *awake* are those who are *alive*, the survivors, the ones who according to 4:15 are "left until the coming of the Lord." And those who are *sleeping* are the *dead*, the departed, the ones who according to 4:15 "fell asleep" (namely, *in* or *through* Jesus Christ).[101]

11. The relation between 5:10 and 11 is a close parallel to that between 4:17 and 18. Just as in chapter 4 the clause, "And so shall we always be

---

there and also here it occurs in a context of exhortations, I see no good reason to depart from the translation favored by most of the versions.

[101] It is simply impossible to interpret the verb *to sleep* here in 5:10 as in verses 6 and 7. Clearly, here in verse 10 the verb has reference to believers ("we"), but in verse 6 it refers to the lost condition of unbelievers, that is, of "the rest," those who are not watchful and sober; and in verse 7 it has reference to the natural repose of sleep. It is also true, of course, that the verb here used for *to sleep* (first pers. pl. pres. subj. of καθεύδω) is not the same as the one used in 4:13-15 (gen. pl. pres. pass. part., and acc. pl. aor. pass. part. of κοιμάω). The latter verb has reference to blessed departure, falling asleep in and through Jesus. In distinction from it, the verb used here in 5:10 refers merely to being physically *dead* at Christ's return. And similarly — for it stands to reason that the two verbs must correspond — it will not do to derive the meaning of the verb *to wake* (first pers. pl. pres. subj. of γρηγορέω) from verse 6 (*to be watchful* morally and spiritually). Here in 5:10 the meaning is simply to be physically *alive* when Jesus comes. Cf. Rom. 14:8. The translators have caught the distinction in the use of these verbs. Hence, for example, in verse 6 they translate "let us *watch*" but in verse 10 (the same verb) "whether we *wake*" (thus A.V., A.R.V., and somewhat similarly most modern translators). Though some interpreters find fault with this, we cannot join them.

with the Lord" was followed by "Therefore encourage one another with these words," so here in chapter 5 the clause "In order that . . . we may live in fellowship with him" is followed by **Therefore encourage one another and build up one the other, as in fact y o u are doing.**

That last expression, "as in fact y o u are doing" has been explained in connection with 4:10. By instructing one another and by encouraging one another with the comfort which is found in the preceding paragraph (such comfort as is contained in assurances like "Y o u are not in darkness," "Y o u are all sons of day," "For God did not appoint us for wrath but for the obtaining of salvation through our Lord Jesus Christ . . . in order that we may live in fellowship with him"), believers at Thessalonica will be doing very valuable personal work: *building up* one the other; for the church and also the individual believer is God's edifice, God's temple, I Cor. 6:19.

Synthesis of 4:13 – 5:11

See p. 108. *Instruction. Paul writes to the Thessalonians instructing them how Christ will come again*

4:13-18 *with impartiality toward all believers, sothat survivors will have no advantage over those who have fallen asleep*

The conversion of the Thessalonians was of very recent date. The danger of a relapse, be it ever so temporary, into *pagan customs* was not imaginary. One of these was the manner of grieving for the dead. As most pagans saw it, there was no hope *at all* for the dead body and no *substantial* hope for the departed soul. Moreover, whatever flickering expectation there may have been of a happy life hereafter – and the inscriptions on tombstones, the letters of condolence, etc., voice despair rather than confidence – there was no solid foundation for it. And in this latter sense it was absolutely true that the heathen had *no hope!*

But surely the man who believes in a Jesus "who died *and arose again*" should not "grieve as do the rest, who have no hope." He should accept the precious truth that there is a glorious future in store for every Christian, and this not only for the soul but also for the body. "Those who *fell asleep* (entered upon their rest from labor, with the certainty of a glorious awakening) through Jesus God will bring with him." In no sense whatever will those who remain alive, who are left until the coming of the Lord, have any advantage over them. When Christ at his descent from heaven shouts the command for the dead to arise and when the archangel by sounding God's trumpet issues a similar order, and proclaims the final and everlasting meeting of God with his people, then *first of all* the spirits of the already departed believers will rejoin their bodies which will arise gloriously, *and not until this has happened* will those children of God who at Christ's coming are still living on earth begin to "rise to worlds unknown." The survivors "shall be caught up *together with*" those who previously fell asleep. *Together* – there is here no favoritism or partiality of any kind! – they shall ascend in clouds to meet the Lord in the air. And *so* – that is, glorious in soul and body, as *one* Church Universal and Triumphant – shall they always be with the Lord. The readers should encourage each other with these words.

5:1-11 *with suddenness, taking people by surprise, though believers will be (and should ever exert themselves to be) fully prepared*

In addition to worry with respect to a possible disadvantage which departed believers might suffer at Christ's return, there was also curiosity anent the exact time when that coming again would take place. *How long* did God's children still have to wait? Just *when* was Jesus going to arrive?

Basing his answer on previous teaching which had come straight from the mouth of the Lord, Paul states that the readers have no need of further information on this subject. If they will but reflect, they will recall that they have been repeatedly shown that, according to the word of the Lord (Matt. 24:43), the day of his return will be "like a thief in the night." He will come very suddenly, taking people by surprise.

As to the wicked, the Lord will come upon them while they are saying, "Peace and safety." They will be *wholly unprepared*. Hence, sudden destruction will come upon them.

In this respect *believers* are different. Moreover, they should *endeavor* to be different, for by God's grace they are filled with the light of salvation. Says Paul, "We belong neither to night nor to darkness," the night and the darkness of sin and unbelief. He continues, "Accordingly, let us not sleep as do the rest, but let us remain *watchful* and *sober*." He means, "Let us be prepared, spiritually alert, firm in faith, courageous, strong, calmly and with glad anticipation looking forward to the future day." Thus, believers will be putting on "the breastplate of faith and love, and for a helmet the hope of salvation." They must never hesitate to keep alive this glorious hope, ever bearing in mind that "God did not appoint us for wrath but for the obtaining of salvation through our Lord Jesus Christ, who died for us, in order that whether at his return we are still living on earth or have fallen asleep in the Lord, we may live forever in fellowship with him."

Summary of I Thessalonians 5:12-28

Paul Writes to the Thessalonians

Exhorting Them How They Should Conduct Themselves
This Section comprises *the Apostle's Exhortation*. Proper Behavior:

5:12, 13 with respect to the elders of the church

5:14 with respect to:
the disorderly
the fainthearted
the weak
"everyone"

5:15 with respect to those who have injured them

5:16-18 with respect to God

5:19-22 with respect to the Holy Spirit and his gifts (also: with respect to would-be prophets)
This is followed by

5:23, 24 a solemn wish for sanctification and preservation, the wish being immediately followed by the promise;
Next comes:

5:25-28 a trio of urgent requests:
for intercessory prayer
for extending greetings by means of the holy kiss, and
for the public reading of this letter. The Benediction.

12 Now we request y o u, brothers, to appreciate those who labor among y o u
and are over y o u in the Lord and admonish y o u, 13 and to esteem them very
highly in love because of their work. Be at peace among yourselves.
14 And we urge y o u, brothers, admonish the disorderly, encourage the faint-
hearted, help the weak, exercise patience toward everyone.
15 See to it that no one renders to anyone evil for evil, but always pursue that
which is good with reference to one another and with reference to all.
16 Always be joyful.
17 Ceaselessly pray.
18 In all circumstances give thanks, for this is the will of God in Christ Jesus
for y o u.
19 The Spirit do not quench.
20 Prophetic utterances do not despise, 21 but test all things: to the good hold
on; 22 from every form of evil hold off.
23 And may he, the God of peace,
sanctify y o u through and through,
and without flaw may be y o u r spirit,
and y o u r soul-and-body
without blame at the coming of our Lord Jesus Christ
may it be kept.
24 Reliable is the One who calls y o u, who will also do it.
25 Brothers, do pray for us.
26 Greet all the brothers with a holy kiss.
27 I solemnly charge y o u before the Lord to have this epistle read to all the
brothers.
28 The grace of our Lord Jesus Christ be with y o u.

5:12-28

5:12, 13. Now we request y o u, brothers, to appreciate those who labor among y o u and are over y o u in the Lord and admonish y o u, and to esteem them very highly in love because of their work.

For the relation of 5:12-28 to 4:1-12; 4:13-18; and 5:1-11 see on 4:1. The watchfulness and soberness enjoined in the immediately preceding paragraph (5:1-11) must become evident in every walk of life. That is the gist of the present section. Detailed directions follow. They are striking because of their brevity. Paul knows how to say much in few words. Though it is, perhaps, impossible to separate the church as an organization from the church as an organism, and to say: *this* instruction pertains to the former and *that* to the latter, yet it may be safely affirmed that at least in verses 12 and 13 it is the church viewed as an organization that receives special attention.

The opening words, "We request y o u, brothers," are similar to what is found in 4:1; see on that verse. In order to understand what follows it must be borne in mind that Timothy had just returned (3:6) and had given a detailed report on "The Thessalonian Situation." It has already become clear that most of what he reported was very favorable. However, it has also been shown that some of the news was of a different nature. See on 4:1-8, 11. Moreover, also here in chapter 5 the immediate context speaks about "disorderly persons" (verse 14). Evidently some of them were loathe to obey the rules laid down by the religious authorities (see also on 4:8). This is the reason why Paul writes, "We request y o u, brothers, *to appreciate* [102] those who labor among y o u," etc. It is clear that the two verbs "to appreciate" and "to esteem (very highly)" are used synonymously.

When Paul speaks about "those who labor among y o u and are over y o u in the Lord and admonish y o u" he has in mind not three different kinds of leaders but one and the same group. The use of only one article preceding all three participles points in this direction. These leaders are characterized as:

a. *laborers or toilers,* that is, men who exert themselves in the interest of their brothers, performing much spiritual labor (explaining the gospel, applying it to concrete situations, warning, admonishing, helping, encouraging, etc.) for their benefit and amid great difficulty. Paul often used this verb (κοπιάω) when he was thinking of work that required strenuous effort and resulted in weariness. He used it in connection with manual labor (I Cor. 4:12; Eph. 4:28; II Tim. 2:6; cf. the noun in I Thess. 1:3; 2:9; II Thess. 3:8) and also with reference to religious work (Rom. 16:12 twice; I Cor. 5:10; Gal. 4:11; Phil. 2:16; 16:16; I Tim. 4:10; 5:17). In the Pauline phraseology not only the church-officer but also the voluntary worker, Col. 1:29, and in a sense every wide-awake member, is a *laborer.* His *exertion* is prompted by love.

b. *superintendents or managers* ("those who are over y o u"), and this "in the Lord," that is, by virtue of appointment by him and qualifications derived from him. Cf. I Tim. 3:4, 12 for an analogous use.

c. *admonishers,* that is, those who *put* (their brothers) *in mind* (νουθετέω from νοῦς and τίθημι) to obey God's ordinances. In the New Testament Paul is the only one who uses this word (besides 5:12, 14 and II Thess. 3:15 also Acts 20:31; Rom. 15:14; I Cor. 4:14; Col. 1:28; 3:16). The admonisher may be Paul himself (Acts 20:31) or any member of the church (Rom. 15:14; Col. 3:16).

Although, as has become evident, the first and the third participles (that is, *laborers* and *admonishers*) apply not only to men who have been invested with an office in the church but also to any other wide-awake member, yet the use of the second participle together with its modifier (*super-*

---

[102] The meaning *to appreciate* (for εἰδέναι) is paralleled in extra-canonical literature (see M.M. p. 440), though this is not what the verb generally signifies. It most frequently indicates *to know by reflection, based on intuition or information;* in distinction from γινώσκω which means *to know by observation or experience.* See also N.T.C. on John 8:28. However, it is easy to see how the meaning *to appreciate* developed from the basic connotation.

intendents, "those who are over y o u in the Lord") would seem to point in the direction of officers. We seem to have a parallel passage in I Tim. 5:17, where those who *rule* well (perfect participle of the same verb) are *the elders.* Note also how in that passage (just as here in I Thess. 5:12) these elders are further described as "those who *labor,*" namely, in the word and in teaching.

It will not do to say that I Tim. 5:17 cannot be adduced as proof because the system of church-organization by then had reached a much higher and more complicated development. To offset that argument it should be borne in mind that Paul was a great organizer (Acts 20:17; Phil. 1:1; Titus 1:5), and that even on his First Missionary Journey he was already appointing "elders in every church" (Acts 14:23). Certainly, if there were elders in the church at Thessalonica – and it is highly probable that there were! – these are meant here in I Thess. 5:12; at least they are included.

Paul requests that *because of their work* (and not solely because they are divinely appointed leaders) these men be esteemed *very highly,*[103] and this in the spirit of love.

Be at peace among yourselves,[104] Paul continues. In connection with what immediately precedes, this must mean, "Stop y o u r carping. Instead of continually criticizing the leaders, follow their directions, sothat peace (here: absence of dissension) results."

14. In view of the fact that in urging the Thessalonians to show respect for their leaders Paul was thinking especially about the disorderly persons who had made this admonition necessary, it is not surprising that the next instruction begins as it does: **And we urge y o u, brothers, admonish the disorderly, encourage the fainthearted, help the weak, exercise patience toward everyone.**

In the congregation at Thessalonica there were three groups that needed special attention: the disorderly, the fainthearted, and the weak.

The words *disorderly* (ἄτακτος-οι, III Macc. 1:19 in the LXX) and *fainthearted* (ὀλιγόψυχος-οι – the "little souls"[105] –, Is. 35:4 in the LXX) occur nowhere else in the New Testament. The word *weak* (ἀσθενής-εῖς, i.e., without strength) occurs frequently, and is used with respect to both physical debility (Matt. 25:39, 43, 44; Luke 10:9; Acts 4:9; 5:15, 16) and moral and spiritual illness (Rom. 5:6; 14:1; I Cor. 8:7, 9, 10; 9:22; 11:30; etc.).

---

103 The Greek adverb is very picturesque: ὑπερεκπερισσῶς over-abundant (also used in 3:10 and in Eph. 3:20). Note the piling up of prefixes in this word: the ocean of esteem having reached its outermost *peri*meter, reaches even *higher* and begins to flow *outward,* overflowing its banks.

104 That the reading, "Be at peace *with them*" (i.e., with the leaders) is better than the one preferred by N.N. has not been proved.

105 Cf. German *die Kleinmüthigen,* Dutch *de kleinmoedigen.*

We have met each group before. Thus, *the disorderly* persons – that is, those who are out of step, like soldiers who do not keep the ranks – are the fanatics, meddlers, and loafers (4:11, 12; 5:12, 13; and cf. II Thess. 3:10). *The fainthearted* are probably those who worried about their departed friends and relatives and/or about their own spiritual condition (4:13-18; 5:4, 5, 9). And *the weak* could well be those who were characterized by a tendency toward immorality (4:1-8). Thus interpreted, each passage is explained in the light of others within the same epistle, and no novelties are introduced. It is, of course, readily admitted that this representation may not be exact. Thus, for example, the third group ("the weak") may also have included individuals who, though spiritually immature, were not particularly in danger of trespassing the bounds of propriety in matters pertaining to sex. Besides, the three groups may overlap to some extent.

It is clear as day that these admonitions are addressed to *the entire congregation* – note the word *brothers* (see on 1:4) – that is, in each case, to all the members except those specifically mentioned in the admonition. Thus, all except the disorderly must admonish the disorderly; all except the fainthearted must encourage the fainthearted, etc. Mutual discipline must be exercised by all the members. It is wrong to leave all this to pastors and elders.

As to the present imperatives [106] here employed, first of all Paul bids the brothers *to admonish* the disorderly. For the verb see on verse 12 above. The admonition might take the form suggested by Paul himself in 4:11, 12; 5:12, 13. It stands to reason that the faint-hearted must be *encouraged* (see on 2:11 and N.T.C. on John 11:31). The weak must be *helped,* that is, must not be abandoned. The brothers should "cling to" [107] them, rendering all the necessary spiritual and moral assistance.

Thus instead of quickly rejecting anyone, whether he be disorderly, faint-hearted, or weak, *patience* (or *longsuffering,* μακροθυμία) should be shown to everyone. Cf. Gal. 5:22; Eph. 4:2.[108]

---

[106] It is tempting to render all of these as durative, progressive, or linear, as is done by several commentators and translators. This would yield the rendering, "Keep on admonishing the disorderly, continue to encourage the fainthearted, never stop helping the weak," or something similar. However, in crisp imperatives of this character it is not always established that the continuative idea is predominant. In certain cases the present tense may be aoristic.

[107] The verb is ἀντέχω. See my doctoral dissertation, "The Meaning of the Preposition ἀντί in the New Testament," p. 68. The original notion of being *opposite* or *in front of* a person or object (oppositeness, the local sense), by an easy transition leads to that of being physically close, which in turn may suggest the idea of moral and spiritual closeness. This closeness may be one of attitude (for example, love or loyalty), or of practical helpfulness, the one not excluding the other. Cf. Matt. 6:24; I Thess. 5:14; Tit. 1:9.

[108] Trench (*op. cit.* liiii) has a fine discussion on the three synonyms μακροθυμία (longsuffering), ὑπομονή (endurance), and ἀνοχή (forbearance). He defines the

15. Not only is it the duty of the entire membership to exercise this virtue, patience or longsuffering, but the brotherhood must also see to it that each individual member cultivates it and manifests this grace toward everyone. Hence, there follows: **See to it that no one renders to anyone evil for evil, but always pursue that which is good with reference to one another and with reference to all.**

The impatient person retaliates when he is injured. He *"renders* (ἀποδῷ: gives back) evil for[109] evil." Paul condemns this practice (see also Rom. 12:17, 19; cf. I Cor. 4:12; 6:7) and so does Peter (I Peter 3:9), in complete harmony with the injunction of Jesus: to love not only those who love us but even those who hate us and who are, in that sense, our enemies (Matt. 5:44).

It is not true, however, that in forbidding the exercise of pesronal vengeance Jesus laid down a principle that was *entirely* new and in striking contrast with the spirit and teaching of the Old Testament. The commandment – "eye for eye, tooth for tooth, hand for hand, foot for foot, burning for burning, wound for wound, stripe for stripe" (Ex. 21:24, 25; cf. Lev. 24:20; Deut. 19:21) – relates to the *public* administration of criminal law (see Lev. 24:14), and was issued in order that the practice of seeking *personal* revenge might be discouraged. What Jesus is opposing in Matt. 5:38-42 was not the Old Testament law but its Pharisaic misinterpretation. What the Lord taught, and what Paul in substance repeats, *is entirely in line with* (is a further development of) such Old Testament passages as Lev. 19:18; Deut. 32:35; Prov. 20:22; and 24:20. To be sure, there is an advance here (i.e. in Matt. 5:43-48). Revelation also in this respect is progressive. The idea that one should never render evil for evil, no not to *anyone,* was never as strikingly expressed as it was by Jesus when he said, "Love y o u r enemies." Also in this respect Jesus "came to fulfil" the law (Matt. 5:17), and also in this respect Paul (here in I Thess. 5:15) enforces a principle which he derived from the Lord.

Instead of "rendering evil for evil" it is the believer's duty to pursue that which is *good* – that is, *beneficial* –, and this not only with reference

---

first (used here in I Thess. 5:14) as "patience in respect of persons," while the second is "patience in respect of things."

From the passages in which Paul uses μακροθυμία (longsuffering) it is clear that he views it as being not only *a divine attribute* (one pertaining to *God,* Rom. 2:4, or to *Christ,* I Tim. 1:16), of which even "vessels of wrath" are the objects (Rom. 9:22), but also *a Christian virtue* (II Cor. 6:6; Eph. 4:2; Col. 1:11; 3:12), which should adorn every believer, and specifically also every Gospel-worker, whether he be an apostle (like Paul, II Tim. 3:10) or his special representative (II Tim. 4:2). As a Christian virtue it is, of course, a fruit of the Spirit (Gal. 5:22).

[109] As I have pointed out in my doctoral dissertation, "The Meaning of the Preposition ἀντί in the New Testament," pp. 92, 93, ἀντί has here the sense "in exchange (or: in return) for" as in Gen. 44:4 and many other passages in which it is the equivalent of the Hebrew *tachath.*

to one another (fellow-believers) but even with reference to all (believers and unbelievers alike; cf. 3:12). This good which the believers must *pursue* (eagerly seek after) is *love,* as is clear from a comparison of the present passage with 3:12; Rom. 13:10; and I Cor. 14:1.

16-18. While in verses 12-15 Paul has shown what should be the attitude of the Thessalonians toward their leaders, to fellow-members characterized by particular shortcomings, to those who have injured them, and finally to one another and to all, in verses 16-18 he sets forth what should be their inner attitude and how this inner attitude should express itself with reference to God. Hence, we now have the following three beautiful, closely related, and tersely expressed admonitions:

Always be joyful.
Ceaselessly pray.
In all circumstances give thanks.

The Thessalonians were no strangers (see on 1:6) to the "joy unspeakable and full of glory" (I Peter 1:8), the "great joy" which resulted from the incarnation of Christ and from the redemption wrought through his cross. Yet with persecution from without and disturbances within, there was a danger (humanly speaking, of course!) that this joy would disappear. Hence, Paul, who himself again and again rejoiced in the midst of persecution and hardship (3:7-9; cf. Phil. 3:1; 4:4, 10), urges his readers to *always* be joyful.

Of course, in seasons of distress and grief he alone is able to find relief and even be joyful (in view of Rom. 8:28, 35-39) who at the Father's throne makes all his wants and wishes known. Hence, the directive "Always be joyful" is immediately followed by "Ceaselessly pray." The most comprehensive word for *prayer* (προσευχή, προσεύχομαι) is used here. For synonyms see the striking passage Phil. 4:6. What Paul means is: there must be no decline in the regularity of the habit of "taking hold on God" in the midst of all circumstances of life. Cf. Rom. 12:12; Eph. 6:18; Col. 4:2. The apostle could afford to say this, for he himself gave the example (3:10; II Thess. 1:11; Eph. 1:16; 3:14).

When a person prays without giving thanks, he has clipped the wings of prayer, sothat it cannot rise. Hence, the trio of admonitions concludes with, "In *all circumstances* give thanks." This phrase *in everything* (ἐν παντί probably with χρήματι understood) includes affliction, for even in the midst of all *these* things ("tribulation, anguish, persecution, famine, nakedness, peril, or sword") believers are not merely conquerors but "more than conquerors" (super-invincibles), inasmuch as all these things actually help them to reach their predestined goal! See Rom. 8:35-37.

For this is the will of God (not merely the word of Paul, Silas, and Timothy) **in Christ Jesus for you.** The will of God, as clearly set forth by means of the redemptive work and revelation of Jesus Christ, is this very thing, namely, that believers should always be joyful, should ceaselessly pray, and should in all circumstances give thanks.

19-22. The next little series of admonitions has to do with the Holy Spirit and his gifts:

The Spirit do not quench.

Prophetic utterances do not despise, but test all things: to the good hold on; from every form of evil hold off.

Upon the early church the Holy Spirit had bestowed certain *special gifts* or *charismata.* Among them were: ability to perform miracles of healing, speaking in tongues, and prophesying.

Although according to some interpreters there was nothing miraculous about the latter, we do not share this opinion.[110] The Church in its infancy had no complete Bible (Old and New Testament). It had no extensive body of Christian literature, such as we have today. Christian hymnology, too, was still in its infancy. Numerically also, the Church was rather insignificant. It was, moreover, the object of scorn and derision from every side. In that situation God graciously provided special supports or endowments, until the time would arrive when these were no longer needed. One of these gifts was that of prophesying.

As the term – and its derivatives – implies (for in this case the etymological sense continues to cling to it), a *prophet* (προφήτης from πρό *forth,* and φημί to *speak*) is "a person who speaks forth." And what he speaks forth or openly declares is the will and mind of God. He is [111] a "forth-teller," and not necessarily (though sometimes also) a "fore-teller."

Now, although this particular gift of prophesying was one of the greatest of the charismata, ranking even above that of the ability to speak in tongues – for, the prophet's message as contrasted with the utterance of the man who spoke in a tongue, was readily understandable (I Cor. 14:1, 2, 4, 5, 6) –, yet it was held in low esteem by some of the members of the Thessalonian church. This was deplorable in view of the fact that by making light of prophetic utterances these members missed the "edification, encouragement, and consolation" (I Cor. 14:3) brought by the prophet. Moreover, by means of despising the prophetic utterances, their Giver, the Holy Spirit, was being dishonored. In the early Church the

---

[110] Lenski (*op. cit.,* p. 360), for example, denies that prophesying belongs to the extraordinary charismata. He points to the fact that in Rom. 12:7 this kind of prophesying heads the list of gifts, none of which were miraculous. But over against this stands the fact that in I Cor. 12:10 prophesying is mentioned in one breath with such gifts as the working of miracles and the ability to speak in tongues; and according to I Cor. 14:24, 25 by means of prophesying the secrets of the heart of the outsider who enters the religious meeting are laid bare, so that he falls on his face and declares, in utter astonishment, "God is really among y o u."

[111] See A. T. Robertson, *Word Pictures,* Vol. IV, pp. 37, 38.

gift of prophesying was like a brightly burning flame. It must not be *quenched* or *extinguished!* (for the verb cf. Matt. 12:20; 25:8; Mark 9:48; Eph. 6:16; Heb. 11:34). Hence, we read, "The Spirit do not quench. Prophetic utterances do not despise." The objects are placed first for the sake of emphasis. It is as if Paul were saying, "By making light of the utterances of the prophets among you, you are belittling the work of no One less than the Holy Spirit."

The reason for this disparagement of prophetical utterances can readily be surmised. Wherever God plants wheat, Satan sows his tares. Wherever God establishes a church, the devil erects a chapel. And so, too, wherever the Holy Spirit enables certain men to perform miracles of healing, the evil one distributes his "lying wonders." And wherever the Paraclete brings a *true* prophet upon the scene, the deceiver presents his *false* prophet. The easiest – but not the wisest – reaction to this state of affairs is to despise *all* prophesying. Add to this the fact that the fanatics, the meddlers, and the loafers at Thessalonica may not have appreciated some of the utterances of the true prophets, and it is readily understood why by some in the congregation prophetic utterances had fallen into disfavor.

Paul, therefore, states what course of action the congregation should take: "Prophetic utterances do not despise, but *test* (on the verb see I Thess. 2:4) all things." The standard by which the true prophet can be distinguished from the false is that the former will declare nothing that is contrary to what God has made known previously, in his special revelation.[112] Cf. Deut. 13:1-5; Rom. 12:6. In the new dispensation the criterion would be the revelation of God through the testimony of Christ and of the apostles. Besides, in the early Church some men seem to have been gifted with rare proficiency in separating genuine from false prophesying (see I Cor. 12:10: "and to another the ability to distinguish between spirits").

Once a true verdict has been reached, the practical rule must apply: "to the good *hold on* (κατέχετε); from every *form* (or *kind,* not *appearance* here) of evil *hold off* (ἀπέχεσθε). Note: *every* form, whether the wicked and uninspired utterance concerns doctrine or life. It is probable that this *every* is even broader, to be taken absolutely.

When verses 19-22 are studied together, as a unit, it becomes apparent immediately that the rule "*Test* all things" cannot mean "Try everything once," or "Enter every place of wickedness and find out for yourselves what it is." In the given context it simply means that, instead of despising each and every prophetical utterance, one should test whatever presents itself as such. The good should be accepted; *every* kind of evil (without any

---

[112] Cf. G. Ch. Aalders, *De Profeten Des Ouden Verbonds,* Kampen, 1918, pp. 224-235. On the indicated pages the author discusses the pro and the con of the various criteria that have been suggested as means for distinguishing the true prophet from the false.

exception; hence, whether it be *evil advice* – given by a false prophet – *or any other form of evil*) must be avoided.

What follows is a concluding wish and a few urgent requests, such as one expects to find at the close of this letter; then the benediction.

23. And may he, the God of peace,
sanctify y o u through and through,
and without flaw may be y o u r spirit,
and y o u r soul-and-body
without blame at the coming of our Lord Jesus Christ
may it be kept.

In this passage the author points to the source of power for the believer. It is as if he wished to say, "In y o u r own strength y o u cannot fulfil the precepts which I have just issued. Y o u need God, *the God of peace* (cf. Rom. 15:33; 16:20; II Cor. 13:11; Phil. 4:9; II Thess. 3:16; Heb. 13:20), a peace established through the cross, a peace which implies spiritual prosperity in the fullest sense (see on 1:1). May this God *sanctify* y o u, that is, may he separate y o u from the life of sin and cause y o u to be dedicated to him (cf. Rom. 15:16; I Cor. 1:2; 6:11; 7:14; Rev. 22:11; and see above on 3:13; 4:3, 7; also N.T.C. on John 17:17, 19) *through and through.* This "through and through" (ὁλοτελεῖς, from ὅλος *whole,* and τέλος *end*) is a rare word, occurring only here in the New Testament. It is a plural adjective, sothat the literal meaning of the word in connection with the noun which it modifies is *y o u whole,* that is, "the whole of each of y o u, every part of each of y o u" (A. T. Robertson, *Word Pictures,* Vol. IV, p. 38). (M.M., p. 447, points out that both here in I Thess. 5:23 and in a decree of Epaminondas the adjective has adverbial force.)

Now this process of sanctification occurs during the present life, the life here on earth. Paul expresses a closely related wish which pertains to the judgment day. The two thoughts constitute a unit. He expresses the wish – which has the solemnity of a prayer – that also "at the coming of our Lord Jesus Christ" (see on 2:19), when others will be sentenced to everlasting damnation for both soul and body (the entire person), the spirit of the believers at Thessalonica (together with all other believers, of course) may be without flaw; indeed that their soul-and-body may be preserved from this terrible condemnation, that is, may be kept *blamelessly* (2:10; cf. 3:13).

So far there is no great difficulty. The *main* idea is clear. The problem arises in interpreting the details. See grammatical footnote [113] which because of its length has been placed at the end of this chapter (on pp. 146-150). If one wishes an answer to the question, "Was Paul a trichotomist?" "Does I Thess. 5:23 teach that man consists of three parts, spirit, soul, and body?" he should read that note.

The *entirety-idea* is stressed throughout the passage. This is shown by the forward position of the word "entire" or "without flaw," and also by such expressions as "through and through" and "y o u r soul and body." Though certain people in Greece and Macedonia might hold the body in low esteem and might consider it to be merely a prison from which the soul must be liberated, and though the Thessalonian believers, mourning the loss of dear ones, might be wondering whether the buried bodies would in any way come to share in the glory of Christ's return (see on 4:13-18), Paul assures the readers that God in Christ is a perfect Savior.

24. A wonderful expression of assurance follows. What Paul has expressed so strikingly is a wish, indeed, but not a *mere* wish. It is a wish which, by God's sovereign grace, will attain certain fulfilment:

Faithful is he who calls y o u, who will also do it.

The Thessalonians need have no fear. The One who *calls* (ὁ καλῶν timeless present participle) them (see on 2:12; 4:7; II Thess. 2:14) will also certainly complete what he has begun with respect to them (cf. Phil. 1:16). He will surely sanctify and preserve them. He is *faithful* (πιστός), to be trusted (cf. I Cor. 1:9; 10:13; II Cor. 1:18; II Thess. 3:3; II Tim. 2:13). What he promises he does.

25. The man who, in the midst of his herculean labors, in II Cor. 11:29 exclaims, "Who is weak, that I am not weak?" and who prefaces that remark with a long list of sufferings and hardships which he had to endure, feels the need of prayer. The circumstances which surround him at Corinth are by no means easy. See on 3:7. Besides, he (together with Silas and Timothy, of course) believes in the efficacy of prayer. It is, therefore, not surprising that here (and in several of the epistles) we find this stirring request, **Brothers, do pray for us.** Cf. II Thess. 3:1; Rom. 15:30; Eph. 6:19; Col. 4:3. The emphatic position of the word "Brothers" (see on 1:4) – sothat the propriety of the request is based, as it were, upon the love which obtains between those who are members of the same spiritual family – adds to its earnest and urgent character.

26. Greet all the brothers with a holy kiss.

Just as someone living today will write, "Tender my kindest greetings to" this or that person, so Paul, Silas, and Timothy ask that they be remembered to "all the brothers," that is, to every member of the congregation, including even those who were displaying tendencies in the direction of fanaticism or of meddlesomeness or of idleness. None is to be skipped.

The form of this greeting is the "holy kiss" (cf. Rom. 16:16; I Cor. 16:20; II Cor. 13:12). This was the kiss *of love* (cf. I Peter 5:14) and *of peace* (see *Constitutions,* quoted below). It was *holy* because it was a symbol of spiritual oneness in Christ. It was, moreover, a seal of *Christian* affection, the feeling which members of one and the same spiritual household cherish for one another.

Among the early references to this kind of kiss are the following:

"As many as are convinced and believe that what we teach and say is true, and pledge themselves to be able to live accordingly, are instructed to pray and to entreat God with fasting for the remission of their past sins, while we pray and fast with them. Then they are brought by us to a place where there is water, and they are regenerated in the same manner in which we ourselves were regenerated. For, in the name of God, the Father and Lord of the universe, and of our Savior Jesus Christ, and of the Holy Spirit, they then receive the washing with water. . . . After we have thus baptized the one who has been convinced and has given his assent to our teaching, we bring him to the place where those who are called *brothers* are gathered, in order that we may offer hearty prayers in common for ourselves, for the baptized person, and for all others in every place. . . . *Having ended the prayers, we salute one another with a holy kiss.* Then bread and a cup containing wine mixed with water are presented to that one of the brothers who was presiding" (Justin Martyr – about the middle of the second century A. D. – *First Apology.* LXI. LXV).

"Who [i.e., what *un*believing husband] will, without some suspicion, dismiss her [i.e., his wife who is a believer] to attend that Lord's Supper which they defame? Who will permit her to creep into prison, *to kiss a martyr's bonds? nay, indeed, to meet any one of the brothers to exchange the kiss?"* (Tertullian – about 207 A. D. – *To His Wife* II. iv).

"Let the younger women also sit by themselves, if there be a place for them; otherwise, let them stand behind the women. Let married women who have children be placed by themselves; but let the virgins and the widows and the old women stand or sit before all the rest. And let the deacon be the disposer of the places, that every one who enters may go to his proper place, and may not sit at the entrance. In like manner, let the deacon watch the people, that nobody whispers or sleeps or laughs or nods. . . . After this let all arise together, and looking toward the east . . . pray to God eastward. . . . After the prayer is over, let some of the deacons attend upon the oblation of the Eucharist. . . . Let other deacons watch the multitude and keep them silent. But let that deacon who is at the highpriest's right hand say to the people, 'Let no one have any dispute with another; let no one come in hypocrisy.' *Then let the men give the men, and the women give the women, the Lord's kiss"* (*Constitutions of the Holy Apostles* – about the third century A. D. – II. vii).

"And after this [prayer for the faithful] let the deacon say, Let us attend. And let the bishop salute the church, and say, The peace of God be with y o u all. And let the people answer, And with thy spirit."

"And let the deacon say to all, *Salute one another with a holy kiss. And let the clergy salute the bishop, the men of the laity salute the men, the women (salute) the women.* And let the children stand by the reading-desk. And let another deacon stand by them, that they may not be disorderly" (*Constitutions of the Holy Apostles,* VIII. xi).

"Let us salute one another with a holy kiss. Let us bow our heads to the Lord" (*"The Divine Liturgy of James, the Holy Apostle and Brother of the Lord"* – date, origin, and authorship disputed –, II).

Of interest, in this connection, is also the remark of Augustine: "People complain about being led out of the dark night of ruinous unbelief into the light of life-giving faith. Held fast by the evil spirit, they grumble because other people stream into the church to render a pure worship to God, where, for the sake of modesty, men are on one side and women on the other" (*Concerning the City of God* – written 413-426 A. D. –, II. xxviii).

27. I solemnly charge you before the Lord to have this epistle read to all the brothers. This solemn charge or adjuration is not surprising. The contents of the epistle is important, both with respect to teaching (for example, anent the Second Coming) and with respect to admonition. It is very well possible that some of the disorderly persons, upon hearing that a letter from the missionaries had arrived and suspecting that it contained some admonitions intended especially for them, might wish to be absent when it was read aloud to the congregation. So Paul stresses the fact that by all means *every* person in the church must hear the letter! The adjuration implies a threat of divine punishment if this be not done. Yet, the charge contains no bitterness, note the term of endearment: *brothers.*

28. The grace of our Lord Jesus Christ be with you. With variations this benediction occurs *at* or *near* the close of *all* of Paul's epistles (i.e., *all* if its occurrence in Rom. 16:20 is authentic). It is entirely in harmony with the spiritual character of the salutation at the beginning. For the various concepts and for the force of both see on 1:1.

Synthesis of 5:12-28

See p. 132. *Exhortation. Paul writes to the Thessalonians, exhorting them how they should conduct themselves with respect to all classes and at all times.*

A close study of I Thessalonians reveals the fact that a mighty conflict between the forces of light and those of darkness is presupposed throughout. At times (in certain words and phrases) it arises to the surface.

Arrayed on one side are, first of all, God the Father, the Lord Jesus Christ, and the Holy Spirit; then Paul, Silvanus, and Timothy, who are carrying on their spiritual labors by means of this letter and also through the elders of the church. Finally, there is the brotherhood in general.

Here again a distinction is made between those whose faith, love, and hope are bearing much fruit (and who are therefore examples to others), and those who, though regarded as brothers, are characterized by shortcomings that call for special consideration. Thus, there are the disorderly persons (fanatics, meddlers, and loafers), the fainthearted, and the weak.

But there are also those who had been endowed with special gifts, for example, that of prophesying, and – as could be expected – there were the would-be prophets.

Furthermore, reference is made to "those who believe in Macedonia and Achaia" and to "the churches of God that are in Judea." From this it is clear that the various local churches, though autonomous, do not stand entirely by themselves. There is an organic bond between them, the bond of faith, love, and hope. The idea of the *one,* holy, catholic Church (the theme of Ephesians) begins to emerge already in I Thessalonians! See especially 1:7-9; 2:14; 2:19; 4:10. The Thessalonian believers love (and have become an example to) those in Macedonia and Achaia. They have become imitators of those in Judea and are enduring the same hardships. Along with others, moreover, they constitute Paul's glory-wreath. Here is the idea of the Church Militant.

But the Church Militant, in turn, stands in the closest possible relation to the Church Triumphant. At Christ's Return those who previously fell asleep, *together with* those who are then still living on earth will be caught up in clouds to meet the Lord in the air, and to remain with him forever.

On the other side are Satan, the idols, the pagans who afflict believers, and those who instigate the pagans. These pagans "do not know God," are living in darkness, are morally and spiritually asleep, have no firmly-anchored hope, and are destined for sudden destruction (everlasting punishment).

The wicked instigators are the impenitent Jews, who are "contrary to all men" and on whom the wrath of God has come "to the uttermost."

Such are the two armies. Again and again believers receive the bracing assurance of complete victory at the coming of the Lord Jesus Christ.

Now the present, closing section of I Thessalonians contains specific exhortations showing what should be the attitude of the Thessalonians with respect to several of the groups and persons mentioned in the preceding, namely, towards:

verses 12, 13	the elders of the church
verse 14	the disorderly
	the fainthearted
	the weak
	"everyone"
verse 15	those who have injured them
verses 16-18	God

verses 19-22	the Holy Spirit and his gifts (also: would-be prophets). This is followed by
verses 23, 24	a solemn wish for sanctification and preservation, the wish being immediately followed by the promise; by
verses 25-28	a trio of urgent requests (for intercessory prayer, for extending greetings by means of the "holy kiss," and for the public reading of this letter); and finally by the benediction.

---

113 If a. the nominative, singular, neuter *adjective* "without flaw" or "entire" or "sound" (ὁλόκληρον) is either treated as an adverb (some call it an adverb) or as an adjective belonging to all three nouns (spirit, soul, body); and b. this word is given a totally different place in the sentence than it has in the original, being now placed next to the word "without blame" (or "blamelessly"), as if also in the original the two occurred in close co-ordination, a rendering results which changes a *little* problem into a *big* one. The rendering to which I refer is:

"And may your spirit and soul and body be preserved entire, without blame. . . ." (A.R.V., cf. A.V. and R.S.V. neither of which is any better).

Naturally, the question now arises, "Did Paul believe that human nature consists of three parts: spirit, soul, and body? In other words, was he a trichotomist?" The deeper question is, "Just what did Paul mean when he wrote I Thess. 5:23 (especially the words in dispute)?"

Among the answers or solutions which have been offered the following are, perhaps, the most important:

a. Paul was evidently a trichotomist. He clearly divides human nature into spirit, soul, and body.

b. Paul's readers were trichotomists. Paul accommodates himself to their view. Had he simply written, "And may your soul and body be kept sound and blameless," the readers would have asked, "Must not our *spirits* be preserved also?" In order to avoid this erroneous conclusion — that *the spirit* did not need to be guarded — the apostle writes as he does.

c. Paul does not distinguish at all between *spirit* and *soul* in the present passage. He is speaking rhetorically. We do the same thing today when we tell an audience to put its "heart and soul" into a certain worthwhile project.

d. Paul, in using the word *spirit,* meant the Holy Spirit, or that portion of the divine Spirit which dwells permanently in each regenerated individual. To this Holy Spirit, who dwells in (but is never part of) the human nature, he, as a true dichotomist, adds "soul and body" as constituting the human nature.

e. When Paul mentions both spirit and soul, he indicates *not two* substances but *one* and the same immaterial substance. However, he views this substance first from the aspect of its relation to God — as a recipient of divine influences and as an organ for divine worship ("spirit") —, then from the aspect of its relation to the lower realm — as the seat of sensations, affections, desires, etc. ("soul"). To this *one* immaterial substance, viewed from *two* aspects, *Paul adds the body*. It is in this sense that he writes, "and may your spirit and soul and body be kept sound and blameless."

f. Paul does not have in mind a series of three co-ordinate elements: "spirit and soul and body." On the contrary, the first concept is "your entire person." To this, by way of explanation, the apostle adds, "both your soul and body."

With respect to these six theories our own opinion is as follows:

Theory a.

This can be dismissed at once. The fact that Paul was not a trichotomist is clear from such passages as the following: Rom. 8:10; I Cor. 5:5; 7:34; II Cor. 7:1; Eph.

so; rejects idea that Paul wrote Hebrews (see Heb. 4:12

2:3; Col. 2:5. Apart from I Thess. 5:23 he nowhere employs trichotomistic language with respect to the nature of man. The conclusion seems valid that also in the present passage he does not write as a trichotomist.

Theory b.

This accommodation theory, besides being questionable as to the ethics implied, lacks a solid historical basis. The readers surely were not Neo-Platonists!

Theory c.

The illustration employed is not very appropriate. When we tell an audience to put its "heart and soul" into a certain project, we immediately recognize the synonymous character of these two terms. But when *within one and the same clause* (as this theory implies) we co-ordinate *three* terms, *the third of which is clearly of a totally different nature from the second* (the third being *body*, the second being *soul*), the question is legitimate whether perhaps the first (*spirit*) should not also be distinguished in meaning from the others. Besides, Paul elsewhere frequently uses the term *soul* (ψυχή, whence ψυχικός "natural" or "unspiritual" I Cor. 2:14) in a sense different from *spirit* (πνεῦμα, whence πνευματικός "spiritual" I Cor. 2:15). It must not be taken for granted, therefore, that every distinction between *spirit* and *soul* is *here* (in I Thess. 5:23) completely absent from his mind.

The summary of the first table of the law, Mark 12:30, far from proving theory c. to be correct, would rather seem to establish the very opposite, for certainly here heart, soul, mind, and strength do not all mean exactly the same thing!

Theory d.

This is definitely wrong, though we admit that it is advanced by really great exegetes. Paul, Silas, and Timothy would not be expressing the wish that the Holy Spirit (or "a portion of the Holy Spirit") might be kept sound and blameless! Nor would they be hoping that the third person of the Trinity might be without a flaw!

Theory e.

This is probably the best of those so far reviewed. It has much in its favor: it permits Paul to remain a dichotomist, which is correct (as has been shown). It is also correct in indicating that the first and the second terms of the triad (hence, πνεῦμα and ψυχή) are at times to be distinguished in the manner stated in the theory. If we had to choose between the five theories discussed so far, this would be our choice. In fact, as we see it, in some respects this theory is also better than theory f. (below), for example, in that it does not render the adjective *sound* (ὁλόκληρον) as if it were in the attributive position.

Nevertheless, the *translation* proposed here ("and may your spirit and soul and body be kept sound and blameless") has the following debatable features:

(1) It co-ordinates the words "sound" and "blameless," placing them next to each other, which does not seem to harmonize with the intention of the original.

(2) It interprets the conjunction "and" (καί) which occurs between the second and the third terms of the triad as *adding* two different substances (soul, body), but it views the "and" (καί) which connects the first and the second as merely indicating that *the same substance* is considered from two different aspects. Although this may be possible, it is not the usual manner in which one would interpret two identical conjunctions in an expression consisting of three terms which one considers to be co-ordinate, *all occurring in the same clause,* and which one thus translates: "your spirit *and* soul *and* body."

(3) It connects the adjective *sound* with all three nouns (spirit, soul, body), but it does not show why in the original it is *in the singular!* (However, this objection is not formidable. It happens more often that in such a series, the number of the adjective which modifies all the nouns in the series simply agrees with the first or last noun mentioned.) Or if the word "sound" is considered to be an adverb modifying the verb "be kept" (some interpreters view it as such), it is not made

clear why it should be an adverb *here* while elsewhere in the Greek Bible it is always an adjective (see in the LXX: Lev. 23:15; Deut. 27:6; Josh. 9:2; Ezek. 15:5; Zech. 11:16; Wisd. Sol. 15:3; I Macc. 4:47; IV Macc. 15:17: *whole* stones, *entire* righteousness, *complete* sabbaths, etc.).

I accept theory e. in part, not entirely.

Theory f.

According to this theory, proposed long ago, and recently presented in strengthened form by Charles Masson in a well-written article ("Sur I Thessaloniciens 5:23," *RThPh* 33 (1945), 97-102) the passage in question should be translated somewhat as follows:

"And may the God of peace himself
sanctify y o u wholly;
and may y o u r entire person,
y o u r soul and y o u r body,
be kept irreproachable
for the day of the coming
of our Lord Jesus Christ."

This theory avoids many of the objectionable features of the others but, as I see it, introduces some new difficulties. The points which distinguish it from the preceding are the following: it experiences no difficulty with respect to the number and gender of the word *sound* or *entire* (ὁλόκληρον); it views that word as an adjective, which is probably correct. However, it considers πνεῦμα, as used here in I Thess. 5:23, to mean *person,* and it offers as proof the parallelism between
"The grace of our Lord Jesus Christ be with y o u r *spirit*" (Gal. 6:18; Phil. 4:23; Philemon 25)

and

"The grace of our Lord Jesus Christ be with *y o u*" (I Thess. 5:28), noting that in such liturgical passages (and it considers I Thess. 5:23 to belong to this category) "y o u r spirit" means "y o u" or something closely akin to it (the entire person of the believer, both soul and body). It seeks support from the immediately preceding line ("sanctify y o u wholly" corresponding to "may y o u r entire person . . . be kept"); and it considers καί . . . καί to mean "both . . . and" (cf. Rom. 11:33).

A final feature, which requires special mention, is the fact that, according to Masson, when the original is read as he reads it, verse 23 "divides itself into two strophes, each containing two stitches, whose parallelism in the number of syllables, as also in the assonances of initial and final syllables, compose an easily perceptible rhythm."

While we acknowledge our indebtedness to Masson and to those before him who have advanced this view, we, nevertheless, cannot go along with them all the way. In addition to minor differences in translation, which become immediately evident when our rendering for the entire verse is compared to that offered by the proponents of this theory, two differences stand out above all the rest:

The first is this: *in the Greek original* the word which Masson, etc., correctly render "entire" is in the predicate position. Hence, as I see it, the original does not really say, "And may y o u r entire spirit," but "And entire (or "and without flaw") may be y o u r spirit." The Berkeley Version correctly retains the predicate position of the adjective when it translates: "May your spirit be without flaw and your soul and body maintained blameless."

The second point which requires additional comment concerns the theory's rendering of the term πνεῦμα. It favors the translation "person" in the sense of *soul and body*. But does this Greek word πνεῦμα ever have that meaning anywhere else in the New Testament? The simple fact is that it does not.

It will be profitable in this connection to give a review of the uses of the two terms in question, namely, πνεῦμα and ψυχή. (The third term, σῶμα, is clear enough.)

(1) There is first of all the meaning *wind* (John 3:8; Heb. 1:7 plural). The original has πνεῦμα.

(2) The closely related concept *breath, breath of life, life, animating principle* is represented both by πνεῦμα (II Thess. 2:8, fig.; Rev. 11:11; 13:15?; and cf. Matt. 27:50; Luke 8:55; 23:46; John 19:30; Acts 7:59; James 2:26) and by ψυχή (Matt. 2:20; 6:25a; 6:25b; 16:26a; 16:26b; Mark 3:4; Luke 6:9, etc.), though mostly by the latter.

(3) The meaning *living being, self, person,* especially frequent in passages which can be traced back to Hebrew originals, but by no means confined to such passages, is always ψυχή. Under this heading some would include only the following: Matt. 11:29; Mark 8:36; Acts 2:41, 43; 3:23; 7:14; 27:37; Rom. 2:9; 13:1; I Cor. 15:45; I Peter 3:20; and Rev. 16:3. Others, on the basis of a comparison of parallel passages, would add such references as Matt. 20:28; Mark 10:45, cf. I Tim. 2:6; John 10:11, 15, 17; and many more (note "my soul" is "I" in Matt. 12:18; and "my soul" is "thy Holy One" and is "he" in Acts 2:27, 31).

(4) *Soul* or *spirit.* The original has ψυχή and πνεῦμα.

(5) *Incorporeal* or *disembodied being.* With the possible exception of the disputed meaning of ψυχή in Rev. 6:9 and 20:4 (which, as I see it, properly come under this heading, but not all agree) this meaning is in the New Testament everywhere represented by πνεῦμα. The following subdivisions can be recognized: spirit in general (Acts 23:8, 9), God as Spirit (John 4:24), Christ as Spirit (I Cor. 15:45), the human soul apart from the body (Heb. 12:23; I Peter 3:19), ghost (Luke 24:37, 39), angel (Heb. 1:14), demon, more than forty passages for this last subdivision of (5) (Matt. 8:16; 10:1; 12:43, etc.).

(6) *The Holy Spirit and/or his gifts.* There are about one hundred twenty passages in which "the Holy Spirit" ("Spirit of God," — "of the Lord," — "of Jesus," — "of Christ," — "of Jesus Christ," "the seven Spirits") is definitely mentioned. In an approximately equal number of passages the term "Spirit" in all probability refers to the Holy Spirit, though in several cases this is disputed. In all cases which come under this sixth heading the word used is πνεῦμα (Matt. 1:18, 20; 3:11; 12:32; etc.).

(7) *Frame of mind, disposition, efficient source, influence, life-imparting energy.* With the exception of a couple disputed instances where one of these closely related connotations may be represented by ψυχή, the word is always πνεῦμα (Matt. 5:3; Luke 1:17; I Cor. 4:21; Gal. 6:1, etc.).

With the exception of (1) all these meanings are also found in the writings of Paul. At present, however, we are concerned only with (4). It is striking that Paul nearly always uses πνεῦμα when this concept is indicated. Yet he also uses ψυχή (I Thess. 2:8, unless this should fall under heading 3; I Thess. 5:23).

The question arises, Did Paul distinguish between πνεῦμα and ψυχή? The two words have in common that both refer to the invisible element in man, viewed as the principle of thinking, willing, desiring. It must be granted that there are several passages in the New Testament where the distinction in meaning is so small that the two may be said to be interchangeable or nearly so. Nevertheless, close study of these terms in all their occurrences points to the fact that *basically* there is a distinction between them. Whenever this distinction has not yet faded away, it amounts to this, that when πνεῦμα is used *mental* activity comes into prominence, while ψυχή frequently points in the direction of *emotional* activity. It is the *spirit* (πνεῦμα) which perceives (Mark 2:8), plans (Acts 19:21), and knows (I Cor. 2:11). It is the *soul* (ψυχή) that is sorrowful (Matt. 26:38). The *spirit* (πνεῦμα) prays (I Cor. 14:14), the ψυχή loves (Mark 12:30). Also, ψυχή is often more general, broader in scope, indicating the *sum-total* of life which rises above the physical, while πνεῦμα is more restricted, indicating the human spirit in its relation to *God,* man's self-consciousness or personality viewed as the subject in acts of worship or in activities related to worship, such as praying, bearing witness, serving the Lord.

In my study of all the Pauline passages in which πνεῦμα is used I have not found a single one in which it has the meaning "person," in the sense of one's soul and body.

It has become evident that I am not satisfied (at least not *wholly* satisfied) with theory f.

Having now discussed the six theories, none of which I am ready to accept in its entirety, though I admit that some contain valuable elements, I will state my own view:

a. The trichotomistic appearance of the passage is considerably reduced as soon as it is seen that the words in dispute are found not in one clause but in two clauses:

hence not: "And may your spirit and soul and body be kept . . ."

but

"And without flaw may be y o u r spirit,
And y o u r soul-and-body
. . . .
May it be kept."

But thus rendering the passage we can do justice to its grammatical syntax and even to its word-order (see the original).

b. Every trace of trichotomy which still remains can be obliterated in one of two ways:

(1) by considering the word "soul" to have the same meaning as "spirit," the change from "spirit" to "soul" having been introduced for stylistic reasons. This eliminates trichotomy.

(2) by accepting the position that although both "spirit" and "soul" refer to *the same* immaterial substance (hence, no trichotomy here either!), this substance is viewed first (in one clause) from the aspect of its relation to *God* — the "spirit" being man's power of grasping divine things, his invisible essence viewed as a recipient of divine influences and as an organ of divine worship — ; then, in the next clause, from the aspect of its relation to *the lower realm,* as the seat of sensations, affections, desires. This could well be the true element in theory e.

If a choice must be made, I would prefer this second alternative. It is in harmony with the distinction between the two words which is present elsewhere (as has been shown). There is also an interesting parallel in a somewhat similar passage, Heb. 4:12, where it is obvious that the two words have distinct meanings.

The main point has been proved, namely, that, either way, every trace of trichotomy has disappeared!

Commentary
on
II Thessalonians

Outline of II Thessalonians 1

Theme: *The Revelation of the Lord Jesus from Heaven* has a twofold purpose:

(1) To be glorified in the saints, including those at Thessalonica, for whom, because of their increase in faith and love, and their continued endurance amid persecution, Paul feels impelled to thank God, and for whom he prays.

(2) To render vengeance to the disobedient.

CHAPTER I

II THESSALONIANS 1:1, 2

1 1 Paul and Silvanus and Timothy to the church of the Thessalonians in God
our Father and the Lord Jesus Christ; 2 grace to y o u and peace from God
the Father and the Lord Jesus Christ.
3 We are obliged to give thanks to God always for y o u, brothers, as is fitting, because y o u r faith is growing beyond measure, and the love of each single
one of y o u for one another is constantly increasing, 4 so that we on our part boast
of y o u in the churches of God, of y o u r endurance and faith in all y o u r persecutions and in the afflictions under which y o u are holding up, 5 an evident indication of God's righteous judgment, in order that y o u may be deemed worthy of
the kingdom of God, for which y o u, too, are suffering; 6 (God's *righteous* judgment, we say) if, indeed, (it is) righteous in God's estimation (as it certainly is) to
repay with afflictions those who afflict y o u, 7 and (to grant) y o u who are being
afflicted rest with us at the revelation of the Lord Jesus from heaven with the
angels of his power in flaming fire, 8 inflicting vengeance on those who do not
know God, even on those who do not obey the gospel of our Lord Jesus, such as
will pay the penalty of everlasting destruction away from the face of the Lord and
from the glory of his might, 10 when he comes in order to be glorified in his saints
and to be marveled at in all who believe – for our testimony to y o u was believed
– in that day.
11 With this in view we are also praying always for y o u, that our God may
count y o u worthy of the call, and that he by his power may bring to fulfilment
(y o u r) every resolve prompted by goodness and (y o u r every) work resulting from
faith, 12 in order that the name of our Lord Jesus may be glorified in y o u, and
y o u in him according to the grace of our God and of the Lord Jesus Christ.

1:1-12

1:1, 2. Paul and Silvanus and Timothy to the church of the Thessalonians in God our Father and the Lord Jesus Christ; 2 grace to y o u and peace from God the Father and the Lord Jesus Christ.

This superscription differs from that found in I Thess. 1:1 in two respects only:

(1) It has *"our* Father" instead of *"the* Father." Thus the fact that both writers and readers have one and the same Father is here definitely expressed, though it was also implied in I Thess. 1:1.

(2) After the clause "grace to y o u and peace" it adds a phrase which

makes explicit *the source* of grace and peace, showing that it comes *"from* God the Father and the Lord Jesus Christ." In I Thess. 1:1 this source was implied in the statement that the church was (founded and still existing) *"in* God the Father and the Lord Jesus Christ."

For the rest, see on I Thess. 1:1.

3. We are obliged to give thanks to God always for y o u, brothers, as is fitting.

For the meaning of, "We give thanks to God always," see on I Thess. 1:2. However, here in II Thess. 1:3 the writers do not state, "We give thanks to God always," but *"We are obliged"* (ὀφείλομεν) to do so. They feel impelled to express their gratitude to God. They cannot do otherwise. And this subjective necessity is in harmony with the objective necessity: "as is *fitting*" (ἄξιον).

The idea advanced by some commentators that the substitution of, "We are obliged to give thanks," for "We give thanks" implies a degree of reluctance or hesitancy, and that this "somewhat faltering manner of expression" must be explained in the light of 2:2; 3:6, 10, 11 – passages which indicate that the mental attitude and conduct of some had grown worse instead of better – impresses us as an instance of reading too much into the text. Also open to serious question is the view according to which the replacement of "for y o u *all*" (I Thess. 1:2) by the simple "for y o u" (here in II Thess. 1:3) must be explained similarly. That Paul is not trying to omit any true "brother" is rather clear from what immediately follows (note the words "each single one of y o u"): **because y o u r faith is growing beyond measure, and the love of each single one of y o u** (literally, "of each one of y o u all") **for one another is constantly increasing.** Clearly in this entire passage – whether it be read in the original or in the translation makes no difference – the writers reveal themselves as men who are elated (see also on 2:13; 3:4) rather than reluctant, exuberant rather than hesitant. The presence in the congregation of a few members who were not living in accordance with the rules cannot be denied. In fact, it constituted a real problem, more so even than when the first epistle was written. But in the jubilant passage which we are now discussing the disorderly persons are kept in the background for the moment. What we have here is irrepressible joy, a joy which in the form of sincere and humble thanksgiving is directed to the Giver of all good things.

The reason for the constant thanksgiving is that the faith of the Thessalonians *is growing beyond measure* (ὑπεραυξάνει) or *very much,* and that the love of each single brother *is constantly increasing* (πλεονάζει), which was exactly what Paul had wished and prayed for so earnestly (see on I Thess. 3:12; 4:1, 10). It is true that in the present passage *faith* and *love* are mentioned, *not hope.* Contrast I Thess. 1:3, where all three are mentioned. But to infer from this omission (as some interpreters do) that in Paul's judgment the Thessalonians had lost their hope is unwarranted. Such a conclusion brings one into conflict with what is clearly stated in II Thess. 2:16: "who gave *us* (both readers and writers) *good hope.*" Besides, Paul immediately adds (verse 4) that he boasts of the *endurance* which the readers are showing; and is not *endurance* inspired by hope? See on I Thess. 1:3.

It is certainly true that the Thessalonians needed further instruction with respect to things to come (see 2:1-12), but their hope was by no means dim. On the contrary, it was buoyant, and it sustained them sothat they were able to endure persecution. Verse 3 must not be interpreted as if verse 4 did not exist! *The only correct way to interpret a passage is to read on and on.* If that is done, we shall not commit the error of saying that Paul praises the Thessalonians for their faith and love but not for their hope.

4. One of the results of the readers' growth in faith and increase in love is now stated: **sothat we on our part boast of y o u in the churches of God, of y o u r endurance and faith in all y o u r persecutions and in the afflictions under which y o u are holding up.**

The perfectly natural and easy manner in which the term *endurance* is here introduced seems to imply that it was already presupposed in verse 3. Faith full-grown implies hope, and hope produces endurance.

Paul, Silas, and Timothy *are boasting* (i.e., they *"spoke with pride"*) about the Thessalonians. In connection with this boasting four facts are pointed out:

(1) *Its authors:* "we on our part" (αὐτοὺς ἡμᾶς). Cf. Rom. 9:3; 15:14; II Cor. 12:13. The idea seems to be one of contrast, not one of resemblance. In other words, the meaning is not, "we, like others who have heard about y o u" (in which case we would have expected καὶ ἡμᾶς), nor is it "we of our own accord," but "we on our part over against y o u on y o u r part." The missionaries must have heard from the Thessalonians since the first epistle was written. Naturally, the genuine believers in the recently established church were rather restrained in speaking about their own spiritual condition. They were humble, ready to admit that even the most devout among them were still far removed from the goal of spiritual perfection, and that some in the congregation conducted themselves in such a manner that the others felt ashamed. Over against this, Paul, by way of encouragement, says, *"We on our part* boast of y o u."

(2) *Its personal object:* "y o u," i.e., the Thessalonians.

(3) *Its impersonal object:* "y o u r endurance and faith in all y o u r persecutions and in the afflictions under which y o u are holding up."

This indicates *the qualities* in the readers which had given rise to the boasting. The missionaries spoke with pride about the Thessalonians because they *were holding up under* (they manifested the grace of ὑπομονή, endurance; see on I Thess. 1:3; 4:14) all their distresses, armed, as they were, by faith in God and in his promises. These distresses are here characterized as *persecutions* (used by Paul also in Rom. 8:35; II Cor. 12:10; II Tim. 3:11), which is the more specific term, and *afflictions,* which is the more general term. The latter may also indicate the result of the persecutions. These afflictions are the "tribulations" caused by the pressure which the enemy exerts upon the children of God. See N.T.C. on John 16:33. Paul commends the Thessalonians for *holding up* (ἀνέχεσθε) under these trials. The expression *"all* y o u r persecutions" seems to indicate that of late these hardships had increased rather than decreased.

(4) *Its place or sphere:* "the churches of God." See on I Thess. 1:7, 8; 2:14. That Paul was in rather close contact with these churches appears again and again. Anxiety for all the churches pressed upon him daily (II Cor. 11:28). Is he thinking here of other churches in Macedonia, of Corinth and other churches in Achaia (cf. II Cor. 1:1), and of the churches in Asia Minor? We do not know. We do know that it was Paul's custom to boast of one church to another (II Cor. 8:1-6; 9-2; contrast Phil. 4:15).

5. an evident indication of God's righteous judgment, in order that y o u may be counted worthy of the kingdom of God, for which y o u, too, are suffering.

Paul calls this unflinching attitude on the part of the Thessalonians (their endurance and faith amid all persecutions and afflictions) an *indication* (ἔνδειγμα) or "proof positive" of God's righteous judgment. The very fact that God *rewards* his children with fortitude indicates that he is a *righteous* God, who, accordingly, will also manifest this righteousness in the final judgment, which judgment will have as its purpose to state openly that his loyal followers are worthy of entering his everlasting kingdom.

For the sake of this kingdom not only Paul, Silas, Timothy and many others *outside* of Thessalonica are suffering but so are also the believers *at* Thessalonica. They gladly endure tribulation in order that one day they may enter into the kingdom of perfection, in which God will be all in all, and his sovereign rule will be joyfully recognized and obeyed.[114]

---

[114] The exegesis here given is based upon the following conclusions with respect to points of grammar.

a. ἔνδειγμα is either accusative in apposition with verse 4b (somewhat like λατρείαν in Rom. 12:1) or else it is to be regarded as a predicate nominative (after ὅ ἐστιν understood). In either case it refers not to the persecutions and afflictions as such, as if Paul were saying that these tribulations which believers had to endure were an evidence of God's righteous judgment, but to the believers' faith and endurance amid all their persecutions and afflictions.

b. The κρίσις refers, indeed, to the *final* judgment, and not to God's verdict here and now with respect to the genuine character of the endurance and faith of the

Let not the Thessalonians doubt this benevolent purpose of God with respect to them, namely, to count them worthy of entering the kingdom. Let them have no fear (cf. I Thess. 5:4, 5, 9). Let them bear in mind that God is not only Judge but *righteous* Judge, who rewards faith and obedience, and who ever keeps his promise. The righteous character of God's judgment is emphasized in the immediately following verses:

6, 7. (God's *righteous* judgment, we say) if, indeed, (it is) righteous in God's estimation (as it certainly is) to repay with afflictions those who afflict y o u, and (to grant) y o u who are being afflicted rest with us at the revelation of the Lord Jesus from heaven.

Here Paul shows that God's kindly purpose with respect to the Thessalonians (to count them worthy of entering the kingdom) is in harmony with the basic principle of recompense, according to which those who persecute God's people will suffer punishment, and those who are persecuted because of their faith will receive a reward.

The apostle is so thoroughly convinced of the absolutely indisputable character of this basic principle that he can afford to say, "If . . ." Note, however, that he does not merely say, "If," but "If, *indeed!*" (εἴπερ), and that the condition is assumed to be true (first class conditional sentence). Hence, clearly to convey the full force of the original, one should add to the words, "If, indeed, (it is) righteous in God's sight" something like "as it certainly is."

Even today we use *such* if-clauses again and again. We use them when we are sure that the statement included in the if-clause is beyond dispute; for instance:

Thessalonians. (On the noun *judgment* and the verb *to judge* see N.T.C. on John 3:19, 17.)

Proof: the following verses (6-10) clearly indicate that Paul is thinking of the judgment "at the revelation of the Lord Jesus from heaven." *One should read on and on.*

c. εἰς τό, as often in Paul, is best taken in its telic sense; cf. the parallel thought expressed in verse 10. The judgment day arrives in order that the saints may be deemed worthy of the kingdom, and in order that Christ may be glorified in his saints.

d. The verb καταξιόω means not "make" but "count" worthy. For evidence see M.M., p. 330.

e. As in I Thess. 2:12 (see on that verse) so also here the expression "the kingdom of God" indicates the redeemed society of the future which will gladly recognize and obey God's rule. This future sense is clear from the entire context (verses 6-10). Also elsewhere in Paul's epistles this kingdom is an inheritance which believers will receive by and by, and from which those who practice immorality, uncleanness, etc., will be excluded (I Cor. 6:9, 19; Gal. 5:21; Eph. 5:5). Flesh and blood cannot inherit it (I Cor. 15:50). Nevertheless, this future kingdom is foreshadowed in the present, into which believers have been translated (Col. 1:13). Its citizens even now possess "righteousness and peace and joy in the Holy Spirit" (Rom. 14:17). It is "not in word but in power" (I Cor. 4:20).

f. For the meaning of ὑπέρ see N.T.C. on John 10:11.

"If the sun rose yesterday, it will rise tomorrow."

"If I am poor, I am not dishonest."

"If the mail was delivered yesterday, it will be delivered today." In each case such an "if" means "on the valid assumption that."

Hence, the sense of verses 6 and 7 in relation to verse 5b is: "On the valid assumption that it is a divine rule that the persecutor is punished and that the persecuted is rewarded, God will reward y o u on the coming judgment-day by counting y o u worthy to enter his glorious kingdom."

God's righteousness is manifested in a twofold manner. On the one hand, it is *retributive:* God *repays* (*gives in return;* see on I Thess. 3:9) with *afflictions* (see N.T.C. on John 16:33) those who afflict believers. On the other hand, it is *remunerative:* he grants those who are being afflicted *rest* (ἄνεσιν, from ἄνεσις, literally *let-up*), gracious *relief* (II Cor. 2:13; 7:5; 8:13) from all the hardships they have borne on account of their valiant battle for the truth.

In a touching manner the passage is so worded that association with others *in suffering* for the cause of Christ (note verse 5: "y o u, *too,* are suffering") is balanced by association with others *in enjoyment of rest* ("rest *with us,*" that is, with Paul, Silas, Timothy, and, of course, with all other believers).

This rest – freedom from every form of bondage, and everlasting peace in the presence of the God of love – will be granted to believers "at the revelation of the Lord Jesus from heaven."

Paul is fond of this word *revelation* (ἀποκάλυψις, literally *uncovering, the removal of the veil*). Often he uses it in the sense of a disclosure of divine truth (Rom. 2:5; 16:25; I Cor. 14:6, 26; II Cor. 12:1, 7; Gal. 1:12; Eph. 3:3). In the present instance, however, the term has reference to the glorious manifestation of the Lord at his second coming. So also in I Cor. 1:7. Then the veil which now hides him from our view will be taken away, for we shall see him in his majestic descent *from heaven* (see on I Thess. 4:16). The expression "at the revelation of the Lord Jesus from heaven" means "when the Lord Jesus will be revealed, coming from heaven." [115]

---

[115] It is clear that I take the genitive to be objective or perhaps objective-subjective; certainly not only subjective (as Van Leeuwen maintains, *op. cit.,* p. 409) as in Gal. 1:12. The Lord Jesus (for the meaning of "Lord" and "Jesus" see on I Thess. 1:1) is represented here in II Thess. 1:7 as being revealed. My reasons for accepting this position are as follows:

(1) This is in harmony with the context (see verse 10: he comes "to be marveled at").

(2) It agrees with Christ's own manner of speaking (which must have been transmitted to Paul). Thus according to Luke 17:30 Jesus spoke about "the day when the Son of man *is revealed.*"

(3) "The revelation of the Lord Jesus" (cf. similar expressions in I Peter 1:7, 13) is "the revelation *of his glory.*"

It is true, of course, that the Lord reveals himself. Hence, it is a revelation of

This is the Parousia (see on I Thess. 2:19; see also N.T.C. on John 21:1). **With the angels of his power in flaming fire** ("in fire of flame" = "flaming fire" is perhaps the best reading; contrast Acts 7:30 "flame of fire").

That the Lord at his coming will be accompanied by the angels (in whom his power is made manifest) had been proclaimed by Jesus himself (Matt. 13:41, 42; 25:31; cf. Jude 15; Rev. 14:19). Their function will be twofold: "first, to gather the weeds, binding them in bundles to be burned," and also "to gather the wheat into my (the Lord's) barn."

The addition of the phrase "in flaming fire" indicates the Lord's holiness manifested in judgment (cf. Ex. 3:2; 19:16-20; Is. 29:6; 66:15, 16; Ps. 50:3; 97:3). The passage which must have been vividly present to Paul's consciousness when he wrote this is Is. 66:15, 16:

"For behold, Jehovah will come with fire, and his chariots will be like the whirlwind; to render his anger with fierceness, and his rebuke with flames of fire. For by fire will Jehovah execute judgment. . . ."

The picture is very vivid. We can almost see the angelic host, the Lord himself in the center. Moreover, this is not merely a picture; it is reality! It is by no means established that the mass of fire with its flames shooting in all directions is a "mere" symbol of judgment. To be sure, not until these events become actual history shall we know how much of this description must be taken literally and how much figuratively, and it is useless to speculate. On the other hand it is also true that the seer on Patmos describes how at Christ's coming the earth and the heaven flee away (Rev. 20:11); and II Peter 3:7, 11, 12 states that the universe will be purged completely by a great conflagration ("the heavens being on fire shall be dissolved, and the elements shall melt with fervent heat"). To explain the phrase "in flaming fire" as indicating that the descending host of angels will itself be a flaming fire does not satisfy. The "in" is that of investiture: the host – with Christ leading in the center – is invested in, surrounded by, fire. The three prepositional phrases are clearly parallel. The revelation of the Lord Jesus is:

a. from heaven
b. with the angels of his power
c. in flaming fire.

To speak about a "mere" symbol in such connections is never right. The reality which answers to the symbol is always far more terrible (or far more glorious) than the symbol itself. Human language is stretched almost to

---

himself, by himself (objective-subjective), but the emphasis is on the idea that it is a revelation in which his glory *is disclosed* (objective).

(4) Thus viewed we get an antithesis between the Christ and the Antichrist: Christ is revealed when he returns in glory, and then also the Antichrist ("the man of sin," "the lawless one") will be revealed (see on II Thess. 2:3, 6, 8).

its breaking-point in order to convey the terrible character of the coming of the Lord in relation to the wicked:

8. inflicting vengeance on those who do not know God, even on those who do not obey the gospel of our Lord Jesus.

The Lord comes in order to "inflict vengeance" (cf. Deut. 32:35; Is. 59:17; Ezek. 25:14). On whom? Two answers are possible, depending on what translation one adopts, whether, "inflicting vengeance on those who do not know God, *and on those* who do not obey the gospel of our Lord Jesus," or "inflicting vengeance on those who do not know God, *even on those* who do not obey the gospel of our Lord Jesus." In the former case two classes are indicated: a. pagans who have never heard the gospel and b. Jews and pagans who have rejected the gospel. In the latter case the reference is to only one class, namely, those who, having heard the gospel, refuse to obey it. In view of the fact that in the entire context the blind heathen who have never come into contact with the message of salvation are never alluded to, and that those who in their wilful disobedience persecute God's children are definitely in the apostle's mind (see verses 4, 6, 9), we accept the latter alternative.

Not ignorance of the gospel but disobedience was the sin of the persecutors. It is true that the wicked are here described as "those who *do not know* God." They do not know him as their own God. They do not call on his name. They hate him; hence, they also hate *his gospel* (the gospel which proclaims him, and which he proclaims). Cf. Jer. 10:25; then N.T.C. on John 7:17; II Thess. 3:14; Rom. 10:16.

9. With reference to the persecutors Paul continues: **such as will pay the penalty of everlasting destruction away from the face of the Lord and from the glory of his might.**

The attention is once more focussed on the cruel individuals who, in their hatred of God and of the gospel, make life hard for sincere believers. They are *such people as* (οἵτινες is a qualitative relative pronoun, not the same as "who") will pay the penalty of *everlasting* (actually never-ending; see N.T.C. on John 3:16) *destruction.* The very fact that this "destruction" (cf. I Thess. 5:3; I Cor. 5:5; I Tim. 6:9) is "everlasting" shows that it does not amount to "annihilation" or "going out of existence." On the contrary it indicates an existence "away from the face of the Lord and from the glory of his might."

While "everlasting life" manifests itself in the blessed contemplation of the face of the Lord, sweet fellowship with him, closeness to him (Rev. 22:4; cf. Ps. 17:15; Matt. 5:8), a most wonderful together-ness (I Thess. 4:17), "everlasting destruction" – which is the product of God's *vengeance* (see verse 8 above) – is the very opposite. Just as the "blessing" (?) of Esau consisted in this, that his dwelling would be *away from* the fatness of the earth, and *away from* the dew of heaven (Gen. 27:39 correctly translated), so the punishment which all the persecutors of God's people will suffer will be everlasting existence *away from* (ἀπό) Christ, banished forever from his favor. Cf. Rom. 9:3. The language employed here reminds one of the recurring refrain of Is. 2:10, 19, 21, or of the well-known stanza:

"To live apart from God is death,
'Tis good his face to seek;
My refuge is the living God,
His praise I long to speak." (Based on Ps. 73:27.)

This banishment from loving fellowship with Christ implies expulsion from "the glory (radiant splendor) of his might" as it is manifested in the salvation of the saints.

10. The terrible separation will become publicly evident **when he comes in order to be glorified in his saints and to be marveled at in all who believed – for our testimony to you was believed – in that day.**

The meaning of Christ's second coming for those who by sovereign grace have placed their trust in him is here set forth. In a sense this may be viewed as a continuation of the thought begun in verse 7. According to that verse, God's children will receive *rest* when the Lord Jesus is revealed. Here in verse 10 we are shown that this rest which they will enjoy means glory for *him*. He will be glorified *in* (not merely *among*) them; that is, they will reflect his light, his attributes as, in principle, they do even now (II Cor. 3:18). Every vestige of sin will have been banished from their soul. They will mirror forth his image and walk in the light of his countenance (Ps. 89:15-17). In this *he* will rejoice. In this the angels, too, in seeing it, will rejoice. And in this each of the redeemed, seeing the reflection of Christ's image in all the other redeemed, will rejoice. Moreover, not only will Christ rejoice in the reflection of his own image in them, but he will also rejoice in their joy! Cf. Zeph. 3:17. And his rejoicing in *their* joy will reflect glory on him! Thus, take it in any sense, he will be glorified in his saints. Cf. Is. 49:3; see also N.T.C. on John 12:28. He *will be marveled at* (viewed with glad astonishment and with grateful wonder; hence, *praised*) in all who believed.

On the one hand, the redeemed are here viewed as *saints* (set apart by God for his service); on the other, as *believers,* men who have placed their trust in the Lord. The first term emphasizes the fact that *their* salvation is basically *God's work*. The second sets forth that *they,* nevertheless, *actively embrace* the Christ.

"When (ὅταν) he comes" means "when he returns on that day which to us is indefinite." Yet to God it is well-known: it is *that specific day* (note emphatic position at the end of the sentence), namely, the day of Christ's

return unto judgment. Cf. Is. 2:11, 17, 20; Matt. 24:36; II Tim. 1:12, 18; 4:8.

The expression "For our testimony (cf. I Cor. 1:6; 2:1) to y o u was believed" is clearly parenthetical. What Paul, Silas, and Timothy wish to say may be paraphrased as follows:

"The enemies of God who so bitterly persecute y o u will pay the penalty of everlasting destruction, away from the face of the Lord and from the glory of his might, when he comes in order to be glorified in his saints and to be marveled at in *all* who believed; and please notice that we said, 'In *all* who believed.' That includes *y o u*, Thessalonians; yes, it includes both those of y o u who have already fallen asleep in Jesus and those (if any) who will remain alive until the return of the Lord. It includes *all* sincere believers without exception. Hence, it includes y o u, for our testimony to y o u was believed."

This was a word of comfort for the congregation as a whole, but especially for those who wondered about the state of their salvation and about the lot of those believers who had departed from this life. See on 4:13-5:11.

11. With this in view we are also praying always for y o u, that our God may count y o u worthy of the call. That is, with a view to the realization of the expectations mentioned in verses 5-10 (namely, that on the day of judgment y o u may be counted worthy of entering the kingdom, that y o u may then receive rest, that he may at his coming be glorified in y o u, etc.) Paul, Silas, and Timothy are *giving thanks* not only (see on verse 3 above) but are *also* (καί) *praying*. They do not skip a single day — note praying *always*, and see on I Thess. 1:2 — but are continually remembering the needs of the Thessalonians before the throne of grace.

Now it stands to reason that if on the day of judgment the Thessalonians are to be counted worthy of inheriting the kingdom, they must *here and now* conduct themselves in harmony with the Gospel-call [116] which they have received. If our life is Christ, our future will be gain; otherwise not. Hence, *the content* (naturally also the purpose) of the prayer is "that God may count y o u worthy" (see on verse 5 above) of his gracious invitation extended to y o u by means of the preaching of the gospel, already in principle savingly applied to y o u r hearts by the Holy Spirit; in other words, that in the estimation of God y o u may live and act as it becomes those who have received the call which y o u have received. Cf. Eph. 4:1.

But since *in their own power* men are unable to live in such a manner

[116] In the New Testament κλῆσις is always the divine call to salvation: Rom. 11:29; I Cor. 1:26; 7:20; Eph. 1:18; 4:1, 4; Phil. 3:14; II Tim. 1:9; Heb. 3:1; II Peter 1:10. In agreement with Lenski (*op. cit.*, p. 394) we see no need of interpreting the term as used here in II Thess. 1:11 in any other way than as indicating the effective Gospel call. For a different interpretation see Van Leeuwen, *op. cit.*, p. 414.

that God can count them worthy of the call, it is immediately added, **and that he by (his) power may bring to fulfilment (your) every resolve prompted by goodness and (your every) work resulting from faith.** Note the combination: *resolve and work.* The first is incomplete without the second. *Delight* (εὐδοκία, used by Paul also in Rom. 10:1; Eph. 1:5, 9; Phil. 1:15; 2:13, *good pleasure*) in doing something that is to God's honor, even to the point of *resolve* or *determination* to do it, is fine; but it must be translated into *action;* it must be brought to fulfilment. For the type of genitive employed in such expressions as "resolve *prompted by goodness* (ἀγαθωσύνης admiration for the good)" and "work *resulting from* (and sustained by) *faith* (πίστεως)" see on I Thess. 1:3. It is hardly necessary to point out that Paul has in mind *the believer's resolve* (cf. in Rom. 10:1; Phil. 1:15) and *the believer's* (not God's) work. If that is the meaning when the latter phrase is used in I Thess. 1:3 (see on that passage), why not here? Moreover, since the two phrases ("resolve prompted by goodness" and "work resulting from faith") form a pair, it follows that not only the latter but also the former refers to the Thessalonians, not to God; (εὐδοκία refers to *God's* good pleasure in Eph. 1:5, 9; Phil. 2:13; cf. Matt. 11:26; Luke 2:14; 10:21).

In thought the word *every* (πᾶσαν, feminine) must be connected both with *resolve* (εὐδοκίαν, feminine) and with *work* (ἔργον, neuter): "every resolve" and "every work." The missionaries are constantly praying that in the case of the Thessalonians no resolution that springs from the good disposition which the Holy Spirit has created in their souls be left unfulfilled, and that no faith-inspired work be left unfinished. They are praying that God may accomplish this "by (his) power" (ἐν δυνάμει), the power of his grace working within them. Cf. Rom. 1:29; Col. 1:4; I Cor. 1:24; and see on I Thess. 1:5.

It is foolish to ask, "But if Paul already knew from the evidences – faith, love, endurance (see verses 3, 4 above) – that God on the day of judgment would count them worthy of entering the kingdom, then why does he with a view to this final verdict still pray for their further sanctification?" The answer is not, "Because, after all, he was afraid that they might still fall away from grace." In that case he could not have said what he did say in verse 5. The true answer is, "Paul knew from the evidences that *as a result of constant prayer* (their own prayer-life and the prayers of others for them) the Thessalonians would live and act as it becomes those who have received the call, sothat on the day of judgment God would count them worthy of entering the kingdom." In the chain of salvation, which connects one eternity with another, constant prayer and daily sanctification are indispensable links.

12. Moreover, the missionaries are interested in something else besides the salvation of the Thessalonians. They desire that *every* resolve prompted by goodness and *every* work resulting from faith be brought to fulfilment and that the readers may finally be counted worthy of entering the state of ultimate perfection *in order that* (ὅπως) an even higher goal may be attained, as is expressed in verse 12: **in order that the name of our Lord Jesus may be glorified in you, and you in him according to the grace of our God and of the Lord Jesus Christ.**

What it means for our Lord Jesus to be glorified in his disciples (or saints) has been explained in connection with verse 10 above. Here in verse 12, however, it is *the name* of the Lord that is glorified. Christ's name is Christ himself as he has revealed himself: for example, as God's Anointed One, the Savior and Lord of his own. Hence, when they share in his anointing, accept his salvation, and recognize his Lordship, then his *name* is glorified in them. And this, in turn, reflects glory on them. (We accept the rendering "in him," though "in it" – i.e., *in the name* – is also possible, with very little difference in meaning.)

This "he in you" and "you in him" is probably based directly upon the teaching of Jesus. See N.T.C. on John 17:10, 22; then also on John 15:4. It indicates the closeness of the fellowship between the Lord and those who are his own. His work in their hearts reflects glory on him. Their nearness to him means glory for them. Moreover, the glory which they receive is not given according to the standard of human merit, for then there would be none. It is given according to the standard of "the grace of our God and of the Lord Jesus Christ." That *grace* (see on I Thess. 1:1) is derived from God our Father as the Fountain, and, being mediated through *the Lord Jesus Christ* (see on I Thess. 1:1), may be said to be derived also from him.

The translation preferred by some, namely, "according to the grace of our God and Lord Jesus Christ," sothat the entire expression would refer to the second person of the Trinity, and sothat it would be another prooftext for the deity of Christ, has little in its favor. In the epistles to the Thessalonians (I Thess. 1:1, 2; II Thess. 1:2) grace is pictured as proceeding from a twofold source, namely, God our Father and the Lord Jesus Christ. There is no solid reason to introduce a change here. It is definitely not true that grammar necessitates such a change.[117]

---

[117] Sharp's Rule is valuable, but on this one condition: that it be applied only to such cases to which it applies by right, not to proper names which may be definite even without the article. Thus A. T. Robertson, who wrote a delightful chapter on Sharp's Rule ("The Greek Article and the Deity of Christ" in *The Minister and his Greek New Testament,* New York, 1923, pp. 61-68; cf. Gram.N.T., pp. 785, 786) admits that the argument in favor of interpreting what follows the final τοῦ in II Thess. 1:12 as referring to only one person is weakened by the fact that κύριος is often employed as a proper name without the article. See also his *Word Pictures,*

Synthesis of Chapter 1

See p. 152. *The Revelation of the Lord Jesus from Heaven has a twofold purpose: to be glorified in the saints and to render vengeance to the disobedient.*

After the usual introduction (verses 1 and 2) Paul writes that he feels impelled to express his gratitude to God for the readers' growth in faith and love. He (and, of course, his partners with him) boasts of the Thessalonians whenever he contacts anyone from the other churches. He regards the readers' endurance and continued faith amid persecution and affliction to be a reward for their loyalty, according to the usual manner in which God rewards holy endeavor with strength to increase in it. The fact that here and now God fulfills his promise causes the apostle to look forward with courage to the day of the final judgment, fully trusting that also then God's righteousness will become evident, and the readers will be deemed worthy of the kingdom in perfection.

This action on the part of God is in harmony with the divinely established principle that a man reaps what he sows. Accordingly, God afflicts the afflictors, and grants rest to those who rest in his promises. Thus, for unbelievers the revelation of the Lord Jesus from heaven with the angels of his power in flaming fire will have as its purpose the rendering of vengeance. This vengeance will be in the form of "everlasting destruction away from the face of the Lord and from the glory of his might." But for believers its purpose will be that he may be glorified and marveled at in them, the splendor of his attributes being reflected in them. This will be the portion of *all* his saints, including the Thessalonians, for they, as well as others, have accepted the missionaries' testimony.

With a view to "the great assize" and its glorious reward Paul never lets a day go by without praying for the readers, in order that the work in them begun may by God's grace be fully done: that pious resolutions may become actions, and that these actions may be completed. Thus the name of the Lord Jesus will be glorified. And this, too, will be glory for *them,* in accordance with the standard of "the grace of our God and of the Lord Jesus Christ."

Vol. IV, p. 46. We disagree, therefore, with Lenski, *op. cit.,* pp. 398, 399, and we agree with most other interpreters.

Outline of II Thessalonians 2

Theme: *The Revelation of the Lord Jesus from Heaven* will be preceded by the falling away and by the revelation of the man of lawlessness:

2:1-3a The two events that will precede Christ's return: the falling away and the revelation of the lawless one. Groundless alarm condemned.

2:3b-12 The lawless one's:
verse 3b perverse character
verse 4 God-defying activity
verses 6-8a present concealment and future revelation
verse 8b decisive defeat
verses 9, 10a relation to Satan and to Satan's power to deceive
verses 10b-12 sin-hardened, hell-bound followers.

2:13-16 Contrast between the destiny of the lawless one and his followers, on the one hand, and that of the readers, on the other.

CHAPTER II

2 1 Now concerning the coming of our Lord Jesus Christ and our gathering
together to (meet) him, 2 we request y o u, brothers, not to be easily shaken
from y o u r (normal state of) mind or disturbed, either by spirit or by word or by
letter as from us, to the effect that the day of the Lord has arrived. 3 Let no one
deceive y o u in any way; for (that day will not arrive) unless there comes the
apostasy first of all and there be revealed the man of lawlessness, the son of perdition, 4 the one who opposes and exalts himself against everything (that is) called
God or worshiped, so that he seats himself in the sanctuary of God, proclaiming
himself to be God. 5 Do y o u not remember that, while still with y o u, I used
to tell y o u these things?

6 And what is now holding (him) back y o u know, in order that he may be
revealed in his appropriate season. 7 For the mystery of lawlessness is already at
work, (but *as mystery*) only until he who now holds (him) back, be taken out of the
way.[118] 8 And then shall be revealed the lawless one, whom the Lord Jesus will
slay with the breath of his mouth, and will utterly defeat by the manifestation of his
coming; 9 (that one) whose coming is according to the energy of Satan, attended by
all power and signs and wonders of falsehood 10 and by all deceit that originates in
unrighteousness for those who are perishing because they did not accept the love
for the truth that they might be saved. 11 And for this reason God sends them a
deluding energy that they should believe in the falsehood; 12 in order that all may
be condemned who did not believe the truth but delighted in unrighteousness.

2:1-12

2:1, 2. Now concerning the coming of our Lord Jesus Christ and our gathering together to (meet) him, we request y o u, brothers, not to be easily shaken from y o u r (normal state of) mind or disturbed.

Paul had written about the sudden character of Christ's (second) *coming* (Parousia; see on I Thess. 2:19) and about the necessity of being prepared for it (I Thess. 5:1-11). Apparently this message had been misinterpreted, as if "sudden" coming meant "immediate" coming. Paul had also made known to the Thessalonians what the Lord had revealed to him *regarding*

---

118 Or: "only (there is) one who now holds (him) back, until he be taken out of the way." Thus, either the rendering favored by the margin of the A.R.V., or the one found in the text of that version may be correct. Essentially, however, there is no difference: the resultant meaning is the same.

(ὑπέρ, see on John 10:11) the "gathering together to (meet) him" (I Thess. 4:13-18). He had stressed the impartial character of this great future event: survivors would have no advantage over departed ones. *Together* the two groups (now united) would ascend to meet the Lord in the air to be with him forever. But though this teaching must have comforted the readers, the comfort had to some extent been offset by the excitement about the "imminent" coming. Believers were behaving like ships that have become the victim of waves and winds and are being blown hither and thither. It seems that in the case of some the Parousia had become the main subject of conversation, the one important and ever-recurring theme for discussion. People were "losing their heads" over it, sothat some decided to stop working altogether. They were perturbed because of it, terribly "shaken up," yes, *"shaken* (σαλεύω, σαλευθῆναι from σάλος, the rolling swell of the sea, cf. Luke 21:25) from their (normal state of) mind."

Hence, soothingly Paul addresses the readers as "brothers" (see on I Thess. 1:4), and *requests* them (cf. I Thess. 4:1; 5:12) not *to be suddenly shaken* (aor. infinitive) or, as a result, *continually disturbed* (present infinitive, cf. Matt. 24:6; Mark 13:7; Luke 24:37); specifically, not to be alarmed *so easily,* that is, **either by spirit or by word or by letter as from us.**[119] It seems that after I Thessalonians had been read to the assembled congregation, there was no dearth of "interpreters." One individual would be telling everybody about an "inspired message" or "prophetic voice" ("spirit") which he had received (or so he thought); another would draw attention to himself by asserting, "Paul must mean this, for I heard the *word* from his own lips while he was here with us," and a third would circulate the news that "someone" had received *a letter* from Paul, in which the latter expressed his views in such or such a manner. In view of 3:17 the idea that someone had even sent a forged letter (a letter purporting to be from Paul) – though open to certain objections – cannot be lightly dismissed.

The substance of all these would-be interpretations (whether by spirit or by word or by letter as from us) is expressed in the words: **to the effect that the day of the Lord has arrived.** These excited people were convinced that "the day of the Lord" (that is, of his return for judgment and of the signs which would *immediately* precede that arrival) was here already. A few more days, weeks, or months at the most, and Jesus *himself* would make his appearance upon the clouds of heaven. His "day" had arrived.

3a: Says Paul, **Let no one deceive you in any way.** The cause of the agitation which menaced the hearts and minds of the Thessalonians was doctrinal error. They were being *deceived, led astray, deluded* (ἐξαπατάω,

---

[119] It is impossible to determine whether "as from us" modifies the immediately preceding item only ("by letter as from us"), the two preceding items, or all three. *The preceding two* seems most natural, but certainty is lacking.

used only by Paul – Rom. 7:11; 16:18; I Cor. 3:18; II Cor. 11:3; I Tim. 2:14 –, though the form without the strengthening prefix ἐκ occurs also in James 1:26). Hence, they are warned that they should not allow themselves to be misled *in any way,* whether by "spirit, word, letter" or anything else whatever.

The reason why the readers should not allow themselves to be deceived and alarmed is stated in the words: **for (that day will not arrive) unless there comes the apostasy first of all.** The words included between parentheses are not found in the original, but can easily be derived from the preceding context. We have here another instance of abbreviated expression.

The fact that the day of the Lord would be preceded by *the* apostasy (falling away, rebellion) – an apostasy about which the readers had received previous instruction (see on verse 5) – had been clearly predicted by the Lord while he was still on earth (Matt. 24:10-13). During the old dispensation the predicted final apostasy had been foreshadowed again and again by defection of Israel from the living God. A most striking instance of apostasy occurred during the reign of that cruel and wicked forerunner of the Antichrist, namely, Antiochus Epiphanes (who ruled from 175-164 B. C.). He was determined to wipe out the religion of Israel root and branch:

"In those days there came forth out of Israel transgressors of the law, who persuaded many, saying, Let us go and make a covenant with the Gentiles that are round about us. . . . And they made themselves uncircumcised, and forsook the holy covenant, and joined themselves to the Gentiles, and sold themselves to do evil. . . . And many of Israel consented to his worship, and sacrificed to the idols, and profaned the sabbath. . . . And the king's officers, *that were enforcing the apostasy,* came into the city of Modein to sacrifice" (I Macc. 1:11, 15, 43; 2:15).

Here at Modein, not far from Jerusalem, there lived at that time an aged priest, Mattathias. When the commissioner of Antiochus requested that he take the lead in offering a pagan sacrifice, he not only refused to do this but slew both the commissioner and an apostate Jew who was about to comply with the request. That deed of courage marked the beginning of the splendid era of Maccabean revolt.

What the apostle Paul is now saying, here in II Thess. 2:3, amount to this: Just like the first coming of Christ was preceded by a period of apostasy, so also the second coming will not occur until a similar apostasy has taken place. In this case, however, the apostasy will be a falling away from (yes, and open rebellion against) the God who climaxed his love by a deed of infinite sacrifice in the interest of sinners, namely, the giving of his only-begotten Son.

The passage with reference to the coming apostasy by no means teaches that those who are God's genuine children will "fall away from grace."

There is no such falling away. The Good Shepherd knows his own sheep, and no one shall ever snatch them out of his hands (see N.T.C. on John 10:28; see also on I Thess. 1:4). But it does mean that the faith of the fathers – a faith to which the children adhere for a while in a merely formal way – will finally be abandoned altogether by many of the children. In that sense the apostasy will be very real, indeed.

It will be a defection on the part of those who have been reached by the gospel (cf. I Peter 4:17; Ezek. 9:6), and it will be on a large scale: "*many* shall stumble . . . *many* false prophets shall arise and shall lead *many* astray . . . the love of *many* shall wax cold" (Matt. 24:10-13).[120] The use of the term *apostasy* here in II Thess. 2:3 *without an accompanying adjective* points to the fact that, by and large, the visible Church will forsake the true faith.

3b, 4. . . . And there be revealed the man of lawlessness,
the son of perdition,
the one who opposes and exalts himself against everything (that is) called God or worshiped,
sothat he seats himself in the sanctuary of God,
proclaiming himself to be God.

The movement of apostasy will soon have a leader, namely, "the man of lawlessness" (ὁ ἄνθρωπος τῆς ἀνομίας). This is probably the best reading, though there is also rather strong support for the reading "the man of sin" (ἄνθρωπος τῆς ἁμαρτίας). In view of the fact that "sin is lawlessness" (I John 3:4), this makes no essential difference. It is important to note, in this connection, that just like the apostasy will not be merely passive but active (not merely a falling away from but also a rebellion against God and his Christ), so also the man of lawlessness will be an active and aggressive transgressor. He is not called "lawless" because he never heard God's law, but because he openly defies it!

A few misconceptions with reference to this "man of sin" must be removed first of all.

(1) *He is not to be identified with Satan.*

The very fact that his coming is "according to the energy of Satan" (verse 9) shows that he is not himself Satan. To call him "the devil incarnate" is wrong.

---

[120] Both of these points are also stressed by Calvin:
Apostasiam ergo vocat Paulus perfidam a Deo defectionem: nec eam unius hominis vel paucorum, sed quae longe lateque in maiore hominum multitudine grassetur. Nam quum apostasia sine adiectione nominatur, non potest restringi ad paucos. Iam non alii possunt intelligi apostatae, quam qui prius nomen Christo et evangelio dederunt. Praedicit ergo Paulus generalem quandam visibilis ecclesiae defectionem (*op. cit.*, pp. 196, 197).

(2) *He must not be identified with "the beast out of the sea" of Rev. 13 and 17.*

There is, indeed, a close connection between these two:

a. "The man of lawlessness" stands in close connection with Satan, and so does "the beast out of the sea" (II Thess. 2:9; cf. Rev. 13:4).

b. "The man of lawlessness" opposes God and exalts himself, proclaiming himself to be God; similarly "the beast out of the sea" opens his mouth for blasphemies against God, and welcomes the honor of being worshiped by a sinful world (II Thess. 2:4; Rev. 13:5-8).

c. "The man of lawlessness" is a "son of perdition" and suffers total defeat when Christ appears upon the clouds of heaven; so also the beast out of the sea goes into perdition (II Thess. 2:8; cf. Rev. 17:8; 19:20).

It is not surprising, therefore, that many authors simply identify the two. Yet this identification is "wholly without foundation." [121] In Revelation the four beasts of Daniel's prophecy (Dan. 7) are combined into one composite beast. Now it should be evident that if even the separate beasts of Daniel's prophecy certainly indicate *kingdoms,* and *not only* individuals (the reference to individuals is not *entirely* absent), the *composite* beast of Revelation cannot refer to only one person. On the contrary it must refer to antichristian government whenever and wherever it manifests itself.[122]

To get the complete picture we must therefore combine II Thess. 2 and Rev. 13 and 17. It then becomes clear that in all ages antichristian power manifests itself, and it is our duty to resist it with might and main. Again and again this dominion of antichrist suffers defeat. It will suffer its greatest defeat at the end of this present age when, symbolized under "the beast out of the sea" under its eighth head, it will be under the control of a terrible blasphemer, namely, the man of lawlessness, the personal antagonist mentioned and described in II Thess. 2. Revelation (chapters 13 and 17) and II Thess. (chapter 2) supplement each other. The one pictures a movement, the other its final leader. This brings us to the more general proposition:

(3) *He is not an abstract power or a collective concept, but definitely an eschatological person.*

The principle of lawlessness, always present, will finally become embodied in "the man of lawlessness." But this does not mean that the two – the principle and the man – are one and the same. It is true that the

---

[121] A. Pieters, *The Lamb, the Woman, and the Dragon,* Grand Rapids, Mich., 1937, p. 205.

[122] See my Commentary on the book of Revelation, namely, *More Than Conquerors,* Grand Rapids, Mich., seventh edition 1954, pp. 175-179, 199-206; also my article "Is the Beast out of the Sea the Personal Antichrist?" in *The Banner,* April 7, 1950. Also J. E. H. Thomson "Antichrist," article in I.S.B.E.; S. Greydanus, *Kommentaar op het Nieuwe Testament,* Vol. XIV, p. 406; K. Dijk, *Het Rijk der Duizend Jaren,* Kampen, 1933, p. 236. Contrast the view expressed by V. Hepp, *De Antichrist,* 1919.

real and final "man of lawlessness" has his precursors; but what is pictured here in II Thess. 2 is not a precursor but "the man of sin" himself.

We base this view not so much on the terms *"man* of sin" or *"son* of perdition" which expressions because of their Semitic character and meaning may not be conclusive for the thesis that "the man of lawlessness" here in II Thess. is a *person,* but on the fact that the entire description which is here given is of a personal character. The man of lawlessness "opposes," "exalts himself," "seats himself in the temple of God," "proclaims himself to be God," and will be "slain." Also, there is every reason to believe that the man of lawlessness described by Paul is the same person as the antichrist mentioned by John. Now Christ is a person. Hence, in all probability, the antichrist ("counter-Christ") is also a person. Therefore, "the man of lawlessness," being the antichrist, is also very likely a person. Like Christ himself, "the man of lawlessness" performs signs and wonders, has his "Parousia" and his "revelation." It would be strange, therefore, if "the man of sin" were not a person. But *is* "the man of lawlessness" to be identified with the antichrist? Our reasons for identifying the two are as follows:

a. "The man of lawlessness" will be revealed immediately before the coming of Christ. The antichrist *concerning whom the readers have received previous information* will come "at the last hour" (II Thess. 2:8; I John 2:18).

b. The "mystery of lawlessness" is already at work. Even now "there are many antichrists" (II Thess. 2:7; I John 2:18). In both cases the thought is as follows: though believers are correct in expecting one definite individual at the end of the age, an individual in whom wicked opposition to Christ will become crystallized, they should rather fix their attention upon the "many" antichrists already present in their own day and age, upon the fact that the mystery of lawlessness is in operation even now.

c. The coming of "the man of lawlessness" is according to Satan's energy, with great signs and miracles, all of them false. Similarly, antichrist is called the liar and deceiver (II Thess. 2:9; I John 2:22; II John 7).

However, not only is "the man of lawlessness" a person; he is a person who belongs to the *end*-time; hence, he is an *eschatological* person. This is clear from verses 3 and 8.

To be sure, by speaking about a whole *line* of antichrists one is doing justice to a Scriptural idea (I John 2:18; cf. II Thess. 2:7). Moreover, this idea has a practical advantage over that of *the one, final* antichrist. The *line*-idea – antichrists in *every* age – against which the church must *ever* be on its guard, furnishes a very useful and proper theme for sermonizing. But a careful reading of II Thess. 2:3, 4, 8, and 9 should suffice to convince anyone that we are here dealing with a precise prediction of a certain, definite person who will receive his doom when Christ returns. Other explanations may be philosophical; they are not exegetical.

This naturally leads to the next proposition:

(4) *He is not to be identified with the line of Roman emperors.*

Here for once I cannot agree with Dr. B. B. Warfield, staunch defender of the faith, whose views on matters theological generally command the utmost respect. It was his opinion that the man of lawlessness is to be identified with the line of such Roman emperors as Caligula, Nero, Vespasian, Titus, and Domitian (see his *Biblical and Theological Studies,* edited by S. C. Craig, Philadelphia, 1952, p. 472). But, as has been indicated, the entire context here in II Thess. 2 is eschatological. It has to do with "the end" of the present dispensation. The "man of lawlessness" is the one who will immediately precede Christ's second coming (verse 3), and will be "slain by the breath of Christ's mouth" when the Lord returns gloriously (verse 8). This fact is an insurmountable obstacle in the path of the "Roman emperor" theory. It also annihilates the theories discussed below, namely, that "the man of lawlessness" is Nero Redivivus, the pope, or some vague mythological figure.

(5) *He is not Nero Redivivus* (Nero brought back to life).

Neither the entire line of Roman emperors nor any one particular Roman emperor is meant here. Thus, for example, Antichrist is not Nero.

It was Kern (in *Tübinger Zeitschrift für Theologie,* 2 [1839], p. 145 ff.) who revived the *old* theory — Augustine was acquainted with it! — : "the man of lawlessness is Nero Redivivus." He thought that the origin of the idea was the widespread and superstitious fear in the early church that the monster of cruelty was about to reappear upon the scene. The Nero Saga seems to have manifested itself in two forms. According to the first, the emperor did not really *die* in 68 A. D., but merely *hid* himself; according to the second (which became prevalent especially after 88 A. D.), he was really dead, but would rise again.

But in addition to the cogent argument already presented (see under (4) above), the most decisive answer is this, that the theory, according to which whoever wrote II Thess. 2 actually meant to say that Nero would return and that he was being held in check temporarily by Vespasian and his son Titus, must be considered "impossible of acceptance" by anyone who believes in an infallible Bible, for Nero never returned! This is the answer which we give to Kern, Baur, Weizäcker, Holtzmann, Schmiedel, and all their followers.

But if "the man of sin" is not the Roman *emperor,* could he be the Roman *pope?*

This introduces the next proposition:

(6) *He is not the pope.*

The notion according to which the antichrist is the pope can be traced to . . . the pope himself! It was Gregory I ("the Great," 550-604) who said that whoever arrogates to himself the title of "universal priest" is a forerunner of antichrist. He made this statement in an epistle in which he denounced the claims of the contemporary "patriarch" of the East. The idea was kept alive throughout the middle ages, and was uttered in whispers here and there whenever any occupant of the papal See manifested his arrogance or lust for power. Wyclif even wrote a treatise *Concerning Christ and his Adversary, Antichrist.* He defended the proposition, The pope is the antichrist, giving twelve reasons.

Naturally, the idea was eagerly seized upon by many of the leaders of the Reformation. Thus, on October 11, 1520, Luther wrote that he felt much more at ease since he had become thoroughly convinced that the pope is the antichrist. The marginal explanations of the Dutch "authorized" or "official" version (Staten-Bijbel) of 1637 are very interesting in this respect. (We happen to own one of these heavy, antique Bibles with covers of wood and hinges of brass; ours was published in 1643 at "Amstelredam" = Amsterdam.) At times the comments become almost amusing, so consistently is everything that pertains to "the man of sin," "the antichrist," "the beast out of the sea," "the beast out of the earth" (Revelation, chapter 13) applied to the pope and his entire machinery. Thus, the fire which the "beast" causes to come down out of heaven is said to represent the pope's excommunication-edict. The "miracles" of which the Roman Catholic boasts, its sacraments, and especially (among these) the mass, are all read back into the pages of Holy Writ. And the number "666" (Rev. 13:18) is interpreted to mean "Lateinos," for the pope is the head of the Latin church!

But if one should find this a bit amusing, it certainly is not any more so than is the statement in the *Preface* to our own A.V. in which "the most high and mighty prince, James, by the grace of God, king of Great Britain, France, and Ireland, Defender of the Faith, etc." is given credit for having by means of a tract dealt "such a blow to that Man of Sin [meaning the pope] as will not be healed."

The Westminster Confession speaks very positively, "There is no other head of the Church but the Lord Jesus Christ: nor can the Pope of Rome, in any sense be the head thereof; but is that Antichrist, that man of sin and son of perdition, that exalteth himself in the Church against Christ, and all that is called God" (XXV. vi).

But though the proposition "the pope is the antichrist" is still being defended, it finds no support on II Thess. 2. It stands to reason that if the man of sin is a definitely eschatological person, he cannot be the first pope, nor the second, nor the third, etc., neither can he be the collective concept "the papacy." It is true, of course, that any man (be he a religious or a political dictator) who arrogates to himself attributes and prerogatives which pertain to deity possesses *anti-christian traits.* He may be called "an antichrist," one among many of the final antichrist's precursors.

In such a man the mystery of lawlessness is already at work. But to call the pope *the* antichrist is contrary to all sound exegesis. Though we Protestants justly deplore whatever idolatry, Maryolatry, superstition, and worship of tradition is found in the Roman Catholic Church, evils against which we must warn with increasing vigor and earnestness, we have no right to condemn *everything* that is found in that church. We should strive to be fair and just, lest while condemning the evils of Rome we close our eyes to the many and very serious evils that are creeping into all sections of the Protestant Church. The proposition, "The pope is *the* antichrist," while inexcusable – though understandable! – even during the days of intense struggle which marked the birth of Protestantism, is no less inexcusable today. And the verdict of some, namely, that those who are not ready to identify the man of sin of II Thess. 2 with the pope have never experienced in their hearts and lives the truth of "justification by faith" impresses us as a rather unkind judgment.

In liberal circles the tendency to interpret Biblical concepts in the light of uncanonical and even pagan origins has asserted itself also with respect to the term now under discussion. This brings us to the final proposition:

(7) *He is not the Chaos-dragon of the Babylonians nor is he to be identified with the apocryphal and pseudepigraphical perversion of the term "Belial."*

To begin with the first, this refers to the Babylonian creation-epic with its story of the struggle between the Chaos-dragon, Tiamat, on the one hand, and the god of light, Marduk, on the other. It has been pointed out again and again, however, that the legendary elements which characterize this wholly mythical and "impossible" tale contrast most strongly with the sober description that is found in the Bible with reference to God's great opponents, Satan and antichrist. In this connection, moreover, one should ever distinguish between *form* and *contents,* between a *term* and the *use* which is made of it. To be sure, inspired authors make use at times of the terminology of ancient and current superstition. Thus, the author of the book of Revelation introduces a *dragon.* But this dragon is not Tiamat, whom Marduk cleaves asunder like a fish, after he has with a javelin cut her heart in pieces. (By the critics reference is also made to such passages as Ps. 74:13; 89:10; Job 41:1, but each passage should be interpreted in the light of its own specific context and background.)

Moreover, of late the entire attempt to derive Biblical teachings from *Babylonian* sources, an attempt which was never very successful and has been refuted more than once, has received another jolt in the discovery of the *Ras Shamra* tablets. These were found in 1929 at the ancient Phoenician city of Ugarit on the coast of Syria. These tablets present a wealth of information with respect to the *Canaanite* background of the Old Testament. They contain several variations on the theme of the slaying of a dragon. Hence, now the critics are beginning to revise their views once more, and are saying that, after all, the religion of Israel may have been influenced more directly by that of Canaan than by that of Babylon. One wonders what theory will be advanced next?

There is also the closely related one which attempts to derive the "man-of-sin" concept from apocryphical and pseudepigraphical perversions of the Old Testament term Belial or Beliar (I Sam. 2:12; II Chron. 13:7; cf. II Cor. 6:15). After a thorough study G. Vos comments as follows:

"This recurrence upon the apocalyptic and pseudepigraphical literature to discover the antecedants of the antichrist figure does not carry much convincing force. Of course, it cannot *a priori* be denied that an amount of superstitious folklore was current in Jewish circles before the Pauline epistles were written. Only that these current beliefs of such gross and rudimentary form were the source from which the N.T. antichrist doctrine was drawn and from which it can be satisfactorily explained is hard to believe. . . . *No clearly traceable and safe road leads back into the past to discover the man-of-sin concept except that via the prophecy of Daniel."* [123]

Having reviewed the various misconceptions regarding the nature of "the man of sin" and the origin of the idea, it can now be positively stated that the apostle's use of the concept is capable of being traced to a canonical book. It is, indeed, true, as conservatives have always maintained, that many of the features in Paul's description of the great and final prince of wickedness are derived from the book of Daniel:

(1) "The man of lawlessness," cf. Dan. 7:25; 8:25.

(2) "the son of perdition," cf. Dan. 8:26.

(3) "the one who opposes," cf. Dan. 7:25

(4) "and exalts himself against everything (that is) called God or worshiped," cf. Dan. 7:8, 20, 25; 8:4, 10, 11.

(5) "sothat he seats himself in the temple of God, proclaiming himself to be God," cf. Dan. 8:9-14.

---

[123] G. Vos, *The Pauline Eschatology,* Princeton, 1930, pp. 103-105. See also *Sib. Or.,* book III; IV *Esdras* 5:4, 6; *Apoc. Bar.,* ch. 40; and *Asc. Isa.,* ch. 4.

For the "Babylonian-derivation" theory see F. Delitzsch, *Babel and Bible* (translation of *Babel und Bibel*), New York, 1903, especially pp. 47-49; then, E. König, *Die moderne Babylonisierung der Bibel,* Stuttgart, 1922, especially pp. 22-26.

And for information with respect to the *Ras Shamra* texts see R. de Vaux, "Les textes de Ras Shamra et l'Ancient Testament," *RB* 46 (1937), 526-565; René Dussaud, *Les découvertes de Ras Shamra et l'Ancien Testament,* Paris, second edition, 1941, vol. I; A. Lods, "Quelques remarques sur les poèmes mythologiques de Ras Shamra et leurs rapports avec l'Ancien Testament," *RHPR* 16 (1936), 112-117; Julian Obermann, *Ugaritic Mythology,* New Haven, 1948; H. F. Hahn, *Old Testament in Modern Research,* Philadelphia, 1954, especially pp. 110-117. This author points out that the *distinctive* features of Old Testament religion were of greater significance than those which it had in common with other religions, and that even those elements which might be called derivative had been transformed into vehicles for *distinctive* beliefs.

This is not surprising, for "the little horn" of *Dan. 7,* the one which came up after the ten horns, is the antichrist, and "the little horn" of *Dan. 8,* the one which came up out of one of the four notable horns, is Antiochus Epiphanes, antichrist's most notorious forerunner, the one who desecrated Jerusalem's temple by erecting a pagan altar over the altar of burnt-offering, and by sacrificing upon it (which was an "appalling horror" in the estimation of every true believer).

Moreover, in Matt. 24:15 (cf. Mark 13:14) "the desolating abomination" ("appalling horror") of which Jesus speaks is derived from Dan. 11:31; 12:11 (probably not directly from 9:27). History, in a sense, repeats itself. Better: prophecy attains multiple fulfilment. The underlying thought is ever the same. God's city and sanctuary are desecrated, whether by Antiochus Epiphanes and his sacrilegious offerings (Dan. 8:9-14; cf. "Gog" in Ezek. 38, 39), by Roman armies with their idolatrous standards (Luke 21:20; Mark 13:14); or finally by the antichrist himself.

Now with respect to the final antichrist as pictured by Paul, our present passage (II Thess. 2:3b, 4) states the following:

He is "the man of lawlessness" (a Semitism), that is, the man in whom opposition to God's law will as it were be embodied, the very personification of rebellion against God's ordinances.

He is also "the son of perdition" (another Semitism), the final Judas, see N.T.C. on John 17:12. Cf. David's remark to Nathan, "The man who has done this is *a son of death*" (i.e., must certainly die); and cf. also Matt. 23:15: "a son of hell." The man of lawlessness is pictured here as the utterly lost one, designated unto perdition. Contrast "sons of light" in I Thess. 5:5.

Furthermore, he is described as "the one who opposes." This word (ἀντίκειμαι, here ὁ ἀντικείμενος) is found eight times in the New Testament (Luke 13:17; 21:15; I Cor. 16:9; Gal. 5:17; Phil. 1:28; II Thess. 2:4; I Tim. 1:10; I Tim. 5:14). It is used both as a verb (finite) and as a participial substantive (so here). The man of sin is *the adversary* of God, of God's law, of God's people, etc. As such he immediately reminds one of his master, Satan, who is "the great adversary."

In very close connection with this opposing activity stands the fact that this adversary who will appear in the end-time "exalts himself against everything (that is) called God or worshiped." In his reckless audacity and ferocious insolence he *uplifts* himself (ὑπεραιρόμενος) not only against the only true God who has revealed himself in Jesus Christ and against all so-called gods, but also against all sacred objects, against whatever stands in connection with religious cults. The reference is probably to such objects as temples, places set aside for divine worship, altars, religious statues. He rages against them all. He recognizes only one god (*he* would spell it with a capital: God), namely, himself! Hence, he seats himself in *the sanctuary* (the term ναός in its primary sense, in distinction from ἱερόν, generally refers to the shrine itself rather than to the entire building-complex) of God, that is, *in the church* (see I Cor. 3:16; 6:19; II Cor. 6:16; Eph. 2:21; and see N.T.C. on 2:19-22), for the term ναός is here clearly used metaphorically. He arrogates to himself authority over God's true people. Of course, they will not recognize this violent usurper, and will refuse to render homage to him. The result will be great tribulation for them (Matt. 24:15, 21, 22, 29). "Standing where he ought not" he *proclaims* or *publicly declares* himself to be God. In the Greek of that day and age the verb (ἀποδείκνυμι) is used of proclaiming an appointment to public office. Thus we are told, "The expectation and hope of the world, Nero!, has been *declared* (ἀποδέδεικται) Emperor" (M.M., p. 60), a quotation which also illustrates emperor-worship. But even Antiochus Epiphanes, that is, "Antiochus (the) Illustrious (God)" or "Antiochus (the) God who reveals himself," demanding divine homage but not altogether ignoring Zeus, was not as blasphemous as the final man of lawlessness will be, for the latter will recognize only *one* deity, namely, himself, will seat *himself* (will *not merely* deposit *his image*) in God's shrine, and will demand divine adoration for himself alone.

It is instructive to note that the explanation which I have given with respect to the "man of sin" passage is in line with that which was favored by the earliest ecclesiastical writers. These understood it as being a prophecy with reference to a definite person who would live on earth at the close of history and would be utterly discomfited by Christ at his return. The church should never have departed from this interpretation. Here are a few quotations:

The *Didache* ("Teaching of the Twelve Apostles")

". . . As lawlessness increases they shall hate each other and shall persecute and betray, and then shall appear the deceiver of the world as a Son of God, and shall do signs and wonders. . . . And then shall appear the signs . . . first, the sign spread out in heaven, then the sign of the sound of the trumpet, and thirdly the resurrection of the dead" (XVI. iv-vi).

Justin Martyr, *Dialogue with Trypho*

"What brainless men! For they have failed to understand what has been proved by all these passages, namely, that two advents of Christ have been announced, the first, in which he is shown as suffering, without glory, without honor, subject to crucifixion, and the second, in which he shall come from the heavens in glory, when the man of apostasy who utters arrogant things against the Most High, will boldly attempt to perpetrate unlawless deeds against us Christians" (CX).

Augustine, *De Civitate Dei* ("Concerning the City of God")

Commenting on II Thess. 2:1-11 he says: "There can be no doubt that what is here said refers to Antichrist and the day of judgment, or as Paul calls it, the day of the Lord. . . ." (XX. xix).

In the same chapter he points out that even in his day the interpretation which points away from *the one, final* antichrist to a whole multitude of antichrists was beginning to become popular; also, that he regards the Nero Redivivus theory, in both forms, to be farfetched.

Having now discussed the nature of the man of sin at some length, we may summarize the idea expressed in verses 3 and 4 as follows:

The day of Christ's glorious coming will not arrive until the apostasy has become a fact and the man characterized by utter disrespect for law, the man who is most certainly doomed, is revealed, sothat both he himself and his program of activities are there for all to see, *the veil* which now hides him from view (for as yet he is only an idea in the mind of Satan) *having been removed.*

5. Hence, the Thessalonians must not be deceived into thinking that the day of the Lord is here. In fact, they have no excuse for so thinking. Says Paul, **Do you not remember that, while still with you, I used to tell you these things?**

This is a kind of mild rebuke. It is as if Paul is saying, "If you had only reflected more often and more earnestly on what I repeatedly told you while still with you, you would not have been so confused with reference to this point, and you would not have become so excited and unsettled." Note: *"I used to tell"* (not merely, "I told"). Evidently the doctrine concerning such matters as the apostasy, the man of sin, the coming of Christ, and the rapture had received more than scant attention in the preaching of Paul at Thessalonica. The singular pronoun implied in the verb (*"I* used to tell" and not *"We* used to tell") shows that although Silas and Timothy are intimately associated with Paul in writing this letter, as they had also been in bringing the gospel to Thessalonica, it is nevertheless, Paul who in both of these activities is to be regarded as the leading spirit.

6, 7. Paul continues: **And what is now holding (him) back you know, in order that he may be revealed in his appropriate season. For the mystery of lawlessness is already at work, (but *as mystery*) only until he who now holds (him) back be taken out of the way.**

Grammatically it is also possible to translate: "And now you know what is holding him back." So the question is, "Does *now* modify the participle (holding back) or the verb (you know)?" The logic of the entire passage (cf. verse 7 with verse 6) seems to point in the direction of connecting it with the participle. The contrast seems to be between the two concepts "*now* held back or restrained" and "*then* revealed."

That "the mystery of lawlessness" is already at work we understand readily. Even in Paul's day rebellion against God and his ordinances was present in the world. Yet, it was not evident that one day this spirit of lawlessness would become incarnate in "the man of lawlessness." This was still a *mystery* (cf. Rom. 11:25; I Cor. 15:51; Eph. 5:22); that is, a truth unknown apart from divine special revelation. In the wicked opposition to the gospel, shown by some of those who knew the way, Paul, as a result of divine special revelation and illumination, saw a clear sign of that sinister movement which one day would culminate in the reign of the antichrist. What the apostle writes may be compared with John's statement that the spirit of the antichrist is in the world already, and that even now there have arisen many antichrists (I John 4:3; 2:18).

Far more difficult to answer is the question, "What is meant by *that which* or *he who* is now holding (him) back" from becoming revealed as "the man of lawlessness"?

In order to approach this question properly, it is necessary first of all to determine the right translation. In the works of commentators the verb in question (κατέχω) has been translated in three different ways: a. *to hold back* or *restrain,* b. *to hold* or *hold fast,* and c. *to hold sway* or *rule.*

Beginning with the last, the meaning might then become:

"And what is now holding sway (namely, the mystery of lawlessness) y o u know, in order that he (Christ) may be revealed in his appropriate season. For the mystery of lawlessness is already at work, only until he who now holds sway (namely, Satan) be taken out of the way."

We can dismiss this at once. Not only is it hard to fit this meaning into the present context, but also: although the verb is of rather frequent occurrence in the New Testament, not once (in any of the other New Testament passages) does it have this meaning (*to hold sway*).

The second meaning (*to hold fast*) and the first (*to hold back, to restrain*) are closely related, and in the end probably yield the same resultant interpretation of the entire passage. With an appeal to such passages as Job 7:12 (placing a guard over a sea-monster), Rev. 20:1-3 (binding the dragon for a thousand years), and passages from the apocrypha, the view is defended that the man of lawlessness is here compared to a mythological being (a dragon or a sea-monster) which is being held fast for the time being. However, it should be borne in mind that the "dragon" in Rev. 20 is a symbol, and represents not Satan's *instrument* but Satan *himself.* And even then the resultant meaning of the symbol is the *restraint* upon Satan, sothat he can deceive the nations no more until the thousand years are finished. Hence, an appeal to Rev. 20, *if* legitimate, would seem to support the translation *hold back, restrain* as readily as *hold, hold fast.* Something similar can be said with reference to the Job 7:12 passage; while the apocryphal passages yield little that is of any value in this connection. Besides, if the man of sin is being *held fast,* he is being held fast with a purpose, and in the present context (in view of what immediately follows in verses 8 and 9) that purpose is *to restrain* him for the present from being revealed.

In the New Testament the various meanings of the verb may be classified as follows (though with respect to a few there is some doubt):

(1) *to possess, have, hold:* I Cor. 7:30; II Cor. 6:10.

(2) *to take possession of:* Luke 14:9.

(3) *to hold fast or keep:* Luke 8:15; Rom. 7:6 (but some would classify this under the fourth heading); I Cor. 11:2; 15:2; I Thess. 5:21 (see on that passage); Heb. 3:6, 14; 10:23. It is possible that the sense of the word as used in Acts 27:40 is not far removed from this. They "held for" (or "made for") the beach.

(4) *to hold back, restrain, detain:* Luke 4:42 (the multitude *would have held him back,* to prevent him from leaving them); Rom. 1:18 (wicked men *hold back* or *suppress* the truth); Philemon 13 (Paul would have liked *to detain* Onesimus). In the present context this meaning makes excellent sense. It has abundant support in the papyri (see M.M., pp. 336, 337).

Adopting meaning (4) as the most natural in the present context, we are face to face with the problem of identifying the restrainer. On this point, however, the Thessalonians were ahead of us in their knowledge of eschatology. *They* knew. *We* do not. Augustine in his day frankly confessed that even with the best efforts he was not able to discover what the apostle meant (*Concerning the City of God.* XX. xix).

Some interpretations are wrong even on the surface (such as, "Paul," "God," "the Holy Spirit"). God or the Holy Spirit are not "taken out of the way" (which, in spite of objections that have been advanced, is probably a good English equivalent of the Greek idiom ἐκ μέσου γίνεσθαι); cf. also Col. 2:14.

Of all the theories advanced so far the one which seems to have most in its favor is that according to which the restrainer is "the power of well-ordered human rule," "the principle of legality as opposed to that of lawlessness" (see Ellicott's *Commentary* on this passage). According to this view Paul intends to say that as long as law and order still obtain, the man of lawlessness is unable to appear upon the scene of history with his program of unprecedented unrighteousness, blasphemy, and persecution. In favor of this view note the following:

a. It has the context somewhat in its favor: "the man of *lawlessness*" is being held back by the reign of *law.*

b. It explains how Paul can speak both of *"that which* restrains" and *"he who* restrains." Think of the empire and the emperor, of justice and the judge, of law and the one who enforces it.

c. It (or something on this order) is the most frequently expressed view of the church fathers. Tertullian, commenting on this passage, states: "What obstacle is there but the Roman state?" (*On The Resurrection of the Flesh* XXIV).

d. It receives support from the fact that Paul was proud of his Roman citizenship, which helped him again and again, also right here in Corinth where the letter was written (Acts 18:12-17). Moreover, in a well-known chapter of another epistle he speaks of the power of the Roman state as "a minister of God to thee for good," and of the rulers as "a terror not to good but to evil conduct" (Rom. 13).[124] We may safely say, therefore, that the apostle viewed government and its administrators as a restraint upon evil.

e. It is a reasonable theory also in view of the fact that in a sense Roman law and order did not die when Rome fell. In the civilized world of today it is still in force. However, when the basic structure of justice disappears, and when fake-trials and fake-confessions become the order of the day, the stage is set for the revelation of the man of lawlessness.

The theory according to which Michael[125] or some other angel binds, restrains, or holds back the antichrist (those who favor it appeal to such passages as Dan. 10:13 and Rev. 20:1-3) does not explain how such an angel can be called both "he who" and "that which" restrains. Nevertheless, the two theories last mentioned – namely, a. that the restrainer is law and order and those who enforce it, and b. that the restrainer is an angel – may not be as far apart as they appear to be. Are not the dispositions of rulers influenced by angels? (See Dan. 10:13, 20.)

We repeat, however, that the view which we have characterized as being in our opinion the best which has been offered so far may not be the right one. Certainty on this point is not available.

Accordingly, the sense of the entire passage (verses 6 and 7) seems to be this: Satan, while perfectly aware of the fact that he cannot himself become incarnate, nevertheless would like to imitate the second person of the Trinity also in this respect as far as possible. He yearns for a man over whom he will have complete control, and who will perform his will as

---

[124] Some have even discovered a word-play in the fact that Claudius was the reigning emperor when this was written; so they connect Claudius with the verb *claudo,* to close, stop, *restrain,* making Claudius the restrainer! This impresses us as being rather far-fetched.

[125] V. Hepp, *De Antichrist,* p. 102, criticized by A. Pieters, *op. cit.,* p. 197.

W. Neil (in *The Moffatt New Testament Commentary)* is of the opinion that the restrainer is perhaps Michael, perhaps Elijah, "more probably someone or something somehow" (The Epistle of Paul to the Thessalonians, New York, 1950, pp. 172, 173).

thoroughly as Jesus performed the will of the Father. It will have to be a man of outstanding talents. But as yet the devil is being frustrated in his attempt to put this plan into operation. Someone and something is always "holding back" the deceiver's man of lawlessness. This, of course, happens under God's direction. Hence, for the time being, *the worst* Satan can do is to promote the spirit of lawlessness. But this does not satisfy him. It is as if he and his man of sin bide their time. At the divinely decreed moment ("the appropriate season") when, as a punishment for man's willingness to cooperate with this spirit, the "some one" and "something" that now holds back is removed, Satan will begin to carry out his plans:

8. And then shall be revealed the lawless one. This "then" is in contrast with the "now" of verse 6: "now" "the lawless one" is being held back, but "then" he will be revealed. "The lawless one" is the same as "the man of lawlessness" introduced in verse 3, that is, the final antagonist, the one who openly defies all of God's ordinances, the antichrist. When the proper time arrives, Satan's scheme will become outwardly realized. *The mystery* will be replaced by *the man.* The lawless one will appear on earth and will become revealed in his words and actions.

In order to encourage believers, who might otherwise be filled with unjustifiable alarm, Paul immediately adds: **whom the Lord Jesus will slay with the breath of his mouth, and will utterly defeat by the manifestation of his coming.**

There will not be a long drawn-out conflict, with victory now apparently with the lawless one, then with the Christ, this "round" going to Satan, that to the Christ. The issue will be settled in a moment. The Lord Jesus (see on I Thess. 1:1) will very summarily and decisively put an end to antichrist and his program. The entire description is symbolical. The two clauses are parallel, though this does *not* necessarily mean that they are *completely identical* in meaning. The first clause stresses what will happen to the lawless one himself: he will be slain (which in this connection has been interpreted to mean that he will be punished with everlasting death, but the idea that he will first be put to death physically must not be excluded). The Lord will merely blow upon him, so swift will be his destruction. The second clause also indicates what will happen to him, perhaps with the added idea: in relation to his program of activities. Also in this respect he will be "abolished," "utterly defeated," "put out of commission," "rendered useless," "made inoperative or inactive" (καταργέω; a verb very frequently used by Paul and almost confined to him in the New Testament; for the particular shade of meaning in the present connection see especially such passages as Rom. 3:31; 4:14; I Cor. 1:28; Gal. 3:17; Eph. 2:15; II Tim. 1:10). In parallel relationship to "breath of his mouth" stands "manifestation of his coming." The very *appearance* (ἐπιφάνεια, epiphany, elsewhere in the New Testament only in the pastorals: I Tim. 6:14; II Tim. 1:10; 4:1, 8; Titus 2:13) of Christ's coming (Parousia; see on I Thess. 2:19), the first gleam of the advent, will suffice to abolish the lawless one, to put him out of commission.

The *thorough, swift,* and *sudden* character of antichrist's defeat is here pictured in symbolic language. The decisive character of his downfall is the one, main thought. Merely by Christ's *breath and appearance* "the man of lawlessness" will be discomfited. More should not be read into the passage. For example, one should not begin to embellish the interpretation by arguing that "the breath of his (Christ's) mouth" means the Word of God, that this Word is always effective, etc. If further commentary is needed, one should read Is. 11:4 and Rev. 1:16.[126]

9, 10. Having comforted the readers with the thought of the decisive intervention of the Lord Jesus when he comes to judge, sothat the passage with reference to the final antagonist has been robbed of its terror for those who believe, Paul now gives a further description of the character of the lawless one and of his activity. One might say that the description already begun in verse 4 is here continued; however with this difference: while verse 4 pictured antichrist's relation to the realm divine, verses 8 and 9 set forth his relation to the kingdom of evil:

(that one) whose coming is according to the energy of Satan, attended by all power and signs and wonders of falsehood and by all deceit that originates in unrighteousness for those who are perishing because they did not accept the love for the truth that they might be saved.

The coming or parousia of the lawless one (for the meaning of the term see on I Thess. 2:19) *is* (prophetic present: it will certainly be) in complete accordance with the powerful activity of Satan, his master. That "energy of Satan" will be its standard of comparison. Hence, this coming will be attended by (or: invested with) all power and signs and wonders; that is, there will be a mighty display of *power* (δύναμις cf. *dynamite*); there will be *signs* (σημεῖα), supernatural feats which point away from themselves to the one who performs them, namely, the devil-controlled antichrist (see also N.T.C. on John 2:11); and *wonders* or *marvels* (τέρατα), the same astonishing performances viewed now from the aspect of their unusual character and their effect upon those who behold them. But all of this display (power, signs, wonders) will spring from *falsehood,* from the desire to deceive.[127] Hence,

---

[126] On the latter passage I have commented as follows: "Do not destroy the unity of the symbol. For example, do not interpret the sharp two-edged sword that proceeds out of Christ's mouth as indicating the sweet and tender influences of the Gospel in its mission of conversion. Notice that in 2:16 we read: 'and I will do battle against them with the great-sword of my mouth.' This is addressed to those who *refuse* to repent" (*More Than Conquerors,* p. 71).

[127] There is no good reason to restrict "of falsehood" to the noun which immedi-

there follows, "and by all *deceit* that originates in unrighteousness." The noun *deceit* is also used by Paul in Col. 2:8 ("philosophy and vain deceit"; and see the compound verb, derived from the same stem, in II Thess. 2:3). The deceit will be inspired by *unrighteousness.* This is not surprising, for the antichrist is energized by the devil himself. See also N.T.C. on John 8:44.

Now this coming of the final antagonist, with his lying power, signs, and wonders, though observed by both believers and unbelievers, has the effect of deceiving *those who are perishing* (i.e., those who then will be perishing); cf. I Cor. 1:18; II Cor. 2:15; 4:3. The cause of their perishing lies not in God but in themselves. They are perishing *because* [128] they *did not accept* (past tense from the aspect of the days just before the final judgment) the love for the truth.

But what is meant by the expression "the love for the truth"? We answer as follows:

When the Gospel is proclaimed, the hearers are urged to accept *Christ and all his benefits.* These benefits are not only objective, such as heaven, the resurrection-body, etc., but also subjective, such as love and hope. Those hearers who perish do so because they have rejected what they have been urged to accept, in this case: "the love *for the truth*" (objective genitive) as it is in Christ (the Gospel-truth). The purpose of their accepting it would have been "that they might be saved." It is true that in his own power no man can accept "the love for the truth." That, however, is not the emphasis here. Here what is stressed is *man's guilt.* When man is lost, it is ever his own fault, never God's.

11. And for this reason God sends them a deluding energy, that they should believe the falsehood. That is, the men of the end-time, who will harden themselves against the earnest exhortation to repent and to receive the love for the truth, will suffer the penalty of being hardened. God sends (i.e., will certainly send) them an "energy of (i.e., unto) delusion." It will be a power working mightily within them, leading them even farther astray, sothat they will believe antichrist's lie. See N.T.C. on John 12:36b-43.

God is love. He is not a cruel monster who deliberately and with inward delight prepares people for everlasting damnation. On the contrary, he

---

ately precedes or to two of the three nouns. It is true that *power* is singular, and that *signs* and *wonders* are plural, but all three terms are co-ordinated by ". . . and . . . and . . ." They evidently constitute one group.

[128] Van Leeuwen states that ἀνθ' ὧν is of infrequent occurrence in the LXX (*Kommentaar op het Nieuwe Testament,* Vol. X, p. 435). It occurs about eighty times, however, and is the Greek equivalent of more than fifteen Hebrew words or phrases with meanings such as: on account of, because, according as, forasmuch as, after that, inasfar as, as a consequence of the fact that, in return for the fact that, in consequence of, as often as. The predominant meaning is *because,* i.e., *in return for the fact that.* One thing is given in the place of another.

earnestly warns, proclaims the gospel, and states what will happen if people believe, also what will happen if they do not believe. He even *urges* them to accept the love for the truth. But when people, of their own accord and after repeated threats and promises, reject him and spurn his messages, then – and not until then – he hardens them in order that those who were not willing to repent may not be able to repent but may believe the falsehood that "the man of lawlessness" is God, the only God, and that everyone should obey him.

When Pharaoh hardens his heart (Ex. 7:14; 8:15, 32; 9:7), God hardens Pharaoh's heart (Ex. 9:12). When the king of Israel hates God's true prophets, then the Lord permits him to be deceived by placing a lying spirit in the mouth of other prophets (II Chron. 18:22). When men practice impurity, God gives them up in the lusts of their hearts to impurity (Rom. 1:24, 26). And when they stubbornly refuse to acknowledge God, he finally gives them up to a base mind and to unclean behavior (Rom. 1:28).

12. So it will also be in the end-time. God will send a deluding energy into the hearts of those who stubbornly refused to accept his redemptive truth; and this in order that they may be condemned: **in order that all may be condemned who did not believe the truth but delighted in unrighteousness.**

This refers to the final judgment. Then all the deluded ones *shall be judged,* i.e., *condemned* (for the verb κρίνω see N.T.C. on John 3:17). This sentence of condemnation will be just and fair, for those upon whom it is pronounced, far from consenting to the redemptive truth of God, *have placed their delight* (εὐδοκήσαντες see on 3:1) in its very opposite, namely, *unrighteousness* (see on verse 9 above). This very antithesis between *truth* and *unrighteousness* (see also Rom. 1:18; 2:8; I Cor. 13:6) indicates that man's intellect cannot be separated from his will and his emotions. When a person really accepts God's truth, he will practice righteousness; when he does not but accepts the lie of antichrist (neutrality is impossible!), he will *delight in* unrighteousness.

The true believer must never be afraid of belonging to the minority. It is the remnant that shall be saved. *All* others will be condemned.

---

13 But we are obliged to give thanks to God always for y o u, brothers beloved by the Lord, because God chose y o u from the beginning to salvation through sanctification by the Spirit and belief in the truth; 14 to which (salvation) he also called y o u through our gospel, with a view to obtaining the glory of our Lord Jesus Christ. 15 So then, brothers, stand firm and cling to the traditions which y o u have been taught by us, whether orally or by letter.

16 Now may he, our Lord Jesus Christ and God our Father, who loved us and graciously gave (us) everlasting encouragement and good hope, encourage y o u r hearts and strengthen (them) in every good work and word.

2:13, 14. But we are obliged to give thanks to God always for y o u, brothers beloved by the Lord, because God chose y o u from the beginning to salvation through sanctification by the Spirit and belief in the truth; to which (salvation) he also called y o u through our gospel, with a view to obtaining the glory of our Lord Jesus Christ.

Over against (note δέ) *the damnation* which awaits Satan's followers stands *the salvation* which is in store for God's children. This thought is developed in the present passage, which is full of rich concepts. However, as all of these have been discussed before, and some at considerable length, a reference to the place where this material can be found should suffice:

For "we are obliged to give thanks to God always for y o u" see on II Thess. 1:3.

For "brothers beloved by the Lord" cf. on I Thess. 1:4.

For "because God chose y o u" see on I Thess. 1:4.

For "salvation" see on I Thess. 5:8, 9.

For "sanctification" see on I Thess. 4:3, 7.

For "belief" see on II Thess. 1:3, 4, 11; I Thess. 1:3.

For "truth" see on II Thess. 2:10, 12.

For "calling" see on I Thess. 1:5; 2:12; 4:7; 5:24.

For "with a view to obtaining" see on I Thess. 5:9.

For "glory" see on I Thess. 2:12.

For "our Lord Jesus Christ" see on I Thess. 1:1.

On the basis of the explanation of these various concepts and of the context here in II Thess. 2:13, 14, we can now paraphrase the thought of the present passage as follows:

"We – Paul, Silas, and Timothy – cannot do otherwise than ceaselessly thank God for y o u, brothers in the faith (who are the objects of God's special love), because in his sovereign, immutable election God from the beginning chose y o u to salvation – which is negatively, rescue from the guilt, pollution, and punishment of sin; positively, the entrance into the inheritance reserved for God's children – ; a salvation which becomes y o u r possession through the work of the Holy Spirit, that is, *through sanctification* – a process of causing y o u to become increasingly detached from the world and attached to Christ until his image is completely formed in y o u – *and through y o u r active, vital consent* to the body of redemptive truth revealed in Christ; to which final and complete salvation God also called y o u, having effectively applied to y o u r hearts the gospel which we preached to y o u and which we urged y o u to accept in order that y o u might one day share in the glory of our Lord Jesus Christ."

We accept the reading, "God chose y o u *from the beginning*" (ἀπ' ἀρχῆς) and not, "God chose y o u *as first-fruits*" (ἀπαρχήν). Both readings are well attested, and the conception of believers as "first-fruits" is entirely Biblical

(Jas. 1:18; Rev. 14:4 [129]) and even Pauline (Rom. 8:23; 11:16; 16:5; I Cor. 15:20, 23; 16:15). However, Paul never uses it in connection with the idea of election or choosing. On the other hand, the idea that God *chose* his own (or *decreed* something) "before the ages" (I Cor. 2:7), "from the ages" (Col. 1:26), "before the foundation of the world" (Eph. 1:4) is definitely Pauline. To this would correspond the rendering "chose y o u from the beginning" (i.e., from eternity) here in II Thess. 2:14. Also, the thought here expressed, namely, that God *called* men to a salvation to which *he had before chosen* them is both logical and Pauline (Rom. 8:30).

15. Paul is now summing up and drawing a conclusion. **So then, brothers, stand firm and cling to the traditions which y o u have been taught by us, whether orally or by letter.**

In view of all that has been said (note "so then"), particularly with respect to dangers from the side of Satan and with respect to the blessed prospect of those who adhere to the faith, the Thessalonians are now urged to lay aside their doubts and fears and to *stand firm* (Rom. 14:4; I Cor. 16:13; Phil. 1:27; 4:1) and *cling* — that is, to remain standing firm and to keep on clinging (note present imperatives which here as often are undoubtedly continuative) — to *the traditions,* that is, to the authoritative teachings that have been handed down (I Cor. 11:2; Gal. 1:14; Col. 2:8; and see on 3:6), whether *orally,* that is, by word of mouth while Paul, Silas, and Timothy were working among them and afterward while Timothy visited them, or *by letter* (I Thessalonians, but note "by *us,*" hence, not by any letter *purporting* to come from Paul; see on verse 2 above).

For the idea of *standing firm* see the beautiful passage I Cor. 16:13; also on I Thess. 3:8. On the matter of transmitting traditions or teaching that has been received see also Rom. 6:17; 16:17; I Cor. 15:1-11; Phil. 4:9; Rev. 2:14, 15.

16, 17. Now may he, our Lord Jesus Christ and God our Father, who loved us and graciously gave (us) everlasting encouragement and good hope, encourage y o u r hearts and strengthen (them) in every good work and word.

Now (δέ is here only slightly adversative; it can be translated *now*) the Thessalonians will not be able to stand firm and to cling to the traditions unless God in Christ encourages and strengthens their hearts. It is for that reason that the command is here followed by the expression of a solemn and effective wish. For the combination "our Lord Jesus Christ" and "God our Father" with singular verb to stress the unity of essence and of purpose,

[129] For the Old Testament background of the idea of the first-fruits and for its meaning in Rev. 14:4 see my *More Than Conquerors,* Grand Rapids, Mich., seventh edition, 1954, pp. 183-185. Naturally those who favor the idea that II Thessalonians was addressed to "the Jewish community" favor "first-fruits" here. See footnote 7.

see on I Thess. 3:11. However, here in II Thess. 2:16, 17, "our Lord Jesus Christ" is mentioned first (before "God our Father"), perhaps because of the reference to Christ in the almost immediately preceding context (verse 14).

Although it is certainly true that the aorist participles ("the One having loved" and "graciously having given") comprehend all the blessings of redemption without exception – beginning from eternity and never ending –, nevertheless this does not mean that in the mind of Paul certain central facts did not stand out clearly; such as, "he chose us," "he gave his Son (also *himself*) for us," "he gave us the Holy Spirit," etc. The main idea, however, is that, as a result of these gifts, "the-Lord-Jesus-Christ-and-God-our-Father," conceived as One, has given everlasting (that is, never-ending) *encouragement* and *good hope* to the readers. In view of their fears and doubts (see on 2:1-12; cf. I Thess. 4:13-5:11) this *help* was, indeed, needed. For the meaning of the word *encourage* (παρακαλέω) see on I Thess. 2:3; also N.T.C. on John 14:16. The encouragement is not only for the present life. It will also be imparted on the final day of judgment. In fact, although *comfort* or *consolation* amid sorrow will not be needed nor imparted in heaven – the land of never-ending delight –, nevertheless even there God in Christ will ever "encourage" the redeemed by giving them glory upon glory. The *good* hope of which Paul speaks is a hope that is well-founded, namely, upon God's promises, Christ's redemptive work, etc., is full of joy, never ends in disappointment, and has its object in God Triune. When, by God's sovereign grace, the words of II Thessalonians (for example, with respect to the *"rest"* in store for God's children, the *"victory"* of Christ over Satan, the divine *"election"* and *"calling"* of the readers) are taken to heart, the readers will experience everlasting encouragement and good hope. Objectively (also subjectively, but only *to a certain extent*) they have it even now. Subjectively it will *then* be applied to their hearts *in full measure.* Of course, such encouragement and good hope never ends in man. Here, too, the circle must be completed. Everlasting encouragement and good hope result in gratitude and a desire to please the Giver. Hence, Paul writes, "Now may he . . . encourage y o u r hearts (the central organ of y o u r life) *in every good work and word.*" Such works and words are those which redound to God's honor. Thus, the circle has again been completed. What came from God has, by way of thanksgiving, returned to him!

Synthesis of Chapter 2

See p. 166 *The Revelation of the Lord Jesus From Heaven will be preceded by the falling away and by the revelation of "the man of lawlessness."*

The latter's destiny and that of his followers contrasted with that of the readers.

Verses 1-3a *The two events that will precede Christ's Return*

In this chapter the apostle warns the readers against acting as if the end of the world had arrived, and against believing that he himself had said or written anything that could have lent color to this notion. He declares that two events will occur first, namely, a. the apostasy — that is, the world-wide falling away from (and rebellion against) God's ordinances — and b. the arrival of "the lawless one."

Verses 3b-12 *The lawless one*

a. His perverse character (verse 3b)

He will be the hell-bound, personal embodiment of the spirit of antagonism to God's law.

b. His God-defying activity (verse 4)

He will strive to dethrone God and to enthrone himself. In his reckless audacity and ferocious insolence he will uplift himself not only against the true God and all so-called gods but also against all sacred objects. He will endeavor to wield dominion over God's people. He has his prototype in everyone who aspires to be God, for example, in the king of Babylon (Is. 14), the king of Tyre (Ezek. 28), and especially Antiochus Epiphanes.

c. His present concealment and future revelation (verses 6-8a)

At present he is being held back. Though present in the mind of Satan, something and someone (perhaps law and order and those who enforce it) is for the time being preventing the antichrist from appearing on the scene of history. However, the spirit of lawlessness, interpreted in the light of God's revelation which clears up this mystery, holds in its womb the lawless one. It cannot but issue in his revelation when the proper time arrives. As soon as the restrainer is taken out of the way, the predicted final antagonist will be seen. When law and order, founded on justice, are removed, then the man of lawlessness will be made manifest.

d. His decisive defeat (verse 8b)

The Lord Jesus, returning on the clouds, will intervene decisively in the interest of his people. Messiah's very breath (cf. Is. 11:4), the first gleam of his advent, will suffice to destroy the lawless one and to cut short the realization of the latter's program. (This indicates that the lawless one belongs to the end-time.)

e. His relation to Satan and to Satan's power to deceive (verses 9, 10a)

The coming of the great opponent will be attended by astounding performances, aimed to delude the masses on their way to perdition. The energy of the devil will operate in and through the son of perdition.

f. His sin-hardened, hell-bound followers (verses 10b-12)

His followers will perish by their own fault, for they will have willfully rejected the love for the truth, and of their own accord will have taken delight in unrighteousness. God, accordingly, will punish them by sending them a deluding energy that they should believe antichrist's falsehood and should suffer everlasting damnation.

Verses 13-16 *Contrast between the destiny of the lawless one and of his followers, on the one hand, and that of the readers, on the other*

These verses are transitional in character. Inasfar as they draw a sharp contrast between the perdition of antichrist and his followers (see the preceding verses), on the one hand, and the everlasting salvation of the "brothers beloved by the Lord," on the other, they belong to the present section. Nevertheless, the change in style (from didactic and revelatory to congratulatory and hortatory) shows that this paragraph may also be considered in connection with the contents of chapter 3. Note the similarities:

a. Expression of thanks to God and (by implication) of confidence in the readers (2:13, 14; cf. 3:4)

b. Exhortation (2:15; cf. the exhortations in 3:1, 6, 12-15)

c. Expression of a wish which has the solemnity of a prayer (2:16; cf. 3:5, 16).

In dividing the material of II Thessalonians into sections or thought-units it is therefore not an error either to consider 2:13-16 along with the preceding twelve verses of chapter 2, or along with the contents of chapter 3. There is overlapping here.

Paul comforts the readers with the thought that the sentence of condemnation will not rest on *them*, for *they* have been chosen from eternity. In this sovereign election *not only the end* was foreordained but *also the means* through which it would be brought about. The end is salvation, and the means are "sanctification by the Spirit and belief in the truth." In fact, the divine, inward calling may also be considered as one of the means, for the readers had been called "with a view to obtaining the glory of our Lord Jesus Christ."

Accordingly, the brothers are urged to stand firm and to cling to the traditions which they have been taught by the writers, whether orally or by letter.

The pendulum swings back once more to emphasis upon the divine factor. The wish expressed in verse 16 (see the explanation) is very touching.

Outline of II Thessalonians 3

Theme: *The Revelation of the Lord Jesus from Heaven*

is a firmly anchored hope whose contemplation should result not in disorderliness but in calm assurance, stedfast endurance, and strength-imparting peace.

3:1 and 2	A request for intercession
3:3-5	Calm assurance and stedfast endurance required and promised
3:6-15	Disorderliness condemned
3:16-18	Conclusion: "Now may he, the Lord of peace, give you this peace." Closing benediction.

CHAPTER III

3 1 For the rest, brothers, pray for us, that the word of the Lord may run its race and be crowned with glory [130], just as it did among you; 2 and that we may be rescued from those unrighteous and evil men, for (true) faith is not everyone's portion. 3 Yet, faithful is the Lord, who will strengthen you and guard you from the evil one. 4 Moreover, we have confidence in the Lord about you, that what we command, you are doing and will continue to do. 5 And may the Lord direct your hearts to the love of God and to the endurance of Christ.

6 Now we command you, brothers, in the name of the Lord Jesus Christ, that you stay away from every brother who conducts himself in a disorderly manner and not in accordance with the tradition which you received from us. 7 For you yourselves know how you ought to imitate us, because we did not conduct ourselves in a disorderly manner (when we were) among you, 8 neither did we eat anyone's bread without paying for it, but with toil and hardship we were working for a living by night and by day, in order not to be a burden to any of you; 9 not because we have no right (to be supported by you) but in order that we might offer ourselves as an example for you to imitate. 10 For also when we were with you, *this* we used to command you, "If anyone does not want to work, neither let him eat." 11 For we hear that some among you are conducting themselves in a disorderly manner, not busy workers but busybodies. 12 Now such people we command and urge in the Lord Jesus Christ that by quietly working for a living they eat their own bread. 13 But as for you, brothers, do not become weary in well-doing. 14 Now if anyone does not obey our word expressed in this letter, note that man, and do not get mixed up with him, in order that he may become ashamed. 15 And do not consider him an enemy, but admonish him as a brother. 16 Now may he, the Lord of peace, give you this peace at all times and in all ways. The Lord (be) with you all.

17 The greeting by the hand of me, Paul, which is a token of genuineness in every epistle; so I write. 18 The grace of our Lord Jesus Christ (be) with you all.

3:1, 2. For the rest, brothers, pray for us, that the word of the Lord may run its race.

The expression "for the rest" (cf. I Thess. 4:1; then II Cor. 13:11; Phil. 4:8) is certainly very appropriate when a letter is drawing to a close; though it is not restricted to this use (see, for example, I Cor. 1:16; 4:2;

---

[130] Or simply: *be glorified.*

7:29; Phil. 3:1). It is as if Paul, having finished chapters 1 and 2, read what he had written, and then decided that there were a few important matters which must not be left unmentioned. So, to the wish for divine encouragement and strengthening (2:16, 17) he now adds some closing admonitions. In Paul's writings the divine and the human, God's decree and man's responsibility, constantly occur side by side. Thus also here in chapter 3 one series of expressions, stressing the former – "Faithful is the Lord, who will strengthen you and guard you," "May the Lord direct your hearts," "May he, the Lord of peace, give you this peace," "The Lord be with you all," "The grace of our Lord Jesus Christ be with you all" – is interwoven with another, stressing the latter – "Pray for us," "Stay away from disorderly persons," "We command that they eat their own bread," "Do not become weary in well-doing," "Note that man," "Admonish him as a brother." We hasten to add, however, that in Paul's teaching as in that of Jesus the qualifying power which enables man to do what God commands is ever from God, of whom and through whom and unto whom are all things. Thus also in the present passage the word of the Lord runs its race in answer to prayer. It is ever God who provides the blessing.

As has been noted previously, Paul sets much store by the intercession of fellow-believers for himself and his fellow-workers (see on I Thess. 5:25; cf. Rom. 15:30-32; II Cor. 1:11; Phil. 1:19; Col. 4:2; Philem. 22). It is not improbable that here the present tense has continuative force: "Continue to pray for us," or "Pray constantly for us." Note, however, that the prayer is not so much for personal blessings as it is for the progress of the gospel by means of the work of the missionaries, though the latter does not exclude the former. Paul prays that *the word of the Lord* (called thus because it proceeds from him and refers to him, that is, to the Lord Jesus Christ) *may run* (or *may run its race*) without hindrance and constant interference from the side of the enemy. That this is the meaning is shown by the immediate context. The apostle adds: **and be crowned with glory** (or simply: "and be glorified"). The fact that he is here employing a figure is evident at once, for in the literal sense of the term "the word of the Lord" does not "run." It is surely entirely in line with Pauline usage to suggest that, as in many other passages so also here, the apostle is borrowing a metaphor from the race-track (cf. Rom. 9:16; I Cor. 9:24-27; Gal. 2:2; 5:7; Phil. 2:16). The author of Hebrews makes use of the same figure (Heb. 12:1, 2). However, the verb "and be glorified" which can be somewhat freely translated "and be crowned with glory" also indicates that in his mind the reality emerges out from under the figure. The word of the Lord is glorified when it is accepted by true faith, sothat it begins to adorn the lives of believers. Now this "word of the Lord" had been successful in Thessalonica. Hence, Paul adds: **just as it did among you** (see the first chapter of both epistles).

The first object-clause is elucidated by the second: **and that we may be rescued from those unrighteous and evil men.**

Note the definite article: "the" or "those" unrighteous and evil men. Paul has a definite, concrete situation in mind, namely, the situation at Corinth. To say that the reference cannot be to the episode before Gallio, recorded in Acts 18:12-17, because this took place a little later, misses the point. What is described in that paragraph is the final flare-up. But surely, the opposition from the side of the Jews did not *begin* then (see, for example, Acts 18:5, 6). In the light of I Thess. 2:15, 16 (see on that passage), it is immediately clear that Paul is referring to the Jews when he speaks of *unrighteous* (literally *out of place*) and *evil* men. The modifying clause, which accounts for the existence of these wicked men, is a characteristically Pauline litotes: **for (true) faith is not everyone's portion** (or simply: "for not all have (true) faith"). The meaning is: "Most people have and show in their conduct the very opposite of faith, namely, unbelief, vicious opposition to the truth." Lack of faith explains the hostile attitude to Christ, his gospel, his ambassadors.

3. Now over against those who lack *faith* stands the *faithful* Lord (note the play upon the words *faith . . . faithful*), ever ready to protect his people: **Yet, faithful is the Lord, who will strengthen you and guard you from the evil one.**

By a very natural transition Paul, having dwelt for a moment upon the theme of his own conflict at Corinth, returns to the very similar battle which the Thessalonians are waging. Inwardly the young, struggling church is in need of strengthening. Outwardly – for Satan is surely an outsider! – it needs to be guarded. Paul now assures the readers that what he had wished with respect to them (see on 2:16, 17) will also come to pass. They will be both "encouraged and strengthened" (2:16, 17) or, as the apostle now expresses it "the Lord will both strengthen and guard" them. This *guarding* will prevent the Thessalonian believers from falling into the snares of the evil one, such as fanaticism, loafing, meddlesomeness, neglect of duty, defeatism (see verses 5-8).

It is from "the evil one" that the readers will be guarded. Though the noun used here (τοῦ πονηροῦ) can also be translated "evil," yet in all probability Paul has reference to the personal devil. That is in harmony with the entire trend of the epistle and of the one that precedes it (see on I Thess. 2:18; 3:5; II Thess. 2:9) and also with Eph. 6:16; Matt. 6:13; 13:19, 38 (and see N.T.C. on John 17:15).

Between the *strengthening* and the *guarding* there is a very close relationship. By being positively strengthened in faith, love, every good work and word (I Thess. 3:2, 12, 13; II Thess. 2:17) believers will be guarded against the sin of capitulating to Satan.

In all this the Lord (Jesus Christ) will manifest his *faithfulness* (cf. I Thess. 5:24). His promise never fails. He ever completes that which he began (Phil. 1:6).

But, as already indicated (see above on verse 1), in this process of spiritual strengthening believers are not passive. On the contrary, they become very active.

It is exactly as is stated in the Canons of Dort:

"Moreover, when God accomplishes this his goodpleasure in the elect, or works in them true conversion, he not only provides that the gospel should be outwardly preached to them, and powerfully illumines their mind by the Holy Spirit, that they may rightly understand and discern what are the things of the Spirit of God, but he also, by the efficacy of the same regenerating Spirit, penetrates into the innermost recesses of man, opens the closed, softens the hardened, and circumcizes the uncircumsized heart, infuses new qualities into the will, and makes that will which had been dead alive, which was evil good, which had been unwilling willing, which had been refractory pliable; and actuates and strengthens it, that as a good tree it may be able to bring forth fruit of good works. . . . The will, being now renewed, is not only actuated and moved by God, but being actuated by God, itself also becomes active. Wherefore the man himself, through this grace received, is rightly said to believe and repent" (Third and Fourth Heads of Doctrine, Articles XI and XII, my translation).

4. Hence, turning from the work of God to the action of the believer, which action is used by God as a means for the accomplishment of the divine design, the apostle continues: **Moreover, we have confidence in the Lord about you, that what we command, you are doing and will continue to do.**

Apart from "the Lord" (that is, Jesus Christ; see on I Thess. 1:1) confidence in the readers and in their future conduct would have lacked a firm basis. One never knows what mere men are going to do. But *by virtue of union with the Lord* (for that is the meaning of "in the Lord") the confidence which Paul has is well-founded, for the Lord perfects that which he has begun (cf. Gal. 5:10; Phil. 1:6). By means of obedience to the commandments (cf. I Thess. 4:11) – those issued before and also those which Paul is about to issue (in verses 6-15) – spiritual strengthening and protection is and will be attained. The readers are doing and are going to do what they are told to do.

Verse 4 does not begin a new section. It is very closely related to the preceding verse, as we have shown. It also prepares for the things that immediately follow. It shows delicate, admirable tact. The commandment will not sound nearly as harsh when those who issue it (principally Paul, but also Silas and Timothy) are kind enough to preface it by saying, "We have confidence . . . that what we command, you are doing and will continue to do." Verse 4 is therefore a window through which we can look into the wise, kind, and considerate soul of Paul.

5. But although the missionaries have full confidence in the readers, they realize, nevertheless, that it is only with the help of the Lord that men will be disposed to keep the commandments. Hence, the pendulum swings back once more (see on verse 1 above) from the human to the divine: **And may the Lord direct your hearts to the love of God and to the endurance of Christ.**

When the love which God has for the Thessalonians and which he is constantly showing to them becomes *the motivating force* in their lives and when the endurance exercised by Christ in the midst of a hostile world becomes their *example,* then they will do and will continue to do whatever God through his servants demands of them.

Both "of God" and "of Christ" are to be considered subjective genitives. Not "their love for God" but "God's love for them" is what is meant. That is regular Pauline usage (see Rom. 5:5, 8; 8:39; II Cor. 13:14; cf. Eph. 2:4). This is "the love of God which has been shed abroad in our hearts." It is "his own love toward us." It is "the love of God in Christ from which nothing shall be able to separate us." It is "his great love with which he loved us."

"Thy love to me, O Christ,
  Thy love to me,
Not mine to thee I plead,
  Not mine to thee.
This is my comfort strong,
This is my joyful song,
  Thy love to me."

(Mrs. M. E. Gates, 1886)

This love is strong, sovereign, unconditional (i.e., not dependent in its origin on foreseen love coming from us, but creating love in our hearts), never-ending, and above all human comprehension. See also N.T.C. on John 21:15-17.

When human *hearts* (see on I Thess. 3:13; II Thess. 2:17) are *directed* (see on I Thess. 3:11) to this love, obedience results; for this love is not only a divine attribute, or that plus a favorable attitude toward believers, but also a divine, dynamic force within them, a principle of life in their innermost being.

The "endurance of Christ" must not be interpreted as meaning the wonderful *longsuffering* which Jesus showed to his friends, for example, to

Peter. *Endurance* (ὑπομονή) *is the grace to bear up under.* It amounts to *stedfastness,* no matter what may be the cost. In nearly every case in which the apostle employs the term he also uses a word which indicates the hostility directed against Christ and his followers or the trials and hardships which they have to endure. Note the following examples:

Rom. 5:3, 4: endurance in the midst of tribulation
Rom. 15:4, 5: endurance in the midst of reproach (cf. verse 3)
II Cor. 1:6: endurance in the midst of suffering
II Cor. 6:4: endurance in the midst of affliction
II Cor. 12:12: endurance in the midst of persecution, distress
II Thess. 1:4: endurance in the midst of persecution
I Tim. 6:11: endurance in the midst of "the good fight of faith" (see verse 12)
II Tim. 3:10: endurance in the midst of persecution, suffering (see verse 11)

See also on I Thess. 1:3. Though the two kinds of patience, namely, *endurance* (ὑπομονή) and *longsuffering* (μακροθυμία, often *slowness to wrath*) are very closely related (cf. Col. 1:11), they must not be confused. See on I Thess. 5:14. We *endure* amid adverse *circumstances;* we show *longsuffering* with (or: we exercise patience toward) *people.*[131] *Endurance* is *the bravery of perseverence* in faith and in all good works even then when all things seem to be against us.

In the present context this mention of *endurance* is very fitting. The meaning is this: just like Christ ran the race with endurance of stedfastness – enduring the cross, despising shame –, so we (in this case, the Thessalonians) in the midst of our afflictions should follow the same course. We should "look unto Jesus," and follow his example. (The idea here in II Thess. 3:5 immediately suggests Heb. 12:1-4.) Hence, there should be no forsaking of duty, no fanaticism or inexcusable excitement sothat one lays down his work, thinking, "What's the use of working, if Christ's return is just around the corner?" *Jesus* persevered. *He* never resorted to idleness, loafing. *He* adhered to his appointed task to the very end. So should *we.*

Paul expresses the solemn wish that "the Lord" (that is, Jesus Christ; see on I Thess. 1:1) may direct the hearts of the readers to this love of God and to this endurance or stedfastness of Christ.

6. By means of this expression of confidence (verse 4) and this solemn wish (verse 5) Paul has prepared the reader for what follows in verses 6-15: **Now we command you, brothers, in the name of the Lord Jesus Christ, that you stay away from every brother who conducts himself in a dis-**

---

[131] Hence, I cannot agree with the interpretation given by Lenski, *op. cit.,* p. 452.

orderly manner and not in accordance with the tradition which you received[132] from us.

The command which follows is given "in the name of" – that is, on the basis of the authority of and in accordance with the teaching (revelation) of – *the Lord Jesus Christ* (see on I Thess. 1:1). He alone is the Anointed Lord and Savior of the Church, and in that capacity has the right to issue commands.

The command has to do with individual cases of "disorderly conduct." The expression "every brother" would seem to indicate that the instances were rather isolated: here one and there one. The congregation as a whole was sound in faith and practice. The "disorderly conduct" probably consisted of such things as:

a. *loafing* (see verse 11: "do nothing-ers"), in view of the conviction that Christ would return any day now;

b. *spreading* all manner of exciting *gossip* about Christ's imminent return (cf. 2:2);

c. *asking to be supported by the church* (see verse 12: "they eat *their own* bread," which implies that this was what they did not want to do); and

d. *meddlesomeness,* perhaps interfering with the business that properly belonged to the officers (see verse 11: "busybodies").

The fact that a rather lengthy paragraph (verses 6-15) is devoted to this sin would seem to indicate that the evil here signalized had grown worse since the first epistle was written (see on I Thess. 4:11, 12; 5:14; then also I Thess. 2:9). Such conduct was certainly far removed from "the tradition" (see on 2:15) which the Thessalonians had received from the missionaries. This "tradition" was the teaching which Paul, Silas, and Timothy, on the basis of the authority vested in them, had passed along to the congregation. It included such instructions as this one: "If anyone does not want to work, neither let him eat" (verse 10). The Thessalonians had received it from the missionaries during their first visit (verse 10), and also subsequently by letter (I Thess. 2:9; 4:11; 5:14). No doubt Timothy, on his visit, had stressed the same thing.

In the case of some individuals all this instruction had been in vain. Hence, somewhat stronger methods must now be used. When *admonition* does not succeed, *segregation* must be resorted to, at least to a limited extent. Note that the severe measure mentioned in I Cor. 5:5 is not yet contemplated here in II Thess. The "brothers" (see on I Thess. 1:4) are told *to stay away* (cf. II Cor. 8:20) from such a "brother" (note that the disorderly persons are still referred to by this name!). Even this *staying*

---

132 Whether the text as originally written had "*you* received" or "*they* received" makes little essential difference. If *you* received it, then *they* (the disorderly ones) also received it.

away however, is qualified. It does not imply complete ostracism, for verse 15 states expressly that such a one must be admonished as a brother. It does mean, however, that the rest of the congregation should not "get mixed up with him" (verse 14), that is, should not associate with such a person on intimate terms, agreeing with him and following his example.

7, 8. Not only was the disorderly conduct contrary to *the instructions* which had been delivered to the Thessalonians, both orally and in writing; it was also in conflict with *the example* which the missionaries had given them:

For y o u yourselves know how y o u ought to imitate us, because we did not conduct ourselves in a disorderly manner (when we were) among y o u, neither did we eat anyone's bread without paying for it, but with toil and hardship we were working for a living by night and by day, in order not to be a burden to any of y o u.

In the light of the immediately preceding context (verse 6), the present passage (verses 7 and 8), in which several thoughts have been compressed together in a few words, may be paraphrased as follows:

"Now we command y o u, brothers . . . that y o u stay away from every brother who conducts himself in a disorderly manner and not in accordance with the tradition which y o u have received from us. We have a right to remind y o u of the teaching which we transmitted to y o u, for y o u know, of course, what that was; also y o u know how y o u ought to *imitate* (μιμεῖσθαι cf. our "mimic," used by Paul only here and in verse 9; also in Heb. 13:7; III John 11; cf. I Thess. 1:6; 2:14) the manner in which we practiced what we preached. We feel free to add this because we did not conduct ourselves in a disorderly manner when we were among y o u. Specifically, we did not eat anyone's bread *without paying for it* (gratis or "as a gift" δωρεάν, adverbial accusative) but with toil and hardship we were working for a living (or "were working at a trade") by night and by day. We did this in order not to be a burden to any one of y o u."

The clause "With toil and hardship we were working for a living by night and by day, in order not to be a burden to any of y o u" occurs also in I Thess. 2:9; see on that passage.

Truly, what the disorderly persons were doing was the very opposite of what the missionaries had done. The latter had been preaching the gospel and working at a trade besides! The former did not do a stitch of real work in either direction. They were loafers and spongers! Instead of being a help they were a hindrance to the progress of the gospel.

9. Why did the missionaries "work for a living by night and by day"? One reason has already been given, namely, "in order not to be a burden to any of y o u." Another reason, closely connected with the first, is now added: "in order that we might offer ourselves as an example for y o u to imitate." The statement which contains this second purpose clause is as follows: **not because we have no right (to be supported by y o u) but in order that we might offer ourselves as an example for y o u to imitate.**

Again and again Paul insists on his rights, but again and again, in the interest of the kingdom, he is willing to waive the use of these rights. This (in connection with his stand on the question of received remuneration) has been discussed in detail; see on I Thess. 2:9 (the ten propositions).

The desire of the missionaries was that the Thessalonians, each in his own way and with the opportunities given him, might *imitate* (see on verse 7) the example of *unselfish devotion* given by those from whose lips they had heard the glorious message of salvation. Since the example of Christ had been imitated by Paul, he now in turn feels free to ask others to imitate his example (and that of his associates). For this thought (specifically for the concepts *to imitate* or *to become imitators* and *example*) see on I Thess. 1:6, 7. Not only in "welcoming the word with Spirit-imparted joy amid great tribulation" but also in whole-hearted self-surrender, the example given by Paul and his fellow-workers must be imitated. That the great majority of the readers had done the former is the thought expressed in I Thess. 1:6, 7. That some refused to do the latter is implied here in II Thess. 3:9.

10. The Thessalonian "irregulars" could not excuse their conduct by saying, "Y o u never taught us any different." They knew the way, because the missionaries:

a. had given them *an example* of unselfish devotion (verses 7, 8, 9)

b. had *also* (note καί at the beginning of verse 10) given them a definite *precept,* namely, "If anyone does not want to work, neither let him eat" (verse 10).

Hence, the conjunction *for* in verse 10 really refers back to verse 7, the thought being, "Y o u yourselves know . . . *for* when we were with y o u (in addition to teaching y o u by means of example) this we used to command y o u," etc. In a sense this *for* refers all the way back to verse 6: "the tradition which y o u received from us."

For also when we were with y o u, *this* we used to command y o u, If anyone does not want to work, neither let him eat. No true parallel to this word of Paul has been found anywhere else. A maxim such as, "If they do not work, they have nothing to eat," is no parallel. That is a mere truism, an axiom so obvious to all except the rich that its very expression seems a bit superfluous. But what Paul had been saying again and again while in Thessalonica, and what he reaffirms here, is something else. It concerns the pious (?) sluggard *who does not want to work,* and who proceeds from the idea: "The church owes me a living." Substitute "world" or "government" for "church" and the passage would fit many people living today, both inside and outside the church!

The command which Paul, by inspiration of the Holy Spirit, was constantly issuing was this, "Do not permit such a person to eat," that is, "Do not supply his material needs." If he refuses to work, let him go hungry. That may teach him a lesson.

Paul keeps perfect balance. While, on the one hand his heart goes out to those who are really in need, and he is the kind of a man who is even willing to undertake a missionary journey that will have as one of its purposes the energetic promotion of a collection for the needy saints in Judea (see II Cor., Chapters 8 and 9; cf. Rom. 15:26-29; Gal. 2:10), on the other hand he has no sympathy whatever with the attitude of people who refuse to do an honest day's work. It is necessary to grasp the deep root of this labor-philosophy. As we see it, the apostle is not (at least not *merely*) "borrowing a bit of good old workshop morality, a maxim applied no doubt hundreds of times by industrious workmen as they forbade a lazy apprentice to sit down for dinner," [133] but is proceeding from the idea that, in imitation of Christ's example of self-sacrificing love for his own, those who were saved by grace should become so unselfish that they will loathe the very idea of unnecessarily becoming a burden to their brothers, and, on the other hand, that they will yearn for the opportunity to share what they have with those who are really in need. While it is certainly true that every man in whom any sense of justice is left will assent to the justice and wisdom of the maxim here expressed ("If anyone does not want to work, neither let him eat"), it is nevertheless also true that for the believer this maxim has added force, for selfishness and the truly Christian life are direct opposites.

11. The apostle now states the reason for being under the necessity of saying these things: **For we hear that some among y o u are conducting themselves in a disorderly manner, not busy workers but busybodies.**

Though it is hardly possible for us who are living in a day of fast transportation and air-mail and of telegraphic, telephonic, and televisic communication to imagine the difficulties connected with the very slow method of receiving and conveying messages which prevailed in the first century A. D., nevertheless we must not exaggerate this contrast. Messages did come through even in the days of Paul. The highways and sea-lanes were often crowded with travelers. Tidings kept reaching Paul and his associates. Hence, by this time he was well aware of one fact, namely, that some "among" the readers (let them take note of the preposition "among," in the deepest sense not really "of" unless they repent) were conducting themselves in the manner outlined above, in connection with our discussion

[133] Thus A. Deissmann, *op. cit.,* p. 314.

of verse 6; see on that passage. Paul says that these disorderly individuals were "nothing working but working (i.e. gadding) about." In the original there is here a play upon words. We read μηδὲν ἐργαζομένους ἀλλὰ περιεργαζομένους. In order to retain the flavor of the original, at least to some extent, we have translated this: "not busy workers but busybodies." It is easy to picture these persons – there were *some,* not many – laying down their tools, running from one "brother" to another with fantastic stories about Christ's immediate Return – the "day" had already arrived! – making extravagant claims for the truthfulness of their thrilling tales, returning home without the day's wages to buy food, then attempting to sponge on others or even on "the benevolence-fund" of the church, meddling in the affairs of the authorities, etc.

12. **Now such people we command and urge in the Lord Jesus Christ that by quietly working for a living they eat their own bread.**

For such irregular people Paul has a formal, objective *command,* a *message* sent *along* or transmitted (the first verb is παραγγέλλω, just as in verses 4, 6, and 10; cf. I Thess. 4:11) from the Head of the Church, who is the Chief Commander. This command, moreover, is at the same time a warm, personal *admonition* (the second verb is παρακαλέω: *admonish, urge,* I Thess. 2:11; 4:1, 10; 5:14; cf. a slightly different sense in I Thess. 3:2, 7; 4:18; 5:11: *encourage, comfort;* and see N.T.C. on John 14:26).

The missionaries do their commanding and urging "in the Lord Jesus Christ," i.e., by virtue of union with him, his Spirit speaking through them. For the full title "the Lord Jesus Christ" see on I Thess. 1:1.

The substance of the command and admonition is that by "calmly working for a living" these irregulars shall "eat their own bread." Instead of gadding about feverishly, running in circles and agitating, spreading excitement and alarm on every side, these people must work *calmly* (literally "with calmness"). This last expression immediately recalls I Thess. 4:11 ("be ambitious to live calmly"); see on that passage and also on I Tim. 2:2.

If they will obey this commandment and heed this admonition, they will not only be doing *themselves* a favor, and this both spiritually and materially, but also *others.* No longer will they be annoying other people. They will be "eating their own bread," providing their own sustenance.

13. Over against the irregular conduct of the few, Paul urges the many to persist in doing whatever is excellent: **But as for y o u, brothers, do not become weary in well-doing.** They must not *begin to behave badly* or *become weary* (ἐγκακήσητε, aorist subjunctive ingressive, cf. Luke 18:1; II Cor. 4:1, 16; Gal. 6:9; Eph. 3:13) in the matter of *well-doing.* As a compound verb (here nominative plural, masc. present participle καλοποιοῦντες) *well-doing* (one word) or *well doing* (two words) makes little, if any, dif-

ference. The two words (three if the article is counted when it occurs: τὸ καλὸν ποιοῦντες) occur in II Cor. 13:7; Gal. 6:9; Rom. 7:21. The point to note is that in each of these passages the meaning is general; that is, it is not specifically "giving to the poor" that is meant, but performing what accords with God's will in every walk of life. Doing the *excellent, honorable,* or *beautiful* (καλός-ή-όν) thing (hence, the *good* deed, cf. Mark 14:6) simply stands over against doing *(the) evil.* Note the following:

II Cor. 13:7: "Now we pray God that you may not do evil . . . that you may do the good."

Gal. 6:9: "And with respect to doing the good (or simply: "in well doing") let us not grow weary."

Rom. 7:21: "I find then the law that to me who would do the good, the evil lies close at hand."

It is probably not necessary to depart from this general meaning here in II Thess. 3:13. It is true that something can be said for the idea favored by several leading commentators, that what Paul meant in the present context was this:

"Do not become so exasperated by the troublesome conduct of a few loafers that you will begin to tire of exercising charity with respect to those who are deserving." But nothing in the context forbids us from interpreting the meaning to be:

"Do not be misled. Do not let a few people who neglect *their* duty keep *you* from doing *yours.* Never grow tired of doing what is right, honorable, excellent."

Since this interpretation, in addition to fitting into the present concrete situation and context, is also the one demanded in the other passages (as has been shown), we accept it to be the right one.

For the concept *brothers* see on I Thess. 1:4.

14, 15. Doing the good and honorable thing means obeying the will of God as revealed by his servants. Some, however, refuse to obey. Hence, Paul continues: **Now if anyone does not obey our word expressed in this letter, note that man for yourselves, do not get mixed up with him, in order that he may become ashamed.**

Paul and his associates provide for the possibility that there will be those who refuse to obey "our word expressed in this letter." The writers are probably thinking especially of those members who were making themselves guilty of disorderly conduct: laying down their tools, rushing away to spread Parousia-gossip, and sponging on (as well as meddling in the affairs of) other people.

These members had been repeatedly warned with respect to these matters: first, during the personal presence of the missionaries when the gospel was brought to Thessalonica (II Thess. 3:10). No doubt Timothy, on his mission, had reiterated the warning. Then, by means of the first letter (both by implication, I Thess. 2:9; 5:14, and directly, I Thess. 4:11, 12) and now in this second letter they had been admonished again, in clear and forceful language (II Thess. 3:6-12). They had been called "busybodies, not busy workers" (3:11). One might expect that Paul would long ago have lost his patience with them, and would now advise their excommunication. However, we find nothing of the kind. The apostle still regards them as "brothers" (see verse 15), though *erring* brothers. To be sure, Paul and his fellow-workers are conscious of their authority, and they believe in discipline, personal, mutual, and church (discipline). But they do not believe in harsh intolerance, rash action, precipitate decision which cannot tolerate the light. They believe in honesty and integrity, and in the exercise of genuine love and patience! Hence, what they desire – and they are speaking by inspiration! – is this, that if all previous admonitions fail to effect their purpose, sterner measures must be resorted to. But even these measures are reformatory in character. They aim to reclaim, to lead to repentance, to save; not to destroy:

The person who persists in his disobedience must now be *marked* or *noted.* "Note that man for yourselves" (second person plural, present imperative middle), he says. This is addressed to *all* the faithful brothers at Thessalonica, not only to the consistory of the church. Or shall we assume that though the pronoun *y o u* in verse 13 and again in verse 16 refer to *all,* yet the similar *y o u* (implied in the verb) in the intervening verses (14 and 15) does not apply to the congregation but only to the consistory? The idea of some, namely, that what the writers have in mind is this: "Let the consistory display this disobedient person's name on a blackboard or bulletin-board" is simply *read into* the text. One cannot find it there, not even when reference is made to certain papyri where the verb ("note" or "mark" or "signify") does occur, but in connections that shed little or no light on its use here in II Thess.

What is actually meant is probably this: The congregation, having listened carefully to the public reading of II Thessalonians, a letter in which the character and conduct of the disorderly members are clearly indicated, must take definite notice of the persons described. In the future these individuals must not be treated as if nothing had happened. On the contrary, to a certain extent *the obedient members* must "withdraw themselves" from such disobedient ones. That the writers have this in mind is clear from the fact that it is exactly what they have already said in verse 6 (see on that verse). Writers should be allowed to explain their own words! Here in verse 14 the command is, "Let there be no intimate association with him" (i.e., with such a recalcitrant member) or "Do not get mixed up with him."[134] The disobedient members must not associate with such an individual *on intimate terms.* They should not welcome him into the company of *close friends,* agreeing with him, approving of his conduct, etc.

The purpose of this limited segregation or ostracism is "in order that he may become ashamed" (cf. I Cor. 4:14; see on Titus 2:8). Clearly this purpose is reformatory. It springs from love, from the desire to heal, not from the desire to get rid of an individual whom one does not happen to favor.

The *shame* will probably result when the individual in question begins to reflect on the patient and loving manner in which, in spite of his own grievous error which is pointed out to him (see verse 15), this "discipline" is being exercised. This man is not being excommunicated, at least not yet and probably never. That will depend on *his own* subsequent behavior. The writers' approach to the subject (here in II Thess. 3:14, 15) is not that *the person* in question *should be barred or banished,* but that *the obedient members* should withdraw themselves from him! It is exegetically unjustifiable to superimpose I Cor. 5:13 ("Put away that wicked man") or I Cor. 5:11 ("do not even eat with him") upon II Thess. 3:14, 15. The present case is different. To be sure, it *may develop* into something analogous to the stern disciplinary measure demanded in the fifth chapter of I Corinthians, but that stage has not been reached here. And even with respect to the Corinthian passages one should bear in mind that, according to what many regard as the most probable interpretation, the stern disciplinary measure there imposed had its wholesome effect, sothat Paul was happy to follow up his earlier commands by saying, "Forgive him, comfort him . . . confirm y o u r love toward him" (II Cor. 2:5-11).

That the "shunning" of the disobedient person was not intended to be absolute is shown by the words: **And do not consider him** (or "Do not regard him *as";* ὡς is pleonastic, perhaps a Hebraism; cf. Job 19:11) **an enemy, but admonish him as a brother.**

This beautiful exhortation which affords an insight into the fatherly heart of Paul – and into the Father-heart of God! – immediately reminds

---

[134] Whether one adopts the imperative or the somewhat better attested infinitive makes little difference. It cannot be denied that, from Homer down, Greek at times carried on an imperative by means of an infinitive with imperative meaning. See Gram.N.T., pp. 943, 944. Here in II Thess. 3:14 (συναναμίγνυσθαι) we probably have an instance of such an infinitive in which the imperative sense of the preceding verb (σημειοῦσθε) is carried on. That would seem to be the simplest explanation. Basically nothing changes when the weaker reading (συναναμίγνυσθε) is adopted, for this is an imperative. But even if one should agree with some interpreters who favor the infinitive but who regard it as an infinitive of *purpose* ("note that man for yourselves *in order not* to have intimate fellowship with him") or of *result* ("note that man for yourselves *so as not* to have intimate fellowship with him"), the basic idea – namely, that either directly or by implication, the readers are here ordered not to have intimate fellowship with such a disobedient person – remains the same.

one of Rom. 12:20 ("If your *enemy* is hungry, feed him; if he is thirsty, give him to drink"), and via Paul leads the mind back to Christ in Matt. 5:44 or Luke 6:27 ("Love y o u r *enemies*"). In all these cases the same word is used, namely, *enemy* (ἐχθρός, which according to some is derived from ἐκτός; hence, basically *an outsider, stranger;* then, a person with a hostile disposition toward one: *an enemy;* cf. the Latin *hostis, a stranger, foreigner,* and finally *enemy*).

But though Rom. 12:20, Matt. 5:44 and Luke 6:27 have as their starting-point the actual existence of an enemy, II Thess. 3:15 warns against positing an enemy where there should be none. The person in question, though heedless with respect to all previous admonitions and even with respect to the earnest counsel given in II Thessalonians, must *not* be placed on the list of enemies . . . no, *not yet* at least! It is as if we hear the vine-dresser say, "Lord, let him alone this year also" (cf. Luke 13:8). "And do not consider him an enemy, but *admonish* (νουθετεῖτε) *him as a brother.*" See on I Thess. 5-12, where the verb *to admonish* has been discussed. For *brother* see on I Thess. 1:4. That this work of *admonishing* must be performed by *the entire congregation* is clear from I Thess. 5:14 (and cf. Rom. 15:14; Col. 3:16). That *the elders* take the lead is clear from I Thess. 5:12, 13.

The question is asked, "But what happens when the person whose conduct is here criticized persists in his refusal to give heed to loving counsel and admonition?" No doubt, such a one would finally have to be excommunicated, for he would be revealed in his true character as a factious person (cf. Titus 3:10). Christian tolerance has its limits (cf. Matt. 18:17; Rev. 2:14-16; 2:20-23), yet, until it is absolutely necessary it is well for the congregation not even to think of this possibility. Hence, Paul here in Thess. 3:15 says *nothing* about it! The erring one must be looked upon and treated not as a possible *reprobate* but as an erring *brother!*

16. Thoroughly convinced that in their own strength the readers cannot fulfil the precepts contained in the preceding verses, the writers add: **Now may he, the Lord of peace, give y o u this peace at all times in all ways.** The Lord of peace is the Lord Jesus Christ. It is he who established peace through his cross. It is he who not only pronounces it but actually *imparts* it. Hence Paul writes, "Now may he . . . *give*" (δῴη, 3rd. per. sing., aor. optative active). This *peace* or spiritual *prosperity* will prevail when the disorderly persons begin to live calmly, attending to their duties both earthly and heavenly (that is the immediate context here), when the faint-hearted go to the depths of God's promise, no longer worrying about their departed friends and about their own spiritual condition, and when the weak gain strength through sanctification. It is needed "at all times, in all ways," that is, in every circumstance of life. The peace here indicated is of a very special character. Note the article in the original (literally, "Now may he, the Lord of *the* peace"). Objectively, it is the condition of being reconciled, God's wrath having been removed. But here the subjective must not be dissociated from the objective. It is the reflection of God's smile in the heart of the believer who, by sovereign grace, has received the blessed assurance of this state of reconciliation. This, truly, is prosperity! Note also the similar expression toward the close of the first epistle (see on I Thess. 5:23; also on I Thess. 1:1, for the meaning of *peace;* and see N.T.C. on John 14:27).

Implied in *the peace* is *the fellowship,* which, however, because of its superlative worth, merits special mention. Hence, there follows **The Lord** (i.e., the Lord Jesus Christ) **with y o u all** (with the verb "be" understood). Note: *y o u all,* not even the disorderly ones are excluded! Did not the writers proceed from the idea that the censored persons were, after all, *brothers?* Cf. I Cor. 16:24; II Cor. 13:13.

17. An autographic conclusion follows, as a token of the fact that the letter is an authentic product of the mind and heart of the great apostle: **The greeting by the hand of me, Paul, which is a token of genuineness in every epistle; so I write.** It was customary in those days that the man who dictated a letter – as Paul, no doubt, dictated this one – would add a few words of greeting, etc., with his own hand, as a sign of authenticity.[135] That this was also Paul's habit is clear from the present passage and from I Cor. 16:21; Col. 4:18. Cf. also Philem. 19. The apostle never failed to do this. It was, indeed a *token of genuineness* (σημεῖον) in *every* epistle. This, of course, does not mean that Paul always *called attention* to it! Often he did not. But that does not change the fact. Thus, we may assume that the benediction at the close of II Corinthians was written by Paul's own hand, even though he does not there expressly state this.

The words, "which is a token of genuineness *in every epistle*" are not difficult to understand if one bears in mind the following facts:

a. Paul had already written I Thessalonians and probably also Galatians.

b. He no doubt intended to write many more letters. Moreover, in God's wise providence, not all the letters written by Paul have come down to us (see I Cor. 5:9). Perhaps, the apostle had even now written more letters.

Why did the apostle, here in II Thess. 3:17, call special attention to this mark of genuineness? The following reasons have been suggested and may well point in the right direction:

a. To prevent the disorderly persons from being able to say, "We admit that the letter which was read to us during the service (II Thessalonians) contained some rather uncomplimentary things with respect to us, but we

---

[135] See A. Deissmann, *op. cit.,* pp. 171, 172.

do not believe that it actually represents the thought of Paul. We deny that he either wrote or dictated it."

b. To discourage the spread of spurious epistles and/or the claim that someone had in his possession (or had seen) a letter from Paul stating that the day of the Lord had already arrived; see on 2:2.

18. The closing benediction **The grace of our Lord Jesus Christ (be) with y o u all** is exactly the same as in I Thess. 5:28 (see on that passage), with the sole exception that here, at the end of the second epistle, the word *all* is added. Was this word added in order to make sure that the individuals who had received a rebuke would feel that, in Paul's great and loving heart, there was room even for them?

Synthesis of Chapter 3

See p. 192. *The Revelation of the Lord Jesus From Heaven is a firmly anchored hope whose contemplation should result not in disorderliness but in calm assurance, stedfast endurance, and strength-imparting peace.*

Verses 1 and 2. *Request for intercession*

Being a firm believer in the power of intercessory prayer, Paul requests that the Thessalonian brothers will remember in their devotions the men who had brought them the glorious gospel of salvation. He makes this request in order that not only in Thessalonica but also at Corinth, where Paul, Silas, and Timothy are staying while this letter is being written, the word of the Lord may run its race and be crowned with glory, and God's servants may be rescued from "those unrighteous and evil men," which expression probably has reference to the Jewish opponents.

Verses 3-5. *Calm assurance and stedfast endurance required*

Over against faith-*less* men stands the ever faith-*ful* Lord, who will inwardly strengthen and thus (as well as in other ways) guard the readers from the evil one. Paul expresses his complete confidence in the obedience of the group which he is addressing. He expresses the hope that the Lord may direct the hearts of the readers to the love which issues from the heart of God, and to the endurance which was shown by Christ in the midst of his own bitter suffering. When this love becomes the motivating force in the lives of the Thessalonians and when that endurance becomes their example, spiritual victory is assured.

Verses 6-15. *Directives with respect to "every brother who conducts himself in a disorderly manner" (Disorderliness condemned)*

Reminding the readers of his own example (and that of Silas and Timothy) while at Thessalonica, an example of bustling activity and industry ("with toil and hardship we were working for a living by night and by day"), and of the order which he had repeatedly issued at that time ("if anyone does not want to work neither let him eat"), Paul rebukes the "busybodies" who refuse to work. He commands and urges them in the Lord Jesus Christ "that by calmly working for a living they eat their own bread." He counsels the congregation not to copy their evil example, that is, not to fall behind in doing whatever is noble and honorable. If "disorderly" individuals disobey the word expressed in the present letter, they must be shunned, but not entirely. The other members must contact them for the purpose of admonishing them. However, as long as the idlers continue in their sinful course, the rest of the membership should refuse to associate with them on intimate terms. The purpose of admonishing them and of the refusal on the part of the others to get "mixed up" with them and their deeds is that the erring ones may become ashamed and thus brought back to a healthy outlook upon life.

Verses 16-18. *Conclusion*

The apostle expresses the ardent wish that upon the struggling church at Thessalonica, oppressed by persecution from without and plagued by fanaticism from within, the peace established by Christ may rest, that peace which alone is able to impart strength and courage. He continues, "The Lord be with y o u *all,*" that is, not only with those who are not in need of special instruction or admonition but also with mourners, with those who are on the way to become martyrs, with the weak, yes even with fanatics, busybodies, and loafers, who repent of their sins.

In order to add weight to the contents of the divinely inspired letter, to prevent the spread of false rumors, and to pronounce upon the readers, assembled for worship, the most precious of all gifts, there follows, "The greeting by the hand of me, Paul, which is a token of genuineness in every letter: so I write. The grace of our Lord Jesus Christ be with y o u all."

SELECT BIBLIOGRAPHY

An attempt has been made to make this list *as small as possible.*

Calvin, John, *Commentarius In Epistolam Pauli Ad Thessalonicenses I et II, (Corpus Reformatorum, vol. LXXX),* Brunsvigae (apud C. A. Schwetschke et Filium), 1895; English translation (in *Calvin's Commentaries*), Grand Rapids, 1948.

Frame, James E., *A Critical and Exegetical Commentary on the Epistles of St. Paul to the Thessalonians* (in *The International Critical Commentary*), New York, 1912.

Milligan, George, *St. Paul's Epistles to the Thessalonians,* London, 1908; reprint Grand Rapids, 1952.

Van Leeuwen, J. A. C., *Paulus' Zendbrieven aan Efeze, Colosse, Filemon, en Thessalonika* (in *Kommentaar op het Nieuwe Testament*), Amsterdam, 1926.

GENERAL BIBLIOGRAPHY

Only those books and articles are listed to which reference has been made in this volume. Many more books have been used, but these are not listed.

Aalders, G. Ch., *De Profeten Des Ouden Verbonds,* Kampen, 1918.

Alford, H., *The Greek New Testament,* Boston, 1878.

Alger, W. R., *A Critical History of the Doctrine of a Future Life,* New York, 1866.

Ante-Nicene Fathers, The, ten volumes, reprint Grand Rapids, Mich., 1950.

Auberlen, C. A. and Riggenback, C. J., *The Two Epistles of Paul to the Thessalonians* (in *Lange's Commentary*), reprint Grand Rapids, 1950.

Bacon, B. W., *An Introduction to the New Testament,* New York, N. Y., 1900.

Barnes, A., *Notes on the New Testament, Explanatory and Practical,* reprint Grand Rapids, 1951.

Barnes, A., *Scenes and Incidents in the Life of the Apostle Paul,* reprint Grand Rapids, 1950.

Barnett, A. E., *The New Testament, Its Making and Meaning,* New York, 1946.

Baur, F. C., *Paulus,* Stuttgart, 1845.

Bavinck, H., *Gereformeerde Dogmatiek,* third edition, Kampen, 1918.

Bavinck, H., *The Doctrine of God* (translated by William Hendriksen), Grand Rapids, Mich., 1951.

Bengel, J. A., *Gnomon Novi Testamenti,* London, 1855.

Berkhof, L., *New Testament Introduction,* Grand Rapids, 1915.

Berkhof, L., *Systematic Theology,* Grand Rapids, 1949.

Bible, The Holy. In addition to the original for both Testaments, various New Testament translations have been consulted (the familiar English modern-language translations; also translations in Dutch, both old and new, French, German, Latin, Swedish, and Syriac).

Blackwood, A. W., *The Fine Art of Public Worship,* Nashville, 1939.

Blair, E. P., "The First Epistle to the Thessalonians," *Int.* vol. II, No. 2 (April, 1948).

Bornemann, W., *Die Thessalonicherbriefe,* Göttingen, 1894 (translation in *Meyer's Critical and Exegetical Commentary on the New Testament*), London, 1928.

Calvin, John, *Commentarius In Epistolam Pauli Ad Thessalonicenses I et II* (*Corpus Reformatorum,* vol. LXXX), Brunsvigae (apud C. A. Schwetschke et Filium), 1895; (English translation in *Calvin's Commentaries*), Grand Rapids, 1948.

Conybeare, W. J., and Howson, J. S., *The Life and Epistles of St. Paul,* reprint Grand Rapids, 1949.

Deissmann, A., *Light From the Ancient East* (translated by L. R. M. Strachan), New York, 1922.

Denney, James, *The Epistles to the Thessalonians* (in *The Expositor's Bible*), reprint Grand Rapids, 1943.

Dijk, K., *Het Rijk der Duizend Jaren,* Kampen, 1933.

Eadie, John, *A Commentary on the Greek Text of the Epistles of Paul to the Thessalonians,* London, 1877.
Ellicott, C. J., *St. Paul's Epistles to the Thessalonians,* London, 1880.
Erdman, Charles R., *The Epistles of Paul to the Thessalonians,* Philadelphia, 1935.
Fausset, A. R., *The First and Second Epistles of Paul the Apostle to the Thessalonians* (in Jamieson, Fausset, Brown Commentary on the Old and New Testament), reprint Grand Rapids, Mich., 1945.
Findlay, G. G., *The Epistles to the Thessalonians* (in Cambridge Greek Testament), Cambridge, 1904.
Frame, J. E., *A Critical and Exegetical Commentary on the Epistle of St. Paul to the Thessalonians* (in the *International Critical Commentary*), New York, N. Y., 1912.
Free, J. P., *Archaeology and Bible History,* Wheaton, Ill., 1950.
Gesenius' *Hebrew Grammar* (edited and enlarged by E. Kautzsch, second English edition, revised by A. E. Cowley), Oxford, 1910.
Goodspeed, E. J., *Paul,* Philadelphia and Toronto, 1947.
Greijdanus, *Bizondere Canoniek,* two volumes, Kampen, 1949.
Grosheide, F. W., *De Handelingen der Apostelen* (in *Korte Verklaring der Heilige Schrift met Nieuwe Vertaling*), Kampen, 1950.
Hahn, H. F., *Old Testament in Modern Research,* Philadelphia, 1954.
Harris, J. R., "A Study in Letter Writing," *The Expositor,* Series 5, volume 8 (September, 1898).
Hawkins, R. M., *The Recovery of the Historical Paul,* Nashville, 1943.
Hendriksen, W., *More Than Conquerors, An Interpretation of the Book of Revelation,* Grand Rapids, Mich., seventh edition, 1954.
Hendriksen, W., *Bible Survey,* Grand Rapids, Mich., fourth edition, 1953.
Hendriksen, W., *The Meaning of the Preposition ANTI in the New Testament* (unpublished doctoral dissertation submitted to Princeton Seminary), 1948.
Hendriksen, W., *Lectures on the Last Things,* Grand Rapids, 1951.
Hendriksen, W., *New Testament Commentary, The Gospel of John,* two volumes, Grand Rapids, Mich., 1953-1954.
Hepp, V., *De Antichrist,* Kampen, 1920.
Heyns, W., *Liturgiek,* Holland, Mich., 1903.
Hooper, J. S. M., "Translation of Biblical Terms: An Illustration," *BTr.* vol. 4, No. 3 (July, 1953).
International Standard Bible Encyclopaedia, The, five volumes, edition published in Grand Rapids, 1943.
Kepler, T. S. (editor of) *Contemporary Thinking About Paul,* New York, Nashville (no date).
Knap, J. J., *The Resurrection and Life Eternal,* Grand Rapids, Mich., 1928.
Knox, John, *Chapters in a Life of Paul,* New York and Nashville, 1946.
Kuyper, A., Sr., *Onze Eeredienst,* Kampen, 1911.
Kuyper, A., Sr., *De Engelen Gods,* Kampen, 1923.
Kuyper, A., Sr., *Het Werk van den Heiligen Geest,* Kampen, 1927.
Kuyper, A., Sr., *Dictaten Dogmatiek,* five volumes, Kampen, 1910.
Lenski, R. C. H., *The Interpretation of St. Paul's Epistles to the Colossians, to the Thessalonians, to Timothy, to Titus, and to Philemon,* Columbus, Ohio, 1937. Other volumes in the series of Lenski's Commentary have also been consulted.
Loeb Classical Library, New York (various dates). The Latin-English volumes have been consulted for the translated writings of Augustine, Cicero, Horace, Lucretius, Pliny, Tertullian, and Virgil; the Greek-English for Aeschylus, The

Apostolic Fathers, Diogenes Laertius, Epictetus, Euripedes, Eusebius, Homer, Philo, and Plato.

Machen, R., *The Origin of Paul's Religion,* Grand Rapids, 1947.

Milligan, George, *St. Paul's Epistles to the Thessalonions,* London, 1908; reprint Grand Rapids, 1952.

Moffatt, James, *An Introduction to the Literature of the New Testament,* New York, 1917.

Moffat, James, *The First and Second Epistles of Paul the Apostle to the Thessalonians* (in The Expositor's Greek Testament), reprint Grand Rapids, Mich. (no date).

Moulton, W. F., and Geden, A. S., *A Concordance to the Greek New Testament,* Edinburgh, third edition, 1950.

Moulton, J. H., and Milligan, G., *The Vocabulary of the Greek New Testament,* New York, 1945.

Neil, William, *The Epistle of Paul to the Thessalonians* (in Moffatt Commentary), London, 1950.

Perry, A. M., "Translating the Greek Article," *JBL* 68 (December, 1949).

Plummer, A., *A Commentary on St. Paul's First Epistle to the Thessalonians; . . . Second Epistle to the Thessalonians,* London, 1932.

Pieters, A., *The Lamb, The Woman, and The Dragon,* Grand Rapids, Mich., 1937.

Postma, F., *Paulus,* Pretoria, 1949.

Quimby, C. W., *Paul for Everyone,* New York, 1944.

Ramsay, W., *St. Paul the Traveler and the Roman Citizen,* reprint Grand Rapids, Mich., 1949.

Ramsay, W., *The Cities of St. Paul,* reprint, Grand Rapids, Mich., 1949.

Richardson, A. (editor of) *A Theological Word Book of The Bible,* New York, 1952.

Robertson, A. T., *The Epistles of Paul* (in Word Pictures in the New Testament), New York and London, 1931.

Robertson, A. T., *Grammar of the Greek New Testament in the Light of Historical Research,* New York, 1923.

Robertson, A. T., *The Minister and his Greek New Testament,* New York, 1923.

Smith, David, *The Life and Letters of St. Paul,* New York, N. Y., 1920.

Stewart, R. W., *The Epistle to the Thessalonians* (in The Speaker's Bible), Aberdeen, 1951.

Trench, R. C., *Synonyms of the New Testament,* edition Grand Rapids, 1948.

Van der Vies, A. B., *De Beide Brieven aan de Thessalonicensen,* Leiden, 1865.

Veldkamp, H., *In de Schemering van Christus Wederkomst,* Kampen, 1928.

Vos, G., *The Pauline Eschatology,* Princeton, N. J., 1930.

Vos, G., *The Self-Disclosure of Jesus,* New York, 1926.

Warfield, B. B., *Biblical and Theological Studies* (edited by Samuel G. Craig), Philadelphia, Pennsylvania, 1952.

Westminster Dictionary of the Bible, by J. D. David (revised and rewritten by H. S. Gehman), Philadelphia, 1944.

Westminster Historical Atlas to the Bible (edited by G. E. Wright and F. V. Filson), Philadelphia, 1945.

Wuest, K. S., *Golden Nuggets from the Greek New Testament,* Grand Rapids, 1939.

NEW TESTAMENT COMMENTARY

NEW TESTAMENT COMMENTARY

By

WILLIAM HENDRIKSEN

Exposition

of

The Pastoral Epistles

TABLE OF CONTENTS

LIST OF ABBREVIATIONS

The letters in book-abbreviations are followed by periods. Those in periodical-abbreviations omit the periods and are written in italics. Thus one can see at a glance whether the abbreviation refers to a book or to a periodical.

A. *Book Abbreviations*

A.R.V.	American Standard Revised Version
A.V.	Authorized Version (King James)
Gram.N.T.	A. T. Robertson, *Grammar of the Greek New Testament in the Light of Historical Research*
I.S.B.E.	*International Standard Bible Encyclopedia*
L.N.T.	Thayer's *Greek-English Lexicon of the New Testament*
M.M.	*The Vocabulary of the Greek New Testament Illustrated from the Papyri and Other Non-Literary Sources,* by James Hope Moulton and George Milligan (edition, Grand Rapids, 1952)
N.N.	*Novum Testamentum Graece,* edited by D. Eberhard Nestle and D. Erwin Nestle (most recent edition)
N.T.C.	W. Hendriksen, *New Testament Commentary*
R.S.V.	Revised Standard Version
W.D.B.	*Westminster Dictionary of the Bible*
W.H.A.B.	*Westminster Historical Atlas to the Bible*

B. *Periodical Abbreviations*

EQ	*Evangelical Quarterly*
JBL	*Journal of Biblical Literature*
JThS	*Journal of Theological Studies*
GThT	*Gereformeerd Theologisch Tijdschrift*
WThJ	*Westminster Theological Journal*
ZNTW	*Zeitschrift für die Neutestamentliche Wissenschaft*

Please Note

In order to differentiate between the second person singular and the second person plural (without reverting to the archaic "thou" and "ye" except where it is proper to do so), we have indicated the former as follows: "you"; and the latter, as follows: "y o u."

Introduction
to
The Pastoral Epistles

I. Why Should We Study Them?

A thorough study of the Pastoral Epistles is necessary for the following reasons:

(1) Because they shed much needed light on the important problem of *church-administration.* Do these letters contain any directions regarding Public Worship which we do well to heed? What qualities must a man possess in order to be a good pastor? A worthy elder? A conscientious deacon? To what extent should women be employed in the work of the church? Upon whom does the primary responsibility rest of providing for the needy? How should a minister deal with aged men who are in need of pastoral counseling? With aged women? With young men? With young women?

(2) Because they stress *sound doctrine.* Is it true that it makes no difference *what* a person believes as long as he is *sincere* in what he believes? Is the Bible "the Word of God" as it lies there, or does it merely *become* the Word of God when it "touches" you? How must one deal with heretics? Is it possible to pay too much attention to their errors?

(3) Because they demand *consecrated living.* Is it possible for a person to be "doctrinally *sound*" but "corrupt in practice"? Must evil men be disciplined? How soon? With what purpose in mind?

(4) Because they answer the question, *"Are creeds of any value?"* Did the church in the transition-period believe in creedal formulations, pithy sayings, and other means of transmitting the truth of the gospel to enquirers and to the youth? Were there any hymns? Is the slogan, "No Creed But Christ" in harmony with the teaching of The Pastorals?

(5) Because they tell us about *the closing activities in the life of the great apostle Paul.* Does the book of Acts give a full account of all his journeys? Were there really two Roman imprisonments?

(6) Because they are *a valuable source for the understanding of the history of the church in the third quarter of the first century A. D.* (See M. C. Tenney, *The New Testament, A Survey,* p. 354).

(7) Because *in these epistles* as well as in the others *God speaks to us.*

II. Who Wrote the Pastorals?

The term "pastoral epistles," as a common title for I Timothy, II Timothy, and Titus, dates from the early part of the eighteenth century.[1] Now these letters do indeed furnish worth-while directions for pastors. Yet, the title is not exact. Timothy and Titus were not "pastors" in the usual, present-day sense of the term. They were not ministers of local congregations, but rather vicars apostolic, Paul's special envoys or deputies sent by him on specific missions. They were entrusted with concrete assignments according to the need of the hour. Their task was to perform their spiritual ministry here or there, carrying forward the work which had been started, and then reporting to the apostle their findings and accomplishments.

Marcion, in the middle of the second century, rejected these three letters. Tertullian states, "I am surprised, however, that when he (Marcion) accepted this letter (Philemon) which was written but to one man, he rejected the two epistles to Timothy and the one to Titus, which all treat of ecclesiastical discipline" (*Against Marcion* V. xxi). Now in a man like Marcion, who preached the strictest asceticism, denied the lawfulness of marriage, and issued rigid rules for fasting, such a rejection of the Pastorals, in which asceticism is condemned (I Tim. 4:3, 4; Tit. 1:14, 15), is altogether natural. A heretic does not like a writing which directly or indirectly condemns his or a somewhat similar heresy.

In the nineteenth century (1807 to be exact) F. Schleiermacher rejected the Pauline authorship of I Timothy. F. C. Baur in his work on the Pastoral Epistles (Stuttgart and Tübingen, 1835) defended the position that it is inconsistent to accept II Timothy and Titus but to reject I Timothy. All three must be considered in the class of pseudepigraphic literature. Many enthusiastic disciples — the Tübingen School — endorsed his view. Today this position is accepted by many, though some have adopted a somewhat more conservative view (see p. 17).

Can it be truthfully maintained that in this negative attitude the critics are as thoroughly objective as they claim to be? Is it just possible that the manner in which these three little gems deal with "some of the fondest shibboleths of the modern mind" [2] has something to do with the decisive way in which their Pauline authorship is denied? The Pastorals place particular emphasis on such matters as *the reality and importance of ecclesiastical offices* (I Tim. 3; Tit. 1), *the inspiration of the written word* (II Tim. 3:16), *the necessity of maintaining doctrinal soundness* (I Tim. 4:1-6;

---

[1] P. Anton called his work, *"Exegetische Abhandlung der Pastoralbriefe."* He first suggested the term in 1726.

[2] Cf. Edmund K. Simpson, "The Authenticity and Authorship of the Pastoral Epistles," *EQ* 12 (1940), 311.

II Tim. 3:14; 4:3; Tit. 2:1), *the reality of the resurrection* (II Tim. 2:18), *and the divine requirement that faith shall make itself militantly manifest* (II Tim. 4:2, 7, 8).

Now, whether or not subjective bias has asserted itself, one conclusion becomes inescapably clear when the facts are examined: the critics have failed to prove their thesis that Paul cannot have written the Pastorals.

The arguments of the critics may be summarized as follows: [3]

---

[3] Anyone who reads the following literature – a selection from among hundreds of books and articles on this subject – will have both the arguments of the critics and the answers of those who cling to the traditional view with reference to the authorship of the Pastorals. *We acknowledge indebtedness to all of the following:*

Bouma, C., *I, II Timotheus en Titus* (in *Korte Verklaring der Heilige Schrift met Nieuwe Vertaling*), second edition, Kampen 1953, especially pp. 13-35.

Bouma, C., *De Brieven van den Apostel Paulus aan Timotheus en Titus* (in *Kommentaar op het Nieuwe Testament*), Amsterdam, 1942, especially pp. 17-60.

Brooks, A. E., "The Problem of the Pastoral Epistles," *JThS* 23 (1922).

Dibelius, M., *Die Pastoralbriefe,* second edition, Tübingen, 1931.

Easton, Burton Scott, *The Pastoral Epistles,* New York, 1947, especially pp. 29-35.

Goodspeed, E. J., *Paul,* Philadelphia, Toronto, 1947, p. 238.

Greydanus, S., *Bizondere Canoniek,* Kampen, 1949, Vol. II, pp. 205-226.

Harrison, P. N., *The Problem of the Pastoral Epistles,* Oxford, 1921.

Hawkins, R. M., *The Recovery of the Historical Paul,* Nashville, Tenn., 1943, p. 13.

Holtzmann, H. J., *Die Pastorale Briefe,* Leipzig, 1880.

Knox, John, *Chapters in a Life of Paul,* New York and Nashville, 1946, p. 20.

Lock, W., *A Critical and Exegetical Commentary on the Pastoral Epistles* (in *International Critical Commentary*), New York, 1924, pp. xxv-xxxi.

Michaelis, W., "Pastoralbriefe und Wortstatistik," *ZNTW* 28 (1929), 69-76.

Michaelis, W., *Pastoralbriefe und Gefangenschaftbriefe. Zur Echtheitsfrage der Pastoralbriefe,* 1930.

Moffatt, J., *Introduction to the Literature of the New Testament,* New York, 3rd ed., 1918.

Nageli, Th., *Der Wortschatz des Apostels Paulus, Göttingen,* 1905, pp. 85-88.

Parry, John, *The Pastoral Epistles,* 1920.

Pherigo, Lindsey P., "Paul's Life After the Close of Acts," *JBL* 70 (December, 1951), 277-284.

Plummer, Alfred, *The Pastoral Epistles* (in *The Expositor's Bible*), reprint Grand Rapids, Mich., 1943, vol. 6, pp. 389-392.

Riddle, W. and Hutson, H. H., *New Testament Life and Literature,* Chicago, 1946, pp. 203-208.

Robertson, A. T., *Word Pictures in the New Testament,* New York and London, 1931, Vol. IV, pp. 555-558.

Schleiermacher, F., *Ueber den Sogenannten Brief von Paulus an den Timotheus,* 1807.

Schweitzer, A., *The Mysticism of Paul the Apostle,* New York, 1931, p. 42.

Scott, E. F., *The Literature of the New Testament,* 6th ed., New York, 1940, pp. 191-197.

Scott, E. F., *The Pastoral Epistles* (in *The Moffatt Commentary*), New York and London, no date.

Simpson, E. K., "The Authenticity and Authorship of the Pastoral Epistles," *EQ* 12 (October, 1940), 289-311.

Simpson, E. K., *The Pastoral Epistles,* London, 1954, pp. 1-23.

Torm, F., "Ueber die Sprache in den Pastoralbriefen," *ZNTW* 18 (1918), 225-243.

(1) *In vocabulary the three epistles are very similar to each other, but entirely different from the other ten epistles which are traditionally assigned to Paul, namely, Romans, I Corinthians, II Corinthians, Galatians, Ephesians, Philippians, Colossians, I Thessalonians, II Thessalonians, and Philemon.*[4]

The following points are emphasized under this general heading, some critics stressing one point, others another:

a. The great similarity in the vocabulary of the three Pastorals.

b. The contrast between the vocabulary of the Pastorals and that of the ten.

At times it would almost seem that a single glance at Harrison's well-known diagrams (in his book, *The Problem of the Pastoral Epistles,* Oxford, 1921) was enough to convince some that Paul could not have written I Timothy, II Timothy, and Titus. Is not the number of new words, *per page* (!) of Greek text, introduced by the author of these three letters, completely out of proportion to the much smaller number of new words per page used by Paul in his ten epistles? If the apostle wrote the latter, is it at all possible that he also wrote the former?

Besides, do not such expressions as the following clearly point away from Paul: "guard the deposit" (τὴν παραθήκην φύλαξον I Tim. 6:20; II Tim. 1:12, 14); "follow doctrine" (a form of παρακολουθέω with τῇ διδασκαλίᾳ, I Tim. 4:6; II Tim. 3:10); "profane chatter" (βέβηλοι κενοφωνίας, I Tim. 6:20; II Tim. 2:16); "man of God" (ἄνθρωπος θεοῦ, I Tim. 6:11; II Tim. 3:17)?

And, on the other hand, is it not true that many words that are used again and again in the ten are absent from the three: "to do wrong" (ἀδικέω), "blood" (αἷμα), "uncircumcision" (ἀκροβυστία), "works of the law" (ἔργα νόμου), etc.? Burton Scott Easton points out that the real Paul uses "Spirit" about 80 times; the author of the Pastorals only 3 times!

c. The presence of entirely new or greatly expanded word-families in the Pastorals.

Is it not true that the Pastorals present, either for the first time or with unparalleled ramification, not only many single words but even whole families of words? To give just one example: the family of compounds which center about the common idea of teaching or *did*actics:

Van Oosterzee, J. J., *The Pastoral Epistles* (in *Lange's Commentary on the Holy Scriptures*), reprint, Grand Rapids, Mich., no date, pp. 2-6.

White, N. J. D., *The First and Second Epistles to Timothy and the Epistle to Titus* (in *The Expositor's Greek Testament*), reprint, Grand Rapids, Mich., no date, Vol. 4, pp. 57-82.

Zahn, Th., *Einleitung in das Neue Testament,* 1897-1900, Vol. II, p. 85 ff.

[4] See, for example, E. F. Scott, *Literature of the New Testament,* New York, 1932, p. 193. Also the same author, *The Pastoral Epistles* (in The Moffatt Commentary), p. xxi.

Occurring nowhere in the ten are the following:

διδακτικός	*apt at teaching,* I Tim. 3:2; II Tim. 2:24
νομοδιδάσκαλος	*a teacher of the law,* I Tim. 1:7
καλοδιδάσκαλος	*a teacher of that which is good,* Tit. 2:3
ἑτεροδιδασκαλεῖν	*to teach differently, to teach a different doctrine,* I Tim. 1:3; 6:3

Occurring also in two or three of the ten are:

διδάσκαλος	*a teacher,* I Tim. 2:7; II Tim. 1:11; 4:3
διδασκαλία	*teaching,* in the Pastorals occurring with great frequency, in both the active and the passive sense (*doctrine*)
διδαχή	*teaching,* II Tim. 4:2; *doctrine,* Titus 1:9

Occurring also in six of the ten are:

διδάσκω	*to teach,* I Tim. 2:12; 4:11; 6:2; II Tim. 2:2; Tit. 1:11.

d. The absence of Pauline word-families.

This is the obverse of the preceding.

e. The fact that several words found in I Timothy, II Timothy, and Titus, but not in the ten, occur in the vocabulary of the Apostolic Fathers, and the complementary fact that a large percentage of genuinely Pauline words which do not occur in the three have also dropped out of the vocabulary of the Apostolic Fathers. It is argued that for the Pastorals this points to a date early in the second century.

In this connection it is also usually pointed out that during the second century there was a revival of classical diction. It is maintained that this explains the presence of a considerable number of classical words in these letters.

f. The frequent use of Latin words and idioms.

It is said that this indicates that the author of the Pastorals cannot have been Paul but must have been someone living in or near Rome. Or, if this conclusion is not stated in so many words, the argument from Latinisms occurring in the Pastorals is at least enlisted in the cause of skepticism.

g. The totally different meaning which in the Pastorals is carried by words that are common to them and to the ten.

Examples: *faith,* in the Pastorals used objectively = what is believed, the true religion; but by Paul in the sense of subjective trust.

to take up, used in I Tim. 3:16 of Christ's ascension, but in Eph. 6:13, 16 of "taking up" spiritual weapons.

letter, used in an unfavorable sense by Paul, but *letters* used in favorable sense in II Tim. 3:15 = *the sacred writings.*

h. Finally, the fact that not only "the stones" differ from those used by Paul but also "the clamps and the mortar" (particles of transition and inference, which abound in the ten but are largely lacking in the Pastorals).

It is not difficult to show that the value of this argument and of its ramifications has been greatly over-estimated.

As to a., to a certain extent the very opposite is the truth. Of new words (*new* in the sense that they do not occur in the ten) only a very few are found in *all* three letters; only 9 out of a total of 306! Hence, *if dissimilarity in new vocabulary proves different authorship, something can be said for the proposition that a different author would have to be posited for each of the Pastorals!* Of new words I Timothy has 127, II Timothy has 81 others, and Titus has 45 others. *Together* I Timothy and II Timothy have only 17; I Timothy and Titus have only 20; II Timothy and Titus have only 7; all three together only 9. (Yet both vocabulary and style, taken as a whole, point rather to *unity* of authorship.)

As to b., fact is that slightly over one-fourth of the total vocabulary of Paul's epistle to the Romans is "new" in the sense that these words do not occur in the other nine epistles. The percentage of new words, in proportion to total vocabulary, in II Timothy (words not occurring in the ten) is hardly any higher than in Romans. The same holds for Titus. In I Timothy about one-third of the words are new. Surely, on the basis of these facts the thesis of the critics, namely, that Paul cannot have written the Pastorals, does not follow! [5]

In each epistle Paul uses the (Spirit-inspired) words which he needs in order to express his (Spirit-inspired) thoughts regarding the specific subject with which he deals. For this reason it is not surprising that certain words, found in the ten, are lacking in the three. As an example, let us take the first three words mentioned in Harrison's list on p. 31, taking them just as they come. The first is ἀδικέω: to do wrong, to commit unrighteousness. The second is αἷμα: blood. The third is ἀκροβυστία: uncircumcision. Now this entire subject of *righteousness,* obtained for the sinner by the *blood* of Christ and not by means of rites such as *circumcision,* belongs to such

[5] Proportion of new words to total vocabulary is given by Michaelis and Greydanus as follows:

Romans:	261:993	= 26.3%
II Timothy:	114:413	= 27.6%
Titus:	81:293	= 27.6%
I Timothy:	173:529	= 32.7%

See Michaelis, the article cited, p. 73; Greydanus, *op. cit.,* p. 210.

This harmonizes with the figures given by Harrison, *op. cit.,* p. 140. Bouma, *Kommentaar op het Nieuwe Testament,* p. 54, stresses the fact that of the 582 words that occur in the ten but not in the Pastorals, no less than 469 are found *in only one* letter; and that, accordingly, *these 469 are lacking in the other nine as well as in the Pastorals!*

epistles as Romans, Galatians, and to some extent I Corinthians. Hence, it is in these epistles that we must look for such or similar words. But surely the apostle did not need to expound in detail to Timothy and Titus, his intimate friends and fellow-workers, the doctrine of justification by faith! Hence, it is altogether natural that these three words do not occur here, though the doctrine itself is not completely absent; see Titus 3:5-7. The same holds for the other words given by Harrison on pp. 31 and 32 of his book. The absence of not a single one of them from the Pastoral epistles is strange, though in one case it is more immediately apparent why a word should not be found than in another. Moreover, if the Pauline authorship of the Pastorals must be rejected because the word "Spirit" occurs only 3 times, must we not also reject the Pauline authorship of Colossians, II Thessalonians, and Philemon?

As to c. and d., this is a sword that cuts both ways, for one might also say that the very presence of entire word-families *here in the Pastorals just as in the ten,* points in the direction of identical authorship. That the basic word around which the word-family has developed is not the same in the different epistles is easily explained: in the letters to Timothy and to Titus, who were definitely in need of good counsel with respect to their own specific task of *imparting instruction,* the word-family which centers about the idea of *teaching* is certainly not at all surprising.

Besides, it can be shown that if the presence or absence of certain words and word-families is decisive in determining authorship, it will not be easy for the critics to defend the Pauline authorship of *all* the ten, for in Harrison's list of 41 words which occur in *five Pauline* epistles but not in the Pastorals (*op. cit.* p. 31), only *one* word out of the first 22 occurs in II Thessalonians! Some, of course, would be perfectly willing to drop II Thessalonians also!

As to e., our knowledge of actual vocabulary in use during the second half of the first century A. D., in comparison with the first half of the second century A. D., is far too scanty to be able to serve as a trustworthy criterion. How often has it not happened that words which were formerly considered "late" suddenly turned up in newly discovered writings of a much earlier date? The idea that the use of "classical" words indicates a second century A. D. author looks like begging the question. Why should it be accounted unreasonable to assume that Paul himself wrote the Pastorals, and that he derived his knowledge of "classical" vocabulary from his own reading or listening? Had he not been a student in his youth? Did Gamaliel's curriculum provide nothing in the line of ancient and contemporary literature? Is it not true that the Paul whom we have learned to know from the ten recognized epistles must have had a rather extensive knowledge (direct or indirect) of Greek authors, so that he was able to quote Menander (I Cor. 15:33) and Aratus (Acts 17:28)? Is it absurd to posit the possibility that during his lengthy first imprisonment (and according to some perhaps even during his second imprisonment, cf. II Tim. 4:13) the apostle added to this knowledge by now and then making excursions into extra-canonical literature? We know, at any rate, that some of the words not found elsewhere in the New Testament but used both by the author of the Pastorals and by writers of the second century A. D. were also used by the apostle's contemporaries. Who will dare to maintain that many other words may not also have been in common use as early as the first century A. D. or even earlier? [6]

The similarity in vocabulary which appears when the Pastorals are compared with *Christian* writings of the second century A. D. does not necessarily mean that whoever wrote I Timothy, II Timothy, and Titus flourished in the days of the Apostolic Fathers and Apologists. It could also mean that these second century Christian authors had read, studied, and to a certain extent copied or paraphrased Paul!

As to f., the frequent use of words and idioms derived from the Latin, this argument hangs by a slender thread! The critics are able to point to a total of no more than *two* Latin words in the three Pastorals, namely, μεμβράνα (Latin *membrana*), *parchment,* II Tim. 4:13; and (same passage) φελόνης (Latin *paenula*), which has been variously interpreted as *cloak, book-cover, brief-case.* But Latin words also occur in those epistles which even by the critics are ascribed to Paul: θριαμβεύω, to lead in triumph (cf. Latin *triumphus*), II Cor. 2:14; Col. 2:15; μάκελλον, meat-market (Latin *macellum*), I Cor. 10:25; and πραιτώριον, Praetorian Guard (Latin *praetorium*), Phil. 1:13. Besides, in his Gospel and Acts, Luke, who had been Paul's companion, and who, according to II Tim. 4:11, was again with him during the apostle's second imprisonment, uses almost half of a total of about thirty different Latin words that occur in the New Testament. If Paul's frequent companion can use Latin words, why cannot Paul do the same?

It is true that echoes of the Latin have also been heard in such expressions as:

δεσπότης	*(dominus),* I Tim. 6:1, 2; 2:21; Tit. 2:9, master, lord
δίλογος	*(bilinguis* in one of its meanings), I Tim. 3:8, double-tongued
ἑδραίωμα	*(firmamentum),* I Tim. 3:15, support, bulwark, foundation
εὐσέβεια	*(pietas),* I Tim. 2:2; 4:7, 8, piety, reverence, devotion, godly living, godliness, religion

---

[6] See W. Lock, *op. cit.* p. xxix, and especially E. K. Simpson, the *Pastoral Epistles,* pp. 16-18; 103, 104.

ματαιολογία	*(vaniloquium),* I Tim. 1:6, futile talk
οἱ ἡμέτεροι	*(nostri),* Tit. 3:14, "our folk," our people
πρόσκλισις	*(inclinatio),* I Tim. 5:21, inclination, partiality
πρόκριμα	*(praeiudicium),* I Tim. 5:21, pre-judging, prejudice
σεμνότης	*(gravitas),* I Tim. 2:2; 3:4; Tit. 2:7, dignity, respectability, gravity, seriousness
χάριν ἔχειν	*(gratiam habere),* I Tim. 1:12, to acknowledge gratitude

But in connection with this, observe the following:

1. Words and phrases which remind one of parallels that are very common in Latin are also found in other New Testament writings.[7]

2. Even during the first century A. D. Greek and Latin had reached the stage of mutual loaning and back-and-forth translation.

3. What may look like a copied idiom may be simply the result of parallel development in cognate languages.

Besides, even though one should admit a considerable measure of influence from the Latin upon the Greek of the Pastorals, would this in any way prove that *Paul* could not have written them? Is it not entirely natural that a man who had at last reached the world's metropolis, where very recently he had spent not less than two years, a man, moreover, who was highly susceptible to environmental influences and eagerly desirous of becoming all things to all men, would now begin to make even fuller use of "Roman" diction and phraseology than he had done heretofore? On this point the argument of the critics would seem to break down completely!

With respect to g., these illustrations readily vanish upon closer examination. Thus, it is claimed that Paul uses the term *faith* in the subjective sense (reliance on God and on his promises), but that the author of the Pastorals uses it in the objective sense (creed, body of truth). But, to begin with the Pastorals, the expression "faith and love that are in Christ Jesus" (I Tim. 1:14) indicates the exercise of these virtues. "To continue in faith and love and holiness" (see I Tim. 2:15) also illustrates the subjective use. And when the author teaches that one obtains "salvation through faith in Christ Jesus," everyone immediately understands that he is speaking about the attitude and exercise of trust in the Redeemer (hence, again subjective sense). See also I Tim. 3:13; 6:11, 12 and II Tim. 1:13; 3:10; 4:7. – And as to the ten epistles, their author does not always use the term in the subjective sense. Thus, in Gal. 1:23 he speaks about "preaching the faith." In Gal. 6:10 he uses the expression, "those who are of the household of the faith." And Phil. 1:27: "striving for the faith of the gospel," furnishes another excellent example of the objective use. Moreover, it is

---

[7] See Gram. N.T., p. 109.

not at all surprising that in the Pastorals Paul, being a man who is about to depart from this life, should be concerned about the preservation of "the truth," and should, accordingly, frequently employ the term "faith" in this objective sense (I Tim. 1:19; 3:9; 4:1; 5:8; 6:10; II Tim. 3:8; Titus 1:13).

As to the other examples that are supposed to prove that when the author of the three uses a Pauline word it frequently attains an altogether different meaning, thus proving that the apostle cannot have written the three, it is not at all clear why one and the same author would not be able to use the verb "to take up" both with respect to the "taking up" of spiritual weapons and the "being taken up" of Jesus into heaven. Similarly, the fact that the expression "the letter," singular, is used in one sense, but the term "letters," plural, in a different sense, is not so strange. Many languages contain idioms of this character: for example, to take in fresh *air,* singular, is very necessary, but to give oneself *airs,* plural, is not advisable. And is it not true that in those epistles which even by the critics are assigned to Paul the terms "flesh" and "law" are used in more than one sense, just as the author of the Fourth Gospel uses the term "world" in several senses?

Finally, anent h., in *expository or argumentative discourses* – think especially of Romans, I and II Corinthians, Galatians – we can naturally expect a much wider use of *particles of transition and inference* than in a *manual of warnings* and *directives* for "pastors." In the latter we look for and find the imperative mood.

In brief, here is *Paul,* "the aged" (thus self-styled already in Philemon 9), writing a letter. Does a man of advancing years use the vocabulary of a younger person? In spite of vigorous denials, is it not possible that age and the experience of imprisonment, whether in the recent past or at the very moment of writing, might have something to do with vocabulary and/or grammar?

The author of the Pastorals is writing to *intimate fellow-workers,* his own *deputies.* Today when a minister of a large congregation gives advice to his "assistant" with whom he is on good terms, does he employ the Sunday pulpit-oratory style?

In writing to his assistants the author advises them how the church should be organized, what kind of elders should be appointed, what should be done about heretics, etc. Do *subjects* of this nature require the vocabulary which one would use in expounding to the congregation the doctrine of "justification by faith" (Romans) or of "the unity of all believers in Christ" (Ephesians)? N. J. D. White, *op. cit.,* pp. 63, 65, 66, accounts for some of the new words that occur in the Pastorals by showing that their presence is quite natural in letters which condemn heresies. He places such terms under the heading "Polemical phraseology in reference to false teaching." An example is "profane chatter."

In conclusion, we would like to ask the critics, At the beginning of his writing-career was the apostle handed a list of words with the requirement that, no matter what the circumstances might be, either of himself or of the readers, and no matter what might be the purpose of any epistle or the subject on which he would write, he must invariably use *these* words, and *only* these words, and, in addition, must distribute them in equal proportion over all his letters, like the spots on a polka-dot dress? In actual, physical compass the literary heritage which Paul has left us is not at all imposing: a mere 138 small pages of print in N.N. (for the *ten* epistles). Do we have any right to assume that what is written on these 138 pages (reduced to 67 larger pages in the English Bible that lies on my desk) comprises Paul's *total* vocabulary and syntax, so that any deviation (either in words or in grammar) which one encounters in the Pastorals proves that the latter must be ascribed to another author? Has any person the right to apply to Paul's writings a criterion which would do away with much of Milton, Shelley, and Carlyle, if it were applied to *their* writings?

The argument based on vocabulary and grammar leads nowhere. Even the staunchest defender of the authenticity of the Pastorals will readily grant that there is a remarkable difference in vocabulary, when these three are compared to the ten, just as there is considerable variation when each of the three is compared with either or both of the others. It is entirely possible that the explanations which have been given — such as, Paul's age and imprisonment (past or present), the character of the readers, the subjects covered, the purpose — do not fully account for these differences. Other factors may also have been operative, for example, the rapid advance and development of the church as a new entity, growing, changing, vigorous, and of necessity developing a new phraseology. Such expressions as "guard the deposit," "follow doctrine," and "man of God" are by White considered to belong to this category. Here, we may assume, Paul is using phraseology which he hears round about him. It has also been suggested that Paul's "secretary" or "secretaries" may have influenced the final product to some extent. On this point see footnote 193.

The point to note, however, is this: *the burden of proof rests entirely on the negative critic!* It is not the conservative believer who claims that vocabulary and grammar *prove* Paul to have been the author, but *it is the critic who now loudly proclaims that vocabulary and grammar indicate that Paul could not have been the author. The literary critics of the early centuries, who were well aware of grammar and style peculiarities, and therefore called in question the Pauline authorship of Hebrews, never had any such difficulty with the Pastorals!* The modern critic has failed completely to prove with respect to even a single word of the total Pastoral vocabulary, that Paul could not have written it! I have worked this out in detail in connection with the vocabulary of the second chapter of Titus. See footnote 193.

(2) *The style of the Pastorals betrays their forged origin.*

Some, in speaking about "style," use this term in a sense which approaches "vocabulary," "diction." This has already been discussed. Others, however, give a broader connotation to the term, and under this heading discuss *what* the author of the Pastorals says and especially *how* he says it, *the general character* of his thoughts and particularly *the manner* in which he expresses them. We shall here take the term in this broader sense.

On *one* matter the critics are agreed, namely, on the proposition that the style of the Pastorals points away from Paul. But as soon as the question is raised, "Why is this true?" the answers divide and become contradictory, some asserting that the style itself is altogether un-Pauline, others that it reminds one at so many points of Paul that a forger, a conscious imitator, must have been at work. He must have had a copy of Paul's genuine epistles in front of him. From these he copied phrase upon phrase, acting as if he were Paul!

From this confusion in the camp of the critics there is only one safe retreat, namely, a candid examination of the actual facts. *These point to Paul as the author.* Observe the following:

We find in these short letters the same kind of a person as is revealed in the ten. It is the character of *Paul* which is here reflected, just as, for example, in I Thessalonians and II Thessalonians. See N.T.C. on I and II Thessalonians, p. 22. The author of the Pastorals is deeply interested in those whom he addresses, namely, in Timothy and Titus, displaying warm affection for them (I Tim. 1:2; 5:23; 6:11, 12; II Tim. 1:2, 5, 6, 7; 2:1, 2, 15, 16; 4:1, 2, 15; Tit. 1:4). He shares their experiences and is fond of commending whatever is good in them (II Tim. 1:8; 3:10-15; 4:5-8; Tit. 1:4). He ascribes to the sovereign grace of God whatever good there is in himself or in those addressed (I Tim. 1:12-17; 4:14; II Tim. 1:6, 7, 13, 14; 2:1). He shows wonderful tact in counseling (I Tim. 1:18; 4:6, 11-16; 5:1; 6:11-16; II Tim. 1:2-7; Tit. 1:4; 2:7). He takes up, one by one, matters of special concern to Timothy and Titus (evident to anyone who reads these three short letters from beginning to end). He is anxious to see them (II Tim. 1:4; 4:9, 11; Tit. 3:12).

He is, moreover, fond of the figure of speech called *litotes,* that is, affirmation by negation of the opposite. This may be viewed as a kind of *understatement* or *miosis.* Thus, instead of saying that he is "proud" of preaching Christ, he states that he is "*not* ashamed" of the One whom he has believed (II Tim. 1:12; cf. 1:8, 16). Similarly he affirms that the Word of God is "not chained" (II Tim. 2:9) and that God is the One who does "*not* lie" (Tit. 1:2). This reminds strongly of Paul, the man who declared that he was a citizen "of *no* mean city" (Acts 21:39); that he had "*not* been disobedient" to the heavenly vision (Acts 26:19); that he was *"not* ashamed of the gospel" (Rom. 1:16); that his entering in among the Thessalonians was *"not* emptyhanded" (I Thess. 2:1); that his appeal did *"not* spring from delusion" (I Thess. 2:3); that he does *not* want the readers to be in ignorance (I Thess. 4:13); and that they "must *not* become weary in well-doing" (II Thess. 3:13).

He is fond of enumerations. Thus, he groups virtues or vices, listing them in series (I Tim. 3:1-12; 6:4, 5; II Tim. 3:2-5; 3:10, 11; Tit. 3:3). This is exactly what Paul does in the other epistles (see Rom. 1:29-32; II Cor. 12:20; Gal. 5:19-23).

He is not averse to introducing here and there a "play upon words." Thus he admonishes the *rich* to fix their hope on him who gives *richly* (I Tim. 6:17). He contrasts "lovers of pleasure" with "lovers of God" (II Tim. 3:4). He informs us that one of the purposes of the inspired writings is "that the man of God may be *complete* (or *equipped*), furnished *completely* (or *thoroughly equipped*) for every good work" (II Tim. 3:17, a passage where the R.S.V., by its translation, misses the evidently intentional play upon words). And he admonishes Timothy that in preaching the Word he must "be on hand in season, out of season."

Here again one thinks inevitably of Paul and his fondness for the same stylistic characteristic. It is Paul who, cognizant of the fact that the name *Jew* (cf. Judah) indicates "let him (that is, *God*) be praised," writes, "But he is a *Jew* . . . whose *praise* is not of men but of God" (Rom. 2:29). It is also Paul who makes use of the fact that the name of a fugitive slave, namely, Onesimus, means *useful, beneficial, profitable:* "I appeal to you in the interest of my child . . . Onesimus, who once was *unprofitable* (or *useless*) to you, but now is profitable (or *useful*) to you and to me."

Again, Paul likes "compendious compounds" (E. K. Simpson). He often chooses terms that are composed of several words (often one or more prepositions plus a verb). Thus, it is he who says that the Holy Spirit *helps* us in our weakness. Now this word *help* originally meant *"he lays hold of* (λαμβάνεται) *along with* (σύν) a person, either *facing* that person or else *taking his turn,* so that he carries the burden *instead of* (ἀντί) that person. The entire verb is συναντιλαμβάνεται.[8]

Here also the Pastorals resemble the ten, witness such compounds as καταστρηνιάσωσιν (they grow wanton, I Tim. 5:11), διαπαρατριβαί (mutual altercations or incessant friction, I Tim. 6:5), εὐμετάδοτοι (ready to share with others, generous, I Tim. 6:18), θεόπνευστος (God-breathed, II Tim. 3:16), and αὐτοκατάκριτος (self-condemned, Tit. 3:11).

Paul's love for phrases "in apposition" – see, for example, Rom. 12:1, "to

[8] I have discussed this verb in my doctoral dissertation, "The Meaning of the Preposition ἀντί in the New Testament," pp. 83, 84.

present yourselves as a living sacrifice . . . (which is) your service according to reason (or *reasonable worship*)" – is well-known and can be illustrated by several passages from the ten epistles. Similar instances of apposition occur throughout the Pastorals. See, for example, I Tim. 1:17; 3:15, 16; 4:10, 14; 6:14, 15; II Tim. 1:2; 2:1; Tit. 1:1, 10; 2:14.

The sudden breaking in of doxologies, which feature one has met in studying the ten (see Rom. 9:5; 11:36; 16:27; Eph. 1:3 ff.; 3:20) appears once more in the Pastorals (I Tim. 1:17; 6:15, 16; II Tim. 4:18; and cf. other instances of elevated style – "near-doxologies" – in I Tim. 3:16; Tit. 2:13, 14).

The expression of personal unworthiness (Eph. 3:8; I Cor. 15:9) recurs in I Tim. 1:13; the "if not . . . then how" phraseology (I Cor. 14:6, 7, 9) is found also in I Tim. 3:5; moreover, who but the Paul whom we have learned to know from the ten could have penned that intensely personal and exuberant line, "I have fought the noble fight, I have finished the course, I have kept the faith," etc. (II Tim. 4:7, 8)?

A glance at those phrases in the Pastorals which Harrison has underscored (to indicate that they are also found in the ten) adds to the accumulation of evidence *in favor* of Pauline authorship, though it was not Harrison's intention to bolster that conclusion.

The argument according to which Paul cannot have written the Pastorals because the style of *certain passages* in the ten is not characteristic of I Timothy, II Timothy, and Titus proves either *nothing* or *too much.* Is there *any* author of note who *always,* under *all* circumstances, at *every* period of his life, and *no matter to whom or on what subject* he writes, employs *the same unvaried* style?

We admit, of course, that there is a striking contrast between the lengthy and involved sentence-structure of such passages as Eph. 1:3-14; Phil. 2:5-8, on the one hand, and many short and pithy admonitions of the Pastorals, on the other. But is this comparison fair? Lengthy sentences are not entirely wanting in the Pastorals (see I Tim. 1:5-7; 1:8-11; 1:18-20; 2:5-7; etc.). Brief statements abound in the ten.

Neither is it fair to contrast the exuberant tone of certain paragraphs in the ten with the much calmer and more matter-of-fact manner of expression which characterizes much of the material of the Pastorals. One should not compare I Tim. 2:8-15 with the vigorous climax of Romans 8 but with the somewhat similar paragraph: I Cor. 11:1-16. Neither should one place Tit. 3:9-14 next to I Cor. 13 but next to I Thess. 5:12-22. If variation in style proves different authorship, then the author of I Cor. 13 cannot have written the letter to Philemon, and the author of Romans 8 cannot even have written Romans 13!

Moreover, is it not entirely natural that the man who was well along in years when he wrote the Pastorals should *now,* as the race was drawing to a close, employ a more reserved style? Are we surprised that rather often in the Pastorals we notice that the rugged fervor and fiery vigor of earlier years has disappeared?

When the Pastorals are compared with those sections in the ten which form the basis for legitimate comparison, it becomes evident – as has been indicated by numerous examples – that their style is characteristically Pauline. In fact, so signally Pauline is the style of these three short letters that several critics are willing to make a concession. They grant that here and there one encounters genuinely Pauline material; for example, the personal notes found in II Tim. 4:6-22. In that paragraph Timothy is urged to come before winter and to take along the prisoner's "cloak" and books, especially the parchments. Demas is represented as a renegade, Luke as true-blue. There is a brief sketch of the "first defence." And personal greetings are extended to several individuals. – A somewhat similar passage is Tit. 3:12.

Now though some critics (especially some of the earlier ones) have been bold enough to consider also these personal notes to be the work of a clever falsifier, who tried to lend color and verisimilitude to his crafty literary product, and who invented unreal – but seemingly real – situations in order to attain this end, meanwhile breathing the air of profoundest regard for the truth, this solution has not found general acceptance.

It is objectionable from many an angle. It is hardly probable that a forger would have used so many personal names. Moreover, he would have been hard-pressed to make his personal notes sound so real and lifelike. He surely would not have spoken in such an uncomplimentary tone about Demas (II Tim. 4:10), who by Paul elsewhere is never pictured as a deserter, a man who had fallen in love with the world (contrast Col. 4:14; Philemon 24).

But is the alternative which other negative critics propose any better? That alternative would make of the author of the Pastorals a second century dove-tailer who took certain genuine Pauline passages, fitted them into his own composition, and thus created the impression that Paul was the author of the whole.

But this theory does not explain how it is that the transitions from genuine to forged material are so unobtrusive. As has been remarked, one would expect the seams to show! And besides, is it not strange that of the earlier correspondence between the great apostle and his associates only a few genuine personal notes have remained? In brief, the theory is vulnerable from several aspects, and today is rejected by many of the negative critics themselves. Albert Schweitzer who, as one could have expected, denies the Pauline authorship of the Pastorals, remarks that the repeated attempts to discover in them "short notes written by Paul" is "in vain." [9]

Now, the true alternative to the "scissors and paste" or "jigsaw-puzzle" theory of the critics is not total denial of Pauline authorship but, in conformity with the data which have been presented, acceptance of Pauline authorship for the *entire* contents. The argument from style, when all the facts are examined, points in only *one* direction, namely, to Paul as the author of the Pastorals.

3. *The theology is not that of Paul. The cross is no longer in the center. There is undue stress on good works.*

One stands amazed that this argument is still being repeated. Any reader of the English Bible who carefully studies the Pastorals from beginning to end, and who is acquainted with Paul's doctrine as unfolded in the other ten epistles can easily answer the critics on this point.

It is true, of course, that here in the Pastorals there is no *detailed exposition* of the doctrine of salvation through faith in Jesus Christ apart from the works of the law. Nevertheless, that doctrine is clearly stated in more than one passage, and is assumed throughout.

The truth is that the doctrine which is taught and presupposed in the Pastorals is clearly the same as that which is held before us in the ten:

The redeemed have been chosen from eternity. They are called *the elect* (II Tim. 2:10; cf. Eph. 1:4; I Thess. 1:4).

Their salvation is due to the grace of God in Christ, and not to human works (I Tim. 1:14; II Tim. 1:9; Tit. 3:5; cf. Gal. 2:16; Rom. 3:21-24).

Christ is God (Tit. 2:13; cf. Rom. 9:5; Phil. 2:6; Col. 2:9).

He is the Mediator between God and man, himself man, our Lord Jesus Christ (I Tim. 2:5; cf. Rom. 9:5; I Cor. 8:4, 6).

His purpose in coming into the world and assuming the human nature was to save sinners, of whom Paul considers himself chief (I Tim. 1:15; cf. II Cor. 8:9; I Cor. 15:9; Eph. 3:8).

Men are saved through faith in this divine and human Mediator Jesus Christ (II Tim. 1:12; cf. Rom. 1:17; Eph. 2:8).

This faith implies mystic union with Christ: dying with him, living with him; enduring with him, reigning with him (II Tim. 2:11, 12; cf. Rom. 6:8; 8:17).

Good works are necessary (I Tim. 2:10; 6:11, 18; II Tim. 2:22; 3:17), and are to be viewed as the fruit of God's grace (hence, also the fruit of faith) operating in the believer (Tit. 2:11-14; 3:4-8; cf. Gal. 5:22-24; Eph. 2:10).

The glory of God is the chief purpose of man (I Tim. 6:16; II Tim. 4:18; cf. Rom. 11:36; 16:27).

---

[9] A. Schweitzer, *The Mysticism of Paul the Apostle* (translated into English by William Montgomery), New York, 1931, p. 42.

Where, in all this, is there contrast in doctrine, a contrast supposedly so marked and definite that the author of the ten cannot have been the author of the three? When, even in recent literature, such a thoroughly unwarranted position is still being defended, and *no evidence of any kind is furnished,* one is led to ask, "Is the higher criticism scholarly?"

Most appropriately God, in his providence, has seen to it that in Paul's *final* three epistles *the fruit* (good works) of faith is emphasized, the *nature* of faith and its *necessity* over against law-works having been fully set forth in the letters which preceded. The tree is first; then comes the fruit.

4. *The Pastorals controvert second century gnosticism, especially Marcionism. Now Marcion was expelled from the Roman church in the year 144 A. D. Hence, the Pastorals must have been written about this time, that is, not earlier than the second quarter of the second century. This shows that Paul cannot have been the author.*

To lend support to the view that whoever wrote the Pastorals is here combating the views of second century gnostics the following points are usually emphasized:

(a) The "genealogies" (I Tim. 1:4; Tit. 3:9) are the second century gnostic "aeons" which emanate from the bosom of God.

(b) The "fables" or "myths" (Tit. 1:14) represent second century gnostic speculations.

(c) The ascetic practices against which the author issues a warning when he condemns the views of those who forbid marriage and who enjoin abstinence from foods (I Tim. 4:3) point to Marcion who practiced the strictest asceticism, revolting from marriage, meat, and wine.

(d) The denial of a physical resurrection (II Tim. 2:18) was a feature of second century gnostic dualism.

(e) The affirmation that *all* Scripture is inspired and useful (II Tim. 3:16), and that there is only *one* God (I Tim. 2:5) cannot fail to remind one of Marcion, who rejected all the books of the Old Testament and drew a sharp *antithesis* between the merely *just* Jehovah of the Old Testament and the *gracious* God of the (i.e., of *Marcion's* mutilated edition of the) New Testament.

(f) The "very title of Marcion's book" ("Antitheses") in I Tim. 6:20, clinches the argument! Surely one who mentions the title of the work of an author who flourished in the *second* century cannot have been Paul, who died in the *first* century!

It is, indeed, very strange that by some this six-point argument, which has been so often and so ably refuted, is still being repeated, either as a whole or in part, as if it contained at least a considerable element of value. The answer is clear and simple:

With respect to (a): The "genealogies," in the light of the entire context, are clearly *Jewish* in character. One is immediately reminded of those which are found in the book of Genesis (cf. also Chronicles). Embellishing speculations with reference to Old Testament names and stories abound in the *Book of Jubilees*. The Jews were past masters in the art of *eisegesis* (introducing one's own thoughts and sentiments into a passage; opposed to *exegesis:* bringing out the author's own meaning). Now Marcion himself fails to discuss *aeons*. One must not confuse his teaching with that of Valentinus. But *nowhere* in gnostic literature is the term "genealogy" used as a synonym for "aeon."

With respect to (b): The "fables" or "myths" are definitely called *Jewish* (Tit. 1:14). Hence, it simply is not fair to equate them with the vagaries of second century gnosticism.

With respect to (c): The critics seem to forget that the apostle Paul warned against similar ascetic tendencies in Col. 2:16-23. Must we conclude, then, that Colossians also belongs to the second century?

Besides, we may readily grant that I Tim. 4:3 warns against ascetic gnosticism, such as that of Marcion. But that does not prove that the author was Marcion's contemporary. There is nothing here that disproves the fact that a first century author, namely, Paul, was able, under the guidance of the Holy Spirit, to predict a second century development of an error which, in its incipient form, was present already in his own day.

With respect to (d): Denial of a physical resurrection is "as old as the hills." It manifested itself in different forms. Sometimes the idea that the body will rise again was frankly and directly rejected. At other times the rejection was by implication, just as in our own day: a spiritual meaning was assigned to the term *resurrection*. This was done, for example, by the heretics described in II Tim. 2:18. In any event, in view of Paul's lengthy argument in I Cor. 15 against those who said, "There is no resurrection of the dead," it is evident that the statement, "The resurrection is past already" (II Tim. 2:18) does not prove what the critics are trying to prove. It does not prove that Paul cannot have written the Pastorals!

With respect to (e): The passages to which reference is made should be read in the light of their own specific contexts. Then it becomes clear that when the author is speaking of *one* God, he is not contrasting a New Testament God with an Old Testament "demiurge." Neither is he placing the Old Testament in antithetical relationship to the New when he uses the expression "all Scripture." He is contrasting the wrong with the right use of Scripture. If proper use is made of Scripture so that one abides in its clear teaching, the conclusion will prove inescapable that "*all* Scripture is inspired of God and profitable."

Finally, with respect to (f): If this has any value, it would amount to the syllogism:

Major Premise: The author of the Pastorals makes use of the term "antitheses."

Minor Premise: Marcion, a second century heretic, also makes use of the term "antitheses," using it as the title of a book which he wrote.

Conclusion: Therefore, the author of the Pastorals must have been acquainted with Marcion's book.

Similarly, one might say:

Major Premise: The author of the book of Genesis writes about Paradise, the river, the tree of life, the serpent.

Minor Premise: The apostle John, a late first century A. D. author, employs these same terms in his book of Revelation.

Conclusion: Hence, the author of the book of Genesis must have read the book of Revelation!

Now anyone who reads I Tim. 6:20 with an unbiased mind and in the light of the entire epistle will easily reach the conclusion that in speaking of "antitheses" what the author has in mind is not Marcion's contrast between Christianity and Judaism but *the conflicting opinions* of those who speculated in Jewish genealogies! Surely, *a merely verbal coincidence* between a word used by one author and a title used by another cannot do duty as a convincing argument with respect to authorship.

In addition to what has been said in answer to the argument of the critics, note the following:

It is being increasingly recognized today that gnosticism did not arise full-blown in the second century but had its origin much farther back in history. Besides, it is not an organically unified system but a speculative religious syncretism or accretion, to which not only Platonic philosophy but also Oriental mysticism, Cabbalistic Judaism, and Christianity contributed. Hence, though it is certainly true that the heresy condemned in the Pastorals *had certain traits in common with* second century gnosticism, this by no means identifies the two.

The error against which the Pastorals warn is both *present* (I Tim. 1:3-7, 19; 4:7; 6:4, 5, 9, 10, 17; II Tim. 2:16-18; Tit. 1:10-16; 3:9) and *future* (I Tim. 4:1-3; II Tim. 3:1-9) – taken together it spans the entire new dispensation until Christ's return – ; both chiefly *doctrinal* (I Tim. 4) and chiefly *moral* (II Tim. 3); both *within* and *without* the gate.

One fact, however, is very evident, namely, that *in the main,* the error which is here condemned has reference to *the Old Testament law and its interpretation* (see I Tim. 1:7; cf. 6:4, 5; II Tim. 4:4; Tit. 1:14; 3:9). Here lies the emphasis. And it was exactly this law with which second century gnosticism would have nothing to do! Hence, there is nothing here which compels one to hunt for a second century author. On the contrary, everything points to the first century and to Paul's day and age.

For the reasons indicated it is not surprising that even among the critics the more careful authors no longer mention "the argument based upon the heresy that is here condemned." It seems that they would like to forget that it was ever seriously used against the Pauline authorship of the Pastorals.

(5) *The Pastorals reveal a marked advance in ecclesiastical organization, far beyond the time of Paul. In his day there was as yet no official ministry. When the Pastorals were written, on the other hand, there was a rather complex organization, with salaried officials whose qualifications had become standardized.*

One critic calls this "the chief argument" proving that Paul cannot have written the Pastorals. Some try to "strengthen" it by affirming that *the beginning* of pyramidal organization is evident from the fact that while the Pastorals recognize only *one* "bishop" (I Tim. 3:1, 2; Tit. 1:7), they speak of *many* "presbyters" or "elders" (Tit. 1:5) who are evidently serving under him.

Other critics, however, scrupulously avoid making reference to the argument in any form. Apparently also in this case they would like to forget that anyone ever brought it up. And, indeed, among the many poor arguments that have been presented in defence of the thesis that Paul cannot have written the Pastorals this is one of the poorest. The *facts* are as follows:

(a) The entire conception according to which ecclesiastical *office* (divine commission with implied authority over life and doctrine) was a late development is erroneous. It simply is incorrect to say that at first there was nothing else than spontaneous leadership based only on spiritual endowment, and that at a later time this made way for elective office. See N.T.C. on the Gospel of John, Vol. II, pp. 461, 462. It is true, of course, that the extraordinary offices were gradually replaced by the ordinary. The Pastorals are Paul's *last* writings. It is not surprising, therefore, that the "ordinary" office of "overseer" or "elder" comes into prominence here.

(b) The notion that in Paul's day there was as yet no official ministry is in conflict with the facts mentioned by Scripture. Jerusalem had its *deacons* (men who "served tables") long before Paul went on his missionary journeys (Acts 6:1-6). From very early times the church also had its *elders* (Acts 11:30), an office which in a way was a natural outgrowth of the institution of elders in ancient Israel. Already on his first missionary journey Paul "appointed for them elders in every church" (Acts. 14:23). It has been indicated that in one of the earliest letters written by Paul there is definite mention of "those who labor among y o u and are over y o u in the Lord and admonish y o u" (see N.T.C. on I Thess. 5:12, 13). On the return from his third missionary journey Paul "calls to him the elders of the church" (of Ephesus or of Ephesus and surroundings). He characterizes them as "overseers" over God's flock, even the church "which the Lord purchased with his own blood" (Acts 20:17, 28). In a prison-epistle both "overseers and deacons" are mentioned (Phil. 1:1).

Now on the basis of all this it surely should cause no surprise that in the epistles which the apostle wrote just before his death the office of "overseers" or "elders" is recognized as well-known. It is also very natural that Paul, about to depart from this earthly realm, should specify certain qualifications and regulations for office, so that the church might be guarded against the ravages of error, both doctrinal and moral.

(c) In the Pastorals the term "elder" (or "presbyter") and "overseer" (or "bishop") are clearly synonymous, as is proved by Tit. 1:5-7 (cf. I Tim. 3:1-7; Phil. 1:1; I Peter 5:1, 2). See on that passage.

(d) The episcopate, a system of ecclesiastical government in which the bishop rules over the presbyters, seems to have arisen during the obscure transition period: the end of the first and the beginning of the second century. It emerges step by step and becomes evident first of all in the epistles of Ignatius of Antioch (who was sent to his martyrdom about the year 110 A. D.), where it appears as congregational (not diocesan) episcopacy.[10] Now this very fact indicates that *the Pastorals,* in which the "overseer" or "bishop" is simply another name for the "elder" or "presbyter," *point back to the first century and away from the second.*

(6) *Since Paul was not released from his one and only Roman imprisonment but was put to death at the end of it, and since the book of Acts, which tells the story of his life from the time when he persecuted the church until the end of his imprisonment, leaves no room for the journeys that are implied in the Pastorals, therefore Paul cannot have written these letters.*

J. Moffatt boldly declares that as a matter of fact Paul *was not released from his imprisonment.*[11] This view has been advocated both before and especially after him by many others.

Now if that be correct, then the critics have won the argument, for it is indeed true that the Pastoral Epistles imply a number of journeys which cannot be fitted into the itineraries of Paul that are recorded in the book of Acts, and, in fact, for which no room can be found in the life-span of the apostle as covered in Acts. The following will make this clear:

As to I Timothy, the author reminds Timothy of the fact that the latter had been instructed to stay behind *in Ephesus* while the author was headed *north-westward from Ephesus toward Macedonia* (I Tim. 1:3). He also informs him (Timothy) that he (the author) hopes to come to him *shortly* (I Tim. 3:14).

---

[10] For a summary of the entire argument regarding the rise of the episcopate see P. Schaff, *History of the Christian Church,* New York, 1924, Vol. II, pp. 132-148.
[11] See his *Introduction to the Literature of the New Testament,* third edition, 1918, p. 417.

Now according to Acts, on his first missionary journey Paul never crossed over into Europe (toward Macedonia) at all. On his second journey: on the outward-bound trip the Holy Spirit prevented him from speaking the word in Asia (Acts 16:6); hence, he was not in Ephesus; and on the homeward-bound trip he went from Corinth in an *easterly* direction to Ephesus, then toward the *south-east,* by way of Cesarea to Antioch (Acts 18:18-23). On the third journey, outward-bound, Paul did, indeed, perform a mighty task in Ephesus (Acts 19). He continued there for a long time (three years, Acts 20:31) and he also afterward crossed over into Macedonia (Acts 20:1). But this time *Timothy was not left behind in Ephesus,* but was sent to Macedonia and Corinth (Acts 19:21, 22; I Cor. 4:17; 16:10), and soon is back with Paul in Macedonia (II Cor. 1:1). With Paul he then goes to Corinth, returns with him to Macedonia, awaits him at Troas, and is probably with him in Jerusalem (Rom. 16:21; Acts 20:3-5; I Cor. 16:3). Finally, on the trip to Rome, Ephesus was left far to the north. Arrived in Rome, the two-year imprisonment followed. And with the recording of that event the book of Acts closes. It is clear that nowhere in this account in Acts is there any room for the journey presupposed in I Timothy.

With respect to Titus the situation is similar. According to this Pastoral Epistle the writer has left Titus in Crete to complete the organization of churches on that island (Tit. 1:5). He now instructs his fellow-worker to meet him at Nicopolis (in Epirus on the east coast of the Ionian Sea), where he expects to spend the winter (Tit. 3:12).

But according to Acts, on none of his three missionary journeys did Paul get anywhere near Crete. And on the journey to Rome, though he and Luke did sail "under the lee of Crete," and did reach Fair Havens, the apostle is pictured as *a prisoner,* who is not carrying on any evangelistic work on the island and who has nothing whatever to say about the place where he expects to spend the winter or where he desires to meet Titus (see Acts 27:7-15).

And finally, II Timothy pictures a prisoner (in Rome, cf. II Tim. 1:17), considered "a malefactor" (II Tim. 2:9), on the eve of his execution. The prospect, *humanly* speaking (but see II Tim. 4:7, 8!), is very gloomy. Only after diligent search does Onesiphorus succeed in finding Paul (II Tim. 1:16, 17). Release is nowhere in sight. Nearly everyone has left him. Luke alone is with him (II Tim. 1:15; 4:10, 11). The time of departure from the earthly scene has (or has just about) arrived (II Tim. 4:6, 18).

In sharp contrast with this, the description of the *Roman* imprisonment which is recorded *in Acts and in Paul's prison-epistles* (*previous* imprisonments certainly do not enter into the picture in this connection) closes hopefully (see also p. 26). The apostle is living in his own hired dwelling, and expects to be released shortly (Acts 28:30; Phil. 1:25, 26; 2:24; Philemon 22).

The conclusion is inescapable: if *Paul* wrote the Pastorals, he must have been released from that Roman imprisonment which is recorded in the book of Acts. He must have made further journeys, and he must have been imprisoned once more.

For a long time critics (intimidated by the prestige of Moffatt?) either denied the historicity of such a release or at least remained agnostic with respect to the subject. Of late, however, there seems to be the beginning of a return to the conservative position. In a recent issue of the *Journal of Biblical Literature* L. P. Pherigo argues strongly in favor of the position that Paul was actually released from the imprisonment recorded in Acts and that he labored a few years longer.[12]

Now, it should be evident to anyone who is willing to examine the evidence, that the arguments against the position that Paul was released are very weak. For example, the contention that had he been released, the author of Acts would have said so – as if Acts were Paul's biography! –, is met by the counter-argument, "Had he *not* been released, Luke *certainly* would have thus indicated, for the favorable note on which his account ends has caused the readers to expect Paul's release" (Acts 28:30, 31). – And the conclusion that Paul never returned to Ephesus, hence, cannot have written I Tim. 1:3, an inference which is drawn from the apostle's statement to the Ephesian elders, namely, "I know that y o u all, among whom I went about preaching the kingdom, will see my face no more" (Acts 20:25, cf. verse 38), is not warranted. In that passage from Acts the apostle did not say, "I know that I will never return to Ephesus," but predicted that making the rounds of Asia Minor, confirming all the churches, going from place to place preaching the gospel of the kingdom and thus seeing believers everywhere he went, would never be resumed by him personally. Paul did not even say, "I know that *none* of y o u, elders here at Ephesus, will ever see my face again," but he said, "I know that *y o u all among whom I went about preaching the kingdom* will see my face no more." The apostle was addressing the elders *as representatives of the churches of Asia Minor.* An occasional brief visit to Ephesus is not excluded. What *is* excluded is anything comparable to three years of day-by-day Kingdom-activity in the Ephesus-region (see *the context,* Acts 20:31).[13]

The arguments in favor of the traditional (and, as we see it, *correct*) position that Paul was, indeed, released from his first Roman imprisonment, made some more journeys, on one of which he wrote I Timothy

---

[12] L. Pherigo, "Paul's Life After the Close of Acts," *JBL* LXX (December, 1951), 277-284. See also the doctoral dissertation of N. G. Veldhoen, "Het Proces van den Apostel Paulus," Leiden, 1924. And see *GThT,* Vol. 55, No. 2, 3 (1955), pp. 60, 61.

[13] Thus also F. W. Grosheide in his comments on this passage in *Korte Verklaring.* For a different solution of the problem regarding Acts 20:25 see R. C. H. Lenski, *Interpretation of the Acts,* pp. 843, 844.

and Titus, was imprisoned for the second time, during which final imprisonment he wrote II Timothy, and was then executed, are as follows:

a. The book of Acts leads the reader to expect Paul's release, and *may* even imply this release.

Luke constantly emphasizes the relative fairness, at times even the friendliness and helpfulness, of the Roman authorities. Rescued by the military tribune out of the hands of the murderous mob at Jerusalem, Paul is permitted to make his defence, first before the people, then before the Jewish council (Acts 21:31-23:9). By the tribune he is rescued once more, this time out of the hands of quarreling Pharisees and Sadducees (Acts 23:10); and even a third time, now from a band of more than forty oath-bound Jews. He is brought to Cesarea. Claudius Lysias writes a letter in his favor (Acts 23:12-35), addressing it to the governor Felix. The latter also permits Paul to make his defence, but desiring to do the Jews a favor, leaves him in prison. When Festus succeeds Felix, the apostle appeals to Cesar. Festus tells King Agrippa that Paul had done nothing worthy of death, and permits him to make his defence before the king. On board a ship on his way to Rome, the apostle is treated kindly by the Roman centurion, Julius (Acts 27:3), who also subsequently saves his life (Acts 27:43). After the storm and the shipwreck, having first been hospitably entertained by the chief of the island of Malta (Acts 28:7), and having afterward covered the final leg of the journey, he arrives at Rome, where he is permitted to stay by himself with a soldier to guard him (Acts 28:16). Though he is a prisoner awaiting trial, he is allowed considerable personal liberty as well as opportunity to preach the gospel (Acts 28:30, 31). — Surely, the notion that he was then *condemned and executed* is completely out of harmony with the entire preceding account. In fact, it has even been suggested (see the article by Pherigo above referred to) that the expression, "And he lived two whole years" in his own hired dwelling (or "at his own expense") *may* have a *legal* meaning, namely, he waited *the full two years* (the limit established by law?) during which the accusers had the opportunity to press their charge. No one appearing (does Acts 28:21 hint in this direction?), the trial ended by default, and Paul was released, the legal requirement of two years having come to an end. — Whether or not this interpretation is correct has not been established. The *main point* is: the closing chapters of Acts point toward release, not toward execution.

b. Paul's prison-epistles show that he expected to be released (Phil. 1:25-27; 2:24; Philemon 22).

c. The very fact that the Pastoral Epistles, which presuppose journeys that require such a release and re-imprisonment, survived and were accepted by the early church as authentic and inspired, would seem to point in the direction of a strong and early tradition to this effect.

d. Even long before the Roman imprisonment recorded in Acts, the apostle had cherished the desire to go to Spain (Rom. 15:24, 28).

e. That he actually was released, went to Spain, was afterward reimprisoned, and having borne witness before the authorities, was executed, is certainly the most natural interpretation of the much-disputed passage of Clement of Rome, who, writing about the last decade of the first century A. D., *from Rome,* the *hub* of the empire, to the Corinthians, admonishing them to put an end to their striving engendered by jealousy, says:

"Paul . . . having taught righteousness to the whole world, *and having gone to the limits of the West,* and having given testimony before the rulers, thus passed from the world and was taken up into the Holy Place, having become the outstanding model of endurance" (First Epistle of Clement to the Corinthians V. vii).

The expression *"the limits of the West,"* especially when used by some- one who is writing *from Rome, the heart and center of the empire,* most naturally refers to the extreme western part of Europe.[14]

Similarly, the Muratorian fragment mentions Paul's journey to Spain.[15] And the great church-historian Eusebius states significantly:

"Luke also, who handed down the Acts of the apostles in writing, brought his narrative to a close by the statement that Paul spent two whole years in Rome in freedom, and preached the word of God without hindrance. Tradition has it that the apostle, having defended himself, was again sent upon the ministry of preaching, and coming a second time to the same city, suffered martyrdom under Nero. While he was being held in prison, he composed the second epistle to Timothy, at the same time signifying that his first defence had taken place and that his martyrdom was at hand" (*Ecclesiastical History* II. xxii. 1, 2). Later tradition also accepts a second Roman imprisonment (Chrysostom, Jerome, Theodore of Mopsuestia, etc.).

It has become clear, accordingly, that the so-called "historical" argument against the possibility that Paul could have written the Pastorals has no more substance than have any of the others. Better reasons will have to be found if the weight of tradition is to be counterbalanced.

---

[14] Thus Herodotus, in the 5th century B. C., described the Celts as the *Western* nation. Theodoret, in the 5th century A. D., speaks of the people of Spain, Gaul, and Britain as "those who dwell in the bounds of the West." Strabo's usage is similar. See the article by Pherigo, above referred to; also Lightfoot, *St. Clement of Rome,* London, 1869, pp. 49, 50. See also E. G. Kraeling, *Rand McNally Bible Atlas,* New York, Chicago, San Francisco, 1956, p. 462.

[15] The Latin is corrupt: lucas obtime theofile comprindit (for: Lucas optimo Theophilo comprehendit) quia sub praesentia eius singula gerebantur sicuti et semote (semota) passione petri (Petri) evidenter declarat sed et profectione pauli (Pauli) ab urbe ad spania (Spaniam) proficiscenti (proficiscentis); that is, "Luke relates them for the most excellent Theophilus because in his presence the individual events transpired, as he clearly declares by omitting the passion of Peter as well as the departure of Paul when the latter proceeded from the city to Spain." "The city" is Rome, of course.

Enough has been said to indicate the inadequacy of the arguments of the critics. On the supposition that the Pastorals were the last of Paul's epistles, written after his first Roman imprisonment, with a purpose quite different from that of the other ten letters, the main problem has been solved, at least to a considerable extent.

According to the information furnished by the Epistles themselves the author was:

(1) A man by the name of "Paul, an apostle of Christ Jesus" (I Tim. 1:1; II Tim. 1:1), or "Paul, a servant of God and an apostle of Jesus Christ" (Tit. 1:1). Thus we see that these three letters are self-attested, in contrast with Hebrews which does not mention the name of its author. In this respect the three are like the ten.

(2) Not only does the writer *name* himself; he also *describes* himself. This description agrees with that which is found in Acts and in the ten *with respect to Paul:*

a. The "Paul" of both used to be a blasphemer and persecutor (I Tim. 1:12-17; cf. Acts 8:3; 9:1, 2; 22:4, 5; 26:9-11; I Cor. 15:9).

b. Converted, he was divinely appointed to be a preacher and apostle (I Tim. 1:1, 11; 2:7; II Tim. 1:1, 11; Tit. 1:1; cf. Acts 9:15; 22:14, 15; 26:16-18; II Cor. 12:12; Gal. 1:1; 2:7).

c. In the defence of the truth he suffered much, for example, on his journey through Antioch, Iconium, and Lystra (II Tim. 1:12, 13; 3:10, 11; cf. Acts 14; II Cor. 11; I Thess. 1:6; 2:2).

(3) This man writes three letters which, with minor variations, are similar *in structure* to the ten Pauline epistles. For the nature of Paul's letter-plan, see N.T.C. on I and II Thess., p. 20. As an example let us take II Timothy. Here we find:

a. The mention of the writer's name and office (1:1)
b. The designation of the one to whom the letter is addressed (1:2a), with brief description of that person
c. The opening salutation (1:2b)
d. The thanksgiving, blending into the body of the letter (1:3 ff)
e. The concluding salutation, in the present instance rather detailed (4:19-21)
f. The benediction.

Even in such a minor detail as e: the presence or absence of words of greeting at the end of the letter, *these three letters* exactly resemble the variation which is found among *the ten.* Thus I Timothy has a closing benediction (6:21b: "Grace be with y o u") but no greetings. This reminds one of Galatians (6:18). In II Timothy those who wish to be remembered are mentioned one by one, and there are several names (4:19-21). This resembles what is found at the close of Romans (chapter 16) and of I Corinthians (16:19-21). In Titus, the closing salutation is very general (3:15: "All who are with me send greetings to you"). With this, one should compare II Corinthians (13:13).

(4) These three letters point to the same relation between the writer and the addressed (Timothy and Titus) that we know from letters commonly ascribed to Paul and (in the case of Timothy) from Acts.

It was a relationship of one who is in authority writing to one who recognizes this authority, of spiritual "father" to spiritual "son," of friend to friend (implying both affection and confidence).

In this connection, for Paul's relation to *Timothy* one should compare I Tim. 1:2; II Tim. 1:2 with I Cor. 4:17; 16:10; Phil. 2:19-23; Col. 1:1; I Thess. 3:2; and Philemon 1; and for his relation to *Titus* one should compare Tit. 1:4 with II Cor. 2:13; 7:6, 13; and 8:17, 23.

(5) These three letters mention by name certain individuals whom, from other sources, we have learned to recognize as companions and co-laborers of *Paul.* See on II Tim. 4 and on Tit. 3.

(6) They reveal an author whose warm interest in the churches which he had established, whose style, and whose theology point clearly to Paul, as has been shown (see pp. 14-19).

The testimony of the early church is in harmony with the conclusion which has been derived from the three epistles themselves.

Thus Eusebius, having made a thorough investigation of the literature at his command, states: "But clearly evident and plain are the fourteen (letters) of Paul; yet it is not right to ignore that some dispute the (letter) to the Hebrews" (*Ecclesiastical History* III. iii. 4, 5). Obviously Eusebius, writing at the beginning of the fourth century, knew that the entire orthodox church accepted the Pastorals as having been written by Paul. We have already observed that he makes specific mention of II Timothy as having been composed by the great apostle "while he was being held in prison," having come for the second time to the same city (*Ecclesiastical History* II. xxii. 1, 2; and cf. III. ii). The negative attitude of a few heretics (Basilides and Marcion) with respect to all three, and of Tatian and some like-minded persons with respect to I Timothy and II Timothy, was probably due to the fact that the teaching of these men was out of harmony with the contents of the Pastorals. That, at least, is the explanation given by Tertullian, Clement, and Jerome. Surely the opinion of a few heretics must not be placed above the considered judgment of the entire church!

From Eusebius we can go back to Origen (fl. 210-250), who quotes ever so many passages from the Pastorals (for example, in his work *Against Celsus:* I Tim. 2:1, 2; 3:15, 16; 4:1-5, 10, 17, 18; 6:20; II Tim. 1:3, 10; 2:5; 3:6-8; 4:7, 11, 15, 20, 21; Tit. 1:9, 10, 12; 3:6, 10, 11), and ascribes them to

Paul: "Moreover, Paul, who himself also subsequently became an apostle of Jesus, says in his epistle to Timothy: This is a faithful saying, that Jesus Christ came into the world sinners to save, of whom I am chief" (quoting I Tim. 3:15, *Against Celsus* I. lxiii).

From Origen we can go back still farther, to his teacher, Clement of Alexandria (fl. 190-200). The latter quotes the passage with reference to the "knowledge falsely so called" (I Tim. 6:20, 21), ascribing this passage to "the apostle" (*Stromata* II. xi). He also quotes the prediction that "in later times some will fall away from the faith" (I Tim. 4:1, 3), referring it to "the blessed Paul" (*Stromata* III. vi). A look at the Textual Index of Clement's works (for example, in *The Ante-Nicene Fathers,* reprint 1951, Grand Rapids, Mich., Vol. II) and an actual reading of these passages in the original or even in a good translation suffices to prove that in the works of this early Father there are numerous references to – and actual quotations from – the Pastorals, regarded as having been written by the apostle Paul.

About the same time Tertullian (fl. 193-216), in the short compass of a few lines, quotes several passages from I and II Timothy (I Tim. 6:20; II Tim. 1:14; I Tim. 1:18; 6:13; II Tim. 2:2, in *Prescription Against Heretics* XXV), definitely declaring that "Paul addressed this expression to Timothy." We have already seen that he frowns upon Marcion's rejection of the Pastorals (*Against Marcion* V. xxi).

Earlier by a few years, but still for a long time a contemporary of Clement of Alexandria and of Tertullian, was Ireneus. He opens his work *Against Heresies* (about 182-188) with a quotation from I Tim. 1:4 (the passage about the "endless genealogies" which fail to edify), which he definitely ascribes to *the apostle* (see the Preface to the aforementioned work by Ireneus). In the same work he quotes or alludes to several other passages, for example, I Tim. 1:9 (IV. xvi. 3); 2:5 (V. xvii. 1); 3:15 (III. i. 1); 4:2 (II. xxi. 2), and not only from the first but also from the second epistle to Timothy (II Tim. 2:23; cf. *Against Heresies,* IV. Preface, 3), and from Titus (Tit. 3:10; cf. *Ag. Her.,* I. xvi. 3). Note especially that in the last passage Ireneus states that it is *Paul* who commands us to avoid men who give heed to fables.

Now when Ireneus ascribes the Pastorals to "the apostle" namely to "Paul," his word should carry considerable weight. He had traveled widely, was intimately acquainted with almost the entire church of his day, and had been a pupil of a pupil (Polycarp) of one of the apostles (John).

The Muratorian Fragment (about 180-200), a survey of New Testament books, states that "the blessed Paul . . . writes . . . out of affection and love one to Philemon, and one to Titus, and two to Timothy . . . held sacred in the honorable esteem of the church universal in the regulation of ecclesiastical discipline."

INTRODUCTION

Among the orthodox writers who flourished at one time or another during the period 90-180 we find that toward the close of that era Theophilus of Antioch refers to "the water and laver of regeneration" (*To Autolycus* II. xvi), which may be regarded as a collation of Eph. 5:26 and Tit. 3:5. He definitely quotes I Tim. 2:2: "that we may lead a tranquil and quiet life" (Same work, III. xiv).

Athenagoras – sometimes called "the Christian philosopher from the Athenian Agora" (cf. his name *Athen – agoras*) –, was an Athenian who has been pictured as having one day sauntered into the market-place where the Christians were being mocked, and then, moved by curiosity, having begun to read the Scriptures in order to refute them. It is claimed that in the process of this Scripture-study he was converted. He, a contemporary of Theophilus, describes God as "light inapproachable" (*A Plea For the Christians* XVI). This certainly reminds one of I Tim. 1:16.

Writing some time between 155 and 161, Justin Martyr also showed that he was acquainted with the Pastorals. It is true that not all the seeming resemblances between certain passages in his writings and the Pastorals have evidential value. Thus, for example, the expression "this very Christ . . . the Judge of all the living and the dead" (*Dialogue with Trypho* CXVIII), while reminding one of II Tim. 4:1 ("Christ Jesus who shall judge the living and the dead"), from which, indeed, it *may* have been derived, was probably a "faithful saying" which had gained currency at a very early stage of Christian belief (see also Acts 10:42; I Peter 4:5; cf. Matt. 25:31-46; John 5:25-29; II Cor. 5:10), so that no argument can be based upon it to prove that Justin knew the Pastorals. However, his reference to "the kindness of God and his love toward man" – note God's *philanthropy!* – is almost certainly derived from Tit. 3:4 ("But when the kindness of God . . . and his love toward man appeared").

Also when we come to Polycarp (probably writing some time between 100 and 135), we feel that we are on firm ground. The fact that he knew the Pastorals and quoted from them would seem to be indisputable. Let the reader judge for himself:

POLYCARP *(To the Philippians)*	THE PASTORALS
"But the beginning of all evils is the love of money" (IV).	"For a root of all the evils is the love of money" (I Tim. 6:10).
"Knowing therefore that we brought nothing into the world and that we can take nothing out of it, let us arm ourselves with the armor of righteousness" (IV).	"For nothing did we bring into the world . . . neither are we able to carry anything out of it" (I Tim. 6:7).

POLYCARP *(To the Philippians)*	THE PASTORALS
"Likewise must the deacons be . . . not doubletongued, not lovers of money, temperate in all things . . ." (V).	"Deacons similarly must be . . . not doubletongued, not addicted to much wine, not greedy of shameful gain" (I Tim. 3:8).
"We shall also reign with him, if, indeed, we have faith" (V).	"If we endure, we shall also reign with him" (II Tim. 2:12).
"For they did not fall in love with the present world" (IX).	"For Demas has deserted me because he fell in love with the present world" (II Tim. 4:10).
"May the Lord grant them true repentance" (XI Lat.).	". . . in the hope that possibly God may grant them conversion" (II Tim. 2:15).
"Pray also for the rulers and for potentates and for princes . . ." (XII Lat.).	"First of all, then, I urge that supplications, prayers, intercessions, thanksgivings be made in behalf of all men, in behalf of kings and all who are in high positions" (I Tim. 2:1, 2).

Here, clearly, one writer is using the words of another, varying the language somewhat as the need requires. It is surely most natural to conclude that when one writer states "Demas . . . fell in love with the present world," and the other refers to persons who *"did not* fall in love with the present world," it is the latter writer who is borrowing from the former, and not vice versa. Moreover, if *the pupil,* Ireneus, ascribed the Pastorals to Paul, as has been shown, is it not probable that the *teacher,* Polycarp, did the same?

Ignatius (not later than 110), in urging Polycarp to be pleasing to him for whom he is soldiering (*To Polycarp* VI), immediately reminds one of II Tim. 2:4. (Other assumed resemblances are less convincing.)

Because of their debatable character we pass by a few possible allusions to the Pastorals in the *Epistle of Barnabas,* and we come, last of all, to Clement of Rome (90-100). The clearest resemblances are the following:

CLEMENT OF ROME *(To the Corinthians)*	THE PASTORALS
"You were . . . ready for every good work" (11).	"Remind them to be ready for every good work" (Tit. 3:1).

CLEMENT OF ROME (*To the Corinthians*)	THE PASTORALS
". . . those who with a pure conscience serve his excellent name" (XLV)	"I acknowledge gratitude to God whom I, like my forefathers serve with a pure conscience" (II Tim. 1:3).

Summing up the entire argument regarding authorship we may now safely state the following:

(1) The arguments of the negative critics have been examined in detail and have been found wanting; that is, these critics have failed to prove that Paul could not have written the Pastorals.

(2) According to the evidence of the epistles themselves the author was no one else than the apostle Paul.

(3) Within the orthodox church there is a uniform tradition ascribing the Pastorals to the apostle Paul. This tradition can be traced back from Eusebius at the beginning of the fourth century to Ireneus and the Muratorian Fragment at the close of the second. Moreover, the Pastorals are included not only in *this* list (the Muratorian) but in *all* the ancient lists of Pauline epistles, and also in *all* the manuscripts and versions that have come down to us.

(4) Even in the period A. D. 90-180 we find clear evidence that I and II Timothy and Titus were already in existence, were held in high esteem as the very word of God, and were being frequently quoted and paraphrased. It is true that these early witnesses do not mention Paul by name as the author. Not mentioning authors of New Testament books by name is rather characteristic of them. They and their readers were living so close to the time of the apostles that this was not considered necessary.

The very fact that already in the days of these earliest witnesses – Theophilus of Antioch, Athenagoras, Justin Martyr, Polycarp, Ignatius, and Clement of Rome – the Pastorals have attained this high fame and wide circulation shows that their date of origin must go back to a period that is still earlier by several years. Hence, all the historical evidence points to Paul as the one who during the period 63-67 A. D. was in a real sense the responsible author of these three little gems of inspired truth.

III. To Whom Were They Addressed?

It is natural to turn from the sender to the addressees: Timothy and Titus.

A most remarkable person was Timothy or Timotheus, meaning: honoring or worshiping *god,* originally a heathen name of very common occurrence,[16] adopted by devout Jews and by Christians, with changed reference, namely, to *their God*. His character was a blend of *amiability* and *faithfulness in spite of natural timidity*. Paul loved Timothy and admired his outstanding personality-traits.

As to Timothy's *amiability*, it is concerning him that the apostle wrote these touching words: "Now I hope in the Lord Jesus to send Timothy to you soon, so that I also may be cheered when I get to know about your condition. Indeed, I have no one of similar disposition, who will be genuinely interested in your welfare. For they all look after their own affairs, not those of Jesus Christ. But you know his proved worth, how as a child (serves) with (his) father, so he served with me in the gospel" (Phil. 2:19-22). Indeed, Timothy was the apostle's "beloved child" (II Tim. 1:2).

As to his unswerving *faithfulness* and unwavering readiness for the sake of the gospel to sacrifice whatever may have looked like his own immediate interests, this is evident not only from the passage just quoted but also from the fact that none of Paul's companions is mentioned as often and is with him as constantly as is Timothy. In the very last chapter from prison the great apostle writes: "Do your utmost to come to me soon . . . do your utmost to come before winter" (II Tim. 4:9, 21). Paul knew that he could depend on Timothy, just as he knew that he could depend on Luke (II Tim. 4:11).

This dependability is also evident from the fact that in spite of his *youth* – he was Paul's junior by several years (cf. I Tim. 4:12; II Tim. 2:22) –, his natural *reserve* and *timidity* (I Cor. 16:10; II Tim. 1:7), and his *"frequent ailments"* (I Tim. 5:23), he was willing to leave his home to accompany the apostle on dangerous missionary journeys, to be sent on difficult and even perilous errands, and to remain to the very end a worthy servant of Jesus Christ (Rom. 16:21; see also on I Thess. 3:2).

Timothy is first mentioned in Acts 16:1, from which passage it may probably be inferred that he was an inhabitant of Lystra (cf. Acts 20:4). He was the offspring of a "mixed marriage": a Greek pagan father and a devout Jewish mother, Eunice (Acts 16:1; II Tim. 1:5). From the days of his childhood he had been instructed in the sacred writings of the Old Testament (II Tim. 3:15). In all probability Paul, on his first missionary journey (about 47 A. D.), had been the means of Timothy's conversion, so that from that day on he could be referred to as Paul's (spiritual) "child" (I Cor. 4:17; I Tim. 1:2; II Tim. 1:2). Hence, it is not strange to read that he was acquainted with the persecutions and sufferings which the missionaries had experienced on this *first* journey (II Tim. 3:11), that is, *before* Timothy himself had joined Paul in active work. Though Paul was Timothy's spiritual father, it is not at all improbable that grandmother

---

[16] Cf. A. Sizoo, *Uit De Wereld van het Nieuwe Testament,* p. 190.

Lois and mother Eunice, whose conversion to the Christian faith preceded that of Timothy (II Tim. 1:5), co-operated very effectively to bring about this happy event.

When Paul and Silas, on the second journey, came to Derbe and Lystra, Timothy responded favorably to the request of the apostle to join the group in missionary labors. This must have occurred about the year 51. From Acts 16:2 we learn that he was "well spoken of" by the people of his own community. Because it was well-known that Timothy's father was a Greek, so that the young man's influence among the Jews would be reduced to almost zero unless something were done to bring out clearly his own devotion to the sacred writings of the covenant people, he was, accordingly, circumcised (Acts 16:3). In all probability another important event also took place at this time: by the elders of the local church (which had been established and organized on the first journey) Timothy was now ordained for his new task, Paul himself taking part in this solemn "laying on of hands" (Acts 14:23; and see on I Tim. 1:18; 4:14; II Tim. 1:6).

Along with the other missionaries Timothy subsequently crossed over into Europe, Luke having by this time joined the company. We have already stated our reasons for believing that though Luke stayed behind at Philippi (contrast "we" in Acts 16:11, 13 with "they" in Acts 17:1), Timothy went along with Paul and Silas to (or at least soon joined them at) Thessalonica (see N.T.C. on I and II Thessalonians, p. 5). He also helped the others in the next place to which they came, namely, Berea, where he and Silas were left behind in order to give spiritual support to the infant church, while Paul himself, escorted by some of his friends, made his way to the coast and finally reached Athens (Acts 17:10-15). Acting upon the request of Paul, Timothy left Berea and found the apostle while the latter was still in Athens (I Thess. 3:1, 2). He was sent back to Thessalonica for the purpose of strengthening and encouraging the brothers there (see N.T.C. on I Thess. 3:1, 2). After Paul had left Athens and had begun his labors in Corinth, both Silas and Timothy "came down from Macedonia" to rejoin the apostle (Acts 18:1, 5; see on I Thess. 3:6).

At Corinth Timothy carried on his missionary labors with Paul and Silas. Hence (and because he was well-known in Thessalonica) his name is associated with theirs in the addresses of the two epistles to the Thessalonians, sent from Corinth (see on I Thess. 1:1; II Thess. 1:1).

On the third missionary journey (53/54-57/58 A. D.) Timothy is with the apostle during the latter's lengthy ministry at Ephesus. From here he is sent to Macedonia and to Corinth (Acts 19:21, 22; I Cor. 4:17; 16:10). As Timothy went by the land route – i.e., to Corinth by way of Macedonia – Paul expected that his fellow-worker would arrive in Corinth after I Corinthians had reached its destination.

When Paul arrives in Macedonia, Timothy has rejoined him, as is evident from the fact that his name is associated with that of the apostle in the letter which was now sent to Corinth (II Cor. 1:1). It is also clear that the assistant and partner accompanied the apostle to Corinth (Rom. 16:21), and that together with others he is with Paul on his return to Macedonia (Acts 20:3, 4), and is waiting for him at Troas (Acts 20:5). He was probably also with Paul in Jerusalem (I Cor. 16:3).

For a little while we lose sight of Timothy, but during Paul's first imprisonment at Rome the two are in close contact with each other again, as is evident from Phil. 1:1; Col. 1:1; Philemon 1:1. When the apostle expects to be released in the very near future (Phil. 2:24), he tells the Philippians that he hopes to send Timothy to them soon (Phil. 2:19).

Again there is a gap in the information that has come down to us. The next time we hear of Timothy he is at Ephesus, where Paul has joined him. The apostle, on leaving, asks Timothy to remain at this place (I Tim. 1:3). While there Timothy one day receives the letter which we now call I Timothy.

Many months pass, during which nothing is heard with reference to Timothy. Then another letter arrives, in which Paul, writing from Rome as a prisoner facing death, urges his friend to do his best to come to him before winter (II Tim. 4:9, 21). Whether the two ever actually saw each other's face again is not recorded. (The enigmatical statement regarding Timothy in Heb. 13:23 cannot be discussed here.) That Timothy *tried* to see the apostle may be taken for granted. It is in line with his entire character. Though he is hesitant and reserved, yet his love for Paul and even more for the Lord Jesus Christ and for his cause always win out in the end. He may *shrink* for a moment (cf. I Cor. 16:10), he never *refuses*. His is a character to be admired. In his becoming diffidence the dynamic aggressiveness of Paul finds its true counterpart. It is not surprising that Paul and Timothy are friends!

Timothy and Titus have in common unwavering loyalty to the cause of the Gospel, willingness to be sent on difficult missions, high regard for their friend and superior, Paul. Yet, in one respect the two differ. Titus is more of a leader; Timothy is a follower. Titus is the type of man who is able not only to take orders but also to go ahead of his own accord (II Cor. 8:16, 17). Timothy needs a little prodding (II Tim. 1:6), though here the emphasis must fall on "a little" and not on "prodding." Titus is resourceful, a man of initiative in a good cause. One finds in him something of the aggressiveness of Paul. Timothy is co-operative, a man who shows this spirit even when such co-operation requires him to do things which run counter to his natural shyness. That is the way these two characters are exhibited in the Art Gallery of Holy Writ.

Now as to Titus, nowhere in the book of Acts does his name appear, but elsewhere in the New Testament it is found thirteen times: twice in Galatians (2:1; 2:3), once in II Tim. (5:10), once in Titus (1:4), and no less than nine times in II Corinthians (2:13; 7:6; 7:13; 7:14; 8:6; 8:16; 8:23; 12:18; and again 12:18). Yet the first *implied* reference to Titus is found in the book of Acts, though there his name is not mentioned. By comparing Acts 15:2 ("some of the others") with Gal. 2:1, 3 ("taking Titus along with me . . . even Titus who was with me") we learn that when, after the first missionary journey, Paul and Barnabas were sent to Jerusalem in order to help the church in reaching a conclusion regarding the question whether Christians from among the Gentiles should be circumcised, they were accompanied by "some of the others," among whom was "Titus." In all probability Titus was one of the apostle's converts, being called his "genuine child in a common faith" (Titus 1:4). Some are of the opinion that Syrian Antioch was his home and that he had been converted during the signally blessed gospel-campaign conducted at that place by Paul and Barnabas (Acts 11:19-26; cf. Acts 14:26; 15:2; Gal. 2:1, 3), but this is no more than a plausible conjecture.

Titus, then, becomes a person of great importance for the progress of the Christian faith. He is taken along to "the apostles and elders" at Jerusalem as *a test case,* a definite challenge to the Judaizers. Titus is a Greek (Gal. 2:3), *both* of his parents being Gentiles (contrast Timothy whose mother was a Jewess). Naturally the Judaistic party at Jerusalem demands that he be circumcised. But Paul does not yield even for a moment (Gal. 2:5), and the matter in dispute is decided in favor of the free admission of Gentiles into the church, solely on the basis of faith in Christ, without being required to keep the Jewish law (Acts 15:13-29). The significance of this victory for Christian liberty and for the progress of Christianity can hardly be over-estimated.

Nothing further is heard about Titus until Paul's third missionary journey is reached (probable date 53/54 – 57/58). During this journey Paul's faithful helper is sent to Corinth on more than one occasion, though commentators differ with respect to the question whether he was sent two or three times.[17] Probably the simplest reconstruction of his journeys is also the best. I shall assume that on this third missionary journey Titus made only two trips to Corinth, one *from Ephesus* (was he then the bearer of I Corinthians?), and one *from Macedonia,* when he carried II Corinthians to its destination.

Returning now to that first trip (Ephesus to Corinth), it was Titus who was charged with the difficult and delicate task of solving "the Corinthian

---

[17] This is not the proper place to discuss the question in detail. It involves exegesis of such passages as II Cor. 2:4; 8:6, 10.

Situation" (party-strife, fornication, etc.; see I Cor. 1:11; 5:6; 16:17). True, his arrival in Corinth seems to have been followed almost immediately by that of Timothy, but nothing at all is reported with reference to the latter's accomplishments in that city. The Corinthians were told, however, to see to it that when Timothy arrived, he would be with them "without fear" (I Cor. 16:10). As to Titus, the apostle had expected that he would meet this returning emissary at Troas. When Paul did not find him there, his mind had no rest. So he departed from Troas and crossed over into Europe (Macedonia, II Cor. 2:13). Here his spirit was refreshed and his heart filled with joy when he not only met Titus but heard from his lips a report which, *on the whole,* was favorable (II Cor. 7:6, 13, 14).

The mission which Titus had been called to perform had been successful to a considerable extent. It seems that at Corinth he had acted on the principle that the best way to overcome evil is "with good." So, while there he had made a beginning of setting in motion again the work of collecting funds for the needy saints at Jerusalem. This important work, which had been started several months earlier (II Cor. 8:10), had been lagging of late. Titus in his own dynamic manner had given fresh impetus to it.

As already indicated, the report which Titus brought was *not altogether* favorable. Paul's enemies had not taken kindly to the rebuke which they had received. They assailed Paul's apostleship, and charged that he was fickle because he had changed his traveling-plans (II Cor. 1:15-24); that he displayed a boastful courage which veiled an inner cowardice; and that even when he preached the gospel without remuneration his motives were not pure. Accordingly, from Macedonia (Philippi?) Paul now writes II Corinthians, which is delivered by (the same man who brought I Corinthians to its destination? namely) Titus. He was the proper man to deal with a difficult situation. At the same time he would be enabled to complete the work of collecting for the Jerusalem poor. This time Titus is accompanied by two others, one of whom was a noted preacher (II Cor. 8:16-24). Titus, true to his character, was eager to go on his mission (II Cor. 8:16, 17). In *him* one discovers no hesitancy.

There follows a long interval (perhaps from about 56 to about 63 A. D.) during which we hear nothing of Titus. The next time his name is mentioned, he is in charge of a church (or churches) in Crete. Paul, having been set at liberty from his first Roman imprisonment and being now on an eastward journey, has left him there in order to carry out the mandate described in Titus 1:5 (see on that passage). We shall meet Titus again (see points 2, 5, 6, and 10, pp. 39, 40).

A comparison between I Tim. 4:12 ("Let no one despise your youth") and Titus 2:15 ("Exhort and reprove with all authority. Let no one despise thee") would seem to indicate that Titus was older than Timothy. He loved the Corinthians. He loved his Lord. He loved the work of the

Lord, and gave ample evidence of this in the spontaneous manner in which he shouldered his task at Corinth. He breathed the spirit of Paul, and followed closely in his steps (II Cor. 12:18). He was original, tactful, courageous, loyal, a close and trusted friend of the great apostle, the latter's true representative in the cause of Christ.

IV. What Is Their Historical Background and Purpose?

It has been established (see pp. 23-27) that all the historical evidence points in the direction of Paul's release from his first Roman imprisonment. Where did he go immediately after his release? We simply do not know with any degree of certainty. The Pastorals, to be sure, imply a number of journeys, but these are merely "links" which can be joined together in ever so many different ways. Did Paul go *at once* to Spain? Did he go from Rome to Philippi, and from there to Ephesus, as is held by some, or vice versa (Rome – Ephesus – Philippi), as is held by others? Just *when* did he travel to Spain? Did Timothy ask Paul for permission to leave Ephesus, which permission was refused? If so, where was the apostle when this request came? Was he somewhere on his way back from Spain to Macedonia, as some have supposed? Or – and this to me seems preferable – should we drop the entire idea of *a request* coming from Timothy, and should we perhaps place *Paul at Ephesus with Timothy,* when the younger man was urged to remain at his post, while the apostle goes on his way to Europe? Similar questions can easily be added. Among the many possible combinations the following scheme is perhaps as good as any. It has the advantage of suggesting a natural line of travel. See a good Bible-map of the Roman world as it was in Paul's day (I suggest W.H.A.B., Plate XV); also the excellent map in the December, 1956, issue of *The National Geographic Magazine,* the map which bears the title "Lands of the Bible Today." *I emphasize, however, that certainty is entirely lacking:*

1. Immediately after his release Paul sends Timothy to Philippi with this good news (Phil. 2:19-23). The date 63 A. D. cannot be off very far. After July 19-24 of the year 64 A. D. (the burning of Rome) release would have been very improbable.

2. Paul himself starts on his journey toward Asia Minor, and on the way to that destination leaves Titus on the island of Crete to bring to completion the organization of the church (or churches) which had been established there (cf. Acts 2:11; Titus 1:5).

3. The apostle arrives at Ephesus, travels on until he reaches Colosse just as he had intended (Philem. 22), and returns to Ephesus.

4. Here he is joined by Timothy who brings news from the congregation at Philippi (see 1 above). On leaving, Paul asks Timothy to remain at Ephesus, which was in need of his ministry (I Tim. 1:3, 4).

5. Paul himself goes to Macedonia, just as he had planned (Phil. 2:24; I Tim. 1:3). He hopes to return to Ephesus shortly, but rather *expects* that his absence may be prolonged (I Tim. 3:14, 15). From Macedonia (Philippi?) he writes two epistles which resemble each other very closely: I Timothy and Titus. In his letter to Titus he requests that beloved brother to meet him at Nicopolis (Tit. 3:12).

6. Accordingly, the apostle journeys to Nicopolis (in Epirus), located on the east coast of the Ionian Sea. Here he spends the winter (Tit. 3:12) and is joined by Titus.

7. Paul journeys to Spain (Rom. 15:24); according to some "taking Titus with him," but of this there is no hint anywhere. The mere possibility that, if Paul went to Spain at this time, Titus went along must be granted. As to Titus, there is nothing definite until we reach II Tim. 4:10 (see Number 10).

8. Having returned from Spain, Paul proceeds to Asia Minor (see 5 above), and leaves Trophimus sick at Miletus, south of Ephesus (II Tim. 4:20). Did the apostle also meet Timothy again, and did the tearful separation (II Tim. 1:4) take place at this time or very shortly afterward?

9. At Troas he visits Carpus, at whose home he leaves his cloak (II Tim. 4:13). By way of Corinth, where Erastus remained (II Tim. 4:20) he goes to Rome. He is rearrested. (Where the arrest occurred – Troas, Corinth, Rome, or elsewhere – is not known.) Cruel Nero is reigning. This is the monster who had murdered his step-brother, *his own mother,* his wife (Octavia), his tutor (Seneca), and many others. When Rome was burned in the year 64, the people accused Nero of having set the city on fire. He sought to turn attention away from himself and placed the blame on the Christians. Frightful was the carnival of blood which followed.

10. Accordingly, Paul, having returned from Spain, no longer enjoyed a measure of political protection. His second Roman imprisonment is severe and brief (II Tim. 1:16, 17; 2:9). Luke only is with him. Demas has forsaken him, having fallen in love with "the present world," and has departed for Thessalonica. Crescens has gone either to Galatia or to Gallia (Gaul), Titus to Dalmatia (see on II Tim. 4:10, 11). Urging Timothy to come to him quickly, he asks him to take Mark with him. These details are found in II Timothy, the letter which was written when death was already staring the apostle in the face (II Tim. 4:6-11). He is condemned to death and beheaded on the Ostian Way, about three miles outside of the capital. Whether Timothy and Mark reached Rome before the apostle's death we do not know.

Let us now return to 4 and 5 above. At Ephesus the Judaists were spreading their strange doctrines, placing great stress upon such things as endless genealogies, profane and old wives' fables, and posing as teachers of the law (I Tim. 1:4, 7; 4:7). According to many interpreters – and they may be right – these errorists also assumed that matter was evil or at least the seat of evil, and therefore recognized only a spiritual resurrection (II Tim. 2:18). Soon they would also prohibit marriage and the use of certain foods (I Tim. 4:3). We have already shown that the errors condemned were partly present, partly future, partly present and future (see above, p. 21).

In addition, to advocating false doctrine and ethics, these sinister teachers (and perhaps others with them) seem to have made it necessary for Paul to lay down some very "plain rules" regarding proper conduct at *public worship* (see especially chapter 2). The ladies also stood in need of special instruction with respect to this point.

The situation was really serious. This becomes evident when two additional facts are borne in mind: a. from such passages as I Tim. 1:6, 20; 3:3, 6; 5:17-25 it may probably be assumed that prominent church-members – including some with a "superiority-complex" ("puffed up" persons) – were among the errorists; and b. Timothy himself, as we have seen, was by nature of the very opposite disposition. He seems to have been a man with an "inferiority-complex." For *such* a man to cope with *such* a situation was, indeed, difficult.

Hence, about the year 63 Paul, having recently departed from Ephesus, where he had left Timothy, and being now in Macedonia (I Tim. 1:3), tells Timothy *how to administer the affairs of the church.* Specifically, he writes in order:

(1) To bolster the spirit of Timothy, reminding him of the "gift" which he had received (see on I Tim. 4:14), of his "good confession" (see on 6:12), and of "the deposit" which had been entrusted to him (see on 6:20).

(2) To impart guidance in the critical conflict against soul-destroying errors that were being spread in the church at Ephesus, and to exhort Timothy to continue in the "sound doctrine" (1:3-11; 1:18-20; ch. 4; ch. 6). Such guidance would be all the more necessary if the apostle's absence should be prolonged (see on I Tim. 3:14, 15). In connection with this battle against the spread of error, stress is laid on the importance of *proper organization:* choosing the right kind of leaders (especially elders and deacons), and of admonishing them if they go astray (ch. 3; ch. 5).

(3) To give directions for proper conduct during *public worship* (see on ch. 2).

Returning once more to point 5, we note that Paul, now in Macedonia (Philippi?), also writes to Titus, whom he had left at Crete and whom he wishes to meet at Nicopolis. The reputation of the Cretans was none too good. The need of thorough-going *sanctification* in congregational, individual, family, and public life had to be stressed here even more than elsewhere. The elders who are to be appointed must be "blameless" (1:5, 6). The mouths of unruly individuals, vain talkers and deceivers, must be stopped (1:10). People (especially church-members!) must be taught to abstain from worldly lusts and to live moderately and righteously and godly in the present world, in the expectation of the Redeemer's glorious appearing (2:11-14). In public life they should be obedient to the authorities and should deport themselves properly toward all (3:1, 2). Impenitent trouble-makers should be disciplined (3:10). On the other hand, sincere gospel-workers (such as Zenas and Apollos), whose itinerary would include Crete, and who probably carried with them Paul's letter addressed to Titus, must receive every assistance (3:13).

Accordingly, the letter to Titus was written with this threefold purpose in mind:

(1) To urge Titus to come to Paul at Nicopolis, as soon as a substitute has taken over the work in Crete (3:12).

(2) To speed on their way Zenas the law-expert and Apollos the eloquent evangelist (3:13).

(3) To give directions for the promotion of the spirit of *sanctification* in congregational, individual, family, and social relationships.

Of these three purpose-items the last covers by far the most territory.

When we leave I Timothy and Titus and turn to II Timothy, we immediately notice that the entire atmosphere has changed. When the apostle wrote I Timothy and Titus, he was a free man, able to make traveling-plans. When he writes II Timothy, he is a prisoner, facing death. Crete (Tit. 1:5), Ephesus (I Tim. 1:3), Macedonia (I Tim. 1:3; cf. Phil. 2:24), and Nicopolis (Tit. 3:12) are the places mentioned by name in I Timothy and Titus (taken together), and they form an easily traceable route on the map. Though no one knows whether the apostle actually journeyed to these places *in that order,* every one will have to admit that such a line of travel is natural. Miletus (II Tim. 4:20), Troas (II Tim. 4:13), Corinth (II Tim. 4:20; cf. Rom. 16:23), are the places which Paul visited on the journey(s) presupposed in II Timothy, until he reached Rome and final imprisonment (cf. II Tim. 1:8; 4:6). Here also, *if* the order in which we have arranged these "stations" is correct, the route is logical. It is therefore natural to assume that the journey to Spain intervened between these two courses of travel, that is, between the route presupposed in I Timothy and Titus, on the one hand, and the route that is probably indicated in II Timothy, on the other.[18]

For the reason given it is probably incorrect to say that Tit. 3:12 and II

---

[18] See also R. C. H. Lenski, *op. cit.,* pp. 473-480.

Tim. 4:21 refer to the same "winter," and then to date Titus accordingly, bringing it as close as possible to II Timothy. It must be borne in mind that the apostle had made definite plans as to the place where he, as a *free man,* would spend "the winter" referred to in Tit. 3:12 (namely, at Nicopolis). No such plans were possible with respect to the place where Paul, *the prisoner,* would spend "the winter" indicated in II Tim. 4:21. These two winters are not the same! When II Timothy is written, the entire picture has changed. See the situation as described under point 10 above (p. 40). *This* is the winter of A. D. 65 or 66 or 67. It is Paul's *last* winter on earth. The great apostle, writing from his prison in the world's metropolis, and being in doubt whether his assistant will be able to reach Rome before his death, admonishes Timothy that, whatever happens, he must keep clinging to *the sound doctrine* and must defend it unceasingly against every adversary.

Though II Timothy does not state where *Timothy* was when it was written, yet there are several passages which point to Ephesus. Thus Paul says that Timothy knows that "all who are in Asia" had turned away from the apostle (1:15). If the one addressed was laboring in Ephesus, which was in "Asia," it is understandable that he would know about this situation. Similarly, Paul writes that Timothy "knows better" than the apostle, or "knows very well," how many services Onesiphorus had rendered, and takes for granted that Timothy "at Ephesus" (1:18), is able to convey Paul's greetings to the family of this "profit-bringer" (4:19). There is another reference to Ephesus in 4:12: "But Tychicus I am sending to Ephesus." Moreover, if Timothy is living in Ephesus, it will not be too difficult for him to "bring with him the cloak" which Paul had "left *at Troas* with Carpus" (4:13). And we would not be at all surprised to find Priscilla (or Prisca) and Aquila (4:19) back again in Ephesus (though the place is not mentioned), where they had been living previously (Acts 18:18, 19, 24, 26; cf. I Cor. 16:19). It is true that subsequent to their first stay in Ephesus they had returned to Rome (Rom. 16:3), but with a persecution of Christians raging fiercely in Rome it is not strange that they had again left the capital. Once before, and for a somewhat similar reason, they had departed from Italy (Acts 18:2).

One additional item in the circumstantial evidence linking Timothy with Ephesus when this letter was written is the nature of the heresy which is here condemned (see on II Tim. 2:14-18). To a certain extent it resembles that which was exposed in I Timothy (addressed to Timothy while he was *at Ephesus,* I Tim. 1:3).

We may suppose, then, that Timothy has not yet left *Ephesus, where error and persecution of believers are raging* (1:8; 2:3, 12, 14-18, 23; 3:8, 12).

Accordingly, Paul's purpose in writing II Timothy may be summarized as follows:

(1) To urge Timothy to come to Rome as soon as possible in view of the apostle's impending departure from this life (4:9, 21; cf. 4:6-8).

(2) To admonish him to keep clinging to the *sound doctrine,* defending it against all error, and enduring hardship as a good soldier.

This second item is characteristic of the entire letter.

Commentary
on
I Timothy

Outline of I Timothy

Theme: *The Apostle Paul, Writing to Timothy, Gives Directions For the Administration of the Church*

Chapter I

The Apostle Paul

A. Salutes Timothy.
B. Repeats his order that Timothy remain at Ephesus to combat the error of those who refuse to see *their sinful condition* in the light of God's holy law, and who pretend to be law-experts.
C. By contrast, thanks God for having made him, *"chief of sinners,"* a minister of the gospel.

Chapter II

Directions with respect to Public Worship

A. Prayers must be made "in behalf of all men."
B. In connection with public worship both the men and the women must behave properly:
   1. The men, in every place of public worship, must lift up holy hands;
   2. The women, in getting ready "to go to church," must dress becomingly, and at the place of public worship must show that they understand and have accepted their divinely ordained position.

Chapter III

Directions with respect to the Institution of the Offices

A. Incentive for becoming an overseer: the glorious character of the work. Directions regarding the necessary qualifications of overseers.
B. Directions regarding the necessary qualifications of deacons and of women who assist them.
   Incentive for faithful performance of the task of deacons and of deacons' assistants.
C. The reasons for conveying these instructions in written form.

Chapter IV

Directions with respect to Apostasy

A. Description of this apostasy and proof of its dangerous character.
B. How Timothy should deal with it.

Chapters V and VI

Directions with respect to Certain Definite Groups and Individuals

Chapter V
- A. Old(er) men, young(er) men, old(er) women, young(er) women
- B. Widows in distress
- C. Widows engaged in spiritual work
- D. Elders and prospective elders

Chapter VI
- E. Slaves
- F. Novelty-teachers who aspire to fame and riches
- G. Timothy himself ("Keep the commission")
- H. People who are rich in terms of this present age
- I. Timothy himself ("Guard the deposit")

Outline of Chapter 1

Theme: *The Apostle Paul, Writing to Timothy, Gives Directions For the Administration of the Church*

The Apostle Paul

1:1, 2 A. Salutes Timothy

1:3-11; 18-20 B. Repeats his order that Timothy remain at Ephesus to combat the error of those who refuse to see *their sinful condition* in the light of God's holy law, and who pretend to be law-experts;

1:12-17 C. By contrast, thanks God for having made him — *"chief of sinners"* — a minister of the gospel.

CHAPTER I

I TIMOTHY 1:1

1 1 Paul, an apostle of Christ Jesus by order of God our Savior and Christ
Jesus our Hope, 2 to Timothy (my) genuine child in faith; grace, mercy,
peace from God the Father and Christ Jesus our Lord.

1:1, 2

1. As was customary, the sender mentions his own name first; then the name of the person addressed. Hence, **Paul . . .** to Timothy. In a world held together politically by Rome and culturally by Greece it was natural that the writer should use his Greek-Roman name *Paul* instead of his Jewish name *Saul.* (For further details on the meaning and use of these names see N.T.C. on I Thess. 1:1.)

Perhaps in order to make it easier for Timothy to carry out the instructions which Paul is about to give him, and also in order to add weight to the words of encouragement contained in this letter, the writer adds to his name the words **an apostle of Christ Jesus.**

Timothy needs to know that this letter is not just a substitute for a friendly, confidential chat, a tête-a-tête; even though its tone is naturally very cordial, for a friend is indeed writing to a friend. The letter, however, rises above the purely human level. The writer is a friend, to be sure, but also an apostle of Christ Jesus.

Now in the broadest sense an *apostle* (ἀπόστολος a term derived from a verb which means *to send, to send away on a commission, to dispatch:* ἀποστέλλω) is any*thing* which is sent or by which something is sent, or any*one* who is sent or by whom a message is sent. Thus, in classical Greek the term could refer to a naval expedition, and "an apostolic boat" was a cargo-vessel. In later Judaism "apostles" were envoys sent out by the Jerusalem patriarchate to collect tribute from the Jews of the Dispersion. In the New Testament the term takes on a distinctly religious sense. In its widest meaning it refers to any gospel-messenger, anyone who is sent on a spiritual mission, anyone who in that capacity represents his Sender and brings the message of salvation. Thus used, Barnabas, Epaphroditus, Apollos, Silvanus, and Timothy are all called "apostles" (Acts 14:14; I Cor. 4:6, 9; Phil. 2:25; I Thess. 2:6, cf. 1:1; and see also I Cor. 15:7). They represent God's cause, though in doing so they may also represent certain definite churches whose "apostles" they are called (cf. II Cor. 8:23). Thus Paul and Barnabas represent the church of Antioch (Acts 13:1, 2), and Epaphroditus is Philippi's "apostle" (Phil. 2:25). Under this broader connotation some would include also Andronicus, Junius (Rom. 16:7), and James, the Lord's brother (Gal. 1:19), but the exact meaning of the passages in which, together with the term "apostles," these men are mentioned is disputed.

But in determining the meaning of the term "apostle" here in I Tim. 1:1 it will be far better to study those passages in which it is used in its more usual sense. Occurring ten times in the Gospels, almost thirty times in Acts, more than thirty times in the Pauline epistles (including the five occurrences in the Pastorals), and eight times in the rest of the New Testament, it generally (but note important exception in Heb. 3:1 and the exceptions already indicated) refers to the Twelve and Paul.

In that fullest, deepest sense a man is an apostle *for life* and *wherever he goes.* He is clothed with *the authority of* the One who sent him, and that authority concerns both *doctrine and life.* The idea, found in much present-day religious literature, according to which an apostle has no real office, no authority, lacks scriptural support. Anyone can see this for himself by studying such passages as Matt. 16:19; 18:18; 28:18, 19 (note the connection!); John 20:23; I Cor. 5:3-5; II Cor. 10:8; I Thess. 2:6.

Paul, then, was an apostle in the richest sense of the term. His apostleship was the same as that of the Twelve. Hence, we speak of "the Twelve and Paul." Paul even stresses the fact that the risen Savior had appeared to *him* just as truly as he had appeared to Cephas (I Cor. 15:5, 8). That same Savior had assigned to him a task so broad and universal that his entire life was henceforth to be occupied with it (Acts 26:16-18).

Yet Paul was definitely *not* one of the Twelve. The idea that the disciples had made a mistake when they had chosen Matthias to take the place of Judas, and that the Holy Spirit later designated Paul as the real substitute, hardly merits consideration (see Acts 1:24). *But if he was not one of the Twelve yet was invested with the same office, what was the relation between him and the Twelve?* The answer is probably suggested by Acts 1:8 and Gal. 2:7-9. On the basis of these passages this answer can be formulated thus: The Twelve, by recognizing Paul as having been specially called to minister to the Gentiles, were in effect carrying out through him their calling to the Gentiles.

The characteristics of full apostleship – the apostleship of the Twelve and Paul – were as follows:

In the first place, the apostles have been chosen, called, and sent forth by Christ himself. They have received their commission directly from him (John 6:70; 13:18; 15:16, 19; Gal. 1:6).

Secondly, they are qualified for their tasks by Jesus, and have been ear-

and-eye witnesses of his words and deeds; specifically, they are the witnesses of his resurrection (Acts 1:8, 22; I Cor. 9:1; 15:8; Gal. 1:12; Eph. 3:2-8; I John 1:1-3).

Thirdly, they have been endowed in a special measure with the Holy Spirit, and it is this Holy Spirit who leads them into all the truth (Matt. 10:20; John 14:26; 15:26; 16:7-14; 20:22; I Cor. 2:10-13; 7:40; I Thess. 4:8).

Fourthly, God blesses their work, confirming its value by means of signs and miracles, and giving them much fruit upon their labors (Matt. 10:1, 8; Acts 2:43; 3:2; 5:12-16; Rom. 15:18, 19; II Cor. 12:12; I Cor. 9:2; Gal. 2:8).

Fifthly, their office is not restricted to a local church, neither does it extend over a short period of time; on the contrary, it is for the entire church and for life (Acts 26:16-18; II Tim. 4:7, 8).

Now Paul is here called an apostle *of Christ Jesus.*[19] He belongs to Christ, is sent and commissioned by him, and has accordingly received his authority from him. It is, in the final analysis, Christ himself who binds and makes loose. It is he who is operating in Paul. Paul's message is Christ's message. Paul's authority is Christ's delegated authority.

The personal name *Jesus,* meaning either "he will certainly save" (cf. Matt. 1:21), or "Jehovah is salvation," is preceded by the official designation *Christ* (Anointed), showing that this Person to whom Paul owes his apostleship was *ordained* and *qualified* by God to carry out the task of providing salvation for his people, a salvation which Paul, as apostle, takes joy in

---

[19] The question is asked, "Why Christ Jesus" instead of "Jesus Christ"? It is probably correct to say that no special significance attaches to the exact order in which these two names occur. It would seem that in the New Testament there are about 127 instances in which the order is "Jesus Christ," and about 91 cases in which it is "Christ Jesus." In Paul's epistles the order "Christ Jesus," though not so prominent at first, gradually takes over, so that in the end the order "Jesus Christ" becomes the exception and "Christ Jesus" the rule. In the earlier epistles (Galatians, I Thessalonians, II Thessalonians; I Corinthians, II Corinthians, and Romans) the figures are (or are approximately): 32 instances of "Christ Jesus" to 54 instances of "Jesus Christ." In the epistles of the first Roman imprisonment — Ephesians, Colossians, Philemon, and Philippians — they are: 31 "Christ Jesus" to 13 "Jesus Christ." In the last-written epistles, the Pastorals: 25 "Christ Jesus" to only 5 "Jesus Christ." To account for this phenomenon it has been suggested that at first the Aramaic "Jesus, the Christ" was rendered into the Greek rather literally, supplying the order in which the proper name Jesus is followed by the appelative Christ, indicating his office. After a while the term Christ began to be felt increasingly as a second proper name next to Jesus. Being now on a par with the name Jesus, the flexible character of the Greek language made it possible to reverse the order; hence, "Christ Jesus" or "Jesus Christ," with no difference in meaning. See on the entire subject S. Vernon McCasland, "Christ Jesus," *JBL* 65 (December, 1946), 377-383. We would add that to the early church the designation "Christ" was never a "mere" name, meaningless as so often among us. Whenever it was pronounced, his followers thought of him as the Anointed. One might compare the name "Christ Jesus" to the somewhat similar one "President Eisenhower." In both cases the designation of office is followed by the personal name.

proclaiming. (Further details on the meaning of "Jesus" and "Christ" are found in N.T.C. on I Thess. 1:1.)

No usurper was Paul. Had he not been appointed to be an apostle, he would never have been one. But he had been *appointed,* and this appointment had come not from men but directly from God. It is for this reason that he calls himself an apostle of Christ Jesus **by order of God our Savior and Christ Jesus our Hope.** It was God in Christ who had separated him from his mother's womb and through his grace had called him (Gal. 1:15); had chosen him in order that he might make known God's name before the Gentiles and kings and children of Israel (Acts 9:15); and had sent him to distant nations (Acts 22:21).

Paul says, *"God* our Savior" here, also in I Tim. 2:3; 4:10; Titus 1:3; 2:10; 3:4; but elsewhere he uses "Savior" with reference to "Christ" (Eph. 5:23; Phil. 3:20; II Tim. 1:10; Titus 1:4; 2:13; 3:6). Yet the expression *"God* our Savior" in the Pastorals but nowhere in the earlier epistles does not mean that Paul cannot have written the Pastorals. In fact, that line of reasoning, were it valid, would mean that an unknown author wrote I Timothy (here the Savior is *God*); that Paul wrote II Timothy (here the Savior is *Christ*); and would leave Titus a question-mark (here the Savior is both *God* and *Christ*).

The fact that here in the Pastorals the name Savior is frequently applied to God is, after all, not at all surprising, for even in his earlier epistles Paul frequently ascribes the work of *saving* man to "God"; for example, "It was *God's* good-pleasure through the foolishness of the preaching *to save* those who believe" (I Cor. 1:21); "but *God* . . . made us alive together with Christ . . . for by grace *have* y o u *been saved* through faith; and that not of yourselves, it is *the gift of God"* (Eph. 2:4, 5, 8); "y o u r *salvation,* and that *from God"* (Phil. 1:28). To "God" he also ascribes the distinct acts in the program of salvation. It is God who spared not his Son but delivered him up for us all. It is God who sets forth his Son as a propitiation for our sins. It is he who commends his love toward us. It is God who blesses us with every spiritual blessing in the heavenly places in Christ. Foreknowledge, foreordination, calling, justification, glorification are all ascribed to *him.* It is *he* who chose us. It is *he* who causes the gospel to be proclaimed. It is *he* who bestows his grace upon us. Faith is *his* gift (Rom. 1:16; 3:24-26; 4:17; 5:8, 15; 8:3, 4, 11, 28-30, 31-33; 9:10, 11; 15:5, 13; I Cor. 1:9, 26-31; 15:57; II Cor. 2:14; 4:7; 5:5, 8, 19, 20, 21; 9:15; Gal. 1:15; 3:26; 4:4-7; Eph. 1:3-5; 2:4, 5; Phil. 2:13; 3:9; Col. 3:3). In view of all this we can almost say that it would have been strange if somewhere in his epistles the apostle would not have called *God* "our Savior." [20] Calling God "our Savior" is

[20] See the more detailed discussion of the concept Soter (Savior, Deliverer, Preserver) in connection with I Tim. 4:10.

entirely proper. And since for Paul God ever saves *through Christ,* verse 1 is also a fitting prelude to verse 15: "Christ Jesus came into the world sinners to save."

Amid circumstances which to man might seem *hopeless* Christ Jesus is pictured as "our Hope," that is, the very foundation for our earnest yearning, our confident expectation, and our patient waiting for the manifestation of salvation in all its fulness (cf. 1:16; 6:14-16, 19). It is he who made this hope possible and actual. It is he who revitalizes it from day to day. The Source as well as the Object of this hope is he (cf. Acts 28:20; Col. 1:27).

2. To Timothy (my) genuine child in faith.

Apostolic authority and tender love are beautifully blended, for the apostle of Christ Jesus calls the addressee "Timothy (my) genuine child in faith." Though some commentators write at great length in order to prove that the omission of the possessive *my* in the original indicates that Paul was thinking of Timothy not as *his* child but as *God's* child, the effort must be considered futile. The omission of the possessive in such a case is not at all unusual; and II Tim. 2:1, where it does occur, surely indicates that here in I Tim. 1:2 and elsewhere (see verse 18; also II Tim. 1:2) it is implied. Timothy was Paul's *child* (Greek τέκνον from τίκτω to beget, bring forth), because it was to the apostle as a means in God's hand, that he owed his spiritual life (cf. I Cor. 4:15; Gal. 4:19). The great change in Timothy's life had taken place on Paul's first missionary journey, as has been explained on p. 34. If we are careful to stress the fact that Paul was Timothy's father in a secondary sense only, the apostle functioning as God's instrument, so that God himself remains the *real* Father, we shall have no difficulty with other passages of Scripture, such as "And call no one on earth y o u r Father: for One is y o u r heavenly Father" (Matt. 23:9; and cf. John 1:13; I John 3:9). It is exactly as Calvin has pointed out: though God—he *alone!*—is the Father of all believers because he has regenerated them by his Word and Spirit and because no one but himself bestows faith, yet his ministers have a subordinate right to this title.[21]

The designation "child" was a very happy one, for it combined two ideas: "I have begotten you," and "you are very dear to me." Timothy was,

---

[21] Sed qui conveniet hoc cum sententia Christi: Nolite vobis patrem vocare in terra (Matt. 23:9)? . . . Respondeo, Paulum ita sibi usurpare nomen patris, ut Deo nullam honoris sui particulam abroget aut minuat. . . . Unicus in fide pater omnium est Deus, quia omnes verbo suo et spiritus sui virtute regenerat: quia solus est qui fidem confert. Sed quibus ad eam rem dignatur uti ministris, eos in honoris sui communicationem etiam admittit, nihil tamen sibi derogando. Erat ergo Deus spiritualis Timothei pater: et quidem solus, proprie loquendo. Sed Paulus, qui minister fuerat Dei in gignendo Timotheo, quasi subalterno iure titulum sibi vindicat (John Calvin).

moreover, a *genuine* child, not a bastard son, not a merely nominal believer. Timothy was no Demas! See on II Tim. 4:10. Not, of course, in the physical sense but *with respect to,* or *in the sphere of,*[22] *faith* the apostle had begotten Timothy. It is probably best to take *faith* here in the subjective sense, a true knowledge of God and of his promises and a hearty confidence in him and in his only-begotten Son. This corresponds with such phrases as ". . . if they continue in faith and love" (I Tim. 2:15); "in love, in faith, in purity" (I Tim. 4:12); "Hold the pattern of sound words which thou hast heard from me in faith and love which is in Christ Jesus" (II Tim. 1:13).

Upon his genuine child in the sphere of faith the apostle now pronounces **grace, mercy, peace from God the Father and Christ Jesus our Lord.** *Grace* is God's unmerited favor in operation in the heart of his child, and *peace* is that child's consciousness of having been reconciled with God through Christ. *Grace* is the fountain, and *peace* is the stream which issues from this fountain (cf. Rom. 5:1). This grace and this peace have their origin in God the Father, and have been merited for the believer by Christ Jesus, their Lord. (All this has been treated much more fully in N.T.C. on I Thess. 1:1. Hence, both for the nature of the salutation and for the meaning of the concepts "grace" and "peace" and of the divine names I refer to what is given there.)

In one important respect this salutation differs from others. Nowhere except in his letters to Timothy does Paul in his salutations use the *three* substantives: grace, mercy, and peace. This triad is, however, also employed by John in one of his salutations (II John 3; cf. Jude 2: "mercy, peace, and love").

When the question is asked, Why did Paul insert *"mercy"* between "grace" and "peace" the probable answer is:

a. The term "mercy" is very fitting in this context, in which Paul has just shown his *affectionate interest* in Timothy, calling him "(my) genuine child." The very essence of "mercy" is *warm affection* which includes but must not be restricted to *tender compassion.*

b. Timothy was in a difficult situation. He faced problems which were all the more trying for a man of his disposition. Hence, God's *tender love toward those in need* was definitely required.

All this will become even clearer when the concept "mercy" is given further study. Paul uses this word ten times: five times outside the Pas-

---

22 The phrase "in faith" in the sense of "in the sphere of faith" is not un-Pauline, and does not prove that Paul cannot have written the Pastorals. It occurs *with* the article in I Cor. 16:13 and II Cor. 13:5; *without* the article in Gal. 2:20. It *is* true that it is found with greater frequency in the Pastorals (I Tim. 1:2, 4; 2:7, 15; 3:13; 4:12; II Tim. 1:13; Titus 1:13; 3:15; and in connection with I Tim. 2:15 cf. Acts 14:22).

torals (Rom. 9:23; 11:31; 15:9; Gal. 6:16; and Eph. 2:4), and five times in the Pastorals (I Tim. 1:2; II Tim. 1:2, 16, 18; Titus 3:5).

The usual way of distinguishing between *grace* and *mercy* is to say that grace pardons while mercy commiserates; grace is God's love toward the guilty, mercy his love toward the wretched or pitiable; grace concerns the state, mercy the condition. To a considerable extent this distinction is correct. The term "mercy" frequently occurs in a context of extending help to those in misery. It is the word that is used in the parable of The Good Samaritan (Luke 10:37; cf. 10:33). There it describes what that noble character did for the man who had fallen among robbers, had been stripped and wounded and was left lying by the road-side half dead. Similarly the Lord says in Is. 54:7, "With great mercies will I gather thee," where "mercies" (LXX ἔλεος) translates the Hebrew raḥamîm: tender feeling, motherly kindness, compassion, pity (here plural). So also when from among the mass of mankind viewed as fallen and in a condition of misery God chooses some, these are called "vessels of mercy" (Rom. 9:23; cf. 11:31).

Nevertheless, the word employed in the original (ἔλεος) is often somewhat broader in scope. It indicates not only the actual outpouring of *pity* upon those *in distress* but also the underlying lovingkindness of which God's creatures, particularly his people, are the objects, regardless of whether in the given context they are viewed as being "in deep misery" or more generally "in need of help." In the latter case the person concerned is usually viewed as God's child, dependent in all things on the heavenly Father, who cherishes toward him a feeling of *tender affection* and is *ever ready to help* him. Timothy, upon whom mercy "drops as a gentle rain from heaven," furnishes an excellent example of the use of the term in this somewhat broader sense.[23] The salutation, accordingly, assures him not only of pardoning grace, operating as a spiritual dynamic in his life, but also of the closely related divine *lovingkindness* in his present difficulties and in every situation of life. When this *grace* and this *mercy* or *kindness*

---

[23] In the Old Testament, which forms the basis of Paul's use of terms, this broader connotation is illustrated in such passages as the following, in each of which the Septuagint has ἔλεος as a translation for the Hebrew ḥeṣedh:

"Jehovah showed *kindness* to him (Joseph)" (Gen. 39:21).

". . . showing *lovingkindness* to thousands of them that love me" (Ex. 20:6; cf. Deut. 5:10).

"But my *lovingkindness* shall not depart from him (David)" (II Sam. 7:15).

". . . who keeps *covenant and lovingkindness*" (Neh. 1:5 = LXX II Esdras 11:5). (Note close connection between God's convenant and his lovingkindness!)

See further various passages in the Psalms, such as those which in our English versions are found in Ps. 5:7; 36:5, 7, etc.

The term God's "mercy," accordingly, may be translated either *kindness, lovingkindness* (cf. German Herzensgüte, Huld; Dutch "goedertierenheid") or *compassion, pity* (cf. German Barmherzigkeit; Dutch "barmhartigheid"). It all depends upon the specific context in which the word is used. The two meanings, moreover, blend into each other as do the colors of the rainbow.

are present, *peace* naturally follows. That which was broken and severed by sin is made whole and bound up by grace. The resulting sense of *wholeness, tranquility,* and *assurance* is *peace.* (By some the Greek word for *peace* – εἰρήνη – is traced to a verb which means *to bind* or *join;* cf. Latin *sero;* English *series.*)

---

3 As I urged you when I was on my way to Macedonia, do stay on at Ephesus,[24] in order that you may charge certain individuals not to teach differently, 4 nor to devote themselves to endless myths and genealogies which foster disputes rather than faith-centered stewardship required by God; 5 whereas the purpose of the charge is love (which springs) from a pure heart and a conscience good and a faith without hypocrisy; 6 from which objectives certain individuals, having wandered away, have turned aside to futile talk, 7 yearning to be law-teachers, although they understand neither the words which they are speaking nor the themes on which they are harping with such confidence. 8 Now we know that excellent is the law if one makes a lawful use of it, 9 bearing this in mind, that not for a righteous man is law enacted, but for lawless and insubordinate, for impious and sinful, for unholy and profane men, for murderers of fathers and murderers of mothers, for those who kill their fellows, 10 for immoral men, sodomites, kidnapers, liars, false swearers, and for whatever else is contrary to the sound doctrine, 11 (which is) in harmony with the glorious gospel of the blessed God, (the gospel) with which I have been entrusted.

1:3-11

3. As I urged you when I was on my way to Macedonia, do stay on at Ephesus.

Writing, then, to his trusted friend, Paul gives immediate expression to what he considers the most pressing necessity, namely, that Timothy by all means stay on duty at Ephesus in order to continue the battle for the truth. It is hardly necessary to point out that the apostle was not interested in Timothy's mere *staying* in Ephesus, but in his remaining there *in order to* straighten out what was wrong.

It should be noted that Paul urges Timothy *to stay on* at Ephesus. This is the stronger way of expressing it (stronger than *to stay*) and probably also implies that the two had been together at Ephesus.[25]

---

[24] Or: "I urge you now, as I did when I was traveling to Macedonia, to stay on at Ephesus, in order" etc. Cf. the Swedish: "Jag bjuder dig, nu sasom när jag for astad till Macedonien, att stanna kvar i Efesus, och där . . ." (Bibeln eller Den Heliga Skrift, Konungen 1917, edition Stockholm, 1946).

[25] Although the construction of the sentence is not easy, the most natural explanations yield the same resultant meaning. Whether we read the sentence as an anacoluthon, "As I urged you when I was on my way to Macedonia to stay on at Ephesus, in order," etc., with "so do I now" (or "so do") understood; or whether *the infinitive* "to stay on" be immediately interpreted as *an imperative;* or, finally, whether *the very act of writing* be itself considered a substitute for the "omitted"

"Timothy," says Paul, "you must stay on in Ephesus," and with this purpose: **in order that you may charge certain individuals not to teach differently.**

"Certain individuals," says Paul. Does he purposely omit their names from a desire *to spare them?* The fact that he definitely mentions names in verse 20 but not here in verse 3, has led to the opinion that these "certain individuals" of verse 3 do not include men as far advanced in error as were Hymenaeus and Alexander. And it is, indeed, true that the apostle was a very tactful person, and may have expressed himself thus indefinitely for the reason given by these interpreters. (One might compare II Thess. 3:11, 15, where the "busybodies" with respect to whom Paul expresses the wish that they be treated as "brothers" are referred to in a similar indefinite manner; see N.T.C. on that passage.) Nevertheless, the argument in favor of excluding Hymenaeus and Alexander is hardly conclusive. *By reading on and on* – an exegetical rule to which reference is made repeatedly in the present set of commentaries – one rather arrives at the conclusion that the expression "certain individuals" here in verse 3 is broad enough and strong enough to include even the men mentioned in verse 20. For, it should be noted that what is said in verses 6 and 7 about these "certain individuals" of verse 3 is by no means mild: "yearning to be law-teachers, although they understand neither the words which they are speaking nor the themes on which they are harping with so much confidence." Moreover, in verse 19 the apostle is *still* (or *again*) speaking about "certain individuals." He continues, "of whom are Hymenaeus and Alexander" (verse 20). It is natural to believe that the "certain individuals" of verse 3 and the "certain individuals" of verse 19 are the same people, and that of this group Hymenaeus and Alexander are the worst representatives, the ring-leaders. On this supposition, the indefinite reference (both in verse 4 and in verse 19) is probably due to one or more of the following reasons:

a. The group includes not only some who must be named but also several who need not be named as yet, the milder cases.

b. Timothy, living right among these people in Ephesus, is naturally better able than is Paul (in Macedonia) to tell who belongs to the group and who does not.

c. The group is not large; hence, "certain individuals" or simply "some," not "many."

d. Those who belong to the group are not as important as they think they are. They are not "big shots" but merely "certain individuals." This explanation tallies with what the apostle says about them in verse 7.

---

words, there is no substantial difference in sense: Paul, alarmed by the encroachment and influence of dangerous doctrines, once more impresses upon Timothy the idea that this surely is not the time for him to leave Ephesus!

Now though these "certain individuals" yearn to be "*law*-teachers" (verse 7), in reality they are nothing but *novelty*-teachers. They are teaching *differently,* that is, they are teaching "something different" or translated somewhat freely, "different doctrine." (cf. I Tim. 6:3; also Ignatius, *To Polycarp* III.) One is immediately reminded of Paul's stern message to the Galatians:

"I am astonished that so quickly y o u are changing over from the One who called y o u in the grace of Christ, to *a different* — which is not an *other* — gospel" (Gal. 1:6, 7).

Some people are ever anxious to welcome whatever is *new* or *different.* Like the Athenians of old "they devote their leisure-time to nothing else than telling or hearing something new" (Acts 17:21). They like to pit their strength against whatever is by them considered to be fuddy-duddy. One finds this tendency at times on the college or seminary campus, where some immature minds, having hardly begun a systematic study of the old and established, loudly acclaim the new about which they know nothing. Quite generally what they consider "new" is old heresy in a new dress. To strike the proper balance between being on the alert for any new discovery by which knowledge is really advanced, and being eager to preserve all that is good in the old, requires much grace. The errorists at Ephesus lacked this sense of careful scrutiny and cautious reflection.

For such people, then, Paul has a *message* which Timothy is urged to *pass along* to them (note the verb παραγγέλλω). He must *charge* or *command* them to desist.

4. Not only must they desist from wrong *teaching* but also from wrong *thinking,* for the former is the result of the latter. The individuals in question were occupying their minds with a dangerous fad. Hence Paul continues: **Nor to devote themselves to endless myths and genealogies.** That was the trouble! These would-be law-doctors were engaged in the business of *turning* (their minds) *to* (from προσέχω with νοῦν implied) "myths and genealogies."

The expression "myths and genealogies" is *one.* It must not be divided, as if Paul were thinking, on the one hand, of myths, and on the other, of genealogies. The apostle refers undoubtedly to man-made supplements to the law of God (see verse 7), mere myths or fables (II Tim. 4:4), old wives' tales (I Tim. 4:7) that were definitely Jewish in character (Titus 1:14). Measured by the standard of *truth,* what these errorists taught deserved the name *myths.* As to *material contents* these myths concern *genealogical narratives* that were largely *fictitious.*

We feel at once that here we have been introduced into the realm of typically *Jewish* lore. It is a known fact that from early times the rabbis would "spin their yarns" — and *endless* yarns they were! — on the basis of what they considered some "hint" supplied by the Old Testament. They would take a name from a list of pedigrees (for example, From Genesis, I Chronicles, Ezra, Nehemiah), and expand it into a nice story. Such interminable embroideries on the inspired record were part of the regular bill of fare in the synagogue, and were subsequently deposited in written form in that portion of *The Talmud* which is known as *Haggadah.*

The Book of Jubilees (also called *The Little Genesis*) offers another striking example of what Paul had in mind. It is a kind of *haggadic* commentary on the canonical Genesis; that is, it is an exposition interspersed with an abundant supply of illustrative anecdotes. The book was probably written toward the close of the second or at the beginning of the first century B. C. It covers the entire era from the creation until the entrance into Canaan. This long stretch is divided into fifty jubilee-periods of forty-nine (7×7) years each. In fact, the entire chronology is based on the number 7, and heavenly authority is claimed for this arrangement. Thus not only does the week have 7 days, the month 4×7 days, but even the year has $52 \times 7 = 364$ days, the year-week has 7 years, and the jubilee has $7 \times 7 = 49$ years. The separate events regarding the patriarchs, etc., are pin-pointed in accordance with this scheme. The sacred narrative of our canonical book of Genesis is embellished, at times almost beyond recognition. Thus, we now learn that the sabbath was observed already by the arch-angels, that the angels also practised circumcision, that Jacob never tricked anybody, etc.

In every age there are people who love to indulge in such strange mixtures of truth and error. They even treat these adulterations as being the all-important thing. They carry on lengthy debates about dates and definitions. Instead of brushing aside all such syncretistic rubbish, they discover fine distinctions and engage in hairsplitting disputes. They pile myth upon myth, fable upon fable, and *the end* is never in sight. Thus the law of God is made void by human tradition (cf. Matt. 15:6), and the picture drawn in the sacred original becomes grossly distorted.

In our own day the same error occurs, and in many different forms. Instead of studying the infallible Word, some resort to all kinds of millennial fancies, or prefer to see on a screen an unscriptural embellishment of the story of Joseph, with special emphasis, of course, on that famous incident in connection with Potiphar's wife; or an equally unscriptural supplement to the story of Samson, with exaggerated stress, naturally, on his Delilah.

Now there is, indeed, a legitimate place for the exercise of the gift of the imagination. There is room for dramatization, yes even for fables and fairy-tales. Grown-ups as well as children can enjoy Hans Andersen's "Fir Tree" and can take its lesson to heart. But one who begins to mix sacred history with fiction and this for the purpose of theatrical effect, gross enjoyment, intoxicating thrill, or the satisfaction of vain curiosity, tampers with the very essence and purpose of the inspired record. God's law was not given in order that those who arrogate to themselves the name "law-teachers" might "shine" in the eyes of the public, or in order that the public itself might be "entertained" with endless myths and fictitious genealogical histories **which foster disputes rather than faith-centered stewardship required by God** (literally, "the stewardship of God, the one in faith").

It has been correctly observed that a person's teaching should be judged by its fruits. Whatever fails to promote stewardship should be rejected, even though it have no other fault. And everything which arouses nothing but disputes deserves double condemnation.[26]

The true objective of every leader and gospel-teacher, the aim and goal of all his striving, should be "faith-centered stewardship required by God." This stewardship [27] is *the care* which the Lord has ordained with respect to the house or household of God, the wise *administration and distribution* of the gospel-mysteries unto the edification of the church. The term *stewardship* is undoubtedly used here in the same sense as in I Cor. 9:17: "I have a stewardship entrusted to me." See also Titus 1:7, where the overseer is called God's steward; and I Cor. 4:1, 2 where the apostle refers to himself and his associates as "stewards of the mysteries of God," and states that the chief qualification of a steward is that he be faithful.

The New Testament passages in which the term *stewardship* occurs are Luke 16:2-4; I Cor. 9:17; Eph. 1:10; 3:2, 9; Col. 1:25 and I Tim. 1:4 (the passage now under discussion). The term seems to refer to the office with which the steward has been entrusted and/or to the active administration of affairs by the one who holds that office. A "steward" (οἰκονόμος) is literally the manager of a household or of an estate (Luke 12:42; 16:1, 3, 8; I Cor. 4:2; Gal. 4:2). The figurative meaning usually shines through, however. In the highest sense of the term, the steward is an administrator of spiritual treasures (I Cor. 4:1; Titus 1:7).[28]

5. Now such a divinely ordained stewardship, a stewardship that originates in God and is, accordingly, required by him, centers in the active

---

[26] Says John Calvin similarly, *op. cit.* p. 252: Aestimat a fructu doctrinam. Quaecunque enim non aedificat, repudianda est, etiamsi nihil aliud habeat vitii: quaecunque vero ad concertiones solum excitandas valet, duplici damnanda est.

[27] The best reading has οἰκονομίαν (stewardship), not οἰκοδομήν (building up, edifying).

[28] Uses of the term that require special comment are the following:
a. In Rom. 16:23 the οἰκονόμος is a *treasurer,* which meaning of the term finds abundant support in extra-canonical Koine literature (see M.M., p. 443).
b. In I Peter 4:10 the metaphorical meaning is broadened and applied to believers generally.
c. In Eph. 1:10 and related passages the meaning of the term is disputed. The sense "dispensation" when that term is defined as *"a period of time* during which a particular divine arrangement of things is operative" is debatable.

exercise of *faith,* whose fruits it seeks to multiply. Hence, its goal is *love* rather than a vain show of speculative *learning.* So Paul continues: **whereas the purpose of the charge is love.** Timothy had been urged to deliver a *charge* to the church at Ephesus, *to pass along a message* which had special reference to "certain individuals" (see on verse 3). This charge, we may be sure, was not strictly limited to negative injunctions, such as, "*Do not* teach that which differs from the sound gospel, and *do not* waste your time on genealogical fables and fancies." The negative naturally implied the positive: "*Do* bear witness to the sound gospel, and *do* exercise living faith in the Lord Jesus Christ, a faith which operates by means of love." Thus viewed, this charge is in reality the sum and substance of *all* Christian admonition, specifically of all admonitory preaching. *Love* is the fulfilment of the law (*both* tables, Mark 12:30, 31) as well as the essence of the gospel. Hence, what is stated in the present passage is in exact harmony with that other great saying of Paul, "For in Christ Jesus neither circumcision nor uncircumcision has any validity, but faith working through love" (Gal. 5:6). Note also the emphasis on love in such other passages in I Timothy as 1:14; 2:15; 4:12; 6:11.

This love may be described as a personal delight in God, a grateful outgoing of the entire personality to him, a deep yearning for the prosperity of his redeemed, and an earnest desire for the temporal and eternal welfare of his creatures. Far better, however, is Paul's own description of its meaning in I Cor. 13.

Now not everything that is called love *is* really love. Hence, the apostle specifies that he is thinking of love which springs **from a pure heart, and a conscience good, and a faith without hypocrisy.**

When a sinner is drawn to Christ, *the heart* is first of all regenerated. The result is that the man's *conscience* begins to plague him in such a manner that, having come under conviction, he is happy to embrace the Redeemer by means of a conscious, living *faith.* Hence, the sequence *heart, conscience, faith* is entirely natural. Moreover, it is clearly evident why the apostle states that these three – and in that order – *give rise to love.* When the God *of love* (love is his very name, I John 4:8) implants his own new life in man's *heart,* the latter naturally becomes a *loving* heart. A *conscience* cleared of guilt and made obedient to God's law will begin to approve only such thoughts, words, and deeds, past or contemplated, which are in harmony with the one, summarizing aim of that law, namely, *love.* And genuine *faith,* which embraces Christ and all his benefits, will result in genuine *love* for the Benefactor and for all those who are embraced in his love. – Hence, Paul speaks of "love *from* (or "out of") a pure heart, and a conscience good, and a faith without hypocrisy."

The heart is the fulcrum of feeling and faith as well as the mainspring of words and actions (Rom. 10:10; cf. Matt. 12:34; 15:19; 22:37; and see

N.T.C. on John 14:1). It is the core and center of man's being, man's inmost self. "Out of it are the issues of life" (Prov. 4:23). "Man looks on the outward appearance, but Jehovah looks on the heart" (I Sam. 16:7). Now the purpose of the gospel-charge is love out of a *pure* heart. The heart is *pure* when it experiences the cleansing work of the Holy Spirit (Ps. 51:10, 11). When this happens, fervent love begins to rise to the surface (I Peter 1:22).

Conscience is man's moral intuition, his moral self in the act of passing judgment upon his own state, emotions, and thoughts, also upon his own words and actions whether these be viewed as past, present, or future.[29] It is both positive and negative. It both approves and condemns (Rom. 2:14, 15).

The word used in the original and in (closely or remotely) related languages has the same meaning when analyzed etymologically. It means *knowledge along with, joint-knowledge,* or *co-knowledge:* Greek συνείδησις, Latin *con-scientia,* English (from Latin) *con-science,* Swedish *sam-vete,* Danish *Sam-vittighed.* But how must this *co-knowledge* be interpreted? Some say, "It is man's knowledge along with God's knowledge, man's own inner voice in the act of repeating God's voice, his own judgment endorsing God's judgment, his own spirit bearing witness with God's spirit." Others reason somewhat as follows, "It is man's *moral* self echoing his *cognitive* self."

This difference of opinion is not very important, just so it is borne in mind that whatever be the true story of the manner in which *the term* originated, its *meaning,* according to Scripture, is by no means obscure. The fact that "con-science is the response of man's moral consciousness to the divine revelation concerning himself, his attitudes, and his activities" cannot be doubted (see Rom. 2:14, 15).

It is *in the believer* that conscience attains its highest goal. For the regenerated individual *God's will,* as expressed in his Word, becomes "the Lord of conscience, its Guide and Director" (I Peter 2:19). The "conscience *good*" of which the apostle speaks here in I Tim. 1:5 is more than merely a *"clear* conscience." Rather, it is the conscience which:

a. is guided by God's special revelation as its norm;

b. pronounces judgments that are accepted, and issues directives that are obeyed;

c. produces "godly sorrow which works repentance unto salvation" (II Cor. 7:10), a salvation by means of which "the love of God is spread abroad

---

[29] Though *the term conscience* does not occur in the Old Testament, *the idea* certainly is found there (Gen. 3:7, 10; 39:9; I Sam. 24:17; 26:21; II Sam. 24:10; Job 42:5, 6; Is. 6:5; Dan. 9:19). In the New Testament the word occurs twice in Acts (23:1; 24:16); five times in Hebrews (9:9; 9:14; 10:2; 10:22; 13:18); three times in I Peter (2:19; 3:16; 3:21); and at least twenty times in Paul's writings. In the Pastorals it is found in I Tim. 1:5, 19; 3:9; 4:2; II Tim. 1:3; Titus 1:15).

in our hearts through the Holy Spirit" (Rom. 5:5). And God's love evokes the response of love.

The positive aspect of a really "good" conscience is *faith,* for a good conscience not only abhors the wrong but embraces the right. *Such* faith is true and genuine. It is not mere play-acting, "a vile conceit in pompous words expressed," a mere *mask,* like the one which an actor puts on and *under* which he hides his real self. Was Paul contrasting living faith with the "faith"(?) of the ring-leaders among the errorists? However that may be, the *faith* which he has in mind is "a *true* knowledge of God and of his promises revealed to us in the gospel, and a *hearty* confidence that all my sins are forgiven me for Christ's sake" (Compendium to the Heidelberg Catechism, answer 19). Such faith results in love.

The substance, accordingly, of verse 5 is this: the essence of the charge given to you, Timothy, which you by public preaching and private admonition must convey to the Ephesians is, "Pray and strive daily to obtain a pure heart, a conscience good, and a faith without hypocrisy, in order that these three, working together in organic co-operation, may produce that most precious of all jewels, *love.*"

6. Now whenever this chief aim of all preaching and of the entire work of the Christian ministry is lost sight of, sad results follow, as the apostle points out when he continues: **from which objectives certain individuals, having wandered away, have turned aside to futile talk.**

These "certain individuals" are the people to whom reference was made in verse 3 (see on that passage). They are said to have *wandered away* or *deviated* (see also on I Tim. 6:21 and on II Tim. 2:18) from their proper objectives: the pure heart, the conscience good, and the faith without hypocrisy. Naturally, they also missed the true *destination,* the final goal, namely *love.* They are like marksmen who miss their target, like travelers who never reach their destination because they have taken the wrong turn and have failed to look for the familiar signs along the road. The path which these people have taken is not even a detour. It is more like a dead-end street beyond which lies a swamp, in their case the swamp of "futile talk," useless reasoning, argumentation that gets nowhere (cf. Titus 1:10), dry as dust disputation, a wrangling about fanciful tales anent pedigrees! Yes, their vaunted learning has finally landed them in the no-man's land of ceremonious subtleties, in the dreary marsh of ridiculous hair-splitting. And the owner of that quagmire is . . . Satan, who heads the welcoming-committee (I Tim. 5:15).

7. And why have these men *turned aside* to futile talk? Because they want to shine! Says Paul: **yearning to be law-teachers.** Now in itself the desire to be a teacher of the Old Testament, particularly the law of Moses, is not bad. But the trouble with these men is that they desire to reach this goal

although they understand neither the words (or things) which they are speaking nor the themes (or subjects) on which they are harping with such confidence (or on which they lay so much stress).

With relish these would-be law-doctors flourished their highfaluting words, their ponderous phrases. But all this was pure bombast, rant and cant. Whenever they would hear a jaw-breaker, they would be sure to commit it to memory and to use it in spinning their tedious tales; but they themselves did not know the meaning of the latest addition to their vocabulary. Worse even, they failed to understand the very subjects on which they lectured with such cock-sureness (cf. Titus 3:8).

8. However, lest anyone should think that Paul under-estimates daily teaching and study of the law, he adds: **Now we know that excellent is the law if one makes a lawful use of it.** The best comment on this is Rom. 7:7, 12, "What then shall we say? 'The law is sin?' Of course not! In fact, sin I would not have recognized except through the law; for instance, covetousness I would not have known had not the law said, 'You shall not covet.' . . . Accordingly, the law (is) holy, and the commandment (is) holy and just and good."

"We *know,*" says Paul. In other words, he wishes to impress upon Timothy – and through him upon the Ephesians, particularly upon those who were promoting erroneous doctrines – that the proposition, "Constant law-study is an excellent thing," is not new. "This proposition," says the apostle as it were, "is a widely recognized principle, something we all know very well." Read Ps. 19; Ps. 119; Matt. 5:17, 18.

Of course, Paul does not mean that "any and all" use of the law is admirable. No, only then is the law of great practical value "if one makes a lawful use of it." Thus one might also say that preaching is an excellent thing, but surely not *all* preaching. It is an excellent thing on the supposition that one knows how to preach!

When the law is buried under a load of "traditions" which nullify its very purpose (Matt. 15:3, 6; Mark 17:9; then Matt. 5:43) or when it is used as a "take-off" point for spell-binders about ancestors, it loses its power. Just as in the public games only that man received the wreath of victory who played according to the rules (cf. II Tim. 2:5), so also only that person can expect to receive a blessing from the law who uses it as it should be used. Hence, Paul continues:

9a. bearing this in mind, that not for a righteous man is law enacted. That was the very point which these false teachers in Ephesus were forgetting. The reason why they wasted their time on all kinds of fanciful tales regarding ancestors was that they had never learned to know themselves as *sinners* before God. They were "puffed up," arrogant, boastful, haughty, self-righteous (see on verse 7 above; also on I Tim. 6:4, 20; II

Tim. 3:2; and cf. Titus 1:10; 3:5). That was their big sin, as Paul points out repeatedly. They lacked humility, the consciousness of guilt.

These people could study God's holy law with its basic precepts and injunctions, and could remain very calm under it all, as if it did not touch them. They would simply read on (or go back) until they came to some proper name or perhaps some ceremonial detail. *Then* of a sudden they would become enthused! *Now* they could shine with their stories and spiritualizations.

Instead, they should have been *crushed* by the law, as was, for instance, Paul (see below, on verse 15, and see also Rom. 7, especially the closing verses). But *these* people considered themselves to be *good* by nature, not bad. They were "righteous" in their own eyes, just like the Pharisees, with reference to whom Jesus said, "I came not to call the righteous but sinners" (Matt. 9:13; and cf. Luke 15:7 and 18:9). In fact, it is very well possible that the apostle had that Matt. 9:13 *saying* of the Savior in mind when he wrote as he did. (The actual date when the Gospels were written has nothing to do with this, of course.) This possible conclusion is strengthened somewhat by what he says in verse 15 of the present chapter:

"Reliable is the saying, and entitled to full acceptance, that Christ Jesus came into the world *sinners* to save, foremost of whom am I." Cf. also Titus 3:5.

Now it stands to reason that for "a righteous" man *law* – *any* law, to be sure (that is, any law touching morals), but here with special reference to the Mosaic law – has not been enacted. If I am so good that I just naturally keep the law, then I do not need the law (whether it be a traffic law or the law of the ten commandments). One of the main purposes of the Mosaic law was to bring *sinners* to the point where they would feel utterly crushed under the load of their sins. But granted, for the sake of argument, that these Ephesian would-be leaders and those who cluster around them, are what, according to Paul's description, they consider themselves to be; granted that they are in themselves good and righteous, then surely *law* is wasted on them.[30] How can it be *a bridle* (Mark 10:20; Ps. 19:13)

---

30 The idea that Paul here teaches that "the justified Christian" has "nothing to do with the law" is burdened by the following objections:

a. It is totally foreign to the context, in which the apostle (barring the salutation which pertains to the entire letter) as yet has said nothing about justified Christians.

b. Here in verse 9 he is speaking entirely in general about "a (notice *a,* not *the*) righteous person; and he is saying that for such *a* righteous person *law* is not laid down.

c. A word is often explained by its antonyms. Here "a righteous person" stands over against persons who are "lawless, insubordinate, impious, sinful, unholy, profane, murderers of fathers, murderers of mothers," etc., all of which terms have to do with sins in the moral-spiritual realm, sins of attitude and conduct, sins against the moral law of the Ten Commandments. Hence, it certainly seems very probable that we are here in the moral, not in the forensic realm.

for those who feel that they need no restraint? How can it be a *dirt-revealing mirror* (source of the knowledge of sin, Rom. 3:20; then Gal. 3:24) for those who think that they show no filthy specks that must be washed away? How can it be *a guide* (Ps. 119:105; 19:7, 8; cf. Rom. 7:22) to point out avenues of gratitude for deliverance from sin, for those who in their pride and arrogance (of which Paul speaks again and again) are convinced that they have not lost the way?

9b, 10. No, not for these people is law enacted, **but for lawless and insubordinate, for impious and sinful, for unholy and profane men, for murderers of fathers and murderers of mothers, for those who kill their fellows, for immoral men, sodomites, kidnapers, liars, false swearers, and for whatever else is contrary to the sound doctrine.**

It would seem that the apostle, in referring to people for whom law (here with particular reference to the divine moral law) was laid down, first describes them in general – as being lawless and insubordinate, impious and sinful – and then descends to particulars, more or less following the order of the ten commandments.

The Ephesian errorists should have asked themselves, "Does not this description fit us?" Paul admitted that it applied to himself. The teachers of false doctrine in the Ephesus region admitted *nothing*. That was the difference!

The first descriptive term which he uses is *lawless*. Lawless persons (pl. of ἄνομος) are not here persons who are ignorant of the law but those who live as if there were no law (see N.T.C. on II Thess. 2:3). They "live themselves out," doing as they please. They thus live apart from the law and contrary to its basic demand. Was Paul thinking at all of himself (as included in this group) and his own former life? (Cf. Rom. 7:9.) In order that the proper exegesis may be given to this portion, one must bear in mind that in the immediate sequel the apostle refers repeatedly to himself and his own sinful life (verses 13, 15, 16). A text, after all, should be interpreted in the light of its context. Otherwise our interpretation lacks unity. – Now, lawless persons are, of course, also *insubordinate*. They refuse *to range themselves under* (note the word: pl. of ἀνυπότακτος) the rule of the God who laid down the law. In practical, every-day life, this means that such people are, *negatively* speaking, *impious*, irreverent, ungodly (pl. of ἀσεβής), a word which in Pauline usage applies even to the elect as long as (or to the extent in which) they are still living in harmony with the principle of unbelief. There are, accordingly "ungodly," though by God's sovereign grace they are (or sometime during their life are going to be) justified (Rom. 4:5; 5:6). Paul would certainly place himself among them. *Positively* speaking, such people are by nature *sinners* (pl. of ἁμαρτωλός), those who have missed the mark or goal of their existence, namely, the conscious glorification of God. Paul very definitely and explicitly tells us that he includes himself, note verse 15 (which must already have been in the mind of the writer when he wrote verse 9): ". . . Christ Jesus came into the world *sinners* to save, *foremost of whom am I.*"

The law, then, was laid down for lawless and insubordinate, for ungodly and sinful persons, in order that it might shake them to the very depths of their being, might frighten them out of whatever self-complacency remained in them. *It was enacted to make the disturbed even more disturbed so that they would cry out in self-despair, "Wretched man that I am, who shall deliver me?"* (Rom. 7:24, and cf. Rom. 3:20).

The apostle now gives a summary of the law of the Ten Commandments. That summary shows clearly that there is no room for *anyone (least of all for the Ephesian errorist)* to sit at ease in Zion, to be filled with a sense of security, so that with perfect composure he can now begin to use the law as a kind of crossword puzzle or as raw material for the fabrication of interesting stories about ancestors.

First, accordingly, the apostle states that law has been enacted ἀνοσίοις καὶ βεβήλοις

"for unholy and profane men."

The term *unholy* (ἀνόσιος), in the New Testament occurring only here and in II Tim. 3:2, and linked here in verse 9 with *profane,* is very suitable in a context which describes those who are careless of their duties *toward God.* In his *Gorgias* (507 B) Plato represents Socrates as saying, "And again, when one is doing what is fitting with respect to *men,* he does things that are *just* (δίκαια); (when he does what is fitting) with respect to *the gods,* (he does things that are) *holy* (ὅσια).[31] Similarly, in II Macc. 7:34 Antiochus Epiphanes, who tried his utmost to destroy the religion of Jehovah, is called an "unholy man."

What is stated negatively in the adjective "unholy" is expressed positively in the adjective *profane* (βέβηλος from βαίνω, to walk, step, tread). That which is "profane" *can be trodden.* It is, as our English word implies, "in front of the temple," that is, "*outside* the temple" (*pro* = before or in front of; *fane* = temple, sanctuary). A *profane person* is one who does not refrain or hesitate *to trample* on that which is holy. The adjective is used with respect to *things* in I Tim. 4:7; 6:20; II Tim. 2:16 (see on these passages) and with respect to *persons* in our present passage and

---

[31] I do not mean that the adjectives ὅσιος and ἀνόσιος are restricted so that *in every* instance they refer to man's attitude with respect to his duties under the first table of the law. Trench is correct when he points out that Scripture recognizes no such arbitrary division between the first and second tables. What I *do* mean is that in the present passage the very use of the word *unholy* in immediate connection with *profane* seems to point in the direction of the classical distinction. For the rest see R. C. Trench, *op. cit.* lxxxviii; also M.M., 45, 460.

in Heb. 12:16. The latter passage mentions the typically *profane* person, namely, Esau, who for a single meal sold his birthright with its Messianic implications.

It is therefore altogether natural to suppose that when Paul mentions *unholy and profane* persons, he is thinking of those who ridicule the very idea that there is only one true God, and of those who deny that this God is the Spirit of infinite perfection, that his name, or the name of Christ, should be reverenced, and that his day should be observed. Those who are unholy and profane flout the four commandments of the first table of the law. Let no one say that Paul excluded himself (see verse 13, also Acts 26:11), or any other *sinner*.

Secondly, this law has been laid down

"for murderers of fathers and murderers of mothers."

The sin here indicated is a flagrant violation of the next commandment of the Decalogue, "Honor your father and your mother, that your days may be long in the land which the Lord your God gives you" (Ex. 20:12). Moreover, the law specifically stated, "And he who strikes his father or his mother shall surely be put to death" (Ex. 21:15). Now if even the *striking* of one's father or one's mother incurred the death-penalty, how much more the *smiting* (striking with a destructive blow, murdering)! Yet the greater sin, in each instance, includes the lesser. *Any* failure to honor one's parents is here condemned. *No sinner escapes.*

Thirdly, this law was intended

"for those who kill their fellows."

Literally, the original has here "for men-slayers." However, in English this term is rather ambiguous, and could be taken to refer exclusively to those who kill *unintentionally* though unlawfully (those guilty of "manslaughter"). The original, however, refers to any one who wrongfully takes the life of another. It has reference to *any and all homicides.*

The commandment violated is the sixth, "You shall not kill" (Ex. 20:13). See Christ's interpretation, Matt. 5:21-26. How it must have hurt Paul to write this. It brought back to his mind memories of the past, *Paul's own* past (Acts 9:1, 4, 5; 22:4, 7; 26:10).

Fourthly, this law was established

"for immoral persons, sodomites."

This clearly refers to those who transgress the seventh commandment, "You shall not commit adultery" (Ex. 20:14).

Note that here also (just as in the phrases "for impious and sinful," "for unholy and profane") the negative description (immoral) precedes the positive (sodomites). The violation indicated is, first, very inclusive "fornication" or immorality; secondly, very flagrant, "sodomy." With respect to the first term (fornication), it is not true that this is always strictly confined to illicit sexual intercourse between *unmarried* persons. As is true with respect to our own word *fornication,* so also with respect to the Greek word, the sense, though restricted at first, gradually acquires a more inclusive meaning, so that in the present passage it is simply *sexual immorality* in whatever form it may occur. That it may even include *adultery* (illicit sexual intercourse between persons at least one of whom is married) is clear from Matt. 5:32; 19:9. In Eph. 5:5 the fornicator or immoral person is mentioned in one breath with the impure or unclean. Cf. also Heb. 13:4. According to Matt. 5:27, 28 every unclean thought is a form of "adultery." *What sinner is not guilty?* A most gruesome instance of immorality is described by Paul in I Cor. 5:1. The heathen world was full of such vices, but the case mentioned in Corinthians is described as one "not found even among pagans."

Immediately after "immoral persons" Paul mentions "sodomites." The word employed in the original is composed of two parts: *male* and *bed* (particularly, marriage-bed). The reference is, therefore, *directly* to *male* homosexuals, in other words to sodomites (cf. Gen. 19:5), "abusers of themselves with men" (Rom. 1:27; I Cor. 6:9); *indirectly,* the reference is to *all* homosexuals, male and female.

Fifthly, the law was instituted

"for kidnapers."

In the New Testament the word (ἀνδραποδιστής) occurs only here. Its origin is rather uncertain, though in view of its component elements some derive it from the verbal idea "to catch a man by the foot." But whatever be its origin, it clearly refers primarily to "slave-dealers" (the word ἀνδράποδον means slave) and then, by extension, to *all* "men-stealers" or "kidnapers." The apostle has in mind a gross violation of the eighth commandment, "You shall not steal" (Ex. 20:15; on stealing *men* see Ex. 21:16; Deut. 24:7). Certainly also those who enter into the homes of Christians, dragging out those who are of "The Way," whether they be men or women, are included, in spite of the fact they may carry with them letters from the high-priest (cf. Acts 9:1, 2)! Yes, men-stealers of every hue or color are meant. Paul is included, and by a legitimate extension of the idea so is every one who has ever infringed on the rights or liberties of his fellow-men. *What sinner goes free?*

Sixthly, this law was made

"for liars, false swearers."

The apostle certainly has in mind the ninth commandment, "You shall not bear false witness against your neighbor" (Ex. 20:16). As Paul sees it, however, not only are *the Cretans* liars (Titus 1:12) but by nature *every man* is a liar (Rom. 3:4). The liar, according to the scriptural usage of the term, is not only the person who actually tells an untruth, but also he whose actions and attitudes are out of harmony with his confession (I John

2:4; 4:20). The arch-liar of all is the devil (see N.T.C. on John 8:44, 55). His most ardent disciple, antichrist, naturally is also a liar (I John 2:22; and see N.T.C. on II Thess. 2:9, 10).

"False swearers" are those who are guilty of *solemnly* ("by my name," Lev. 19:2) asserting that which is false, with the intention of hurting their neighbor; or those who, while making a solemn vow, do not intend to keep it. This is a most shocking form of the sin against the ninth commandment, just like kidnaping is a most shameful manifestation of the sin against the eighth, and sodomy a gross example of sin against the seventh commandment. Of course, as in the case of the preceding violations against the moral law, so here: *the sin mentioned includes the sins which lead to it and all kindred sins.* The selfish design of the Pharisees to restrict the meaning of the evil so that only those would be accounted guilty of perjury who failed to keep *that promise in connection with which the name of God had been literally taken upon the lips,* was exposed by the Lord (Matt. 5:33-37).

If we bear in mind that the sin of swearing falsely was sometimes committed with a view to obtaining possession of the neighbor's property, it becomes clear that the theory is not too far-fetched that in making mention of this particular violation of the moral law Paul is thinking not only of sin against the ninth but also of sin against the tenth commandment, "You shall not covet your neighbor's house . . . or anything that is your neighbor's (Ex. 20:17). *False swearing* often (perhaps we can even say *always*) has as its root *covetousness.*

Having now given both a general and a more detailed description of those people for whom the law was intended, the apostle adds "and for whatever else is contrary to the sound doctrine." *No sinner and no sin can escape,* least of all the errorists at Ephesus, *as God saw them!* The only one for whom the law was not laid down was the *righteous* person, the errorist *as he sees himself!* See on 1:9a. For the rest, the law condemns each and all, causing its sentence of condemnation to be felt! It is *laid down* (κεῖται) for whatever is *laid against* (ἀντίκειται) the sound doctrine. This *doctrine* touches both theory and practice. Hence, *every* sin is a sin against sound doctrine. And this doctrine is called *sound*[32] (ὑγιαινούσῃ, whence we have our word "hygienic") because it promotes spiritual health. See also II Tim. 4:3; Titus 1:9; 2:1; then Titus 1:13; lastly I Tim. 6:3; II Tim. 1:13. This is not surprising, for this teaching is:

[32] The idea that Paul cannot have written the Pastorals because the word "sound" is used here, and that this word must mean "in harmony with reason," must be rejected. "Soundness" is not a purely intellectual concept; and the metaphorical use of the word was surely known to Paul, for example, from the LXX rendering of Prov. 13:13, second line. Cf. footnote 193.

11. in harmony with the glorious gospel of the blessed God.

The sound doctrine demands that man *must* keep God's law. It also declares that by nature he *cannot* keep it. Hence, it reveals his utterly lost, his thoroughly *sinful* condition. This, of course, exactly matches (is "according to" or "in harmony with") *the gospel,* for the latter's central thrust is, "Christ Jesus came into the world *sinners* to save" (verse 15). What a *glorious* gospel! [33] It is glorious because it displays the radiance of the divine attributes. (See N.T.C. on John 1:14.) It declares the righteousness, grace, love, etc., of "the blessed God." With respect to this divine blessedness a great theologian wrote as follows:

"Now *blessedness* when ascribed to God comprises three elements: In the first place it expresses the fact that God is absolute perfection, for blessedness is the property of every being that is perfect or complete: that has life, and is free from disturbance, whether inwardly or outwardly. . . . Because of the fact that God is absolute perfection, the sum-total of all virtues, the highest essence, the supreme of goodness and truth, in other words, because he is absolute life, the fountain of all life, he is the God of absolute blessedness. . . . Secondly, the word *blessedness* when applied to God implies that this absolute perfection is the object of God's knowledge and love . . . God knows himself with a knowledge that is absolute, and he loves himself with a love that is absolute. Hence, the word *blessedness* when applied to God implies thirdly that God delights in himself in an absolute sense, that he rests in himself, that he is perfectly self-sufficient. His life is not a continual development, a mere striving and becoming, as is taught by pantheism, but an uninterrupted rest, an eternal peace" (H. Bavinck, *The Doctrine of God,* my translation, Grand Rapids, Mich., 1951, p. 248).

The word employed in the original to express this blessedness is μακάριος. It is the same word which occurs in The Beatitudes, for example, "*Blessed* are the poor in spirit" (Matt. 5:3), elsewhere in the Gospels (see N.T.C. on John 13:17), in James, I Peter, and Revelation. Paul uses it in Rom. 4:7, 8 (quotations from Ps. 32); 14:22; I Cor. 7:40; our present passage; also I Tim. 6:15; and Titus 2:13.[34]

---

[33] In agreement with the A.V., Berkeley Version, Goodspeed, Moffatt, R.S.V., Weymouth, Williams, etc., we construe the genitive "of the glory" as adjectival. (II Cor. 4:4 proves nothing to the contrary.) It is not true that when δόξης is preceded by the article it cannot be adjectival. Cf. "steward of the unrighteousness" in Luke 16:8. Moreover, in biblical Greek the adjectival genitive is of frequent occurrence, due, no doubt, to the Semitic background.

There is no need of searching for a remote connection for the phrase under discussion. It is the immediately preceding "sound doctrine" which is "according to" or "in harmony with" the glorious gospel of the blessed God.

[34] A close synonym of μακάριος is εὐλογητός. The former is the equivalent of the Hebrew *'ashrey,* which as a construct plural may be rendered, "O the blessedness of . . . !" It occurs, for example, with reference to men who have communion with God, are the recipients of God's special benefits, particularly, of the blessing of for-

In mentioning "the glorious gospel of the blessed God" the apostle naturally thinks of his own relation to it. Hence, he continues **(the gospel) with which I have been entrusted.** Paul was deeply conscious of this "trust." He refers to it again and again (I Cor. 9:17; Gal. 2:7; and see N.T.C. on I Thess. 2:4). It is for that very reason that he calls himself "an apostle of Christ Jesus" (see above, on verse 1). It is for that same reason that he is able to commit a "charge" to Timothy (see on verse 3). Now Timothy himself was fully conscious of this sacred trust with which Paul had been entrusted. Others, however – think of the teachers of strange doctrine at Ephesus – need a reminder!

Yet, it is not primarily the desire to remind others of his authority that prompts the apostle to write about this trust. Rather, he mentions it here in order to make a transition to a paragraph (verses 12-17) in which he is going to express his gratitude to God, who made *him,* the chief of sinners, a minister of the gospel! According to the context, therefore, the true sense of the closing clause of verse 11 is this, "the glorious gospel of the blessed God, (the gospel) with which I, *thoroughly unworthy of such a great privilege,* have been entrusted."

---

12 I acknowledge my gratitude [35] to him who gave me strength, Christ Jesus our Lord, that [36] he considered *me* trustworthy and appointed *me* for himself [37] to (this) ministry, 13 though previously I was a blasphemer and a persecutor and a wanton aggressor. But I was accorded mercy because I acted ignorantly in unbelief. 14 And it superabounded (namely) the grace of our Lord, with faith and love (which center) in Christ Jesus. 15 Reliable (is) the saying, and worthy of full acceptance, that Christ Jesus came into the world sinners to save, foremost of whom am I. 16 But for this reason I was accorded mercy, in order that in me as foremost Jesus Christ might exhibit all his longsuffering as a sketch for those who would come to rest their faith on him with a view to life everlasting. 17 So to the King of the ages, the imperishable, invisible, only God (be) honor and glory forever and ever! [38] Amen.

---

giveness (Ps. 32:1; cf. Rom. 4:8). The latter translates the Hebrew *baruk,* and means "to be praised," or "worthy of praise" (Mark 14:61; Luke 1:68; Rom. 1:25; 9:5; II Cor. 1:3; 11:31; Eph. 1:3; I Peter 1:3).

[35] Or simply, "I thank him," etc. But χάριν ἔχω is perhaps a trifle stronger than εὐχαριστέω. It seems to mean, "I both feel and express my gratitude." See also p. 11; and cf. Luke 17:9; Heb. 12:28.

[36] Or "because." Whether ὅτι is taken as declarative or as causal makes very little difference here.

[37] The original has θέμενος, nominative, sing., masc., second aor. participle, *middle,* from τίθημι; hence, "having appointed me for himself," but in such cases – the action expressed by the participle being simultaneous with the action expressed by the finite verb – the meaning can be conveyed by using two finite verbs connected with "and."

[38] Literally "for the ages of (the) ages."

1:12-17

12. I acknowledge my gratitude to him who gave me strength, Christ Jesus our Lord, that he considered *me* trustworthy and appointed *me* for himself to (this) ministry.

The personal reference in the last clause of verse 11 is now expanded. Beautifully the apostle combines two ideas: a. I, though entirely unworthy, have been commissioned to proclaim the gospel of God's grace; and b. that grace and mercy was most gloriously displayed in my own conversion.

In this short paragraph (verses 12-17) we find not the usual stiff, stereotyped, and formal "thanksgiving to the gods or to a particular deity" which in ancient letters ordinarily follows the opening address. Instead, here we meet an outburst of gratitude, sincere and warm. Issuing from a heart that is filled with intense emotion, it rises to a higher and higher pitch until it ends in a sublime doxology (verse 17). What we actually see here is Paul as a radiant example of what God's law, lawfully used, can accomplish in the life of a former persecutor. Let the false teachers at Ephesus take note of this, so that they may no longer look upon the law as a toy, or as a tool for the aggrandizement of their own ego.

Deeply conscious is the apostle of his own inability to give adequate expression to his feeling of fervent gratitude. And this thankfulness is rendered not "to the gods," but "to Christ Jesus our Lord" (cf. verse 2).

Paul acknowledges his gratitude to Christ for three closely related benefits: a. for having imparted strength to him (he calls Christ his Enabler or Qualifier), b. for having judged him to be trustworthy or reliable, and c. for having "appointed" – this combines *destination* and *duty* (cf. N.T.C. on I Thess. 5:9) – him to the "ministry" (of the apostleship), a service rendered to the Lord in the spirit of love and personal devotion (for that is the meaning of the word διακονία; see Eph. 4:12; Col. 4:17; Heb. 1:14; also N.T.C. on I Thess. 3:2. For the technical sense see on I Tim. 3:10). Of course, these *three* ideas blend into *one*. It may be paraphrased as follows, "I thank him, Christ Jesus our Lord, my Strength-Imparter (cf. II Cor. 12:9; Phil. 4:13; II Tim. 4:17), who in his sovereign mercy considered me trustworthy – looking not at what I was in myself but at what his grace was doing within me (cf. I Cor. 4:7; Eph. 2:8) –, and accordingly for his own purpose appointed me to the ministry of the apostolic office." The *enabling*, the *favorable judging*, and the *appointing* were simultaneous. They all occurred when Paul was converted on the way to Damascus. See his *own* vivid account in Acts 9:15, 16; 22:1-21; 26:16-18; cf. Acts 13:1-4; and see N.T.C. on I Thess. 2:4.

13. He did this for such a one as I, **though previously I was a blasphemer and a persecutor and a wanton aggressor.**

That exactly was the astounding fact, namely, that on *such* a sinner *such* mercy had been bestowed.

"I know not why God's wondrous grace to me he hath made known,
Nor why, unworthy, Christ in love, redeemed me for his own."

Such mercy! for, note well: this very great sinner was not only *saved,* but was even deemed worthy to be entrusted with the ministry of the apostleship! All this happened though previous to his conversion the apostle had belonged to the very category of terrible sinners whom he has just described (see on verses 9b, 10 above): unholy and profane persons, etc. Yes, with reference to the first table of the law the apostle had been a *blasphemer* (Acts 26:11), ridiculing the name of Christ; and with reference to the second he had been a *persecutor* (see N.T.C. on I Thess. 3:12; II Thess. 1:4; cf. Acts 9:1, 4, 5; 22:4, 7; 26:10; Gal. 1:13). Moreover, in persecuting the church of God "beyond measure" he had persecuted Christ himself. "Saul, Saul, why do you persecute *me?*" Jesus had asked him. (Hence, in reality, here as always, man sins against *both* tables at once!) So violent and outrageous had been his attack upon believers – his very breath had been a threat of murder (Acts 9:1) – that he had been nothing less than "a wanton aggressor," one who committed outrage upon outrage against those who were of "The Way." We must never forget that the man who after his conversion (at Philippi) was "shamefully treated" had himself previous to his conversion "shamefully treated" the followers of Christ.

Thus this retrospect of sins reaches its sad climax: "blasphemer, persecutor, wanton aggressor." It was thus that grace had found this sinner. Surely, had this grace not been *sovereign, unconditional,* it would never have found *him!* **But I was accorded mercy because I acted ignorantly in unbelief.** Though his past conduct had been frightful, it had not amounted to the sin against the Holy Spirit, the wilful sin against better knowledge (Heb. 10:26). For such a sin there is no pardon (Matt. 12:31, 32; Heb. 6:4-6; I John 5:16; cf. Num. 15:30), nor does the one who lives in it have any desire for pardon. But *Paul's* case was different. During his campaign of aggression the apostle, in his state of "unbelief" with respect to the truth in Christ, had actually thought that he was offering service to God (see N.T.C. on John 16:2). He had been thoroughly convinced that he "ought to do many things contrary to the name of Jesus of Nazareth" (Acts 26:9). So, for *him* there was forgiveness, just as for the same reason there was forgiveness for the men of Israel who had killed the Prince of life (Acts 3:17; cf. also Luke 23:34). Yes, *mercy* – divine pity (see above, on verse 2) – had been accorded to this former member of a group of legalists – the Pharisees! – who were always bragging about "showing mercy" ("donating alms") to others. (Note that in the original the noun "alms" in

Matt. 6:2-4 and the verb "was accorded mercy" here in I Tim. 1:13 are derived from the same root.)

14. This *mercy,* as always, was united with *grace.* Grace abounding, yes super-abounding! Says Paul, **And it super-abounded (namely) the grace of our Lord, with faith and love in Christ Jesus.**

The transition from verse 13 to verse 14 is that from abounding sin to super-abounding grace. Here in verse 14 the emphasis is on the great change which by this grace was brought about in the life of the apostle. Note the position of the verb at the head of the sentence, for the sake of emphasis: "And it super-abounded, (namely) the grace of our Lord." *Grace,* here as in 1:2, is God's unmerited favor bestowed on the elect, producing consecrated lives (see N.T.C. on I Thess. 1:1). The verb *super-abounded* clearly points to *Paul* as the author of the Pastorals, for nowhere in the New Testament do we find such constant emphasis on the "super" character of redemption in Christ. It is Paul who declares:

"Where sin abounded, grace *super*-overflowed (overflowed all the more, Rom. 5:20)."

"Faith *super*-increases (is growing beyond measure, II Thess. 1:3)." So does love.

"I *super*-overflow (overflow abundantly) with joy (I am overjoyed, II Cor. 7:4)."

"We are praying *super-abundantly* (with intense earnestness, I Thess. 3:10)."

"The peace of God *sur* (-super)-passes all understanding (Phil. 4:7)."

"Esteem them (the leaders) *super*-abundantly (very highly) in love (I Thess. 5:13)."

"In order that I might not *super*-exalt myself (uplift myself to an excessive degree), there was given me a thorn in the flesh" (II Cor. 12:7).

It is clear that this "super" vocabulary is characteristic of Paul.

The phrase "with faith and love" indicates the effect of grace in Paul's heart and life. Grace *kindles* faith and love, floods the soul with these divine gifts. The apostle is fond of this combination (see N.T.C. on I Thess. 1:3 and 5:8). With him grace is ever *the root,* faith and love are *the trunk,* and good works are *the fruit* of the tree of salvation. That holds for the Pastorals as well as for the other epistles (Rom. 4:16; 11:6; Gal. 5:22-24; Eph. 2:4-10; II Thess. 2:13; Titus 2:11-14; 3:4-8). For the concepts "faith" and "love" see N.T.C. on I Thess. 5:8. This faith and this love are "in Christ Jesus," that is, they are centered in him. Paul possesses these graces because of his mystic union with Christ, the Savior.

15. Moreover, what holds for Paul holds for all saved sinners. Hence, there is first the statement of a truth applicable to *all* sinners whom Christ came to save. This is followed immediately by a clause of *personal* appro-

priation. **Reliable (is) the saying, and worthy of full acceptance, that Christ Jesus came into the world sinners to save, foremost of whom am I.**

Paul's saying with respect to the glorious purpose of Christ's first coming, this is the theme of the marvelous declaration which may be regarded as the very core of the gospel, its sum and substance. (It is comparable to John 3:16, on which see N.T.C.).

The *saying* is viewed from three aspects: 1. its reliability, 2. its contents, and 3. its personal appropriation.

1. *Its reliability*

Simple and great, like a granite rock, stands the word *reliable,* at the head of the sentence, without any connecting particle. It indicates that the proposition which it introduces has sustained the very crucial, fiery test of experience. It is not a mere *formula* but a considered *judgment.* It has been passed from mouth to mouth, as such sayings have the habit of doing, and, having embedded itself in the heart of the Christian community, where all the fears, hopes, struggles, and joys of these early Christians played around it, has survived gloriously. It has, in fact, become a sparkling epigram, a pithy, current commonplace, demanding and receiving the immediate, spontaneous, and enthusiastic assent and endorsement of all believers who hear it. The saying is the testimony of Christian experience, and is now also the utterance of the Holy Spirit.

The Pastorals contain five of these *reliable sayings:* I Tim. 1:15; 3:1; 4:8, 9; II Tim. 2:11-13; Titus 3:4-8. Although the clause, "Reliable is the saying," occurs only in these five passages of the Pastorals, and exactly in that form nowhere in the other ten epistles, this does not give anyone the right to conclude that Paul cannot have written the Pastorals. Surely no reason can be shown why the one who wrote, "Reliable (is) God," (I Cor. 1:9) and "Reliable (is) the One who calls y o u," (I Thess. 5:24) could not have written the grammatically exactly similar statement, "Reliable (is) the saying."

The famous saying, having been subjected to the flames of persecution and ridicule of Satan, had emerged from this crucible more sparkling and glorious than ever. Though not even four decades had elapsed since the death of the Savior, it had become even at this early date an unshakable conviction, "worthy of full acceptance," that is, entitled to wholehearted and universal *personal appropriation* with no reservations of any kind (or as we say colloquially "with no strings attached").

2. *Its contents*

The saying is, "That Christ Jesus came into the world sinners to save." Something should be said, first, about the *form* of this statement; then, about its *meaning.*

As to *the form,* it is asserted by several commentators that the saying is distinctly Johannine, since only John speaks of the Savior as "coming into the world." Some, even among those who regard *Paul* as the author of the Pastorals, proceed farther, and do not hesitate to connect this Johannine character of the language with the fact that the destination of I Timothy and II Timothy was *Ephesus* (where Timothy was carrying on his work as Paul's special envoy), *the very headquarters of John!* Accordingly, it is maintained that Timothy and the membership of the Ephesian church (on the assumption that the epistle was also read to the church), having become used to John's style, through his labors in their city, would appreciate such phraseology more than would believers who lived elsewhere.

However, this representation is open to the following objections:

a. The name "Christ Jesus" is Pauline rather than Johannine (it is never found in John's writings, often in Paul's).

b. It would seem altogether probable that the apostle John did not reach Ephesus until *after* Paul's death, hence also *after* the date of composition of I Timothy. The fact that Peter had received his "inheritance" in the heavens, and Paul his "crown" may have induced John to take charge of the orphan churches of Asia Minor. When we surmise that John reached Ephesus in the year 67 or 68, we cannot be far amiss (see also N.T.C. on John, vol. I, p. 29). But Paul wrote I Timothy in the year 63 or 64!

c. To a considerable extent the phraseology is, indeed, Johannine, but only in this sense that John has *preserved* and *transmitted* it. He did not *coin* it! It was *Jesus himself* who, according to the Fourth Gospel, again and again referred to himself as having "come into the world" (John 3:19; 9:39; 12:46; 16:28; 18:37). His earliest disciples learned it from him and copied it. Hence, it is not surprising that "the disciple whom Jesus loved" began to use it (John 1:11); and so did others, for example, Martha (John 11:27). Accordingly, here in I Tim. 1:15 Paul is simply making use of the Savior's own way of speaking about himself, and is employing language which, having been adopted from his lips by the earliest disciples, had been spread far and wide. It is only natural – in view, for example, of the close contact between Jerusalem and Ephesus, and of the "scattering" of the disciples due to persecution – that the saying had also reached Ephesus. And in this connection it is not at all improbable that the great apostle John, *before leaving Palestine,* had contributed his share toward perpetuating it.

As to the *meaning* of the expression, the combination "Christ Jesus" has already been explained (see N.T.C. on I Thess. 1:1, and footnote 19 in the present Commentary). The fact that this divinely anointed Savior "came into the world" indicates *not merely a change of location,* a "descent" from one place to another (from heaven to earth), but *a change of state and of moral and spiritual environment.* Hence, it implies the supreme *sacrifice,* the climax of condescending grace. From the infinite sweep of eternal delight in the very presence of his Father, Christ was willing to descend deeper and deeper into the realm of sin and misery. (The "coming into the world" includes incarnation, suffering, death.) In the original the word *sinners* immediately follows the word *world;* hence, not as most versions have it, ". . . came into the world to save sinners," but ". . . came into *the world sinners* to save." The juxtaposition of *world* and *sinners* shows that *world* is an *ethical* concept. For the meaning of *world* see also N.T.C. on John 1:10, 11, including footnote 26. The Lord of glory, so pure and holy that before his presence even the most consecrated men fall down as though dead (Rev. 1:17; cf. Is. 6:1-5), voluntarily entered the sphere to which he does not seem to belong, namely, the sphere in which the curse reigns. The reason for his entrance into this realm of sin is given in the words "sinners to save." This shows that the paradoxical *coming* was, after all, fully justified and gloriously motivated.

It took a former Pharisee to pour full and terrible meaning into that word *sinners.* As Pharisees saw it, even to eat with *sinners* was scandalous (Mark 2:16; Luke 5:30; 15:1, 2). With *a sinner* a prophet was not supposed to have any dealings (Luke 7:39). When the Pharisees wanted to heap insults upon Jesus, they would call him "a glutton, a drinker, *a friend of* (tax-collectors and) *sinners*" (Luke 7:34). They divided mankind into two groups: "the righteous," which was tantamount to saying, "ourselves," and "sinners," that is, "everybody else," "the riffraff," "the scum," "the people of the soil," "those who do not know the law." The Holy Spirit through Paul takes this opprobrious epithet "sinners," and applies it to *all* persons who are brought under conviction through the proper use of God's law. For them, for them *alone,* Christ Jesus came (Matt. 9:13; Luke 15:7; 19:10):

"Come, ye sinners, poor and needy,
  Weak and wounded, sick and sore;
Jesus ready stands to save you,
  Full of pity, love, and power;
He is able, He is able,
  He is willing, doubt no more;
He is able, He is able,
  He is willing, doubt no more.

"Come, ye weary, heavy-laden,
  Bruised and mangled by the fall;
If you tarry till you're better,
  You will never come at all;
Not the righteous, not the righteous,
  Sinners Jesus came to call.
Not the righteous, not the righteous,
  Sinners Jesus came to call."

(Joseph Hart)

If those in Ephesus who were using the law *un*lawfully were ever going to be saved, they would have to experience a fundamental change. These "righteous" persons would have to become "sinners" before God. Thus it is seen that verse 15 stands in close connection with *everything* that precedes (not only with verses 12-14 but also with verses 3-11).

It was *to save* sinners that Christ Jesus came into the world. He did not come to help them save themselves, nor to induce them to save themselves, nor even to enable them to save themselves. He came *to save* them!

In Paul's writings the expression *to save* means:

NEGATIVELY	POSITIVELY
to rescue men from sin's:	to bring men into the state of:
a. guilt (Eph. 1:7; Col. 1:14)	a. righteousness (Rom. 3:21-26; 5:1)
b. slavery (Rom. 7:24, 25; Gal. 5:1)	b. freedom (Gal. 5:1; II Cor. 3:17)
and	and
c. punishment:	c. blessedness:
(1) alienation from God (Eph. 2:12)	(1) fellowship with God (Eph. 2:13)
(2) the wrath of God (Eph. 2:3)	(2) the love of God "shed abroad" in the heart (Rom. 5:5)
(3) everlasting death (Eph. 2:5, 6)	(3) everlasting life (Eph. 2:1, 5; Col. 3:1-4).

Note that over against each evil stands a corresponding blessing. To be saved, then, means to be emancipated from the greatest evil, and to be placed in possession of the greatest good. The state of salvation is opposed to the state of "perishing" or being "lost." Cf. Luke 19:10; John 3:16.

3. *Its personal appropriation*

"... Christ Jesus came into the world *sinners to save, foremost of whom am I.*" This final clause (beginning with the word "foremost") has caused a wider variety of interpretation than almost any other in Paul's writings. The difficulty is this: it does not seem right that one who himself declares that before his conversion to the Christian faith he had lived according to the strictest sect of his religion as a Pharisee (Acts 26:5), should now call himself "chief of sinners." For various interpretations which I reject, and the reasons why I reject them, see the footnote.[39]

---

[39] The apostle means:

1. "I *belong to that group* of persons which consists of *foremost sinners.*" In Acts 28:17 the word "foremost" is used as a plural. Hence, what the apostle means is, "I am *one of the greatest* of sinners" (not necessarily *the greatest*). Moreover, he does not use the definite article. Hence, he does not really say, "I am *the* chief of sinners."

Objection: The presence or absence of the article makes very little difference, as is shown by the fact that the New Testament contains several passages in which "foremost" (or "first"), though without the article, has the absolute meaning: Matt.

Complete objectivity in exegesis demands that we state that the immediate context would seem to leave room for only *one* explanation, and that this explanation is the very one which the ordinary student of Scripture in reading his Bible, in quiet meditation, and also in song, generally gives to it. When the apostle, his heart troubled by the vivid recollection of the gruesome deeds of the past, gives written expression to the deeply rooted conviction and the poignant sorrow of his inner soul, and states, "Christ Jesus came into the world sinners to save, foremost of whom am I," he must have meant, "Of all sinners whom Christ Jesus came into the world to save, I am the greatest."

In fact, he not only states but *emphasizes* that no one else than he himself is "the chief of sinners." In the original he reserves for the first personal pronoun singular a place at the very end of the clause. I can see

---

10:2; John 8:7; 20:4; Eph. 6:2; I John 4:19. – In the present case the immediately following context (verse 16) also shows that the apostle describes himself as the *one* person who leads the procession.

2. "I am the chief of sinners, that is, the greatest sinner." But this is simply a figure of speech: *hyperbole,* as is, for example, the statement in II Kings 17:10, according to which the children of Israel set up idolatrous pillars "on every high hill and under every green tree."

Objection: verse 16 clearly shows that the apostle consistently carries through the idea contained in "foremost." Hence, this is no rhetorical exaggeration.

3. *"Historically* I am sinner No. 1. In course of time others will follow."

Objection: Even though there is perhaps *a small element* of truth in this explanation (see verse 16), it certainly does not account for the intensity of feeling which is expressed in the famous clause, and which causes it to end in a doxology! What Paul says is clearly nothing less than an instance of self-reproach and praise of God's infinite, incomprehensible mercy!

4. "I am *the most important sinner,* since as an apostle I have labored more abundantly than all the others" (cf. I Cor. 15:10).

Objection: This interpretation is foreign to the context, in which Paul, far from commending himself, describes himself as a former blasphemer, persecutor, and wanton aggressor (verse 13).

5. "I am the worst sinner." This is clearly what the apostle meant. It shows what a humble man he was, and how his past sins troubled him. However, though psychologically such self-reproach is understandable and to a certain extent justifiable, it is not necessary for us to agree with Paul's estimate of himself. He was actually a far better man than he thought he was.

Objection: This view under-estimates the seriousness of Paul's life as a persecutor, and fails to do full justice to Scripture's infallibility.

6. "Of *all* men, past, present, and future, I am the worst." The statement must be taken in its most absolute sense.

Objection: Then the apostle would be saying that he considers himself even worse than Judas and also even worse than "the man of lawlessness." The context does not point in this direction, and we cannot believe that the man who wrote II Thess. 2 would render such a verdict concerning himself.

7. "I am the worst of men." This self-abasement is morbid. Paul cannot have written these words. They sound insincere and point to another author.

Objection: The fact is that this self-reproach or self-condemnation is so characteristic of *Paul* (see what he says about himself in I Cor. 15:8, 9; Eph. 3:8) that others have exclaimed, "No one except Paul could have written it."

no good reason for radically changing this word-order. The translation should be, "of whom foremost am *I*," or "foremost of whom am *I*." Paul fixes the attention upon himself as a clear illustration of the depth of human *sin,* in order that in verse 16 he may return to that wonderful theme on which he has just dwelt (see verses 12-14), namely, the exaltation of the power of divine *grace, mercy* and *longsuffering.*

This interpretation of the disputed clause not only suits the context but is also in line with what Paul says about himself elsewhere:

"For I am the least of the apostles, not fit to be called an apostle, because I persecuted the church of God" (I Cor. 15:9).

"To me, the very least of all saints, was this grace given, to preach to the Gentiles the unsearchable riches of Christ" (Eph. 3:8).

In both these cases, just as here in I Tim. 1:15, the apostle is making a comparison between himself and other people whom Christ came to save (whether they were destined to become apostles or believers not clothed with any special office), and he makes the humble confession that he is *the least* of all saints, *the foremost* (or "chief") of sinners whom Christ came to save.

Taken in that sense and as a description of what *Paul* felt, the words of the familiar hymn are entirely correct:

"Chief of sinners though I be,
Jesus shed his blood for me;
Died that I might live on high;
Lives that I may never die."
(William McComb)

That the apostle, who certainly knew his own past, was able in all sincerity to describe himself as being "of sinners foremost" is less difficult to grasp if the following facts are borne in mind:

When, years before this, Paul for the first time heard the good tidings of salvation in Christ, he disbelieved. This disbelief he shared with many. Had his attitude to the Christian faith remained on this level, namely, one of unbelief, he would probably never have called himself, "of sinners *foremost.*" However, he became *a persecutor,* and not only "a" persecutor but *the most bitter persecutor of all!* His entire soul was wrapped up in the work of annihilating the church. He breathed threats and slaughter (Acts 9:1). Ruthlessly he bound and imprisoned both men and women. He did not confine his efforts to Jerusalem but was bent on uprooting the new religion wherever it was found, even if this would necessitate a trip all the way to Damascus. He was busy persecuting God's people "unto death," as he himself subsequently declared (Acts 22:4, 5). Had his plan succeeded, the church would have been smothered in its very birth; God's eternal decree would have been annulled; and Satan would have triumphed.

Indeed, so very great was his sin that, had it not been done in ignorance (see on verse 13), it would have been unpardonable.[40] Accordingly, when the apostle now says, "... sinners to save, foremost of whom am I," we must not begin to attenuate the meaning of "foremost." We should permit this glorious confession to stand within its own context, without either adding to it or subtracting anything from it.

Paul writes *"am* I," not *"was* I." This indicates that even now, years after his conversion, he deeply regrets his past. Besides, even a fully pardoned sinner is a sinner.

16. The *purpose* of God's marvelous grace is now stated: *proximate* purpose, verse 16; *ultimate* purpose, verse 17. **But for this reason I was accorded mercy, in order that in me as foremost Jesus Christ might exhibit all his longsuffering.** Chief of sinners, *nevertheless* the recipient of infinite mercy! That accounts for the "but." In fact, the magnitude of the sin made it necessary for mercy, if it was to be shown at all, to superabound. That is the very point which the apostle makes here in verse 16. For the expression "I was accorded mercy" see on verse 13. The purpose clause, "in order that in me as foremost," in connection with what follows, indicates that the apostle considers himself not only the chief of sinners but *also* — and in a certain sense *for that very reason* — the most glorious illustration of Christ's longsuffering. Here in verse 16 two ideas blend into one: Paul is "foremost" as an example of what Christ's longsuffering can accomplish. He is at the same time "foremost" as the head of a procession of persons to whom that longsuffering is shown. *Longsuffering* indicates the divine patience with respect to persons, by virtue of which wrath is withheld, the sinner is spared, and mercy is shown (for further details see N.T.C. on I Thess. 5:14). In the case of Paul this longsuffering had been exhibited *in full measure* (note "all his longsuffering," or as one might say, "the whole of it"), forgiving his frightful crimes, appointing him to the apostleship, and giving him strength for each day. This longsuffering had been thus exhibited **as a sketch for those who would come to rest their faith on him with a view to life everlasting.** In his gallery of grace the Artist-Savior had, as it were, drawn and put on exhibition *a sketch* (ὑποτύπωσις, acc. — ιν, used only here and in II Tim. 1:13), just like a master will first draw a rough pencil-sketch before attempting his final work. This sketch revealed Paul, as an illustration, pattern or model, of the type of work sovereign grace was going to perform in the lives of all those who through its efficacy *would come to* (cf. Acts 13:48: "had been ordained to") *rest their faith* (note durative present infinitive πιστεύειν) *on* (note ἐπί) Christ, the solid rock or the precious cornerstone (Matt. 7:24, 25; Is. 28:16;

---

[40] See J. Van Andel, *Paulus' Brieven aan Timotheus,* Leiden, 1904, p. 28.

cf. Rom. 9:33; 10:11; I Peter 2:6), with a view to *life everlasting,* a life that is opposed to "corruption" (Gal. 6:8) and "death" (Rom. 6:22). Death is *wages;* life everlasting is *a free gift* (Rom. 6:22, 23). It manifests itself in fellowship with God in Christ (John 17:3), partaking of the love of God (John 5:42), of his peace (John 16:33), and of his joy (John 17:13). It is also actually what its name indicates ever-lasting, never-ending life.

17. "And from my smitten heart with tears,
Two wonders I confess:
The wonders of his glorious love
And my own worthlessness."
(Elizabeth C. Clephane)

The contemplation of these "two wonders" which Paul has been discussing leads naturally to a doxology, which is all the more exuberant because in the present case the attention is riveted on Christ's incomprehensible longsuffering exhibited not only to *one* sinner but to an entire procession of sinners whom Christ came to save: Paul "the foremost" and those who followed him. Through Christ, accordingly, God displays his glorious attributes *in every* age, for he is "the King of the ages." This accounts for the form in which this doxology is cast: **So to the King of the ages, the imperishable, invisible, only God (be) honor and glory forever and ever! Amen.**

Man proposes; God disposes. Man – for instance Paul before his conversion – may try *to destroy* the church; God will *establish* it. And for that purpose he will use the very man who tried to destroy it! Hence, though man is a mere *creature* of time, God is *the King* of the ages, over-ruling evil for good; directing to its predetermined goal whatever happens throughout each era of the world's history. His "dominion endures throughout *all* generations" (Ps. 145:13).

This implies that he is the eternal God, and as such "imperishable" [41] (the best reading). *His* arms never become tired (Deut. 32:27). *He* never grows weary (Is. 40:28). Decay and death are not applicable to *him* (Ps. 103:15-17). *He* never changes (Mal. 3:6). On the contrary, *he* is the inexhaustible reservoir of strength, ever new, for his people (Is. 40:29-31). For the doctrine of God's *imperishability* see also Rom. 1:23; and cf. the synonym *immortality* (see on I Tim. 6:16).

When one thinks of God as the *im*perishable, the mind inevitably turns

---

[41] Although it is true that the idea of God's "imperishability" is also found in the works of Greek and later Jewish philosophers, to speak of Paul's "borrowing" or "deriving" the idea from them is highly precarious, and this for two reasons: a. the doctrine of God's imperishability is taught and presupposed throughout the Old Testament; b. the philosophical idea and the scriptural idea are not identical (see on I Tim. 6:16).

to those objects that are perishable, for example, grass, the flowers of the field (Ps. 103:15-17), man's body, birds, quadrupeds, creeping creatures (Rom. 1:23). These are all visible. God, being imperishable, is also *invisible,* "whom no one has seen or can see" (I Tim. 6:16). It is only in his Image (Col. 1:15, 16) that man "sees Him who is invisible," and then only *by faith* (Heb. 11:27), and in a finite manner. Never shall we be able to "find out the Almighty unto perfection" (Job 11:7, 8). Paul surely was not able to comprehend the grace of God which had been shown to him. Here all reasoning stops. There is room only for doxologies!

Such a God, finally, is the "only" God; not merely in the coldly abstract sense that numerically there is but *one* God, but in the warm, scriptural sense, namely, that this *one* God is "unique, incomparable, glorious, lovable" (Deut. 6:4, 5; Is. 40:12-31; Rom. 16:27; I Cor. 8:4, 5).

Out of the wellsprings of Paul's spontaneity issues the exclamation – it is a veritable outburst coming from a heart that has experienced what it means to have *such* a God as one's own God – that "for the ages of (the) ages," that is, "forever and ever," *honor and glory* (praise and adoration) be rendered to the God who in his being and attributes is so wonderful. The doxology ends with the word of solemn assent and emphatic confirmation, "Amen" (see N.T.C. on John 1:51).

---

18 This charge I commit to you, my child Timothy, in agreement with the previous prophetic utterances concerning you, in order that with their aid you may war the good warfare, 19 holding on to faith and a good conscience, (the kind of conscience) which some have discarded and have suffered shipwreck with reference to their faith; 20 among whom are Hymenaeus and Alexander, whom I have handed over to Satan, in order that they might be disciplined not to blaspheme.

1:18-20

18. This charge I commit to you. The charge referred to has been clearly set forth in the entire preceding section, especially in verses 3-11. It is the "mandate" or "instruction" (see N.T.C. on I Thess. 4:2) that Timothy stay on at Ephesus in order that he may teach certain individuals not to make misuse of the law but to use it lawfully, unto conversion to Christ, *the sinners'* Savior.

Paul *commits* or *entrusts* (cf. Luke 12:48; 23:46) this charge to one whom he calls **my child Timothy.** This expression of endearment is not strange if the following three facts are borne in mind: a. under God, Timothy owed his conversion to Paul, who was therefore his spiritual father; b. the disciple was the apostle's junior by several years; c. he was amiable, dependable, and co-operative even to the extent of performing tasks that ran counter to his natural disposition.

The charge was not new, arbitrary or unfair, but entirely **in agreement with the previous prophetic utterances concerning you.** The construction of this compound phrase is difficult, and has led to widely different interpretations.[42]

The previous prophetic utterances include *at least* the following:

a. The Spirit-guided recommendations whereby on the *second* missionary journey, about the year 51, Paul's attention had *once more* been turned to Timothy (Acts 16:1-3). – It should be borne in mind that previously Paul and Barnabas had themselves been "separated" by the church, with the co-operation of certain *prophets* (Acts 13:1-3). Timothy's *conversion* to the Christian faith seems to have occurred on the *first* missionary journey.

b. The inspired words which had been spoken in connection with Timothy's ordination (see especially on I Tim. 4:14. Cf. I Tim. 6:12; II Tim. 2:2; Acts 14:23).

These previous prophetic utterances had probably been of the following nature. They singled out Timothy for special service in God's kingdom, summarized his duties, predicted his suffering, and strengthened him with the promise of divine help in all his trials. At least, such were the prophetic utterances in connection with *Paul's own* call to duty (Acts 9:15, 16; 22:14, 15, 21; 26:16-18). We may assume that in Timothy's case words of somewhat similar character had been spoken.

"My child Timothy, I wish to remind you of these prophetic utterances," says Paul as it were, **in order that with their aid you may war the good (or noble or excellent) warfare.** Timothy is viewed as a high-ranking officer, who has received his "orders," and is "warring his warfare" (see I Cor. 9:7; II Cor. 4:4; 19:3) against evil, particularly against the Satan-inspired perversion of doctrine described in verses 3-12 (cf. I Tim. 6:12; II Tim. 4:7; Eph. 6:10-20). In this warfare reflection on former prophecies can be very encouraging (see N.T.C. on John 16:1, 4). They remind one of the fact that nothing happens contrary to the eternal decree of God, that one is engaged

---

[42] The original has κατὰ τὰς προαγούσας ἐπὶ σὲ προφητείας. In the New Testament the verb προάγω means *to lead* (or *to bring*) *out* or *forth* (Acts 12:6; 16:30; 17:5; 25:26); or *to precede* (Matt. 2:9; 14:22; 21:9; 21:31; 26:32; 28:7; Mark 19:32; 14:28; 16:7). In all the instances mentioned so far the verbal form has an immediately following pronoun-object. However, at times either the object is not mentioned, though implied, or the verbal form may even become entirely intransitive (Mark 6:45; 11:9; Luke 18:39; I Tim. 5:24). The intransitive connotation would seem to be especially present in such cases as II John 9 ("whoever *goes ahead*") and Heb. 7:18 (in which case the participle has the force of an adjective: "a foregoing commandment" = "a *former* commandment"). In the passage under study (I Tim. 1:18) no pronoun-object is expressed, and probably none is implied. We seem to have an intransitive use similar to that in Heb. 7:18. Hence, we translate, "the preceding prophetic utterances with respect to you," or "the previous prophetic utterances concerning you." The fact that ἐπί with acc. may mean "concerning" is clear from Mark 9:12.

in a battle which is not merely his own but the Lord's, and that courage and faithfulness will certainly be rewarded.

19. The manner in which this warfare must be carried on is now set forth: **holding on to faith and a good conscience.**

Timothy is admonished *to hold* faith, that is, *to hold on* to it. In warring his warfare against errors and errorists he must keep clinging to *the truth* of the gospel. The fact that the word *faith* here in verse 19 means *truth* is clear from II Tim. 2:17, 19. By living and teaching in accordance with this truth, remaining firm and stedfast in the midst of all opposition, Timothy will be obeying the voice of *conscience*. For the meaning of "a good conscience" see on verse 5. Paul continues: **(the kind of conscience) which certain individuals have discarded and have suffered shipwreck with reference to their faith.**

A Christian must be both a good soldier and a good sailor. Now a good sailor does not *thrust away* or *discard* the rudder of the ship. The good conscience – one that obeys the dictates of the Word as applied to the heart by the Holy Spirit – is the rudder, guiding the believer's vessel into the safe harbor of everlasting rest. But "certain individuals" (the Ephesian heretics; see on verse 3) have discarded that rudder.[43] The inevitable result was that with reference to their *faith* – the truth which they had confessed with their lips; the name of Christ which they had named (see on II Tim. 2:17-19) – they *suffered shipwreck*. If even literal shipwreck is agonizing, as Paul had experienced (Acts 27:39-44; II Cor. 11:25), how much more to be feared is *religious* shipwreck!

20. The ringleaders among the shipwrecked are now mentioned: **Among whom are Hymenaeus and Alexander.** The name of the first is derived from Hymen, the god of marriage. This Hymenaeus is also mentioned in II Tim. 2:17. Associated with him was Alexander, which means "defender of men." Then as now it was a very common name. Hence, there is no good reason to identify the Alexander to whom Paul refers here in I Tim. 1:20 with the one mentioned in Acts 19:33, 34, who on the occasion of the Ephesian riot tried to turn the anger of the mob away from the Jews; nor with the one mentioned in II Tim. 4:14, 15, who was a metal-worker *in*

---

[43] Paul does not definitely say that he regards conscience to be *the rudder*. In the abstract he may have been thinking of conscience as the ship's furniture, tackle, or cargo. In that case the verb which we have translated "discarded" may be rendered "thrown overboard" (cf. Acts 27:18, 19, 38). He may even have been thinking of the ship's anchor. However, if, as seems probable, his reference to shipwreck as a result of "pushing away" conscience implies that he is thinking of conscience under the symbolism of some object pertaining to the ship, what figure would be more logical than that of a *rudder?* Cf. Rom. 2:14, 15, in which passage conscience is represented as a law which one obeys (for example, just like a ship obeys its rudder). – Also, a ship without a rudder may readily suffer shipwreck.

Rome. The Hymenaeus and Alexander to whom Paul refers here in I Tim. 1:20 were leaders among the Ephesian *heretics.* They were self-righteous persons who yearned to be law-teachers, although they understood neither the words which they were speaking nor the themes on which they were harping with such confidence (see on verse 7). As has been indicated (see on verse 4), they specialized in myths and fanciful stories about family-trees. See also on II Tim. 2:17.

So far did these heretical teachers advance in error that they even railed at the true presentation of the gospel. Hence, Paul declares **whom I have handed over to Satan in order that they may be disciplined not to blaspheme.** The expression "handed over to Satan," which also occurs in I Cor. 5:5, is somewhat obscure. That it refers to expulsion from the church ("excommunication") — a sentence to be carried out by the congregation under the direction of its elders — seems certain (cf. I Cor. 5:2, 7). Did it imply even more than this, for example, *bodily* suffering or disease? Though this is denied by some,[44] the evidence, nevertheless, seems to favor the idea. Let anyone study Job 2:6, 7; I Cor. 5:5; 11:30; Rev. 2:22; then also Acts 5:1-11; 13:11. This extraordinary gift, namely, to commit a person to Satan's power, in order that he might suffer anguish not only in soul but also in body, may strike us as unbelievable, but is it, after all, so strange that added to the charismatic gift of bodily *healing* was the power to inflict bodily *suffering?* If we deny the latter, should we not also deny the former?

However, even when this extreme measure was resorted to, its purpose was *remedial.* Not damnation but reclamation was the object, "in order that they may be *disciplined* (cf. II Tim. 2:25) not to blaspheme." Here speaks the same loving heart as in II Thess. 3:14, 15 (see N.T.C. on that passage) and in II Cor. 2:5-11. The apostle is earnestly desirous that the discipline — the divine pedagogy — imposed may have a salutary effect on Hymenaeus and Alexander. He is hoping and praying that by means of this dire affliction these false teachers may come to see themselves as grievous sinners and may be brought to genuine repentance, so that they will no longer rail at the truth and thereby revile its Author.

Synthesis of Chapter 1

See the Outline at the beginning of the chapter.

Paul salutes Timothy. In this salutation the apostle shows that he belongs to Christ Jesus who has entrusted him with the task of preaching the gospel. His authority is equal to that of the Twelve. Beautifully blending apostolic authority and tender love, Paul calls Timothy his genuine child in the sphere of faith, and pronounces upon him grace, mercy, and

[44] For example, by Lenski, *op. cit.,* p. 534.

peace, springing from the twofold source, "God the Father and Christ Jesus our Lord."

He charges Timothy to stay on at Ephesus in order to combat the errors of novelty-teachers, who instead of being crushed by God's moral law, here summarized, use that law as a take-off point for fictitious narratives about ancestors. The apostle calls their argumentations "futile talk," and accuses them of selfish ambition. He indicates the essence of the charge which Timothy must deliver to the churches of Ephesus and vicinity, namely, "love which springs from a pure heart, a conscience good, and a faith without hypocrisy."

Paul thanks God who has made him – *"chief of sinners"* – a minister of the glorious gospel of salvation full and free.

In this connection he introduces the first of five "reliable sayings." Taken together, the five comprise a summary of doctrine (from Theology to Eschatology) as confessed by the early church.

The Five Reliable Sayings

"Reliable (is) the saying, and worthy of full acceptance, that Christ Jesus came into the world sinners to save." Paul adds the words of personal appropriation, "foremost of whom am I" (I Tim. 1:15).

"Reliable is the saying, If anyone aspires to the office of overseer, he desires a noble work" (I Tim. 3:1).

"(For) while physical training is of *some* benefit, godly living is of benefit *in every way*. Reliable is that saying and worthy of full acceptance" (I Tim. 4:8, 9).

"Reliable is the saying:
(For) if we died with (him), we shall also live with (him);
if we endure, we shall also reign with (him);
if we shall deny (him), he on his part will also deny us;
if we are faithless, he on his part remains faithful" (II Tim. 2:11-13).

"(But) when the kindness of God our Savior and his love toward man appeared, he saved us, not by virtue of works which we ourselves had performed in (a state of) righteousness, but according to his mercy, through the washing of regeneration and renewing by the Holy Spirit, which he poured out upon us richly through Jesus Christ our Savior, in order that, having been justified by his grace, we might become heirs-in-hope of life everlasting. Reliable (is) this saying" (Titus 3:4-8a).

Outline of Chapter 2

Theme: *The Apostle Paul, Writing to Timothy, Gives Directions For the Administration of the Church*

Directions with respect to Public Worship

2:1-7 A. When the congregation gathers for worship prayers must be made "in behalf of all men."

2:8-15 B. Both the men and the women must behave properly:

1. The men, in every place of public worship, must lift up holy hands;
2. The women, in getting ready "to go to church," must dress becomingly, and at the place of worship must show that they understand and have accepted their divinely ordained position.

CHAPTER II

I TIMOTHY 2:1

2 1 First of all, then, I urge that supplications, prayers, intercessions, thanksgivings be made in behalf of all men, 2 in behalf of kings and all who are
in high positions, that we may lead a tranquil and calm life in all godliness and
gravity. 3 This is excellent and acceptable in the sight of God our Savior, 4 who
desires all men to be saved and to come to the acknowledgment of the truth. 5 For
(there is) but *one* God and (there is) but *one* Mediator between God and men, the
man Christ Jesus, 6 who gave himself as a ransom for all, the testimony (to be
borne) in due season; 7 for which purpose I was appointed a herald and apostle —
I am telling the truth, I am not lying — a teacher of Gentiles in (the realm of) faith
and truth.

2:1-7

A new subject begins here: Directions for Public Worship:

1. First of all, then, I urge that supplications, prayers, intercessions, thanksgivings be made in behalf of all men.

Paul has something to "urge" upon Timothy. He is, as it were, "calling him aside" in order to exhort him with respect to a matter of utmost significance (note "first of all"). It concerns the relation of the church to the state. If churches are to flourish spiritually, public worship is highly desirable, to say the least; but such public worship cannot be conducted to the best advantage (calmly, without disturbance; see on verse 2b) unless the church does its duty with respect to the state. Besides, the church is a light shining in the darkness. It must seek to win others for Christ and his kingdom. Is it possible that Paul, on his visit to Ephesus, had noticed that prayer for rulers was being neglected?

So the apostle urges his representative to see to it that wherever in the Ephesian territory God's people may gather for public worship, kings and all that are in high positions be remembered in prayer, in fact that supplications, prayers, intercessions, thanksgivings be made in behalf of *all* men.

The four synonyms that are used here do not amount to meaningless repetitions.

The first word, *supplications,* means petitions for the fulfilment of certain definite needs which are keenly felt. Fully aware of his complete dependence on God, one asks that *this* particular illness may be removed, or that *these* disturbing tidings may be over-ruled for good, etc. Supplications, then, are humble requests which one makes in the light of this or that concrete situation in which God, he alone, can furnish the help that is needed.

The next word, *prayers,* is more general in meaning. As often used, it covers *every* form of reverent address directed to the Deity. Whether we "take hold on God" by means of confession, intercession, supplication, adoration, or thanksgiving, we can in each instance speak of being engaged in *prayer.* Both the Greek and the English word have that general meaning. However, in view of the fact that the word is here used as one of a list of four synonyms, and since it is clear that each of the other three stresses a particular aspect of prayer-life, the conclusion seems warranted that its meaning in this particular passage (and probably also in I Tim. 5:5 and Phil. 4:6) must be somewhat restricted. I venture the thought that it here refers to requests for the fulfilment of needs that are *always* present (in contrast with *supplications* in *specific* situations): the need for more wisdom, greater consecration, progress in the administration of justice, etc. Even when thus interpreted, the meaning is still very broad.

The noun *intercessions* occurs only here and in I Tim. 4:5. I have hesitated a long time before adopting as my own (for the *present* passage) the translation of the A.V., A.R.V., R.S.V., and many others. It is perhaps impossible to find *one* word in the English language which will be the full equivalent of the original. I might begin by stressing the fact that it is by no means true that the noun (used in the original: ἔντευξις) in and by itself (that is, apart from the context) necessarily conveys the thought which we *today* generally associate with the word *intercession:* "a pleading in the interest of others." In the only other New Testament passage in which it is used (I Tim. 4:5) it does *not necessarily* have that meaning. And the related *verb* (ἐντυγχάνω) can be used in connections in which (together with a preposition) it indicates a pleading *against* rather than a pleading *in behalf of* (Rom. 11:2; and cf. Acts 25:24).

The basic idea contained in both verb and noun is rather that of "falling in with," "meeting with in order to converse freely," hence, "freedom of access." A person (or *P*erson) finds himself in the very audience-chamber of God the Father. The privilege of having a sacred interview with him is *his own,* whether *by nature,* as in the case of Christ or of the Holy Spirit, or *by grace,* as in the case of a believer.

But though this is the basic idea of the word, the particular context in which it is used changes the meaning slightly. Thus it is indeed true that the *verbal* form in the New Testament passages not yet referred to indicates a confident interview which is "in the interest of others." Hence, it takes on the meaning of *intercession.* According to Rom. 8:27 the Holy Spirit, having come to our assistance, *intercedes* for us. Christ, upon his heavenly throne, remembers us similarly (Rom. 8:34). In fact, he *evermore lives to intercede for us* (Heb. 7:25). In our present passage (I Tim. 2:1) this meaning — namely, pleading in the interest of others, and doing this without "holding back" in any way — fits exactly, as is shown by what immediately follows: "in behalf of all men, in behalf of kings and all who are in high positions."

The final word, *thanksgivings* (that is, completing the circle, so that the blessings that come from God return to him again in the form of *expressed gratitude*) is clear enough. Nevertheless, it must be borne in mind that not only supplications, prayers, and intercessions but also thanksgivings must be made *in behalf of all men,* including kings, etc.

Indeed, such invocations must be made "in behalf of" or "for" (see N.T.C. on John 10:11, for the meaning of the preposition) *all men.* Several expositors feel certain that this means every member of the whole human race; every man, woman, and child, without any exception whatever. And it must be readily admitted that *taken by itself* the expression *all men* is capable of this interpretation. Nevertheless, every calm and unbiased interpreter also admits that *in certain contexts* this simply cannot be the meaning.

Does Titus 2:11 really teach that the saving grace of God has appeared to every member of the human race without any exception? Of course not! It matters little whether one interprets "the appearance of the saving grace" as referring to the bestowal of salvation itself, or to the fact that the gospel of saving grace has been preached to every person on earth. In either case it is impossible to make "all men" mean "every individual on the globe without exception."

Again, does Rom. 5:18 really teach that "every member of the human race" is "justified"?

Does I Cor. 15:22 really intend to tell us that "every member of the human race" is "made alive in Christ"?

But if that be true, then it follows that Christ did not only *die* for every member of the human race, but that he also actually *saved* every one without any exception whatever. Most conservatives would hesitate to go that far.

Moreover, if, wherever it occurs, the expression "all men" or its equivalent has this absolutely universalistic connotation, then would not the following be true:

(a) Every member of the human race regarded John the Baptist as a prophet (Mark 11:32).

(b) Every member of the human race wondered whether John was, perhaps, the Christ (Luke 3:15).

(c) Every member of the human race marveled about the Gadarene demoniac (Mark 5:20).

(d) Every member of the human race was searching for Jesus (Mark 1:37).

(e) It was reported to the Baptist that all members of the human race were flocking to Jesus (John 3:26).

And so one could easily continue. Even today, how often do we not use the expression "all men" or "everybody" without referring to every member of the human race? When we say, "If everybody is ready, the meeting can begin," we do not refer to everybody on earth!

Thus also in the present passage (I Tim. 2:1), it is *the context* that must decide. In this case the context is clear. Paul definitely mentions *groups* or *classes* of men: kings (verse 2), those in high position (verse 2), the Gentiles (verse 7). He is thinking of rulers and (by implication) subjects, of Gentiles and (again by implication) Jews, and he is urging Timothy to see to it that in public worship not a single group be omitted. In other words, the expression "all men" as here used means "all men without distinction of race, nationality, or social position," not "all men individually, one by one."

Besides, how would it even be possible, except in a very vague and global manner (the very opposite of *Paul's* constant emphasis!), to remember in prayer *every person on earth?*

2. In explanation of the expression "in behalf of all men" the apostle continues: **in behalf of kings and all who are in high position.**

How necessary, this admonition! Even today! The apostle is probably thinking, first of all, of sovereign rulers of states, as they succeed one another in the course of history; and of all other functionaries subject to them. He must have had in mind the then-reigning emperor Nero, and further: the proconsuls (Acts 19:38), Asiarchs (Acts 19:31), the town-clerk (a rather influential position, Acts 19:35), etc.

However, had the emperor been Augustus or Tiberias or Caligula or Claudius, had he been Vespasian or Titus or Domitian; had those who ruled under them been *kings* properly so called, as for instance Herod the Great, tetrarchs such as Herod Antipas, ethnarchs such as Archelaus—even emperors, tetrarchs, and ethnarchs were sometimes called *kings* (John 19:15; Matt. 14:9; Matt. 2:22) —; had they been procurators such as Pontius Pilate, or had they been invested with any other political office, the charge, "Pray for them," would have been exactly the same. It is a commandment which holds for every age and for every region. President Eisenhower, Queen Elizabeth, Queen Juliana, etc., etc., the Holy Spirit via Paul bids us to remember them all before the throne of grace. The present precept is as general as is the closely related one found in Rom. 13:1.

And the purpose is hinted in the words which follow: **that we may lead a tranquil and calm life in all godliness and gravity.** The rare adjectives *tranquil* and *calm* (the former occurring only here; the latter only here and in I Peter 3:4) differ but slightly in meaning. The first seems to refer to a life which is free from *outward* disturbance; the second, to a life which is free from *inner* perturbation. Paul exhorts the Thessalonians to be ambitious about "living calmly" (see N.T.C. on I Thess. 4:11).

Of course, this merely "hints" at the real purpose of praying for the rulers. Paul certainly does not mean to encourage a life of ease. His aims are never selfish. Rather, the idea is this: freedom from disturbances, such as wars and persecutions, will facilitate the spread of the gospel of salvation in Christ to the glory of God. One must read the present passage in the light of the immediately following context (verses 3 and 4), of other passages from the Pastorals (I Tim. 1:15; 4:16), and of passages from Paul's other epistles (I Cor. 9:22; 10:31).

Included in the purpose of Paul's prayer is also this, that believers, leading a life of tranquility and calm, may do nothing to create unnecessary disturbance, and may conduct themselves "in all godliness and gravity," that is, "in all *piety* and *respectability* or *dignity,"* striving to be blameless in their conduct or attitude both *toward God* and *toward men.* See also pp. 10, 11 on these two words. For the first see on I Tim. 3:16; for the second, I Tim. 3:4, 8, 11.

3, 4. How such prayers are viewed by God is now stated: **This is excellent** (or **beautiful, admirable) and acceptable in the sight of God our Savior, who desires all men to be saved and to come to the acknowledgment of the truth.**

To *the eye* of God such praying is excellent or admirable. To *his heart* it is acceptable, most welcome. This stands to reason, for his name is "God, our Savior" (see on I Tim. 1:1). Though *men* may at times feel inclined to skip prayer for kings and those who are in authority, especially when the co-operation from the side of princes is not what it should be, in God's sight the matter looks differently. He does not see things as we see them (I Sam. 16:7). In more ways than one, conditions of tranquility and calm promote the spread of the gospel of salvation. And it is he "who desires all men to be saved." The expression "all men" here in verse 4 must have the same meaning as in verse 1; see the discussion there. In a sense, salvation is universal, that is, it is not limited to any *one* group. Churches must not begin to think that prayers must be made for subjects, not for rulers; for Jews, not for Gentiles. No, it is the intention of God our Savior that "all men without distinction of rank, race, or nationality" be saved.[45] What

[45] On the question, "Did Christ die for each individual human being, including Judas and the antichrist, actually atoning for the guilt and paying the debt of each and everyone?" see N.T.C. on John, Vol. II, p. 111, and the excellent discussions in the following works:

L. Berkhof, *Vicarious Atonement Through Christ,* Grand Rapids, Mich., pp. 151-178.

this "being saved" implies has been shown in connection with I Tim. 1:15.

Now in the process of *being saved* (taken as a whole) men are not passive. On the contrary, they become active. It is God's will that they come to the acknowledgment of *the truth,* that is, of the way of salvation which is revealed in the Word. Such *acknowledgment* is more than intellectual *knowledge* (γνῶσις). It is joyful *recognition* (ἐπίγνωσις), deep, spiritual *discernment.* See its use in Phil. 1:9; Col. 1:9; 2:2; 3:10. Thus we can also understand the expression "repentance unto the acknowledgment of the truth" (II Tim. 2:25). It is possible for a person to learn a good many things in a merely intellectual fashion, and yet never really come to a *recognition* or *appropriation* of the truth (II Tim. 3:7). There is a "knowing" which is different from a "knowing fully" (see the related verb in I Cor. 13:12). The purpose of prayer for all men, without distinction of rank,

---

L. Boettner, *The Reformed Doctrine of Salvation,* Grand Rapids, 1932, pp. 150-161.

A source-document for the Arminian position is "the remonstrance" or "Five Arminian Articles" (A. D. 1610). P. Schaff, in *Creeds of Christendom,* New York, fifth edition 1919, Vol. III, pp. 545-549, gives the original Dutch text, a Latin, and an English translation, in parallel columns. Here we read, ". . . Jesus Christ, the Savior of the world, died for all men and for every man, so that he has obtained for them all, by his death on the cross, redemption and the forgiveness of sins; yet . . . no one actually enjoys the forgiveness of sins except the believer." On the whole, in this historic document the Arminians express themselves with restraint. (For other literature on this question, presenting either side — or both sides —, see the bibliographies in R. L. Dabney, *Systematic and Polemic Theology,* Richmond, 1927, p. 579; H. Bavinck, *Gereformeerde Dogmatiek,* Kampen, third edition, 1918, Vol. III, pp. 519-521; and the works listed at the end of the article "Arminius and Arminianism," in *The New Schaff-Herzog Encyclopaedia of Religious Knowledge,* Vol. 1, pp. 296, 297. Also *The Writings of Arminius* (3 vols.).

The dispute between the followers of Arminius and those of Gomarus was brought to a head at the Synod of Dort. Here the position of those who favored the limited Atonement won the day. See "The Canons of the Synod of Dort, held A. D. 1618, 1619," in P. Schaff, *Creeds of Christendom,* Vol. III, pp. 550-597. The second head of doctrine declares that the design of the Atonement is limited to the elect, but that the promise of the gospel should be published to all nations, and that the sacrifice of Christ is *sufficient* for everyone without exception. Among the various works in which the proceedings of the Synod of Dort are discussed I have found L. H. Wagenaar, *Van Strijd En Overwinning* to be especially informative. In their *conduct* both sides seem to have gone too far at times. Extreme "Remonstrants" (they preferred this name to "Arminians") branded the decisions of the Synod as "the devil's triumph." They grossly misrepresented the Calvinistic position, just as some of their followers are doing even today. And on the other hand, one finds it hard to defend the manner in which the Synod's strictly Calvinistic president dismissed the Arminian opponents. Brusquely gesturing for them to leave, the on the whole highly respected Rev. Johannes Bogerman reminded them that they had begun with lies and ended with lies. Then, in a voice of thunder, he shouted, "You are dismissed. Get going."

The Arminian position on this and related doctrinal points gained many adherents, especially during the eighteenth century. It is said to have leavened religious thinking in America. A strong advocate of the unrestricted atonement view is Lenski in his commentaries.

race, and nationality, is that they may be saved, and may come to "full knowledge," a knowledge in which not only the mind but also the heart partakes. The purpose of such praying corresponds with God's own sovereign desire.

5. The position, "God desires *all* men – men from *every* rank and station, tribe and nation – to be saved" is true, **For (there is but) *one* God, and (there is but) *one* Mediator between God and men, the man Christ Jesus.**

There is not one God for this nation, one for another; one God for slaves and one for free men; one God for rulers, one for subjects. Paul is his own best interpreter: "For in one Spirit were we all baptized into one body, whether Jews or Greeks, whether bond or free; and were all made to drink of one Spirit" (I Cor. 12:13). Again, "or is God the God of Jews only? Is he not the God of Gentiles also? Yes, of Gentiles also: if it be true (and it certainly is true) that God is *one* . . ." (Rom. 3:29). That the apostle is actually thinking of the distinction "ruler . . . subject" follows from the immediately *preceding* context (I Tim. 2:2a). That he has in mind the distinction "Jew . . . Gentile" is apparent from the immediately *following* context (I Tim. 2:7b).[46]

Not only the realm of creation but also that of redemption is united under *one* Head. Hence, not only is there only *one* God; there is also only "*one* Mediator *of* (here in the sense of *between*) God and men." The present is the only passage in which Paul speaks of *Christ* as "Mediator." However, in Gal. 3:19, the apostle also uses the term, with probable reference to Moses, who as mediator transmitted God's law to the people. In Gal. 3:20 he speaks in general about "a mediator." It is the author of the epistle to the Hebrews who discusses at some length the position of Christ, our heavenly Highpriest, as Mediator (Heb. 8:6; 9:15; 12:24), "the Mediator of a new covenant." By derivation the word simply indicates someone who stands "in the middle." The purpose for which he takes this in-between position must be derived, in each single case, from the context, or from parallel passages. In the present case it is not open to legitimate doubt that the apostle takes his *point of departure* in the fact that Christ is the One who has voluntarily taken his stand between the offended God and the

[46] It is not at all necessary here to regard *one* as subject and *God* as predicate, so that we should have to translate "For *one* is God; *one* also is Mediator," etc. Dr. C. Bouma in his comment on this passage is entirely correct when he points out that Paul's argument is not here directed (except by implication) against polytheism, but rather against one of the practical consequences of polytheism, namely, that each nation has its own God who is concerned especially with that nation. No, there is *one* God who cares for all his people gathered from all over the world!

What we have here, accordingly, is simply an instance of abbreviated expression. The words, "There is but" are easily supplied. The very context requires them. On "abbreviated expression" see N.T.C. on John 5:31.

offending sinner, in order to take upon himself the wrath of God which the sinner has deserved, thereby delivering the latter. This is clear because the entire context speaks of *salvation* (verse 4), and of Christ as a *ransom* (see on verse 6). A striking explanation is found in Gal. 3:13, "Christ redeemed us from the curse of the law, having become a curse *for* (or *over*) us." In that passage the Savior is pictured as standing *over* us, that is, *between* us and the curse of the law, so that the curse falls on him, and we are saved.[47] However, it is clear that in the present passage (I Tim. 2:5) the concept *Mediator* is even slightly broader. Not only does Christ in this capacity restore sinners to the right legal relationship to God, but he also brings them to *"the knowledge* of the truth" (verse 4); and causes *the testimony* of this glorious truth to be borne to them (verse 6). Hence, *he both establishes peace and reveals it to men,* persuading them to accept the good news. He stands revealed as Mediator in this *twofold* sense.[48]

Note the manner in which the identity of this Mediator is revealed: *"one* Mediator between God and *men, the man* Christ Jesus." To think of *men* in this connection means to think of *man,* the man Jesus Christ. Hence *men* and *man* are juxtaposed. Had salvation been intended only for one particular group – say, only for the Jews – the apostle would have written, *"the Jew* Christ Jesus." Since it was intended for both Jew and Gentile, that is, for men in general, without distinction of race or nationality, he writes *"the man* Christ Jesus." (By no means is this a denial of Christ's *deity.* That he is the object of faith and worship is clear from I Tim. 3:16. The word *man* here in I Tim. 2:5 is not contrasted with *God* but with *Jew* or *Gentile.*)

6. Prayer must be made in behalf of all men (verses 1 and 2) because:
a. salvation was intended for all, regardless of rank, station, race, or nationality (verses 3 and 4);
b. there is but one God and one Mediator for all (verse 5), not one for each group; and now:
c. there is but one ransom for all: **who gave himself a ransom for all.**

That is the basic element in Christ's position as Mediator, which Paul has just mentioned. By his suffering and death Christ paid the penalty which God's law demanded, thereby rendering satisfaction. He gave himself as "a substitute-ransom" (ἀντίλυτρον). See on Titus 2:14, for a list of

---

[47] See A. T. Robertson, *The Minister and His Greek New Testament,* New York, 1923, p. 39.

[48] Excellent with respect to this twofold Mediatorship are the words of L. Berkhof, *Systematic Theology,* Grand Rapids, Mich., fourth edition, 1949, pp. 282, 283. – It is immediately clear that the meaning "arbiter" (or "arbitrator") in legal disputes, a sense which the word often has in the papyri, is much too superficial to suit the context *here.* Christ not only *"talks* peace" but *establishes* it: lays the foundation for it by his active and passive obedience; *then* persuades men to accept it. On the sense in the papyri see M.M., p. 399.

pertinent passages. Christ's vicarious death, his sacrifice of himself *in the place of* others, is taught here as clearly as words can possibly convey it.[49]

By adding the preposition "for" or "in behalf of" (on which see N.T.C. on John, Vol. II, p. 110) to the preposition "in exchange for" Paul conveys the twofold idea that Christ's *substitutionary* death was *to the advantage of* all. It merited not deliverance from wrath only, but salvation full and free (see on I Tim. 1:15) for *all men,* regardless of rank, station, race, or nationality.

The second element in Christ's position as Mediator is now indicated: **the testimony (to be borne) *in due* season.** Christ's death as a ransom, to satisfy God's justice, *must be proclaimed.* It was the intention of God that when "the appropriate seasons" or "favorable opportunities" arrived, the fact that God desires *all men* to be saved and to come to the acknowledgment of the truth, should be made known. Whatever is contained in verses 4-6 must be published. The "due season" (see footnotes 102 and 105) comprises the entire *new* dispensation. It is a "due season" or an *"appropriate* season" because it corresponds with God's eternal plan with respect to it. Moreover, at its beginning the ransom was brought, and this *for all;* and the Holy Spirit was poured out, again *upon all flesh.* (See also N.T.C. on John 7:6 and on I Thess. 5:1.) Hence, the proper moment for the publication of *the testimony* (especially by those whose eyes have seen and whose ears have heard; see N.T.C. on John 1:7, 8) had arrived. Not during the old dispensation but only during the new can the mystery be fully revealed that *all men,* Gentiles as well as Jews, are now on an equal footing; that is, that the Gentiles have become "fellow-heirs and fellow-members of the body and fellow-partakers of the promise in Christ Jesus through the gospel" (Eph. 3:6; cf. Eph. 2:11-22).

7. Now it was exactly for this purpose, namely, to bear testimony to *all men,* that Paul had been appointed "a teacher *of the Gentiles*" (with all the emphasis on this last phrase). Hence, he continues: **for which purpose I**

---

[49] From my doctoral thesis, *The Meaning of the Preposition* ἀντί *in the New Testament,* unpublished doctoral dissertation submitted to the Graduate School of Princeton Seminary, 1948, pp. 74, 75, I quote the following:

"That the prefix ἀντί (in ἀντίλυτρον) has here the substitutionary sense is clear. It means *in exchange for.* This conclusion is based on the following considerations:

"(1) The concept *substitution* is in harmony with the idea that is immediately suggested by the base-word to which ἀντί is prefixed. A λύτρον is a ransom; that is, it is the amount paid for the release of a person from captivity or slavery. Cf. I Peter 1:18, 19, which shows that the blood of Christ was understood to be the price.

"(2) The term ἀντίλυτρον in I Tim. 2:6 seems to be based on the expression λύτρον ἀντὶ πολλῶν (ransom for many) in Matt. 20:28; Mark 10:45. Moreover, if the independent preposition ἀντί in these Synoptic passages has the substitutionary sense, it is certainly probable that when the preposition is used in composition with the noun it has the same meaning."

was appointed a herald and apostle – I am telling the truth, I am not lying – a teacher of Gentiles in (the realm of) faith and truth.

Once it is seen that the expression "all men" in verses 1 and 3 indicates "all men regardless of social, national, and racial distinctions" and not "one by one every member of the entire human race, past, present, and future, including Judas and the antichrist," the logic of the entire paragraph becomes clear. *All men,* in the sense explained, must be remembered in prayer and thanksgiving (verse 1), rulers as well as subjects (verse 2), because God desires that all men be saved and come to acknowledge the truth (verses 3 and 4). There is not *one* God for this group, *another* for that group; there is not *one* Mediator for this nation, *another* for that nation, but only *one* God for all men, and only *one* Mediator for all men, the *man* Christ Jesus (verse 5), who gave himself as a ransom not just for this *one* particular group or nation but *for all,* to which good news testimony was to be borne when the favorable opportunity arrived (verse 6). Hence, I, Paul, was appointed to be a teacher *of Gentiles,* in order that not only Jews but also Gentiles – hence, *all men on an equal footing* – might come to accept the truth by a living faith (verse 7).

In order that God's plan for the salvation of men from every tribe and nation (not only from the Jews but also from the Gentiles) might be carried out, Paul had been divinely *appointed.* He was no usurper, no claimer of authority which was not his by right. He had not *forced* his way to the front, but had been *called* to office by no one less than God himself. Moreover, he was God's chosen vessel "to bear (Christ's) name before the Gentiles and kings and the children of Israel" (not *only* before the children of Israel, but also – yes *especially* – before the Gentiles and kings). He was to be a witness to "all men." He was sent to the Gentiles to open their eyes, that they might receive remission of sins and an inheritance among them that are sanctified by faith in Christ. All this is plainly stated in Acts 9:15; 22:15, 21; 26:17, 18.

It is very clear that Paul did not view the church as an exclusive, esoteric group with carefully guarded "secrets" that must be "concealed" from the public. What a difference between his inspired teaching and the "order" which we find in *The Manual Of Discipline* which was discovered recently in a cave near the Dead Sea. According to that Manual "the counsel of the law" must be "concealed" from "the men of error." If a question is asked about the belief of a member of the community, he must refuse to answer. See Millar Burrows, *The Dead Sea Scrolls,* New York, 1956, pp. 333, 377, and 383. Paul, on the contrary, had been appointed to proclaim the truth publicly.

At times this matter of having been divinely appointed had been called in question by the enemies (Gal. 1:1, 12). It is only natural to surmise that also at Ephesus the teachers of false doctrine would begin to raise questions with reference to it, *especially* with reference to the apostle's appointment to proclaim *to the Gentiles* the gospel of abundant grace. It is for this reason that he injects the words, "I am telling the truth, I am not lying" (cf. Rom. 9:1; II Cor. 11:31; Gal. 1:20).

Now this matter about which Paul is telling the truth and not lying is that he had been divinely appointed as a herald and apostle, a teacher of the Gentiles in the realm of faith and truth.

In the ancient world a "herald" was the person who by order of a superior made a loud, public announcement. Thus, in public games it was his function to announce the name and country of each competitor, and also the name, country, and father of the victor. According to Dan. 3:4, 5 the herald cried aloud, "To y o u it is commanded . . . that whenever y o u hear the sound of . . . all kinds of music, y o u fall down and worship the image which Nebuchadnezzar the king has set up . . ." It has been claimed that the gospel gave this title "of a subordinate official in connection with public and other gatherings" a "strange dignity and world-wide importance." [50] But it is probable that the dignity and importance which attached itself to the term preceded the era of the New Testament. Certainly it was the voice of *the herald* which, as predicted long before the beginning of the new dispensation, cried out, "Prepare in the wilderness the way of Jehovah; make ready in the desert a highway for our God" (Is. 40:6-9, and see N.T.C. on John 1:23). Just as in Isaiah's prophecy Jehovah promised to visit with new tokens of his grace those who are pictured as having returned from the Babylonian captivity, and employs a herald to announce the coming of the King of kings and to command the people to make straight the Lord's highway that leads into their hearts, so Paul is God's *herald* (only other New Testament occurrences: II Tim. 1:11; II Peter 2:5) and ambassador, proclaiming to the nations, "We beseech y o u, on behalf of Christ, be reconciled to God" (II Cor. 5:20). That is the very heart of "preaching," that is, of "heralding." Rebels – for sin is rebellion – who had deserved a message of *woe* receive good tidings of *weal.* The picture is beautiful. It is not the rebellious city which sends out an ambassador to sue for peace-terms, but the offended King of kings who sends his own herald to proclaim peace through a ransom, and that ransom: the blood of his own dear Son!

Paul had been appointed to be not only a herald but also an apostle, representing Christ, fully clothed with delegated authority over doctrine and conduct, an authority continuing for life and extending over the entire church, wherever it existed on earth. It was in this broad capacity as apostle that Paul was a herald. For the meaning of the term *apostle,* especially as applied to Paul, see on I Tim. 1:1.

Having been appointed to be a herald and apostle, Paul was "a teacher

---

[50] M.M., p. 343.

of the Gentiles in (the realm of) faith and truth," that is, he and his message were used by God as means to bring to the minds and hearts of the Gentiles living faith in the truth of the gospel.

---

8 I will then that in every place the men offer prayer, lifting up holy hands without wrath and evil deliberation.

9 Similarly, that women adorn themselves in adorning attire with modesty and good sense, not in braids and gold or pearls or expensive clothing, 10 but – as is proper for women who profess to be God-fearing – (that they adorn themselves) by means of good works. 11 Let a woman learn in silence with complete submissiveness. 12 But to teach I do not permit a woman, nor to exercise authority over a man, but to remain silent. 13 For Adam was formed first, then Eve. 14 And it was not Adam who was deceived, but it was the woman who was indeed deceived and fell into transgression. 15 She will, however, be saved by way of her[51] child-bearing, if they continue in faith and love and sanctification along with good sense.

2:8-15

Having made clear that prayers must be offered for all men, the apostle proceeds to indicate who should offer these prayers and in what spirit they should be offered. This naturally concerns the conduct of *men* in public worship (verse 8). By a natural transition he then gives directions with respect to the proper behavior of *women* in public worship (verses 9-15).

8. I will then that in every place the men offer prayer.

Paul, exercising his full authority as an apostle of Jesus Christ, continues to give directions. The translation of the A.V. "I will" fits the context and suits the word that is used in the original. The word *then* (either loosely inferential or continuative; cf. N.T.C. on John, Vol. II, p. 386, footnote 246) connects this paragraph with the preceding. Prayers must be offered in behalf of all people (verses 1-7); hence, let these prayers be offered; not, however, by *the women* but by *the men* (verse 8). It is clear that the verb *offer prayer* or simply *pray* must here be taken in the broadest sense, including every form of invocation mentioned in 2:1 (see on that passage).

Such prayers must be offered "in every place" of public worship. Often a large room in the house of one of the members would be used for that purpose. There were probably several places of worship in Ephesus and surroundings. In order and manner of worship the customs prevailing in the synagogue were followed as far as possible. The idea that the *men* should lead in prayer cannot have surprised those who were used to the synagogue, except in so far as Paul's emphasis on the equality of the sexes "in Christ" (Gal. 3:28) may have caused some to wonder whether this

---

[51] Literally "by way of the."

spiritual emancipation of women might not imply a change in their position in public worship. Moreover, it must be borne in mind that many of the converts had been gathered from the *Gentile* world. And the church was still very young, with new centers of worship being established right along. Moreover, the possibility that false teachers had been spreading erroneous ideas with respect to the respective roles of *men* and *women* "in church" must not be entirely dismissed. However this may have been, Paul knew, at any rate, that instruction was necessary with respect to this point. He emphasizes that the Christian faith does not call for a complete break with the past. The *presence* of women in the religious assembly is, of course, assumed. Paul's point is that these women should pray as Hannah did, "She spoke *in her heart;* only her lips moved, but her voice was not heard" (I Sam. 1:13).

As for *the men,* they should offer prayer, **lifting up holy hands without wrath and evil deliberation.** Posture in prayer is never a matter of indifference. The slouching position of the body while one is supposed to be praying is an abomination to the Lord. On the other hand, it is also true that Scripture nowhere prescribes one, and only one, correct posture during prayer. Different positions of arms, hands, and of the body as a whole, are indicated. All of these are permissible as long as they symbolize different aspects of the worshipper's reverent attitude, and as long as they truly interpret the sentiments of the heart. Note the following *Prayer Postures:*

(1) *Standing:* Gen. 18:22; I Sam. 1:26; Matt. 6:5; Mark 11:25; Luke 18:11; Luke 18:13. (Note the contrast between the last two passages. It makes a difference even *how* and *where* one stands.)

(2) *Hands Spread Out or/and Lifted Heavenward:* Ex. 9:29; Ex. 17:11, 12; I Kings 8:22; Neh. 8:6; Psalm 63:4; Psalm 134:2; Psalm 141:2; Is. 1:15; Lam. 2:19; Lam. 3:41; Hab. 3:10; Luke 24:50; I Tim. 2:8; James 4:8. (Compare the "Orantes" of the Catacombs. And see A. Deissmann, *Light From the Ancient East,* translated by L. R. M. Strachan, fourth edition, New York 1922, pp. 415, 416.)

(3) *Bowing the Head:* Gen. 24:48 (cf. verse 13); Ex. 12:27; II Chron. 29:30; Luke 24:5.

(4) *The Lifting Heavenward of the Eyes:* Psalm 25:15; Psalm 121:1; Psalm 123:1, 2; Psalm 141:8; Psalm 145:15; John 11:41; John 17:1; cf. Dan. 9:3; Acts 8:55.

(5) *Kneeling:* II Chron. 6:13; Psalm 95:6; Is. 45:23; Dan. 6:10; Matt. 17:14; Mark 1:40; Luke 22:41; Acts 7:60; Acts 9:40; Acts 20:36; Acts 21:5; Eph. 3:14.

(6) *Falling Down with the Face Upon the Ground:* Gen. 17:3; Gen. 24:26; Num. 14:5, 13; Num. 16:4, 22, 45; Num. 22:13, 34; Deut. 9:18, 25, 26; Jos. 5:14; Judg. 13:20; Neh. 8:6; Ezek. 1:28; Ezek. 3:23; Ezek. 9:8;

Ezek. 11:13; Ezek. 43:3; Ezek. 44:4; Dan. 8:17; Matt. 26:39; Mark 7:25; Mark 14:35; Luke 5:12; Luke 17:16; Rev. 1:17; Rev. 11:16.

(7) *Other Postures:* I Kings 18:42 (bowing, with face between the knees); Luke 18:13 (standing from afar, striking the breast).

As is clear from this final reference, the indicated postures and positions of members of the body may occur in various combinations. In Luke 18:13 (1) and (7) are combined. I Kings 8:22 (Solomon) combines (1) and (2). Neh. 8:6 combines (1) and (3). John 11:41 (see verse 38) links (1) with (4). In addition to being combined with (1), number (2) may also be combined with (5), "Solomon arose from the altar of Jehovah, from kneeling on his knees, with his hands spread forth toward heaven" (I Kings 8:54; cf. Ezra 9:5). Moreover, the *bow* (3) was often so deep that the person would fall prostrate upon the ground (6). See, for example, Num. 22:31. In fact, a favorite method of prostration among Orientals has always been falling upon the knees (5), then gradually inclining the body, bowing the head until it touches the ground (3), which may become (6). And even in most cases where Scripture does not definitely indicate this, it may be gathered from the context that the man who spread out or lifted up his hands was *standing*. That is the case also in our present passage (I Tim. 2:8).

Now all these postures were appropriate. The standing position (1) indicates reverence. The lifting up or spreading out of the hands (2) – arms outstretched, with palms upward – is a fit symbol of utter dependence on God and of humble expectancy. Bowing the head (3) is the outward expression of the spirit of submission. The lifting heavenward of the eyes (4) indicates that one believes that his help comes from Jehovah, from him alone. Kneeling (5) pictures humility and adoration. Falling down with face toward the ground (6) is the visible manifestation of awe in the divine presence. Striking the breast (7) beautifully harmonizes with the feeling of utter unworthiness.

The present custom of closing the eyes while folding the hands is of disputed origin. Though unrecorded in Scripture and unknown to the early church, the custom may be considered a good one if properly interpreted. It helps the worshipper to shut out harmful distractions and to enter the sphere where "none but God is near." It is, at any rate, far better than some postures of the body that prevail among moderns when prayer is being offered.

What is stressed, however, throughout Scripture and also in the passage now under study, is not the posture of the body or the position of the hands but *the inner attitude of the soul.* The hands that are lifted up must be *holy,* that is, they must be hands unpolluted by previous crimes. A man who has just committed a murder or an act of adultery or a theft must not think that without pardon and restitution, when this "making good" is possible, his hands can now be lifted up in a prayer that is pleasing to God. See Psalm 24:3, 4; cf. Matt. 5:23, 24.

Moreover, this lifting up of hands must be done "without wrath and evil deliberation." *Wrath* (cf. N.T.C. on John 3:36), that is, *settled indignation* against a brother, the attitude of the unmerciful debtor of the parable (Matt. 18:21-35), makes prayer unacceptable (see also, in this connection, Matt. 6:14, 15; Eph. 4:31, 32; Col. 3:8; Jas. 1:19, 20). And so does *evil deliberation* of any kind whatever. The word used in the original is related to our English word *dialogue.* The soul of man is so constituted that it can carry on a dialogue with itself. Thus a man can debate within himself whether he shall do *this* to his neighbor or *that, balancing* one thought against another (our word *deliberate* – from Latin *de* and *libra* – literally means *to thoroughly weigh, libra* being *a balance*).[52] Although the word used in the original does not in itself brand the *dialoguing* as being *evil* (see Luke 2:35, in which passage the deliberations referred to are not necessarily evil), yet it is worthy of note (cf. Gen. 6:5; 8:21) that in almost every passage in which it is used the deliberation referred to is clearly of a sinful nature (Matt. 15:19; Mark 7:21; Luke 5:22; 6:8; 9:46, 47; Rom. 1:21; 14:1; I Cor. 3:20; Phil. 2:14. In Luke 2:35 it indicates *doubting, questioning*). Here in I Tim. 2:8 the use of the word in conjunction with *wrath* makes this meaning certain.

The sum and substance, therefore, of the present admonition is that in public worship *the men,* not the women, should stand with uplifted hands and offer prayer aloud. The elders naturally would take the lead (I Tim. 5:17). These hands, however, must be holy, and the prayer must be offered in the proper spirit. If the heart of a person is filled with wrath or malice against his brother, so that he is planning evil against him, prayer will not be acceptable.

9. Similarly, that women adorn themselves in adorning attire with modesty and good sense.

The word *similarly* shows that Paul is continuing his remarks about conduct in connection with *public worship.* Just as *the men* must make the necessary preparations, so that with prepared hearts and without previous disposition to evil they "come to church," able to lift up holy hands, so also *the women* must give evidence of the same spirit of holiness, and must show this while they are still at home, getting ready to attend the service.

They should, accordingly, "adorn themselves in adorning attire." Thus

---

[52] In Demosthenes (Athenian orator of the fourth century B. C.) and in other writers the word διαλογισμός indicates a *balancing of accounts;* cf. the etymological meaning of our *de-liberation.* It is easy to see that out of this literal meaning grew the figurative: mental balancing, calculation, consideration, etc. The suffix – μός is an action-ending; hence, primary sense, deliberat*ing;* then, delibera*tion.*

the sentence will have to be rendered if the alliteration of the original is to be preserved. We readily grant that alliteration cannot always be reproduced without changing the sense of the original. In the present instance, however, we believe that the alliteration of the original should be retained in the translation. Moreover, the argument employed by several commentators, to the effect that the adjective used in the original must here mean *virtuous* or *honorable,* because in non-literary sources it is used in that sense (see M.M., p. 356), ignores the fact that it has that meaning when it describes the *character* of a person (just as in I Tim. 3:2). Such references are of little value when the adjective modifies a noun which indicates not character but "dress." Surely in the latter case the more literal sense "adorning" immediately suggests itself. Women, then, must adorn themselves in *adorning* — that is, *becoming* — *attire* (καταστολή, literally "something let down").

It is clear, therefore, that the apostle does not condemn the desire on the part of girls and women — a desire created in their souls by their Maker — to adorn themselves, to be "in good taste." But if a woman's robe is to be truly such, it will be expressive of modesty and good sense. Hence, Paul writes, "in adorning attire with modesty and good sense." *Modesty* (αἰδώς) indicates *a sense of shame,* a shrinking from trespassing the boundaries of propriety; hence, *proper reserve.* The next word, which we have rendered *good sense,* means literally *soundness of mind* (σωφροσύνη). In getting dressed for church women must practise *sanity.* They must dress in *sensible* attire. They must not try to show off, to be "all the rage," wearing flashy apparel so as to make others jealous of them. They should *adorn* themselves, to be sure. They do not have to balk at fashion, unless a particular fashion happens to be immoral or indecent. They must not look decidedly old-fashioned, awkward, or queer. It must ever be borne in mind that a proud heart is sometimes concealed behind a mask of pretended modesty. That too is sin. Extremes must be carefully avoided. That is what "good sense" implies. The robe must be expressive of inner modesty and of a sane outlook on life, the outlook of the Christian. Applied to our own day and age this means that Pope's well-known lines should be pondered. They contain food for thought:

> "Be not the first by whom the new is tried,
> Nor yet the last to lay the old aside." [53]

Now to adorn oneself in adorning attire with modesty and good sense will mean that a woman does **not** adorn herself **in braids and gold or pearls or expensive clothing.**

---

[53] On this entire subject see W. A. Maier, *For Better Not For Worse,* St. Louis, Mo., 1935, pp. 205-219. This excellent book should be in every church-library and in every home that can afford it.

Paul has been criticized severely for these words, as if he did not want the members of the fair sex to look their loveliest. It has been remarked, "Think of it, he is even opposed to hair-braids! What is wrong with them?" Such criticism is, however, entirely unjustified. The very combination of the word "braids" with "and gold or pearls or expensive clothing" should have sufficed to inform the reader that the apostle is thinking of the sin of extravagance in outward adornment. As to these "braids," the sense is not that under any and all circumstances women throughout all future generations are here forbidden to wear their hair braided. Not at all. The following points must be borne in mind:

a. In view of the context (see verse 10) Paul means this: the Christian woman must understand that her real adornment is not coiffure or jewelry or splendid attire but something else, which the apostle is about to mention, namely, the doing of good works which are the fruits of character transformed by the Holy Spirit.

b. But what about these *braids* which were popular in the world of Paul's day? No expense was spared to make them dazzling. They actually sparkled. The braids were fastened by jewelled tortoise-shell combs, or by pins of ivory or silver. Or the pins were of bronze with jewelled heads, the more varied and expensive the better. The pin-heads often consisted of miniature images (an animal, a human hand, an idol, the female figure, etc.).[54] *Braids,* in those days, often represented *fortunes.* They were articles of luxury! The Christian woman is warned not to indulge in such extravagance.

Similarly, a woman who is a believer must not try to make herself conspicuous by a vain display of ornaments of *gold.* Also, she will not yearn for *pearls,* obtained (at that time) from the Persian Gulf or from the Indian Ocean. These were often fabulously priced and thus way beyond the purchasing power of the average church-member. In order to obtain a pearl of great value a merchant might have to sell all his possessions (Matt. 13:46). Yet someone who was living in Paul's day said, "I have seen Lollia Paulina [wife of emperor Caligula] covered with emeralds and pearls gleaming all over her head, hair, ears, neck, and fingers, to the value of over a million dollars."

A woman of faith will not (at least *should not*) crave *costly garments,* for example a most expensive and showy robe. The robe or mantle worn by the lady resembled a man's toga. However, it was often the product of finer

---

[54] See the picture and description in T. G. Tucker, *Life in the Roman World of Nero and St. Paul.* New York, 1922, p. 311. Also, *The Good News, The New Testament Of Our Lord and Savior Jesus Christ, With Over 500 Illustrations and Maps,* published by The American Bible Society, 1955; the illustration in connection with the text of I Timothy, p. G 19. Finally, *Everyday Life In Ancient Times,* published by The National Geographic Society, Washington, D.C., pp. 244, 245.

workmanship, and was characterized by richer ornamentation, and greater color-variation.[55]

Vain display on the part of women was and is offensive to what is best in Oriental taste. What is more important, it also offends the Creator. In a woman who professes to be a believer such pursuit of the cult of beauty and personal adornment is doubly unbecoming. It offends the Creator *and* the Redeemer. See also Is. 3:16-24 and I Peter 3:3, 4. Though always wrong, it is most reprehensible in a woman who is getting ready to attend church; for showy clothes ill befit broken and contrite hearts, the kind of hearts which God welcomes at the service of the Word and sacraments.

10. "I will then that . . . the women adorn themselves . . . not in braids and gold or pearls or expensive clothing, **but – as is proper for women who profess to be God-fearing – by means of good works.**

For women genuine adornment is attained by means of the performance of *good works* (cf. I Tim. 6:11, 18; II Tim. 2:22; 3:17). Divine grace brings into existence the tree of faith on which these good works grow as so many fruits. That is the apostle's doctrine both here in the Pastorals (Titus 2:11-14; 3:4-8) and elsewhere (Gal. 5:22-24; Eph. 2:10). Now for women to adorn themselves by means of good works is the *proper* thing to do, inasmuch as they *profess* to be *God-fearing*. Literally Paul says, "who profess *God-fearingness.*" The verb rendered *profess* has the root-meaning *to convey a message loudly, clearly;* hence, *to proclaim*. Such a proclamation may be in the form of *a promise* or of *a profession;* generally the former (Mark 4:11; Acts 7:5; Rom. 4:21; Gal. 3:19; Titus 1:2; Heb. 6:13; 10:23; 11:11; 12:26; James 1:12; 2:5; I John 2:25), but here and in I Tim. 6:21 the latter. The noun *God-fearingness* (see LXX: Gen. 20:11) occurs nowhere else in the New Testament; but see the adjective in John 9:31.

The entire idea reminds us at once of I Peter 3:3, 4: "whose adorning let it not be the outward adorning of braiding the hair and of wearing jewels of gold, or of wearing robes, but . . . the hidden man of the heart with the imperishable jewel of a meek and quiet spirit which in the sight of God is very precious."

11, 12. Next, the apostle gives a few directions with respect to the relation of women to *gathering* and *imparting knowledge (learning* and *teaching),* again with special reference to public worship. He writes,

Let a woman learn in silence with complete submissiveness. But to teach I do not permit a woman, nor to exercise authority over a man, but to remain silent.

Though these words and their parallel in I Cor. 14:33-35 may sound a

---

[55] On the entire subject see A. Sizoo, *De Antieke Wereld En Het Nieuwe Testament,* Kampen, 1948, II. 62-64; T. G. Tucker, *op. cit.,* pp. 289-313.

trifle unfriendly, in reality they are the very opposite. In fact, they are expressive of a feeling of tender sympathy and basic understanding. They mean: let a woman not enter a sphere of activity for which by dint of her very creation she is not suited. Let not a bird try to dwell under water. Let not a fish try to live on land. Let not a woman yearn to exercise authority over a man by lecturing him in public worship. For the sake both of herself and of the spiritual welfare of the church such unholy tampering with divine authority is forbidden.

In the service of the Word on the day of the Lord a woman should *learn, not teach.* She should *be silent, remain calm* (see N.T.C. on I Thess. 4:11 and on II Thess. 3:12). She should *not cause her voice to be heard.* Moreover, this learning in silence should not be with a rebellious attitude of heart but "with complete *submissiveness*" (cf. II Cor. 9:13; Gal. 2:5; I Tim. 3:4). She should cheerfully *range herself under* God's law for her life. Her full spiritual equality with men as a sharer in all the blessings of salvation (Gal. 3:28: "there can be no male and female") does not imply any basic change in her nature *as woman* or in the corresponding task which she *as a woman* is called upon to perform. Let a woman remain a woman! Anything else Paul *cannot permit. Paul* cannot permit it because *God's holy law* does not permit it (I Cor. 14:34). That holy law is his will as expressed in the Pentateuch, particularly in the story of woman's creation and of her fall (see especially Gen. 2:18-25; 3:16). Hence, *to teach,* that is, to preach in an official manner, and thus by means of the proclamation of the Word in public worship to *exercise authority* over a man, *to dominate him,* is wrong for a woman. She must not assume the role of a master.

13, 14. As already indicated, these directives regarding the woman's role in connection with public worship are based not on temporary or contemporary conditions or circumstances but on two facts that have meaning for all time, namely, the fact of *creation* and the fact of *the entrance of sin.* Accordingly, Paul writes: **For Adam was formed first, then Eve. And it was not Adam who was deceived, but it was the woman who was indeed deceived and fell into transgression.**

In *forming* or *moulding* (cf. Rom. 9:20) the human pair, God first made Adam; afterward Eve. Not only that, but he made Eve *for the sake of* Adam, to be his helper (Gen. 2:18-25), and his glory (I Cor. 11:7-9). Neither is complete without the other (I Cor. 11:11). But in his sovereign wisdom God made the human pair in such a manner that it is natural for *him* to lead, for *her* to follow; for *him* to be aggressive, for *her* to be receptive; for *him* to invent, for *her* to use the tools which he invents. The tendency *to follow* was embedded in Eve's very soul as she came forth from the hand of her Creator. Hence, it would not be right to reverse this order in connection with public worship. Why should a woman be encouraged to do things that are contrary to her nature? Her very body, far from *preceding* that of Adam in the order of creation, *was taken out of* Adam's body. Her very name — *Ish-sha* — *was derived from* his name — *Ish* (Gen. 2:23). It is when the woman recognizes this basic distinction and acts accordingly that she can be a blessing to the man, can exert a gracious yet very powerful and beneficent influence upon him, and can promote her own happiness, unto God's glory. Longfellow was right when he said:

> "As unto the bow the cord is,
> So unto the man is woman;
> Though she bends him she obeys him,
> Useless each without the other!"
> (Hiawatha)

Added to this fact of *creation* is that of the entrance of *sin*. Eve's fall occurred when she ignored her divinely ordained position. Instead of *following* she chose *to lead*. Instead of remaining submissive to God, she wanted to be *"like* God." *She* — not Adam — *was indeed* (or *was completely*) *deceived or deluded.*[56]

Eve "was indeed deceived," but Adam "was not deceived." Of course, this cannot be taken absolutely. It must mean something on this order: Adam was not deceived in the manner in which Eve was deceived. See Gen. 3:4-6. *She* listened directly to Satan; *he* did not. *She* sinned before *he* did. *She* was the leader. *He* was the follower. She led when she should have followed; that is, she led in the way of sin, when she should have followed in the path of righteousness.

And so she fell *into transgression,* into the fatal *stepping aside* from the path of obedience. And now that which before was an unmixed blessing — namely, that Eve, by virtue of her creation, constantly followed Adam — is an unmixed blessing no longer; for now she who, by her sinful example, chose *to rule* him who at that moment was still her *sinless* husband, *must obey* the creature of her own designing, namely, her *sinful* husband. Hence, let none of her daughters follow her in reversing the divinely established order. Let none assume the role that was not intended for her. Let not the daughter of Eve teach, rule, lead, when the congregation gathers for worship. Let her learn, not teach; obey, not rule; follow, not lead.

---

[56] Though it is true that Paul uses the verbs ἀπατάω and ἐξαπατάω to express the same basic idea (see N.T.C. on II Thess. 2:3a), yet when, as here in I Tim. 2:14, he uses the strengthened and the unstrengthened form side by side, it is reasonable to assume that he intends to convey a difference in meaning. Hence, *was not deceived . . . was indeed deceived* (or: *was completely deceived*).

15. She will, however, be saved by way of her child-bearing.

Not by way of preaching to *adults* (see on verse 12) but by way of bearing *children* does a woman attain to real happiness, to *salvation,* with stress on its positive aspect (see on I Tim. 1:15). The path that leads to salvation is ever that of obedience to God's ordinances. It is his will that the woman should influence mankind "from the bottom up" (that is, by way of *the child*), not "from the top down" (that is, not by way of *the man*). She must choose to do that for which by God's creation-ordinance she is naturally equipped, both physically and spiritually. She must reach her goal *by way of* (διά) *her child-bearing.*

Again, not by way of *exercising dominion* over men but by way of *submission* does a woman reach the state of true freedom and blessedness (see on verses 11 and 12). Now the curse which was pronounced upon Eve included two elements: a. *submission* to her (now sinful) husband, and b. painful *child-bearing* (mentioned in reverse order in Gen. 3:16). It is therefore not at all surprising that Paul, thoroughly at home in The Law and writing by inspiration, immediately mentions *child-bearing* after having mentioned *submission.* He sees what Adam also saw. Paul, however, sees it more clearly. Adam already perceived that by God's grace *the curse* of child-bearing (think of its *painful* character) was changed into *a blessing* (Gen. 3:20). Because of the prospect of child-bearing Adam's wife was named *Eve,* that is "Life" (the mother of all *living*). Paul takes up this thought and develops it. Child-bearing will mean *salvation* for the Christian mother, for what Christian mother does not experience inner delight, joy, blessing, and glory in seeing the image of her Savior reflected in little ones who belong to him? In *bearing children* (here *the noun: child-bearing; the verb* is used in I Tim. 5:14) the Christian mother by faith in God's covenant promise (Gen. 17:7; Acts 2:38, 39) looks forward to all the joys of Christian motherhood unto the glory of God. This to her is *salvation.*[57]

When Paul says *she* (in the clause "She . . . will be saved by her child-bearing"), he is thinking of "the woman" of verse 14. This referred first of all to Eve, but then also to any Christian mother taken as a representative of *the entire class* to which she belongs. Hence, it is not strange that

---

[57] I reject the following explanations:

(1) "She will be saved by means of The Childbirth" (that is, the Birth of Christ).

(2) "She will come safely through child-birth."

Objection: both of these ideas are foreign to the present context. In addition, Number (2) assigns a meaning to the verb which in the present context is not warranted. See the verb in 1:15 and 2:4.

(3) "By means of bearing children she will be rescued from everlasting damnation and will merit everlasting glory."

Objection: this idea of making child-bearing a meritorious act strikes at the very heart of Paul's theology as expressed both in the Pastorals and elsewhere (see pp. 18, 19). Besides, the immediately following words (". . . if they continue in faith," etc., suffice to rule it out).

the apostle now shifts from the singular to the plural (from "she" to "they") as he continues: **if they continue in faith and love and sanctification along with good sense.** Not child-bearing as such procures salvation. The love of God shed abroad in the heart, the peace which passes all understanding, the delight which is experienced when one submits to God's ordinances, the joys of truly *Christian* motherhood, all these are experienced only if women "continue in faith," etc. Faith comes first. It is the product of God's sovereign grace. To be truly blessed, women must *continue* in it. The matter of salvation is regarded here from the side not of God but of the human individual. It is true, indeed, that once a woman (or a man, but the present passage deals with women) is truly saved, she remains saved forever; yet, God does not keep a woman on the way of salvation without exertion, diligence, and watchfulness on her part. The strength thus to persevere in the faith is ever from God, from him alone (see also N.T.C. on John, Vol. II, p. 299).

The nouns used in the present passage have all been explained. For *faith* and *love* see on I Tim. 1:5. For *sanctification* (the daily dying unto sin and being renewed unto holiness; here perhaps with special emphasis on active opposition to all immorality or uncleanness in thought and act, sins so often associated with the married state) see N.T.C. on I Thess. 4:3-8. And for *good sense* see on I Tim. 2:9. The complete thought is therefore as follows: if the women members of the church will abide in faith and love and sanctification, meanwhile exercising proper self-control and reserve, they will find their joy and salvation in bearing children to God's glory, yes, in all the duties and delights of Christian motherhood.

Synthesis of Chapter 2

See the Outline at the beginning of the chapter.

When the congregation assembles for public worship, *all* must be remembered in prayer, that is, rulers as well as subjects, for:

a. salvation is intended "for all," regardless of rank, station, race, or nation;

b. there is but one God and one Mediator, not one God and one Mediator for *this* group, and one for *that* group;

c. there is but *one* ransom;

d. hence Paul had been appointed to be a teacher *of Gentiles,* in order that not only Jews but also Gentiles might come to accept the gospel by a living faith.

At public worship *the men* – not the women – should stand with uplifted hands, offering prayer aloud. For such praying there should be adequate preparation, so that the heart may not be filled with malice against a brother or with predisposition to evil.

The women, too, must prepare themselves adequately when they are about to go to church. They must avoid all extravagance in outward adornment, bearing in mind that their true adornment is the doing of good works. In the place of public worship women should realize that their duty is to learn, not to teach; to obey, not to rule; to follow, not to lead. If they abide in faith and love and sanctification, meanwhile exercising proper self-control and reserve, they will find their joy and salvation in the delights of Christian motherhood. (To be sure, Priscilla – as well as Aquila – taught Apollos, but *not from the pulpit.* Read Acts 18:26.)

This teaching regarding the place which women should occupy when the congregation gathers for worship is based not on any temporary condition but on Adam's priority in creation and Eve's priority in transgression.

In this connection it should be pointed out that though the apostle definitely ascribes to women a *different* position than to men, he does not regard their role in church-affairs to be in any way less important than that filled by men.

The Dignity of Women in the Pauline Epistles

(1) He mentions with favor the following, to many of whom he sends greetings: Phoebe, Prisca, "Mary," Tryphena and Tryphosa, Persis, Julia, the sister of Nereus, Apphia, Lois and Eunice (see Romans 16; Phil. 4; II Tim. 1; Philemon).

(2) He employs women in the service of the gospel (Rom. 16:1-3; Phil. 4:3); specifically, the older widows (I Tim. 5:9, 10), deacons' assistants (I Tim. 3:11), women who are able to support others (I Tim. 5:16). Cf. what the book of Acts says with reference to Lydia (16:14, 40), Dorcas (9:36), Mary, the mother of John (12:2), and the daughters of Philip (21:8, 9).

What a difference between the status of women in the early church, on the one hand, and in the Qumran sect, described in the Dead Sea Scrolls, on the other. In the church women were given an honorable status. In the Qumran sect women played hardly any part. See Millar Burrows, *op. cit.,* pp. 233, 244 and 333.

(3) He emphasizes that "in Christ" there is neither male nor female (Gal. 3:28). In relation to him there is perfect equality.

(4) He recommends marriage, even for widows, and he praises the joys of *Christian* wifehood and motherhood (I Cor. 7:39; I Tim. 5:14; then I Tim. 2:15; 4:3). There are circumstances, however, under which Paul considers it better "not to marry" (I Cor. 7:26, 27).

(5) Anyone who maintains that Paul holds women in low esteem should read the following passages. If they are honestly interpreted, one will have to admit that in many ways no man is ever able to bestow upon a woman the full honor which according to Paul's teaching should be bestowed upon her:

"For the unbelieving husband is sanctified through his wife, and the unbelieving wife is sanctified through her husband" (I Cor. 7:14).

"The wife does not have power over her own body, but the husband has; and similarly, the husband has no power over his own body, but the wife has" (I Cor. 7:4).

"The woman is man's glory" (I Cor. 11:7).

"In the Lord neither is woman without (the) man, nor is man without (the) woman" (I Cor. 11:11).

"Husbands, love y o u r wives, even as Christ also loved the church, and gave himself up for it; that he might sanctify it . . . Even so ought husbands also to love their own wives as their own bodies. . . . Let each one of y o u love his wife as he loves himself; and let the wife see to it that she respects her husband" (Eph. 5:25-33).

Paul's practical attitude to women kingdom-workers is expressed in this beautiful, concise order:

"HELP THESE WOMEN" (Phil. 4:3).

Outline of Chapter 3

Theme: *The Apostle Paul, Writing to Timothy, Gives Directions For the Administration of the Church*

Directions with respect to the Institution of the Offices

3:1-7 A. Incentive for becoming an overseer; the glorious character of the work.
Directions regarding the necessary qualifications of overseers.

3:8-13 B. Directions regarding the necessary qualifications of deacons and of women who assist them.
Incentive for faithful performance of the task of deacons and of women who assist them: their glorious reward.

3:14-16 C. The reasons for conveying these instructions in written form:
1. Though I hope to see you soon, I fear that I may be delayed.
2. Yet, the matter permits of no delay, for it concerns God's house, the church, which is great because of its exalted Head, Jesus Christ. Hymn in adoration of the Christ.

CHAPTER III

3 1 Reliable is the saying, "If anyone aspires to the office of overseer, he desires a noble work." 2 The overseer therefore [58] must be above reproach, one wife's husband, temperate, self-controlled, virtuous, hospitable, qualified to teach; 3 not (one who lingers) beside (his) wine, not given to blows, but genial, not contentious, not fond of money, 4 managing well his own household, with true dignity keeping his children in submission 5 (for if a person does not know how to manage his own household, how will he take upon himself the care of God's church?), 6 not a recent convert, in order that he may not become befogged by conceit and fall into the condemnation of the devil. 7 He must also have a favorable testimony from outsiders, lest he fall into reproach and a snare of the devil.[59]

Public worship generally precedes the institution of the offices. Hence, it is not surprising that Paul, having discussed the former, now proceeds to give directions regarding the latter. In the present chapter he shows that elders, deacons, and women who render auxiliary service must be spiritually and morally qualified in order to perform their tasks in the church of Jesus Christ, the One "who was made manifest in the flesh . . . taken up in glory."

3:1-7

1. Accordingly, the apostle begins by writing: **Reliable [60] is the saying, If anyone aspires to the office of overseer, he desires a noble work.**

---

[58] Something can be said in favor of the rendering "however" (for οὖν). But the more usual meaning of the Greek particle (inferential "therefore") makes excellent sense: *"in view of the fact that* the overseership is such a noble work, the man who fills this office must be above reproach. The continuative meaning ("now," "then") is also possible. See further N.T.C. on John, Vol. II, p. 386, footnote 246.

[59] With respect to possible parallels (to such a list of requirements) in secular literature see on Titus 2:1.

[60] The reading "popular" or "human" (ἀνθρώπινος) is the saying, is weakly attested; see N.N. It may possibly be ascribed to a scribe's hesitancy to prefix the profound introductory clause, *"Reliable* is the saying" to a statement which fails to give expression to a paramount essential of the Christian faith.

Possibly for the same reason some would construe this clause with the preceding paragraph (thus, for example, Lock and A. T. Robertson). But it is hard to see how anything in the immediately preceding paragraph (which deals with the behavior of women, their proper attire with a view to church-attendance, etc.) could have become "a watchword of Christian wisdom." The saying, moreover, harmonizes beautifully with the entire paragraph which follows.

This is the second of five "reliable sayings" or trustworthy current proverbs, wisdom maxims. For their general character see on I Tim. 1:15.

It is sometimes maintained that the present saying is not only devoid of great significance or value but is even harmful, encouraging sinful aspiration to office! But this opinion results from the fact that the saying is read in the light of later conditions. Some interpreters reason as follows, "It is decidedly wrong for anyone *to stretch out his hand* (note the verb ὀρέγω) in order to lay hold on the holy office. Such sinful ambition deserves *to be condemned.* The office should seek the man, not the man the office. Hence, it is very strange that Paul seems to have a word of praise for such sinful striving." But over against this the following two points deserve emphasis:

a. Although it is true that praise for the man who aspires *is implied* in the saying, it is not definitely *expressed.* The apostle simply says, *"If* anyone aspires." It is *the office* rather than the striving that is definitely described as being *excellent* or *noble* ("a noble work").

b. Though it is nevertheless true that praise for the aspirant *is implied,* it must be borne in mind that *in the early history of the church willingness to serve as an overseer meant sacrifice.* Again and again persecution would rage, from the side of the Jews, of the Gentiles, or, as often, of both. False teachers did their utmost to undermine the true foundation. Truly, in *such* a time and amid *such* circumstances an *incentive to overseership and a word of implied praise* for the man who indicated a willingness to serve in this high office were not at all out of place. And the office itself was surely "a noble work." It still is, but it was never more so than in the early decades!

When Paul speaks about the office of *overseer* (ἐπισκοπή, — ῆς), he has in mind the divinely authorized task of the *elders,* as has been (and will be) indicated (see also on Titus 1:5-7). These overseers or elders constituted a presbytery or board of presbyters or elders. With respect to age and dignity its members were called *presbyters* or *elders,* just as in Israel. With respect to the nature of their task they were called *overseers* or *superintendents.*

The manner in which, on the whole, these men conducted themselves in the sacred office, and their willingness to suffer innumerable hardships for the cause of Christ, justified the current saying, "If anyone aspires to the office of overseer, he desires a noble task." Let no one look down upon the overseer! Let no one despise him because he does not have *all* the special gifts. He is eager to give of his time and energies, and is even willing to sacrifice his physical ease and safety for the noble work of "feeding the church of the Lord which he purchased with his own blood" (Acts 20:28). May the glorious character of the work be *an incentive* to all who are considering overseership, so that they may eagerly desire it!

But just because the work is so noble and the task so grand certain qualifications are stipulated. In order that these qualifications may be seen as the apostle groups them, the following verses are here printed together according to what appears to be their intended and natural classification:

2-7.

2. The overseer therefore must be
above reproach
one wife's husband
temperate
self-controlled
virtuous
hospitable
qualified to teach
3. not (one who lingers) beside (his) wine
not given to blows
but genial
not contentious
not fond of money
4. managing well his own household, with true dignity
keeping his children in submission; 5. (for if a person
does not know how to manage his own household, how will
he take care of God's church?)
6. not a recent convert, in order that he may not become beclouded by conceit and fall into the condemnation of the devil.
7. He must also have a favorable testimony from outsiders,
lest he fall into reproach and a snare of the devil.

It is immediately clear that according to Paul's inspired teaching the prospective overseer must have a favorable testimony from two groups: (a) *insiders,* that is, church-members, and (b) *outsiders,* that is, those who are outside the church.

As was to be expected, the emphasis falls on the first, the reputation which the man has among church-members. The various items which belong to this first classification are divided into two sets of seven items each. However, the very first item – "above reproach" – may be considered a kind of caption or heading for all the items in both sets of this *first* classification. The *second* classification is summarized somewhat similarly, but without a list of detailed requirements.

Beginning with the first category, as far as his standing or reputation *with the members of the church* is concerned, the overseer must accordingly be *without* (or "above") *reproach.*

Note that the first set of seven characteristics is *positive* (except for the caption itself: *without* – or *above* – reproach or *un*-assailable). The second set is largely *negative.* Five times we read *not* (of these five, three have μή;

two have ἀ -privative). Thus, in all there are eight (6 plus 2) requirements expressed positively, six (1 plus 5) expressed negatively.

It must not escape our attention that the very first and the very last of the eight *positive* requirements describe the qualified person's relation to *his family*. That relationship is again emphasized in connection with the deacons. Paul (and the Holy Spirit speaking through Paul) must have regarded this family-relationship as being of great importance.

In the first set of seven requirements the subdivision is as follows: under the caption "above reproach" we find first a set of four requirements having to do with the man's attitude to *Christian morality in general:* he must be maritally pure, temperate, sensible, virtuous. Then, two requirements describing the man's attitude toward (and influence upon) people who stand in some definite relation to *the church*. How does he treat guests from other churches, etc.? Is he hospitable? What influence for good does he exert on those who require guidance or instruction? Is he qualified to teach?

In the second set of seven requirements we see the man in his *daily life,* rubbing elbows with his *fellow-men* at work and everywhere. The item "not (one who lingers) beside (his) wine" easily merges with the next one, namely, "not given to blows," for drunkenness often leads to blows. Over against this stands the positive requirement *genial*. Paralleling it is "not contentious." The contentious person is generally selfish, hence "fond of money." The question, accordingly, is this, "Can the candidate under review be trusted with the church's *funds?*" (Note how here, just as at the close of the first set of seven requirements, the attention is focused once more on the man's relation to *the church*.) Also, can he take care of its *affairs?* How does he manage his own family? That ought to show whether he can take upon himself the care over the affairs of the church! And finally, can it be reasonably expected that he will command the respect of its *members,* the experienced as well as those recently converted? But in that case he himself must be a man of some experience in Christian living. He must not be *a novice*.

We see, therefore, that the items in the list are not just thrown together in haphazard fashion. They follow each other logically and are neatly arranged.

A few remarks will now be made with reference to each of the fifteen (7 plus 7 plus 1) requirements. The *first set of seven* is as follows: The overseer must be:

1. *"Above reproach"* in the estimation of fellow church members

See also I Tim. 5:7 and 6:14. The word used in the original literally means "not to be laid hold of," hence *irreprehensible* or *unassailable*. Enemies may bring all manner of accusations, but these charges are proved to be empty whenever fair methods of investigation are applied. With the church and in accordance with the rules of justice, this man not only *has* a good reputation but *deserves* it.

Example of a man who was "above reproach":
Simeon

"And there was a man in Jerusalem, whose name was Simeon; and this man was righteous and devout, looking for the consolation of Israel, and the Holy Spirit was upon him" (Luke 2:25). Cf. Job 1:8.

The particulars with respect to which he is "above reproach" follow:

2. In *marital relationship* "one wife's husband"

See also I Tim. 5:9 ("one husband's wife"). This cannot mean that an overseer or elder must be a married man. Rather, *it is assumed* that he is married — as was generally the case —, and it is stipulated that in this marital relationship he must be an example to others of faithfulness to his one and only marriage-partner. Infidelity in this relationship is a sin against which Scripture warns repeatedly. That this sin and those related to it (sexual immorality in any form) were of frequent occurrence among the Jews and certainly among the Gentiles, is clear from ever so many passages (among many others: Ex. 20:14; Lev. 18:20; 20:10; Deut. 5:18; 22:23; II Sam. 12; Is. 51; Prov. 2:17; Prov. chapter 7; Jer. 23:10, 14; 29:23; Hos. 1:2; 2:2; 3:1; Matt. 5:28; John 8:3; Rom. 1:27; 7:3; I Cor. 5:1, 9; 6:9-11; 7:2; Gal. 5:19. See also N.T.C. on I Thess. 4:3-8). And let us not forget what Paul says in this very epistle (see on I Tim. 1:10).

Accordingly, the meaning of our present passage (I Tim. 3:2) is simply this, that an overseer or elder must be a man of unquestioned morality, one who is entirely true and faithful to his one and only wife; one who, being married, does not in pagan fashion enter into an immoral relationship with another woman.

In view of this, the attempt on the part of some to change the meaning of the original — making it say what it does not say — is inexcusable. In harmony with the views of *some* Church Fathers (for example, Tertullian and Chrysostom), and in disagreement with the explanations favored by others (for example, Jerome and Origen), these translators and commentators are of the opinion that Paul is here referring to men who, having been widowers, remarried. The translation (?) then becomes, "An overseer must be a man *who was married only once.*" [61] One can *understand* how men who reject or soft-pedal Scripture's infallibility — who, accordingly no longer feel obliged to accept as most certainly true the words, *"Paul . . .* to Timothy" (I Tim. 1:1, 2) — can also take the next step, and, assuming that the Pastorals reflect conditions which prevailed *after* Paul's departure from this earth, at a time when by many celibacy and the virgin-state began to be exalted above marriage, can read their private reconstruction of the

---

[61] Thus, or in similar fashion, Parry, Goodspeed, Moffatt, R.S.V., etc.

formation of these letters into the text, so that they think of the author of the Pastorals as a man who considered marriage and certainly *remarriage* to be sinful or nearly so. One *cannot excuse* an attempt to make a text say what it does not actually say in the original. The original simply says, "He must be . . . one wife's husband" (δεῖ — μιᾶς γυναικὸς ἄνδρα).[62]

The real author of the Pastorals, namely, Paul, did not oppose remarriage after the death of the marriage-partner (see especially I Tim. 5:14; then 4:3; cf. Rom. 7:2, 3; I Cor. 7:9), though *under certain specified conditions* he considered continuation in the unmarried state to be wiser than marriage (I Cor. 7:26, 38). Paul, we may be sure, was in entire agreement with the author of Hebrews, who said, "Let marriage be held in honor among all." (Heb. 13:4).

Example of a man who gives every evidence of having been true to his one and only wife, and of the beautiful harmony between the two, also in religious matters:

Aquila

"But when Priscilla and Aquila heard him (Apollos), they took him unto them, and expounded to him the way of God more accurately" (Acts 18:26).

3. In *mode of living (tastes and habits),* "temperate"

See also I Tim. 3:11; Titus 2:2. For the related verb see N.T.C. on I Thess. 5:6, 8 and see on II Tim. 4:5. Other possible translations of the adjective would be *sober* (not, however, in the sense of *somber* or *sad*), *circumspect.* Such a person lives deeply. His pleasures are not primarily those of the senses, like the pleasures of a drunkard for instance, but those of the soul. He is filled with spiritual and moral earnestness. He is not given to excess (in the use of wine, etc.), but moderate, well-balanced, calm, careful, steady, and sane. This pertains to his physical, moral, and mental tastes and habits.

Example of such a well-balanced, sober, careful, temperate person:

Luke

". . . having investigated them all carefully from the beginning" (Luke 1:3). Even those who cannot be counted among the company of believers are at times not altogether devoid of this virtue; note the town-clerk at Ephesus, who subdued the tempers of the crowd (Acts 19:35).

---

[62] It is correctly rendered by the following (among others): Syriac (published by British and Foreign Bible Society, London, 1950, I. 142); Latin (Theodori Bezae, "unius uxoris virum"); English (A.V., A.R.V., Weymouth, Lenski, Berkeley; the same idea, Williams: "must have only one wife"; Riverside: "true to one woman"); Dutch (Statenvertaling: "eener vrouwe man"; Nieuwe Vertaling: "de man van een vrouw"); Frisian; South African; French (Version D'Ostervald); German (Luther and subsequent versions); Swedish authorized in 1917, edition Stockholm 1946).

4. In *manner of judging and of acting on these judgments,* "self-controlled"

See also Titus 1:8; 2:2, 5; and see on I Tim. 2:9, 15 for the related noun. The *self-controlled* or *sensible* man is the man *of sound mind.* He is *discreet,* sane; hence, not swayed by sudden impulses over which he exercises no mastery, nor is he at all ready to accept the nonsense which was being disseminated by the errorists at Ephesus (see on I Tim. 1:3, 4, 6, 7). The sensible person is always ready and willing to learn.

Example of such a sane individual:

Apollos

Though he was a gifted orator, mighty in the Scriptures and instructed in the way of the Lord, still he was willing to be taught by Priscilla and Aquila, in order to learn the way of God more accurately (Acts 18:26, quoted above, under 2).

5. In *morals in general,* "virtuous"

See also I Tim. 2:9. The overseer must be a man "of inner moral excellency and of outward *orderly* behavior." It is an epithet of honor. See M.M., p. 356. The adjective naturally has a slightly different shade of meaning when applied to *character* than when applied to *clothes* or *outward appearance* (as in I Tim. 2:9). The root-meaning of the related noun is *order.* See N.T.C. on John, Vol. I, p. 79, footnote 26.

Example of a virtuous person, a person of moral strength:

Ruth

"All . . . know that thou art a virtuous woman" (a woman of worth, LXX: cf. strength, Ruth 3:11).

Further: Job (Job 1:8); Zechariah and Elizabeth (Luke 1:5, 6); Simeon (Luke 2:25); Anna (Luke 2:37).

6. In hospitality, "hospitable"

See also Titus 1:8; then Rom. 12:13; Heb. 13:2; I Peter 4:9. A hospitable person is literally a *friend of strangers* (φιλόξενος). He "communicates to their necessities." We can well imagine how deeply appreciated was such hospitality in a day when organized *social* welfare on any large scale was virtually non-existent; when widows and orphans were dependent on the kindness of relatives and friends; when persecutions with their imprisonments raged fiercely; when poverty and hunger were far more in evidence than they are today in the countries of the West; when messages from one section of Christendom to another had to be delivered by personal messenger, necessitating a great deal of travel; and when lodging with unbelievers was less than desirable. Hence, if hospitality was a requirement for *every* Christian according to his ability and opportunity to furnish it, it was all the more a requirement for the overseer.

Example:

Onesiphorus

"Onesiphorus . . . often refreshed me, and was not ashamed of my chain" (II Tim. 1:16). See also Gen. 18:1-8; I Kings 17:8-16; I Kings 18:13; II Kings 4:8; Heb. 13:2.

7. In teaching-ability, "qualified to teach"

See also I Tim. 5:17; II Tim. 2:2; 2:24; 3:14; then I Cor. 12:29. Every overseer or elder should possess this gift to some extent. No one, moreover, will be *able to teach* (διδακτικός) unless he himself is *taught* (διδακτός). Having been instructed by "faithful witnesses" one imparts this instruction to others, who in turn must teach still others.

But though all the overseers must have this ability in a certain degree, so that they can counsel those who seek their advice, some have received *greater* or *different* talents than others. Hence, even in Paul's day the work of the elders was divided, so that, while all took part in ruling the church, some were entrusted with the responsibility of laboring in the word and in teaching (I Tim. 5:17). Accordingly the distinction arose between those overseers who today are generally called "ministers" and those who are simply called "elders."

Example:

Ezra and his helpers

"He (Ezra) was a ready scribe in the law of Moses . . . Ezra the priest, the scribe, and the Levites who taught the people, said to all the people, This day is holy to Jehovah y o u r God" (Ezra 7:6; Neh. 8:9). See also Acts 6:10.

And now *the second set of seven requirements.* The overseer must also be *above reproach* in the following respects. He must be:

(1) "not (one who lingers) beside (his) wine"

See also I Tim. 3:8; Titus 1:7, and see on I Tim. 5:23. (The original has acc. of πάροινος.) With respect to drinking wine Scripture avoids extremes. The same inspired author who advises Timothy to use a little wine for the sake of his stomach and frequent illnesses (I Tim. 5:23), also clearly declares that one who fails to practise moderation has no right to a place in the presbytery. A wine-bibber, tippler, or drunkard cannot be a worthy overseer.

Example of those who were guilty of the sin here condemned:

Some Communicants at Corinth

"one is hungry and another is drunk" (I Cor. 11:21). Cf. I Sam. 25:36: Nabal. See also Gen. 9:20-27.

(2) "not given to blows"

See also Titus 1:7. Literally Paul says, "not a striker." He is thinking of a man who is ever ready with his fists, a bellicose person, a spitfire or fire-eater. Think of the backwoodsmen of former days who literally wore a chip on their shoulder as a challenge to fight anyone who would dare to knock it off, whence our expression, "He carries a chip on his shoulder."

Between the immoderate use of wine and the eagerness to engage someone in combat there is but a small step. Hence, these two follow each other here in the list of negatively expressed requirements for overseership. Seneca said, "Wine kindles wrath" (Vinum incendit iram). And the same close relationship is indicated in Prov. 23:29, 30. Hence, examples are:

The men against whom the author of Proverbs issues his warning

"Who has woe? Who has sorrow? Who has contentions? Who has wounds without cause? Who has redness of eyes?

"Those who tarry long over the wine,

"Those who go to try the mixed wine" (Prov. 23:29, 30). See also Gen. 4:23: Lamech; Gen. 49:5, 6: Simeon and Levi.

(3) "genial"

See also Titus 3:2; then Phil. 4:5; James 3:17; I Peter 2:18. The person here indicated is the very opposite of the spitfire. Though he never compromises with respect to the truth of the gospel, he is willing to yield when it comes to his own rights, in the spirit of I Cor. 6:7, "Why not rather suffer wrong?" The rendering "yielding" or "ceding" — which also corresponds with the root-idea of the word used in the original — expresses the meaning in part. However, it may be doubted whether any single word or expression in the English tongue is the complete equivalent of the original. The qualities of yieldedness, fairness, sweet reasonableness, gentleness, helpfulness, and generosity are combined in this *conciliatory, considerate, genial,* better than *debonair,* individual.

One who, but for what is recorded in Acts 15:39, approaches this ideal is

Barnabas

"And Joseph, who by the apostles was surnamed Barnabas (which being interpreted means *son of encouragement*) a Levite, a man of Cyprus by race, in possession of a field, sold it, and brought the money, and laid it at the apostle's feet. . . . But Barnabas took him (Paul), and brought him to the apostles. . . . He was a good man, and full of the Holy Spirit and of faith" (Acts 4:36, 37; 9:27; 11:24). Other examples: Abraham as pictured in Gen. 13:8, 9; Isaac (Gen. 22; 26:12-22); Joseph (Gen. 50:15-21); Moses (Num. 12:3); Jonathan (I Sam. 18:1); Timothy!

(4) "not contentious"

See also Titus 3:2. Note how "genial" is interposed between "not given to blows" and "not contentious," the reason being that it is contrasted with both. The requirement "not contentious," literally "averse to fighting," probes even deeper than "not given to blows." A person might not be eager to come to blows, but being disputateous, as were no doubt the errorists at Ephesus (see I Tim. 1:4), he would still be lacking one of those characteristics which are needed by an overseer.

In addition to the false teachers at Ephesus, who certainly were contentious persons, think also of:

The Corinthian Quarrelers

"Each one of y o u says, I am of Paul; and I of Apollos; and I of Cephas; and I of Christ" (I Cor. 1:12).

(5) "not fond of money"

See also I Tim. 3:8 and Titus 1:8. Not only must the overseer be a man who is far removed from the Judas-like attitude (John 12:6) of trying to enrich himself by dishonest means (the sin indicated in I Tim. 3:8 and in Titus 1:8), but he must also be far removed from making the acquisition of earthly treasure his chief goal in life even though the means employed should be honest. Paul must have been thinking first of all of some men in Ephesus where Timothy was carrying on his ministry (I Tim. 6:9, 10). In addition one can think of:

The Rich Fool

"Thou fool, this night is thy soul required of thee; and the things which thou hast prepared, whose shall they be?" (Luke 12:20). And think of the Rich Man in the parable of The Rich Man and Lazarus (Luke 16:19-31).

(6) "managing well his own household"

See also I Tim. 3:12; 5:17; then Rom. 12:8; I Thess. 5:12. The overseer, it being assumed that he is a married man with children, must be gifted with the ability to oversee, to preside, to manage. Paul reasons from the less to the greater, in this twofold sense:

a. If a man cannot even preside over or *manage,* how will he be able to *take upon himself* (that is, upon his heart) *the care of* anything? The latter activity indicates a watchful regard that is even more solicitous and incessant than the former.

b. If a man cannot discharge his responsibility with respect to *his own* family, how will he do this with respect to *God's* family, that is, the church (the local congregation), the family which has God as its Father?

Now this ability to manage or govern well his own family becomes evident when the father keeps his *offspring in submission* (see on I Tim. 2:11).

The so-called "progressive" idea of permitting the child to do as he pleases finds no support in Scripture. But though authority must be exercised, this must be done "with true dignity," that is, it must be done in such a manner that the father's *firmness* makes it *advisable* for a child to obey, that his *wisdom* makes it *natural* for a child to obey, and that his *love* makes it *a pleasure* for a child to obey.

Imagine how ideal must have been that early family-life which in later years blossomed forth into the relationship pictured in Acts 21:9:

Philip the evangelist

"And he had four virgin daughters who prophesied." And see the beautiful family-life portrayed in Ps. 128:3. Cf. Gen. 18:19; Is. 78:3, 4; 105:8-10; Luke 2:51; Acts 2:39; 16:14, 15; 16:33.

(7) "not a recent convert"

A member of the congregation may, however, possess all the characteristics mentioned in the preceding, and still not be qualified to serve as an overseer. He may be *a beginner,* one who was converted only recently, whether old or young. He lacks the maturity and prestige that is required in an overseer. He is *a novice.* Literally the apostle says, "not *a neophyte* (acc. of νεόφυτος, *newly planted;* hence, *young plant:* Job 14:9; Ps. 128:3; 144:12; Is. 5:7). The church is God's *field* (I Cor. 3:9). The believers are his *plants* (I Cor. 3:6). By a slight change of metaphor Paul also says that they have become "one-plant-with-Christ" (Rom. 6:5). Cf. N.T.C. on John 15:1-8.

The choosing of a neophyte might have disastrous results for himself; hence, also for the church. So, a novice must not be elected, "in order that he may not become beclouded (or: blinded) by conceit." The verb means literally "wrapped up in smoke," the smoke of arrogance in this case. See I Tim. 6:4; II Tim. 3:4. The result would be: "and fall into *the condemnation* (κρίμα) of the devil." This undoubtedly means "the condemnation pronounced upon the devil." [63] Cf. II Tim. 2:26. We read

---

[63] The idea that διαβόλου when in verse 6 it is used in the expression "condemnation of the devil" must be a subjective genitive because this same word when in verse 7 it occurs in the phrase "snare of the devil" is a subjective genitive, impresses me as being superficial. In determining the nature of these genitives, one question is paramount. It is this: What is the scriptural usage? Is it more scriptural to represent the devil as pronouncing a sentence of condemnation, or to represent him as being condemned? Of course, the latter! See the following passages: Gen. 3:15; Is. 14:12 (by implication); Zech. 3:2; Matt. 4:10; 12:29; Luke 10:18; John 12:31; Rom. 16:20; Eph. 6:11; James 4:7; II Peter 2:4; Jude 6; Rev. 12:7-9; 20:10. Hence, "the condemnation of the devil" means "the condemnation pronounced (and executed) upon the devil" (objective genitive).

Similarly, is it the more usual scriptural representation to speak of the devil as striving to lure others into his snares, or is he more generally described as becom-

about this sentence of condemnation in II Peter 2:4 (and see footnote 63). Pride ever leads to the fall. In order to prevent this from happening, the church must not choose a beginner to be an overseer.

In harmony with this rule, on his first missionary journey Paul did not appoint elders in every church until he revisited the churches (Acts 14:23). Also note that Timothy himself, upon his conversion, was not immediately ordained. Having been led to Christ on Paul's first missionary journey, he was not ordained until later (on the second journey at the earliest). The rule, "Whenever possible no neophytes shall be chosen to overseership in the church," was also adhered to in the case of

Joseph called Barsabbas and Matthias:

"Of the men who have accompanied us all the time that the Lord Jesus went in and went out among us . . . one must be chosen to become with us a witness of the resurrection" (Acts 1:21, 22). In fact, Paul himself, after his conversion in 33/34 A. D., spent three years in Arabia before doing effective work at Tarsus and Antioch, and was not commissioned to go on his first missionary journey until ten years after his conversion! See my *Bible Survey,* Grand Rapids, Mich., fourth printing 1953, pp. 189-195.

Having finished the list of requirements that pertain to the estimation in which the brother is held by his fellow church-members, the apostle proceeds now to the opinion of outsiders (those who do not belong to the church) with respect to him:

(1) Above reproach in the estimation of outsiders

"He must also have a favorable testimony from outsiders." Even with them the prospective overseer, and also the overseer who is already in office, must have a good reputation. The necessity of adding this requirement follows from the fact that often such "outsiders" know more about the man in question than do the members of the church. It frequently happens, for example, that most or all of those associated with him in his daily occupation are unbelievers. Their judgment is of some importance. Besides, the church seeks to exert a powerful influence for good upon the world, leading sinners to Christ. An overseer's bad reputation with the world will not be of any help in achieving this purpose.

Now it is a fact that frequently the world's adverse opinion of the Christian is motivated by hatred of the Christ (Rom. 15:3; Heb. 13:12, 13). But

---

ing himself ensnared? Of course the former. It is the devil who, also in the Pastorals, is depicted as setting snares. II Tim. 2:26 settles this point. Cf. I Tim. 6:9. Hence, "the snare of the devil" means "the snare which he sets" (subjective genitive).

it is not *this* light esteem that Paul has in mind. What he means is that in order to be an effective overseer a brother must be known even to worldly people with whom he is (or has been) in contact as *a man of character,* a man against whom it is not possible to level any *just* charges of *moral* turpitude. It must be possible to say with reference to him, "He conducts himself properly with respect to outsiders" (see N.T.C. on I Thess. 4:12. Cf. Col. 4:5).

A person who does not have this favorable testimony and who is nevertheless chosen to be an overseer in the church may easily "fall into reproach." But here for once "the reproach of the world" is not to the church-member's credit. It is not now an honor, as it is in the other passages where the same word "reproach" is used (Rom. 15:3; Heb. 10:33; 11:26; 13:13). We can imagine how, on the morning after this undeserving person's election to office, the men who work with him will greet him with the mocking exclamation, "What do we hear now? Have they actually made *you* an elder . . . *you?*" And *the devil* will rejoice.[64]

Moreover, such a person may easily become very bold, thinking, "If I can get away with this conduct of mine, and still be elected overseer, I can get away with anything." Thus he will fall into the devil's *snare,* that is, into the devil's *trap,* hence, into his *power.* See especially II Tim. 2:26; then also I Tim. 6:9; finally, Luke 21:35; Rom. 11:9; and for a synonym N.T.C. on John 6:61.

To have a good reputation even with those who are outside the church, is, under the most favorable circumstances, to be considered a blessing.

Example:

Cornelius

"well spoken of by the entire Jewish nation" (Acts 10:22).

---

8 Deacons similarly (must be) dignified, not double-tongued, not addicted to much wine, not greedy of shameful gain, 9 keeping hold of the mystery of our faith with a pure conscience. 10 And let these also first be tested; then let them render service, if they are blameless.

11 Women similarly (must be) dignified, no slanderers, temperate, reliable in all matters.

12 Let a deacon be one wife's husband, managing well his children and his

---

64 This is true whether or not the word "reproach" as well as "snare" be construed as modified by "of the devil." Either is grammatically possible, arguments to the contrary (as in Lenski, *op. cit.,* p. 591) notwithstanding. The non-repetition of the preposition (εἰς) argues in favor of linking "of the devil" with both nouns, but does not absolutely settle the question. Materially, however, there is little if any difference in meaning. When the world reproaches, the devil, too, reproaches. When Lenski says that the devil is the last one to reproach a Christian for his faults, is he not forgetting Zech. 3:1-3?

own household. 13 For those who have served well acquire for themselves a noble standing and great confidence in the faith (which centers) in Christ Jesus.

3:8-12

8-12. Note how the qualifications of women who render auxiliary service are wedged in between the requirements for deacons.

Though the New Testament contains but few specific references to *deacons* (besides our present passage also Phil. 1:1, and of course Acts 6:1-6,[65] where however the term "deacon" does not occur), this does not mean that the work of the deacon was considered to be of inferior value. It was and is a glorious task. It is based upon Christ's loving concern for his people. So close to his heart is this tender solicitude that he regards what is done to the least of his brothers as if it had been done to himself (Matt. 25:31-46).

From Acts 6 we learn that deacons were chosen because the elders did not have the time and energy to take upon themselves the care of the poor and needy in addition to performing all their other work: governing the church, preaching the Word, administering the sacraments, leading the congregation in prayer, etc. The deacons, accordingly, were chosen in order to "serve tables." Their special task is to gather the offerings which God's people in gratitude make to their Lord, to distribute these gifts in the proper spirit to all who are in need, to prevent poverty wherever it is possible to do this, and by means of their prayers and words of Scripture-based comfort, to encourage the distressed.

Now in order to carry out so worthy a task, they, as well as the elders, must be men full of faith and of the Holy Spirit (Acts 6:5).

Accordingly, deacons similarly (must be):

(1) **Dignified**

See also Titus 2:2; cf. Phil. 4:8. For the noun see on I Tim. 2:2; Titus 2:7. This refers not only to their necessary decorum or propriety of manner and conduct but also to the fact that in their inner thoughts and attitudes they must be men of Spirit-wrought gravity and respectability. Such a serious-minded man was

Stephen

"a man full of faith and of the Holy Spirit" (Acts 6:5).

Moreover, when such a man administers cheer, he means what he says. Hence,

---

[65] Other references, such as Rom. 12:7; 16:1; I Cor. 12:28; and I Peter 4:11, would seem to be of a more general nature. They do not — or in some cases, do not exclusively — refer to the office and work of the deacon.

(2) **Not double-tongued** [66]

He does not say one thing to one person and something different to another. He does not "talk out of both sides of his mouth." He does not *say* one thing and *know* another, like:

Gehazi (II Kings 5:19-27) or *Sanballet and Geshem* (Neh. 6:2) or *Ananias and Sapphira*

"And she said, Yes, for so much" (Acts 5:8).

(3) **Not addicted to much wine**

Cf. "not (one who lingers) beside (his) wine" in verse 3. The qualified deacon is moderate in his use of wine if he drinks any. He is no

Nabal

"He was very drunk" (I Sam. 25:36).

(4) **Not greedy of shameful gain**

Cf. Titus 1:7; I Peter 5:2; also "not fond of money" in verse 3. However, here in verse 8 the emphasis is slightly different. A man who is fond of money is not necessarily an embezzler. But it is the embezzler or pilferer and the man who joins a good cause for the sake of material advantage whom Paul has in mind here in verse 8. It is the man with the mercenary spirit who goes all out in his search for riches, anxious to add to his possessions regardless of the method, whether fair or foul. Think of

Judas

"Now this he said, not because he was concerned about the poor, but because he was a thief and as he had the money-box he used to take what was put in it" (John 12:6). And cf. Simon the Sorcerer (Acts 8:9-24).

(5) **Keeping hold of the mystery of our faith with a pure conscience**

A good deacon, accordingly, is attentive to duty for Christ's sake. He is conscientious. Were he undignified, double-tongued, addicted to much wine, and greedy of shameful gain, he would not be the kind of man who with *a conscience* purified by the Holy Spirit (see on I Tim. 1:5) "keeps clinging to the mystery of *our* (literally, "of *the*") faith." It is hard to believe that the expression "the mystery of our faith" here in I Tim. 3:9 means something different than "the mystery of our religion" in verse 16. Hence, see on that verse. *For Christ's sake* the qualified deacon watches himself scrupulously, doing all in his power to remain in the closest possible

---

[66] Here one might have expected a form of δίγλωσσος, as in the apocryphal book Eccles. 5:9, where "the man who winnows with every wind" is so characterized (cf. Prov. 11:13 in the LXX). The word which Paul actually employs (acc. masc. pl. of δίλογος), and which elsewhere occurs with a different sense ("one who repeats," see M.M., p. 163), reminds one of the Latin *bilinguis* in one of its meanings. Does this mean that the author of the Pastorals borrows from the Latin? See pp. 10, 11.

union with *him,* that is, with the most sublime of all divinely disclosed mysteries, namely, "God revealed in the flesh" for the salvation, on equal terms, of Jew and Gentile.

The trait here described finds a beautiful illustration in

Joseph

who, *for God's sake,* remained on the straight path.

"How then can I do this great wickedness, and sin against God?" (Gen. 39:9).

(6) **And let these also first be tested; then let them render service, being blameless**

Cf. I Tim. 3:6. What holds for the overseers holds also for the deacons. No neophytes must be chosen. Only *tested* men should *serve* (see on verse 13) in this capacity. This does not mean that a prospective deacon must first serve a trial-period, but rather that by means of a consecrated life he must furnish a testimonial of character. He must be able to sustain the test of having the eyes of the whole church (plus the outsiders!) focused upon him. If he succeeds, he is then *blameless* (literally, "not to be called to account," a close synonym of "above reproach" or "irreprehensible" in verse 2).

This method of selecting deacons is surely far removed from the one which is suggested at times, namely, "May-be if we make him a deacon, he'll stop his criticizing. Let's place him on the nomination for deacons. If elected, we can perhaps make something of him."

The Seven Men of Good Report

who became the first deacons of the early church furnish an excellent example of the manner in which deacons should be chosen.

"Therefore, brothers, look around for seven men from among you of good reputation, full of the Spirit and of wisdom" (Acts 6:3).

The section with respect to deacons is interrupted by a passage stating the requirements in the case of *women.* That these women are not "the wives of the deacons" nor "all the adult female members of the church" is clear from the syntax: "The overseer therefore *must be* . . . Deacons similarly (must be) . . . Women similarly (must be) . . ." One and the same verb coordinates the three: the overseer, deacons, women. Hence, these women are here viewed as rendering special service in the church, as do the elders and the deacons. They are a group by themselves, not just the wives of the deacons nor *all* the women who belong to the church.

On the other hand, the fact that no special and separate paragraph is used in describing their necessary qualifications, but that these are simply wedged in between the stipulated requirements for deacons, with equal clarity indicates that these women are not to be regarded as constituting a third office in the church, the office of "deaconesses," on a par with and endowed with authority equal to that of deacons.

It is true that from early times, in justification of "the-office-of-deaconess-theory," an appeal has been made to such passages as the one now under consideration (I Tim. 3:11); I Tim. 5:9; and Rom. 16:1. But as to I Tim. 5:9, see on that passage. As to Rom. 16:1, no adequate reason has been given to prove that there the term used in the original does not have its far more usual meaning *servant* (correctly thus rendered in A.V. and in the text of the A.R.V.) or *assistant,* one who *ministers lovingly* (see N.T.C. on John, Vol. I, pp. 116, 119); in this case, to the cause of the gospel.

Nothing can erase the fact that according to Scripture, and particularly also according to Paul's epistles, women perform very important ministries in the church. It is also true that the extent and value of the service which they are able to render has not always been fully recognized or appreciated. See on I Tim. 5:9. But it is contrary to the spirit of Paul's remarks concerning women and their place in the church (see on I Tim. 2:11, 12; and cf. I Cor. 11:1-16; 14:34, 35), and contrary also to the significance of the manner in which the apostle here in I Tim. 3:11 *parenthesizes* the requirements for women-helpers, to regard their task as a third office, to be co-ordinated with that of the overseers and with that of the deacons.

The simplest explanation of the manner in which Paul, not yet finished with the requirements for the office of deacon, interjects a few remarks about women, is that he regards these women as the *deacons' assistants* in helping the poor and needy, etc. These are *women who render auxiliary service,* performing ministries for which women are better adapted. Here again we refer to our explanation of I Tim. 5:9. A few simple words indicate their necessary qualifications. Says Paul: **Women similarly (must be) dignified, no slanderers, temperate, reliable in all matters.**

For *truly respectable* or "dignified" see on verses 4 and 8. For *temperate* or *sober* see on verse 2. Also the requirement of thorough-going "reliability" or *trustworthiness* holds for the women as well as for elders and deacons (implied for the latter two groups in verses 6 and 10). Hence, these three virtues do not need to be discussed again.

It is also easily understood why Paul would emphasize that women who do the rounds of the church in performing loving ministries must not be gossipers. "No scandal-mongers please!" he says as it were. Those who *slander* imitate the evil one, whose very name is *diabolos,* that is, slanderer.

Lengthy is the list of truly respectable, temperate, trustworthy women who are mentioned in Scripture. Among them are, in greater or lesser degree, the two Deborah's (Gen. 35:8; Judg. 4:4); Jochebed (Heb. 11:23), Naomi and Ruth (Ruth 1:15-18), Hannah (I Sam. 1:15, 16; 1:22-2:10),

Ichabod's mother (I Sam. 4:21), Abigail (contrasted with her *intemperate* husband, I Sam. 25:3, 25, 36), the widow at Zarephath (I Kings 17), the Shunammite woman (II Kings 4:8), Huldah (II Kings 22:14), Queen Esther (the book of Esther), Elizabeth (Luke 1:5, 6), Mary the mother of Jesus (Luke 1:46-55; 2:19; Acts 1:14), Anna (Luke 2:36, 37), Mary and Martha (Luke 10:38-42; John, ch. 11; 12:1-8), the women who followed Jesus and ministered to him, such as Jesus' aunt Salome, Mary the wife of Clopas, Mary Magdalene, Johanna, (Luke 23:55; 24:1, 10; John 19:25), Dorcas (Acts 9:36-43), Lydia (Acts 16:14, 15, 40), Priscilla (Acts 18:26), Phoebe (Rom. 16:1), Tryphosa and Tryphaena (Rom. 16:12), and last but not least Lois and Eunice (II Tim. 1:5). In spite of weaknesses which Scripture does not conceal, the names of Sarah (Gen. 12:5, and note her name in the list of heroes of faith Heb. 11:11, 12), Rebecca (Gen. 24) and Rachel (Gen. 29) – also Leah (Gen. 29:35) – should be added to the list. How sharp was the contrast between *these* women and some females of Timothy's acquaintance (II Tim. 3:6, 7)!

Opposed to the lengthy list of *noble* women, Scripture mentions such *evil slanderers* as Potiphar's wife (Gen. 39:7-33) and Jezebel (I Kings 21:5-10).

What Paul means, accordingly, is this, "Timothy, see to it that the deacons' assistants be carefully selected. They should be Ruths and Lydias, not 'silly women,' nor the kind that remind one of Jezebel!"

The enumeration of qualifications for deacons is now continued and concluded:

(7) **Let a deacon be one wife's husband, managing well his children and his own household.** See on I Tim. 3:2, 4.

13. The apostle proceeds to show how he knows that deacons *must* be all this. He is deeply convinced of it, and this not only because of direct divine revelation but also because of the manifest special reward by means of which it pleases God to crown the deacons' efforts. The sense of the words which immediately follow is, "I know this is true, **For those who have served well acquire for themselves a noble standing and great confidence in the faith (which centers) in Christ Jesus."**

This is at the same time *an incentive* for deacons so that they may labor faithfully. It is not unscriptural to speak of such incentives. *It is* unscriptural not to recognize them (Matt. 19:29; II Tim. 4:7, 8; Heb. 12:2; Rev. 2:7, 10, 17, 26-29; 3:5, 6, 12, 13, 21, 22; etc.). Looking forward to a reward is not at all sinful, provided one plans to use this reward for the glory of God and for even greater service (if possible) in his kingdom.

It is entirely right and natural to regard the reward which is here promised as pertaining to *the deacons and their helpers.* The apostle has been speaking about *them,* and about no one else, in verses 8-12. The connection, moreover, is very close, being introduced by the word, "for." It will hardly do, therefore, to say that Paul is still thinking about *the overseers,* introduced in verse 1, and that he includes these in the reward here promised. To be sure, to these overseers also an incentive has been given, namely, the incentive based on the glorious character of their task (see verse 1). We may even go farther and admit that the blessing described in verse 13 will actually be enjoyed by elders as well as by deacons and their assistants. And we must probably accept as correct the position that the first verb used in the original here in verse 13 (cf. verse 10) should not be rendered *"have served* (well) *as deacons"* but simply *"have served* (well)." [67]

But though all this be freely granted, it still remains true that in the present passage the apostle is in all probability speaking about the persons mentioned in the immediately preceding context (verses 8-12). In verse 1 the incentive for the elders was indicated: their *task* is glorious. Verse 13 now adds the incentive for the deacons: their *reward* is rich. Let no one, permitting himself to be misled by the fact that it is the deacons' task *to serve* and not (like the elders) *to rule,* begin to think lightly of them and of their office. Let it be remembered that those deacons who have served well acquire for themselves a noble *standing.* The church will think highly of them because they have performed their tasks in a worthy manner. (Incidentally, the word rendered *standing* has the primary meaning *a step,* say of a staircase. Since such a staircase with its steps could be used to measure the sun's shadow, see II Kings 20:9-11 in the LXX, the meaning *degree* — cf. the "degrees" on a sun-dial — is not strange. Hence, in some such way the figurative meaning *degree, rank, standing* is easily reached.)

Moreover, the very consciousness of the fact that with the help of God he has done his best, so that he is not vexed by pangs of conscience, will give the deacon great *confidence.* He will not hold back, but will *tell all* (παρρησία is derived from πᾶς, *all,* and ῥῆσις *telling, speech*). This confidence has reference to *the faith* (subjective sense here) which centers in Christ Jesus. It is concerning *him* that the deacon will freely and gladly testify.

---

14 These things I am writing to you though I am hoping to come to you shortly, 15 but (I am writing them) in order that if I should be delayed, you may know how you should conduct yourself in God's house, which is the church of the living God, (the) pillar and foundation of the truth. 16 And confessedly great is the mystery of (our) devotion,

---

[67] Nowhere else in the New Testament does διακονέω mean *serve as deacon.* It means *to serve, to minister, to care for one's needs* (Matt. 20:28; Mark 10:45; Luke 10:40; 22:26, 27; John 12:2; II Tim. 1:18; I Peter 4:11; etc.) or *to supply by ministering:* (I Peter 1:12; 4:10). The mere fact that Paul has just been speaking about deacons would seem to be hardly sufficient to ascribe to the verb a technical sense which it has nowhere else in Scripture.

Who was manifested in the flesh,
Vindicated by the Spirit,
Seen by angels,
Heralded among (the) nations,
Believed in by the world,
Taken up in glory.

3:14-16

14. Paul now states the reasons for conveying these instructions (2:1-3:13) *in writing.* They are:

(1) Though I hope to see you soon, I fear that I may be delayed.

(2) Yet, the matter permits no delay, for it concerns *God's* house.

These things I am writing to you though I am hoping to come to you shortly. Did he mean, "I hope to come to you even before wintering at Nicopolis"? See p. 40.

15. But (I am writing them) in order that if I should be delayed, you may know how you should conduct yourself in God's house.[68]

Timothy must know how to supervise worship and the election of officers. Moreover, he must bear in mind that he has been entrusted not with a private business but with *God's house!* "House" is correct here, not "household" as in verses 4, 5, 12. Believers are God's *house* or *sanctuary* (I Cor. 3:16; 6:19; II Cor. 6:16) because *God dwells in them.* Hence, Paul continues: **which is**[69] **the church of the living God** (*not the temple of dead idols!* Cf. N.T.C. on I Thess. 1:9, 10), **the pillar and foundation of the truth.** Having been called "God's *house,*" we now note that the church is next compared to a pillar and foundation. As *the*[70] *pillar* supports *the roof,* even better (note the climax!) as *the foundation supports the entire superstructure,* so the church supports the glorious *truth* of the gospel. Cf. II Tim. 2:19; then Matt. 16:18. It supports the truth by:

---

[68] Condition of third class (stating the purpose after ἵνα). Protasis has ἐάν with first person sing. present active subjunctive of βραδύνω (cf. II Peter 3:9; and see the related adjective *slow* in Luke 24:25). Apodosis has second person sing. perfect active subjunctive of οἶδα.

Literally, "...how it is necessary in God's house *to conduct oneself* (ἀναστρέφεσθαι present middle infinitive of ἀναστρέφω, *to turn up and down, to conduct oneself, to behave*). This may mean either "how it is necessary *for anyone* to conduct himself," or "how it is necessary *for you* to conduct yourself." Note context: "I am writing *to you* . . . I am hoping to come *to you* . . . in order that *you* may know." Hence, "how it is necessary *for you* to conduct yourself" seems to be natural here.

[69] ἥτις (attracted to the gender of ἐκκλησία) ἐστιν "because it is," or "it being."

[70] The omission of the article does not make the nouns "pillar" and "foundation" indefinite, but stresses their qualitative force: the church is nothing less than the truth's *pillar;* better still, it is the truth's very *foundation.*

H earing and *H* eeding it (Matt. 13:9)
H andling it rightly (II Tim. 2:15)
H iding it in the heart (Ps. 119:11), and
H olding it forth as the Word of Life (Phil. 2:16).

Or, if one prefers, by

D igesting it (Rev. 10:9). That takes study and meditation.
D efending it (Phil. 1:16)
D isseminating it (Matt. 28:18-20)
D emonstrating its power in consecrated living (Col. 3:12-17).

The heart of this gospel and of our whole devotion is *Christ.* Hence, Paul continues:

16. And confessedly great is the mystery of our devotion.

Great is the church because great is its exalted Head, Jesus Christ. That the expression "the mystery of our devotion" refers to *Christ* is clear from the fact that whatever follows in verse 16 refers to him. It is he who is great, and this *confessedly,* that is, thus acknowledged by the church in its daily witness, its preaching, and, as here, its hymns.

"The mystery of our devotion" is "the mystery of our faith" (verse 9), meaning that it pertains to our faith, to our devotion. By faith we embrace him. By means of our devotion we glorify him. The word used in the original (εὐσέβεια, — ας) occurs here in a sense slightly different from *piety* or *godliness* when this is viewed as a *quality* or *condition* of the soul. It is here used in a more active sense. It is *piety in action* ("operative piety," M.M., p. 265), *godly living* (as in 4:7) the conscientious *devotion* of our lives to God in Christ, the fear of God, (cf. the German "Gottesfurcht," and the Dutch "godsvrucht").

Christ is called *the mystery* of our devotion, not only because had he not been revealed to us, we would not have known him (a "mystery" being "a revealed secret"), but also because he transcends our comprehension (Eph. 3:18, 19). The more we know him, the better will we be able to discern the mysterious, unfathomable character of his love and of all his attributes.

It is exactly this *immeasurable greatness of the Christ* which forms the subject of the hymn from which Paul now quotes six lines. That theme was a familiar one in the early church, as is shown by passages such as the following: Acts 2:22-36; 4:11, 12; 10:38-43; 13:26-41; Rom. 8:31-39; I Cor. 1:30; 15:1-20, 56, 57; Eph. 1:20-23; Phil. 2:5-11; Col. 1:12-20; II Thess. 1:7, 8; 2:8; Titus 2:13; Heb. 1:1-4; 7:23-8:2; 9:24-28; 10:5-25; 12:1-3; Rev. 5:6-14; 12:10-12; 19:6-8.

Depending on an antecedent such as *Logos* (Word) or *Christ(os),* or Theos

(God)[71] the hymn continues: "who" or "he who" (ὅς) was made manifest in the flesh, etc.

The Six Lines in their Chiastic Arrangement

(1) Who was manifested in the flesh (2) **Vindicated by the Spirit**

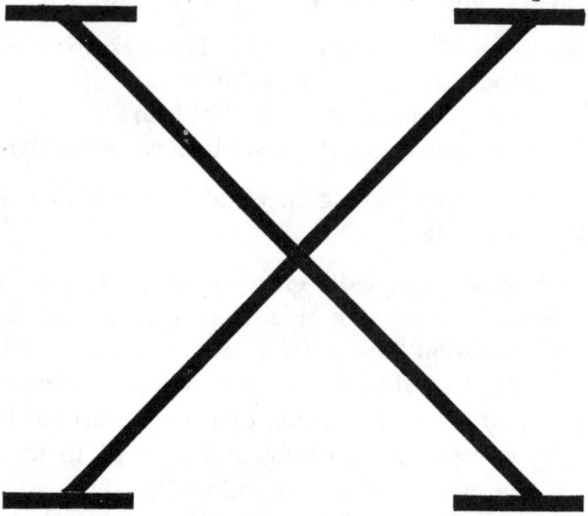

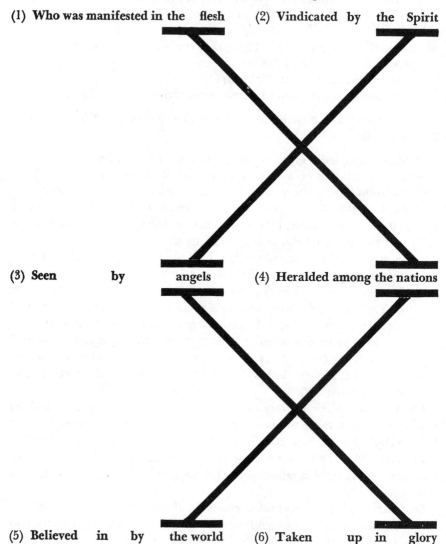

(3) Seen by angels (4) **Heralded among the nations**

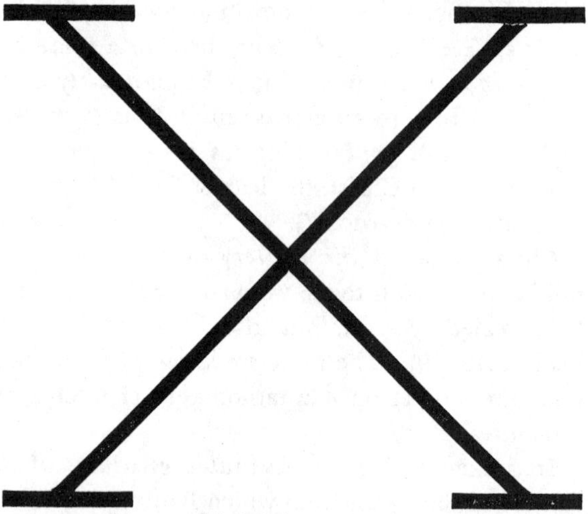

(5) Believed in by the world (6) **Taken up in glory**

[71] Nevertheless, the reading θεός here in I Tim. 3:16 is regarded by many as weakly attested. It is defended by E. F. Hills, *The King James Version Defended,* Des Moines, Iowa, 1956, pp. 59, 60. The Western reading ὅ instead of ὅς is probably the result of a scribal attempt to make the relative agree with the gender of μυστήριον. But the relative agrees with whatever was its antecedent *in the hymn from which* the quotation was made!

The movement of thought is:

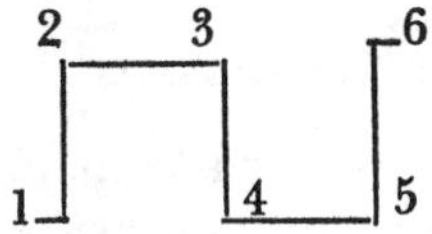

From the

(1) lower realm (the flesh)

to the

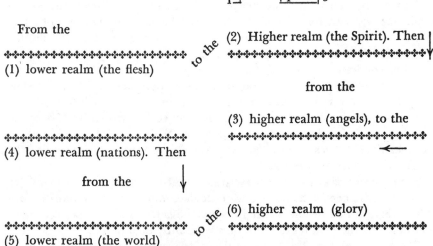

(2) Higher realm (the Spirit). Then

from the

(3) higher realm (angels), to the

(4) lower realm (nations). Then

from the

(5) lower realm (the world)

to the

(6) higher realm (glory)

By drawing connecting-lines between the words which indicate realities that belong to the same realm, *flesh, nations,* and *world* are linked; and so are *Spirit, angels,* and *glory.* See these lines on p. 138. Thus the X – which is the twenty-second letter of the Greek alphabet and is called *chi* – is drawn twice. We may say, therefore, that the six lines are arranged *chi*-astically.

The six lines of this *Hymn in Adoration of the Christ* begin with a line about *Christ's lowly birth* and end with a reference to *his glorious ascension.* It is clear that if in such a humiliation-to-exaltation hymn the chiastic thought-movement is to be maintained, there must be not less than six lines.

The contrasts are clearly drawn:

Weak flesh (line 1) contrasted with *strength-imparting Spirit* (line 2)
Heavenly angels (line 3) over against *earthly nations* (line 4)
The world below (line 5) over against *glory above* (line 6).

Yet, the beauty of it is this, that though the hymn pictures these regional contrasts, the thought is throughout that of *glory* and *adoration.* To be sure, the word *flesh* in line 1 indicates Christ's *humiliation;* but the expression "*manifested* in the flesh" ("veiled in flesh the Godhead see") points to his exalted, glorious nature. His glory is also indicated by the expressions "vindicated by the Spirit," "seen (with adoration) by angels," "heralded (joyfully) among the nations," "believed in (unto salvation) by the world," and "taken up (for exaltation) in glory." Hence what we have in these six lines is not antithetic parallelism (in the sense in which that term is usually employed), but *chiastic, cumulative parallelism.*

The Six Lines Considered Separately:

(1) "Who was manifested in the flesh." [72]

Into the human nature, weakened by the curse, came Christ, the Son of God. He was sent forth by God (Gal. 4:4); hence, Virgin-born. The fact that One so glorious in his pre-existence was willing to adopt the human nature in that curse-laden, weakened condition, was a manifestation of infinite, condescending love. Cf. John 1:1-14; II Cor. 8:9; Phil. 2:5-11. Hence, this voluntary self-concealment was at the same time a self-revelation. From the very beginning of his coming into the *flesh* self-concealment and self-disclosure walked side by side in connection with this "Mystery of our devotion." For the meaning of "flesh" see N.T.C. on John 1:14; and for the meaning of "was manifested" see N.T.C. on John 21:1, footnote 294.

(2) "Vindicated by the Spirit."

Not everyone saw his glory. "He was despised, and rejected of men" (Is. 55:3). By his enemies his claims were denied, and he himself was cast out (Heb. 13:12). But by the Spirit he was vindicated: his own perfect righteousness and the validity of his claims were fully established.

The A.V. and the R.S.V. are entirely correct in spelling Spirit with a capital letter, as referring to the Holy Spirit. The combination "flesh" and "Spirit" has scriptural warrant. Note: "And the Word became *flesh,* and dwelt among us as in a tent. And we beheld his glory, a glory as of the only begotten from the Father, full of grace and truth . . . And John testified, saying, I beheld *the Spirit* like a dove descending from heaven, and he remained on him" (John 1:14, 32; cf. 3:34). Having been thus anointed by the Holy Spirit (Ps. 2:2; 45:7; Matt. 3:16; Mark 1:10; Luke 3:22; Acts 4:27; 10:38), he was able, while in the "flesh" (the weakened human nature), to perform miracles, to cast out demons, etc. (Matt. 12:28). By means of every deed of power his *justice* was established, for surely the Holy Spirit would not have given this power to a sinner (John 9:31). But it was especially by means of *his resurrection from the dead* that the Spirit *fully* vindicated the claim of Jesus that he was the Son of God (Rom. 1:4).

(3) "Seen by angels."

The greatness of Christ *in his resurrection* stands out in the early preaching of the apostles. That resurrection was his complete vindication. It was also in connection with that resurrection that he was "seen by angels" (Matt. 28:2-7; Mark 16:5-8; Luke 24:4-7; John 20:12, 13). To be sure, angels had

[72] The six verbs are all third person singular passive *aorists.* The use of this tense indicates that each of the six indicated actions is viewed as a single whole, regardless of the time-element involved. Thus, though the statement, "He was manifested in the flesh," indicates not only Christ's *birth* but the entire period of earthly sojourn, from birth to burial, yet this entire manifestation in the flesh is viewed as *one fact.* The same holds with respect to the other five verbs.

shown an interest in his birth (Luke 2:9-14), and in his triumph over Satan when the latter tempted him in the desert (Matt. 4:11). Angels, moreover, addressed the disciples after his ascension (Acts 1:10, 11). Angels welcomed him back to heaven (Rev. 5:11). They were and are intensely interested in the whole program of redemption (I Peter 1:12). But although none of these great events need be excluded from the meaning of the line "seen by angels," the reference to Christ's glorious *resurrection,* a redemptive fact which stood out in the consciousness of the early church, is clear as daylight.[73] While the eyes of *men* – and *women* too! – were beclouded by the mist of "little faith" and, in a sense, lack of faith (Mark 16:11, 13, 14; Luke 24:10, 11; John 20:8, 9, 15, 24, 25), *angels* saw him clearly. They knew him as their glorious Lord.

(4) "Heralded among the nations."

It was *the resurrected Christ* who, *before his ascension,* issued The Great Commission, "Go, therefore, and make disciples of all the nations" (see Matt. 28:18-20: The Great Claim, The Great Commission, The Great Presence). And so the One who was not esteemed, the Despised One (Is. 53:3), began to be universally *heralded* or *proclaimed* (see on II Tim. 4:2) as The Savior of the World. Though this happened on and after Pentecost, *the "great commission" was issued before the ascension!*

(5) "Believed in by the world."

This, of course, was the direct result of the pre-ascension mandate. Men from every tribe and nation begin to worship him as their Lord and Savior, as had been predicted (Ps. 72:8-11, 17; 87; cf. Gen. 12:3; Am. 9:11, 12; Mic. 4:12).

(6) "Taken up in glory."

Having been manifested in the flesh, vindicated by the Spirit, seen by angels, and having issued the order which resulted in the proclamation of his name among the nations and the outgathering of a spiritual harvest from the world, he "was taken up." This is the same verb as is used in Mark 16:19 and in Acts 1:2. Luke 24:51 has "he parted from them," and Acts 1:9, "he was lifted up." While the echo of men's voices, "Crucify, crucify," had scarcely died, heaven opened wide its portals, and, upon receiving back its victorious King, resounded with the echoes of the jubilant anthem, sung by ten thousand times ten thousands and thousands of thousands, "Worthy is the Lamb." Truly, he was taken up *in glory.*

How great is the church which has such an exalted Head! Let Timothy bear this in mind as he goes about his task of supervision.

---

[73] Hence, I cannot agree here with interpreters who see little if any reference to the *resurrection*-activities of the angels; e.g., C. Bouma, *Kommentaar op het Nieuwe Testament* (Timotheus en Titus), pp. 149, 150. When Lenski says, in explanation of this line, "Angels saw him risen indeed," he is certainly right, *op. cit.,* p. 614.

Synthesis of Chapter 3

See the Outline at the beginning of the chapter.

We have here a list of requirements for office; also a statement regarding the glorious character of such work and its crowning reward. The qualifications of overseers and deacons (and in the latter connection, of deacons' female assistants) are stated. The emphasis falls on such qualities as reliability, dignity, temperance, helpfulness, proper relationship to one's family, and to some extent, Christian experience.

The lists reveal two facts:

On the one hand, the requirements for office are high enough so that persons with outstanding moral defects are excluded from office and in fact from any position of considerable responsibility in the church.

Yet, on the other hand, these requirements are low enough so that almost any member in good standing and of deserved reputation can qualify. Sinlessness, material riches, exceptional cultural attainment, these are not required.

Accordingly, a group of converts which displays a manifest lack of such qualities as are here mentioned is not yet ready to be organized into a congregation.

In stating his reasons for transmitting these lists *in written form,* Paul quotes from a beautiful early Hymn in adoration of the Christ, confessing the latter's glory from his incarnation to his coronation. Here we have proof of the fact that there was at least *a beginning* of hymnody during this early period. On the subject of psalm-singing and hymn-singing in the days of the apostle see also Acts 16:25; I Cor. 14:26; Eph. 5:19; and Col. 3:16. And do not forget the Old Testament Psalter, with its many cries for rescue, songs commemorating deliverance, and anthems of praise.

Outline of Chapter 4

Theme: *The Apostle Paul, Writing to Timothy, Gives Directions For the Administration of the Church*

Directions with respect to
Apostasy

4:1-5 A. Description of this apostasy and proof of its sinister nature.

4:6-16 B. How Timothy should deal with it:

1. By nourishing himself on the words of faith, and training himself for godly living;
2. By shunning profane and old-womanish myths;
3. By continuing stedfastly in positive exhortation and teaching, based upon the Word.

CHAPTER IV

I TIMOTHY 4:1

4 1 But the Spirit expressly says that in later seasons some will depart from the faith by giving heed to seducing spirits and doctrines of demons, 2 (embodied) in (the) insincere utterance of those who speak lies, whose own conscience is seared, 3 forbidding (people) to marry, and (enjoining them) to abstain from foods which God created in order that those who believe and acknowledge the truth may partake of them with thanksgiving. 4 For, every creature of God is good, and nothing is fit to be thrown away if it is received with thanksgiving; 5 for it is consecrated by the word of God and prayer.

Though the church be ever so glorious, reflecting the radiance of its precious Lord and Savior (I Tim. 3:15, 16), apostasy is just around the corner, for not all who belong outwardly to the church belong to it inwardly.

The present chapter deals with this apostasy.

4:1-5

1. But the Spirit expressly says that in later seasons some will depart from the faith.

"The Spirit says," that is, "is now saying." To whom was the Spirit speaking? Acts 20:29, 30 leads me to think that the apostle meant "to myself" (perhaps also to others). The Spirit, then, is saying that "in later seasons" – eras of this new dispensation, eras definitely marked out in God's foreknowledge – some will *depart* or *apostatize* from *the faith* (objective sense), the body of redemptive truth, the Christian religion.

The Spirit was saying this *expressly* ("in stated terms"). There was neither doubt nor vagueness about it. A half dozen years ago Paul, addressing the elders of the churches located in the very region where Timothy was now laboring, had spoken as follows: "I know that after my departure grievous wolves will enter in among y o u, not sparing the flock; and from among y o u r own selves men will arise, speaking perverse things, to draw away the disciples after them." A few years after that speech recorded in Acts 20, the apostle, writing to the Colossians from his first Roman imprisonment, had warned them against accepting the error that faith in Christ's atoning work has to be supplemented by ascetic beliefs and practices (Col. 2). And now, writing to Timothy from Macedonia, he is distinctly informed by the Holy Spirit that the error, *already present* in its incipient form, *will grow and develop* in the manner indicated in verse 3.

Men will depart from the faith by **giving heed to seducing spirits and doctrines of demons.** As the context indicates (and see also I John 4:6 where "the spirit of seduction" is contrasted with "the Spirit of truth"), these *spirits* are not men but *demons.* Like *planets* that seem *to wander* back and forth among the constellations, these spirits wander; moreover, they *cause men to wander.* They *seduce, lead astray.* By giving heed to them one is giving heed to *doctrines of demons* (cf. II Cor. 4:4; Rev. 13:11, 14).

2. These doctrines are **(embodied) in (the) insincere utterance** (literally, *in hypocrisy*) **of those who speak lies.** As Satan made use of a serpent to deceive Eve, and this by means of *an insincere utterance* (Gen. 3:1-5: he was hiding his real objective; for while he pretended to raise Eve to a higher level of glory, so that she would be "like God," his real aim was to dethrone God and enthrone himself), so these seducing spirits or demons make use of *men who speak lies,* and who talk piously and learnedly in order to cover up their own arrogance or immorality.

These hypocrites are described as the men **whose own conscience is seared** (literally, *"who are cauterized as to their own conscience"*). By constantly arguing with conscience, stifling its warnings, and muffling its bell, they at last have reached the point where conscience no longer bothers them. *Grieving* the Holy Spirit has led to *resisting* him, and *resisting* him to *quenching* him. Then, through their own rebellion and obstinacy, their conscience will have been rendered (and thus will be permanently) *seared.* It will have been made callous. A good example is Balaam (Num. 22:12, 19, 21, 22, 32; 25:1-3; II Peter 2:15; Rev. 2:14).

3. Their teaching is – or will be – as bad as their character: **forbidding (people) to marry, and (enjoining them) to abstain from foods.**

Principles bear fruit. The false teachers who are here described, probably accept as one of their starting principles the thesis: Anything physical or sensuous is contaminating. It is not difficult to see how such a principle would in course of time cause the errorists to frown on *marriage. Foods,* too, would be condemned, though, of course, not absolutely. Fasting would be praised.

An early fulfilment of the prophecy came in the second century. It is not difficult to understand how Jewish ritualistic scruples, *already* in evidence in near-by Colosse as well as elsewhere (see Col. 2 and cf. Rom. 14), would ally itself with dualistic heathen philosophy. They had in common *Asceticism,* the renunciation of the comforts of life with a view to attaining happiness and perfection.

The second century syncretistic cult (see p. 20) in which the prophecy was partly fulfilled, was *Gnosticism,* which elevated *gnosis,* that is, *knowledge,* to a position of prominence above *pistis,* that is, *faith.* According to this system, the good God – the God of the new dispensation – could not have created the world, for the world is matter, and matter is the seat of evil. It was the Jehovah of the Old Testament, the Demiurge, who created the world, the human body, matter. These are our enemies. They must be conquered. Hence, all Gnostics favored "the abuse of the flesh." But this abuse of the flesh can express itself in two diametrically opposite imperatives: a. "Shun it"; b. "Overcome it by indulging in it." The first was advocated by *Ascetic Gnostics,* such as Marcion, Saturninus, and Tatian (see Tertullian, *Against Marcion,* I. xxix; Irenaeus, *Against Heresies,* I. xxviii); the second by *Antinomian* or *Licentious Gnostics,* such as the Nicolaitans. The apostle Paul, here in I Tim. 4, predicts and warns against the former. The apostle John (I John 3:4-10; Rev. 2:15, 20, 24), the apostle Peter (II Peter 2:12-19), and Jude (verses 4, 8, 11, and 19) combat the latter. But the two are never far apart. Paul in reality combats *both* varieties, for we have not only his statements here in I Tim. 4 but also that in II Tim. 3:1-9. (For the Cerinthian application of the basic thesis of Gnosticism see N.T.C. on John, Vol. I, pp. 33, 83, 84.)

But this is only *one* fulfilment. Others follow; for though in its ancient forms Gnosticism has passed away, its spirit has been in evidence again and again throughout the centuries. Also in our own day, whenever the Old Testament is frowned upon, whenever human reason is exalted above Christian faith, whenever the thesis: "Sin is real and is in its essence rebellion against God" is rejected, or whenever man's ability to save himself is proclaimed (which is a denial of Christ as the only and perfect Savior), the ghost of Gnosticism stalks again.

Gnosticism despises God's ordinances, for example, the marriage-ordinance (Gen. 2:24) and the ordinance concerning food (Gen. 1:29, 30; and especially Gen. 9:3). These errorists, whose coming Paul in a measure *describes* but even more *predicts,* order men to abstain from foods **which God created in order that those who believe and acknowledge the truth may partake of them with thanksgiving** (literally, *which God created for participation with thanksgiving by those who believe and who acknowledge the truth).*

These words pertain to *foods,* not to *marriage.* Of course, by implication they apply to both, but *directly* only to foods. The apostle has expressed his favorable view of *marriage and the family* in such passages as I Tim. 2:15; 3:2, 4, 12. With respect to foods, then, note that God – the only true God, who is the same in both dispensations – has created them. Hence, they cannot be bad or contaminating. And he has created them with a definite purpose, namely, "for participation with thanksgiving" (I Cor. 10:31), so that the circle may again be completed, and what came from God may, in the form of thanksgiving, be returned to him. But the *natural* man is not able to pour out his heart in thanksgiving unto God. Hence, Paul adds, "by those who believe and acknowledge the truth." Such joyful acceptance of the truth leads not to asceticism but to partaking with thanksgiving. This thought receives further emphasis as Paul continues:

4. For every creature of God is excellent, and nothing is fit to be thrown away if it is received with thanksgiving. This sentence confirms the preceding passage. Foods that were created for consumption with accompanying thanksgiving are excellent. In fact, *every* creature of God is excellent: "And God saw everything that he had made, and behold, it was very good" (Gen. 1:31). Nothing is fit to be thrown away, as if it were evil or the seat of evil. Of late, science is beginning to discover that what used to be regarded as of no direct value to man may prove to be a source of great blessing; may, in fact, help to solve the food-problem of future generations; think, for example, of "plant-food from the ocean."

Every creature of God is excellent:

(a) For the very reason that God *created* it

and

(b) Because he also *consecrated* it.

Hence, Paul continues:

5. For it is consecrated by the word of God and prayer. By means of God's *blessing* upon it and by means of our *confident prayer,* it has been *consecrated* (cf. II Tim. 2:21), that is, set apart for holy use, lifted into the spiritual realm. For the Christian, eating and drinking are no secular activities (I Cor. 10:31). While, before partaking of food, *he* utters his petition and thanksgiving, *God* at the same time pronounces his word of blessing (cf. Deut. 8:3). He remembers his gracious covenant (Ps. 11:5).

---

6 By submitting these matters to the brothers you will be an excellent minister of Christ Jesus, nourished on the words of the faith and of the excellent doctrine which you have been following. 7 But profane and old-womanish myths shun. Train yourself for godly living. 8 For, while physical training is of *some* benefit, this godly living is of benefit *in every way,* as it holds promise of life both for the present and for the future. 9 Reliable is that saying and worthy of full acceptance. 10 For to this end we toil and strive, because we have set our hope on the living God, who is the Savior of all men, especially of those who believe.

11 Command these things and teach (them). 12 Let no one despise your youth, but become the believers' model in speech, in conduct, in love, in faith, in purity. 13 Until I come, attend to the (public) reading (of Scripture), to the exhorting and to the teaching. 14 Do not grow careless about the gift that is in you, which was granted to you through prophetic utterance with the laying on of the hands of the presbytery. 15 Let these things be your constant care; in these things be (absorbed), so that your progress may be evident to everyone. 16 Look to your-

self and to the teaching, persevere in them, for by doing this you will save both yourself and those who hear you.

4:6-16

6. By submitting these matters to the brothers you will be an excellent minister of Christ Jesus.

Timothy must warn against coming danger. He must point out what will be the outcome of certain errors which in their initial form were manifesting themselves even now but which as to their further development belonged to the future. He must make plain to the leaders and to the people of Ephesus and surroundings what the Spirit has distinctly revealed as to the nature of the approaching falsehood and as to the way in which it should be combated. Hence, the expression "these matters" refers to the things touched upon in verses 1-5. Timothy must *submit* these things to the brothers, that is, he must *place* a firm foundation *under* their feet (note the verb ὑποτίθημι only here and in Rom. 16:5).

The apostle writes that these things must be submitted to "the brothers" (cf. 5:1; 6:2; II Tim. 4:21). Paul is fond of this term (see N.T.C. on I Thess. 1:4). Though he is never afraid to assert his *authority* as an apostle of Jesus Christ, nevertheless, he places the emphasis on *love.* Believers in the Ephesus-community are *brothers,* members of Paul's (and of God's!) spiritual family. *Paul* loves them. *God* loves them.

Now, by submitting these things to the brothers, Timothy will prove himself to be "an excellent *minister* of Christ Jesus." For "minister" the original uses the term "diakonos," from which we have derived the word "deacon." In I Tim. 3:8, 12 its meaning is "deacon." But in I Tim. 1:12 the closely related "diakonia" does not mean *deaconate* but *ministry,* and it is probable that the related verb, wherever it is used in the New Testament (see on I Tim. 3:13), does not mean "to function as deacon" but "to minister," or "to supply by ministering." "An excellent minister" is one who, in loving devotion to his task, to his people, and above all to his God, warns against departures from the truth and shows how to deal with error. Such a man truly represents (and belongs to) Christ Jesus. "Doing your duty, you, Timothy," says Paul, will fit this description, being **nourished on the words of the faith and of the excellent doctrine which you have been following.**

"The words" are the ones which embody "the faith" and "the excellent teaching" of the church, true Christian doctrine. The apostle may be thinking of certain summaries of doctrine which (perhaps in the form of current "reliable sayings" and other fixed formulations of truths) could be considered good spiritual nourishment. Timothy had been and is still following this excellent doctrine or teaching. If he is to remain a highly qualified minister of Jesus Christ, he must be *constantly nourished* by (or "on") this kind of food. A minister who neglects to study his Bible and the doctrine based upon it *atrophies* his powers by disuse.

7a. Timothy must be nourished. Of course he must use the *proper* victuals. He must not feed on trash. So Paul continues: **But profane and old-womanish myths shun.** Note that the apostle definitely continues to tell Timothy what the latter should do in order to be and remain an excellent minister. The expressions: "being nourished on the words of the faith," "shun profane and old-womanish myths," "train yourself in godly living," belong together. Doing the one and shunning the other is, of course, a contrast. Hence, the translation "but" (for δέ) here at the beginning of verse 7 fits excellently.[74]

The profane and old-womanish myths which the apostle tells Timothy to shun are the "endless myths and genealogies" mentioned in I Tim. 1:4. In contrast with the heresy against which Paul warned Timothy in the section which has just been discussed (I Tim. 4:1-5), a heresy which had reference largely, though not exclusively, to *the future,* these inane Jewish anecdotes, by means of which errorists were trying to embellish the law, pertained to *the present.* Timothy should refuse to be bothered with them (cf. II Tim. 2:23). He should "beg off." These myths are *profane,* fit to be trodden under foot (see on I Tim. 1:9). They are nothing but drivel, and belong to the category of silly superstitions which *old women* sometimes try to palm off on their neighbors or on their grandchildren.

7b, 8. In continuing his advice with respect to Timothy's spiritual advancement and the means which he should use to that end, Paul says:

Train yourself for godly living. For while physical training is of *some* benefit, this godly living is of benefit *in every way.*

The figure which underlies the passage is, of course, that of the Greek *gymnasium* (or its popular imitation), comprising grounds for running, wrestling, etc. It was a place where *stripped* youths by means of physical training would try to promote the grace and vigor of their bodies. Timothy, then, is told *to gymnasticize.* But, in keeping with the immediately preceding context, which pictured him as being nourished on the words of

---

[74] I agree here with A.V., A.R.V., and in fact with very many versions and commentators. I cannot follow the reasoning of Lenski on p. 629 of his Commentary. Verse 6 and verse 7 mark a clear contrast. Verse 6 implies: "Continue to be nourished on the words of the faith." Verse 8 states, "But profane and old-womanish myths shun." Paul is not merely telling Timothy how to deal with those myths, but he is also, and at the same time, advising his young colleague what to do for his own spiritual and professional advancement in order to become an even more useful minister of Jesus Christ. That interpretation harmonizes beautifully with what follows directly in verse 8, with respect to training for godly living versus physical training.

faith and as shunning profane myths in order that thus he may be (and may continue to be) "an excellent minister of Christ Jesus," he is told to train himself with a view to *godliness* or *godly living.* The *exercise* which he is urged to take is to be of a *spiritual* character.

What Paul had in mind, accordingly, must have included *one or more* of the following comparisons:

(a) Just as a youth in the gymnasium exerts himself to the utmost, so you, too, by God's grace and power, must spare no efforts to attain your goal.

(b) Just as that youth discards every handicap or burden in order that he may train the more freely, so you, too, should divest yourself of everything that could encumber your spiritual progress.

(c) Just as that youth has his eye on a goal – perhaps that of showing superior skill on the discus range, that of winning the wrestling match or boxing-bout in the palestra, that of being the first one to reach the post which marked the winning-point on the running track, at least that of improving his physique – so you should be constantly aiming at your spiritual objective, namely, that of complete self-dedication to God in Christ.

It is not at all surprising that the apostle, with this figure of the gymnasium or its less pretentious substitutes in mind, now draws a comparison between the value of *physical training* (literally "bodily gymnastics") and *training for godly living.* He states that the former is *of some benefit.* It is useful for something. The latter, however, is of benefit *in every way.* It is useful for all things. He is by no means belittling the value of physical exercise. He is saying two things: a. that the boon which bodily training bestows, however great it may be, is definitely inferior to the reward which the godly life promises. The former at best bestows health, vigor, beauty of physical form. These things are wonderful and to be appreciated. But the latter bestows life everlasting! b. that the sphere in which bodily training is of benefit is far more restricted than that in which godly living confers its reward. The former concerns the here and now. The latter concerns the here and now but also reaches far beyond it.

That this is, indeed, what he means is clearly shown by what follows in verse 8, after the words, "this godly living is of benefit in every way," namely, **as it holds promise of life both for the present and for the future.**

The essence and contents of the promise is *life,* fellowship with God in Christ, the love of God shed abroad in the heart, the peace of God which passes all understanding. (See also N.T.C. on John, Vol. 1, pp. 71-73, 141.) Complete devotion, godliness, or godly living, itself the fruit of God's grace, results in the increasing *possession and enjoyment* of this reward, according to the teaching of Scripture throughout (Deut. 4:29; 28:1-3, 9, 10; I Sam. 15:22; Ps. 1:1-3; 24:3-6; 103:17, 18; I John 1:6, 7; I John 2:24, 25; Rev. 2:10, 17; 3:5, 12, 21).

God has promised this, and he always fulfils his promise. And this *life* which God bestows, and which surpasses all other blessings in value, is both for the present and for the future, for the age that *now* is and for *the coming* age. It can never cease.

The explanation of I Tim. 4:7b, 8 which I have given departs in some points from that which is favored by others. See the footnote.[75]

9. Over against the widely proclaimed value of *physical* training, the church confessed its faith in the infinitely superior value of *spiritual* training. Hence, with reference to the significant declaration which we have just studied – namely, "While physical training is of *some* benefit . . . godly living is of benefit *in every way*, as it holds promise of life both for the present and for the future" – believers were constantly saying, **Reliable is that saying and worthy of full acceptance** (see on I Tim. 1:15, where exactly the same formula occurs).

10. That Paul and also Timothy are indeed deeply convinced of the reliability of the declaration regarding the gift of life, now and in the future, to be enjoyed by all those who live godly lives, follows from what the apostle now states: **For to this end we toil and strive, because we have set our hope on the living God.**

It is true that we are deeply convinced of the truth expressed in the faithful saying, *for* otherwise we missionaries (I, Paul, and you, Timothy) would

---

[75] The divergent explanations are legion. I shall mention only two of the main differences between my own explanation and that of others. They are:

(1) Some interpret the expression "bodily gymnastics" as referring to ascetic practises, whether they be those referred to in verse 3, or those pertaining to "Christian asceticism" (keeping the appetites in control).

Objections:

a. Here in verses 7b, 8 the apostle is no longer thinking of the heresy which to a large extent is still future (verses 1-5), but of the heresy of the present (see verse 7a), and even that is not his main thought. The point which he stresses is what Timothy must do in order to grow in spiritual and professional efficiency as a minister of Christ Jesus. This emphasis naturally suggests the figure of the athlete, for he, too, is trying to improve his skill.

b. The very term *gymnastics* brings to the mind physical training rather than fasting. To call abstention from food "bodily gymnastics" seems rather inappropriate.

c. Paul frequently borrows metaphors from the sphere of athletics (Rom. 9:16; I Cor. 9:24-27; Gal. 2:2; 5:7; Phil. 2:16; II Thess. 3:1).

d. He definitely derives illustrations from that sphere *in the Pastorals* (I Tim. 6:12; II Tim. 2:5; 4:7, 8). It is therefore entirely reasonable to conclude that he is doing the same here in I Tim. 4:7b, 8.

(2) Some translate the final clause of verse 8 as if it read: "having promise for the present life and for the one to come" (or something similar).

Objection:

That is obviously not what the apostle writes. He does not use the dative "for the life" but the genitive of quality "of the life." Life in its fullest, most blessed meaning, is ever the content of the promise (John 3:16; I John 2:24, 25). And that holds both for the age that now is and for the one which is to come.

not be toiling and striving so hard. That seems to be the connection between verses 7b, 8, 9, on the one hand, and 10, on the other.

The end or purpose for which Paul and Timothy are toiling and striving is, of course, this, that men from all over the world, be they Jews or Gentiles, shall hear the blessed gospel of salvation, and better still, shall accept it and obtain everlasting life. It is this *life,* that is, *salvation,* that God has promised (verse 8).

These missionaries *labor* or *toil.* They exert themselves to the utmost in the work of bringing the gospel, applying it to concrete situations, warning, admonishing, helping, and encouraging, generally amid great difficulties. Paul uses this word *labor* or *toil* with reference to manual labor (I Cor. 4:12; Eph. 4:28; II Tim. 2:6; cf. the noun in I Thess. 1:3; 2:9; II Thess. 3:8) and also in connection with religious work (Rom. 16:12 twice; I Cor. 5:10; Gal. 4:11; Phil. 2:16; 16:16; I Thess. 5:12; I Tim. 5:17; and in our present passage).

They *strive,* that is, in the spiritual arena they struggle against the forces of darkness, in order that they may bring men out of the darkness into the light. They suffer *agonies.* Cf. I Tim. 6:12; II Tim. 4:7; then Col. 1:29; 4:12. See N.T.C. on I Thess. 2:2.

They gladly carry on this difficult task because they have their hope set not on idols, which can neither make nor keep promises, for they are *dead,* but on the *living* God (see N.T.C. on I Thess. 1:9, 10), **who is the Savior of all men, especially of those who believe.**

This clause has given rise to a variety of interpretations. Here one should tread very carefully. Some explanations, as I see it, are wrong even on the surface:

(1) God is the Savior of all men in the sense that ultimately he *actually* saves *every human being* who has ever lived on the earth.

Objection: This is contrary to all biblical teaching. Not all men are saved in that full, spiritual sense. Moreover, if this were true, why would Paul have added, "*especially* of those who believe"? That last phrase would make no sense.

(2) He *actually* bestows salvation – in the full, evangelical sense of the term – on *all kinds of people.* He gives to them all everlasting life.

Objection: This explanation, too, is impossible in view of the final phrase, "*especially* of those who believe."

(3) He *wants* all men to be saved (see I Tim. 2:3), but in the case of some his will is "frustrated" by obstinate unbelief. (Lenski's explanation is along this line; *op. cit.,* p. 639.)

Objection: The present passage, however, does not say that he *wants* to save, but that he *actually* saves; he is *actually* the Savior (in some sense) of all men. Also, "*frustration*" – in the absolute, ultimate sense – of the divine will is impossible. Otherwise God would not be God!

(4) He *is able* to save all men; but though all *can* be saved, only the believers are *actually* saved. (See N. J. D. White, *The Expositor's Greek Testament* on this passage.)

Objection: That is not what the text says. It says, "He *is* the Savior of all men."

The true explanation is found, it would seem to me, by making a thorough study of the term *Savior* in a passage of this kind. The final phrase "especially of those who believe" clearly indicates that the term is here given a twofold application. Of *all* men God is the Savior, but of *some* men, namely, believers, he is the Savior in a deeper, more glorious sense than he is of others. This clearly implies that when he is called the Savior of all men, this cannot mean that he imparts to all everlasting life, as he does to believers. The term *Savior,* then, must have a meaning which *we today* generally do not immediately attach to it. And that is exactly the cause of our difficulty. One must study this term in the light not only of the New Testament but also of the Old Testament and of Archaeology.[76]

Now in the LXX version of the Old Testament the word *Soter* which is used here in I Tim. 4:10, and which is usually rendered *Savior,* is at times employed in a sense far below that which we generally ascribe to it. So, for example, the judge Othniel is called a *Soter* or "savior" or "deliverer" because he *delivered* the children of Israel from the hands of Cushan-rishathaim, king of Mesopotamia (Judg. 3:9). See also II Kings 13:5: "And Jehovah gave Israel a savior (deliverer), so that they were delivered from the hands of the Syrians." In a sense all the judges of Israel were "saviors," (deliverers), just as we read in Neh. 9:27, "Thou gavest them saviors (deliverers) who saved (that is, *delivered*) them out of the hand of their adversaries." Cf. also a somewhat similar use of the word in Obadiah verse 21, "And saviors (deliverers) shall come up on mount Zion to judge the mount of Esau, and the kingdom shall be Jehovah's."

It is not strange that especially Jehovah would be called Savior, for it was he who again and again rescued or delivered his people (Deut. 32:15; Ps. 25:5). He "did great things in Egypt . . . terrible things by the Red Sea," being, accordingly, "God, their Savior" (Ps. 106:21).

Having delivered Israel from the oppression of Pharaoh, he had been the Savior of that entire multitude that went out of Egypt. Yet, "with

---

[76] See the following:
Deissmann, A., *op. cit.,* p. 363, and see his Index; I.S.B.E. on "Saviour"; M.M., pp. 621, 622; Ramsay, W., *The Bearing of Recent Discovery on the Trustworthiness of the New Testament,* reprint Grand Rapids, Mich., 1953, pp. 172-198; Taylor, F. J., on "Saviour" in *A Theological Word Book Of The Bible* (edited by Alan Richardson), New York, 1952; W.D.B., on "Saviour"; Wendland, "Soter," *ZNTW,* Number 5 (1904), p. 335 ff.

most of them God was not well pleased" (I Cor. 10:5). *In a sense,* therefore, he was the Savior or Soter of all, but *especially* of those who believed. With the latter, with them alone, he was "well pleased." All leave Egypt; not all enter "Canaan."

It is especially in certain beautiful passages of Isaiah that the word Soter is given a rich, spiritual content: Jehovah is Israel's Savior, and this not only because he delivers his people from oppression but also because *collectively* he *loves* them. Yet, even in these exalted passages the meaning which we today generally attach to the word has not been reached. The passages cannot be interpreted to mean that he gave everlasting life to all the individuals in the group. Note Is. 63:8-10:

"For he said, Surely they are my people, children who will not deal falsely: so he was their Savior. In all their affliction he was afflicted, and the angel of his presence saved them: in his love and in his pity he redeemed them; and he bare them, and he carried them all the days of old. But they rebelled and grieved his Holy Spirit: therefore he was turned to be their enemy, and he himself fought against them. . . ." Cf. Is. 43:3, 11; 45:15, 21; 49:26; 60:16. Cf. Jer. 14:8; Hos. 13:4. (In the last reference note especially the context: "besides me there is no Savior" preceded by "Jehovah thy God from the land of Egypt," and followed by, "I knew thee in the wilderness.") According to the Old Testament, then, God is *Soter* not only of those who enter his everlasting kingdom but in a sense also of others, indeed, of all those whom he delivers from temporary disaster.

Besides, the Old Testament teaches everywhere that God's kind providence extends to all men, in a sense even to plants and animals: Ps. 36:6; 104:27, 28; 145:9, 16, 17; Jonah 4:10, 11. He provides his creatures with food, keeps them alive, is deeply interested in them, often delivers them from disease, ills, hurt, famine, war, poverty, and peril in any form. He is, accordingly, their *Soter* (Preserver, Deliverer, and in *that* sense Savior).

In the New Testament this teaching is continued, as was to be expected. In his love, kindness, and mercy the heavenly Father "makes his sun to rise on the evil and on the good, and sends rain on the just and the unjust" . . . "is kind toward the unthankful and evil" (Matt. 5:45; Luke 6:35). The wickedness of evil men consists partly in this that they have not given thanks for this goodness of God (Rom. 1:21). It is he who "gives to all life and breath and all things" (Acts 17:25). It is he "in whom we live and move and have our being" (Acts 17:28). He preserves, delivers, and in that sense *saves,* and *that* "saving" activity is by no means confined to the elect! On the Voyage Dangerous (to Rome) God "saved" not only Paul but all those who were with him (Acts 27:22, 31, 44). There was no loss of life.

Moreover, God also causes his gospel of salvation to be earnestly proclaimed to *all men,* that is, to men from every race and nation. Truly, the kindness of God extends to all. There is no one who does not in one way or another come within the reach of his benevolence,[77] and even the circle of those to whom the message of salvation is proclaimed is wider than the circle of those who accept it by a true faith.

This is really all that is needed in clarification of our present passage, I Tim. 4:10. What the apostle teaches amounts, accordingly, to this, "We have our hope set on the living God, and in this hope we shall not be disappointed, for not only is he a kind God, hence the *Soter* (Preserver, Deliverer) of all men, showering blessings upon them, but he is in a very special sense the *Soter* (Savior) of those who by faith embrace him and his promise, for to them he imparts salvation, everlasting life in all its fulness (as explained in connection with I Tim. 1:15; see on that passage).

It is *this living God* who in Jesus Christ is the Savior! In classical and in Koine Greek the term *Soter* was used as a designation of various gods (Zeus, Apollo, Hermes, Ascelepius), Roman emperors, and leading officials, inasmuch as these were viewed as delivering men from this or that calamity, supplying this or that physical need, or bestowing general health or "well-being." But according to Paul, back of every real deliverance stands God, the living One. The most glorious "well-being" of all (for the soul but in the end also for the body), and that everlasting, is promised and given by him to all who believe. For them, *for them alone,* God is the *Soter* in the sense in which the term is also used in I Tim. 1:1; 2:3; Titus 1:3; 2:10; 3:4. Them he rescues from the greatest evil, and upon them he bestows the greatest good. It is in that full, evangelical sense that the term is applied to God also in Jude 25 (and, according to some, also in Luke 1:47).

Though as a title for God Paul did not use the term until he wrote the Pastorals, the *idea* that God is the *Soter* is certainly present in his earlier writings, as has been shown (see on I Tim. 1:1). It is probable that the closer Paul and believers in general came into contact with the Roman world and with the epithet *Soter* as applied to its gods and leaders, the more they began to make use of that same term *Soter* as a designation for the true and living God, basing *the contents* of this conviction not on anything which the world round about them offered but upon special revelation as given in the Old Testament and in the teaching of the Lord.

11. Command these things and teach (them).

Timothy is told *to command* (or: to keep on commanding) *and teach* (or: to keep on teaching; both verbs are present imperatives) these things. He must *command* such things as, "Profane and old-womanish myths shun,"

---

[77] Says Calvin, *op. cit.,* on this passage: Intelligit Dei beneficentiam ad omnes homines pervenire. Quod si nemo est mortalium, qui non sentiat Dei erga se bonitatem eiusque sit particeps, quanto magis eam experientur pii qui in eum sperant? Somewhat similar is the explanation given by Chrysostom, Bengel, Barnes, Lock, J. Van Dyk, C. Bouma, J. Van Andel (see Bibliography for titles).

"Train yourself (and yourselves) for godly living" (verse 7). Orders such as these apply not only to Timothy himself but to all the presbyters, yes, and even to all Christians. It is probable that the expression "these things" in connection with "command" refers also to *implied* commands, such as, "Never reject what God has intended for use, but partake of it with thanksgiving" (verses 3, 4), "Nurture yourself (yourselves) on the words of faith and sound doctrine" (verse 6), "Rely on the living God and on his promise to all who live the godly life and who accept him by genuine faith" (verses 8, 9).

Timothy must *teach* such things as, "Apostasy is coming, in the form of asceticism" (verses 1-3), "*That* error is an insult to God and to his work of creation" (verses 4, 5), "An excellent minister is one who is nourished on sound doctrine which he transmits to others" (verse 6), "The benefit which accrues from godly living transcends that which results from physical training (verses 8-10).

12. Let no one despise your youth.

It may be assumed that about the year 51, when Timothy joined Paul who was on his *second* missionary journey, the former had reached the age of 22-27 years of age. It is hardly probable that the apostle would have permitted a man even younger than that to join him in such a difficult task. Besides, we know that Timothy must have reached a degree of maturity even during Paul's *first* missionary journey, for it was then that he had "confessed his faith." If this calculation be correct, then Timothy is *now* – i.e., about the year 63 – somewhere between 34 and 39 years of age. According to Ireneus, the first stage of life embraces thirty years and extends onward until forty years (*Against Heresies,* II. xxii). Hence, Timothy was still "a young man." Besides, he must have been considered *very young for the position* which he occupied: apostolic representative and as such chief over all the *presbyters* in the churches of Ephesus and surroundings. These *presbyters* (as the very name implies), in ancient Israel, in the later synagogue, and also in the early church – which in many ways copied the synagogue – were generally *old* or at least *elderly* men. And here is Timothy, a much younger man and moreover a person of natural reserve and timidity, wielding authority over those who were his seniors by perhaps 10-40 years! Hence, the command, "Let no one *look down* upon you" – the Greek idiom says, "Let no one *think down* upon you" – was called for. Timothy must not permit anyone to despise him because of his youth. He must see to it that he is respected because of his office. But he must attain this end not by "acting big" or bragging about his credentials, but by conducting himself as a man of sage counsel and consecrated, practical wisdom. Respect for *the man* will mean respect for his *office!* Hence, Paul continues, **But become the believers' model in speech, in conduct, in love,**

in faith, in purity. In an altogether natural and organic manner he must win the respect of all the believers. Note that Paul does not really say that Timothy should become a model *for* the believers, that is, for them to follow (see N.T.C. on I Thess. 1:7; II Thess. 3:9), but that ever increasingly he should become a model *of* what the believers are; and this in five respects:

a. *in speech,* that is, in personal conversation (for *preaching* see the next verse).

b. *in conduct,* that is, in customs, habits, ways of dealing with people, etc.

c. *in love,* that is, in deep personal attachment to his brothers and in genuine concern for his neighbors (including even his enemies), always seeking to promote the welfare of all.

d. *in faith,* that is, in the exercise of that gift of God which is the root from which love springs (note: *love* here probably indicates the horizontal relationship; *faith,* the vertical).

e. *in purity* (see also I Tim. 5:2), that is, in complete conformity, both in thought and act, with God's moral law.

13. Reaffirming the directive of verse 11 Paul continues, **Until I come, attend to the (public) reading (of Scripture), to the exhorting and to the teaching.**

"Until I come" is the correct translation, and harmonizes with 3:14 ("hoping to come to you shortly"). The idea is, "If and when I return, I will give you new instructions." Perhaps Paul had in mind some other mission on which Timothy could then be sent.

During the apostle's absence, then, his representative is given instructions anent his duty with respect to public worship in the entire district. He must see to it that in all the churches of Ephesus and surroundings three elements receive due prominence, namely,

a. *the public reading of Scripture* (just as in the synagogue, Luke 4:16; Acts 13:15; II Cor. 3:14; but now not only the reading of law and prophets, but in addition portions of the growing New Testament, Col. 4:16; I Thess. 5:27; Rev. 1:3).

b. *exhorting.* This includes warning (for example, against error in doctrine and morals), advice, and encouragement. See further the discussion of the word in N.T.C. on Thessalonians, p. 62, and on John, Vol. II, p. 276.

c. *teaching.* It *does* make a difference *what* one believes! The *attitude* of heart is not everything. There are certain *facts* with respect to doctrine and morals which must be taught, and which one must accept and embrace, so that one's life is founded upon them. See, for example, John 3:16, and all the teaching in the present epistle.

This is not a complete summary of the essentials which comprise public worship. For instance, *prayer* is not mentioned. But it did not need to be mentioned, for Paul had dwelt on this in detail in chapter 2. So much is clear: if there be no pulpit-reading, exhorting, and teaching, *divine worship* is a misnomer. In the early church, when very few individuals owned private copies of the sacred writings, and all such material had to be copied by hand, one can imagine how important was the *public reading* of Scripture. But even today the careful selection, and clear and interpretive reading of an appropriate portion of Holy Writ is "the most important part of public worship." [78] And even today if the choir takes so much time that little is left for exhorting and teaching, something is wrong. Timothy, then, must *continue to devote his attention* to these important matters.

Is there not another hint here that has value for today as well as for the times of Paul and Timothy, namely, that a minister should strive to effect a proper balance between the reading of Scripture, exhorting, and teaching? Some never exhort. Others never teach. And the reading of Scripture is prone to be regarded merely as a necessary preface to what the preacher himself is going to say!

14. Timothy had been specially gifted for his task. Hence, Paul continues, **Do not grow careless about the gift that is in you.** That gift of discernment between the true and the false, and consequently of being able to exhort, teach, and guide, Timothy must employ to the best advantage. He must make use of it when he himself administers the Word and he must also exercise it when he tells others how to preach. He must *never grow careless* about it or neglect it. It is a precious *charisma,* that is, a special gift of God's grace bestowed upon him by the Holy Spirit. Hence, Paul continues: **which was granted to you through prophetic utterance with the laying on of the hands of the presbytery.** In all probability this refers to what had happened at Lystra on Paul's second missionary journey. It was then that Timothy by the operation of the Holy Spirit had been amply endowed with this gift. Of this and of the character of his task he had been made aware *through* (διά) *prophetic utterance* of inspired bystanders. Moreover, all this was *in association with* (or *accompanied by:* μετά) the imposition of the hands of *the presbytery* (used elsewhere to indicate the Sanhedrin – Luke 22:66; Acts 22:5 –, but here for *the college of elders* or, in that sense, *the consistory of the church*). Paul's own hands had also rested upon him (II Tim. 1:6). This imposition of hands symbolizes *the transfer* of a gift from the Giver to the recipient. In the present instance it signifies that gracious act of the Holy Spirit whereby he confers

---

[78] See A. W. Blackwood, *The Fine Art Of Public Worship,* Nashville, 1939, chapter VII, "The Public Reading of the Scriptures," pp. 128-141; note especially the excellent suggestions on pp. 140, 141.

his special favor upon Timothy, enabling him to carry out the duties of his important office as apostolic representative (cf. also Acts 6:6; 8:17; 13:3, 4).

15. Let these things be your constant care. Over against "Do not grow *careless,*" Paul places, "Let these things be your constant care" (cf. verses 14 and 15). By the expression "these things" he is thinking of the entire contents of chapter 4 (that defection is on the way, against which Timothy must warn others; that even now there are those who would substitute profane myths for the true gospel; that Timothy must be nourished on the words of the faith, and must train himself for godly living; that he must so conduct himself that no one will despise his youth; that he must not neglect but must exercise and cultivate his special gift; etc.). **In these things be (absorbed).** "Be *in* them," says the apostle, as if to say, "Be *in* them with your whole heart, with all your soul; be completely wrapped up in them." The contemplated result will be **so that your progress may be evident to everyone.** We accept the usual interpretation of these words to be the correct and natural one, namely, that if Timothy will devote himself completely to his task, as indicated, *all* (especially those in the church, but to some extent even outsiders who come into close contact with believers) will take note of his spiritual and professional advancement, to the glory of God. Cf. Phil. 1:12, 25. The closing words of the chapter are:

16. Look to yourself and to the teaching, persevere in them.

Holy living and sound teaching must go together if Timothy (or, for that matter, any apostolic representative, any minister, any elder, etc.) is to be a blessing. Hence, Paul admonishes Timothy to continue *to focus* (*his mind,* understood) *on himself,* that is, on his own duties, his own gift, his own privilege to go to the depths of God's promise; particularly also upon *the* teaching (his own and that of others in the Ephesus district). He must *stay on* or *persevere* in them, that is, in holy living and in vigilance with respect to teaching. The promise is: **"for by doing this you will save both yourself and those who hear you."** To be sure, a man is saved by grace, through faith; not by works (Titus 3:3; cf. Eph. 2:6-8); yet, since holy living and sound teaching are a fruit of faith, Paul is able to say that "by doing this" Timothy will save himself and his hearers. It is *along the path of* holy living and diligence in teaching and in watching over the life and teaching of others, that *salvation* (both present and future; see on I Tim. 1:15) is obtained. Besides, God promises a special reward to his faithful ministers, yes, to *all* his faithful witnesses (Dan. 12:3; Matt. 13:43; James 5:20); and threatens with severe punishment the unfaithful ones (Ezek. 33:7, 8).

Synthesis of Chapter 4

See the Outline at the beginning of the chapter.

Though the Christ be ever so exalted (see the close of Chapter III), and the church ever so glorious, apostasy is just around the corner. The instigators are the seducing spirits who invade the hearts of deceivers. These deceivers will forbid people to marry, and will order them to abstain from certain foods, as if salvation could be attained by practices such as these, practices, moreover, which detract from Christ as the one and only Savior. As to the foods in question, these are excellent because God created them and because he in answer to our prayers consecrates them.

Timothy, in combating such developing errors, which will grow worse and worse, must make himself strong. Hence, he must use *positive* weapons. He should not concentrate his attention and energy on *myths*. Rather, he should nourish himself on the words of faith, and continue stedfastly in the public reading of Scripture, exhortation and teaching.

Yes, let Timothy train himself for godly living. Positive living and positive teaching are the best means of spiritual self-development and also the best weapons against error. As to this training for godly living, it confers a blessing far greater than physical training can ever confer. It brings everlasting life, which is a boon for the present and for the future. If Paul and his helpers had not been thoroughly convinced of this, they would not have labored so hard. But they have placed their complete confidence in a God who will not disappoint them, for he is the God of love. He preserves not only man and beast but especially his people. Let Timothy then attend faithfully to his ministerial duties. Let him conduct himself in such a manner that no one will look down upon him, thinking, "He is still so young." By using to the full the gift which he received when he was ordained, and by being absorbed in such things as the public reading of Scripture, exhortation, and teaching, he will save both himself and those who hear him.

Note especially the words:

"While physical training is of *some* benefit, godly living is of benefit *in every way.*"

The Greeks worshiped at the shrine of beauty and physical culture. Long before the days of Paul they had already established their Olympian, Isthmian, and Pythian games. In Paul's time contests of this character were held in many of the Roman provinces.

Now in this comparison between the value of bodily training and the value of training in godly living, one important item must not be overlooked. Physical exercise, especially with a view to partaking in the public contests, was closely connected with *pagan religion.* In fact, in the popular mind, the two were almost inseparable. The Olympian games were held in honor of Zeus; the Isthmian games in honor of Poseidon; and the Pythian in honor of Apollo. *Roman* athletic contests were preceded by processions in which the statues of the gods were carried on beautiful chariots. *Their* most important contests were held in honor of such gods as Jupiter, Apollo, Diana, etc. And even in connection with the execution of criminals in the amphitheater the stories with reference to the pagan deities were often made vivid to the public and re-enacted in the manner in which the death-sentence was carried out. On this whole subject see *Everyday Life in Ancient Times,* published by the National Geographic Magazine, pp. 209, 227; also Erich Sauer, *In the Arena of Faith,* Grand Rapids, 1955, pp. 30-68.

In view of all this, is it any wonder that Paul says, "Physical training is of *some* benefit." It benefited the body, to be sure. Before it could even contribute in its own small way to the welfare of the soul, it would have to be placed in an entirely different context.

Outline of Chapter 5

Theme: *The Apostle Paul, Writing to Timothy, Gives Directions For the Administration of the Church*

Directions with respect to
Certain Definite Groups and Individuals

5:1, 2 A. Older men, younger men, older women, younger women

5:3-8 B. Widows in distress

5:9-16 C. Widows engaged in spiritual work

5:17-25 D. Elders and prospective elders

CHAPTER V

5 1 An old(er) man do not treat harshly, but admonish him as you would a father; young(er) men as brothers; 2 old(er) women as mothers, young(er) women as sisters, in all purity.

Up to this point Paul has imparted counsel with respect to matters most of which touched the entire Christian community which had its center in Ephesus. He has stated the reason why Timothy had been left in Ephesus (chapter 1), has given directions for the conduct of both men and women in connection with public worship (chapter 2), has stipulated the qualifications of elders and deacons (chapter 3), and has pointed out the path which Timothy (and the presbyters under his supervision) must tread in order to cope with apostasy and to grow in efficiency as minister(s) of Christ (chapter 4).

To a large extent – but with important personal digressions – all this was quite general. Now the apostle begins to direct his attention more especially to *individuals* and *groups* within the Christian community. See the Outline.

It must be borne in mind, however, that this is a genuine letter, and that the divisions are never rigid. Thoughts continually overlap. Ideas once stated return in slightly altered form. The Outline covers the contents and marks the divisions *in general.*

5:1, 2

1. An old(er) man do not treat harshly, but admonish him as you would a father.

In the course of his pastoral work Timothy will at times have to correct the faults of certain church-members. These individuals can be distinguished as to age and sex: old(er) man, young(er) men; old(er) women, young(er) women. The comparative idea (*older* instead of *old; younger* instead of *young*) has almost vanished.

None of these must be treated harshly, least of all the senior members of the congregation. See Lev. 19:32; Prov. 20:29; Lam. 5:12b. The verb used in the original literally means *to strike at;* then *to treat harshly.* The word which we have rendered "old(er) man" is πρεσβύτερος. Elsewhere in

The Pastorals (I Tim. 5:17, 19; Titus 1:5) it means *an elder* or *presbyter.* Here it is used in its primary sense of a man of advanced age (cf. Acts 2:17), as the context clearly shows.

Instead of dealing harshly with those who need correction, Timothy must *admonish.* The verb used in the original means *to call aside.* This calling aside may be for the purpose of encouraging, comforting, exhorting, entreating, appealing to, or admonishing. It is obviously the latter thought which is predominant in the present passage.

Now it should be emphasized that also here Paul maintains beautiful balance. On the one hand, he does not want Timothy to spare the older people, permitting them to "get away" with their sins. On the other hand, he desires that they be treated with due respect. Timothy must admonish an old man as if the latter were *his own father.* How considerately, with what tact, what gentleness and moderation, would he deal with one who stood so close to him! Let him then treat this erring one with the same humility, love and tenderness. For, after all, the Christian community *is* a family, the most glorious family of all (Matt. 12:49, 50); and it *does* indeed consist of fathers, mothers, brothers, and sisters . . . *in the Lord!* Hence, old(er) men must be treated as fathers, that is, with respect; **young(er) men as brothers,** that is, in the spirit of equality, an equality of persons, which does not exclude the exercise of authority on the part of him who administers the admonition.

2. Old(er) women as mothers.

Female members of the congregation must not be excluded from the sphere of private pastoral counseling with respect to sin. Though this task may at times prove to be delicate, it must not be shunned. But when Timothy admonishes the old(er) women, he must deal with them as a good and loving adult son deals with his erring mother! To correct one's own mother surely requires deep humility, genuine searching of heart, wrestling at the throne of grace, wisdom! It is in that spirit that Timothy must proceed when he feels duty-bound to admonish old(er) women who have erred.

Young(er) women as sisters, in all purity.

Young(er) women, too, are the objects of pastoral care. They should be admonished *as sisters;* hence, *in all purity.* When one seeks to help *his sister* to overcome a certain blemish of character, *impurity* (at least in the more popular sense of the word) is completely absent. Let Timothy treat the young ladies and the young married ladies who are under his spiritual care in that same fashion, just as if they were his own sisters, for they really are . . . *in the Lord!* In agreement with Calvin, we believe that the phrase "in all purity" belongs to the immediately preceding clause: "admonish . . . young(er) women as sisters." Now it is certainly true that here as well as in 4:12 the phrase "in all purity" means "in complete conformity in thought and word with God's moral law," and is not to be restricted to *sexual* purity. Nevertheless it would be incorrect to say that the idea of sexual purity is excluded from it. That the command was altogether in place as a word not only for Timothy but for all "ministers" in every age is clear to anyone who will take the trouble to read the sad accounts which describe what happens when it is not heeded.[79]

It is true, of course, that the direction which Paul gives in these two verses is not for Timothy *only* but also for his assistants in the various churches of Ephesus and vicinity. On the other hand, the very language employed clearly indicates that it is wrong to regard Timothy as a "superintendent" without any pastoral duties of his own. Even his superior, Paul, *was a real pastor,* deeply concerned about every member (Acts 20:20; and see N.T.C. on I Thess. 2:7-11). Then why not Timothy?

---

3 As widows, honor those (who are) really (what is implied in the name) *widows.* 4 But if a widow has children or grandchildren, let these first learn their religious duty to their own family and make a real return to their parents; for this is acceptable in the sight of God. 5 Now the real widow, the one who was left all alone, has set her hope on God, and continues in her supplications and her prayers by night and by day; 6 but the one who is giving herself up to luxury, though living, is dead.

7 These things, too, you must command, in order that they may be above reproach. 8 Now if any one does not provide for his own, and especially for the members of his own family, he has denied the faith and is worse than an unbeliever.

5:3-8

3. As widows, honor those (who are) really (what is implied in the name) widows.

Distressed widows are discussed in verses 3-8; *those employed by the church* in verses 9-16.

If older women must be treated as *mothers,* as Paul has just stated (see verse 2), and if mothers must be honored (Ex. 20:12; Deut. 5:16; Eph. 6:2), it follows that distressed widows must also be honored.

Such widows (described in verse 5), must be *honored,* that is, treated with high regard, with great consideration, and this implies that those who are in need must receive material support. See also on I Tim. 5:17.

Strikingly beautiful is what Scripture teaches with respect to widows:

(1) God is "a father of the fatherless, and a judge of the widows" (Ps. 68:5).

---

[79] See for example, C. Chiniquy, *Fifty Years In The Church Of Rome,* pp. 580-602; also his work *The Priest, The Woman, and The Confessional.*

They are under his special care and protection (Ex. 22:23; Deut. 10:18; Prov. 15:25; Ps. 146:9).

(2) By means of the tithe and "the forgotten sheaf" he provides for them (Deut. 14:29; 24:19-21; 26:12, 13). At the feasts which he has instituted, they too should rejoice (Deut. 16:11, 14).

(3) He blesses those who help and honor them (Is. 1:17, 18; Jer. 7:6; 22:3, 4).

(4) He rebukes and punishes those who hurt them (Ex. 22:22; Deut. 24:17; 27:19; Zech. 7:10; Job 24:3, 21; 31:16; Ps. 94:6; Mal. 3:5).

(5) They are the objects of Christ's tender compassion, as is clear from the Gospels, especially from the Gospel according to Luke (Mark 12:42, 43; Luke 7:11-17; 18:3, 5; 20:47; 21:2, 3).

(6) In the early church they were not forgotten. It was the neglect of certain widows which led to the appointment of the first deacons, so that in the future widows might receive better care (Acts 6:1-6). And according to James, one of the manifestations of a religion that is pure and undefiled is this: "to visit the fatherless and widows in their affliction" (James 1:27).

Timothy, then, certainly knows what Paul means when he says, "Honor . . . those who are really (what is implied in the name) widows."

There is here a play upon words, for in the original the word *widow* means the one *bereaved, deprived* (of her husband; hence, often without means of support). Hence, what the apostle is saying amounts to this, "As *deprived* ones, honor those (who are) really *deprived*" (or "As *destitute,* honor those who are really *destitute*"). If certain etymologists are correct (not all agree), then we could have a similar play of words in English, for the word "widow" = Latin *vidua,* is by them linked with such words as *void* and *devoid.* Hence, one might say, "As *viduae* (widows), honor those who are really de*void* (of means of support)."

Gainful employment for widows was scarce. Besides, some widows were too old to provide for themselves. Hence, those who had no other means of support must be provided for by the church.

4. There are, however, widows who do not fall within this category. Hence, Paul continues, **But if a widow has children or grandchildren, let these [80] first learn their religious duty to their own family and make a real return to their parents; for this is acceptable in the sight of God.**

The church must not be unnecessarily burdened. Yet, that is not the main reason for the present command. It is rather this: Children and

---

80 The idea that the expression "Let *these* first learn" refers to *the widows* and not to the children — an idea favored even by Calvin — must be considered erroneous. Note the order of the words in the sentence, the use of the plural verb (the singular is weakly attested), the natural and entirely scriptural idea that children shall honor their parents, that in doing this they are "making a return," etc.

grandchildren should honor their progenitors! That is their first religious (cf. Acts 17:23) duty toward those who brought them up. They should strive to make a *real return* (acc. pl. of ἀμοιβή, plural of intensity) for all the care that was so lovingly bestowed upon them. Note, "Let these first *learn*" this lesson. By nature children are often disinclined to provide for their needy parents. According to a Dutch proverb it frequently seems easier for *one* poor father to bring up *ten* children than for *ten* rich children to provide for *one* poor father. But even if it means self-denial, this lesson must be *learned.* It is certainly implied in the fifth commandment. Moreover, it should be done with gladness, in the spirit of love, as a token of appreciation for that which the children have themselves received from their parents. Joseph's genuine concern for the welfare of his father should serve as a lesson for all time: "I am Joseph; is my father still alive?" (Gen. 45:3). Note with what tenderness and whole-hearted devotion he provided for *his father* (Gen. 45:9-13; 46:28-34; 47:7, 27-31; 50:1-14). And read also the words of the crucified Christ with respect to *his mother* (see N.T.C. on John 19:26, 27). Surely, when children honor their parents and grandparents, such conduct is acceptable in the sight of God! His *promise* is bound to be fulfilled.

5. The apostle now returns to the discussion of *the real widow* (see verse 3), the one who does not have children and/or grandchildren who can support her. Says he, **Now the real widow, the one who was left all alone, has set her hope on God.**

The real widow, then, has nowhere else to go! Her refuge is the living God, for on earth she is no one's dependent. She was left *all alone,* and abides in that condition. There is no child or grandchild or anyone else whose duty it would be to support her. On God she has permanently fixed her hope (third per. sing. perfect indic.). Her expectation is of him (Ps. 123:1, 2).

This hope is real and vital. Hence, Paul adds: **and continues in her supplications and in her prayers by night and by day.**[81] The terms *"supplications and prayers"* have been explained before (see on I Tim. 2:1). In the present instance the original has the article with each noun: *"the* supplications . . . *the* prayers." In other words, they are *her* very own, the outpourings of her own soul. Moreover, she prays not only by day, at set times and whenever the need arises, but also by night: every night, and perhaps especially, when, vexed with anxiety, she cannot sleep, during nightly vigils, etc. The emphasis rests on the fact that, with her, praying is not a "now and then" affair; she *continues* in her supplications and in her pray-

---

81 "Night and day" (instead of "day and night") is the order also in I Thess. 2:9; 3:10; II Thess. 3:8; II Tim. 1:3; cf. Jer. 14:17; contrast 16:13.

ers. Part of every night and part of every day is spent in supplication and prayer. She reminds one of the widow Anna (Luke 2:36, 37).

This is a truly beautiful description of "the real widow." The apostle does not repeat that such a widow should be "honored" by the church. Timothy will, of course, link verses 3 and 5. The obvious does not have to be repeated.

6. Our admiration and high regard for "the real widow" grows when we compare her with her "opposite" as now described by Paul: **but the one who is giving herself up to luxury, though living, is dead.** This widow is living luxuriously, perhaps even riotously (cf. James 5:5), like the daughters of Sodom (Ezek. 16:49). She is gay, frivolous, dissolute, pleasure-mad, "a merry widow." Whatever interest in religious matters she may have displayed at one time is now completely gone. Like the seed that fell among the thorns and was choked by them (Matt. 13:7, 22), so also in this woman's case, the word of God, to which at one time she listened outwardly, was choked by her delight in riches and pleasures. She reminds us of Kipling's Widow at Windsor with "ships on the foam and millions at home." Though *physically alive,* she *has actually died* and *is therefore now dead to all higher interests.* Of course, she never was a real Christian, but she used to pay her respects to *religion.* She went to church, and seemed to listen to the reading of the Word. Her lips used to move in prayer, and she was even emotionally stirred at times. Today, however, all *that* belongs definitely to the past. She is dressed in her gayest attire, and her purpose is "to have fun" and, perhaps, "to make a good catch." It is not necessary for Paul to add, "Do not honor such widows."

7. These things, too, you must command, in order that they may be above reproach.

Timothy is to urge obedience not only to the things referred to in I Tim. 4:11 ("Command these things and teach them") but also to the things which Paul has just now been saying. Surely, the most natural view is that the expression "these things" refers to the entire paragraph (verses 3-6). Timothy must see to it that the church honors really dependent and deserving widows (verses 3 and 5); that children and grandchildren do their duty to their parents (verse 4); and that everyone knows how to distinguish between the widow who should be honored and the widow who should not be honored (implied in verses 5 and 6).

If all the interested persons obey these commands, they will be above reproach both from the side of the world and from the side of the church.

8. Now if anyone does not provide for his own, and especially for the members of his own family, he has denied the faith and is worse than an unbeliever.

What has been stated positively in verse 4 is now stated negatively, more inclusively, and with greater force. The sin here censured is present in every community and in every age. Hence, the rule "Bear one another's burdens, and so fulfil the law of Christ" (Gal. 6:2) has validity for all time, particularly with reference to those whom one should consider "his own." Does this expression "his own" as here used mean "his own close relatives," for example, a widowed mother or grandmother, an aged and infirm father or grandfather, a physically or mentally ill cousin, an uncle or aunt on the verge of collapse? Are *friends* included or only *relatives?* No doubt, indefiniteness is here a virtue. Each case must be judged on its own merits, according to the need which exists and the ability to render assistance. But John 13:34; 15:12; Gal. 6:2 are always applicable.

However, within this rather indefinite (not sharply delimited) circle of dear ones there is a smaller one which is far more definite: "and especially for the members of his own family." Here the immediate family is meant, that is, immediate in the sense indicated in verse 4.

The apostle, then, has a word of rebuke for the person who neglects his duty toward "his own," and especially for him who fails to support the members of his immediate family. Such a neglectful individual *"has denied* the faith." (Same verb with same meaning in II Tim. 2:12; but see also on Titus 2:12.) He has denied it not by means of *words* necessarily but (what is often far worse) by means of his *sinful negligence.* Lack of positive action, the sin of omission, gives the lie to his profession of *faith* (subjective sense). Though he professes to be a Christian, he lacks the most precious of all the fruits that grow on the tree of a truly Christian life and conduct. He lacks *love.* Where this good *fruit* is absent, there cannot be a good *tree.*

Such a person is said to be "worse than an unbeliever." This is true for the following reasons:

(1) Most "unbelievers" (in the sense of "outsiders") have never heard about *the specific precept* found in John 13:34; 15:12; Gal. 6:2. But he who has been instructed in the Christian religion has heard this command again and again.

(2) Most "unbelievers" are complete strangers to *Christ's glorious example* of love for his own (including the love for his mother). But the church-member has become acquainted with the story of his infinite love.

(3) "Unbelievers," in general, know nothing about the promise of an *enabling power,* namely, the power of the Holy Spirit operating in the believer's heart. But he who professes to be a Christian has witnessed the evidences of this power in the lives of others.

(4) Yet, in spite of this threefold lack, "unbelievers" do often show some affection toward those who belong to their family-circle, in wider or more restricted sense. Frequently they do actually provide for their widowed mothers and grandmothers, and pagan reverence for ancestors is a well-

known religious phenomenon. Hence, the person who wishes to be viewed as a Christian but who, in spite of the clearer light and the many privileges which he has received, does not perform his religious duty with respect to those whom God has placed within the sphere of his special responsibility, is, indeed, "worse than an infidel."

---

9 A widow, in order to be placed on the list of widows, must not be less than sixty years of age; (she must have been) one husband's wife, 10 well-attested for noble deeds. (She can be placed on the list) if she has reared children, if she has practised hospitality, if she has washed the feet of saints, if she has assisted the afflicted, if she has been devoted to every kind of good work.

11 But younger widows you must refuse (to place on the list); for often when, contrary to (their pledged devotion to) Christ, they grow restless with desire, they want to get married (again); 12 incurring guilt because they have repudiated their former pledge. 13 At the same time they also learn to be idle, gadding about from house to house, and not only idle but also gossipy and meddlesome, saying things which they should not (say).

14 So I would have young widows marry (again), bear children, manage a home, and give the adversary no occasion whatever for slandering. 15 For even now some have turned aside after Satan. 16 But if any believing woman has widows, let her assist them, and let the church not be burdened, so that it may assist those who are really (what is implied in the name) widows.

5:9-16

9. A widow, in order to be placed on the list of widows, must not be less than sixty years of age.

The subject of verses 9-16 differs in one important respect from that treated in verses 3-8. *There* the theme was "Widows and *their Need.*" *Here* Paul discusses "Widows and *their Work.*" *That* section dealt with widows in general; *this* one has to do with "widows that are placed on a list" or "catalogued."

With respect to the question, "Who are these widows?" there are, in the main, four views:

(1) They are the deaconesses (Schleiermacher).

Objections:

a. Note the age: not under sixty (verse 9).

b. "Deaconesses" (rather, "deacons' assistants," "women who minister") have been discussed previously (see on 3:11).

(2) They are those widows who are entitled to material support from the church (Chrysostom, Calvin, N. J. D. White in *The Expositor's Greek Testament,* Dibelius, and many others). The theories vary. Some think of *all* the widows of 60 and above, who possess the qualities that are mentioned. Others believe that only such widows are meant who were willing to *work* for the church. They think of a contract, "We, older widows, promise to

render service to the church." – "We, the church-authorities, promise to provide for y o u when the need arises."

Objections:

a. Would the church refuse to support widows *under* sixty, *with small children?*

b. Does not verse 10 indicate that the widows of which this section speaks were comparatively well-to-do?

c. Is it not true that the question, "Which widows should receive aid from the church, and which should not?" has already been discussed (verses 4, and by implication, 5, 7, and 8)? Why would another set of restrictions be added now, and those "of so very exclusive a nature" (Ellicott); see verse 10?

(3) The question must be left unanswered (Lenski).

Objection:

Though I share Lenski's objections to the second view, I do not agree with his argumentation against view Number (4).

(4) These are the widows who possessed the necessary qualifications for the performance of certain spiritual and charitable functions in the church (C. J. Ellicott, A. T. Robertson, E. F. Scott, C. Bouma, and many others).

I believe that this is the correct view. Reasons:

a. The qualifications for inclusion in the list point in the direction of *work* to be done, just as did the list of qualifications for "women-helpers" in 3:11, and the lists for elders and for deacons in 3:1-10, 12.

b. Let it be granted that most widows over sixty might be considered too old to take care of orphans – Lenski's objection, *op. cit.*, p. 669 – the answer to this (aside from the fact that *some* women at that age are still *not* too old, and, in fact, insist on performing work of that kind!) is simple: *verse 10 does not state that they must take care of orphans but that they must have reared children!* Surely, widows who have successfully brought up children are the very ones who can impart good advice to younger women. They can train them "to love their husbands and to love their children" (Titus 2:4), and can give them all kinds of valuable hints!

c. There is sufficient evidence to show that in the early church such a body of *widows, with definite functions* actually existed. Thus Tertullian (possibly about the year 204), referring definitely to I Tim. 5:9 ("sixty years"), states that the task of these women was, "that their experienced training in all the affections may have rendered them capable of readily assisting all others with counsel and comfort" (*On The Veiling Of Virgins*, IX).

In the early church such a widow was called "the intercessor of the church," "the keeper of the door," and "the altar of God."

Their duties seem to have been: giving good counsel to the younger women, praying and fasting, visiting the sick, preparing women for baptism, taking them to communion, and giving guidance and direction to widows and orphans who were supported by the church (see article "Woman" in I.S.B.E., IV. 5, Vol. V, p. 3103).

d. If even today, as any minister who has served large churches knows, older women are at times consulted and sent on missions in which *they* excel, and which may be too delicate for others to perform, it is readily understandable that *in Bible-lands* (and particularly *at that time,* but to a degree even today), with their social and psychological barriers between men and women (see N.T.C. on John 4:27) there would be much work which these widows were able to perform with greater effectiveness than anyone else (especially work *among women*). And there would be plenty of somewhat similar work left for the younger *married* women. The reasons why *the younger widows* – those less than sixty years of age – were to be excluded from the performance of much of this work is stated by Paul in verses 11-15.

As a second requirement Paul states: **(she must have been) one husband's wife** (see on I Tim. 3:2, 12). Of course, this cannot mean, "She must not have been a widow who subsequently remarried, and who then lost also her second husband," for had Paul meant that, he would have been contradicting himself. Such a widow would have done the very thing which the apostle wanted young widows to do – he wanted them to remarry (verse 14) –, and it surely would have been unjust afterward to bar them from The Widow's List! The expression "one husband's wife" must simply mean that while married she had been faithful to her one husband. Other qualifications follow:

10. well-attested for noble deeds. Anyone who performs church-work must have a good reputation (see on I Tim. 3:2, 7, 10; cf. Acts 6:3; 16:2; Heb. 11:2).

There follow five "if" or "whether" clauses. We have here another instance of *abbreviated discourse* (which we have discussed in N.T.C. on John 5:31, Vol. I, p. 206). One can fill in the implied words in either of two ways, with very little difference in resultant meaning:

Either:

One should enquire whether she has reared children, *whether* she has practised hospitality, etc.

Or:

She can be placed on the list if she has reared children, *if* she has practised hospitality, etc.

In either case the meaning is: she should not be placed on the list unless her record shows that she has been diligent in these matters.

The items themselves are readily understandable. Surely a woman who is to perform the work which has been indicated (see on verse 9) must have the qualifications that are implied in the five clauses:

a. **(She can be placed on the list) if she has reared children.** She must be experienced in this line if she is to give counsel and direction to others.

b. **if she has practised hospitality.** See on I Tim. 3:2. This grace was practised beautifully by the widow of Zarephath who "sustained" Elijah (I Kings 17:9), by the Shunammite woman ("a great woman") who lodged Elisha (II Kings 4:8-11), and by Lydia (Acts 16:40).

c. **if she has washed the feet of saints.** Perhaps meaning literally, that this service was rendered by her or under her supervision; surely figuratively: that she has rendered humble service to traveling preachers. See Gen. 18:6; I Sam. 25:41. On the entire matter of footwashing see N.T.C. on John, Vol. II, pp. 219-241, especially p. 236 and the footnote there.

d. **if she has assisted the afflicted.** The early Christians were persecuted, oppressed. Cf. John 16:33; I Thess. 1:6; II Thess. 1:4. They needed relief, help (same verb in verse 16). Burdens must be shared (Gal. 6:2).

e. **if she has been devoted to every kind of good work.** This may be viewed as a re-iteration of "well-attested for noble deeds" at the beginning of the verse. However, it is possible that the thought is somewhat strengthened here: not only must this widow *have a reputation for noble deeds;* she must actually *have been diligently devoted to (she must have followed) every kind* of *good work!* Reputation is a fine thing, but sometimes it is undeserved. To be placed on the list, it must have been deserved!

11, 12. The apostle now proceeds to give two reasons why younger widows should be excluded from the list. The first reason is stated in verses 11 and 12: **But younger widows you must refuse (to place on the list); for often when, contrary to (their pledged devotion to) Christ, they grow restless with desire, they want to get married (again).**

For much of the work which Paul has in mind (see on verse 9) older women would be required, women with experience, who had the time and the opportunity, *old widows* therefore. But the possibility existed that also younger widows might *apply.* However, the importance of the work required whole-hearted devotion. If the interests are divided, so that the widow's mind, even during the performance of her spiritual functions, is pre-occupied with the idea of finding a suitable husband, her efficiency will suffer. This is *often* the case (note the indefinite ὅταν). This is one of the reasons why the application of *younger* widows (those under sixty) should be rejected.

Of course, Paul finds no fault whatever with the idea that younger widows should wish to marry again. In fact, he *wants* them to do just that (see verse 14). But he definitely finds fault with young widows *who have pledged themselves to an important spiritual ministry* and who then, nevertheless, break their pledge by marrying again! The apostle says, "contrary to . . . Christ." That he means "contrary to their pledged devotion to Christ" (that is, to the work of Christ which they have pledged to perform) is clear from verse 12.

Such young widows, as Paul must have noticed again and again, tend to *grow restless with desire.* Because their minds are occupied with other matters (for example, with respect to the next husband), they become bored with their church-duties, and begin to rebel against them. The verb καταστρηνιάω is used only in this one passage. It seems to mean "to exercise one's youthful vigor against" (see M.M., p. 593). The uncompounded verb is also found in Rev. 18:7, 9, where Babylon and the kings of the earth are said to have "waxed wanton" with wealth and pleasure. The upsurge of feeling which is indicated here in I Tim. 5:11 is not necessarily evil. It is natural for a young widow to cherish the desire to remarry. She is young, throbbing with life, longing for a husband. Let her then get married again if the opportunity presents itself, but as long as she is a young widow let her not be placed on the list of widows who perform special services in the church. Paul was a very practical man!

He continues: **incurring guilt because they have repudiated their former pledge.** The idea of several commentators that these young widows have rejected their *faith* in Jesus Christ, that they wish to marry *pagans,* and that they consequently suffer the judgment of "everlasting damnation" is surely foreign to the entire context. The apostle is writing about Christian young widows, who love the Lord sufficiently that they have applied for a position of special service in his kingdom! That they might subsequently become pre-occupied with the idea of remarriage is, after all, quite natural. Only, in that case they would be *repudiating* (as in Luke 10:16) their former (πρώτην) *pledge* (πίστιν) to the church, namely, to continue in the work of the Lord. This would involve them in *a judgment,* that is, in *guilt* (κρίμα). Paul wishes to spare them, and to promote the spiritual and charitable work of the church. Hence, he advises that such young widows be not placed on the list, but that they marry again (verse 14).

13. The second reason why such young widows should not be placed on the list is now stated: **At the same time they also learn to be idle, gadding about from house to house, and not only idle but also gossipy and meddlesome, saying things which they should not** (say).

Of course, Paul does not mean that *all* young widows are like that. He does mean that this is likely to happen, and surely the church cannot afford to "take a chance."

Writing, then, about a certain type of young widows, the apostle's description becomes very vivid.

First, he says, they "learn to be" (μανθάνουσιν; the Greek idiom does not require εἶναι) idle: they get into habits of idleness. This idleness is brought about by their "gadding about from house to house" (literally, "making the circuit of the houses"; cf. Acts 19:13; 28:13). Now this business of "going from house to house" was in all likelihood included in their work (see on verse 9), the purpose being to render assistance and impart counsel. But these *young* widows would tend "to make *everything*" of this *one* phase of their task, and a person can easily guess why: they were the sociable type. They enjoyed boon companionship. They liked to be entertained at (what in our day would be called) a "tea-party." And so they made a purely *social affair* of their assignment! They would become not only *idle* but *chatty* and *meddlesome.* (Note the play upon words: ἀργαί περίεργοι. One might translate: "not busy workers but busybodies" as were some people in Thessalonica; see N.T.C. on II Thess. 3:11.) The description is so very vivid that one cannot help thinking that young widows had been tried out for this kind of work, and that this was what had happened. Of course, the result was that thus they might easily be doing more harm than good. In the midst of their vivacious chatter they would often "say things which they should not (say)," *creating* problems for the church instead of *solving* any!

14, 15. What, then, should young widows do? The answer is: **So I would have young widows marry (again), bear children, manage a home.**

Paul does not favor asceticism. He does not want young widows to remain unmarried. This surely indicates that the apostle does not regard celibacy as a higher form of Christianity. There is a wide gulf between Paul and Tertullian. The latter came to regard second marriage as "successive polygamy." In the early church (second century and afterward) there were many who took a somewhat similar view, though they did not always advance so many and such lengthy arguments in favor of absolute monogamy as did Tertullian.

Paul wants these young widows to be entirely happy, and to fulfil their natural calling. Hence, not only does he desire that when a good opportunity presents itself they get married again (always "in the Lord," of course, I Cor. 7:39), but also that they *bear children* (the verb occurs only here, but for the related noun see I Tim. 2:15). Moreover, he wants them to assume their divinely ordained role in the rearing of these children. He wants them to "manage a home" or "rule a household" (this verb, too, occurs nowhere else in the New Testament; but see M.M., p. 441).

It is clearly evident that Paul is seeking to promote the welfare not only of the church but also of these young widows. He does not want them to do what is unbecoming. Let them accept the offer of marriage if they can conscientiously do so. Let them not waste their time in idle gossip. Let them adorn their confession with a life to God's honor. Hence, he adds:

and give the adversary no occasion whatever for slandering (or: favorable to slandering). Paul is thinking of a human adversary, whether he be a Jew or a Gentile. Such a person would always be ready to rail or revile (cf. I Peter 3:9). Thus not only would the reputation of the widow suffer, but God's name would be dishonored. With sadness of heart the apostle adds: **For even now some have turned aside after Satan.** He is still thinking about *young widows.* The meaning is, "It is necessary that I emphasize this, namely, that the adversary must not receive any occasion for slandering, *for* I know of concrete cases where this has already taken place." These widows had *turned aside* from the right path (see on I Tim. 1:6), and were now following *Satan* instead of obeying Christ's command, "Follow *me*" (John 21:19).

16. Is there, then, no work in the kingdom for a young widow with means and with the desire to help the good cause? O yes there is! In addition to what she is able to do in a strictly personal way (for example, pray for the church and for all those in need, make a *personal* visit to those in need, etc.), there is another way in which she can help the church. And not only *she* but *any believing woman* (πιστή is the best reading here; see N.N.) who has the means can do the thing which Paul expresses in these words: **But if any believing woman has widows, let her assist them.**

Here, let us say, is a lady like Lydia, who has a spacious home. She has a servant, a friend, or a relative, who happens to be a widow. Perhaps she can provide a home for that widow, or even for more than one widow. Or else she can help the widow financially or by providing work. Let her then do her Christian duty so that God may be glorified, so that this gracious lady may herself experience in her heart the peace which results from divine approval of deeds well done, and so that the needy one may be relieved. Paul, however, gives expression not to these objectives but to another. Says he: **And let the church not be burdened, so that it may assist those who are really (what is implied in the name) widows.**

Here the apostle returns to the thought expressed in verses 3 and 4. Needy widows are *first of all* the responsibility of those who are nearest to them; for example, children, grandchildren, women of means who stand in a relation of closeness to them. Let them then do their duty. Not only is this morally the right thing to do, but there is also a very practical consideration. The church has its hands full as it is. It does not count many rich people among its members (Mark 10:25; cf. I Cor. 1:26). Hence, it should not be *burdened* (weighed down with too heavy a load; for the verb see also II Cor. 1:8; 5:4; then Matt. 26:43; Luke 9:32; 21:34). Without this extra burden it will be able to assist "those who are really (what is implied in the name) *widows.*" This last clause has already been explained (see on verse 3). These are the widows who are completely destitute, having no one to support them. If everyone does his part, it will be so much easier for the church to care for *these* widows. Truly, a lesson also for today!

---

17 Let the elders who rule well be counted worthy of double honor, especially those who labor in preaching and teaching. 18 For the Scripture says, "A threshing ox you shall not muzzle," and "Worthy of his pay (is) the worker." 19 Never entertain an accusation against an elder unless (it is) supported by two or three witnesses. 20 Those who do wrong you must rebuke in the presence of all, so that also the others may be filled with fear.

21 I charge (you) in the sight of God and of Christ Jesus and of the elect angels that you observe these instructions (or: these things) without prejudice, doing nothing from partiality. 22 Do not lay hands (of ordination) upon anyone hastily, neither be a partaker in the sins of others: keep yourself pure. 23 No longer drink water (only), but use a little wine for the sake of your stomach and your frequent ailments.

24 The sins of some men are clearly evident, proceeding ahead of them to judgment, but the sins of others follow after (them). 25 Similarly, the noble deeds (are) clearly evident, and even those that are otherwise cannot remain hidden.

5:17-25

17. Let the elders who rule well be counted worthy of double honor, especially those who labor in preaching and teaching.

Honor due to widows suggests honor due to elders. Moreover, just as the word *widow* was used first in a general sense (verse 3), but later (verse 9) in the sense of those whose names had been entered upon a list and who performed certain functions in the church, so also the word *presbyter* occurs first in the general sense of *old man* (5:1), but now as a synonym of *overseer,* the latter term indicating the character of the man's work, the former his age and the dignity which pertains to him because of his age and office.

It is clear that by the terms *overseer* and *elder* the same person is indicated, for in both cases we are told that these men *rule* and *teach* (cf. I Tim. 3:2, 5 with 5:17). That an overseer would be called a *presbyter* or *elder* is not strange, for in ancient Israel, in the synagogue, and also in the early church, the *older* men were clothed with this office. Very fittingly the term *overseer* is used when the emphasis is on their *work* (I Tim. 3:1), the term *elder* when the emphasis is on the *honor* that is their due (the present passage, I Tim. 5:17).

It is worthy of note that Timothy is here instructed to see to it that "the excellently ruling elders" (thus literally) are honored by the congregation. The apostle must have been aware of the fact that in many cases church-members are apt to forget this. They are prone to believe that the overseers are living on Easy Street, "especially those who labor in preaching and teaching," or that if any honor is to be bestowed it should be by means of the funeral-sermon! Is it surprising that so many ministers suffer nervous breakdowns? And that among them there are several who were doing their work conscientiously?

The words "especially those who labor in preaching (literally *in word*) and teaching" show that already in Paul's days a distinction began to be made between those whom today we call "ministers" and those whom we still call "elders." *All* rule, and to a certain extent *all* teach, but *some* (in addition to ruling) *labor* in *preaching* (expounding the Word to the assembled congregation), and *teaching* (imparting instruction to the youth, to enquirers, and to all who stand in need of it). They specialize in it, working hard at it. It requires much of their time and effort: preaching, teaching, and preparing for it.

Now all the excellently ruling elders must receive "double honor." But what is meant by this expression? Interpretations vary:

(1) honor and honorarium. They should receive both honor and material reward (Chrysostom, C. Bouma).

(2) ample pay, better remuneration, twice the salary they get (along this line, but with individual variations, Moffatt, White in *Expositor's Greek Testament,* Williams).

(3) twice as much "honor" as widows, or twice as great a portion of the firstfruits as widows (*Constitutions of the Holy Apostles* II. xxviii; in that same direction Calvin, Lock).

(4) honor as brothers and honor as rulers; or honor on account of age and honor on account of office (Tertullian, Bengel).

(5) honor as elders, extra honor as those who rule excellently (Lenski).

I believe that this last interpretation is the correct one, and I endorse the statement of Lenski that the context itself explains "twofold honor." Nevertheless, this double honor must not be so interpreted as if any idea of remuneration is completely excluded from it, and as if in connection with verse 18 the thought conveyed is simply this: Excellently ruling elders should receive their due, namely, double honor; just like the threshing ox receives its due, namely, wisps of grain; and just like the laborer receives his due, namely, wages (see Lenski on verse 18). In this way every notion of financial remuneration would be completely excluded from the "double honor" due to the elders who serve well and are in need of it. But that can hardly be correct, for also in the case of the widows the *honor* due them was immediately linked with that of material support (verses 3 and 4), and the analogies which Paul uses in verse 18 certainly point in the same direction as far as the elders are concerned. The true explanation, therefore, would seem to be this:

An elder deserves to be honored; particularly if his labor excels in quality. This honor is due especially to those who labor in preaching and teaching. And this implies, of course, that wherever it is necessary (and it would be necessary especially in the case of the "minister") the work should also be rewarded in a material way. A man who spends all his time and effort in kingdom-work (a "minister") certainly deserves "a good salary." *Not* that the word "honor" in and by itself has here the meaning *honorarium.*[82] It means *honor.* But it would be evidence of *lack* of honor if the church should demand of a man who devotes himself entirely to spiritual work that he do this gratis.

The explanation which I have given does not imply that *every* elder, or even *every* excellently ruling elder receive a salary. *All* who rule well deserve double honor, and in the case of those who devote themselves entirely to church-work this implies the right of remuneration. (And it implies more than that; see verses 19, 20, 22.)

18. For the Scripture says,

A threshing ox you shall not muzzle

and

Worthy of his pay (is) the worker.

The two sayings are clearly co-ordinate. If the first is "scripture," so is the second. Thus a word spoken by Jesus is here placed on a par with a saying from the Old Testament canon.

The first saying is quoted from Deut. 25:4. Paul makes a similar use of it in I Cor. 9:8-12. The picture is that of a threshing-floor: a circular piece of level ground, exposed to the wind. Sometimes it is a flat rock on top of a hill. The sheaves of grain have been unbound and lie on this floor, arranged in circles. Oxen are driven over them, so that by the trampling of their hoofs the ripe grain may be shaken out of the ears (Hos. 10:11; Mic. 4:13). Or, for the same purpose the oxen may be harnessed to a rough sledge on which the driver stands or sits, as he guides the oxen around and around (Judg. 8:7; Is. 28:27; 41:15). This sledge or drag is a kind of sled consisting of two heavy boards, fastened side by side, and curved upward in front. To the bottom of it sharp pieces of stone are attached, to loosen the kernels of grain.[83]

Now cruel pagans would at times muzzle such threshing oxen, but Je-

---

[82] In the New Testament the word τιμή *never means wages or pay or salary.* Rather, it has the meaning *price* (Matt. 27:6, 9; Acts 5:2, 3; 7:16; I Cor. 6:20; 7:23; pl. Acts 4:34; 19:19), and *esteem, honor* (Rom. 12:10; 13:7; I Cor. 12:23, etc.). This corresponds with the connotation of the word in the papyri (M.M., p. 635). In classical Greek the word has a variety of meanings: worth, value, price; compensation, satisfaction, recompense; penalty; worship, dignity; lordship, office; reward, present, offering; esteem, honor.

[83] See W.D.B., pp. 604, 605, the picture and the article. Excellent pictures of the threshing dredge or drag and of threshing with oxen are found in I.S.B.E., art. "Agriculture"; see also art. "Threshing-floor." Also Thomson, *The Land and The Book,* Vol. II, p. 314; M.S. and J. L. Miller, *Encyclopaedia of Bible Life,* the article on p. 19, and the fine illustration opposite p. 15 and p. 22.

hovah had distinctly forbidden Israel to do this. The purpose of this injunction was that men might see the kindness of God; particularly, that they might discern this basic principle, namely, that *to every worker* (be that worker an ox, a common laborer, or a minister of the gospel) God has given the right to partake of the fruits of his work. (The context in Deuteronomy deals with *men,* not with animals. Cf. I Cor. 9:9, 10.) In the present instance this would mean that "those who proclaim the gospel should make their living by the gospel" (I Cor. 9:14).

The second saying, "Worthy of his pay is the worker" is found in this precise form in Luke 10:7. (In Matthew 10:10 the saying occurs in a slightly different form: "Worthy of his *food* is the worker.") Paul and Luke were friends, and were often together. Luke had been with Paul during the latter's first Roman imprisonment (Col. 4:14; Philemon 24). It is not impossible that Luke's Gospel had just been brought to completion. Hence, if that be true, the apostle was able to quote from it. Or else he may here be quoting from a collection of sayings which presumably was used as a source of Luke's Gospel.[84]

By combining the two quotations, and viewing them in the light of preceding context, we notice that Paul is emphasizing that the respect of which excellently ruling elders are worthy implies that those among them who devote themselves entirely to gospel-work have a right to wages, and that these wages should not be withheld.

19. Now this "honor" which is the elder's due should express itself also in another way: **Never entertain an accusation against an elder unless (it is) supported by two or three witnesses.**

An accusation against an elder must be *upon* — that is, must be based *upon* the oral testimony of — two or three witnesses. Note that though of old *any* Israelite was safeguarded against *indictment and sentencing* unless two or three reliable witnesses testified against him (cf. Deut. 17:6; cf. Num. 35:30; and see N.T.C. on John 5:31; 8:14), here (I Tim. 5:19) *presbyters* are safeguarded even against *having to answer a charge* (cf. Ex. 23:1 in LXX), unless it be at once supported by two or three witnesses. Lacking such support, the accusation must not even be *taken up* or *entertained.* The reputation of the elder must not be unnecessarily damaged, and his work must not suffer unnecessary interruption.

20. Nevertheless, at times a charge against an elder will have sufficient support to be *entertained,* and will afterward even be *sustained* by the facts. What then? Says Paul: **Those who do wrong you must rebuke in the presence of all, so that also the others may be filled with fear** (literally: *may have fear*).

[84] On the subject of probable dates when the New Testament books were written, and on the Synoptic Problem see my *Bible Survey,* p. 325, 383-394.

Elders who walk in sinful ways must not be spared. In fact, their sin must be punished even more severely than that of others. The law made the same distinction (Lev. 4:22, 27). Timothy must not only *bring their sin home to their conscience,*[85] but in *their* case he must do this *not privately* or in the presence of just a few (Matt. 18:15-17), *but publicly,* that is, in the presence of the entire consistory, so that the remaining elders may also become filled with godly fear of wrong-doing (cf. Gen. 39:9; Ps. 19:13).

21. Now in the matters discussed in verses 19 and 20, and, in fact, in any matter touching the discipline of church-leaders, one is easily influenced by purely subjective considerations. But this can spell ruin for the church and for all those concerned. Timothy, as apostolic delegate in the churches of Ephesus and vicinity, must not allow this to happen to him. Even today biased judges, ecclesiastical "machines," so-called "investigating-committees" manned by job-hunters, "buddy-ism," and the like can easily destroy a denomination. Corruption generally begins "at the summit." Church History furnishes many examples. The man in the pew does not know what happened "while he slept." When he wakes up – if he ever does! – it is generally too late.

Hence, absolute impartiality and unimpeachable honesty in all such matters are essential. It is for that reason that the charge which the apostle now lays on Timothy is so very grave. *Everything* is at stake! The church of the twentieth century may well take to heart these solemn words: **I charge (you) in the sight of God and of Christ Jesus and of the elect angels that you observe these instructions without prejudice, doing nothing from partiality.**

That the verb used in the original cannot *here* mean "I Solemnly *testify*" (as, for example, in I Thess. 4:6) but "I charge," that is, "I solemnly *admonish,*" or "I solemnly *order*" or even *"adjure,"* is clear from the clause which it introduces: "that you observe these instructions." Paul emphasizes that it is under the very eye and with the full approval of God that these directives (verses 19 and 20) have been issued. This is the very God who through Christ Jesus *will one day judge all men.* And these are the angels who will be associated with Christ in the final judgment. Hence, the apostle is, as it were, putting Timothy *under oath* to comply with the mandate which he has received (in the spirit of Gen. 24:3, 9). One who breaks the oath *will be judged.* That, in giving this charge, Paul is actually thinking of *the final judgment* is clear from a comparison with the similar language of II Tim. 4:1. Note the particulars that are mentioned here in I Tim. 5:21:

The Judge is *God* (Gen. 18:25; Heb. 12:23). The addressed must be

---

[85] For detailed discussion of the verb here used see N.T.C. on John, Vol. II, pp. 324-326.

deeply conscious of the fact that Paul in issuing and Timothy in dealing with this charge are acting in the sight of God, the Judge!

Yet, God judges not directly but through *Christ Jesus.* It is upon the Mediator that the honor of judging was conferred as a reward for the atonement which he rendered (Matt. 25:31-46; John 5:22, 23, 27; Acts 19:42; 17:31; II Cor. 5:10; Phil. 2:10, 11; II Tim. 4:1; Rev. 14:14-16).

Associated with Christ in this work of judging will be *the angels,* as is taught everywhere in Holy Writ (Dan. 7:10; Matt. 13:27, 41, 42; 16:27; 24:31-33; 25:31; II Thess. 1:7; Heb. 12:22; Rev. 14:15, 17-20). They will gather the redeemed and will drive the wicked before the judgment-seat.

These are God's *elect* angels, in distinction from the angels "who did not keep their own position" (Satan and his demons; cf. Jude 6). In his sovereign, inscrutable decree, which transcends all human understanding, God from all eternity decided that to *these* angels (here called *elect*) would be given the grace of perseverance, so that they would remain standing. Being *elect,* they are of course also *beloved.* (For the doctrine of election *of men,* as taught by Paul, see N.T.C. on I Thess. 1:4.) [86]

It is not strange that the apostle mentions also these *angels.* He wants Timothy *to obey* the all-important charge concerning the discipline of elders; that is, he wants him to resemble the angels *in obedience.* Besides, these angels are spectators of Timothy's actions and will accompany Christ at the final judgment when everything that was hidden will be revealed, and oath-breaking will be punished. According to Paul, and in harmony with all the rest of Scripture,

ANGELS ARE:

A ttendants of Christ (II Thess. 1:7), their exalted Head (Eph. 1:21, 22; Col. 2:10)

B ringers of good tidings concerning our salvation, having seen the Lord not only in his birth but also in his resurrection and post-resurrection glory (see on I Tim. 3:16; cf. Luke 2:14; 24:4; Acts 1:11)

C horisters of heaven (I Cor. 13:1; cf. Luke 15:10; Rev. 5:11, 12)

D efenders of God's children (II Thess. 1:7-10; cf. Ps. 91:11; Dan. 6:22;

---

[86] From the analogy of the election *of the angels* it has been argued that also in the case *of men* election must be conceived of as supralapsarian, so that, in listing under each other the elements which pertain to the decree, God's decision to reveal his mercy in the salvation of some men, and his justice in the perdition of others, would have to be placed *above* (supra) his decision to permit *the fall* (lapsus). However, the legitimacy of this reasoning from analogy is not granted by all. Most theologians would probably agree that, as far as predestination has to do with *men,* both supralapsarianism and infralapsarianism are one-sided. For this entire subject see L. Berkhof, *Systematic Theology,* pp. 118-125 (note the literature on p. 125); also my translation of H. Bavinck, *The Doctrine of God,* pp. 382-394.

10:10, 13, 20; Matt. 18:10; Acts 5:19; Rev. 12:7), though the latter outrank them and will judge them (I Cor. 6:3; cf. Heb. 1:14)

E xamples in obedience (I Cor. 11:10; cf. Matt. 6:10)

F riends of the redeemed, constantly watching them, deeply interested in their salvation, and rendering service to them in every way, also in executing the judgment of God upon the enemy (Gal. 3:19; I Cor. 4:9; II Thess. 1:7; cf. Matt. 13:41; 25:31, 32; Luke 16:22; I Peter 1:12; Heb. 1:14; Rev. 20:1-3).

Accordingly, since Timothy's actions are scrutinized by God, by Christ Jesus (both *divine,* note the *one* article in the original) and by the angels (*creatures,* note repetition of the article), and this with a view to the final judgment, let him observe (stand guard over) the given instructions "without prejudice," that is, uninfluenced by any sinful subjective considerations, guided only by the objective standard of the truth as revealed by God, and "doing nothing from partiality (or favoritism)," *leaning* neither *toward* this nor toward that side, neither toward the accuser nor toward the accused, until all the important facts in each concrete case have been fully established.

22. Much trouble can be avoided if in the matter of ordaining men to office Timothy will exercise the necessary precaution. Hence, Paul continues: **Do not lay hands (of ordination) upon anyone hastily, neither be a partaker in the sins of others: keep yourself pure.**

The symbolical indication of the impartation of gifts which one will need in discharging the duties of his office has been mentioned before (see on I Tim. 4:14), and will be mentioned again (II Tim. 1:6). This work must not be done "in a hurry." The qualifications of the men who are being considered must be fully examined before they can be nominated for office. This is in harmony with what the apostle has been saying in I Tim. 3:2, 7, 10. Ordination without preceding thorough investigation would render Timothy co-responsible for the wrongs which such elders might subsequently commit. This, in turn, would add to the difficulty of disciplining them. Timothy must strive to "keep himself *pure*" (in full conformity with God's moral law) with respect to this and all other matters. (For the related noun, *purity,* see on I Tim. 4:12; 5:2.)

23. The precept, "Keep yourself pure" was of a personal nature. This leads to another remark which is also personal: **No longer drink water (only), but use a little wine for the sake of your stomach and your frequent ailments.**

Timothy was a conscientious person. He did not want to be accused of being the kind of individual who "lingers beside his wine" (see on I Tim. 3:3). Hence, he had formed the habit of drinking nothing but water. However, in the Orient the water is often far from "safe." Those who have been there – including, for example, those who were there while serving in the armed forces – know this. If one insists on drinking nothing but unboiled water, attacks of dysentery may result. In fact, something worse might happen! Consequently, for the sake of helping Timothy to overcome his stomach-troubles and related ailments, which seem to have been coming to him "thick and fast," Paul advises him to stop being purely a water-drinker. Timothy must use some *wine*, not *much* wine, but *some* wine. That will do him good physically.[87] Paul is here speaking of wine as a *medicine*, not as a *beverage*, as Wuest correctly observes.

24, 25. Returning now to the subject of necessary caution before ordaining men to office (see verse 22), Paul says:

The sins of some men are clearly evident, proceeding ahead of them to judgment, but the sins of others follow after (them).

Similarly, the noble deeds (are) clearly evident, and even those that are otherwise [88] cannot remain hidden.

Of the many explanations the most reasonable would seem to be this one:

In verse 24 Paul is speaking about sins, namely, the sins of men who are unfit for office. In verse 25 he is speaking about noble deeds (or excellent works), namely, the noble deeds of men who are fit for office.

By implication he divides the first main group – the sins of men unfit for office – into two subdivisions:

a. the clearly evident sins of some men;

b. the not clearly evident sins of other men (this is implied rather than expressed).

---

[87] Note that with respect to the use of wine Paul avoids extremes. On the one hand he warns against the man who "lingers beside his wine" or is "given to much wine" (I Tim. 3:3, 8). On the other hand, he believes that in Timothy's case the use of some wine for the purpose of promoting health, and that caution in the use of water (probably because of the danger of pollution) is advisable.

Many have given their views on the subject of the sinister effects of social wine-drinking and drinking of other alcoholic beverages. Very recently there appeared an article, "Negative or Positive" in *The Foundation Issue* of July, 1955, published by The Michigan Temperance Foundation, with headquarters in Lansing, Mich.; also another article, "Hereditary Consequences of Alcoholism," in *Christian Economics* of September 6, 1955. Similar literature is being distributed regularly, no doubt with many wholesome effects.

On the other side, the value of wine as food and medicine is discussed by Dr. Salvatore in his recently published book *Wine As Food And Medicine,* Blakiston Co. This was summarized and reviewed in the magazine *Newsweek,* the issue of July 19, 1954.

In the present day and age a vigorous campaign against *every* form of intemperance is certainly in order. Paul's word must be interpreted in the light of conditions prevailing in the Orient and in the light of *Timothy's* physical condition.

[88] ἔχω *plus adverb* means here *to be in a certain condition.* For this idiom see also Matt. 4:24; Mark 5:23; 16:18; John 4:52; Acts 7:1; 15:36; 21:13; 24:25; and II Cor. 12:14.

Expressly he divides the second main group – the noble deeds of men fit for office – into two similar subdivisions:

a. the clearly evident noble deeds of some men;

b. the not clearly evident noble deeds of other men.

With respect, then, to the first group Paul says that the sins of some men are so *clearly evident* (πρόδηλοι, see also Heb. 7:14), so conspicuous or obvious, that in their case thorough examination in order to reach a *decision* or *judgment* (see N.T.C. on John, Vol. I, pp. 142, 143) is hardly even necessary. The sins precede the man! This does not merely mean that the man in question has a bad reputation (for that, after all, might be based on slander), but that he *is bad:* his evil-doing is out in the open. It is there, for all to see. The very idea of nominating such men for office is preposterous.

In the case of other men the situation is different. *Their* sins *follow* them (literally *follow after* them, or *follow them up*). When their case is considered in order that a decision may be reached, they are found, after *thorough examination,* to be unfit for office. *Before* their case comes up, Timothy and perhaps several presbyters consider these men to be possible candidates for office. *After* thorough examination and the rendering of a judgment, things take on an altogether different aspect. The sins of these men have now been uncovered, so that, the judgment having been rendered, there is no longer any doubt about their unfitness for office.

The situation with respect to men who are spiritually fit for office is similar in this respect, namely, that also in their case Timothy, as a rule, need not be afraid that hidden qualities will remain hidden. In general, the noble deeds (or excellent works) which adorn the lives of these men will be clearly evident. And even in such exceptional cases in which they are not at once evident, they cannot remain hidden. Proper questioning and investigation will bring them to the surface.

For the encouragement of Timothy, who, as has been shown (see p. 34), was rather timid, Paul is trying to establish this point: if he will but exercise due caution, and will not be hasty in ordaining men to office (see verse 22), he will have good elders in the churches of Ephesus and vicinity; the rule being that even in the case of such men whose unfitness or fitness for office is not immediately clear, careful examination will lead to valid conclusions. And, in any case, Timothy will then not become involved in the sins of other men.

Synthesis of Chapter 5

See the Outline at the beginning of this chapter, which may be paraphrased as follows:

As to *those members who are in need of pastoral counseling or correction,* you (Timothy) should deal with them as their age and sex requires:

Admonish an old(er) man as you would a father, young(er) men as brothers, old(er) women as mothers, young(er) women as sisters in all purity.

As to *widows and their distress,* those who are really destitute should be honored and assisted in every way. They should receive both moral and physical support. The Object of their constant hope and prayer will by means of the church provide for them.

However, there are also widows who have children or grandchildren that can support them. These should discharge that debt which they owe to those who brought them up. God is pleased with this. If they neglect their duty, they are worse than infidels. It is the widow who has no means of support who should be assisted *by the church.*

There are some widows, however, who are living luxuriously. These, though physically alive, are spiritually dead. It is not even necessary to add that such widows do not deserve to be honored by the church. Constantly stress these regulations regarding the duty of the church and of children and grandchildren toward widows.

Now as to *widows and their work,* in order to qualify for such work as giving good counsel to younger women, preparing them for baptism, taking them to communion, giving guidance to orphans, etc. (this is a *conjecture* as to the nature of their work), such widows must not be less than sixty years of age, must have been faithful wives, wise mothers, good hosts, kind benefactresses; in fact, must have given proof of fitness for such a position.

For this type of work you must *not* engage *young* widows, for experience has shown that in many cases these become restless and break the work-pledge which they have made to the church, thereby incurring guilt. Also, they often place social affairs above kingdom-affairs, so that when they make the rounds of the various homes, ostensibly to help and to guide, they actually do nothing but gossip and meddle in other people's affairs. Thus they do more harm than good, and scandals will arise. Now these should be prevented by all means. Hence, instead of being engaged for such kingdom-work, let young widows fulfil their natural desire. When a good opportunity presents itself, let them marry again. Let them have a family and manage it properly. This is honorable, and will remove suspicion and slander. It is necessary that I add this, for I know of certain widows who have turned aside from the honorable course in order to follow *Satan.*

Nevertheless, this does not mean that for young widows there is no opportunity to perform kingdom-work. There is work for everyone, also for every woman. For example, if there be any believing woman of means, who stands in some relation of responsibility toward widows in distress, let her assist them, so that the church may not be burdened but may be better able to help those widows who are not being supported by anyone.

As to *elders and prospective elders,* note the following:

An elder should be honored for the sake of his office; and he should receive *double* honor if he does his work well. This holds with special emphasis with respect to "ministers," men who labor in preaching and teaching. Respect them highly and provide generously for them, for the Scripture says:

"A threshing ox you shall not muzzle" (Deut. 25:4)
and
"Worthy of his pay is the worker" (Luke 10:7).

As to an accusation against an elder, it should not even be entertained unless it is supported by two or three witnesses. But if the wrong has been definitely established, the man who committed it must be reproved in the presence of the entire consistory, so that the remaining elders may become filled with godly fear of wrong-doing. Now in connection with all such matters I charge you in the sight of God and of Christ Jesus and of the elect angels that you observe these instructions without prejudice. You must never allow yourself to be influenced by subjective considerations. Do not be in a hurry to ordain a man. Then you will not be co-responsible for the wrongs which he may afterward commit. Keep yourself pure. (Incidentally, take care of your body also. No longer drink water only, but use a little wine for the sake of your stomach and your frequent ailments.)

In connection with men who are being considered for office, you need not be unduly concerned *if you exercise due caution.* In the case of men who are *unfit,* their *sins,* which render them unfit, are often evident even before an investigation into their character is begun; and if they are not evident *before,* they will become evident *upon* investigation. And in the case of men who are *fit,* their *noble deeds,* which show that they are qualified, are generally clearly evident even prior to investigation; and if not before, then afterward.

Outline of Chapter 6

Theme: *The Apostle Paul, Writing to Timothy, Gives Directions For the Administration of the Church*

Directions with respect to
Certain Definite Groups and Individuals (continued)

6:1, 2	E.	Slaves
6:3-10	F.	Novelty-teachers who aspire to fame and riches
6:11-16	G.	Timothy himself ("Keep the commission!")
6:17-19	H.	People who are rich in terms of this present age
6:20, 21	I.	Timothy himself ("Guard the deposit!")

CHAPTER VI

6 1 Let as many as are under (the) yoke, namely, slaves, regard their own [89] masters as worthy of all honor, in order that the name of God and the doctrine be not reviled. 2 And those who have believing masters, let them not, because these (masters) are brothers, look down upon them, but let them serve all the better because *believers* are the latter and *beloved ones,* who reciprocate this kind service. These things teach and urge.

Continuing his admonitions with respect to groups within the Christian community, Paul says:

6:1, 2

1. Let as many as are under (the) yoke, namely slaves, regard their own masters as worthy of all honor.

It is clear that in *this* passage the word used in the original (δοῦλοι) means *slaves,* not *servants.* It frequently has the latter meaning, and even in the present passage the apostle is trying his level best to change the *slave* into a beloved *servant.* (See further N.T.C. on John, Vol. II, p. 306, footnote 184.) In our passage, then, he starts out by talking about real *slaves,* as is clear from the fact that he defines the concept by saying, "as many as are under (the) yoke." The power of a master over his slave was almost absolute, like that over his *yoke*-animals.

The Roman world was full of slaves. It has been estimated that in Rome itself at one time about a third of the inhabitants belonged to this social class! They had become slaves: a. as prisoners of war, or b. as condemned men, or c. through debt, or d. through kidnaping (which evil reportedly is still continuing in certain parts of the world) or, e. as those who had been sold into slavery by their parents. Besides, many *were born* into slavery. Often slaves had their own slaves.

Among all these slaves there were some who had attained to a degree – sometimes a *high* degree – of culture. Not only the barber, the butler, and the cook but even the family-physician might be "under the yoke."

Roman law did not forbid the master to treat his slaves harshly. They could be condemned to hard labor, chained, severely lashed, branded upon the forehead (for instance, if they were considered thieves or runaways),

---

[89] Or simply "their," for ἴδιος (here ἰδίους) has lost some of its force.

or even crucified. Public opinion, however, often asserted itself as a kind of restraint upon intolerable unfairness and cruelty. Besides, in several recorded instances Romans treated their subordinates with eminent fairness, providing liberally for them, and even becoming their friends (cf., for example, the friendship of Pliny for his "slave" Zosimus). Manumission was not uncommon. A slave might be permitted to buy his freedom with a sum of money which he had been able gradually to accumulate through the liberality of the master or as a result of "extra" services, and which by this slave was then, amid ceremonies occurring on the day of emancipation, given to the god, from whom, as it were, he received his freedom and to whom he felt himself thereafter forever indebted. Often slaves were set free by the master's last will.

With the entrance of the Christian religion into the fabric of Roman society, difficult problems arose. It is not surprising, therefore, that Paul deals with various phases of slavery in passages such as the one now under consideration and also in Eph. 6:5-9; Col. 3:22-4:1; Titus 2:9; and in the letter to Philemon.

His way toward a solution commends itself by reason of its evident wisdom. It avoids extremes which would have resulted in much harm both to the slave and to his master, and would have reflected dishonor upon the cause of the Christian religion. *He advocated neither outright revolt by the slaves nor the continuation of the status quo.* Instead of recommending either of these he aimed by the law of indirection to destroy *the very essence* of slavery, with all its attendant evils. This method, though for a while maintaining "slavery" in outward form, was, nevertheless, the surest and most commendable way of working toward the final goal of complete abolition of this gruesome, inhuman institution. It aimed to destroy slavery without waging a war to do so! "Let the slave honor his master, and let the master be kind to his slave. Let both bear in mind that with God there is no respect of persons." That was the principle. Thus the ill-will, dishonesty, and laziness of many slaves would be replaced by willing service, integrity, and industry. Thus also the cruelty and brutality of many masters would melt into kindness and love. The grace of Christ, working *from within outward* — which is ever the way of the kingdom of God! — would become a penetrating leaven, tending to transform the whole lump.

Let then those who are under the yoke regard their *masters* (plural of "despot," cf. II Tim. 2:21; Titus 2:9, a word which even more than *kurios* stresses the *authority* which the slave-owner wielded over his slave) [90]

---

[90] See on these synonyms R. C. Trench, *Synonyms Of The New Testament,* par. xxviii. Because of the stress which this word "despot" places on unrestricted authority it is also used with respect to *God* (Luke 2:29; Acts 4:24; Rev. 6:10) and *Christ* (II Peter 2:1; Jude 4).

as worthy of all *honor* (see footnote 82). Whenever it is at all possible thus to respect the master, let the slave do so, **in order that the name of God and the doctrine be not reviled** (literally, *be not blasphemed;* for the related noun, *blasphemy,* see on I Tim. 6:4). God's redemptive revelation in Christ, in other words God's *name,* and also his *instruction,* the teaching of the gospel, would become contemptible in the eyes of the masters if the slaves treated them with disdain and the spirit of rebellion. And nothing is more important than God's *name* and his *doctrine!* These must not be exposed to ridicule or abuse (cf. Is. 52:5; Rom. 2:24).

2. A peculiar problem presented itself with respect to believing slaves who had *believing* masters. Says Paul: **And those who have believing masters, let them not, because these (masters) are brothers, look down upon them, but let them serve all the better because believers are the latter and beloved ones, who reciprocate this kind service.**

A Christian slave who had a Christian master might be inclined to say in his heart, "If my master is really a Christian, how can he keep me *as his slave?* His religion must not amount to very much. Besides, how can I be *equal* to my master *in church* (Gal. 3:28), and yet *inferior* to him *at home?"* Such an attitude would lead to trouble all around. So the apostle recommends the very opposite attitude: if the slave is in an exceptionally privileged position, having a believing master, let him render exceptional service! Christian masters are *brothers* in Christ. They are *believers, beloved, loved* both by their fellow-believers and by God (see N.T.C. on I Thess. 2:8). And not only for *this* reason should slaves serve such masters all the better, but also because the latter are gentle and considerate. Christian employers are the ones who "reciprocate [91] this *kind service"* (literally, *the good deed*). They are *taking upon themselves* (λαμβανόμενοι) the responsibility of giving *a return* (ἀντί; hence the entire participle is ἀντίλαμβανόμενοι) for the ready and enthusiastic co-operation of their slaves. But shall we still say *slaves;* have not the *slaves* become *servants* now?

These things teach and urge (Or: *keep teaching and urging*).

---

[91] In the New Testament this verb occurs three times (in the middle voice). In Luke 1:54 and Acts 20:35 it means *to help* (probably: to take hold of by oneself *in turn;* but see A. T. Robertson, Gram. N.T. for a different explanation). Very closely related to this is the meaning which may be ascribed to the verb here in I Tim. 6:2: *to re-ciprocate.* Thus, justice is done to the idea contained in the prefix ἀντί.

Interpretations which I cannot accept are:

(1) *to be devoted to, exert oneself in.* This wanders too far away from the idea contained in the prefix.

(2) *to benefit by.* The translation proposed is, "because those who benefit by their service are believers and beloved." But this changes a predicate into a subject. The clause "who reciprocate this kind of service" is clearly in the predicate, in apposition with "believers" and "beloved," which words are in the predicate position.

What Paul has been saying with reference to slaves (in verses 1 and 2) must be dinned into the ears of the people. Timothy must *teach* these things. However, not only upon *the minds* of the people and of their presbyters must he make an impression but also upon their *wills.* He must *urge* as well as *teach* these things. In *this* connection the present imperatives for both verbs probably point in the direction of the necessity of constant repetition: *keep on teaching* and *keep on urging.* The second verb has the basic meaning: to call to one's side. See also I Tim. 1:3; 2:1; 5:1; II Tim. 4:2; Titus 1:9; 2:6; 2:15. Derived meanings are: to appeal to or to entreat, to admonish, to exhort, to urge, to encourage or to comfort. Here the meaning *urge* best fits the context.

What is especially important in this connection is that, wholly contrary to certain present-day trends, the apostle is definitely *not* of the opinion that all propositions touching religion and ethics are necessarily subjective and relative, and that the only justifiable method of arriving at some measure of truth is that of *asking questions, such as,* "Brother Brown, what do you think of this?" and "Brother Smith, what is your opinion about that?" *Paul has accepted certain definite propositions which he considers to be the truth of God! He wants these to be taught! And he requests that Timothy urge their acceptance and application to life!* See also 4:11 and 5:7.

---

3 If anyone teaches differently and does not come over to the sound words of our Lord Jesus Christ and to the doctrine that harmonizes with godliness, 4 he is blinded with conceit, knowing nothing, but possessed with a morbid craving for controversies and word-battles, (the sources) out of which proceed envy, wrangling, revilings, base suspicions, 5 and mutual altercations between men depraved in mind and deprived of the truth, who imagine that the (practice of) godliness is gain.

6 And it *is* a great gain, namely, the (practice of) godliness *with soul-sufficiency.*[92] 7 For nothing did we bring into the world, (just as it is evident) that neither are we able to carry anything out of it. 8 But having nourishment and shelter, we shall regard these as sufficient.[93]

9 But those who are eager to be rich fall into temptation and a snare and numerous senseless and hurtful cravings, such as plunge the members of the human race into ruin and destruction. 10 For, a root of all the evils is the love of money, and some people, reaching out after it, have wandered away from the faith, and have pierced themselves with numerous pangs.

6:3-10

3-5. If anyone teaches differently and does not come over to the sound words of our Lord Jesus Christ and to the doctrine that harmonizes with godliness, he is blinded with conceit.

---

[92] Or: "with contentment." See also footnote 94.
[93] Or: "with these we shall be content."

From the sound and intensely practical doctrine of Paul – samples of which have just been given – to the unfruitful disputations of false teachers, was, indeed, a far cry. The very contrast causes Paul to return to the subject of chapter 1 (see especially in that chapter verses 3-7, 19, 20). Note the similarity between the two paragraphs:

Chapter 1:	Chapter 6:
certain individuals (verse 3)	anyone (verse 3)
teaching differently (verse 3)	teaching differently (verse 3)
disputes (verse 4)	controversies (verse 4)
sound doctrine (verse 10)	sound words (verse 3)

Novelty-teachers and hair-splitters! The apostle was fully acquainted with them. He emphasizes that any peddler of ponderous platitudes about the law of Moses, any specialist in specious speculations about ancestors, is "blinded with conceit." Such a person is "full of smoke," besmoked, befogged, beclouded (see on I Tim. 3:6). Two ideas are combined here: moral-spiritual *denseness* and *conceit*. The first is the result of the second. This description is true with respect to every dissenter who "does not *come over to* the sound words of our Lord Jesus Christ." The verb used in the original (προσέρχεται which is favored by textual evidence both internal and external) has here a meaning not far removed from its primary sense: *come to, approach*. Here it seems to mean *come over to*, that is, *join, fall in with*. This is a little stronger than *consent to* or *agree with*. A *mere* listener may mentally *agree with* the words of a speaker. An *enthusiastic* listener will *come over to* or *join* the speaker. He will not only *agree*, but he will *express* that agreement. He will "chime in." He will eagerly come to the same fountain and will drink the same water. He will take to heart and will begin to proclaim "the sound words of our Lord Jesus Christ," the pure and perfect "unimpaired," "uninfected," and in that sense "healthy," "sound" *truths* which issued from Christ's mouth and were exemplified in his life and death. Viewed as a whole, these "words" constitute "the doctrine that harmonizes with godliness." This doctrine is the expression of the inner attitude of "complete devotion to God," that is, of *godliness* (for this noun see on I Tim. 2:2; 3:16; 4:7, 8; 6:5, 6, 11; II Tim. 3:5; Titus 1:1. Cf. the verb, I Tim. 5:4; and the adverb, II Tim. 3:12; Titus 2:12).

Now the person who, in his blind conceit and obstinate dissent refuses to come over to such doctrine which tallies with godliness, is prevented from knowing anything. Living in a mental, moral, and spiritual world of his own making, he is now completely out of touch with reality. Hence, Paul continues: **knowing nothing, but possessed with a morbid craving for controversies and word-battles, (the sources) out of which proceed envy, wrangling, revilings, base suspicions, and mutual altercations between men depraved in mind and deprived of the truth.**

When a person rejects *sound* or *healthy* words, *sickness* results. This sickness reveals itself in a "morbid craving for controversies and word-battles" (see on I Tim. 1:4). The man stricken with such a disease will make mountains out of molehills. Somewhat after the fashion illustrated in The Talmud, he will get "all excited" about questions like this one, "Is it permissible on the Sabbath to throw away the pits of dates?" One person might answer, "The pits of dates to which some of the meat adheres may be thrown away. Other pits must not be thrown away." Another person would disagree and express his contrary opinion in no uncertain terms. Again, the question might be asked, "If it be permissible to throw them away, *where* and *how* should they be thrown?" And the answer might be, "They should be thrown outside." To which another might reply, "No, indeed, they should be thrown under the bed." Or, he might say, "The person confronted on the Sabbath with the problem of what to do with datepits should turn his face toward the back of the bed and throw out the pits with his tongue."

At times a mere *name* of some ancestor might start a controversy. The name might be changed into several anagrams, one anagram suggesting this, the other that. Or, the name might cause one to recall a story which had been transmitted by oral tradition. But *one* story would contradict *another* story, and this, too, might lead to a heated argument.

Thus, broken cisterns which hold no water would be substituted for the living fountain of God's Word.[94]

Some people seem to take delight in such quibbling, such, *word-battles*. Hence, Paul sets forth its bitter fruits:

a. *envy*. One disputant, smarting under defeat, begins to waste away. He is filled with malignant ill will, with poisonous spite against the victor.

b. *wrangling*. This results from envy. The person who was worsted in the argument is unwilling to admit defeat. Bitter discord follows. One man is constantly contradicting the other. If we were to speak in the language of mythology, we might say that Eris, the goddess of strife, who was considered to be closely related to Ares, the god of war, has a field-day.

---

[94] One might compare the largely futile controversies in Reformed circles — only yesterday! — between extreme Infralapsarians and extreme Supralapsarians. Or, the still continuing "hot" debates about the age of the earth.

Now in discussions of this nauseating character the two opponents sometimes *mean* the same thing, but *express* it differently. To use a present-day illustration, one man may assert, "Obtaining salvation is *conditioned* on faith." Another insists with equal firmness, "Scripture recognizes *no conditions.*" Yet, if only the first disputant would be ready to admit that God supplies what he demands, so that the exercise of faith is ever the result of the divine gift; and if only the second disputant would be willing to grant that (at least in the case of those who have arrived at years of discretion) the exercise of faith is *indispensable* unto salvation, and that it is *man* — not God — who believes, it would soon become clear that the dispute was *a battle of words.*

c. *revilings.* The Greek word used is *blasphemies.* But in Greek this word has a somewhat broader meaning than in English. While in our language it refers to abusive language with respect to God or things religious, that is, to *defiant irreverence* (see on verse 1 above), in the original it refers to insults directed either against God or against man. In the present instance the latter is clearly meant: scornful and insolent language directed against a human opponent, slander, defamation.

d. *base suspicions.* "All looks yellow to the jaundiced eye" (Pope). The mind of the envious individual is haunted by mistrust and foreboding. He begins to suspect his opponent's every action, word, and even gesture. He imagines that there is "an occult reason" behind every move of the person whom he considers his adversary. This disease, moreover, is contagious.

e. *mutual altercations* or *incessant frictions.* When the "mad" novelty-dispenser meets his opponent again, to discuss other "religious" matters, he either glares and glowers, or else he smoulders within but puts on an act by the seeming imperviousness of his demeanor. Underneath, however, he "boils." He is vengefully nettled, convulsively agitated, thirsting for "blood." The two men *"rub* each other the wrong way" (note root-idea in the original). Their "religious" discussions frequently assume the nature of *diatribes,* in the unfavorable sense of that term (in the original "dia-para-tribes"). Such disputations are full of scurrilous abuse, stinging insult, and heated invective, or else of covert insinuation, malicious innuendo, and thinly veiled disdain.

Such conduct and its bitter fruits mark the men who are "depraved in mind and deprived of the truth." It is God himself who endowed man with intelligence, so that he is able to reflect on the higher things of life. Yet, with respect to this precious gift, namely, the intelligence, the errorists at Ephesus and vicinity have corrupted themselves, so that they have now entered the *abiding* state of being "depraved in mind." The depraved mind opposes the truth and welcomes the lie, until at last those who possess such a mind become completely and permanently separated from *the truth:* God's objective revelation as revealed in his Word. Envy, wrangling, revilings, base suspicions, and mutual altercations lead to mental, moral, and spiritual *sterility.* Those who practise such things are so completely occupied with themselves and their own interests that in their hearts there is neither time nor room for God and his revealed truth. This selfishness is clear also from the fact that the apostle describes them as being men **who imagine that the (practice of) godliness is gain.** For the sake of *becoming rich* (not merely for the sake of gaining a livelihood) they outwardly practise "godliness." They make a show of their "religion" (see on I Tim. 3:16). In the meantime they charge exorbitant fees for the "instruction"(?) which they impart. (For Paul's attitude with respect to the question of receiving remuneration for evangelistic labor see N.T.C. on I and II Thessalonians, pp. 66, 67.)

6, 7. The *truly* godly person is not interested in becoming rich. He possesses *inner resources* which furnish riches far beyond that which earth can offer. Hence, with respect to this genuine godly life Paul continues: **And it *is* great gain, namely, the (practice of) godliness *with soul-sufficiency.*** This is the life of true devotion to God. It is "of benefit in every way," (see on I Tim. 4:8). Such Christian living springs from the source of – and is accompanied by – *soul-sufficiency.*[95]

The truly pious individual has peace with God, spiritual joy, assurance of salvation, the conviction that "to them that love God all things work together for good, even to them that are called according to his purpose" (Rom. 8:28). Hence, he feels no need of "ample (earthly!) goods stored up for many years," which can never satisfy *the soul* (Luke 12:19, 20). He is *content* with what he has. Cf. Phil. 4:10-13. **For,** earthly possessions do not pertain to the "self," which is clear from the fact that **nothing did we bring into the world, (just as it is evident) that** [96] **neither are we able to carry anything out of it.**

---

[95] The word used in the original might be more literally translated "self-sufficiency" were it not for the fact that in English this word is ambiguous, as it may be used either in a favorable sense (inherent and adequate capacity for this or that activity) or in an unfavorable sense (self-satisfaction or extreme self-confidence). Used in the unfavorable sense, the antonym of the English word would be *humility.* In the favorable sense, its antonym is *spiritual impotence* or *soul-poverty.* It is in the favorable sense that the word is employed in the New Testament. By an easy transition this admirable *soul-sufficiency* begins to include the element of *contentment.* New Testament occurrences: only here and in II Cor. 9:8.

[96] Literally, the original reads, "For, nothing did we bring into the world, ὅτι neither are we able to carry anything out of it." The question is, Just what must we do with the particle ὅτι? Proposed solutions:

(1) The particle is superfluous (E. F. Scott).

Objection: This is an easy way out. Scott does not explain how that superfluous word crept in, nor how it is that even the earliest attempts to "correct" the text *retained* the particle.

(2) The particle should be taken in the causal sense: "Because we are not able to carry anything out of the world, we did not bring anything into it" (Along this line Belser, Weiss, Lenski).

Objection: This fits neither the present thought-connection nor the evident source of the saying in the Old Testament.

(3) The particle is recitative or has the meaning "for the proverb says." This is mentioned by Lock as one of several possibilities.

Objection: In that case we would have expected it at the beginning (and not in the middle) of the paraphrase from the Old Testament.

(4) ὅτι οὐδε should be οὐδ' ὅτι: "not to speak of being able to carry anything out." (This is favored by Parry; cf. also Lock.)

Objection: This, too, is not in keeping with the evident Old Testament source of the saying. Besides, it has the textual evidence against it. The textual evidence, both external and internal, favors not only the retention of ὅτι but also its position before οὐδε, exactly as the text of N.N. has it.

(5) The two clauses of the compound sentence are loosely co-ordinated, so that ὅτι must here be construed as meaning something like "just as." This is the solution proposed by Dibelius and Bouma.

The apostle is clearly thinking of Job's famous saying, "Naked came I out of my mother's womb, and naked shall I return" (Job 1:21; cf. Eccl. 5:14, 15).

8. Hence, we shall not strive after earthly riches. **But having nourishment and shelter, we shall regard these as sufficient** (or: *with these we shall be content*).

For "nourishment and shelter" the original has the plural (cf. "victuals and coverings"). Our word "nourishment" is sufficiently comprehensive to include all the articles of food that are necessary to support physical life, just as our word "shelter" indicates whatever is necessary for the outward protection of the body. The rendering "food and *clothing*" is less exact. The original ("shelter" or "coverings") in all probability, includes *the dwelling* in which a man resides as well as *the garment* which he wears. The Lord does not demand of us that, having clothing, we do not even look for a tent or a house in which to live. The desire to meet *the needs* of the body is not criticized. It is the yearning for *material riches,* as if these could satisfy the soul, that is here condemned, as is evident also from that which follows, namely,

9. But those who are eager to be rich fall into temptation and a snare and numerous senseless and hurtful cravings.

Paul does not condemn "desire" as such. He is not a Stoic but a Christian. What he condemns is the desire *to be rich.* Such people fall into *temptation.* (The word in the original means either *trial* or *temptation.* Classic example illustrating first the one and then the other meaning is James 1:2, 12. In the present instance the meaning *temptation* is clear from the context.) As a *snare* (see on I Tim. 3:7) keeps an animal imprisoned, so the ungovernable passion for wealth fastens its clutching tentacles about "those who pant after the dust of the earth" (Am. 2:7). Cf. Ps. 39:6; Prov. 28:20; Matt. 6:19-21, 24-26; 19:24; James 5:1-6.

Moreover, Sin never walks alone. The desire to become rich causes the man who, in today's terminology, is "an incarnation of fat dividends" to fall into numerous cravings. One kind of craving easily leads to another.

Comment: This solution is not open to the objections advanced against the others. It may be the correct one. It is either this or (6), with little difference in resultant meaning.

(6) We have here another instance of abbreviated expression. Note elliptical use of ὅτι in John 6:46 (see N.T.C. on John, Vol. I, pp. 54, 206). Fully rendered, the thought might be reproduced as follows: "For, nothing did we bring into the world, *just as it is evident* that neither are we able to carry anything out of it" (the words in italics being implied). While later texts wrongly inserted the word *evident* or *true,* as if the original contained such a word, they probably correctly discerned the thought which the apostle (who often abbreviates!) intended to convey. See also A.V., based on Textus Receptus.

The person who craves riches generally also yearns for honor, popularity, power, ease, the satisfaction of the desires of the flesh, etc. All spring from the same root, selfishness, which, being the worst possible method of *really* satisfying the "self," is both senseless and hurtful (cf. Matt. 20:26-28; see N.T.C. on John 12:25, 26).

In the original the sentence is conspicuous by virtue of its beautiful alliteration. The constantly recurring letter p (π) strikes the eye and then the ear, and probably serves to fix the saying more firmly in the mind, as if we were to say:

"Those who desire to be opulent precipitate themselves into evil promptings and perilous pitfalls and into numerous precarious passions."

These cravings, passions, or lusts of which the apostle speaks are described as **such as plunge the members of the human race into ruin and destruction.**

Instead of the *gain* which they were seeking (see verse 5), the men whose hearts are set on riches experience only *loss*. In the original the words *ruin* and *destruction* are both derived from a verb whose secondary meaning is *to lose*.

Note the progressive and climactic character of the movement which is portrayed here. First, these men are described as *desiring* the wrong thing, namely, material wealth. Soon they lose their footing and *fall* into temptation and a snare and numerous senseless and hurtful cravings. Finally, these cravings *plunge* them into ruin and destruction. Wretched men! They have guided their vessel to the very brink of the cataract, which, in its turn, plunges them into the awesome depths. For examples see the next verse.

10. The situation as described is correct, **For a root of all the evils is the love of money.**[97]

The apostle does not say that the love of money is *the* (one and only) root of all existing evils, but that it is *a* root. Though it is true that a word does not always have to be preceded by the article *the* to be definite, it surely is not wise to apply the exception when this would bring Paul's words into conflict with the facts of daily experience and with other passages of Scripture. There are other roots or sources of evil besides the love of money, for example, "bitterness" (Heb. 12:15; cf. also James 1:15). But avarice is, indeed, *a* root "of all the evils," or "of all kinds of evil." It caused the man with very many flocks and herds (in Nathan's parable) to steal the poor man's one little ewe lamb, the rich young ruler to turn away from Christ, the rich fool (of Christ's parable) to deceive himself into think-

---

[97] The inspired saying reminds one of others, for example: "The love of money is *the metropolis of every evil* (or: of all the evils)," which has been ascribed to Bion and to Democritus; and "Expel *avarice, the mother of all wickedness,* who, always thirsty for more, opens wide her jaws of gold" (Claudianus). That Paul was "undoubtedly quoting" a current secular proverb cannot be proved.

ing that all was well, the rich man (of another parable told by the Lord) to neglect poor Lazarus, Judas to betray his master and commit suicide, Ananias and Sapphira to tell lies, and the rich oppressors of James' epistle (cf. Amos 2:6, 7) to exploit those who worked for them. None of these escaped punishment. The desire for riches, moreover, has been the cause of innumerable frauds, dollar-sign marriages, divorces, perjuries, robberies, poisonings, murders, and wars. And in the heart of man this sinful craving has led to "numerous pangs" (see below).

In the present connection Paul is thinking especially of church-members, as is also clear from what follows: **and some people, reaching out after it,[98] have wandered away from the faith, and have pierced themselves with numerous pangs.**

People who thus *reach out after* (or "aspire after," see on I Tim. 3:1) money are like the *planets.* They have *wandered* away from, literally "*planeted* away from" (ἀπεπλανήθησαν) the faith. The word *planet* means *wanderer,* for that is exactly what a planet is. Not in the sense that the earth or the other planets are "thrown out of their appointed orbits." Their orbits have been fixed, so that it is possible by means of six or seven "elements of a planetary orbit" to predict exactly where in the sky each planet will be. But in relation to the "fixed" stars, the planets, revolving around the sun, seem to wander about. This accounts for their name.

Now it is from *the faith,* the truth as confessed by the church (for this objective sense of the term *faith* see p. 11), that these people have wandered away. They have gone astray in inner attitude, in outward conduct, and even in the profession of the lips, that is, in the things which they are now teaching. But in so doing they have pierced themselves (as a man pierces himself with a spear) with *numerous pangs.* Among these pangs are unrest, boredom, dissatisfaction, gloom, envy. — In the pocket of a rich man who had just committed suicide was found $30,000 and a letter which read in part: "I have discovered during my life that piles of money do not bring happiness. I am taking my life because I can no longer stand the solitude and boredom. When I was an ordinary workman in New York, I was happy. Now that I possess millions I am infinitely sad and prefer death" (Quoted by W. A. Maier, *For Better Not For Worse,* p. 223).

---

98 Literally, "*which* (ἧς) some reaching out after," etc. Cf. A.V. and A.R.V. The question is, To what does ἧς refer? Some interpreters (C. Bouma, R. C. H. Lenski) answer that it refers to φιλαργυρία. Bouma explains this as follows: consciously these avaricious people reach out after *money,* but unconsciously they reach out after *the love of money.* — But relative pronouns (especially in Koine Greek) are flexible. The rules which govern them are not at all rigid. Hence, the more natural explanation is to be preferred. Though grammatically ἧς agrees with φιλαργυρία yet in actual meaning it refers to ἀργύριον, which concept by the mind has been abstracted from φιλαργυρία. Thus also N. J. D. White (*The Expositor's Greek Testament,* Vol. IV, p. 144).

11 But you, O man of God, flee away from these things, and run after righteousness, godliness, faith, love, endurance, gentleness. 12 Fight the noble fight of the faith; take hold of that everlasting life to which you were called when you confessed the beautiful confession [99] in the presence of many witnesses. 13 In the presence of God who endues all things with life, and of Christ Jesus who while testifying before Pontius Pilate made the beautiful confession,[100] 14 I charge you to keep the commission [101] without spot and above reproach until the appearing of our Lord Jesus Christ, 15 which in due season [102] he will display, (even he) the blessed and only Sovereign, the King of kings and Lord of lords, 16 the only One possessing immortality, dwelling in light unapproachable, whom no human being has (ever) seen or is able to see; to whom (be) honor and strength eternal. Amen.

6:11-16

11. Over against the vices which Paul has just condemned (see verses 3-10) stand the virtues which Timothy is urged to cultivate: **But you, O man of God, flee away from these things, and run after righteousness, faith, love, endurance, gentleness.**

Timothy is urged to *flee away from* such things as wickedness, gold-hunger, error, envy, wrangling, reviling; and to *run after, pursue* or *eagerly seek after* (see N.T.C. on I Thess. 5:15; cf. Rom. 12:13; I Cor. 14:1; Phil. 3:12) their opposites, namely, righteousness, godliness, faith, love, endurance, gentleness. This befits him as a "man of God." In the old dispensation this was a designation of the person who by God had been entrusted with a high office (Moses, Deut. 33:1; Ps. 90:1; David, II Chron. 8:14; Elijah, II Kings 1:9; the prophets, I Sam. 2:27). In the new dispensation, now that *every* believer is viewed as a partaker of the anointing of the Holy One, and therefore as a prophet, priest, and king (I John 2:20; cf. I Peter 2:9), the description is used with respect to any and every believer, as is clear from II Tim. 3:17. And surely, if *every* Christian is a "man of God," Timothy, having been placed in a position of great responsibility, is this in a special sense. Now a "man of God" is God's peculiar possession, his special ambassador. He is, accordingly, the very opposite of the man whose owner is Mammon, whose commands he obeys.

Timothy, then, as a "man of God," must *"run after" righteousness,*[103] the state of heart and mind which is in harmony with God's law, and will lead

---

[99] Literally, "to which you were called and confessed the beautiful (or *excellent* or *noble*) confession."
[100] Literally, "who witnessed (or *attested*) before Pontius Pilate the beautiful confession."
[101] Or, "the precept," "the mandate." See N.T.C. on John, Vol. II, pp. 252, 253.
[102] Or, "in its (or his) own season." See also footnote 105.
[103] I have tried thus to reproduce both the sense of the original and the alliteration: *r* un after *r* ighteousness represents δίωκε δικαιοσύνην. Thus also in II Tim. 2:22.

to godliness, the godly life, truly pious conduct. "Faith, love, and *endurance*" belong together [104] (Titus 2:2; cf. II Tim. 3:10 then I Thess. 1:3) just like "faith, love, and *hope*" (Col. 1:4, 5; cf. "faith, hope, and love," I Cor. 13:13), for *endurance* is the fruit of *hope* (I Thess. 1:3). It is the grace *to bear up under* adversities; for example, persecution. It amounts to *stedfastness* no matter what may be the cost, in the full assurance of future victory. (For a word-study of *endurance* and its synonyms see N.T.C. on I Thess. 1:3; 5:14 – footnote 108 – ; II Thess. 1:4; 3:5). As to *faith,* this concept is here used in the subjective sense, active reliance on God and his promises. And *love,* with Paul, is broad as the ocean, having as its object God in Christ, believers, and in a sense "everyone" (I Tim. 1:5, 14; 2:15; 4:12; II Tim. 1:7, 13; 2:22; 3:10; Titus 2:2; cf. I Thess. 3:12). When these virtues are present, *gentleness* of spirit will certainly result. The word thus translated is found only here in the Greek Bible. Comparison with II Tim. 3:10 indicates that it is akin in meaning to *longsuffering* (patience with respect to persons).

12. Comparing the Christian life with a contest, the apostle continues his admonition in these words: **Fight the noble fight of the faith.** The sense is that Timothy must *continue to* fight this noble fight, just as he must *continue to* flee away from the vices of his opponents and to pursue the opposite virtues. It is true that literally the words in the original are: "*Contend* (in) the noble *contest* of the faith," and that the word *contest* (ἀγών, a. *gathering,* especially for games or contests; b. the *contest* itself; c. the *agony,* anguish or anxiety that is connected with it; and d. agony, anguish, anxiety, concern or *solicitude,* in general) may refer to *any* kind of contest or conflict, whether physical – for example, a *race* (Heb. 12:1) – or spiritual (Phil. 1:30; Col. 2:1; and see N.T.C. on I Thess. 2:2). It is also true, however, that when *Paul* (in distinction from the author of the epistle to the Hebrews) is comparing the Christian life with a *race,* he makes this very clear by using such words as *running, race, stadium* (I Cor. 9:24; II Tim. 4:7). It is safe to conclude that when he compares the Christian life with any *contest* (using either the noun or the verb or both) except a *race,* the underlying figure is that of a *boxing-bout* or *wrestling-match* or something similar (see especially I Cor. 9:24-27). Therefore, the rendering, "Fight the good fight of the faith" (A.R.V., R.S.V., cf. A.V.) is not really wrong but approaches very nearly what the apostle had in mind. The passage, I Tim. 6:12, reminds one of the slightly different figure. "War the good (or *noble* or *excellent*) warfare" (I Tim. 1:18). (For Paul's use of metaphors borrowed from the sphere of athletics see on I Tim. 4:7b, 8.)

---

[104] Hence, I cannot agree here with Meinertz, Wohlenberg, and Lenski who divide the six into three groups of two each.

In distinction from the *word-battles* of the opponents (see on I Tim. 6:4), Timothy must carry on the *noble* fight that springs from and is inspired by his *faith* (probably the same sense as in the preceding verse).

Paul continues: **take hold of that everlasting life to which you were called when you confessed the beautiful confession in the presence of many witnesses.**

By putting up a successful fight, one is already *getting a firm grip on* (note the aorist tense now, in distinction from the present in the clause which precedes) *everlasting life.* This life pertains to the *future* age, to be sure, to the realm of glory, but in principle becomes the possession of the believer even here and now. It is actually *ever-lasting,* never-ending, life. Yet, though whenever the life so qualified pertains to man the *quantitative* idea is not excluded, the emphasis is on the *qualitative*: this is the life which manifests itself in fellowship with God, in partaking of his holiness, love, peace, and joy. (See N.T.C. on John 3:16.)

The idea that this everlasting life is here pictured as being *wholly* future – a kind of reward which one does not receive in any degree until the conflict is over –, hardly does justice to the flavor of the imperative, and would also seem to be in conflict with the words which immediately follow: "to which you were called when you confessed the beautiful confession in the presence of many witnesses." Note: *to which,* that is, this calling makes one a possessor of everlasting life. When, on Paul's first missionary journey, Timothy was "called" (both externally and internally), he had in connection with his baptism professed his faith publicly. While even today such a confession is "beautiful," or "noble" (καλή), it must have seemed more so at a time when practically the entire world was opposed to the gospel of Christ.

The admonition, "Fight the noble fight of the faith; take hold of that everlasting life to which you were called," does not imply that Timothy was remiss or lax in carrying out his religious duties. Every believer needs this admonition every day. A *timid* nature like Timothy, confronted with determined and subtle opponents, is especially in need of it. Let Timothy then remember the "many witnesses" who have heard his confession!

13 and 14. With impressive solemnity, which reminds one of I Tim. 5:21, the apostle continues: **In the presence of God who endues all things with life, and of Christ Jesus who while testifying before Pontius Pilate made the beautiful confession, I charge you to keep the commission without spot and above reproach until the appearing of our Lord Jesus Christ.**

Paul says, "I charge," or "I command," that is, "I pass along an authoritative message" (see on I Tim. 1:3; 4:11; 5:7). He presents two reasons why Timothy should do as he has just been told:

(1) Let him not fear for his life, for the charge is given and received under the very eyes of that God who is the Bestower and Preserver of life, the "life-generating" God. Cf. Luke 17:33; Acts 7:19.

(2) Let him remember what *Christ Jesus* (see on I Tim. 1:1; especially footnote 19) did when *he* was testifying before an enemy of the truth. Before Pontius Pilate he stood firm, and, bearing witness before him by *word* and *deed* (Matt. 17:1, 2, 11-31; Mark 15:1-20; Luke 23:1-7, 13-25; John 18:28-19:16), thus made the beautiful confession, thereby proving himself to be "the faithful witness" (Rev. 1:5; 3:14).

Hence, let Timothy *keep* – that is, stand guard over, protect, and preserve – his commission. That *commission, precept,* or *mandate,* comprises *all* that he has been ordered to do with respect to the ministry of the gospel and the government of the church. Cf. I Tim. 6:20; then Matt. 28:20. He must, moreover, take care that his attitude and conduct is such that this commission remains "without spot" (see James 1:27; II Peter 3:14; cf. Eph. 5:27) and "above reproach" (see on I Tim. 3:2; literally, "not to be laid hold of," hence, "irreprehensible," "unassailable").

A similar command comes to all those upon whom similar responsibility has been conferred. Every one must keep his commission untainted and unsullied until the very day of his death, or, if the consummation of the ages should occur before that time – Paul never sets dates; see N.T.C. on I Thess. 5:1, 2 –, then "until the appearing of our Lord Jesus Christ." This *appearing* or *manifestation* is literally Christ's *epiphany,* the first gleam of *the dawn,* namely, that dawn to which the believer looks forward with eager anticipation, *the rising* (never more to set!) of "the sun of righteousness with healing in its wings." Cf. Mal. 1:11; 4:2; Is. 60:1-3; Luke 1:78, 79; Rev. 1:7; and for the word *epiphany* itself see N.T.C. on II Thess. 2:8; and cf. II Tim. 1:10; 4:1, 8; Titus 2:13.

15, 16. With reference to this *appearing* Paul continues: **which in due season he will display, (even he)**

	Old Testament Parallels
a. the blessed and only Sovereign	Deut. 6:4; Ps. 41:13; Is. 40:12-31; Dan. 4:35
b. the King of kings	Ezek. 26:7; Dan. 2:37; Ezra 7:12
and	
c. Lord of lords	Deut. 10:17; Ps. 136:3
d. the only One possessing immortality	Ps. 36:9; Is. 40:28; Dan. 4:34
e. dwelling in light unapproachable	Ex. 24:17; 34:35; Ps. 104:2

f. whom no human being has (ever) seen or is able to see Ex. 33:20; Deut. 4:12; Is. 6:5

g. to whom (be) honor and strength eternal. Amen. Neh. 8:6; Ps. 41:13; 72:19; 89:52

To the two reasons which have been given, indicating why Timothy should "keep the commission without spot and above reproach" a third is now added, but only by implication, namely, that he will receive his reward when Jesus returns in glory. However, the idea of reward for Timothy is pushed into the background by the rapturous contemplation and consequent exaltation of the majestic attributes of the One who, *in due season* (or: "in its – or *his* – own season"),[105] the season designated by the Father from eternity (Acts 1:7; 3:20, 21; cf. Gal. 4:4), will exhibit that great event to which, in a sense, the entire universe looks forward (cf. Rom. 8:19): the *epiphany* or visible shining forth of Jesus Christ upon clouds of glory. Just as, in Paul's thinking, it is *God* (I Cor. 6:14; Eph. 1:20), or more particularly, *God the Father* (Rom. 6:4; Gal. 1:1; cf. I Peter 1:3) who *raises* the Son (though it is also true that Christ arose through his own power, John 10:18), so it is *God* who displays the Son's *epiphany*. He *displays it as proof* (for the verb in this sense see John 2:18) to the world, for this is the public vindication of the Son and of his people.

The doxology in praise of God is one of the finest in Scripture. For its origin one must not look to pagan philosophy. Though some of its phrases have parallels in extra-canonical Jewish literature,[106] it should certainly be

---

[105] The original has the plural "seasons," here as well as in I Tim. 2:6; Titus 1:3. However, this is probably an idiomatic plural, to be rendered as a singular. Cf. for this use Jer. 5:26 (27:26 LXX); see also pl. of χρόνος as used in Luke 20:9; 23:8).

[106] S.BK. III, 656. Commentators have made the following guesses with respect to the origin of this doxology:

1. It was an element in a eucharistic prayer which Paul was wont to utter.
2. It was a Christian adaptation of a synagogue doxology.
3. It was taken from an early Christian hymn.
4. Part of it (especially b. and c.) was derived from pagan sources; particularly from the formulae of the imperial cult.

To begin with the last, the usurpation of divine titles by earthly rulers may have been *one* of several reasons why early Christians spoke of *their* Lord as (the only) King of kings and Lord of lords. See A. Deissmann, *op. cit.*, pp. 362-366. Also E. Stauffer, *Christ and the Caesars* (translated by K. and R. Gregor Smith), Philadelphia, 1955; esp. pp. 95, 150, 240. Over against idols and emperors who *are called* gods, he is the one and only *real* God. I Cor. 8:5, 6 points in that direction. Yet, the title as such was not derived from paganism. The Old Testament was the real source.

As to the suggestions made in 1, 2, and 3, these, even if true, do not point to the *original written* source, which must have been the Old Testament. Between that ultimate source and the mind of Paul there may have been many avenues, both direct and indirect. It should, however, be clear that what we have here in I Tim. 6:15, 16 is not mere copy-work but a spontaneous outburst of praise!

regarded as a spontaneous outburst coming from the heart of a devout believer in Jesus Christ, an apostle who, while he is writing or dictating, is thoroughly conscious of the loving presence of his Lord and who in his youth had made a thorough study of the Old Testament, so that its phraseology was embedded in his soul. The parallels from the Old Testament have already been indicated (see the incomplete list of references above, next to the quoted passage). It is possible to duplicate the sense – and in most cases the very words – of the doxology without departing from the text of the Old Testament. Thus, quoting throughout from the Old Testament, one might paraphrase the doxology as follows:

"the blessed and incomparable One, who does according to his will in the army of heaven and among the inhabitants of the earth, the King of kings and Lord of lords, with whom alone is the fountain of life, who covers himself with light as with a garment, whom no human being shall (ever) be able to see, whose glorious name be blessed forever, Amen and Amen."

It was to be expected that just as the contemplation of the *first* coming of Christ led to a doxology (I Tim. 1:17), so also the meditation upon the *second* coming (here in I Tim. 6:15, 16) would lead to a *similar* and *expanded* doxology.

The present doxology consists of seven terms descriptive of Deity. In the original, as in our translation, a., b., and c. are nouns; d. and e. are participial modifiers; and f. and g. are relative clauses.

As to thought-content, every element in this doxology stresses the transcendence or incomparable greatness of God. He is *Sovereign* (a word applied to human rulers in Luke 1:52; Acts 8:27; and to God in II Macc. 3:24; 12:15; 15:4, 23; but see Dan. 4:35). As Sovereign he is altogether *blessed.* See on I Tim. 1:11. He is, moreover, the *only* Sovereign (cf. Jude 25); hence, absolutely incomparable in his right to do as he pleases, for example, to choose the appropriate season for Christ's epiphany (note preceding context). Thus, "the blessed God" (of I Tim. 1:11) and "the only God" (of I Tim. 1:17) are here combined. Whatever titles *men* may bear, either rightfully or by usurpation, he – *he alone!* – is the real King of kings and Lord of lords. Literally, the original has, "the King of those kinging and the Lord of those lording" (Rev. 17:14; 19:16, used both times with reference to *Christ,* have the simpler form). The lengthened (participial) form probably adds freshness and vigor to the meaning.

Having set forth God's relation to the universe and particularly to all earthly rulers, Paul in the last four terms (d., e., f., and g.) dwells on the divine essence itself, the majestic *being* of God.

He alone possesses *immortality.* This must not be confused with "endless existence." To be sure, that, too, is implied, but the concept *immortality* is far more exalted. It means that God is life's never-failing Fountain. On the concept *life* as applied to God see N.T.C. on John 1:4. This immortality is the opposite of *death,* as is clear from the derivation of the word both in English and in Greek. *Athanasia* is deathlessness. It is fulness of life, *imperishable* (cf. I Tim. 1:17) blessedness, the inalienable enjoyment of all the divine attributes. The only human beings who, *as far as it is possible for creatures to do so,* share this immortality, and thereby become "partakers of the divine nature" (II Peter 1:4), are *believers,* though also unbelievers *exist* endlessly. It is *through the gospel* that immortality or imperishability was brought to light (II Tim. 1:10). For the believer immortality is therefore a redemptive concept. It is *everlasting salvation.* For God it is *eternal blessedness.* But while the believer *has received* immortality, as one receives a drink of water from a fountain, God *has* it. It belongs to his very being. He *is* himself the Fountain.

The idea of life, implied in immortality, naturally leads to that of *light.* "In him was life, and that life was the light of men" (John 1:4). Now, this light is like the sun. We need it to see by, yet we cannot look into it, for it is too intensely brilliant. In that sense, God, too, dwells in light *unapproachable.* The metaphor is even stronger than that employed in Ps. 104:2 ("He covers himself with light as with a garment"). Like a dwelling conceals its occupants, and hides them even more when it is *unapproachable,* so God's very essence, by virtue of what it is, conceals him. Hence, the term *light* as here used re-emphasizes his incomparable greatness. "Verily, thou art a God that hidest thyself, O God of Israel, the Savior" (Is. 45:15). "Behold, God is great."

This greatness of God has as its corollary, ". . . and we know him not" (Job 36:26). Similarly, here in I Tim. 6:16 the line, "dwelling in light unapproachable," already implies and is immediately followed by, "whom no human being has (ever) seen or is able to see." Cf. I Tim. 1:17, in connection with which the sense in which God is *invisible* has been explained. See also N.T.C. on John 1:18; and cf. I John 4:12.

The devout contemplation of this majestic Being, who has wonderful blessings in store for his children, leads to the climax, "to whom be honor and strength eternal. Amen." Truly, such a God is worthy of all *honor:* reverence, esteem, adoration (see footnote 82 above). He is also worthy of eternal *strength,* that is, power manifested in action, to the discomfiture of his enemies and to the salvation of his people. Paul's expressed wish is that God may receive this honor and may manifest this eternal strength. This wish is very deep-seated, for the apostle loves God very, very much. Hence, as in I Tim. 1:17, he seals the wish with the solemn word of affirmation or confirmation: Amen (cf. Num. 5:22; Neh. 8:6; Ps. 41:13; 72:10; 89:52; and see N.T.C. on John 1:51).

17 As for those (who are) rich in terms of this present age, charge them not to be high-minded, nor to set their hope on (the) uncertainty of riches, but on God, who richly provides us with everything for (our) enjoyment. 18 (Charge them) to do what is good, to be rich in noble deeds, to be quick to give, ready to share, 19 (thus) storing up a treasure for themselves, (which will form) an excellent foundation for the (age) to come, so that they may take hold of the real life.

6:17-19

17. Truly, believers are rich in terms of the age to come, that age which will be ushered in by Christ's glorious epiphany! What a contrast between them and those who are rich *only* in terms of this *present* age. Let wealthy church-members beware lest the word "only" should apply to them! Paul does not *say* that their wealth is limited to this earthly sphere, but he *warns* them. Says he:

As for those (who are) rich in terms of this present age, charge them not to be high-minded, nor to have their hope set on (the) uncertainty of riches, but on God, who richly provides us with everything for (our) enjoyment.

Not those who are eager to become rich, as in verse 9, are here addressed, but those who are actually rich. By immediately adding, "in terms of this present age" (an expression used only here and in II Tim. 4:10; Titus 2:12), the apostle is already beginning to fix the mind of the reader and hearer upon the transitory character of earthly wealth. He means, "this present era which will soon be past." Timothy, then, must tell these people: (a) what should *not* be their attitude (verse 17a); and (b) what should be their attitude (verses 17b, 18, 19).

As to a., they must not be *high-minded* but humble (Eph. 4:2; Col. 3:12); and they must not *have their hope set* [107] on the uncertainty of riches, that is, on their riches, which, as a matter of fact, are very uncertain. Rich church-members, then, must be neither snobbish nor smug.

As to b., they should have their hope fixed on *God* (this is the best reading; better than, "on the living God"). This God is ever true to his promise. He is the God of love. He *richly* provides. Note play on words: "As for those (who are) *rich,* charge them . . . not to have their hope set on . . . *riches,* but on God, who *richly* provides." Not only is God rich (Ps. 50:10-12), so that with him *wishing* and *having* are one and the same, but he ever gives *"according to* his riches" (Eph. 1:7; cf. Titus 3:6), not only *"of* his riches." For God's munificence, by virtue of which he provides us with

---

[107] Note ἠλπικέναι, perfect active infinitive of ἐλπίζω, emphasizing that this action of hoping, having begun in the past, has continued until by this time it has become a fixed state. Rich church-members, accordingly, are warned not to get to the point where they will have rested the weight of their confidence on earthly treasures.

all things necessary both for body and soul, for time and eternity, see also Acts 14:17; James 1:17; and innumerable passages in the Psalter, such as 37:25; 68:19; 81:19b; and see Psalms 103, 104, 107, 111, 116, 145, etc. Moreover, all these things are given to us in order that we may not only "partake of" them (I Tim. 4:3), but may also *enjoy* them. When *we* sing, *God* sings along with us (Zeph. 3:17).

18. What should be the attitude of the rich is continued, with this difference: in verse 17b their proper attitude *toward God* has been pointed out; now in verse 18 their correct relation toward *other people,* particularly toward other believers is set forth. Says Paul: **(Charge them) to do what is good, to be rich in noble deeds, to be quick to give, ready to share.**

A rich church-member should strive to be rich in noble deeds, in "beautiful works," as was Mary of Bethany. He should be *quick to give,* being ever *ready to share* what he has with others who belong to the *fellowship* or *community* of believers in Christ. He should do this in the spirit of Acts 2:42-44; 4:34-37.

19. The result of following this proper procedure will be: **(thus) storing up a treasure for themselves, (which will form) an excellent foundation for the (age) to come, so that they may take hold of the real life.**

By practising the grace of sharing, a person is storing up a treasure for himself. *Gifts are investments.* By giving materially one enriches himself spiritually, and assures himself of future reward. "Sell whatever you have, and give to the poor, and you will have treasure in heaven" (Mark 10:21). That "treasure" in heaven consists of the following:

a. a good conscience (cf. I Tim. 1:5),

b. an enthusiastic reception by those who have been benefited (Luke 16:9),

c. in general, the entrance into all the joys and glories of heaven.

This treasure will be an excellent *foundation* [108] upon which to build when, in the age to come (particularly in the great Judgment Day), the believer's works are taken into account. His having been with Jesus in heaven is a *solid basis* for confidence in that great day. The believer himself will not have to give a review of his good works. In fact, if they were

---

[108] To say that the word used in the original means both *foundation* and *fund* affords little help in this connection, may even be confusing. It cannot very well have both meanings at the same time in the same passage. Paul's thought is, after all, simple and clear. Good works (the fruit of faith; hence, of grace) performed here below are rewarded with treasure above. And the consciousness of having enjoyed this heavenly treasure will be a firm foundation for the expectation of everything good on the Day of Judgment. — The apostle may have been thinking of Christ's utterances in the Sermon on the Mount, for there, too, the two ideas — *treasure* and *good foundation* — are found side by side (Matt. 6:19, 20; 7:24, 25).

really *good* works, he will not even be able to do so. Christ will do it for him (Matt. 25:34-40). With respect to both body and soul the believer, having listened to the words of approval which issue from the lips of Christ, will then enter into the fullest enjoyment of that life which alone is life indeed. Paul's teaching here in I Tim. 6:19 is in exact accord with Christ's in Matt. 25:34-40, 46b. Salvation, to be sure, is entirely *by grace through faith* (Eph. 2:8; Titus 3:5), but the reward is *according to works* (Dan. 12:3; II Cor. 5:10; Rev. 20:12).

---

20 O Timothy, what has been entrusted to you guard,[109] turning away from the profane empty-chatter and contradictions of what is falsely styled "Knowledge," 21 for by professing it [110] certain individuals have wandered away with respect to the faith.

Grace [111] (be) with you.

6:20, 21

20. O Timothy, what has been entrusted to you guard.

Having reached the end of the letter, Paul addresses his friend and fellow-worker with solemn earnestness: "O Timothy." [112] Timothy, then, is admonished to guard *the trust* or *deposit;* that is, he must faithfully watch over *that which has been committed to his care.* It is as if God had made a "deposit" in Timothy's bank. The word employed in the original is related to a verb meaning "to place by the side," hence, "to deposit," "to commit to (someone)." See M.M. for illustrations of the meaning "deposit," "pledge," "security."

Moreover, the object which has been thus given into his charge for protection is *the gospel,* as is clear from II Tim. 1:11. It is *God's redemptive truth* entrusted to him by the Holy Spirit (see II Tim. 1:14). But here the term "gospel" must be taken in its widest sense, as embracing "all (sacred) scripture" (II Tim. 3:16). This *includes,* of course, what the apostle is writing in the present letter: all the orders given to Timothy and all the teaching which this epistle contains. The point, then, is that this gospel belongs not to Timothy but *to God.* Cf. Rom. 3:2 (the Jews had been entrusted with "the oracles *of God*"). *He* has made it possible through the sending

---

109 Literally, "the entrusted (thing) guard." One might also say, "Guard the deposit."

110 Literally, "which certain individuals professing."

111 Literally, "The grace."

112 "O" with vocatives is not very common in Greek. The addition of the interjection strengthens the vocative. Other instances in Paul: I Tim. 6:11; then Rom. 2:1, 3; 9:20; 11:33; Gal. 3:1. It is also Paul who uses it in Acts 13:10; 27:21; Luke, in Acts 1:1; Gallio, in Acts 18:14. Jesus used it a few times: Matt. 15:28; 17:17 (cf. Mark 9:19; Luke 9:41); Luke 24:25.

of *his* Son. *He* has revealed it. *To God* Timothy will have to give an account as to what he has done with it. Ministers are God's "stewards" (Titus 1:7). The "talents" which they employ in performing their tasks are not their own, but *God's* property (Matt. 25:14-30). They must be used to the best advantage in the promotion of *his* cause and the progress of *his* Kingdom.

This implies that Timothy must continue to proclaim the pure gospel, and like a dauntless, vigilant *sentinel* (note Greek verb) must rush to the defence whenever its precious truths are attacked or misrepresented, as was the case in the Ephesus region. It is with this in mind that Paul continues: **turning away from the profane empty-chatter and contradictions of what is falsely styled *Knowledge.***

Timothy must avoid one mistake. He must not waste any time on *the inanities* of those false teachers who "understand neither the words which they are speaking nor the themes on which they are harping with such confidence" (I Tim. 1:7). Such *profane* (unholy, unclean, II Tim. 2:16; Lev. 10:10) "empty-jabberings" he must simply *shun* (I Tim. 4:7). He must *turn away* from them in disgust. Why should he concern himself with "endless myths and genealogies" (I Tim. 1:4), with "idle talk" (I Tim. 1:6)? Why should he meddle with the "contradictions" or "word-battles" in which those men engage each other who are "depraved in mind and deprived of the truth" (I Tim. 6:5)? To be sure, these false teachers rave about their systems of "Knowledge." But their vapid mouthings are "Knowledge *falsely so called.*" It should be *avoided* like the pestilence. Paul's inspired advice, by means of which, having reached the end of the letter, he returns to the theme which he had mentioned at the beginning, should be taken to heart by the church in every age. Also *today* far too much attention is being paid to the "empty jabberings" of men who, in the final analysis, reject God's infallible revelation! Paul's command addressed to Timothy is ever up-to-date. And the apostle John is in thorough agreement with him (II John 10). One *guards* the truth by *turning away from* all insipid ranting.

21. Against this pseudonymous "Knowledge," there follows a word of warning which emphasizes the necessity of heeding the admonition expressed in verse 20: **for, by professing it certain individuals have wandered away with respect to the faith.** Here are those "certain individuals" again. We have already seen that the manner in which they are here pictured is in perfect harmony with their description in I Tim. 1:3, 4, 6, 7, 19, 20. The "profane empty jabberers" of our present passage are the "futile talkers" of I Tim. 1:6. Even the same verb is used in both places to describe them. They are said to *have wandered away* (I Tim. 1:6; 6:21).

Now these "certain individuals," in *professing* (see on I Tim. 2:10), that is, proclaiming and making propaganda for, their vaunted "Knowledge," have wandered away from *the faith,* that is, from *the truth* (cf. I Tim. 6:10, 12; II Tim. 2:18). But this does not mean that they had all broken with "the church." There were *then,* as there are *now,* individuals *in* the church who have forsaken the truth. They prefer not to leave the church, but to drag it along with them into ruin.

Nowhere in Paul's letters is there a shorter benediction: **Grace (be) with y o u.** But though brief, it is rich in meaning, for *grace* is the greatest blessing of all. It is God's favor in Christ toward the undeserving, transforming their hearts and lives and leading them to glory. The apostle, who in his opening salutation had spoken of *grace,* as the first element in the series "grace, mercy, peace," now closes the letter by pronouncing *this* grace (note the article; hence really "the grace") upon . . . well, upon whom? The reader who is unacquainted with the original is almost sure to reason that the words "Grace be with you," of the A.R.V., mean, "Grace be with *you, Timothy."* The R.S.V. has not improved matters any. And the A.V. is based upon an inferior reading; hence has "with thee." This shows how necessary it is in our translation to distinguish carefully between "you" (singular) and "y o u" (spaced letters, plural), for surprisingly, *it is the plural* that is used here! Though the epistle is addressed to just *one* person, Timothy, the latter would certainly see to it that its contents reached others. God's grace, accordingly, is pronounced upon *the entire Christian community.*

Synthesis of Chapter 6

See the Outline at the beginning of this chapter, which may be paraphrased as follows:

Let as many as are under the yoke, namely, slaves, regard their own masters as worthy of all honor. Otherwise the blame will be placed on the gospel, and the name and doctrine of God will be evil spoken of. Those slaves who happen to be in the exceptionally privileged position of having believing masters should render exceptional service. The fact that their masters are brothers is no reason for these slaves to look down upon them. Let them rather bear in mind that these beloved ones will reciprocate the kindness of their slaves.

Keep on teaching and urging these things.

If anyone is a teacher of novelties – hair-splitting so-called "deductions" from the law of Moses, fanciful stories about ancestors – and does not chime in with the sound words of our Lord Jesus Christ, the doctrine that promotes true piety, such a man is blinded with conceit. Though he may boast about his superior "Knowledge," in reality he does not know a thing. A morbid craving for controversies and word-battles has taken possession of him; and these, in turn, breed envy, wrangling, revilings, base suspicions, and mutual altercations between men depraved in mind and deprived of the truth. These men imagine that the real aim of being religious is to make a profit.

Now genuine religion, which exists when the soul is no longer empty but filled with grace and contentment, is actually profit-bearing. Material possessions, however, can never impart true riches to the soul, as is evident from the fact that no matter how rich a person may become in earthly goods, he will leave this world as devoid of them as he entered it. Hence, when we, believers, have nourishment and shelter, we shall regard these as sufficient.

But those who are eager to be rich fall into temptation and a snare and into numerous cravings. These cravings are senseless and hurtful because they defeat their very purpose. Instead of making men really rich and happy they make them poor and wretched, for they plunge men into ruin and destruction. For, a root of all the evils is the love of money; and some people, reaching out after it, have wandered away from the faith, and have pierced themselves with numerous pangs: unrest, worry, boredom, dissatisfaction, gloom, envy.

But you, O man of God, continue to flee away from such things as gold-hunger, envy, wrangling; and run after righteousness – the state of mind and heart which is in harmony with God's law –, godliness, faith, love, endurance, gentleness. Fight the noble fight of the faith. Get a firm grip on that everlasting life to which you were called when on the occasion of your baptism you confessed the beautiful confession in the presence of those many witnesses who heard it. Do not be afraid to lose your life. Remember that your mandate is given and received in the presence of a God who is the Bestower and Preserver of life, and of a Christ Jesus who while testifying before that enemy of the truth, Pontius Pilate, made the beautiful confession. Therefore you also must courageously cling to your commission with respect to preaching and discipline; yes, you must stand guard over it so that it remains unsullied and completely free from every possibility of justified criticism. Keep it then until the day when our Lord Jesus Christ shines forth brilliantly, the day of his appearing. God himself will display that great event. He, moreover, is the blessed and only Sovereign, the King of kings and Lord of lords, the only One possessing *immortality – not* just *endless existence* but *real life* possessed eternally –, dwelling in light unapproachable, whom no human being has (ever) seen or is able to see; to whom (be) honor and strength eternal. Amen.

As for those who are rich in material possessions, charge them not to be uppish nor to have their hope fixed on the uncertainty of riches but on God, who richly provides us with everything for our enjoyment. Charge them to do what is good, to be rich in noble deeds, to be quick to give, ready to share. Remember: gifts are investments. Hence, these givers are really storing up a treasure for themselves. They will not have only a good conscience but also, when soul and body separate, an enthusiastic reception in the glories of heaven. What a solid foundation this will be for the age to come, particularly for the day of the final judgment. With respect to both body and soul they will then begin to enter upon the fullest enjoyment of that life which alone is life indeed and which will never end.

O Timothy, guard as a most precious deposit the gospel which has been entrusted to you. Turn away meanwhile from the profane empty-chatter and contradictions of what is falsely styled "Knowledge," those endless myths and genealogies, those word-battles about the law. Remember that by making propaganda for it certain individuals have wandered away from the path of God's redemptive truth. The grace of God be with you, and not only with you but with the entire Christian community in whose midst you dwell.

Commentary
on
II Timothy

Outline of II Timothy

Theme: *The Apostle Paul Tells Timothy What To Do in the Interest of Sound Doctrine*

No brief outline can do full justice to the rich, varied, and overlapping contents of a letter which is as personal as is II Timothy. The dominant note, however, is clear: "Timothy, do not be ashamed, but by God's grace exert yourself to the utmost, being willing to endure your share of hardship in preserving and promoting sound doctrine."

There are no sharp divisions. Rather, the emphasis gradually shifts from one point to another. When a new point is made, the old one is not entirely relinquished. The thoughts overlap like shingles on a roof. For example, a key-passage in chapter 1 is, "Do not be ashamed" (verses 8, 12, 16). The idea recurs, however, in chapter 2 (verse 15). Similarly, a key-passage in chapter 2 is, "Suffer hardship along with us" (verse 3; cf. verse 9). But this has been anticipated in chapter 1 (verse 8).

I have called "Do not be ashamed" *a* key-passage. It can hardly be called *the* key-passage, at least not in the sense that Paul's main idea in the first chapter would be *negative.* "Do not be ashamed" is, of course, an example of the figure of speech called *litotes:* "strong affirmation by means of negation." Hence, the predominant idea of chapter 1 is "Be very courageous. Whatever happens, *hold on* to the precious doctrine of the church."

Similarly, in chapter 2 the predominant idea is not simply that Timothy must be willing to suffer hardship along with Paul and others, but that he must be willing to do this *in connection with* all the work pertaining to the gospel-ministry, one phase of which is emphasized in this chapter, namely, that of *teaching:* imparting proper instruction in the Word over against heresy.

In chapter 3 the admonition to *abide in* the true doctrine obtains its justified emphasis from the observation, "Grievous times will come."

And in chapter 4 the exhortation, *"Preach* (literally, "Herald") the word," is introduced very solemnly, as an authoritative charge, "I charge you."

In view of all this the main line of thought running through II Timothy can be briefly indicated in the following manner (note the overlapping):

AS REGARDS SOUND DOCTRINE:

HOLD ON TO IT — Chapter 1
TEACH IT — Chapter 2
ABIDE IN IT — Chapter 3
PREACH IT — Chapter 4

Main Divisions with Key-Passages

Chapter 1: HOLD ON TO IT
"Stir into full flame that gift of God" (verse 6)
"Do not be ashamed" (verse 8; cf. verses 12, 16)
"Hold on to . . . the sound words" (verse 13)
"That precious deposit guard" (verse 14)

Chapter 2: TEACH IT
"The things which you have heard . . . entrust to faithful men . . . able to teach others also" (verse 2)
"Suffer hardship along with (us)" (verse 3; cf. verse 9)
"The Lord will give you understanding in all things" (verse 14)
"A servant of the Lord must be . . . qualified to teach" (verse 24)

Chapter 3: ABIDE IN IT
"Grievous seasons will come" (verse 1)
"But you have followed my teaching, conduct, purpose" (verse 10)
"Continue in the things which you have learned" (verse 14)

Chapter 4: PREACH IT
"I charge you" (verse 1)
"Preach (or "Herald") the word" (verse 2)
"Do the work of an evangelist; your duties as a minister discharge to the full" (verse 5).

Outline with Divisions and Subdivisions

Chapter 1: HOLD ON TO IT "Do not be ashamed."

A. As did Lois and Eunice.
B. As I do, never ashamed of the gospel.
C. As did Onesiphorus, not ashamed of my chain.

Chapter 2: TEACH IT "Suffer hardship along with (us)."

A. It brings great reward; is glorious in contents.
B. Vain disputes, on the contrary, serve no useful purpose.

Chapter 3: ABIDE IN IT "Grievous times will come."

A. Knowing that enemies will arise, who have its form, not its power.
B. Knowing that it is based on the sacred writings, as you learned from trustworthy persons.

Chapter 4: PREACH IT "I charge you."

A. In season, out of season, for apostasy is coming. Remain faithful, in view of the fact that I am about to set sail.
B. Items of personal information, requests, greetings.

Outline of Chapter 1

Theme: *The Apostle Paul Tells Timothy What To Do in the Interest of Sound Doctrine*

Hold On To It "Do not be ashamed"

1:1-7 (Hold on) as did Lois and Eunice. Verses 1 and 2 contain the address and salutation.

1:8-14 As I do, never ashamed of the gospel.

1:15-18 As did Onesiphorus, not ashamed of my chain. Contrast "all that are in Asia," who deserted me.

CHAPTER I

II TIMOTHY **1:1, 2**

1 1 Paul, an apostle of Christ Jesus through the will of God in harmony
with the promise of life (which centers) in Christ Jesus, 2 to Timothy (my)
beloved child; grace, mercy, peace from God the Father and Christ Jesus our Lord.
3 I acknowledge gratitude to God, whom I, like my forefathers, serve with
a pure conscience, just as I cherish that constant recollection of you in my supplication by night and by day; 4 longing to see you, as I revive in my memory your
tears, in order that (seeing you again) I may be filled with joy; 5 having received
a reminder of your unfeigned faith, the kind (of faith) which first dwelt in your
grandmother Lois and in your mother Eunice, and, I am convinced, also in you. 6
For this reason I remind you to stir into a living flame that gift of God which is
within you through the laying on of my hands. 7 For God gave us not a Spirit of
timidity but of power and love and self-discipline.

1:1-7

1, 2. Paul, an apostle of Christ Jesus through the will of God in harmony with the promise of life (which centers) in Christ Jesus, 2 to Timothy (my) beloved child; grace, mercy, peace from God the Father and Christ Jesus our Lord.

The opening phrases of the two letters addressed to Timothy resemble each other rather closely, as anyone can see for himself. In the columns below, the words that differ are printed in italics:

I Tim. 1:1, 2	II Tim. 1:1, 2
Paul, an apostle of Christ Jesus *by order* of God *our Savior* and Christ Jesus *our Hope,* to Timothy (my) *genuine* child *in faith;* grace, mercy, peace from God the Father and Christ Jesus our Lord.	Paul, an apostle of Christ Jesus *through the will* of God *in harmony with the promise of life* (which centers) *in* Christ Jesus, to Timothy (my) *beloved* child; grace, mercy, peace from God the Father and Christ Jesus our Lord.

Hence, for a more detailed discussion of the material that is common to the two passages I refer to the explanation of I Tim. 1:1, 2.

Briefly, then, the meaning of II Tim. 1:1, 2 is as follows:

Paul introduces himself as the official representative of Christ Jesus. He has a right to say "of Jesus Christ," for by the latter he has been set apart for his high office. To *him* he belongs, and in *his* service he functions. Moreover, not self-appointed is Paul but invested with his authoritative commission "through the will of God" (cf. "by order of God," I Tim. 1:1). Though he is but a prisoner, his word has divine sanction! Cf. Eph. 1:1; Col. 1:1, also written from prison.

Now this apostleship by the will of God was "in harmony with (or "in accordance with") the promise of life," that is, it was a result of that promise, in the sense that had there been no such *promise* there could have been no *divinely willed apostle* to proclaim the promise. This promise and assurance is the one already implied in Gen. 3:15 and definitely stated in Ps. 16:11; 138:7, 9; John 3:16; 6:35, 48-59; 14:6. It was the promise "of life," that is, the promise which has *everlasting life* as its contents. It is very fitting that Paul, the prisoner who faces *death,* should rivet the attention on the promise of indestructible *life!* This is, indeed the life which *is* or *centers* (implied) "in Christ Jesus," for apart from *his* atonement and intercession no one would ever be in possession of that *life,* that *salvation* (see N.T.C. on John 3:16).

Paul is addressing his letter "to Timothy (my) beloved child." Cf. II Tim. 2:1; 3:14. As, in a secondary sense, a child owes his natural life to his earthly father, so Timothy owed his spiritual life to Paul (see p. 34). Moreover, as a child serves (with) his father, so Timothy served (with) Paul in the gospel. See Phil. 2:19-22, which passage also indicates why the apostle calls Timothy his *beloved* or *dear* (cf. I Tim. 1:2, "genuine") child. Moreover, the term of endearment is natural on the lips of one who, facing death, in his mind and heart reviews his entire past association with the precious young friend and helper whose life had been mingled with his own in so many ways.

Upon this "beloved child" Paul pronounces *grace* (unmerited pardoning and transforming favor), *mercy* (warm and tender affection shown to the one who is in a difficult situation), and that blessing which flows forth from grace and mercy just as a stream issues from a fountain, namely, the blessing of *peace* (the consciousness of having been reconciled to God through the accomplished mediatorial work of Christ).

These gifts are regarded as having as their source "God the Father and Christ Jesus our Lord." The Father bestows them. The Son has earned them.

3-5. When Paul adds to the words of introduction an expression of sincere and humble thanksgiving to God, he is following a custom (see N.T.C. on I and II Thessalonians, p. 45). With respect to the letters written by Paul the statistics are as follows:

"I (or *we*) thank God"	"I acknowledge gratitude"	"Blessed be . . ."	Absence of introductory thanksgiving or doxology
Rom. 1:8	I Tim. 1:12 ("to Christ Jesus")	II Cor. 1:3	Galatians
I Cor. 1:4	II Tim. 1:3 ("to God")	Eph. 1:3	Titus
Phil. 1:3			
Col. 1:3			
I Thess. 1:2			
II Thess. 1:3 ("We are obliged to give thanks")			
Philem. 4			

But though, as has been shown, the apostle was used to adding words of thanksgiving or praise, with him this was never *merely* a custom. Rather, we should view the situation as follows: Sitting in his gloomy dungeon and facing death, Paul, far from complaining, as many people in similar circumstances would have done, meditates on blessings past and present, and sincerely desires to express his gratitude. This is the background of the words:

I acknowledge gratitude to God, whom I, like my forefathers, serve with a pure conscience, just as I cherish that constant recollection of you in my supplication by night and by day; longing to see you,

a. as I revive in my memory your tears,

b. in order that (on seeing you again) I may be filled with joy;

c. having received a reminder of your unfeigned faith, the kind (of faith) which first dwelt in your grandmother Lois and in your mother Eunice, and, I am convinced, also in you.

Paul states that he *acknowledges gratitude to God.* Though he will soon die the death of a criminal, he is not afraid to speak of *serving*[113] God, for in proclaiming the gospel he has done what his *conscience, purified* by the Holy Spirit, had told him to do. (For the meaning of *conscience* see on I Tim. 1:5; and for *pure conscience* see on I Tim. 3:9.) In this respect he was like his *forefathers* or *ancestors* (cf. I Tim. 5:4, but in that passage the word is used with reference to *still living* progenitors). They, too, served the same God, and they, too, did it with a pure conscience. The thought is the same as that which is expressed in Acts 24:14, 15:

"But this I confess to thee, that after the Way which they call a sect, so

[113] The original uses the verb λατρεύω here, not λειτουργέω. The latter always has an *official* connotation; the former embraces a wider area, and may denote either official or unofficial service or worship. See R. C. Trench, *op. cit.*, XXXV.

serve I the God of *our fathers,* believing all things which are according to the law and which are written in the prophets; having hope (which is directed) toward God . . . that there shall be a resurrection both of the just and the unjust."

The "forefathers" of our present passage are, in all likelihood, the "fathers" of the passage in Acts. The *service* rendered is the same in both instances.

What Paul stresses, therefore, is that he has not introduced a *new* religion. *Essentially* what he now believes is what Abraham, Isaac, Jacob, Moses, Isaiah, and all the pious ancestors also believed. There is continuity between the old and the new dispensation. The forefathers believed in the resurrection; so does Paul. They looked forward to the coming Messiah; Paul proclaims the same Messiah, who had actually made his appearance. It is *Rome* that has changed its attitude. It is *the government* which, after the burning of its capital in the year 64, has begun to persecute Christians. Paul's conscience is *pure. The prisoner* enjoys peace of heart and mind!

Literally Paul writes, "whom I *from* my forefathers serve." He means, "whom I serve with a faith *derived from* my forefathers," that is, with a faith which had its roots in their religion, and is therefore similar to theirs. Hence, the translation, "whom I, like my forefathers, serve," is justified.

By adding, "just as I cherish that constant recollection of you in my prayers by night and by day," Paul is saying that whenever he thinks of Timothy he views him as a man who *likewise* serves the true God with a pure conscience. It is in his *supplications by night and by day* (see on I Tim. 5:5) that the apostle cherishes this ever-recurring recollection of Timothy. These supplications are *accompanied by* (and probably to a certain extent even *caused by*) ardent *longing*: "longing to see you."

For this deep yearning there are two expressed motivations: one comes from within, the other from without. The motivation *from within* is stated in the words, "as I *revive in my memory* (or: recall to mind) [114] your tears."

---

[114] The present passage, verses 3-5, contains *three* different expressions that have to do with *the memory.* Adding verse 6, there are *four.* They should, however, be carefully distinguished, which is not always done (see the various versions and commentaries). Note the following:

a. "I have or cherish the (constant) recollection (of you)" or "I hold (you) in (constant) memory." Thus we would render ἔχω τὴν περὶ σοῦ μνείαν. This corresponds to the Latin: *(continuam tui) memoriam teno.* See N.T.C. on I Thess. 3:6, same idiom. This should not be confused with, "I make mention (of you)." That is the proper translation of μνείαν ὑμῶν ποιοῦμαι; Latin: mentionem facio. See N.T.C. on I Thess. 1:2; also see Rom. 1:9; Eph. 1:16; Philem. 4.

b. "reviving in my memory," or "recalling to mind." The original has μεμνημένος, nom. sing. masc. part. perf. "reflexive," from μιμνήσκω. In the New Testament this verb never occurs in the active voice, always middle or passive. Hence, μιμνήσκομαι; and perfect with present significance: μέμνημι; whence the participle used here. It may be freely translated, "as I revive in my memory," or, "as I recall to mind." Cf. the same middle or reflexive idea in the Dutch: "als *ik mij* (uw tranen) herin-

It is entirely probable that when Paul and Timothy had parted *for the last time,* the latter had shed tears. Paul himself, no doubt, had done the same thing, but he does not now refer to his own tears but to those of Timothy. This parting was not the one referred to in I Tim. 1:3, but a much later one which in all probability took place after the apostle's return from Spain. See p. 40, not item 4 but item 8. By means of his tears the younger man had shown how wholehearted and genuine was his devotion to Paul, how warm and tender his affection, and how deep and poignant his sorrow at the thought of separation, especially under the circumstances then obtaining. Remember: it was a time of religious persecution; in fact, Paul was about to be captured. The memory of Timothy's loving tears motivated Paul's longing to see him again. The apostle was eager to have his friend come and visit him in his dungeon at Rome.

The motivation *from without* is somewhat obscure. All Paul says is, "having received a reminder of your *unfeigned* (literally: *unhypocritical*) *faith.*" Just how this reminder from without had reached Paul we do not know. Some interpreters are of the opinion that in Rome something had just now happened which had reminded the apostle of Timothy's early faith. Others believe that Paul had received a letter from Timothy. Still others suggest that someone who knew "all about" the younger man's childhood days and subsequent conversion had visited the apostle in prison, and that this friend had recited from memory incidents long past in the life of absent Timothy. Whatever may have been the precise nature of the reminder from without, one fact is certain: as a result of both motivations, the one from within and the other from without, Paul's soul is filled with longing *to see* Timothy.[115]

Paul is convinced that Timothy is no fair-weather believer, but that the faith of this "beloved child" is "the kind" (ἥτις) which first dwelt in his grandmother Lois and in his mother Eunice.

The apostle does not say that Timothy's grandmother and mother had "served God with a pure conscience," but that *faith* had *first* taken up its place of residence in *their* hearts; *afterward* in the heart of *Timothy.* What does he mean here by *faith?* Was it nothing more than "Old Testament Israelitish faith," or was it faith in Jesus Christ, as the fulfilment of the

---

ner." Similarly, the German has the idiom: ". . . wenn *ich mich* recht erinnere" (if my memory serves me right).

c. "having received a reminder." Thus should be rendered ὑπόμνησιν λαβὼν (τῆς ἐν σοὶ ἀνυποκρίτου πίστεως).

d. "I remind you." The original has ἀναμιμνήσκω.

115 See the passage (verses 3-5) as printed on p. 225. As I construe it, a. and c. modify "longing to see you," but b. modifies only the last part of that expression, namely, "to see you." *Seeing* Timothy again, will fill the cup of Paul's joy. For a different view as to the grammatical construction of b. see C. Bouma, *op. cit.,* p. 243.

Old Testament promises? I believe that the latter view has probability on its side:

(1) Acts 16:1 clearly teaches that as soon as Timothy's mother is introduced, at the beginning of the second missionary journey, she is called "a *believing* Jewish woman." That adjective ("believing") is the one which, in a slightly modified sense ("faithful"), is used in the same chapter with respect to *Lydia* (Acts 16:15). That was *after* Lydia's baptism. *Before* that conversion to the Christian faith she was called, "one who worshiped God" (Acts 16:14).

(2) The same chapter also teaches that after the jailer had obeyed the missionaries' exhortation, he is spoken of as a *believer*. (Acts 16:31, 34.)

(3) In Paul's terminology "believers" are those of the old dispensation who trusted in the Christ-centered promises – for example, Abraham –, and those of the new dispensation who accept Christ as the fulfilment of these promises (Rom. 4:12; Gal. 3:9). As far as the new dispensation is concerned, "believers" are *Christians* (II Cor. 6:15). According to Luke, Jews converted to the Christian faith are "believers from among those circumcised" (Acts 10:45).

It would seem, therefore, that, at a date not later than Paul's first missionary journey, grandmother Lois (living, perhaps, with her daughter?) and mother Eunice had been converted, so that they saw in Christ the fulfilment of the promises, and placed their trust in him; and that these two women, in turn, had co-operated with Paul in that glorious work of grace which resulted in Timothy's conversion.

6, 7. On the basis, then, of this faith which dwells in Timothy's heart, just as it had previously established its home within the hearts of Lois and Eunice, Paul is able to continue: **For this reason I remind you to stir into a living flame that gift of God which is within you through the laying on of my hands.**

Paul knew that the fire of Timothy's *charisma* (the gift of God's grace which enabled the younger man to become the apostle's chosen representative) was burning low. Once before, in the earlier letter, the apostle had written, "Do not grow careless about the gift that is within you, which was granted to you by prophetic utterance with the laying on of the hands of the presbytery" (I Tim. 4:14; see on that passage). The repetition, in slightly altered form, of this exhortation is really not surprising. We should bear in mind the following:

a. Timothy was handicapped by frequent physical ailments (I Tim. 5:23).

b. He was naturally timid ("Now if Timothy comes, see to it that he is with you without fear," I Cor. 16:10).

c. He was, in a sense, "a young man" (I Tim. 4:12; cf. II Tim. 2:22).

d. The Ephesian errorists who opposed him were very determined (I Tim. 1:3-7, 19, 20; 4:6, 7; 6:3-10; II Tim. 2:14-19, 23).

e. Believers were being persecuted by the State. Think of Paul (I Tim. 4:6).

Of course, we do not know whether *all* or only some of these factors contributed to the expressed result, namely, that the flame of Timothy's ministerial office needed attention, nor do we know to what extent each contributed. The main idea, however, is clear. So Paul, having carefully selected the most gentle verb, *reminds* Timothy to "stir (up) into a living flame" the divine gift of ordination. The flame had not gone out, but it was burning slowly and had to be agitated to white heat. The times were serious. Paul was about to depart from the scene of history. Timothy must carry on where Paul was about to leave off. The gift of the Spirit must not be quenched (cf. I Thess. 5:19). Timothy loves Paul. Let Timothy remember, then, that at the time of his ordination *Paul's* hands, too, had rested upon him as a symbol of the impartation of the Spirit's gift!

The ministry is, indeed, the gift of the Holy Spirit, and this is the Spirit *of power* (Acts 1:8; 6:5, 8). Accordingly, Paul continues, **For God gave us not a Spirit of timidity but of power and love and self-discipline.**

In this passage some (in agreement with A.V., A.R.V., R.S.V.) spell Spirit with a small letter ("spirit"), while others capitalize. The former sometimes argue that the descriptive genitive (". . . of power and love and self-discipline") rules out any reference to the Holy Spirit.[116] But the use of such a genitive does not in itself settle the question, for a similar modifier is also used in passages which undoubtedly refer to the Holy Spirit. Thus, Jesus, in speaking about the coming Helper or Comforter, calls him "the Spirit *of truth*" (John 14:17; 15:26; 16:13). There are other similar phrases in which many interpreters find a reference to the Holy Spirit (Is. 11:2; Zech. 12:10; Rom. 8:2; Eph. 1:17; Heb. 10:29). Moreover, the idiom, "not the Spirit of . . . but (the Spirit) of . . ." is used by Paul in other passages which, in the light of their specific contexts, seem to refer to the Holy Spirit, though not every interpreter is ready to grant this (Rom. 8:15; I Cor. 2:12). And besides, do not *charisma* (verse 6) and *pneuma* (verse 7), in the sense of Holy Spirit, go hand in hand?

The gist of Paul's argument, then, would seem to be as follows:

"My dear child, Timothy, fight that tendency of yours toward fearfulness. The Holy Spirit, given to you and me and every believer, is not the Spirit of timidity but of power and love and self-discipline. Avail yourself of that limitless, never-failing *power* (δύναμις cf. our "dynamite"), and you will proclaim God's *truth;* of that intelligent, purposeful *love* (ἀγάπη see N.T.C. on John, Vol. II, pp. 494-501), and you will comfort God's *children,* even to

[116] Cf. Lenski, *op. cit.*, p. 755.

the extent of visiting me in my Roman prison; and of that ever-necessary *self-discipline* or *self-control* (σωφρονισμός, note the suffix; hence, *sound-mindedness in action,* a word used only here in the New Testament, see footnote 193), and you will wage God's *battle* against cowardice, taking yourself in hand."

If a person *fears* Satan's persecuting power more than he *trusts* God's ability and ever-readiness to help, he has lost his *mental balance.* Surely, Timothy has not reached that point! Let him then *hold on* to the truth. Let him *cling* to it by *giving it away* . . . as did Lois and Eunice!

---

8 Do not be ashamed, therefore, of the testimony concerning our Lord nor of me his prisoner, but in fellowship with (me) suffer hardship for the gospel, according to (the) power of God, 9 who saved us and called us with a holy calling, not according to *our* works but according to his own purpose and grace, which was given to us in Christ Jesus before times everlasting, 10 but has now been manifested through the appearing of our Savior Christ Jesus, who, on the one hand, utterly defeated death,[117] and, on the other hand, brought to light life and incorruptibility through the gospel, 11 for which I was appointed herald and apostle and teacher.

12 For this reason I am also suffering these things, but I am not ashamed, for I know him in whom I have placed my trust, and I am convinced that he is able to guard with a view to that day that which I have entrusted to him.

13 As a pattern of sound words hold on to those which you have heard *from me,* (and do this) in (the spirit of) faith and love (which center) in Christ Jesus.
14 That precious thing which was entrusted to you guard through the Holy Spirit who dwells within us.

1:8-14

Timothy should think of Lois and Eunice . . . *and of Paul.* The latter thought is stressed in this section (verses 8-14) in which the apostle refers to himself specifically no less than ten times: his willingness to suffer hardship for the gospel, his divine appointment, his trust in God, his stand on doctrine, and his method of proclaiming the message ("in faith and love"). Paul has supplied the "outline," or "rough sketch." Timothy should fill in the details. But in doing this he should be absolutely faithful to the "pattern." He should *hold on* to that which he has received from Paul. Similarly, a minister today should be up-to-date in his preaching. In his *application* he should figure with present-day conditions. But *the truth* which he applies should be the "old-fashioned" doctrine of Scripture, not some "liberal" substitute!

The rather lengthy section may be divided into three paragraphs (verses 8-11; verse 12; verses 13, 14). In the first paragraph the mention of *the*

---

[117] Literally, "the death," that well-known death, in its most comprehensive sense, which is the result of sin.

gospel, for which Paul suffers hardship and for which Timothy should be willing to suffer hardship along with him, leads the apostle to introduce his "beautiful digression" with reference to the work of redemption: *its character, motivation,* and *results.* Here we meet with an interesting style-characteristic, namely, *duadiplosis,* by which is meant that the clauses are joined to one another like overlapping shingles,[118] somewhat as follows:

After saying that Timothy should suffer hardship for the gospel according to the power of
GOD, Paul continues:
WHO saved us
and
called us with A HOLY CALLING
NOT (A CALLING) according to our works
but
according to HIS GRACE
WHICH was given to us in Christ Jesus before times everlasting
but
has now been manifested through the appearing
of OUR SAVIOR CHRIST JESUS
WHO on the one hand defeated death
and
on the other hand brought to light
life and incorruptibility through
THE GOSPEL
FOR WHICH I was appointed. etc.

8. Timothy has no legitimate excuse. The gift of God is within him (verse 7). So Paul continues: **Do not be ashamed, therefore, of the testimony concerning our Lord nor of me his prisoner.** The *testimony "concerning our Lord"* (objective genitive; cf. I Tim. 2:6) is, of course, the gospel, as the very parallelism of the compound clause indicates. "Do not be ashamed of *the testimony* concerning our Lord," is explained by, "But, in fellowship with (me) suffer hardship for *the gospel.*" And cf. Rom. 1:16. In the gospel we find the testimony concerning the works and words of the Lord (John 15:26, 27). Not to be ashamed of the gospel means to be proud of it.

---

118 Another striking but slightly different type of example is found in the Epistle of James, especially 1:3-6. See my *Bible Survey,* Grand Rapids, Mich., third edition 1953, pp. 329 and 332. The difference is that James carries on the thought by means of the repetition of a word; Paul mostly by means of modifying participles, which can be rendered into English by relative clauses.

Since *Paul* is so intimately associated with the gospel, it does not surprise us to read, "Do not be ashamed of the testimony concerning our Lord *nor of me his prisoner.*" Not *Nero's* prisoner is Paul, though it may seem that way, but "our Lord's." The apostle *always* emphasizes that thought in connection with the idea of being a prisoner (Eph. 3:1; 4:1; Philem. 1, 9). Now, the expression, "his prisoner" does not only mean that it was for the defence of "our Lord's" gospel that Paul had been imprisoned, but also that whatever pertained to his incarceration was entirely safe in the hands of the Sovereign Disposer of destinies.

So, Paul continues: **But in fellowship with (me) suffer hardship for the gospel, according to (the) power of God.** Timothy must be willing *to bear ill treatment* (cf. II Tim. 2:3) *along with* Paul. He must be willing to take his share of persecution; and this not in his own power, which would be impossible, but "according to (the) power of God." That power is infinite. It will enable a person to endure even unto death. It is the power of *that* God:

9. who saved us and called us with a holy calling. The result of the operation of the divine power within all believers (including Paul and Timothy) is characterized here according to a. its nature ("who saved us"), and b. its purpose ("and called us with a holy calling"). What is meant by *saving* us has been explained in detail in connection with I Tim. 1:15; see on that passage. Briefly, God has delivered us from the greatest of all evils and he has placed us in possession of the greatest of all blessings. But in saving us he made us the recipients of *the effective gospel call* (see N.T.C. on I and II Thess., p. 162, footnote 116), which is always "a *holy* calling," for not only does it reveal God's holiness but it is also distinctly a call unto holiness of life, unto a holy task, and unto a condition of everlasting sinlessness and virtue (Eph. 4:1; Phil. 3:14; II Thess. 1:11).

Now as to its *juridical basis* and glorious *motive,* this calling (and, in general, this act of saving us) was **not according to our works but according to his own purpose and grace.** This is the thought which occurs over and over again in Paul's epistles, especially in Romans and Galatians (Rom. 1:17; 3:20-24, 28; 10:5, 9, 13; 11:6; Gal. 2:16; 3:6, 8, 9-14; 6:14, 15; Eph. 2:9; Titus 3:5). Salvation is not based on our accomplishments but on God's sovereign *purpose* (Rom. 8:28; 9:11; Eph. 1:11), his wise (not arbitrary), fixed, and definite plan; and therefore on his *grace* or sovereign favor. And if it be by *grace,* it cannot be by *works.* This is clear from two considerations: a. grace, by virtue of its very nature, is something that is *given* to us, *cannot be earned by* us (though it is, indeed, merited *for* us); and b. grace *precedes* our works, for ideally we were already its objects before time began. Hence, Paul continues: **which was given to us in Christ Jesus before times everlasting** (literally, "before times of ages"). Time, "like an ever-rolling stream," flows *on and on and on.* But *before* it even began we were already included in the gracious purpose of God.[119]

10. This grace which was *given* to us, that is, *designated* for us (cf. Eph. 1:11) "before times everlasting," has *now* been clearly revealed. Hence, Paul continues: **but has now been manifested through the appearing of our Savior Christ Jesus.**

That grace of God which was hidden from before the foundation of the world and was only dimly discerned in the old dispensation "has now been revealed or manifested." The verb *manifested* is of frequent occurrence in the Gospel according to John (see N.T.C., Vol. II, p. 476, especially footnote 294). Paul also uses it several times (Rom. 1:19; I Cor. 4:5; II Cor. 2:14; 11:6; Col. 4:4; Titus 1:3). It was through the *epiphany* or *appearing* (employed everywhere else to designate the Second Coming – II Thess. 2:8; I Tim. 6:14; II Tim. 4:1, 8; Titus 2:13 –, but here to indicate the First Coming), that is, through the *"rising* of the Sun of righteousness with healing in its wings" (Mal. 4:2; cf. Luke 1:78, 79; cf. Titus 2:11), that God's grace toward his people has become manifested. Note the Lord's title: "our Savior Christ Jesus." Cf. Titus 2:13. When one thinks of *grace,* he naturally also thinks of *our Savior,* divinely *anointed by God* (hence, called *Christ,* Anointed One) for the specific task of *saving* (think of the name *Jesus:* "he will certainly save") his people from their sins (Matt. 1:21). By means of that *entire* First Coming of his (from conception to coronation) the grace of God had been revealed. – What Christ did for sinners, in need of grace, is beautifully summarized in the words: **who, on the one hand, utterly defeated death, and, on the other hand, brought to light life and incorruptibility through the gospel.**

In connection with his first coming he *utterly defeated, put out of commission, rendered ineffective* (see N.T.C. on II Thess. 2:8) death. As a result of Christ's Atonement, for the believer *eternal death* no longer exists. *Spiritual death* is vanquished more and more in this life and completely at the moment when the soul departs from its physical enclosure. And *physical death* has been robbed of its curse and has been turned into gain (John 11:26; then Phil. 3:7-14; then I Cor. 15:26, 42-44, 54-57). *That* he did *on the one hand;* and *on the other hand* he *brought to light* (see N.T.C. on John 1:9) life and incorruptibility. He brought it to light by exhibiting it in his own glorious resurrection; most of all, he brought it to light by means of *his promise;* hence, through *the gospel.* The two concepts "life and incorruptibility" probably constitute a hendiadys; hence, *incorruptible* (or imperishable) *life.*

---

[119] Hence, I cannot agree here with C. Bouma, who, in commenting on this verse (*op. cit.,* p. 255), expresses the view that the expression πρὸ χρόνων αἰωνίων means "immediately after the fall in Paradise." Rom. 16:25 and Titus 1:2, properly interpreted, do not militate against my interpretation. See on Titus 1:2.

This is the *immortality* (cf. I Tim. 1:17) which in the gospel is promised to believers. It transcends by far mere endless existence or even endless conscious existence. The gospel of our Savior Christ Jesus is far better than anything Plato ever excogitated!

It is clear, of course, that though even here and now the believer receives this great blessing *in principle,* and in heaven *in further development,* he does not *fully* receive it until the day of Christ's re-appearance. Until that day arrives, the bodies of all believers will still be subject to the laws of decay and death. *Incorruptible life, imperishable salvation,* in the full sense, belongs to the new heaven and earth. It is an inheritance stored away for us.

11. Reflecting on *the good news* which proclaims this wonderful blessing and which invites men to receive it by faith, Paul continues: **for which I was appointed herald and apostle and teacher.** This is the same thought as expressed in I Tim. 2:7; see on that passage (also on II Tim. 4:2). As a *herald* Paul must announce and loudly proclaim that gospel. As an *apostle* he must say and do nothing except that which he has been commanded to say and to do. And as a *teacher* he must impart carefully instruction in the things pertaining to salvation and the glory of God, and he must admonish unto faith and obedience. For this threefold gospel-task Paul has been *divinely appointed* or *commissioned.*

12. Thus the trend of thought has returned to that of verse 8: Paul's faithfulness to the gospel, as an example for Timothy. Accordingly, the second paragraph of the present section is very personal in character. Says the apostle: **For this reason I am also suffering these things.**

Because of the fulfilment of my assignment as an apostle of Jesus Christ I suffer here in this terrible Roman prison – a dismal underground dungeon with a hole in the ceiling for light and air –, with the prospect of execution as a criminal! **But I am not ashamed.** Though Paul has been subjected to ignominy, he has not disgraced himself. Along with others, such as Joseph, Jeremiah, Daniel, John the Baptist, and Peter, he has joined the ranks of prisoners for the best cause. After all, the place of dishonor may be the place of highest honor. Was not Jesus crucified between two malefactors? and cf. I Peter 4:16!

The reason why Paul is not ashamed is stated in these memorable words: **For I know him in whom I have placed my trust, and am convinced that he is able to guard with a view to that day that which I have entrusted to him.**

Paul has once for all placed his trust in the sovereign God (see verses 8, 9 above). One might also translate with the A.V., "for I know whom I have believed," i.e., I know God who revealed himself in his precious Son, "our

Savior Christ Jesus" (verse 10). The apostle has become abidingly convinced of God's infinite power, tender love, and absolute faithfulness.

Literally translated, the apostle says, ". . . and I am convinced that he is able to guard *my deposit* (τὴν παραθήκην μου) with a view to (or unto: εἰς) that day." This leads to the question on which commentators are hopelessly divided: Just what is meant by *my deposit?* Is it "that deposit which he has entrusted to me," or is it "that deposit which I have entrusted to him"? [120] Or, putting it differently, Is it *the gospel* or is it *myself and my complete salvation?*

As I see it, the latter view deserves the preference, for the following reasons:

(1) Clearly, *not Paul but God* (in Christ) *guards* this deposit ("*he* is able to guard"). Hence, the view that it is the deposit which Paul has entrusted to God has probability on its side. In verse 14 (see on that verse) and also in I Tim. 6:20 it is not God but Timothy who must do the guarding. Hence, in *that* case it is the deposit which God has entrusted to (Paul and to) Timothy.

Now if verse 12 has to do with the deposit which Paul has entrusted to God, then the view that the reference is to *my soul* or *my spirit* or *myself and my complete salvation* has logic on its side. Here some commentators favor *my soul;* others, *my salvation.* But the difference is not very important: "myself and my complete salvation" includes both.

(2) The immediate context favors this interpretation. Paul has just written, "I know whom I have believed," meaning, in the light of the clause which follows: "I know that this God in whom I have placed my confidence is dependable, and will certainly keep in perfect safety that which I have entrusted to him for safe-keeping and protection."

(3) The words of verse 10 also support this view. The apostle has just referred to "life and incorruptibility." But, as was noted in the explanation of verse 10, the believer does not *fully* receive this blessing until the day of Christ's glorious Return. Hence, the idea of verse 12 is that this truly immortal life possessed even now *in principle,* and deposited with God for safe-keeping, will be returned to Paul *more gloriously than ever* on "that day," the day of the great consummation (cf. verse 18 below; also II Tim. 4:8; then II Thess. 1:10).

(4) The idea of a treasure that is guarded by God is also found elsewhere; sometimes in a slightly different sense (I Peter 1:4).

---

[120] In favor of the former translation are, among others, the following: A.R.V. margin, R.S.V. text, Dutch (new version); Chrysostom, Gealy (in *Interpreter's Bible*), Koole, Lenski, Phillips, Scott, Van Dyk, Wuest. In favor of the latter are, among others, A.V., A.R.V. text, R.S.V. margin, Goodspeed, Verkuyl (Berkeley Version), Weymouth, Williams, Dutch (old version); and further: Barnes, Bouma, Calvin, Lock, Robertson, Simpson, Van Andel, Van Oosterzee (in Lange's Commentary), White (in *Expositor's Greek Testament*).

(5) Cf. the words of our Lord as he died on the cross (Luke 23:46; cf. Ps. 31:5; I Peter 4:19). Christ's spirit, having been *committed* to the Father, is on the third day re-united with the body, now gloriously resurrected.

The arguments of those who defend the opposite view are answered in footnote.[121]

13. Paul has been speaking about himself and his faithful Lord who is going to reward him in the Day of days. Let Timothy, then, copy Paul. Let him fill out the details of the sketch which Paul has outlined. So, in the third brief paragraph (verses 13, 14) of this section (verses 8-14) the author turns once more to the matter of Timothy's duty. Says Paul: **As a pattern of sound words hold on to those which you have heard *from me*, (and do this) in (the spirit of) faith and love (which center) in Christ Jesus.**[122]

As an artist has his *sketch* (see on I Tim. 1:16), so Timothy also had his model to go by. This sketch, model, or pattern consisted of the words which he had heard from Paul. Let him hold on to these, ever using them as his example, never departing from them. This is important, for Paul's teaching consisted of *sound* words. Note the emphasis on Paul's teaching (over against that of the Ephesian errorists): literally, "which *from me* you have heard." And it is exactly the necessity of remaining *sound* and of

---

[121] These arguments are as follows:

(1) If *deposit* means *the gospel* in I Tim. 6:20 and in II Tim. 1:14, why not here in II Tim. 1:12?
Answer: Because the "setting" of the word is entirely different. In the other passages *Timothy* is the guard; here in II Tim. 1:12 *God* is the guard. – Besides, a word does not always have the same reference. For example, the apostle has just used the word *appearing* (verse 10) with reference to Christ's *First* Coming, whereas everywhere else he uses it with reference to the *Second* Coming!

(2) The addition of "my" to the word "deposit" does not suffice to change the reference.
Answer: We agree. "My deposit" might conceivably mean either: a. "that which I have deposited," or b. "that which has been deposited with me." But that is neither here nor there. The argument either way should not be based on the word "my."

(3) The reference to "myself and my complete salvation" does not fit the words which follow, namely, "with a view to that day."
Answer: It fits beautifully, as we have shown in the text.

[122] The construction of the sentence is as follows: Subject: *you* (understood). Predicate: *hold on to* or *ever have.* Modifying phrase: *in* (the spirit of) *faith and love.* Hence, "ever have . . . in faith and love." Modifier of "in faith and love": (which center) *in Christ Jesus.* Direct object of the main verb: *those (words) which you have heard from me.* Predicate object in apposition with this direct object: *as a pattern of sound words.* Literal translation: "As a pattern of sound words ever have those which from me you have heard, in faith and love." Here ὧν may be construed as having been "attracted to the case of its antecedent" (so Lenski and many others), but this is not necessarily true. There is no hard and fast rule about the case of the object of ἀκούω, as Robertson has shown. See his *Word Pictures,* Vol. III on Acts 9:7, p. 118.

transmitting *sound* doctrine that is stressed throughout the epistle and, to a certain extent, in all the Pastorals (cf. I Tim. 1:10; 6:3; II Tim. 4:3; Titus 1:9, 13; 2:1, 2, 8). The slogan, so popular today, "It does not matter *what* you believe, just so you are serious in whatever you believe," is flatly contradicted in the Pastorals! Nevertheless, *the spirit* in which one clings to the truth and passes it along to others does matter. Hence, the apostle adds, "(Do this) in faith and love (which center) in Christ Jesus." Faith in God and his redemptive revelation, love toward him and the brotherhood is the spirit in which Timothy must hold on to the true doctrine. That these center "in Christ Jesus" is self-evident. Apart from his merits, his Spirit, and his example, there can be no faith and love.

14. Parallel with the thought just expressed is that contained in verse 14: **That precious** (or: **excellent**) **thing which was entrusted to you guard through the Holy Spirit who dwells within us.**

The "precious deposit" is, of course, *the gospel,* taken in its widest sense (see on I Tim. 6:20). It consists of "the sound words" which Timothy has heard from Paul (see the preceding verse). It is *precious* or *excellent* because it belongs to God and results in his glory through the salvation of those who accept it by sovereign grace (see verses 8-10 above). Again (as in I Tim. 6:20) Timothy is urged once for all to guard this deposit. He must defend it against every attack and never allow it to be changed or modified in the slightest degree.

But since the enemy is strong and Timothy is weak, Paul very wisely adds the thought that this guarding cannot be done except "through the Holy Spirit who dwells within us," that is, within Paul, Timothy, all believers (Rom. 8:11).

Timothy, then, should hold on to the pure gospel, the sound doctrine, as Paul has always done.

---

15 You are aware of this, that all those in Asia turned away from me, among whom are Phygelus and Hermogenes. 16 May the Lord grant mercy to the household of Onesiphorus, for he often refreshed me and was not ashamed of my chain. 17 On the contrary, when he was in Rome he diligently searched for me and found me. 18 May the Lord grant him to find mercy from the Lord in that day! And what services he rendered in Ephesus you know better (than I).

1:15-18

15. Timothy should imitate Lois and Eunice. He should also copy the example of Paul. There is one more pattern he should follow, namely, that of Onesiphorus. In every respect this wonderful man was true to the meaning of his name. He was, indeed, a "profit-bringer," a messenger of courage and cheer. The beauty of his character and the nobility of his actions stand out clearly upon the dark background of the sorry behavior of "all those in Asia."

In view of the fact that Timothy was right now living in the Roman province of Asia, Paul was able to say: **You are aware of this, that all those in Asia turned away from me, among whom are Phygelus and Hermogenes.** It is probable that several leading Christians in the province of which Ephesus was the capital had been asked by Paul to come to Rome in order to appear on the witness-stand in his favor. However, with the possible exception of the one to be mentioned in verses 16-18, no one had complied with the request. In all likelihood fear had held them back. That was true also with respect to two among their number, namely, Phygelus and Hermogenes, known to Timothy but not to us, there being no further reference to them in Scripture. Are these two singled out for special mention because *their* failure to function as "friends in need who are friends indeed" was especially surprising?

16. It would seem, however, that there was *one* significant exception. It must be admitted, however, that it is not even certain that he was one of those to whom Paul *had appealed.* Certain is the fact that he came, whether by request or entirely of his own accord. With warmth and enthusiasm Paul exclaims: **May the Lord grant mercy to the household of Onesiphorus, for he often refreshed me and was not ashamed of my chain.** Onesiphorus had shown mercy to Paul in his dungeon at Rome. Accordingly, may the Lord (Jesus Christ) grant mercy in return! This is in accordance with the rule laid down in Matt. 5:7. But why "to *the household* of Onesiphorus" (both here and in II Tim. 4:19), instead of simply "to Onesiphorus"? Here one can only guess. Some of the possibilities are as follows:

(1) Onesiphorus, having appeared in defence of a prisoner accused of a capital crime and having shown great interest in his case, was himself arrested and imprisoned. Hence, Paul's heart, filled with sympathy for the hero's *family,* utters the wish that the Lord may show mercy to these dear ones.

(2) Paul knows that the departure of Onesiphorus – from Ephesus to Rome – had caused worry to those whom he had left behind, but that they had nevertheless readily consented. Hence, not only Onesiphorus but also his household deserved to be specially mentioned by Paul. Besides, in circumstances that were "trying" for all the members of the family, the Lord's mercy was needed by all.

(3) Onesiphorus was no longer alive (having been executed?). Hence, Paul expresses the wish that the Lord might grant mercy to *his household!* (But if this be true, it would seem somewhat strange that not a word is

mentioned concerning the death of this hero. However, even for that fact – if it was a fact – a reason can be suggested.)

The very enumeration of some of the possibilities indicates that we are here in the realm of conjecture. We just do not know.

Paul states that Onesiphorus had *refreshed* him, *had,* as it were, *caused him to breathe more easily.* And Onesiphorus had done this not only once but frequently. Just how the visitor had carried out this bracing and cheering ministry is not stated. Perhaps by his very presence, a presence which implied self-sacrifice and love; furthermore, by bringing news to Paul concerning individuals and churches; by encouraging him on the basis of God's promises; by bringing him food, drink, literature. One is reminded of the services which, with great danger to himself, Jonathan rendered to David (I Sam. 18, 19, 20). Even Paul, a man of dauntless courage and amazing faith, could use encouragement at times. That was true also with respect to David, Elijah, Jeremiah, and John the Baptist. It is comforting to know that though the treatment which the apostle received was far less considerate than that which was accorded him during his first imprisonment, the privilege of receiving visitors and "refreshments" had not been completely taken away. Cf. II Tim. 4:13.

The fact that Onesiphorus had not been ashamed of Paul's *chain* filled him with gratitude. In all probability this *chain* must be taken literally; at least the literal meaning must be *included* (cf. Mark 5:3, 4; Luke 8:29; Acts 12:6, 7; 21:33; 28:20; Eph. 6:20; Rev. 20:1). Note in this chapter the meaningful recurrence of the expression "not ashamed." Timothy must not be ashamed (verse 8). Paul is not ashamed (verse 12). Onesiphorus was not ashamed (verse 16). Readiness to suffer, if need be, for the cause of Christ is the mark of the Christian (II Tim. 3:12; then John 16:33; Rom. 8:17).

17. Far from being ashamed, Onesiphorus had conducted himself in the very opposite manner. Hence, Paul says: **On the contrary, when he was in Rome he diligently searched for me and found me!** As soon as Onesiphorus had arrived in Rome he started the search for Paul. But why did he have to *search* for him? Several answers are given, and in some or all of them there is no doubt an element of truth. For example, a. Onesiphorus had never been in Rome; hence, did not know his way around. b. Part of the city had been destroyed by the great fire. This caused confusion. c. For a while the place of Paul's imprisonment was not known even to believers in Rome. d. Believers in Rome had been greatly reduced in numbers due to persecution and flight, and not even all who were left were eager to disclose "to a stranger" their spiritual affinity with "the prisoner of the Lord." And so one could continue. However that may be, it required *diligent* searching to find Paul. The words, "and he found me" sound like an exclamation.

Having located the "prison," it may not have been easy for Onesiphorus to gain immediate access to Paul. The present imprisonment was grim (cf. II Tim. 1:9). All the more credit to Onesiphorus! Hence, Paul continues:

18. May the Lord grant him to find mercy from the Lord in that day! The apostle utters a devout wish that *on the great day of judgment* (see verse 12 above; cf. II Tim. 4:8; then II Thess. 1:10) the Lord (Jesus Christ) may grant that the man who had gone to a great deal of trouble to *find* Paul may, in turn, *find* mercy (note wordplay), and this "from the Lord," which probably means, "from God the Father." [123]

Does the fact that Paul expresses the wish that Onesiphorus may find mercy "in that day" (contrast what is said about *the household* of Onesiphorus, verse 16) mean that this true and loyal friend had already departed from this earth, so that he could no longer receive mercy in *this* life? It is possible, but in view of the fact that the apostle does at times express the wish that eschatological blessings be granted to those who, while the apostle is writing, are still living on earth (for example, I Thess. 5:23b), the conclusion that Onesiphorus had actually died is not necessary. Here again we must confess our ignorance.

In reviewing the services which Onesiphorus had rendered, Paul begins with the most recent ones ("he often refreshed me," verse 16), then moves back the clock of his memory ("when he was in Rome he diligently searched for me and found me!" verse 17), and now (verse 18b) moves it back still farther: **And what services he rendered in Ephesus you know better (than I).**[124] Even before he went on his mission to Rome, Onesiphorus, still in Ephesus, had rendered many valued services to the cause of the gospel. This labor of love had been performed under the very eyes of Timothy. Hence, Paul says, "You know better than I."

Timothy, then, should show similar stedfastness, loyalty, and courage!

---

[123] I cannot follow Lenski's reasoning here (*op. cit.*, p. 775). If Paul had meant to say, "May the Lord grant unto *him* (Onesiphorus) to find mercy from the Lord in that day," with "Lord" referring to Jesus Christ in both cases, he could very well have substituted "from *him*" for "from *the Lord*." This substitution of a pronoun (this time in a different case than a moment before) would not have been ambiguous. Onesiphorus certainly could not find mercy "from *himself*." The true antecedent, namely, "Lord" (Jesus Christ) would have been obvious.

[124] For *better* the original has βέλτιον. Cf. τάχιον in the sense of "faster" (John 13:27; 20:4). Nevertheless, the elative use of βέλτιον here in II Tim. 1:18 (see also Acts 10:28 in D) cannot be entirely ruled out. Timothy knows "very well" what services Onesiphorus had rendered in Ephesus. See also M.M., 1. 108.

Synthesis of Chapter 1

See the Outline at the beginning of the chapter.

After another "grace, mercy, and peace" salutation, Paul acknowledges gratitude to the God of the forefathers who is also Paul's and Timothy's God. He tells his "beloved child" that his heart yearns to be filled with the joy of seeing him again; and that this yearning has been strengthened by the memory of the latter's tears shed when the two last separated, and by a recent reminder of his unfeigned faith in Christ.

As to that *faith,* Paul "recognizes" it, for he has seen it first in Timothy's grandmother *Lois* and mother *Eunice.* Let *Timothy* then cling to it as *they* had done. Yes, let him stir into a living flame the divine gift which he had received. Does Timothy love Paul? Of course, he does. Let him then bear in mind that at the time of his ordination *Paul's* hands, too, had rested upon him, as a symbol of the impartation of the gift of the Spirit; and that the latter is the Spirit not of timidity but of power and love and self-discipline.

Let Timothy then hold on to his faith as *Paul* had done and is still doing. Let him never be ashamed of the gospel, nor of "the Lord's prisoner" (note: *not* "Nero's prisoner"!), as the writer calls himself.

For the sake of the gospel Timothy must be willing to bear ill treatment along with Paul. God's infinite power will sustain him, for it was this very God who had included both Paul and Timothy (along with all the chosen ones) in his gracious purpose from eternity. Their salvation, the precious treasure which through the effective gospel-call has become their possession, can never be taken away from them. Reason: it rests not on *human works* but on *divine grace.* And this grace "was given to us in Christ Jesus before times everlasting, but has now been displayed through the appearing (First Coming) of our Savior Christ Jesus." And for his own comfort and strengthening, Timothy should bear in mind that it was this very Christ who on the one hand utterly defeated *death,* and, on the other hand, brought to light *life and incorruptibility* through the gospel. Let Timothy then look forward with joy to the prospect of one day entering upon the possession of this incorruptible life for both soul and body. Paul himself rejoices in the fact that with respect to the good news he has been appointed herald and apostle and teacher. To be sure, loyalty to such a commission results in suffering. Reflecting on this, Paul exclaims, "But I am not ashamed, for I know whom I have believed . . ." Prof. E. K. Simpson writes (*op. cit.,* p. 127) that when Dr. James Alexander of Princeton lay on his death-bed, his wife quoted these words inexactly — "I know *in* whom I have believed" — ; and that the dying man then gently corrected her version, because he was unwilling to let even a preposition creep between his soul and his Savior.

Paul continues, "and am convinced that he is able to guard with a view to that day that which I have entrusted to him." The apostle has deposited his soul and his complete salvation with God for safe-keeping. In that respect, too, he was following the example of Jesus who committed his spirit into the Father's hands (Luke 23:46). On the third day the deposit was returned to Jesus, as it were "with interest": a glorious spirit housed in a now glorious body. So, too, on *that* great day, namely, the day of the final judgment, Paul's soul, having been kept in safety in the Father's mansions above, would be clothed with a body like unto Christ's glorious body. Immortal life, in its full meaning (that is, for both body and soul) would take over from then on.

Encouraged by the certainty of a future so glorious, let Timothy then *hold on* to the pattern of sound words which Paul has given him; and let him do it in the spirit of faith and love centering in Christ Jesus. Yes, let him once for all guard the precious deposit of the gospel-ministry which God has left with him. The indwelling Holy Spirit will qualify him.

Another excellent example for Timothy to copy is *Onesiphorus*. When the apostle thinks of him, he exclaims, "May the Lord grant mercy to his house," and a little later, "May the Lord grant him to find mercy from the Lord in that day." When all those in Asia turned away from Paul, no one — not even Phygelus and Hermogenes — being willing to come to Rome in order to appear on the witness-stand in his favor, Onesiphorus had come, perhaps even before being asked. In various ways he had often refreshed Paul, not being ashamed of the apostle's chain. On arriving in Rome, Onesiphorus had searched for the prisoner and after considerable difficulty had found him. And even before starting out for Rome from Ephesus, this wonderful "profit-bringer" had rendered many valuable services to the gospel, as Timothy, in Ephesus, knew even better than Paul.

Outline of Chapter 2

Theme: *The Apostle Paul Tells Timothy What To Do in the Interest of Sound Doctrine*

Teach It "Suffer hardship along with (us)"

2:1-13 Though this teaching brings hardship, it also brings great reward.

2:14-26 Vain disputes, on the contrary, serve no useful purpose.

CHAPTER II

II TIMOTHY **2:1, 2**

2 1 You then, my child, be strengthened in the grace (that is) in Christ
Jesus; 2 and the things which you have heard from me among many witnesses, these things entrust to reliable men, such as will be qualified to teach others
as well. 3 As a noble soldier of Christ Jesus suffer hardship along with (us). 4 No
soldier on active duty gets himself entangled in the business-pursuits of civilian
life, since his aim is to please the officer who enlisted him. 5 Again, if anyone is
competing in an athletic event, he does not receive the victor's wreath unless he
competes in compliance with the rules. 6 The hard-working farmer should be the
first one to take his share of the crops. 7 Put your mind on what I say, for the
Lord will give you understanding in all matters. 8 Keep in memory Jesus Christ
as raised from the dead, of the seed of David, according to my gospel, 9 for which
I suffer hardship even to bonds as an evil-doer; but the word of God is not bound.
10 On account of this I endure all things for the sake of the elect, in order that
also they may obtain the salvation (which is) in Christ Jesus with everlasting glory.

11 Reliable is the saying:

For if we have died with (him), we shall also live with (him);
12 if we endure, we shall also reign with (him);
if we shall deny (him), he on his part will also deny us;
13 if we are faithless, he on his part remains faithful,
for to deny himself he is not able.

2:1-13

1, 2. You then, my child, be strengthened in the grace (that is) in Christ Jesus; and the things which you have heard from me among many witnesses, these things entrust to reliable men, such as will be qualified to teach others as well.

In view then of all that has been said in chapter 1 – the examples of faith and stedfastness (Lois and Eunice, Paul himself, Onesiphorus), the Holy Spirit's gift to Timothy, the great salvation that awaits him who perseveres, the wonderful calling – let Timothy *be strengthened* (cf. II Tim. 1:6-8, 14; and for the word itself see Acts 9:22; I Tim. 1:12; II Tim. 4:17, then Rom. 4:20; Eph. 6:10; Phil. 4:13) in that Christ-centered grace which, as was pointed out, had been given to him "before times everlasting" (see on II Tim. 1:9). Timothy's strength in the sphere of grace will grow if he cultivates *the gift* which grace has bestowed on him. The appeal is again couched in the language of the tender affection of a father for his son; note the emphasis "*you* then," and the appeal to *the heart,* "my child" (see on II Tim. 1:2). What the (spiritual) father (Paul) wants the child (Timothy) to do is found in verses 1-7. What the father, as the child's example, is doing is described in verses 8-10a. What *all believers* should constantly remember with respect to the manner in which faithfulness to Christ is rewarded, and unfaithfulness punished, is stated most clearly in verses 10b-13, and is already implied in verses 4-6.

Now, *one* sure way of being strengthened in grace is to transmit to others the truths which have embedded themselves in one's heart and have become enshrined in the memory. Accordingly, let Timothy be a teacher. Even more, let him produce teachers! Timothy needs this experience, and what is far more important, the church needs the teachers! Paul is about to depart from this life. He has carried the gospel-torch long enough. Hence, he hands it to Timothy, who, in turn, must pass it on to others. The *deposit* which was entrusted to Timothy (I Tim. 6:20; II Tim. 1:14) must be deposited with *trustworthy* men. They must be men, moreover, who will be *qualified to teach* others (cf. I Tim. 3:2), so that these others *as well* as their teachers will have been instructed in God's redemptive truth.

This redemptive truth or gospel of salvation, which Timothy is asked to transmit, is here described as "the things which you have heard from me among many witnesses." This expression undoubtedly refers to the entire series of sermons and lessons which the disciple had heard from the mouth of his teacher during all their association from the day when they first met.

Many had been *the witnesses* [125] of this preaching and teaching. Let Timothy bear in mind that the message which he has heard from the mouth

---

[125] The word used in the original has various shades of meaning. The exact connotation is sometimes difficult to determine. At times not much more than *a spectator and/or auditor* seems to be meant; one, however, who is able, if he so desires, to give competent testimony (cf. I Tim. 6:12). Then again, the idea of *actually giving testimony* of that which one has seen and/or heard seems to be reached. Similarly, in our own language a "witness" may be a. a person who is competent to give testimony whether or not he does it, or b. a person who actually gives testimony. In the present passage (II Tim. 2:2) the latter is probably the sense in which the word is used. The *witnesses* of whom Paul speaks were not merely silent observers and listeners. They were obedient to the exhortation, "Let the redeemed of Jehovah *say* so." It is easy to see how the legal sense in which the term *witness* is used is related to this meaning (see Acts 6:13; 7:58). Finally, the word may signify a *martyr* (see also N.T.C. on John, Vol. I, p. 7), one who has sealed his testimony with his blood. Thus, for example, Stephen and Antipas were *martyrs.* Nevertheless, even when these are called μάρτυρες, the question is debatable: In Acts 22:20 and Rev. 2:13 should we choose as English equivalent the word *witness* or *martyr?* Often, as in their case, the faithful *witnesses* became *martyrs.* This also applies to the *witnesses* mentioned in Rev. 11:3; see verse 7; and in Rev. 17:6.

of Paul had been given *among* or *in the midst of* [126] many persons who were ever ready *to lend their support* to the apostle's testimony.

3. The business of entrusting the gospel to reliable men (and, in fact, the gospel-ministry in general) entails *hardship* (verse 3). Yet, when a man fights wholeheartedly for the good cause, competes according to the rules, and works energetically, he will receive a glorious reward (verses 4-6; cf. 10b-13).

Says Paul: **As a noble soldier of Christ Jesus, suffer hardship along with (us).**

Timothy, then, as a *noble* or *excellent soldier* of Christ Jesus, belonging to him and engaged in that warfare in which "the cross of Jesus" is ever "going on before," must not shrink back but must be willing to *suffer hardship* (see on II Tim. 1:8; 2:9), which in this connection means even more than to "rough it" as soldiers do. It implies *suffering persecution* (II Tim. 3:12). He must be willing to endure this, says Paul, "along with. . . ." The question arises: along with *whom?* In view of the fact that in the preceding verse Paul has just referred to himself and the many witnesses, it is best to translate: "along with *us*," and not "along with *me*," as in II Tim. 1:8.[127]

4, 5, 6. These verses contain a threefold figure, beginning with the soldier-simile, continued from verse 3. The three illustrations clearly belong together, and must be seen as a unit in order to be understood:

(a) **No soldier on active duty gets himself entangled in the business-pursuits of civilian life,**[128] **since his aim is to please the officer who enlisted him.**

---

[126] I cannot follow Gealy (*The Interpreter's Bible,* Vol. II, pp. 478, 479) on this passage. Certainly διά does not have to mean *through.* The meaning *among* or *in the midst of* is easily accounted for. The preposition seems to have been derived from the number *two* (cf. δύο and διά). From this it developed into *be-tween* ("by two's"), which, slightly modified in meaning, easily slides into *among* or *in the midst of* (and by a different semantic shift, into *through*). Cf. the use of διά in II Cor. 2:4. In this connection it should be noted that the meaning *in the midst of* is not only "late Greek," as is sometimes maintained. Homer already uses the preposition in that sense (*Iliad* IX, 468; *Odyssey* IX, 298). – In this note I have indicated only a few semantic shifts. It is high time that more intensive study be devoted to the origin and evolution of New Testament prepositions. I have tried to do this with respect to ἀντί. See my doctoral thesis *The Meaning of the Preposition* ἀντί *in the New Testament,* Princeton Seminary Library. For διά what is found in Gram. N.T., pp. 580-584 is a good *beginning.*

[127] A.V., "endure hardness" rests on an inferior reading. A.R.V., "Suffer hardship with *me,*" adds the wrong pronoun. The context favors *us.* Another translation (R.S.V. and others), "Take your share of suffering," though somewhat less literal, is good.

[128] This, by necessity, is a somewhat free translation. Literally the passage reads: "No one soldiering entangles himself (or "gets entangled") in the business-pursuits

(b) **Again, if anyone is competing in an athletic event, he does not receive the victor's wreath unless he competes in compliance with the rules.**

(c) **The hard-working farmer should be the first to take his share of the crops.**

Paul compares the Christian minister (here with particular reference to Timothy, but cf. Phil. 2:25; Philem. 2) to a soldier, an athlete, and a farmer. I Cor. 9:6, 7, 24-27 presents the same threefold figure but with a different application. The resemblance, here in II Tim. 2, is as follows:

a. First, like a soldier on active duty, perhaps even engaged in a campaign, Timothy must perform his task *wholeheartedly*. If a soldiering person should pursue a business on the side, one that would really absorb his interests, so that he becomes "implicated" in it, he would not be able to really "give" himself to his appointed task as a soldier.[129]

The soldier in the field has just *one* purpose, namely, to satisfy the officer who enlisted him. Similarly, Timothy – and, for that matter, any "minister" – must realize that his exalted task "demands his soul, his life, his all." *One* holy passion must fill his frame. He must devote himself completely to his Lord who appointed ("enlisted") and qualified him for his task. Every true and faithful servant of Christ Jesus will *actually* devote himself thus wholeheartedly to his task, in order *to please* his Master (cf. I Cor. 7:32-34; cf. I John 3:22; and see N.T. on I Thess. 2:4). "No enlisted soldier," says Paul, will do differently!

The thought is implied: by way of reward, Timothy's Superior will surely provide for him! That implied thought is expressed with increasing clarity in the figures which follow:

b. *Wholehearted devotion* is not all that is required. *Rules* must be obeyed. In this respect the best figure is always that of a man who is competing in an athletic event. Paul pictures him in the very act of competing.[130] Now, unless such an athlete (for a fuller description see on I Tim.

(or, "in the affairs") of the βίος." M.M., p. 532, shows that πραγματεία may have either the more restricted meaning "business which provides a livelihood," or the wider meaning "matter," "affair." The word βίος may have one of several meanings depending on the context: mode of life, livelihood, the world we live in, biography, settled or civilian life, etc. Here in II Tim. 2:4 the context seems to draw a contrast between military and civilian life; hence, the rendering *civilian life* seems best. It is either that or "livelihood." In the latter case the entire phrase would be, "business of making a livelihood."

[129] It is true that Paul made tents, but this was not a business-pursuit in which he was engaged in order to *establish* himself financially. His heart was in his one, great endeavor. In order to gain the best results for Christ and his kingdom, he made good tents. See N.T.C. on I and II Thessalonians, p. 66.

[130] With respect to the grammatical implications of the tenses in this sentence, I beg to differ (respectfully, of course!) with two authorities: First, I do not believe that the present active subjunctive (ἀθλῇ) necessarily implies that the apostle has in mind *a professional athlete*. It is true that he *may* have been thinking of such

4:7b, 8) competes *lawfully,* that is, in accordance with the established rules, he does not receive *the victor's wreath,* the chaplet of leaves or of leaflike gold. Similarly, unless the man who performs special service in God's kingdom observes the rules – for example, to preach and teach *the truth,* and to do this in *love;* to exercise discipline in the same spirit; and see especially verses 10-12 below –, he will not receive the wreath of righteousness (II Tim. 4:8) and of glory (I Thess. 2:19; cf. I Peter 5:4; James 1:12; Rev. 2:10; see A. Deissmann, *op. cit.,* pp. 309, 369).

c. Timothy, then, must *fight wholeheartedly* for the good cause. He must also *compete according to the rules.* And now, thirdly: *he must toil energetically,* like *the* (generic use of the article) hard-working farmer (cf. I Cor. 3:9). He must be the very opposite of the "sluggard" pictured vividly in Prov. 20:4; 24:30, 31. If the farmer works hard, he should be the first to take his share of the crops (Deut. 20:6; Prov. 27:18). Similarly, if Timothy (or any worker in God's vineyard) exerts himself to the full in the performance of his God-given spiritual task, he, too, will be the first to be rewarded. Not only will *his own* faith be strengthened, his hope quickened, his love deepened, and the flame of his gift enlivened, so that he will be blessed "in his doing" (James 1:25), but in addition he will see in the lives of *others* (Rom. 1:13; Phil. 1:22, 24) the beginnings of those glorious fruits that are mentioned in Gal. 5:22, 23. See also Dan. 12:3; Luke 15:10; James 5:19, 20.

7. Put your mind on what I say, for the Lord will give you understanding in all matters.

Since several beautiful thoughts had been compressed into a terse threefold figure, and no explanation had been furnished, Timothy is told to *put his mind on* (νόει present, active imperative of νοέω; cf. νοῦς *mind*) that which [131] Paul has just said (in verses 4, 5, 6). Mere *reading* is not enough. What has been written must be *pondered.* What has been spoken must be *digested* (cf. Matt. 11:29; 13:51; 15:17; 16:9, 11; I Cor. 10:15; and especially Rev. 10:9, 10). Timothy need not fear that such mental activity will be fruitless. Has not the Lord given his definite promise? See Luke 19:26; John 14:26; 16:13. Surely in all matters with respect to which Timothy is

---

a person, but the present tense could also be used of anyone else. It simply pictures the action as *in progress.* For the opposite view see Bouma, *op. cit.,* p. 273.

Secondly, I do not believe that the first aorist active subjunctive (ἀθλήσῃ) necessarily means, "unless in a particular contest he contends," as A. T. Robertson maintains (*Word Pictures,* Vol. IV, p. 617). The aorist tense simply summarizes the action, takes a snapshot of it, instead of picturing it as being in progress. It is only fair to add that elsewhere Robertson himself states this; see Gram. N.T., p. 832.

[131] The textual apparatus in N.N. clearly indicates that ὃ is to be preferred here to ἅ. It also shows that "will give" (δώσει) is the best reading. It is not difficult, moreover, to account for the variants.

in need of understanding (σύνεσις, comprehension, insight), it will be given to him if he will but apply himself. Let Timothy then compare a scripture with scripture. Let him pray for wisdom (James 1:5). Let him reflect on his own past experience and the experience of other children of God. Let him listen to what these others have to say. By such means as these the Holy Spirit will give him all the guidance he will need in the performance of his task. He will be able to apply to himself and his office the rich meaning of the threefold figure, and he will derive from it the comfort which it affords.

8. In view of raging persecution, comfort was certainly needed. Faithful adherence to duty meant hardship (verses 3-6). Let Timothy not lose courage. Let him not even fear death. Let him rest his confidence on One who "utterly defeated" this terrible enemy (II Tim. 1:10). Accordingly, Paul continues, **Keep in memory Jesus Christ as raised from the dead, of the seed of David, according to my gospel.**

Note here "Jesus Christ," instead of "Christ Jesus" as elsewhere in II Timothy. If this be more than a stylistic variation, the possible reason for it may well have been this, that the apostle wished to turn Timothy's attention first of all to the historical, curse-laden *Jesus* (Gal. 3:13; 4:4, 5), in order that next he may remind him of the fact that this Jesus "was made" (was openly revealed as) *Christ* as a reward for his obedience unto death, yea the death of the cross (Acts 2:36; Phil. 2:5-11; see also footnote 19). Let Timothy then rivet his attention upon the resurrection; nay rather, let him keep his thought concentrated on *the resurrected Lord himself*. "Keep in memory Jesus Christ as raised from the dead," says Paul. Having been raised once for all from the realm in which death reigns, Jesus Christ now remains forever the risen One; hence, the living One (Rev. 1:17, 18). Coordinated with this exhortation is the one: "Keep in memory Jesus Christ as the seed of David." This follows very naturally; for, *the risen One* is surely also *the reigning One!* (cf. Matt. 28:18; I Cor. 15:20-25; Heb. 2:9; Rev. 22:1-5). Notice how also in verses 11 and 12 *living* and *reigning* follow one another.

Jesus Christ is "of the seed of David" (II Sam. 7:12, 13; Ps. 89:28; 132:17; Acts 2:30; Rom. 1:3; Rev. 5:5; and cf. Matt. 1:20; Luke 1:27, 32, 33; 2:4, 5; John 7:42).[132] He is "the Son of David" (Matt. 1:1; 9:27; 12:23; 15:22; 20:30, 31; 21:9, 15; 22:42-45; Mark 10:47, 48; 12:35; Luke 18:38, 39; 20:41). It is as the rightful, spiritual heir of David, David's glorious Antitype, that he sits enthroned at the Father's right hand.

The implied comfort is: "Timothy, if you and I and all other believers have died with him, we shall also *live with him*. If we endure, we shall

---

[132] I have discussed the genealogical problem with respect to the Davidic origin of Christ's human nature, in my *Bible Survey*, pp. 135-139.

also *reign with him.*" What is *implied* here is *expressed* in verses 11 and 12.

More than this, however, is implied, namely, "Timothy, constantly remember that, as living and reigning Lord, Jesus Christ is able as well as willing to help you and to carry you through. Not Nero but Jesus Christ, exalted at the right hand of the Father, has the reins of the universe in his hands and will continue to govern all things in the interest of the church and unto the glory of God. Hence, whatever happens, never lose courage. We know that to them that love God all things work together for good."

Now this presentation of Jesus Christ as the ever-living and reigning One is "according to (or "in harmony with") my gospel," says Paul. It was *Paul's* gospel, for: a. he had received it by immediate revelation (Gal. 1:12); b. he continues to proclaim it even in this letter, for he had been appointed its herald, apostle, and teacher (II Tim. 1:11); and c. he still clings to it with his whole heart, even now that he is facing death.

9. Exactly as in II Tim. 1:10-12, so also here the mention of Paul's *gospel,* is immediately followed by a statement about his *suffering.* Says Paul, **for which I suffer hardship even to bonds as an evil-doer.** Note in the preceding chapter "suffering" (verse 12), here "suffer hardship" (cf. II Tim. 1:8). The hardship which Paul is now suffering extends "even to bonds as an evil-doer." The rendering "bonds" (A.V., A.R.V.) has the same flexibility of meaning as has the word used in the original. It may refer to literal *shackles, chains,* or *fetters* (Luke 13:16; Acts 16:26); but also to all the hardship of *imprisonment* (Acts 20:23; 23:29; 26:31; Col. 4:18; Philem. 10, 13). Paul generally uses it in the latter, more general, sense. Nevertheless, the "chain" is certainly *included* in the meaning of the term (II Tim. 1:16), as used here. It would have been impossible for the apostle not to think of it!

"Even to bonds as an evil-doer," says Paul. "Evil-doer" (or "evil-worker," "*malefactor*") is a good, literal translation. A free rendering would be *criminal.* One thinks immediately of the "malefactors" who were crucified with Jesus (Luke 25:32, 33). This second imprisonment of Paul must have been very harsh!

However, in the midst of all his suffering and shame, there were two considerations which afforded him much comfort: First, "The way of the cross leads home," for the watchful eye of Jesus Christ who lives and leads is constantly upon me. He is able to guard my deposit with a view to that day (II Tim. 1:12). Secondly, Though I am bound, **the word of God is not bound.** Others will carry on when I leave this earthly scene. The authorities have put *me* in this dungeon, but they cannot imprison *the gospel.* It will triumph. It will perform its pre-ordained mission on earth. No enemy can thwart it. See the beautiful commentary which Scripture itself supplies in such well-known passages as Is. 40:8; 55:11; Phil. 1:12-14; and II Tim. 4:17.

One is reminded of Luther's immortal hymn *Ein feste Burg ist unser Gott,* the last two stanzas:

The German:

Und wenn die Welt voll Teufel wär'
Und wollt uns gar verschlingen,
So fürchten wir uns nicht zu sehr
Es soll uns doch gelingen.
Der Fürst dieser Welt,
Wie sau'r er sich stellt,
Thut er uns doch nichts;
Das macht, er ist gerecht't;
Ein Wörtlein kann ihn fällen.

Das Wort sie sollen lassen stan
Und kein'n Dank dazu haben.
Er ist bei uns wohl auf dem Plan
Mit seinem Geist und Gaben
Nehmen sie den Leib,
Gut, Ehr', Kind und Weib;
Lass fahren dahin,
Sie haben's kein'n Gewinn;
Das Reich muss uns doch bleiben.

Translation by Thomas C. Porter:

Did devils fill the earth and air,
All eager to devour us,
Our steadfast hearts need feel no care,
Lest they should overpower us.
The grim Prince of hell,
With rage though he swell,
Hurts us not a whit,
Because his doom is writ:
A little word can rout him.

The Word of God will never yield
To any creature living;
He stands with us upon the field,
His grace and Spirit giving.
Take they child and wife,
Goods, name, fame, and life,
Though all this be done,
Yet have they nothing won:
The kingdom still remaineth.

10. The triumph of the gospel causes Paul to continue with these courageous words, **On account of this I endure all things for the sake of the elect.** Even more literally one might translate: "*On account of* (διά) this I endure all things *on account of* (again διά) the elect." *On account of* the fact that the word is not bound, Paul does not lose courage but perseveres in faith and witness-bearing even in the midst of bitter trial. And this all the more *on account of* the elect, that they may obtain salvation. The two considerations which cause him to continue stedfastly in the course which he is pursuing are really *one:* the glorious and deeply-rooted conviction that the word of God will certainly triumph in the lives and destinies of the elect! Though Paul is in this dungeon, he does not despair. Victory is written on his banner.

The apostle endures *all things,* that is, all his manifold trials, for the sake of the gospel (cf. II Cor. 11:16-33; cf. Rom. 8:35-39; note "all these things," Rom. 8:37). He *endures* them, that is, he exercises the bravery of *bearing up under* them, the courage of positive perseverance and stedfastness even then when all things seem to be against him (cf. I Cor. 13:7). *To endure* means more than *not to complain.* It means more than *acquiescence.* It means going right ahead (believing, testifying, exhorting) though the load under which one is traveling on life's pathway has become very heavy. See further N.T.C. on I and II Thess. pp. 49, 50.

The apostle, then, endures all things "for the sake of the elect." (For a summary of Paul's doctrine of election see N.T.C. on I and II Thessalonians, pp. 49, 50. Cf. N.T.C. on John, Vol. II, p. 307.) *These elect are those on whom God has set his peculiar love from eternity.* Cf. Col. 3:12. They are the objects of his sovereign goodpleasure, chosen not because of their foreseen goodness or faith but because God so willed. It was not man's faith which caused election; but election which caused man's faith. If anyone wishes to see this for himself he should read such passages as the following: Deut. 7:7, 8; Is. 48:11; Dan. 9:19; Hos. 14:4; John 6:37, 39, 44; 10:29; 12:32; 17:2; Rom. 5:8; 9:11-13; I Cor. 1:27, 28; 4:7; Eph. 1:4; 2:8; I John 4:10, 19.

These references clearly teach that God did not choose his own because they are more numerous, but *for his own sake;* that he loves them *freely;* that they are *given* to the Son by the Father, *drawn* by the Father and the Son; and that with respect to them God exercises *his own* very unique kind of love. They teach that this predestinating love has as its objects *sinners,* viewed in all their foolishness and weakness; that it bestows its favor on those who have *nothing* and will never have anything except what they *receive;* on those who differ from other people for the simple reason that God in effectuating his decree of election *causes them to differ;* on those who, far from being chosen on account of their unblemished character, are chosen *in order that they may be* without blemish and unspotted before him; yes, *on those who will love him because he first loved them!*

Instead of *condemning* this doctrine, a person should first of all prove that it is not scriptural! It fits beautifully into the present context. Paul courageously endures all things because he knows that the word of God will certainly triumph in the hearts and lives of the elect. Cf. Eph. 3:13; Phil. 2:17. If it were true that their salvation had its deepest root in *their own works,* would the apostle have been able to face death with such fortitude? [133]

But even though for the elect, salvation is certain from all eternity, *it must be obtained.* The scriptural doctrine of election, far from putting

---

[133] Lenski, *op. cit.,* p. 791, in connection with the present passage, assails the Calvinistic doctrine. It is to be commended in him that he shows where he stands. But he does not furnish proof that this doctrine is unscriptural. Besides, if his attack on the Calvinistic position means that the Calvinist fails to point out that believers "should make their calling and election sure (II Peter 1:10)," then we answer that this is a point which the well-balanced Calvinist *emphasizes.* See L. Berkhof (surely a Calvinist!), *The Assurance Of Faith,* Grand Rapids, Mich. 1928, the whole book!

any restrictions on the exercise of human freedom, points to the One who makes man free indeed! The God who in his sovereign love chooses a person, in time powerfully influences his will, illumines his mind, floods his heart with love in return for God's love, so that these "faculties," under the constant guidance of the Holy Spirit, begin to function to God's glory in their own right. The decree of election includes the means as well as the end. God chose his people to salvation "through sanctification by the Spirit and belief in the truth." And to this salvation they are "called through our gospel" (see N.T.C. on II Thess. 2:13, 14).

Hence, the apostle, here as so often combining the divine decree and human responsibility, continues, **in order that also they may obtain the salvation (which is) in Christ Jesus with everlasting glory.**

Paul is interested not only in his own salvation (II Tim. 1:12) but *also* in that of others, namely, in the salvation of those who even now (while he is writing) are believers in Christ, and those who will afterward be brought to believe. He endures in order that *also they* may obtain that salvation which was merited by Christ, proclaimed by him, and experienced in living communion with him (hence, "the salvation *in* – or *centering in* – Christ Jesus"). He has in mind nothing less than *full salvation.* (For the meaning of *salvation* see on I Tim. 1:15.) Though believers even in this life enjoy salvation *in principle* (II Tim. 1:9; cf. Luke 19:9), they will not receive it in perfection (for both body and soul) until the great day of the consummation of all things (see on II Tim. 1:10-12; cf. Rom. 13:11). And this word *salvation* has two modifiers: a. it is a salvation "in Christ Jesus," as already explained; and b. it is a salvation "with everlasting glory" (Col. 1:27; 3:4). The second follows from the first. Union with Christ Jesus makes one *radiant,* both as to the *soul* (as explained in II Cor. 3:18) and as to the *body* (as set forth in Phil. 3:21). And this glory, in connection with the eternal One, never ends (John 3:16). Both in quality and in duration it differs from earthly glory.

11-13. Accordingly, Paul is willing to endure *all things* – hardship even to bonds, with the prospect of death – in order that through his stedfast ministry the elect may obtain their full, everlasting, Christ-centered salvation (see verses 3, 9, 10). It is necessary to keep this connection in mind. Otherwise what follows may be misinterpreted.

In harmony with what the apostle has just stated, he now introduces the fourth of five "reliable sayings" (see on I Tim. 1:15). The opinion that the lines which he quotes were taken from an early Christian hymn, a cross-bearer's or martyr's hymn, is probably correct. It is evident that he does not quote the entire hymn (unless γάρ here is not "for"; but in the present case "for" is probably right). Now, the word "for" indicates that in the hymn something preceded. The probability is that the unquoted line which preceded was something like, "We shall remain faithful to our Lord even to death," or, "We have resigned ourselves to reproach and suffering and even to death for Christ's sake." In either case the next line, the first one quoted by Paul, could then be: *"For,* if we have died with (him), we shall also live with (him)." Note that this feature of the quotation is similar to that which we encountered in connection with the lines quoted in I Tim. 3:16. Also in that case something that was not quoted must have preceded the quoted portion. In that case the line which presumably immediately preceded the beginning of the quotation probably ended with the word Logos or Christos or Theos (see on that passage).

Here in II Tim. 2:11-13, after the introductory formula (explained in connection with I Tim. 3:16):

Reliable is the saying,

the quoted lines are as follows:

For if we have died with (him), we shall also live with (him);
if we endure, we shall also reign with (him);
if we shall deny (him), he on his part will also deny us;
if we are faithless, he on his part remains faithful.[134]

In the first two lines the if-clause describes the attitude-and-action which proceeds from *loyalty* to Christ: we have died with (him), we endure (re-

---

[134] Grammatically the four lines are similar in that all are First Class Conditional Sentences. In this case the condition *is assumed to be* true to fact. Whether it is *actually* a fact has nothing to do with the form of the conditional clause.

In this kind of sentence we find εἰ with any tense of the indicative in the protasis. In the four lines which are quoted the apodosis, too, is constantly in the indicative. However, in the first three lines the apodosis is in the form of a prediction (future tense); in the last it is in the form of a statement of fact (present tense).

Summary:

	Protasis	*Apodosis*
Line 1:	First person plural aorist indicative.	First person plural future indicative
Line 2:	First person plural present indicative.	First person plural future indicative
Line 3:	First person plural future indicative.	First person singular future indicative
Line 4:	First person plural present indicative.	Third person singular present indicative

I do not agree with Lenski, *op. cit.,* p. 793, when he maintains that the use of the aorist tense shows that, since neither the apostle nor Timothy had as yet died physically, Paul in writing "If we have died with him," cannot have been thinking of physical death. The aorist tense does not necessarily indicate that an action has taken place in the actual past. It simply views an action *as a whole.* Accordingly, the interpretation, "For if at any time we have (or "shall have") died with (him), we shall also live with him," is not grammatically impossible.

main stedfast). *In the last two lines* the if-clause describes the attitude-and-action which proceeds from *disloyalty.*

The first two lines are clearly illustrations of synthetic or constructive parallelism. They do not express an identical thought, but there is progressive correspondence between the two propositions. As to the if-clauses, the persons who are assumed to have died with Christ are also the ones who endure, being faithful to death. And as to the conclusions, not only will such persons *live* with Christ, but they will also *reign* with him. These two go together. Note that in all the four clauses of these two lines the subject is *we* ("we . . . we . . . ; we . . . we").

The last two lines, describing the course of disloyalty, differ *in form* from the first two. Here we have not "we . . . we," but twice "we . . . *he.*" In the third line ("If we shall deny him, he on his part will also deny us"), the conclusion is the *expected* one (just as in lines one and two). In the fourth line, however, the conclusion comes as somewhat of a surprise. It takes careful reflection before we realize that the surprising conclusion is, after all, the only possible one. Once we grasp its meaning, we understand that also lines three and four express a parallel thought, and are illustrations of synthetic parallelism.

Before a detailed analysis of these four lines is attempted, it should be stressed that taken as a whole they convey *one* main thought, namely, *Loyalty to Christ, stedfastness even amid persecution, is rewarded, and disloyalty is punished.* This is in harmony with the idea of the entire chapter (see the Outline).

The meaning of the individual lines:

Lines 1 and 2:

After the connective "For," which has been explained, *line 1* immediately confronts us with a difficulty. There are *two main* lines of interpretation – there are also others which we shall pass by because even on the surface they are unreasonable – ; and the first of these two main lines is subdivided into two main branches or forms:

The first main line of interpretation, *in its first form,* is as follows: "If we have (that is, "If we shall have," or, "If at any time we have") experienced physical death, having been put to death because of our loyalty to Christ, we shall also live with him in glory." The reference in the if-clause would then be to a violent death, the kind of death Christ also suffered. In the case of believers this would be *the martyr's death.*[135]

This interpretation is surely possible. It does not clash with the context. The apostle desires that Timothy be willing to endure bonds along with

---

[135] Bouma, *op. cit.,* pp. 283, 284, interprets the passage in this manner.

other faithful servants of God (verse 3). Paul has just stated that he himself is suffering hardship even to bonds as an evil-doer, and that he endures all things for the sake of the elect (verses 9, 10). All this suffering has been imposed from without. Hence, when now in verse 11 he continues, "For if we *have died* with (him)," he could well have been thinking of that final form of physical affliction (the martyr's death) which may at any time be imposed upon Christ's loyal servants.

It is possible, however, that this interpretation is in need of some modification. This brings us to *the second form* in which the first main line of interpretation presents itself. Here, too, just as in the first form of this main line, *the martyr's death* is in the picture. But according to this view the sense would not be that believers (including Paul and Timothy) are pictured as having at any time already experienced the martyr's death but rather as being fully resigned to it and to all the afflictions which precede it. Paul then would be saying, "For Christ's sake and in harmony with his example we have given ourselves up once for all to a life that involves exposure to pain, torture, reproach, and finally to the martyr's death. We have, accordingly, *died to* worldly comfort, ease, advantage, and honor. If, then, we have in that sense died with (him), we shall also live with (him), here and now, even more by and by in heavenly glory, and especially after the Judgment Day in the new heaven and earth." Along this line Calvin, Ellicott, and Van Andel (for titles see Bibliography).

In favor of this interpretation are the following considerations:

(1) This also is not in conflict with the context which, as was noted, describes deprivation to which believers are exposed.

(2) It is in complete harmony with the line which immediately follows, for the person who has given up earthly ambition and has resigned himself for Christ's sake to reproach, suffering, and if need be to violent death, is the very man who "endures," that is, who "remains stedfast to the end."

(3) It is in agreement with Paul's thought as expressed elsewhere. See especially II Cor. 4:10: "*always* bearing about in the body the *dying* of Jesus, so that *the life* of Jesus may also be manifested in our bodies." With this compare I Cor. 15:31, "I die daily" (explained by verse 30: "we stand in jeopardy every hour").

If this be the correct interpretation – and I believe that it has much in its favor –, the thought which Paul, in quoting from the hymn, is conveying, is the one with which we ourselves are familiar. It has been expressed poetically in the beautiful lines:

"Hence with earthly treasure!
Thou art all my pleasure,
Jesus, all my choice.
Hence, thou empty glory!

Naught to me thy story,
Told with tempting voice.
Pain or loss or shame or cross
Shall not from my Savior move me,
Since he deigns to love me.

Hence, all fear and sadness!
For the Lord of gladness,
Jesus enters in.
Those who love the Father,
Though the storms may gather,
Still have peace within.
Yea, whate'er I here must bear,
Thou art still my purest pleasure,
Jesus, priceless treasure."
(Johann Frenck, 1653; translated by Catherine Winkworth, 1863)

The interpretation given, in either of its two forms, is surely preferable to *the second main line of interpretation,* according to which here in II Tim. 2:11 the apostle is referring *in general* (without any reference to the martyr's death) *to the process of dying unto sin,* that process of conversion and sanctification which is symbolized by the rite of baptism. This is a very popular view, in support of which an appeal is usually made to the similar-sounding passage, Rom. 6:8.[136]

But the present passage, II Tim. 2:11, *occurs in an entirely different context.* Romans 6 deals, indeed, with "death unto sin." The theme of the beginning of that chapter is that of spiritual renewal ("What shall we say then? Shall we continue in sin that grace may abound? God forbid. We who died to sin, how shall we any longer live in it? . . . Our old man was crucified with him that the body of sin might be destroyed," etc.) And from verse 10 on to the end of that chapter the word *sin* (noun or verb) or its synonym occurs in every verse!

Accordingly, the contexts of the two passages (Rom. 6:8; II Tim. 2:11) are entirely different. The one deals with sanctification in general; in the other cross-bearing and the martyr's death are in view. – Things which differ should not be confused!

Line 2 is not difficult once line 1 has been correctly interpreted. It means, "If we *remain stedfast* to the very end (for the meaning of *endurance*

---

136 Among the many commentators who share this view, in one form or another, are Barnes, Gealy (in *The Interpreter's Bible*), Lenski, Lock (in *The International Critical Commentary*), Scott (in *The Moffatt New Testament Commentary*), Van Oosterzee (in *Lange's Commentary*), and White (in *Expositor's Greek Testament*).

see N.T.C. on I and II Thessalonians, p. 198), we shall be kings in close association with him."

If Interpretation 1, Form 1, is adopted, the living and reigning would have to refer solely to the believer's existence *after* death. If Interpretation 1, Form 2, is preferred, the living and reigning pertains in principle even to the period before death, but comes to fruition immediately after death (cf. Matt. 10:32; Rev. 20:4), reaching its everlasting climax on and after the Judgment Day, when the saints will live and reign with Christ with respect to both body and soul (Dan. 7:27; Matt. 25:34; Rev. 22:5).

To live with Christ means *to be* with him, to have fellowship with him, to delight in him, to be like him, to love him, and to glorify him (see, for example, John 17:3; Phil. 2:5; Col. 3:1-4; I John 3:2; 5:12; Rev. 14:1; Rev. 19:11, 14; 22:4).

To reign with Christ means to experience in one's own life the restoration of the royal office. By virtue of creation man held the threefold office of prophet, priest, and king. As prophet his *mind* was illumined so that he knew God. As priest his *heart* delighted in God. As king his *will* was in harmony with God's will. This threefold office, lost through the fall, is restored by God's grace. The joyful response of the believer's will to the will of Christ, that response which is true freedom, is the basic element in this *reigning* with Christ. Moreover, even during the period before death Christians rule the world by means of their prayers, in the sense that again and again judgments occur in answer to prayer (Rev. 8:3-5). In heaven they are even closer to the throne than are the angels (Rev. 4:4; 5:11). In fact, they sit with Christ on his throne (Rev. 3:21), sharing his royal glory. And when Christ returns, the saints sit and judge with him (Ps. 149:5-9; I Cor. 6:2, 3).

Lines 3 and 4:

Having stated in the first two lines what will happen to those who endure or are willing to endure hardship even to violent death, the last two lines of the quoted portion of the hymn take up the case of those who, having confessed Christ (at least with the lips), become disloyal to him. "If we shall *deny* (cf. I Tim. 5:8) him, he on his part will also deny us." When a person, because of unwillingness to suffer hardship for the sake of Christ and his cause, *disowns* the Lord ("I do not know the man!"), then, unless he repents, *he will be disowned* by the Lord in the great day of judgment ("I do not know you"). See Matt. 26:72; then Matt. 25:12; also Matt. 10:33.

To deny Christ means *to be faithless.* (The parallelism and also the conclusion – "he . . . remains faithful" – show that here the meaning of the verb used in the original cannot be: to be unbelieving.) Hence, the hymn continues: "If we are faithless, he on his part . . . ," but obviously the continuation cannot be "will also be faithless." One *can* say, "If we shall deny him, he on his part will also deny us," but one *cannot* say, "If we are faithless, he on his part will also be faithless." Nevertheless, the conclusion of the fourth line corresponds *in thought* with that of its parallel, the third line; for, the clause "he on his part remains faithful" (line four) is, after all, the same (even more forcefully expressed!) as, "he on his part will also deny us," for *faithfulness* on his part means carrying out his threats (Matt. 10:33) as well as his promises (Matt. 10:32)! Divine faithfulness is a wonderful comfort for those who are loyal (I Thess. 5:24; II Thess. 3:3; cf. I Cor. 1:9; 10:13; II Cor. 1:18; Phil. 1:6; Heb. 10:23). It is a very earnest warning for those who might be inclined to become disloyal.

It is hardly necessary to add that the meaning of the last line cannot be, "If we are faithless and deny him, nevertheless he, remaining faithful to his promise, will give us everlasting life." Aside from being wrong for other reasons, such an interpretation destroys the evident implication of the parallelism between lines three and four.

The final clause of verse 13 is probably to be regarded as a comment by Paul himself (not a part of the hymn): **. . . for to deny himself he is not able.** If Christ failed to remain faithful to his threat as well as to his promise, he would be denying *himself,* for in that case he would cease to be The Truth. See also Num. 23:10; Jer. 10:10; Titus 1:2; Rev. 3:7. But for him to deny himself is, of course, impossible. If it were possible, he would no longer be God!

---

14 Remind them of these things, charging them in the presence of the Lord not to wage thoroughly useless word-battles, which upset the listeners. 15 Do your utmost to present yourself to God approved, a workman who has nothing to be ashamed of, rightly handling the word of the truth. 16 But profane empty-chatter shun, for they (who indulge in it) will advance to an increase of ungodliness. 17 And their word will devour like a gangrene. Among them are Hymenaeus and Philetus, 18 the kind of people who have wandered away from the truth, saying that (the) resurrection has already occurred, and they upset the faith of some. 19 Nevertheless, the solid foundation of God stands firm, having this seal:

The Lord knows those who are his,

and

Let every one who names the name of the Lord stand aloof from unrighteousness.

20 But in a large house there are not only gold and silver utensils, but also wooden and earthen, and some (are) for honor, some for dishonor. 21 So, if anyone will effectively cleanse himself from these, he will be a utensil for honor, sanctified, very useful to the Master, prepared for every good work. 22 But from the desires of youth flee away, and run after righteousness, faith, love, peace with those who call upon the Lord out of pure hearts. 23 But those foolish and ignorant inquiries reject, knowing that they breed quarrels. 24 And the Lord's servant must not quarrel, but be gentle to all, qualified to teach, patient under injuries, 25 with mildness correcting the opponents, in the hope that possibly God may grant them

conversion (leading) to acknowledgment of (the) truth, 26 and they may return to soberness, (being delivered) out of the snare of the devil, by whom they had been taken captive to (do) his will.

2:14-26

14. The subject of verses 1-13 is continued, the difference being that what was stated positively in the previous paragraph is stated negatively now (cf., for example, verse 2, "These things entrust to reliable men, such as will be able to teach others as well," with verse 14, "charging them . . . *not* to wage thoroughly useless word-battles"; see also verses 16, 21, 22, 23, 24).

Says Paul, **Remind them of these things, charging them in the presence of the Lord not to wage thoroughly useless word-battles** [137] **which upset the listeners.**

Timothy is told to remind the "reliable men" ("ministers") to remain stedfast in the performance of their God-given tasks of teaching, preaching, etc. Amid their many afflictions let them always look up to Jesus Christ, the risen and reigning Savior, who imparts strength to his faithful ones, and rewards them. It is clear that the expression "these things," refers especially to the entire preceding paragraph (verses 1-13), and perhaps even more directly to verses 8-13.

Timothy, then, has a "charge" for these leaders, just as Paul had a charge for Timothy. In both cases it was a charge "in the presence *of God*" or (in the present instance) *"of the Lord"* (see on I Tim. 5:21; II Tim. 4:1). Thus solemnly Timothy must warn the ecclesiastical leaders of "The District Ephesus and Surroundings" not to wage thoroughly useless word-battles (literally, "not to-wage-word-battle for nothing useful"). For such word-quibbling see on I Tim. 6:4 (*there* the noun is used; *here* the infinitive; in both cases the only instance of its use in the New Testament). Such word-battling is "unto the catastrophy (up-setting) of the listeners." Paul is referring, of course, to the quarrels arising from investigations into "endless

---

[137] *Note on the textual variants in II Tim. 2:14.* Though N.N. favors τοῦ θεοῦ instead of τοῦ κυρίου, the textual evidence in favor of the former is not sufficiently preponderant to rule out the idea that it may have been substituted for τοῦ κυρίου to bring the phrase into exact, verbal agreement with I Tim. 5:21; II Tim. 4:1. But essentially the difference is unimportant.

As to the remaining variants, the readings adopted by N.N. are probably the best. The *infinitive* (λογομαχεῖν) is natural in the present construction. As to the difference between the two ἐπί -phrases, the first followed by *the accusative* (an adverbial phrase: "to-wage-word-battles *for nothing useful*"), the second by *the dative* (indicating result: "unto the catastrophy of the listeners"), the attempts to eliminate this difference in construction after the same preposition (either by causing ἐπί to be followed by the dative both times, or by substituting εἰς for the first ἐπί) evidently stem from a desire for less rugged syntax.

myths and genealogies" (I Tim. 1:3, 4), "profane and old-womanish myths" (I Tim. 4:7a), the kind of drivel that was exposed earlier (see on I Tim. 1:3-7; 4:7a; 6:3-10). It is evident that during the period which had elapsed between the writing of the two epistles to Timothy religious conditions in the Ephesus region had not improved! The leaders and future leaders had to be warned not to be sidetracked into the devious by-ways of futile debates.

15. Timothy's personal example must serve as a powerful weapon against error: **Do your utmost to present yourself to God approved.** Timothy must exert every effort so to conduct himself that even now *before the bar of God's judgment* [138] he stands *approved,* that is, as one who, after thorough examination by no one less than the Supreme Judge, has the satisfaction of knowing that the latter is well-pleased with him and commends him (note synonyms in Rom. 14:18 and II Cor. 10:18). Now this happy result will be achieved if Timothy is found to be:

a. **a workman who has nothing to be ashamed of,**

accordingly also:

b. **rightly handling the word of the truth.**

Timothy, then, must be a *workman,* not a *quibbler.* His work, moreover, must be such that it does not reflect shame on him and that he does not need to fear that shame will cover him when he hears the divine verdict with respect to it.

This means, of course, that he is the kind of leader who is engaged in "rightly handling the word of the truth." This word of the truth is "the testimony concerning our Lord" (II Tim. 1:8), "the gospel" (same reference and see Eph. 1:13), "the word of God" (II Tim. 2:9). It is God's redemptive truth. The modifier "of *the truth*" emphasizes the contrast between God's unshakeable special revelation, on the one hand, and the Ephesian errorists' worthless *chatter* on the other.

The expression "rightly handling" has caused much controversy. It is true that "to cut" is the primary meaning of the main element (the *base*) of the composite verb from which this present masculine participle (ὀρθοτομοῦντα) is derived. Nevertheless, the view that *the composite verb* retains either this literal sense or the near-literal sense "divide" (A.V.) is debatable. In a composite verb the meaning-emphasis may shift to the prefix, until in the semantic process the literal sense of the base is lost. Thus straight-*cutting* begins to mean *straight*-handling, handling *aright.* It is not so strange that, by an easy transition from the physical to the moral sphere,

---

138 The word παρίστημι seems to have the judicial sense here (and also in Acts 27:24; Rom. 14:10; I Cor. 8:8) which it has at times in the papyri. See M.M., pp. 494, 495.

some such notion as "cutting a straight road or path" led in the course of time to the exclusively moral use of the term. Thus Prov. 11:5 (LXX) informs us that "the righteousness of the perfect *cuts his way straight,*" meaning: *"keeps his way straight,"* causes him to do what is *right.* Cf. Prov. 3:6 (LXX). Thus it is understandable that here in II Tim. 2:15 the meaning is, "handling aright."[139]

That the base ("to cut") should lose its original, literal meaning when a prefix ("straight") is added is not strange. Even *without* any affix the word "to cut" is frequently used in a non-literal sense. Thus, the Greek speaks of *"cutting* (taking) an oath," *"cutting* (diluting) a liquid," *"cutting* (working) a mine," etc. He also uses the expression "cutting short" (bringing to a crisis), and "cutting the waves," just as we do today. And compare our idioms "cutting a strange figure," "cutting droll capers," "cutting a pack of cards," etc.

Returning to the *composite verb,* I would emphasize that *the context* confirms the meaning which nearly all authorities ascribe to it. In the light of verses 14 and 16 the idea which Paul wishes to convey is clearly this, *"Handle* the word of the truth *rightly* instead of waging thoroughly useless word-battles which upset the listeners, and instead of paying any attention to profane, empty-chatter."

The man who handles the word of the truth properly does not change, pervert, mutilate, or distort it, neither does he use it with a wrong purpose in mind. On the contrary, he prayerfully interprets Scripture in the light of Scripture. He courageously, yet lovingly, applies its glorious meaning to concrete conditions and circumstances, doing this for the glory of God, the conversion of sinners, and the edification of believers.

16-18. The proper handling of the word of the truth implies the rejection of whatever is in conflict with its contents and meaning. Hence, Paul continues: **But profane empty-chatter shun, for they (who indulge in it) will advance to an increase of ungodliness. And their word will devour like a gangrene.**

This "profane empty-chatter" has been dealt with earlier (see on I Tim. 1:4; 4:7a; 6:4, 20). The term refers to the unholy, useless disputes about fictitious genealogical histories ("old womanish myths") and hair-splitting

---

[139] One possible reason why this verb has caused some difficulty to English readers may have been that *in English* the expression "cutting straight" or even "rightly dividing" is not immediately clear as an idiom which must be interpreted figuratively. On the other hand, those who are familiar with *the Dutch Bible* (Statenvertaling) experience no difficulty, for that language has the idiom: "die het Woord Gods *recht snijdt,*" "he who cuts the Word of God straight," which is immediately understood to mean, "he who handles the Word of God in the proper, straightforward manner."

debates about niceties in the law of Moses. Verse 18 seems to indicate that the men who were afflicted with this disease subjected the teachings of Paul to the same abuse. They began to "interpret" them into oblivion, just as is happening even in our own day and age.

Here, as in I Tim. 6:20, Paul uses the plural, so that one might translate "empty-jabbering*s*." Whenever Timothy encounters them, he must *turn himself about* in order *to avoid* them. Engaging the errorists in debate will make them worse, for *they* (not the jabber*ings* but the jabber*ers,* as the rest of the sentence shows) will *advance!* Do these would-be teachers claim to be advancing, to be making progress? "True," says Paul! "They will advance . . . *to more of ungodliness!"* A strange way to advance! They will "chop forward" steadily, removing every obstacle, making for the goal: *an increase of wickedness!* Paul surely knew how to use *irony* effectively!

And their *word* or *talk* will *devour.* It will "have pasture," [140] just like cattle "have pasture," eating away in every direction. The foolish disputes of the jabberers will resemble a *gangrene* or *malignant tumor.* Not only does the cancer eat away the healthy tissue, but in doing so it also aggravates the condition of the patient. Similarly heresy, advertised by too much attention, will develop both extensively and intensively. By adversely affecting an ever-increasing proportion of the membership it will tend to destroy the organism of the church.

The ringleaders are now mentioned by name: **Among them** (literally, "among whom") **are Hymenaeus and Philetus, the kind of people who have wandered away from the truth, saying that the resurrection has already occurred, and they upset the faith of some.**

The Dangerous Error of Hymenaeus and Philetus. The facts with respect to them may be summarized as follows:

(1) They were teachers of heresy in the Ephesian district.

(2) Hymenaeus was possibly the leader. At least, in both passages in which he is mentioned, his name occurs first. In I Tim. 1:19, 20 (see on that passage) Paul associates him with Alexander; here in II Tim. 2:16-18, with Philetus. We do not know why Alexander is no longer mentioned along with Hymenaeus. Had he moved away? Had he died? Had he repented? About Philetus (meaning "beloved") nothing is known except what is found here.

(3) Hymenaeus and Philetus were *the kind of* (οἵτινες) people who had *wandered away* (see on I Tim. 1:6; 6:21) from *the truth,* that is, from the true doctrine of salvation in Christ. It is immediately evident that Paul is not discussing a minor difference of opinion among men who basically thought alike. On the contrary, he refers to capital error.

---

140 This looks like a medical term. Cf. II Tim. 4:11: *Dr.* Luke was with Paul!

(4) Their error consisted in this, that they said, "The [141] resurrection has already occurred." In this they resembled those present-day liberals who, while refusing to be caught saying, "There is no resurrection," allegorize the concept. Now it must be admitted that Paul, too, believed in a *spiritual* resurrection, the act of God whereby he imparts the new life to those who are dead in sins and trespasses (Rom. 6:3, 4; Eph. 2:6; Phil. 3:11; Col. 2:12; 3:1; and cf. Luke 15:24). But the apostle also most definitely taught *the resurrection of the body* (I Cor. 15; Phil. 3:21), just as Jesus had done (John 5:28). According to Paul's teaching, *denial of the bodily resurrection implies the complete overthrow of faith,* for "if there is no resurrection of the dead, then Christ has not been raised either; and if Christ has not been raised, then our preaching is in vain, y o u r faith is in vain, . . . and y o u are still in y o u r sins" (I Cor. 15:13, 14, 17).

(5) What made matters worse was that Hymenaeus and Philetus professed to be Christians. The context – see verse 19b – seems to indicate that they were among those who "named the name of the Lord." Until their excommunication (for which cf. I Tim. 1:20) they had been members of the church!

In fact, these false prophets pretended to be "experts" in all matters touching religion. They yearned to be law-teachers, although "they understood neither the words which they were speaking neither the themes on which they were harping with so much confidence" (I Tim. 1:7). They perverted both the law and Paul's teaching.

(6) Their denial (by implication at least) of the bodily resurrection probably stemmed from pagan dualism, according to which whatever is spiritual is good, and whatever is material is evil. Their reasoning may well have been: "Since matter is evil, our bodies must be evil. Hence, they will not be raised." The same basic error would lead to other erroneous deductions (see on I Tim. 4:3).

(7) In view of their conviction that in their own case "the resurrection" – the only one they recognized, namely, from sin to holiness, from error to knowledge – had already occurred, why should they worry any longer about *sin?* They were self-righteous and conceited ("puffed up"). Hence, God's law did not "crush" them. They used it as an instrument for adding to their fame as teachers, as has been explained (see on I Tim. 1:9).

---

141 It is true that the textual evidence somewhat favors the omission of the article. Nevertheless, the context shows that pernicious, fundamental error is meant. Had Hymenaeus and Philetus merely taught that there was *a* resurrection which was past already, the apostle would not have been disturbed in the least, for that would have been a thoroughly scriptural (also *Pauline*) doctrine. But these heresy teachers totally denied the physical resurrection. Hence, as to the article, either: we must accept the reading of A.C., Koine text, D pl., or we must assume that ἀνάστασις can be definite even without the article.

(8) This indifference to sin resulted in their "advance" from ungodliness to "more of ungodliness" (see the context, verse 16; and cf. verse 19b, "unrighteousness").

(9) For example, they even *blasphemed* – railed at – the true gospel (I Tim. 1:20).

(10) Their false teaching "incipient gnosticism") was contagious. "They *upset* the faith of some." They "turned upside down" (see N.T.C. on John 2:15, Vol. I, pp. 122, 123) the religious convictions of these church-members. Perhaps, as yet *not many* had been infected with this terrible heresy (note, *"of some"*), but this was only the beginning. As a malignant tumor eats away the healthy flesh, so this wicked teaching eats away the Christian "faith."

19. Does this mean then that God's true church can be destroyed? Says Paul, **Nevertheless, the solid foundation of God stands firm, having this seal:**

The Lord knows those who are his,

and

Let everyone who names the name of the Lord stand aloof from unrighteousness.

False prophets shall lead many astray (Matt. 24:11). In fact, if it were possible, they would lead astray even the elect (Matt. 24:24). But the Good Shepherd *knows* his sheep, and gives everlasting life to them, and *they* shall certainly never perish, and no one shall snatch *them* out of his hands (John 10:14, 28). Since God is in the midst of her, God's city shall not be moved (Ps. 46:5). His kingdom cannot be shaken (Heb. 12:28). Though Paul has just pointed out that certain individuals have wandered away from the truth and have upset the faith of some (verse 18), it must ever be borne in mind that they are not all Israel that are of Israel (Rom. 9:6), and that, in spite of defections, "all Israel" shall be saved (Rom. 11:26; cf. I John 2:19).

In similar vein he now writes, "Nevertheless, the *solid* (or *compact;* cf. I Peter 5:9; Heb. 5:12, 14) foundation of God *stands firm"* (ἕστηκεν third per. sing., perfect indicative). But what is meant by this "solid foundation"? Among the many answers that have been given – such as, the Old and New Testaments, the bodily resurrection, the Christian religion, etc. – the following are, perhaps, the most important: (1) Election from eternity; (2) Christ himself; (3) the church.[142]

[142] For the first view see on this passage Calvin; also J. L. Koole; for the second, C. Bouma; for the third, Gealy, Lenski, Van Dyk, White, and Wuest. For titles see Bibliography. Bouma, commenting on II Tim. 2:19, flatly rejects the idea that *the foundation* indicates the church, *op. cit.,* p. 297 (even more definitely in his *Korte Verklaring,* p. 150). Nevertheless, *op. cit.,* p. 146, commenting on I Tim. 3:15, he states, "The Church of the Lord is a pillar; what is more, it is a foundation."

With respect to (1): This idea cannot be altogether discarded. Paul has just made mention of election (verse 10). No doubt the idea of the divine predestinating love does enter in – notice especially the words, "The Lord knows (from everlasting) those who are his" – ; nevertheless, nowhere else does the apostle call election a *foundation.* Besides, the second inscription on the seal (verse 19b) is hardly in keeping with this interpretation, and the context does not demand it.

With respect to (2): It is true that Christ is called the *foundation* in I Cor. 3:10-12. Nevertheless, this does not settle the matter. One cannot always ascribe exactly the same meaning to Paul's metaphors. Thus, in Eph. 2:20 Christ is not called the foundation but "the chief cornerstone." Here in II Tim. 2:19 there is nothing to suggest that Christ is regarded as the foundation.

With respect to (3): I consider this view to be correct. *The church, established upon the bedrock of God's predestinating love, is his foundation, his building well-founded.* Reasons for adopting this view:

a. This harmonizes most beautifully with the context: God's *true* church consists of those who are his, those who stand aloof from unrighteousness (note the seal!). By calling the church "God's *solid foundation,*" Paul stresses its permanency and immobility. Some, indeed, have wandered away, etc., but the *true church* is immovable!

b. This is consistent with I Tim. 3:15. There, too, the church is called "the *foundation*" or "the *support*" (there ἑδραίωμα, here in II Tim. 2:19 θεμέλιος).

God's foundation has *a seal* (not *merely* an inscription!). Now a seal may *indicate authority* and thus may *protect* or at least *warn* against all tampering. Thus, the tomb of Jesus was sealed (Matt. 27:66). Again, it may be *a mark of ownership.* "Set me as a seal upon thy heart" (Song of Solomon 8:6). Or it may *authenticate* a legal decree or other document, *certifying* and *guaranteeing* its genuine character. Thus, the decree of Xerxes was sealed (Esther 3:12; cf. I Cor. 9:2).

When we now read that God's solid foundation, the church, has a seal, it is probably unwarranted to apply only *one* of these three ideas to *this* seal. The seal by which believers are sealed protects, indicates ownership, and certifies, all three in one! [143] Cf. Rev. 7:2-4. God the Father *protects* them, so that none are lost. He has *known* them as his own from all eternity (the context calls for this idea). God the Son *owns* them. They were *given* to him. Moreover, he *bought* or *redeemed* them with his precious blood. This idea of ownership is clearly expressed here ("the Lord knows *those who are his*"). And God the Holy Spirit *certifies* that they are,

---

143 Thus also D. M. Edwards in his excellent article "Seal" in I.S.B.E.

indeed, the sons of God (Rom. 8:16). This divine protection, ownership, and certification *seals* them!

But how do believers experience the comfort of the seal? The answer is: by taking to heart what is written on the seal! The seal bears two closely related inscriptions. *God's* decree and *man's* responsibility receive equal recognition:

The first inscription deals the deathblow to *Pelagianism;* the second, to *fatalism.*

The first is dated *in eternity;* the second, *in time.*

The first is a declaration which we must *believe;* the second, an exhortation which we must *obey.*

The first exalts *God's predestinating mercy;* the second emphasizes *man's inevitable duty.*

The first refers to the *security;* the second to the *purity* of the church (Wuest, in agreement with Vincent).

Between the two there is a very close connection. That connection is interpreted beautifully in I Cor. 6:19b, 20: "Y o u are not y o u r own, for y o u were bought with a price (cf. the first inscription); glorify God therefore in y o u r body" (cf. the second inscription).

The close relationship between the two inscriptions is evident also from the fact that the words of both were probably derived from the same Old Testament incident; namely, the rebellion by Korah, Dathan, and Abiram (Numbers 16). Hymenaeus and Philetus, in their rebellion against true doctrine and holy living, resembled these wicked men of the old dispensation. In both of these instances of rebellion against constituted authority there was disbelief of what God had clearly revealed. In both cases the leaders involved others in their crime. The implication is that just as the rebellion under Korah, etc., ended in dire punishment for those who rebelled and for their followers, so also will the present rebellion of Hymenaeus and Philetus terminate in disaster for them and their disciples, unless they repent.

The similarity between the Old Testament references and Paul's words will be seen by placing them in parallel columns:

Numbers 16:5, 26 (LXX):	II Tim. 2:19:
"God . . . knows those who are his."	"The Lord knows those who are his."
"Separate yourselves from the tents of these wicked men . . . lest y o u be destroyed along with them in all their sin."	"Let everyone who names the name of the Lord stand aloof from unrighteousness."

It is probable, however, that in addition to the story of rebellion so vividly portrayed in Numbers 16, Paul was thinking of other Old Testament references. Thus, the following (and other similar passages) may also have served as a basis for the first inscription: the Lord *knows* Abraham (Gen. 18:19), Moses (Ex. 33:12, 17), those who take refuge in him (Nah. 1:7). The aorist tense here in II Tim. 2:19, "The Lord *knows* or *knew* (ἔγνω)," may be called *timeless. By virtue of his sovereign grace he from eternity acknowledged them as his own, and consequently made them the recipients of his special love and fellowship (in the Spirit).* Cf. John 10:14, 27; Rom. 8:28. Hence, they are perfectly safe. They can never be lost (John 10:28).

But this security does not become their possession in any arbitrary or mechanical fashion. *The first inscription has no meaning at all apart from the second, nor the second apart from the first.* The Lord will tell *the wicked* that he has never *known* them (Matt. 7:23; Luke 13:27). The two inscriptions always go together if anyone is ever to become a truly *sealed* person. Security and purity dovetail. Read in this connection, II Thess. 2:13: "God chose y o u from the beginning to salvation through sanctification by the Spirit and belief of the truth." Cf. I Peter 1:1, 2: "Elect . . . according to the foreknowledge of God the Father, in sanctification of the Spirit, unto obedience," etc.

Hence, the second inscription follows hard upon the first. On the seal the two stand next to each other; or *one* on one side, *the other* on the other side. Compare an American coin, with its two sides, an inscription upon each, one pointing to God as the source of our liberty, the other reminding us of the fact that though there are many States, yet there is only one nation, and implying that all should co-operate. *Obverse:* IN GOD WE TRUST; *Reverse:* E PLURIBUS UNUM.

Basic to the words of the second inscription ("Let everyone who names the name of the Lord stand aloof from unrighteousness") are, in addition to Num. 16:26, such Old Testament passages as Is. 26:13 (LXX: "We name thy name"); Ps. 6:8; and Is. 52:11; cf. II Cor. 6:17 (exhortations to depart from evil and from evil-workers). Whether the apostle derived the thoughts embodied in the two inscriptions *directly* from the Old Testament, or whether they had first become embodied in a Christian hymn, as some think, is a question that cannot now be answered, and is of little importance.

The meaning of the second inscription is this: expressed reliance on God must reveal itself in a life that is consecrated to God's glory. A person's confession must exemplify itself in a holy walk and conduct. The person who in prayer and praise "names the name of the Lord" thereby declares that he embraces God's revelation of himself in the realm of nature (Ps. 8) and of redemption (John 16:24). Such a person must be consistent! That very consistency is what Hymenaeus and Philetus lacked. They named the name of the Lord, and promoted unrighteousness! Literally Paul says "Let everyone who names the name of the Lord *apostatize.*" But in this connection it must be borne in mind that the Greek uses this verb (to apostatize, stand aloof, withdraw oneself from) both in a favorable and in an unfavorable sense. Let him *apostatize* . . . not from *the faith* (I Tim. 4:1), but from *unrighteousness* of every variety.

20. But, although God's elect never perish, **in a large house there are not only gold and silver utensils, but also wooden and earthen, and some for honor, some for dishonor.**

Timothy must not be surprised about the fact that there is such a thing as defection! He must bear in mind that it is with the *visible* church as it is with "a *large* house." Such a *large* house contains all kinds of *utensils;* that is, furniture, vases, pots and pans, etc., in short, all those material objects which one expects to find in a mansion, the entire "household contents"; hence, not only gold and silver but also wooden and earthen vessels; not only articles to be kept and displayed, but also those which are taken to the dump or junk-yard when they have served their purpose. In passing, note that Paul must say *large* house, because a *small* house might not contain gold and silver utensils. — Similarly, the visible church, as it manifests itself on earth, contains *true believers* (some more faithful, comparable to gold; others less faithful, comparable to silver) and *hypocrites.* Cf. Matt. 13:24-30: wheat and tares. The genuine members are destined for *honor* (see Matt. 25:34-40); the others, for dishonor (see Matt. 25:41-45). Cf. I Sam. 2:30b; Rom. 9:21.[144]

21. How can one be sure of being a utensil for honor? The answer is: **So, if anyone will effectively cleanse himself from these, he will be a utensil for honor, sanctified, very useful to the Master, prepared for every good work.**

Close and intimate association with hypocrites may easily lead to moral and spiritual contamination (I Cor. 15:33; and see N.T.C. on II Thess.

---

144 Reference to I Cor. 3:10-15 or to I Cor. 12:12-31 only serves to confuse matters. The first discusses building-materials (works, teachings); the second, distribution of talents. But II Tim. 2:20, 21 describes *church-members,* genuine and false. Scott (*op. cit.,* p. 114) says that the writer of II Timothy uses a clumsy simile that becomes more and more confused. Bouma (*Korte Verklaring,* p. 152) thinks of this *house* of verse 20 as built upon *the foundation* mentioned in verse 19. That is *one* reason why he cannot identify the foundation with the church, for how can the church be built upon the church? But verse 20 does not say that *the house* of verse 20 is built on *the foundation* of verse 19. Both of these interpreters fail to do justice to the fact that each metaphor must be given its own distinct interpretation. This is often the case in Scripture. The church is *both* a house *and* a foundation (thus also in I Tim. 3:15, though the words used in the original vary slightly from those used here in II Tim. 2:19, 20). In *one* sense it is like a house; in another sense it is like a foundation. Thus also in John 10 Jesus is both the door and the Good Shepherd. His enemies are strangers, thieves, *and* hirelings. And in the book of Revelation the church is *both* a bride *and* a city. See N.T.C. on John, Vol. II, p. 102. These are not *mixed* metaphors, but *different* metaphors.

3:14). The temptation to fall into this trap must be avoided. The sin of accepting the doctrines and/or of copying the example of such wicked men (whether the latter be thought of as still in the church or as already out of the church) must be avoided (cf. verse 19b); and if committed, must be confessed, and the evil must be overcome with good. Thus, a person must "effectively" or "thoroughly" cleanse himself "from these," that is, from evil men ("utensils for dishonor") and their defiling doctrines and practices; from such men as Hymenaeus and Philetus and their disciples, and from their false teachings and evil habits.

Now if anyone will thus effectively cleanse himself, he will be a utensil for honor.[145] The reality rises above the figure: a cheap dish will always remain a cheap dish, but God's grace enables a sinner to become a saint, "a utensil for honor." Such a person, having cleansed himself, is *sanctified.* Through the purifying operation of the Holy Spirit he has now become "a saint in experience as well as position" (K. S. Wuest, *Golden Nuggets,* p. 72), having been wholly *set apart* for the Lord and his work, and this abidingly. Accordingly, he is now "very useful" to his *Master,* the One who exercises full authority over him (cf. I Tim. 6:1, 2; Jude 4; Rev. 6:10), namely, Jesus Christ. Once for all he is *prepared* for *every* good work (cf. II Tim. 3:17; Titus 1:16; 3:8, 14; then II Cor. 9:8).[146]

22. The way to cleanse oneself is to become *de*tached from that which is evil and *at*tached to that which is good. Hence, Paul continues: **But from the desires of youth flee away, and run after righteousness, faith, love, peace with those who call upon the Lord out of pure hearts.**

When Paul wrote these words, Timothy must have been 37-42 years of age (see on I Tim. 4:12). He was still rather young, especially in relation to the position of trust and responsibility which he occupied. So the apostle warns him against "the (or "those well-known," note the article) *desires* of youth." But just what does he mean? [147]

---

[145] The construction is regular: a future more vivid conditional sentence, using ἐάν with the aorist subjunctive in the protasis, and the future indicative in the apodosis. The condition is conceived as a probable future reality. See N.T.C. on John, Vol. I, pp. 42, 43. The expression "utensil for honor" has three modifiers: "sanctified" and "prepared" are perfect passive participles; "very useful" is an old verbal adjective.

[146] This, however, does not necessarily mean that the "utensils for *dis*honor" serve no useful purpose in the church. They *do,* and this in spite of themselves! Study Rom. 9:17, 22, 23. Even Pharaoh was of some use (Ex. 7:4, 5; 9:16; 10:1, 2). Cheap dishes serve a useful purpose even though they are soon discarded!

[147] The word "desire" (ἐπιθυμία) has the following uses: (1) Legitimate desire: Luke 22:15 (Christ's desire to eat the Passover with his disciples); Phil. 1:23 (Paul's desire to depart and be with Christ); I Thess. 2:17 (the desire of Paul, etc., to re-visit the Thessalonians).

(2) Illegitimate or sinful desire (the desire for wrong things, or simply the wrong kind of desire):

The word *desire* that is used in the original, whether in a favorable or unfavorable sense, always indicates *strong yearning.* As the footnote indicates, it is used far more often in an unfavorable than in a favorable sense. In the present passage, it is definitely *sinful* desire that is meant ("From the desires of youth *flee away*"). Such sinful desires, as the footnote also proves, can be classified more or less after the manner of modern psychology (though here these yearnings would hardly be called *sinful*), as follows:

(1) *P*leasure, etc., the inordinate craving for the satisfaction of the physical appetites: the "lust" for food and drink, pleasure-madness, uncontrolled sexual desire (Rom. 1:24; Rev. 18:14, etc.)

(2) *P*ower, etc., the ungoverned passion to be Number 1, the lust to "shine" or be dominant. This results in envy, quarrelsomeness, etc. This sinful tendency is included prominently in such references as Gal. 5:16, 24; II Peter 2:10, 18; Jude 16, 18.

(3) *P*ossessions, etc., uncontrolled yearning for material possessions and for the "glory" that goes with them (see I Tim. 6:9 in its context).

Objectively speaking, Christ triumphed over the first when in the first temptation he said, "Man shall not live by bread alone, but by every word that proceeds out of the mouth of God" (Matt. 4:1-4); over the second, when in the second temptation he refused to cast himself down from the pinnacle of the temple (Matt. 4:5-7); and over the third, when in the third temptation he refused to receive as a gift out of Satan's hand "the king-

---

a. With the emphasis definitely on sins in the realm of sex: (Rom. 1:24; I Thess. 4:5).

b. With the emphasis more general, the context at times indicating one or more of the following: the closely related sins of sex and of idolatry, the liquor-mania, inordinate craving for material possessions, self-assertiveness (hence, quarreling, jealousy, vanity, the lust to dominate): Mark 4:19 (the "thorns" which choke the good seed); John 8:44 (Satan's desires); Rom. 6:12 (unrighteous desire versus righteousness); Rom. 7:7, 8 (covetousness); Rom. 13:14 (note synonyms); Gal. 5:16, 24 (sex, idolatry, self-assertiveness in several manifestations, drunkenness, etc.); Eph. 2:3 (with probably the same mental context as Gal. 5:16, though *there* the context is more specific); Eph. 4:22 (versus "righteousness, holiness, and truth"); Col. 3:5 (cf. Gal. 5:16); I Tim. 6:9 (money-lust and its results); II Tim. 2:22 (the passage under discussion); II Tim. 3:6 ("various impulses," see on that passage); II Tim. 4:3 (very general: desiring "teachers after their own lusts"); Titus 2:12 ("worldly passions"); Titus 3:3 ("malice, envy," etc.); James 1:14, 15 (probably the same mental context as Gal. 5:16); I Peter 1:14; 2:11 (for context see I Peter 2:1: "wickedness, guile, hypocrisy, envy, evil speaking"); I Peter 4:2, 3 (sins of sex and idolatry, drunkenness and its results); II Peter 1:4 (very general); II Peter 2:10, 18 (sex, self-assertiveness and kindred sins); II Peter 3:3 (emphasis on mockery); I John 2:16, 17 ("lust of the flesh and lust of the eyes"); Jude 16, 18 (mockery, sinful desire for advantage, animal-desires, the dissatisfied spirit, arrogance); Rev. 18:14. Probably this also belongs here (inordinate desire for ripe fruits, crowding out desire for spiritual things).

R. C. Trench, *op. cit.*, par. lxxxvii, has shown that while πάθος represents the more passive aspect of evil desire, ἐπιθυμία expresses the active side, and is also far more comprehensive in its *New Testament* usage.

doms of the world and their glory" (Matt. 4:8-10). As a result of his triumph he in a far more glorious sense received from his heavenly Father the very things with which the devil had tempted him. (In *Christ's* case, however, the temptations were entirely *objective;* there were no *subjective,* sinful tendencies.)

Since these inordinate desires often assert themselves more turbulently in youth than in old age – as he grows older a Christian rises above them through the sanctifying grace of the Holy Spirit, bringing him gradually to spiritual *maturity* –, they are here fittingly called "the desires *of youth*" (literally, "the youthful desires").

Two extremes should be avoided. First, it is wrong to construe the reference to be, either exclusively or predominantly, to uncontrolled *sexual* desire. Secondly, it is not necessary to exclude this evil entirely from view. The term, as here used, must probably be taken in its most general sense, as indicating *any sinful yearning to which the soul of a young or relatively young person is exposed.* If, within this general connotation, any element of special emphasis must be found, it should be derived from the context. In the present case there was, perhaps, the tendency of the younger man to be somewhat impatient with those who stood in the way. Timothy's high moral character, coupled with his youthful years, might induce him to act somewhat inconsiderately toward those who were opposing the truth. A person of natural reserve, timidity, and general amiability, such as Timothy, can at times act rather impulsively when at last, contrary to his natural tendency, he is aroused to action. But whether or not in Paul's mind there was any special reference to *this* particular danger of youth cannot now be determined. The sinful desires of youth may best be regarded in the most general sense, and thus as the antonyms of the virtues now mentioned: "righteousness, faith, love, and peace."

Grammatically it is also possible to interpret Paul's words as meaning no more than this: "Timothy, continue to do exactly as you have always been doing. Keep on in your present course, fleeing away from the desires of youth and pursuing righteousness, faith, love, peace," etc.[148] But, though the tense used in the original *permits* this interpretation, it does not *require* it. It is, moreover, in line with Paul's very practical bent of mind to assume that these crisp commands bear some reference to reality, and were warnings that were actually needed, yes needed even by Timothy because of certain character-weaknesses, however unpronounced they may have been. In our desire to do full justice to the beauty of Timothy's character, let us not equip him with wings!

Paul's youthful associate, then, must constantly flee away from the sinful propensities of youth, and must cultivate the habit of running after the

---

[148] Lenski interprets along this line, p. 812.

virtues that are here enumerated. Note the alliteration – *"run* after *right*-eousness" (here as in I Tim. 6:11) – and the *chiastic* sentence-structure, with *the vices and the virtues* (the last one, "peace," expanded into a compound phrase) at either end of the sentence; and *the opposite actions* – "flee away from," "run after" – next to each other in the middle.

Since most of the concepts here mentioned have occurred before, the reader is referred to the more detailed explanation in I Tim. 4:12 and I Tim. 6:11. Briefly, then, what Paul has in mind may be paraphrased as follows:

From the sinful tendencies of youth flee away, and *run after* (steadily pursue) the following: a. that state of heart and mind which is in harmony with God's law ("righteousness"); b. humble and dynamic confidence in God ("faith"); c. deep personal affection for the brothers, including in your benevolent interest even the enemies ("love"); and d. undisturbed, perfect understanding ("peace") with all *Christians* (those who in prayer and praise "call upon" the Lord Jesus Christ – cf. Joel 2:32; Rom. 10:12; I Cor. 1:2 – out of pure hearts). The "pure hearts" (the original has the singular where English prefers the plural) are the inner personalities of those who "stand aloof from unrighteousness" (verse 19) and "have effectively cleansed themselves" (verse 21).

23. To the admonition of verse 22 a second is now added: **But those foolish and ignorant inquiries reject, knowing that they breed quarrels.**

See what has already been said with reference to this in our comments on verse 14 above, and on I Tim. 1:4; 4:7; 6:4; cf. also Titus 3:9. Not only must Timothy refrain from waging thoroughly useless word-battles (verse 14), but he should even refuse, politely but definitely, to bother with *the* well-known (note the article) *enquiries* that would result in such word-battles. Such enquiries are *foolish.* They are senseless, the kind of investigations which one associates with morons. They are *ignorant,* "uneducated" or "uninstructed"; that is, they are the work and the mark of ignorant men. The person who has been *properly* educated in God's redemptive truth is able to distinguish between the worth-while and the worthless, and does not conduct such worse than useless enquiries (into genealogical and other Jewish-tradition lore). Timothy must *constantly refuse* to have anything to do with them, for he knows that they breed or generate *quarrels.*

24-26. These three verses clearly form a unit. The mention of *quarrels* in verse 23 leads Paul to re-inforce his admonition that Timothy must refuse to become involved in foolish and ignorant enquiries. Such enquiries breed quarrels, which are exactly the obstacles which ministers must avoid. Says Paul:

And the Lord's servant must not quarrel, but be gentle to all, qualified to teach, patient under injuries, with mildness correcting the opponents,

in the hope that possibly God may grant them conversion (leading) to acknowledgment of (the) truth, and that they may return to soberness, (being delivered) out of the snare of the devil, by whom they had been taken captive to (do) his will.

Timothy is *the servant* (this is a better rendering than *slave;* see N.T.C. on John, Vol. II, footnote 184) *of the Lord* (Jesus Christ; cf. Rom. 1:1; Phil. 1:1; then also James 1:1). As such he should resemble his Lord, who was meek, lowly, restful; who did not cry or lift up his voice or cause it to be heard in the street; who when he was oppressed and afflicted opened not his mouth, but was like a lamb that is brought to the slaughter; and who refused to revile those who reviled him (Is. 42:2; 53:7; Zech. 9:9; Matt. 11:29; 12:19; 21:5; I Peter 2:21-24). True, *the Lord's servant* – the term and the admonition apply not only to Timothy but to every "minister" – must be *an excellent soldier* (see verses 3 and 4 above), but he must *not* be *a quarreller,* a mere *quibbler* about farcical questions regarding family-trees and rabbinical law-interpretations.

Instead of finding in these words additional proof that Paul cannot have written the Pastorals, one should find in them the very opposite. It was *Paul* who also wrote I Thess. 2:7-12!

The Lord's servant, then, must be *gentle* (this is the best reading, both here and in I Thess. 2:7, the only New Testament occurrences), that is, affable, easy to speak to, approachable in his demeanor; *not* irritable, intolerant, sarcastic, or scornful, not even toward those who err. He must try to *win* them. Hence, he must be gentle *to all!*

Gentleness is necessary, for the Lord's servant must be *qualified to teach,* capable of imparting counsel and instruction.

His gentleness will, however, not always be reciprocated or even appreciated. His teaching will at times meet with ridicule and abuse, with insult and injury. When this happens, he must be *patient under injuries.* He must *hold up under evil* (cf. I Peter 2:21-24).

Not only must he be *gentle* in outward demeanor; he must also be *mild* or *meek* in inner attitude or disposition, "with *mildness* (see also Titus 3:2; then I Cor. 4:21; II Cor. 10:1; Gal. 5:23; 6:1; Eph. 4:2; Col. 3:12; James 1:21; 3:13; I Peter 3:15) correcting the opponents"; cf. Christ's example (Matt. 11:29). Note here the play on words in the original. The *opponents* ("those who are constantly placing themselves in opposition") never ceased to come up with ignorant or *"uninstructed"* enquiries (verse 23). So the apostle tells Timothy to instruct these uninstructed ones, to educate the uneducated, to discipline (in this case, with the discipline of *teaching;* contrast I Tim. 1:20) the undisciplined, to inform the uninformed. Instead of entering into their foolish enquiries, he must gently show them why one should not even bother with these things, and he must then immediately proceed to impart positive instruction, so that the opponents may thus receive *correction.*

The purpose of all this didactic and pastoral work is now stated: "in the hope that possibly God may grant them *conversion,* leading to acknowledgment of the truth, and they may return to soberness . . ." This hope may have been expressed in such a hesitant manner ("possibly . . . may grant") because with the errorists *contradicting* had become a habit. It had become hard for them even to listen to the truth. If there was to be a change, no one less than *God* would have to bring it about. It is Paul's earnest longing that this great transformation may still be effected.

The word used in the original to indicate this basic change (μετάνοια) means more than *repentance.* It is *conversion* (cf. II Cor. 7:8-10), a term which looks forward as well as backward, whereas *repentance* mainly looks backward. *Conversion,* moreover, affects not only the emotions but also the mind and the will. In fact, it *is first of all* (as the derivation of the word implies) *a complete change-over in mental and moral outlook.* It is *a radical change of view that leads to a radical change of life.* Thus, it is here described as leading to "acknowledgment of (the) truth." Paul hopes that the adherents of false doctrine will be converted from their habit of majoring on minors, and that they will recognize and confess the great and wonderful truth as revealed in the gospel and as centered in Christ.

He hopes, accordingly, "that they may return to soberness" (ἀνανήψωσιν). (This is the only occurrence of this compound verb in the New Testament. But see also footnote 193.) Through the work of the ministry may the adversaries be brought back to their senses; may they be aroused from their dull stupor, being delivered "out of the snare of the devil," that is, out of the snare set by the devil, the snare into which he had lured them, that they might do his will (see on I Tim. 3:7). That this is the meaning is clear from the words which immediately follow: "by whom they had been taken captive to (do) his will" (literally, "having been taken captive by *him* (that is, by the devil), for *that one's* (the devil's) will").[149]

True conversion, then, is a radical change:

(1) from ignorance to acknowledgment of the truth (verse 23, verse 25);

---

[149] It is difficult to see why there is so much disagreement about the pronouns αὐτοῦ and ἐκείνου. The antecedent of αὐτοῦ is naturally the nearest noun *(the devil);* and the antecedent of ἐκείνου is the nearest pronoun *(him,* that is, *the devil).* This makes excellent sense. It is the devil who captures men, and endeavors to hold on to them. Note the perfect passive participle: "having been captured (primary meaning: *caught alive*) once for all." The devil does not intend to release them! Attempts to connect these pronouns with remote antecedents in order to prove that one or both of them refer to *God* or to *the Lord's servant* impress me as being unsuccessful. Hence, I cannot agree here with Robertson, *op. cit.,* p. 622; Lenski, *op. cit.,* p. 818; Scott, *op. cit.,* p. 117; Lock, *op. cit.,* p. 103; etc.

(2) from intoxication and stupor to soberness (verse 26a); and
(3) from slavery to freedom (verse 26b).

Synthesis of Chapter 2

See the Outline at the beginning of the chapter.

In view, then, of the examples and of the gift which he has received, let Timothy – Paul's "child" – be strengthened in the grace that is in Christ Jesus. In order to become strong himself and to benefit the church, let him *teach* men who, in turn, are qualified to teach others. To such men let him entrust those teachings which he – among many others, "witnesses" all – has heard from the lips of Paul throughout their years of association with each other.

Now this activity of *teaching* – in fact, *all* the work of the ministry – will not be easy, but will result in hardship for Timothy. Let him then be a noble soldier and suffer hardship along with Paul and the witnesses just mentioned. Let him be encouraged by the fact that only the soldier who fights wholeheartedly, only the athlete who competes according to the rules, and only the farmer who works hard, will receive their reward. Thus also Timothy will receive *his* reward. Let him rely on his Lord, who will give him understanding in all matters. Let him, moreover, keep in memory Jesus Christ. He, too, performed his task *wholeheartedly, obediently* – never breaking any divine rule –, and *diligently*. And did he not receive his reward? Was he not raised from the dead, and does he not reign on high as the rightful spiritual heir of David? Is this not true according to the gospel which Paul cherishes as his very own ("*my* gospel")?

For this gospel Paul suffers hardship, even to bonds, as if he were a criminal. But he is greatly comforted by the fact that though he himself is bound, the word of God which he proclaims is not bound but accomplishes God's pleasure in the hearts and lives of all the elect, in order that they may obtain the salvation which centers in Christ Jesus with everlasting glory.

Four lines of what was probably an early-church hymn are now quoted. These show that *loyalty* to Christ and stedfastness even in the midst of bitter persecution are ever rewarded by the privilege of living and reigning with Christ; while, on the contrary *denial and disloyalty* are punished by being rejected by him who ever remains faithful to his threats as well as to his promises, *not being able* (adds Paul) to do otherwise.

In the second part of this chapter the apostle shows that word-battles, profane empty-chatter, and foolish inquiries serve no useful purpose and breed quarrels. Timothy must do his utmost to win God's approval, as a workman who has nothing to be ashamed of, one who rightly handles the word of the truth. The errorists will make progress, indeed, but what kind of progress? They will advance . . . to an increase of ungodliness! Their word will "have pasture," eating its way like a malignant tumor. Among the ring-leaders of these false teachers are Hymenaeus and Philetus, men who teach that the only resurrection is the spiritual one, which, they say, *has already occurred!* But though these do upset the faith of *some,* God's *true* church remains stedfast. It is his solid foundation. Its members are protected by the Father, owned by the Son, and certified by the Spirit. In other words, they are *sealed.* And on that seal there are two inscriptions, one stressing the *divine* side of their salvation: "The Lord knows who are his"; and the other bringing out the *human* side: "Let every one who names the name of the Lord stand aloof from unrighteousness."

With the visible church, however, it is as with a large house: not everything in it is equally valuable: some "vessels" are destined for honor; others for dishonor. Hence, it should not cause any surprise that men like Hymenaeus and Philetus have a following. But if anyone will effectively cleanse himself from men of this type and their evil influences, he will be . . . very useful to the Master, prepared for every good work. This applies also to Timothy.

Now in order to become thus thoroughly qualified, Timothy must also flee away from the sinful desires that pertain to the younger generation. Positively, he should stedfastly pursue faith, love, etc. He must not be quarrelsome but gentle to all. Only in this way will he be *qualified to teach.* Such teaching will require that he exercise great patience, even under injuries. When opposed, he should correct his opponents with mildness, in the hope that possibly God may grant them conversion, a complete mental, moral, and spiritual turn-about which leads to acknowledgment of the truth and to soberness. Thus they will have been delivered from the snare set by the devil, by whom they had been taken captive to do *his* (that is, the devil's) will.

Outline of Chapter 3

Theme: *The Apostle Paul Tells Timothy What To Do in the Interest of Sound Doctrine*

Abide in It — "Grievous times will come"

3:1-9 Knowing that enemies will arise, who have its form, not its power.

3:10-17 Knowing that it is based on the sacred writings, as you learned from trustworthy persons.

CHAPTER III

3 1 But understand this, that in (the) last days grievous seasons will set in; 2
for the people will be self-loving, money-loving, boasters, overbearing, blasphemers, disobedient to (their) parents, unthankful, unholy, 3 unfeeling, unforgiving, slanderers, unrestrained, untamed, unloving toward the good, 4 traitors,
reckless, blinded with conceit, pleasure-loving rather than God-loving, 5 having a
form of piety but denying its power; and from such people turn away.
6 For out of these circles come those who are infiltrating the homes and are
taking captive weak-minded women loaded down with sins, swayed by various impulses, 7 ever learning and never able to arrive at the acknowledgment of (the)
truth. 8 And just as Jannes and Jambres opposed Moses, so do also these men oppose the truth, men corrupt in mind and reprobate with respect to the faith. 9
But they will not get very far, for their folly will be obvious to everyone, as also
that of those (two men) got to be.

3:1-9

1. To be gentle, patient, and mild (see II Tim. 2:24-26) will not be easy, as the apostle now proceeds to show: **But understand this, that in (the) last days grievous seasons will set in.**

There are two things which Paul wants Timothy to do, according to the lengthy sentence which extends all the way from 1:1 to the end of verse 5. He tells his dearly-beloved representative that he:

a. must constantly realize that in the last days grievous seasons will set in; and

b. must constantly turn away from the kind of people who will make these seasons so grievous.

These two commands are connected by the conjunction "and." Hence, when most of the explanatory material that intervenes between the commands is omitted, there remains this: "But *understand* this, that in (the) last days grievous seasons will set in; for the people will be self-loving . . . *and* from such people *turn away*."

Once this connection is understood, it also becomes clear that the expression "in the last days," as here used, cannot be limited to the days which will immediately precede Christ's second coming.[150] It would have been

---

[150] Scott *op. cit.*, p. 118, simply states that this is the meaning, but does not offer any proof or any word-study of the concept. Bouma, *op. cit.*, p. 311, who inter-

senseless to tell Timothy to avoid people who would never bother him at all! And it is not warranted to "solve" the difficulty by saying: "The writer expected Christ's return any moment!" (See N.T.C. on II Thess., chapter 2). – The key to the correct interpretation is the contextual explanation of the expression "in the last days."

Now in the Old Testament this expression (Gen. 49:1; Num. 24:14; Deut. 4:30; Is. 2:2; Jer. 23:20; 30:24; 48:47; 49:39; Ezek. 38:16; Dan. 2:28; 10:14; Hos. 3:5; Mic. 4:1) refers to "the days to come," "the future." What is included in that "future" must be determined in each separate instance by the context.[151] That it cannot in every instance refer exclusively to the days that will immediately precede Christ's second coming is clear at once from the context of such a passage as Gen. 49:1. Jacob, in blessing his sons, was not thinking primarily of what would happen at the end of the world, nor was he even thinking of a period which for each tribe would begin at the Messiah's first advent. On the contrary, he was describing the events that were to take place in the lives of his sons and in the history of the tribes of Israel. And even from the context of such a passage as Dan. 2:28 it is evident that the expression "in the last days" covers a period which *begins* with the Babylonian sovereignty, long before the days of Christ's first advent, and which includes also the entire new dispensation. In fact, in a sense, the period covered never ends, for a kingdom is predicted "which will last forever."

As the context shows, in passages such as Is. 2:2; Micah 4:1 (cf. 5:2) the expression "in the last days" refers to *the age ushered in by Christ's appearance on earth.* This is the age of the fulfilment of the Messianic promises, promises which attain their even more glorious realization at the consummation.[152]

This is clearly also the meaning in Acts 2:17 (quotation from Joel 2:28), where the events that occurred on the day of Pentecost are included in "the last days." (Cf. the use of the expression in James 5:3, variously interpreted.) The rather similar expression "at the end of these days" in Heb. 1:2 (see context) also clearly refers to a period which began with the coming of Christ into the flesh. Moreover, the apostle John knew that "the last hour" *had already arrived* (I John 2:18).

Accordingly, Paul's words here in II Tim. 3:1 are best interpreted as meaning, "Timothy, constantly realize that in these last days – this lengthy dispensation – *in which we are now living* there will be grievous seasons."

---

prets similarly, states that John in his Gospel often uses this expression. But this is incorrect. Christ's "at the last day" (sing., see John 6:39, 40, 44, 54; 11:24; 12:48) must not be confused with Paul's "in the last days" *(plural).*

[151] See G. Ch. Aalders, *Het Herstel Van Israel Volgens Het Oude Testament,* pp. 13, 14, 39, 46.

[152] The Old Testament, however, does not sharply distinguish between the two comings, but treats them as if they were one.

These seasons will come and go, and the last will be worse than the first. They will be seasons of ever-increasing wickedness (Matt. 24:12; Luke 18:8), which will culminate in the climax of wickedness, the revelation of "the man of lawlessness" (II Thess. 2:1-12; cf. Matt. 24; Mark 13; Luke 21).

"There will *set in* (approaching like a thunder-storm, until fully present) seasons grievous." Thus the passage reads literally, with some emphasis on the adjective *grievous, hard* or *painful* (to endure). These *seasons,* then, are eras of duress for the true church, difficult time-periods of the new dispensation, definitely marked out in God's eternal decree.

As was true with respect to the closely related "later seasons" prophecy (I Tim. 4:1-5), so also the present prediction has "multiple fulfilment." But while I Tim. 4:1-5 warned against the coming of *Ascetic* Gnostics and their followers throughout the course of history, the present prophecy deals more emphatically with the coming of *Antinomian* or *Licentious* Gnostics and with those throughout the centuries who, although dropping some of their weird basic theories, copy their worldly example.

2-5. Grievous seasons will set in, **for the people will be. . . .** It is *the people* (the members of the human race; *the men* generically, not the "men" as distinguished from the "women") living during these grievous seasons who will cause all the grief. A catalogue of their sinful characteristics follows. It should be compared with the list in Rom. 1:29-31. Note in both lists: a. *boasters, overbearing* (or *haughty*); b. *unsubmissive* or *disobedient to parents;* and c. *unfeeling* (or *without natural affection*). Note also synonyms: Romans has *whisperers* and *defamers* ("backbiters"); II Timothy, *slanderers;* Romans, *haters of God;* II Timothy, *pleasure-loving rather than God-loving;* Romans *unmerciful;* II Timothy, *unforgiving* (or *implacable;* literally; *admitting of no truce*); etc.

Here in II Tim. the list has nineteen items (if the modifiers "pleasure-loving rather than God-loving," and "having a form of piety but denying its power" each be regarded as *one* item).[153] Whether Paul had any division in mind, so that the nineteen can be divided into groups, each group emphasizing one central idea, cannot be determined. It is true, however, that items 6-10 form an unbroken series, in the sense that all of these begin with the prefix *un-* or *dis-* (ἀ -privative in the original). This would divide the entire catalogue into three groups (items 1-5; 6-10; 11-19), structurally considered. Note, however, that three of the items in the last group also begin with the negative prefix.[154]

---

[153] I cannot follow Lenski's arithmetic, *op. cit.,* p. 821. He counts "eighteen" items, and then seems to divide these 18 into three groups, containing respectively 5, 3, and 12 items. But that would make 20 in all, not 18! Hence, his allegorical interpretation of the figures (5, three 4's, and a final 3) also looks rather dubious.

[154] It is true, of course, that ἀ -privative does not need to be rendered by a similar negative prefix like *un-* or *dis-* or *in-* or *non-*. One may try the suffix *-less;* or one

The list, then, is as follows:

self-loving, money-loving, boasters, overbearing, blasphemers, disobedient to (their) parents, unthankful, unholy, unfeeling, unforgiving, slanderers, unrestrained, untamed, unloving toward the good, traitors, reckless, blinded with conceit, pleasure-loving rather than God-loving, having a form of piety but denying its power.

These people, then, are, first of all *self-loving.* Cf. Titus 1:7: "self-pleasing." Trench (par. xciii) borrows the illustration of the hedgehog which a. rolls itself up in a ball, keeping the soft, warm wool for itself (φίλαυτος, self-loving, selfish); and b. presents the sharp spines to those without (αὐθάδης, self-pleasing, arrogant).

Since they are self-loving, they are naturally also *money-loving* (lovers of silver). Think of the Pharisees as described in Luke 16:14.

They are *boastful* or *boasters* (cf. Rom. 1:30). This word originally referred to a person who wanders about the country. He may be peddling medicine, boasting about its healing virtue; hence, a "quack." But in the present passage boasting in general is meant.

While boasting about themselves and their "wares," accomplishments, or talents, these people are *overbearing* (cf. Rom. 1:30; then Luke 1:51; James 4:6; I Peter 5:5) in their attitude to others. They are the *haughty* type, "uppish."

It is not surprising that such people are also described as being *blasphemers.* When they *speak,* they *hurt* or *injure.* They use scornful language, insulting God and man (see on I Tim. 6:4). The group of words formed around this stem has many examples in the New Testament. For the adjective *blasphemous* (here in II Tim. used as a substantive, *blasphemers*) see also Acts 6:11; II Peter 2:11 (cf. Jude 9). For the related verb *(to blaspheme)* see on I Tim. 1:20; for the related noun *(blasphemy),* see on I Tim. 6:4.

These people are *lacking* in such excellent qualities as submissiveness, thankfulness, holiness, affection for their own families, and the forgiving attitude. It is implied that in each case they possess the very opposite attitude; that is, they are not only *disobedient* but definitely *rebellious;* not only *untamed* but *fierce;* not only *unholy* but *wicked,* etc. Taking these five characteristics one by one, these people are described as being, first of all, *disobedient* toward their parents (cf. Rom. 1:30; then Luke 1:17; Acts 26:9; Titus 1:16; 3:3).

This shows that they are *unthankful* (cf. Luke 6:35), not appreciative of the many acts of kindness which their parents have bestowed upon them,

---

may even substitute a positive for a negative word; for example, "fierce" for "untamed." I have chosen *un-* or *dis-* for all the ἀ -privatives in the list in order to remain as close as possible to the flavor of the original without changing the sense of the entire word.

and not appreciative toward other people either, nor toward God (cf. Rom. 1:21, "neither gave thanks"). Though blessings are common enough, there is in this world no "common gratitude." "Common *grace*" (God's kindness toward all his creatures, Ps. 145:9, 17; Jonah 4:10, 11; Matt. 5:43-45; Luke 6:35), yes; "common *gratitude,*" no!

With respect to things which have divine sanction, they are *unholy* or *impious* (cf. I Tim. 1:9). They do not reverence the established sanctities. This implies that they are *unfeeling,* or *unsympathetic, heartless, lacking* even in natural affection such as parents have for their children, and children for their parents (cf. Rom. 1:31).

They show that same callousness all around, also in their relation to their fellowmen. Their feuds never end. In their camp no libation is ever poured out to signify that those who had been at variance with each other have consented to a truce. They are *implacable, irreconcilable.*

The final group shows how these inner attitudes or deficiencies express themselves outwardly in words of hatred and deeds of cruelty.

These people, then, hurl false and/or hostile epithets and charges at each other. They are *slanderers, false accusers,* imitators of the great Diabolos (I Tim. 3:6, 7; Eph. 4:27; 6:11; etc., a word of frequent occurrence in the New Testament). They have never learned to control themselves; hence, are *unrestrained,* "uninhibited," thoroughly lacking in self-control, devoid of power to check their own drives and impulses. Having never "settled down," they are *untamed, savage, fierce.* They despise virtue, are *unloving toward the good.* By them their associates, even *before* the latters' ruin is evident, have been *given over* to the enemy. They are *traitors,* therefore, receiving their pay beforehand, just like Judas (cf. Luke 6:16; Acts 7:52). Nothing stops them. Rashly they plunge ahead in their wickedness, being *reckless* or *precipitate* in their deeds of violence (cf. Acts 19:36). No one can tell them anything, for they "know it all," so *blinded with conceit* (see on I Tim. 3:6; 6:4) are they. This blindness, moreover, has a moral, spiritual cause. Its root is in the heart and in the will, for these people are utterly selfish (note how the description in reaching a climax returns to its starting-point: "self-loving"). They are *pleasure-loving rather than* (or *more than*) *God-loving.* This definitely does not mean that they also love God to some extent. It means that they do not love God at all (for "rather than" or "more than" in this sense see also John 3:19; 12:43; Acts 4:19; 17:11; I Tim. 1:4; cf. somewhat similar idioms in Luke 15:7; 18:14). Not only does one find these people outside of the church. They have infiltrated the church (and not only the church, see verse 6). And even should they be excommunicated, they will still pretend to be eminent Christians. They are described as having a *form,* a mere *semblance* or *appearance* (cf. Rom. 2:20) of *piety* (see on I Tim. 2:2; 3:16; 4:7, 8; 6:3, 5, 6, 11), but *denying* (literally, "having once for all denied") its power.

These people lack spiritual dynamite. They have no love for God, nor for his revelation in Jesus Christ, nor for his people. Hence, since they are not Spirit-filled men, it is not surprising that they lack power.

And from such people turn away, says Paul (for explanation see pp. 281, 282). Cf. II John 10.

6, 7. The reason why Timothy must turn away from such people is now pointed out: **For out of these circles come those who are infiltrating the homes and are taking captive weak-minded women.**

Out of the circles (for the Greek idiom see N.T.C. on John 1:24) of the men described in verses 1-5 come those false prophets who specialize in the art of captivating *women.* They are not successful with *all* the women, of course. Many women are far too sensible to become the dupes of false prophets. Paul thought very highly of such noble women and made good use of their talents (see on I Tim. 3:11; and on I Tim. 5:9, 10). But every age also has its *fickle* women (see on I Tim. 5:13), and these are found both *in* the church and *outside* of it.

Probably when their husbands are not at home, the women are visited by these peddlers of strange doctrines. There was a beginning of this evil practice in Paul's day — or shall we go back all the way to Paradise? (Gen. 3:1-6a) — ; it was going to become worse in days to come. We of the twentieth century know that exactly this practice is going on today, and that the false prophets who engage in it show a close resemblance to those of Paul's day and age. Also today, as many can testify, the men who visit the women in order to ensnare them fail to take sin seriously, often deny everlasting punishment, and in general proclaim a religion which satisfies "the flesh."

These men, then, worm their way into *the homes* (pl. of οἰκία, *dwelling; then home, household, family*). Why is it that they seek out *women?* Is it because they know that women (especially women of this particular brand) are easier to mislead than men? Is it that they reason thus: Once we have the women on our side, the men will come of their own accord? (Again see Gen. 3.) By methods either fair or foul these men *are getting into* (not necessarily in every case: are sneaking into) the family-units. By means of the very novelty of their doctrines, which offer "an easy way out" for anyone who is bothered by sin, these infiltrators *are taking captive* (original sense: *taking with the spear;* but here more general and metaphorical, *captivating*) *weak-minded women.* To describe these women, the original uses a diminutive with contemptuous meaning. This is hard to reproduce in English. Cf. the German *Weiblein,* and the Dutch *vrouwtjes;* "little women" would hardly do. Probably "weak-minded women" or "weak-natured women" or "silly women" (A.V., A.R.V.) will do; cf. the colloquial "softies." These are, at any rate, women "who do not amount to much," "easy marks" for the false prophets.

By means of three participial phrases, the last one a compound phrase, these weak-minded women are further described: **loaded down with sins, swayed by various impulses, ever learning and never able to arrive at the acknowledgment of (the) truth.**

First of all, then, these women are "heaped up with sin" (for the verb see Rom. 12:20). They are *very wicked,* and the fact that they welcome the smooth talkers seems to indicate that their sins have given them an uneasy feeling, though not in the sense of Rom. 7:24. These women are probably *afraid* of the consequences of their sins, but are not necessarily *ashamed* of them.

Secondly, they are "swayed by various *impulses*" (or *"desires,"* see explanation of II Tim. 2:22 for word-study). What these evil incentives are is not stated. Perhaps we may think of such things as the following: the desire to find an easy way out of their guilt-complex, the desire to gain recognition, to be considered "well-informed," to satisfy their curiosity, to have attention bestowed upon them by "prominent" representatives of the opposite sex, etc.

Thirdly, these weak-minded women are *ever learning.* Eager disciples are they, "taking it all in," as with rapt attention they sit down to listen to their licentious teachers and to admire them. But their unwillingness openly to confess and to resist the evil promptings of their nature results in their being *"never able* to arrive at the acknowledgment of (the) truth" as revealed in the gospel (cf. I Tim. 2:4; II Tim. 2:25).

By making propaganda for their nefarious doctrines, going from home to home in order to enlist women-disciples and women-helpers, these false teachers become manifest to all true believers as adversaries of God and of his truth. This also has its present-day fulfilment, for the well-known "witnesses" (or by whatever name they may be called) are always denouncing the orthodox churches and their ministers.

8. Says Paul, **And just as Jannes and Jambres opposed Moses, so do also these men oppose the truth, men corrupt in mind and reprobate with respect to the faith.**

When Moses told Pharaoh, "Let my people go" (Ex. 5:1), and when he proved his divine commission by performing genuine miracles through the power of God (Ex. 7:10, 20, etc.), Pharaoh's magicians performed their counter-miracles (Ex. 7:11, 22; 8:7; but see also 8:18, 19). From Jewish tradition,[155] with which Paul was very familiar (having been a student of

[155] The names Jannes and Jambres occur frequently in late Jewish, pagan, and early Christian literature. For specific references see the article "Jannes and Jambres" in *The New Schaff-Herzog Encyclopaedia of Religious Knowledge,* Vol. VI, p. 95.

Gamaliel, Acts 22:3), he cites the example of those two ring-leaders among the magicians who, whatever their real names may have been, were known to the Jews as "Jannes and Jambres" (Aram. probably: "he who seduces and he who makes rebellious"). The apostle had in mind the following comparison:

Just as Jannes and Jambres *opposed* God's representative, Moses, so do also these licentious leaders *oppose* the truth of God as revealed in his Word and as proclaimed by Paul, Timothy, etc.

This point of comparison is definitely stated. (For another undoubted third of comparison see below, on verse 9.) Whether here in verse 8 any further resemblances are implied cannot be proved. The following are mere possibilities:

(1) Jannes and Jambres were deceivers; so are the purveyors of strange doctrine against whom Paul warns Timothy.

(2) If Jewish tradition can be credited in this respect, Jannes and Jambres became proselytes, faking "conversion" to the Jewish religion. When they saw that they could not prevent Israel's exodus from Egypt, they are said to have joined the departing multitude. Later (according to Jewish tradition!) *they* were the ones who induced the people to make a golden calf and to worship it. They were pretenders, therefore; hypocrites, and as such very dangerous. – Similarly, the false leaders whom Paul describes are all the more dangerous because they pretend to be genuine converts to the Christian religion.

Paul calls the men whom he is describing "corrupt in mind" (perfect passive participle; cf. I Tim. 6:5). In their case the very organ that was given to men in order that he might be able to receive and reflect on spiritual realities has become thoroughly and permanently defiled. As a result, with respect to "the faith" (objective sense), these men have been found to be worthy of emphatic disapproval; hence, *reprobate,* condemned as worthless, unfit, disqualified, utterly *rejected.*

9. There is, however, one reason for encouragement. Says Paul: **But they will not get very far, for their folly will be obvious to everyone, as also that of those (two men) got to be.**

To be sure, the enemies of the faith advance to constantly increasing ungodliness, and their word devours like a gangrene (II Tim. 2:16, 17), so that for a while it may seem that their purpose is going to be achieved and that the entire organism of the church will be destroyed. But this never happens, not in any of the many periods of the church's history, not even toward the end of the age. The purpose is always to lead astray: *if possible,* even the elect (Mark 13:22), but this is ever *impossible!* The thought here is like that in II Tim. 2:17, 18, followed by the comforting verse 19. God's solid foundation remains standing. And in that sense it is true that the errorists "will not get *very far*" (for ἐπὶ πλεῖον in this sense consider also Acts 20:9). Their *folly* (lack of understanding, senselessness) will become *entirely clear to all.* No doubt, God's true children see this folly first of all. Afterward, others too will see it; for worldly people have a tendency to follow first one deceiver, then another. For example, those who yesterday *glorified* Stalin, today *condemn* him in no uncertain terms! Exactly that same thing happened in the case of Jannes and Jambres.

---

10 *You,* however, followed my teaching, my conduct, my purpose, my faith, my longsuffering, my love, my endurance, 11 my persecutions, my sufferings, what kind of things happened to me at Antioch, at Iconium, (and) at Lystra, what kind of persecutions I underwent; yet from them all the Lord rescued me! 12 In fact, all who desire to live devoutly in Christ Jesus will be persecuted. 13 Evil men and impostors, moreover, will proceed from bad to worse, deceiving and being deceived. 14 *You,* however, must continue in the things which you have learned and of which you have become convinced, knowing from w h o m you learned (them), 15 and that from infancy you have known (the) sacred writings, which are able to make you wise for salvation through that faith (which is) in Christ Jesus. 16 All scripture (is) God-breathed and useful for teaching, for reproof, for correction, for training in righteousness, 17 that the man of God may be equipped, for every good work thoroughly equipped.

3:10-17

10, 11. Now in view of the fact that grievous seasons will set in, in which wicked men and impostors will proceed from bad to worse, Timothy, who has hitherto followed Paul's teaching, etc., should exert himself the more to *abide in* this sound doctrine, which he has learned from trustworthy persons and which is based upon those divinely inspired writings in which from the days of infancy he has been instructed. Says Paul, ***You,* however, followed my teaching, my conduct, my purpose, my faith, my longsuffering, my love, my endurance, my persecutions, my sufferings, what kind of things happened to me at Antioch, at Iconium, (and) at Lystra, what kind of persecutions I underwent.**

Between the false teachers and Timothy there had been a sharp contrast, so that Paul is able to exclaim, "*You* (with great emphasis on this pronoun), however, followed my teaching," etc. The verb *followed,* in Greek as well as in English, when it is used in a figurative sense, can mean either *watched, observed, investigated* (cf. Luke 1:3); or *took as a model, adhered to, copied.* Though the latter meaning will do very well when associated with "my teaching, my conduct, my purpose, my faith," etc., it will not do nearly as well with "the things which happened to me at Antioch," etc. Probably what the apostle means is this, "Timothy, in contrast with our opponents, *you* took a deep, sympathetic interest in my teaching, my conduct," etc. So interpreted, the verb implies that Timothy had actually taken Paul as his model, and had also listened to him with keen interest when he related his experiences, in some of which (for example, those at Lystra) the younger man had become intimately involved.

Paul, soon to die, clearly is looking back upon his whole life of service to Christ, especially upon that part of it which began with his first missionary journey and extended to this very day here in the Roman dungeon. With respect to that entire long journey he says, in summary, "You . . . followed my teaching, conduct," etc.[156]

In the original each of the particulars with respect to which Timothy has "followed" Paul is definite. Hence, the correct rendering is not "my teaching, conduct, purpose," etc. (A.V. and A.R.V.), but "my teaching, my conduct, my purpose," etc., with "my" repeated before each item.

Does the list of nine particulars show any definite order or grouping? It is impossible to answer this question categorically. Surely, if any sequence is pointed out, it should be a natural one, characteristic (at least to some extent) of Paul.[157] An arbitrary division is of no help whatever. It must be admitted, however, that we today cannot be sure that *our* attempt to point out why one item in the list follows another corresponds with *Paul's own* reasoning. If it be permissible, nevertheless, to make such an attempt — with the definite understanding that it is merely an attempt, which may or may not be entirely successful — I would suggest the following:

All the items express or imply *obedience to the Lord.* The seven items in verse 10 are the manifestations of *active* obedience (even *endurance,* that is, "stedfast perseverance," is active; and so is *longsuffering,* "the exercise of patience toward others"). The two items in verse 11 are the manifestations of a more *passive* type of obedience: a person is *persecuted;* as a result, he *suffers.*

In the first group of seven there are four items which probably go together ("my faith, my longsuffering, my love, my endurance"). The linking of *faith, love,* and *endurance* is characteristic of Paul (I Thess. 1:3; I Tim. 6:11; Titus 2:2). Sometimes *hope* appears in the place of *endurance,* the latter being the fruit of the former: Col. 1:4, 5 ("faith, love, hope"); I Cor. 13:13 ("faith, hope, love"). Here in II Tim. 3:10 it is not strange to find *longsuffering* in a subdivision which also lists *endurance.* In both of these the Christian's *patience* is expressed (for the distinction see below).

---

[156] This, it would seem to me, is a more natural explanation than that favored, among others, by Bouma, *op. cit.,* p. 323, according to which the aorist would be ingressive, and would mean, "You *became* my follower when you changed from the Jewish to the Christian faith."

[157] Hence, I cannot agree with the grouping presented by Lenski, *op. cit.,* p. 831. Paul would not thus separate *faith* and *love.*

We arrive, accordingly, at the following grouping which *may* have been in the author's mind:

A. *Expressions of Active Obedience* (verse 10)

1. my teaching, my conduct, my purpose (as to the possible relation of these three see below)
2. my faith, my longsuffering, my love, my endurance

B. *Expressions of Passive Obedience* (verse 11)

my persecutions (those which I experienced), my sufferings.

As to the separate items, note the following:

a. *my teaching.* Logically this comes first, for it was *the teaching* of Paul, *the gospel* which he preached, which had first of all impressed Timothy, and had been sanctified to his heart unto conversion (cf. Acts 14:12). On this word *teaching* see also pp. 6, 7, 9.

b. *my conduct.* Paul's consecrated walk of life (cf. I Cor. 4:17), his completely unselfish behavior, giving all honor to God and refusing to receive any honor for himself, had also left its imprint upon Timothy (cf. Acts 14:13-18). Moreover, not only at the beginning but throughout their association with each other Paul's teaching and his conduct in harmony with that teaching had constantly been watched with sympathetic interest by the younger man. In his own life these two (teaching and conduct) had borne fruit.

c. *my purpose.* A man's real, inner purpose is not clearly evident the first time you meet him. Though his words may be very fine, he may be a deceiver. But when, as in the case of Paul, teaching and conduct are in beautiful harmony, no legitimate doubt remains as to the purpose of one's life. Already at the time of Paul's first visit to Lystra, Timothy, no doubt, had become persuaded about this purpose and had made it his own. The apostle's subsequent heroic return (on this same first missionary journey) to the very city which had stoned him almost to death must have made that glorious purpose even clearer (see especially Acts 14:22), and even more a matter to be copied. Later experiences had served to further clarify and intensify this "aim in life."

Turning now to the group of four items which seem to belong together (as has been shown), the one first in this list is:

d. *my faith.* Occurring between "my purpose" and "my longsuffering," the expression "my faith" is best interpreted in the subjective sense, "the faith in God (and in his redemptive truth) which I exercise." This, too, had exerted its powerful effect upon Timothy and had been reproduced in his own heart and life.

e. *my longsuffering.* This "patience with respect to *people*" (as distinguished from *endurance,* which is "patience amid *adverse circumstances,*" see N.T.C. on I and II Thess., p. 198), yes even with respect to *persecutors,* Paul had exhibited again and again, from the very day when Timothy had first met him at Lystra.

f. *my love,* probably in this connection especially with respect to *people,* including *enemies.*

g. *my endurance.* For definition see under e. above. Stedfast perseverance amid trying circumstances, the grace to hold up under, had been characteristic of Paul throughout his glorious missionary-career. To a certain extent, Timothy had caught the spirit.

As to Paul's passive obedience (also reflected in Timothy), the apostle continues:

h. *my persecutions,* those which I endured; and last of all, their natural effect or consequence:

i. *my sufferings,* for the sake of Christ, of course (Rom. 8:17, 18; II Cor. 12:10; Col. 1:24). To see what kind of persecutions and sufferings Paul endured one should read the list in II Cor. 11:21-33. In some of these Timothy had shared.

It is not at all surprising that in connection with persecutions and sufferings Paul says, "what kind of things happened to me at Antioch, at Iconium, (and) at Lystra," for these were the very places which he had visited on his first missionary journey, the journey on which Timothy had first met the apostle and had been converted. Timothy had heard Paul's preaching at Lystra, had probably witnessed the miraculous cure of the born-cripple, the manner in which Paul (and Barnabas) had restrained the multitude from worshipping him, and the stoning. Very vividly Timothy must have recalled how the people, believing that Paul was dead, had dragged him out of the city (*Timothy's* native city, in all probability). Read Acts 14. On this occasion or shortly afterward the new convert must also have learned about the tribulations which the missionaries had endured just before entering Lystra, namely, at Antioch (expulsion), and at Iconium (the minds of the Gentiles poisoned against them by the Jews, and the threat of physical harm). By saying "what kind of things happened to me," and "what kind of persecutions I underwent," the apostle indicates: a. the character or nature of these woeful experiences (they were very severe, very bitter), and probably b. the fact that many similar hardships for the sake of the gospel had followed in their train, until this very moment.

The vivid recollection of these afflictions, which march in rapid procession before Paul's mind's eye, causes him by way of contrast to exclaim, **Yet** (καί is undoubtedly adversative here) **from them all the Lord rescued me!** Let timid Timothy take this to heart (Ps. 27:1-5; Ps. 91; Ps. 125; Is.

43:2; Nah. 1:7). The Lord *ever* rescues his people, frequently *from* death, sometimes *by means of* death. Either way, nothing ever separates them from his love (Rom. 8:38, 39).

12. The fact that believers are intimately united with Christ means that *essentially* (though not in degree) *all* must suffer Christ's reproach. Says Paul, **In fact, all who desire to live devoutly in Christ Jesus will be persecuted.**

The idea of the godly, pious, or devout life occurs again and again in the Pastorals (see p. 10; then for the noun also on I Tim. 2:2; 3:16; 4:7, 8; 6:3, 5, 6, 11; II Tim. 3:5; Titus 1:1; for the related verb see I Tim. 5:4. Here in II Tim. 3:12 and also in Titus 2:12 the adverb is used). But though the words built on this stem occur at times in a very general sense and are applied also to pagan religious life (see M.M., pp. 265, 266), Paul speaks distinctly about those who desire to live devoutly *in Christ Jesus*. The people whom he has in mind have made it their earnest resolution, with God's help and by his grace, to live the life of devotion *to Christ*. They live in close fellowship *with him* (John 15:4, 5; Gal. 2:20; Phil. 3:10).

Now the apostle makes the definite statement that *all* those who desire to live devoutly in Christ Jesus *will be persecuted*. Paul's own experience (see verse 11 above) is by no means peculiar. Scars are the price which *every* believer pays for his loyalty to Christ. They are also his *credentials* before God.

The reason why persecution awaits all those who are firmly resolved to adorn their confession with a truly Christian life is that in the midst of contradictions coming from every side they refuse either to stop their ears or to cringe and compromise. Instead, they face the foe and challenge him to combat. They go right ahead, boldly defending the faith against every attack, and courageously assaulting the fortress of unbelief. The result is persecution, at times very bitter.

This inescapable character of persecution is a truth which Scripture proclaims everywhere (especially in such passages as Matt. 5:10-12; 10:28; John 15:17-20; 16:1-4, 33; I Thess. 3:4). The fact that Timothy knows beforehand that also this is included in God's decree and takes place within the realm of God's providence which is ever causing good to come forth out of evil, should be a source of comfort to him and to all true believers. The comfort becomes even greater when verse 12 is read in the light of the immediately preceding verse: even in the midst of bitter persecution the interests of every believer are perfectly secure with him whose name is Rescuer.

13. Between verses 12 and 13 there is no contrast. Not until verse 14 is reached is a contrast introduced, similar in nature to that which is found at the beginning of verse 10 (in both cases, *"You,* however") – Persecution is the lot of every believer; hence, will continue. That is the idea which the apostle has conveyed in verse 12. And now the reason why it continues is stated: the wicked will never desist, but will increase in wickedness. Says Paul, **Evil men and impostors, moreover, will proceed from bad to worse, deceiving and being deceived.** These "wicked men" and "impostors" are the ones described in verses 2-9. They must not be thought of as two mutually exclusive groups (one group consisting of nothing but "wicked men," the other of nothing but "impostors"). It is *one and the same* group, *one* predicate applying to everyone included in the group, though in the subject *two* descriptive terms are used to characterize this group. These persons are called: a. *evil men* (cf. I Cor. 5:13; II Thess. 3:2), men whose attitudes, desires, words, and works are wicked (see verses 1-9), and whose master is "the evil one" (II Thess. 3:3; then Matt. 6:13). b. These persons are also called *impostors* (γόητες, used only here in the New Testament). They are deceivers, shrewd and crafty individuals. In that respect – not necessarily in the ability to work magic – they remind one of Jannes and Jambres (see on verse 8 above).

These evil men and impostors, who persecute sincere believers and who strive to lead everyone astray, "will proceed from bad to worse," that is, *inwardly:* morally and spiritually, "deceiving (see on verses 6-8) and being deceived." [158] The implication may well be that while they are engaged in deceiving others, they themselves are being deceived. A "deluding energy" is the punishment which those receive who would delude others. Delusion is their weapon; by delusion they are slain. They believe, or try to make themselves believe, that the falsehoods by means of which they would ensnare others will gain for themselves complete happiness and ultimate victory. In this they will be bitterly disappointed. (See N.T.C. on II Thess. 2:11.) Nevertheless, the emphasis in the present passage is not on "being deceived" but on "deceiving," as is clear from the words which immediately follow. While some fall for this deception, let Timothy be on his guard. Let *him* remain firm and stedfast. Says Paul:

---

[158] The expression is almost proverbial. Cf. Philo, *On The Migration Of Abraham,* XV, "intending to deceive, they are deceived." Ovid, *Metamorphoses,* XIV. 81, "Being herself disappointed, she disappointed all." Augustine, *Confessions,* VII. 2, "deceived deceivers."

Having erected an instrument of death for Mordecai, Haman discovers too late that it is going to be the instrument for his own execution. Perillos of Athens, desiring to bake others to death by means of his "metal bull" is himself baked to death in it. Hugues Aubriot, having built the Bastille for the imprisonment of others, is himself the first one to be confined in it. The bishop of Verdun, having invented the Iron Cage for the punishment of others is himself the first man to be shut up in it. And Rebent Morton is the first to lose his head to The Maiden (a kind of guillotine) which he himself devised for the decapitation of others.

14, 15. *You,* however, must continue in the things which you have learned and of which you have become convinced.

You (note emphatic position in the original, at the very head of the sentence, just as in verse 10) must pursue a course which is the very opposite of that which was followed by the false teachers and their adherents. Timothy, then, is here admonished *to continue* or *abide* in "the things" (the doctrines based on Holy Writ, see verses 15, 16) which he has learned and of which he has become convinced. When did he learn them? And when had he become convinced of them? The tense used in the original does not specify. It simply *states* the historical fact that Timothy has learned and has become convinced.[159] From the context (verse 15) we gather that the two activities (learning and becoming convinced) had begun already in very early childhood. It is natural to suppose that they had continued up to this very moment while Paul is admonishing him to remain in these things. Learning had increased throughout the years, and conviction had been deepened.

Note that *learning* is not enough. What has been learned must be applied to the heart by the Holy Spirit, so that one also *becomes convinced,* with a conviction that transforms life.

According to the most natural grammatical construction, Paul states *two* reasons why Timothy must continue in the things which he learned and of which he became convinced. *In reality* the two reasons are only *one,* for the testimony of human beings with respect to matters of faith means nothing apart from the Word; nevertheless, since it pleased God *by means of devout human individuals* to convey to the mind and heart of Timothy the message of the Word, it is entirely proper to speak of *two* reasons:

a. The trustworthy character of those who had instructed Timothy in these doctrines (verse 14b); and

b. The super-excellence of the sacred writings on which these doctrines are based (verse 15).

The first reason is expressed in these words: **knowing from whom you learned them.** Timothy must never forget that he had learned these things from no less a person than Paul himself (see verses 10 and 11 above) and, going back even farther, from those highly esteemed worthies: grandmother Lois and mother Eunice (II Tim. 1:5), women who, before their conversion to the Christian faith, had instructed the little child Timothy in "the sacred writings," and who, having once accepted Jesus as their Lord and Savior, had been used as instruments in God's hand to co-operate with

---

[159] The theory of some interpreters, namely, that the aorist tense expresses that Timothy had learned and had become convinced of these things at a definite time (for instance, "before he became a Christian," Bouma, *op. cit.,* p. 328) is questionable. Far better is the view of Lenski, *op. cit.,* p. 836: both aorists are simply constative. They simply summarize the past, without indicating any definite time.

Paul in the important task of leading the young man to see in Christ the fulfilment of the Old Testament promises.

It is clear that Paul, Lois, Eunice, and any others who may have nurtured Timothy, are not viewed as independent authorities, apart from the Word, but as secondary or intermediate sources of knowledge, avenues of instruction, and even this *only because they accepted Scripture!* – Hence, not Tradition *and* Scripture (which really means Tradition *superimposed upon* Scripture) are here viewed as *basically* authoritative. *Scripture alone* (see verses 15 and 16) *is final authority,* and Tradition is important only in the measure in which it adheres to and imparts Scripture. When it does this, then it is of considerable significance, and this especially in the education of children who as yet are not able to read and/or interpret Scripture itself!

Accordingly, the second – the only really *basic* – reason why Timothy should abide in the things which he learned and of which he had become persuaded is: **And that from infancy you have known (the) sacred writings, which are able to make you wise for salvation through that faith (which is) in Christ Jesus.**

Principles and Methods of Education in Israel
Background for the Understanding of II Tim. 3:15

(1) Among the Jews education was definitely *God-centered* as to principles, contents, and methods. *The devout Israelite taught his children because Jehovah commanded him to do so.* And he instructed them *with respect to* the *verba et gesta Dei* (words and deeds of God), *as recorded in "the* sacred writings." This is evident throughout the Old Testament (Gen. 18:19; Ex. 10:2; 12:26, 27; 13:14-16; Deut. 4:9, 10; 6:7, 9; 11:19; 32:46; Is. 38:19; and many other passages; cf. also Josephus, *Antiquities,* IV. viii. 12).

(2) Naturally *the content* of this body of God-centered education was, "The fear of Jehovah is the beginning of (knowledge and of) wisdom, And the knowledge of the Holy One is understanding" (Prov. 1:7; 9:10). That was also its *purpose:* "This is the end of the matter . . . Fear God and keep his commandments; for this is the whole duty of man" (Eccl. 12:13).

(3) *At first,* as is clear from many of the passages cited, the physical-mental-moral-spiritual nurture of the child was centered *solely in the home,* both father and mother taking part in this. Little children, both boys and girls, were taught by their mother, to whom also the education of the older girls was entrusted. The boys, on the other hand, were soon placed under the care of the father. *Even in later times* (when father and mother received outside help in the rearing of their children; see (14)) the influence

of godly parents and their efforts to train their children in the fear of the Lord remained paramount.

(4) *Children,* in turn, were admonished to give heed to their father's instruction, and not to reject their mother's teaching (Prov. 1:8; 6:20). They *were taught to honor and obey* their parents (Ex. 20:12; 21:15-17; Lev. 20:9; Deut. 21:18; Prov. 30:17; cf. Eph. 6:1-3). The soul-destructive falsehood that the child should be permitted to do "just as he pleases" is refuted by Scripture. Godly parents did not inflict this cruelty upon their immature offspring!

(5) The reason why everything was not simply left to the child was that *the little one was viewed as being* not only immature (that were reason enough in itself) but also *sinful by nature,* hence incapable of itself to choose the good (Ps. 51:5).

(6) Realizing that no human wisdom or piety is ever able to cope with the tremendous ravages of sin, *godly parents committed their children to God* and to his kindly care (Job 1:5).

(7) In Israel God-centered education was begun when the child was still very, very young (I Sam. 1:27, 28; 2:11, 18, 19; cf. Josephus, *Against Apion,* I. 12; Susanna 3; IV Macc. 18:9). The purpose of beginning early is expressed beautifully in the words of Prov. 22:6, "Train up a child in the way he should go (literally, "according to his way"), And even when he is old he will not depart from it."

(8) In the midst of the difficult task of properly training their children, *Israelites received much encouragement from God's covenant-promise:* "I will establish my covenant between me and thee and thy seed after thee throughout their generations for an everlasting covenant, to be a God unto thee and to thy seed after thee" (Gen. 17:7; Ps. 74:20; Ps. 105:8, 9), a promise which is organically realized in the hearts and lives of all those who through the enabling power of God's sovereign grace are firmly resolved to surrender themselves completely to him. (Cf. Acts 2:38, 39; Gal. 3:9, 29.)

(9) In view of the fact that the child was regarded as by nature sinful but by grace capable of inner change, *discipline was not cast aside* as unprofitable or unjust. The rod of correction was not spared, yet was used with discretion, since wise reproof was considered generally better than a hundred stripes (Prov. 13:24; 23:13, 14; then 17:10).

(10) Above all, *parents loved their children,* and nurtured them in the spirit of love (Ps. 103:13). Jewish children were not forced to devote all their time to work and study. They had their games (Zech. 8:5; Matt. 11:16-18).

(11) Though *godly Israelites* made many decisions *for* their children, they *prepared them to choose for themselves* (Josh. 24:15).

(12) *Education* in Israel *was* of a *very practical* character. It would seem

that even the smaller children were in many cases taught to read and write (Is. 10:19; cf. Josephus, *Against Apion.* II. 25), though it is impossible to determine the extent of this ability (cf. Is. 29:11, 12). That boys were taught an occupation, and that craftsmanship was encouraged is well-known.

(13) As to methodology, the Israelites were not, as a rule, afflicted with memorization-phobia. To a certain extent, necessity even demanded and common sense dictated that committing to memory receive its prominent place in the system of education (Is. 28:10). At times this method may have received undue emphasis, just as today it certainly receives *too little* emphasis.

The notion that educators should merely ask questions to which no one except the child (!) has the right to supply answers was favored only by men like Eli ("Why do y o u do such things?" I Sam. 2:23), who failed miserably in the task of bringing up his children. *God demanded that when questions were asked, definite answers should be given* (Ex. 13:8; Deut. 6:7; 6:20-25; 11:19; Josh. 12:26-28); that children should be *taught* Jehovah's statutes; that a body of truth with respect to the words and deeds of Jehovah should be handed down from generation to generation.

(14) Although at first the education of the child was viewed as the sole task and responsibility of the parents, at a later period priests and Levites, prophets, special tutors (especially in the case of the well-to-do, Numbers 11:12; II Sam. 12:25; II Kings 10:1; I Chron. 27:32; Is. 49:23), "wise men," scribes, and rabbis, all contributed their share in raising the cultural level of youth and of the nation.

After the Exile (especially from the time of Simon ben Shataḥ, about 70 B. C.), due to scribal influence, a new order of educational institutions or "schools" gradually arose. The school was called a "house" or "place" (Hebrew *Beth*). The lower or elementary school was called *Beth Ha-Sefer* ("place of writing"), the school attended by talented youths was called *Beth Ha-Midrash* ("place of study"), while for the masses there arose the *Beth Ha-Keneseth* ("place of assembly"). In course of time this "place (or "house") of assembly" began to be known by its Greek name, of similar meaning, "synagogue."

(15) That the system of home-centered religious nurture, both *formal* (imparting specific, systematic instruction) and *informal* (teaching *by example*) — in connection with the feasts, formal and informal education coalesced —, actually "worked" is evident from the book of Daniel. Even in the lands of the exile, youths who had been brought up in Jehovah's ways refused, at the risk of losing their lives, to defile themselves or to render homage to anyone or anything other than the God of their fathers. Thus, throughout the dark night of the captivity and foreign domination, the example of parental piety, the indoctrination in Jehovah's statutes (Ps

119:33), served as a lamp unto the feet and a light upon the path (Ps. 119:105). It also served to bind the people together, and wherever it was practised diligently, it prevented them from losing their spiritual distinctiveness, and made them, in many instances, a blessing to their heathen neighbors.[160]

Accordingly, in the manner of devout Israelites, grandmother Lois and mother Eunice had instructed "little" Timothy (II Tim. 1:5). Note the expression "from infancy." Literally Paul says, "from *an infant.*" In some passages the word used in the original refers to *an unborn child* (Luke 1:41, 44); elsewhere simply to *a very small child,* a babe or infant (Luke 2:12, 16; 18:15; Acts 7:19; I Peter 2:2). Nevertheless, when Paul writes, *"You,* however, must continue in the things which you have learned and of which you have become convinced because . . . *from infancy* you have known (the) sacred writings," he is not thinking only of Timothy's *early childhood,* but is referring to Timothy's life from the days of his infancy *to this very*

---

[160] In addition to Scripture itself the following references with respect to education among the Jews have been consulted:

Abrahams, Israel (editor), *Hebrew Ethical Wills,* Philadelphia, 1926, esp. ch. III, "A Father's Admonition" (by Judah ibn Tibbon).

Bavinck, H., *Paedagogische Beginselen,* Kampen, 1904, esp. pp. 26, 27.

Benzinger, I., art. "Family and Marriage Relations," esp. par. 15, *The New Schaff-Herzog Encyclopaedia of Religious Knowledge,* Vol. IV, p. 277.

Berkhof, L., *Biblical Archaeology,* Grand Rapids, Mich., 1915, p. 68.

Day, E., *Social Life of the Hebrews,* New York, 1901.

Drazin, N., *History of Jewish Education from 515 B.C.E. to 220 C.E.,* Baltimore, 1940.

Edersheim, A., *The Life and Times of Jesus the Messiah,* two volumes, New York, 1897, esp. Vol. I, pp. 226-234.

Finkelstein, Louis (editor), *The Jews, Their History, Culture, and Religion,* New York, two volumes; see especially Vol. II, chapter 21, "The Role of Education in Jewish History" (by Julius B. Maller).

Gispen, W. H., "Bijbelsche Archaeologie," in *Bijbelsch Handboek,* two volumes, Kampen, 1935; see Vol. I, pp. 252, 253.

Guignebert, Charles, *The Jewish World in the Time of Jesus,* translated by S. H. Jooke, London, 1938.

Kuiper, A., Jr., "De Opvoeding in het Huisgezin," in *Christendom En Opvoeding* (composite authorship), Baarn, pp. 33-75.

Leipziger, *Education of the Jews,* New York, 1890.

Mackie, G. M., *Bible Manners and Customs,* London, 1898.

Marcus, Samuel, *Die Paedagogik des israelitischen Volkes,* two volumes, Vienna, 1877.

Meyer, H. H., art. "Education" in I.S.B.E.

Miller, M. S. and J. L., *Encyclopedia of Bible Life,* New York and London, 1944, pp. 390-392.

Schuerer, Emil, *A History of the Jewish People,* Edinburgh, 1893, esp. Vol. II, "The Scribes," "School and Synagogue."

Seeley, *History of Education,* New York, Cincinnati, Chicago, 1914, Chapter V, "The Jews" (pp. 44-49).

Strack, Hermann L., *Introduction to the Talmud and Midrash,* Philadelphia, 1931.

moment. Throughout that entire period Timothy had known the sacred writings, having learned to know them better and better right along.

This also indicates that the term "sacred writings" does not merely mean "the ABC which you learned from the Bible when you were a little child" (as several commentators interpret it). By "sacred writings" the apostle simply means *The Old Testament.* Words have a history. The fact that γράμμα has the primary meaning "that which is drawn or traced," hence, *character, letter, script,* does not in any way compel us to accept that meaning *here.* See N.T.C. on John 7:14, 15. In Josephus "sacred writings" means The Old Testament (*Antiquities,* X. x. 4; *Against Apion,* I. 10). He gives the list of the books belonging to it in *Against Apion,* I. 8. This list shows that his Old Testament was the same as ours (see the explanation in my *Bible Survey,* pp. 19, 20).

Paul uses the expression "sacred writings" here in verse 15, but "all scripture" in verse 16, for the simple reason that he wishes to draw a distinction between the Old Testament (verse 15) and *whatever* has a right to be called divinely inspired scripture (verse 16). The latter comprises more than the former. Yet, Paul would have been incorrect had he said that Timothy had been instructed in *"all* scripture" *from the days of his infancy,* for when he was a small child Lois and Eunice knew only the Old Testament. But it was definitely true that from very early childhood until the moment when Paul is writing these words Timothy had been constantly adding to his knowledge of *the Old Testament.* Let him then remain firm in the faith. Let him keep clinging to that which he has learned so thoroughly and of which he has become persuaded in his heart!

That this is the correct explanation is also clear from the words which follow, namely, "the sacred writings . . . which are able to make you wise for salvation." Letters of the alphabet (even when they are learned from the Bible!), the mere ABC, cannot make one wise for salvation; the sacred writings can! It is "the testimony of Jehovah" and his "commandments" which *make a man wise* (Ps. 19:7; 119:98; in both cases the same verb is used in the Septuagint as is used here in I Tim. 3:15; see LXX Ps. 18:8; 118:98). It is these that lead a person to choose the best means in order to achieve the highest goal. And *that* is real wisdom! Note: "wise *for salvation"* (Rom. 11:11; Phil. 1:19; 2:12, etc.). What is included in this rich concept has been explained in connection with I Tim. 1:15.

Now this wonderful work of God whereby sinners are emancipated from the greatest evil and made possessors of the highest good is not brought about in a mechanical fashion, through the mere hearing, reading or study of "the sacred writings." One must learn to see Christ Jesus in the Old Testament. One must *surrender his life* (note: "through the faith") to the Anointed Savior, apart from whom "the sacred writings" have no meaning (on Christ as the fulfilment of the Old Testament see Luke 24:27, 32,

44; John 5:39, 46; Acts 3:18, 24; 7:52; 10:43; 13:29; 26:22, 23; 28:23; I Peter 1:10).

16, 17. Paul now expands the idea which he has just expressed. He does this in three ways:

a. Not only are "the sacred writings" (verse 15) of inestimable value; so is also *"all* scripture."
b. Not only does this sacred literature "make wise for salvation" (verse 15) but it is definitely God-breathed and as such capable of thoroughly qualifying a person "for every good work."
c. Not only will it benefit *Timothy* (verse 15), but it will do the same for *every* "man of God."

Accordingly, Paul writes, **All scripture** [161] **(is)** [162] **God-breathed and useful for teaching, for reproof, for correction, for training in righteousness.** *All scripture,* in distinction from "(the) sacred writings" (for which see on verse 15) means everything which, through the testimony of the Holy Spirit in the church, is recognized by the church as canonical, that is, authoritative. When Paul wrote these words, the direct reference was to a body of sacred literature which even then comprised more than the Old Testament (see on I Tim. 5:18; also footnote 160). Later, at the close of the first century A. D., "all scripture" had been completed. Though the history of the recognition, review, and ratification of the canon was somewhat complicated, and virtually universal acceptance of all the sixty-six books did not occur immediately in every region where the church was represented – one of the reasons being that for a long time certain of the smaller books had not even *reached* every corner of the church –, it remains true, nevertheless, that those genuine believers who were the original recipients of

---

[161] It is not true that the absence of the article compels us to adopt the translation of the A.R.V., "Every scripture." The word Scripture can be definite even without the article (I Peter 2:6; II Peter 1:20). Similarly πᾶς Ἰσραήλ means "all Israel" (Rom. 11:26). See Gram. N.T., p. 772. But even if the rendering "every scripture" be accepted, the resultant meaning would not differ greatly, for if "every scripture" is inspired, "all scripture" must be inspired also.

[162] The most natural rendering of θεόπνευστος καὶ ὠφέλιμος is "God-breathed and useful." I can see no compelling reason for inserting a copula between the two modifiers, resulting in: "God-breathed *is also* useful." Moreover, if *God-breathed* is attributive, καί in the sense of *also* would be superfluous: "All scripture God-breathed is useful," etc., would suffice.

In the abstract, another possibility presents itself, namely, that we adopt the rendering "God-breathed and useful," but regard both as attributive; hence, "All scripture God-breathed and useful for teaching," etc. However, when this is done, the sentence dangles. It "hangs in the air," having no predicate.

It is clear, therefore, that with respect to grammatical construction there is no solid reason for departing from the view which forms the basis of the A.V. Though not the only possible view, it seems to be the most natural. Its translation, "All scripture is given by inspiration of God," is excellent. So is also the almost identical rendering found in the text of the R.S.V.

the various God-breathed books regarded them at once as being invested with divine authority and majesty. What should be emphasized, however, is that not because the church, upon a certain date, long ago, made an official decision (the decision of the Council of Hippo, 393 A. D.; of Carthage, 397 A. D.), do these books constitute the inspired Bible; on the contrary, the sixty-six books, by their very contents, immediately attest themselves to the hearts of all Spirit-indwelt men as being the living oracles of God. Hence, believers are filled with deep reverence whenever they hear the voice of God addressing them from Holy Writ (see II Kings 22 and 23). All scripture is canonical because God made it so!

The word *God-breathed,* occurring only here [163] indicates that "all scripture" owes its origin and contents to the divine breath, the Spirit of God. The human authors were powerfully guided and directed by the Holy Spirit. As a result, what they wrote is not only without error but of supreme value for man. It is *all* that God wanted it to be. It constitutes the infallible rule of faith and practice for mankind.

The Spirit, however, did not suppress the personality of the human writer, but raised it to a higher level of activity (John 14:26). And because the individuality of the human author was not destroyed, we find in the Bible a wide variety of style and language. Inspiration, in other words, is organic, not mechanical. This also implies that it should never be considered apart from those many activities which served to bring the human author upon the scene of history. By causing him to be born at a certain time and place, bestowing upon him specific endowments, equipping him with a definite kind of education, causing him to undergo predetermined experiences, and bringing back to his mind certain facts and their implications, the Spirit prepared his human consciousness. Next, that same Spirit moved him to write. Finally, during the process of writing, that same Primary Author, in a thoroughly organic connection with all the preceding activity, suggested to the mind of the human author that language (the very words!) and that style, which would be the most appropriate vehicle for the interpretation of the divine ideas for people of every rank and position, age and race. Hence, though every word is truly the word of the human author, it is even more truly the Word of God.[164]

Though the word *God-breathed* — that is, inspired by God — occurs only here, the idea is found in many other passages (Ex. 20:1; II Sam. 23:2; Is. 8:20; Mal. 4:4; Matt. 1:22; Luke 24:44; John 1:23; 5:39; 10:34, 35;

---

[163] θεόπνευστος does not mean "God-breathing," "breathing the divine spirit," but is passive: "God-breathed." Cf. II Peter 1:21. See the detailed argument in B. B. Warfield, *The Inspiration and Authority of the Bible,* Philadelphia, Pa., 1948, pp. 245-296.

[164] See J. Orr, *Revelation and Inspiration,* London, 1910; H. Bavinck, *Gereformeerde Dogmatiek,* third ed., Vol. I, p. 464.

14:26; 16:13; 19:36, 37; 20:9; Acts 1:16; 7:38; 13:34; Rom. 1:2; 3:2; 4:23; 9:17; 15:4; I Cor. 2:4-10; 6:16; 9:10; 14:37; Gal. 1:11, 12; 3:8, 16, 22; 4:30; I Thess. 1:5; 2:13; Heb. 1:1, 2; 3:7; 9:8; 10:15; II Peter 1:21; 3:16; I John 4:6; and Rev. 22:19).

Now by virtue of the fact that "all scripture" is God-breathed, it is *useful* or *beneficial* or *profitable*. It is a very practical, yes an indispensable, instrument or tool *for the teacher* (implied here). Timothy should make good use of it:

a. *for teaching*. What is meant is the activity of imparting knowledge concerning God's revelation in Christ. See on I Tim. 5:17. This is ever basic to everything else.

b. *for reproof* (cf. Ps. 38:14; 39:11). Warnings, based on the Word, must be issued. Errors in doctrine and in conduct must be refuted in the spirit of love. Dangers must be pointed out. False teachers must be exposed (cf. I Tim. 5:20; Titus 1:9, 13; 2:15; then Eph. 5:18; and see N.T.C. on John 16:8-11).

c. *for correction* (see M.M., p. 229). If *reproof* stresses the negative aspect of pastoral work, *correction* emphasizes the positive side. Not only must the sinner be warned to leave the wrong path, but he must also be directed to the *right* or *straight* path (Dan. 12:3). This, too, "all scripture" is able to do. The Word, especially when it is used by a consecrated servant of God who is diligent in the performance of his pastoral duties, is *restorative* in character (cf. John 21:15-17).

d. *for training in righteousness* (cf. II Tim. 2:22). The teacher must train his people. Every Christian needs to be disciplined, so that he may prosper in the sphere where God's holy will is considered normative. Such is the character of *training in righteousness* (cf. Titus 2:11-14).

The teacher (in this case Timothy, but the word applies to everyone to whom the souls of men are entrusted) needs "all scripture" in order to enable him to perform his fourfold task (teaching, administering reproof, correction, training in righteousness), with a glorious purpose in mind, a purpose which in his own way and at his own time God will cause to be realized in the hearts of all his people: **that the man of God may be equipped, for every good work thoroughly equipped.**

The man of God (see on I Tim. 6:11) is the believer. *Every* believer, viewed as belonging to God, and as invested with the threefold office of prophet, priest, and king, is here given this title. To function properly in this threefold office the believer must become *equipped* (note the emphasis of the original; literally, ". . . that equipped may be the man of God"); yes, once for all *thoroughly equipped* (cf. Luke 6:40) "for every good work" (I Tim. 5:10; II Tim. 2:21; Titus 3:1). Paul (and the Holy Spirit speaking through him) is not satisfied until the Word of God has fully accomplished its mission, and the believer has reached "the measure of the stature of the fulness of Christ" (Eph. 4:12, 13).

The ideal to be realized is glorious, indeed! The power to reach it is from God. Hence, let Timothy remain stedfast. Let him *abide* in the true doctrine, applying it whenever opportunity presents itself.

Synthesis of Chapter 3

See the Outline at the beginning of this chapter.

Timothy must *abide* in the sound doctrine. He must put forth every effort to do so in view of the fact that in these last days – that is, in the age ushered in by Christ's First Coming – grievous seasons will set in. Let him realize this. Are not the peddlers of sinister falsehoods beginning to make their appearance even now? Such individuals are characterized by love of *self* and of their own pleasures instead of love for *God,* by disobedience toward their superiors, unthankfulness with respect to their benefactors, an unforgiving attitude to those whom they dislike, and an unwillingness to restrain their own evil desires. Yet, they put on a religious front. They are fakers, for though they maintain a facade of religion, they deny its power. From such people Timothy should turn away.

Out of circles such as these come the men who worm their way into the homes of church-members with the purpose of making a prey of weak-minded women, women who are burdened with an evil conscience, yet are impenitent, being swayed by various impulses; and who, in spite of all the "instruction" they receive, are never able to arrive at the acknowledgment of the truth.

As to these women-baiters and the other men who belong to the same circles, they remind one of Jannes and Jambres, men who according to tradition were the two ringleaders among Pharaoh's magicians. As they *opposed* Moses, so these *oppose* the truth. They are corrupt in mind and utterly useless and disqualified as far as the faith is concerned. However, they will not get very far, for their folly will become as obvious to everybody as did that of Jannes and Jambres.

Another reason why Timothy must by all means endeavor to *abide* in the sound doctrine is the fact that it is based on the most reliable foundation, as he has learned from trustworthy persons. Has not Timothy had the apostle as a model of obedience both active ("*my* teaching, *my* conduct," etc.) and passive ("*my* persecutions, *my* sufferings")? Has he not taken a keen interest in the persecutions which Paul underwent, beginning with the first missionary journey – Antioch, Iconium, and Lystra! –, the journey which had meant so much to Timothy himself? How vividly Paul recalls especially this fact, which should encourage Timothy, namely, that though persecution is the lot of everyone who desires to live a sincere Christian life, inasmuch as evil men and impostors proceed from bad to worse, deluding and being deluded, nevertheless the Lord protects his faithful ones! Did he not rescue Paul from all these persecutions? Let Timothy then *abide* in the things he has learned and of which he has become convinced, constantly bearing in mind from what kind of people his knowledge has come, namely, from those who had been his wise monitors from the days of his earliest infancy. From infancy until this very day he had known the sacred writings – the Old Testament –, having learned to know them better right along. These are the writings which are able to make a man wise for salvation through faith in Christ Jesus. This, moreover, holds not only with respect to the inspired writings of the Old Testament but also with respect to God's further special revelation that has been deposited in written form. In fact, *all* such scripture (today we would say: both the Old and the New Testament) is God-breathed and *useful* – indispensable to the teacher! – for teaching, for warning the sinner to depart from unrighteousness, for leading him in the path of righteousness; hence, for training him in righteousness; in order that, as a result, "the man of God," that is, the believer, thus instructed and guided, may be equipped, yes *fully* equipped for every good work.

Outline of Chapter 4

Theme: ***The Apostle Paul Tells Timothy What To Do in the Interest of Sound Doctrine***

Preach It "I charge you"

4:1-8 In season, out of season, for apostasy is coming.
Remain faithful in view of the fact that "I am about to set sail."

4:9-22 Items of personal information, requests, greetings.

CHAPTER IV

II TIMOTHY **4:1**

4 1 I charge you in the sight of God and of Christ Jesus, who will judge the
living and the dead, and by his appearing and his kingdom: 2 herald the
word; be on hand in season, out of season; reprove, rebuke, admonish, with all
longsuffering and teaching. 3 For the season will arrive when men will not endure
the sound doctrine, but, having itching ears, will accumulate for themselves teachers to suit their own fancies; 4 and will turn away their ears from the truth, and
will turn aside to the myths.

5 As for yourself, however, be sober in all matters, suffer hardship, do the
work of an evangelist, your ministry discharge to the full.

6 For I am already being poured out as a drink-offering, and the season of
my departure has arrived. 7 The grand fight I have fought, the race I have finished,
the faith I have kept. 8 For the future, there is safely stored away for me the
wreath of righteousness, which the Lord, the righteous Judge, will award to me on
that day, and not to me alone but to all who have loved his appearing.

4:1-8

1. Underlying the thought expressed in the opening paragraph of chapter 4 are the "grievous seasons" of departure from the faith, which were described in chapter 3. Though, in a sense, these seasons are certainly future (3:1; 4:3, 4), they must not be thought of as wholly separate from and unrelated to conditions present even now, while Paul is writing. The very fact that Paul admonishes Timothy to fulfil his ministry, reproving and rebuking whenever this is necessary, and remaining sober in the midst of all untoward circumstances, shows that future heresy is viewed as the outgrowth of present error. The coming apostasy is a further stage in the development of the already present deviation from the truth.

But though the background of chapters 3 and 4 is the same, a difference of approach is, nevertheless, discernible. Chapter 3 stresses the fact that Timothy, confronted with developing opposition to the truth, must *abide* in the true doctrine. Chapter 4 brings into prominence Timothy's duty *to proclaim* this doctrine. Let him "speak out" while people are still willing to listen. They will not always be willing. Let the "herald" of the gospel discharge his ministry to the full!

Accordingly, Paul writes, **I charge you in the sight of God and of Christ Jesus, who will judge the living and the dead, and by his appearing and his kingdom.**

For the meaning of "I charge[165] you in the sight of God and of Christ Jesus" see on I Tim. 5:21. It is on the eve of his death that Paul delivers this final, most solemn charge. He directs Timothy's attention to God and to Christ Jesus, in whose presence the charge is issued and received. He places Timothy under oath to comply with the charge. It is to God and to the Anointed Savior that Timothy (Paul, too, of course!) will have to render an account. And this is the Christ who "is about to" judge! In a sense, even now his approaching footsteps can be heard. He is on the way. Paul stresses the certainty of his coming and its impending character, but does not fix any date.

Now this Christ Jesus will judge "the living," that is, those who will still be living on earth at the moment of the Second Coming, and "the dead," that is, those who will have died by that time. (See also Matt. 25:31-46; Luke 18:8; John 5:27-29; I Cor. 15:51, 52; I Thess. 4:13-18; Rev. 20:11-15.)

The idea that Christ is coming to judge is of frequent occurrence in Paul (Rom. 2:16; I Cor. 4:5; II Cor. 4:5; II Thess. 1:7-9; cf. Acts 17:31). The expression, "He will judge the living and the dead" may already have become a fixed formula, as would appear from similar statements in Acts 10:42 and I Peter 4:5. It was probably part of a baptismal confession, explained to the catechumens and afterward confessed by them at baptism. Out of such formulas as these *The Apostles' Creed* arose.[166]

Paul furthermore adjures Timothy by Christ's future, glorious *appearing*, that is, by his brilliant Second Coming, viewed as the rising of the sun (see also verse 8; I Tim. 6:14; Titus 2:13; see on II Tim. 1:10; also N.T.C. on II Thess. 2:8; and cf. Mal. 4:2), and *by*[167] his *majestic kingship*, the rulership into which he will then fully enter. (With reference to this perfected reign see also verse 18; then N.T.C. on I Thess. 2:12 and on II Thess. 1:5, especially footnote *e*.) If Timothy obeys, he will share in (and if he disobeys, he will miss) the glory of the Epiphany and of the Reign (I Thess. 4:13-18; cf. 3:13; II Tim. 2:12; Rev. 3:21; 22:5).

2. By means of five brisk imperatives (all of them aorists) the content of the charge is now set forth: **herald the word; be on hand in season, out of season; reprove, rebuke, admonish, with all longsuffering and teaching.**

---

[165] The rendering "charge" (A.V., A.R.V., R.S.V.) is correct. The context requires this rendering *charge* or *adjure*, not *solemnly testify*; for what follows (in verse 2) *is a charge*, not a *testimony*. For the opposite view see Robertson (*Word Pictures*, Vol. 4, p. 629), and Lenski, *op. cit.*, p. 850.

[166] See P. Schaff, *Creeds of Christendom*, three volumes, New York and London, edition 1919, Vol. I, pp. 16-23.

[167] The accusative of the nouns *epiphany* and *kingdom* (or "kingship") has been called that of "adjuration" or "conjuration" (cf. Mark 5:7; Acts 19:13; I Thess. 5:27; cf. LXX on Deut. 4:26; 30:19; 31:28).

a. "Herald[168] the word." This is basic to the other four imperatives. The rendering *"Preach* the word" is entirely correct, *if* the verb *preach* be understood in its primary, etymological meaning (from the Latin *praedicare*): *to proclaim before the public,* and not in the weakened sense which today is often attached to it: "to deliver a moral or religious discourse of any kind and in any way." The word employed in the original means *proclaim* (cf. Matt. 10:27); literally, *herald,* make known officially and publicly a matter of great significance. Of course, all preaching should be heralding (Rom. 10:14, 15). Paul calls himself a *herald* (see footnote 168). By order of his Superior he made an authoritative, open, forceful declaration. He here commands Timothy to be a herald also.

According to Scripture, then, *"heralding" or "preaching" is generally the divinely authorized proclamation of the message of God to men. It is the exercise of ambassadorship.*[169]

This is evident from the following examples. These men are all said to have "heralded":

Noah

"God will destroy the world. Turn away from y o u r sins!" Or similar words (II Peter 2:5; cf. I Peter 3:19).

Jonah

"Yet forty days, and Nineveh shall be overthrown!" (Jonah 3:4; Matt. 12:41; Luke 11:32).

John the Baptist

"Repent, for the Kingdom of heaven is at hand!"

"Look, the Lamb of God, who is taking away the sin of the world!" (Matt. 3:1, 2; John 1:29).

The Healed Gerasene Demoniac

"God has done great things for me!" (Luke 8:39).

---

[168] In Paul *the verb* "to herald" (κηρύσσω) occurs in the following passages: Rom. 2:21; 10:8, 14, 15; I Cor. 1:23; 9:27; 15:11, 12; II Cor. 1:19; 4:5; 11:4; Gal. 2:2; 5:11; Phil. 1:15; Col. 1:23; I Thess. 2:9; I Tim. 3:16; II Tim. 4:2. It is also of frequent occurrence in the Synoptics and in Acts. It is found once in Peter (I Peter 3:19); once in Revelation (5:2). *The noun* "herald" (κῆρυξ) is found in I Timothy 2:7 and II Tim. 1:11. In the New Testament outside of Paul it occurs only in II Peter 2:5. "Proclamation by the herald" or "heralding" (κήρυγμα) is found in Rom. 16:25; I Cor. 1:21; 2:4; 15:14; II Tim. 4:17; Titus 1:3. In addition to its occurrences in Paul this noun also occurs in Matt. 12:41 and in Luke 11:32.

Synonyms are εὐαγγελίζω (to announce good tidings), and in certain contexts καταγγέλλω (to proclaim, declare).

[169] Words have a history. It is, therefore, not surprising that also this verb, like so many others, is at times used in a more general sense, namely, with respect to a proclamation or heralding that is *not* divinely authorized, Mark 1:45; 7:36.

The Apostle Paul

"Jesus is the Christ!" (Acts 9:20).

"Far be it from me to glory, except in the cross of our Lord Jesus Christ!" (Gal. 6:14).

"But now has Christ been raised from the dead, the first-fruits of them that are asleep!" (I Cor. 15:20; cf. verses 55-58; I Thess. 4:13-18).

Similarly the twelve, Philip the evangelist, Peter at Cesarea, "a strong angel," etc., are said to have "preached" ("heralded"). The verb is even used in connection with Christ, for he, too, was bringing God's message to man.

The herald brings *God's* message. Today in the work of "heralding" or "preaching" careful exposition of the text is certainly included. But genuine heralding or preaching is lively, not dry; timely, not stale. *It is the earnest proclamation of news initiated by God. It is not the abstract speculation on views excogitated by man.*

The somewhat timid Timothy must never be afraid to herald *the word,* that is, *the gospel* (see on II Tim. 2:8, 9; cf. Mark 1:14; 16:15; I Thess. 2:9). It is *the true* message of redemption in Christ, and as such stands over against all *falsehood* (see verse 4). Moreover, in sharp contrast with the oft stealthy *infiltration* practised by Satan and his servants (II Tim. 3:6) is this open-and-above-board *proclamation* by one who brings good tidings and publishes peace (Nah. 1:15; Rom. 10:15).[170]

How this heralding must be done is indicated by the four imperatives which follow:

b. "Be on hand in season, out of season." Welcome or not welcome, Timothy must ever be "on the spot" [171] with the message from God. He must "buy up the opportunity" (Eph. 5:16).

---

170 One must not ascribe qualities to "heralding" which do not properly belong to it. The view — held by some (see, for example, Alan Richardson, article "Preach, Teach" in *A Theological Word Book of the Bible,* New York, 1952, pp. 171, 172) — that the term "heralding" and its synonyms have nothing to do with the delivery of sermons to the converted, but always indicate the proclamation of the good news to *the non-Christian world,* is incorrect. To be sure, when the church was still in its infancy, and when even in the Roman world most people had never heard of the gospel, great emphasis was placed on missionary-activity. And the missionary's audience would naturally consist exclusively or largely of unbelievers, whether Jews or Gentiles. But this does not mean that when *believers* are being established in the faith, the message which they hear ceases to be "kerugma" (see Rom. 16:25), and that the messenger ceases to be a "herald."

171 Since everywhere else in the New Testament the verb has the sense "arrive," "come near," "be present," "be on hand," (or the very closely related meaning "come upon," "come on"), a meaning which also suits the present context, I see no reason to adopt a different sense here (like "keep on," or "be urgent").

c. "Reprove" or "Convict." See on II Tim. 3:16 for the related noun. Sin must be brought home to the sinner's consciousness in order that he may repent. See the detailed discussion of this verb in N.T.C. on John 16:8, especially footnote 200.

d. "Rebuke." In the process of reproving or convicting the sinner, the latter must be sharply reprimanded. His sin must not be toned down.

e. "Admonish." Nevertheless, the demands of love must be fully satisfied. Hand in hand with pertinent rebuke there must be tender, fatherly admonition. See N.T.C. on I Thess. 2:7-12, and for detailed explanation of the verb "admonish" see on I Tim. 5:1.

Modifying each of the three imperatives is the beautiful phrase, "with all longsuffering and teaching," meaning "with utmost longsuffering and with most painstaking teaching-activity." Cf. a similar combination in II Tim. 2:24, "gentle to all, qualified to teach."

Such longsuffering is a distinctly Christian virtue (II Cor. 6:6; Eph. 4:2; Col. 1:11; 3:12; and see N.T.C. on I Thess. 5:14), as well as (elsewhere) a divine attribute (Rom. 2:4; I Tim. 1:16). Note that *longsuffering* (slowness to wrath, gentle patience with people who have erred) and *teaching-activity* go together. Neither is complete without the other. The manner in which Paul dealt with the Corinthian fornicator illustrates what he means by "reprove, rebuke, admonish, with all longsuffering and teaching" (I Cor. 5:1-8, 13; II Cor. 2:5-11). A much earlier example is Nathan's treatment of David (II Sam. 12:1-15).

3 and 4. A reason is now given, showing why Timothy must be diligent in the work of heralding the gospel and of reproving, rebuking, and admonishing: **For the season will arrive when they will not endure the sound doctrine.**

In every period of history (see on II Tim. 3:1) there will be a season during which men refuse to listen to sound doctrine. As history continues onward toward the consummation, this situation grows worse. Men will not endure or tolerate the truth, the doctrine which because it promotes spiritual health is called *sound* (see on I Tim. 1:10). **But, having itching ears, will accumulate for themselves teachers to suit their own fancies.** It is not the herald of the gospel that is at fault, but *the hearing* of the fickle men who make up the audience! They have ears that *are itching* (from a verb which in the active means *to tickle;* hence, in the passive, *to be tickled,* and thus *to itch,* fig. "to have an irritating desire"). Their craving is for teachers to suit their *fancies* or *perverted tastes* (see on II Tim. 2:22). So great is that hankering that they pile up teacher upon teacher. This reminds one of Jer. 5:31, "The prophets prophesy falsely . . . and my people love to have it so," and of Ezek. 33:32, "And lo, thou art unto them as a very lovely song of one who has a pleasant voice and can play well on an instrument; for they hear thy words, but they do them not." The people here pictured are more interested in something different, something sensational, than they are in sober truth. And when sober truth is presented (as it surely was by Ezekiel), they are not interested in the truth itself, but only in *the way* in which it is presented, the preacher's "style," "oratory," . . . the preacher *himself,* his voice, bearing, looks, mannerisms. Here in II Timothy 4:3, 4 the emphasis is on the craving for fascinating stories and philosophical speculations: **and will turn away their ears from the truth, and will turn aside to the myths.** God's redemptive truth, which deals with sin and damnation, with the necessity of inner change, etc. (cf. II Tim. 3:15-17) they cannot stomach. They *turn away* (as in II Tim. 1:15) from it, and *turn aside* (as in I Tim. 1:6) to "the myths," those familiar old womanish myths mentioned earlier (see on I Tim. 1:4, 7; 4:7; Titus 1:14; cf. II Peter 1:16) or anything similar to them. There are always teachers that are willing to "scratch and tickle the ears of those who wish to be tickled" (Clement of Alexandria, *The Stromata,* I. iii).

5. As for yourself, however . . . Cf. 3:10, 14. Note the sharp and double contrast. Verse 5 is both the climax of verses 1-5 and the introduction to verses 5-8. *As a climax,* it draws a contrast between Timothy and the fickle multitude described in verses 3 and 4. *As an introduction,* it draws a contrast between Timothy, still in the thick of the fight, and Paul who *has fought* the grand fight. In the beginning of the verse the first of these two contrasts predominates; at the end, the second.

Paul writes, **be sober in all matters, suffer hardship, do the work of an evangelist, your ministry discharge to the full.** The sober person is calm, steady, and sane (cf. I Peter 4:7; see N.T.C. on I Thess. 5:6, 8). He is not intoxicated with morbid craving for whatever is sensational or sentimental. He does not turn away his ears from the truth and turn aside to the myths. The apostle demands that Timothy shall show this calm and well-balanced attitude "in all matters." This means, of course, that also with respect to suffering for the sake of the gospel Timothy must neither court such suffering, on the one hand, nor complain about it, on the other. He must simply "do the work of an evangelist" (gospel-preacher, Acts 21:8; Eph. 4:11), perfectly willing to bear ill-treatment whenever it is his lot so to suffer, even rejoicing that he is counted worthy to suffer dishonor for the name of Christ (Acts 5:41; on the verb see II Tim. 2:9; cf. the similar verb in II Tim. 1:8). He must permit nothing to stop him, but must discharge his gospel-ministry *to the full:* heralding the word, being on hand in season, out of season, reproving, rebuking, admonishing, with all longsuffering and teaching.

6-8. Timothy, then, must "preach the word," etc., not only because apostasy is coming (verses 1-4), but also in view of the fact that Paul is about to set sail to the shores of eternity. When the older man is called to higher spheres, the younger man must fill the breach. He must take the torch and carry it onward. This second thought explains the conjunction "for" at the beginning of verse 6.

In one of the most sublime and moving passages, which with respect to grandeur of thought and stateliness of rhythm is probably unsurpassed anywhere in Paul's epistles, the apostle lifts this letter – and his apostolic career – to its wonderful finale:

For I am already being poured out as a drink-offering, and the season of my departure has arrived.

The grand fight I have fought, the race I have finished, the faith I have kept.

For the future there is safely stored away for me the wreath of righteousness, which the Lord, the righteous Judge, will award to me on that day, and not to me alone but to all who have loved his appearing.

A possible theme for this passage would be:

In Three Tenses Paul, the Lord's Prisoner, Triumphantly Expresses His Faith

This is divided as follows:

1. Verse 6: His Faith-Appraisal of the Present
2. Verse 7: His Faith-Summary of the Past
3. Verse 8: His Faith-Exultation regarding the Future

1. *His Faith-Appraisal of the Present*

When Paul writes, "For I am already being poured out as a drink-offering," he is making a *profession of faith.* He does not call his present horrible imprisonment, with the issue no longer in doubt, *death,* but a *drink-offering,* comparable to the libation of wine which was poured out beside the altar. According to the law (Num. 15:1-10), when a lamb was sacrificed, the drink-offering consisting of one-fourth of a hin of wine (1 hin = slightly more than 1 gallon); when the offering was a ram, the prescribed libation was one-third of a hin; and for a bull it was one-half of a hin. Since this wine *was gradually poured out,* was *an offering,* and was *the final act* of the entire sacrificial ceremony, it pictured most adequately *the gradual ebbing away* of Paul's life, the fact that he was presenting this life to God as *an offering,* and the idea that while he viewed his entire career of faith as "a living sacrifice" (Rom. 12:1; cf. 15:16), he looked upon *the present* stage of this career as being *the final sacrificial act.*

Similarly, when the apostle adds, "And the season of my departure has arrived," he is again making a *profession of faith.* The word *season* (καιρός) is entirely proper in this connection, for: a. the apostle is thinking not only of the moment of execution but of this entire final imprisonment which was about to end in execution; and b. he views this final period under the symbolism of the unmooring of a ship which in its coming and going is bound to the seasons (cf. Acts 27:12).

Now this appropriate time or season is here called "the season of my departure." The primary meaning of the phrase used in the original is "of my *loosening*" or "of my *release.*" Think of the loosening of the ropes or cables of a ship when weighing anchor. Hence, the word *loosening* acquired the secondary meaning *departure* (cf. M.M., p. 36). Accordingly, Paul says that the season of his departure *has arrived* (perfect tense of the verb that was used in verse 2, where it was rendered "be on hand," see footnote 171). Even now *the season* is already here. The weighing of the anchors and the loosening of the ropes has begun. Soon the blast of the wind will be in the sails, and then, almost immediately, the haven of everlasting bliss will have been reached.

It is only by faith that *present circumstances* can be so appraised. Similarly, in other passages the apostle speaks of the believer's demise as: a departure to be with Christ (Phil. 1:23), and to be at home with the Lord (II Cor. 5:8); gain (Phil. 1:21); very far better (Phil. 1:23); a falling asleep in Jesus (I Thess. 4:14).

Elsewhere Scripture calls it: precious in the sight of Jehovah (Ps. 116:15); a being carried away by the angels into Abraham's bosom (Luke 16:22); a going to paradise (Luke 23:43); a going to the house with many mansions (John 14:2).

2. *His Faith-Summary of the Past*

When the apostle continues, "The grand fight I have fought," he is again using the language *of faith;* for it is clear that an unbeliever, describing Paul's post-conversion life, would have characterized it as "foolish" or even "insane," sheer "madness" (cf. Acts 26:24), certainly not "the *grand* fight." But Paul, by means of the very word-order which he selects (placing each of the three objects before its verb; see my translation), emphasizes that it was, indeed, *the* "beautiful," *grand,* or noble, *fight* which he had fought; that it was not the path of chance but *the scheduled race* which he had run; and that this life of his, now viewed as finished, had been ruled not by the whim or caprice of the moment but by *that personal faith* which by God's grace he had kept to the very end.

When Paul thus summarizes his past, he is not boasting, except "in the Lord." He is recording what grace has achieved in the heart of "the chief of sinners." Hence, not on the pronoun "I" does he place the emphasis – as one might mistakenly infer from the usual translation, which causes each of the three brief clauses to begin with *"I"* —, but on "the grand fight," "the race," "the faith."

When the apostle summarizes his life as a Christian under the symbolism of "the grand fight," the underlying figure is probably a wrestling-match, boxing-bout, or similar contest (see on I Tim. 4:7b, 8; 6:12). The third of comparison is prodigious exertion of energy against a very powerful foe.

It had been a fight against Satan; against the principalities and powers, the world-rulers of this darkness in the heavenlies; against Jewish and pagan vice and violence; against Judaism among the Galatians; against fanaticism among the Thessalonians; against contention, fornication, and litigation among the Corinthians; against incipient Gnosticism among the Ephesians and Colossians; against fightings without and fears within; and last but not least, against the law of sin and death operating within his own heart.

But triumphantly Paul is able to say, "the grand fight *I have fought.*" It is vain to say that this is not strictly true because Paul had not as yet actually reached the execution-block. When death is very near and very certain, it is easy for the mind to project itself into that near-by future moment from which it then looks back upon the past, and rejoices not only in that past but in the present blessing which that past has produced.[172] Our Lord used similar language, which must be explained similarly (see N.T.C. on John 17:4).

When the apostle adds, "the race I have finished" — an obstacle-race, indeed! —, he stresses the fact that in his life as a believer he has fully accomplished that ministry to which the Lord had called him (the passage which sheds light on this is Acts 20:24); his eye, like that of a skilled runner, having been riveted at all times upon the finishing post: the glory of God by means of the salvation of sinners (Gal. 2:2; 5:7; Phil. 2:16; cf. Heb. 12:1, 2).

That Paul was, indeed, a man with *this one holy passion,* with *this* one objective in mind, so that the figure of *the race* is very appropriate, is evident from such words as the following:

"I have become all things to all men, *that I may by all means save some* . . . Even so *run* that y o u may attain . . . Therefore, whether y o u eat or drink, or whatever y o u do, do it all to *the glory of God* . . . just as I also please all men in all matters, not seeking my own profit but the profit of the many, *that they may be saved.*" (I Cor. 9:22-24; 10:31-33) And cf. 3:7-14.

In summarizing the past, Paul finally drops every metaphor, and writes,

---

172 Hence, I cannot agree with Lenski (*op. cit.*, p. 860) who criticizes Robertson's graph (Gram. N.T., p. 895) for the three perfect tenses in "I have fought, I have finished, I have kept."

"The faith I have kept." Here, as in I Tim. 6:12, the meaning is probably not, "I have kept the pledge" (or "fidelity") nor "I have maintained *the true doctrine*" ("faith" in the objective sense), but, in harmony with the present context, "I have retained my personal trust in God, my confidence in all his Christ-centered promises. In the spiritual arena of life I have not only *fought hard* and *run well,* but I have also been sustained to the end by the deeply rooted *conviction* that I shall receive the prize, the glorious reward" (see next verse).

3. *His Faith-Exultation regarding the Future*

Having discussed the present and the past, Paul turns his eye to the future. This, as has become evident, is altogether natural; for, the noble fight, successfully waged, the race satisfactorily run, and the faith stedfastly exercised, call for the reward of grace. Accordingly, the apostle writes, *"For the future,*[173] and then tells us what he confidently expects. Says he, "There is *safely stored away for me* (note the force of the compound Greek verb ἀπόκειται), so that no enemy will ever be able to deprive me of it, *the wreath* – the *victor's* wreath (see on II Tim. 2:5) – *of the righteousness,*[174] that is, the wreath to which I am *entitled* as a reward for the life which in principle has been in conformity with God's law (see on I Tim. 6:11; II Tim. 2:22; 3:16; Titus 3:5). That this wreath is Paul's *by right,* a right founded upon grace, is evident; for:

a. To those who fight the grand fight, run the race, and keep the faith (in other words, to Paul and others like him) *God has promised* to give the wreath (I Tim. 6:12; James 1:12; I Peter 5:4; Rev. 2:10).

b. *Christ has earned* it for them (see on Titus 3:5, 6).

Now the present passage simply states that the wreath or award is a righteous one, but does not indicate its nature. From other passages we

---

[173] The objection advanced by Lenski against the futuristic rendering of ἀπόκειται (*op. cit.,* p. 862), namely, that the verb which is here introduced is present tense with perfect meaning ("there has been laid up"), is not valid. It is the sense of the entire verse (verse 8), and not of the one verb, that determines the meaning of the adverb. English, too, allows such usage; for example, "As to the future, a job *has been* provided for me!" For other examples of λοιπόν (with or without the article) in the futuristic sense see Acts 27:20; I Cor. 7:29; Heb. 10:13. The meaning "for the rest" is represented by the following passages: a. without the article: I Cor. 1:16; 4:2; I Thess. 4:1; b. with the article: Phil. 3:1; 4:8.

[174] This is "a righteous wreath," a wreath *justly* bestowed upon the righteous. It *springs from* righteousness, just like in I Thess. 1:3 work springs from (results from) faith, exertion springs from (is prompted by) love, and endurance springs from (is inspired by) hope. For this *genitive of source* see N.T.C. on I and II Thessalonians, pp. 46, 47, footnote 35. Others (e.g. Robertson, *op. cit.,* p. 631) consider this to be a *genitive of apposition,* which, however, yields a very difficult meaning in the present context.

learn that it means *everlasting life* (I Tim. 6:12; cf. James 1:12; I Peter 5:4; Rev. 2:10), here (in II Tim. 4:8) as possessed and experienced in the new heaven and earth.

The apostle continues, "which the Lord, the righteous Judge, will award to me on that day." This Lord and Judge is Christ Jesus (see on verse 1). And this Judge or Umpire respects the contest-rules which he himself has laid down. He is the *righteous* Judge, who on that notable day, the day of his return (see on II Tim. 1:12, 18; cf. II Thess. 1:10) *will give whatever is due* (note the verb used in the original, on which such passages as Matt. 20:8, 13; Rom. 2:6 shed much light). For all such people who, like Paul, are unjustly condemned, the idea of the coming judgment day when they will be vindicated by a *just* Judge is full of comfort.

This righteous Judge, says Paul, will award the wreath of righteousness *to me.* Yet, not to me alone, but *to all who love his appearing,* his brilliant second coming (as in verse 1). Note the word *love,* not *fear,* for perfect love casts out fear (I John 4:18). When the Spirit and the bride say, "Come," every person who really loves the Lord will also say, "Come." And when the Lord answers, "I am coming quickly," the immediate reply will be, "Amen, come, Lord Jesus." Of all the indications that one loves the Lord, this earnest longing for his return is one of the best, for such a person is thinking not only of himself and of his own glory but also of his Lord and of the latter's public vindication. For all such persons the wreath is waiting. And *this* wreath, unlike earthly wreaths, is imperishable (I Cor. 9:25).

---

9 Do your best to come to me quickly; 10 for Demas has deserted me, because he fell in love with the present world, and has gone to Thessalonica; Crescens (has gone) to Galatia, Titus to Dalmatia. 11 Luke is the only one with me. Pick up Mark and bring him with you, for he is very useful to me for (the) ministry. 12 Now Tychicus I am commissioning for Ephesus. 13 The cloak which I left in Troas with Carpus bring along when you come; also the books, especially the parchments.

14 Alexander, the metal-worker, did me much damage. The Lord will repay him in accordance with his deeds. 15 You, too, be on your guard against him, for he vigorously opposed our words.

16 At my first defence no one was at my side, but all deserted me; may it not be charged against them! 17 But the Lord stood at my side, and gave me strength, in order that through me the message might be fully heralded, and all the Gentiles might hear it, and I was rescued out of (the) mouth of (the) lion. 18 And the Lord will rescue me from every evil work, and save me (bringing me) to his heavenly kingdom; to him (*be* or *is*) the glory forever and ever. Amen.

19 Greet Prisca and Aquila and the family of Onesiphorus. 20 Erastus remained at Corinth, but Trophimus I left at Miletus sick. 21 Do your best to come before winter. Eubulus greets you, as do Pudens and Linus and Claudia and all the brothers.

22 The Lord (be) with your spirit. Grace (be) with y o u.

4:9-22

The present paragraph consists, in general, of items of personal information, requests, and greetings. It can be divided into five sub-paragraphs, as follows:

a. verses 9-13: Paul gives expression to the loneliness which he feels, and the need of more kingdom-workers, asks for his cloak, for books and parchments, and for the speedy arrival of Timothy.

b. verses 14, 15: He warns Timothy against Alexander, the metal-worker.

c. verses 16-18: From the manner in which the Lord had strengthened him during his "first defence" Paul derives comfort for the present and for the future.

d. verses 19-21: Greetings to and from certain individual believers, items of information with reference to others, repetition of request for Timothy's speedy coming.

e. verse 22: Benediction.

9, 10, 11a. Do your best to come to me quickly.

Paul, writing from a cold, dank dungeon in Rome, and facing death, longs for the presence of his "beloved child" Timothy. He wants him to come quickly, that is, "before winter" (see on verse 21). The reason for the apostle's feeling of loneliness is as follows: **for Demas has deserted me, because he fell in love with the present world, and has gone to Thessalonica; Crescens (has gone) to Galatia, Titus to Dalmatia. Luke is the only one with me.**

Demas had at one time been Paul's assistant in the gospel-ministry (Philemon 24). During the first Roman imprisonment Demas, too, had been in Rome. Twice the apostle had mentioned him in one breath with Luke, the beloved physician (Col. 4:14; Philemon 25). It would seem to be a safe inference from the present passage that also during the second Roman imprisonment Demas had been in Rome, and had rendered service in the kingdom. Hence, all the more pathetic are these plaintive words, "Do your best to come to me quickly, for Demas has deserted me." The verb used in the original implies that Demas had not merely *left* Paul (on this or that legitimate mission), but had *left him in the lurch,* had abandoned, forsaken him. The separation was not merely local but spiritual. Paul is deeply disappointed with Demas. Demas left *because he fell in love*[175] with the present age, the "world" on this side of the grave, the transitory era which, in spite of all its pleasures and treasures, will soon be past (see

[175] By means of the translation, "because he fell in love," I have tried to do justice to two facts: a. the participle used in the original is aorist, and b. it is undoubtedly causal in the present connection.

on I Tim. 6:17). Much can be said in support of the view that Demas, in love with the present world, never belonged to the company of those who love Christ's appearing. Note the sharp and probably intentional contrast between the lover of the present world (verse 9) and the lovers of the Epiphany (verse 8). Moreover, nowhere is there a word about the restoration of Demas. Demas should probably not be placed in a class with Mark! Though we have no solid ground for speaking with certainty about this matter, nevertheless, the spirit of the present passage and of its context rather points in the direction of Matthew 7:22, 23, as a general indication of the class to which Demas belongs. Just why Demas went *to Thessalonica,* and not to some other place, is not known. Perhaps he thought that the deepest desires of his soul could be better satisfied there than elsewhere. Did he leave Rome because this capital was at that time the most dangerous place for a Christian to be? Did he have business, friends, or relatives in Thessalonica? We do not know.

Paul adds, "Crescens (has gone) to Galatia." Instead of *Galatia* another reading has *Gallia.* This would then be the region which today is called France plus certain surrounding territories. It is impossible to determine which of these two readings is correct. Hence, we do not know where Crescens went.[176] Nor do we have any *reliable* information about Crescens except that which is supplied by the present passage.

---

[176] The problem with reference to *Galatia* or *Gallia* is complicated. About the year 400 B. C. certain Gauls or Celts migrated to northern Italy. Some of the tribes moved farther eastward, entering Macedonia and Thrace. In the year 278 B. C. 20,000 Gauls crossed the Hellespont and moved into Asia Minor. Here they prospered and increased greatly in numbers. Though subsequently subjugated by the Romans, they were permitted to keep their own kings. The Roman province *Galatia,* named after them, comprised: a. the territory in central and northern Asia Minor in which most of *these* Gauls were now living, and b. certain districts to the south of this Celtic territory.

Since Paul must be regarded as the author of the Pastorals, and he was in the habit of using the official names of Roman political units or provinces — "Asia" (I Cor. 16:19); "Achaia" (II Cor. 1:1); and "Macedonia" (II Cor. 8:1) — I believe that in I Cor. 16:1; Gal. 1:2; and also in our present passage (II Tim. 4:10) *if the reading "Galatia" is here authentic,* it is the Roman province of Galatia (in Asia Minor) that is meant. (The fact, mentioned by several commentators, that certain Greek writers — Polybius, Plutarch, etc. — use the term "Celtic Galatia" to designate Gaul proper, has nothing to do with the argument. It is *Paul's* usage that interests us.) *The Constitutions of the Holy Apostles,* VII. xlvi (see the context) favors Galatia in Asia Minor as the province to which Crescens was sent.

However, if the reading "Gallia" is, after all, authentic, it becomes easier to account for the tradition which ascribed to Crescens the founding of the church at Vienne near Lyons. Eusebius, moreover, says that Crescens was sent to Gaul, *Ecclesiastical History,* III. iv. The possibility that it was Gaul in Europe and not Galatia in Asia must be granted. On the assumption that Paul had visited Spain, it is logical to believe that he may also have established churches in Southern Gaul, and that Crescens may have been sent to strengthen what had been started there. Accordingly, the answer to the question, "Where did Crescens go?" depends on

"Titus (has gone) to Dalmatia," continues Paul. It seems that after Titus' visit to Jerusalem as a test-case (Gal. 2:21), all his missions were to provinces in Europe. Whenever, away from Paul, he was on a mission, he was never very far from the east coast of the Adriatic Sea or its southern extension, the Ionian Sea. Being able, courageous, and consecrated, he knew how to handle the quarrelsome Corinthians, the mendacious Cretans, and the reputedly pugnacious Dalmatians. Cf. Rom. 15:19. In contrast with Demas who had deserted Paul, we must believe that both Crescens and Titus had gone where duty called them. See also on Titus 3:12.

"Luke is the only one with me." The author of the third Gospel was a remarkable person. He was "the beloved physician" (Col. 4:14), always loyal to Paul, to the gospel, to the Lord. Frequently he had been Paul's companion in travel, as is indicated by the "we" sections in Acts (16:10-17; 20:6-16; 21; 27; 28). He had been with Paul on the second missionary journey, at Troas and at Philippi. He had evidently been left behind at the latter place (Acts 16:17-19). Toward the close of the third tour he seems again to have joined Paul at Philippi (Acts 20:60), and he accompanied him to Jerusalem. For a while we do not see him. But suddenly he re-appears, for he is in Paul's company on the long and dangerous sea-journey from Palestine to Rome (Acts 27). He is with the apostle during both the first and the second Roman imprisonments (Col. 4:14; Philemon 24; II Tim. 4:11). Paul needed a doctor and a friend. Luke was both, and *directly or indirectly* may also have served in the capacity of Paul's secretary.

Luke and Paul had much in common. Both were educated men, men of culture. Both were big-hearted, broad-spirited, sympathetic. Above all, both were believers and missionaries.[177]

But if Luke was such a wonderful friend, why does Paul say, "Luke is the only one with me"? The following answer may be suggested: a. The very presence, off and on, of no one else besides Luke made the absence of all the others all the more conspicuous, especially in contrast with Paul's circumstances during the *first* imprisonment when he was permitted to

---

the answer to that other question, "What is the correct reading here in II Tim. 4:10?" Is it "Galatia" or is it "Gallia"? And the textual evidence is too nearly even to answer this question with any degree of finality.

[177] Several authors have attempted to write a Biography of Luke; for example, W. Ramsay, *Luke The Physician;* A. T. Robertson, *Luke The Historian In The Light of Historical Research,* New York, 1923, chapter II: "A Sketch of Luke's Career"; D. A. Hayes, *The Most Beautiful Book Ever Written,* New York, 1913, pp. 3-54. The accounts are all very interesting; nevertheless, there is scarcely enough reliable first-hand information for a biography. There are many possibilities and some probabilities, but there are few certainties. Authorities are not even in agreement on the place of Luke's birth, though much can be said in favor of Antioch in Syria. See *The Anti-Marcionite Prologue to the Third Gospel.*

receive all who came to him (Acts 28:30). Also, b. There may be more here than an expression of *loneliness.* It is entirely possible that the apostle also wishes to stress the fact that he is short on help, that there were not enough reapers; perhaps not even a sufficient number to provide adequately for the spiritual needs of those believers who were still in Rome.

It must be emphasized that whatever is stated in verse 10 and 11a, in connection with Demas, Crescens, Titus, and Luke, has the purpose of urging Timothy to do his best to come quickly.

11b, 12, 13. With a view to this coming of Timothy, the apostle continues, **Pick up Mark and bring him with you, for he is very useful to me for (the) ministry.** The home of Mark was in Jerusalem (Acts 12:12). It was he who had deserted Paul and Barnabas on the first missionary journey. Paul, therefore, had refused to take Mark with him on the second tour. So Barnabas had taken Mark and had sailed away to Cyprus (Acts 15:36-41). Subsequently, however, we find Mark again in the company of Paul at Rome during the apostle's first imprisonment (Col. 4:10; Philemon 24). Afterward he is with Peter in Rome (I Peter 5:13). Tradition supports the idea that there was a close connection between Peter's preaching in Rome and the writing of Mark's Gospel. After Peter's martyrdom Mark seems to have become *Paul's* assistant once more. At Paul's request and in co-operation with Timothy he may have been making a tour of the churches in Asia Minor while Paul was writing II Timothy. Timothy, leaving for Rome, is urged to "pick him up," because Paul knows that by this time Mark is very useful to him "for ministry." The implication is probably this: since Mark has experienced a change for the better, having taken to heart the lesson which his earlier failure had taught him, and since he is well acquainted with Rome and with the condition of the church in that city, hence *in Rome* he will be the right man in the right place. The context indicates that when Paul uses the term *ministry* or *service,* he is thinking of kingdom-work, service in the interest of the gospel, and does not merely mean, "He can perform certain duties to make life easier for me personally."

Continuing, then, along this same line, the man who even in the dungeon is the great superintendent of missions adds, **Now Tychicus I am commissioning** (probably an epistolary aorist) **for Ephesus.** Tychicus (Greek proper name, meaning "fortuitous") was a beloved brother, faithful minister and fellow-servant in the gospel, a man worthy of all confidence. He was one of several intimate friends who had accompanied the apostle when at the close of his third missionary journey he was returning from Greece through Macedonia into Asia, with the purpose of going to Jerusalem on a charitable mission (Acts 20:4). Also later, during the first Roman imprisonment, Tychicus had been with Paul. He had been commissioned by the apostle to carry to their destinations the epistle to the Ephesians, the one to the Colossians, and probably also the one to Philemon. He was, moreover, the right person to supply the necessary "atmosphere" – more detailed information about Paul's circumstances –, so that the letters which he delivered could be understood all the more readily (Eph. 6:21; Col. 4:7). During the interval between the first and second Roman imprisonments Tychicus is again (or *still*) working in close cooperation with Paul (see on Titus 3:12). And now, during the second Roman imprisonment, Paul finds that Tychicus is the logical person to send to Ephesus with this letter (II Timothy). In addition, he is also the right man to serve for a while as director of affairs in the churches of Asia Minor, as a substitute for Timothy during the latter's absence, which would be of rather lengthy duration, since Timothy would not be able to return to Ephesus until at least April (see on verse 21).

Timothy, then, must not hesitate to leave Ephesus. Under another trusted leader, namely, Tychicus, the work will be continued. The *cause* will not have to suffer. When Timothy leaves for Rome, he must, moreover, take with him a few things needed by Paul: **The cloak which I left in Troas with Carpus bring along when you come; also the books, especially the parchments.**

The word translated "cloak" (φαιλόνης = , by metathesis from φαινόλης, a transliteration of the Latin *paenula*) indicates a kind of blanket of coarse wool that was used as an outer garment to protect against the cold and the rain. It had a hole in the middle for the head to pass through. There were no sleeves. In Latin this is the more usual (though not the only) meaning of the word. In Greek it is this meaning that has abundant papyri support. The connotation *briefcase, bookwrap,* or *satchel,* a receptacle for important documents and/or "books," is found at times, and there have always been those who assign this meaning to the word in the present passage.[178] But the apostle does not seem to be asking for his "satchel with documents" but for two different kinds of articles: a. "the paenula," and b. "the books, especially the parchments." It is possible that both a. and b. were in one class in *this* sense only, that they were rather troublesome to carry along at all times; for example, in hot weather. So, Paul may have left them with Carpus (otherwise unknown to us), intending soon to return in order to pick them up. Whatever may have been the reason

[178] Milligan formerly defended this view, but changed his opinion (M. M., p. 665). A recent defender is A. Sizoo, in his own, very interesting, manner. See his valuable book, *De Antieke Wereld En Het Nieuwe Testament,* Kampen, 1948, pp. 90, 91. His argument in defence of the position that here the word can hardly mean "cloak" is that Paul, the great traveler, would not have left his rain-coat behind, an article which was necessary not only in winter but in certain regions also during the summer. – However, for reasons unknown to us, it may not have been feasible or even possible for Paul to get his belongings together.

why this was not done, the apostle in his cold, damp dungeon, with winter just around the corner, feels the need of this cloak, and asks Timothy to bring it along when he comes. Troas was not far from Timothy's headquarters at Ephesus.[179]

And let Timothy also bring "the books, especially the parchments." The "books" were in all probability papyrus-rolls; the "parchments" or "membranes" were skins of sheep, lambs, goats, or calves, especially prepared for writing. Paul wants the books but above all the parchments! What was written in these books and parchments? Is it not natural to assume that the Lord's prisoner desired above all else to spend his few remaining weeks or months in meditating upon the Word of God? For the rest, as to exact contents, we simply do not know, and it is useless to add to the guesses that have been made.[180]

It is clear that the believer in his yearning to provide for his intellectual and spiritual needs (books, parchments) is not called upon to ignore the needs of the body ("the cloak"). One is reminded of the very similar entreaty which, under analogous circumstances, was penned by another notable warrior of the cross many centuries later. It was William Tyndale, the well-known Bible translator, who from his cold prison-cell at Vilvoorde made request that *in view of the approaching winter* (how like Paul!) a cloak, woollen shirt, warm cap, and most of all, his Hebrew Bible, grammar, and vocabulary be brought to him.

14, 15. We come now to the second sub-paragraph (see p. 318), a warning against a bitter enemy of the faith: **Alexander, the metal-worker, did me much damage.**

It is not easy to reconstruct the circumstances under which Alexander

---

[179] On the basis of the reference to Troas, Scott argues that these verses must be assigned to a much earlier letter, because Paul had not been in Troas for several years (*op. cit.*, p. 138). But Scott's argument has value only if the book of Acts (see 16:8; 20:5) and Paul's other epistles (see II Cor. 2:12) give us a complete itinerary. Specifically, it has value only if there cannot have been a release from a first Roman imprisonment and, following upon this release, a second Roman imprisonment. Such assumptions are precarious.

[180] There are those who think that *the rolls* contained portions of the Old Testament, or Jewish commentaries, or copies of his own letters, or of certain writings of pagan philosophers or poets. The following are a few among the many conjectures with respect to *the parchments:* the Septuagint, the words of Jesus which preceded the Gospels, Paul's own notations, legal documents or certificates (for example, a certificate of Roman citizenship) which the apostle needed for his coming (?) trial, etc. This last view is especially in favor among those commentators who are convinced that verses 16-18 imply that Paul is still awaiting a formal trial. Thus the reader is being gradually conditioned for what I consider to be a rather questionable interpretation of these verses. There are also those who adopt the view that neither books nor parchments had any writing on them. The apostle, then, is simply asking for something to write on!

opposed Paul and the good cause which the latter represented. It can, however, be stated with well-nigh certainty that there had been a trial (this, in the light of the trial-context; see verse 16, though the trial referred to there is probably not the same as the one in which Alexander was involved; see on that verse). In this trial Alexander had been an accuser or a witness for the prosecution. Who was this Alexander? His name was as common then as are the names Brown, Jones, or Smith today (Mark 15:21; Acts 4:6; 19:33, 34; I Tim. 1:19, 20; II Tim. 4:14, probably five different Alexanders). From the context it would appear that *this* Alexander is living in Rome; for it stands to reason that it was especially in Rome that he was able to oppose Paul, who was also in that city. Now if that inference be correct, he must probably not be identified with the Alexander mentioned in I Tim. 1:20 nor with the one to whom Acts 19:33, 34 refers, for these Alexanders lived in the Ephesus region.[181]

---

[181] A. Those who, nevertheless, favor the identification of "Alexander the metal-worker" or "metallurgist" (II Tim. 4:14, 15) with "Alexander the Ephesian heretic" (I Tim. 1:19, 20) base this theory upon the supposition that what Paul means in the passage now under discussion is, "On my recent visit to Ephesus, Alexander the metal-worker did me much damage by vigorously opposing my proclamation of the gospel. So, Timothy, as long as you remain in Ephesus, be on your guard against him." Cf. John Rutherford, art. "Alexander," in I.S.B.E., Vol. I., see esp. p. 91. *Objections:*

(1) If the Alexander of II Tim. 4:14, 15 is the one of I Tim. 1:19, 20, Timothy would know him. If any further description were needed, in addition to the mention of his name, would it not be in terms of the passage in the earlier epistle? The addition "the metal-worker" points *away from* the Alexander mentioned in I Tim. 1:19, 20.

(2) As the context indicates (see verse 16), the apostle is not now thinking principally about opposition to the proclamation of the gospel but about opposition to "words" of defence in the court-room.

(3) The setting in our present passage is Rome, not Ephesus.

B. Those who favor identification of "Alexander the metal-worker" (II Tim. 4:14, 15) with "Alexander the Jew" thrust forward, in connection with a riot, to shield the Ephesian Jews (Acts 19:33, 34), an identification favored, among others, by F. W. Grosheide, *Korte Verklaring, Handelingen,* Vol. II, p. 100, do so because they like to associate Demetrius *a silversmith* (Acts 19:24) with Alexander *the coppersmith.* On the basis of this theory an interesting story can then be fabricated. For example, at the occasion of the Ephesian riot Alexander can be imagined to say, "We Jews are not guilty of opposing Diana of the Ephesians. Why, I myself, as a coppersmith, make the shrines which Demetrius plates with silver. So, please do not take this out on us. Punish this fellow Paul and his companions Gaius and Aristarchus." The *possibility* that the two ("Alexander the metal-worker" and "Alexander the Ephesian Jew") were the same person must be granted, but the belief that this is more than a mere *possibility* is faced with the following difficulties:

(1) The account in Acts tells us nothing about the occupation of *that* Alexander.

(2) In order to clinch this identification, Alexander the Jew of Ephesus must be brought to Rome. Now, of course, this may have happened; but there is nothing in the account to raise this mere possibility to the level of a probability. — Or else the *opposition* of which Paul speaks (II Tim. 4:14, 15) must be regarded as having taken place in Ephesus. This would seem to be in conflict with the present context.

The present Alexander, then, is probably a different person. He is *the metal-worker* (primary meaning is *coppersmith;* then *metal-worker* in general; cf. Gen. 4:22 LXX). Now, in connection with the trial, Alexander, by means of *deeds* (verse 14) and *words* (verse 15), had succeeded in damaging Paul. No doubt he had helped to bring about an adverse court-decision with respect to the apostle, though we do not know whether the sentence, "Condemned to death" had already been announced or conveyed to the apostle. We *do* know, however, that this sentence was now *certain,* and that Paul knew this. He knew that he was about to die (see on 4:6, 7, 8; also on verse 18). But instead of avenging himself upon Alexander, he leaves the matter of retribution entirely to the Lord (Deut. 32:35; cf. Rom. 12:17-19; I Peter 2:23). Hence, he immediately adds, **The Lord *will repay*** (best reading) **him in accordance with his deeds.** When Christ returns to judge (see on verses 1 and 8), he will not forget what Alexander has done, but *will give him his due* (same verb as in verse 8, where it is used in a favorable sense). See Ps. 62:12; Prov. 24:12; Matt. 25:31-46; John 5:28, 29; Rom. 2:6; II Cor. 11:15; Rev. 2:23; 20:13.

Paul continues, **You, too, be on your guard against him, for he vigorously opposed our words.** "Forewarned is forearmed." Let Timothy, in coming to Rome, be constantly on his guard against this wicked Alexander, who will try his utmost to harm the disciple even before the latter has reached his master. Let him take the necessary precautions so that he will know what to say and what to do if and when he should be confronted with Alexander. And, prayer being at all times the best prophylactic, let him pray about this matter, in order that the proper words may be given to him when he needs them, and the proper actions may be suggested to him.

This Alexander was a relentless persecutor, one who *vigorously* (upon this word rests the emphasis) *stood over against* – hence, *resisted, opposed* (Matt. 5:39; Luke 21:15; Acts 6:10; 13:8; Rom. 9:19; Gal. 2:11; Eph. 6:13; II Tim. 3:8; 4:15; James 4:7; I Peter 5:9) – "our words," that is, the arguments for the defence, a defence in which the apostle had been assisted by others (Onesiphorus, Luke?; see on II Tim. 1:15, 16; 4:11), as the modifier *our* indicates.

16-18. That word *our* ("our words"), instead of *my,* brings up the past. There had been another trial. In that *first* defence no one had taken Paul's side. It is readily understood why Paul speaks of the trial as a *defence* (literally "apology" in the sense of speech in vindication from accusation), for that had been *his* part in it. In that former trial, then, Paul had stood alone. *Entirely* alone? No, for the Lord had caused *his* presence to be felt in a remarkable manner. From the way in which the Lord had then strengthened him Paul derives comfort for the present and for the future. Let Timothy also take courage. – This, in general, is the sense of the third sub-paragraph (see p. 318) which follows.

I shall treat it first *positively,* giving the interpretation which by many is considered to be "the most natural one," even though today it is not the most widely accepted one; then *negatively,* stating the difficulties which beset the opposite interpretation.

At my first defence no one was at my side, but all deserted me.

Paul, being in a reminiscent mood, as one is prone to be when he reaches the end of his life here on earth and has an opportunity to look back, vividly recalls this other trial, the one which, if these interpreters are correct, had taken place a few years earlier. At that time no one had come to *stand beside* him in his defence. That was during the period of the first Roman imprisonment. What a difference between then and now, *as to the actual trial! Now,* during this second Roman imprisonment, *Demas* had *deserted* him (see on verse 10), and "all those in Asia" had *turned away from* him (see on II Tim. 1:15). But Onesiphorus had come from Asia, and Luke had remained faithful. But during that previous imprisonment *not a single person* had presented himself as a witness for Paul's defence. *All had deserted.* Why? Had fear held them back? Or possibly the feeling: The apostle does not need us, for the Romans are favorably inclined to him, and no accuser has appeared in order to press his charge? See pp. 26, 27. However that may be, to a certain extent Paul had suffered a disappointment. But he knows how to forgive. Hence, he continues: **May it not be charged against them.** This prayerful wish is entirely in harmony with the spirit of Christ (Luke 23:34), of Stephen (Acts 7:60) and . . . of Paul himself (I Cor. 13:5).

But the Lord stood at my side and gave me strength. That, during his first imprisonment, this had indeed been Paul's blessed experience is clear from Phil. 4:13. The Lord (Jesus Christ) had stood by him and *had strengthened* (cf. I Tim. 1:12; the same word as in Phil. 4:13; and cf. Acts 9:22; Rom. 4:20; Eph. 6:10) him, and this not only *during* that imprisonment but even *on his way* to it (Acts 23:11; 27:23). And the purpose had been: **in order that through me the message might be fully heralded** (literally, "in order that through me *the heralded message* – or "preaching," "kerugma," see on verse 2 – *might be fulfilled* or accomplished"), **and all the Gentiles might hear it.**

The following interpretation is natural: I was set at liberty in order that after my acquittal I might complete my task of heralding the gospel of salvation, so that not only the Gentiles *east* of Rome but also those *west* of Rome might hear it. – Paul's gospel-message, the heralded word as spoken by him, must reach the limits of the West. Spain could not be omitted (Rom. 15:24, 28).

And I was rescued out of (the) mouth of (the) lion. Probably this is simply an idiomatic way of saying, "I was delivered out of the jaws of death" (*ex faucibus mortis,* Calvin), and not a specific reference to Satan, Nero, or a literal lion of the amphitheater. In all probability this, as is clear from Ps. 22:21, 22 (the passage upon which Paul's figurative expression is based) means *complete* deliverance. Paul had been enabled to declare the name of the Lord far and wide. His first Roman imprisonment had ended in full acquittal and in more missionary journeys.

From this experience of the past the apostle draws encouragement: **And the Lord will rescue me from every evil work, and save me (bringing me) to his heavenly kingdom.**

Note the parallel:

At my first defence *all deserted* me (verse 16). Now Demas *has deserted* me (verse 10). Same verb in both cases.

At my first defence *I was rescued* (verse 17). Now, "the Lord *will rescue* me" (verse 18). Again the same verb both times.

The stress falls on this divine rescuing activity. *In the past* there had been danger. *Now,* too, there was that which men would consider danger. But in the past the Lord had intervened; now again he will *intervene decisively for deliverance* (which is the meaning of *rescue,* as in I Thess. 1:10). In the past Paul had been rescued *from* death. Now he will be rescued *by means of* death. In neither case does his soul perish. He is never separated from the love of God in Christ.

To destroy Paul spiritually and to annihilate the kingdom of Christ is, nevertheless, at all times exactly what Satan intends to do. All the efforts which he puts forth to achieve this sinister purpose constitute his *evil work.* But Paul is convinced that, as in the past so also now, "the Lord will rescue me from every evil work," though not from all physical harm. The man who wrote II Cor. 11:22-33 does not expect immunity from injury to the body! But *the Lord* (Jesus Christ) *will save me to* (this is either a pregnant expression meaning "will save me, bringing me to," or means "will save me *for,*" the two interpretations yielding about the same resultant sense) *his heavenly kingdom.* The Lord is going to bring Paul to heaven, that is, to that kingdom which, though seen on earth in shadow, has its seat in heaven, and belongs to heaven as to its essence and fulness (see on verse 1).

The expression "the Lord . . . will save me to (or *for*) his heavenly kingdom" implies that Paul expected to go to heaven immediately upon death. This is Scripture's doctrine throughout. Thus, the psalmist expects to be welcomed into the realm of glory when he dies (Ps. 73:24, 25). "Lazarus" is immediately carried by the angels into Abraham's bosom (Luke 16, see especially verse 22). The penitent thief enters Paradise at once, together with his Lord (Luke 23:43). Paul is convinced that when the earthly tent is destroyed, the building from God, "eternal in the heavens" will be ready to receive the believer (II Cor. 5:1); that death is "gain" (Phil. 1:21), which would not be true if it meant extinction of being or passing into oblivion; and that to depart from this earth means to be with Christ, a condition which is "better by far" than continued life here below (Phil. 1:23). And the book of Revelation pictures the souls of the martyrs as having been translated immediately into heaven, and as being very happily and busily occupied in that region of bliss (Rev. 7:13-17).

Not filled with dismay is Paul when he thinks of imminent departure from this earth. On the contrary, since this departure is better by far than remaining on earth, his soul is filled with rapture. Hence, not surprising is the doxology: **To him the glory forever and ever. Amen.** Cf. Gal. 1:5; but here in II Tim. 4:18 the never-ceasing glory is ascribed to *Christ, the Lord.* Cf. Rom 9:5; 16:27. By adding the word of solemn affirmation or confirmation, "Amen" (on which see N.T.C. on John, Vol. I, p. 111, footnote 51), the apostle shows that he most heartily *desires* (if the omitted verb is "be") or definitely *declares* (if "is" must be understood, as in I Peter 4:11 and in those texts of Matt. 6:13 which contain the doxology of the Lord's prayer) that Christ's *glory* – the radiating splendor of all his marvelous attributes – be (or "is") his possession world without end.

The interpretation that has been presented, according to which the expression "my first defence" refers to the first Roman imprisonment, particularly to the trial which then took place and which resulted in Paul's acquittal and more journeys, is supported by the testimony of tradition. That Eusebius thus interprets the passage is clear from the quotation which has been given (see p. 27). Cf. also Chrysostom (Hom. XI).[182]

Many commentators, however, favor an interpretation which differs radically from the one supported by tradition. They feel that the latter is out of harmony with the favorable conditions of the imprisonment recorded in the book of Acts. Their view may be briefly summarized as follows:

(1) "My first defence" means: "my first appearance in court," "the preliminary investigation" (prima actio) in *the present trial.*

(2) "No one was at my side" means: no *patron* ("friend" at court, a man of importance in the eyes of the Romans) accompanied me to the courtroom, attesting by his very presence that I am a respectable person.

Similarly, "all deserted me" means: all those potential *patrons* abandoned me.

(3) The sentence, "But the Lord stood at my side and gave me strength, in order that through me the message might be fully heralded" means: the

---

[182] Among others who have accepted this view or, while admitting some doubt, have expressed a preference for it, are the following: Barnes, Bouma, Lock, Zahn (for titles see Bibliography).

Lord strenghtened me in order that by means of my defence in the court-room my message might reach its climax (or: so that by that means it got to be fully completed).

(4) "And all the Gentiles might hear it" means: and in order that the crowd of Roman grandees in the court-room, as representing the entire heathen world, might hear my defence (or: so that this crowd got to hear my defence).

(5) "And I was rescued from the mouth of the lion" means: and I was kept from being executed that day.[183]

In fairness to those who favor this view it must be said that some, though wishing to be counted among its defenders, express serious misgivings and doubts about it. This is not surprising. Note the following:

With respect to point (1) above. The fact that the statement, "Alexander, the metal-worker, did me much damage" is followed by *"At my first defence* no one was at my side," may imply that the damage wrought by Alexander was *not* done "at my first defence," but more recently. Paul may be comparing the present with the past. *If so, he is retracing his steps,* drawing lessons and analogies from the experiences of former years. *This, at any rate, is entirely in line with what he is doing in other passages of the same epistle* (1:5; 2:2; 3:14, 15; 4:7).

With respect to (2). Paul mentions Luke who is with him, and Demas who has deserted him. About "patrons" not a word. Also, if there has been a trial of any kind ("preliminary" or otherwise) *during this present imprisonment,* it is hard to believe that Paul intended to say that Luke was either absent or not qualified to serve as patron.

With respect to (3). The idea that *the fully accomplished proclamation* refers simply to a court-room defence does not seem as reasonable as is the view that it refers to the hope of *proclaiming the gospel* to the whole world, that is, to the West (Spain) as well as to the East.

With respect to (4). To say that the clause, ". . . and that all the Gentiles might hear it" means no more than, "and that the whole court-room crowd might hear it" would seem to do violence to the text (as Gealy admits). To view this crowd as *representing* "the entire heathen world" looks like forced exegesis in the interest of a theory.

And finally, with respect to (5). In the light of the passage of which Paul, no doubt, was thinking, namely, Ps. 22:21, 22, which describes a deliverance of the most thorough-going character, it can be said with little possibility

---

183 Among those who accept or lean toward this view are the following, with individual variations as to details of interpretation: Dibelius, Ellicott, Feine, Gealy, Jűlicher, Lenski, Robertson, Scott, Simpson, and White (see Bibliography for titles). It must be stressed, however, that the summary which has been given does not necessarily do full justice to the view of any one particular interpreter. See the separate Commentaries and Introductions for more complete information.

of successful contradiction that rather unsatisfactory is the view according to which *rescue from the lion's mouth* means nothing more than this, namely, that immediately after his preliminary hearing Paul, instead of being executed, was led back, as a chained prisoner, to his horrible dungeon, there to await *certain* death (cf. II Tim. 4:6).

It is safe to say, therefore, that if there be a better interpretation than that which was offered by the early church, it has not yet been presented. It must be freely admitted that the traditional view has its difficulties. But are not the difficulties with which the opposite view is confronted even more formidable?

19. The fourth sub-paragraph (greetings, etc., verses 19-21; see p. 318) begins as follows: **Greet Prisca and Aquila and the family of Onesiphorus.**

As to Prisca and Aquila, note that in four of the six references to this wonderful team the name of the wife precedes (Acts 18:18; 18:26; Rom. 16:3; and here in II Tim. 4:19). In two references the order is reversed (Acts 18:2; I Cor. 16:19). Guesses as to the reason why Aquila is usually mentioned *last* (and Prisca *first*) are:

a. Prisca excelled her husband in loyalty and zeal with respect to the work of the Lord.

b. Prisca sprang from a more distinguished family.

c. Prisca had been the "noble hostess," and as such had bestowed much sympathetic care upon Paul and his helpers.

If the underlying assumption be correct, namely, that a writer bestows special honor or higher rating upon the person whom he most often mentions first – an assumption which is *not* granted by all! – then the last-mentioned reason might well be the correct one; but we do not know.

Note also that Paul says *Prisca* ("earnest – or *old* – woman"), but Luke says *Priscilla* (same meaning with "little" added as a suffix; cf. Dutch "oudje"). *Aquila* means *eagle.* These are Latin names.

Aquila was "a man of Pontus by race," who had lived for a while in Rome. As a result of an outburst of anti-Semitism on the part of emperor Claudius, Aquila and his wife had left Rome and had settled in Corinth. He was a tentmaker as was Paul. Soon the two men were working together. (Acts 18:1-3.) The inference would seem to be justified that it was through Paul that his host and hostess were brought to Christ. When, homeward bound from the second missionary journey, the apostle made a brief stop at Ephesus, Aquila and Prisca were traveling with him, and "he left them there" (Acts 18:18, 19). It was here that they proved to be a God-send to that fervent preacher Apollos, to whom "they expounded the way of God more accurately" (Acts 18:24-26). When Paul on his third missionary journey sends I Corinthians from Ephesus, he appends a fervent greeting from Aquila and Prisca and from "the church that is in their house" (I

Cor. 16:19). When on this same journey Paul finally arrives in Corinth and sends a letter to the Romans, he causes the salutation to Prisca and Aquila to be the first of a lengthy list. (The theory that this list does not belong here, though strongly argued, has never been proved. I cling firmly to the belief that it is an authentic part of the epistle to the Romans.) Not only is this greeting the first, it is also the fullest and the warmest. It now appears that the devoted couple had "risked their necks" for Paul. Once more, as in Ephesus, the home of Aquila and Priscilla, who are now back in Rome, is the meeting-place for the Christian congregation (Rom. 16:3-5). Finally, it appears from our present passage (II Tim. 4:19) that the two have again left Rome and have returned to Ephesus. The reason for this return to Ephesus may have been the Neronian persecution. With what warmth of feeling Paul must have sent this greeting – penning it with his own hand! See on II Thess. 3:17 – to his loyal friends and fellow-workers Aquila and Prisca!

The apostle also sends greetings to "the family of Onesiphorus" (see on II Tim. 1:16).

20. Paul is about to convey "best regards" from certain believers here in Rome with whom he had maintained a degree of contact (see verse 21), no doubt through Luke (see on verse 11). Before he does this, however, he is careful to indicate the reason why two persons have been prevented from sending greetings. This reason is that they are not in Rome. The apostle wants Timothy to know this, so that he may not begin to wonder about the omission. Says Paul: **Erastus remained at Corinth, but Trophimus I left at Miletus sick.** Since in the book of Acts both of these *names* occur in close proximity, in connection with Paul's third missionary journey, a journey in which he was accompanied by Timothy much of the way (see pp. 35, 36), and since here in II Tim. 4:20 the apostle mentions these names as those of men well-known to Timothy, so that no further designation is necessary, it may be safely assumed that Erastus is the one who on the third missionary journey (outward bound) was sent *with Timothy* to Macedonia (Acts 19:22),[184] and that Trophimus was the one who on that same journey

---

[184] Whether the Erastus mentioned in Rom. 16:23 was the same person as the one mentioned in the other two references (Acts 19:22 and II Tim. 4:20) cannot be determined. Those who reject the identification reason that the treasurer of the city of Corinth would not have been able to find time to be Paul's constant assistant, so as to be with him in Ephesus, ready to be sent on various missions.

Those who favor the identification answer:

a. Timothy and Erastus are sent by way of Macedonia *to Corinth* (cf. Acts 19:22 with I Cor. 16:10), and according to Rom. 16:23 Erastus is "the treasurer of the city," that is *of Corinth.*

b. Also, according to both Rom. 16:23 and II Tim. 4:20 Erastus has something to do with *Corinth.* According to the first, he is Corinth's treasurer; according to the second, he "remained at Corinth."

(homeward bound), *with Timothy* accompanied Paul (Acts 20:4, 5). It was this same Trophimus, an Ephesian, who became the innocent cause of Paul's seizure by the mob in Jerusalem (Acts 21:29).

It is reasonable to assume that, in his notes regarding Erastus and Trophimus, the apostle is recounting recent experiences. It was only shortly ago, while Paul, perhaps returning from Spain, was traveling east, then north, then west (via Miletus, Troas, Corinth, to Rome; see a map; also pp. 39, 40) that Erastus had remained at Corinth, and that Trophimus had been left at Miletus sick. Hence, neither of these men is now able to send greetings from Rome.

It must have been hard for Trophimus to be left behind at Miletus, only thirty-six miles south of his home at Ephesus. And it must have been a sorrowful experience for Paul to discover that he did not at this occasion receive from his Lord the power to heal. In God's sovereign providence believers, too, become ill (Elisha, II Kings 13:14; Hezekiah, II Kings 20:1; Paul, Gal. 4:13; Epaphroditus, Phil. 2:25-27; Timothy, I Tim. 5:23; Trophimus, II Tim. 4:20). They even die! The passage, "With his stripes we are healed," does not mean that they have been exempted from the infirmities of the flesh. Often, to be sure, it pleases God to heal them, a blessing which arrives in answer to prayer (James 5:14, 15). But even if God's will be otherwise, theirs is ever the comfort of such passages as Ps. 23; 27; 42; John 14:1-3; Rom. 8:35-39; Phil. 4:4-7; II Tim. 4:6-8; Heb. 4:16; 12:6, to mention only a few among many references.

21. For a true appreciation of the depth of feeling, the pathos, which underlies the request which now follows, one must bear in mind that to the list of *absent fellow-workers* mentioned in verse 10 those which have just now been named (Prisca, Aquila, Erastus, Trophimus, and where was Onesiphorus? still on earth?) must now be added. Hence, not at all surprising are the words: **Do your best to come before winter.** The winter-season (Feast of Tabernacles to Feast of Passover; in other words, October to April) was approaching. Then navigation ceased, or, if attempted at all, became very dangerous, as Paul knew by experience (read Acts 27). Besides, the apostle was aware that the day of execution was fast approaching (II Tim. 4:6). If Timothy delayed his coming, the two would never

c. On his third missionary journey Paul *was collecting funds* to help the needy brothers in Jerusalem. A man such as the Erastus of Rom. 16:23, expert in financial affairs, would therefore be the right person to go along with Timothy (Acts 19:22).

d. It is not impossible that a man who traveled with Paul as financial expert could become city-treasurer, perhaps for one year. This office, moreover, was not regarded as one of great prominence. Even a slave or freedman could become city-treasurer.

On the entire question see also H. J. Cadbury, "Erastus of Corinth," *JBL* 50 (1931), 42-58. For myself the matter remains in doubt.

meet again on earth. And, with winter approaching, Paul needed his cloak (see on verse 13).

Probably through Luke as go-between, certain believers who have resisted the urge to flee away from Rome and its bloody persecution ask to be remembered: **Eubulus greets you, as do Pudens and Linus and Claudia and all the brothers.** Even legend has nothing to say with reference to *Eubulus,* a Greek proper name meaning "good counselor," "prudent person." Among the Greeks *Linus* (meaning "flaxen-haired") was the name of a mythical minstrel. The Linus to whom Paul refers seems to have been simply a believer in Rome, not a past companion of Paul. Tradition has it that after Peter's death this man was appointed to the bishopric of the church at Rome (Irenaeus, *Against Heresies* III. iii. 3; Eusebius, *Ecclesiastical History* III. iv). Whether this tradition rests upon any basis of fact is open to doubt. The apostle does not seem to regard him quite so highly. According to legend *Pudens* ("modest") was a Roman senator converted by Peter; and *Claudia* ("lame") was the mother of Linus. These last two (Pudens and Claudia) are common Latin names. Except for these brief notices here in II Tim. 4:21, we have no definite and reliable knowledge about any of the four persons mentioned here.[185] Neither do we know who are meant by "all the brothers." For example, we do not know whether these brothers belonged to the original, predominantly Gentile congregation or to one of the subsequently established assemblies of believers drawn from the Jewish element in Rome.[186]

22. The closing salutation, which is the fifth sub-paragraph (see p. 318) has two parts. The first part is addressed to Timothy alone: **The Lord (be) with your spirit.** "The Lord" means "the Lord Jesus Christ" (cf. Gal. 6:18; Phil. 4:23). The predicate "(be) with your spirit" implies that the spirit of Timothy needs to be strengthened, so that he will fully discharge his ministerial task and in the fulfilment of his duties will even be able to endure suffering for the sake of Christ, and this without protest. The second part is addressed not only to Timothy but also to all those who will hear or read the letter: **Grace (be) with y o u.** See on I Tim. 6:21.

Synthesis of Chapter 4

See the Outline at the beginning of this chapter.

Timothy must *preach* the sound doctrine. This is the final, most solemn charge which the apostle issues as he directs his assistant's attention to God and to Christ Jesus, who will judge the living and the dead, and in whose

---

[185] For the unreliable legends with respect to Pudens and Claudia see Edmundson, *The Church in Rome,* note C.
[186] See my *Bible Survey,* pp. 427-432.

presence the charge is issued and received. Thus he places Timothy under oath to comply with the charge. If Timothy obeys, he will share in (and if he disobeys he will miss) the glory of Christ's Epiphany and Reign.

Timothy, then, must be a herald. He must forcefully and faithfully proclaim the divinely authorized message of salvation. Welcome or not welcome, he must ever be on hand with his good news. In this connection, he must reprove, rebuke, and admonish, doing all this with utmost longsuffering and painstaking teaching-activity. Let him bear in mind that the season will arrive – every age has such a season, but these seasons grow progressively worse – when men will not tolerate the sound doctrine. To be sure, they will still want to have teachers; in fact, "heaps of them." But these teachers will be the kind that suit the fancies of men whose ears itch to hear interesting stories instead of the truth. Let Timothy then be sober, willing to suffer hardship, while he discharges to the full his evangelistic ministry. Let him do this all the more in view of the fact that Paul, who has fought the grand fight, has finished the race, and has kept the faith, is about to depart to the shores of eternity, in order that he may receive the wreath which he can justly claim as his own, and which the Lord, the righteous Judge will award to him on the day of judgment, and not to him alone but to all those who have been looking forward with love and longing to the moment of their Lord's appearing, his brilliant second coming.

The closing paragraph (4:9-22) has been summarized on p. 318.

Commentary
on
Titus

Outline of Titus

Theme: *The Apostle Paul, Writing to Titus, Gives Directions for the Promotion of the Spirit of Sanctification*

Chapter 1: In Congregational Life.

A. The Address and Salutation.

B. Well-qualified elders must be appointed in every town.

C. Reason: Crete is not lacking in disreputable people who must be sternly rebuked.

Chapter 2: In Family and Individual Life

A. All classes of individuals that compose the home-circle should conduct themselves in such a manner that by their life they may adorn the doctrine of God, their Savior.

B. Reason: to all, the grace of God has appeared unto sanctification and joyful expectation of the appearing in glory of our great God and Savior, Jesus Christ.

Chapter 3: In Social (i.e. Public) Life

A. Believers should be obedient to the authorities. They should be kind to all men, since it was the kindness of God our Savior – not our own works! – which brought salvation.

B. On the other hand, foolish questions should be shunned, and factious men who refuse to heed admonition should be rejected.

C. Concluding directions with respect to kingdom-travelers (Artemas or Tychicus, Titus, Zenas, Apollos) and Cretan believers in general. Greetings.

Outline of Chapter 1

Theme: *The Apostle Paul, Writing to Titus, Gives Directions for the Promotion of the Spirit of Sanctification*

In Congregational Life

1:1-4 The Address and Salutation.

1:5-9 Well-qualified elders must be appointed in every town.

1:10-16 Reason: Crete is not lacking in disreputable people who must be sternly rebuked.

CHAPTER I

TITUS **1:1**

1 1 Paul, a servant of God and an apostle of Jesus Christ in the interest
of (the) faith of God's elect and of (their) acknowledgment of the truth which
accords with godliness, 2 (based) on the hope of life everlasting, which the never-
lying God promised before times everlasting 3 – but in due season he revealed his
word by that proclamation which by order of God our Savior was entrusted to
me –; 4 to Titus (my) genuine child in terms of (the) common faith; grace and
peace from God (the) Father and Christ Jesus our Savior.

1:1-4

1. Paul, a servant of God and an apostle of Jesus Christ in the interest of (the) faith of God's elect and of (their) acknowledgment of the truth which accords with godliness.

These are the opening words of a lengthy salutation. In Paul's epistles only two are longer. For the sake of comparison note the following list which, arranged in an ascending series, indicates the number of words *in the original* for each salutation:

I Thessalonians	19	II Corinthians	41
II Thessalonians	27	Philemon	41
Colossians	28	I Corinthians	55
Ephesians	28 (or 30)	**Titus**	**65**
II Timothy	29	Galatians	75
Philippians	32	Romans	93
I Timothy	32		

The present salutation (verses 1-4) resembles that in Romans more than it does any other. Here as in Romans Paul calls himself both *servant* and *apostle* (cf. II Peter 1:1), and speaks about a *promise* now fulfilled. Also, as in Romans and in several other epistles, he traces *grace* and *peace* (not "grace, mercy and peace" as in I and II Timothy) to the same twofold source, though the wording varies.

Here as elsewhere (especially in lengthy salutations) the salutation is in line with the character and purpose of the epistle. Thus, it comes as no surprise that in Titus, which stresses the idea that *sound doctrine goes hand in hand with the life of sanctification and the doing of good works,* the very salutation already mentions *godliness* ("the truth which accords with godliness"), and over against the *mendacious* character of the Cretans (Titus 1:12) makes mention of the *never-lying God.*

Paul is *God's servant*[187] ("servant" also in Rom. 1:1; Phil. 1:1; cf. James 1:1; II Peter 1:1, but note variation in modifiers), and has received his authoritative commission directly from *Jesus Christ,* being therefore his *apostle.*

The service and apostleship are exercised "in the interest of" (that seems to be the meaning of κατά here; cf. John 2:6; II Cor. 11:21) the faith of God's elect and (their) acknowledgment of the truth which accords with godliness; that is, they are carried out *in order to further or promote* the reliance of God's chosen ones upon him, and their glad recognition or confession of the redemptive truth which centers in him; a truth which, in sharp contrast with the vagaries of false teachers, *accords with* (or here also "is in the interest of," "promotes") godliness, the life of Christian virtue, the spirit of true consecration.[188]

2. Now *all* that has been said so far – Paul's service and apostleship in the interest of the faith of God's elect and of their acknowledgment of the truth which accords with godliness – rests **on the hope of life everlasting, which the never-lying God promised before times everlasting.**[189] This hope is an

---

[187] Translators and commentators will probably never reach agreement with respect to the question whether δοῦλος, as used here and in similar passages, should be rendered *slave* or *servant.* In favor of *slave* is the fact that Paul's Master *has bought* him, hence *owns* him, and that the apostle *is completely dependent* upon this Master, a relation of which he is fully aware. On the other hand, this very rendering is jarring to our ears because the word "slave" generally conveys to our minds the idea of *involuntary service* and *harsh treatment.* All in all, it would therefore seem that if the choice is between *slave* and *servant,* the rendering *servant* deserves the preference here. See also N.T.C. on John, Vol. II, p. 306, footnote 184. However, it must be admitted that here, as happens frequently, no translation is able *in one word* to convey the full, rich meaning of the original.

[188] Various concepts in this verse have been discussed more fully elsewhere. For the idea of *apostleship* see on I Tim. 1:1. For the idea of *election* see N.T.C. on I Thess. 1:4. For the expression "Jesus Christ" see the comments on I Tim. 1:1; cf. N.T.C. on I Thess. 1:1. And for *godliness* see on I Tim. 2:2; 3:16; 4:7, 8; 6:3, 5, 6, 11; and II Tim. 3:5.

[189] Does the expression "on the hope of life everlasting" really modify the entire first verse? In other words, is *hope* here viewed as a kind of energizing cause both of Paul's apostolic ministry and of the elect's complete devotion to God? This would seem to be the most natural view. Also, it harmonizes with Paul's teaching elsewhere:

Thus, with respect to a. *hope viewed as a spur to faithfulness in the performance of his own task* (and that of Timothy), he says, "For to this end we toil and strive, because we have our hope set on the living God" (see on I Tim. 4:10).

And with respect to b. *hope viewed as an incentive for holy living of believers in general,* the passage Titus 2:11-14 is very clear. (Other passages proving a. or b. or both are the following: I Tim. 1:16; 6:19; II Tim. 1:12; 2:5, 11, 12; 4:1, 7, 8, 18; then also Acts 26:6, 7; Rom. 4:18; 8:20; I Cor. 9:10; 15:58; I Thess. 1:3, 9, 10; 2:12; 4:13.) Surely, if even Jesus "for the joy that was set before him" endured the

earnest yearning, confident expectation, and patient waiting for "life everlasting," salvation in its fullest development (cf. John 17:24; Rom. 8:25). It was this salvation which the God *who cannot lie* (I Sam. 15:29; Heb. 6:18; cf. II Tim. 2:13; contrast Titus 1:12) "promised before times everlasting."

Just as God's grace was given to us in Christ Jesus "before times everlasting" (II Tim. 1:9), so also everlasting life was promised "before times everlasting." Before the ages began to roll along in their never-ending course, that is, "before the world began" (A.V.), hence "from eternity," the grace was given and the life was promised. When God decides to call into being a people for his own possession, the fulfilment of this decree is so certain that the grace which they will receive can be spoken of as having been already given, just as the life is described as having been already promised. Besides, strictly speaking, the text does not say, "God promised *to them,*" but simply, "God *promised.*" Nevertheless, the context (see verse 1) definitely implies that it is *for the benefit of the elect* out of Jews and Gentiles that this promise is made. That in the covenant of redemption from eternity such a promise (of the Father to the Son in the interest of all the elect) was actually made is clearly implied in the fact that believers are viewed as "given" to Christ by the Father, in order that they may inherit life everlasting in its most glorious manifestation (John 17:6, 9, 24; cf. also Ps. 89:3, based on II Sam. 7:12-14; cf. Heb. 1:5). Note especially John 17:24, "Father, I desire that they also, whom thou hast given me, be with me where I am, in order that they may gaze on my glory which thou hast given me, for thou lovest me *before the foundation of the world*" (John 17:24).

This "before the foundation of the world" doctrine, the exact phrase-

---

cross (Heb. 12:2), believers have a right to regard their future salvation as a legitimate (though not as the only!) incentive for a life of consecrated service here below.

But several commentators accept only a. as far as the present passage is concerned. They interpret as follows:

Paul's ministry and apostleship are:

(1) "in the interest of the faith of God's elect," etc.,

and

(2) "based on the hope of life everlasting, which," etc.

The phrases (1) and (2) are viewed as co-ordinate modifiers of "Paul, a servant of God and an apostle of Jesus Christ."

Though this view may be correct, it would seem to be exposed to the following objections, making it less probable:

In the first place, in that case would not (2) be more naturally introduced by some specifying particle?

Secondly, thus narrowly conceived, is not the antecedent of the expression "(which is based) on the hope" rather remote?

Thirdly, when the words which immediately precede this expression mention other things (furtherance in faith, acknowledgment of the truth, the exercise of godliness) which according to Paul's consistent teaching are *also* stimulated by this living hope, as has been shown, what good reason is there to say that *only* Paul's apostolic ministry is based on it?

Other views of the construction are even less satisfactory.

ology, is not only Johannine but also definitely Pauline. Note Eph. 1:4, "He elected us for himself in him (i.e., in Christ) *before the foundation of the world.*"

Thus interpreted, Titus 1:2 is entirely in harmony with Pauline thinking, which regularly traces the salvation of believers to its origin in God's redemptive plan from eternity (besides II Tim. 1:9 and Eph. 1:4 see also Rom. 8:29, 30; I Cor. 2:7; II Thess. 2:13; and see N.T.C. on I Thess. 1:4 [190]).

3. Verse 3 is really a parenthesis: – **but in due season he revealed his word by (that) proclamation which by order of God our Savior was entrusted to me –.**

From eternity God *promised* life everlasting, but "in due season" (here used as in I Tim. 2:6; 6:15; see footnotes 102 and 105; cf. also Gal. 4:4) he *revealed* it. Strictly speaking, however, it was not life everlasting itself in its glorious heavenly phase that was revealed to earth-dwellers (how could it be?), but *the word* of God with respect to it. Hence, the change from "life everlasting" in verse 2, to "his word" in verse 3. In the form of (or: by means of) the *good news* which Paul proclaimed and which by order of "God our Savior" (see on I Tim. 1:1) had been *entrusted* to him (see on I Tim. 1:11-13), this *word* or *message* of God with respect to Christ and his gracious gift had now been made manifest.

This parenthetical statement is in complete harmony with Paul's teaching throughout. That teaching may be summarized as follows:

Full salvation in Christ for both Jew and Gentile, considered as equals, a salvation viewed as based solely upon Christ's merits appropriated by faith, was:

a. objectively *given* and *promised* from eternity (I Cor. 2:7; Eph. 1:4; II Thess. 2:13; II Tim. 1:9; Titus 1:2);

b. *hidden* – i.e., the message with reference to it was hidden – in preceding ages and from the eyes of former generations (Rom. 16:25; Eph. 3:5, 6, 9; Col. 1:26a); hidden, namely, in the sense that it was not *fully* proclaimed, nor *fully* realized, nor *fully* understood by the men of the old dispensation, though it had been foreshadowed (Gen. 3:15; 12:3; cf. Gal. 3:8; Is. 60; 61;

---

190 The objections that have been raised against this explanation are as follows:
(1) It cannot be truly said that life everlasting *was promised* from all eternity. This objection has already been answered.
(2) He who in this connection thinks of God's eternal decree is forced to conclude that God gave the promise *before eternity*.
Answer: Not at all; he gave it "*before* times everlasting," that is, "*from* eternity."
(3) The verb *promised* is in the *aorist tense* (middle voice). Hence, it must refer to just one event, probably to the promise in Gen. 3:15.
Answer: It is not true that the aorist tense necessarily refers to only one *event*. Rather, its function is to summarize, to give a "capsule view." But even if it did refer to only one event, that event could be the (humanly conceived) promise of God in the covenant of redemption.

Joel 2:28, 29; Amos 9:11, 12; Micah 4:12; Mal. 1:11; also Ps. 72:8-11, 17; 87);
c. now fully *manifested* – i.e., the message with reference to it was fully manifested – by means of universal gospel-proclamation (see on II Tim. 1:10, 11; cf. Rom. 16:26; Eph. 3:3-9; Col. 1:26b-29). For "proclamation" or "preaching" (literally "heralding," "kerugma") see on II Tim. 4:2.

The glorious fact that the proclamation of the good news concerning life everlasting had actually been entrusted to one so unworthy as Paul, a fact which caused the heart of the apostle to overflow with gratitude, accounts for this interruption in the steady flow of the sentence.

4. To Titus (my) genuine child in terms of (the) common faith; grace and peace from God (the) Father and Christ Jesus our Savior.

The words of address closely resemble those in II Tim. 1:2 and even more closely those in I Tim. 1:2. Note how here, too, apostolic authority (Titus 1:1) and tender love ("my genuine child") are beautifully blended.

Titus was Paul's *child* because it was to the apostle as a means in God's hand that he owed his spiritual life, though the time, place, and circumstances of his conversion have not been revealed (see p. 37). The designation *child* is a happy one, for it combines two ideas: "I have begotten you," and "You are very dear to me." Titus was, moreover, a *genuine* child, natural (not adopted), not a bastard son, not merely a nominal believer. Paul considers himself the father of Titus, not in the physical sense but "in terms of the common faith," that is, with respect to the faith common to Paul and Titus. The phrase "in faith" ("my genuine child in faith") in I Tim. 1:2 has virtually the same meaning. It is probably best to take *faith,* as here used, in the subjective sense, a true knowledge of God and of his promises revealed in the gospel and a hearty confidence in him and in his redemptive, Christ-centered love.

Upon this genuine child the apostle now pronounces *grace and peace* (cf. "grace, mercy, and peace" in I Tim. 1:2 and in II Tim. 1:2). *Grace* is God's unmerited favor in operation in the heart of his child. It is his Christ-centered pardoning and strengthening love. *Peace* is that child's consciousness of having been reconciled with God through Christ. *Grace* is the fountain, and *peace* is the stream which issues from this fountain (cf. Rom. 5:1).

This grace and this peace have their origin in God the Father, and have been merited for the believer by Christ Jesus. These two are the *one* source of grace and peace (the preposition *from* is not repeated). But though in all the other salutations of Paul (Rom. 1:7; I Cor. 1:3; II Cor. 1:2; etc., including the Pastorals: I Tim. 1:2; II Tim. 1:2) Christ is called *Lord,* he is here called "our Savior." For the meaning of this word *Savior,* which occurs as often in Titus as in all the other Pauline epistles put together (six times: Titus 1:3, 4; 2:10, 13; 3:4, 6), and in this letter is used both with reference to "God" and to "Christ," see on I Tim. 4:10. Here in Titus 1:4 the term is used in its full, redemptive meaning. Christ Jesus is the One who rescues from the greatest evil and bestows upon the rescued ones the greatest good. For the meaning of *salvation* see on I Tim. 1:15.

In view of the close similarity between Titus 1:4 and I Tim. 1:2, the reader is referred to the explanation of I Tim. 1:2 for a more detailed discussion. And see also N.T.C. on I and II Thessalonians, pp. 37-46.

---

5 For this reason I left you behind in Crete, that you might straighten out the things that remain to be done, namely, that you might appoint elders in each city in such a manner as I gave you directions. 6 A person (can be appointed) if he is blameless, one wife's husband, having believing children (who are) not open to the charge of dissolute behavior nor unsubmissive. 7 For the overseer, as God's steward, must be blameless, not self-pleasing, not hot-tempered, not (one who lingers) beside (his) wine, not given to blows, not greedy of shameful gain, 8 but hospitable, loving the good, self-controlled (or sensible), fair, pious, master of himself, 9 holding on to the trustworthy word which is in line with the doctrine, in order that he may be able both to encourage (others) by means of his sound teaching and to refute those who contradict (it).

1:5-9

5. In order that congregational life in the various cities of Crete may flourish, well-qualified elders must be appointed: **For this reason I left you behind in Crete, that you might straighten out the things that remain to be done, namely, that you might appoint elders in each city in such a manner as I gave you directions.**

Evidently, on a certain journey by sea Paul and Titus had been together in Crete. The gospel had been proclaimed, little groups of disciples had been gathered, meeting-places had been arranged, but no official organization had been effected, or, if anything worthy of this name had been initiated, it had been left far from finished.

If the *conjecture* be correct that the stop-over in Crete occurred immediately after Paul's release from his first Roman imprisonment, the following problem had at that time presented itself:

a. After a lengthy absence from his friends the apostle was anxious to see the old familiar faces and to revisit the churches previously established. This is understandable, for he was an intensely human, warm-hearted person. Also, he loved his Lord and longed to promote the good cause in every possible way. Moreover, he had made what might be considered *promises* of early visits (Philemon 22; Phil. 1:25, 26). Accordingly, for Paul himself a lengthy delay in Crete was out of the question.

b. Nevertheless, in Crete the business of organizing the various churches was far from finished, and undue haste in appointing men to office was contrary to Paul's principles (I Tim. 3:6; 5:22).

The solution was: Paul must be on his way, and Titus must be *left behind* (cf. II Tim. 4:13, 20) in the island to straighten out the things that remained to be done, *namely* (κατά here used in that sense), to establish presbyteries. The apostle, who likes to stress the fact that *God* does not leave *his* work of grace unfinished (Phil. 1:6; I Thess. 5:23), is a true imitator of God also in this respect; for Paul, too, abhors unfinished business (see I Tim. 1:3 and I Thess. 3:10 for different applications of this same principle). And with respect to Titus, one could almost say that for him no task was too difficult to be attempted and no challenge too formidable to be met, in dependence on divine strength and wisdom (see pp. 36, 39).

The text implies that the apostle had given directions as to *just how* (ὡς = abbreviation for *in such a manner as*) elders must be appointed. This refers to *the requirements for office* which must be considered in appointing men to office. Since the verses which follow refer only to *elders* but it is clear from I Timothy 3 that it was Paul's conviction that (at least in course of time) a church would also need *deacons,* we may assume that the apostle means that when the work to be done became too heavy for the elders, deacons should be appointed similarly (cf. Acts 6:1-6).

Accordingly, the directions as to the requirements for the office of presbyter or elder are here re-stated. They had been given orally while Paul and Titus were still together in Crete, and they are now repeated in written form: *"For this reason* (anticipative τούτου χάριν followed by ἵνα, as in Eph. 3:1, 14-16) I left you behind in Crete, that you might . . . appoint elders *in each city"* ("down the line," hence, "city by city"). For the practice see Acts 14:23, and for this use of the preposition see Luke 8:1; Acts 10:23.

Possible reasons for the repetition in written form of a directive which earlier had been given orally:

(a) For the convenience of Titus, to assist his memory;

(b) For the confirmation of his authority in the event that this should be disputed;

(c) For future ages.

Though Paul says, "that *you* might appoint," he by no means excludes the responsible co-operation of the individual congregations (see Acts 1:15-26; 6:1-6, note same verb in Acts 6:3).

6-9. The list of requirements for elders or presbyters is introduced by the words: "If anyone is . . ." We have here another instance of *abbreviated discourse* (see N.T.C. on John 5:31, Vol. I, p. 206). Here as in I Tim. 5:10 it is not difficult to fill in the implied words. The meaning, as required by the preceding context, is, "If anyone is blameless, etc. . . . , *he can be appointed,"* or as I have translated: **A person (can be appointed) if he is,** etc.

The requirements listed occur in three groups:

(1) The person who is going to occupy such an important post must be of deservedly high reputation and if married (which will generally be the case) a good family-man (verse 6).

(2) He must *not* be the type of person who in his desire to please himself has lost interest in other people (except to vex them!) and who, if embroiled in a quarrel, is ever ready with his fists. A list of *negative* characteristics is given: qualities which the overseer must *not* have (verse 7).

(3) All his actions must give evidence of the fact that both in *deed* and in *doctrine* he wishes to be a blessing to others. A list of *positive* characteristics is given: qualities which the overseer must have (verses 8 and 9).

The three groups of requirements pertain to people who as to their age and dignity are called *elders,* and as to their task are called *overseers.* Though it is true that the text has the singular "the overseer," this "the" is generic, one member representing the entire class viewed from the point of view of a definite characteristic (see N.T.C. on I and II Thessalonians, p. 55, footnote 41). One might paraphrase the meaning as follows, "For, *any* overseer, by reason of the very fact that he should live up to his name of *overseer* and should manage God's own house, (being God's *steward;* see on I Tim. 1:4; cf. I Cor. 4:1; I Peter 4:10), must be blameless," etc. That for the author of the Pastorals the terms *elder* and *overseer* indicate the same person also follows from the fact that essentially the same requirements for an elder as are given here in Titus 1:5, 6 – that he be blameless, one wife's husband, and have well-behaved children – are listed with reference to the *overseer* in I Tim. 3:2, 4. The hierarchical idea – the *several* "priests" and their "parishes," outranked and governed by the *one* "bishop" and his "diocese" – is foreign to the Pastorals.

To avoid unnecessary duplication and at the same time to show the relation between the two rather similar lists of requirements (Titus 1 and I Timothy 3), I give the explanation of verses 6-9 in the form of a Table. *Whenever the stipulated requirement has already been treated elsewhere (particularly in I Tim. 3) the reader is referred to the fuller explanation which can be found there.*

Column 1 contains the list of requirements for elders or overseers as found in Titus 1. Column 2 gives the meaning in brief of each of these requirements. Column 3 lists those requirements *of the Titus 1 list* which are paralleled (either exactly or by means of a synonym) in *the overseer-requirements-list* as found in I Tim. 3. Column 4, similarly, shows the parallels in *the deacon-requirements-list* of I Tim. 3. And Column 5 lists antonyms of four overseer-requirements which find no parallel in I Tim. 3. These antonyms occur in the II Tim. 3 list of character-traits of people living "in the last days" (see the explanation of II Tim. 3:1-5).

1 *Titus 1*	2 *Meaning*	3 *I Timothy 3-* *Overseers*	4 *I Timothy 3-* *Deacons*	5 *II Timothy 3*
Elders				
blameless	not to be called to account (particularly with respect to the points to be mentioned in verses 6-9)	cf. above reproach (verse 2)	blameless, (verse 10)	
one wife's husband	faithful in the marriage-relationship	one wife's husband (verse 2)	one wife's husband, (verse 12)	
having believing children (who are) not open to the charge of dissolute behavior nor unsubmissive	having children who share the Christian faith of their fathers and who adorn that faith with a godly conduct. A man whose children are still pagans or behave as pagans must not be appointed elder. cf. Eph. 5:18	cf. managing well his own household, with true dignity keeping his children in subjection, etc. (verses 4, 5)	cf. managing well his children and his household (verse 12)	
Overseers				
For the overseer as God's steward must be blameless, (This has already been explained.) **not self-pleasing**	(explanation of "not self-pleasing") not self-indulgent to the point of showing arrogance to others (cf. II Tim. 3:2 and II Peter 2:10)			contrast and cf. "self-loving" (verse 2)
not hot-tempered	not given to outbursts of wrath	cf. not given to blows, not contentious (verse 3)		

1 *Titus 1*	2 *Meaning*	3 *I Timothy 3-Overseers*	4 *I Timothy 3-Deacons*	5 *II Timothy 3*
not (one who lingers) beside (his) wine	no wine-bibber, tippler, or drunkard	not (one who lingers) beside (his) wine (verse 3)	cf. not addicted to much wine (verse 8)	
not given to blows	not eager to use his fists, not bellicose, no spitfire	not given to blows (verse 3)		
not greedy of shameful profit	no embezzler, pilferer, Simonite (cf. Titus 1:11; also cf. I Peter 5:2 adverb)	cf. not fond of money (verse 3)	not greedy of shameful profit (verse 8)	
but hospitable	"loving strangers"; here, especially, ready to befriend and to lodge destitute, traveling, or persecuted believers (cf. I Peter 4:9)	hospitable (verse 2)		
loving the good	loving goodness, virtuous, ready to do what is beneficial to others			contrast and cf. "unloving toward the good" (verse 3)
self-controlled or sensible	of sound mind, discreet, sane (cf. Titus 2:2, 5)	self-controlled (verse 2)		
fair	performing one's duty toward man			
pious (or "holy")	performing one's duty toward God (cf. I Tim. 2:8)			contrast and cf. "impious" or "unholy" (verse 2)

master of himself	possessing *the moral strength* to curb or master one's sinful drives and impulses (cf. Gen. 39:7-9; 50:15-21)			contrast and cf. "unrestrained" (verse 3)
holding on to the trustworthy word which is in line with the doctrine	clinging to and applying himself to the sacred tradition which is in harmony with the sound doctrine, that is, with the doctrine which, in turn, is based on Scripture		cf. keeping hold of the mystery of our faith with a pure conscience (verse 9)	
in order that he may be able both to encourage (others) by means of his sound teaching and to refute those who contradict it	to the end that every overseer may be able by means of his sound teaching to incline will and heart to the joyful service of God, and to expose the errors of those who rebel; that is, to withstand these opponents, if at all possible bringing *them* to an acknowledgment of their error and to repentance; at least, convincing *believers* that these adversaries are wrong. Not all the overseers or elders are actually called upon to perform this task (see on I Tim. 5:17), but *all must be able* to perform it.	qualified to teach (verse 2)		

10 For there are many insubordinate men, futile talkers and mind-deceivers, especially those of the circumcision-party, 11 whose mouths must be stopped, since (they are) such as upset entire families by teaching, for the sake of shameful profit, what is not proper. 12 One of them, a prophet of their own, made the statement:

"Cretans (are) always deceivers, evil brutes, bellies inactive."

13 This testimony is true. Therefore reprove them sharply in order that they may be sound in the faith 14 instead of devoting themselves to Jewish myths and injunctions of men who turn their backs on the truth.

15 All things (are) pure to those who are pure; but to those who are contaminated and unbelieving nothing (is) pure; on the contrary, contaminated are even their minds and their consciences. 16 God they profess to know, but by their actions they deny (it), because they are despicable and disobedient and for every good work unfit.

1:10-16

10. The reason why men so highly qualified for spiritual office are *especially* necessary in Crete is now stated:

For there are many insubordinate men, futile talkers and mind-deceivers, especially those of the circumcision-party.

This group (verses 10-14a) is the same as is mentioned in I Tim. 1:3-11; note similarities:

Titus 1	I Timothy 1
insubordinate men (verse 10)	insubordinate men (verse 9)
futile talkers (verse 10)	certain individuals . . . have turned aside to futile talk (verse 6)
teaching what is not proper (verse 11)	in order that you may charge certain individuals not to teach differently (verse 3); cf. 6:3
always liars (verse 12)	liars (verse 10)
in order that they may be sound in the faith (verse 13)	contrary to the sound doctrine (verse 10); cf. 6:3
devoting themselves to Jewish myths (verse 14)	not to devote themselves to endless myths and genealogies (verse 4); cf. 4:7a.

These men are present here in Crete *in alarming numbers* ("*many* insubordinate men"; contrast the "certain individuals" in I Tim. 1:3). This may have been due to the fact that their peculiar faults were in line with the Cretan national character and that they were under the strong influence of Jewish rabbis (*outsiders,* verses 14b-16). They are *insubordinate;* that is disobedient to the Word of God. Also, they are *futile talkers,* achieving no *useful* purpose, with their fictitious tales about Adam, Moses, Elijah, etc., and with their legalistic hair-splitting (cf. I Tim. 1:6); yet *deceiving the minds* (see M.M., p. 675) of the weak. Especially "those of the circumcision-party," that is, Jewish church-members (cf. Acts 10:45; Gal. 2:12), belong to the class of futile talkers and mind-deceivers. They probably regarded their circumcision as a mark of superior excellence, entitling them to be heard and looked up to by others.

11. But Paul, disagreeing sharply with their opinion of themselves, says with respect to them and also with respect to the rest of the futile talkers and mind-deceivers: **whose mouths must be stopped, since (they are) such as upset entire families by teaching, for the sake of shameful profit, what is not proper.**

In telling Titus what should be done with such people, Paul uses a rare verb (see M.M., p. 246) which has as its primary meaning "to stop the mouth by means of a bridle, muzzle, or gag." The deceivers, then, must not be tolerated but be silenced, and this should be done *by Titus and by the elders,* as the context would seem to indicate (verses 5-9).

Just *how* this silencing should be done is not indicated in the present passage. See, however, on I Tim. 1:3, 4; 1:20; 4:7; II Tim. 2:16, 21, 23; 4:2; Titus 1:13b; 3:10. At first the errorist should be tenderly admonished so that he may be won for the truth. If he refuses, he must be sharply reprimanded and told to desist. The person who persists in his evil ways must be shunned by the church and disciplined. The supreme measure, excommunication, may have to be employed in order to safeguard the church and in order to bring the sinner to repentance. In the church of God there is no such thing as "freedom of *misleading* speech." Reason: it would be too dangerous. The teachers of false doctrine "upset (cf. John 1:15) entire families," causing them to wander away from the truth (see on II Tim. 3:6). They do this by teaching "what is not proper," that is, "Jewish myths and injunctions of men" (see on verse 14). And their purpose is to acquire *shameful profit,* profit that is shameful because the men who are after it are anxious to enrich themselves even at the expense of the downfall of others. They are utterly selfish, aiming at nothing but money and prestige. (Cf. I Tim. 3:3, 8; 6:5; Titus 1:7; and on the entire subject of remuneration for spiritual work see N.T.C. on I Thess. 2:9.)

12. These *Jewish church-members* of the Pharisaic type and tinged with incipient gnosticism, which led at times to licentiousness and at times to asceticisms (see on I Tim. 4:3, 4), were *Cretans* – there were many Jews in Crete (cf. Acts 2:11) – , and, in addition to being influenced by unbelieving Jews (see on 14b-16), had absorbed the worst character-traits of their non-

Jewish countrymen. This had not been a chore, for the Jew and the Cretan had something in common. The employment of trickery or deception for selfish advantage characterized both (cf. John 1:47 with Titus 1:12). An honest Jew or an honest Cretan seems to have been an exception. And certainly the combination *Cretan-Jew* was not a happy one.

As to the Cretans, they were condemned "out of their own mouth." Says Paul, **One of them, a prophet of their own, made the statement:**

Cretans (are) always deceivers, evil brutes, bellies inactive.

A prophet *of their own* would be more apt *to brag* about his countrymen to others than *to condemn* them. Yet, condemn them is exactly what their own prophet had done. By Clement of Alexandria (*Stromata* I. xiv. 59) and by Jerome the devastating characterization is attributed to a poet and reformer whose date is variously given as somewhere between 630 and 500 B. C. His name was Epimenedes, a native of Cnossus near Iráklion (= Candia) on Crete's northern shore, where even today one can visit the museum that contains the unique treasures of the Minoan Age. In a hymn "To Zeus" Callimachus (about 300-240 B. C.) had quoted the first words, "Cretans (are) always deceivers." To the question whether or not Paul himself *had actually read* Epimenedes not all give the same answer. Some hold that since the quotation is really a proverb, it may have been derived by Paul from widely disseminated oral tradition. Others believe that it is not necessary to confine Paul's *reading*-knowledge within such *narrow* limits.[191]

Now by the ancients Epimenedes was considered *a prophet,* "a divinely inspired man" (thus Plato), "a man dear to the gods" (thus Plutarch). Paul does not mean to say that the Cretan reformer was actually a prophet in the Scriptural sense. He means, "a man who by them and by others was considered a prophet, a spokesman of the gods." With reference to Epimenedes' so-called *prophetic* activity Plato (*Laws* I. 642 D and E) wrote as follows:

"That divinely-inspired man Epimenedes . . . was born in Crete, and ten years before the Persian War, in accordance with the oracle of the god, went to Athens . . .; and when the Athenians were filled with fear by reason of the Persians' expeditionary force, he made this prophecy: They will not come for ten years, and when they do come, they will turn back again, having accomplished nothing that they had hoped (to accomplish), and having suffered more woes than they will have inflicted."

By many Epimenedes was regarded as one of "the seven wise men" of the ancient world. These seven were: Bias of Priene, Chilon of Sparta, Cleobulus of Lindus, Pittacus of Mitylene, Solon of Athens, Thales of

---

[191] Cf. R. Stob, *Christianity and Classical Civilization,* Grand Rapids, 1950, pp. 61, 62, and A. T. Robertson, "Paul the Apostle," in I.S.B.E., especially IV, 3.

Miletus, and Epimenedes of Crete or Peiander of Corinth or Anacharsis the Scythian (see Plutarch, *Lives, Solon* XII. 4-6; cf. Clement of Alexandria, *Stromata* I. xiv).

It was this same Epimenedes who according to Diogenes Laertius advised the Athenians to sacrifice "to the appropriate god," which advice may have led to the erection of that well-known "altar to an unknown god" which provided a starting-point for Paul's proclamation of *the living God* (Acts 17:23).

The quotation from Epimenedes here in Titus 1:12 is a line which consists of six metrical feet (hexameter verse), somewhat like Longfellow's (*Evangeline*):

"This is the forest primeval. The murmuring pines and the hemlocks . . ."

I have tried to preserve the rhythm, and have therefore rendered the line as follows:

"Cretans are always deceivers, evil brutes, bellies inactive."

Their representation as *deceivers* or *liars* may have arisen from their claim that they had on their island the tomb of Zeus. But the reputation of the Cretans for telling lies for selfish purposes (notice context, verse 11) was so widely spread that it had given rise to the noun "Cretism," meaning "Cretan behavior," that is, "lying" (Plutarch, *Aemilius* 26); and to the verb "to Cretize" or "to speak like a Cretan," which meant "to tell lies," "to deceive" (e.g. Polybius VIII. 19). Cf. "to Corinthianize," meaning "to live a profligate life like a Corinthian."

The expression "evil brutes" describes the savage and cruel character of the Cretans of the days of Epimenedes and of the days of Paul and Titus. They would push everyone out of the way in order to gain an advantage for themselves. Some see in this descriptive epithet an allusion to the mythical Cretan Minotaur, half bull half man, whom Minos hid in the Cretan labyrinth, where, until Theseus slew this monster, he devoured the Athenian youths and maidens sent as a tribute every nine years.

"Bellies inactive" marks the Cretans as lazy gluttons, sluggish and sensual gormandizers.

The Cretans, then, are *untruthful, selfish,* and *pleasure-loving.* Now some writers consider the action of Paul in quoting this devastating verdict with respect to the character of the Cretans as singularly untactful, a "smear" upon the good name of an entire population. However, the character of the Cretans displayed itself so clearly that confirmation of the severe judgment comes from every direction and is not limited to a single century. The reader should see this for himself. In addition to the noun "Cretism" = *lie,* and to the verb "to Cretize" = *to deceive, to tell lies,* we have the following (the dates given are mostly approximate):

Polybius, Greek historian (203-120 B. C.):

"So much in fact do love of shameful profit and greed prevail among them that among all men Cretans are the only ones in whose estimation no profit is ever disgraceful" (*The Histories* VI. 46).

Cicero, Roman orator, statesman, and philosopher (106-43 B. C.):

"Indeed, (men's) moral principles are so divergent that the Cretans . . . consider highway-robbery (or "brigandage") to be honorable" (*Republic* III. ix. 15).

Livy, Roman historian (59 B. C.-A. D. 17):

"The Cretans followed (Perseus) in hope of cash" (XLIV. xlvi).

Plutarch, Greek essayist and biographer (A. D. 46-120):

"Of his soldiers (only) the Cretans followed him, not through being favorably disposed (toward him), but because they were as devoted to his riches as are bees to their honeycombs. For he was carrying along vast treasures, and he had handed out for distribution among the Cretans drinking-cups and mixing bowls and other utensils of gold and silver, valued at fifty talents" (*Aemilius Paulus* XXIII. 4). Werner Keller, *The Bible as History,* New York, 1956, pp. 172, 173, hints that the ancient Cretans were "powerful drinkers" and submits interesting archaeological evidence: the fact that large numbers of wine cups and beer mugs, the latter fitted with filters, were found in the settlements of the Philistines who, as Scripture says (Amos 9:7), came from Caphtor, that is, Crete.

13 and 14. It is not surprising therefore that Paul says, **This testimony is true.** The character of the mendacious, grasping Cretans was so clearly displayed by their actions that Paul cannot do anything else than confirm the judgment that was expressed in Epimenedes' hexameter.

An attempt has been made to show that the verdict of Epimenedes and of Paul is really a self-contradiction. This is done by means of the following bit of sophistry:

"A Cretan, Epimenedes, said that Cretans always lie. He must therefore himself have lied when he said this. Therefore it is not true that the Cretans always lie. Or (even worse): Therefore, the Cretans do not lie. But if the Cretans do not lie, then Epimenedes, a Cretan, must have spoken the truth. But then he, too, being a Cretan, was a liar when he said that Cretans always lie." And so we are back at the place from which we started.

But certainly all that was meant by Paul was that *Crete was notorious for its many constant liars.* His statement leaves ample room for the following propositions:

a. Even Cretan liars sometimes speak the truth.

b. Some Cretans are not outstanding liars.

c. This particular Cretan, namely Epimenedes, spoke the truth when he described Cretans as being, generally speaking, constant liars.

Therefore reprove them sharply in order that they may be sound in the faith. The errorists and those who listen to them must be *reproved* (cf. II Tim. 4:2) *sharply* (cf. II Cor. 13:10), decisively, and this not only by the elders (see on verse 9 above) but also by Titus himself, in order that they may be (that is, *may become*) what at present they are not, namely, *sound* (cf. I Tim. 1:10) in their stand with respect to the truth as revealed in Christ.

Paul continues: **instead of devoting themselves to Jewish myths and injunctions of men who turn their backs upon the truth.**

To escape the impact of the law of God the errorists were devoting themselves (see on I Tim. 1:4) to "Jewish myths," that is, to fanciful stories about ancestors; and to "injunctions of men," that is, to man-made commands. These, too, were probably to a large extent Jewish in character. To the extent in which they were, *they were said to be* based on the law of God. *Actually,* however, they obscured the real intent and meaning of the law. Cf. Matt. 5:43; 15:3, 6, 9; Mark 7:1-23; Luke 6:1-11; and see N.T.C. on John 5:1-18.

The Cretan deceivers, accordingly, busied themselves with Talmudic anecdotes and hair-splitting legal decisions for which the claim was made that they were derived from the law. The injunctions which they praised and tried to force upon others were actually the commands of "men who turn their backs upon the truth." By these men *the Jews* are meant, particularly Jewish rabbis and scribes. The situation, then, was as follows:

The stedfast believers in the island of Crete mingled daily with other church-members who were not so stedfast but were willing to lend an ear to loud-mouthed Judaistic deceivers, tinged with gnosticism. These false teachers, in turn, were under the influence of men who stood entirely outside the church, namely, Jews, Pharisaic propagandists, who completely rejected Christ, turning their backs upon God's redemptive truth as revealed in his Son.

15. The nature — at least in part — of the subversive doctrine that was literally being *sold* (taught by false teachers with a view to "shameful profit") in Crete is suggested by the words of verse 15. The deceivers, who in turn were being deceived by outside-deceivers, namely, by the Jews, were *denying* that: **All things (are) pure to those who are pure; but to those who are contaminated and unbelieving nothing (is) pure; on the contrary, contaminated are even their minds and their consciences.**[192]

---

[192] In agreement with most commentators I regard the proverb "All things (are) pure to those who are pure" to be part of Paul's own teaching. It was either coined by himself or else it had been phrased by another (perhaps by Jesus Christ himself; cf. Luke 11:38-41) and then taken over by him and quoted over against the Jewish differentiation between "pure" and "impure."

Other interpreters (for example, J. Van Dijk, *Paraphrase Heilige Schrift, Tim-*

The false teachers inside the churches of Crete were trying to reconcile Jewish bondage (ceremonialism) with Christian freedom. Many of them, no doubt, had been trained from early childhood in the religion of the shadows, and it was hard for them to understand that with the coming and death of the Lord these shadows had disappeared. Influenced, as they certainly were, by the impenitent Jews outside the church, they attach a degree of *saving* value (a value which even the law itself had never taught) to ceremonial ordinances – and even more to Pharisaic refinements of these ordinances – concerning what was "clean" and what was "unclean" with respect to articles of food, pieces of furniture, the human body, etc. They regarded purity as being an attribute not of the mind and conscience of man but of material things. As was shown in connection with I Tim. 4:3, they were probably also strengthened in this error by pagan dualism which regarded matter as being sinful in itself. But the main sinister influence here in Crete seems to have come from the Jews.

Jesus had combated this error vigorously. He had said, "Not what goes into a man but what comes out of him defiles him, for from within come evil thoughts" (see Matt. 15:11, 15-20; Mark 7:14-22; Luke 11:38-41; and cf. Prov. 4:23). The early church had followed where Christ had led (as is implied in Acts 10:9-16; 11:1-18; 15:20). Paul, too, in his other epistles had consistently defended the thesis that "nothing is unclean in itself" (Rom. 14:14, 20; cf. I Cor. 6:12; 10:23; Gal. 2:11-21; Col. 2:16-23), and that it is the disposition of the heart and the purpose of the mind which render a matter clean or unclean (Rom. 14:23; I Cor. 10:31). In Romans and I Corinthians this basic truth had been applied in one direction (to eat without regard to the weaker brother is sinful); here it is applied in another direction (to eat with an unbelieving mind or contaminated conscience is defiling).

"All things (are) pure to those who are pure; but to those who are contaminated and unbelieving nothing (is) pure." The expression "all things" is best explained by Paul himself. It amounts to "every creature of God" (I Tim. 5:5), that is, everything that was created by God for consumption as food. It is not the impure thing which makes men impure, as the Jews erroneously held (see N.T.C. on John 18:28), but it is impure men who make *every* pure thing impure, a truth foreshadowed in Hag. 2:13.

Pure men are those who have been cleansed from their guilt by the

---

otheus, Titus en Philemon, p. 68) regard it as a saying of the false teachers as an excuse for their immoral teaching and conduct.

But that view fails to reckon with the fact that these errorists were for the most part "of the circumcision" (verse 10), people who esteemed very highly the Jewish *Halacha* (verse 14; cf. also verse 16 and 3:9). Their rules regarding morals were far more likely to be rigid than loose (see I Tim. 4:3; cf. Col. 2:21). – Besides, if Rom. 14:14, 20 and I Tim. 4:4, 5 contain positive Pauline teaching, why not Titus 1:15?

blood of Christ and, having been regenerated by the Holy Spirit, are being constantly cleansed by that same Spirit from the pollution of their sins (see on Titus 3:5; then Matt. 5:8; John 3:3, 5; I Cor. 6:11; Eph. 1:7; 5:26, 27; I John 1:7, 9; see also N.T.C. on John 13:10; 15:3). These are the ones who do not reject what God has created as good foods but "partake of them with thanksgiving" (see on I Tim. 4:3, 4).

On the other hand, those who are contaminated, befouled, or polluted, namely, the Jews, and having rejected Christ are at the same time unbelieving, have thereby defiled *all* of God's pure gifts. Even their *minds,* those organs which reflect on things spiritual and guide the will, and their *consciences,* that is, their moral selves in the act of passing judgment upon their deeds, *are* – and unless God's grace intervenes, *remain;* note perfect passive indicative – *contaminated.* (For the concept *conscience* see on I Tim. 1:5.) This is evidenced by the fact that their moral judgments are perverted and that they do not arrive at godly sorrow.

16. The description of "men who turn their backs upon the truth," a description begun in verse 14b, continues. Referring, then, to *the Jews* (particularly, the Pharisaic leaders who, though outsiders, are exerting a sinister influence upon the false leaders within the churches of Crete), Paul adds: **God they profess to know.** As did their fathers long ago (Deut. 6:4), so also these Jews proclaim to all who are willing to listen that they know the one true God as their own God (see N.T.C. on John 8:54, 55; and cf. Rom. 2:17). "We know him," they declare; and they mean, "with a knowledge intuitive and direct" (note the verb used in the original).

Now it was indeed true that to their forefathers God had revealed himself in a very special way, as to no other nation (Ps. 96:5; 115; 135; 147:19, 20; Amos 3:2; Rom. 3:1, 2; 9:1-5); but instead of realizing that greater opportunity implies greater responsibility, especially with respect to those *who do not know God* (cf. Gal. 4:8; I Thess. 4:5), they had become boastful and had completely rejected the Messiah. Hence, Paul is able to assert that though these Jews profess to know God, yet **by their actions they deny (it).** Their actions *belie* their profession. (The verb *deny,* though not occurring in the earlier epistles of Paul, is found again and again in the Pastorals; see on I Tim. 5:8; II Tim. 2:12, 13; 3:5; Titus 2:12.) For a vivid account of the actions of the Jewish leaders whom Paul has chiefly in mind see Matt. 23. These actions may be summarized in two words: hypocrisy and rejection of the Christ. By wrongly influencing false teachers in Crete they are continuing to reject him.

The reason why they commit these evil acts is now stated: **because they are despicable and disobedient and for every good work unfit.**

They *do* what they do because of what they *are* in their inner nature. It is not surprising that Paul characterizes those who are "defiled in mind and conscience" (see on verse 15) as being *despicable, detestable,* or *abominable* in the eyes of God. Again, they are despicable because, *in spite of* being such sticklers for man-made rules and regulations (cf. Is. 1:12-15; Jer. 6:20; Amos 5:21-23; Matt. 23:23-33; Luke 18:11, 12) – or shall we not rather say: *because* of this very fact? – they are *disobedient* to *God's* holy law. Hence, instead of being "men of God for every good work thoroughly equipped" (see on II Tim. 3:17; cf. II Tim. 2:21), they are the very opposite: "for every good work *unfit*" (after testing rejected as worthless), completely incapable of performing any work that proceeds from faith, is done according to God's law, and redounds unto his glory.

Synthesis of Chapter 1

See the Outline at the beginning of this chapter.

In addressing this letter to Titus, here described as Paul's genuine child in terms of the common faith, the apostle introduces himself as a servant of God and an apostle of Jesus Christ. He declares that he fulfils this mission in order to promote the faith of God's elect and their acknowledgment of the truth which harmonizes with (or: which furthers) the life of Christian devotion. He regards *his* apostleship and *their* devotion as being based on the hope of life everlasting. It is that hope which encourages both Paul and believers in general to be true to their calling. The God who, in sharp contrast with the Cretans, never deceives anyone, promised life everlasting before the never-ending time-process began; that is, he made that promise "from eternity." In due season his word with respect to this great salvation began to be fully and authoritatively proclaimed in the "preaching" (kerugma, proclamation) of Paul, to whom it had been entrusted.

Upon Titus, Paul pronounces "grace and peace from God the Father and Christ Jesus our Savior."

It was in the interest of promoting the spirit of sanctification in the life of the congregations that Paul had left Titus behind in the island of Crete. With this purpose in mind Titus is now being reminded *in writing* of the order which previously had been given to him *orally,* namely, that he should straighten out what remained to be done, and should accordingly appoint elders in each city. The requirements for the office of elder have been summarized on pp. 345-349.

That the idea of *sanctification* in congregational life is, indeed, uppermost in the apostle's mind as he pens this chapter is clear from *the reason* which he gives, showing why men so highly qualified for office are *especially* necessary in the churches of *Crete.* He speaks of *false teachers* within the bosom of the churches, insubordinate men, futile talkers, mind-deceivers, men interested in shameful profit; of *Cretans* whom he describes as "always deceivers, evil brutes, bellies inactive"; and of a certain class of *Jews* whom he pictures as "men who turn their backs upon the truth," and are *"contaminated* in mind and conscience." Accordingly, wise leadership and saving discipline is a "must," in order that *sanctification* may replace *contamination.*

Interesting recent articles on Crete are the following: "Greece, The Birthplace of Science and Free Speech," in *Everyday Life in Ancient Times,* published by The National Geographic Society, Washington, D. C., 1953, see especially pp. 189, 191, 202, 203; and "Crete, Cradle of Western Civilization," in The National Geographic, November, 1953, pp. 693-706. See also E. G. Kraeling, *op. cit.,* p. 463.

Outline of Chapter 2

Theme: *The Apostle Paul, Writing to Titus, Gives Directions for the Promotion of the Spirit of Sanctification*

In Family and Individual Life

2:1-10 All classes of individuals that compose the home-circle should conduct themselves in such a manner that by their life they may adorn the doctrine of God, their Savior.

2:11-15 Reason: to all the grace of God has appeared unto sanctification and joyful expectation of the appearing in glory of our great God and Savior, Jesus Christ.

CHAPTER II

TITUS **2:1**

2 1 But as for you, speak what is consistent with the sound doctrine: (2) (urge) aged men to be temperate, dignified, self-controlled, sound in their faith, in their love, (and) in their endurance; 3 (urge) aged women similarly (to be) reverent in demeanor, not slanderers and not enslaved to much wine, teachers of that which is excellent, 4 so that they may train the young women to be loving toward their husbands and loving toward their children, 5 self-controlled, chaste, workers at home, kind, submissive to their own husbands, in order that the word of God may not be reviled. 6 Similarly urge the young(er) men to exercise self-control in every respect, 7 showing yourself a model of noble deeds; in your teaching (showing) incorruptibility, dignity; (8) (your) speech (being) sound, incensurable, so that he that is on the opposite (side) may be put to shame, having nothing evil to report concerning us. 9 (Urge) slaves to be submissive in every respect to their own masters, to be eager to please (them), not talking back, 10 not pilfering, but evincing the utmost trustworthiness, so that in every respect they may adorn the doctrine of God our Savior.[193]

2:1-10

1. Directions for the promotion of the spirit of sanctification in *congregational life* have been given. Titus has been urged to complete the organization of the various churches in the island, in order that, by means of the work of truly consecrated elders, the voice of persons who by their false doctrines and practices were defiling the churches might be silenced, and congregational life might flourish. That was the substance of chapter 1.

Now in chapter 2 Paul focuses the attention of Titus upon *family and individual life.* He issues commands relative to the proper conduct of five classes of individuals: *aged men, aged women, young married women, young men* (Titus himself to set the example), *and slaves.* The emphasis upon *the family* is evident especially from verses 4 and 5: "so that they (the aged women) may wisely train the young women to be loving toward their husbands, loving toward their children," etc.

For Paul's teaching with respect to The Christian Family see also I Tim. 5:1-8; then Gal. 3:28; Eph. 5:22-6:4; Col. 3:18-21. On Slaves and Their

---

193 Because of its length this footnote has been placed at the end of the chapter.

Masters (considered members of the family) see also I Tim. 6:1, 2; then Eph. 6:5-9; Col. 3:22-4:1; Philemon.[194]

Since Titus is the man who must deliver Paul's instructions with respect to the five groups, the apostle begins by writing, **But as for you, speak what is consistent with the sound doctrine.** Note the word of contrast, *"But,* as for you." Cf. a similar contrast in I Tim. 6:11; II Tim. 3:10, 14; 4:5. The life and teaching of Titus must contrast sharply with that of "the contaminated and unbelieving" enemies of the faith who were doing such damage in Crete (as shown in chapter 1). Not only must these errorists be reproved sharply (Titus 1:13), but *evil must be overcome with good.* Not only must *the elders* do their duty over against teachers of false religion (chapter 1), but *Titus himself* must give the example! Even in his informal daily *conversation* he must "speak" what is consistent with sound doctrine. Note the verb "speak" or literally "talk" (λάλει), which indicates informal vocal utterance.

Now to talk "what is consistent with (or "proper to," cf. I Tim. 2:10; Eph. 5:3) the sound doctrine" certainly means that, as the author conceives of it, *doctrine and life must harmonize.* This is the key to all that follows in verses 2-10. Accordingly, the position defended by some, namely, that the morality urged here is *in no sense* specifically Christian, is in conflict with Paul's declaration. It is true, of course, that even outside of the church some of the character-traits here mentioned – for example, *being temperate or sober, being self-controlled or sensible* – are given in lists of moral requirements for those who occupy certain important positions in life: the Stoic philosopher, the general, etc.[195] Even an unbeliever has "some regard for virtue and for good outward behavior," a truth which should never be denied (see on I Tim. 3:7; and *Canons of Dort,* Third and Fourth Heads of Doctrine, art. 4; note, however, the qualification at the end of that article). But when these same qualities are mentioned here in this letter (or in I Tim. 3), they must not be lifted out of their context, nor must they be dissociated from the general teachings of Scripture. Titus 2:1, 2 must not be separated from Titus 2:12, 13. As soon as the question is asked, "What is the source of these virtues, how are they motivated, according to what standard is their exhibition to be judged, and for what purpose are they to be used?" the great contrast immediately appears. Accordingly, the qualities that are mentioned in the verses which follow are *specifically Christian* virtues in this sense, namely, that they presuppose the

---

[194] For a fine summary of biblical teaching with respect to The Christian Home one may consult (in addition to various works on Ethics, Encyclopedia-articles, and special treatises) the excellent topical outlines in the Index of Thompson's *New Chain Reference Bible,* pp. 62-66, article "Home."

[195] See the lists on p. 201 of Burton Scott Easton's *The Pastoral Epistles,* New York, 1947.

dynamic of God's grace working in the heart, are motivated by the example of Christ, are measured by God's holy law, and have God's glory as their goal.

2. The first rule has reference to "aged men." [196] Says Paul, **that aged men be temperate, dignified, self-controlled, sound in their faith, in their love, (and) in their endurance.**

The greybeards should have the same moral characteristics as the elders and the deacons. Titus must *urge* (here in verse 2 the verb of verse 6 is probably implied) them to be *temperate* or *sober,* that is, moderate with respect to the use of wine (see verse 3) and in all their tastes and habits (cf. I Tim. 3:2, 11). They must also be *dignified,* that is grave, venerable, serious, respectable (cf. I Tim. 3:5, 8, 11); *self-controlled* or *sensible,* that is, men of mature judgment and proper restraint (cf. Titus 1:8; then I Tim. 3:2); and *sound* (see on verse 1; especially footnote 193); not *morbid* (cf. I Tim. 6:4; then Rom. 14:1), but healthy and even health-imparting: spreading health, moral and spiritual, in every direction (cf. Titus 1:9, 13; then I Tim. 1:10; 6:3; II Tim. 1:13; 4:3).

This soundness must be shown with respect to *the* faith, *the* love, and *the* endurance. Here the article is perhaps best rendered by the possessive *their . . . their . . . their.* Their faith, in order to be sound, must be neither luke-warm nor mixed with error (cf. Titus 1:14). Their love must not deteriorate into sentimentality nor must it be permitted to wax cold (Matt. 24:12; Rev. 2:4). And their endurance must not be replaced by either faint-heartedness on the one hand or obstinacy on the other.

In their attitude *toward God* let the aged men show *soundness in their faith.* Let them rely wholly on him and his revealed truth. In their attitude *toward the neighbor* let them evince *soundness in their love.* And in their attitude *toward bitter trials* let them reveal *soundness in their endurance* or *stedfastness* (for a word-study of this term see N.T.C. on I and II Thessalonians, pp. 136-137 – footnote 108 – ; 155, 156; and pp. 197, 198).

---

196 Titus has the sequence: *aged men, aged women, young women, young(er) men,* a chiastic arrangement. I Tim. 5:1, 2 has: *old(er) man, young(er) men, old(er) women, young(er) women.* Note that three of the words in the first list differ from the three corresponding words in the second list. "Aged man" (πρεσβύτης cf. Philem. 9) cannot mean church-elder, but the word which in I Tim. 5:1 has been rendered "old(er) man" (πρεσβύτερος) has elsewhere in the Pastorals the meaning church-elder (I Tim. 5:17, 19; Titus 1:5). "Aged woman" (πρεσβῦτις) is fem. of πρεσβύτης, the prose form of πρέσβυς, but "old(er) woman" is compar. adj. as subst. Finally, "young woman" is the adj. *young, youthful,* with fem. ending, as subst.; but "young(er) woman" is the compar. of the same adj. However, as remarked in connection with I Tim. 5:1, at times the comparative idea seems to have almost vanished.

3. To the four requirements for aged men four somewhat similar requirements for aged women are now added: **(urge) aged women similarly (to be) reverent in demeanor, not slanderers and not enslaved to much wine, teachers of that which is excellent.**

In their entire bearing (hence, not only in their *dress,* I Tim. 2:9) as well as in their deportment, aged women must be *reverent,* conducting themselves as if they were servants in God's temple, for such, indeed, they are! Cf. Rev. 1:6. The theme-song of these aged women (as well as of all members of the Christian family) must ever be:

"Fill thou my life, O Lord my God,
In every part with praise,
That my whole being may proclaim
Thy being and thy ways.
Not for the lip of praise alone,
Nor e'en the praising heart,
I ask, but for a life made up
Of praise in every part.

"Praise in the common words I speak,
Life's common looks and tones,
In intercourse at hearth or board
With my beloved ones,
Enduring wrong, reproach, or loss,
With sweet and stedfast will,
Loving and blessing those who hate,
Returning good for ill."

(Horatius Bonar, 1866)

Note how "not *slanderers*" (on which see I Tim. 3:11) and *"not enslaved by much wine"* are combined. Wine-drinking and malicious gossip often go together. (For *wine-drinking* see the remarks on I Tim. 3:8 and on I Tim. 5:23.) Aged women, then, must be temperate, just like aged men. They must not become *enslaved to* (for this figurative sense see also Rom. 6:18, 22; I Cor. 9:19; Gal. 4:3) much wine. On the contrary, by their godly example they must be "teachers of that which is excellent" (cf. I Peter 3:1, 2).

4 and 5. Such "teaching by way of example" has as one of its purposes the "training" of the younger married women. Hence, Paul continues: **so that they may train the young women to be:**

a. **loving toward their husbands** (or **husband-lovers**) **and**

b. **loving toward their children** (or **children-lovers**),

c. **self-controlled,**

d. **chaste,**

e. **workers at home,**

f. **kind,**

g. **submissive to their own husbands.**

One understands immediately that no one – not even Titus – is better able to train a young woman than an experienced, older woman. Note the emphasis on *love.* The Christian young woman must be trained *to love* her husband and *to love* her children. Was it not *love* that saved her? See John 3:16. This love, coming from heaven, being shed abroad in the heart, must "flow out" toward others; and certainly among those "others" a young woman's own husband and her own children should occupy a very prominent place. Moreover, the Christian virtue of *self-control* – that same virtue which is demanded not only of overseers (Titus 1:8; then I Tim. 3:2) but also of aged men in general (verse 2 above), and which is implied in what is demanded of aged women (verse 3 above) – is a most necessary requirement for any practical Christian wife and mother. Such younger women must scrupulously avoid any immorality in thought, word, and action. Their attention, moreover, must be concentrated on their own families. Hence, not only must they be *chaste* but also *workers at home* (see on I Tim. 2:10 and especially on I Tim. 5:13). The two virtues quite obviously are related. Now, while performing their tasks in the family, these young women must take care that the constant strain of domestic duties does not make them irritable or cruel. They must pray for grace to remain *kind,* and this not only to husbands and children but also to slaves.[197] Moreover, lest Christian women should begin to think that their equality in spiritual standing before God and the great liberty which has now become their portion as believers (Gal. 3:28) entitles them to forget about God's creation-ordinance regarding the relation to their husbands (Gen. 3:16), Paul, inspired by the Holy Spirit, adds that they must be "submissive to their own husbands" (see also on I Tim. 2:11-15, and cf. Rom. 7:2; I Cor. 7:4; 14:34, 35; Eph. 5:22-24, 33; Col. 3:18; I Peter 3:1-6). Surely, in the light of Gen. 24:67; Eph. 5:22-33; Col. 3:19; I Peter 3:7, when the husband too is a believer, this is not a burden. And when he is not, then "as unto the Lord" makes the burden bearable.

A purpose-clause, in all probability qualifying not only the last requirement but all seven, is now added: **in order that the word of God may not be reviled.** See on I Tim. 6:1. This is characteristically Pauline language; cf. Rom. 2:24. He, in turn, borrowed it from the Old Testament (Is. 52:5).

---

[197] It is possible to accept a different punctuation, so that instead of the rendering "workers at home, kind," we would have to translate (with Bouma and others): "*good workers* at home." But the former is more in keeping with the entire list of requirements. Note that none of the four preceding ones has a modifier; each is a single word: loving-toward-their-husbands (just one word), loving-toward-their-children (again only one word in the original), self-controlled, chaste.

Wrong conduct on the part of the young married women would easily lead to slanderous remarks with respect to the gospel. Not only do *the Greeks* judge a doctrine by its practical effect upon everyday life (Chrysostom), but so does the world in general. If young mothers, professing to be Christians, should manifest lack of love for their husbands and for their children, lack of self-control, of purity, domesticity, kindness, and submissiveness, they would cause the message of salvation to be evil spoken of by outsiders. It must be borne in mind, moreover, that when Paul says "in order that the word of God *may not be reviled,*" he means, "in order that the word of God *may be honored.*" This, too, as noted earlier, is a typically Pauline way of speaking (see pp. 14, 15).

6. The admonition which must be passed along to "the young(er) men" of the various congregations is brief, but in its very brevity it is all-inclusive: **Similarly urge the young(er) men [198] to exercise self-control in every respect.** The fact that this admonition is very brief makes it all the more probable that the phrase "in every respect" belongs here and must not be construed with verse 7. *In every respect,* therefore, whether the attention is focused upon morals or upon doctrine, *young men* must place themselves under the discipline of the gospel, and must guard themselves against being led astray either by the evil promptings of their own sinful nature or by the opinions and customs which prevail in the pagan world round about them. Let them never place their own conclusions, feelings, or ambitions above the will of God (cf. Rom. 12:3; cf. II Cor. 10:5). Let them learn to master themselves. The verb translated "to exercise self-control" is from the same stem as the adjective rendered "self-controlled." Hence, young men are here urged to exercise the same virtue which is demanded of the overseer (Titus 1:8; cf. I Tim. 3:2), of aged men (Titus 2:2), of the young women (verse 4), and, by implication, of aged women (verse 3).

7 and 8. Since Titus, though not as young as Timothy (see p. 38), must probably still be reckoned among the "young(er) men," it is logical that Paul urges him to be an example for the group mentioned in the preceding verse. Says Paul: **showing yourself a model of noble deeds; in your teaching (showing) incorruptibility, dignity; (your) speech (being) sound, incensurable.**

---

[198] What age-limit does the apostle have in mind when he refers to these "young(er) men"? Is he thinking only of those under forty? (See on I Tim. 4:12 and II Tim. 2:22.) But then, if by "aged men" those of 60 and over are indicated, there would remain a large group — those of 40-60 — for which he has no admonition at all. Hence, "young(er) men" may here indicate all those under 60; or else the age-limit separating the two classes — "aged" and "young(er)" — may have to be lowered somewhat, say to 50 years of age. See Irenaeus, *Against Heresies* II. xxii, 5; also John 8:56, 57.

A similar admonition was addressed to Timothy. He also had been admonished to be *the believers' model* (in speech, in conduct, in love, in faith, in purity). The word *model,* too, is exactly the same; hence, see on I Tim. 4:12 (cf. II Thess. 3:9; Phil. 3:17). Note the beautiful co-ordination: Titus must a. *admonish* the young(er) men (verse 6), and b. *give them a good example* (verses 7 and 8). *Precept and example must go hand in hand.* Precept alone will never do, for often "*Example* draws where *Precept* fails." [199] The young(er) men of the various congregations entrusted to the care of Titus must be able to see in their leader what *noble deeds* really are. Note the constant emphasis in the Pastorals on these *noble deeds* or *good works.* May this not be considered a reaction, on the part of Paul, to the misrepresentation and abuse of his doctrine of "salvation by grace"?

In his teaching, Titus must show *incorruptibility.* He must give such clear and courageous instruction in the well-balanced truth of the gospel that it is evident to all that he has not been and cannot be *infected* with the lies and distortions of the adversaries. Moreover, his attitude and the manner in which he presents his teaching must be that of *dignity* or *seriousness.* Not only must his more formal teaching be characterized by purity of contents and gravity of method, but his entire *speech* (his *word* whenever and wherever it is spoken), whether it is uttered in the form of a sermon, a lesson, a message of consolation, or even an ordinary daily conversation, must be *sound* and *incensurable,* that is, not open to just rebuke (cf. synonym in I Tim. 6:4).

Now the intended result or purpose of such conduct is: **so that (or: in order that) he that is on the opposite (side) may be put to shame, having nothing evil to report concerning us.** As to the expression "on the opposite (side)" or "of the opposite (party)" – the ellipse is obscure –, note that it was the centurion who stood "over against" or "facing" Jesus on the cross (Mark 15:39). We read of *contrary* winds (Matt. 14:24; Mark 6:48; Acts 27:4). In the passage under discussion the ἀντί-compound is used in a metaphorical sense; opposition here amounts to *hostility* (cf. Acts 26:9; 28:17; I Thess. 2:15). The one on the opposite (side) is the spiritual *adversary* (cf. I Tim. 5:14; II Tim. 2:25). The reference is especially to any one of the Cretan errorists described in Titus 1:10-16.

Now when the opponent begins to notice that his shrewd little plan of spreading malicious gossip about Titus or of preferring formal charges against him miscarries, because the irreproachable conduct of Paul's representative completely disproves the insinuations and accusations that were aimed against him, this enemy of the truth will be put to shame (as in

---

[199] Nam parum alioqui autoritatis habebit doctrina, nisi in vita episcopi, tanquam in speculo, vis eius et maiestas eluceat. Vult ergo doctorem esse exemplar, cui se discipuli conforment (John Calvin on this passage).

II Thess. 3:14; I Cor. 4:14). He will look foolish, "having nothing *evil* (cf. II Cor. 5:10) to report concerning" . . . here we expect that the next word will be "you" (Titus), but it actually is "us," for the antagonism is directed not against Titus as a separate individual but against him as a disciple of Christ; hence, really against Christ himself and all his messengers.

9 and 10. To the family belonged also *slaves.* In his first epistle to Timothy the apostle distinguishes between slaves who had believing masters and those who did not (I Tim. 6:1, 2). Here in Titus no such distinction is made. The command is to be transmitted to all slaves who hear the gospel; no doubt especially to all *believing* slaves. Says Paul, **(Urge) slaves to be submissive in every respect to their own masters, to be eager to please (them), not talking back (or: not rebellious), not pilfering, but evincing the utmost trustworthiness.**

For a discussion of the slavery-question in Paul's day see on I Tim. 6:1, 2. Had all masters and slaves everywhere taken to heart the inspired words of Paul anent slavery, this institution would have perished from the earth without blood-baths. – A superficial glance at the passage now under discussion might cause one to think that their author is hardly fair to the slave, neglecting to point out the equality of slave and master before God, and apparently condoning the sins of the master. But this inference would be erroneous, for it overlooks two important facts: a. Titus 2:9, 10 contains only *part* of Paul's teaching with respect to the master-slave relationship (see also Eph. 5:8, 9; Col. 3:25; 4:1; Philem. 16); and b. even here in the Titus-passage the immediately following context (note particularly verse 11) stresses the full equality of *all* believers, bond and free, from the aspect of God's redeeming grace.

The verb of verse 6 is again implied; hence, "*Urge* or *admonish* slaves." The three points with respect to which slaves must be admonished are:

(1) *D*eportment.

The slave must comply with the wishes of his master, and this "in every respect" (cf. Col. 3:22; then Eph. 5:24). From morning until evening and in every category of work the slave must be submissive to his master. It is hardly necessary to add that this phrase "in every respect" must not be taken in the absolute sense, as if the apostle meant to say that even then when the master demanded of the slave that he tell a lie or commit thievery, adultery, or murder, the latter must obey. The purpose-clause at the close of verse 10 implies a restriction, for surely by agreeing to sin the slave would never be able to "adorn the doctrine of God our Savior." And see also Acts 4:19; 5:29; Eph. 5:21.[200]

---

[200] I see no need, therefore, of adopting the view of Bouma and others, that ἀγαθήν (verse 10, the best text) is a limiting word and must be translated "with respect to

(2) *D*isposition

External compliance with the will of the master is not enough, however. Growling and grumbling underneath are also forbidden. The sullen disposition has never yet won a soul for Christ. Slaves, accordingly must be *eager to please, well-pleasing*. This adjective is typically Pauline: elsewhere the apostle uses it no less than *seven* times, while in all the rest of the New Testament it occurs only *once* (Heb. 13:21). And even if we add to this one occurrence the number of times Hebrews employs the cognate verb and adverb (fairness requires that we make this addition!), the frequency-ratio is still 7-5 (or if the reference in Titus is included 8-5) in favor of Paul.

The negative aspect of being well-pleasing is *not talking back*. This ἀντί-compound occurs nine times in the New Testament: Luke 2:34; 20:27; John 19:12; Acts 13:45; 28:19; 28:22; Rom. 10:21; Titus 1:9; 2:9. The cognate noun occurs in four passages: Heb. 6:16; 7:7; 12:3; and Jude 11. Although the basic meaning is that of *talking back,* it often conveys the overtone of *active disobedience, resistance, rebellion, strife*. See, for example, Rom. 10:21; Heb. 12:3; Jude 11. It probably has that coloring here also. Thus interpreted, the two expressions make a fitting pair: "well-pleasing" and "not rebellious" in disposition.

(3) *D*ependability.

When the master's back was turned, petty larceny was often committed. Such pilfering or purloining, whereby the slave secretly *holds back* (cf. the use of the verb in Acts 5:2, 3) or *withdraws* (sets apart for himself) a portion of that which belongs to his master, must not be excused by saying, "The master owes me much more than this, for he has taken away my freedom and he is robbing me of my strength and talents, all without adequate compensation." The slave must show "the utmost *trustworthiness*" (or "fidelity," Rom. 3:3b; cf. I Tim. 5:12; then Gal. 5:22).

Now the reason for the demand that slaves display a submissive deportment, an ingratiating disposition, and utmost dependability is this: **so that in every respect they may adorn the doctrine of God our Savior.** A sanctified life, which brings into clear perspective all the fruits of transforming grace — obedience, cheerfulness, integrity, etc. — scintillating like so many precious jewels, is an ornament to "the doctrine of *God our Savior*" (see on I Tim. 1:1), the Christian faith. It should cause masters to exclaim, "If the Christian religion does this even for slaves, it must be wonderful!"

---

that which is good." More natural would seem to be the construction which gave rise to the rendering found in the A.V. and A.R.V.: "showing all good fidelity." One might regard the original as an idiom for "evincing the utmost trustworthiness." Cf. the original in Titus 3:2; II Tim. 4:14.

11 For the grace of God has appeared, bringing salvation to all men, 12
training us in order that, having renounced ungodliness and those worldly passions, we in the here and now may live lives of self-mastery and fairness and devotion, 13 while we are waiting for the blessed hope, the appearing of the glory of
our great God and Savior Christ Jesus, 14 who gave himself for us in order to
redeem us from all lawlessness and to purify for himself a people, his very own,
with a zest for noble deeds.
15 These things keep on telling (them) and urging (upon them) and reproving with all authority. Let no one slight you.

2:11-15

11-14. *The grace of God considered as the reason why every member of The Christian Family can and should live a Christian life,* this is the theme of one of the richest passages of Holy Writ. Note the four main thoughts:

1. verse 11 *The Grace of God in Christ is the Great Penetrator, Dispelling the Darkness for All and Bringing Salvation to All.*

Says Paul, **For the grace of God has appeared, bringing salvation to all men.**

God's grace is his active favor bestowing the greatest gift upon those who have deserved the greatest punishment. (For a word-study of the concept *grace* see N.T.C. on I Thess. 1:1.) This grace has *penetrated* our moral and spiritual darkness. It "has appeared." The verb used in the original is related to the noun *epiphany,* that is, *appearing* or *manifestation* (for example, of the sun at sunrise). Upon those sitting in the darkness and in the shadow of death the grace of God had suddenly dawned (see also Mal. 4:2; Luke 1:79; Acts 27:20; and Titus 3:4). It had arisen when Jesus was born, when words of life and beauty issued from his lips, when he healed the sick, cleansed the lepers, cast out demons, raised the dead, suffered for man's sins, and laid down his life for the sheep in order to take it again on resurrection-morning. Thus, grace had "shed on the world Christ's holy light" and had "chased the dark night of sin away." The sun of righteousness had arisen "with healing in its wings." The grace of God had appeared *"saving* (σωτήριος) for all men." Everywhere else in the New Testament this word *saving,* when preceded by the article and used as a noun, means *salvation* (Luke 2:30; 3:6; Acts 28:28; Eph. 6:17), in the spiritual sense of the term. Hence, also here in Titus 2:11 the meaning is: God's grace made its appearance "salvation-bringing." Grace came to rescue man from the greatest possible evil, namely, the curse of God upon sin; and to bestow upon him the greatest possible boon, namely, the blessing of God for soul and body throughout all eternity. (For a word-study of the concept *salvation* see on I Tim. 1:15.)

It brought this salvation to "all men." For a detailed explanation of this expression see on I Tim. 2:1. Here in Titus 2:11 the context makes the meaning very clear. Male or female, old or young, rich or poor: *all* are guilty before God, and from them *all* God gathers his people. Aged men, aged women, young women, young(er) men, and even slaves (see verses 1-10) should live consecrated lives, *for* the grace of God has appeared bringing salvation to men of *all* these various groups or classes. "All men" here in verse 11 = "us" in verse 12. Grace did not bypass the aged because they are aged, nor women because they are women, nor slaves because they are merely slaves, etc. It dawned upon *all,* regardless of age, sex, or social standing. Hence, no one can derive, from the particular group or caste to which he belongs, a reason for not living a Christian life.

2. verse 12 *The Grace of God in Christ is the Wise Pedagogue.*

The words which convey this thought are: **training us in order that, having renounced ungodliness and those worldly passions, we in the here and now may live lives of self-mastery and fairness and devotion.**

Grace *trains.* See on I Tim. 1:20. The verb used in the original is from the same stem as is the noun *pedagogue.* A pedagogue leads children step by step. Thus, grace, too, gently leads and guides. It does not throw things into confusion. It does not suddenly and forcefully upset the social order. For example, it does not abruptly order masters to free their slaves; nor does it unwisely command slaves to rebel forthwith against their masters. On the contrary, it gradually causes masters to see that the encroachment upon the liberty of their fellows is a great wrong, and it convinces slaves that resort to force and vengeance is not the solution to every problem. Grace *trains* by teaching (Acts 7:22; 22:3), chastening (I Tim. 1:20; II Tim. 2:25; then Luke 23:16, 22; I Cor. 11:32; II Cor. 6:9; Heb. 12:6-11; Rev. 3:19), counseling, comforting, encouraging, admonishing, guiding, convicting, rewarding, restraining, etc.

The purpose of all this is stated first negatively, then positively (which is a Pauline style-characteristic). *Negatively,* it induces us to *renounce* or *reject* (the verb has here the same meaning as in Acts 3:13; 7:35) *ungodliness,* impiety, wickedness (see on II Tim. 2:16). Study the vivid description of "ungodliness" in Rom. 1:18-32 (note the very word in Rom. 1:18; cf. 11:26). Such ungodliness is *idolatry* plus *immorality,* both terms taken in their most comprehensive meaning. When grace takes over, the sinner repudiates ungodliness. This repudiation is a definite act, a decision to give up that which is displeasing to God. No one *sleeps* his way into heaven. Rejecting ungodliness implies the renunciation of "those worldly passions" – strong, sinful desires – as well. (See word-study of the term *passion* or *desire* in connection with the exegesis of II Tim. 2:22.) According to scriptural usage, such worldly or sinful desires include the following: inordinate sexual desire, the liquor-mania, excessive yearning for material possessions, self-assertiveness (hence, quarrelsomeness, vanity, the lust to dominate), etc. Briefly, it refers to inordinate longing for pleasure, power, and possessions. See also I John 2:16, and on Titus 3:3.

Positively, grace trains us in order that "in the here and now" (*this present age;* cf. I Tim. 6:17; II Tim. 4:10; then Rom. 12:2; I Cor. 1:20; II Cor. 4:4; contrasted with *the coming age* in Eph. 1:21; cf. Mark 10:30) we may live lives which display a changed relation:

a. *to oneself:* "selfmastery," making the proper use of such desires or drives as are not sinful in themselves, and overcoming those that are sinful;

b. *to the neighbor:* "fairness," honesty, justice, integrity in dealing with others;

c. *to God:* "devotion," godliness, true piety and reverence with respect to him who alone is the proper Object of worship.

3. verse 13 *The Grace of God in Christ is the Effective Preparer.*

We – aged men, aged women, young women, young men, slaves, etc. – should live a Christian life because through the power of God's grace **we are waiting for the blessed hope, the appearing of the glory of our great God and Savior Christ Jesus.**

The grace of God trains us in order that we may *live* consecrated lives, *while we are waiting for* [201] the blessed hope. The *waiting for* or *patient looking forward to* modifies the *living,* of which it is an attendant circumstance or further explication. It is "the blessed hope" for which believers are waiting. This is metonymy for *the realization of that hope* (that is, the realization of our earnest yearning, confident expectation, and patient waiting). We find a similar metonymy in Gal. 5:5; Col. 1:5 (to which some interpreters would add Heb. 6:18).

This hope is called *blessed.* It imparts bliss, happiness, delight, and glory. The adjective *blessed* is used in connection with *God* in I Tim. 1:11; 6:15; see on these passages.

Now, even *the possession* of the hopeful spirit and *the exercise* of hope is blessed, because of hope's:

(1) immovable foundation (I Tim. 1:1, 2; then Rom. 5:5; 15:4; Phil. 1:20; Heb. 6:19; I Peter 1:3, 21);

---

[201] The present participle προσδεχόμενοι is here used in a sense in which Luke often (and Paul never elsewhere) employs the word (Luke 2:25, 38; 12:36; 23:51). Paul uses it in the sense of *receiving favorably, welcoming* (Rom. 16:2; Phil. 2:29; thus also Luke in Luke 15:2). But this is no valid argument against the Pauline authorship of the Pastorals or the Lucan authorship of Luke 15:2. Luke and Paul were friends. Besides, if Paul's nephew could use the word in the sense of *waiting for* (Acts 23:21), why not Paul himself? And, if the answer to this should be, "But it is Luke, and not Paul's nephew, who is responsible for the word in Acts 23:21," the reply to this is once again, "Luke and Paul were friends!"

(2) glorious Author (Rom. 15:13; cf. II Thess. 2:16);

(3) wonderful object (everlasting life, salvation, glory: Titus 1:2; 3:7; then I Thess. 5:8; then Rom. 5:2; Col. 1:27);

(4) precious effects (endurance, I Thess. 1:3; "boldness of speech," II Cor. 3:12; and purification of life, I John 3:3);

(5) and everlasting character (I Cor. 13:13).

Then surely *the realization* of this hope will be blessed, indeed! Read Dan. 12:3; Matt. 25:34-40; Rom. 8:20b; I Cor. 15:51, 52; I Thess. 4:13-18; II Thess. 1:10; Rev. 14:14-16; 19:6-9. In fact, the certainty of the realization imparts strength to the hope, and results in the graces mentioned under (4) above.

Now the realization of the blessed hope is "the appearing in glory." [202] Note the two appearings. There had been *one* (see on verse 11; cf. II Tim. 1:10). There is going to be *another* (see N.T.C. on II Thess. 2:8; cf. I Tim. 6:14; II Tim. 4:1, 8). It will be the appearing of . . . well, of whom? Throughout the history of interpretation that question has divided grammarians and commentators. Are we waiting for the appearing in glory of *one* Person or of *two Persons?*

Those who endorse the *one-Person* view favor the rendering:

"of our great God and Savior Christ Jesus." (Another reading has "Jesus Christ," but that makes no difference in connection with the point at issue.) Now if that view be correct, those who accept Scripture's infallibility have in this passage an additional prooftext for the deity of Christ; and even those who do not accept Scripture's infallibility but who do accept the *one-Person* rendering must admit that at least the author of the Pastorals (perhaps erroneously, according to them) held Jesus to be one in essence with God the Father. The *one-Person* rendering is favored by the A.R.V. margin, Weymouth, Goodspeed, Berkeley Version, R.S.V., and many commentators: Van Oosterzee, Bouma, Lenski, Gealy, Simpson, etc. The great New Testament grammarian A. T. Robertson has given a strong defence of this view, from the standpoint of grammar, basing his arguments upon Granville Sharp's rule.

Among others, John Calvin was unwilling to choose between the *one-Person* and the *two-Persons* rendering. Yet, he emphasized that on either view the purpose of the passage is to state that when Christ appears, the

---

[202] Literally the text reads "the appearing of the glory." Some (for example, A.V., Berkeley Version, Goodspeed) prefer the rendering "the glorious appearing." Others (for example, Lenski and White) object to this rendering. Yet, I cannot see that the objection is very formidable. If the expression "the steward of the unrighteousness" (Luke 16:8) means "the unrighteous steward," why cannot the phrase "the appearing of the glory" mean "the glorious appearing"? But whether a person translates one way or the other, the resultant meaning is about the same, namely, "the appearing in glory" (as Weymouth renders the phrase and as Bouma and others interpret it). Cf. Matt. 25:31; Mark 13:26; II Thess. 1:10.

greatness of the divine glory will be revealed in him (cf. Luke 9:26); and that, accordingly, the passage can by no means give any comfort to the Arians in their attempt to prove that the Son is less divine than the Father.

The *two-Persons* theory is represented, with minor variations, in the versions of Wyclif, Tyndale, Cranmer, A.V., A.R.V. (text), Moffatt, and R.S.V. (margin). It has been supported by a long list of commentators (among whom are De Wette, Huther, White [in *The Expositor's Bible*], E. F. Scott, etc.) and especially by the grammarian G. B. Winer.

The rendering then becomes:

"of the great God and the (or "and of the") Savior Jesus Christ."

Winer was willing to admit that his endorsement of this view was based not so much upon grammar — which, as even he admitted, *allowed* the one-Person rendering — as upon "the dogmatic conviction derived from Paul's writings that this apostle cannot have called Christ *the great God.*" (Such argumentation encounters difficulty in interpreting Rom. 9:5; Phil. 2:6; Col. 1:15-20; Col. 2:9; etc.) But he should have noticed that even the very context (verse 14) ascribes to *Jesus* functions which in the Old Testament are ascribed to *Jehovah,* such as *redeeming* and *purifying* (II Sam. 7:23; Ps. 130:8; Hos. 13:14; then Ezek. 37:23); and that the word *Savior* is in each of the three chapters of Titus ascribed first to *God,* then to *Jesus* (Titus 1:3, 4; 2:10, 13; 3:4, 6). It is therefore evidently the purpose of the author of this epistle (namely, Paul!) to show that Jesus is fully divine, just as fully as is Jehovah or as is the Father.

The *one-Person* rendering must be considered the correct one. It is supported by the following considerations:

(1) Unless in any specific instance there are strong reasons to the contrary, the rule holds that when the first of two nouns of the same case and connected by the conjunction *and* is preceded by the article, which is not repeated before the second noun, these two nouns refer to *the same person.* When the article is repeated before the second noun, *two persons* are indicated. Examples:

a. The article, preceding the first of two nouns and *not* repeated before the second: "*the* brother y o u r and fellow-partaker." The two nouns refer to *the same person,* John, and the expression is correctly translated, "y o u r brother and fellow-partaker" (Rev. 1:9).

b. Two articles, one preceding each noun: "Let him be unto you as *the* Gentile and *the* tax-collector" (Matt. 18:17). The two nouns refer to *two persons* (in this case, each representing a class).

Now, according to this rule the disputed words in Titus 2:13 clearly refer to *one* Person, namely, Christ Jesus, for when translated word for word the phrase reads:

"of *the* great God and of Savior our Christ Jesus." The article before the first noun is not repeated before the second, and therefore the expression must be rendered:

"of our great God and Savior Christ Jesus."

No valid reason has ever been found which would show that the (Granville Sharp) rule does not apply in the present case.[203] In fact, it is generally admitted that the words which in the original occur at the close of II Peter 1:11 refer to *one* Person, and must be rendered, "our Lord and Savior Jesus Christ." But if that be true, then why should not the *essentially* identical idiom in II Peter 1:1 and here in Titus 2:13 be rendered, "our God and Savior Jesus Christ" (or "Christ Jesus")?

(2) Nowhere in the entire New Testament is the term *epiphany (appearing* or *manifestation)* used with respect to more than *one* Person. Also, the *one* Person to whom it refers is always Christ (see II Thess. 2:8; I Tim. 6:14; II Tim. 4:1; II Tim. 4:8; and II Tim. 1:10, where the reference is to the First Coming).

(3) The phraseology here in Titus 2:13 may well have been framed in reaction to the type of language that was often used by the heathen with respect to their own idol-gods, whom they regarded as "saviors," and particularly to the phraseology in connection with the worship of earthly rulers. Was not Ptolemy I called "Savior and God"? Were not Antiochus and Julius Cesar addressed as "God Manifest"? [204] Paul indicates that believers look forward to the Appearing of the One who is *really* God and Savior, yes "our great (exalted, glorious) God and Savior, namely, Christ Jesus."

The real "point" of the passage, in connection with all that has preceded, is that our joyful expectation of the appearing in glory of our great God and Savior Christ Jesus *effectively prepares* us for the life with him. How does it do this? First, because the Second Coming will be so altogether glorious that believers will not want to "miss out on" it, but will want to "be manifested with him in glory" (Col. 3:4). Secondly, because the blissful expectation fills believers with gratitude, and gratitude produces preparedness, by God's grace.

4. verse 14 *The Grace of God in Christ is the Thorough-going Purifier.*

---

[203] See Gram. N.T., pp. 785-787; also same author (A. T. Robertson), *The Minister And His Greek New Testament,* New York, 1923, pp. 61-68. Now if it could be established that not only is σωτῆρ a proper name but that in addition Paul generally refers the epiphany to two Persons, we would have something parallel to the expression "of *the* God our and of Lord Jesus Christ" where in spite of the *one* article the reference is in all probability to *two* Persons, and the phrase can be rendered: "of our God and of the Lord Jesus Christ" (II Thess. 1:12). See N.T.C. on I and II Thessalonians, p. 164, the last paragraph, and also footnote 117 on that page. But II Thess. 1:12 and Titus 2:13 are not identical.

[204] See E. Stauffer, *Christ and the Caesars,* Philadelphia, 1955 (reviewed in *WThJ,* XVIII, Number 2 (May, 1956), pp. 171-176. And see also footnote 76.

Our great God and Savior Christ Jesus to whose appearing in glory believers look forward with such hope and joy is the One **who gave himself for us in order to redeem us from all lawlessness and to purify for himself a people, his very own, with a zest for noble deeds.**

For the meaning of "who gave himself for us in order to redeem us" see on I Tim. 2:6, "who gave himself a ransom for all." Anyone who doubts the necessary, objective, voluntary, expiatory, propitiatory, substitutionary, and efficacious character of the act of Christ whereby he gave himself for us should make a diligent, contextual study of the following passages: [205]

Old Testament	*New Testament*		
Gen. 2:16, 17	Matt. 20:28	I Cor. 7:23	Heb. 9:28
Ex. 12:13	Matt. 26:27, 28	II Cor. 5:18-21	I Peter 1:18, 19
Lev. 1:4	Mark 10:45	Gal. 1:4	I Peter 2:24
Lev. 16:20-22	Luke 22:14-23	Gal. 2:20	I Peter 3:18
Lev. 17:11	John 1:29	Gal. 3:13	I John 2:2
II Sam. 7:23	John 6:55	Eph. 1:7	I John 4:10
Psalm 40:6, 7	Acts 20:28	Eph. 2:16	Rev. 5:12
Psalm 130:8	Rom. 3:25	Eph. 5:6	Rev. 7:14.
Isaiah 53	Rom. 5	Col. 1:19-23	
Zech. 13:1	I Cor. 6:20	Heb. 9:22	

He gave nothing less than *himself,* and this *for us,* that is, in our interest and in our stead. The contemplation of this sublime thought should result in a life to his honor. Furthermore, by his sacrificial death he merited for us the work of the Holy Spirit in our hearts. Apart from that Spirit it would be impossible for us to live the sanctified life.

Christ gave himself for us with a twofold purpose: the first negative (see Ps. 130:8), the second positive (see II Sam. 7:23). Negatively, he gave himself for us "in order to redeem us," that is, in order to ransom us from an evil power. The ransom-price was his own precious blood (I Peter 1:18, 19). And the power from which we are delivered is that of "lawlessness" (see N.T.C. on II Thess. 2:3), that is, indwelling disobedience to God's holy law, in whatever form that disobedience makes itself manifest ("*all* lawlessness").

Positively, he gave himself for us "in order to purify for himself a people," that is, in order by means of his blood and Spirit to purify us (Eph. 5:26; Heb. 9:14; I John 1:7, 9), so that, thus purified, we are fit to be a people, *his very own* (see footnote 193 and cf. Ezek. 37:23). Formerly *Israel* was Jehovah's peculiar people; now *the church* is. And just as Israel was characterized by zeal for the law (Acts 21:20; cf. Gal. 1:14), so now

---

[205] Read also A. A. Hodge, *The Atonement,* Philadelphia, 1867; and L. Berkhof, *Vicarious Atonement Through Christ,* Grand Rapids, Mich., 1936.

Christ purifies his people with this very purpose in mind, namely, that it shall be a people for his own possession "with a zest for noble deeds," deeds which proceed from faith, are done according to God's law and unto his glory (cf. I Peter 3:13).

In summary, verses 11-14 teach us that the reason why every member of the family should live a life of self-mastery, fairness, and devotion is that the grace of God in Christ has penetrated our moral and spiritual darkness and has brought salvation to all men; that this grace is also our Great Pedagogue who leads us away from ungodliness and worldly passions and guides us along the path of holiness; that it is the Effective Preparer who causes us to look forward with eagerness to the Appearing in glory of our great God and Savior Christ Jesus; and, finally, that it is the thorough-going Purifier, so that, redeemed from all disobedience to God's law, we become Christ's peculiar treasure, filled with a zest for excellent deeds.

15. As a fitting conclusion to the entire chapter (in a sense to both chapters) Paul adds: **These things keep on telling (them) and urging (upon them) and reproving, with all authority.**

Titus must never grow slack in his duty. He must continue to do what he has been doing all along. He must constantly *talk* (see on verse 1) about this glorious life of sanctification as a thank-offering presented to God for his wonderful grace in Christ. He must *urge* it upon the people, doing this whenever the occasion presents itself, *admonishing* (see on verse 6) those who are in need of special admonition, and even *reproving* (see on Titus 1:9, 13) those who have merited reproof. All this he must do "with all authority," the authority of Christ whom he represents.

Let no one slight you. Cf. I Tim. 4:12. Titus must conduct himself in such a manner that no one will "think around" him; that is, that no one will in his heart and mind "by-pass," disregard or ignore Titus, thinking, "Never mind what *he* has said about this or that matter." Though this command is addressed *directly* to Titus who must take it to heart, it will also *indirectly* help him in the performance of his duties, namely, when it is read to the various presbyters and congregations.

---

[193] Because of its many words or expressions that occur only once — *hapax legomena* — the second chapter of Titus is among those portions of the Pastorals on which the critics concentrate in order to prove that Paul cannot in any sense have been the author. But do *the facts* support this conclusion? *I am convinced that they do not.* A long list of such words may look very impressive, but in the final analysis it is not the mere *number* of such words that counts but their *nature.*

By means of the summary which follows, I wish to show that *every word* of this chapter is of such a character that no one has a right to say, "Paul cannot have written it." The vocabulary of Titus 2 may be summarized as follows:

(1) Many of the words used in this chapter are more or less common in the Greek language or at least in Koine Greek. Surely, no argument against Pauline authorship can be based upon them.

(2) Then, among the remaining words there are those which elsewhere in the New Testament are used only by Paul. How can they prove that Paul could not have written the Pastorals?

(3) Again, there are those which elsewhere are used only by Paul's frequent companion and close friend, Luke, or elsewhere only by Luke and by Paul. No argument against Pauline authorship can be derived from them either, as is obvious.

(4) Among the words which in the New Testament occur only here in the second chapter of Titus or only in the Pastorals, there are those which are known to have been used by other authors living in or very close to Paul's own time. How can it be argued that Paul could not have used those words which he heard round about him? Or, some of the words were known to Paul because he had found them in the LXX.

(5) There are also words which, though occurring only once or only a few times in the Pastorals, and nowhere else in the New Testament, are close cognates of words used by Paul and/or by Luke. Now if an author has written "nicely," is it impossible for him to use the word "nice"?

In this same connection, there are words which, though occurring only here, follow a typically Pauline pattern. Let us imagine that a certain author, John Brown, in works which by common consent are ascribed to him, has been using a series of substantives in which the word *snow* occurs as a component element; e.g., "snow-field," "snow-flake," "snow-pigeon," "snow-flower," etc. Now, in a writing of disputed authorship the word "snow-ball" is used. Would it be reasonable, in such a case, to argue as follows: "John Brown cannot have written this particular book, for the word *snow-ball* does not occur in any of his recognized literary products"? Would it not be more reasonable to say, "It is surely *possible* that John Brown wrote this book, for he is the very man who is fond of combinations containing the word *snow*"?

Analysis of the Words Occurring in Titus, Chapter 2

A. *Words of more or less Common Usage*

All the words of verse 1 belong to this class. Such words as "But," "you," "speak," and "the," are, of course, very common.

As to "being sound," this, too, is an expression that is by no means limited to the Pastorals. Luke and John also use it. Much has been made, however, of the following three arguments:

(1) In the Pastorals this word is used in a superphysical sense; elsewhere in a merely physical sense.

(2) In the Pastorals the word has a philosophical meaning. It means "in accordance with reason." It is in that sense that one's teaching or doctrine must be "sound." Hence, *Paul* cannot have written the Pastorals, for he asserted that *his* gospel is not based on human reason but is "foolishness" to the world (I Cor. 2:6, 14). An unknown author borrowed words and concepts from the Hellenistic literature of his own day. (See M. Dibelius, *Die Pastoralbriefe,* second edition, Tübingen, 1931, p. 14.)

(3) In the Pastorals this word is used with great frequency.

But over against this threefold argument against Pauline authorship stands the following:

In answer to (1). See Prov. 13:13 (LXX). Here "being sound" cannot be restricted to man's physical frame.

In answer to (2). In the Pastorals "being sound" is not an antonym of "being irrational" but of "being morally and spiritually perverted," as appears most clearly from Titus 1:12, 13. It is true, of course, that man's intellect, too, is beclouded when he resists the will of God.

In answer to (3). The frequency with which a certain term is used does not necessarily prove difference in authorship. It may simply prove difference in subject-matter and general situation. Is it really impossible to picture *Paul,* the aged, deeply concerned about the question whether the church will remain loyal to "sound" doctrine?

The final word of verse 1 – namely, "doctrine" – is also rather common. Matthew and Mark both use it. So does Paul in Rom. 12:7; 15:4; Eph. 4:14; and Col. 2:22.

Hence, nothing whatever against Pauline authorship can be based upon any of the words found in verse 1. And the same holds with respect to the "more or less common words" used in the rest of the chapter. It would be a waste of time, therefore, to pay any further attention to words of that class in this brief summary.

B. *Words which elsewhere in the New Testament occur only in Paul's Epistles*

Thus, "dignified" or "honorable," aside from its use in Titus 2:2 and I Tim. 3:8, is in the New Testament found only in Phil. 4:8; "appearing" (Titus 2:13; cf. I Tim. 6:14; II Tim. 1:10; 4:1, 8) occurs only in II Thess. 2:8; and the word translated "authority" (Titus 2:15; cf. 1:3; I Tim. 1:1) is found only in Rom. 16:26; I Cor. 7:6, 25; II Cor. 8:8, though the cognate verb also occurs in Mark, Luke, and Acts.

Such words would seem to point *toward* Paul rather than *away from* him.

C. *Words which elsewhere in the New Testament are found only in Luke or only in Paul and Luke*

The word "aged man" (Titus 2:2) is found only in Philem. 9 and in Luke 1:18; "embezzle" or "purloin" (Titus 2:10) occurs only in Acts 5:2, 3; "appeared" (Titus 2:11; cf. 3:4) is found only in Luke 1:79; and "bringing salvation" (Titus 2:11) appears elsewhere only in Eph. 6:17; Luke 2:30; 3:6; Acts 28:28, though in these several instances it is neut. as subst. "salvation."

Interesting, although not entirely confined to Paul and Luke, is also the word "waiting for" (see on verse 13). Does the sense in which it is here used betray Lucan influence?

This group of words offers nothing in support of the theory that Paul cannot have written the Pastorals.

D. *Words which in the New Testament occur nowhere outside the Pastorals, but which do occur in earlier and/or contemporary sources*

Verse 3 contains the word "demeanor." It occurs also in Josephus, *Jewish Antiquities* XV. vii. 5. He makes mention of the alleged intrepid *demeanor* of Mariamne, the wife of Herod the Great. It was one of the causes which led to her death by order of her cruel husband. Plutarch (A. D. 46-120) also has the word.

In verse 7 the word "incorruptness" or "incorruptibility" is used. "Untaintedness" or "purity" would be another good rendering. In the sense of *pure* or *chaste* the cognate adjective is found in Esther 2:2 (LXX): "Let *chaste* maidens (virgins), beautiful in form, be sought for the king."

Verse 14 has the expression "people for his own possession." Here περιούσιος is from the verb περίειμι *to be over and above;* hence, *to be left over.* It indicates that which remains to oneself; for example, after the price has been paid; hence, anything which one can call "his very own." The expression is a quotation which occurs again and again in the LXX (Ex. 19:5; 23:22; Deut. 7:6; 14:2; 26:18). In Deut. 7:6 the Hebrew original on which the LXX is based has ʻam ṣ ᵉgullah, "peculiar treasure." As that passage proves, it indicates that Israel is Jehovah's "special possession," his "holy people" because he has chosen it. That act of divine grace raised Israel above all other nations.

Paul was, of course, well acquainted with the LXX. Hence, this quotation (cf. Eph. 1:14; then I Peter 2:9) presents no great problem.

E. *Words which in the New Testament occur nowhere outside the Pastorals, but which follow a Pauline word-pattern*

Nearly all the words which follow could also have been included under D. But in addition to being current in the Greek-speaking world of that day, as most of them were, they follow a Pauline word-pattern, as will be shown:

Verse 3 contains the word "aged woman" (πρεσβῦτις). But this is simply the fem.

of πρεσβύτης. See also footnote 196. Not only is this fem. form found also in IV Macc. 16:14 (LXX) and in several other early and later sources, but Paul has himself used the masc. in Philem. 9 (cf. Titus 2:2).

The same verse (Titus 2:3) also contains the word ἱεροπρεπής, "as is proper for those employed in temple-service" (or *in sacred-service*); hence, reverent, pious. This word is found in the stirring Macabbean story of the mother and her seven sons who were martyred for their loyalty to Jehovah. In connection with the death of the eldest son we read, "And having said this, the *pious* youth died" (IV Macc. 9:25; cf. 11:20; cf. Josephus, *Jewish Antiquities* XI. viii. 5). Although the two expressions do not have exactly the same meaning, nevertheless the one here in Titus ("as is proper for those employed in temple-service") and the one in Eph. 5:3 ("as is proper for saints," and cf. I Cor. 11:13) have enough in common to prevent one from saying that the author of the latter could not have been the author of the former.

Once more turning to verse 3 we find the word καλοδιδάσκαλος, "teacher of that which is excellent." Now it was exactly Paul who loved such compounds, and they were not limited to any particular period of his life as an author. See p. 15. So why could not he who in II Thess. 3:13 wrote *"doers* of that which is excellent" also write *"teachers* of that which is excellent"?

Verse 4 contains the verb σωφρονίζω, to moderate, curb, sober down; then, as here, "to train." It was Xenophon (430-355 B. C.), who, in using as an illustration the training of horses, said, "Fear of the spearmen *curbs* them" (*The Tyrant* X). In the New Testament this verb is found only here. And the cognate περιφρονέω "to slight" is found only in verse 15. Another word from the same stem, which also occurs only once in the entire New Testament, is σωφρόνως, "with self-control," sensibly (verse 12). I might add that the cognate adjective "self-controlled" is found only in I Tim. 3:2; Titus 1:8; 2:2, 5; and that the cognate noun "self-control" is found only in II Tim. 1:7.

But does this mean that Paul could not have written the Pastorals? On the contrary, I find that about half of the words listed separately in the Lexicon, and based upon the stem φρήν, that is, *heart, mind, thought,* occur in one or more of the ten epistles commonly ascribed to Paul. The apostle was very fond of words formed on this stem (see, for example, the original of the following passages: Rom. 2:4; 2:20; 8:6; 12:3; I Cor. 10:15; I Cor. 13:11; I Cor. 14:20; II Cor. 2:2; II Cor. 11:1; II Cor. 11:23; Gal. 6:3; Eph. 1:8; and Phil. 2:3). Is it logical to believe that an author who in Rom. 12:3 used the term ὑπερφρονέω, and who in Phil. 2:3-5 used both φρονέω and ταπεινοφροσύνη could not have used περιφρονέω in Titus 2:15? As to the latter, Plutarch describes Fable as at times obviously *disdaining* to make herself convincing (*Parallel Lives,* Theseus I). The word is also found in IV Macc. 6:9; 14:1 (LXX). But long before this, Thucydides already used it.

Verse 4 also contains the expression φίλανδρος καί φιλότεκνος, here in pl., "loving toward their husbands and loving toward their children." Plutarch used both words in the sense here indicated. And see Deissmann, *Light From the Ancient East,* p. 315. Now the Pastorals contain many composites based on φιλ-, and among them there are several which are not found elsewhere in the New Testament (φιλήδονος, φιλόθεος, φίλανδρος, φιλότεκνος, φιλάγαθος, ἀφιλάγαθος, φιλαργυρία, and φίλαυτος). But this use of words based on φιλ- appears also to have been characteristic of Paul and of Luke. Paul, for example, in his other epistles, *is the only New Testament author* who uses the following: φιλόνεικος, φιλοσοφία, φιλόστοργος, and φιλοτιμέομαι; while his good friend and frequent companion Luke is the only New Testament author in whose writings we find φιλανθρώπως, φιλονεικία, φιλόσοφος, and φιλοφρόνως.

Surely, to say that *Paul* could not have written the Pastorals, because it contains many compounds based on the stem φιλ- is hardly convincing.

Verse 5 contains the noun οἰκουργός, home-worker. (I shall consider this the best reading here, as it seems to agree best with the context.) Now is this really an un-Pauline word, showing that the apostle could not have written the Pastorals? (We can safely permit the medical writer of the second century who also used it to rest in peace.) It was exactly Paul who loved word-formations in ἐργ-, either using them freely wherever he finds them or else perhaps even coining them himself. For ἐργ- compounds in Paul examine the original in the following references, each reference pointing to a different form: Acts 14:17 (Paul speaking); Rom. 4:15; Rom. 15:16; Rom. 16:3; I Cor. 3:9; II Cor. 1:11; II Cor. 12:16; II Thess. 3:11. It surely seems indefensible to say that the only New Testament writer who used πανοῦργος (II Cor. 12:16) could not have written οἰκουργός. — Luke also loved ἐργ-compounds. Luke and Paul were friends!

Similarly verse 8 presents the only instance in the New Testament of the word ἀκατάγνωστος uncensurable, irreproachable. In the sense of *uncondemned* the word occurs in II Macc. 4:47 (LXX): "And him who was the cause of all the evil, Menelaus, he discharged from the accusations; but those luckless men who, if they had pleaded even before the Scythians, would have been discharged *uncondemned,* them he sentenced to death." But why would it be impossible for the same author who in Gal. 2:11 used the verb καταγινώσκω to write ἀκατάγνωστος here in Titus 2:8? An un-Pauline word? Not at all!

Similar reasoning holds with respect to other words which in their New Testament usage occur here in Titus 2 and for the rest only in the Pastorals; such words as *temperate or sober* (Titus 2:2; cf. I Tim. 3:2, 11); *piously* (Titus 2:12; II Tim. 3:12); and *dignity or seriousness* (Titus 2:7; cf. I Tim. 2:2; 3:4). Does anyone really wish to maintain that an author who wrote *impious* (Rom. 4:5; 5:6) and *impiety* (Rom. 1:18; 11:26) could not have written *piously;* that the one who wrote *dignified or honorable* (Phil. 4:8) could not have used the word *dignity;* and that he who wrote *awake to soberness* (I Cor. 15:34) could not have written *sober?*

CONCLUSION: *When all the words in the second chapter of Titus have been examined, this conclusion becomes clear: there is not a single one which Paul could not have written.*

Note also that there are here, in Titus 2, several concepts which, though also found elsewhere in the New Testament, are treated *more fully by Paul* in the ten epistles than by any other New Testament writer. I refer to such concepts as are here in Titus 2 indicated by the words: a. *noble* (or excellent, admirable) *deeds* (Titus 2:7, 14; cf. 3:8; I Tim. 3:1; 5:10, 25; 6:18); with which one should compare the expression *good work(s)* (Titus 1:16; 3:1; cf. I Tim. 2:10; 5:10; II Tim. 2:21; 3:17); b. *grace* (Titus 2:11, etc.); and c. *the here and now* or *the present age* (Titus 2:12, in distinction from *the future or coming age*).

It is true that a synonym is sometimes found in addition to or in the place of the word used in the earlier epistles. Thus, in the Pastorals we meet both *noble deeds* (cf. Mark 14:6) and *good works,* while in the earlier epistles the latter expression alone is found. But to base upon grounds as flimsy as this the assertion that Paul cannot have been the responsible author of the Pastorals is certainly unwarranted. Why would it be impossible to assume either that since both expressions were current, the author, in writing extensively on the subject, as he does here in the Pastorals, chose to vary the terminology; or else that here and there his "secretary" is using his own vocabulary, with Paul's full approval? Even in that case the real and responsible author could certainly be *Paul.*

When to all this the various Pauline style-characteristics of Titus 2 are added, to which I have called attention in the commentary proper — and see also pp. 14-18, it will be evident that the burden of proof rests entirely on him who rejects Pauline authorship.

Synthesis of Chapter 2

See the Outline at the beginning of the chapter.

Sanctification in mutual relationships, with emphasis on the Christian family, is the theme of this chapter. Doctrine and life must agree. Hence, Titus must urge aged men to be temperate, dignified, etc.; aged women to be reverent; young men to exercise self-control (Timothy himself being their model); and slaves to be submissive in their deportment, pleasing in disposition, and of unquestionable dependability. Moreover, he wants the older women to instruct the younger ones to love their husbands and their children, to be self-controlled, chaste, domestic, kind, and submissive to their husbands. All these various classes should be motivated by the desire that the Word of God be honored, the sound doctrine adorned, and the enemy of the truth put to shame.

Not a single class or group of society must fail to come under the sanctifying influence of the Holy Spirit. Has not the grace of God appeared, bringing salvation to them all? This grace is the Great Penetrator, which invaded the realm of darkness and brought light, namely, the light of knowledge, holiness, joy, and peace ("salvation"); the Wise Pedagogue, training us to crucify worldly passions and to live lives of Christian devotion; the Effective Preparer, pointing to the realization of our blessed hope when our great God and Savior Christ Jesus returns in glory; and the Thorough-going Purifier, in Christ redeeming us from all lawlessness and transforming us into a people for Christ's own possession, filled with a zest for noble deeds. Titus must constantly talk about this glorious life of sanctification on the part of everybody. It should be presented to God as a thank-offering for his wonderful grace. Let Titus then see to it that no one slights him or his words.

On the question of slavery and race-relations see also the following: *Everyday Life in Ancient Times,* published by the *National Geographic Magazine,* 1953, pp. 175, 302, 303; J. C. Furnas, *Goodbye to Uncle Tom,* New York, 1956, especially pp. 285-388; note extensive Bibliography on pp. 397-418; Frank C. J. McGurk, "A Scientist's Report on Race Differences," *U.S. News and World Report,* Sept. 21, 1956; and the pertinent articles in *Life* magazine, Sept. 3, 1956.

Outline of Chapter 3

Theme: *The Apostle Paul, Writing to Titus, Gives Directions for the Promotion of the Spirit of Sanctification In Social (i.e. Public) Life*

3:1-8 Believers should be obedient to the authorities.
They should be kind to all men, since it was the kindness of God our Savior – not our own works! – which brought salvation.

3:9-11 On the other hand, foolish questions should be shunned, and factious men who refuse to heed admonition should be rejected.

3:12-15 Concluding directions with respect to kingdom-travelers (Artemas or Tychicus, Titus, Zenas, Apollos) and Cretan believers in general. Greetings.

CHAPTER III

TITUS **3:1-8**

3 1 Remind them to be in subjection to rulers (and) to authorities, to be
obedient, to be ready for every good work, 2 to revile no one, not to be
contentious, to be genial, showing all mildness toward all people.
3 For at one time we also were without understanding, disobedient, deluded,
enslaved to various passions and pleasures, living in malice and envy, detestable,
hating each other. 4 But when the kindness of God our Savior and his love toward
man appeared, 5 he saved us, not by virtue of works which we ourselves had performed in (a state of) righteousness, but according to his mercy through the washing
of regeneration and renewing by the Holy Spirit, 6 which he poured out upon us
richly through Jesus Christ our Savior, 7 in order that, having been justified by his
grace, we might become heirs-in-hope of life everlasting. 8 Reliable (is) this saying,
and about these matters I want you to speak with confidence, in order that those
who have their faith fixed on God may be careful to apply themselves to noble
deeds. These matters are excellent and beneficial for (all) people.

3:1-8

To the directions for the promotion of the spirit of sanctification in congregational life (chapter 1) and in family and individual life (chapter 2) are now added:

Directions for the promotion of the spirit of sanctification in public life.

The *positive* part of this section is found in verses 1-8, the *negative* part in verses 9 and 10, while the remaining verses of the chapter form a fitting *conclusion* to the entire letter. As to the positive part (verses 1-8) note:

1. The Reminder: obey the magistrates and be kind to everyone (verses 1 and 2).
2. The Reason: at one time we were like these outsiders, and were it not for the sovereign kindness of God Triune we would be like them today (verses 3-7).
    a. What we were at one time: without understanding, etc.
    b. The sovereign kindness of the Father
    c. The work of the Holy Spirit
    d. The grace of Jesus Christ
    e. The purpose of all this: life everlasting for us.
3. The Re-affirmation: these matters must be asserted with confidence, for they are excellent and beneficial for (all) people (verse 8).

1 and 2. Remind them to be in subjection to rulers (and) to authorities, to be obedient, to be ready for every good work, to revile no one, not to be contentious, to be genial, showing all mildness toward all people.

Although believers, being heavenly-minded, look forward with joy to the day of the glorious appearing of him who bought them with his own precious blood, they must never forget their duty here on earth. Titus must *remind* them of this (cf. II Tim. 2:14), in order that at all times they may be *good citizens* and *good neighbors.*

For the Christian's relation to the State see also on I Tim. 2:1-7; cf. Matt. 17:24-27; 22:15-22; Rom. 13:1-7; I Peter 2:13-17. The expression *"Remind* them to be in subjection," probably implies that Paul had talked to the Cretans about this important matter while he was with Titus on the island (cf. II Thess. 2:5). Moreover, from the writings of Polybius and of Plutarch it appears that the Cretans were fretting and fuming under the Roman yoke. It is *possible,* therefore, that this circumstance had something to do with the precise nature of the present "reminder." It has been pointed out by several commentators that while *Timothy* at Ephesus was ordered to see to it that believers cease not *to pray* for rulers, *Titus* is told to remind the Cretans *to be in subjection* to rulers. But see also Rom. 13:1-7. At any rate, the Christian message will be ineffective unless, in obedience to the fifth commandment in its broader meaning, believers "render unto Cesar the things that are Cesar's, and unto God the things that are God's."

To those, then, who not only actually *rule* but as such have also been invested with divine *authority* (Rom. 13:1) – hence, "to rulers and authorities" – believers must not only in a general way *outwardly subject themselves* but must even be *inwardly obedient,* carrying out with a willing heart *all the particular commands;* for example, those with respect to paying taxes, being orderly in behavior, displaying honesty in business, etc. (The exception referred to in Acts 5:29 holds whenever any human regulation clashes with the law of God.)

Not only that, but whenever the need presents itself – think of epidemics, wars, conflagrations, etc. – believers must be ready to show their good spirit, in thorough co-operation with the government which protects them. Note same connection in Rom. 13:3. They must not only be "thoroughly equipped" but also "ready" and eager for *every good work* (cf. Titus 3:1 and II Tim. 3:17).

The expression "ready for every good work" forms a natural bridge between the duties which believers owe to their government and those which they owe to their neighbors.

In the five requirements which follow, a climax is clearly observable. It stands to reason that believers should never *revile* any one (see on I Tim. 6:4). Not many believers will even need such a reminder. Insulting and abusive language is surely out of place for anyone, certainly for believers.

A more stringent requirement is the one which demands that believers be not even *contentious* or *quarrelsome* (cf. I Tim. 3:3). But more than the absence of a vice is expected of them. A positive virtue must display itself in all their contacts with those outside the church: Christians must be *genial* (also I Tim. 3:3), that is, ready to yield personal advantage, eager to help the needy, kind to the weak, considerate toward the fallen, always filled with the spirit of sweet reasonableness. The climax is surely reached with the words: "showing *all* mildness (cf. II Tim. 2:25) toward *all* people." Note the play on words,[206] reflected also in the A.V. and A.R.V. renderings. Showing *some* mildness toward *some* people might not be so difficult. Nor showing *all* (that is, *complete, thorough-going*) mildness to *some* people, or *some* mildness to *all* people. But to *show all* mildness to *all* people, even to all those Cretan "liars, evil brutes, and lazy bellies," was an assignment impossible of fulfilment apart from God's special grace!

3. The reason why this *must,* nevertheless, be done (and *can* be done) is stated in the beautiful passage beginning with the words: **For at one time we also were without understanding, disobedient, deluded, enslaved to various passions and pleasures, living in malice and envy, detestable, hating each other.**

Reflection upon our own former condition makes it easier for us to be mild and kind toward others. Note, "For at one time *we* also were . . ." *We* means: I, Paul, who write the letter; you, Titus, who receive it; and further, all believers in Crete, and in fact, all believers everywhere. Paul, too, had been a slave of sin. To be sure, he had been "zealous for the traditions," but at the same time he had been "persecuting the church" (see on I Tim. 1:13; then Gal. 1:11-17). As to what Titus had been, read Gal. 2:2, 3. This merciful inclusion of oneself is very effective and appealing. It causes the reader (Titus) and the hearers (the Cretan believers when the letter is read to them) to feel that the writer is standing on common ground with them and understands them (cf. Titus 1:4; then I Thess. 5:9; Rev. 1:9). Moreover, the sharp contrast between what men *were* in their state of sin and what they *have become* since they entered the state of grace encourages gratitude to God; hence also goodwill toward the neighbor who was made in God's image. (The vivid portrayal of this contrast is characteristic of Paul; see I Tim. 1:12-17; then Rom. 6:17-23; I Cor. 6:11; Eph. 2:2-13; 5:8; Col. 3:7; and cf. I Peter 4:3.)

We are not surprised, then, to notice that over against the seven virtues

---

[206] Translations which go too far in their attempt to "westernize" the New Testament *miss* the play on words in this verse, and then, contrary to the original but in harmony with A.V. and A.R.V., *insert* a play on words in the next verse: "hateful, hating one another." In both cases I have attempted to retain in the translation the flavor of the original.

mentioned in verses 1 and 2, showing *what (Cretan) believers should be,* are placed an equal number of vices (verse 3) showing *what we once were.*

We were *without understanding* ("senseless," I Tim. 6:9), not only ignorant, but by nature actually *unable* to discern the things of the Spirit (I Cor. 2:14; cf. Rom. 1:21; Eph. 4:18).

Disobedient to both divine and human authority (Titus 1:6, 10; 3:1; then II Tim. 3:2; Rom. 1:21, 30), heeding neither the voice of conscience nor the admonitions of parents or the laws of civil magistrates.

Deluded (see on II Tim. 3:13), made to wander from the truth, living in a world of unreality, imagining that license is liberty. Though we considered ourselves to be free, we had become slaves:

Enslaved to various passions and pleasures, allowing these strong evil desires to dominate our life and conduct. (For *passions* see on II Tim. 2:22; 3:6, and for *pleasures* cf. Luke 8:14; James 4:1, 3; II Peter 2:13.) The world apart from Christ passes in review, and what a sorry spectacle it is. Here "we" come: the glutton and the toper, the miser and the spend-thrift, the mad-cap and the dotard, the sports-worshiper and the sluggard, the fraud and the fop, the sadist and the rapist, the "tiger" and the "wolf." Cf. Rom. 1:18-32; Gal. 5:19-21. Some serve one master, some another, but by nature all are slaves to those terrible "drives" which they have never learned to control, and which, according to some modern psychologists they should not even try too strenuously to hold down!

Living (literally *"leading,"* with *a life* understood; cf. I Tim. 2:2) *in malice and envy.* This *malice* is not mere "mischief" as in "With Malice Toward *Some.*" No, it is badness, perversity, wickedness; especially the evil disposition of the mind. One of its most soul-destroying manifestations is *envy,* an evil which, as the probable etymology of the Greek word implies, causes one *to waste away.* Has not envy been called that vice whose rage nothing can allay, "the eldest-born of hell"? Does it not "feed on" the living, never ceasing until they are dead? Is it not "the rottenness of the bones"? (Prov. 14:30). See also what *Paul* says about it elsewhere (I Tim. 6:4; then Rom. 1:29; Gal. 5:21; Phil. 1:15) and cf. Matt. 27:18; Mark 15:10; James 4:5; and I Peter 2:1. Our English word *envy* is from the Latin *in-video,* meaning "to look against," that is, to look with ill-will at another person because of what he is or has. (*Jealousy,* it has been well said, is afraid of losing what it has; *envy* hates to see another person have something. Thus, Mr. A. is *jealous* of his own honor, and is *envious* of Mr. B.'s superior skill.) It was envy which caused the murder of Abel, threw Joseph into a pit, caused Korah, Dathan, and Abiram to rebel against Moses and Aaron, made Saul pursue David, gave rise to the bitter words which "the elder brother" (in the Parable of the Prodigal Son) addressed to his father, and crucified Christ. *Love* never envies (I Cor. 13:4).

Detestable, odious, fulsome, offensive, disgusting, repulsive. In the New

Testament the word used in the original occurs only here, but Philo the Jew (20 B. C.-A. D. 50) also uses it. The unconverted sinner by means of his attitude to God and man causes *loathing.* Hence:

Hating each other. This is the natural result when detestable people in all their gruesomeness are nevertheless forced somehow to live with each other and to meet each other in a hundred different ways.

"Such were we at one time," says Paul. Hence, let us not be too hard on the people who are still in that condition, but let us strive by godly conduct to win them for Christ.

4-6. And let us do this from the motive of gratitude for what we ourselves have received. Hence, Paul continues, **But when the kindness of God our Savior and his love toward man appeared, he saved us.** What a striking contrast, a *double* contrast, in fact! (1) Over against "man's inhumanity to man" pictured in verse 3, is portrayed God's *benignity* (a word used *only* by Paul: Rom. 2:4; 3:12; 11:22, etc.) and *love* for man (cf. Acts 28:2). And (2) upon the Stygian darkness of our *past* (verse 3) *dawns* dramatically the light of the Father's kindliness and pity which brought us into the *present* state of grace. (Here again is that glorious *epiphany* mentioned earlier; see on Titus 2:11.)

This, let it be emphasized, is more than an *argument.* It *is* an argument, to be sure, as has already been pointed out. But it is *more* than that. It is the outpouring (in proverbial language; see on verse 8) of a heart which is glowing with love in return for God's love. It must be borne in mind that Paul writes as one who has in his own life *experienced* all this. He does not stand next to his story, but he is himself part of it. Hence, these words about the kindness of God our Savior and his love toward man are as warm and tender as was the heart of this same apostle, a man who was often seen to weep, and who once wrote very touchingly, "The Son of God loved *me,* and gave himself up . . . *for me!*" (Gal. 2:20).

The expression "the kindness and the love toward man" is *one* concept; hence, the verb in the original is singular. The *expression* as such is found also in the works of pagan moralists, but the *content* as used here in Titus 3:4 is unique. Here is not "the kindness and the love" ascribed to some earthly ruler upon whom the praises of men are being showered, praises which he has hardly deserved; but here is the *real* benignity and love. The expression "love-toward-man" is *one* word, exactly the same word as our "philanthropy." Nevertheless, since in present English usage the term "philanthropy" is often understood as referring only to "the work of practical benevolence," a work of which men are the authors as well as the recipients, it is probably best to retain the beautiful rendering which is found in our common English versions; for certainly, as Paul uses the term it combines both the love itself and its generous outpouring upon mankind. By retaining the rendering *"love* toward man" one is immediately reminded of John 3:16, which beautifully expresses the truth which the apostle had in mind.

It was the kindness and the love of *God our Savior* (see on I Tim. 1:1; Titus 1:3; 2:10) which came to man's rescue. It was he, namely, God the Father, who *saved* us, rescuing us from the greatest evil and bestowing upon us the greatest blessing (see on I Tim. 1:15). He saved *us:* Paul, Titus, in fact all those who in course of time become the recipients of this great blessing.

Now, in order to make us all-the-more-ready to help others who as yet are unsaved, and to prevent us from ever saying, "But they *do not deserve* our help," Paul stresses the fact that we, on our part, did not deserve our salvation either. He does this by pointing out that *negatively* the Father saved us **not by works which we ourselves had performed in (a state of) righteousness,** and *positively* **but according to his own mercy.** So strong is Paul's emphasis upon this completely *sovereign* (that is, by us wholly unmerited) character of our salvation, that (as is clear in the original; and see also the renderings of the A.V. and A.R.V.) he causes this entire lengthy compound phrase to *precede* the verb *saved.* Thus, A.V. has:

"4 But after that the kindness and love of God our Saviour toward man appeared, 5 Not by works of righteousness which we have done, but according to his mercy he saved us . . ."

As concerns the word-order, that rendering is correct. The only objection which many have felt is this, that, unless one pays very close attention to the punctuation, he is in danger of mentally construing the compound phrase as if it were a modifier of the verb *appeared,* and not of the verb *saved.*

"Not *by* (i.e., in consequence of, on the basis of; cf. Gal. 2:16) works which we ourselves had performed in a state of righteousness." The implication is: there were no such works. Neither Paul nor anyone else had ever performed such a work, for before God and his holy law *all* – both Jews and pagans – are by nature "under sin" (Rom. 3:9). Hence, if men are ever to be saved at all, it can only be done "according to his (God's) own mercy." Note, not only are men saved *of* or *by* or *on the basis of* his mercy (all this, to be sure, is implied), but *according to* his mercy, the "wideness of God's mercy" being the yardstick which determines the wideness of their salvation (cf. Eph. 1:7). Other passages of Scripture which similarly emphasize the completely sovereign character of God's grace in saving man are quoted on p. 307 of N.T.C. on John, Vol. II.[207] God's

[207] See also Edwin H. Palmer, *The Five Points of Calvinism,* published by The Men's Society of the Christian Reformed Church, 422 E. Exchange St., Spring Lake, Mich.; esp. pp. 21-33.

mercy (for which see on I Tim. 1:2) is his *kindness* and *pity* to those *in need* or *in distress.*

The means employed in saving us is indicated by an additional modifier of the verb *he saved,* namely, **through a washing of regeneration and renewing by the Holy Spirit.** Note "through *a washing*" (λουτρόν, -οῦ), not "through *a laver* or *basin for washing.*" The washing referred to is wholly spiritual. It is that of *regeneration and renewing,* regarded as one concept.

The term *regeneration* as applied to *individuals* occurs only in this one New Testament passage. (Matt. 19:28 has reference to the cosmic regeneration.) Literally it means *new birth,* the being born again (*palin* = again, plus *genesia* = birth; hence, *palin-genesia*). But though *the word* occurs only this once, *the idea* is found in many other passages (John 1:13; 3:3, 5-8; I Peter 1:23; I John 2:29; 3:9; 4:7; 5:1, 4, 18; cf. also II Cor. 5:17; Gal. 6:15; Eph. 2:5; 4:24; and Col. 2:13). I know of no better definition than that which is given by L. Berkhof, namely, "Regeneration is that act of God by which the principle of the new life is implanted in man, the governing disposition of the soul is made holy, and the first holy exercise of this new disposition is secured." [208]

The present passage, in connection with its context, places emphasis on the following particulars in connection with this wonderful work of God:

(1) It is the work of *the Holy Spirit.* This stands to reason, for in Scripture it is especially the third person of the Trinity who is represented as the bestower of life; hence, also of *spiritual* life. Also, it is he, the *Holy* Spirit, who takes the lead, as it were, in the work of making men *holy.*

(2) It precedes and gives rise to the process of *renewing.* While the latter is a life-long activity, the former is a single act, an instantaneous change.

(3) It affects the entire man. Note: "he saved *us.*"

(4) It is a *radical* change, so that those who beforehand were loaded down with the seven vices mentioned in verse 3 are now *in principle* adorned with the seven virtues mentioned in the verses 1 and 2.

The word *renewing* is found also in Rom. 12:2. That passage indicates that although this work, as well as regeneration, is ascribed to the Holy Spirit, nevertheless, there is this difference: *regeneration* is entirely the work of God, but in *renewing* or *sanctification* man as well as God takes part. While *regeneration* is never directly perceived by man, and becomes known to him only because of its effects, *renewal* requires the *conscious* and *continued* surrender of man's whole personality to the will of God.

For the definition I quote once more L. Berkhof (p. 532 of the work mentioned in footnote 208):

"Sanctification is that gracious and continuous operation of the Holy Spirit, by which he delivers the justified sinner from the pollution of sin,

---

208 *Systematic Theology,* Grand Rapids, 1949, p. 469.

renews his whole nature in the image of God, and enables him to perform good works."

It is clear from such passages as John 3:3, 5 and especially Eph. 5:26 (cf. Heb. 10:22) that this "washing of regeneration and renewing" stands in some relation to the rite of baptism. Undoubtedly, also here in Titus 3:5 there is an implied reference to this sacrament. However, discussing that problem *here,* while commenting on a passage in which the *water* is not even mentioned, would take us too far afield. See, however, N.T.C. on John 3:3, 5.

Now, in order to place still more emphasis on the fact that believers do not have a reason for falling short in their duty of winning others for Christ through godly conduct, Paul adds the following words, with reference to the kindness of God in saving us and imparting to us his *enabling* Spirit: **which** (or **whom,** namely, this Spirit) **he** (namely, God the Father) **poured out upon us richly through Jesus Christ our Savior.**

Note how in this passage God the Father, God the Spirit, and God the Son are beautifully combined.

God the Father not only gives his Son but also pours out his Spirit. The reference is to Pentecost (Acts 2:17, 18, 33). Organically speaking, the Spirit was poured out upon the church of the present and of the future; for, that Spirit having once established his personal residence in the church, never leaves it again. Hence, Paul can say, "whom he poured out upon *us.*"

The adverb *richly* indicates the rich supply of spiritual gifts which results from this outpouring. No one has any right to say, "I can do nothing in the kingdom, since God has given me nothing." The beautiful phrase "through Jesus Christ our Savior" indicates that the latter through his atoning sacrifice and prayer secured for his people the gift of the Holy Spirit (John 14:16; 16:7).

7. Our former state, described in verse 3, has ended. The blessings described in verses 4-6 have been and are being received. Their purpose and result is now stated: **in order that, having been justified by his grace, we might become heirs-in-hope of life everlasting.**

The process of reasoning which we find in these verses (verses 3-7) is familiar to the student of Paul's epistles. Note the three stages:

We *were* by nature children of wrath – we *have been made* alive – we *now look forward* by faith to the ages to come when we shall receive even greater glory (Eph. 2:1-10);

We *were* idol-worshippers – we *now* serve the true and living God – we *await* the coming of the Son of God from heaven (I Thess. 1:9, 10), and our everlasting fellowship with him (I Thess. 4:13-18).

We *were* ungodly and ruled by worldly passions – we *have renounced* all this and are now living lives of self-mastery and fairness and devotion — we *are waiting for* the realization of the blessed hope (Titus 2:11-13).

Having just mentioned "Jesus Christ our Savior," Paul, still thinking about the grace of God in Christ, continues, "in order that having been justified by *his* grace" (as effective, meriting cause), etc. Note the aorist passive participle *having been justified.* This does not mean "having been made upright." [209] It means *having been declared righteous.* Justification is that act of God the Father whereby he counts our sins to be Christ's, and Christ's righteousness to be ours (II Cor. 5:21). It is the opposite of *condemnation* (Rom. 8:33, 34). It implies deliverance from the curse of God because that curse was placed on Christ (Gal. 3:11-13). It means *forgiveness* full and free (Rom. 4:6-8). It is God's free gift, the fruit of *sovereign grace,* and not in any way the result of human "goodness" or "accomplishment" (Rom. 3:24; 5:5, 8, 9). It brings peace to the soul (Rom. 5:1), a peace that passes all understanding. It fills the heart with such thanksgiving that it produces in the life of the believer a rich harvest of good works. Hence, justification and sanctification, though ever distinct, are never separate but stand in the closest possible relation to each other (Rom. 6:2; 8:1, 2).

The purpose, then, of the work of God in saving us is "that . . . we might become heirs . . . of life everlasting"; that is, that *even now in this present life* we might have the right as children to look forward to the full possession of that which we now possess only *in principle.* When that future day arrives, we shall rejoice in the richest possible (because sinless!) fellowship with God in Christ (see also N.T.C. on John 3:16; 17:3), basking in the sunshine of his love (John 5:42) and partaking, to the fullest extent possible for man, of his joy and glory (John 17:13). That life differs, accordingly, *in essence* from the "life"(?) of the unbeliever, and *in degree* even from the life of the believer here below. It is, moreover, actually *ever-lasting,* that is, *never-ending.* Of that life as it is in principle we are *now* the possessors; and of that life as it will be in perfection we are *even now* the heirs, but heirs-in-hope, hoping heirs. But this hope will *certainly* be realized (Rom. 5:5).

8. Reflecting on the gospel-summary given in verses 4-7 the apostle continues: **Reliable (is) this saying, and about these matters I want you to speak with confidence, in order that those who have their faith fixed on God may be careful to apply themselves to noble deeds.**

This, then (that is, verses 4-7), was the last of the five great "sayings." See on I Tim. 1:15 for the meaning of the introductory formula, "Reliable is the saying." It is about *these* matters — namely, a. the kindness of the

---

[209] See L. Berkhof, *Systematic Theology,* p. 510.

Father and his love toward man; b. the work of the Holy Spirit in regenerating and renewing man; c. the grace of Jesus Christ considered as the effective cause of our justification; and d. the purpose of all this: that we might become what we are today, heirs-in-hope of life everlasting – that Paul wants Titus *to speak with confidence*. Others, to be sure, speak with confidence about frivolous matters; matters, moreover, about which they know nothing (see on I Tim. 1:7; and see on verse 9 below). Let Titus then stress those matters of which he has become firmly and rightfully convinced, the purpose being that those who have their faith fixed on God (note perfect participle, indicating both the past action and the present abiding result) *may be careful to apply themselves* to noble deeds. They should concentrate their *thought* on such deeds of gratitude, *applying* themselves with diligence to their performance, and making this their chief business. **These matters** – that is, the things just mentioned: the kindness of the Father, the work of the Holy Spirit, etc. – **are excellent and beneficial for (all) people.** Not only are these things excellent in themselves, but they are also *beneficial* (*useful, profitable;* see on I Tim. 4:8; II Tim. 3:16; also in classical Greek and in the papyri). Moreover, when appropriated by faith, they benefit *men in general,* not this or that particular class. They bring life, light, joy, and peace where before there was death, darkness, sadness, and fear.

---

9 But as for foolish inquiries and genealogies and wrangling and skirmishes about the law, shun them, for they are unprofitable and futile. 10 After a first and a second warning have nothing further to do with a factious person, 11 knowing that such an individual is distorted and sins, being self-condemned.

3:9-11

9. A few negative directions are now added: **But as for foolish inquiries and genealogies and wrangling and skirmishes about the law, shun them, for they are unprofitable and futile.**

This is in strong contrast with the preceding: Titus must *do* the one, but *avoid* the other. The order of the words in the sentence (the compound object placed before the verb) and the absence of the article before any of the four nouns, these facts clearly prove that all possible emphasis is placed on the quality and contents of the object. It is exactly *foolish inquiries,* namely, investigations into genealogical lore, that must be avoided. It is precisely *wrangling,* namely, skirmishes about the law, that must be given a wide berth. See also on Titus 1:9, 10, 14. The matters referred to have been described in detail in connection with I Tim. 1:3-7, 19, 20 and I Tim. 6:3-5 (see on these passages). Let Titus then shun (cf. II Tim. 2:16) the Jewish legends and the stipulations, the inquiries and the wrangling.

When he sees them coming, let him turn around and flee! Let him see these things for what they truly are: *unprofitable, futile.* What a sharp contrast between all this *useless* nonsense and the very *useful* matters about which Paul has just spoken in verses 4-7 (see also verse 8). A minister who does justice to the latter will have no time for the former.

10, 11. And what must be the attitude of Titus toward those church-members who are "roped in" by these specialists in genealogical lore and by these law-skirmishers, and who begin to make propaganda for this unworthy cause? Says Paul: **After a first [210] and a second warning have nothing further to do with a factious person, knowing that such an individual is distorted and sins, being self-condemned.**

Paul speaks about a "heretical" person. Originally, the word "heresy" (αἵρεσις) simply meant "that which one chooses for himself," "an opinion." This meaning gave rise to another, namely, "a set of persons professing certain definite principles or opinions," hence a *school* or *party;* for example, the "party of the Sadducees" (Acts 5:17), and "the party of the Pharisees" (Acts 15:5; cf. 26:5).

While in certain contexts this neutral meaning persisted for a while, the term began to be used also in an unfavorable sense. Cf. our English word *faction.* In that sense there were *factions* in Corinth ("I am of Paul," "I am of Apollos," etc.). When Tertullus called Paul "a ringleader of the *faction* (or *sect*) of the Nazarenes," he was not trying to pay him a compliment. Cf. also Acts 24:14 where Paul says, "after the Way which *they* call a *faction* (or *sect*)." And see Acts 28:22.

Accordingly, *a factious person* is here a person who without justification creates division. In the light of the context it is probable that the rendering "a heretic" is not far off. At any rate, the word is moving in that direction. The factious person of whom the apostle is thinking has accepted the sinister philosophy of the Cretan errorists who specialized in foolish inquiries and law-skirmishes (see on verse 9). As has become clear, their error touched both doctrine and life, as is usually the case. It is true, of course, that the term as here used need not be restricted to a particular type of fanatic. *Every* factious person stands condemned here.

The apostle demands that when the time is ripe such a person shall be *rejected.* The expression "Have nothing further to do with" must be taken in the sense of *refuse, reject* (cf. I Tim. 5:11; II Tim. 2:23). There seems to be a reference here to Matt. 18:15-17. Official exclusion from church-membership is probably indicated. This is not surprising, for Titus will know *that such an individual* (cf. Rom. 16:18, etc.), who not only creates division but also after repeated warnings persists in this practice,

---

210 The Koine often substitutes the cardinal for the ordinal; cf. Matt. 28:1; Mark 16:2.

"is distorted" and is sinning. The word rendered "is distorted" is very descriptive. Such a person is not living and seeing *straight*. He is *mentally and morally turned* or *twisted*. He is even worse than the man who colloquially is sometimes called "a screw-ball." He is actually living in sin. What makes his sin very bad is the fact that *he knows* that he is sinning. If his conscience has not already spoken plainly, he has at least been warned, and that not once but twice. Hence, he sins "being self-condemned."

In this connection the qualification is very important, namely, "After a first and a second *warning* (or *admonition*)." Both this noun and the cognate verb (*to warn, to admonish;* literally *to put in mind*) are used elsewhere only by Paul (for the noun see I Cor. 10:11; Eph. 6:4; for the verb, Acts 20:31: Paul speaking; Rom. 15:14; I Cor. 4:14; Col. 1:28; 3:16; I Thess. 5:12, 14; II Thess. 3:15). The qualification indicates that, according to Pauline teaching, discipline must ever spring from love, from a desire to heal, never from a desire to get rid of an individual. Much patience must be shown. Even when the error is very grievous and dangerous, as in the present instance, every effort must be put forth to win the erring one. If the member, having been lovingly warned, refuses to repent and continues his evil work in the midst of the congregation, the church through its officers and by means of the entire membership must redouble its efforts. There must be a second warning. But if even this remedy fails, he must be expelled. Even this extreme measure has as one of its purposes the reclamation of the sinner. This, however, can never be the only purpose. The welfare of the entire church (cf. Matt. 12:25) unto the glory of God must never be lost sight of. That, after all, is the main objective of discipline (see also N.T.C. on II Thess. 3:14, 15).

---

12 As soon as I shall have sent Artemas or Tychicus to you, do your best to come to me at Nicopolis, for I have decided to spend the winter there. 13 Do all you can to help along on their journey Zenas the law-expert and Apollos, so that they may lack nothing. 14 Besides, let also our people learn to apply themselves to noble deeds for these occasions of imperative need, in order that they may not be unfruitful.

15 All those who are with me send you greetings. Greet those who love us in faith. Grace[211] (be) with y o u all.

3:12-15

12. The *body* of the letter (Titus 1:1-3:11) is finished. Was it written by *an amanuensis* who faithfully reproduced Paul's message, retaining in every instance the latter's style, hence also most of his words, but here and there making use of his own vocabulary, the whole having been subse-

---

[211] Literally "the grace," that is, the grace of God.

quently approved by the apostle? And did Paul then add verses 12-15, writing *them* "with his own hand"? See N.T.C. on II Thess. 3:17. However that may be, fact is that, as could be expected, the concluding section consists almost entirely of words which are also found in the Ten (Paul's epistles apart from the Pastorals).[212]

Says Paul: **As soon as I shall have sent Artemas or Tychicus to you, do your best to come to me at Nicopolis, for I have decided to spend the winter there.**

At this moment Paul is probably somewhere in Macedonia (Philippi?). He is certainly not in Nicopolis, though the subscription found in late manuscripts states that it was from that place that the letter to Titus was sent. If that had been true, Paul could not have written, "I have decided to spend the winter *there*."

The apostle desires to spend the winter with Titus. He has decided upon Nicopolis as the meeting-place. Since this name is mentioned without any further clarification, it probably refers to the most well-known of all the Victory Cities, namely, the one situated on the southwest promontory of Epirus, in Greece. Its site was a few miles north of the modern Preveza. The ancient city of Nicopolis had been founded and had been constituted a Roman colony by Augustus, as a memorial to his *victory* over Antony and Cleopatra at nearby Actium (31 B. C.).

Nicopolis was certainly a suitable meeting-place, and this for one or more of several possible reasons, such as:

It was more or less centrally located: Paul would have to travel almost as far southwest as Titus would have to travel northwest. Consult a map.

It was a fine winter-resort. Moreover, the winter-months were not suitable for sea-travel (see also Acts 27:12; 28:11; I Cor. 16:6; and II Tim. 4:21).

It was an excellent "base of operations" for mission-activity in Dalmatia. It seems probable that Titus actually reached Nicopolis, and performed some evangelistic work in Dalmatia, to which he returned at a later time (see on II Tim. 4:10).

It was a fine stepping-stone to places farther west. Did Paul intend to go from there to Spain as soon as the winter-season was over?

But although Titus must *do his best* (or "do his utmost," cf. II Tim. 2:15; 4:9, 21; Gal. 2:10; Eph. 4:3; I Thess. 2:17) to meet Paul at Nicopolis, Crete must not be left without a good leader. Conditions were too serious to permit even a brief period of vacancy. As soon as a replacement arrives,

---

[212] Note, however, that even in this conclusion "noble deeds" replaces Paul's earlier "good works," and the verb προ-ΐστημι is used in a sense which does not attach to it in the Ten. But, as has been noted earlier, the apostle's vocabulary may have changed somewhat. Also, it is not always easy to discover the exact extent of what Paul wrote "with his own hand."

Titus can leave, but not before. Note that Paul does not say, "The Cretans can easily take care of themselves during your absence." He realizes that churches cannot be made "indigenous" over-night. As long as leadership "from the outside" is necessary, it must be provided.

So Paul is going to send either Artemas or Tychicus. Both of these men may be regarded as Paul's co-workers and envoys, performing kingdom-work under his authority and supervision. The name Artemas is probably an abbreviation of Artemidorus, meaning "gift of Artemas," the Greek goddess of hunting, corresponding to the Roman Diana. No further reliable information has come down to us with reference to this man. What is known about Tychicus has been summarized in II Tim. 4:12; see on that passage. His name, meaning "fortuitous" may be connected with that of the Greek goddess Tyche, that is, Fortune ("Fortuna").

There are those who think that when Paul had to make up his mind whom to send to Crete, whether Artemas or Tychicus, he commissioned Artemas for that task. They deduce this from the fact that during his second imprisonment the apostle reports that he has commissioned Tychicus for Ephesus (II Tim. 4:12). This could be a questionable deduction.

13. With reference to the bearers of the letter Paul has a friendly word: **Do all you can to help along on their journey Zenas the law-expert and Apollos, so that they may lack nothing.**

What kind of law-expert was Zenas? Before his conversion to the Christian faith, had he been an expounder of the law of Moses ("teacher of the law," "scribe"), or was he a Roman jurist or "lawyer" with whose assistance a will was made or a lawsuit was instituted? Some prefer the latter view, giving as their reason that the man could hardly have been a Jew since he has a Greek name, a name which is probably an abbreviation of Zenodorus, meaning "gift of Zeus." But there were many Jews with Greek names. Were not *Paulos* and *Apollos Jews* with Greek names? Others, "putting two and two together" in an interesting way, surmise that Zenas as well as Apollos was a Jew, *and* that both of these good Christians who were also experts in Jewish lore were sent to Crete in order to curb the influence of those who specialized in Jewish myths at the expense of the true gospel.

This may be true, but all we really know is that Zenas, in some sense a law-expert, and Apollos, who were in all probability bearers of the letter, were on a journey, and that Titus is ordered to do everything possible *to help them along* (or "set them forth") on this trip. To what ultimate destination? Again, we simply do not know. These men must be provided with food and lodging while in Crete, and must be aided in every way so that, *lacking nothing,* they may be able to continue their travels.

Apollos is a familiar figure. He was a Jew, a native of Alexandria (Acts

18:24), the famous Egyptian library-and-university-city which had been founded by Alexander the Great in the year 332 B. C. He was, moreover, an orator, mighty in the scriptures. Having come to Ephesus, where he spoke boldly in the synagogue, he had been taught the way of God more accurately by Priscilla and Aquila (Acts 18:26). Thus equipped, he had gone to the province of Achaia where he proved to be a great blessing to believers, and powerfully confuted the Jews, and that publicly, showing by the scriptures that Jesus was the Christ (Acts 18:27, 28). Afterward he had returned to Ephesus (I Cor. 16:12). He was a good friend of Paul ("I planted, Apollos watered; but God gave the increase," I Cor. 3:6). We may be sure that both Paul and Apollos were grieved by the party-spirit which plagued the Corinthian church ("I am of Paul," "I am of Apollos," I Cor. 1:12).

14. Titus, then, must help these men along on their journey, but he should not try to shoulder the burden *alone*. Hence, Paul continues, **Besides, let also our people learn to apply themselves to noble deeds for these occasions of imperative need, in order that they may not be unfruitful.**

In the light of the immediate context the meaning must be: Titus, do not fail to encourage *our folks* (see p. 11), that is, the believers on the island of Crete, to co-operate wholeheartedly in all these manifestations of generosity. They should *keep on learning* things of this kind, that is, they should *become experienced* in well-doing (cf. I Tim. 5:4; Phil. 4:11), just as Paul himself had *learned* to be content in whatsoever state he was. This "learning through practice" is the finest self-education anyone could ever desire.

The Cretan believers, then, should learn "to apply themselves to noble deeds" (see on verse 8; cf. verse 1) "for these imperative needs" (thus literally). Cf. Acts 20:34; 28:10. If Paul was at Philippi when he wrote this letter, he did not have far to look in order to point to brilliant examples of men and women who understood this duty and were learning it better and better right along (read Phil. 2:25; 4:16). The purpose is: "in order that they may not be unfruitful" (cf. Matt. 7:15; 13:8, 23; John 15:8; Gal. 5:22). The author of this epistle realizes fully that though grace is *the root* (Titus 3:7; cf. Eph. 2:8), noble deeds are *the fruit* (cf. Eph. 2:10) of the tree of salvation.

15. The farewell greeting consists of three parts: **All those who are with me send you greetings.** All the fellow-workers who are in the company of (μετά) the apostle send greetings to Titus. Cf. II Tim. 4:21; then Acts 20:34. **Greet those who love us in faith.** Titus is asked to convey the greetings of Paul and of his companions to those who are filled with affection for them in the sphere of the Christian faith. **Grace (be) with y o u all.** Upon all the believers who hear this letter when it is read to them "God's favor

in Christ for those who have not deserved it" is pronounced. In their *midst* (μετά) it will dwell, filling their hearts with peace and joy. For details see N.T.C. on I Thess. 1:1.

Synthesis of Chapter 3

See the Outline at the beginning of this chapter.

Sanctification in public relations is stressed in the present chapter. Believers should be obedient to the authorities. They should be kind to all men, since it was the kindness of God our Savior – not our own works! – which brought salvation. For the synthesis of the first eight verses see p. 385. On the other hand, foolish inquiries into genealogical lore and skirmishes about the law should be shunned, for they are unprofitable and futile. Factious men who refuse admonition should be rejected. Such people are mentally and morally turned or twisted. Moreover, they *know* that they are sinning, for if their conscience has not already told them this, they have at least been so informed by the church on the basis of the Word. Hence, they sin against better knowledge.

In his *Concluding Directions* Paul tells Titus that he will provide for the vacancy which will arise when the latter leaves Crete. The apostle is going to send either Artemas or Tychicus to replace Titus on the island. As soon as the substitute has arrived, he wants Titus to do his utmost to meet Paul at Nicopolis, probably the one in Epirus, where the apostle has decided to spend the winter. Also he asks that both Titus and the Cretan believers in general do all in their power to help along on their journey the two Christian friends and helpers who were in all probability the bearers of this letter, namely, Zenas the law-expert, and Apollos the famous orator from Alexandria. Note: not only *Titus* must provide for these men but "our people," too, must learn to apply themselves to noble deeds for such occasions of imperative need, in order that they may not be unfruitful. – All the fellow-workers who are with Paul send greetings to Titus, who, in turn, must convey the greetings of Paul and his companions to those who are filled with Christian affection for them. – A brief salutation concludes the letter: "Grace (be) with y o u all."

SELECT BIBLIOGRAPHY

An attempt has been made to make this list *as small as possible.*

Bouma, C., *De Brieven van den Apostel Paulus aan Timotheus en Titus* (in *Kommentaar op het Nieuwe Testament*), Amsterdam, 1942.*

Calvin, John, *Commentarius In Epistolam Pauli Ad Timotheum I, Ad Timotheum II, Ad Titum* (Corpus Reformatorum, vol. LXXX), Brunsvigae, 1895; English translation (in *Calvin's Commentaries*), Grand Rapids, 1948.

Simpson, E. K., *The Pastoral Epistles,* London, 1954.

---

* In the present commentary "Bouma, *op. cit.*," refers to *this* book, not to Bouma's shorter work on the Pastoral Epistles (in *Korte Verklaring*).

GENERAL BIBLIOGRAPHY

Ante-Nicene Fathers, The, ten volumes, reprint Grand Rapids, Mich., 1950.

Arminius, The Writings of (tr. by James Nichols and W. R. Bagnall), reprint Grand Rapids, Michigan, 1956.

Barnes, A., *Notes on the New Testament, Thessalonians-Philemon,* reprint Grand Rapids, 1949.

Bavinck, H., *Gereformeerde Dogmatiek,* third edition, Kampen, 1918.

Bavinck, H., *The Doctrine of God* (tr. by William Hendriksen), Grand Rapids, Mich., 1951.

Bengel, J. A., *Gnomen Novi Testamenti,* Tübingen, 1742.

Berkhof, L., *The Assurance of Faith,* Grand Rapids, 1928.

Berkhof, L., *Systematic Theology,* Grand Rapids, 1949.

Berkhof, L., *Vicarious Atonement Through Christ,* Grand Rapids, Mich., 1936.

Blackwood, A. W., *The Fine Art of Public Worship,* Nashville, 1939.

Bouma, C., *I, II Timotheus en Titus* (in *Korte Verklaring*), second edition, Kampen, 1953.

Bouma, C., *De Brieven van den Apostel Paulus aan Timotheus en Titus* (in *Kommentaar op het Nieuwe Testament*), Amsterdam, 1942.

Brooks, A. E., "The Problem of the Pastoral Epistles," *JThS* 23 (1922).

Burrows, Millar, *The Dead Sea Scrolls,* New York, 1956.

Calvin, John, *Commentarius In Epistolam Pauli Ad Timotheum I, Ad Timotheum II, Ad Titum* (Corpus Reformatorum, vol. LXXX), Brunsvigae, 1895; English translation (in *Calvin's Commentaries*), Grand Rapids, 1948.

Deissmann, A., *Light From the Ancient East* (tr. by L. R. M. Strachan), New York, 1922.

De Wette, W. M. L., *Kurze Erklärung der Briefe an Titus, Timotheus,* Leipzig, 1844.

Dibelius, M., *Die Pastoralbriefe,* second edition, Tübingen, 1931.

Easton, B. S., *The Pastoral Epistles,* London, 1948.

Ellicott, C. J., *Commentary on the Pastoral Epistles,* London, 1864.

Erdman, Charles R., *The Pastoral Epistles of Paul,* Philadelphia, 1923.

Everyday Life in Ancient Times, published by The National Geographic Society, Wash., D.C., 1953.

Falconer, R., *The Pastoral Epistles,* Oxford, 1937.

Goodspeed, E. J., *Paul,* Philadelphia and Toronto, 1947.

Greydanus, S., *Bizondere Canoniek,* Kampen, 1949.

Grosheide, F. W., *De Openbaring Gods In Het Nieuwe Testament,* Kampen, 1953.

Harrison, P. N., *The Problem of the Pastoral Epistles,* Oxford, 1921.

Hawkins, R. M., *The Recovery of the Historical Paul,* Nashville, Tenn., 1943.

Hendriksen, W., *The Meaning of the Preposition ANTI in the New Testament* (unpublished doctoral dissertation submitted to Princeton Seminary), 1948.

Hendriksen, W., *Bible Survey,* Grand Rapids, Mich., fourth edition, 1953.

Hendriksen, W., *More Than Conquerors, An Interpretation of the Book of Revelation,* Grand Rapids, Mich., eighth edition, 1957.

I-II TIMOTHY AND TITUS

Holtzmann, H. J., *Die Pastoralbriefe,* Leipzig, 1880.

James, J. D., *The Genuineness and Authorship of the Pastoral Epistles,* London, 1906.

Jeremias, Joachim, *Die Briefe an Timotheus und Titus,* Göttingen, 1934.

Keller, Werner, *The Bible as History,* New York, 1956.

Knox, John, *Chapters in a Life of Paul,* New York and Nashville, 1946.

Koole, J. L., *I en II Timotheus en Titus* (in *De Bijbel In Nieuwe Vertaling*), Kampen (no date).

Kraeling, Emil G., *Rand McNally Bible Atlas,* New York, 1956.

Lock, W., *The Pastoral Epistles* (in *International Critical Commentary*), Edinburgh, 1924.

Loeb Classical Library, New York (various dates). The volumes of this set have been consulted for the writings of Homer, Josephus, Menander, Philo, Plato, Plutarch, Thucydides, Xenophon, etc.

Michaelis, W., "Pastoralbriefe und Wortstatistik," *ZNTW* 28 (1929).

Michaelis, W., *Pastoralbriefe und Gefangenschaftbriefe. Zur Echtheitsfrage der Pastoralbriefe,* 1930.

Moffatt, J., *Introduction to the Literature of the New Testament,* New York, 3rd ed., 1918.

Moulton, W. F., and Geden, A. S., *A Concordance to the Greek New Testament,* Edinburgh, third edition, 1950.

Moulton, J. H., and Milligan, G., *The Vocabulary of the Greek Testament,* Edinburgh, 1930.

Nageli, Th., *Der Wortschatz des Apostels Paulus,* Göttingen, 1905.

National Geographic Map, *Lands of the Bible Today,* December, 1956.

Parry, John, *The Pastoral Epistles,* 1920.

Pherigo, Lindsey P., "Paul's Life After the Close of Acts," *JBL* 70 (December, 1951).

Plummer, Alfred, *The Pastoral Epistles* (in *The Expositor's Bible*), reprint Grand Rapids, Mich., 1943, Vol. 6.

Riddle, W., and Hutson, H. H., *New Testament Life and Literature,* Chicago, 1946.

Robertson, A. T., *Word Pictures in the New Testament,* New York and London, 1931, Vol. IV.

Robertson, A. T., *The Minister and his Greek New Testament,* New York, 1923.

Robertson, A. T., *Grammar of the Greek New Testament in the Light of Historical Research,* New York, 1923.

Sauer, E., *In the Arena of Faith,* Grand Rapids, 1955.

Schlatter, A., *Die Kirche der Griechen im Urteil des Paulus,* Stuttgart, 1936.

Schleiermacher, F., *Ueber den Sogenannten Brief von Paulus an den Timotheus,* 1807.

Schweitzer, A., *The Mysticism of Paul the Apostle,* New York, 1931.

Scott, E. F., *The Literature of the New Testament,* 6th ed., New York, 1940.

Simpson, E. K., "The Authenticity and Authorship of the Pastoral Epistles," *EQ* 12 (October, 1940).

Simpson, E. K., *The Pastoral Epistles,* London, 1954.

Sizoo, A., *De Antieke Wereld en het Nieuwe Testament,* Kampen, 1946.

Sizoo, A., *Uit de Wereld van het Nieuwe Testament,* Kampen, 1948.

Spicq, P. C., *Saint Paul, Les Épîtres Pastorales,* Paris, 1947.

Tenney, Merrill C., *The New Testament, A Survey,* Grand Rapids, 1953.

The Good News, The New Testament with over 500 Illustrations and Maps, published by the American Bible Society, New York, 1955.

Torm, F., "Ueber die Sprache in den Pastoralbriefen," *ZNTW* 18 (1918).

Trench, R. C., *Synonyms of the New Testament,* edition Grand Rapids, 1948.
Tucker, T. C., *Life in the Roman World of Nero and St. Paul,* New York, 1922.
Van Andel, J., *Paulus' Brieven Aan Timotheus,* Leiden, 1904.
Van Dijk, *Paraphrase van de Eerste Brief aan Timotheus,* Franeker (no date).
Veldhoen, N. G., *Het Proces van den Apostel Paulus* (unpublished doctoral dissertation submitted to the university of Leiden), 1924.
Warfield, B. B., *The Inspiration and Authority of the Bible,* Philadelphia, Pa., 1948.
Westminster Dictionary of the Bible, by J. D. Davis (revised and rewritten by H. S. Gehman), Philadelphia, 1944.
Westminster Historical Atlas to the Bible, Philadelphia, 1945.
White, N. J. D., *The First and Second Epistles to Timothy and the Epistle to Titus* (in *The Expositor's Greek Testament*), reprint Grand Rapids, Mich., vol. 4 (no date).
Wohlenberg, G., *Die Pastoralbriefe,* Leipsig, 1906.
Wuest, Kenneth S., *The Pastoral Epistles in the Greek New Testament* (Twelfth in the Series of *Word Studies*), Grand Rapids, 1954.
Wuest, Kenneth S., *Golden Nuggets from the Greek New Testament,* Grand Rapids, 1939.
Zahn, Th., *Einleitung in das Neue Testament,* 1897-1900, Vol. II.

New Testament Commentary

New Testament Commentary

Exposition of the Epistle to the Hebrews

Simon J. Kistemaker

Contents

Abbreviations

ASV	American Standard Version
ATR	*Anglican Theological Review*
BA	*Biblical Archaeologist*
Bauer	Walter Bauer, W. F. Arndt, F. W. Gingrich, and Frederick Danker, *A Greek-English Lexicon of the New Testament*, 2d ed.
BASOR	*Bulletin of the American Schools of Oriental Research*
BF	British and Foreign Bible Society, *The New Testament*, 2d ed.
Bib	*Biblica*
BibLeb	*Bibel und Leben*
Bov	Jose M. Bover, *Novi Testamenti Biblica Graeca et Latina*, 4th ed.
BS	*Bibliotheca Sacra*
CBQ	*Catholic Biblical Quarterly*
CTJ	*Calvin Theological Journal*
I Clem.	First Epistle of Clement
Dial.	Justin Martyr, *Dialogue with Trypho*
Epid.	Irenaeus, *Epideixis*
EvQ	*Evangelical Quarterly*
ExpT	*Expository Times*
GNB	Good News Bible
Heresies	Irenaeus, *Against Heresies*
HTR	*Harvard Theological Review*
Interp	*Interpretation*
JBL	*Journal of Biblical Literature*
JB	Jerusalem Bible
JETS	*Journal of the Evangelical Theological Society*
JTS	*Journal of Theological Studies*
KJV	King James Version
LB	The Living Bible
LCL	Loeb Classical Library edition
LXX	Septuagint
Merk	Augustinus Merk, ed., *Novum Testamentum Graece et Latine*, 9th ed.
MLB	The Modern Language Bible

Moffatt	The Bible: A New Translation by James Moffatt
NAB	New American Bible
NASB	New American Standard Bible
NEB	New English Bible
Nes-Al	Eberhard Nestle; Kurt Aland, rev., *Novum Testamentum Graece,* 26th ed.
NIDNTT	*New International Dictionary of New Testament Theology*
NIV	New International Version
NKJV	New King James Version
NovT	*Novum Testamentum*
NTS	*New Testament Studies*
Phillips	The New Testament in Modern English
4Q *Florilegium*	Collection of biblical texts from Qumran Cave 4
1QSa	Rule of the Congregation *(serekh hayaḥad)* from Qumran Cave 1
RefR	*Reformed Review*
RSV	Revised Standard Version
RV	Revised Version
ScotJT	*Scottish Journal of Theology*
SB	H. L. Strack and P. Billerbeck, *Kommentar zum Neuen Testament aus Talmud und Midrasch*
StTh	*Studia Theologica*
Talmud	The Babylonian Talmud
TB	*Tyndale Bulletin*
TDNT	*Theological Dictionary of the New Testament*
TR	Textus Receptus: The Greek New Testament According to the Majority Text
Tyn H Bul	*Tyndale House Bulletin*
TS	*Theological Studies*
TZ	*Theologische Zeitschrift*
WH	B. F. Westcott and Fenton Hort, *The New Testament in the Original Greek*
WTJ	*Westminster Theological Journal*
ZNW	*Zeitschrift für die Neuentestamentliche Wissenschaft*
ZPEB	*Zondervan Pictorial Encyclopedia of the Bible*
ZTK	*Zeitschrift für Theologie und Kirche*

Preface

When Dr. William Hendriksen died in January 1982, he had completed commentaries in the New Testament Commentary series on the four Gospels and on all of Paul's epistles with the exception of I and II Corinthians. He set the goal of writing as many commentaries as he was able.

I have been given the challenge to continue this task. Although my style may differ somewhat from that of Dr. Hendriksen, the format, design, and purpose are those of my predecessor. My commentary on Hebrews has been written for the benefit of the pastor and the lay person.

The commentary on the text itself is free from technical terms and phrases, so that the lay person can read the explanation of a text without difficulty. For the student who knows Greek, I have placed the explanation of Greek words, phrases, and constructions at the conclusion of each section of the text.

Introductory statements, comments about doctrinal considerations, and a summary are part of every chapter. And throughout the commentary the reader finds numerous practical helps and applications. Last, a Scripture index in the concluding pages proves to be of great value for quick reference and consultation.

Spring 1984 Simon J. Kistemaker

Introduction

Outline

A. What Are the Characteristics of Hebrews?
B. Who Wrote This Epistle?
C. What Is the Message of Hebrews?
D. Why Was This Letter Rejected in the Early Centuries?
E. When Was Hebrews Written?
F. Who Were the First Readers?
G. How Can Hebrews Be Outlined?

If there is one book of the New Testament that exhorts the Christian to remain faithful "in the last days," it is the Epistle to the Hebrews. This epistle has a special message for a day marked by apostasy; it addresses the believer who, facing unbelief and disobedience, must stand firm in the faith. The letter to the Hebrews, then, is an exhortation to faithfulness. Granted that Hebrews teaches the superiority of Christ over angels, Moses, Joshua, Aaron, and Melchizedek, the exhortations that are freely interspersed among the doctrinal sections set the tone. The admonitions reveal the warm heart and deep concern of the pastor-writer.

Constantly in the epistle the author pleads with the reader to remain faithful to the gospel and not to drift away (2:1; 3:12; 4:11; 6:11–12; 10:22–25; 12:25). He stresses corporate responsibility: fellow believers are exhorted to take care that not one believer is allowed to turn away from the living God (3:12–13; 4:1, 11). The consequences of falling away are indeed unimaginable, for, says the writer, "It is a dreadful thing to fall into the hands of the living God" (10:31).

The writer of Hebrews counsels the believer to listen obediently to the Word of God (4:2–3, 6, 12). He exhorts the believers to "worship God acceptably with reverence and awe" (12:28). And he concludes that "our God is a consuming fire" (12:29)—in case this exhortation is disregarded.

In an age in which apostasy is commonplace and "the secret power of lawlessness is already at work," as Paul puts it in II Thessalonians 2:7, the message of Hebrews is most relevant. We simply cannot ignore the warning that accompanies "such a great salvation" (2:3), because we are unable to escape if we do. Therefore, we do well to listen attentively.

A. What Are the Characteristics of Hebrews?

Many translations of the Bible call Hebrews "the Epistle to the Hebrews." But is this New Testament book really an epistle? If we compare it with the epistles of Paul, James, Peter, Jude, and John, we must say that it is not. Greetings customary in these letters—with the exception of I John—are absent in Hebrews.

1. Letter or Epistle?

In the letter itself, however, the writer includes a few references to the conduct and possessions of the readers (6:10; 10:32–34). And in chapter 13 he becomes rather intimate with the recipients. He calls Timothy "our brother" and mentions that Timothy, having been released from prison, will accompany him to visit the readers (13:23). The letter ends with greetings (13:24), and therefore in view of this last chapter Hebrews is indeed a letter.

The beginning of Hebrews has something in common with the First Epistle of John. Both have an introduction that in many respects serves as a summary statement for the succeeding chapters. The name of the author is absent in Hebrews and in I John. Also, specific mention of the addressees, greetings, and prayers are missing. These elements are characteristic of the rest of the New Testament epistles.

To say that Hebrews is a treatise in order to avoid the use of the words *epistle* or *letter* is not too satisfactory. A treatise consists of an exposition of or discourse on one topic, but Hebrews teaches a number of doctrines and intersperses them with pastoral exhortations. We admit that whatever word is used to describe this book of the New Testament, difficulties remain. One solution to the problem is to call the book Hebrews, as some of the more recent translations do. Yet Hebrews itself is one of the general Epistles of the New Testament.

As an epistle Hebrews is similar to some of the writings of Paul; it contains doctrine and exhortation. Paul's custom, however, is to set forth doctrine first; toward the end of his epistles, Paul gives his exhortations. Hebrews differs in this respect. The writer mingles doctrine and pastoral admonition; for example, in the midst of his teaching on the Son's superiority to the angels, the author exhorts the reader to "pay more careful attention" to the Word of God (2:1–4).

2. Pastoral or Doctrinal?

Is Hebrews a pastoral or doctrinal epistle? We can easily answer, "It is both." Yet we admit that on balance the purpose of the writer of Hebrews is to convey a pastoral exhortation to the recipients. He strengthens his admonitions with doctrines about Christ's superiority, the priesthood, the covenant, and faith.

Nowhere in the entire New Testament except in the letter to the Hebrews are the doctrines of Christ's priesthood and the covenant explained. We find but a passing reference to the priesthood of Christ in Romans 8:34, "Christ Jesus, who died—more than that, who was raised to life—is at the right hand of God and is also interceding for us." Paul merely mentions the intercessory work of Christ and thus implies Christ's priesthood. But in all his epistles Paul refrains from writing about this doctrine. Although Paul's theological training included the doctrine of the covenant as an integral part of Old Testament teaching, he mentions the word *covenant* nine times (Rom. 9:4; 11:27; I Cor. 11:25; II Cor. 3:6, 14; Gal. 3:15, 17; 4:24; Eph. 2:12). In Galatians 4:24 he is somewhat specific: "These things may be taken figuratively, for the women represent two covenants. One covenant is from Mount Sinai and bears children who are to be slaves: This is Hagar." Yet even in this setting, Paul's treatment is rather scant. The writer of Hebrews, on the other hand, teaches the doctrines of the priesthood and the covenant in full.

3. Revelation and Inspiration

The author gives the reader God's revelation. For him the primary author of Scripture, namely, the Holy Spirit, is all important, for God addresses the reader through his Word. Thus, not the secondary author but God is the speaker in the introductory phrases to the numerous quotations from the Old Testament. In chapter 1, God is the One who utters the citations from the Psalms, the Song of Moses (Deut. 32:43, LXX), and II Samuel 7:14. With variations the phrase *God says* occurs constantly (1:5, 6, 7, 8, 10, 13; 2:12, 13; 3:7; 4:3; 5:5, 6; 7:21; 8:8; 10:5, 15, 17; 13:5). And because the secondary author is unimportant for the writer of Hebrews, his own name also has been deleted, perhaps purposely, in this letter. By focusing attention on the Triune God as speaker, the author teaches that Scripture is divinely inspired. He has heard not the voice of man but the voice of God.

Interestingly, however, when the author quotes from the Old Testament he uses the Greek translation (the Septuagint) of the Hebrew text. And this translation in places differs from the original. Here are two examples. First, Psalm 8:5 has: "You made him a little lower than the heavenly beings [or: than God]," and Hebrews 2:7 reads: "You made him a little [or: for a little while] lower than the angels." Second, the wording of Psalm 40:6 is: "Sacrifice and offering you did not desire, but my ears you have pierced." However, Hebrews 10:5 gives this reading: "Sacrifice and offering you did not desire, but a body you prepared for me."

Why did the author use a translation that differed from the Old Testament text? Possibly the writer did not know Hebrew, had learned the Scriptures through a Greek translation, and wrote to readers who themselves used this translation. Does this mean that the so-called Septuagint translation was inspired? Of course not. The Hebrew text of the Old Testament, not the translation, was inspired by God. But this does not mean that the writer of Hebrews was forbidden to quote from a translation, even from one that showed some variation. However, at the moment the author wrote his letter, the inspiration of the epistle, including the Old Testament quotations, took place. Guided by the Holy Spirit, the writer was free to take his material from a translation that differed from the Hebrew text; he did not have to correct the translation to make it conform to the reading of the Hebrew original. He wrote to Hebrews who were familiar with the Septuagint; that, for them, was the Bible.

4. The Old Testament

We who are accustomed to owning personal copies of the Bible should not think that this was true for the readers of Hebrews in the second half of the first century. Copies of the Old Testament books were kept in the local synagogue and church. These were used during the worship services for the instruction of the people. But the people attending the worship services did not possess these books. They treasured the Word in their hearts and minds by committing the psalms and hymns to memory. Also they learned messianic passages of the Old Testament by heart. They sang the well-known psalms and hymns in church or at home, and they recited particular verses from the Old Testament.

The author of Hebrews chose his citations carefully. For instance, in chapter 1, five quotations are from familiar psalms, one from the Song of Moses, and one from a messianic passage. The author appeals to the memory of his readers and thus communicates the Word clearly and effectively.

5. Style

A final characteristic of Hebrews is the choice of words, the balanced sentences, the rhetorical rhythm in the original Greek, and the excellent style. Even in translation the reader today perceives something of the magnificence of the author's literary ability. Take, for example, the author's pithy definition of faith: "Now faith is being sure of what we hope for and certain of what we do not see" (11:1). Or analyze this sentence for balance: "If we deliberately keep on sinning after we have received the knowledge of the truth, no sacrifice for sins is left, but only a fearful expectation of judgment and of raging fire that will consume the enemies of God" (10:26–27). The author reveals himself as an educated person who chose his words carefully and who was thoroughly familiar with the teaching of the Old Testament.

B. Who Wrote This Epistle?

When questioned about the authorship of Hebrews, the third-century theologian Origen said, "But who wrote the epistle, to be sure, only God knows." And that was in A.D. 225. If scholars at the dawn of the Christian era did not know who wrote Hebrews, we certainly will not rise above them.

1. Apollos

Of course, scholars have suggested possible candidates, but they must resort to hypotheses. Martin Luther, for example, thought that Apollos was the author of Hebrews. He based his hypothesis on Acts 18:24–26, "Meanwhile a Jew named Apollos, a native of Alexandria, came to Ephesus. He was a learned man, with a thorough knowledge of the Scriptures. He had been instructed in the way of the Lord, and he spoke with great fervor and taught about Jesus accurately, though he knew only the baptism of John. He began to speak boldly in the synagogue. When Priscilla and Aquila heard him, they invited him to their home and explained to him the way of God more adequately."

Luther pointed out that Alexandria was a great educational center, where Apollos learned to express himself masterfully in the Greek language. Apollos used the Septuagint translation of the Old Testament because the Septuagint was first published in Alexandria.

Apollos had become acquainted with the Christian faith, had heard Paul preach in Ephesus, and had been instructed "in the way of God more adequately" by Priscilla and Aquila. He possessed a "thorough knowledge of the Scriptures," "taught about Jesus accurately," and became an outstanding speaker. For Martin Luther, Apollos was most qualified to write the Epistle to the Hebrews.

The hypothesis is attractive indeed and answers many questions. However, the silence of the centuries is telling. We would expect that Clement of Alexandria, about A.D. 200, says something about this matter, but he omits the name *Apollos.* Instead Clement ascribes Hebrews to Paul.

2. Paul

Was Paul the author of Hebrews? For centuries numerous people have accepted the Pauline authorship of this epistle. From the first publication of the King James Version in 1611 to the present, many people have taken the title verbatim: "The Epistle of Paul the Apostle to the Hebrews." But in the margin of some Bibles of this version the reader is told: "Authorship uncertain, commonly attributed to Paul."

The uncertainty of Pauline authorship stems from the difference between the epistles of Paul and Hebrews. To begin with the language of Hebrews, we see a distinct difference. Nothing in Hebrews reminds us of the style, diction, word choice, and material of Paul's letters. The language in Hebrews simply is not that of Paul.

The doctrines expressed in Hebrews find no echo in any of Paul's epistles. Usually in these letters cross-references to major doctrines are evident. Not so in Hebrews. The doctrines of Christ's priesthood and the covenant are prominent in Hebrews, but absent from the letters of Paul.

The use of names referring to Jesus in Hebrews differs from that of Paul. In his earlier epistles Paul refers to the Lord as Jesus Christ, but in his later epistles this combination is reversed: Paul calls him Christ Jesus. He seldom writes *Jesus* (II Cor. 11:4; Phil. 2:10; I Thess. 4:14). The author of Hebrews, by contrast, repeatedly calls the Lord by his given name *Jesus* (2:9; 3:1; 4:14; 6:20; 7:22; 10:19; 12:2, 24; 13:15). Three times the author of Hebrews uses the combination *Jesus Christ* (10:10; 13:8, 21), and only once he says *Lord Jesus* (13:20). The Epistle to the Hebrews, however, lacks the combination *Christ Jesus.*

The most significant point in considering whether Paul wrote the Epistle to the Hebrews has to do with Hebrews 2:3. The writer, who includes himself in his warning to pay attention to the Word of God, says, "This salvation, which was first announced by the Lord, was confirmed to us by those who heard him." In schematic form, we have the following sequence:

This salvation which

1. was first announced by the Lord
2. by those who heard him
3. was confirmed to us

The conclusion may be drawn that the writer had not heard the Lord personally but had to rely on the reports of others. Paul, of course, states categorically that he did not receive the gospel from anyone but Jesus Christ (Gal. 1:12). Paul heard the voice of Jesus on the Damascus road (Acts 9:4; 22:7; 26:14). And Jesus spoke to him afterward (Acts 18:9–10; 22:18–21). Paul, therefore, could not have written the words of Hebrews 2:3.

3. Barnabas

Tertullian, around A.D. 225, suggested that Barnabas was the writer of Hebrews. He did this in light of Barnabas's credentials given in Acts 4:36–37: "Joseph, a Levite from Cyprus, whom the apostles called Barnabas (which means Son of Encouragement), sold a field he owned and brought the money and put it at the apostles' feet." As a Levite, Barnabas was fully acquainted with the Levitical priesthood. Besides, he came from the island of Cyprus where he presumably learned the Greek language well. He was familiar with the church and its needs. Thus, he was eminently qualified to write the Epistle to the Hebrews, according to Tertullian. The weakness of this position is that it has not found any support in the history of the canon. Tertullian has not gained any followers and his suggestion has been viewed as a curiosity.

4. Priscilla

Last among the names that have been proposed for solving the question of authorship is the name of Priscilla. She with her husband Aquila instructed Apollos (Acts 18:26). But Priscilla could not have written Hebrews because in the original Greek of Hebrews 11:32, the writer uses a participle with a *masculine* ending when he refers to himself: "I do not have time to tell about Gideon. . . ."

What is the conclusion of the matter? We simply say with Origen, "But who wrote the epistle, to be sure, only God knows." In the final analysis, authorship is not important. The content of the epistle is what matters.

C. What Is the Message of Hebrews?

A cursory glance at the Epistle to the Hebrews tells the readers that its content is strengthened by numerous quotations from the Old Testament; next, the author constantly exhorts the readers pastorally; and last, the development of the doctrinal part follows a logical sequence. We begin our survey of the content with a discussion of the Old Testament citations in Hebrews.

1. Old Testament Quotations

Estimates of the number of direct quotations in the Epistle to the Hebrews vary. For example, some scholars count all the direct citations and come to a total of thirty-six.[1] Others find twenty-four direct quotations from the Old Testament and add another five passages "which are used verbally though not formally quoted." They recognize twenty-nine citations.[2]

Although we realize that the author of Hebrews did not have to provide introductory statements for each Old Testament quote, we still think that a direct citation is one with an introductory formula. We find twenty-six quotations, to which we add five that lack an introduction. This brings the total to thirty-one passages.

The Psalter was a favorite book for the writer of Hebrews. One-third of his direct quotations have been taken from the Book of Psalms. Most of them are located in Hebrews 1. One citation comes from the Hymn of Moses, Deuteronomy 32, in the Septuagint version.

Direct Quotations

	Old Testament	*Hebrews*
1.	Psalm 2:7	1:5a; 5:5
2.	II Samuel 7:14	1:5b
3.	Deuteronomy 32:43	1:6b
4.	Psalm 104:4	1:7
5.	Psalm 45:6–7	1:8–9
6.	Psalm 102:25–27	1:10–12
7.	Psalm 110:1	1:13
8.	Psalm 8:4–6	2:6–8a
9.	Psalm 22:22	2:12
10.	Isaiah 8:17	2:13a
11.	Isaiah 8:18	2:13b
12.	Numbers 12:7	3:2, 5
13.	Psalm 95:7–11	3:7–11
14.	Genesis 2:2	4:4
15.	Psalm 110:4	5:6; 7:17, 21
16.	Genesis 22:17	6:14
17.	Genesis 14:17–20	7:1–2
18.	Exodus 25:40	8:5
19.	Jeremiah 31:31–34	8:8–12
20.	Exodus 24:8	9:20
21.	Psalm 40:6–8	10:5–7
22.	Deuteronomy 32:35a	10:30a
23.	Deuteronomy 32:36a; Psalm 135:14a	10:30b
24.	Isaiah 26:20; Habakkuk 2:3–4	10:37–38

1. Ceslaus Spicq, *L'Épître aux Hébreux,* 2 vols. (Paris: Gabalda, 1952), vol. 1, p. 331.
2. B. F. Westcott, *Commentary on the Epistle to the Hebrews* (Grand Rapids: Eerdmans, 1950), pp. 469–74.

25. Genesis 21:12	11:18
26. Proverbs 3:11–12	12:5–6
27. Exodus 19:12–13	12:20
28. Deuteronomy 9:19	12:21
29. Haggai 2:6	12:26
30. Deuteronomy 31:6	13:5
31. Psalm 118:6	13:6

The writer of Hebrews appeals to his readers by quoting familiar passages from the Old Testament. These passages presumably had been memorized by the readers, so that when they heard the Epistle to the Hebrews read to them in a worship service, they could relate to its content. The Old Testament Scriptures, therefore, were of great importance to the author and the readers of this epistle. In the words of the writer, "the word of God is living and active. Sharper than any double-edged sword" (4:12). And that Word has been quoted, alluded to, and used in Hebrews more than in any other New Testament book.

2. Pastoral Admonitions

Repeatedly the author admonishes his readers to "pay more careful attention" to the Word of God (2:1). He calls that word preached to the Israelites in the desert "the gospel" (4:2), and he states that these rebellious people died in the desert because they failed to combine the Word they had heard with faith.

Is the epistle predominantly pastoral? Or is it doctrinal? Differently stated, the question is whether the author's admonitions result in theological teaching or, vice versa, whether doctrines lead to admonitions.[3] If we look at the numerous passages that exhort the readers, we see a remarkable consistency in approach. The author writes pastorally and encourages the Hebrews to remain faithful to God and his Word. "See to it, brothers, that none of you has a sinful, unbelieving heart that turns away from the living God" (3:12). This admonition is the key to understanding the pastoral concerns of the writer. It is basic to the warnings that precede and follow. In sequence, here are a number of admonitions that make up the content of the Epistle to the Hebrews:

2:1–4	"We must pay more careful attention, therefore"
3:1	"Therefore, holy brothers, . . . fix your thoughts on Jesus"
3:12–19	"See to it, brothers"
4:1–3	"Therefore, . . . let us be careful"
4:11	"Let us, therefore, make every effort"
4:14–16	"Therefore, . . . let us hold firmly to the faith"

3. F. W. Grosheide, *De Brief aan de Hebreeën en de Brief van Jakobus* (Kampen: Kok, 1955), p. 43.

6:1–3	"Therefore let us leave the elementary teachings"
6:11–12	"We want each of you to show this same diligence"
10:19–39	"Therefore, brothers, . . . let us draw near to God"
12:1–28	"Therefore, . . . let us throw off everything that hinders"
13:1–25	"Keep on loving each other as brothers"

The appeal of the writer comes to the readers in phraseology that borders on repetition. The message is clear: keep the faith, be obedient, remain strong, come to God, and claim your salvation. The author warns the reader against the sin of unbelief that eventually takes its toll and ends in apostasy.

As the writer exhorts so he teaches. He expresses his concern that the readers obey the Word of God, and thus he exhorts them. He also wants his readers to know the Word, and thus he teaches them.

3. Doctrinal Sequence

In the opening verses of his introduction (1:1–2), the author defines the extent and the range of the Word of God: in the Old Testament era God spoke through his prophets; in New Testament times, he has spoken through his Son. He expected his people to obey his Word when it was communicated to them "by angels" (2:2), for disobedience resulted in "just punishment." How much more, then, are the people of the New Testament era to obey God's Word that was proclaimed not by angels but by the Son of God. And this Son is far superior to the angels because he is the Prophet who spoke the Word (1:2), the Priest who "provided purification for sins" (1:3), and the King who "sat down at the right hand of the Majesty in heaven" (1:3). Furthermore, this Prophet, who is Priest and King as well, demands strict obedience to the Word that proclaims salvation (2:3).

The superiority of the Son of God in relation to the angels is confessed in psalm and song. The psalm and hymn writers portray the Son as King, God, Creator, and one whose "years will never end" (1:12). In distinction from the angels, the Son took upon himself man's human nature (2:14) and is not ashamed to call his people brothers and sisters, for he and they "are of the same family" (2:11–12). Because of this close identity with his brothers and sisters, Jesus became their "merciful and faithful high priest in service to God," and thus he made "atonement for the sins of the people" (2:17). For this reason, says the writer of Hebrews, I exhort you to "fix your thoughts on Jesus, the apostle and high priest whom we confess" (3:1).

Jesus is greater than Moses. Moses was a faithful servant in God's house; Jesus is a faithful son over God's house (3:5–6). In the time of Moses the Israelites refused to obey God's Word and consequently perished in the desert (3:17). The believer today is exhorted to listen to "the gospel" and to make every effort to enter the rest God has promised (4:3, 6, 11). Take the living and active Word of God to heart, counsels the author, because it may be compared with a double-edged sword (4:12).

Also, Jesus is far greater than Aaron. Aaron was a high priest, but a sinner; Jesus is the great high priest, yet without sin (5:3; 4:14–15). Jesus became high priest in the order of Melchizedek (5:10). The readers should have known this fact by searching the Scriptures. Therefore, the author of Hebrews reproves them for their indolence (5:11–13). He exhorts them to advance in the "teachings about Christ" (6:1); refusal to advance leads to spiritual death (6:4–6, 8). He encourages the believers with the reassuring word that God is true to his promise. That promise God confirms with an oath, so that his word is unchangeable (6:17–18).

The writer shows the readers from the Old Testament Scriptures that Jesus, belonging to the high-priestly order of Melchizedek, is superior to the Levitical priests (chap. 7). Priests in the Aaronic order were appointed by law, were sinners, and were subject to death (7:23, 27–28). When God swore an oath, Jesus became priest and thereby indicated the unchangeableness of his priestly office (7:21). He is sinless and is priest forever.

Jesus is priest-king, but he does not serve in an earthly tabernacle; he has gone to serve in "the true tabernacle set up by the Lord, not by man" (8:2; see also 9:11, 24). There in the Most Holy Place he obtained eternal redemption for his people, and there he serves as "the mediator of a new covenant" (9:15). Christ offered himself once for all and thereby "made perfect forever those who are being made holy" (10:14) and have the law of the new covenant in their hearts and written on their minds.

The second part of the epistle begins with 10:19 and is pastoral throughout. The writer encourages the readers "to draw near to God," to meet together for worship, and to await the coming Day (10:22, 25). Once more he stresses that deliberate sin cannot be forgiven (6:4–6; 10:26–29). The result of willful sin is that one "fall[s] into the hands of the living God" (10:31).

Chapter 11 is a consideration of the heroes of faith depicted in the Old Testament. The author has been selective and devotes most of the discussion to Abraham the father of believers (11:8–19). He exhorts the readers to fix their attention on Jesus, the "author and perfecter" of their faith (12:2), to strengthen their "feeble arms and weak knees" (12:12), and "to live in peace with all men and to be holy" (12:14). Chapter 12 concludes with an exhortation to "worship God acceptably with reverence and awe" (12:28). The last chapter of Hebrews is a series of concluding exhortations with an eloquent benediction (13:20–21) and personal greetings (13:22–25).

D. Why Was This Letter Rejected in the Early Centuries?

1. First Century

The history of the Epistle to the Hebrews in the Christian church of the first few centuries is rather varied. The letter was accepted in the West and quoted by Clement of Rome in his epistle, known as I Clement, to the church of Corinth. First Clement was written about A.D. 96 and contains segments from Hebrews (see especially I Clem. 36:1–5; 17:1, 5; 19:2; 27:2; 43:1;

56:2–4). Clement's use of Hebrews in the last decade of the first century is sufficient evidence that the Epistle to the Hebrews circulated widely.

2. Second Century

Irenaeus, about A.D. 185, quotes from Hebrews. He was bishop of the churches of Vienne and Lyon in southern France. Tertullian, a North African writer who died in A.D. 225, quotes Hebrews 6:4–8. He introduces the lengthy quotation as follows:

> For there is extant withal an Epistle to the Hebrews under the name of Barnabas—a man sufficiently accredited by God. . . . Warning, accordingly, the disciples to omit all first principles, and strive rather after perfection, and not lay again the foundations of repentance from the works of the dead. . . .[4]

The church of the West (Italy, France, and Africa), during the latter part of the second century, had reservations about the place of Hebrews in the canon of the New Testament. For example, the list of New Testament books known as the Muratorian Canon that presumably dates from A.D. 175 does not include the Epistle to the Hebrews.

The reason for these reservations can be traced to the doctrinal controversies of the second and third centuries. In A.D. 156, Montanus, a self-proclaimed theologian from Asia Minor, practiced asceticism and expected his followers to live a life of holiness. He applied Hebrews 6:4–6 to anyone who indulged in worldly matters and thus denied such a person the possibility of repentance. Then in A.D. 250 Emperor Decius instigated persecutions against the Christians, many of whom under duress denied the Christian faith. Novatian, a native of Phrygia in Asia Minor, used Hebrews 6:4–6 against all Christians who had fallen away because of these persecutions. Novatian was of the opinion that it was impossible for them to come to repentance; they were cut off from the church and denied readmission. The application of this Scripture passage in the rigorous manners of the Montanists and the Novatians did not meet with approval in the church. Because of these schismatic movements and their abuse of this particular passage, the Epistle to the Hebrews was not placed among the canonical books of the New Testament in the West.

3. Third Century

The church of the East (Egypt and Syria), however, applied the rule that for a New Testament book to be canonical it had to be apostolic. The Epistle to the Hebrews was thought to be written by Paul, who was an apostle, and therefore Hebrews was accepted as canonical. Already in A.D. 175 Pantaenus said that Paul omitted his name in the epistle for several reasons: his mod-

4. Tertullian, "On Modesty," *Ante-Nicene Fathers* (Grand Rapids: Eerdmans, 1965), vol. 4, chap. 20, p. 97.

esty, his respect for the Lord, and the superabundance of his writing.[5] Although these reasons are unconvincing, they indicate that Pantaenus harbored a degree of uneasiness about Pauline authorship.

His successor Clement of Alexandria, in approximately A.D. 200, expresses the same uneasiness.

> And as for the Epistle to the Hebrews, [Clement] says indeed that it is Paul's, but that it was written for Hebrews in the Hebrew tongue, and that Luke, having carefully translated it, published it for the Greeks. . . . The [words] "Paul an apostle" were naturally not prefixed. For, says he, "in writing to Hebrews who had conceived a prejudice against him and were suspicious of him, he very wisely did not repel them at the beginning by putting his name."[6]

An Alexandrian papyrus manuscript, listed as P^{46} and dated approximately A.D. 200, places the Epistle to the Hebrews among those of Paul. In fact, Hebrews comes after Romans and before I Corinthians. And Athanasius, bishop of Alexandria, writes in A.D. 367 about Hebrews and places it between II Thessalonians and I Timothy.

In the Western church, Hebrews was eventually accepted in the fourth century. Some scholars ascribed it to Paul, but others doubted whether Paul was the author. At any rate, the councils of that century placed Hebrews in the canon. The Council of Hippo Regius in A.D. 393 provides this interesting note: "Thirteen epistles of Paul, and one by the same to the Hebrews." And the Council of Carthage in A.D. 397 includes Hebrews in the epistolary of Paul and simply ascribes fourteen epistles to Paul.

E. When Was Hebrews Written?

Because of I Clement, we can say that Hebrews was composed before A.D. 96. In that year Clement of Rome wrote his epistle to the Corinthian church and incorporated a number of quotations and allusions from Hebrews in his epistle. The outer limit of dating the Epistle to the Hebrews is sure: sometime before A.D. 96. To determine a starting point for the composition of the epistle is difficult.

1. Internal Evidence

In Hebrews 2:3, the author places himself among the readers as second-generation Christians. That is, he himself had not heard the gospel from the lips of Jesus but with the readers had to rely on the preaching of those who had heard Jesus. The author, then, was a follower of the apostles, many of whom could still be alive at the time the writer composed his epistle. Numerous passages in Hebrews reflect a time in which the Christians' ardent love for Christ had waned and the enthusiasm of a former period had disappeared.

---

5. Eusebius, *Ecclesiastical History*, 6.14.4 (LCL).
6. Eusebius, *Ecclesiastical History*, 6.14.2–3 (LCL).

The readers of Hebrews were in danger of drifting away from the gospel they had heard (2:1). Some of them might run the risk of being hardened by the deceitfulness of sin (3:13). Some were in the habit of no longer attending the worship services (10:25). Others were faltering in their spiritual zeal (12:12).

The author rebukes the readers for having failed to learn the doctrines of Scripture. "In fact, though by this time you ought to be teachers, you need someone to teach you the elementary truths of God's word all over again" (5:12). Also their leaders who had taught the Word of God had died (13:7).

In earlier days the readers had endured persecution after they "had received the light" (10:32). They had experienced suffering, insults, and confiscation of their property (10:33). The author fails to provide an indication when the persecution took place. Although we are inclined to think of the time following the burning of Rome in A.D. 64—after which the Neronian persecutions were instigated—the author says nothing more than "remember those earlier days."

The frequent exhortations—to pay attention (2:1), to encourage one another (3:13), to persevere (10:36), to run with perseverance (12:1), and to resist sin (12:4)—leave the impression that the recipients of the epistle lived in a period of religious peace. They no longer seemed to suffer for being Christians, as they had on earlier occasions. And because of the peaceful times, religious backsliding had become a distinct threat to the people to whom Hebrews was addressed.

2. Historical Setting

If we look at the historical setting of the second half of the first century, we note that Nero acceded to the imperial throne in A.D. 54. A decade later the persecutions against the Christians began; they lasted until Nero committed suicide in A.D. 68. Within a year in short succession, Galba, Otho, and Vitellius ruled the Roman empire. But in A.D. 69 Vespasian, who at the time functioned as general of the Roman army that surrounded the city of Jerusalem, became emperor. He loved peace and stability; he was a virtuous man, upright in character.[7] During his ten-year rule, peace returned to his worldwide domain, and consequently persecutions against the Christians belonged to history.

Vespasian's son, Titus, who took his father's place as general of the army in Judea, also followed in his footsteps as emperor in A.D. 79. His brief reign of two years was marked by the same desire for peace and tranquility. When Titus' brother, Domitian, began to rule the empire in A.D. 81, the peaceful trend established by Vespasian and continued by Titus endured for the next decade. Toward the end of his reign, Domitian introduced persecutions that may have caused the exile of John to the isle of Patmos (Rev. 1:9).

---

7. Michael Grant, *The Twelve Caesars* (New York: Scribner's, 1975), p. 219.

History verifies that a decline of religious fervor occurs more often in a period of peace and prosperity than in times of persecution and hardship. I venture to say that the Epistle to the Hebrews reflects a period of sustained peace during which the Christians had relaxed spiritually. The writer of the epistle, then, felt obliged to write words of exhortation and occasional rebuke. His reference to the persecution the readers had endured in "those earlier days" may refer to that of Nero in the years A.D. 64–68. The epistle probably was written in the early 80s.

3. Religious Context

However, a much more weighty consideration relates to the author's discussion of the high priesthood of Christ. When the writer is about to discuss the topic of Jesus as high priest in the order of Melchizedek, he says that this subject "is hard to explain because you are slow to learn" (5:11). The word *hard* had overtones that reverberated in the Hebrew community. For the Jew, the Aaronic priesthood was sacrosanct because God had ordained it by law (7:11–12). No Jew would dare suggest that the Levitical priesthood ought to be "set aside because it was weak and useless" (7:18) and assert that "the law made nothing perfect" (7:19). Should he say such a *hard* thing, he would bring the wrath and indignation of the Hebrew community on his head.

The fact that the author of the epistle boldly writes about the setting aside of the Levitical priesthood can best be understood when we place the time of composition a decade or more after the destruction of the temple and the cessation of the Aaronic priesthood. The writer, therefore, had the freedom to express himself on this matter without incurring the anger of the Jewish people. Perhaps this is one of the reasons that the other New Testament writers refrained from discussing the priesthood of Christ. For example, in spite of the vow of purification that Paul took to show the Jews in Jerusalem that he was living in obedience to the law (Acts 21:22–26), he was accused of teaching doctrines against the Jewish people, the law, and the temple (Acts 21:28). What Paul could not do regarding the priesthood, the writer of Hebrews was able to do in a time in which the priesthood and the law concerning it belonged to the past.

Nowhere in the Epistle to the Hebrews do we find any mention of the temple in Jerusalem. The writer discusses the tabernacle and priesthood of the forty-year period in the wilderness. Because he deletes any reference to the temple or the destruction of Jerusalem, he may imply that the priestly services had come to an end. And for that reason, he turns his attention to the initial stages of the Levitical priesthood and the construction of the tabernacle.

The conclusion to these observations is that a date for Hebrews of a decade after the destruction of the Jerusalem temple and the cessation of the priesthood is not at all improbable. Perhaps Hebrews was composed between A.D. 80 and 85.

F. Who Were the First Readers?

The recipients of the Epistle to the Hebrews were Jewish Christians. Where these Hebrews lived, the author fails to say. If he had only given some indication as to the epistle's place of destination, we would not need to work with a hypothesis. Many place names have been suggested: Jerusalem, the Qumran settlement near the Dead Sea, Alexandria, Rome—to mention no more.

1. Israel

If we accept a date of composition after A.D. 70, automatically Jerusalem and the Qumran community are ruled out. After the Romans destroyed the city of Jerusalem, they eventually renamed it Aelia Capitolina and forbade the Jews from resettling there. Also, the Qumran community evacuated during the years of Roman occupation.

2. Alexandria

Scholars who favor Alexandria as the place where the Hebrews lived base their supposition on the fact that Alexandria for centuries had been the home of many Jewish people. Here the Septuagint originated to aid the Greek-speaking Jews in their Scripture reading. And according to Acts 18:24, Alexandria was the place from which Apollos came. But no writer of the first few centuries testifies to an Alexandrian destination or to a possible authorship of Apollos. We need to look elsewhere for a place of destination.

3. Rome

Many factors point to Rome. The final greeting of the epistle mentions Italy. "Those from Italy send you their greetings" (13:24). Granted that the preposition *from* can be interpreted to mean *in*—that is, "those who are in Italy send you their greetings"—the commonly understood meaning *away from* Italy seems to be preferred. Christians from Italy who were away from their homeland conveyed greetings to their loved ones in Italy, presumably Rome.

Did the writer of Hebrews address his letter to the same congregation that received Paul's letter to the Romans? Not necessarily. Many congregations flourished in the imperial city in view of the early beginnings of the church in Rome. (For example, archaeologists have unearthed a funerary inscription in Rome that bears the name of a Christian lady, known as Pomponia Graecina, who was buried in A.D. 43.) We assume that in the course of time the church continued to increase in numbers. The author of Hebrews makes a distinction between "leaders" and "people" when he writes, "Greet all your leaders and all God's people" (13:24). He seems to leave the impression that he addresses his epistle to a particular congregation in Rome.

Next, Clement of Rome quoted from the epistle soon after it was written. Although the letter could have been composed elsewhere and in time brought to Rome, a letter addressed to the Hebrews in Rome would circulate among the congregations in that city and thus be available to Clement.

And last, Jewish people were most numerous in the imperial city, as Roman historiographers and Flavius Josephus attest. An inscription bearing the word *Hebrews* and dating from the second century after Christ has been found in Rome.

We feel comfortable with the choice of Rome, although we admit that we can only use a hypothesis. And yet the accumulated facts seem to point to this choice. Perhaps the intention of the author of Hebrews in omitting the place of destination may have been to indicate that his epistle has a message for the church universal. Especially in our day in which we hear the expression *the end time* repeatedly, the message of the Epistle to the Hebrews is most relevant.

G. How Can Hebrews Be Outlined?

A concise outline of Hebrews can easily be committed to memory with the following seven points:

1:1–4	1. Introduction
1:5–2:18	2. Jesus Is Superior to Angels
3:1–4:13	3. Jesus Is Greater Than Moses
4:14–7:28	4. Jesus Is the Great High Priest
8:1–10:18	5. Jesus Is the Mediator of a New Covenant
10:19–12:29	6. Jesus' Work Is Applied by the Believer
13:1–25	7. Conclusion

Here is a more detailed outline:

1:1–2:18	Jesus' Superiority and His Role as Savior and High Priest	
	A. Introduction	1:1–4
	B. Jesus' Superiority to Angels	1:5–14
	C. Jesus, Savior and High Priest	2:1–18
3:1–4:13	Jesus' Superiority to Moses	
	A. A Comparison of Jesus and Moses	3:1–6
	B. A Warning Against Unbelief	3:7–19
	C. An Invitation to Enter God's Rest	4:1–13
4:14–5:10	Jesus' High Priesthood	
	A. Encouragement for the Readers	4:14–16
	B. Enablement of the High Priest	5:1–3
	C. Fulfillment of the High-priestly Office	5:4–10

5:11–6:20	Exhortations	
	A. Do Not Fall Away	5:11–6:12
	B. Hold on to God's Promise	6:13–20
7:1–28	Jesus: High Priest like Melchizedek	
	A. Melchizedek, King and Priest	7:1–10
	B. Melchizedek's Superior Priesthood	7:11–19
	C. Christ's Superior Priesthood	7:20–28
8:1–10:18	Jesus: High Priest and Sacrifice	
	A. The Heavenly Sanctuary	8:1–2
	B. Jesus the Mediator	8:3–6
	C. God's New Covenant	8:7–13
	D. The Earthly Sanctuary	9:1–10
	E. Jesus' Sacrificial Blood	9:11–28
	F. Jesus' Effective Sacrifice	10:1–18
10:19–39	More Exhortations	
	A. An Exhortation to Persevere	10:19–25
	B. A Warning to Pay Attention	10:26–31
	C. A Reminder to Continue	10:32–39
11:1–40	The Heroes of Faith	
	A. A Definition of Faith	11:1–3
	B. Three Examples of Faith: Abel, Enoch, and Noah	11:4–7
	C. The Faith of Abraham	11:8–19
	D. The Faith of Isaac, Jacob, and Joseph	11:20–22
	E. The Faith of Moses	11:23–29
	F. Faith at Jericho	11:30–31
	G. Known and Unknown Heroes of Faith	11:32–40
12:1–13:25	Admonitions and Exhortations	
	A. Divine Discipline	12:1–13
	B. A Divine Warning	12:14–29
	C. Communal Obligations	13:1–6
	D. Ecclesiastical Duties	13:7–17
	E. Prayers and Benedictions	13:18–21
	F. Final Greetings	13:22–25

Commentary

1

Jesus' Superiority and His Role as Savior and High Priest, *part 1*

1:1–14

Outline

1:1–4	A. Introduction	
	B. Jesus' Superiority to Angels	
1:5		1. Psalm 2:7
1:5		2. II Samuel 7:14
1:6		3. Deuteronomy 32:43
1:7		4. Psalm 104:4
1:8–9		5. Psalm 45:6–7
1:10–12		6. Psalm 102:25–27
1:13		7. Psalm 110:1

1 1 In the past God spoke to our forefathers through the prophets at many times
and in various ways, 2 but in these last days he has spoken to us by his Son, whom
he appointed heir of all things, and through whom he made the universe. 3 The
Son is the radiance of God's glory and the exact representation of his being, sustaining all things by his powerful word. After he had provided purification for sins, he sat
down at the right hand of the Majesty in heaven. 4 So he became as much superior to the
angels as the name he has inherited is superior to theirs.

A. Introduction
1:1–4

The writer of Hebrews dispenses with the usual greetings and salutations that are typical of Paul's letters and those of James, Peter, John, and Jude. (The First Epistle of John does not give any greetings in the introduction nor in the conclusion, and for that reason is technically not an epistle.) In the conclusion of Hebrews, however, the author uses the first person pronoun *I* a few times; mentions that if Timothy, who has been released from prison, arrives soon, he will accompany the writer on a visit to the recipients of the epistle; and conveys greetings to all God's people.

Why would the writer not address the readers in the customary way by making himself known, specifying the addressees, and pronouncing a salutation of grace, peace, and mercy? The answer must be that the author wants to focus attention primarily on the ultimate revelation of God—Jesus Christ, his Son. This revelation is contrasted with the piecemeal revelation that God, through the prophets, gave to the forefathers for many centuries. The author stresses the theme of the person, offices, and function of Jesus, the Son of God.

The writer does not address the original readers by name or place even though he intimately uses forms of the first person pronoun ("we," "us," and "our") throughout his epistle. The title of the epistle may have been added later, for the writer nowhere in his letter refers to Hebrews. We may assume that the epistle, although written to a specific congregation originally, was intended for the church universal. The message conveyed is addressed to the church of all ages and places. To put it differently, if there is any epistle in the New Testament that addresses the church universal in the days prior to Jesus' return, it is the Epistle to the Hebrews.

The failure of the author to identify himself at all in his writing is in keeping with the time in which he lived. It was customary for a writer to display modesty by omitting his name; for example, the Gospel writers do not refer to themselves by name, and among the writers of epistles, John refrains from using his name in the three letters attributed to him.

The author of Hebrews does not call attention to himself or to the recipients of his epistle, but to Jesus, who completed through his appearance the revelation of God to man.

1. In the past God spoke to our forefathers through the prophets at many times and in various ways.

In sonorous tones and in a somewhat musical setting, the author begins his epistle with an introductory sentence that is elegant in style, diction, and word choice. Some translators have tried to convey the dignity and alliteration of the original, but most of them have been ineffectual in capturing the exact intonation of the opening sentence of Hebrews.[1]

God spoke to the forefathers in the ages preceding the birth of Jesus and communicated to them his revelation. God is the originator of revelation. He is the source, the basis, the subject. God used the prophets in the Old Testament era to make his Word known to the people. But he was not limited to speaking through the prophets; this first verse states that God brought his revelation to his people at many times and in various ways. The words *times* and *ways* have a prominent place in the original Greek: they stand first in the sentence. Among the forefathers who received God's revelation were Adam, Abel, Enoch, Noah, Abraham, Isaac, Jacob, Joseph, and Moses. God spoke to Adam "in the cool of the day" (Gen. 3:8); to Abraham in visions and visits—in fact, Abraham was called God's friend (James 2:23); to Jacob in a dream; to Moses "face to face" (Exod. 33:11) as a man speaks with a friend.

Through the prophets, from Moses to Malachi, God's revelation was recorded in written form as history, psalm, proverb, and prophecy. The prophets were all those saints called by God and filled with his Spirit to speak the Word as a progressive revelation that intimates the coming of Christ. In his first epistle, Peter refers to them:

> The prophets, who spoke of the grace that was to come to you, searched intently and with the greatest care, trying to find out the time and circumstances to which the Spirit of Christ in them was pointing when he predicted the sufferings of Christ and the glories that would follow. It was revealed to them that they were not serving themselves but you, when they spoke of the things that have now been told you by those

---

1. Among the translations that most successfully reflect the emphasis and the alliteration of the original are the Dutch translation of 1637, *Staten Vertaling* ("God, voortijds veelmaal en op velerlei wijze tot de vaderen gesproken hebbende door de profeten, heeft in deze laatste dagen gesproken door de Zoon") and the Spanish translation of 1602 ("Dios, habiendo hablado muchas veces y en muchas maneras en otro tiempo á los padres por los profetas, en estos postreros días nos ha hablado por el Hijo").

who have preached the gospel to you by the Holy Spirit sent from heaven. [1:10–12]

The prophet did not bring his own message, his own formulation of religious truth. Inspired by the Holy Spirit, he spoke the Word of God, which did not have its origin in the will of man (II Peter 1:21) but came from God (Heb. 3:7).

2a. But in these last days he has spoken to us by his Son.

Although the contrast between the times before the coming of Christ and the appearance of Christ as the completion of God's revelation is striking in verses 1 and 2, the continuity of this revelation is also significant. Both parts of God's revelation form one unit because there is but one Author. There is but one God who reveals, and there is but one revelation. The Word spoken by God to the forefathers in the past does not differ basically from the Word spoken to us by his Son.

Yet in many ways the contrast between the first and the second verse is obvious. We may show the contrast graphically:

God has spoken
in the

	OLD TESTAMENT ERA	NEW TESTAMENT ERA
how?	at many times and in various ways	
when?	in the past	in these last days
to whom?	to our forefathers	to us
by whom?	through the prophets	by his Son

The figure appears to be incomplete: the "how" on the Old Testament side does not have a New Testament counterpart. The phrase "at many times and in various ways" lacks a parallel. The writer is pointing out that the fullness of revelation is unique, final, and complete. He is not implying that the piecemeal revelation given through the prophets was inferior and that the revelation provided by the Son was without variation. Not at all. The many-sided revelation of God that came repeatedly to the forefathers in the ages before the birth of Christ was inspired by God. It was a progressive revelation that constantly pointed toward the coming of the Messiah. And when Jesus finally came, he brought the very Word of God because he *is* the Word of God. Therefore, Jesus brought that Word in all its fullness, richness, and multiplicity. He was the final revelation. As F. F. Bruce aptly remarks, "The story of divine revelation is a story of progression up to Christ, but there is no progression beyond Him."[2]

2. F. F. Bruce, *The Epistle to the Hebrews,* New International Commentary on the New Testament series (Grand Rapids: Eerdmans, 1964), p. 3.

Jesus himself did not write a single verse of the New Testament; men designated by him and filled with the Spirit wrote God's revelation. Jesus, the living Word, speaks to us because no one else possesses equal authority; "for there is no other name under heaven given to men by which we must be saved" (Acts 4:12). By his Son, God addresses all believers. In these last days God has spoken to us by his Son. The phrase *in these last days* is set over against the phrase *in the past* and refers to the age in which the fulfillment of the messianic prophecies has taken place. This age waits for the liberation "from its bondage to decay" to be "brought into the glorious freedom of the children of God" (Rom. 8:21).

In the first two verses of Hebrews there is a contrast between the prophets, who were a distinct group of people chosen and appointed by God to convey his revelation, and the Son of God, who surpasses all the prophets because he is Son. In fact, all the emphasis in verse 2 falls on the word *Son.*[3] There is, strictly speaking, only one Son of God; all others are created sons (angels) and adopted sons (believers). As God has spoken by his Son, so the Son has spoken by the apostles who, inspired by the Holy Spirit, wrote the books of the New Testament. The new revelation that God has given us in his Son is a continuation of the revelation given to the forefathers. God's revelation, completed in his Son, is a unit, a harmonious totality in which the Old is fulfilled in the New.

2b. Whom he appointed heir of all things, and through whom he made the universe.

To express the excellence of the Son of God, the writer of Hebrews describes what God has done.

God appointed his Son heir of all things. An heir rightfully inherits whatever the father has stipulated in his will. As the one and only Son, Jesus thus inherits everything the Father possesses. Incomprehensible! Unfathomable!

The time when God appointed the Son heir of all things cannot be determined. The Son may have been appointed heir in God's eternal plan. Or Jesus may have been appointed heir when in the fullness of time he entered the world, or when he pronounced the Great Commission: "All authority in heaven and on earth has been given to me" (Matt. 28:18).

The writer of Hebrews immediately clarifies the term *all things* by saying that God made the universe through his Son. The phrase obviously refers to the creation account in the first chapters of Genesis. Many people think that the New Testament, which speaks about redemption, has nothing to say about creation. However, the New Testament is not entirely silent on this subject; both Paul and the writer of the Epistle to the Hebrews teach that Jesus was active in the work of creation. In his discussion about the supremacy of Christ, Paul teaches: "For by him all things were created . . .; all things

---

3. The RSV gives the literal translation *by a Son.* But the noun is used in an absolute sense of the word and is equivalent to a proper name. See John Albert Bengel, *Gnomon of the New Testament,* ed. Andrew R. Fausset, 7th ed., 5 vols. (Edinburgh: Clark, 1877), vol. 4, p. 339. The definite article in the Greek is omitted, as it is in Heb. 1:5; 3:6; 5:8; and 7:28.

were created by him and for him" (Col. 1:16). And John in his Gospel confirms the same truth: "Through him all things were made; without him nothing was made that has been made" (1:3).[4]

Through his Son, God made the universe. It is impossible for man to understand the full import of this statement, but complete understanding is not the objective at this point. However, it is important to recognize the majesty of the Son of God, who was present at creation and is the sovereign Lord of all created things. He is God.

The word *universe* signifies primarily the cosmos, the created world in all its fullness, and secondarily all the stars and planets God has created. But the meaning is much more comprehensive than this, because it involves all the events that have happened since the creation of this world. It concerns the earth and its history throughout the ages. The word has been interpreted as "the sum of the 'periods of time' including all that is manifested in and through them."[5] It refers not to the world as a whole but to the entire created order that continued to develop in the course of time.

3. The Son is the radiance of God's glory and the exact representation of his being, sustaining all things by his powerful word. After he had provided purification for sins, he sat down at the right hand of the Majesty in heaven.

a. "The Son is the radiance of God's glory." The word *radiance* is to be preferred to variations of the word *reflection,* which many translations provide.[6] The moon receives its light from the sun and simply reflects these light beams to the earth. The moon itself does not possess nor emanate light, because it does not produce light. The sun as a heavenly body radiates its light in all its brightness and power to the earth. By way of comparison, we may see Christ as the radiant light coming from the Father as sunlight emanates from the sun.[7]

Jesus said, "I am the light of the world" (John 8:12); he is light, and in him there is no darkness. He radiates the light of God's glory, perfection, and majesty. Philip Edgcumbe Hughes observes that Jesus' radiance "is not so much . . . the glory of the Son's deity shining through his humanity, but . . . the glory of God being manifested in the perfection of his manhood completely attuned as it was to the will of the Father."[8]

Jesus' radiance is derived from the Father, even though he himself is the light. The Son causes the radiance of the Father to shine forth. As John writes in the prologue to his Gospel, "We have seen his glory, the glory of

---

4. See also Ps. 33:6; Rom. 11:36; I Cor. 8:6; Rev. 3:14.

5. B. F. Westcott, *Commentary on the Epistle to the Hebrews* (Grand Rapids: Eerdmans, 1950), p. 8.

6. GNB, MLB, *Moffatt,* NAB, RSV.

7. Gerhard Kittel, *TDNT,* vol. 1, p. 508; Ralph P. Martin in *NIDNTT,* vol. 2, p. 290, writes, "On balance, the act[ive] sense of 'radiance' is to be chosen in preference to 'reflection.' "

8. Philip Edgcumbe Hughes, *Commentary on the Epistle to the Hebrews* (Grand Rapids: Eerdmans, 1977), pp. 41–42.

the One and Only, who came from the Father, full of grace and truth" (1:14). The Son's radiance, therefore, is an extension of God's glory.

b. "And the exact representation of his being." The Son is the perfect representation of God's being. That is, God himself stamped upon his Son the divine imprint of his being. The word translated as "exact representation" refers to minted coins that bear the image of a sovereign or president. It refers to a precise reproduction of the original. The Son, then, is completely the same in his being as the Father.[9] Nevertheless, even though an imprint is the same as the stamp that makes the impression, both exist separately. The Son, who bears "the very stamp" (RSV) of God's nature, is not the Father but proceeds from the Father and has a separate existence. Yet he who sees the Son has seen the Father, as Jesus explained to Philip (John 14:9).

The word *being* is really a parallel of the word *glory,* for both terms describe the essence of God.[10] Although existing separately, the Son, as the exact representation of the Father's being, is a perfect copy of God's nature. The Son is the mediator who possessed God's glory by nature before he assumed his mediatorial role. The Son bears the exact imprint of the Father's being from eternity.

c. "Sustaining all things by his powerful word." The Son is not only the Creator of the universe (1:2); he is the upholder of all things as well (1:3). The two passages complement each other and reveal the divine power of the Son. He speaks, and by his word all things are sustained, preserved, upheld.

This part of the verse in the original is closely connected to the preceding portion by means of the particle *and,*[11] which unfortunately many translations omit. It directly ties the participial phrase to the verb *is* in the first part of the sentence.

The first part of the verse stresses the person of Christ; the second, the work of Christ. From a discussion about the being of the Son, the writer proceeds to an explanation of the Son's activity, which involves caring for all things. In fact, the word that has been translated as "sustaining" basically means carrying. That word in itself signifies a forward motion, although not in the sense of an Atlas whose movement is torturously slow because the weight of the globe nearly crushes him.

The Son carries "all things" to bring them to their destined end. And he does this by a mere utterance ("by his powerful word"). Christ, the ruler of the universe, utters a word, and all things listen in obedience to his voice. No other motions are necessary, for the spoken word is sufficient.

d. "After he had provided purification for sins, he sat down at the right

---

9. The writer of the Wisdom of Solomon says of wisdom: "For she is a breath of the power of God, and a pure emanation of the glory of the Almighty; therefore nothing defiled gains entrance into her. For she is a reflection of eternal light, a spotless mirror of the working of God, and an image of his goodness" (7:25–26, RSV). *The Apocrypha of the Old Testament,* ed. Bruce M. Metzger (New York: Oxford University Press, 1965).

10. Helmut Köster, *TDNT,* vol. 8, p. 585.

11. Westcott, *Hebrews,* p. 13.

hand of the Majesty in heaven." This sentence indicates a sequence in the redemptive deeds of Christ.

He performed his mediatorial work by completing and yielding his earthly life as a sacrifice on the cross for the removal of sins. In a rather pithy phrase the high-priestly work of Christ is summarized: Christ himself "provided purification for sins." According to the Mosaic law the high priest had to make atonement on the Day of Atonement to cleanse the people of Israel of all their sins (Lev. 16:29–34). The Aaronic high priest was a sinner and therefore did his work imperfectly, whereas Christ as the sinless One and the true High Priest completed the work of purification perfectly. The high priest in the Old Testament era needed animal sacrifices, first to cleanse himself and afterward to remove the sins of the people. Christ was simultaneously the High Priest and the sacrifice when he offered himself for the purification of the sins of his people. The Son once for all offered himself up on the cross in order to atone for our sins. The plural is used for the concept *sin* (see Eph. 1:7; Col. 1:14; II Peter 1:9).

After his mediatorial work was completed, the Son ascended to heaven and took his rightful place of honor next to God the Father. In typical Hebraic style, perhaps to avoid offending any of his Jewish readers, the author refers to God as the Majesty in heaven. Of course, elsewhere in the epistle he freely uses God's name.

e. "He sat down at the right hand of the Majesty in heaven" (cf. Rom. 8:34; Eph. 1:2; Col. 3:1). The expressions *sat down* and *the right hand* must not be taken literally, but rather symbolically. The idea of sitting at the right hand of someone signifies a privilege granted to a highly honored person. In this instance it means that the Son now has authority to rule his worldwide kingdom on earth and is enthroned above all spiritual powers "in heavenly places." The kingdom belongs to him and God has given him "the name that is above every name, that at the name of Jesus every knee should bow, in heaven and on earth and under the earth, and every tongue confess that Jesus Christ is Lord, to the glory of God the Father" (Phil. 2:9–11).

4. So he became as much superior to the angels as the name he has inherited is superior to theirs.

The writer of Hebrews has portrayed the Son as

1. the Prophet through whom God has spoken
2. the Creator who made the universe
3. the Heir of all things
4. the Representation of God's being
5. the Upholder of all things
6. the Priest who provided purification for sins
7. the King who sat down at his place of honor

Now the author compares the Son with angels, those created beings that constantly surround the throne of God. They of all creatures are closest to

God; they serve as his messengers; they are appointed to be busy in the work of providing man with God's revelation and in the work of redeeming fallen man (Acts 7:38, 53; Gal. 3:19; Heb. 2:2). In many respects, angels are higher than man, who was crowned with glory and honor as king in God's creation (Ps. 8:5).

Even if angels are in a certain sense higher than man, they are in no sense superior to the Son, because "he has inherited" a name that is superior to theirs. Thus far the Son has not been introduced by name, either as Jesus or as Christ. The name of the Son does not refer to a specific personal name but to his designation as the Son. He is known as the Son of God, the one and only Son. He is also Lord and Savior. The prophet Isaiah calls him "Wonderful Counselor, Mighty God, Everlasting Father, Prince of Peace" (9:6). By contrast, angels are referred to as "messengers" (Ps. 104:4); they are designated "ministering spirits" (Heb. 1:14).

The name of the Son came to him by inheritance, because the Father appointed him heir (Heb. 1:2). The angels have been created to be servants and are excluded from being heirs. They minister to those who shall inherit salvation (Heb. 1:14), but they themselves do not share in any inheritance.

Angels may be called "sons of God" (Job 1:6; 38:7), "mighty ones" (Ps. 29:1), or "holy ones" (Ps. 89:6), but remain created beings, in contrast to the Son, who is their Creator.

Christ inherited the name, which was foreordained in the counsel of God; and when he completed his mediatorial work on earth, he received the inheritance so that he could say, "All authority in heaven and on earth has been given to me" (Matt. 28:18). The permanence of his inheritance can be seen in Paul's description of the resurrection and the ascension of Christ, who is seated at the right hand of God "in the heavenly realms, far above all rule and authority, power and dominion, and every title that can be given, not only in the present age but also in the one to come" (Eph. 1:20–21).

Doctrinal Considerations in 1:1–4

The revelation that God had given to the believers in the Old Testament era was completed in the New Testament era by the Son of God. There are not two revelations, one for the Old Testament believers and one for New Testament believers. God's revelation is one, although given in two phases. During the first phase God's revelation came often and in a variety of ways. The second phase constitutes the fulfillment of God's revelation in the person of his Son. The Old Testament is the promise of the coming of the Son; the New Testament is the fulfillment of that promise. These familiar lines summarize the unity of God's revelation in the Scriptures:

The New is in the Old concealed,
The Old is in the New revealed.

The writer of Hebrews demonstrates his high regard for the Scriptures by stating unequivocally that God is the author of his revelation. God spoke in the past and has now spoken in his Son. And because it is God who has spoken, no one ought to question the authority of his written Word. God has spoken last of all in his Son, and that revelation is final.

The threefold office of prophet, priest, and king is spelled out in the first few verses of this brief introduction. The Son is the Prophet, for God in these last days has spoken in him; he is the Priest who has provided purification for sins; and he is the King who sustains the world by his powerful word and is seated at the right hand of God in heaven. These few introductory verses are a summary of what the writer is about to teach in the remainder of his letter.

The author's teaching about the supremacy of Jesus Christ (Heb. 1:4) is preceded by three verses that stress the divinity of the Son. The theme in Hebrews 1:3 is similar to that which Paul develops in Colossians 1:15, 17, 20.

Hebrews 1:3	*Colossians 1:15, 17, 20*
The Son is the radiance of God's glory and the exact representation of his being, sustaining all things by his powerful word.	He is the image of the invisible God, the firstborn over all creation.
	He is before all things, and in him all things hold together.
After he had provided purification for sins, he sat down at the right hand of the Majesty in heaven.	and through him [God was pleased] to reconcile to himself all things, whether things on earth or things in heaven, by making peace through his blood, shed on the cross.

The construction of Hebrews 1:3–4 indicates that the verses were an early Christian confession, perhaps used for liturgical and catechetical purposes. The short participial phrases in the original remind the reader of similar confessions that are recorded in Philippians 2:6–11 and I Timothy 3:16.

Greek Words, Phrases, and Constructions in 1:1–4

Verse 1

λαλήσας—aorist active participle, which may denote concession.

ἐν τοῖς προφήταις—the preposition ἐν is followed by the instrumental dative. Because of the definite article, the word προφήταις should be taken in its broadest possible sense.

Verse 2

ἐπ' ἐσχάτου τῶν ἡμερῶν τούτων—although translated as "in these last days," the Greek literally says, "at the end of these days." The adjective ἐσχάτος is singular.

ἐλάλησεν—aorist active, to be taken in the culminative sense. Note that, as in verse 1, the verb λαλεῖν is used instead of λέγειν to indicate that the emphasis falls on the act of speaking and not on the content.

ἐν υἱῷ—the preposition ἐν implies a locative and an instrumental meaning. The definite article is lacking because the absolute sense of the noun is stressed: Jesus Christ is the one and only Son.

κληρονόμος—the word is a combination of κλῆρος (lot) and νέμομαι (I possess) with the meaning *one who received by lot.* The word occurs fourteen times in the New Testament, three of which are in Hebrews (1:2; 6:17; 11:7).

Verse 3

ὤν—present active participle of εἰμί, denoting time.

ἀπαύγασμα—the noun is derived from the verb ἀπαυγάζω (I emit brightness). A related noun is αὐγή (brightness). The ending -μα in ἀπαύγασμα generally indicates the result of an action.

χαρακτήρ—from χαράσσω (I engrave, inscribe). The noun refers to the exact expression, the precise reproduction of an original. See I Clement 33:4. A related noun is χάραγμα (a stamp or imprinted mark); this word is used in Acts 17:29; Revelation 13:16, 17; 14:9, 11; 15:2; 16:2; 19:20; 20:4.

ὑπόστασις—the word finds its root in ὑφίσταμαι (I stand under). The meaning of the noun includes the idea of substance, nature, or essence.

φέρων—present active participle denoting time.

τε—an adjunct particle that links this clause closely to the preceding one.

τὰ πάντα—note the definite article used to emphasize the concept by making it all-inclusive.

τὸ ῥῆμα—the use of τὸ ῥῆμα instead of ὁ λόγος stresses the act of speaking more than the content of the spoken word.

ποιησάμενος—aorist middle participle. The aorist is used to show that the Son accomplished the task of purification; the middle indicates that he himself was the agent.

Verse 4

τοσούτῳ—the dative of degree of difference, followed by ὅσῳ. See Hebrews 7:20–22; 10:25. The word is a pronoun of degree referring to size and quantity.

κρείττων—comparative adjective.

γενόμενος—aorist middle participle that may have a causal or a temporal meaning.

τῶν ἀγγέλων—genitive of comparison. The definite article points to the class or the category of angels.

διαφορώτερον—comparative form from διάφορος (excellent, surpassing). The word is derived from the verb διαφέρω (I bear or carry through).

κεκληρονόμηκεν—perfect active indicative to state that the inheritance has been, is, and will be in effect.

---

5 For to which of the angels did God ever say,
"You are my Son;
today I have become your Father"?
Or again,
"I will be his Father,
and he will be my Son"?
6 And again, when God brings his firstborn into the world, he says,
"Let all God's angels worship him."
7 In speaking of the angels he says,
"He makes his angels winds,
his servants flames of fire."

8 But about the Son he says,
"Your throne, O God, will last for ever and ever,
and righteousness will be the scepter of your kingdom.
9 You have loved righteousness and hated wickedness;
therefore God, your God, has set you above
your companions
by anointing you with the oil of joy."
10 He also says,
"In the beginning, O Lord, you laid the foundations
of the earth,
and the heavens are the work of your hands.
11 They will perish, but you remain;
they will all wear out like a garment.
12 You will roll them up like a robe;
like a garment they will be changed.
But you remain the same,
and your years will never end."
13 To which of the angels did God ever say,
"Sit at my right hand
until I make your enemies
a footstool for your feet"?
14 Are not all angels ministering spirits sent to serve those who will inherit salvation?

B. Jesus' Superiority to Angels
1:5–14

5. For to which of the angels did God ever say,

> **"You are my Son;**
> **today I have become your Father"?**

Or again,

> **"I will be his Father,**
> **and he will be my Son"?**

The reader of Hebrews is immediately struck by the numerous citations from the psalms that the author uses to strengthen his teaching about the superiority of Jesus Christ. In the first chapter alone he includes five quotations from the Psalter and two from other books. And in the following chapter, quotations from the Psalms occur rather frequently; they almost become the hallmark of this epistle.

The recipients of the letter had become familiar with the Psalms in the local worship services in which the congregation sang "psalms, hymns and spiritual songs" (Eph. 5:19; Col. 3:16). They possessed a store of knowledge that had been communicated orally in the worship services and committed to memory. "It is not surprising at all that the author [of Hebrews], in an attempt to reach perfect communication, strengthens not only his whole Epistle with quotations from the Psalter known in the liturgy of the Church: indeed in his first chapter he avails himself of five passages from the Psalms and one from the Hymn of Moses (Deut. 32)."[12] The quotations are from Psalm 2:7 and II Samuel 7:14 in verse 5; Deuteronomy 32:43 (according to the readings in the Dead Sea Scrolls and the Septuagint) in verse 6; Psalm 104:4 in verse 7; Psalm 45:6–7 in verses 8–9; Psalm 102:25–27 in verses 10–12; and Psalm 110:1 in verse 13.

1. Psalm 2:7
1:5

For to which of the angels did God ever say, "You are my Son; today I have become your Father"? The writer obviously links this verse to verse 4, in which he introduces the teaching of the Son's superiority to angels. He does not intend to by-pass the significance of the first three verses, but in verse 4 he makes the point of comparing the Son with the angels and stating his superiority. With the help of quotations from the Old Testament, specifically from the Book of Psalms, the author indicates that the Son has fulfilled the Scripture passages that he quotes.

One of these passages, Psalm 2, is probably of Davidic origin. This assumption is predicated on information in Acts 4:22–26, which indicates that the Jerusalem church handed down an ancient tradition concerning the authorship of this psalm.[13] The Jewish people understood Psalm 2 to be messianic, and their use of the psalm in the synagogue reflected that understanding.[14] The individual writers of the New Testament also interpreted messianically all the quotations and references from the second psalm. For example, when Paul preached in Pisidian Antioch, he said, "What God promised our fathers he has fulfilled for us, their children, by raising up Jesus. As it is written in the second Psalm: 'You are my Son; today I have become your Father' " (Acts 13:32–33). Quotations from Psalm 2 are given in Acts 4:25–26; 13:33; Hebrews 1:5; 5:5; Revelation 2:26–27; 19:15. Allusions to verses 2, 7, 8, and 9 can be discerned in Matthew, Mark, Luke, Acts, Hebrews, II Peter, and Revelation.

As Psalm 2:7 asks, did God ever say to any of the angels, "You are my son; today I have become your Father"? The answer to this rhetorical question obviously is negative, even though angels are called sons of God (see especially Job 1:6; 2:1; 38:7). The status described in this verse has never been conferred on the angels, and no angel has ever been given the title *Son of God* anywhere in the Scriptures.[15]

In the same way, Solomon, the son of David, never completely fulfilled the words of the psalm. Why, for example, would a son of a king receive the

---

12. Simon J. Kistemaker, *The Psalm Citations in the Epistle to the Hebrews* (Amsterdam: Van Soest, 1961), pp. 14–15.

13. Jan Ridderbos, *De Psalmen,* 2 vols. (Kampen: Kok, 1955), vol. 1, p. 21.

14. SB, vol. 3, pp. 675–77; 1QSa 2.11.

15. Westcott, *Hebrews,* p. 20. The title *Son of God* is never given to a person in the Old Testament. Only the nation Israel is called "my son" (Hos. 11:1) and "my firstborn son" (Exod. 4:22).

title *son*? It would be more fitting to call him king at the time of his accession to the throne (as in Psalm 2:6, "I have installed my King on Zion, my holy hill"). This son is a type of the Son of God. The believers in the Old Testament era, then, were given a representative who foreshadowed the Messiah.

Obviously the earthly king, called Son, was unable to fulfill the words of Psalm 2, for the passage referred to the Messiah who in the fullness of time gave the psalm its ultimate significance. (In the prophecy of Isaiah, the Messiah is revealed as a Son: "for to us a child is born, to us a son is given" [9:6]). The words of Psalm 2 apply ultimately to the Son of God. His appointment to the office of Son—specifically, his appearance in the flesh—is reflected in the clause "today I have become your Father." (The word *today* ought not be taken literally but should be understood generally to refer to the time of Jesus' work on earth.) But the clause does not say that at the moment of Jesus' birth he became the Son or at the time of his resurrection (Acts 13:33) God became his Father. Rather, the words *I have become* indicate that God the Father from eternity has begotten and continues to beget the Messiah, his Son. The Athanasian Creed of the fourth century summarizes this succinctly in its twenty-first and twenty-second articles:

> The Father is made of none, neither created nor begotten, the Son is of the Father alone; not made nor created, but begotten.[16]

The words of Psalm 2:7 could have been fulfilled by neither David nor Solomon but only by Jesus Christ.

Or again. The writer uses a second selection from the Old Testament to show that God has never been called Father of angels and that no angel ever addressed God as Father. Archangels, including Michael and Gabriel, never experienced that honor.

2. II Samuel 7:14
1:5

I will be his Father, and he will be my Son. The context of the quotation reflects David's desire to build a house for the Lord God. The word of the Lord is given to Nathan the prophet, who informs David that not he but his son is to build God's house. Declares the Lord, "He is the one who will build a house for my Name, and I will establish the throne of his kingdom forever. I will be his father, and he will be my son" (II Sam. 7:13–14; I Chron. 17:12–13). The words of the Lord were directed to David's son Solomon, who indeed built the temple in Jerusalem. But through his mediatorial work the Son of God completely overshadowed Solomon.

The author of Hebrews evidently chose this Old Testament passage be-

16. The Nicene Creed states, "[I believe] . . . in one Lord Jesus Christ, the only-begotten Son of God, begotten of the Father before all worlds." And the Belgic Confession says, "We believe that Jesus Christ . . . is the Son of God, not only from the time that he assumed our nature but from all eternity" (art. 10).

cause of its messianic significance. The allusions to II Samuel 7 in the New Testament (especially in Luke 1:32–33; and in John 7:42) indicate that the passage was applied to the Messiah.[17]

3. Deuteronomy 32:43
1:6

6. And again, when God brings his firstborn into the world, he says, "Let all God's angels worship him."

From a well-known messianic psalm and a similar passage from a historical book the writer of Hebrews turns to the Hymn of Moses, recorded in Deuteronomy 32 and used in temple services and local synagogues. The Jews considered the concluding verses of this hymn to be messianic.[18]

This quotation is introduced by the phrase *and again,* which is followed by the clause "when God brings his firstborn into the world." The subject is God the Father, who brings his Son into the world. But when did or will this take place? The question remains: should the translation from the Greek read, "And again, when God brings his firstborn into the world" or "But when God shall bring again his firstborn into the world"?[19]

The first translation is a reference to the birth of Jesus, when a multitude of the heavenly host praised God in the fields near Bethlehem (Luke 2:13). The second translation is an amplification of Jesus' discourse on the end of the age. At the end of time "he will send his angels with a loud trumpet call" (Matt. 24:31); that is, the angels of God will worship the Son when he returns at the close of this age. However, why does the writer of Hebrews speak of a second coming of Jesus when he has not said anything in the immediate context about Christ's first coming? It seems more appropriate to prefer the first translation, for it logically follows the quotations in verses 5 and 6.

The word *firstborn* in verse 6 (see also Luke 2:7; Rom. 8:29; Col. 1:15, 18; Heb. 11:28; 12:23; Rev. 1:5) qualifies the word *Son* and is a title given to Jesus. We cannot determine when that title was given, because the writers who use the term apply it to creation, resurrection, dignity, and honor. The psalmist records a blessing upon David when God said, "I will also appoint him my firstborn" (Ps. 89:27). The Son, as the firstborn, enters the inhabited world of men. The word *world* is Hellenic and was used in ordinary speech to refer to the populated world.[20]

a. The quotation itself shows that "not only is the Son greater than angels,

---

17. In 4Q *Florilegium,* II Sam. 7:14 is quoted and interpreted in a way that calls attention to the Messiah.

18. F. W. Grosheide, *De Brief aan de Hebreeën en de Brief van Jakobus* (Kampen: Kok, 1955), p. 69.

19. See ASV, NASB. A number of commentators, including Westcott, Grosheide, Franz Delitzsche, and R. C. H. Lenski, feel that the Greek word order should be followed. Scholars who think that the adverb *again* modifies the verb *bring* interpret the clause as a reference to the return of Christ; others think that the clause refers to the resurrection.

20. *TDNT,* vol. 5, p. 157; *NIDNTT,* vol. 1, p. 519.

but He is worshipped by angels."[21] The Son is the Creator of the angels, and God orders these creatures to show homage to his Son. The angels, because they are created, must serve the Son and "those who will inherit salvation" (Heb. 1:14).

b. The origin of the quotation seems to be a Greek translation of the Hymn of Moses (Deut. 32:43). The translation based on the Hebrew text is rendered:

> Rejoice, O nations, with his people,
> for he will avenge the blood of his servants;
> he will take vengeance on his enemies
> and make atonement for his land and people.

The Septuagint and the Dead Sea Scrolls show an addition to the first line of the verse.

> Rejoice, O nations, with his people,
> and let all the angels worship him,
> for he will avenge the blood of his servants.

In the Septuagint version of Psalm 97:7 (Ps. 96:7, LXX) we read the exhortation: "Worship him[,] all you his angels." The translation based on the Hebrew text reads, "Worship him, all you gods!"

c. The Hymn of Moses is quoted and alluded to more than any other portion from the Book of Deuteronomy. The writer of Hebrews quotes twice from this hymn (Heb. 1:6; 10:30). In his letter to the Romans, Paul cites the hymn three times (Rom. 10:19; 12:19; 15:10). Allusions to this hymn are found in Matthew, Luke, John, Acts, Romans, I Corinthians, II Corinthians, Ephesians, Hebrews, I John, and Revelation. John records in Revelation 15 that the victorious saints were given harps by God and "sang the song of Moses the servant of God" (Rev. 15:3). This reference to the heavenly use of the Hymn of Moses reflects its liturgical use in the church on earth. And in the church on earth the hymn was sung in languages other than Hebrew. The Jews living in dispersion used the Greek rendition of this song, from which the author of Hebrews quoted a line that describes the superiority of the Son over the angels.

The addressee in Deuteronomy 32:43 is the Lord God, who must be worshiped by his angels. This homage the writer of Hebrews (having clearly established the divinity of Jesus) transfers to the Son. The quotation reinforces the author's teaching about the deity of Christ.

Doctrinal Considerations in 1:5–6

Angels do not share in God's promises; they have no part in the inheritance that is accorded to believers ("we are heirs—heirs of God and co-heirs with Christ"; Rom. 8:17). Scripture does not say that any angel is God's Son; therefore an angel,

---

21. Bengel, *Gnomon,* vol. 4, p. 344.

although exalted by being in the presence of God, is in no way equal to, nor can in any way be compared to, the Son of God.

The writer of Hebrews quotes from the Hymn of Moses as it was rendered in the Septuagint. The Greek translation of Deuteronomy 32 was well known to him and his audience because in the dispersion the Jews used the Septuagint in the synagogues. The early Christians adopted the liturgy with variations to express the Christian emphasis.

The author's use of a quote from the Septuagint that is without an exact equivalent in the Hebrew text in our possession does not mean that the doctrine of inspiration has been undermined. The Holy Spirit, who is the primary author of Scripture and inspired every human writer, directed the author of Hebrews to select a quote from the Hymn of Moses in the Greek. When the author incorporated the line into his epistle, that line became inspired Scripture.

The word *today* (v. 5) is not limited to designating a specific time but ought to be understood in a broader sense. For example, the declaration of Christ's sonship was effective not only on the day of his resurrection, but also on the day of his ascension and his session at the right hand of God the Father (Heb. 1:4).

Greek Words, Phrases, and Constructions in 1:5–6

Verse 5

οἱ ἄγγελοι—in the Septuagint the phrase ἄγγελοι θεοῦ occurs frequently. The definite article points to the angels as a class.

υἱός—without the definite article the noun is to be understood in the absolute sense: "My Son you are"; not "You, too, are my son."

μου . . . σύ, ἐγὼ . . . σε—the use of the personal pronouns shows the emphasis the writer wishes to express in this rather short sentence.

γεγέννηκα—the use of the perfect of γεννάω conveys the idea of a completed state, constitutes a declaration of sonship, and relates an action that continues perpetually and eternally.

Verse 6

εἰσαγάγῃ—the aorist active subjunctive of εἰσάγω. The aorist signifies single occurrence of an action but says nothing about the time itself.

προσκυνησάτωσαν—the verb προσκυνέω means "to bow down, to show respect, to worship by falling down." The verb form is the aorist active imperative, which implies command as well as consent.

---

4. Psalm 104:4
1:7

7. In speaking of the angels he says,
"He makes his angels winds,
his servants flames of fire."

The contrast between the Son of God and the angels is evident to the writer. Nowhere in Scripture are angels given a title that indicates they are equals of the Son. Instead, as creatures they are servants of God and stand ready to do his bidding.

Psalm 104 is a nature psalm, well known to Jewish and early Christian worshipers, who sang the psalm in synagogues and churches. In the liturgy of the synagogue the psalm was sung on Friday evenings and Saturday mornings.[22] The synoptic Gospels quote Psalm 104:12 (Matt. 13:32; Mark 4:32; Luke 13:19). The great multitude that praises God in heaven makes use of Psalm 104:35 (Rev. 19:1, 3, 6). In the early church the psalm was not unknown.

The writer of Hebrews quotes from the Greek translation of this psalm because of the key word *angels.* In most translations of Psalm 104:4, the word *angels* does not appear. The verse is translated

> He makes winds his messengers,
> flames of fire his servants.[23]

The psalmist ascribes splendor and majesty to God, who as the Creator "stretches out the heavens like a tent and lays the beams of his upper chambers on their waters" (Ps. 104:2–3). Clouds and winds stand at his call because they are (figuratively) his means of transportation. Winds are his messengers; bolts of lightning, his servants. God is in perfect control of his creation.

However, in the Septuagint, the word *angels* is predominant because it is the first of two direct objects (that is, the word *angels* comes before the term *winds,* not vice versa). For the writer of Hebrews, who had the Greek translation at his disposal, the text read: "He makes his angels winds," not "He makes winds his messengers."

The writer uses the quotation from Psalm 104 to emphasize the subservient state of the angels. They are like winds and bolts of lightning, which are part of God's creation and completely obedient to his will. The text compares angels to winds and flames of fire to indicate that their deeds are as transient as changes in nature.

God uses angels to execute his will, and they serve him in a mighty way, forceful as the wind and destructive as a streak of lightning. When their task is completed, however, they return to him as humble and obedient servants. Although they perform mighty deeds, they remain lowly attendants.

The comparison between the Son and the angels is a further elaboration of the first four verses of chapter 1. God appointed the Son "heir of all things, and through [him] made the universe" (Heb. 1:2). The words *he makes* in the sentence *he makes his angels winds* point to the Creator who made all things and who by implication relegates angels to the status of created beings.

---

22. Ernst Werner, *The Sacred Bridge* (London: D. Dobson, 1959), p. 150.

23. English translations have the reading *messengers,* although footnotes may give the word *angels* as an alternative. The LXX as well as the Targum Jonathan and the ancient rabbis read Ps. 104:4, "He makes his angels winds." See SB, vol. 3, p. 678.

5. Psalm 45:6–7
1:8–9

8. But about the Son he says,
"Your throne, O God, will last for ever and ever,
and righteousness will be the scepter of your kingdom."

The contrast between angels and Son is expressed most characteristically by means of the two quotations from the Psalter.

The first quoted psalm (104) is a nature psalm that extols the works of God in creation and in the fourth verse, according to the Greek translation, speaks about the angels' role as servants.

The second psalm (45) portrays an earthly king who celebrates his wedding. After the introduction (v. 1), the psalmist describes the excellence and grace of the king (vv. 3–4), his victory in battle (v. 5), his rule of justice and righteousness (vv. 6–7), and his joy in his palace and in the daughters of kings (vv. 8–9). The second part of this psalm (vv. 10–15) concerns the bride and her companions. The conclusion follows in verses 16–17.[24]

The psalm is typological of the Messiah. Only in the advent of the Son of God is the description of the king's wedding completely fulfilled. The Jewish rabbis understood this psalm as a nuptial hymn composed for the occasion of the marriage of a king of Israel.[25] An Aramaic translation or paraphrase, Targum Jonathan (which dates from the first centuries of the Christian era), gives this rendition of Psalm 45:2: "Your beauty, O king Messiah, is greater than that of the sons of men."[26] That Christians of the first and second centuries considered that Jesus Christ fulfilled the words of the psalm is obvious from the context and the application in Hebrews 1 and from such writers as Justin Martyr and Irenaeus, who quote Psalm 45:6–7 numerous times.[27]

The person addressed in the first chapter of Hebrews is called the Son; thus far no other name has been given to him. The author of the epistle writes, "But about the Son he [God] says." The Son, divine and eternal (as the author has shown earlier), is the king seated at the right hand of the Majesty in heaven.

The writer selects verses 6–7 of Psalm 45 and applies them to the Son to emphasize the deity of the Son. These particular words form the core of

---

24. Ridderbos, *Psalmen,* vol. 2, p. 32.

25. John Calvin and other scholars have interpreted the psalm as describing a wedding of King Solomon. The Jerusalem Bible, in a footnote to Ps. 45, states, "According to some scholars, this psalm may be a secular song to celebrate the marriage of an Israelite king, Solomon, Jeroboam II, or Ahab (whose bride was a Tyrian princess, 1 K 16:31). But Jewish and Christian tradition understand it as celebrating the marriage of the messianic King with Israel. . . ."

26. For further details consult SB, vol. 3, pp. 679–80. Franz Delitzsch, in his *Commentary on the Epistle to the Hebrews,* 2 vols. (Edinburgh: Clark, 1877), vol. 1, pp. 76–77, "regards the forty-fifth Psalm as a not merely typico-Messianic, but as a directly prophetico-Messianic Psalm."

27. Justin, *Dial.* 63, 56, 86; and Irenaeus, *Heresies,* 3.6.1; 4.33.11; *Epid.* 47.

Psalm 45 because of their message to the king: "Your throne, O God, will last for ever and ever" (v. 6). The reference to the perpetual stability of the king's throne may point to the Davidic line.

Of much greater importance is the appellation *O God,* which teaches the divinity of the Son. The question raised by translators of Psalm 45:6 and Hebrews 1:8 is whether the word *God* is an address or a predicate construction that should be translated "Your throne is God."[28] According to ancient translations of Psalm 45:6, the address *O God* makes excellent sense, and the author of Hebrews uses this address to express the deity of Christ.[29]

To reveal the stability of the king's throne—that is, the throne of the Son—the writer of Hebrews quotes the rest of the verse: "and righteousness will be the scepter of your kingdom." The scepter in the hand of the Son is a scepter of righteousness to administer justice and equity. Says John Calvin, "But righteousness in the kingdom of Christ has a wider meaning; for he by his Gospel, which is his spiritual scepter, renews us after the righteousness of God."[30]

9. "You have loved righteousness and hated wickedness;
therefore God, your God, has set you
above your companions
by anointing you with the oil of joy."

The divine kingship could not be assumed by any Israelite monarch; only the Son of David, Jesus Christ, fulfilled the words of the psalm. He has loved righteousness and hated wickedness, as he demonstrated during his earthly ministry. The question, however, is whether the words of the quotation can be applied to a particular event or period in Jesus' ministry. We ought not limit the verse to designating any particular moment in the life of Christ, but rather understand it as a description of his nature. Jesus loves righteousness and desires that the people in his kingdom also love righteousness and hate wickedness. Righteousness is the foundation of his kingdom. Thus he exhorts his followers to seek first the kingdom of God and his righteousness (Matt. 6:33).

It is because of Christ's love for righteousness that God has anointed Jesus with the oil of joy. Obviously, Jesus Christ is the Anointed of God from eternity to eternity. There is no particular moment at which Jesus began his love for righteousness and after which he was anointed.

We do well to understand the phrases *scepter of righteousness* and *oil of joy* as Hebraic idioms that were translated literally into Greek.

---

28. Some translations apparently wish to avoid reference to the divinity of the king. Examples are NEB ("Your throne is like God's throne, eternal"); GNB ("The kingdom that God has given you will last forever and ever"); and *Moffatt* ("Your throne shall stand for evermore").

29. These ancient translations include the Sahidic and the Vulgate. Refer to James Moffatt, *Epistle to the Hebrews,* International Critical Commentary series (Edinburgh: Clark, 1963), p. 13.

30. John Calvin, *Epistle to the Hebrews* (Grand Rapids: Eerdmans, 1949), p. 46.

a. Thus, the phrase *scepter of righteousness* actually means that the king holds in his hand a scepter, which symbolizes royal authority. The king can hold out the scepter to invite someone to approach his throne, or he can sway his scepter to demand silence. By means of this instrument the king rules. How does the king execute his rule? Justly!

b. Likewise, the phrase *oil of joy* is not a symbolic description of either the baptism of Jesus in the Jordan River or his ascension and session at the right hand of God; rather, it describes the constant administration of his just rule. The application of his justice fills him with joy and happiness, and constitutes his anointing. It is the anointed Son who, set above his companions, shares his happiness with them (Isa. 61:3).

c. The word *companions* implies that the companions of Jesus share in his righteousness and joy. The word is used not of angels but of Jesus' followers, who "share in the heavenly calling" (Heb. 3:1).[31] "Hence he is the Christ, we are Christians proceeding from him, as rivulets from a fountain."[32] Therefore Jesus is not ashamed to call his companions brothers (Heb. 2:11). They, too, "have an anointing from the Holy One," says John in his first epistle. And he continues, "As for you, the anointing you received from him remains in you" (I John 2:20, 27).

A sixteenth-century catechism asks the penetrating question, "But why are you called a Christian?" and gives the revealing answer:

> Because by faith I am a member of Christ
> and so I share in his anointing.
> I am anointed
> to confess his name,
> to present myself to him
> as a living sacrifice of thanks,
> to strive with a free conscience
> against sin and the devil in this life,
> and afterward to reign with Christ
> over all creation
> for all eternity.[33]

Greek Words, Phrases, and Constructions in 1:7–8

Verse 7

πρὸς μέν . . . πρὸς δέ—the contrast between verse 7 and verse 8 is clear and unequivocal because of the particles μέν and δέ. The contrast is between the angels on the one hand and the Son on the other. The preposition πρός followed by the accusative case conveys the idea *with reference to*.

τοὺς ἀγγέλους αὐτοῦ πνεύματα—the two accusatives are double, depending on

---

31. Moffatt, in *Hebrews*, p. 14, understands the term *companions* to refer to "angels (Heb. 12:23) rather than human beings (Heb. 3:14)."

32. Calvin, *Hebrews*, p. 46.

33. Heidelberg Catechism, question and answer 32.

the present participle ποιῶν, which conveys the thought that God is constantly using and sending them. Of the two direct objects, ἀγγέλους has the definite article and therefore comes first in translation.

τοὺς λειτουργοὺς πυρὸς φλόγα—the double accusative gives priority to the word λειτουργούς because of the definite article; φλόγα, therefore, takes second place. The singular accusative φλόγα (from φλόξ) is used collectively. The reading πυρὸς φλόγα seems to be an integral part of the New Testament wording; the combination of πῦρ and φλόξ occurs six times (Acts 7:30; II Thess. 1:8; Heb. 1:7; Rev. 1:14; 2:18; 19:12).

Verse 8

τὸν υἱόν—the definite article preceding υἱόν is balanced by the definite article in the introduction of verse 7, καὶ πρὸς μὲν τοὺς ἀγγέλους.

σου/αὐτοῦ—the reading αὐτοῦ is supported by excellent witnesses, although the text of Psalm 45:7 (Ps. 44:7, LXX) reads σου. The word αὐτοῦ is preferred by some commentators: F. W. Grosheide, Ceslaus Spicq, and B. F. Westcott. "Thus, if one reads αὐτοῦ the words ὁ θεός must be taken not as vocative (an interpretation that is preferred by most exegetes), but as the subject (or predicate nominative), an interpretation that is generally regarded as highly improbable."[34]

---

6. Psalm 102:25–27
1:10–12

10. He also says,
"In the beginning, O Lord, you laid the foundations of the earth,
and the heavens are the work of your hands."

The sixth quotation from the Old Testament is taken from Psalm 102:25–27. The psalm, actually a prayer of a believer who is grieving for Zion, ends with a song of praise about the unchangeableness of God. The writer of Hebrews applies this song of praise to Christ, the eternal Son of God. The author needed the words of this psalm to explain the introduction to his epistle: "But in these last days [God] has spoken to us by his Son, whom he appointed heir of all things, and through whom he made the universe. The Son is the radiance of God's glory and the exact representation of his being, sustaining all things by his powerful word" (Heb. 1:2–3). The sixth quotation therefore was prompted by the introduction, in which the writer set forth the doctrine of the eternity of the Son, through whom everything was created and through whom all things are sustained. What formerly was said of Israel's God has now been applied to Jesus Christ. The Son of God is Creator and Upholder of the universe and as such is far superior to angels. For that reason, the writer of Hebrews emphasizes the pronoun *you* to express the contrast between the "Lord, [who] laid the foundations of the earth, in the beginning" and the angels, who serve only as God's messengers.

In the original Hebrew text of Psalm 102:25, the address *Lord* is lacking;

---

34. Bruce M. Metzger, *A Textual Commentary on the Greek New Testament* (London and New York: United Bible Societies, 1975), p. 663.

the Greek translators supplied the word, which was used as a title of respect by those who addressed Jesus. The author of Hebrews, who relied on the Greek translation of the Old Testament, understandably applied this section of Psalm 102 to the Christ, because the title *Lord* appeared in the Greek text.

The phrase *in the beginning* immediately calls to mind the creation account in Genesis. And the words "laid the foundations of the earth" are a figure of speech, a synonym for creation.[35] The creation of the heavens and the earth is recorded in Genesis 1. It is but natural that for reasons of balance and completion the psalmist says, "And the heavens are the works of your hands." Paul summarized all of these comments by saying of the Christ that "by him all things were created: things in heaven and on earth" (Col. 1:16).

11. "They will perish, but you remain;
they will all wear out like a garment.
12. You will roll them up like a robe;
like a garment they will be changed.
But you remain the same,
and your years will never end."

The message of this portion of the psalm is the unchangeableness of God, a characteristic that the writer of Hebrews ascribes to the Son. Everything changes, deteriorates, passes away—except the Creator. Henry F. Lyte captured the thought when he wrote:

> Change and decay
> in all around I see;
> O Thou who changest not,
> abide with me.

Although heaven and earth have been created by the Son who is eternal, they do not share his eternity. They are and will remain temporal. The heavens and certain parts of the earth (for example, the mountains) seem to exhibit timelessness. Yet they are subject to change, as Isaiah prophesies: "Lift up your eyes to the heavens, look at the earth beneath; the heavens will vanish like smoke, the earth will wear out like a garment and its inhabitants die like flies. But my salvation will last forever, my righteousness will never fail" (51:6).

Everything the Creator has made bears the mark of time. The psalmist uses the illustration of a garment that changes, gradually deteriorates, is eventually rolled up and discarded. The Creator, however, lives forever; he is the same because his years never end. His years never end inasmuch as they never began. The Son has no beginning and no end. Certainly this can never be said of angels, who may live eternally in the presence of God. Their beginning dates from the moment the Son created them.

---

35. Job 38:4; Ps. 24:2; 89:11; 104:5; Prov. 8:29; Isa. 24:18; 48:13; 51:13, 16; Mic. 6:2; Zech. 12:1.

The citation from Psalm 102 teaches the distinguishing characteristics of the Son: he is the Creator, almighty, unchangeable, and eternal. The preexistence of the Son is indicated by the phrase *in the beginning*; his permanence, by the clause *you remain the same*; and his eternity, by the words *your years will never end.*[36]

Doctrinal Considerations in 1:10–12

The comparison in verses 10, 11, and 12 is between the Creator and his creatures. That which is created shall perish, but the Creator transcends time and space and therefore remains forever.

He who is unchangeable is far superior to that which is changeable.

The contrast between the Son and the perishable heaven and earth is intensified by means of the frequent use of personal pronouns (for instance, "*they* will perish, but *you* remain"; italics added).

Greek Words, Phrases, and Constructions in 1:10–12

Verse 10

σύ—the first word in the sentence receives the emphasis. The author has deliberately taken this second person pronoun from its original place and has given it prominence by putting it first in the sentence.

κατ' ἀρχάς—the phrase *in the beginning* (ἐν ἀρχῇ; John 1:1) differs from κατ' ἀρχάς in number. The former, in the singular, denotes a point in time; the latter, in the plural, seems to refer to periods of time.

Verse 11

διαμένεις—some manuscripts accent the verb as a future active indicative διαμενεῖς, but this tense does not suit the context. The present tense, referring to the permanence of the Son, is contrasted with the passing nature of heaven, earth, and the objects of the earth (robe and garment) expressed in future tenses. The verb διαμένεις is a compound with a perfective connotation, denoting the Son's eternity.

Verse 12

ἑλίξεις—the word is the future active indicative of ἑλίσσω (I roll up; Rev. 6:14). A few manuscripts have the reading ἀλλάξεις, the future active indicative of ἀλλάσσω (I change), most likely because of ἀλλαγήσονται, the second future passive indicative, which occurs shortly thereafter.

ὡς ἱμάτιον—although the phrase is omitted in some manuscripts, its inclusion receives strong support from early and varied witnesses. Says Metzger, in his *Textual Commentary,* p. 663, "The absence of the words from most witnesses is the result of conformation to the text of the Septuagint."

---

36. Ceslaus Spicq, *L'Épître aux Hébreux,* 3d ed., 2 vols. (Paris: Gabalda, 1953), vol. 2, p. 20.

7. Psalm 110:1
1:13

13. To which of the angels did God ever say,
"Sit at my right hand
until I make your enemies
a footstool for your feet"?

This introductory sentence resembles the one in Hebrews 1:5. Interestingly, the author of the epistle begins his series of seven quotations with the question, "For to which of the angels did God ever say," and ends the series with the same rhetorical question, which expects a negative answer. The first six quotations lead to the climax in the last one, taken from Psalm 110:1. No angels have ever been given the honor of sitting at God's right hand, although their work may be important. Nowhere does God ever honor an angel by giving him a reward for services performed; nowhere does God promise an angel any gift, distinction, or rank. An angel is an angel and will remain an angel. By contrast, the Son, "after he had provided purification for sins, . . . sat down at the right hand of the Majesty in heaven" (Heb. 1:3). The Son took his place of honor in answer to the Father's invitation to sit at his right hand.

Of all the psalm quotations in the New Testament, Psalm 110:1 is quoted and alluded to most often. It is quoted in Matthew 22:44 and the parallel places Mark 12:36 and Luke 20:42–43, as well as in Acts 2:34–35 and Hebrews 1:13. Writers allude to Psalm 110:1 in Matthew 26:64; Mark 14:62; 16:19; Luke 22:69; Romans 8:34; I Corinthians 15:25; Ephesians 1:20; Colossians 3:1; and Hebrews 1:3; 8:1; 10:12.

a. Jesus himself, in discourse with the Pharisees on the identity of Christ, the Son of David, quoted Psalm 110:1 and asked the revealing question: "If then David calls him 'Lord,' how can he be his Son?" (Matt. 22:45). Obviously, Jesus is the Messiah.[37]

b. Peter, on the day of Pentecost, quoted Psalm 110:1 and, ruling out a possible reference to David, concluded, "Therefore let all Israel be assured of this: God has made this Jesus, whom you crucified, both Lord and Christ" (Acts 2:36).

c. And Paul, in the resurrection chapter of I Corinthians, applied Psalm 110:1 to Christ, who " 'has put everything under his feet' " (I Cor. 15:27).

The command *sit at my right hand* is addressed not to David but to Christ,

---

37. This particular citation from the psalms occupied a prominent place in the writings of the Fathers. Clement of Rome borrowed a passage from Heb. 1 and quoted Ps. 110:1 together with Ps. 2:7 (I Clem. 36:5); the verse is also mentioned in the Epistle of Barnabas (12:10). Justin Martyr cited Ps. 110:1 many times (*Dial.* 32, 33, 56, 82, 127; *Apol.* 1.45), as did Irenaeus (*Heresies,* 2.28.7; 3.6.1; 3.10.6; 3.12.2; *Epid.* 48, 85). During the first century, Ps. 110:1 was understood messianically in the ancient synagogues. (See especially SB, vol. 5, pp. 452–65.) Also, Billerbeck, in his appendix on Ps. 110:1, argues convincingly that the Jews in the first century of the Christian era interpreted the psalm messianically.

who is elevated to a place of honor, seated next to God the Father. Angels are never asked to be seated; they stand around the throne ready to do God's bidding in the interest of "those who will inherit salvation" (Heb. 1:14).

The words *sit at my right hand* are not only a symbolic description for the seat of honor; they also conjure up a picture of an oriental court in which the king, seated on his throne, is surrounded by servants. The servants stand in the presence of the king to show their deference. To be asked by the king to take a seat next to him on his right is the greatest honor one could hope to receive. "To sit near the king at any time, is the emblem of being on terms of familiarity and friendship with him, for all but his peculiar favourites *stand* in his presence; but to sit near him when on the throne, is an emblem of rank, and dignity, and power in the kingdom. A seat on the right hand and a seat on the left of the king are just other words for the two most dignified stations in the kingdom."[38] The mother of John and James, the sons of Zebedee, asked Jesus whether one of her two sons might sit at his right side and the other at his left side in his kingdom (Matt. 20:21).

Of the two seats, one on the left hand and one on the right hand, that on the right hand of the king is more honorable. This is the place Jesus received when he completed his mediatorial work:

> He ascended into heaven,
> and sits at the right hand
> of God the Father Almighty.
> —Apostles' Creed

We do not need to think of Jesus continuously seated at the right hand of the Father. Stephen, before he was dragged out of Jerusalem to be killed, said, "Look, . . . I see heaven open and the Son of Man *standing* at the right hand of God" (Acts 7:56; italics added). Jesus does not quietly spend his time sitting or standing. He is preparing a place for his followers and is subjugating his enemies. "Sit at my right hand until I make your enemies a footstool for your feet" (Ps. 110:1; Heb. 1:13).

The expression "your enemies a footstool for your feet" describes an oriental military practice. A victorious king or general would place his feet on the neck of a defeated king (Josh. 10:24; Isa. 51:23) to demonstrate his triumph over his enemy. Jesus "must reign until he has put all his enemies under his feet" (I Cor. 15:25). When the last enemy, death, has been destroyed, Jesus "hands over the kingdom to God the Father" (I Cor. 15:24).

14. Are not all angels ministering spirits sent to serve those who will inherit salvation?

From the throne of God and from the seat of honor, commands are given to angels to work in behalf of and for the benefit of the believers, who will inherit salvation. Whereas Jesus sits enthroned in majesty and grandeur,

38. John Brown, *An Exposition of Hebrews* (Edinburgh: Banner of Truth Trust, 1961), pp. 66–67. Italics his.

angels are ministering spirits. They must obey and serve. Not a single angel is excluded. Even archangels, including Gabriel and Michael, are sent by God to work in the interest of the saints (Luke 1:11–38; Jude 9).

Scripture teaches that angels are ministering spirits, "sent to serve those [the people of God] who will inherit salvation." Angels announce the law of God (Acts 7:53; Gal. 3:19; Heb. 2:2); deliver messages to God's people (Isa. 6:6–7; Dan. 8:18–19; 9:20–23; 10:12, 14; Luke 1:18–19); minister to the needs of the people of God (I Kings 19:5, 7; Ps. 91:11–12; Matt. 18:10; Acts 7:38; 12:15; I Cor. 11:10); are appointed guardians of cities and nations (Ezek. 9:1; Dan. 10:13, 20–21; 11:1; 12:1); and will gather the elect at the time of Christ's return (Matt. 24:31; Mark 13:27). However, the angels have not been commissioned to teach or preach to the elect. Nor are they given power to govern God's people, although the angels stand in the presence of God and share his plans (Zech. 1:12–13).

The angels constitute a numberless host, for John relates in Revelation that he "heard the voice of many angels, numbering thousands upon thousands, and ten thousand times ten thousand" (Rev. 5:11; see also Dan. 7:10). Their work continues until the time of the judgment, when Jesus, sitting on his throne, will say to the elect: "Come, you who are blessed by my Father; take your inheritance, the kingdom prepared for you since the creation of the world" (Matt. 25:34).

The reference to salvation as an inheritance that the elect will receive on judgment day ought to be understood in the broadest possible sense. When the elect are in the presence of Christ, they will no more experience death, mourning, crying, or pain (Rev. 21:4). They will enter a blessed and glorious state reserved for them and given to them for eternity. They shall be with Christ forever. That is the fullness of inherited salvation.

In this quotation the contrast between the Son and the angels has been brought to a climax: Jesus is sitting on the throne and is sending the angels to serve the believers. The contrast indeed is striking. In spite of their holiness, their status, and their dignity, the angels continue to function as ministering spirits to the inheritors of salvation. In a sense, therefore, angels are inferior to the saints.

Doctrinal Considerations in 1:13–14

In contrasting the Son with the angels, the writer of Hebrews begins and ends his set of seven quotations with rhetorical questions that expect a negative answer. The response to the question, "For to which of the angels did God ever say" (v. 5) is: to no one. The same is true of the question in verse 13. However, in the concluding verse of chapter 1, the writer poses a rhetorical question that expects a positive answer. "Are not all angels ministering spirits sent to serve those who will inherit salvation?" The answer is: Yes, all of them are.

The Son has been given the place of highest honor; that is, he is seated next to God the Father. The throne of God is the throne of Jesus, who rules until all his enemies are conquered.

All angels are ministering spirits. Obviously, the text speaks only of the angels that have not fallen into sin. Every angel, regardless of status, has been ordered to minister to the needs of the saints.

The saints do not have to doubt their salvation. Their inheritance is waiting for them when they, in the last day, stand before the judgment throne.

Greek Words, Phrases, and Constructions in 1:13–14

Verse 13

εἴρηκεν—the perfect active indicative is used here in distinction from the aorist active indicative εἶπεν in Hebrews 1:5. For the use of the perfect see Hebrews 4:3, 4; 10:9; 13:5. Also consult Acts 13:34.

κάθου—the present middle imperative, second person singular of κάθημαι indicates that the Son is indeed seated next to God the Father and is told to continue to do so.

ἐκ δεξιῶν μου—the adjective δεξιός is given in the neuter plural with the noun μέρη (parts) understood. The Greeks used this expression idiomatically, although often in the singular ἡ δεξιὰ [χείρ] (the right hand).

ἕως ἂν θῶ—the temporal construction with the aorist active subjunctive of τίθημι shows the finality of the matter.

Verse 14

οὐχὶ—the strengthened form of οὔ. It introduces a rhetorical question that expects an affirmative reply.

πάντες—because of its position in the sentence, the adjective πάντες is emphatic.

ἀποστελλόμενα—the present passive participle in the neuter plural modifying πνεύματα indicates that angels are constantly being sent out to aid the saints.

διά—the author of Hebrews could have used ὑπέρ (in behalf of). Instead he chose διά with the accusative to show cause.

τοὺς μέλλοντας—although the verb μέλλω is found with the future infinitive (Acts 12:6; Gal. 3:23; Rev. 3:2), it is generally followed by the present infinitive (eighty-four times in the New Testament). The present active participle ("those who are to inherit salvation"), in the context of Hebrews 1:14, conveys the idea of an action that must or certainly will take place.

Summary of Chapter 1

The central figure in chapter 1 is the Son of God, who is introduced not by name but rather as Creator of the universe, Redeemer of his people, and King who rules at God's right hand. The author of Hebrews formulates themes that he develops in the remainder of his epistle.

The Son of God is superior to angels, says the author of Hebrews. He writes not to discredit angels, but to direct attention to the exalted position of the Son. He proves his point by quoting from the Old Testament seven times, chiefly from the Book of Psalms. The author shows that the Son of God is eternal and unchangeable, and rules in royal splendor, seated at God's right hand. Angels, by contrast, are ministering spirits who are told to serve the elect people of God.

2

Jesus' Superiority and His Role as Savior and High Priest, *part 2*

2:1–18

Outline

	C. Jesus, Savior and High Priest
2:1–4	1. An Exhortation
2:5–9	2. Jesus Is Crowned with Glory and Honor
2:10–13	3. Jesus and His Brothers
2:14–18	4. Jesus Is like His Brothers

2 1 We must pay more careful attention, therefore, to what we have heard, so that
we do not drift away. 2 For if the message spoken by angels was binding, and
every violation and disobedience received its just punishment, 3 how shall we escape if we ignore such a great salvation? This salvation, which was first announced
by the Lord, was confirmed to us by those who heard him. 4 God also testified to it by signs,
wonders and various miracles, and gifts of the Holy Spirit distributed according to his will.
5 It is not to angels that he has subjected the world to come, about which we are speaking. 6 But there is a place where someone has testified:

"What is man that you are mindful of him,
the son of man that you care for him?
7 You made him a little lower than the angels;
you crowned him with glory and honor
8 and put everything under his feet."

In putting everything under him, God left nothing that is not subject to him. Yet at present
we do not see everything subject to him. 9 But we see Jesus, who was made a little lower
than the angels, now crowned with glory and honor because he suffered death, so that by
the grace of God he might taste death for everyone.
10 In bringing many sons to glory, it was fitting that God, for whom and through whom
everything exists, should make the author of their salvation perfect through suffering. 11 Both
the one who makes men holy and those who are made holy are of the same family. So Jesus
is not ashamed to call them brothers. 12 He says,

"I will declare your name to my brothers;
in the presence of the congregation I will
sing your praises."

13 And again,

"I will put my trust in him."

And again he says,

"Here am I, and the children God has given me."

14 Since the children have flesh and blood, he too shared in their humanity so that by his
death he might destroy him who holds the power of death—that is, the devil—15 and free
those who all their lives were held in slavery by their fear of death. 16 For surely it is not
angels he helps, but Abraham's descendants. 17 For this reason he had to be made like his
brothers in every way, in order that he might become a merciful and faithful high priest in
service to God, and that he might make atonement for the sins of the people. 18 Because
he himself suffered when he was tempted, he is able to help those who are being tempted.

C. Jesus, Savior and High Priest 2:1–18

1. An Exhortation 2:1–4

One of the links between the first and the second chapters is the author's direct and indirect references to the threefold offices of Christ: prophet, priest, and king. In the first chapter, the writer describes the Son as the person through whom God spoke prophetically (1:2), a high priest who "provided purification for sins" (1:3), and the one who in royal splendor "sat down at the right hand of the Majesty in heaven" (1:3). The author continues this emphasis in the second chapter by portraying Christ as "the Lord" who as a prophet announces salvation (2:3), the king crowned "with glory and honor" (2:9), and "a merciful and faithful high priest in service to God" (2:17).

In chapter 1, the author introduces Jesus as "Son" (vv. 2, 5) or "the Son" (v. 8); in the next chapter he refers to Christ as "the Lord" (2:3) and "Jesus" (2:9).[1] In succeeding chapters the author uses these and other names more frequently.

Throughout his epistle the writer intertwines teaching and exhortation, doctrine and advice about practical matters. After providing an introductory chapter about the superiority of the Son, the author explains the significance of that chapter in a unique and practical manner. In the exhortation he reveals himself to be a loving, caring pastor who seeks the spiritual well-being of all who read and hear the words of this epistle.

1. We must pay more careful attention, therefore, to what we have heard, so that we do not drift away.

In this verse the author reminds us that we have been given a portrait of Christ's eminence and greatness and, therefore, ought to listen to what he says. For the higher a person stands in rank, the greater authority he exerts, and the more he demands the listener's attention. The original, emphatic and expressive, is conveyed well in the New English Bible: "Thus we are bound to pay all the more heed to what we have been told, for fear of drifting from our course." Obviously, refusal to pay attention to the spoken word has detrimental consequences that can lead to ruin. The difference between hearing and listening may be acute. To hear may mean merely to perceive sounds that do not necessarily require or create action. To listen means to pay thoughtful attention to sounds that enter the ear and then

---

1. Throughout the epistle the following names are used: Son (1:2, 5, 8; 3:6; 5:8; 7:28); Lord (2:3; 7:14); Jesus (2:9; 3:1; 6:20; 7:22; 10:19; 12:2, 24; 13:12, 20); Christ (3:6, 14; 5:5; 6:1; 9:11, 14, 24, 28; 11:26); Jesus Christ (10:10; 13:8, 21); Jesus the Son of God (4:14); and the Son of God (6:6; 7:3; 10:29). See the section on divine names in B. F. Westcott's *Commentary on the Epistle to the Hebrews* (Grand Rapids: Eerdmans, 1950), pp. 33–35.

evoke positive results. A child may be told by his parents to attend to some household chore and, if the task is somewhat disagreeable, may dawdle. He has heard his parents clearly but at the moment fails to listen. There is no response.

The author of Hebrews says that we—and he includes himself—must direct our minds toward listening attentively to the divine message.[2] The words may not immediately slip from one's mind because of sloth and failure to pay attention; yet there is always the danger that the words will fall into disuse.[3] Moses taught the people of Israel their creed ("Hear, O Israel: The LORD our God, the LORD is one," Deut. 6:4) and the summary of the Ten Commandments ("Love the LORD your God with all your heart and with all your soul and with all your strength," Deut. 6:5). He instructed the people to impress the words of the creed and the law on their children, to talk about them constantly, to tie them on hands and forehead, and to write them on houses and gates (see Deut. 6:7–9).

2. For if the message spoken by angels was binding, and every violation and disobedience received its just punishment . . .

The expression *the word spoken by angels* refers to the law that God gave to the Israelites from Mount Sinai. Although the Old Testament in general and Exodus in particular give no indication that God used angels to convey the law to the people of Israel (Exod. 20:1; Deut. 5:22), Stephen in his address before the Sanhedrin (Acts 7:35–53) and Paul in his Epistle to the Galatians (3:19) mention the instrumentality of angels. There is, of course, a reference to angels, present at Mount Sinai, in the blessing that Moses pronounced on the Israelites before he died (Deut. 33:2).[4] It is conceivable that oral tradition preserved this information for Stephen, Paul, and the writer of Hebrews.

The text indicates that God was the actual speaker, even though he made use of his messengers, the angels. The Word—that is, the Old Testament law—was binding because behind this Word stood God who made a covenant with his people at Mount Sinai. It is God who gives binding validity to his Word, for he is true to his word.[5] He is the covenant-keeping God of his people. The Word of God (Heb. 1:1–2) remains the same and constitutes one revelation that was entrusted to God's people at various and successive

---

2. The author constantly includes himself in the admonitions by using the first person plural verb forms. He recognizes his own frailty and avoids claiming spiritual superiority for himself.

3. The verb *drift away* may be a nautical term.

4. The Septuagint adds the words "on his right hand angels were with him" to Deut. 33:2. Also, the Targum, the Midrash, the Talmud, and liturgical hymns sung in the ancient synagogues reflect the view that angels mediated the law. See Franz Delitzsch, *Commentary on the Epistle to the Hebrews,* 2 vols. (Edinburgh: Clark, 1877), vol. 1, p. 96.

5. Otto Michel, *Der Brief an die Hebräer,* 10th ed. (Göttingen: Vandenhoeck and Ruprecht, 1957), p. 63.

times. That is, the law of God came to the Israelites by angels from Mount Sinai; the gospel was proclaimed by the Lord.

The Old Testament provides numerous instances that show that "every violation and disobedience received its just punishment." Instead of mentioning specific examples from Old Testament history, the author of Hebrews stresses the principle that transgressing the divine law results in righteous retribution. Every violation is evil; every act of disobedience, an affront to God.

3a. How shall we escape if we ignore such a great salvation?

The key word in this part of the sentence, which began with the preceding verse, is "salvation." The term has already been used in 1:14, in which the readers are told that all angels are ministering spirits that serve believers (the heirs of salvation). The value of salvation ought never be underestimated, for its price was the suffering and death of Jesus. He is called the author of salvation who brings many sons to glory (2:10). Therefore, the believer's salvation is immeasurably great.

As verse 2 states, the message of the Old Testament could not and cannot be violated without suffering the consequences. How much more, then (this verse says), ought we to treasure our salvation. If we ever ignore the message concerning our redemption, it is impossible for us to escape God's wrath and subsequent punishment. The more precious the gift, the greater the penalty if it is ignored.

3b. This salvation, which was first announced by the Lord, was confirmed to us by those who heard him.

The focus of chapter 2, like that of chapter 1, is Jesus, the Son of God, who is Lord even over angels. And verses 2–3 are an example of the principle of arguing from the lesser to the greater, a method the author employs repeatedly in his epistle.[6] These verses remind the readers of the teaching about the Son's superiority (1:4–14); the author's method of argument emphasizes the contrast between angels, who mediated the law, and Jesus, who proclaimed the gospel. Angels merely served as God's messengers when they were present at Mount Sinai, but the Lord has come with the message of salvation, which he proclaimed and which his followers have confirmed by the spoken and written Word.

In this verse (3b) the emphasis is on Jesus, whose word is sure. It is true that the angels brought "the message," whereas Jesus brought "salvation." The author, however, employs a figure of speech called metonymy (in which a concept is brought to mind by the use of a word that describes a related idea. An example is Abraham's comment to the rich man who wants to keep his five brothers out of hell: "They have Moses and the Prophets" [Luke

---

6. The hermeneutical principle *a minore ad maius* (from the lesser to the greater) was originally formulated by Rabbi Hillel (died c. A.D. 20) as *qal wa-homer* (light and heavy). The implication is that particulars that are applicable in the case of minor things certainly hold true for major things. See, for example, Heb. 9:13–14.

16:29]. The intent is to say that they have the Old Testament.). Thus the word *salvation* refers to the gospel of salvation proclaimed by Jesus. This single word encompasses the doctrine of redemption in Christ and in a sense refers to the New Testament. Jesus came not to annul the Law and the Prophets, but to fulfill them (Matt. 5:17). The Old and New Testaments are God's written revelation to man, although the fullness of redemption comes to expression in the New. Jesus, whose name is derived from the name *Joshua* (salvation), was first in proclaiming the riches of salvation. From the moment of his public appearance to the day of his ascension, Jesus unfolded the full redemptive revelation of God. He, who came from heaven and therefore is above all, was sent by God to testify "to what he has seen and heard" (John 3:32). His message of full and free salvation "was the true origin of the Gospel."[7]

However, perhaps the readers would say that they did not hear Jesus proclaim his message, for Jesus' earthly ministry lasted only three years, chiefly in Israel. Countless people never had the opportunity to listen to him. The author of Hebrews immediately counters this objection by saying that the message "was confirmed to us by those who heard him." He himself had not had the privilege of being in Jesus' audience; he too had had to listen to those followers who had heard the word spoken by Jesus.

This statement tells us that these followers were faithful witnesses of the words and works of Jesus. They testified as eyewitnesses to the veracity of the events that had happened and the message that had been preached (Luke 1:1–2). And the author indicates that he and the readers of his epistle belong to the second generation of followers; they had not heard the gospel from Jesus himself. This fact rules out the possibility of apostolic authorship of the letter to the Hebrews. Because the author states that he and his readers had to rely on the reports of the original followers of Jesus, it is reasonable to assume that some decades had passed since the ascension of Jesus.

4. God also testified to it by signs, wonders and various miracles, and gifts of the Holy Spirit distributed according to his will.

The writer of the epistle assumes that his readers are quite familiar with the gospel, in either oral or written form, and have a knowledge of the beginning and the development of the Christian church. For that reason he does not elaborate on the proclamation of the gospel by Jesus (1:3) and the apostles and does not specify what the "signs, wonders, various miracles, and gifts of the Holy Spirit" are. He assumes that his readers are well acquainted with the history of the church, specifically the spread of the gospel accompanied by supernatural signs and wonders. His reference to the gifts of the Holy Spirit seems to imply that the readers are aware of those gifts mentioned in I Corinthians 12:4–11.

Signs, wonders, miracles, and gifts of the Spirit supplemented the proc-

7. Westcott, *Hebrews,* p. 39.

lamation of God's Word in the first few decades of the rise and the development of the Christian church. The Book of Acts is replete with vivid examples of miracles: Peter healed the crippled man at the temple gate called Beautiful (3:1–10), rebuked Ananias and Sapphira (5:1–11), restored a bedridden paralytic (9:32–35), and raised Dorcas from the dead (9:36–43).

Apparently the words *signs and wonders* were somewhat of a stock phrase referring to either the end of the world (when miracles and portents would take place) or the time of the initial growth of the church. The words *signs* and *wonders* were used as synonyms, especially in Acts, where this phrase *signs and wonders* occurs nine of the twelve times it appears in the New Testament.[8] Moreover, the phrase occurs in the first fifteen chapters of Acts, which relate the early growth and spread of the church (2:19, 22, 43; 4:30; 5:12; 6:8; 7:36; 14:3; 15:12). It is found in Jesus' eschatological discourse (Matt. 24:24; Mark 13:22) and in Jesus' word spoken to the royal official of Capernaum (John 4:48).

The terms *miracles* and *miraculous* describe the supernatural deeds of Jesus as recorded especially in the synoptic Gospels (Matt. 7:22; 11:20, 21, 23; 13:54, 58; 14:2; 24:24; Mark 6:2, 14; 13:22; Luke 10:13; 19:37; 21:25 ["signs"]). Peter also used the expression in his sermon at Pentecost: "Jesus of Nazareth was a man accredited by God to you by miracles, wonders and signs, which God did among you through him, as you yourselves know" (Acts 2:22). The word *miracles* (or *powers*) occurs also in Acts 8:13; 19:11; Romans 8:38; 15:13; I Corinthians 12:10, 28, 29; II Corinthians 12:12; Galatians 3:5; Hebrews 6:5; and I Peter 3:22. Among the gifts of the Holy Spirit listed by Paul in I Corinthians 12:4–11 is the gift of "miraculous powers" (I Cor. 12:10).

And gifts of the Holy Spirit [are] distributed according to his will. It does not matter whether we interpret the phrase *according to his will* as referring to the Holy Spirit or to God the Father. The parallel verse, I Corinthians 12:11, says that the Spirit "gives them [the gifts] to each man, just as he determines." Ultimately God is the one who testifies to the veracity of his Word. If we understand the words *according to his will* to include signs, wonders, and miracles, then God himself is the agent who used these divine powers "for the distinct purpose of sealing the truth of the Gospel."[9]

Practical Considerations in 2:1–4

The author is not an ivory-tower theologian; he reveals the heart of a pastor who cares for the church. He warns the readers and the hearers of his epistle to pay close attention to the Word of God. Effectively he includes himself in the warnings and the exhortation.

This passage is a continuation of Hebrews 1:1–2. In the gospel that is proclaimed

---

8. Bauer, p. 748.
9. John Calvin, *Epistle to the Hebrews* (Grand Rapids: Eerdmans, 1949), p. 56.

by the Lord and confirmed by those who heard him, the full revelation of God has now been made known. The message, whether communicated by the angels or proclaimed by the Lord, constitutes God's revelation to man.

In Hebrews 2:1–3 the writer uses many key words that even in translation show a definite sequence:[10]

we	to us
have heard	who heard him
the message	confirmed by those
spoken	announced
by angels	by the Lord
salvation	

Repeatedly the author warns the reader not to turn away from the living God (3:12) and writes that it is dreadful "to fall into the hands of the living God" (10:31), "for our God is a consuming fire" (12:29). Neglect of the Word of God does not appear to be a great sin; yet the writer, by contrasting this sin with the disobedience of people in the Old Testament era, teaches that ignoring God's Word is a most serious offense. Because God has given us his full revelation in the Old and New Testaments, it is impossible for us to escape the consequences of disobedience or neglect.

Salvation announced by the Lord is far greater than God's law that was announced to the Israelites at Mount Sinai. Christ takes away the veil that covers the hearts of those who read the Old Testament (II Cor. 3:13–16).

Signs, wonders, and various miracles were performed only by Jesus and by the apostles who had received authority to act during the establishment and growth of the early church. The gifts of the Holy Spirit, however, are still with the church today.

Greek Words, Phrases, and Constructions in 2:1–4

Verse 1

περισσοτέρως—a comparative adverb of περισσός, which in itself is already a comparative; in effect, the idea of a double comparative is present.

προσέχειν—the present active infinitive is durative; it needs the words τὸν νοῦν to complete the thought: it is necessary to hold the mind to [a matter].

παραρυῶμεν—the second aorist passive subjunctive, first person plural, παραρρέω (παρά and ῥέω, to flow past). The passive voice may be translated "in order that we may be carried past" or (intransitively) "in order that we do not drift away." The latter is preferred. The author does not say that the readers are actually drifting away. The aorist indicates that the danger lies before them and may at once overtake them. The possibility of drifting—hence the subjunctive—is not at all imaginary.

---

10. The diagram is from Pierre Auffret, "Note sur la structure littéraire d' HB II. 1–4," *NTS* 25 (1979): 177. Used by permission of Cambridge University Press.

Verse 2

ὁ λόγος—the word λόγος is used for the giving of the law at Mount Sinai; one would expect the term ὁ νόμος (the law). The choice of λόγος to describe the law was made, as Westcott puts it, "to characterise it as the central part of the Old Revelation round which all later words were gathered."[11]

πᾶσα παράβασις καὶ παρακοή—the adjective πᾶσα governs both nouns. παράβασις refers to the overt deed; παρακόη, the underlying motive. παράβασις, because of the -σις ending of the word, shows that the deed itself is in a state of progression. Transgressing the law is a degenerative process. Of course the lawbreaker must take full responsibility for his behavior.

μισθαποδοσίαν—a combination of μισθός (pay, wages) and ἀποδίδωμι (I recompense). The word can mean "reward" (10:35; 11:26) or "punishment" (2:2).

Verse 3

ἐκφευξόμεθα—the future middle active indicative, first person plural, translated in the active voice, expresses finality.

ἀμελήσαντες—the privative ἀ (not) and the verb μέλω (I care for) in the aorist active participial form may be rendered "neglecting, being unconcerned about something, ignoring." The participle denotes condition: if we ignore.

ἀρχήν—the Lord is the originator of the gospel. Jesus Christ is the ἀρχή (Col. 1:18) and the ἀρχηγός (Heb. 2:10; 12:2).

ἐβεβαιώθη—the verb is used twice in the epistle (2:3; 13:9); the adjective βέβαιος (firm, reliable, stable), five times (2:2; 3:6, 14; 6:19; 9:17). The aorist passive shows that an action was done once for all, and that it was done by others.

Verse 4

συνεπιμαρτυροῦντος—the compound consists of the verb μαρτυρέω (I bear witness) and two prepositions, σύν (together) and ἐπί (upon). The present active participle implies continued action. God continues to testify. The genitive case is the genitive absolute construction.

τε καί—the combination of these conjunctions is used to connect two corresponding concepts; in this verse the conjunctions connect two synonyms.

μερισμοῖς—only in Hebrews is this word used, apart from extrabiblical literature. Here it means "distribution"; in 4:12 the word is translated "division." The subject of the distribution—that is, the agent—is the Holy Spirit.

θέλησιν—in the New Testament, Hebrews 2:4 is the only place where this word occurs. The noun θέλημα (will) is the accepted term. The difference is that the -σις ending shows continued action; hence, θέλησις may be translated "willing." The noun ending -μα indicates result, that which is completed or settled.

2. Jesus Is Crowned with Glory and Honor
2:5–9

5. It is not to angels that he has subjected the world to come, about which we are speaking.

---

11. Westcott, *Hebrews*, p. 37.

After inserting a pastoral word of exhortation and admonition, the writer of the epistle continues the theme he set forth in chapter 1: the superiority of the Son. The angels are creatures subject to their Creator, the Son of God. Angels, as the writer said in 1:14, are ministering spirits sent to serve the believers who will inherit salvation. And in the world to come, not the angels, but the Son, will rule.

This reference to the world to come may surprise us, because from our perspective the Bible speaks primarily about the present world. When we think of the world to come, we imagine Jesus' return and the restoration of the earth. The author of Hebrews, however, looks at the salvation that believers will inherit in the world to come and makes it part of the messianic age in which Jesus rules supreme. This age began when Jesus took his seat at the right hand of the Majesty in heaven (1:3). That is what the author is referring to when he says, "about which we are speaking."

Why does the writer teach that the world to come will not be subject to angels? The author and the original readers were accustomed to reading the Old Testament in the Greek translation, the Septuagint. This translation differs from the Hebrew text: "When the Most High gave the nations their inheritance, when he divided all mankind, he set up boundaries for the people according to the number of the sons of Israel" (Deut. 32:8). The Greek translation relies on another Hebrew reading, which was discovered at Qumran.[12] The text in the Septuagint reads, "according to the number of the angels of God."

Moreover, in Hebrews the writer frequently used quotations from the Psalter and from hymns. By this method he reminded his readers of psalms and hymns that they had memorized during childhood. The Song of Moses (Deut. 32), most likely in the wording of the Septuagint, was familiar to them. Because his readers were accustomed to the wording of the Greek texts, the author acquainted them with the truth that the world to come will be subject not to angels but to the Son.

6a. But there is a place where someone has testified.

Verse 5 is a negative declaration that makes the reader ask to whom the world to come will be subject. The author wishes to answer by letting Scripture speak. However, instead of merely introducing the quotation from Psalm 8, he writes, "But there is a place where someone has testified." He does not reveal ignorance, for as a theologian he knows the Scriptures thoroughly. He wants to call attention not to the place from which the quotation is taken or to David who wrote Psalm 8, but to the content and meaning of the citation. For the author, the Word of God is central.

---

12. See P. W. Skehan, "A Fragment of the 'Song of Moses' (Deut. 32) from Qumran," *BASOR* 136 (1954): 12–15. The RSV, JB, and NAB have the reading *sons of God.* The footnote in the JB explains: "The 'sons of God' (or 'of the gods') are the angels, Jb 1:6+, the heavenly courtiers, cf. v. 43 and Ps 29:1; 82:1; 89:6, cf. Tb 5:4+; in this context they are the guardian angels of the nations, cf. Dn 10:13+. But Yahweh himself takes care of Israel, his chosen one, cf. Dt 7:6+. 'God' Greek; Hebr. 'Israel.' "

6b. What is man that you are mindful of him, the son of man that you care for him?

a. In Psalm 8 David first describes the glory of the heavens, the work of God in creation. He looks at the work of God's hands—the heavens, the moon, and the stars, all set in their places.

b. David then compares these heavenly bodies to man, who is nothing but a speck of dust; yet God is mindful of him and cares for him. Not size and volume but worth and value count, for man has been made in the image and likeness of God (Gen. 1:26–27). Man was given authority over the fish in the sea, the birds of the air, and all creatures that move on the ground.

c. Although this fact is not mentioned in the psalm, we know that because of Adam's fall into sin man's condition changed: he became mortal. David does not mention the mortality of man, but merely writes about the seeming insignificance of man (Ps. 8:4). Nonetheless, man's purpose ("to fill the earth and subdue it and to rule over all God's creatures") remains, even after sin entered the world.

d. Furthermore, God commanded Noah and his sons to "be fruitful and increase in number and fill the earth. The fear and dread of you will fall upon all the beasts of the earth and all the birds of the air, upon every creature that moves along the ground, and upon all the fish of the sea" (Gen. 9:1–2). Abraham also was given authority to rule. These names, then, are representative: Adam, the head of the human race; Noah, the head of post-flood humanity; Abraham, the father of many nations. Thus David, aware of the insignificance of man, can nevertheless speak of man's authority to rule God's great creation.

7–8a. "You made him a little lower than the angels; you crowned him with glory and honor and put everything under his feet."

One of the reasons that the author of the epistle chose verses 4–6 of Psalm 8 may have been that in the Septuagint, which he used, the word *angels* appeared. (The Hebrew text, in translation, reads, "You made him a little lower than the heavenly beings [or: than God]," Ps. 8:5). If the readers relied on the Greek translation, they then needed to reexamine the author's statement that the world to come will not be subject to angels, for this translation meant that man had been placed on a lower level than the angelic beings.

The words *you made him a little lower* do indicate that God has brought man from a higher to a lower position. Man shared immortality with the angels until his fall into sin.[13] At the time of the resurrection, man once again will be equal to the angels: he will be immortal (Matt. 22:30).

However, the term *a little* can be understood to mean either degree (man's position in God's creation) or time (for a short while). In Psalm 8:5 (8:6, LXX) the word signifies degree, but in the context of Hebrews 2 the ref-

---

13. John Brown, *An Exposition of Hebrews* (Edinburgh: Banner of Truth Trust, 1961), p. 93.

erence to time is definitely to be preferred. By applying the text to Jesus (Heb. 2:9), the author seems to favor the temporal interpretation of the term *a little.*[14]

This interpretation means that for a little while, man is placed on a lower level than the angels. Does this indicate that angels are superior to man and have been given authority to rule? Nowhere in Scripture do we read that God has honored angels in the way that he has honored man. Only man has been crowned with "glory and honor." This expression points to man's exalted position: king over God's creation.[15]

Everything that God has made is placed "under [man's] feet." In Hebrews 2:5 the verb *to subject* was used; now, in this last line of the psalm citation, the author seeks to convey the thought that all things, including angels, are subject to man. In the world to come, the author intimates, angels do not rule man; on the contrary, they, as "ministering spirits sent to serve those who will inherit salvation" (1:14), are subject to man.

8b. In putting everything under him, God left nothing that is not subject to him. Yet at present we do not see everything subject to him.

What is man that he should be
Loved and visited by Thee,
Raised to an exalted height,
Crowned with honor in Thy sight!
How great Thy Name!

With dominion crowned he stands
O'er the creatures of Thy hands;
All to him subjection yield
In the sea and air and field.
How great Thy Name!
—*Psalter Hymnal*

Psalm 8 speaks of man's rule over God's creation. At the time man received the mandate to rule all that God had made (Gen. 1:28), nothing was left outside of man's control. He was responsible to God alone. The mandate was given to Adam as the king of creation. He stood at the pinnacle of creation, for God had left nothing that was not subject to him. Such was man before the fall into sin.

Yet verse 8 is, in one sense, ambiguous. Does the writer think of Christ or of man in this particular verse? It is possible that the author meant to say: God put everything under Christ, although at present we do not see every-

---

14. Many translations have adopted this explanation. See, among others, the NASB, NAB, NEB, JB, MLB, GNB, and RSV.

15. The clause "you made him ruler over the works of your hands" (Ps. 8:6) is omitted because of the distinct "probability that the longer reading may be the result of scribal enlargement of the quotation (Ps. 8:7 LXX)." Bruce M. Metzger, *A Textual Commentary on the Greek New Testament* (London and New York: United Bible Societies, 1975), pp. 663–64.

thing subject to Christ. Conversely, some translations of this text show that the emphasis should be on man. They read, "But in fact we do not yet see all things in subjection to man."[16]

Because of the phrase *son of man* in Hebrews 2:6 and the apparent similarity between the quotation from Psalm 110:1 in Hebrews 1:13 ("a footstool for your feet") and the last line of the citation from Psalm 8:6 in Hebrews 2:8 ("and put everything under his feet"), it is possible to interpret 2:8b messianically. However, it is preferable to interpret the psalm citation as referring first to man and second to Christ. B. F. Westcott puts it rather succinctly when he comments on Psalm 8: "It is not, and has never been accounted by the Jews to be, directly Messianic; but as expressing the true destiny of man it finds its accomplishment in the Son of Man and only through Him in man. It offers the ideal (Gen. 1:27–30) which was lost by Adam and then regained and realised by Christ."[17] Certainly Jesus Christ fulfilled the words of Psalm 8, but the original intent of the psalm was to call attention to man's rule in God's creation.

In time, Psalm 8 was interpreted messianically by Paul (I Cor. 15:27; Eph. 1:22). Jesus had quoted the psalm (8:2) when he heard the children in the temple area shout, "Hosanna to the Son of David" (Matt. 21:15–16). And the writer of Hebrews, who was fully acquainted with the Old Testament, may have used Daniel 7:13–14 (with its description of the Son of man who was given authority and dominion) and Luke 22:69 (Jesus' word to the Sanhedrin that "the Son of Man will be seated at the right hand of the mighty God") to make the theological transition from Psalm 110:1 to Psalm 8:4–6.[18]

9. But we see Jesus, who was made a little lower than the angels, now crowned with glory and honor because he suffered death, so that by the grace of God he might taste death for everyone.

a. Jesus fulfilled the message of Psalm 8: "Being found in appearance as a man, he humbled himself and became obedient to death" (Phil. 2:8). Because of his humiliation, especially his death and burial, he was made lower than the angels for a little while. Jesus, then, is portrayed as man, who in effect has accomplished what the first Adam because of sin failed to do. Jesus became man, suffered, died, and was buried. After his humiliation was completed, he was no longer "lower than the angels." His state of exaltation came to full realization when he was crowned with glory and honor; that is, when he ascended to heaven to take his seat at the right side of the Majesty in heaven (Heb. 1:3). Jesus rules supreme as king of the universe!

---

16. See the NEB, GNB, and *Moffatt.*

17. Westcott, *Hebrews,* p. 42.

18. In a perceptive article ("The Son of Man in the Epistle to the Hebrews," *ExpT* 86 [11, 1975]: 328–32) Pauline Giles writes, "The fact that the Son of Man is not used outside the gospels as a title for Jesus, except in the passage under consideration [Heb. 2:6], in Stephen's vision recorded in Acts 7:55, 56, and in the Apocalypse, does not necessarily imply that it was unknown or unimportant." See also Simon J. Kistemaker, *The Psalm Citations in the Epistle to the Hebrews* (Amsterdam: Van Soest, 1961), pp. 81–82.

Because of man's disobedience in Paradise and the curse God placed upon him (Gen. 3:17–19), sinful man could never fully experience the state that is described in Psalm 8. But, says the author of the epistle, we see Jesus. He suffered death and gained the victory. He wears the crown of glory and honor, and rules the universe. In fact, even though the author does not explicitly state it, all things are subject to Christ (see I Cor. 15:27; Eph. 1:22). Jesus said, "All authority in heaven and on earth has been given to me" (Matt. 28:18).

b. Christ is introduced as Son in the first chapter; here he is called Jesus. By using the personal name *Jesus,* the author of the epistle draws attention to the historical setting of Jesus' suffering and death. We assume that the name was vivid in the minds of the first readers of the epistle because of the steady preaching of the gospel. These readers were acquainted with the details of the life, death, resurrection, and ascension of Jesus.

c. The name *Jesus* calls to mind the concept *salvation.* Jesus, the Savior, gained glory and honor for himself and life eternal for his people. The death of Jesus was purposeful in that it provided benefits, as the author writes, "for everyone." This expression does not imply universal salvation, for the writer in the broader context mentions that "many sons" (not all the sons) are brought to glory (2:10) and that they are called Jesus' brothers (2:11–12).

Jesus accomplished the redemption of his people by tasting death, so that his people may live and rule with him. The text does not say that Jesus died, but that he tasted death for everyone. This phrase is not just a Hebraic idiom for the verb *to die,* which also occurs in Matthew 16:28; Mark 9:1; Luke 9:27; and John 8:52.[19] The words *to taste death* are "a graphic expression of the hard and painful reality of dying which is experienced by man and which was suffered also by Jesus."[20]

Jesus experienced death in the greatest degree of bitterness, not as a noble martyr aspiring to a state of holiness, but as the sinless Savior who died to set sinners free from the curse of spiritual death.

d. The phrase *by the grace of God* has been replaced in some manuscripts by the words *apart from God.* The evidence for this latter reading, although not strong, indicates that the phrase may be a reference to Jesus' death on the cross when he cried out, "My God, my God, why have you forsaken me?" (Matt. 27:46).[21] The reading *apart from God* gains support when we see that

19. Brown, *Hebrews,* p. 101.

20. Johannes Behm, *TDNT,* vol. 1, p. 677. Also consult Erich Tiedtke, *NIDNTT,* vol. 2, p. 271; SB, vol. 1, p. 751; and Bauer, p. 157.

21. Some translations (JB, NEB) provide an explanatory footnote on this point. And some commentators have chosen the reading *apart from God* as the original text. Among them is Hugh Montefiore, *The Epistle to the Hebrews* (New York and Evanston: Harper and Row, 1964), pp. 58–59. Gunther Zuntz, in his Schweich lectures published in *The Text of the Epistles* (London: Oxford University Press, 1953), pp. 34–35, argues cogently for the adoption of the reading *apart from God.* In his opinion, the accepted reading "yields what can only be called a preposterous sense in stating that Jesus suffered 'through the grace of God.' " Also see J. K.

twelve of the thirty-eight New Testament uses of the Greek word for "apart" occur in the Epistle to the Hebrews. On the other hand, the phrase *by the grace of God*—with slight variations—is common in the Gospels and in the Epistles.

On the basis of the author's intent, if that can be ascertained, we could defend the reading *apart from God.* And we could argue that it is easier to explain how in the original the word *grace* was substituted for the term *apart* than to explain the converse. But the fact that the earliest manuscript, dating back to A.D. 200, has the reading *grace* is significant. A solution to this rather difficult problem is often sought in conjecture. One theory is that a scribe reading Hebrews 2:8 ("God left nothing that is not subject to him") added a note in the margin that said, "nothing apart from God." He did so because of Paul's comment in I Corinthians 15:27 ("For he 'has put everything under his feet.' Now when it says 'everything' has been put under him, it is clear that this does not include God himself, who put everything under Christ"). According to this theory, then, the note eventually became part of the text when the word *grace* was substituted for the term *apart.*[22] Perhaps the conjecture ought to be taken seriously; yet the phrase *by the grace of God* needs interpretation.

e. What is meant by the phrase "tasting death for everyone by the grace of God"? The grace of God is equivalent to the love of God (by analogy to Rom. 5:15; II Cor. 8:9; Gal. 2:20–21; Eph. 1:7; 2:5, 8; Titus 2:11; 3:7). In the words of John Calvin, "The cause of redemption was the infinite love of God towards us, through which it was that he spared not even his own son."[23]

Doctrinal Considerations in 2:5–9

Angels surround the throne of God and constantly behold the glory of the Lord. They are immortal, do not marry, and in a sense are superhuman because of their power and might. Nevertheless, God has given man dominion over the works of his hands. Authority over every living creature in the world was given to man, not to angels.

In Hebrews 1, the author stresses the divinity of Christ; in the second chapter, he emphasizes Christ's humanity. Jesus Christ, in his divine and human natures, was able to fulfill the mandate originally given to Adam. *Christ shall have dominion.*

Because Christ accomplished his work of atonement and therefore claimed the

---

Elliott, "Jesus apart from God (Heb. 2:9)," *ExpT* 83 (11, 1972): 339–41; and R. V. G. Tasker, "The Text of the 'Corpus Paulinum,' " *NTS* 1 (3, 1954–55): 180–91.

22. Metzger, *Textual Commentary,* p. 664. Also consult F. F. Bruce, *The Epistle to the Hebrews,* New International Commentary on the New Testament series (Grand Rapids: Eerdmans, 1964), p. 32, n. 15. Conjectures, of course, have been proposed before. F. Bleek, in *Der Brief an die Hebräer* (Berlin: Dummler, 1828–40), suggested that the Greek text of the original was not very clear, so that a scribe who was copying the word made a mistake by reading one expression for another.

23. Calvin, *Hebrews,* p. 61.

crown of glory and honor, he is the rightful ruler of God's creation. And by his death he has obtained dominion not only for himself but also for all his followers. We have become heirs and coheirs with Christ.

The parallel between Paul's quote from Psalm 8:6 (and his interpretation in I Corinthians 15:27 and Ephesians 1:22) and the citation of Psalm 8:4–6 by the author of Hebrews in 2:6–8 (and his interpretation) is striking. A key term in both I Corinthians 15 and Hebrews 2 is the verb *to subject.* Both writers demonstrate that God is the agent, that Christ has taken the place of the first man, and that time elapsed before Christ's work came to completion.

Greek Words, Phrases, and Constructions in 2:5–9

Verse 5

οἰκουμένην—the form is actually the feminine present passive participle from οἰκέω (I dwell). The form may be completed with the noun γῆ (earth). The term refers to the inhabited world.

μέλλουσαν—the present active participle from μέλλω (I am about to, I am at the point of). As a participle it has the connotation *about to happen.* The participle has already been introduced in Hebrews 1:14.

Verse 6

μιμνῄσκῃ—the form is a second person singular, middle (deponent), indicative of μιμνῄσκομαι (I remind myself, remember, care for, am concerned about).

ἐπισκέπτῃ—a somewhat synonymous term; a second person singular, middle (deponent), indicative of ἐπισκέπτομαι (look at, visit [especially visiting sick people], look after, care for). Here it signifies "God's gracious visitation in bringing salvation."[24] The quotation is punctuated in two ways: as two questions (Bov, Nes-Al, [25th ed.], BF, KJV, RV, and ASV) or as a single question (TR, WH, Nes-Al [26th ed.], RSV, NEB, NIV, MLB, NAB, and JB).

υἱὸς ἀνθρώπου—the term is used here without definite articles, although in the Gospels and Acts it is always with the two definite articles ὁ υἱὸς τοῦ ἀνθρώπου. The phrase does not occur in Paul's epistles. In Revelation 1:13 and 14:14 it is written without the definite articles as a quote from Daniel 7:13.

Verse 8

ὑποτάξαι—the aorist active infinitive shows single occurrence.

τὰ πάντα—the definite article τά makes the earlier πάντα (2:8a) all-inclusive; it encompasses the whole of God's creation.

ἀνυπότακτον—derived from α-privative and ὑποτάσσω (I subject). It is a verbal adjective with a passive interpretation: it is not made subject.

ὑποτεταγμένα—the form is a perfect passive participle in the neuter plural accusative. The perfect points to an act of God with lasting consequences.

---

24. Bauer, p. 298.

Verse 9

τὸ πάθημα τοῦ θανάτου—the noun with the -μα ending constitutes the result of an action—in this case, suffering. It is debatable whether the genitive should be taken subjectively (suffering that is characteristic of death) or objectively (suffering that leads to death).

παντὸς—the adjective in the genitive singular can either be masculine (everyone) or neuter (everything). The context seems to favor the masculine usage.

χάριτι θεοῦ—the manuscript evidence is early and weighty, whereas the evidence for the reading χωρὶς θεοῦ is late and somewhat scanty—three minuscules and the testimony of church fathers.

3. Jesus and His Brothers
2:10–13

10. In bringing many sons to glory, it was fitting that God, for whom and through whom everything exists, should make the author of their salvation perfect through suffering.

In Hebrews 2:9 the author briefly states that Jesus suffered the agony of death—he tasted death—for everyone. In the next verse he explains the term *everyone* by designating those who are saved as "many sons" and by referring to Jesus as "the author of their salvation." The Son suffered the pains of death, which the sons should have experienced, and was crowned with glory and honor afterward. Because of the redemptive work of the Son, the sons are led into the glory with which the Son is crowned.

a. The subject in verse 10 is God, for whom and through whom everything exists. The wording obviously echoes Romans 11:36, where Paul in a doxology writes, "For from him and through him and to him are all things." The honor, however, is shared with Jesus, as is evident from I Corinthians 8:6: "Yet for us there is but one God, the Father, from whom all things came and for whom we live; and there is but one Lord, Jesus Christ, through whom all things came and through whom we live."[25] (See also Col. 1:16–17.)

b. Jesus is presented as "the author of their [the sons'] salvation." He is actually going ahead of them because he is the pioneer, the founder of salvation.[26] In Hebrews 12:2 Jesus is called "the author and perfecter of our faith." God made him pass through gruesome suffering to bring about perfection. It was God's will that his Son had to suffer in order to effect the salvation of many sons. And when the Son completed his suffering, he became the founder of their salvation. He received the appointment to lead

---

25. Philip Edgcumbe Hughes, R. C. H. Lenski, Ceslaus Spicq, and Westcott directly and indirectly quote or borrow from Thomas Aquinas, who describes God as the efficient cause and the final cause of all things. Says Hughes, "All creation flows from God and all creation flows to God." *Commentary on the Epistle to the Hebrews* (Grand Rapids: Eerdmans, 1977), p. 98.

26. Hans Bietenhard, *NIDNTT*, vol. 1, p. 168; Gerhard Delling, *TDNT*, vol. 1, p. 488. Translations vary: "their leader in the work of salvation" (NAB); "the leader who would take them to their salvation" (JB); "the leader who delivers them" (NEB); "the pioneer of their salvation" (RSV); and "the Leader of their salvation" (MLB).

the elect out of a life of slavery in sin to a life of eternal happiness in which they are considered sons and heirs with Christ.

c. The sequence in Hebrews 2:10 presents a transposition of four concepts, which can be put in the following scheme:[27]

many sons to glory and their salvation	the author's suffering and his perfection

But how can Jesus be made perfect? He is without sin or blemish. The word *perfect* must be understood to mean achieving the highest goal. In the context of the Epistle to the Hebrews, the term *to make perfect* signifies that Jesus removed the sins of his people from the presence of God and thus by his sacrificial death on the cross consecrated the "many sons." The perfection of Jesus, therefore, points to the work of salvation he performed on behalf of his people.[28] In 10:14, for example, the author of the epistle writes that "by one sacrifice he has made perfect forever those who are being made holy."

11. Both the one who makes men holy and those who are made holy are of the same family. So Jesus is not ashamed to call them brothers.

This verse constitutes an explanation of the preceding thought, in that the work of perfecting the "many sons" is a work of holiness. This work of holiness is performed by and through the members of God's family: Jesus, the one who makes men holy, and those who are made holy. This verse clearly teaches the *humanity* of Jesus (by implying his identification with the human race) and alludes to his *divinity* (by noting his sanctifying work).

Jesus is the one who makes men holy, and he continues to do so until the end of time. He is the one who removes the sin of the world (John 1:29) and constantly serves as high priest on behalf of his people. The sanctification of his people is not an isolated event but a lifelong process. The path of sanctification lies in obedience to doing God's will, and that obedience is out of gratitude. But, we may ask, can holy people do God's will perfectly? A sixteenth-century catechism states, "No. In this life even the holiest have only a small beginning of this obedience."[29] If we fall into sin, our holiness is soiled. However, there is no need to stay unclean, for Jesus Christ, who shares our human nature, stands ready to cleanse us and make us holy.

The bond of humanity that links the one who makes holy to those who are made holy is further defined by the word *brothers.* In this holy family the spiritual relationship supersedes the human aspect. Jesus died for his

---

27. John Albert Bengel, *Gnomon of the New Testament,* ed. Andrew R. Fausset, 7th ed., 5 vols. (Edinburgh: Clark, 1877), vol. 4, p. 360.

28. The group of words related to the verb *perfect* occurs in the Epistle to the Hebrews rather frequently (nineteen times). The verb *to make perfect* is used nine times in this epistle (2:10; 5:9; 7:19, 28; 9:9; 10:1, 14; 11:40; 12:23) out of twenty-four occurrences in the entire New Testament.

29. Heidelberg Catechism, answer 114.

own people; he redeemed them from the curse of sin; he forgives their sins; he leads them to glory; and, because of his sacrificial work, he is not ashamed to give them the name *brothers.* The implication is that we, in turn, may call Jesus our brother. What a privilege to be called brothers of the Son of God! He who is seated at the right hand of the Majesty in heaven condescends to sinful man and unashamedly calls him brother (Matt. 28:10; John 20:17).

12. He says,

> **"I will declare your name to my brothers;**
> **in the presence of the congregation I will**
> **sing your praises."**

To prove his bold assertion that Jesus calls his followers *brothers,* the author gleans a verse from the messianic twenty-second psalm. Interestingly, he puts the words of this particular text on the lips of Jesus and introduces the quotation with the words *he says.* In chapter 1 of Hebrews, God is the speaker; in chapter 2 Jesus utters verses from Psalm 22:22 and Isaiah 8:17–18 (quoted in v. 13) with divine authority.

The Messiah proclaims the name of his brothers in the midst of the congregation—that is, in the church. By calling attention to the place in which he will testify, the Messiah limits the appellation *brothers* to those who spiritually make up the church, the body of believers. The psalmist exhorts those who fear the Lord to praise him (Ps. 22:23), for he says:

> [The Lord] has not despised or disdained
> the suffering of the afflicted one;
> he has not hidden his face from him
> but has listened to his cry for help. [Ps. 22:24]

The Messiah is speaking not only in the first part of Psalm 22, well known because of Jesus' words spoken on the cross, but also in the last part of the psalm. This Scripture is fulfilled by the Christ, who rejoices in the midst of his people, the church, of which he is the head. He defends his brothers, upholds them, and listens to their prayers. They can put their trust in him.

13. And again,

> **"I will put my trust in him."**

And again he says,

> **"Here am I, and the children God has given me."**

At this point in the discussion, the writer turns to the prophecy of Isaiah and takes two lines from Isaiah 8:17–18. "I will put my trust in him" is the last part of verse 17; "here am I, and the children God has given me" forms the first portion of verse 18. Isaiah testifies that he "will wait for the Lord, who is hiding his face from the house of Jacob." And the children God has given him "are signs and symbols in Israel from the LORD Almighty, who dwells on Mount Zion."

The context of these two citations is quite important. Chapters 7, 8, and 9 of Isaiah are decidedly messianic in tenor. For example, the name *Immanuel* occurs in Isaiah 7:14 and 8:8, 10. And the birth of a Son is mentioned in Isaiah 7:14–17 and 8:1–4.

Also, the sentence "I will put my trust in him" was incorporated into psalm and spiritual song (II Sam. 22:3; Ps. 18:2; Isa. 12:2) and constituted part of the heritage of God's people.

Further, the words of the prophet Isaiah become the words of Christ. The prophet and the Messiah say that they put their trust in God; the prophet and his children, as well as Christ and his brothers, stand before God. (The children the Lord gave Isaiah are the remnant of faithful Israel. The brothers of Jesus form the church.) As Isaiah was surrounded by his God-fearing countrymen, so Christ is in the midst of his people. And as the faithful remnant in Isaiah's day were God's sign and symbol in a world of unbelief, so the church today functions as lightbearer in a dark and sinful world. Thomas Benson Pollock prayed:

Jesus, with thy Church abide;
Be her Savior, Lord and Guide,
While on earth her faith is tried:
We beseech Thee, hear us.

May her lamp of truth be bright;
Bid her bear aloft its light
Through the realms of pagan night:
We beseech Thee, hear us.

Doctrinal Considerations in 2:10–13

Throughout chapter 2 God is the primary subject: he testified (2:4); he left nothing that is not subject to man (2:8); and he makes perfect the author of salvation (2:10).

The author of salvation is Jesus, crowned with honor and glory because of his suffering and death on behalf of his people.

The world of unbelief rejects the path of suffering and death that Jesus undertook, but in the sight of God Jesus' course of action was most fitting.

Because of his sacrificial death on the cross, Jesus leads his people to glory and identifies himself with them. Together they form the family of God.

Greek Words, Phrases, and Constructions in 2:10–13

Verse 10

ἔπρεπεν—the imperfect active indicative, third person singular impersonal use of πρέπω expresses that which is proper and acceptable. The same form occurs in Hebrews 7:26. Consult Matthew 3:15; I Corinthians 11:13; Ephesians 5:3; I Timothy 2:10; and Titus 2:1 for other forms and usages.

ἀγαγόντα—the participle, in the aorist active accusative singular from ἄγω (I lead, bring), agrees with the noun τὸν ἀρχηγόν. The aorist is ingressive.

τὸν ἀρχηγόν—as a compound (ἀρχή and ἄγω), the term is related to the preceding participle. Gerhard Delling claims that ἀρχηγός means the same thing as τελειωτής and refers to the "crucifixion as the causative presupposition of πίστις."[30]

Verse 11

ὁ ἁγιάζων—the present tense of this participle in the active voice illustrates the work that Jesus progressively performs. The present passive participle ἁγιαζόμενοι shows that sanctification is a process whose implied agent is Jesus and whose subjects are the believers.

Verse 12

ἐκκλησίας—since the word ἐκκλησία is part of the quotation from Psalm 22:22, the author of Hebrews employs this term instead of the more familiar συναγωγή. In the Septuagint, including the Apocrypha, the word ἐκκλησία occurs 100 times; by contrast, συναγωγή, 225 times.[31]

Verse 13

πεποιθώς—the second perfect active participle in conjunction with ἔσομαι forms a future periphrastic construction.

---

4. Jesus Is like His Brothers 2:14–18

14. Since the children have flesh and blood, he too shared in their humanity so that by his death he might destroy him who holds the power of death—that is, the devil— 15. and free those who all their lives were held in slavery by their fear of death.

In an earlier verse (2:11) the author of Hebrews has demonstrated that Jesus and his people belong to the same family; the implication is that Jesus has assumed our human nature.

Now the author indicates that the necessity of delivering his people from their enemies, death and Satan, meant that Jesus had to become man. He had to have a body of flesh and blood and had to be fully human in order to set his people free. Delivering his followers from the curse of sin and the clutches of the devil demanded nothing short of taking the place of those whom God had given him but who stood condemned because of their sin.

> Bearing shame and scoffing rude,
> In my place condemned He stood,
> Sealed my pardon with His blood;
> Hallelujah! What a Savior!
> —Philip P. Bliss

---

30. *TDNT,* vol. 1, p. 488, n. 4.

31. Lothar Coenen, *NIDNTT,* vol. 1, p. 292.

a. Because Jesus is divine, it would have been impossible for him to deliver us from sin unless he himself shared in our humanity. Jesus shared our human nature and, although he was sinless, lived a full life with its weaknesses, ills, desires, needs, and temptations (Heb. 4:15).

Jesus became fully human in such a manner that he is related to us. He is our blood relative. In the original Greek the word order is reversed ("blood and flesh," rather than "flesh and blood"); possibly this is an idiom. But the prominence of the word *blood* indicates that the ties that bind us are blood ties. We can say of Jesus that he is one of us. He is our brother.

b. God the Father desired that Jesus be born of the Virgin Mary, ordained that he should suffer and die, and set him free from the bondage of death by raising him from the dead (Acts 2:23–24). Thus God expressed his love toward his people by delivering his own Son to die a shameful death. And the Son willingly suffered and died in humiliation on behalf of his brothers and sisters, the members of the household of God.

c. The result of Christ's death is twofold: he conquered Satan and set his people free from the fear of death. Satan desired the destruction of God's creation in general and man in particular. After the fall Satan had the power of death over Adam and his descendants and used death as a weapon against us. He had the privilege of coming before God in heaven to accuse the believers (see Zech. 3:1–2), and stood ready to execute the verdict pronounced upon the guilty and to destroy man, who was condemned to death. He, the murderer from the beginning (John 8:44), desired man's death in the fullest sense of the word: physical death and spiritual death (separation from God). He wanted to serve as the angel of death by wielding the power of death.

However, not Satan but God pronounced the curse of death on the human race when Adam and Eve fell into sin. And Satan, who is an angel created by God, is a servant of God. Without permission from God, Satan is unable to do anything.

Jesus, the Son of God, was present at creation, for through him God made the universe (Heb. 1:2). He alone would be able to destroy Satan, and he could do this by means of his death on the cross. That is, Jesus defeated Satan by using the weapon of death. Jesus paid the penalty of sin by giving his life and set us free from the curse of death. And by paying this penalty for us, Jesus took the weapon of death out of Satan's hands. Jesus took away the fear of death.

d. Of course, all men die, including believers, so that Satan still appears to rule supreme. However, the curse of God no longer rests upon the family of God, for Jesus removed it. All those who are his people no longer fear death, for they are free from the bondage of death. We know that nothing, not even death, can "separate us from the love of God that is in Christ Jesus our Lord" (Rom. 8:38–39). By contrast, all those who do not know Jesus as their Lord and Savior face eternal death and thus are eternally held in slavery. Only Jesus sets man free from this slavery.

Since the death of Jesus on Calvary's cross, death has lost its power and its effect. Through death the Christian enters not hell but heaven. And because Jesus' human body was resurrected, the believer's body also shall come forth from the grave in the last day. The believer knows the words of Jesus: "I was dead, and behold I am alive for ever and ever! And I hold the keys of death and Hades" (Rev. 1:18).

16. For surely it is not angels he helps, but Abraham's descendants.

The author of Hebrews is bringing his discourse on Jesus' superiority to angels to a conclusion. He does so by appealing to a self-evident truth: Jesus redeems not angels but the spiritual descendants of the father of believers, Abraham. The name *Abraham* obviously must be understood to mean that all those who put their faith in Jesus are Abraham's descendants.

The translations of this verse vary because of the main verb in the sentence. For example, the King James Version reads, "For verily he took not on him the nature of angels; but he took on him the seed of Abraham." And the Revised Standard Version says, "For surely it is not with angels that he is concerned but with the descendants of Abraham."[32] The New International Version, on the other hand, translates, "For surely it is not angels he helps, but Abraham's descendants."

If Jesus had been an angel, he would be expected to come to the aid of fellow angels. But he helps men instead, thereby giving ample proof of his identity.[33] As the God-man he has come to help Abraham's spiritual children because he has identified himself with them. Jesus is the author not of the salvation of angels, but of the salvation of Abraham's descendants. And they receive his help.

17. For this reason he had to be made like his brothers in every way, in order that he might become a merciful and faithful high priest in service to God, and that he might make atonement for the sins of the people.

In this verse the writer of Hebrews explains the necessity of Christ's identification with man. In order to be of help to sinful man, Jesus had to become like his brothers in all but one way: he was sinless. Full identification was necessary; he was under divine obligation to become like his brothers. In a sense the author of Hebrews repeats himself, for earlier in chapter 2 he has introduced the thought of identity (vv. 9, 14, 15). But now he shows that Jesus had to become man in order to assume his role as a merciful and faithful high priest.

In this verse the term *high priest* occurs for the first time in Hebrews. In no other book of the New Testament is Jesus described as high priest. Only in Hebrews is the doctrine of Jesus' high priesthood fully developed (2:17–18;

32. Other versions read "takes to himself" (NEB) or "took to himself" (JB). The NASB broke rank and translated, "For assuredly He does not give help to angels, but He gives help to the seed of Abraham." In Sir. 4:11 the same Greek verb is used: "Wisdom exalts her sons and gives help to those who seek her" (RSV).

33. Montefiore, *Hebrews,* p. 66.

3:1; 4:14–16; 5:1–10; 6:20; 7:14–19, 26–28; 8:1–6; 9:11–28; 10). The writer calls attention to two of Jesus' high-priestly characteristics: mercy and faithfulness (see 7:26 for additional characteristics).[34]

a. The adjective *merciful* occurs only twice in the New Testament: once in the Beatitudes ("Blessed are the merciful," Matt. 5:7) and once in Hebrews 2:17. In Matthew we read that mercy is to be expressed from man to man; those who practice mercy are promised the mercy of God. In Hebrews 2:17, Jesus is depicted as the high priest who represents man before God, averts God's wrath, heals the brokenhearted, lifts up the fallen, and ministers to the needs of his people.

b. Whereas mercy is directed to man, faithfulness is directed to God. Jesus is a faithful high priest in service to God. Westcott aptly remarks that the word *faithful* actually has two meanings: a person is faithful in performing his duties and is trustworthy toward persons who rely on him.[35] Usually the two meanings merge.

After noting these two characteristics of Christ's high priesthood, the author mentions the purpose of Christ's high priesthood: he makes atonement for his people.[36] The term *atonement* is a theological one with profound meaning; it is often explained by other, even more difficult, terms such as "propitiation" and "expiation."

In the context of Hebrews the word *atonement* means that Jesus as high priest brought peace between God and man. God's wrath was directed toward man because of his sin, and man because of sin was alienated from God. Jesus became high priest. And as the high priest once a year on the Day of Atonement entered the Holy of Holies, he sprinkled blood—first for himself and then for the people—to remove (literally, to cover) sin. In the same way, Jesus offered himself so that the shedding of his blood covered our sins. Thus we might be acquitted, forgiven, and restored. Jesus brought God and man together in inexpressible harmony. In the words of Paul, "Since we have been justified through faith, we have peace with God through our Lord Jesus Christ" (Rom. 5:1).

The marvel of it all is that in the act of reconciliation God himself took the initiative. God, although angry because of man's sin, appointed his Son to become high priest and sacrifice in order to remove sin by his death on the cross. Thus, through Christ the relationship between God and man is restored. "For if, when we were God's enemies, we were reconciled to him through the death of his Son, how much more, having been reconciled, shall we be saved through his life!" (Rom. 5:10).

---

34. R. C. H. Lenski, following Martin Luther, translates the adjective *merciful* as a predicate and the word *faithful* as an attributive. "Hence he was obliged in all respects to be made like his brothers in order to be merciful and a faithful High Priest. . . ." *The Interpretation of the Epistle to the Hebrews and of the Epistle to James* (Columbus: Wartburg, 1946), p. 92.

35. Westcott, *Hebrews,* p. 57.

36. A study on the word *atonement* by C. H. Dodd (*JTS* 32 [1931]: 352–60) elicited strong reactions from Leon Morris (*ExpT* 62 [1951]: 227–33) and R. R. Nicole (*WTJ* 17 [1955]: 117–57).

18. Because he himself suffered when he was tempted, he is able to help those who are being tempted.

That Jesus' humanity is genuine can be demonstrated, says the author of Hebrews, by the fact that Christ was tempted. He personally experienced the power of sin when Satan confronted him and when the weaknesses of our human nature became evident. Jesus experienced hunger when he was tempted by Satan in the wilderness, thirst when he asked the woman at Jacob's well for water, weariness when he slept while the storm raged on the Sea of Galilee, and sorrow when he wept at the grave of Lazarus.

As high priest, through his sacrificial work, Jesus removed the curse of God that rested on man. Because of the forgiveness of sin, God's love flows freely to the redeemed, and Jesus stands ready to help. Those who are being tempted may experience the active support of Jesus. They can expect nothing short of perfect understanding from Jesus, because he himself suffered when he was tempted.

Of course, Jesus did not share with us the experience of sin; instead, because of his sinlessness, Jesus fully experienced the intensity of temptation. He is able and willing to help us oppose the power of sin and temptation. As he said to the sinful woman in the house of Simon the Pharisee, "Your sins are forgiven. . . . Go in peace" (Luke 7:48, 50), so also Jesus shows his mercy, peace, and love to us. He is our sympathetic High Priest.

Doctrinal Considerations in 2:14–18

"Now the prince of this world will be driven out," said Jesus when he predicted his death after his triumphal entry into Jerusalem on Palm Sunday (John 12:31).

Jesus became fully human like his brothers, yet remained the Son of God. Athanasius formulated this doctrine in creedal form:

> 30. For the right faith is that we believe and confess that our Lord Jesus Christ, the Son of God, is God and man.
> 31. God of the substance of the Father, begotten before the worlds; and man of the substance of his mother, born in the world.
> 32. Perfect God and perfect man, of a reasonable soul and human flesh subsisting.
> 33. Equal to the Father as touching his Godhead, and inferior to the Father as touching his manhood.
> 34. Who, although he is God and man, yet he is not two, but one Christ.

The writer of Hebrews develops progressively the doctrine of Christ's high priesthood.[37] In 2:17 we read that Jesus "had to be made like his brothers in every way, in order that he might *become* a merciful and faithful high priest" (italics added). In 5:10 the writer says that once Jesus was made perfect, he "was *designated* by God to be high priest" (italics added). And after Jesus had entered the inner sanctuary, "he . . . *bec[a]me* a high priest forever" (6:20; italics added).

---

37. Bengel, *Gnomon,* vol. 4, pp. 367–68.

Greek Words, Phrases, and Constructions in 2:14–18

Verse 14

κεκοινώνηκεν—the perfect active indicative, third person singular, from κοινωνέω (I share, take part, contribute) shows the continued sharing of flesh and blood by every generation from the days of Adam until the present.

παραπλησίως—the form of this adverb occurs only once in the New Testament, although it is frequently used in other literature. It is translated "similarly," and "it is used in situations where no differentiation is intended."[38]

μετέσχεν—the aorist active indicative, third person singular, of μετέχω (I share, participate) is synonymous with κοινωνέω. The aorist points to a definite time in history. It is followed by the partitive genitive τῶν αὐτῶν. Also see Hebrews 7:13.

καταργήσῃ—the verb in the aorist active subjunctive, third person singular, conveys the meaning *destroy, abolish, bring to an end.* The subjunctive is expressed in a purpose clause introduced by ἵνα; the aorist indicates a single occurrence. See the parallel verses of I Corinthians 15:26; II Thessalonians 2:8; and II Timothy 1:10.

Verse 15

ἀπαλλάξῃ—the aorist active subjunctive, third person singular of ἀπαλλάσσω (I free, release) is a compound verb expressing an intensive meaning—the verb ἀλλάσσω means "I change."

Verse 16

ἐπιλαμβάνεται—the compound verb has a directive sense: ἐπί points to the goal in giving aid and λαμβάνομαι denotes the act of receiving support. The verb is translated "to take hold of, grasp, catch," but in a figurative sense it means "to be concerned with, take an interest in, help." It is used of God, who takes the hand of his people in order to help them.[39]

Verse 17

ὅθεν—this adverb occurs fifteen times in the New Testament, six of which are in Hebrews (2:17; 3:1; 7:25; 8:3; 9:18; 11:19). The word is a compound of the neuter relative pronoun referring to place or fact and the suffix -θεν, which signifies motion away from a place. It is translated "for this reason"; that is, "from the available information the following conclusion is drawn."

ὤφειλεν—the imperfect active indicative, third person singular, of ὀφείλω (I owe, must, ought) is followed by the aorist passive infinitive ὁμοιωθῆναι (to be made like). The word signifies that because of law, duty, custom, or convention, an obligation is placed on a person to attend to a matter under consideration. A distinction, then, between ὀφείλω and δεῖ is that the first expresses obligation; the second, necessity.

ἱλάσκεσθαι—the present tense of the infinitive indicates that the work of atoning

---

38. Bauer, p. 621.

39. Delling, in *TDNT,* vol. 4, p. 9, says that the verb in Heb. 2:16 means "to draw someone to oneself to help," and thus to take him into the fellowship of one's own destiny.

is a continuing activity. Man is being reconciled to God. Says Westcott, "The love of God is the same throughout; but He 'cannot' in virtue of His very nature welcome the impenitent and sinful: and more than this, He 'cannot' treat sin as if it were not sin."[40]

τοῦ λαοῦ—contrasted with τὸ ἔθνος (the nation, the people), the word generally refers to God's elect people.

Verse 18

πέπονθεν—from the verb πάσχω (I suffer), the perfect active indicative, third person singular, brings out the lasting effect of Jesus' suffering.

πειρασθείς—the author of Hebrews has a penchant for using participles describing Jesus and his people (see 2:11). The aorist passive, nominative masculine singular πειρασθείς points to the earthly ministry of Jesus in general and to his temptation in the desert in particular. The present passive πειραζομένοις (dative plural), on the other hand, points to the continued and varied temptations God's people endure.

βοηθῆσαι—in light of the immediate context (2:16), the aorist infinitive of βοηθέω (I help, come to the aid of) is a synonym of ἐπιλαμβάνομαι.

Summary of Chapter 2

The Epistle to the Hebrews is characterized by teaching and pastoral admonition—the writer is a teacher and a pastor. As a spiritual overseer he constantly admonishes his readers to listen attentively and obediently to God's Word. He shows a genuine concern for the spiritual well-being of the recipients of his letter.

One of those readers perhaps asked if Jesus, the divine Son of God, is unacquainted with human nature. The answer is given in the form of a lengthy quotation from Psalm 8. Jesus "was made a little lower than the angels" but now, because of his death, resurrection, and ascension, is "crowned with glory and honor." Jesus fulfilled the words of Psalm 8 and through this fulfillment has obtained salvation for his people. No angel could have fulfilled the task that Jesus accomplished by "tast[ing] death for everyone." He is one with his brothers because together they constitute the family of God. Jesus, the Son of God, is truly human and fully identifies with his brothers. Because of this identity, Jesus has "become a merciful and faithful high priest in service to God." He sets his people free from sin and stands with them in their times of trial and temptation. Jesus sympathetically and at the same time intimately understands the problems believers face.

---

40. B. F. Westcott, *The Epistles of Saint John* (Grand Rapids: Eerdmans, 1966), p. 87.

3

Jesus' Superiority to Moses, *part 1*

3:1–19

Outline

3:1–6 A. A Comparison of Jesus and Moses

B. A Warning Against Unbelief

3:7–11 1. Scripture

3:12–15 2. Application

3:16–19 3. Summation

3 1 Therefore, holy brothers, who share in the heavenly calling, fix your thoughts on Jesus, the apostle and high priest whom we confess. 2 He was faithful to the one who appointed him, just as Moses was faithful in all God's house. 3 Jesus has been found worthy of greater honor than Moses, just as the builder of a house has greater honor than the house itself. 4 For every house is built by someone, but God is the builder of everything. 5 Moses was faithful as a servant in all God's house, testifying to what would be said in the future. 6 But Christ is faithful as a son over God's house. And we are his house, if we hold on to our courage and the hope of which we boast.

A. A Comparison of Jesus and Moses
3:1–6

In the span of two chapters, the author of Hebrews has demonstrated from the pages of the Old Testament that Jesus is superior to angels. Someone among the Hebrews who received the epistle might ask whether Jesus is greater than Moses. The Jews thought that no one was greater than Moses, for he gave the people of Israel two tablets of stone on which God had written the law (Exod. 34). The angels, by contrast, were only intermediaries at the time the law was given (Acts 7:38, 53).

In the preceding chapter the writer described Jesus as high priest (Heb. 2:17) but did not compare him with Aaron. The comparison between Jesus and Moses in this chapter in a sense parallels the comparison of Jesus and the angels.

1. Therefore, holy brothers, who share in the heavenly calling, fix your thoughts on Jesus, the apostle and high priest whom we confess.

The word *therefore* links chapter 3 to the immediately preceding discourse on the unity Jesus has with his brothers. Together they belong to the family of God. The brothers are holy because they are made holy by Jesus (Heb. 2:11), and on that account Jesus is not ashamed to call them brothers.

In 3:1 these people are, for the first time in Hebrews, specifically addressed as "holy brothers." The adjective *holy* reveals that the brothers have been sanctified and may enter the presence of God, for sin has been removed through the suffering and death of Jesus. The term *brothers* also applies to the author of Hebrews. In fact, he is one of them in the family of God (Heb. 3:12; 10:19; 13:22).

The recipients of the epistle are also sharers in the heavenly calling. This is a unique calling, a heavenly invitation to enter the kingdom of God (Rom.

11:29; Eph. 1:18; 4:1, 4; Phil. 3:14; II Thess. 1:11; II Tim. 1:9; II Peter 1:10).

The privilege of being called by God is coupled with a command. The charge is not difficult and complicated, and the brothers are able to comply with it. They are asked to fix their thoughts on Jesus and to do this diligently. Apparently the readers of the epistle are not doing this at the moment, for they seem to drift away. Already in Hebrews 2:1 the writer exhorts them to "pay more careful attention" to the gospel they have heard, for knowledge about Jesus is essential. As the author prepares to teach about Jesus, he does not call Jesus the Christ, the Son of God, the Son of man, or Lord and Savior, but calls him the apostle and high priest. Interestingly, the word *apostle* appears first in this verse, even though we would have expected the expression *high priest* to have precedence because of its use in Hebrews 2:17.

The term *apostle* refers to the one whom God has sent—a concept repeatedly used by the evangelist John in his Gospel (3:17, 34; 5:36–38; 6:29, 57; 7:29; 8:42; 10:36; 11:42; 17:3) and even in his first epistle (I John 4:10). The word *apostle* has the deeper meaning of ambassador. The apostle is not merely sent: he is empowered with the authority of the one who sends him.[1] Furthermore, he can and may speak only the words his superior gives him. He is forbidden to utter his own opinions when they are at variance with those of the one who sends him. Jesus, then, proclaims the very Word of God. He brings the gospel, the good news.

Whereas the term *apostle* relates by comparison to Moses, the designation *high priest* is reminiscent of Aaron. The separate functions of these two brothers are combined and are fulfilled in the one person of Jesus. And in his work Jesus is greater than both Moses and Aaron.

The congregation that received the author's epistle confessed the name of Jesus. I do not think that the church of that time had a standard confession apart from the saying *Jesus is Lord* (I Cor. 12:3) and a few hymns (Phil. 2:6–11; I Tim. 3:16; II Tim. 2:11–13). After all, the author of Hebrews instructs his readers about the apostleship and high priesthood of Jesus. In subsequent years, however, a carefully worded confession may have begun to circulate in the early churches.

2. He was faithful to the one who appointed him, just as Moses was faithful in all God's house.

God the Father appointed Jesus to be the mediator between God and man and to bring the good news of salvation to sinful humanity. God appointed him to be apostle and high priest and expected him to faithfully execute his task, which Jesus did.

---

1. The Hebrew term *shaliach* is an equivalent of the Greek *apostolos*. See Otto Michel, *Der Brief an die Hebräer*, 10th ed. (Göttingen: Vandenhoeck and Ruprecht, 1957), p. 94; Philip Edgcumbe Hughes, *Commentary on the Epistle to the Hebrews* (Grand Rapids: Eerdmans, 1977), p. 127; Ceslaus Spicq, *L'Épître aux Hébreux*, 3d ed., 2 vols. (Paris: Gabalda, 1953), vol. 2, p. 64; Karl Heinrich Rengstorf, *TDNT*, vol. 1, pp. 414–16; Erich von Eicken and Helgo Lindner, *NIDNTT*, vol. 1, pp. 126–28.

The translation employs the past tense, "he *was* faithful" (italics added). However, the author, by using a present participle in the original, intimates that the work God appointed Jesus to do did not terminate when his earthly task was complete, but continues in heaven. Jesus continues to be faithful in his high-priestly work of intercession and in preparing a place for his people (John 14:3). He remains faithful in loving and in perfecting the church of which he is the head. Paul states this eloquently: "In him the whole building is joined together and rises to become a holy temple in the Lord" (Eph. 2:21).

However, the first recipients of the epistle perhaps asked, "Was not Moses faithful to God?" They knew the words God spoke to Aaron and Miriam in the presence of Moses:

> When a prophet of the LORD is among you,
> I reveal myself to him in visions,
> I speak to him in dreams.
> But this is not true of my servant Moses;
> he is faithful in all my house. [Num. 12:6–7]

Observe this parallel:

> Jesus was faithful to God who appointed him
>
> Moses was faithful to God in all his house[2]

The parallelism takes on added meaning when we interpret the word *house* not literally but figuratively. The term *house* is a synonym for the family of God. Moses ministered faithfully to the church of God in the desert during the forty-year journey. Then what is the difference between Jesus and Moses? That question the writer answers in the next verse.

3. Jesus has been found worthy of greater honor than Moses, just as the builder of a house has greater honor than the house itself.

In this verse the author returns his attention to Jesus and deems him worthy of greater honor than Moses. Certainly both Jesus and Moses have been faithful to God, but the difference between the two goes beyond the virtue of faithfulness. Already the writer has called Jesus apostle and high priest; Moses never filled this twofold office. But that point is not under discussion at the moment. To demonstrate this truth the writer uses an illustration from the building trade, an example whose validity everyone acknowledges.

As we know, the builder of a house has greater honor than the house itself has. When a house or a building is erected, people may admire the

---

2. A number of manuscripts (among them papyri documents, Codex Vaticanus, and the Coptic versions) omit the word *all.* Conversely, leading manuscripts (including Codices Sinaiticus, Alexandrinus, Ephraemi, and Bezae, along with the Vulgate, some Old Latin versions, and all the Syriac versions) attest to the reading *all.* Understandably, a few of the more recent translations do not include the adjective *all,* either: see the RSV, NEB, and GNB. Other translations include the adjective: see the NAB, JB, NIV, and NASB.

beauty of the structure and speak words of praise, but they reserve tribute and honor for the architect and for the builder. The architect and the builder stand, figuratively, above the structure they have created. They stand on a different level. By analogy, the author says, God is the architect; Jesus is the builder of God's house; Moses is a servant in God's house.

By making the comparison between Jesus and Moses the author does not minimize the work of Moses. His faithfulness is not in question; indeed, Scripture reveals that God honored Moses in many ways. God himself appeared to Moses face to face (Exod. 33:11) and conferred on him the gift of a long life—to be precise, 120 years. And when Moses died in Moab, God buried him (Deut. 34:6). But the writer of Hebrews is saying that there is no comparison between Jesus and Moses because we really are talking about two different categories. Jesus constructs the spiritual house of God; Moses was a faithful servant in all God's house. Jesus is the founder of God's household (which has its beginning in creation) and Moses himself belongs to that household. In addition, the seat of honor at God's right hand belongs to Jesus. Jesus has been honored by God because through him God made the universe (Heb. 1:2).

4. For every house is built by someone, but God is the builder of everything.

This verse is an explanatory comment and may be placed in parentheses.[3] A house does not grow as a plant does; it is an inanimate object that needs a builder. Every house has a builder. The word *house* may be understood literally, as in verse 3; or it can be used figuratively to refer to the family living in the house.

The emphasis in verse 4 falls on the last part of the sentence. The change of subject is introduced by the conjunction *but.* God is the builder of everything. At first the meaning of this clause seems incongruous with the context, which speaks about Jesus. We would have expected a statement that Jesus builds the house, instead of the comprehensive remark that God builds everything. Of course, no one disputes the truth of the remark, and it directs our attention to God's sovereignty.

The author of Hebrews thus far has shown that he does not make a clear distinction between God and the Son. Rather he teaches that God works through the Son; for example, in creation (Heb. 1:2). Also, God makes Jesus perfect through suffering (Heb. 2:10). God the Father, then, builds everything through his Son. And because Christ constructs God's house, he is worthy of greater honor than Moses.

5–6a. Moses was faithful as a servant in all God's house, testifying to what would be said in the future. But Christ is faithful as a son over God's house.

a. The author repeats what he already said in Hebrews 3:2. There he

3. See, for example, the RSV and *Moffatt.*

compares Moses and Jesus; here he contrasts the two. He literally quotes the Septuagint version of Numbers 12:7, although the word order varies.

b. Moses is called a servant; Christ, a son. The contrast is heightened by the use of two different prepositions: Moses was a servant *in* God's house, whereas Christ is a son *over* God's house.

c. The author chooses the term *servant* to describe Moses. Note that he does not call Moses a slave or an attendant. This word (*servant*) occurs frequently in the Old Testament, but only once in the original Greek of the New Testament (Heb. 3:5). It means that a person is in service to someone who is superior. Also, it connotes one who wishes to serve, in contrast to a slave who must serve.

d. Moses proved faithful in the function God had given him and served honorably with distinction (Josh. 1:1–4). Christ also is faithful, although he occupies a different position. He is the son to whom God has given authority over the house; that is, the household of God (Heb. 10:21).

e. Moses functioned as a prophet and was a prototype of Jesus, the great prophet (Deut. 18:15, 18). He testified to what would be said in the future, specifically the gospel that Jesus proclaimed as the fullness of God's revelation (Heb. 1:2).[4]

6b. And we are his house, if we hold on to our courage and the hope of which we boast.

The metaphor that describes the people of God as a house or a building occurs rather frequently in the New Testament (I Cor. 3:16; 6:19; II Cor. 6:16; I Peter 2:5). We are the house of God, says the author of Hebrews. This means that now the believers in Jesus Christ, not the Jews, constitute the household of God (Eph. 2:19–22; I Tim. 3:15). Only Christians acknowledge Christ Jesus as the chief cornerstone. For only in him "the whole body, supported and held together by its ligaments and sinews, grows as God causes it to grow" (Col. 2:19).

There are two limitations.

a. "If we hold on to our courage." We can no longer be part of the house unless we have courage. For the Hebrew Christians the temptation to return to Judaism was not at all imaginary. They were exhorted to hold on to their faith in Christ against fierce opposition from their Jewish countrymen. But Gentile Christians, too, must be vigilant in the face of persecution (I Thess. 2:14). The word *courage* is significant for the Christian because it relates to his boldness, openness, and frankness in preaching and teaching the gospel.

b. "And the hope of which we boast."[5] If the readers of this epistle do not

---

4. Numerous commentators, including John Calvin, Franz Delitzsch, B. F. Westcott, Hugh Montefiore, and Hughes, interpret the clause to refer to the message "which was first announced by the Lord" (Heb. 2:3).

5. On the basis of a number of influential manuscripts (including Codices Sinaiticus, Alexandrinus, Ephraemi, and Bezae) the KJV, NKJV, RV, ASV, NASB, and *Phillips* add the phrase *firm* [or: steadfast] *unto the end.* Note also that the phrase occurs in Heb. 3:14, where in the original it is grammatically correct; this is not the case in Heb. 3:6.

hold on to the hope of which they boast, then they are no longer part of the household of God. Later in the epistle the writer explains what he means by hope. He speaks of the unchangeable nature of God's purpose and the impossibility that God would lie. Says the author, "We who have fled to take hold of the hope offered to us may be greatly encouraged. We have this hope as an anchor for the soul, firm and secure" (Heb. 6:18–19).

As God is true to his purpose and being, so the Christian must be a true reflection of his Creator and Redeemer. If he fails, he ceases to be part of God's house. Therefore, throughout the epistle, but especially in Hebrews 10:23, the author exhorts his readers to be true to their calling: "Let us hold unswervingly to the hope we profess, for he who promised is faithful."

Doctrinal Considerations in 3:1–6

In the first verse of Hebrews 3, two titles are given to the recipients of the epistle and two to Jesus. Jesus has called the recipients brothers and they confess his name, just as he is not ashamed to declare their names.

The structure of Hebrews 3:1 can be represented in a diagram:[6]

BROTHERS		
	holy	
		and sharers in the heavenly calling
		fix your thoughts on
JESUS		
	the apostle and high priest whom	
WE		
	confess	

Verses 2–6a of Hebrews 3 display a remarkable parallelism in which the symmetry is lucid and logical. See the following outline.

3:2	Jesus	faithful	Moses	house
3:3	Jesus	greater honor	Moses	
			builder	house
3:4	God		builder	
3:5	Moses	faithful	servant	house
3:6a	Christ	faithful	son	house

Greek Words, Phrases, and Constructions in 3:1–6

Verse 1

κατανοήσατε—the aorist active imperative, second person plural of the compound intensive verb (from κατά [down] and νοέω [I put my mind to]) conveys

6. Consult Pierre Auffret's interesting "Essai sur la structure littéraire et l'interprétation d'Hébreux 3, 1–6," *NTS* 26 (1980): 380–96.

the message of thoroughly and carefully noticing someone or something; in this case, Jesus. See Hebrews 10:24.

Verse 2

τῷ ποιήσαντι—a literal translation of this aorist active participle in the dative singular is "to the one who made" him and could refer to the humanity of Jesus. It is better to translate the participle as "to the one who appointed" him. Then it relates to the office of Christ as apostle and high priest.

Verse 5

θεράπων—the word belongs to the family of the verb θεραπεύω (I serve, venerate, care for, cure). The Septuagint uses the noun as a translation of *'ebed* (attendant, servant); the noun θεράπων denotes willing service, whereas δοῦλος or παῖς indicates slavish submission.

Verse 6

παρρησίαν—translated "boldness, frankness, openness, confidence," the noun is a combination of πᾶν (all) and ῥῆσις (speech, word), from ἐρῶ (I speak). It conveys the meaning, therefore, of having the freedom to speak to everyone.[7]

---

7 So, as the Holy Spirit says:

"Today, if you hear his voice,
8 do not harden your hearts
as you did in the rebellion,
during the time of testing in the desert,
9 where your fathers tested and tried me
and for forty years saw what I did.
10 That is why I was angry with that generation,
and I said, 'Their hearts are always going astray,
and they have not known my ways.'
11 So I declared on oath in my anger,
'They shall never enter my rest.' "

12 See to it, brothers, that none of you has a sinful, unbelieving heart that turns away from
the living God. 13 But encourage one another daily, as long as it is called Today, so that
none of you may be hardened by sin's deceitfulness. 14 We have come to share in Christ if
we hold firmly till the end the confidence we had at first. 15 As has just been said:

"Today, if you hear his voice,
do not harden your hearts
as you did in the rebellion."

16 Who were they who heard and rebelled? Were they not all those Moses led out of
Egypt? 17 And with whom was he angry for forty years? Was it not with those who sinned,
whose bodies fell in the desert? 18 And to whom did God swear that they would never enter
his rest if not to those who disobeyed? 19 So we see that they were not able to enter, because
of their unbelief.

---

7. Hans-Christoph Hahn, *NIDNTT,* vol. 2, p. 734.

B. A Warning Against Unbelief
3:7–19

One of the stylistic devices that the author uses to introduce a quotation of the Old Testament is the formula *God says* or *the Holy Spirit says.* The writer refers to the Old Testament writer as only a mouthpiece of God (see, for example, Heb. 4:7). That is, God is the primary author of Scripture, and man is the secondary author through whom God speaks.[8] Scripture, for the author of Hebrews, is God's Word, and that Word is divine. He indeed has a high view of Scripture.

Many times in his epistle the author quotes a passage from the Old Testament without a smooth transition in the context. The author first quotes Scripture, subsequently explains it by applying the words to the readers of his epistle, and afterward at times supports his application with examples taken from biblical history.

Consider, then, the third chapter of Hebrews. In the first six verses the author, in drawing a comparison between Jesus and Moses, declares that Jesus is worthy of greater honor than Moses. Then, without a transition, the writer quotes Psalm 95:7–11. He explains and applies the psalm citation in verses 12–15. And to buttress his application, he provides historical examples (vv. 16–19).

1. Scripture
3:7–11

In the temple ritual and in the synagogue worship services, the use of Psalm 95 was well established. Both Psalms 95 and 96 were known as the psalms of invitation to worship. We may assume that these psalms were a significant part of the early Christian liturgies as well.[9]

a. **7–9. So, as the Holy Spirit says:**
"Today, if you hear his voice,
do not harden your hearts
as you did in the rebellion,
during the time of testing in the desert,
where your fathers tested and tried me
and for forty years saw what I did.

David, whose name is mentioned later in Hebrews 4:7, does not speak. But the Holy Spirit speaks, addressing both the people of God in Old Testament times and the readers of the Epistle to the Hebrews. And it is because of the Holy Spirit, as the author of Hebrews teaches, that Scripture is divinely

8. The author of Hebrews introduces God as speaker in 1:5 (Ps. 2:7); 1:7 (Ps. 104:4); 1:13 (Ps. 110:1); 5:5 (Ps. 2:7). Christ is the speaker in 2:12 (Ps. 22:22); 2:13 (Isa. 8:17); 10:5–7 (Ps. 40:6–8). And the Holy Spirit is the speaker in 3:7–11 (Ps. 95:7–11); 10:15–17 (Jer. 31:33–34).

9. Ernst Werner, *The Sacred Bridge* (London: D. Dobson, 1959), pp. 131, 145, 157. Also see Ismar Elbogen, *Der Jüdische Gottesdienst* (Frankfurt: Kaufmann, 1931), pp. 82, 108, 113.

inspired and addresses people throughout the centuries (see I Tim. 3:16; II Peter 1:20–21).[10] The Holy Spirit speaks to man by means of the inspired Word of God.

Today. God's Word is "living and active[,] sharper than any double-edged sword" (Heb. 4:12). At no point does Scripture become outdated and irrelevant. God spoke to the people of Israel in the desert; David composed Psalm 95, through which God addressed the Israelites; the author of Hebrews quotes a number of verses from that psalm and says that the Holy Spirit speaks to those reading his epistle. God's Word still speaks to us today.

If you hear his voice, do not harden your hearts. The reference is to the original hearers and singers of Psalm 95, and is expressed in the form of a wish in the original Hebrew but in the Greek is given as a conditional sentence. The sentence means: If you should hear God's voice, listen to what he has to say to you. Do not be like your forefathers who turned a deaf ear to the voice of God. Therefore, God is saying to you, "Do not harden your hearts. That is, don't ever ignore my voice, for that spells trouble." James in his epistle puts it succinctly: "You adulterous people, don't you know that friendship with the world is hatred toward God? Anyone who chooses to be a friend of the world becomes an enemy of God" (4:4).

The phrase *harden not your hearts* is Semitic in origin, but no one has difficulty understanding its meaning. In our culture we use the concept *deaf* and say that someone, by ignoring the speaker, deliberately refuses to hear. Nevertheless, by doing this the person takes full responsibility for his willful neglect and refusal to hear.

As you did in the rebellion, during the time of testing in the desert. God speaks to his people Israel, and he calls to mind what happened in the desert during the forty-year journey. He even refers to place names: Meribah and Massah (Ps. 95:8). In the Septuagint, these two names are translated *rebellion* and *testing* respectively. The history lesson, however, is to the point. After the people of Israel (at the beginning of their journey) had left the Desert of Sin near Rephidim, they lacked water. When they quarreled with Moses, God told him to strike a rock. He did, and water gushed forth. Moses called the place Massah, which means testing, and Meribah, which is the word for quarreling (see Exod. 17:7). Near the completion of their forty-year journey, the people of Israel quarreled again because of thirst. This time Moses lost his temper, struck the rock twice instead of speaking to it as God had said, and forfeited his place as leader of the Israelites. Consequently he was not allowed to enter the Promised Land. Moses called the place Meribah (Num. 20:13).

Where your fathers tested and tried me and for forty years saw what I did. From the first year through the fortieth year, the people of Israel tried the patience of God. The history of the Israelites' forty years in the wilderness is replete with examples of the unbelief and faithlessness of young

10. SB, vol. 3, p. 684.

and old.[11] Yet amidst the rebelliousness of the people of Israel, God showed his mighty acts: a pillar of fire by night to shield them from the desert cold, a cloud by day to protect them from the sun's burning rays, manna to satisfy their hunger, and water out of the rock to quench their thirst; furthermore, their clothes and shoes did not wear out (Exod. 13:21; 16:4–5; 17:6; Deut. 29:5). The Lord God of Israel was their rock and shield for forty years.[12]

b. **10. That is why I was angry with that generation,**
and I said, "Their hearts are always going astray,
and they have not known my ways."
11. So I declared on oath in my anger,
"They shall never enter my rest."

God's patience was taxed to the limit by those rebellious people. His anger flared. God was incensed with that generation.[13] Twice God addressed the obstinate Israelites and spoke to them directly.

Their hearts are always going astray, and they have not known my ways. The exact words spoken by God are found in Numbers 14 and Deuteronomy 1, where Moses records the historical narrative of Israel's rebellion. When the people refused to enter the Promised Land, wanted to return to Egypt, and chose another leader, God said to Moses: "How long will these people treat me with contempt? How long will they refuse to believe in me, in spite of the miraculous signs I have performed among them?" (Num. 14:11).

The Israelites did not rebel against God once: after the return of the spies, they put God to the test ten times (Num. 14:22) and refused to listen to his voice. Their hearts were filled with unbelief, and their eyes were blind to the miracles God performed.

They shall never enter my rest. Because the people of Israel treated God with contempt, God solemnly swore: "Not a man of this evil generation shall

11. Israel's history was recounted often by psalmists. For example, see Ps. 78:40–42, where the psalmist speaks of Israel's rebellion in the wilderness and of putting God to the test because the Israelites did not remember God's power. And the prophet Amos asks, "Did you bring me sacrifices and offerings forty years in the desert, O house of Israel?" (Amos 5:25; Acts 7:42).

12. A number of writers see in the words *forty years* an allusion to Jerusalem and the destruction of the temple in A.D. 70, for that event marked the end of a forty-year period of rebellion against Jesus by the obstinate Jews of "this generation." Among those who hold this view are F. F. Bruce, Delitzsch, Hughes, Thomas Hewitt, Westcott, and Theodor Zahn. However, there is no explicit reference in the epistle to the temple and its destruction. Writes Hugh Montefiore, "Our author is throughout his Epistle strangely uninterested in contemporary references" (*The Epistle to the Hebrews* [New York and Evanston: Harper and Row, 1964], p. 76). Therefore, I do not think, on the basis of the reading *this generation* instead of *that generation,* that we have the assurance that the author in this text wished to indicate when he wrote the Epistle to the Hebrews.

13. Although the Hebrew text lacks the demonstrative pronoun before the noun *generation* in Ps. 95:10, the Septuagint reads "that generation." In the New Testament the textual evidence (the papyri manuscripts and leading codices) is very strong for the reading *this generation.* Among the translations the RV, ASV, NASB, and *Phillips* read "this generation"; the others (KJV, NKJV, NEB, NAB, JB, GNB, MLB, NIV, RSV, and *Moffatt*) have "that generation" or a variant that is similar in meaning.

see the good land I swore to give your forefathers" (Deut. 1:35; see also Num. 14:23). God took the promise of rest away from the unbelieving Israelites and told them they would die in the desert. Their children of twenty years and younger would be allowed to enter the land God had promised to the forefathers.

The land the Israelites were to possess is called a rest, for there they would have a permanent and safe dwelling (Deut. 12:9). The land of Israel would be given to those who had not spurned God. In his anger God swore that all the others would not see the land but would die in the desert. God was saying that he would cease being God—as it were—before he would let those rebellious Israelites enter the land of Canaan.

In the context of the Israelites' possession of the land, the concept *rest* was fulfilled only in a limited sense. The way of life for the wandering nomad had ended and the career of the valiant soldier ceased when the land was conquered. However, the word *rest* has a much deeper meaning, which the author subsequently explains in Hebrews 4.

2. Application
3:12–15

The quotation from the psalm is now applied to the recipients of the Epistle to the Hebrews, and its meaning is especially significant for the people who are in danger of turning away from God. The psalm citation serves as an introduction to a stirring appeal not to fall away from the living God. In a sense, Hebrews 3:12 may be called the summary of the pastoral exhortations in the epistle.

12. See to it, brothers, that none of you has a sinful, unbelieving heart that turns away from the living God.

The connection between Hebrews 3:6b and 3:12 is quite natural if we read the lengthy quotation from Psalm 95 as a parenthetical comment. This passage is an illustrative, historical reminder of the obstinate Israelites who died in the desert and were denied entrance to the land God had promised them.[14] The readers are exhorted to hold on to their courage and hope as members of the household of God. They cannot turn their backs on Christ in unbelief, for turning away from Christ is falling away from God.

For Christians, therefore, the experience of the rebellious Israelites must serve as a warning that should not be taken lightly. Christians must thoroughly examine themselves and one another to see whether anyone has a sinful, unbelieving heart.

The author of Hebrews knows from Scripture that a falling away from God finds its origin, development, and impetus in unbelief. Unbelief—characterized by mistrust and unreliability—first comes to expression in disobedience, which in turn results in apostasy. The signs of apostasy are hardening

---

14. The controversy continues: should the first word of Heb. 3:7, *so,* be taken with the command *do not harden your hearts* (Heb. 3:8) or with Heb. 3:12?

of the heart and an inability to repent (Heb. 3:13; 4:1; 6:6; 10:25–27; 12:15). The following series of contrasts can be made:

unbelief—faith
disobedience—hearing obediently
neglect—steadfastness
apostasy—entrance to life
hardening—salvation

The heart of someone who turns away from God is described as sinful, which means evil or wicked. God does not take the sin of unbelief lightly, for he knows that its origin lies in man's evil heart. "The heart is deceitful above all things and beyond cure. Who can understand it?" (Jer. 17:9). Furthermore, the author of Hebrews indicates that it is possible to find persons with sinful, unbelieving hearts in the fellowship of the Christian church.

> Whoever turns from the living God
> must fall;
> It's he who shares his guilt, his lot
> with all:
> Family, kin, nation, state,
> small and great.
>
> Whoever forsakes God is forsaken;
> Whoever rejects God is rejected.
> Frequent voices daily claim:
> Man who's come of age will settle
> down
> But they who say so without God
> drown.
> —Nicholaas Beets

13. But encourage one another daily, as long as it is called Today, so that none of you may be hardened by sin's deceitfulness.

Other portions of Scripture use various metaphors to describe the church. We read that the house of God consists of living stones (I Peter 2:5), not of individual bricks cemented together by mortar. The household to which the believers belong is like a body that is made up of many parts; all the many parts form one body (I Cor. 12:12). Furthermore, all the parts should have equal concern for each other.

These examples provide the background for the exhortation in verse 13. We also are urged to "encourage one another and build each other up" (I Thess. 5:11) so that no member of the church will fall away. If the church were faithful to Jesus individually and collectively, the danger of apostasy would recede to the perimeter of the church. To put it figuratively, we as individual believers, united by faith, have the obligation to expel the forces of unbelief from the sacred precincts of the church, the body of Christ. What salvation, what joy in heaven over one sinner who repents, what victory over Satan if we daily encourage one another and uphold each other in the faith!

> All one body we,
> One in hope and doctrine,
> One in charity.
> —Sabine Baring-Gould

In addition, all of the members of the church are told to exhort one another daily. This in itself is a call to faithfulness. And all members ought to teach and admonish one another with all wisdom (Col. 3:16; see also Acts 14:22; Heb. 10:25).

The author of Hebrews links the exhortation to the lengthy quote from Psalm 95 with the single word *Today.* He calls to mind the experience of the nation Israel in the wilderness; he intimates that the present is a period of grace that God extends until death terminates man's earthly life. And the termination of life may come rather suddenly for some people.

Moreover, the moment will come when God will cease to warn sinful man. When that moment arrives, the day of grace has changed into the day of judgment. Therefore, while there is still time, we are obligated to encourage one another daily, so that no one falls into the deceitful trap of sin.

Finally, the author notes that Satan sends sin as a deceptive agent, singling out individuals here and there, seeking to lead believers astray (Matt. 13:22; Mark 4:19; Rom. 7:11; II Cor. 11:3; Eph. 5:6; Col. 2:8; II Thess. 2:3, 10; II Peter 2:13). Sin enters deceptively by enticing the believer to exchange the truth of God for a lie. Sin presents itself as something attractive and desirable. Because of its appearance—"Satan himself masquerades as an angel of light" (II Cor. 11:14)—sin is an extremely dangerous power confronting the believer. It always attacks the individual, much as wolves stalk a single sheep.

The author of Hebrews is fully aware of sin's deceptive power directed toward individuals. For this reason he stresses the need to pay attention to every person in the church; repeatedly he says "none of you"—that is, not a single one of you (Heb. 3:12–13; 4:1).

Sin is regarded as an agent that hardens man's heart. Note that the verb *to harden* is presented in the passive voice: "so that none of you may be hardened by sin's deceitfulness." Hardening is demonstrated by a refusal to hear the voice of God and a determined desire to act contrary to everything classified as faith and faithfulness. As a sly, deceptive agent of Satan, sin enters the heart of man and there causes the growth and development of unbelief, which becomes evident in hardening of the spiritual arteries.

14. We have come to share in Christ if we hold firmly till the end the confidence we had at first. 15. As has just been said:

"Today, if you hear his voice,

do not harden your hearts
as you did in the rebellion."[15]

The parallel between Hebrews 3:6 and Hebrews 3:14 is striking. The imagery in verse 6 is of the house of God over which Christ has been placed as son and of which we are part. In verse 14 the same relationship is described as a sharing in Christ.[16] And the courage and hope that we should "hold on to" (v. 6) are identified as "the confidence we had at first" (v. 14).

Only those believers who unwaveringly continue to profess their faith in Jesus are saved. Only faith keeps the believers in a living relationship with Jesus Christ. As the writer says in Hebrews 11:6, "Without faith it is impossible to please God." Faith is the basic substance of our sharing in Christ. "Faith is being sure of what we hope for and certain of what we do not see" (Heb. 11:1). The phrase *being sure* is equivalent to "confidence" (Heb. 3:14); this confidence is the basis upon which our faith rests.

What does the author mean when he says, "if we hold firmly till the end the confidence *we had at first*" (italics added)? John Albert Bengel aptly says, "A Christian, so long as he is not *made perfect,* considers himself as a *beginner.*"[17] This confidence is the continual clinging to Christ in faith. As long as our faith in Christ is foundational, we are safe and secure as members of God's household.

To remind us once more of the daily necessity to listen attentively and obediently to the voice of God, the author quotes the now-familiar statement from Psalm 95, "Today, if you hear his voice, do not harden your hearts as you did in the rebellion." Constantly God addresses us by means of his Word, and he expects us who live by faith to give him our undivided attention.

3. Summation
3:16–19

In a concluding paragraph, the author asks a number of rhetorical questions relating to the Israelites who perished in the desert because of unbelief. In a series of self-explanatory questions, the writer makes it clear that unbelief ends in death.

16. Who were they who heard and rebelled? Were they not all those Moses led out of Egypt?

In this first question the author directs attention to the message of the lengthy quotation from Psalm 95, and by means of the second question he provides the answer to the first question. These people had seen the miracles God performed; they had experienced the goodness of God. Day by day

---

15. Punctuation and paragraph division play a role in Greek texts and English translations. Thus, the Nes-Al text places Heb. 3:14 between dashes to indicate a parenthetical thought. The NKJV, MLB, GNB, and NIV end the paragraph with Heb. 3:15. The NASB, RSV, *Moffatt,* ASV, KJV, JB, NAB, and RV end the paragraph with Heb. 3:19. The NEB, Martin Luther, Zahn, R. C. H. Lenski, Delitzsch, Spicq, and Bruce begin a new paragraph with Heb. 3:15.

16. The common translation is "share in Christ." Other versions translate the Greek as "Christ's partners" (NEB) or "partners of Christ" (NAB), or "co-heirs with Christ" (JB).

17. John Albert Bengel, *Gnomon of the New Testament,* ed. Andrew R. Fausset, 7th ed., 5 vols. (Edinburgh: Clark, 1877), vol. 4, p. 376. His italics.

they ate manna, and they could see the presence of God in the pillar of fire by night and in the cloud by day.

By implication the author conveys the message already stated in Hebrews 2:2: "For if the message spoken by angels was binding, and every violation and disobedience received its just punishment, how shall we escape if we ignore such a great salvation?"

17. And with whom was he angry for forty years? Was it not with those who sinned, whose bodies fell in the desert?

Would the behavior of the Israelites have improved in the course of forty years? The answer to this question is given in Exodus and Numbers: Exodus 17 records the first rebellion at the beginning of the forty-year period and Numbers 25 records the grievous sin of immorality at the end of that period. The Israelites had not changed: they remained rebellious and obstinate. The only exceptions, of course, were Joshua and Caleb, who demonstrated their faith and were privileged to conquer and possess the land.

18. And to whom did God swear that they would never enter his rest if not to those who disobeyed?

When the writer asks, "Was it not with those who sinned?" (v. 17), he parallels this question with the clause "if not to those who disobeyed" (v. 18). The verbs *sinned* and *disobeyed* are synonyms: the first verb represents the action followed by just punishment; the second verb reveals the root of the evil. Disobedience is a refusal to hear the voice of God and an obstinate refusal to act in response to that voice. Disobedience is not merely a lack of obedience; rather it is a refusal to obey.

19. So we see that they were not able to enter, because of their unbelief.

The author states, in conclusion, that the rebellious Israelites, in an example that needs no imitation, had to perish in the desert because of unbelief, a sin of openly defying God, refusing to believe, and exhibiting disobedience.

Unbelief is the root of the sin of provoking God. Unbelief robs God of his glory and robs the unbeliever of the privilege of God's blessings. Because of unbelief, rebellious man is denied entrance into the rest that God provides for the members of his household.

Practical Considerations in 3:7–19

Our salvation is of the highest importance and may never be taken lightly. We must heed the admonitions that the author of Hebrews gives us in the form of illustrations from Israel's past (Exod. 17:7; Num. 20:13; Deut. 33:8; Ps. 106:32).

According to Numbers 1, the census of the Israelites took place in the second year after the people came out of Egypt, and the total number of men twenty years and older who were able to serve in Israel's army was 603,550 (Num. 1:46). Double this number (this assumes an equal number of women who were twenty years or older) and divide the total by the number of days the Israelites spent in the wilderness during those thirty-eight years. The result is nearly ninety deaths per day in consequence of God's curse (Num. 14:23; Deut. 1:34–35). A daily reminder of God's anger!

All sins are deviations from the law that God has given his people. The Israelites deliberately chose to follow their own desires and wishes; they demonstrated their devious nature in action and word, in mind and heart. Their attitude stemmed from an evil heart.

Believers have a corporate and an individual responsibility to care for the spiritual well-being of their fellow men. They must consider this responsibility a holy obligation and exhibit utter faithfulness, even if the fruit of their fidelity is not always evident.

We are sharers in Christ when we have accepted the gospel in faith and obedience and show in our lives that what we believe in our hearts we confess with our mouths (Rom. 10:10). Those who consistently fail to confess never shared in Christ and consequently fail to know Christ as their Savior.

Greek Words, Phrases, and Constructions in 3:7–19

Verse 7

τὸ πνεῦμα τὸ ἅγιον—the use of the definite articles before the noun and the adjective occurs in Hebrews 9:8 and 10:15; but also see Hebrews 2:4 and 6:4, where the definite articles are lacking. And see Hebrews 9:14 and 10:29.

ἀκούσητε—the aorist active subjunctive, second person plural of ἀκούω (I hear) indicates the probability that the audience may hear. Also note that the verb is followed by the genitive case φωνῆς instead of the accusative. The genitive calls attention to the sound of the voice and does not necessarily imply understanding or listening obediently to what is said.

Verse 8

σκληρύνητε—the negative prohibition in the aorist subjunctive conveys the meaning that the recipients of the letter had not yet hardened their hearts, but that the possibility was not imaginary.

Verse 12

ἔσται—after the negative μήποτε we would expect the subjunctive. The author uses the future indicative ἔσται in order to express the urgency of listening to his exhortation and the distinct possibility of apostasy.

θεοῦ ζῶντος—definite articles are lacking to focus attention on the absolute power of God to create, uphold, and govern the world. (See II Cor. 3:3; 6:16; I Tim. 4:10; Heb. 9:14; 10:31; 12:22; I Peter 1:23; Rev. 7:2.)

Verse 13

τὸ σήμερον—note the definite article in the neuter singular. The use of τὸ (instead of the usual phrase ἡ σήμερον ἡμέρα) tells the reader that the quotation of Psalm 95 is intended.

Verse 14

ὑπόστασις—in the New Testament ὑπόστασις occurs five times (II Cor. 9:4; 11:17; Heb. 1:3; 3:14; 11:1). In Hebrews the word is theologically important and is translated "being" (1:3), "confidence" (3:14), and "being sure" (11:1).

Verse 18

εἰσελεύσεσθαι—the future middle infinitive is used because of the quotation (Heb. 3:11). The future is the equivalent of an aorist in the sense of a single occurrence.

Summary of Chapter 3

In the first two chapters of the epistle, the author of Hebrews compared Jesus and the angels. In chapter 3 he compares Jesus and Moses. The Jews revered Moses because of his close relationship with God. Moses' career was characterized by faithfulness—no one disputes that fact. However, with a fitting illustration of servant (Moses *in* God's house) and Son (Jesus *over* God's house), the writer of Hebrews clearly demonstrates the superiority of Jesus.

Psalm 95:7–10 is a unique citation, filled with disheartening information about Israel's rebellion and apostasy in the wilderness. The author of Hebrews warns his readers not to fall into the trap of unbelief which leads to a falling away from the living God. The writer stresses the corporate responsibility of the Christian community in warning the individual believer not to turn away from God but to continue to be strong in the faith. The author applies the words of Psalm 95:7–10 directly to his hearers; for him the message is a matter of eternal life or eternal death. In a sense, Hebrews 3:12 may be called one of the nerve centers of the epistle.

4

Jesus' Superiority to Moses, *part 2*

4:1–13

Outline

	C. An Invitation to Enter God's Rest
4:1–5	1. God's Rest
4:6–11	2. God's Day
4:12–13	3. God's Word

4 1 Therefore, since the promise of entering his rest still stands, let us be careful that
none of you be found to have fallen short of it. 2 For we also have had the gospel
preached to us, just as they did; but the message they heard was of no value to
them, because those who heard did not combine it with faith. 3 Now we who have
believed enter that rest, just as God has said,

"So I declared on oath in my anger,
'They shall never enter my rest.' "

And yet his work has been finished since the creation of the world. 4 For somewhere he has
spoken about the seventh day in these words: "And on the seventh day God rested from all
his work." 5 And again in the passage above he says, "They shall never enter my rest."
6 It still remains that some will enter that rest, and those who formerly had the gospel
preached to them did not go in, because of their disobedience. 7 Therefore God again set
a certain day, calling it Today, when a long time later he spoke through David, as was said
before:

"Today, if you hear his voice,
do not harden your hearts."

8 For if Joshua had given them rest, God would not have spoken later about another
day. 9 There remains, then, a Sabbath-rest for the people of God; 10 for anyone who
enters God's rest also rests from his own work, just as God did from his. 11 Let us, therefore,
make every effort to enter that rest, so that no one will fall by following their example of
disobedience.
12 The word of God is living and active. Sharper than any double-edged sword, it penetrates even to dividing soul and spirit, joints and marrow; it judges the thoughts and attitudes
of the heart. 13 Nothing in all creation is hidden from God's sight. Everything is uncovered
and laid bare before the eyes of him to whom we must give account.

C. An Invitation to Enter God's Rest
4:1–13

1. God's Rest
4:1–5

In the third chapter of his epistle, the writer of Hebrews quotes at length from Psalm 95 and speaks of the unbelievers who were cursed by God and died in the desert. Although the author speaks of the unbelievers in chapter 3, he addresses the believers in chapter 4. The admonition of 3:12–14 is now resumed and is substantially enlarged in 4:1–11. The question that is raised is this: Is the promise of entering God's rest, given to the Israelites but forfeited because of unbelief, still valid in our time? The answer is a resounding yes. The message of entering the rest that God promises is the same and still calls for acceptance in faith. The assurance is that "we who have believed enter that rest" (Heb. 4:3).

1. Therefore, since the promise of entering his rest still stands, let us be careful that none of you be found to have fallen short of it.

The first word *therefore* is rather significant because it looks backward to the quotation and the interpretation of Psalm 95, and points forward to the believers who read the Epistle to the Hebrews. The message of 4:1 can be summarized in three words: fear, promise, failure.

a. *Fear.* The author is a pastor who, filled with concern, strives for the spiritual well-being of his people. He does not want to see a single member of the church fall into the same sin (i.e., unbelief) that was displayed by the Israelites who died in the desert. The author is a shepherd, so to speak, who watches over every sheep in the flock.

But the writer is not the only one in the church to care for the members of the congregation. He exhorts the recipients of his epistle to be equally concerned. Thus he writes, "Let us be careful." He shares his pastoral concerns with all the members—all are responsible for the welfare of the church. To be concerned about one's own salvation is commendable; to pray for one's fellow man is praiseworthy; but to strive for the salvation of everyone within the confines of the church is exemplary. We ought to take careful note of members who may be drifting from the truth in doctrine or conduct and then pray with them and for them. We are constantly looking for spiritual stragglers. Says Philip Edgcumbe Hughes in his commentary on this point, "There is no attitude more dangerous for the church than that of unconcern and complacency."[1]

Most translations have the reading *let us fear* or some variation, denoting something that causes concern and anxiety in a person's heart (Acts 23:10; 27:17, 29; II Cor. 11:3; 12:20; Gal. 4:11).

b. *Promise.* God's promises remain the same for all times and for every generation because God is true to his Word (Deut. 3:18–20; Josh. 1:12–18; 21:45; 23:14; I Kings 8:56; Ps. 89:1; I Cor. 1:9; Heb. 6:18). On the basis of this scriptural truth, I prefer the translation "since the promise of entering his rest still stands." We have the assurance that God's promise is still valid today and did not come to an end with the Israelites in the desert. And because of the certainty that the promise of God still stands, we must have special care for and interest in the spiritual growth and development of fellow believers.

Some translations describe the duration of the promise of entering God's rest: "while the promise of entering his rest remains." Others express the concessive idea, namely, "although there is still left a promise to enter into

---

1. Philip Edgcumbe Hughes, *Commentary on the Epistle to the Hebrews* (Grand Rapids: Eerdmans, 1977), p. 155.

his rest."[2] These translations are to the point and accurate—they stress the continuing validity of God's promise to his people. This promise is in a specific sense still incomplete and open.[3] In other words, the promise will lose its significance only at the end of time when in fact the last of the believers has entered God's rest.

c. *Failure.* For the Israelites on their way to the land of Canaan, for David who composed Psalm 95, for the writer of Hebrews and his readers, and for us today the promise of God is firm and spans the centuries. This does not mean, however, that God is obligated to fulfill his promise when faith is lacking. When man fails God by not believing in his Word, God turns the promise into a threat and a curse as he did during Israel's journey in the wilderness.

What then does the writer of Hebrews imply when he tells his readers that they have the promise of entering God's rest? The answer must be that the idea of rest has taken on a much broader meaning, because when the word *rest* was first used it referred to entering Canaan. The concept included rest from harassment by Israel's enemies in neighboring countries; spiritually it related to a blessed life spent in harmony with the law of God. When David spoke of rest, he lived safely in his palace at Jerusalem. For the recipients of the epistle, the term *rest* had spiritual significance.

In the congregation that originally received the epistle, the possibility that someone had fallen short of appropriating God's promise seems to have been real. The expression *to have fallen short* may have been borrowed from the sports arena; it conveys the meaning of being left behind in the race and thus failing to reach the goal.[4] When someone does not reach the goal, he cannot give even the appearance of having arrived. In the eyes of the spectators in the arena, the contestant has failed. He cannot receive a prize and in many cases even forfeits sympathy.

This type of failure to claim the promise of God's rest may not be found in the church. The writer is direct in his appeal "that *none of you* be found to have fallen short" (italics added; see also 3:12; 4:11). The entire congregation ought to be vigilant about possible lack of interest in spiritual matters. No one may let his guard down. No one may be lost. Responsibility for one another's spiritual interest is the obligation of every believer.

2. For we also have had the gospel preached to us, just as they did; but the message they heard was of no value to them, because those who heard did not combine it with faith.

---

2. R. C. H. Lenski, *The Interpretation of the Epistle to the Hebrews and of the Epistle of James* (Columbus: Wartburg, 1946), p. 125.

3. Bauer, p. 413, translates the phrase "a promise that is still open."

4. Joseph H. Thayer, *A Greek-English Lexicon of the New Testament* (New York, Cincinnati, and Chicago: American Book Company, 1889), p. 646, says the expression means "to fall short of the end." William L. Lane (*NIDNTT,* vol. 3, p. 954) speaks of a "broad range of nuances" for the sixteen times that the word occurs in the New Testament. The primary meaning is to arrive too late for an appointed meeting or event. The secondary nuance, obviously a consequence of the first, is that of failure and of lacking something.

The conjunction *for* links the concept of the promise, given to the Israelites but still valid today (v. 1), with that of the gospel preached to the nation Israel in the desert and to us.

Highlights in verse 2 are the following points.

a. The Word of God, although a continuous revelation from the first book in the Bible to the last, is the same. It is good news for the Israelite and for the Christian.

b. The clause "we also have had the gospel preached to us" receives a certain degree of emphasis. The writer does not say, "We have received the gospel." Instead, he states that the Word has been preached to us for a considerable time so that we are fully evangelized.

c. The Israelites traveling from Egypt to Canaan also had the Word preached to them over an extended period.

d. However, the gospel news (I Thess. 2:13) that the desert travelers heard did not do them any good, because they failed to pay attention.

e. Those who heard the Word *did not combine it with faith* (Rom. 10:16–17). And that was their downfall.

The last clause in 4:2, depending on the wording in a number of ancient manuscripts, varies in translation. There are two usual ways of translating the clause. One of these is, "because it [the Word] was not united by faith in those who heard."[5] This translation is by far the more prevalent, frankly because it fits the context and is readily understood. The manuscript evidence, however, favors the second translation, "because they did not share the faith of those who listened."[6] The implication is that among the Israelites in the desert were two people who obeyed the Word of God: Joshua and Caleb. It is rather strange that the writer is not more explicit; he leaves the reader to fill in the historical details and to draw the necessary conclusions.

Differences exist and the difficulties in the passage are undeniable, but in both translations the emphasis is on the faith that was not shared. During the entire period in which the Israelites had the Good News preached to them, they refused to accept it in faith. Their refusal was not a momentary reaction but a continuous rejection of God's written and spoken Word.

God fulfills his promises only in those who accept his Word in faith and trust, whether that happens to be Joshua, Caleb, or "the soul that on Jesus has leaned for repose." No one among the Israelites could complete the desert journey and enter the Land of Promise except the one who demonstrated true faith in God. And no one shall enter God's eternal rest unless his faith is anchored in Jesus, the Son of God.

3. Now we who have believed enter that rest, just as God has said,
"So I declared on oath in my anger,
'They shall never enter my rest.' "
And yet his work has been finished since the creation of the world.

---

5. Representative translations are KJV, NKJV, ASV, NASB, MLB, and RSV.

6. See, for example, RV, NEB, JB, NAB, and GNB.

After comparing the Israelites who wandered in the desert and the recipients of his epistle, the writer of Hebrews confidently asserts, "Now we who have believed enter that rest." He does not use the future tense ("we will enter"). He says, "We who have believed enter," and thus affirms that God's promise has become reality according to his divine plan and purpose.[7] At the moment—in principle but not yet in full realization—we are entering that rest. As long as we keep our eyes fixed on "Jesus, the author and perfecter of our faith" (Heb. 12:2), we enjoy the rest God has promised, and eventually we shall be with him eternally.

This point raises the following questions.

a. Who enters that rest? The author is quite specific. We; that is, those of us who have believed and have demonstrated our faith in Christ by professing his name (Acts 4:32; 16:31; Rom. 10:9; I Thess. 2:13). And we enter because God's promise still stands.

As God's promise does not lose its validity, so God's threat remains true for everyone who does not accept God's Word in faith. God's Word prevails because he has spoken:

> "So I declared on oath in my anger,
> 'They shall never enter my rest.' "

These words not only apply to Israel's experience in the wilderness, but also remind readers of the epistle that God's promise and threat are equally valid today.

b. What is God's rest? The writer of Hebrews has expected this question, it seems. The next sentence, "And yet his work has been finished since the creation of the world," indicates that.[8] The author explains the word *rest* in his own inimitable way by quoting an expression from Genesis 2:2, which he cites in 4:4. This expression (the words *his work*), along with the rest of the sentence, anticipates the reference to the Genesis account. (It is significant that the writer of Hebrews constantly quotes from the Old Testament Scriptures.[9] He never appeals to the words of Jesus or the teachings of the apostles, although he was acquainted with the gospel [Heb. 4:2]. For him and for the recipients of his epistle, the writings of the Old Testament were authoritative.)

After the world was created, the author tells us, God initiated a new period—a period of rest. God rested from his work of creation at the conclusion of the sixth day. Whereas for the six days of creation the concluding words are "there was evening, and there was morning," for the seventh day

---

7. Ceslaus Spicq, *L'Épître aux Hébreux,* 3d ed., 2 vols. (Paris: Gabalda, 1953), vol. 2, pp. 81–82.

8. Numerous texts and translations combine the sentence with the preceding quote and divide the two only by a comma (see Nes-Al; BF; and KJV, RV, ASV, and RSV as examples). Other translators are of the opinion that the sentence should stand separately, serving as a bridge between the quote from Ps. 95 and the one from Gen. 2:2.

9. F. W. Grosheide, *De Brief aan de Hebreeën en de Brief van Jakobus* (Kampen: Kok, 1955), p. 113.

these demarcations of time are lacking. With the seventh day, then, the period of God's rest began.

4. For somewhere he has spoken about the seventh day in these words: "And on the seventh day God rested from all his work." 5. And again in the passage above he says, "They shall never enter my rest."

Once before, in 2:6, the author has expressed himself rather vaguely about a Scripture passage. He does this deliberately to focus attention not on the precise location of the reference, but on the words themselves. Every reader knows that a reference to the seventh day comes from the creation account in Genesis. The quoted words, however, are more important: "And on the seventh day God rested from all his work."

The term *rest* merits attention, especially if we think of Jesus' words when the Jews persecuted him for healing an invalid on the Sabbath: "My Father is always at his work to this very day, and I, too, am working" (John 5:17). Rest for God does not mean idleness; rather it is a cessation from the work of creation. God continues to enjoy this rest now that the work of his creation is completed.

On the combined strength of the two Old Testament passages—one from Psalm 95 and one from Genesis 2:2—the author concludes that only those persons who believe enter God's rest. This rest, to be sure, has become a reality for the believer. Unbelievers have no access to the rest God provides, for by spurning God's Word they have forfeited the privilege of entering his rest.

Note the author's repeated reference to the solemn oath God swore: "They shall never enter my rest" (Heb. 3:11, 18 [with minor variations]; 4:3, 5). This recurring warning ought not be taken lightly by the reader. And no one can ever say, "It will never happen to me." If the Israelites, entering the land of Canaan, had listened to words spoken by Moses (Deut. 28:1–14) and obeyed the commands of God, they would have been the recipients of all the blessings God had promised. They would have been honored above all the nations of the earth, and they would have enjoyed rest by living in God's favor and grace. For them, life in Canaan would have been living in the presence of God. But one generation after the death of Joshua and the elders who outlived him, the people turned their backs on the God of their fathers (Josh. 2:10), and the promise of God turned into a threat and a curse. It is for this reason, vividly documented by historical fact, that the author of Hebrews repeats the verse *they shall never enter my rest.*

Practical Considerations in 4:1–5

The exhortations in 4:1–3 are in effect an application of the lesson learned from history. As in chapter 3 the unbelieving Israelites were mentioned, so in chapter 4 the believers are addressed. The call to faithfulness and mutual care is earnest and sincere.

The gospel is proclaimed to believers and unbelievers, so that no one can claim the excuse of not having heard the promise of God. Man's failure to listen to God's

Word does not terminate the promises: for the unbeliever these become threats; for the believer they remain promises which in due time are fulfilled.

Believers, because of firm faith, enter God's rest, which is a spiritual state of being in the presence of God. The Genevan Reformer John Calvin had a motto, *Coram Deo* (in the presence of God). The believer by faith lives in harmony with his God. As Calvin puts it: "The highest happiness of man is to be united to his God."[10]

Greek Words, Phrases, and Constructions in 4:1–5

Verse 1

φοβηθῶμεν—the author includes himself in the exhortation and thus identifies himself with the readers. The aorist subjunctive expresses the exhortation to watch over one another's spiritual welfare. The author tells the reader to do so without delay.

ἐπαγγελίας—in the epistle this noun occurs fourteen times and the verb an additional four times. There seems to be word play involved in the Greek when the author speaks of promise (ἐπαγγελία) and preaching the gospel (εὐαγγελίζομαι). The latter verb appears only two times in Hebrews (4:2, 6). The noun ἐπαγγελία is in the genitive absolute construction with a causal connotation.

Verse 2

εὐηγγελισμένοι—together with the verb ἐσμεν, the perfect passive participle forms a periphrastic construction that expresses the idea of a continuous activity that began in the past and lasts into the present. Note that the personal pronoun ἡμεῖς is not used, in order to place emphasis on the verb instead.

ὁ λόγος τῆς ἀκοῆς—the genitive is qualitative in nature (see also Rom. 10:17; I Thess. 2:13) and is related to the aorist active, dative plural participle ἀκούσασιν.

Verse 3

οἱ πιστεύσαντες—the aorist active participle and the preceding definite article modify the main verb εἰσερχόμεθα. The aorist is ingressive.

γενηθέντων—the aorist passive (deponent) participle in the genitive and the words τῶν ἔργων form a genitive absolute construction.

---

2. God's Day
4:6–11

The emphatic threat "they shall never enter my rest" does not rule out God's honoring his promise to those who believe. Some enter God's rest.

6. It still remains that some will enter that rest, and those who formerly had the gospel preached to them did not go in, because of their disobedience. 7. Therefore God again set a certain day, calling it Today, when a long time later he spoke through David, as was said before:

> **"Today, if you hear his voice,**
> **do not harden your hearts."**

Note these observations.

---

10. John Calvin, *Epistle to the Hebrews* (Grand Rapids: Eerdmans, 1949), p. 96.

a. *Unalterable fact.* From biblical history the reader knows that Joshua and Caleb entered the land of Canaan. They put their trust in God, who kept his Word. They were privileged to enter the Land of Promise, because God does not break his Word. This fact remains throughout the ages and is unchangeable.

Thus the reader of these verses is exhorted to enter God's rest, because God is true to his Word and does fulfill his promise. A careful reading of the first part of 4:6 shows that the thought expressed is somewhat incomplete. That is, the introductory clause, "it still remains that some will enter that rest," needs a concluding remark, perhaps in the form of an exhortation. And this exhortation is given in 4:11, "Let us, therefore, make every effort to enter that rest."[11] If we accept God's Word in faith and do his will obediently, the promise of rest will be fulfilled for us, too. That fact is unquestionable.

b. *Just reward.* Some enter God's rest; others are denied entrance. This is not a matter of injustice nor of favoring one party over another. Rather, the author of Hebrews perceives that the distinction is just. Says he, "Those who formerly had the gospel preached to them did not go in, because of their disobedience." Those people who heard the voice of God from Sinai and who were given the law of Moses refused to accept the promise. They were without excuse, for although they heard the gospel, they chose to disobey. They received their due when entrance into Canaan was denied. Their unbelief turned into disobedience; heart and hand were willfully opposed to God and his Word.

c. *Repeated promise.* God remains in control; he rules and overrules. His promise, which the Israelites ignored and which was consequently nullified, God repeats. "Therefore God again set a certain day, calling it Today."

The word *Today* emphasizes the characteristics of relevance, timeliness, and newness. The text indicates that God set a certain day and mentions that "a long time later he spoke through David." God spanned the centuries from desert life to Davidic rule, from Moses recording Israel's history in the Pentateuch to David composing his songs for the Psalter.[12] He makes his promise available *today,* which is the time for embracing the gracious offer of salvation. God appeals to readers:

> Today, if you hear [my] voice,
> do not harden your hearts.

d. *Timeless validity.* Why is the promise of God always valid? In at least three different verses of chapter 4 the author gives the answer: God has

---

11. John Brown, in *The Epistle to the Hebrews* (Edinburgh: Banner of Truth Trust, 1961), p. 207, labels Heb. 4:6b–10 parenthetical and maintains that the writer chooses this structure "to establish the principle on which this exhortation proceeds."

12. The Hebrew Bible does not have a superscription for Ps. 95. The Septuagint ascribes the psalm to David. The author of Hebrews quotes exclusively from the Septuagint; this translation was, for him and his readers, Scripture. Thus he considered David the composer.

spoken (vv. 3, 4, 7). The simple phrase *as God has said,* which in the original Greek is in the perfect tense, signifies that what God says has permanent validity (see also Heb. 1:13; 10:9; 13:5). No matter how many centuries elapse, God's Word spans the ages; his message is just as clear, firm, and sure today as it was when first uttered. God's Word is divinely inspired and, as Paul says, "useful for teaching, rebuking, correcting and training in righteousness" (II Tim. 3:16).

8. For if Joshua had given them rest, God would not have spoken later about another day.

The writer clearly appeals to biblical history, specifically to the books of Deuteronomy and Joshua. God promised rest to the wandering Israelites when Moses declared, "But you will cross the Jordan and settle in the land the LORD your God is giving you as an inheritance, and he will give you rest from all your enemies around you so that you will live in safety" (Deut. 12:10; also see Deut. 3:20; 5:33).

This promise was fulfilled literally when Joshua addressed the people of the tribes of Reuben and Gad and the half-tribe of Manasseh: "Now that the LORD your God has given your brothers rest as he promised, return to your homes in the land that Moses the servant of the LORD gave you on the other side of the Jordan" (Josh. 22:4; see also Josh. 1:13, 15; 21:44; 23:1).

The writer demonstrates once again that he knows the Old Testament Scriptures thoroughly, and as an expert theologian he formulates the conditional sentence: "For if Joshua had given them rest—and we know that God fulfilled this promise—God would not have spoken later about another day, as he does in Psalm 95." In other words, the rest of which God speaks is a spiritual rest and has much greater significance than living safely in Canaan.

The rest that God intended for his people transcends the temporal and attains the eternal. It is a spiritual rest that is effected by the gospel, whether proclaimed in Old Testament or New Testament days. It is a rest from sin and evil. As Zacharias Ursinus, with the help of Caspar Olevianus, aptly expressed it:

> that every day of my life
> I rest from my evil ways,
> let the Lord work in me through his Spirit,
> and so begin already in this life
> the eternal Sabbath.[13]

9. There remains, then, a Sabbath-rest for the people of God; 10. for anyone who enters God's rest also rests from his own work, just as God did from his.

From Psalm 95 the author has shown that the rest that the Israelites enjoyed in Canaan was not the rest God intended for his people. The intended

13. Heidelberg Catechism, answer 103.

rest is a Sabbath-rest, which, of course, is a direct reference to the creation account (Gen. 2:2; see also Exod. 20:11; 31:17) of God's rest on the seventh day.[14]

For the believer the Sabbath is not merely a day of rest in the sense that it is a cessation of work. Rather it is a spiritual rest—a cessation of sinning. It entails an awareness of being in the sacred presence of God with his people in worship and praise. John Newton captured a glimpse of what Sabbath-rest is to be when he wrote:

> Safely through another week
> God has brought us on our way;
> Let us now a blessing seek,
> Waiting in His courts today;
> Day of all the week the best,
> Emblem of eternal rest.

The day of rest is indeed an *emblem* of eternal rest! During our life span on earth, we celebrate the Sabbath and realize only partially what Sabbath-rest entails. In the life to come, we shall fully experience God's rest, for then we will have entered a rest that is eternal. " 'Blessed are the dead who die in the Lord from now on.' 'Yes,' says the Spirit, 'they will rest from their labor, for their deeds will follow them' " (Rev. 14:13).

Who then enters that rest? Only those who die in the Lord? The answer is: All those who in faith experience happiness in the Lord because they are one with him. Jesus prays for those who believe in him, "that all of them may be one, Father, just as you are in me and I am in you" (John 17:21). In God we have perfect peace and rest.

> My heart, Lord, does not rest
> Until it rests in Thee.
> —Augustine

However, the text indicates that whoever enters God's rest does so only once. He enters that rest fully when his labors are ended. He then enjoys uninterrupted heavenly rest from which death, mourning, crying, and pain have been removed; at that time God's dwelling will be with men; he will live with them and be their God, for they are his people (Rev. 21:4).

11. Let us, therefore, make every effort to enter that rest, so that no one will fall by following their example of disobedience.

Hebrews 4:6 serves as an introduction to 4:11. With the introductory clause, verse 11 reads: "Since therefore it remains for some to enter, let us, then, make every effort to enter that rest." The intervening verses must be understood as a parenthetical thought.

a. "Let us, therefore, make every effort to enter that rest." From now on,

---

14. H. W. Attridge, in defining God's rest, speaks of type and antitype—rest in Canaan is the antitype of God's rest upon completing the week of creation. Refer to "Let us strive to enter that rest: The logic of Hebrews 4:1–11," *HTR* 73 (1980): 279–88.

says the author, let us exert ourselves to enter God's rest. Let us not take that rest for granted but earnestly strive to live in harmony with God, to do his will, and to obey his law. Paul in his Epistle to the Philippians puts the same thought in different words: "Continue to work out your salvation with fear and trembling" (2:12). This eagerness ought to be the hallmark of every believer and the password of the church. We are not to be fanatical, but are to demonstrate inner assurance in obedience to God's Word. The writer of Hebrews does not cease to warn and to exhort his readers. He is utterly serious when he says, "In your struggle against sin, you have not yet resisted to the point of shedding your blood" (Heb. 12:4).

b. "So that no one will fall." The key word in this clause is the term *fall,* which of course is a direct reminder of the desert journey of the Israelites as it is recorded in the Pentateuch and in Psalm 95. These people sinned, and as a consequence of God's curse, their bodies fell in the desert. The word *fall* must be taken in a broader sense than referring only to physical death; it includes falling away spiritually and thus being completely ruined. Those who fall have lost their salvation and deserve eternal destruction.

As a pastor watching over his flock, the writer of Hebrews admonishes his readers to take care of one another spiritually. He stresses the responsibility of each believer toward the individual members of the church. No one in the Christian community should be neglected and thus, left to himself, be allowed to fall (see Heb. 3:12; 4:1).

c. "By following their example of disobedience." The disobedient Israelites who perished in the desert became an example to their descendants. They became the object lesson of how not to live in the presence of God. Fathers would teach their children (Ps. 78:5–8) what the consequences of disobedience were for the rebellious Israelites on the way to the land of Canaan. And they would warn them not to follow this example.

Implicitly the author of Hebrews is saying to his readers: If any of you falls by following the example of the Israelites in the wilderness, he himself will be an example to his contemporaries, and everyone will take his failure as a warning not to make the same mistake. Rather, the reader must do everything in his power to walk the pathway of obedience and to exhort his brother and sister in the Lord to do likewise.

Unbelief leads to willful disobedience, which results in an inability to come to repentance. And what is the conclusion? The answer is forthright and to the point: eternal condemnation. Therefore, says the writer, let us make every effort to enter God's rest.

Doctrinal Considerations in 4:6–11

If Joshua, leading the Israelites into the land of Canaan, had given them rest, the psalmist would not have had to repeat the promise of rest (Ps. 95:11). The rest promised in Psalm 95 and explained in 4:10 is a copy of God's rest; this rest is attained by the believer in personal repentance and an ardent dedication to obey God. When the believer rests from his evil works, he enters the Sabbath-rest granted to the people of God.

God commands us to remember the Sabbath day by keeping it holy and, referring to the creation week and his rest on the seventh day, instructs us to follow his example (Exod. 20:8–11; also see Deut. 5:12–15). The noun *rest* does not convey the thought of idleness but rather of peace. "It stands for consummation of a work accomplished and the joy and satisfaction attendant upon this. Such was its prototype in God."[15]

One of the motifs in the Epistle to the Hebrews is the author's recurring use of statements that describe a condition contrary to fact (see Heb. 4:8; 7:11; 8:7). The writer employs a conditional sentence in each instance and shows that in the Old Testament era rest (Heb. 4:8) and covenant (Heb. 8:7) were incomplete. Perfection, he writes, could not be attained (Heb. 7:11). But Christ brought fulfillment to promise and prophecy when he delivered the fullness of God's revelation.

The name *Joshua* (Heb. 4:8) is equivalent to the name *Jesus* in the Greek New Testament. Joshua, the son of Nun, led the Israelites across the river Jordan into the Land of Promise where they enjoyed rest and peace from wandering and warfare. Jesus leads his people into the presence of God and grants them the eternal Sabbath-rest.

Greek Words, Phrases, and Constructions in 4:6–11

Verse 6

ἀπολείπεται—the compound verb has a directive connotation: "to leave behind." In 4:6 and 9 it has the meaning *to remain.* The present tense expresses lasting validity.

εὐαγγελισθέντες—the aorist passive participle (compare Heb. 4:2) is preceded by the definite article οἱ to indicate a definite group. Between the article and the participle stands the adverb πρότερον (formerly) for emphasis.

ἀπείθειαν—in Hebrews 3:12 and 19 the noun ἀπιστία occurs; in Hebrews 4:6 and 11 the noun ἀπείθεια. The former (unbelief) leads to the latter (disobedience). Disobedience comes to expression in obstinate opposition to God's will.

Verse 7

ὁρίζει—from the noun ὅρος (boundary) the verb ὁρίζω (I mark, define) is derived. The English derivative is the word *horizon.*

προείρηται—a few manuscripts have the perfect active προείρηκεν (he has said before).

Verse 8

εἰ—this conditional clause is contrary to fact. If Joshua had given the Israelites rest—but he did not provide permanent rest—God would not have spoken later about another day as he did in Psalm 95.

---

15. Geerhardus Vos, *Biblical Theology* (Grand Rapids: Eerdmans, 1954), p. 156.

ἐλάλει—in this statement that is contrary to fact, the use of the imperfect tense is eloquent testimony that God's promise is valid for all generations and that God repeats his offer of eternal rest. For the use of the verb λαλέω, see 1:1, 2.

Verse 9

σαββατισμός—the verb σαββατίζω (I keep the Sabbath) is the basis of the noun σαββατισμός, which occurs only once in the New Testament. The ending -μός signifies the progressive act of keeping the Sabbath.

τῷ λαῷ—modified by the genitive τοῦ θεοῦ (the people *of God*), the noun refers to the believers in the Christian community; that is, the people God has elected for himself (Acts 15:14; 18:10; Rom. 9:25; I Peter 2:10; and see Hos. 1:6, 9; 2:23).

Verse 10

ὁ εἰσελθών—the participle in the aorist indicates that entrance into God's rest happens once.

ὥσπερ—in 4:10 and the immediate broader context, the Greek word order is highly significant. Note that the first word and the last word in the sentence receive the emphasis. Also, the author frequently arranges words in the original Greek (see, for instance, the adjective ἄλλης, which modifies the noun ἡμέρας in Heb. 4:8) in such a way as to accentuate them, much the same as we italicize words for emphasis. Last, the enclitic particle περ adds force to the word ὡς. It means "thoroughly," "indeed," "in fact."

Verse 11

σπουδάσωμεν—this is one of the twelve hortatory subjunctives the author employs in Hebrews. Ten of these are in the present tense; the other two (Heb. 4:1, 11), in the aorist tense.

---

3. God's Word[16]
4:12–13

In the last section of the author's discussion about the rest of God that is reserved for the believers, the focus is on the power of God's Word (v. 12) and on man's inability to hide from that Word (v. 13). Because of the rather striking word order and word choice in these verses, the assumption is that the writer has borrowed a line or two from a poem, circulating in the early church, about the Word of God. This is a possibility. The effect of these two verses, however, is to give the discussion about Sabbath-rest a fitting conclusion by appealing to the nature and authority of the Word of God.

12a. The word of God is living and active.

The writer reminds the reader that God's Word cannot be taken lightly; for if the reader does not wish to listen, he faces no one less than God himself (see Heb. 10:31; 12:29). The Bible is not a collection of religious

---

16. Paragraph division differs in Greek texts and translations. Heb. 4:11–13 is taken as a complete paragraph in Merk, Nes-Al, RSV, MLB, NKJV, and *Moffatt.* On the other hand, the United Bible Society (3d ed.), GNB, NAB, NEB, JB, and NIV put 4:11 with the preceding paragraph and place 4:12–13 separately.

writings from the ancient past, but a book that speaks to all people everywhere in nearly all the languages of the world. The Bible demands a response, because God does not tolerate indifference and disobedience.

In their interpretation of verse 12a, some scholars assert that the phrase *Word of God* is a reference to Jesus.[17] This view is difficult to maintain, even though such a reference exists in Revelation 19:13 (where the rider on the white horse is called the Word of God). The phrase *Word of God* occurs at least thirty-nine times in the New Testament and almost exclusively is the designation for the spoken or written Word of God rather than the Son of God. In the introductory verses of the Epistle to the Hebrews, the writer clearly states that *God* spoke to the forefathers in the past, and in the present he spoke to us in his Son (Heb. 1:1–2). In Hebrews Jesus is called the Son of God, but never the Word of God.[18]

In the original Greek, the participle *living* stands first in the sentence and therefore receives all the emphasis. This participle describes the first characteristic of God's spoken and written Word: that Word is alive! For example, Stephen, reciting Israel's history in the desert, says that Moses at Mount Sinai "received living words" (Acts 7:38), and Peter tells the recipients of his first epistle that they "have been born again . . . through the living and enduring word of God" (I Peter 1:23).

A second characteristic is that the Word of God is active. That is, it is effective and powerful. (The original Greek uses a word from which we have derived the term *energy*.) God's Word, then, is energizing in its effect. No one can escape that living and active Word. Just as God's spoken Word brought forth his beautiful creation, so his Word recreates man dead in transgressions and sins (Eph. 2:1–5). As in the wilderness some Israelites refused to listen to God's Word while others showed obedience, so today we see that "the message of the cross is foolishness to those who are perishing, but to us who are being saved it is the power of God" (I Cor. 1:18).

The Bible is not a dead letter, comparable to a law that is no longer enforced. Those people who choose to ignore the message of Scripture will experience not merely the power of God's Word but its keen edge as well.

12b. Sharper than any double-edged sword.

In the ancient world, the double-edged sword was the sharpest weapon available in any arsenal. And in verse 12b, the author of Hebrews likens the Word of God to this weapon. (In a similar passage [Rev. 1:16] we read about the "sharp double-edged sword" coming out of the mouth of Jesus as John

---

17. Among recent defenders of this view is James Swetnam in "Jesus as *Logos* in Hebrews 4:12, 13," *Bib* 62 (2, 1981): 214–24. The view, although prevalent in the early church and in the Middle Ages, is rejected by modern commentators. Bertold Klappert (in *NIDNTT*, vol. 3, p. 1113) writes, "This word of God, which had its beginning in the words of Jesus (Heb. 2:3) is decisively grounded in the exaltation of Jesus to the right hand of God (Heb. 1:5ff.) and in his installation as eschatological high priest (Heb. 7:1ff.)."

18. Says Henry Alford, *Alford's Greek Testament: An Exegetical and Critical Commentary*, 4 vols. (Grand Rapids: Guardian, 1976), vol. 4, pt. 1, p. 83, "Every where He is the Son of God, not His Word." See also Hugh Montefiore, *The Epistle to the Hebrews* (New York and Evanston: Harper and Row, 1964), p. 87.

saw him on the island of Patmos. Whether this means that the tongue resembles a dagger is an open question.) The symbolism conveys the message that God's judgment is stern, righteous, and awful. God has the ultimate power over his creatures; those who refuse to listen to his Word face judgment and death, while those who obey enter God's rest and have life eternal. Let no one take the spoken and written Word for granted; let no one ignore it; let no one willfully oppose it. That Word cuts and divides, much as the scalpel of a surgeon uncovers the most delicate nerves of the human body.

However, the Word of God also provides protection. Paul in his Epistle to the Ephesians equates the Word with the sword of the Spirit—that is, part of the Christian's spiritual armor (6:17).

12c. It penetrates even to dividing soul and spirit, joints and marrow; it judges the thoughts and attitudes of the heart.

I do not think that the writer of Hebrews is teaching the doctrine that man consists of body, soul, and spirit (I Thess. 5:23). Of course, we can make a distinction between soul and spirit by saying that the soul relates to man's physical existence; and the spirit, to God.[19] But the author does not make distinctions in this verse. He speaks in terms of that which is not done and in a sense cannot be done.

Who is able to divide soul and spirit or joints and marrow? And what judge can know the thoughts and attitudes of the heart? The author uses symbolism to say that what man ordinarily does not divide, God's Word separates thoroughly. Nothing remains untouched by Scripture, for it addresses every aspect of man's life. The Word continues to divide the spiritual existence of man and even his physical being. All the recesses of body and soul—including the thoughts and attitudes—face the sharp edge of God's dividing sword. Whereas man's thoughts remain hidden from his neighbor's probing eye, God's Word uncovers them.

God's Word is called a discerner of man's thoughts and intentions. In the Psalter David says:

> O Lord, you have searched me
> and you know me.
> You know when I sit and when I rise;
> you perceive my thoughts from afar.
> You discern my going out and my lying down;
> you are familiar with all my ways. [Ps. 139:1–3]

And Jesus utters these words:

> As for the person who hears my words but does not keep them, I do not judge him. For I did not come to judge the world, but to save it. There is a judge for the one who rejects me and does not accept my words; that very word which I spoke will condemn him at the last day. [John 12:47–48]

19. For a complete discussion on trichotomy, see William Hendriksen, *I–II Thessalonians,* New Testament Commentary series (Grand Rapids: Baker, 1955), pp. 146–50.

same pages in this vol. in common I Thess. 5:23

The Lord with his Word exposes the motives hidden in a man's heart. In his epistle the author stresses the act of God's speaking to man. For instance, the introductory verses (Heb. 1:1–2) illustrate this fact clearly. And repeatedly, when quoting the Old Testament Scriptures, the writer uses this formula: God, Jesus, or the Holy Spirit says (consult the many quotations, for example, in the first four chapters). The Word is not a written document of past centuries. It is alive and current; it is powerful and effective; and it is undivided and unchanged. Written in times and cultures from which we are far removed, the Word of God nevertheless touches man today. God addresses man in the totality of his existence, and man is unable to escape the impact of God's Word.

13. Nothing in all creation is hidden from God's sight. Everything is uncovered and laid bare before the eyes of him to whom we must give account.

The emphasis in 4:12–13 shifts from the Word of God to God himself. If God's Word uncovers everything, then it follows that God himself is fully aware of all things. It is therefore impossible for man to hide his sinful motives in the dark corners of his heart. God knows. He sees everything; even darkness is as light to him (Ps. 139:12).

Moreover, the past, the present, and the future are all alike to God. While we are bound to time and place, God dwells in eternity and transcends all that he has made in his great creation. He created the magnificent constellations in outer space and hung the stars in place. He also created the tiny spider that busily weaves its web. If then his eye is on the sparrow, does he not know the hidden motives of man? Before we open our mouths to speak, God already knows. If we remain silent, he discerns.

No creature is hidden from God's sight, because with God everything is light—there is no darkness. Man, the pinnacle of God's creation, is invited to walk in that light, so that he may see clearly. Consider these verses:

> Your word is a lamp to my feet and a light for my path. [Ps. 119:105]
>
> I am the light of the world. Whoever follows me will never walk in darkness, but will have the light of life. [John 8:12]

The unbeliever seeks to hide from God but is unable to do so (Jer. 23:24). Secret sins man can hide from his fellow man, but before God sinful man is "uncovered and laid bare." This latter expression, in the original Greek, refers to the neck. The precise meaning of the word, however, is not clear. Perhaps it indicates that a sinner will have his head pushed up and back so that his face and neck will be exposed to view.[20] Whatever the interpretation may have been, the expression itself is sufficiently clear in context. It is synonymous with the word *uncovered* and indicates that God's all-seeing eye rests upon everything.

---

20. Franz Delitzsch, *Commentary on the Epistle to the Hebrews,* 2 vols. (Edinburgh: Clark, 1877), vol. 1, p. 216.

The clause "to whom we must give account" is rather interesting. The books must be audited, and all the bills, payments, and receipts handed over to be checked. Man must give an account of himself before God, the auditor. The books of man's conscience are open before God's eyes. Nothing escapes him.

In the last day sinners may call to the mountains and the rocks, "Fall on us and hide us from the face of him who sits on the throne and from the wrath of the Lamb!" (Rev. 6:16). In the final judgment, everyone must give an account of himself. Only those who are in Christ Jesus will hear the liberating word *acquitted.*

Doctrinal Considerations in 4:12–13

In a sense, 4:12 is a summary statement of earlier references to the spoken and written Word of God. Whether spoken or written, God's Word is a unity. The same voice speaks with clarity and authority to every generation. It addressed the Israelites in the desert, the citizens of Israel in David's day, and the recipients of the Epistle to the Hebrews in the first century. That voice still speaks today.

The Word of God is living and powerful in the hearts and lives of the believers. Unbelievers, however, brazenly reject the very Word that addresses them. They echo the words of William Ernest Henley:

> It matters not how strait the gate,
> How charged with punishments the scroll,
> I am the master of my fate;
> I am the captain of my soul.

Paul writes to the Corinthians that his preaching is to the one the smell of death, to the other the fragrance of life (II Cor. 2:16). And Calvin observes that God "never promises to us salvation in Christ, without pronouncing, on the other hand, vengeance on unbelievers, who by rejecting Christ bring death on themselves."[21]

The expression *double-edged sword* ought not be taken literally and thus interpreted to mean that one edge is directed toward believers and the other toward unbelievers. The writer uses symbolism to imply that the Word of God does indeed "cut to the heart" (Acts 2:37).

God's knowledge is all-comprehensive, including self-knowledge and complete understanding of all events, past, present, and future.[22] Scripture repeatedly refers to God's omniscience (see Deut. 2:7; I Sam. 16:7; I Chron. 28:9, 12; Job 23:10; 24:23; 31:4; 37:16; Ps. 1:6; 33:13; 37:18; 119:168; 139:1–4).

Hebrews 4:12 teaches that God's Word "judges the thoughts and attitudes of the heart." Here, as elsewhere in the epistle, there is no reference to Christ as the judge. Quoting Deuteronomy 32:36 ("The Lord will judge his people" [Heb. 10:30]), the writer concludes, "It is a dreadful thing to fall into the hands of the living God" (Heb. 10:31).

---

21. Calvin, *Hebrews,* pp. 102–3.

22. Louis Berkhof, *Systematic Theology* (Grand Rapids: Eerdmans, 1953), p. 67.

Greek Words, Phrases, and Constructions in 4:12–13

Verse 12

ζῶν—the use of the present active participle teaches that the Word of God does not merely exist; it must be understood as "having in itself energies of action"[23] (see I Peter 1:23).

ἐνεργής—a variant reading in Codex Vaticanus reads ἐναργής (clear, evident). As an adjective from the verb ἐνεργέω (I am effective), ἐνεργής means "effective, powerful."

τομώτερος—this adjective in the comparative occurs once in the New Testament; it is derived from τομός (sharp), which in turn is from the verb τέμνω (I cut).

δίστομος—the compound adjective *double-edged* (δίς [twice] and στόμα [mouth]) appears in the Septuagint in Judges 3:16 and Proverbs 5:4; and in the New Testament in Hebrews 4:12 and Revelation 1:16; 2:12; 19:15 (variant reading).

διϊκνούμενος—this present middle participle from the deponent verb διϊκνέομαι (I penetrate) occurs once in the New Testament, but see Exodus 26:28 in the Septuagint. The form is a compound of the preposition διά (through) and the verb ἵκω or ἱκνέομαι (I come, reach, arrive at).

μερισμοῦ—from the verb μερίζω (I divide), the noun—because of the ending -μός—shows progressive action. In Thayer's *Lexicon,* preference is given to translating the word passively: "*even to the division,* etc., i.e. to that most hidden spot, the dividing line between soul and spirit, where the one passes into the other."[24]

Verse 13

τετραχηλισμένα—as a perfect passive participle of τραχηλίζω (I seize the neck; I expose by bending back), the word has been interpreted in numerous ways. The basic meaning is "to expose." Because the verb occurs only once in the New Testament, the exact meaning cannot be ascertained.

ὁ λόγος—the noun λόγος appears at the beginning of 4:12 and at the end of 4:13. The latter evidently is in the form of an idiom, "we must give an account," while the former refers to the Word of God.

Summary of Chapter 4

The focus in chapter 4 is not so much on the unbelieving Israelites who refused to obey God as it is on the believers who in faith enter God's promised rest. The unbelieving desert travelers failed to listen to God's voice and perished on the way to the land God had promised. The Christian who lives by faith enters into God's rest, the Sabbath-rest for the people of God. And this entrance into rest can be accomplished only by listening obediently to the gospel.

The first thirteen verses of this chapter form an introduction to the author's discussion about the high priesthood of Jesus the Son of God. Already in 2:17–18 the author introduced this subject, which in succeeding chapters he fully develops and explains.

23. B. F. Westcott, *Commentary on the Epistle to the Hebrews* (Grand Rapids: Eerdmans, 1950), p. 102.

24. Thayer, *Lexicon,* p. 400. His italics.

5

Jesus' High Priesthood

4:14–5:10

Outline

4:14–16	A.	Encouragement for the Readers
5:1–3	B.	Enablement of the High Priest
5:4–10	C.	Fulfillment of the High-priestly Office

4 14 Therefore, since we have a great high priest who has gone through the heavens, Jesus the Son of God, let us hold firmly to the faith we profess. 15 For we do not have a high priest who is unable to sympathize with our weaknesses, but we have one who has been tempted in every way, just as we are—yet was without sin. 16 Let us then approach the throne of grace with confidence, so that we may receive mercy and find grace to help us in our time of need.

A. Encouragement for the Readers
4:14–16

In his series of illustrations establishing the excellence of Jesus, the writer now contrasts Jesus with Aaron, the high priest. In Hebrews 2:17 and 3:1, the author introduced Jesus as high priest. With occasional digressions,[1] the author writes extensively about the office and work of the high priest (see Heb. 5:5, 10; 6:20; 7:26; 8:1; 9:11; 10:21).

14. Therefore, since we have a great high priest who has gone through the heavens, Jesus the Son of God, let us hold firmly to the faith we profess.

Note the following points:

a. Because of his sonship, Jesus already is great.
b. Thus, being high priest does not make Jesus great.
c. Jesus excels because he is divine.
d. Only Jesus has gone through the heavens.
e. The difference, therefore, between Jesus and Aaron is immeasurable.

The adverb *therefore* ought not be understood to refer to the immediately preceding context but to Hebrews 2:17, where the subject of Christ's priesthood is first introduced.[2] The author, who briefly referred to the "high priest

---

1. The chapter division is somewhat infelicitous at this juncture. Martin Luther in his Bible translation boldly begins chapter 5 at Heb. 4:14. Most commentators believe that the concluding verses of chapter 4 should be interpreted with the following chapter on the high priesthood of Christ.
2. Franz Delitzsch prefers to connect the word *therefore* with the exhortation: "Let us therefore, having a great high priest who hath passed through the heavens, Jesus the Son of God, hold fast by our confession" (*Commentary on the Epistle to the Hebrews,* 2 vols. [Edinburgh: Clark, 1877], vol. 1, p. 217). However, the adverb *therefore* in the Greek has a variety of meanings, which should be determined on the basis of context, "and at times it may be left untranslated." (See Bauer, p. 592.) Indeed, a number of translations delete the adverb.

whom we confess" in Hebrews 3:1, now is ready to explain the significance of Jesus' priesthood.

Since we have a great high priest. The emphasis falls on the term *great,* which also occurs in Hebrews 10:21 ("since we have a great priest over the house of God") and Hebrews 13:20 (where Jesus is called "that great Shepherd of the sheep"). The adjective *great* indicates that Jesus is superior to earthly high priests and shepherds.[3] He is the *great* high priest, not the one who entered the Most Holy Place once a year and sprinkled blood to atone first for his own sins and then for those of the people. Jesus, as the great high priest, excels earthly high priests.

Who has gone through the heavens. The Jewish high priest entered the inner sanctuary of the temple once a year and stood momentarily in the very presence of God. Jesus, by contrast, has entered the heavens and is always in the presence of God (Heb. 9:24). He has been raised from the dead, has ascended to heaven, and sits at the right hand of God the Father. He has gone through and is "exalted above the heavens" (Heb. 7:26). He is majestic in power and glory because he is the Son of God, human and divine.

Let us hold firmly to the faith we profess. The author of Hebrews uses the earthly name of Jesus to focus attention on his ministry, suffering, death, resurrection, and ascension. Jesus could not be in heaven as the great high priest without having performed his priestly work on earth.

Once more the writer of Hebrews intersperses his teaching with exhortation. This exhortation can be connected logically with the first part of the verse ("since we have a great high priest who has gone through the heavens"). Characteristically, the author includes himself in the exhortation when he writes, "Let us hold firmly to the faith we profess" (see also Heb. 3:1; 10:23).

What then is this faith we profess? Is it a formulated confession of faith? Perhaps. But as Philip Edgcumbe Hughes writes, faith "is the belief that is both inwardly entertained by the heart and outwardly professed before men."[4] This is, of course, a paraphrase of Romans 10:10, "For it is with your heart that you believe and are justified, and it is with your mouth that you confess and are saved." This faith we must continue to profess with heart and mouth, joyfully, openly, so that our fellow man, too, may hear about Jesus the Son of God.

15. For we do not have a high priest who is unable to sympathize with our weaknesses, but we have one who has been tempted in every way, just as we are—yet was without sin.

The recipients of the epistle might have raised an objection to the author's teaching: Because Jesus is the Son of God and is exalted in heaven, far

---

3. C. P. Sherman ("A Great High Priest," *ExpT* 34 [1922]: 235) demonstrates from the Hebrew that two terms were used: "the great priest" and "the chief priest." Ceslaus Spicq, in *L'Épître aux Hébreux,* 3d ed., 2 vols. (Paris: Gabalda, 1953), vol. 2, p. 92, notes that in the time between the accession of Herod the Great and the destruction of the temple there were no fewer than twenty-six high priests.

4. Philip Edgcumbe Hughes, *Commentary on the Epistle to the Hebrews* (Grand Rapids: Eerdmans, 1977), p. 171.

removed from man's daily toils and struggles, his priesthood is of little consequence. The author, however, anticipates objections and in Hebrews 4:15 counters them. Not so, he says, for when I introduced the teaching I stated that we, the brothers of Jesus, have a high priest who is merciful and faithful. And "because he himself suffered when he was tempted, he is able to help those who are being tempted" (Heb. 2:18).

The writer makes his point by stating this truth negatively and positively.

a. *Negatively.* The double negative—we do not have a high priest who is unable to sympathize—expresses a positive idea: yes, we have a highly exalted high priest who can descend to our level.

The original recipients of Hebrews knew that the teaching about Jesus' high priesthood was articulated for the first time in this epistle. Perhaps they had to endure hardship, persecution, and isolation from the Jews if they professed the high priesthood of Jesus. They may have wondered: Would the exalted high priest understand their weaknesses if they failed to profess him publicly? Would he understand their situation? Yes, the author assured them, the heavenly high priest is able to sympathize. If we confess his name publicly, he suffers with us when others reproach, scorn, and insult us.

b. *Positively.* Jesus is not only fully divine; he is also fully human and thus understands our weaknesses and our temptations. Furthermore, Jesus himself experienced weaknesses and temptations. At the onset of his ministry, he was tempted by Satan; he coped with thirst, weariness, desertion, and disappointments throughout his earthly ministry.

Jesus, fully acquainted with human nature, is "touched with the feeling of our weaknesses," as B. F. Westcott puts it.[5] He has been tempted—in extent and range—in every way. Nothing in human experience is foreign to him, for he himself has endured it. And he has been tempted just as intensely as we are. The author adds the qualifying phrase *yet was without sin.*

When he was in the wilderness, Jesus experienced hunger, and the devil tempted him by asking him to make bread out of stones (Matt. 4:2–3). While hanging on the cross, he was mocked by chief priests, teachers of the law, and elders, who said, "Let him come down now from the cross . . . for he said, 'I am the Son of God' " (Matt. 27:42, 43). He endured the full range of temptations, although, as the writer notes, without sinning. Sin is the only human experience in which Christ has no part.

The temptations we endure are given to us in accordance with what we are able to bear. God's watchful eye is always upon us, so that we do not succumb. Says Paul:

> No temptation has seized you except what is common to man. And God is faithful; he will not let you be tempted beyond what you can bear.

---

5. B. F. Westcott, *Commentary on the Epistle to the Hebrews* (Grand Rapids: Eerdmans, 1950), p. 107. And John Calvin classifies as infirmities the physical as well as the spiritual: "fear, sorrow, the dread of death and similar things." See Calvin's *Epistle to the Hebrews* (Grand Rapids: Eerdmans, 1949), p. 108.

> But when you are tempted, he will also provide a way out so that you can stand up under it. [I Cor. 10:13]

We, however, will never be able to fathom the depth of the temptations Jesus endured. Yet he withstood the depth, as well as the force, of these temptations. He overcame them as the sinless One.

Is Jesus (the sinless One) able to sympathize with us (weakened by sin) in our temptations? Because of his sinless nature, says John Albert Bengel, "the mind of the Savior much more acutely perceived the forms of temptation than we who are weak," not only during his earthly ministry but also during his service as the exalted high priest.[6] He anticipates temptations we are going to face, sympathizes fully with us, and "is able to help [us] who are being tempted" (Heb. 2:18).

16. Let us then approach the throne of grace with confidence, so that we may receive mercy and find grace to help us in our time of need.

What encouraging words! The writer throughout his epistle exhorts the readers numerous times, but in this particular verse he has a special word for us. This time he does not exhort believers to rectify their way of life; he commends us for coming in prayer to God and urges us to do so confidently.

a. "Let us then approach the throne of grace with confidence." The invitation to approach the throne of grace implies that the readers are already doing this. The author also uses the same verb in Hebrews 10:22 ("let us draw near to God with a sincere heart in full assurance of faith"). He later repeats the same invitation in slightly different wording (see Heb. 7:25; 10:1; 11:6; 12:18, 22).

The verb *approach* may have a religious connotation, because it often referred to the priests who in their cultic service approached God with sacrifices (Lev. 9:7; 21:17, 21; 22:3; Num. 18:3).[7] In Hebrews 4:16 the writer urges us to come near to the throne of grace in prayer, for the only sacrifice a believer can bring is a broken and a contrite heart (Ps. 51:17). The great high priest has brought the supreme sacrifice in offering himself on the cross on behalf of his people. The merciful and faithful high priest invites the weak and tempted sinner to come to the throne of grace.

What is meant by the phrase *throne of grace*? This is an explicit reference to the kingship of the Son of God (Heb. 1:2–4). Jesus sits at the right hand of God and has been given full authority in heaven and on earth (Matt. 28:18). But the word *grace* implies that the reference is also to the priesthood of Christ. The sinner who comes to the throne of grace in repentance and faith indeed finds the forgiving grace of Jesus.

---

6. John Albert Bengel, *Gnomon of the New Testament,* ed. Andrew R. Fausset, 7th ed., 5 vols. (Edinburgh: Clark, 1877), vol. 4, p. 384.

7. Spicq, *Hébreux,* vol. 2, p. 94. James Moffatt asserts that the verb applies to a court or to authority. See his *Epistle to the Hebrews,* International Critical Commentary series (Edinburgh: Clark, 1963), p. 60.

Moreover, we are exhorted to come to the throne with confidence; that is, we may come boldly (Heb. 3:6; 10:19, 35), not rashly or in fear of judgment, but "in full confidence, openness to God and in the hope of the fullness of the glory of God."[8] Jesus invites his people to approach freely, without hesitation. He holds out the golden scepter, as it were, and says, "Come!"

b. "So that we may receive mercy and find grace." Although the terms *mercy* and *grace* are often interpreted as being synonyms, their difference ought to be noted. Westcott makes the distinction succinctly:

> Man needs mercy for past failure, and grace for present and future work. There is also a difference as to the mode of attainment in each case. Mercy is to be "taken" as it is extended to man in his weakness; grace is to be "sought" by man according to his necessity.[9]

The mercy of God is directed to sinners in misery or distress; they receive God's compassion when they approach him. And whereas God's mercy extends to all his creatures (Ps. 145:9), his grace, as the writer of Hebrews indicates in Hebrews 4:16, extends to all who approach the throne of God. Mercy is characterized as God's tender compassion; grace, as his goodness and love.[10]

c. "To help us in our time of need." Help is given at the right moment in the hour of need. The author is not saying that the help is constant, but rather that it alleviates the need of the moment. That need may be material, physical, or spiritual. When we call on the name of the Lord in faith and approach the throne of God, he will hear and answer. He stands ready to help (see Heb. 2:18).

This aid, in the form of grace, comes when temptation seems to sway us. God provides the means to find a way out of our temptations. God is faithful (I Cor. 10:13).

Doctrinal Considerations in 4:14–16

When the writer states that Jesus "has gone through the heavens" (v. 14), he implies that Jesus has entered the presence of God the Father. The Aaronic high priest, by entering the Most Holy Place once a year, stood in the presence of God. Because Jesus appears before God the Father in heaven, he transcends the Aaronic high priest. Therefore, the author of Hebrews calls him the "*great* high priest" (italics added).

The use of the plural noun *heavens* in the original Greek is rather common in

---

8. Hans-Christoph Hahn, *NIDNTT,* vol. 2, p. 736. This sense of assurance, writes Heinrich Schlier, "works itself out in the confidence and openness which [causes one] not [to] be ashamed when [he] stands before the Judge" (*TDNT,* vol. 5, p. 884).

9. Westcott, *Hebrews,* p. 109. Also see Otto Michel, *Der Brief an die Hebräer,* 10th ed. (Göttingen: Vandenhoeck and Ruprecht, 1957), p. 124.

10. Louis Berkhof, *Systematic Theology* (Grand Rapids: Eerdmans, 1953), pp. 71–72.

the Epistle to the Hebrews (Heb. 1:10 [Ps. 102:25]; 4:14; 7:26; 9:23; 12:23, 25). It is possible that the plural, which is also common in the Septuagint and in the New Testament (especially in Matthew's Gospel), conveys in the Epistle to the Hebrews the idea of completeness. However, the author uses the word *heaven* in the singular, too (Heb. 9:24; 11:12; 12:26 [Hag. 2:6]).

In rabbinic writings and in apocryphal literature, the conception of a multilayered heaven is somewhat common. In fact, Paul even speaks of knowing a man "caught up to the third heaven" and "to paradise" (II Cor. 12:2, 4). It seems that Paradise is located in either the third or the seventh heaven. Speculations about the heavenly Jerusalem, the location of God's throne, and the heavenly altar are numerous.

Because of the scarcity of information on this point in the Epistle to the Hebrews, we do well to refrain from speculation. In 4:14, it is implied that God's dwelling place is not in heaven; that is, "not within his creation to which heaven belongs, but above the heavens."[11] Jesus has transcended the heavens, has come to the throne of God, and has taken his place at God's right hand as the great high priest.

If Jesus endured temptations during his earthly ministry as the Son of God, how do we understand the author's teaching that he "has been tempted in every way, *just as we are*" (v. 15; italics added)? Herman N. Ridderbos, commenting on Jesus' temptation in the desert, raises this question in a slightly different form: Could Jesus fall into sin or was the temptation imaginary? Although Jesus as God's Son surpassed Satan and therefore could not fall, Jesus was not necessarily immune to temptation.[12] We admit that for us it is difficult to understand how the Son of God, who could not sin, was tempted just as we are. From our limited perspective, we are unable to explain the difficulty inherent in the biblical teaching about Jesus' sinlessness and temptation.

Greek Words, Phrases, and Constructions in 4:14–16

Verse 14

ἔχοντες—in the context of the verse, the present active participle may express cause.

διεληλυθότα—the perfect active participle, accusative singular masculine, derives from διά (through) and ἔρχομαι (I go). It denotes completed action in the past with lasting results for the present.

κρατῶμεν—a hortatory subjunctive, as a present active from κρατέω (I hold firmly, I keep faithfully; see Rev. 2:25; 3:11).

---

11. Hans Bietenhard, *NIDNTT,* vol. 2, p. 195.

12. Herman N. Ridderbos, *Mattheüs,* Korte Verklaring, 2 vols. (Kampen: Kok, 1952), vol. 1, p. 68. Geerhardus Vos, in *The Teaching of the Epistle to the Hebrews* (Grand Rapids: Eerdmans, 1956), p. 103, asserts that for Christ "there was as much real *appeal* to sin . . . as there is with us, but in His case there was no *issue* of sin." R. Williams argues that Jesus had to have actual participation in the experience of sinning in order to share fully in the human weaknesses of man. Next, Jesus had to subject himself to the process of learning obedience and thus achieve sinlessness when he offered himself on the cross. See Williams's article in *ExpT* 86 (1974): 4–8. Of course, this reasoning controverts Scripture's unequivocal teaching about Jesus' sinlessness (Isa. 53:9; John 8:46; II Cor. 5:21; Heb. 4:15; 7:26; I Peter 1:19; 2:22).

Verse 15

συμπαθῆσαι—in the New Testament the verb appears only twice: in Hebrews 4:15, referring to Jesus, and in Hebrews 10:34, referring to the recipients of the epistle. In extrabiblical literature it occurs numerous times. The aorist tense is constative; that is, the action of the verb does not refer to duration but rather to entirety.

πεπειρασμένον—the perfect passive participle, instead of the aorist passive πειρασθείς (see Heb. 2:18), indicates continued action in the past until its culmination—Jesus' death.

χωρὶς ἁμαρτίας—the last two words in this sentence emphasize the contrast between man, who is tainted by sin, and Jesus, who is sinless. The adverb χωρίς, serving as a preposition, controls the genitive singular ἁμαρτίας.

Verse 16

προσερχώμεθα—we are exhorted, with the hortatory subjunctive, to approach the throne of grace. The present tense suggests that we in fact are doing so.

λάβωμεν. . .εὕρωμεν—the verse shows chiasmus with two verbs and two nouns. The noun *mercy* follows the verb *to receive,* and the noun *grace* precedes the verb *to find.* Both verbs are in the aorist tense.

---

5 1 Every high priest is selected from among men and is appointed to represent them in matters related to God, to offer gifts and sacrifices for sins. 2 He is able to deal gently with those who are ignorant and are going astray, since he himself is subject to weakness. 3 This is why he has to offer sacrifices for his own sins, as well as for the sins of the people.

B. Enablement of the High Priest 5:1–3

After encouraging his readers, the author continues his teaching ministry by defining the qualifications for the one who serves as high priest. The obvious reference is to the institution of the Aaronic priesthood (Heb. 5:4); the high priest's appointment, duties, and obligations were divinely stipulated and were to be meticulously observed.

1. Every high priest is selected from among men and is appointed to represent them in matters related to God, to offer gifts and sacrifices for sins.

Three points require our attention.

a. A high priest is selected. The writer constructs a beautifully balanced sentence in which he describes the selection, appointment, and duty of a high priest. According to the law of Moses (Exod. 28–29, Lev. 8–10, and Num. 16–18), only Aaron and his sons were permitted to serve at the altar. "The priesthood was therefore a fraternity fenced round with irremovable barriers, for they had been fixed forever by natural descent."[13] From what

---

13. Emil Schürer, *A History of the Jewish People in the Time of Jesus Christ,* 5 vols. (Edinburgh: Clark, 1885), vol. 1, div. 2, p. 209.

we are able to learn about the selection process, a high priest was chosen from the members of relatively few influential priestly families. He did not serve actively as high priest for any length of time, as is evident from the Gospels and the Acts (John 18:13; Acts 4:6). The author of Hebrews, however, is not interested in historical details. Rather, he identifies the principle: the high priest is selected from among men. He writes in terms of biblical regulations and not historical aberrations.

b. A high priest is appointed. Note the passive voice of the verb that is used to describe the process of selection and appointment. The writer wishes to indicate that the high priest does not appoint himself, but by implication is appointed by God. The high-priestly office, therefore, is based on a divine calling (Heb. 5:4), especially in view of the high priest's work. That is, a sinful high priest is appointed to represent sinful people in matters related to God.

c. A high priest is to offer sacrifices. In the original Greek, the phrase *matters related to God* is used in Hebrews 2:17, where the author specifies that this includes the high priest's work of "mak[ing] atonement for the sins of the people." This work consists of representing men before God when the people come with gifts and sacrifices. They bring these gifts and sacrifices to the high priest so that he can offer them to God for the sins of the people.

The author of Hebrews explains this concept in a subsequent verse. The phrase *gifts and sacrifices* occurs again in Hebrews 8:3 and is abridged in the next verse where only the term *gifts* appears. In using this condensation, the author seems to imply that the two terms are synonyms, for every gift to God offered for sin is essentially a sacrifice. These gifts, then, the high priest presents to God to remove sin, to bring about reconciliation, and to gain access into God's grace (Rom. 5:2). The high priest is the intermediary between God and his people.

2. He is able to deal gently with those who are ignorant and are going astray, since he himself is subject to weakness.

The high priest, representing man before God, may never lose patience with the one he represents, in spite of that man's sins and shortcomings. As intercessor, the high priest must exercise moderation in expressing anger or sorrow concerning errors and faults of his fellow man. The high priest in the Old Testament era was a type of mediator whose fulfillment came in Jesus Christ.

However, not every sin can be brought to the high priest for remission. The writer of Hebrews is specific, for he says that the high priest deals gently with those who are ignorant and who go astray. Nothing is said about sin committed purposely to grieve God. By implication, the high priest must know the difference between sins perpetrated to vex God (Ps. 95:7–11) and sins committed because of weakness. Sins of ignorance usually result from a lack of paying attention to God's commandments, whereas intentional sins stem from a rebellious heart and mind fully acquainted with the law of God (Num. 15:22–31; also see Lev. 4, 5, and 22:14).

The high priest ought to deal gently with the people but should neither overlook or condone sin nor rank himself above the people. He himself daily confronted temptation and, because of his own human weakness, committed sin. Because the high priest had to cope with his own sinful nature, he was an equal of the people who sought his intercession for the sins they committed in weakness. Moreover, because of his ability to identify with his fellow man, he could deal gently with them in leading them to God.

The writer of Hebrews portrays the weakness, which the high priest shares with the people he helps, as something that clings to him as a garment covers his body. The realization of his own weakness and yielding to temptation causes the high priest to be moderate in expressing anger or grief.

3. This is why he has to offer sacrifices for his own sins, as well as for the sins of the people.

Verse 3 is an explanatory note in which the writer emphasizes what he already has stated in the preceding verse, where he pointed to the weakness of the high priest. Now, making an obvious reference to Leviticus 9:7 and 16:6, 15–16, he says that Aaron is told to sacrifice a sin offering and a burnt offering for himself and for the people. The writer of Hebrews indicates the obligation that the high priest has to offer a sacrifice for himself and the people he represents.

We should remember that, although the author is drawing a parallel between the Levitical high priest and Jesus the great high priest, not everything in the comparison is equal. The most significant difference is that Jesus "does not need to offer sacrifices day after day, first for his own sins, and then for the sins of the people. He sacrificed for their sins once for all when he offered himself" (Heb. 7:27).

For the moment, however, the author speaks of high priests in the Old Testament era. He alludes to the ritual of the annual entrance of the high priest into the Most Holy Place on the Day of Atonement; that is, on the tenth day of the seventh month, Tishri (approximately equivalent to October). According to Leviticus 16, Aaron had to

1. offer a bull for his own sin offering to atone for his own sin and the sin of his household,
2. enter the Most Holy Place with incense,
3. sprinkle the blood of the bull on the atonement cover of the ark,
4. cast lots over two live goats brought by the people,
5. kill one of the goats for a sin offering for the nation, and sprinkle its blood inside the Most Holy Place,
6. place his hands on the head of the live goat and confess the sins of the people, and
7. send the live goat away into the wilderness.[14]

---

14. Charles L. Feinberg, "Day of Atonement," *ZPEB*, vol. 1, p. 414.

The high priest made intercession for his people by praying that God might forgive the sins he himself and they had committed:

> O God, I have committed iniquity,
> transgressed, and sinned before thee,
> I and my house.
> O God, forgive the iniquities and
> transgressions and sins which
> I have committed and transgressed
> and sinned before thee,
> I and my house.[15]

Greek Words, Phrases, and Constructions in 5:1–3

Verse 1

λαμβανόμενος—the present passive participle indicates continuity. The term of office for the high priest was relatively short, and upon termination a successor had to be appointed. The passive voice shows that a man could not appoint himself to this office.

καθίσταται—the form is a present passive indicative, third person singular, from καθίστημι and καθιστάνω (I appoint, put in charge, ordain; see Heb. 7:28; 8:3). The verb should not be interpreted as a middle, for the words τὰ . . . θεόν do not lend themselves as a direct object.

Verse 2

μετριοπαθεῖν—although the verb is related to συμπαθέω (Heb. 4:15), it ought not be considered a synonym.[16] In the New Testament it occurs only once. In the writings of Philo, Plutarch, and Josephus the word means "to restrain or moderate one's anger."

τοῖς ἀγνοοῦσιν καὶ πλανωμένοις—the use of only one definite article indicates that the two participles ἀγνοοῦσιν (present active) and πλανωμένοις (present passive) describe one group of people. The active voice refers to the mental and spiritual condition of the readers; the passive voice implies an agent.

περίκειται—this compound verb is the present passive of περί (around) and κεῖμαι (I lie). The word appears in Mark 9:42, Luke 17:2, and Acts 28:20, as well as Hebrews 5:2 and 12:1.

Verse 3

ὀφείλει—the verb, in the present active, expresses obligation or necessity. Someone may be obligated, because of legal, conventional, or divine necessity, to act or to be the object of action (e.g., receive punishment). In the context of this verse it means the high priest, because of his office, ought to present sacrifices for himself and for the people.

---

15. *Mishna,* Moed Yoma 3.8, ed. H. Danby (London: Oxford University Press, 1967), p. 165.
16. Wilhelm Michaelis, *TDNT,* vol. 5, p. 938.

4 No one takes this honor upon himself; he must be called by God, just as Aaron was. 5 So
Christ also did not take upon himself the glory of becoming a high priest. But God said to
him,

"You are my Son;
today I have become your Father."

6 And he says in another place,

"You are a priest forever,
in the order of Melchizedek."

7 During the days of Jesus' life on earth, he offered up prayers and petitions with loud cries
and tears to the one who could save him from death, and he was heard because of his reverent
submission. 8 Although he was a son, he learned obedience from what he suffered 9 and,
once made perfect, he became the source of eternal salvation for all who obey him 10 and
was designated by God to be high priest in the order of Melchizedek.

C. Fulfillment of the High-priestly Office
5:4–10

Scholars debate whether Hebrews 5:4 ought to be bracketed with the preceding or the following verse. Does the paragraph end with verse 4, or does a new one begin with that verse? Verses 4 and 5 form a unit for the simple reason that they show parallelism—just as Aaron was, so Christ was also. Therefore, it may be preferable to begin a new paragraph with verse 4.

4. No one takes this honor upon himself; he must be called by God, just as Aaron was. 5. So Christ also did not take upon himself the glory of becoming a high priest. But God said to him,

"You are my Son;
today I have become your Father."

6. And he says in another place,

"You are a priest forever,
in the order of Melchizedek."

In these verses the author of Hebrews focuses on the priesthood of Christ by highlighting the following points.

a. The honor of the office. The office of high priest is an honor that God conferred upon the person who assumed the duties of the office. The high priest, from the time of Aaron to the destruction of the temple in A.D. 70, enjoyed proper recognition from the Hebrew community. Without a doubt, next to the civil leader the high priest held the highest office in the land.

The author, however, stresses that no one takes the honor upon himself for self-gratification. No one fills the office of the high priest merely for the sake of entering into the presence of God on the Day of Atonement, of receiving the respect of the Israelite community, or of wearing the beautiful high-priestly robe and turban (Lev. 8:7–9). The honor associated with the office derives from fulfilling the duties assigned to the high priest. He is to serve God on behalf of the people. He is their representative. He fulfills the mediatorial role of pleading for the remission of sin.

b. The calling by God. Moreover, a high priest must be called by God to this honorable office. Of course, this does not mean that there were no exceptions in Israel's history.[17] But the author of Hebrews is not interested in aberrations; he mentions the name of Aaron to call to mind that God inaugurated the high priesthood in Aaron.

In contemporary terms, this means that no one but he who has been called by God ought to assume the office of minister of the gospel. A seminary president once addressed an incoming class of students and, after words of welcome, said to these aspiring theologians: "Unless the Lord has called you to study for the ministry, we don't want you here."

Anyone inducted into sacred office must be called by God. If this is not the case, he is an affront to God and a provocation to his people. That is, he elevates himself above the people he wants to represent; exhibits a haughty instead of a humble spirit; and, because his concept of holiness is deficient, has a perverted perception of God.

c. Similarity with a difference. The parallelism between Aaron and Christ is expressed in terms of the office they fill. Note, for example, that the author does not use the name *Jesus* but uses *Christ,* the name that describes the office and duty of the Son of God. As Aaron was called and appointed by God (Exod. 28; Num. 16–17) to serve as high priest, so "Christ also did not take upon himself the glory of becoming a high priest." Note that the term *honor* in Hebrews 5:4 is a synonym of the word *glory.*

Yet the difference between Aaron and Christ is profound, because God (as this verse implies) has crowned Christ with glory and honor as high priest. Jesus did not presumptuously appropriate the office of high priest.

d. The Son of God. The author of Hebrews seems to anticipate that someone may raise the objection that Jesus and Aaron, apart from a few similarities pertaining to the office of high priest, have very little in common. That is true, says the writer; and once more he quotes Psalm 2:7, where God says to the Son:

> You are my Son;
> today I have become your Father.

The first time the author uses the quotation to compare the Son with angels (Heb. 1:5). Now the psalm citation indirectly contrasts Christ and Aaron. Jesus is the Son of God, and yet he is called and appointed by God to serve as high priest.

---

17. The history of the high priesthood in Israel from the time of Aaron to the destruction of Jerusalem in A.D. 70 has been recorded, although in summary form, by Josephus in *Antiquities of the Jews* 20.10 (LCL). Numerous men, from the second century before Christ to the cessation of the priesthood, were neither of Aaronic descent nor appointed by God. See especially Schürer, *History of the Jewish People,* vol. 1, div. 2, pp. 195–202. F. F. Bruce, in *The Epistle to the Hebrews,* New International Commentary on the New Testament series (Grand Rapids: Eerdmans, 1964), p. 92, n. 19, lists names and terms of office of persons who were appointed high priest by civil rulers.

In Hebrews 4:14, the writer combines the two concepts of sonship and high priesthood. Says Geerhardus Vos, "He gives exceptionally high value to the high priesthood of Christ, and derives its eminence from the Sonship."[18]

Now it is true that Psalm 2 stresses the royal status of the Son, who received the nations as his inheritance and who rules them with an iron scepter. How then, someone objects, can the Christ be high priest as well? The author expects the question and, as he has done before, uses the Old Testament to give an answer and prove his point.

e. The priest of God. The idea of a king-priest appears in the Old Testament at various places. The first reference we note is Genesis 14:18, where Melchizedek is introduced as king of Salem and priest of God Most High. Next, in Psalm 110:1 David speaks of royalty: "Sit at my right hand until I make your enemies a footstool for your feet." In Psalm 110:4 the reference is to priesthood: "You are a priest forever, in the order of Melchizedek." Finally, Zechariah, who symbolically refers to the Branch (i.e., the Messiah), writes what the Lord Almighty says:

> It is he who will build the temple of the LORD, and he will be clothed with majesty and will sit and rule on his throne. And he will be a priest on his throne. And there will be harmony between the two. [6:13]

The writer of Hebrews was thoroughly familiar with the teaching of the Old Testament. In order to be precise as to the type of priesthood Jesus assumed, he quotes Psalm 110:4, "You are a priest forever, in the order of Melchizedek." We should note that just as God addresses the Son in Psalm 2:7, so he speaks to him in Psalm 110:1 and 4. Thus God announces the kingship and the priesthood of his Son. "The Epistle to the Hebrews stands alone among the New Testament books in calling Christ priest."[19] The cause for this neglect may perhaps be found in the history of the Jewish people. Throughout the ages the Jews had expected a king from David's house. This king would deliver them from foreign oppression. And this king, because David's line was from the tribe of Judah, could not be a priest; priests were descendants of Aaron in the tribe of Levi. Therefore, Jesus was known as *king*. At his birth the wise men called him "king of the Jews" (Matt. 2:2), and this appellation was commonplace during the trial and crucifixion of Jesus. He was not known as *priest*.

Already in the first chapter of Hebrews, the author quoted Psalm 110:1 as irrefutable evidence of Christ's kingship. Now in chapter 5 he cites Psalm 110:4 to describe the unique function and purpose of Christ's priesthood. He makes it clear, although he explains the details in chapter 7, that Jesus' priesthood differs from that of Aaron. Jesus is "a priest forever, in the order of Melchizedek."

---

18. Vos, *Teaching*, p. 77.

19. Ibid., p. 91. The term *priest* occurs 31 times in the New Testament, 14 of which appear in Hebrews. The word *high priest* is featured 123 times in the Gospels, Acts, and Hebrews. The expression does not occur in the Epistles and Revelation. In Hebrews it is used 18 times. In short, it is the writer of the Epistle to the Hebrews who develops the doctrine of the priesthood of Christ.

7. During the days of Jesus' life on earth, he offered up prayers and petitions with loud cries and tears to the one who could save him from death, and he was heard because of his reverent submission.

The writer of Hebrews wants to prove that Jesus did not become a priest after his ascension, but that already during his life on earth the Lord offered up prayers and petitions. The reference to Jesus' earthly life seems to be related to his suffering at Gethsemane. In one sentence the literary artist portrays Jesus in spiritual agony.

a. *Setting.* Although the author has mentioned the name *Jesus* in preceding chapters (Heb. 2:9; 3:1; 4:14), in the present passage he clearly has the Gospel account in mind. He does not quote any specific words of Jesus, but the references are to the experience at Gethsemane (Matt. 26:36–46; Mark 14:32–42; Luke 22:39–46) and to the so-called little Gethsemane incident (John 12:27).

Admittedly, the Gospel writers do not tell us whether Jesus in Gethsemane prayed with loud cries and tears. However, we may infer from the words of Jesus that his agony was intense. Matthew and Mark report that Jesus said, "My soul is overwhelmed with sorrow to the point of death" (Matt. 26:38; Mark 14:34), and Luke writes that Jesus' agony was so acute that "his sweat was like drops of blood falling to the ground" (Luke 22:44).

b. *Function.* At first the phrase *offered up prayers and petitions* seems to be somewhat liturgical. However, the expression, describing Jesus' mediatorial work in the Garden of Gethsemane, must be understood to connote sacrificial activity—Jesus with prayer and petition functioned as priest. On behalf of sinners, whose sin he had taken upon himself, he prayed to God.

The prayers and petitions Jesus uttered cannot accurately be called offerings and have little resemblance to the work of the priest at the altar. But if we consider the function of Jesus' earthly life, especially the last days of his life, we see him offering himself as the sacrificial Lamb of God to atone for the sins of his people. In the Garden of Gethsemane, Jesus prayed, "My Father, if it is possible, may this cup be taken from me. Yet not as I will, but as you will" (Matt. 26:39) and "My Father, if it is not possible for this cup to be taken away unless I drink it, may your will be done" (Matt. 26:42). These prayers and petitions are far removed from liturgical worship. They reveal the depth of Jesus' spiritual and even physical agony expressed by the "drops of blood falling to the ground."

Jesus as the sin-bearer faced the wrath of God against sin. "God made him who had no sin to be sin for us" (II Cor. 5:21). And because of our sins, Christ stood before God as the most wicked of all transgressors. He stood alone as our substitute. The words of Ben H. Price capture this thought poetically:

> It was alone the Savior prayed
> In dark Gethsemane;
> Alone He drained the bitter cup
> And suffered there for me.

Alone, alone, He bore it all alone;
He gave Himself to save His own,
He suffered, bled and died alone, alone.

c. *Manner.* That the evangelists do not record that Jesus uttered his prayers and petitions "with loud cries and tears" does not imply that Jesus' prayers to God were quiet. In fact, his words from the cross were uttered in a loud voice (Matt. 27:46, 50; Mark 15:34, 37; Luke 23:46). Jesus saw the cup of God's wrath handed to him; he felt the curse of God (Gal. 3:13); and he realized that God's judgment was pronounced upon him. He faced death, which for him was not only physical death. If Jesus had died a martyr's death on a cross outside Jerusalem, it would hardly be noteworthy, because numerous people have met equally violent deaths.

However, Jesus died the so-called second death (Rev. 2:11; 20:6, 14; 21:8). What Jesus experienced in the Garden of Gethsemane and on the cross was eternal death. His cry, "My God, my God, why have you forsaken me?" reflected complete separation from God. And that is death unimaginable. We cannot fathom the depth of Jesus' agony when he experienced eternal death. We can only describe it, as the author of Hebrews does. We conclude by saying that Jesus in his separation from God experienced hell itself.

d. *Addressee.* Throughout his earthly ministry Jesus spent much time in prayer, calling God his Father. The intimate relation between Father and Son is especially evident in the high-priestly prayer recorded in John 17. Jesus' prayers uttered in Gethsemane and from the cross also were directed to the Father (Matt. 26:39, 42; Mark 14:36; Luke 22:42; 23:34, 46).

Jesus addressed his prayers "to the one who could save him from death." Many questions can be raised at this point. We could ask why Jesus prayed for deliverance from death when he knew that he was sent to give his life "as a ransom for all men" (I Tim. 2:6). Jesus himself, as the Second Person of the Trinity, had agreed to the decree to redeem mankind by sending the Son of God to earth. His prayer, therefore, did not arise out of ignorance. From one point of view, Jesus knew that the Father had commissioned him to redeem the world through the Son's sacrificial death. From another point of view, Jesus saw the horrors of enduring the indescribable agonies of being forsaken by God and experiencing eternal death.

Jesus fully submitted to the Father's will to enter death in order to remove the curse, fulfill the sentence pronounced against him, and redeem his people. Because of Christ's atoning work and victory over death and the grave, we shall never know the weight of sin, the severity of the curse, the penalty of judgment, or the meaning of eternal death and hell. We have been acquitted and set free because of Jesus, our high priest.

In Gethsemane Jesus prayed that the will of God might be accomplished in respect to the bitter cup of death Christ had to drink. Although this will was done, God did not leave his Son, for "God raised him from the dead, freeing him from the agony of death, because it was impossible for death to keep its hold on him" (Acts 2:24).

e. *Answer.* The prayers and petitions of Jesus were heard. In Luke 22:43 we read, "An angel from heaven appeared to him and strengthened him." This verse follows immediately the account of Jesus' prayer for the removal of the cup. The fact, however, is that the cup of agony was not removed. After Jesus prayed more earnestly, presumably the same prayer, "his sweat was like drops of blood falling to the ground" (Luke 22:44). The question must be raised whether the appearance of the angel constituted support for Jesus or a prolonging of his agony.[20]

How did God answer Jesus' prayer for deliverance from death? The author of Hebrews does not answer this question directly; instead he writes, Jesus "was heard because of his reverent submission." And here is the answer. Jesus accompanied his prayer with the request that the will of God might prevail. Thus, he reverently submitted to the Father's will. He experienced death, but God raised Jesus from the dead (Gal. 1:1).

Translations disagree about the correct rendering of the last clause of Hebrews 5:7. Some give the reading *because of his godly fear.* Others say, "because of his reverent submission."[21] The author of Hebrews uses the same Greek word in Hebrews 12:28, where the translation is "reverence." Moreover, the term occurs only in the Epistle to the Hebrews and nowhere else in the New Testament. On the basis of consistent use in Hebrews, we do well, perhaps, to understand the word to mean "reverent submission." Westcott comments that the expression "marks that careful and watchful reverence which pays regard to every circumstance in that with which it has to deal."[22] Jesus' life was marked by true submission to his Father's will, for even in Gethsemane he prayed that God's will might be done.

8. Although he was a son, he learned obedience from what he suffered 9. and, once made perfect, he became the source of eternal salvation for all who obey him 10. and was designated by God to be high priest in the order of Melchizedek.

Verses 8–10 are closely connected with the preceding verse. Indeed, in the original Greek the main verb in verses 7 and 8 is "he learned." That is where the emphasis falls in this passage. Therefore, numerous translations end verse 7 not with a period, but with a comma. This is correct, for the two verses are closely related and form a unit. Incidentally, the stress on the main verb, "he learned," gives added support to the reading *because of his reverent submission.*

Consider these questions.

a. Would Jesus have to learn obedience? The author introduces this subject by mentioning the divinity of Jesus first and stating this fact concessively:

---

20. Klaas Schilder shows that *after* the arrival of the angel Jesus began to sweat drops of blood. The coming of the angel caused intensified anguish. Refer to *Christ in His Sufferings* (reprint; Minneapolis: Klock and Klock, 1978), p. 358.

21. The earliest translations in Latin that show the difference are the Old Latin, which reads *a metu* (from fear), and the Vulgate, which has *pro sua reverentia* (because of his reverence).

22. Westcott, *Hebrews,* p. 127.

"although Jesus was the Son of God." He does not say that because Jesus was divine he had to learn obedience. Jesus did not have to learn anything concerning obedience, for his will was the same as God's will. However, in his humanity Jesus had to show full obedience; he had to become "obedient to death—even death on a cross!" (Phil. 2:8). As one version has it: "son though he was, he learned obedience in the school of suffering."[23]

b. What was the obedience Jesus had to learn? Translations, for reasons of style and diction, speak of obedience. In the original Greek, however, a definite article precedes the noun so that it reads "*the* obedience"; that is, the well-known obedience expected from the Lord.

When we interpret this verse we are not to think in terms of contrasts. It is true that sinful man needs to correct his ways by listening to God's Word and turning from disobedience to obedience. But Christ, the sinless One, did not learn by unlearning. Rather, through his active and passive obedience, Christ provides eternal life for the sinner and a discharge of man's debt of sin. Says Paul in Romans 5:19, "For just as through the disobedience of the one man the many were made sinners, so also through the obedience of the one man the many will be made righteous."

c. How was Jesus made perfect? The question is legitimate, for Jesus, as the Son of God, is perfect from eternity. But in his humanity, "Jesus grew in wisdom and stature, and in favor with God and men" (Luke 2:52). We see his development in the school of obedience. As the burden becomes more taxing for Jesus, so his willingness to assume the task his Father has given him increases.

In the Garden of Gethsemane and on Calvary's cross, he endured the ultimate tests. Jesus was made perfect through suffering. His perfection "became the source of eternal salvation for all who obey him." The author of Hebrews in effect repeats the thought he expressed in Hebrews 2:10—Jesus, made perfect through suffering, leads many sons to glory. Perfection, therefore, must be seen as a completion of the task Jesus had to perform.

d. What does the writer mean by "the source of eternal salvation"? The writer of Hebrews calls Jesus the "author" of salvation (Heb. 2:10) and the "source" of salvation. These two expressions are synonymous. Jesus is the captain, the chief, the originator, and the cause.

When the author uses the word *source,* he does not open a discussion on the primary cause of salvation; God the Father commissioned his Son to effectuate salvation. Instead the writer uses the term *source* in the context of his discussion about the high priesthood of Christ. By accomplishing his redemptive work, especially in Gethsemane and at Golgotha, Jesus is the source of eternal salvation (Isa. 45:17). Only those people who obey him will share in the salvation Jesus provides. F. F. Bruce describes the concept of

---

23. See the NEB for this translation. Kenneth Taylor paraphrases this verse: "And even though Jesus was God's Son, he had to learn from experience what it was like to obey, when obeying meant suffering" (LB).

obedience adequately when he writes, "The salvation which Jesus has procured, is granted 'unto all them that obey him!' There is something appropriate in the fact that the salvation which was procured by the obedience of the Redeemer should be made available to the obedience of the redeemed."[24]

e. How does the author of Hebrews conclude his discussion about the priesthood of Christ? He states that God designated Jesus to be high priest in the order of Melchizedek. That is significant, because this section about the high priesthood of Christ, beginning with Hebrews 4:14, is presented in terms of Aaron's priesthood. The section continues and concludes with a clear reference to the priesthood of Melchizedek.

Note the following observations.

Not the writer of Hebrews but God designates Christ as high priest in the order of Melchizedek (Ps. 110:4). The writer of Hebrews searches the Old Testament and shows that God addresses his Son as high priest.

The topic of the high priesthood of Christ is important to the author of Hebrews. He introduces the subject in Hebrews 2:17; after a discussion about Israel's disobedience in the desert and the meaning of rest the author returns to the subject in Hebrews 4:14–5:10; and the theme eventually is fully treated in Hebrews 7.

We also note that Jesus fulfilled the priestly duties of Aaron when he, in his submission and suffering, brought the task God had given him to completion. Thus Jesus became "the source of salvation for all who obey him." This could never be said of Aaron or any of the high priests who succeeded him.

The subject of Christ's high priesthood in the order of Melchizedek is deep. In fact, the writer of Hebrews calls it "hard to explain" (Heb. 5:11), although after a pastoral word to his readers he does explain it fully.

Doctrinal Considerations in 5:4–10

In chapter 1 the author introduces the Son as king when he quotes Psalm 110:1 in Hebrews 1:13. But the subject of Jesus' kingship does not need to be explored; the priesthood of Jesus needs attention because the author of Hebrews portrays Jesus as mediator. That role of mediator was given not to a king, but to the priest. In other words, the author explains the priestly office of Christ by quoting directly from the Old Testament.

Among the writers of the New Testament, only the author of Hebrews, an expert student of the Scriptures, teaches the doctrine of Christ's priesthood. Paul, for example, touches on the intercessory work of Jesus (Rom. 8:34) and the concept of mediator (I Tim. 2:5–6). Nowhere in his epistles does he discuss the teaching of Jesus' priesthood. That has been done by the writer of Hebrews.[25]

---

24. Bruce, *Hebrews,* p. 105.

25. Peter calls believers a "holy priesthood" (I Peter 2:5), and John refers to them as "a kingdom and priests" (Rev. 1:6). But neither John nor Peter speaks of the priesthood of Christ. See also John 17:19; Rom. 5:2; I Peter 3:18; and I John 2:1.

Did God appoint Jesus to serve as the Aaronic high priest or to function as a priest in the order of Melchizedek? The Scriptures teach that Christ was appointed in the order of Melchizedek and that he could not serve as priest in the order of Aaron because he belonged to the tribe of Judah and not to the tribe of Levi (Heb. 7:14–17). And yet through his sacrificial death Jesus fulfilled the responsibilities of the Levitical priesthood.

The duties of the Aaronic high priest were to become thoroughly familiar with man's spiritual weakness, to represent him before God, and to offer sacrifices and gifts to God on his behalf. The high priest on the Day of Atonement shed the blood of a sacrificial animal for himself and for the people. Jesus offered himself as "for all time one sacrifice for sins" (Heb. 10:12). Later he sat down as priest and king at the right hand of God.

In Hebrews 5:7–8 the author stresses two conditions that Jesus as high priest has to fulfill: he must bring an offering, and he must learn obedience. The author of Hebrews deliberately repeats the theme about the priesthood of Christ in Hebrews 2:11–18; 5:5–10; and 7:23–28.

Greek Words, Phrases, and Constructions in 5:4–10

Verse 4

καλούμενος—this present passive participle, from καλέω (to call), is followed by the agent *by God.* It constitutes a call to an office; its parallel is in Hebrews 5:10 ("was designated by God to be high priest").

καθώσπερ—the combination of καθώς (just as) and οὕτως (so; see Heb. 5:3) shows contrast and comparison. The two adverbs indicate a link between verses 4 and 5. Note the stress particle περ, which has been added to καθώς as an enclitic.

Verse 5

οὕτως—this adverb finds its antecedent in the preceding καθώσπερ.

γεγέννηκα—the perfect active indicative of γεννάω (to beget). See Hebrews 1:5.

Verse 7

τε καί—two nouns or concepts of similar import are often combined by the adjunct τε with καί. The nouns *prayers* and *petitions* therefore are synonyms.

ἱκετηρία—the substantivized adjective in the feminine used to be followed by either the noun ἐλαία (olive tree, olive branch) or the noun ῥάβδος (rod, staff, stick). Around this branch or rod wool was wound, and then it was used by a suppliant.

σῴζειν—the present active infinitive (to save) must be seen in relation to the noun σωτηρία (salvation; Heb. 5:9). Also, the present tense testifies to God's constant power to save his Son from death.

ἀπὸ τῆς εὐλαβείας—the preposition ἀπό is causal. The noun εὐλαβείας, preceded by the definite article, can mean either reverential fear toward God (see Heb. 12:28, where the word is translated "reverence") or piety. Still others prefer the translation *fear*; that is, horror.

Verse 8

υἱός—the definite article has been omitted deliberately to express the absolute relationship of Father and Son. That is, there is only one Son.

ἔμαθεν. . .ἔπαθεν—it is obvious that the author has a play on words in mind. The first verb is the aorist active from μανθάνω (I learn) and the second is the aorist active of πάσχω (I endure).

Verse 9

τελειωθείς—the author of Hebrews used the verb τελειόω (to complete, finish, perfect) at least three times of Jesus (2:10; 5:9; 7:28). Here the aorist passive participle is given, which refers to Jesus' sacrificial work in Gethsemane and on the cross.

ὑπακούουσιν—note the use of the present tense of the active participle. Not only does the verb have the meaning of obeying, but also in the broader context it conveys the idea of believing in Christ.

Verse 10

προσαγορευθείς—the verb in the aorist passive participle form occurs only once in the New Testament. However, it appears frequently in extracanonical literature and means "to call, name, designate."

Summary of Chapter 5

In the religious life of the Jew, no man received greater esteem than the high priest. Under his supervision were the priests who were commissioned to take charge of routine tasks. The high priest, man's representative before God, entered the Most Holy Place once a year on the Day of Atonement and sprinkled blood for the remission of sin. Aaron was the first high priest to enter into the presence of God behind the curtain in the ancient tabernacle.

However, Jesus is superior to Aaron because Jesus "has gone through the heavens." That is, he entered into the very presence of God, whereas the high priests were accustomed merely to entering the symbolical presence in the tabernacle or temple once a year. In his glorified human nature, Jesus has entered the presence of God. Fully acquainted with human weaknesses and temptations, he intercedes in our behalf when we approach the throne of God in prayer.

The author of Hebrews depicts Jesus in his role of high priest, fulfilling the responsibilities of the high priesthood of Aaron and assuming the priesthood in the order of Melchizedek.[26] As a priest in the order of Melchizedek,

---

26. F. W. Grosheide, *De Brief aan de Hebreeën en de Brief van Jakobus* (Kampen: Kok, 1955), p. 132. The question is raised whether Jesus could be both sacrifice and priest at the same time. In his dying he presents himself as a sacrifice to God. But note that Jesus did not commit suicide; rather his life was taken. Thus he became a sacrifice for sin.

Jesus offered himself as a sacrifice for sin. This fulfilled the requirements of the Old Testament sacrificial system.

God appointed Jesus as high priest not when Jesus entered heaven, but prior to his coming to earth. According to Psalm 110:4 ("You are a priest *forever,* in the order of Melchizedek"; italics added), Jesus' priesthood is eternal. He was already priest before he began his earthly life.

6

Exhortations

5:11–6:20

Outline

	A. Do Not Fall Away
5:11–14	1. Slow Learners
6:1–3	2. Elementary Teachings
6:4–6	3. No Repentance
6:7–12	4. Blessings of God
	B. Hold on to God's Promise
6:13–15	1. The Promise to Abraham
6:16–20	2. Heirs of the Promise

5 11 We have much to say about this, but it is hard to explain because you are slow
to learn. 12 In fact, though by this time you ought to be teachers, you need someone to teach you the elementary truths of God's word all over again. You need milk,
not solid food! 13 Anyone who lives on milk, being still an infant, is not acquainted
with the teaching about righteousness. 14 But solid food is for the mature, who by constant
use have trained themselves to distinguish good from evil.
6 1 Therefore let us leave the elementary teachings about Christ and go on to maturity, not laying again the foundation of repentance from acts that lead to death,
and of faith in God, 2 instruction about baptisms, the laying on of hands, the
resurrection of the dead, and eternal judgment. 3 And God permitting, we will
do so.
4 It is impossible for those who have once been enlightened, who have tasted the heavenly
gift, who have shared in the Holy Spirit, 5 who have tasted the goodness of the word of God
and the powers of the coming age, 6 if they fall away, to be brought back to repentance,
because to their loss they are crucifying the Son of God all over again and subjecting him to
public disgrace.
7 Land that drinks in the rain often falling on it and that produces a crop useful to those
for whom it is farmed receives the blessing of God. 8 But land that produces thorns and
thistles is worthless and is in danger of being cursed. In the end it will be burned.
9 Even though we speak like this, dear friends, we are confident of better things in your
case—things that accompany salvation. 10 God is not unjust; he will not forget your work
and the love you have shown him as you have helped his people and continue to help
them. 11 We want each of you to show this same diligence to the very end, in order to make
your hope sure. 12 We do not want you to become lazy, but to imitate those who through
faith and patience inherit what has been promised.

A. Do Not Fall Away
5:11–6:12

1. Slow Learners
5:11–14

A teacher knows that not every student is quick to learn, is perceptive, and is blessed with a retentive memory. Numerous times the teacher has to repeat his lessons and exercise patience with students who by nature are slow learners. The writer of Hebrews interrupts his explanation of Christ's priesthood in order to admonish his readers to be better students of the Word.

11. We have much to say about this, but it is hard to explain because you are slow to learn. 12a. In fact, though by this time you ought to be

teachers, you need someone to teach you the elementary truths of God's word all over again.

An experienced teacher senses when the students are no longer absorbing the lesson material. He knows that students do not always advance in their learning skills and that sometimes a word of rebuke or correction is very much in place. The words of the author of Hebrews are sharp and pointed. Something has gone drastically wrong in the learning process. By all standards the readers should have graduated, but they have failed their examinations because of a lack of interest, diligence, and adequate preparation.

The author had planned to continue his teaching on the high priesthood of Jesus in the order of Melchizedek.[1] However, the material is too advanced for his readers, his theology is too deep, and his students are too lazy. The subject matter, says the writer, is difficult to explain, not because of the writer's lack of skill, but because of the readers' inability to comprehend. The writer becomes rather personal and says, "You are slow to learn." The author, then, is forced to divert his attention from the topic of the priesthood.

How many years are needed in preparation for teaching the Christian faith? The author does not specify the number of years, but he points out that by the time of his writing the readers should have been teachers. The time allotted to learn the teachings of the faith has been ample; his readers are under obligation to pay dividends—they ought to be able to teach others the teachings of God's Word. But they are unable to do so.

The Christian church must grow in order to exist. Those who have heard the gospel and have accepted it in faith are required to share their knowledge with others who need instruction. When the writer of Hebrews says, "By this time you ought to be teachers," he is not speaking about professionally qualified educators. Rather, he addresses himself to the believer who has heard Bible stories and has been taught the doctrine of salvation, but nevertheless fails to put his ability to work in leading others to a knowledge of salvation in Christ. What a disappointment when a Christian who is given the opportunity to witness for Christ and teach the gospel declines because he feels inadequate! The author of Hebrews speaks to this situation.

You need someone to teach you the elementary truths of God's word all over again. What an admonition! What a rebuke! Writers of catechisms in the time of the Reformation incorporated three Christian documents into their teachings: the Apostles' Creed, the Ten Commandments, and the Lord's Prayer. These they considered the ABC's of the Christian faith. If a believer knew how to explain the basic doctrines of these three elements of Christian belief, he was expected to testify for Christ and teach others.

Although we do not know exactly what the writer of Hebrews means by "elementary truths of God's word," we do not go amiss if we say: the basic

1. The word *this* in verse 11 is rather general and may be interpreted as "this subject" (JB) or "this matter" (GNB).

teachings of the Bible.[2] Of course, he enumerates the elementary teachings of Christ in Hebrews 6:1–2. The author states that if his readers do not know even the elementary truths, someone has to teach them anew.

12b. You need milk, not solid food! 13. Anyone who lives on milk, being still an infant, is not acquainted with the teaching about righteousness. 14. But solid food is for the mature, who by constant use have trained themselves to distinguish good from evil.

The rebuke of the author is comparable to Paul's stern remarks to the believers in Corinth: "Brothers, I could not address you as spiritual but as worldly—mere infants in Christ. I gave you milk, not solid food, for you were not yet ready for it. Indeed, you are still not ready" (I Cor. 3:1–2). Milk is given to the very young, and when they are older they receive solid food. The babes in the faith cannot digest the solid food of God's Word; they need spiritual milk instead.[3]

If there is anything a child dislikes, it is to be called a baby. That is too degrading and goes against his innate desire: to grow up! He wants to become independent. He looks ahead and compares himself constantly with those children who are older and more mature.

The author of Hebrews calls the reader of his epistle "an infant." To him it is incredible that adults in the faith are still nurtured on spiritual milk, not solid food. He uses the word *infant* to put his readers to shame.[4] As a pastor, he is not afraid to rebuke them, to admonish them, and to direct them to a higher level of development. They must realize that growth demands solid food. They will never advance on a diet of milk.

Anyone who lives on milk . . . is not acquainted with the teaching about righteousness. The writer keeps on rebuking his readers. Drawing a logical inference from the illustration of babies who exist on milk alone, the author indicates that just as infants do not know the difference between right and wrong, so the recipients of his letter are unacquainted with "the teaching about righteousness." A mere infant is unaccustomed to making decisions about correct conduct because he needs to be taught on a daily basis (I Cor. 14:20; Eph. 4:14). Of course, we must understand that the writer is using a metaphor in order to make this point.

I do not think that the phrase *teaching about righteousness* within the context of figurative language was meant to convey theological truth.[5] Elsewhere in the New Testament (for example, I Cor. 1:30), the word *righteousness* is

2. See Acts 7:38; Rom. 3:2; I Peter 4:11; these verses relate to the Old Testament. The expression in Heb. 5:12 is broader in scope.

3. Hans Kropatschek, *NIDNTT,* vol. 2, p. 269.

4. The JB uses the word *baby,* and the KJV, NKJV, and *Moffatt* have "babe."

5. Philip Edgcumbe Hughes, Ceslaus Spicq, and B. F. Westcott interpret the phrase theologically. In an explanatory footnote, the JB points out, " 'The doctrine of righteousness' like 'God's oracles' can mean either the O.T., cf. 2 Tm. 3:16, or the whole body of doctrine. Here it seems to mean all that Christ taught about the righteousness of God as applied to mankind, Rm. 3:21–26, and especially about his own priesthood of mediation, prefigured by Melchizedek, the 'king of righteousness', 7:2."

understood implicitly or explicitly as God's righteousness—a concept that is commonly stressed in Paul's letters.[6] We, however, ought to look at the phrase in question not from a theological perspective but from a contextual point of view.[7]

The contrast between infants and adults is shown in verse 14: "But solid food is for the mature, who by constant use have trained themselves to distinguish good from evil." Adults need solid food, not a diet of milk, for nourishment. The writer calls adults mature people—those who are constantly making decisions concerning ethical conduct. Their mental and spiritual training is perpetually put to use when they distinguish between good and evil. These people from childhood to maturity have trained and continue to train their spiritual and moral senses. Adults are repeatedly confronted with moral decisions that need to be made. And because of their experience, adults are able to make wise choices in distinguishing between good and evil.

Adults gain experiential knowledge that is still absent in children. As children mature they, too, will acquire the moral sense of discriminating between good and evil; and for them, too, this skill of differentiating will become second nature.

The author uses the metaphor of milk for infants and solid food for adults to spur his readers to spiritual and intellectual activity. He wants to have them understand the biblical implications of Jesus' high priesthood.

Practical Considerations in 5:11–14

We should guard against being critical of the original recipients of the epistle, for we ourselves show the same characteristics. We who have heard the gospel proclaimed for numerous years—many of us since childhood—often do not demonstrate spiritual discernment. Although we have God's revelation in the Old and New Testaments, we remain slow learners.

Surveys conducted by local pastors or by Christian agencies invariably reveal that church members do not know the basic principles of Scripture or, if they do know, they are unable to apply these basic teachings.

The ABC's of the Christian faith are readily mastered by any sincere believer who, in turn, should be capable of imparting this elementary knowledge to people unacquainted with the gospel. On this elementary level the Christian church fails to communicate effectively and thus stymies growth and development.

Yet the corporate responsibility of the church is to formulate the teachings of the Christian faith. The doctrines of God, man, Christ, salvation, the church, and the end of the age belong to the entire church and not merely to a few gifted theolo-

---

6. Horst Seebass, in a study on the word *righteousness,* concludes: "Hebrews shows scarcely any Pauline influence." Refer to *NIDNTT,* vol. 3, p. 365.

7. The various interpretations of the phrase "not acquainted with the teaching about righteousness" range from "the righteousness of God revealed in Christ" to "[lacking] experience of moral truth." Consult, for further details, Hugh Montefiore, *The Epistle to the Hebrews* (New York and Evanston: Harper and Row, 1964), p. 103.

gians who have been instrumental in drafting the precise wording of these doctrines. The church as a body of believers is the responsible agent in formulating, adopting, teaching, and defending these doctrines of the faith. Therefore, the individual Christian is exhorted to progress beyond the level of "the elementary truths of God's word."

Greek Words, Phrases, and Constructions in 5:11–14

Verse 11

νωθροί—the adjective in the nominative masculine plural, translated "lazy" or "slow to learn," occurs twice in the epistle (5:11; 6:12). It also appears in the Septuagint (Prov. 22:29; Sir. 4:29; 11:12) and in I Clement 34:1, where it refers to a "lazy and careless workman."

γεγόνατε—the use of the perfect tense of γίνομαι (I become) indicates a state that the recipients had acquired in the course of time.

ταῖς ἀκοαῖς—the plural of ἀκοή (the act of hearing) refers specifically to the ears. The dative is a dative of respect.

Verse 12

καὶ γάρ—the combination of καί and γάρ is rather emphatic and is equivalent to "in fact" or "yes, indeed."

τὰ στοιχεῖα—the noun is used four times by Paul (Gal. 4:3, 9; Col. 2:8, 20), twice by Peter (II Peter 3:10, 12), and once in Hebrews. It is derived from στοῖχος (row, rank, line, course). In Hebrews the noun signifies basic lines or principles of elementary doctrines.

ἡ ἀρχὴ τῶν λογίων—the presence of the definite article before ἀρχή (beginning) points to that which is basic. In translation the noun ἀρχή serves adjectivally with λογίων, and is translated "elementary truths."

Verse 14

ἕξις—a noun derived from the verb ἔχω (I have [future, ἕξω]) and given the meaning of exercise, practice, or skill. The -σις ending of the noun indicates process or constant activity. In the New Testament this noun occurs only once; in other literature, half a dozen times.

τὰ αἰσθητήρια—a noun in the neuter plural (translated "senses") that is derived from αἰσθάνομαι (I perceive). The noun is rendered "themselves" (NIV); "faculties" (RSV); or "perceptions" (NEB).

γεγυμνασμένα—the perfect middle participle of γυμνάζω (I exercise, train). The perfect tense shows continuity from the past into the present, and the middle indicates an agent acting upon oneself.

διάκρισις—derived from the verb διακρίνω (I differentiate, discriminate), the noun with the -σις ending reveals a process or an activity in respect to distinguishing "good from evil."

2. Elementary Teachings
6:1–3

A cursory reading of this passage indicates that the author seems to have had second thoughts. In 5:12–14 he states that his readers cannot digest solid food and must live on milk. In 6:1–3 he tells them "to go on to maturity" and proceeds to prepare them to receive deeper spiritual truths. But upon closer examination we see at work an expert psychologist who rouses his audience by inducing shame. The effect of his remarks about their spiritual eating habits is expected to be positive. His readers want to reach maturity, and the author prudently places himself at their level and, in effect, says that he is one with them in striving for maturity.

1. Therefore let us leave the elementary teachings about Christ and go on to maturity, not laying again the foundation of repentance from acts that lead to death, and of faith in God, 2. instruction about baptisms, the laying on of hands, the resurrection of the dead, and eternal judgment.

Instead of teaching the elementary truths of God's Word once more (see 5:12), the author urges his readers to go beyond these truths. They are not ignorant of the basic teachings of Christian doctrine; they need to be stimulated to progress in their understanding of the faith. They ought to review the *elementary* teachings *about Christ,* so that they are ready to receive further instruction.[8]

The introductory word *therefore* is retrospective.[9] In the preceding verses, the writer contrasts the spiritually weak believer with the mature Christian. And the model he holds before his readers is that of the believer who strives for maturity. He exhorts them to go on to perfection after having left the elementary teachings behind. Actually the author is saying, "Let us . . . go forward to adult understanding" (*Phillips*), and together we are able to do this. The verb ("let us go on") that the author employs is a key word because it conveys the idea of actively exerting oneself to make progress. He includes himself and places himself on his readers' level even though he, as the teacher, really occupies a higher position than the recipients of his letter. This implies that the writer has not yet achieved maturity in spiritual matters. Therefore, the author does not explain the "elementary teachings about Christ" but merely outlines them.

A. Foundation of
   1. repentance
   2. faith in God

---

8. J. C. Adams, "Exegesis of Hebrews vi.1f.," *NTS* 13 (1967): 378–85.

9. John Brown, in *An Exposition of Hebrews* (Edinburgh: Banner of Truth Trust, 1961), p. 274, suggests that the word *therefore* is not retrospective but prospective. That is, according to Brown, the author regards the recipients who are spiritually immature (5:11–14) as the same people who are depicted in 6:4–6. However, the author uses the adverb *therefore* (διό) in the Greek nine times (3:7, 10; 6:1; 10:5; 11:12, 16; 12:12, 28; 13:12) and seems to give the adverb the meaning *consequently.*

B. Instruction about
   1. baptisms
   2. laying on of hands
   3. resurrection of the dead
   4. eternal judgment[10]

a. "Not laying again the foundation." Does the author refer to a standard of instruction in the church of the first century? Perhaps. F. F. Bruce points out that the items listed among the elementary teachings are as much Jewish as they are Christian.[11] We assume that these doctrines were given much more prominence in the Christian church than in the Jewish synagogue. These truths also may have been used as a catechism that new converts were required to learn before they were fully accepted.

Because the readers know that to be members in the church they must have a foundation of repentance and faith, the writer states that it is not necessary to lay that foundation anew. He is spelling out for his audience the difference between the basic doctrines (which he calls a foundation) and the deeper truths of Scripture (which believers ought to study in order to progress in their spiritual lives). He concludes that because of their membership believers already have laid the foundation.[12]

b. "The foundation of repentance from acts that lead to death." The first component of the Christian's spiritual foundation is repentance (Acts 2:38; 3:19). This means turning away from something that is detrimental to one's being. Basically repentance constitutes a negative action, in this case a change of mind that results in no longer performing "acts that lead to death." Repentance, then, is an activity that involves the mind and thinking of a person—a complete turnabout in the life of the believer. No longer does he show an interest in activities that lead to his destruction. He now shuns the effects of sin that bring about death (Rom. 5:12, 21; 6:23; 7:11). Consequently, it would not be necessary for the author to ask his readers to lay the foundation of repentance again.

c. "And of faith in God." Laying a foundation of faith in God was a positive action that believers had taken when they accepted Christ in faith. They turned from their "acts that lead to death" to life in Christ through faith. We would expect the author to write "faith in Christ" instead of "faith in

---

10. Another categorization is threefold: repentance and faith; baptisms and laying on of hands; and resurrection and judgment. However, I understand the word *instruction* as an accusative in the Greek; that is, in apposition to the term *foundation.* The manuscript evidence for the accusative form is weighty. Bruce M. Metzger's explanation in *A Textual Commentary on the Greek New Testament* (London and New York: United Bible Societies, 1975), p. 666—that copyists had changed the word *teaching* from a genitive to an accusative for stylistic reasons—does not seem very satisfactory.

11. F. F. Bruce, *The Epistle to the Hebrews,* New International Commentary on the New Testament series (Grand Rapids: Eerdmans, 1964), pp. 112–13.

12. Consult the article by Jürgen Blunck in *NIDNTT,* vol. 1, pp. 660–62.

God," for Jewish converts to Christianity did not need to be instructed in the doctrine of faith in Israel's God. The difficulty disappears, however, when we realize that throughout his epistle the author speaks of God as revealed in Christ (3:1–6; also see Acts 20:21; I Thess. 1:9–10). Indirectly, the author reminds the reader of Jesus' word, proclaimed at the beginning of this ministry: "The time has come. . . . The kingdom of God is near. Repent and believe the good news" (Mark 1:15). This twofold message from the lips of Jesus is repeated by the apostles. For example, Peter on the day of Pentecost called the people to repentance, and as a result three thousand believers were added to the church (Acts 2:38, 41).[13]

Of course, faith is a prominent theme in Hebrews. Chapter 11 with its brief definition of faith and list of the heroes of faith is eloquent testimony to the author's interest in this theme. For the writer, faith constitutes complete trust as demonstrated by Joshua, who because of his faith entered the land God had promised (4:8). Everyone who puts faith in the gospel, says the author of Hebrews, enters God's rest (4:2–3).[14]

d. "Instruction about baptisms." Next to the foundation of repentance and faith comes the instruction about baptisms, laying on of hands, resurrection of the dead, and eternal judgment. The first phase in the believer's instruction is the teaching concerning baptisms. Interestingly enough, the writer uses not the common Greek word *baptisma* (baptism), but rather the term *baptismos* (washing; Mark 7:4; Heb. 9:10).[15] Furthermore, the word is in the plural.

What is the writer saying? Use of the plural provides sufficient reason to assume that he calls attention to washings other than Christian baptism. What these washings are has been debated at length by numerous scholars. I mention only a few interpretations:

1. purification ceremonies (Qumran)
2. triple immersion in the name of the Trinity
3. multiplicity of baptismal candidates
4. baptisms of water, blood, fire, and the Holy Spirit
5. Levitical washings and Christian baptism[16]

The New Testament does refer to the baptism of John the Baptist (Matt. 3:7; Mark 11:30; Luke 7:29; John 3:23; 4:1; Acts 1:22; 10:37; 18:25) that was still practiced more than twenty-five years after his death (Acts 19:3). Also there is the Jewish rite of baptism for proselytes.

---

13. John Calvin, *Epistle to the Hebrews* (Grand Rapids: Eerdmans, 1949), p. 132.

14. Donald Guthrie, *New Testament Theology* (Downers Grove, Ill.: Inter-Varsity, 1981), p. 597.

15. In the Greek text also see the variant reading in Col. 2:12 and the TR reading of Mark 7:8.

16. Philip Edgcumbe Hughes provides an interesting and almost complete list of possible interpretations. See his *Commentary on the Epistle to the Hebrews* (Grand Rapids: Eerdmans, 1977), pp. 199–202.

The word *baptismos* (which signifies "the act alone," whereas *baptisma* is "the act with the result") is a Jewish-Christian term.[17] The expression in the plural probably expresses a "contrast between Christian baptism and all other religious washings . . . known to the readers."[18]

Finally, the four Gospels and Acts mention the baptism with the Holy Spirit (Matt. 3:11 and parallels; Acts 1:5; 11:16). Although this particular form of baptism is different from the washing that the word *baptismos* describes, it has significance for the next phase of instruction, the imposition of hands.

e. "The laying on of hands." In Acts the imposition of hands results in the outpouring of the Holy Spirit. For example, Peter and John visited the believers in Samaria and placed their hands on the Samaritans, who as a consequence received the Holy Spirit (Acts 8:17). Ananias put his hands on Saul (Paul), who received both his sight and the Holy Spirit (Acts 9:17). In Ephesus, Paul laid his hands on some disciples of John the Baptist who were recipients of the Holy Spirit (Acts 19:6).

Other passages show that the practice of laying hands on someone relates to the ceremony of ordination to service: ministering to the needs of the poor (Acts 6:6); proclaiming the gospel (Acts 13:3); or pastoring the church (I Tim. 4:14; II Tim. 1:6).

Apart from the instances that mention the imposition of hands in connection with healing (Matt. 9:18; Mark 5:23; 6:5; 7:32; 8:23; Luke 13:13; Acts 28:8) and with Jesus blessing the children (Matt. 19:13, 15; Mark 10:16), the New Testament is silent.

What did the practice of laying hands on a believer mean to the first recipients of the Epistle to the Hebrews? John Calvin declares that baptized children, after a period of instruction in the faith, received another rite—that of laying on of hands. This rite was intended as confirmation of their baptism and originated in the time of apostles.[19] This may very well be the explanation of the practice, although substantiating evidence is scarce.

f. "The resurrection of the dead." The next phase in the believer's instruction is his knowledge concerning the resurrection of the dead. Already in Old Testament times the doctrine of the resurrection was known (Ps. 16:10; Isa. 26:19; Ezek. 37:10; Dan. 12:2). In the days of Jesus and the apostles, the general public knew the teaching about the resurrection from the dead (John 11:24), and the Pharisees separated themselves from the Sadducees because the two groups disagreed about this doctrine (Acts 23:6–7).

Jesus taught the doctrine of resurrection by claiming it for himself: "I am the resurrection and the life" (John 11:25); the apostles made this teaching the foundation of their gospel proclamation (Acts 1:22; 2:32; 4:10; 5:30;

---

17. Albrecht Oepke, *TNDT,* vol. 1, p. 545.
18. G. R. Beasley-Murray, *NIDNTT,* vol. 1, p. 149.
19. Calvin, *Hebrews,* p. 134.

10:40; 13:37; 17:31–32; 26:23). The author of Hebrews also refers to this doctrine directly (11:35) and indirectly (2:14–15).

g. "And eternal judgment." The two doctrines of the resurrection and of eternal judgment are logically related, but I do not think that we should explain the first as the resurrection of the righteous and the second as the judgment on the wicked. The author does not provide sufficient information, and therefore we do well to understand the words as general references to these teachings.

Hebrews 6:2 is the only text in the New Testament that gives the reading *eternal judgment.* The passage that is somewhat similar is Acts 24:25, which says, "Paul discoursed on righteousness, self-control and the judgment to come." That Jesus returns "to judge the living and the dead" is a basic teaching eventually formulated in the three ecumenical creeds: the Apostles', the Nicene, and the Athanasian.

3. And God permitting, we will do so.

The text because of its brevity fails to communicate clearly what the author intends to say. Thus it has been explained in various ways.

a. The writer plans to visit the readers after the release of Timothy (13:23); then, arriving with Timothy, he will instruct them in the elementary truths about Christ. The objection to this interpretation is indirectly supplied by the author himself, who wants his readers to advance to maturity. Why would he teach them elementary articles of faith after teaching them doctrines that are "hard to explain" (5:11)?

b. The pronoun *we* is used editorially—the author refers to himself as he does in 5:11. However, the main verb in the preceding verses is in the first person plural ("let us . . . go on to maturity"; 6:1), and the writer counts himself an equal of the recipients of his epistle. Using the editorial *we* in 6:3, therefore, would break the flow of thought.

c. The main verb *let us . . . go on* receives the emphasis in 6:1. The author, after stating the exhortation, simply and positively indicates that he and his readers will fulfill the exhortation. He adds the clause *and God permitting.* That is, although the writer of Hebrews takes his task of teaching and pastoring seriously, God has to open the hearts of the people who receive instruction in the truths of God's Word. In fact, this clause may be understood as an introduction to 6:4–6, where the author teaches that for some people repentance has become an impossibility.

Greek Words, Phrases, and Constructions in 6:1–3

Verse 1

ἀφέντες—the second aorist active participle in the nominative plural from the verb ἀφίημι (I give up). Because of its close relationship to the main verb φερώμεθα, the participle may be understood to connote exhortation (let us leave).

τελειότης—this noun occurs twice in the New Testament—Hebrews 6:1 and Colossians 3:14—and means "perfection, maturity." It is derived from the verb τελειόω (I bring to an end) that appears nine times in Hebrews, more than in any other New Testament book. The noun τελειότης in context is the opposite of νήπιος (5:13).

φερώμεθα—the present middle subjunctive, first person plural of the verb φέρω (I carry). The subjunctive is hortatory; the present tense indicates that the author and readers of Hebrews are indeed going to do this; and the middle shows a reflexive action. Interpreting the verb in the passive voice (let us be carried [by God]) seems to diminish emphasis on human responsibility.

Verse 2

ἐπίθεσις—a noun derived from ἐπιτίθημι (I put or lay upon). The -σις ending points to the activity or the ceremony of the imposition of hands.

ἀνάστασις—this noun has its roots in the verb ἀνίστημι (I rise up). Especially in Acts and in the Epistles, the noun is followed by the noun νεκρῶν, with variations.

Verse 3

ποιήσομεν—this verb from ποιέω (I do) is in the first person plural, future active indicative. The textual variant is ποιήσωμεν—the first person plural, first aorist active subjunctive. Manuscript evidence favors the reading of the future indicative. And this reading is more appropriate in the context than the exhortation *let us do so.*[20]

ἐπιτρέπη—the form is the third person singular, present active subjunctive of ἐπιτρέπω (I allow, permit). Although the context and even the verb tense differ, a similar construction occurs in I Corinthians 16:7.

---

3. No Repentance
6:4–6

In chapters 3 and 4 the author of Hebrews discussed the sin of unbelief that resulted in apostasy. Now in one lengthy sentence (6:4–6) he develops that teaching in greater detail. The emphasis in this sentence falls on the main verb *to be brought back to repentance* (v. 6), which is introduced negatively by the phrase *it is impossible.*

4. It is impossible for those who have once been enlightened, who have tasted the heavenly gift, who have shared in the Holy Spirit, 5. who have tasted the goodness of the word of God and the powers of the coming age, 6. if they fall away, to be brought back to repentance, because to their loss they are crucifying the Son of God all over again and subjecting him to public disgrace.

Throughout the epistle the writer has admonished his readers to accept the Word of God in faith and not to fall into the sin of unbelief that results

---

20. Metzger, *Textual Commentary,* p. 666. However, Zane C. Hodges and Arthur L. Farstad have chosen the aorist subjunctive reading. See *The Greek New Testament According to the Majority Text* (Nashville and New York: Thomas Nelson, 1982), p. 656.

in eternal judgment (2:1–3; 3:12–14; 4:1, 6, 11; 10:25, 27, 31; 12:16–17, 25, 29). In 6:4–6 he does not address the recipients of his letter, but instead he states a truth that emerges from an earlier reference to the Israelites' perishing in the desert because of their unbelief. This truth also applies to the Hebrews, even though the author omits the personal reference in 6:4–6.

Before we discuss the details of the passage, we need to look at the major points that divide the text. We ask three questions.

a. Who are the people mentioned in 6:4–6? They are those characterized by four participles that in the original Greek display poetic rhythm: enlightened, tasted, shared, tasted. There is no particular connection among these participles, although some commentators like to see a sequence of baptism, Lord's Supper, ordination, and perhaps even proclamation in this verse.

Those who have once been enlightened. From the second century to the present, writers have associated the verb *enlightened* with baptism.[21] Added weight is given to this interpretation by the restrictive word *once.* And in the broader context of the passage, the term *baptisms* does appear in 6:2. We can point out many similarities between baptism and enlightenment. For example, the early Christian practice of scheduling baptisms at daybreak utilizes the symbolism of the receding night of sin and the rising sun that illumines the baptismal candidate, who enters a new life.

But the verb *enlightened* also has other meanings. The author uses the word again in 10:32, where the expression seems to be synonymous with "knowledge of the truth" (Heb. 10:26). Besides the two occurrences in Hebrews, the verb appears nine times in the New Testament and has a broader meaning than a reference to baptism (Luke 11:36; John 1:9; I Cor. 4:5; Eph. 1:18; 3:9; II Tim. 1:10; Rev. 18:1; 21:23; 22:5).

Who have tasted the heavenly gift. Suppose that someone has attended the worship services of the church, has made profession of faith, has been baptized, and has taken part in the active life of the church; he has tasted the broken bread and taken the cup offered to him at the celebration of the Lord's Supper. Then this new convert has indeed tasted the heavenly gift.

To limit the interpretation of this phrase ("tasted the heavenly gift") however, is decidedly narrow.[22] The New Testament itself provides a broader explanation. Jesus identifies himself as the "gift of God" when he talks to the Samaritan woman at the well (John 4:10). Peter designates the Holy Spirit the gift of God (Acts 2:38; 8:20; 10:45; 11:17). And in his epistles, Paul mentions "the gift of grace" and "the gift of righteousness." He associates these gifts with Jesus Christ (Rom. 5:15, 17; II Cor. 9:15; Eph. 3:7; 4:7).

---

21. The first to identify enlightenment with baptism was Justin Martyr, *First Apology* 61.12–13; 65.1. In place of the verb *enlightened,* the Syriac Peshitta has "who have once descended to the baptismal pool."

22. B. F. Westcott, *Commentary on the Epistle to the Hebrews* (Grand Rapids: Eerdmans, 1950), p. 148, states: "Any special interpretation, such as the Eucharist or more generally forgiveness, peace and the like, falls short of the general idea which is required here."

Who have shared in the Holy Spirit. The original Greek indicates the close connection between the preceding clause and this one. In the general context of 6:4, we may see a link between the phrase *the laying on of hands* (Heb. 6:2) and the sharing in the Holy Spirit, especially if we understand the heavenly gift to be the Holy Spirit.[23]

Sharing in the Holy Spirit implies that this is done in fellowship with other believers. And the Spirit of God manifests himself in various spiritual gifts given to the members of the church (I Cor. 12:7–11).

Who have tasted the goodness of the word of God. The writer of Hebrews does not specify the extent of the Word, only that the Word is good. When God speaks, man receives a good gift. Once more the writer of Hebrews uses the verb *to taste* to indicate the enjoyment of receiving this gift. This enjoyment consists in hearing the Scriptures proclaimed and in obtaining spiritual nourishment from that Word.

And the powers of the coming age. The continuation of tasting the Word of God is experiencing the powers of the age to come. First, note that the author uses the plural form *powers.* That is, they are part of the "signs, wonders and various miracles" that he has mentioned earlier (2:4). These powers belong to the coming age, but already in this age they are evident. The writer does not say what these powers are, although we note that they are directed toward the advancement of the church throughout the world.

The phrase *the coming age* (with slight variations) occurs only six times in the New Testament: three times in the Gospels (Matt. 12:32; Mark 10:30; Luke 18:30) and three times in the Epistles (Eph. 1:21; 2:7; Heb. 6:5). Because the New Testament writers use this phrase rather infrequently, we ought to exercise prudence in interpreting it. In principle we are able to experience in the present age the powers that belong to the future age.[24] When the coming age dawns, we shall fully realize the supernatural powers we now are allowed to observe.

The author of Hebrews has described a number of experiences some persons have had. In a sense he is deliberatively vague, for he merely lists phenomena but does not clarify who experiences them. He continues, however, and relates what happens to these people.

b. What happens to the people mentioned in 6:4–6? The author adds a participle that many translators preface with the conditional particle *if.*[25]

If they fall away. I am not sure that the author intends to say that the Hebrews will never be apostate. In the preceding chapters he spoke of apostasy and illustrated this by quoting from Psalm 95. The Israelites who in the desert fell away had put blood on the doorpost in Egypt and eaten the

---

23. Bruce, *Hebrews,* p. 121.

24. Hermann Sasse, *TDNT,* vol. 1, p. 206. Also consult George E. Ladd, *A Theology of the New Testament* (Grand Rapids: Eerdmans, 1974), p. 576.

25. The KJV, NKJV, RSV, and NIV have the conditional "if"; the RV, ASV, NASB, *Moffatt,* GNB, and NAB have "and then . . ."; JB has "and yet in spite of this"; and the NEB reads "and after all this."

Passover lamb; they had left Egypt, consecrated their first-born males to the Lord, and crossed the Red Sea; they could see the pillar of cloud by day and the pillar of fire by night; they had tasted the waters of Marah and Elim and daily ate the manna God provided; they had heard the voice of God from Mount Sinai when God gave them the Ten Commandments (see Exod. 12–20). Yet these same Israelites hardened their hearts in unbelief, and because of their disobedience they fell away from the living God (Heb. 3:12, 18; 4:6, 11). The author of the Epistle to the Hebrews teaches that apostasy that rises from unbelief results in a hardening of the heart and an inability to repent (3:13; 4:2; 6:6; 10:26; 12:15).

On the other hand, the writer speaks encouraging words to the recipients of his epistle. In the extended context he writes: "Even though we speak like this, dear friends, we are confident of better things in your case—things that accompany salvation" (6:9).

What does the passage (6:4–6) mean for the original readers of Hebrews? Does the author merely sound a warning or does he think that the Israelites' example would be imitated by the people he addresses in his letter? The constant, repetitive, and heartfelt warnings of the author prove conclusively that apostasy can occur (3:12–13; 4:1, 11; 12:15). Repeatedly he places before the readers the responsibility of guarding the spiritual well-being of each other, "so that no one will fall by following their [the Israelites'] example of disobedience" (4:11).

A distinction must be made at this point. The author speaks about falling away, not about falling into sin. For example, Judas fell away from Jesus and never returned to him; Peter fell into sin but soon afterward saw the resurrected Jesus. The two concepts (apostasy and backsliding) may never be confused. In 6:6, the author refers to apostasy; he has in mind the person who deliberately and completely abandons the Christian faith.[26]

Apostasy does not take place suddenly and unexpectedly. Rather it is part of a gradual process, a decline that leads from unbelief to disobedience to apostasy. And when the falling away from the faith happens, it leads to hardening of the heart and the impossibility of repentance.[27] The author, using the example of the Israelites, has shown the process that results in apostasy (3:18; 4:6, 11).

If the Israelites in the days of Moses deliberately disobeyed the law of God and "received its just punishment" (2:2; and see 10:28), "how much more severely do you think a man deserves to be punished who has trampled the Son of God under foot" (10:29)?

Where do the recipients of the epistle fit into this process? The author chides them for being slow to learn (5:11), lazy (6:12), and feeble (12:12).

26. Falling away "must consist in a *total renunciation* [italics his] of all the constituent principles and doctrines of Christianity," writes John Owen in *An Exposition of Hebrews,* 7 vols. in 4 (Evansville, Ind.: Sovereign Grace, 1960), vol. 5, p. 86.

27. F. W. Grosheide, *De Brief aan de Hebreeën en de Brief van Jakobus* (Kampen: Kok, 1955), p. 44.

Constantly he exhorts them to strengthen their faith (4:2; 10:22–23; 12:2). If their faith continues to weaken, they will fall prey to unbelief that leads to disobedience and apostasy.

It is impossible . . . to be brought back to repentance. We notice at least two items in this passage that are purposely vague. First, in the preceding verses (5:11–6:3) and the following verses (6:9–12), the writer uses the first and second person plural pronouns *we* and *you,* but in verses 6:4–6 the third person plural pronouns *those* and *they* occur. Second, the subject of the verb *to be brought back* is missing. The writer does not reveal the identity of the implied agent. Is he saying that God does not permit (6:3) a second repentance? Or does he mean that a person who has fallen away from the living God cannot be restored to repentance because of the sinner's hardened heart? Although the writer does not provide the answer, we assume that both questions could receive an affirmative response.

The use of the pronoun *we* in the broader context of 6:4–6 demonstrates that God never fails the believer who in faith trusts in him. God makes "the unchanging nature of his purpose very clear to the heirs of what was promised" (6:17), and he does so by swearing an oath. And the heirs of the promise are the author and readers of the Epistle to the Hebrews.

Is the Christian church unable to bring a hardened sinner back to the grace of God?[28] Again the writer does not provide an answer in the context of the passage. In another connection, however, he repeats the general sentiment of 6:4–6 and writes: "If we deliberately keep on sinning after we have received the knowledge of the truth, no sacrifice for sins is left" (10:26). The author does not say anything about restoring a hardened sinner; what he refers to is the impossibility of removing sin because the person sins deliberately. The word *deliberately* received all the emphasis in the original Greek because it stands first in the sentence. If a person who is familiar with "the elementary teaching about Christ" sins deliberately, restoration by way of repentance is an impossibility.

c. Why is this so? The writer of the epistle gives two reasons: "to their loss they are crucifying the Son of God all over again" and they are "subjecting him to public disgrace."

Of course the author obviously is using a metaphor; those who have fallen away do not literally crucify the Son of God and put him to open shame. Note that the writer uses not the personal name *Jesus* or the official name *Christ,* but rather the appellation *Son of God* to express on the one hand the divine exaltation of the Son and on the other hand the utter depravity of the sinner who has turned away from, as well as against, the Son of God.

The one who has fallen away declares that Jesus ought to be eliminated. As the Jews wanted Jesus removed from this earth and thus lifted him up

28. Verlyn D. Verbrugge, in "Towards a New Interpretation of Hebrews 6:4–6," *CTJ* 15 (1980): 70, interprets the passage to refer to the congregation the author addresses. Thus he inserts the word *us* in verse 6: "It is impossible for us to restore to repentance those who have fallen away."

from the ground on a cross, so the apostate denies Jesus a place, banishes him from this earth, and metaphorically crucifies the Son of God again. Thus he treats Jesus with continuous contempt and derision and knowingly commits the sin for which, says the author of the epistle, there is no repentance (6:6) and no sacrifice (10:26). The sinner can expect God's judgment that will come to him as a "raging fire that will consume the enemies of God" (10:27).

Doctrinal Considerations in 6:4–6

The connection between verses 3 and 4 should not be overlooked. The words *God permitting* must be seen in relation to the phrase *it is impossible.* Of course, Jesus said in regard to salvation that "with God all things are possible" (Matt. 19:26; Mark 10:27; Luke 18:27). The context here, however, differs. God changes the heart of sinful man to make him receptive to the gospel. But God does not permit willful sin to go unpunished. Thus it is impossible to bring such a person to repentance.

The Old Testament, at various places, speaks about the consequences of sinning willfully against God. For example, in Numbers 15:30–31, God says, "Anyone who sins defiantly, whether native-born or alien, blasphemes the LORD, and that person must be cut off from his people. Because he has despised the LORD's word and broken his commands, that person must surely be cut off; his guilt remains on him."

Acquainted with the teachings of the Old Testament on this subject, the writer of Hebrews compares the man who sinned by rejecting the law of Moses with someone "who has trampled the Son of God under foot" and "has insulted the Spirit of grace" (10:29). He poses a rhetorical question: Will not the person who has offended the Son of God and the Holy Spirit receive more severe punishment than the one who rejected the law of Moses?[29] The answer is: Of course.

God does not permit anyone to despise willfully his Son, his Word, and his Spirit. Deliberately sinning against God in full awareness and knowledge of God's divine revelation constitutes sin against the Holy Spirit (Matt. 12:32; Mark 3:29; Luke 12:10).[30] This sin God does not forgive.

Theological questions about the genuineness of repentance and faith of people who fall away from Christ remain unanswered. The writer refuses to judge people; instead he warns them not to fall into the same error that the Israelites in the desert committed. He encourages his readers to grow spiritually and continue to obey God's Word.

We face a mystery when we see God leading the chosen nation of Israel out of Egypt and then destroying the people who were twenty years old and more in the desert (Num. 14:29); when we see Jesus spending a night in prayer before he appointed Judas as one of his disciples (Luke 6:12, 16) and later declaring that Judas was "doomed to destruction" (John 17:12); and when we see Paul accepting

---

29. Ladd, *Theology of the New Testament,* p. 586.
30. "No apostasy could be more final than this," writes Guthrie, *New Testament Theology,* p. 596.

Demas as a fellow evangelist who years later deserted Paul because Demas "loved this world" (II Tim. 4:10).

The writer of Hebrews observes that disobedient Israelites died in the desert because of unbelief. By analogy, the possibility that individuals who have professed the name of Christ will fall away is real (Matt. 7:21–23). Is it possible for true believers to turn away from Christ? Constantly the author exhorts the recipients of his epistle to remain faithful, for God is faithful. God does not break his good promises to his people. "God is not unjust" (6:10). Therefore, says the writer, "imitate those who through faith and patience inherit what has been promised" (6:12).

Greek Words, Phrases, and Constructions in 6:4–6

Verse 4

ἀδύνατον—this adjective in the neuter singular appears four times in Hebrews (6:4, 18; 10:4; 11:6). As the first word in a lengthy sentence, it receives great emphasis. Note that ἀδύνατον is far removed from its complement ἀνακαινίζειν in 6:6.

ἅπαξ—the word occurs fourteen times in the New Testament, eight of which are in Hebrews. Its placement in 6:4 is significant: between the definite article (those) and the participle (have been enlightened). The word is contrasted with πάλιν (6:6).

φωτισθέντας—it is noteworthy that the first five participles, excluding μέλλοντος (6:5) in 6:4–6 are in the aorist tense and that the last two participles (6:6) are in the present tense. φωτισθέντας is used twice in Hebrews (6:4; 10:32).

γευσαμένους—closely connected to the preceding participial phrase with the adjunct τε is the clause "who have tasted the heavenly gift." The aorist middle participle from the verb γεύομαι (I taste) governs the noun *gift* in the genitive case. In 6:5 the same participle takes the accusative case of the noun *word*. To maintain that the use of the genitive is partitive and that of the accusative holistic in these two instances is not without difficulty. For example, the accusative case is also used in John 2:9 for "the water that had been turned into wine." A holistic interpretation in that verse is impossible.[31] Therefore, I suggest that the variation in Hebrews 6:4, 5 is stylistic.

γενηθέντας—the aorist passive participle is deponent and is therefore translated in the active voice.

Verse 5

ῥῆμα—the word is described as καλόν (good). Generally the translation *goodness of the word* is given to indicate that "the gospel and its promises [are] full of consolation."[32] See the Septuagint reading of Joshua 21:45; 23:15; Zechariah 1:13.

Verse 6

παραπεσόντας—this compound in the aorist active participial form occurs once in the New Testament; it appears in the Septuagint reading of Ezekiel 14:13; 15:8. It is synonymous with the verb ἀποστῆναι (to fall away) in Hebrews 3:12.

---

31. Grosheide, *Hebreeën*, pp. 144–45.

32. Joseph H. Thayer, *A Greek-English Lexicon of the New Testament* (New York, Cincinnati, and Chicago: American Book Company, 1889), p. 332.

ἀνακαινίζειν—not the aorist tense but the present tense is used in this active infinitive to express the progressive idea of the verb. It is introduced by the adjective ἀδύνατον (6:4) and signifies the impossibility of renewing the fallen sinner. The verb occurs in early Christian literature "in connection with regeneration and baptism."[33]

ἀνασταυροῦντας—this active participle, as well as the one that follows, is in the present tense. The tense of the participles reflects the reason why repentance is impossible. Consequently the translation of the participles expresses cause. The prefix ἀνά signifies "again."

παραδειγματίζοντας—the word is a compound from the preposition παρά (beside) and δείκνυμι (I show). It can have a favorable connotation in the sense of "to set forth as an example" and a negative connotation of "to subject to public disgrace." Like the preceding participle, the word appears only once in the New Testament (with the exception of the variant reading in Matthew 1:19).

---

4. Blessings of God
6:7–12

7. Land that drinks in the rain often falling on it and that produces a crop useful to those for whom it is farmed receives the blessing of God. 8. But land that produces thorns and thistles is worthless and is in danger of being cursed. In the end it will be burned.

In the agrarian society of the first century, people lived much closer to the land than many of us in our day. When the writer of Hebrews depicts the rainfall, the crops, the thorns, and the thistles, his readers readily understand the significance of the author's illustration. We are more analytical and like to see the comparison presented schematically.

Land
that drinks in the rain
often falling on it
and

that *produces a crop useful* to those for whom it is farmed *receives the blessing* of God.	that *produces thorns and thistles* is *worthless* and in danger of *being cursed.* In the end it will be burned.

Note the following observations.

a. The rain keeps falling on the land as a continual blessing from God; the land drinks in the rain.

b. One part of the land is being cultivated, and as a result of this diligent labor it keeps on producing the fruit of the field to nourish the people; in full view of everyone God is blessing the land, the laborers, and the persons receiving the crops.

---

33. Johannes Behm, *TDNT,* vol. 3, p. 451.

c. Although the rain keeps falling on the other part of the land, too, no one tills the field, sows seed, and plants seedlings. The owner of the field does not seem to show interest in his land, and therefore thorns and thistles have taken the place of fruit-bearing crops. The useless land eventually will be cleared of these thorns and thistles by burning them.

d. The contrast between productive land and worthless land is expressed in a few places in the Old Testament (Gen. 1:11–12; 3:17–18; Isa. 5:1, 6).

e. Verses 7–8 serve to illustrate the teaching of verses 4–6. When we look at the illustration, we can see the broad lines of the picture; however, the details are somewhat obscure and cannot be distinguished. The lines are these: God's blessings, in the form of rain, keep falling on the land. The structure of the land, together with the diligent labor of the workers, brings forth a crop; but in the absence of laborers working the field, the rain nourishes only thorns and thistles that grow in abundance. By analogy, believers and those who have fallen into unbelief receive continual blessings. If the heart of man is evil, all the blessings of God do not make him prosper spiritually. Instead, God's blessings, when they are rejected by an unbelieving heart, eventually are turned into a curse. And the unbeliever stands condemned.

f. The purpose of the author's illustration is to warn the recipients of his letter that merely observing, tasting, and experiencing the blessings of God cannot save a person unless genuine spiritual rebirth has taken place. When rebirth is evident and God's blessings are received with thanksgiving, spiritual life develops and brings forth fruit. The words of Jesus ("by their fruit you will recognize them" [Matt. 7:20]) tell the story. Not the rain alone, but the rain and the labor expended in tilling the land, determine the crop that the land produces.

9. Even though we speak like this, dear friends, we are confident of better things in your case—things that accompany salvation. 10. God is not unjust; he will not forget your work and the love you have shown him as you have helped his people and continue to help them.

The pastor-teacher speaks words of tender love to his people. He addresses them as dear friends and by this term conveys his pastoral love to them. The writer wants to relate that in his opinion the readers are heirs of the promise of salvation. The recipients of his epistle ought not think that they are the apostates described in the preceding passage. All that the author wants to do in these verses is to warn them to avoid unbelief. Now he encourages his readers by assuring them that they are to receive better things that pertain to their salvation.

Speaking in the plural (the first person *we*), the author says "we are confident." Presumably he employs the word *we* editorially, as he has done at other places (for example, 5:11).[34] He instills assurance in the hearts and

---

34. R. C. H. Lenski, in *The Interpretation of the Epistle to the Hebrews and of the Epistle of James* (Columbus: Wartburg, 1946), pp. 189–90, thinks that the pronoun *we* refers to persons who were with the author when he wrote his epistle.

minds of the readers, and as a faithful pastor he ministers to the needs of his people. He does not drive them to despair. He looks at the positive marks the readers display in their labor of love. Therefore, he writes that he is absolutely positive about their glorious future, for they will receive "things that accompany salvation." What these better things are the author does not say. The context seems to indicate that he contrasts the miserable destiny of the apostate and the glorious inheritance of the believer. Believers are sure of better things to come—things closely associated with salvation.

Someone could raise the question of fairness concerning man's destiny. God is just, counters the writer. He knows exactly what he is doing because he has your spiritual well-being in mind always. He remembers your labor performed in his service as you, out of loving concern, helped others in need.

Scripture teaches that God will forgive wickedness and will no longer remember the sins (Jer. 31:34) of those people who know the Lord and who have his law written on their hearts. Sin God forgets, but deeds of kindness done in the interest of his people he remembers. These deeds may be forgotten by those who perform them, whether these consist of feeding the hungry, welcoming strangers, clothing the poor, or visiting the sick and the prisoner. Jesus' word is to the point: "I tell you the truth, whatever you did for one of the least of these brothers of mine, you did for me" (Matt. 25:40). The labors of love ultimately are performed for Jesus, and deeds of kindness God does not forget.

One of the characteristics of the writer is that he introduces a subject at one point and returns to it later at another place where he provides additional information. In 6:10 he merely states that his readers have done works of love. In 10:32–34 he reminds them of having endured suffering when they helped those who were persecuted, of sympathizing with those in prison, and of rejoicing when their property was confiscated.

The readers demonstrated their love for their neighbors when troubles and hardship were evident, and they continued to show unselfish love. This love is the fruit of a regenerated heart that is always ready to serve God's people. Their lives exemplify the field that brings forth a crop useful for God's people, in marked contrast to the author's picture of a field overgrown with thorns and thistles.

God is just. He does not forget to bless that which is good and to punish that which is evil. On those who have fallen away and have hardened their hearts, he brings judgment; on those who reflect God's virtues, he showers his blessings. And what are these blessings? In this earthly life the believer receives strength to withstand temptation and trials so that his faith continues to grow and develop; in the life of the coming age these blessings consist of being with Jesus eternally and fully appropriating the reality of salvation.

11. We want each of you to show this same diligence to the very end, in order to make your hope sure. 12. We do not want you to become

lazy, but to imitate those who through faith and patience inherit what has been promised.

As a true pastor the writer is concerned about the spiritual life of the individual church member. Throughout his epistle he has taken an interest in the individual (3:12; 4:1, 11) and has stressed the corporate responsibility of the church. He is not satisfied that many believers are developing spiritually; he wants everyone to make progress. Thus he proves to be an imitator of Jesus, who does not wish to see any of his people wander. In short, he is the shepherd tending the spiritual flock.

Once again the author employs the plural pronoun *we* editorially. What he desires ("we want") is that everyone individually show the same diligence in ministering in love to the needs of God's people. He fears that some members of the church are deficient in the virtue of hope. This deficiency will be detrimental to the spiritual development of the believer.

In Hebrews 6:10–12 the writer features three well-known virtues: love, hope, and faith. Mentioned frequently in the New Testament, these three virtues are integrally related to one another.[35] To use an illustration, the Christian's spiritual growth is supported by the tripod of faith, hope, and love. When one of the legs of this tripod bends, the other two legs will fall, and spiritual development ceases.

The apostles constantly urge the believers to grow spiritually. For example, Peter, in his second epistle, encourages his readers to "grow in the grace and knowledge of our Lord and Savior Jesus Christ" (3:18) and to "be all the more eager to make your calling and election sure" (1:10). When the writer of Hebrews exhorts his readers about making their hope sure, he puts into service the word *diligence,* which "expresses something of the greatness of the Christian's responsibility for the development of his life."[36] Believers must show this diligence "to the very end," says the writer. Many desire to have full assurance but fail to put forth any effort toward diligence.

Admonishing the recipients of his letter not to become lazy, the writer resorts to sound psychology. Earlier he indicated that they had not progressed beyond "the elementary truths of God's word" (5:12) and were still infants in the faith. In 6:12 he does not say that they have been lazy; rather, he exhorts them and says, "We do not want you to become lazy." He speaks words of encouragement. He is positive in his evaluation; he exhorts them to imitate those who are inheriting the promises through faith and patience; he directs their attention to the saints who have appropriated God's promises. Claiming these promises always calls for faith and patience.

Although the writer does not specify in 6:12 who the inheritors are, the

---

35. Paul mentions the triad in Rom. 5:1–5; I Cor. 13:13; Gal. 5:5–6; Col. 1:4–5; I Thess. 1:3; 5:8. Peter cites these qualities in I Peter 1:21–22. And the writer of Hebrews refers to them in 6:10–12 and 10:22–25.

36. Wolfgang Bauder, *NIDNTT,* vol. 3, p. 1169.

context reveals that he is thinking of Old Testament saints—Abraham (6:13) and the heroes of faith (chap. 11)—and saints of his own day.

Believers are inheritors of God's promises. The word *inherit* calls attention to the dividing of a legacy; an inheritor is entitled to possess part of that legacy. The legacy in this case consists of God's promises given to all believers. The author of Hebrews tells the readers to imitate the saints in their faithful trust, perseverance, and zeal. He introduces the subject of faith, hope, and love in 6:10–12; and true to form he elaborates on and fully discusses the topic in 10:22–24, 35–39; and 11.

Doctrinal Considerations in 6:7–12

The Christian is familiar with the themes of faith and love, but the theme of hope does not receive the attention the other two topics do. In our day of instant success, hope may seem outmoded. But in the days of Jesus and the apostles, this concept was relevant. Except for Mark, James, II Peter, Jude, and Revelation, the motif of hope appears in all the books of the New Testament. Paul stresses the concept more than any other New Testament writer.[37] Hope teaches endurance and an eager anticipation of that which will become reality. God promises eternal life to everyone who believes in his Son, and the believer expects the promise of eternal life to be fulfilled. Thus hope arises from and supports faith. "There can be no hope without faith in Christ, for hope is rooted in him alone. Faith without hope would, by itself, be empty and futile."[38]

To make his teaching graphic, interesting, and practical, the author applies illustrations taken from the world in which his readers lived. His illustration from agrarian life is apt and speaks to the recipients of his letter because they are able to relate to his teaching.

Greek Words, Phrases, and Constructions in 6:7–12

Verse 7

γῆ—this noun in the nominative singular lacks the definite article, yet it is qualified by participles and adjectives. It is the subject of the verb μεταλαμβάνει (it shares) and is the unifying factor in both verses 7 and 8.

εὔθετον—a two-ending adjective in the accusative singular; it modifies the noun βοτάνην (crop). The adjective is a compound derived from εὖ (well) and θετός (placed; an adjective from the verb τίθημι [I place]). The word contrasts with ἀδόκιμος (worthless) in the next verse. Note also that εὐλογίας (blessing) is contrasted with κατάρας (curse).

---

37. The noun *hope* occurs forty-eight times in the New Testament, thirty-one of which are in Paul's epistles and five in Hebrews. The verb *hope* appears thirty-one times, nineteen times in Paul's letters and once in Hebrews.

38. Ernst Hoffmann, *NIDNTT*, vol. 2, p. 242.

Verse 8

ἀδόκιμος—this two-ending adjective is derived from the privative ἀ (not) and δόκιμος (accepted; from the verb δέχομαι [I accept]). Some translations give the reading *rejected*; however, because this is not a moral issue, it is better to translate the word as "worthless."

καταράς—a noun in the genitive singular. It is genitive because of the adverbial preposition ἐγγύς (near). The noun is composed of κατά (down) and ἀρά (curse).

Verse 9

πεπείσμεθα—the use of the perfect passive (from πείθω, I persuade) instead of the perfect active πεποίθαμεν (we trust) is significant because it expresses the passive idea. The writer indicates that he has gained confidence in his readers on the basis of a lengthy investigation.[39]

ἐχόμενα—a participial form (present middle neuter plural accusative) from the verb ἔχω (I have, hold).[40] In the middle the meaning is to hold oneself to something. The participle, then, signifies closeness, accompaniment, or associations; it controls the genitive case of the word σωτηρίας (salvation).

Verse 10

ἐπιλαθέσθαι—the aorist middle from ἐπιλανθάνομαι (I forget) is followed by the genitive case of ἔργον (work); verbs of remembering and forgetting govern the genitive. The aorist is constative.

ἧς—the genitive case of the relative pronoun in the feminine gender is attracted to the antecedent ἀγάπης on which it depends.

διακονήσαντες—the aorist tense of this active participle relates to a past event. The present tense of διακονοῦντες refers to the deeds of love performed in the time when the author wrote his epistle.

Verse 11

πληροφορίαν—this noun occurs twice in Hebrews (6:11; 10:22), and twice in Paul's epistles (Col. 2:2; I Thess. 1:5). It is derived from the verb πληροφορέω (I fulfill, convince fully) and means "full assurance."

---

13 When God made his promise to Abraham, since there was no one greater for him to swear by, he swore by himself, 14 saying, "I will surely bless you and give you many descendants." 15 And so after waiting patiently, Abraham received what was promised.

16 Men swear by someone greater than themselves, and the oath confirms what is said and puts an end to all argument. 17 Because God wanted to make the unchanging nature of his purpose very clear to the heirs of what was promised, he confirmed it with an oath. 18 God did this so that, by two unchangeable things in which it is impossible for God to lie, we who have fled to take hold of the hope offered to us may be greatly encouraged. 19 We have this hope as an anchor for the soul, firm and secure. It enters the inner sanctuary behind the

---

39. Grosheide, *Hebreeën,* p. 148.

40. A. T. Robertson, in *A Grammar of the Greek New Testament in the Light of Historical Research* (Nashville: Broadman, 1934), p. 485, points out that many verbs in the passive voice "retain the accusative of the thing."

curtain, 20 where Jesus, who went before us, has entered on our behalf. He has become a high priest forever, in the order of Melchizedek.

B. Hold on to God's Promise
6:13–20

1. The Promise to Abraham
6:13–15

If there is anyone in Old Testament times who exemplifies the concept *hope,* it is Abraham. "Against all hope, Abraham in hope believed and so became the father of many nations" (Rom. 4:18). Exhorting his readers to have the full assurance of hope, the author illustrates his admonition by calling attention to Abraham. The patriarch known as the father of believers demonstrates that faith and hope are interrelated. Faith gives birth to hope, and hope in turn strengthens faith.

13. When God made his promise to Abraham, since there was no one greater for him to swear by, he swore by himself, 14. saying, "I will surely bless you and give you many descendants."

Illustrations can be more effective at times than plain teaching. Earlier in chapter 6, the author illustrated the hardness of the unbeliever's heart by using the example of worthless land that was about to be cursed and burned (vv. 7–8). Once more he resorts to an illustration. What better example can he hold before the Hebrews than the life of faith and hope that Abraham lived?

Abraham was seventy-five years old when he received the promise: God would make him into a great nation in the land he would show Abraham (Gen. 12:1–9). God appeared to him at Shechem and promised to give the land to Abraham's offspring (Gen. 12:6–7). God repeated this promise after Abraham and Lot separated (Gen. 13:14–17).

Some years later, Abraham wanted to make Eliezer of Damascus his heir, because God still had not given Abraham a son. God told Abraham that his descendants would be as numerous as the stars in the sky (Gen. 15:5). When Abraham was eighty-six years old, Ishmael was born (Gen. 16:16); but God told him that Isaac, not Ishmael, was the fulfillment of the covenant promise (Gen. 17:21; 21:12). Isaac was born when Abraham was a hundred years old (Gen. 21:5).

Abraham put his hope in God and trusted that God would keep his promise to make Abraham into a great nation. He waited twenty-five years for God to fulfill that promise. Sixty years after the birth of Isaac, Jacob and Esau were born (Gen. 25:26). When these children were 15 years old, Abraham died at the age of 175 (Gen. 25:7). At the time of his death, Abraham had one son of the covenant (Isaac) and one grandson of the covenant (Jacob).

God tested Abraham's faith on a mountain in the region of Moriah by telling him to sacrifice his son Isaac. God rewarded that faith by reiterating, on oath, the promise that Abraham had received: "I will surely bless you and make your descendants as numerous as the stars in the sky and as the sand on the seashore" (Gen. 22:17). God gave Abraham this sworn promise not because he was God's friend (James 2:23), but because Abraham "was singled out as a pattern and example for all believers."[41] As the author of the Epistle to the Hebrews asserts at the conclusion of chapter 11, Abraham was commended for his faith, yet he did not receive "what had been promised" (v. 39). That is, Abraham and all the other heroes of faith lived by faith and hoped for the coming of Christ. But they were not given the privilege of seeing the fulfillment of this promise. The recipients of the epistle, however, no longer lived with the promise. For them Christ fulfilled it.

God spoke to Abraham in human terms when he addressed the father of believers: "I swear by myself, declares the LORD, . . . I will surely bless you" (Gen. 22:16, 17). God did not have to swear to guarantee the trustworthiness of his Word; his Word is true, and God will keep his promise. But God adapted himself to the ways of man and swore by himself (Exod. 32:13; Ps. 95:11; Isa. 54:9).

The writer of Hebrews notes that man always swears by someone greater than himself; however, God has no one to excel him. Therefore, "he swore by himself." The author constantly makes comparisons in his epistle. In this instance, however, he admits that "there was no one greater for [God] to swear by."

God in a sense identified himself with his Word when he swore and gave Abraham the promise. The solemn promise came directly in response to Abraham's faith, but its fulfillment would take centuries. When the fulfilling of a promise takes time, it needs added assurance in order to ward off doubt.

Abraham could see fulfillment of the promise only in Isaac, but that was only the beginning of all that God meant by the promise. Therefore, God swore an oath. The oath assured Abraham that God would keep his Word in spite of the years of waiting that were in store for the recipients of the promise. Abraham indeed would have numerous descendants.

15. And so after waiting patiently, Abraham received what was promised.

Abraham waited for twenty-five years to see the promise of Isaac's birth fulfilled. But he never saw the descendants promised him on oath when God said, "I will surely bless you and give you many descendants." The father of believers saw only a partial fulfillment.[42]

Is there a conflict between 6:15 and 11:39? Hardly. At the end of the author's discussion of the heroes of faith he says, "These were all commended

---

41. Owen, *Hebrews,* vol. 3, p. 223.

42. Ernst Hoffmann, *NIDNTT,* vol. 3, p. 73. The writer of Hebrews "ascribes to the patriarchs an understanding of the promise which looks far beyond all historical foreshadowings and partial fulfillments, to an eternal consummation (11:10–16)."

for their faith, yet none of them received what had been promised" (11:39). When we consider still another passage of Scripture, we gain additional insight. Although the full intent of Jesus' word concerning Abraham is uncertain, Jesus in his controversy with the Jews told them: "Your father Abraham rejoiced at the thought of seeing my day; he saw it and was glad" (John 8:56).[43] Abraham waited patiently for God's specific promise to him (Isaac's birth), saw the next generation when Jacob and Esau were born, and claimed the promise of the coming of the Messiah for himself. Abraham was not only a man of faith, but also a man of hope.

Greek Words, Phrases, and Constructions in 6:13–15

Verse 13

ἐπαγγειλάμενος—the aorist middle participle from ἐπαγγέλλομαι (I promise) appears three times in Hebrews (6:13; 10:23; 11:11). In verb form it occurs once (Heb. 12:26). The aorist tense of the participle may be understood to be contemporaneous with the aorist of the main verb ὤμοσεν (he swore).[44] Because God repeated his promise to Abraham, it is advisable not to be too dogmatic but to understand that the aorist tense of the participle refers to all the incidents relating God's promise to Abraham.

εἶχεν—the imperfect active indicative of ἔχω (I have, hold) combined with the infinitive ὀμόσαι (to swear) has the meaning *was able, could* (see, for example, Matt. 18:25).

Verse 14

εὐλογῶν—this present active participle of εὐλογέω (I bless) together with the future active εὐλογήσω represents a Hebrew infinitive absolute construction that has been carried into the Greek because it is used in the Septuagint. In the Hebrew the combination of participle and verb strengthens the concept expressed; in the Greek the participle is redundant. Also in the sequence πληθύνων πληθυνῶ (multiplying, I will multiply) the emphatic use of the participle is evident. The redundancy is avoided in translation by rendering the participle as "surely": "I will surely bless you and I will surely multiply you."

Verse 15

μακροθυμήσας—the aorist active participle from μακροθυμέω (I have patience), a compound construction from μακρός (long) and θυμός (passion), expresses Abraham's patient expectation. The participle describes Abraham's spiritual disposition.

---

43. Ceslaus Spicq, in *L'Épître aux Hébreux,* 3d ed., 2 vols. (Paris: Gabalda, 1953), vol. 2, p. 160, mentions the possibility of Abraham's receiving some type of revelation about the birth of the Savior. Leon Morris, however, in his *Gospel of John,* New International Commentary on the New Testament series (Grand Rapids: Eerdmans, 1970), p. 472, more cautiously suggests "that Abraham's general attitude to this day was one of exultation, rather than [that Jesus referred] to any one specific occasion in the life of the patriarch."

44. Grosheide, *Hebreeën,* p. 153.

ἐπέτυχεν—the verb ἐπιτυγχάνω (I obtain, attain) occurs four times in the New Testament (Rom. 11:7; Heb. 6:15; 11:33; James 4:2), always in the aorist active tense. It is a compound from ἐπί (on, toward) and τυγχάνω (I obtain, get). The compound is more intensive than the simple verb.

---

2. Heirs of the Promise
6:16–20

After providing the illustration that portrays Abraham as the recipient of the promise, the author of the epistle applies the teaching of the promise to all believers. As God assured Abraham of the veracity of his Word and therefore swore an oath, so also for the believers, called heirs of the promise, God confirms the promise with an oath.

16. Men swear by someone greater than themselves, and the oath confirms what is said and puts an end to all argument.

As the Scriptures reveal, Jewish people resorted quickly to swearing an oath. They might swear by heaven (Matt. 5:34; 23:22; James 5:12), by the earth (Matt. 5:35; James 5:12), by the temple (Matt. 23:16), by Jerusalem (Matt. 5:35), or in the name of the Lord God (Gen. 14:22; Deut. 6:13; 10:20; Judges 21:7; Ruth 1:17; Jer. 12:16).

Most of the oaths were sworn in the name of God or that which was associated with God (heaven, the temple, or Jerusalem). That does not mean that the Jew identified God with the objects used as substitutes, but rather that the Jew of Jesus' day did not take his oaths seriously. Jesus forbade the swearing of an oath (Matt. 5:33–37) because of this sinful practice. He taught that a man's word must be unquestionably true so that, as a consequence, oaths would no longer be necessary.

In a court of law, however, the judge administers an oath in order to uphold the truth. Indeed, "men swear by someone greater than themselves" when they invoke the name of God. They appeal to God because he is the ultimate truth, and thus in case they break the oath they risk divine revenge. In court the truth must be spoken by defendant, plaintiff, and their lawyers.[45] The oath, then, settles the truth in any dispute.

17. Because God wanted to make the unchanging nature of his purpose very clear to the heirs of what was promised, he confirmed it with an oath.

Once again we read an argument that leads from the lesser to the greater. The Epistle to the Hebrews is replete with examples of this type of argument. Man, by appealing to God, establishes the truth in a particular matter. How much more significant, by comparison, is the oath God himself swears to confirm the certainty of fulfilling his promises to those who have received

---

45. The author of Hebrews borrows terminology from Egyptian civil law. Refer to Adolf Deissmann, *Bible Studies* (Winona Lake, Ind.: Alpha Publications, 1979), p. 107.

them. The message that the author of Hebrews conveys is that man can depend on the utter truthfulness of God.

Actually the oath God swears is superfluous, for God himself is truth. Man because of sin confirms the truth of his words by invoking God's name, but God does not need to establish the truth. Jesus' prayer to the Father testifies to this: "Your word is truth" (John 17:17).

Why, then, does God swear an oath? He wants to effectively show the heirs of the promise that they can rely fully on his Word. Accommodating himself to human customs, God swears an oath. He is conscious of man's weak faith. Therefore, to give man added assurance of the complete reliability of God's Word, God provides the extra affirmation.

Reading Genesis 22:16–17, we receive the impression that God gave the promise to Abraham, for he is the one who obtains the blessing. "I will surely bless you," God says to Abraham. But the writer of the Epistle to the Hebrews makes the divine blessing applicable to all believers by calling them heirs of the promise. That means that God's promise to Abraham transcends the centuries and is in Christ as relevant today as it was in Abraham's time (Gal. 3:7, 9, 29). The oath God swore to Abraham was meant for us to strengthen us in our faith.

When the author writes, "God wanted to make the unchanging nature of his purpose very clear," he reminds us that the purpose of God is to make us heirs. Furthermore, according to God's will, this purpose has been determined in eternity (Eph. 1:4–5, 11).[46] God's purpose to save the believers in Jesus Christ is firm, unchanging, and inviolable.

No believer ought to doubt God's will to save him, for God gives him perfect assurance that the nature of God's purpose is unchanging. The believer, who has eternal security because of this unchanging will of God, can sing Fanny J. Crosby's hymn:

> Blessed assurance, Jesus is mine!
> O what a foretaste of glory divine!
> Heir of salvation, purchase of God,
> Born of His Spirit, washed in His blood.

Hebrews 6:17 teaches that God not only made the promise to believers but also is the guarantor of the promise. God makes the promise of salvation, and at the same time he becomes the intermediary who ensures that the promise is fulfilled. The word *intermediary* implies that there are two other parties: the one who gives the promise and the one who receives it. Between these two parties stands God as guarantor.

18. God did this so that, by two unchangeable things in which it is

46. Dietrich Müller (*NIDNTT,* vol. 3, p. 1018) writes, "The purpose of divine election far precedes the act of historical election." Gottlob Schrenk explains that "the purpose of his will" encompasses the foreordination and predestination mentioned in Eph. 1:4–5, 11 and in effect "has the final word." *TDNT,* vol. 1, p. 635.

impossible for God to lie, we who have fled to take hold of the hope offered to us may be greatly encouraged.

The available evidence accumulates, as the author notes. God has given his unchangeable promise and he confirmed this promise with an unchangeable oath. Besides noting these "two unchangeable things," the writer declares that God cannot lie. These statements have a built-in redundancy, for God by nature is the personification of truth. "God is not a man, that he should lie, nor a son of man, that he should change his mind" (Num. 23:19; see also I Sam. 15:29; Ps. 33:11; Isa. 46:10–11; Mal. 3:6; James 1:17).

If then God accommodates himself to man's custom of swearing an oath to establish the truth, the implication is that when a Christian refuses to accept this oath-confirmed promise of salvation and turns to sin or another religion, he risks being blasphemous.[47] This person intimates that God's Word cannot be trusted and that God is a perjurer.

But in this verse the writer stresses the positive, for he returns to the use of the first person plural. Says he, "We who have fled to take hold of the hope offered to us may be greatly encouraged." The author directs his lesson on the unchangeableness of God's purpose to us who believe the Word of God, and he writes to encourage us in our flight from sin. The words *we who have fled* are somewhat vague because the writer does not provide specific place names or circumstances. However, the general context indicates that we who believe have escaped the power of willful unbelief and thus we turn to God "to take hold of the hope offered to us." We are the people who "for refuge to Jesus have fled."

As true heirs of the promise, we take hold of the hope that God offers us. We have fled as fugitives and cling to the one who offers new life. The author uses a figure of speech by which a single word conveys an entire concept.[48] That is, we must understand that the word *hope* refers to the one who gives that hope. God himself has provided hope through the promises of his Word. And we whom the author of Hebrews exhorts "to make [our] hope sure" (6:11) are invited to appropriate the hope that God places in full view before us.

Taking hold of hope is not something that we do halfheartedly. On the contrary, we must attain the hope offered to us with the strong encouragement that we receive from God's Word. In short, God holds out to us hope and at the same time strenuously urges us to accept and appropriate it.

19. We have this hope as an anchor for the soul, firm and secure. It enters the inner sanctuary behind the curtain.

The author, true to form, introduces a certain topic rather briefly in order

---

47. Spicq, *Hébreux,* vol. 2, p. 162.

48. The figure is called metonomy. Louis Berkhof, in *Principles of Biblical Interpretation* (Grand Rapids: Baker, 1950), pp. 83–84, explains the figure as "a mental [relation] rather than a physical one." He provides the example of Paul's reference to the Holy Spirit—"Quench not the Spirit" (I Thess. 5:19, KJV)—by which Paul intends to describe "the special manifestations of the Spirit."

to explain it fully in subsequent verses. In a brief exhortation he presents the subject *hope* (6:11); after discussing the absolute dependability of God's promise to the believer, he explains the significance of hope (6:18–19). Hope, says the writer, is like an anchor; it gives stability and security to the soul.

The imagery is vivid and telling. The author paints a picture of a boat, battered by the waves but held in place by an unseen anchor that clings to the bottom of the sea. So man's soul, buffeted by winds and waves of doubt, has a secure anchor of hope firmly fixed in Jesus.[49] This anchor gives stability to man's soul, and that includes "the whole inner life of man with his powers of will, reason, and emotion."[50] We relate to the image of an anchor and express our feelings in the words of Priscilla J. Owens:

> We have an anchor that keeps the soul
> Steadfast and sure while the billows roll;
> Fastened to the Rock which cannot move,
> Grounded firm and deep in the Savior's love.

But the Hebrews of Old Testament times and the Jews of the first century had a dislike for the sea. A reflection of this fact is that the word *anchor* never occurs in the Old Testament; and only four times in the New Testament, three of which appear in the account of Paul's shipwreck (Acts 27:29, 30, 40). Therefore the author rather abruptly switches metaphors and mentions the veil of the Most Holy Place. The recipients of the Epistle to the Hebrews were much more attuned to the worship services of tabernacle and temple; they knew the construction of the sanctuary; and the clause "it enters the inner sanctuary behind the curtain" was meaningful to them.

The author of the epistle has come to the end of his exhortation that began after he had introduced Jesus as "high priest in the order of Melchizedek" (5:10). He returns to the subject of the high priesthood of Christ with a reference to "the inner sanctuary behind the curtain." The words immediately reminded the readers of the Day of Atonement, when the high priest entered into the presence of God (Lev. 16:2, 12). Moreover, the Hebrews knew from the gospel proclaimed to them that at Jesus' death the curtain of the temple was torn from top to bottom, exposing the Most Holy Place to the view of all who were inside the temple. They understood the reference to the inner sanctuary figuratively and associated it with heaven. Already the writer had called attention to this fact when he wrote, "We have a great high priest who has gone through the heavens, Jesus the Son of God" (4:14).

20. Where Jesus, who went before us, has entered on our behalf. He has become a high priest forever, in the order of Melchizedek.

---

49. "The anchor of hope was a fairly common metaphor in the late Greek ethic," writes James Moffatt in his *Epistle to the Hebrews,* International Critical Commentary series (Edinburgh: Clark, 1963), p. 89. Westcott adds that the symbol of the anchor, often with that of a fish, occurred on gravestones. *Hebrews,* p. 163.

50. Günther Harder, *NIDNTT,* vol. 3, p. 684.

Our hope is pinned on Jesus, who has entered the heavenly sanctuary. An anchor lies unseen at the bottom of the sea; our hope lies unseen in the highest heaven. "For in this hope we were saved," writes Paul. "But hope that is seen is no hope at all" (Rom. 8:24). Our anchor of hope has absolute security in that Jesus in human form, now glorified, has entered heaven. And he has entered heaven in his humanity as a guarantee that we, too, shall be with him. This guarantee is indicated by the phrase *who went before us.* (In the Greek the equivalent expression is the word *prodromos,* which means "forerunner.") He goes ahead and we follow. Also note that the name *Jesus* and not *Christ* (5:5) occurs—a distinct reminder of the earthly life of the Lord. Jesus ascended in his glorified human body to heaven and entered the presence of God. As Jesus' human body has come into God's presence, so our bodies will enter heaven.[51] That is our hope.

Jesus "has become a high priest forever." This rather short sentence is filled with meaning.

a. Jesus *has become* a high priest. He did not become high priest when he ascended into heaven. Rather, he took his place at the right hand of God the Father because he accomplished his atoning work on the cross. He indeed was the sacrificial Lamb of God offered for the sin of the world; as the writer of Hebrews puts it, "Christ was sacrificed once to take away the sins of many people" (9:28).

b. Jesus has become *a high priest.* The writer has called Jesus high priest in Hebrews 2:17; 3:1; 4:14–15; and 5:5, 10. He will explain the concept *high priest* in succeeding chapters, but in 6:20 the author stresses that Jesus entered heaven as high priest, as the one who atoned for the sins of God's people. He opened the door to heaven because of his high-priestly work.

c. Jesus has become a high priest *forever.* An Aaronic high priest served in the capacity of high priest for a limited duration. Jesus serves forever. The high priest entered the Most Holy Place once a year. Jesus is in heaven forever. "Because Jesus lives forever, he has a permanent priesthood" (7:24). Constantly he intercedes for us (Rom. 8:34; Heb. 7:25; 9:24).

By his death on the cross, Jesus fulfilled the responsibilities of the Aaronic priesthood. But as a high priest he had to belong to a different order. The writer of Hebrews showed that according to Psalm 110:4 God designated Jesus as high priest forever in the order of Melchizedek (5:6, 10). The writer will explain this topic in the next few chapters.

Doctrinal Considerations in 6:13–20

Joshua told the elders, leaders, judges, and officials of Israel that God had fulfilled all the promises given to them (Josh. 23:14). Every promise God has fulfilled.

Not only Joshua but also every believer can testify that God keeps his Word. The

---

51. George E. Rice, "The Chiastic Structure of the Central Section of the Epistle to the Hebrews," *Andrews University Seminary Studies* 19 (1981): 243.

promises made to our spiritual forefathers are repeated and given to us in our generation. To Abraham God said, "I will establish my covenant as an everlasting covenant between me and you and your descendants after you for the generations to come, to be your God and the God of your descendants after you" (Gen. 17:7). Throughout Scripture we read the promise *I will be your God.* Because of the redeeming work of Christ, believers are in that covenant God made with Abraham and are Abraham's spiritual offspring (Gal. 3:16).

God's Word is sure. God does not lie, as Paul explicitly states (Titus 1:2). In the Epistle to the Hebrews God's promise is reinforced—as if it needed support—by an oath sworn by God himself. The point is that God's Word is absolutely reliable. After exhorting the recipients to make their hope sure (6:11) and by encouraging them to have their hope anchored in Jesus, the writer continues his exposition about the high priesthood of Christ. This doctrine is basic to the Epistle to the Hebrews.

Greek Words, Phrases, and Constructions in 6:16–20

Verse 16

μείζονος—the comparative adjective from μέγας (great) is in the genitive singular case because the verb ὀμνύω (I swear) is followed by the preposition κατά, which demands the genitive. The gender of the comparative is either masculine or neuter; the masculine means "someone," and the neuter "something." Although it is possible to use the translation *something,* we do well to translate the adjective as "someone."

ἀντιλογία—this noun derived from ἀντί (against) and λέγω (I speak) occurs four times in the New Testament (Heb. 6:16; 7:7; 12:3; Jude 11).

Verse 17

ἐν ᾧ—although the nearest antecedent is the preceding noun ὅρκος (oath), this relative pronoun is dependent on the content of 6:16. Some translators give the prepositional phrase the meaning *and so, thus,* or *wherein*; others leave it untranslated.

βουλόμενος and βουλή—the choice of the present middle participle, nominative singular of βούλομαι (I want) together with the noun βουλή (decision, purpose) is deliberate; these two are coupled together for reinforcement. The present participle denotes God's desire to make known the decision that he had made beforehand.

τὸ ἀμετάθετον—this substantivized verbal adjective is a compound consisting of ἀ (un-, not), μετα (after), and τίθημι (I place, put). The verb μετατίθημι (I change, transfer) occurs in Hebrews 7:12; 11:5. The verbal adjective implies a passive idea with overtones of necessity: that which cannot be changed. In the New Testament, the word is used only by the author of Hebrews in 6:17, 18.

ἐμεσίτευσεν—the aorist active indicative of μεσιτεύω (I mediate) occurs once in the New Testament. It relates to the adjective μέσος (middle) and the noun μεσίτης (mediator).

Verse 18

πραγμάτων—this noun appears eleven times in the New Testament, three of which are in Hebrews (6:18; 10:1; 11:1). Derived from πράσσω (I practice), the noun in 6:18 means "facts." The two facts are the promise and the oath. The preposition διά (through, by means of) requires the genitive case.

τὸν θεόν—a few major Greek manuscripts (for example, Codex Vaticanus and Codex Bezae) omit the definite article to express the meaning *for one who is God.* However, the rest of the manuscripts, including a papyrus document, have the definite article.

καταφυγόντες—the second aorist active participle of the verb καταφεύγω (I flee for refuge) has a perfective connotation;[52] that is, "to escape completely."

κρατῆσαι—the first aorist infinitive of κρατέω (I hold faithfully) is constative; that is, comprehensive. The infinitive is closely linked to the preceding participle καταφυγόντες.

Verse 19

ἀσφαλῆ τε καὶ βεβαίαν—these two descriptive adjectives modify the noun ἄγκυραν. The presence of the particle τε with καί conveys the meaning *not only . . . but also.* ἀσφαλῆ is an adjective derived from ἀ (un-, not) and σφάλλω (I cause to fall, fail). The adjective βεβαίαν is featured five times in Hebrews (2:2; 3:6, 14; 6:19; 9:17) out of a total of nine times in the New Testament (Rom. 4:16; II Cor. 1:6; II Peter 1:10, 19).

τὸ ἐσώτερον—the comparative adjective of the adverb ἔσω (within) may be translated "the inner part" of the sanctuary. Some scholars interpret the adjective as a preposition that controls the genitive case of καταπετάσματος. We do well to translate the phrase as "the inner sanctuary behind the curtain."

Verse 20

πρόδρομος—this noun appears once in the New Testament. Its roots are in πρό (before) and τρέχω, ἔδραμον (I run, ran), and it refers to Jesus, who has entered heaven to prepare a place for those who believe in him (John 14:3).

γενόμενος—in Hebrews 2:17 the author gives the aorist subjunctive form γένηται ("that [Jesus] might become"); in 6:20 γενόμενος is the aorist middle participle, translated "he has become." The aorist is culminative. Jesus' mission on earth has been culminated, yet his activities as interceding high priest continue.

Summary of Chapter 6

The chapter which begins at 5:11 and ends at 6:20 is a lengthy pastoral exhortation. It is an interlude. Before the author explains the doctrine of the high priesthood of Christ in the order of Melchizedek, he exhorts his readers to faithfulness. First, he admonishes them because of their dullness in learning the basic doctrines of God's Word. Next, he delineates what these elementary teachings are: repentance, faith, baptism, ordination, resurrection, and judgment. He exhorts the recipients of his letter to advance in their understanding of these teachings.

Throughout the epistle the author warns the Christians against the sin of

---

52. Robertson, *Grammar,* p. 827.

unbelief (3:12; 4:1, 11; 10:26, 29; 12:15, 28–29). He describes the rebellious Israelites who perished in the desert because of this sin (3:16–19). In 6:4–6 the author pursues that same theme by referring to those persons who have hardened their hearts after receiving a knowledge of the truth. These people continue to crucify Jesus and to despise him. They do so in open rebellion. For such persons, says the author, there is no possibility of being brought back to repentance. They are lost forever.

This observation serves as a warning to the readers not to fall into the sin of unbelief, but to demonstrate their diligence in exhibiting the qualities of faith, hope, and love. The author singles out the virtue of hope and encourages them to make hope a priority in their spiritual lives. He commends them for their loving care shown to people in need and assures them that they are the recipients of the blessings of salvation. He exhorts them to cultivate hope. He points to Jesus, the forerunner who has entered heaven as high priest and who by his presence in heaven guarantees them entrance.

Hope is anchored in the finished work of Christ, who atoned for the sins of his people.

7

Jesus: High Priest like Melchizedek

7:1–28

Outline

A. Melchizedek, King and Priest
7:1–3 1. The History of Melchizedek
7:4–10 2. The Significance of Melchizedek
B. Melchizedek's Superior Priesthood
7:11–12 1. Imperfection of the Levitical Priesthood
7:13–14 2. Inappropriate Service for Judah's Descendant
7:15–19 3. Indestructible Life
C. Christ's Superior Priesthood
7:20–22 1. By Oath
7:23–25 2. For Eternity
7:26–27 3. In Sacrifice
7:28 4. To Perfection

7 1 This Melchizedek was king of Salem and priest of God Most High. He met Abraham returning from the defeat of the kings and blessed him, 2 and Abraham gave
him a tenth of everything. First, his name means "king of righteousness"; then also,
"king of Salem" means "king of peace." 3 Without father or mother, without genealogy, without beginning of days or end of life, like the Son of God he remains a priest
forever.
4 Just think how great he was: Even the patriarch Abraham gave him a tenth of the
plunder! 5 Now the law requires the descendants of Levi who become priests to collect a
tenth from the people—that is, their brothers—even though their brothers are descended
from Abraham. 6 This man, however, did not trace his descent from Levi, yet he collected
a tenth from Abraham and blessed him who had the promises. 7 And without doubt the
lesser person is blessed by the greater. 8 In the one case, the tenth is collected by men who
die; but in the other case, by him who is declared to be living. 9 One might even say that
Levi, who collects the tenth, paid the tenth through Abraham, 10 because when Melchizedek
met Abraham, Levi was still in the body of his ancestor.

A. Melchizedek, King and Priest
7:1–10

1. The History of Melchizedek
7:1–3

After an interlude of exhortations and admonitions, the author returns to the topic of Christ's priesthood that was introduced in 2:17; 3:1; 4:14; and especially 5:6, 10. In chapter 7, he begins to explain the significance of the quotation from Psalm 110:4 ("You are a priest forever, in the order of Melchizedek," 5:6; see also 6:20). The heart of the doctrinal section of the Epistle to the Hebrews lies in the discussion of the high priesthood of Christ recorded in chapter 7. All of the preceding material in this chapter is introductory.[1]

1. This Melchizedek was king of Salem and priest of God Most High. He met Abraham returning from the defeat of the kings and blessed him, 2. and Abraham gave him a tenth of everything. First, his name means "king of righteousness"; then also, "king of Salem" means "king of peace."

---

1. Simon J. Kistemaker, *The Psalm Citations in the Epistle to the Hebrews* (Amsterdam: Van Soest, 1961), p. 98.

Melchizedek is not familiar to us, for his name occurs only twice in the Old Testament (Gen. 14:18; Ps. 110:4). Although the historical account in Genesis 14 provides more information than Psalm 110, the details nevertheless are not elaborate.

First, the name *Melchizedek* has the same ending as that of Adoni-Zedek, the king of Jerusalem who is mentioned in Joshua 10:1, 3. The first part of the name (*Melchi*) means "my king" and the second part (*zedek*) means "righteous"—that is, "my king is righteous." The author of Hebrews interprets the name as "king of righteousness" (7:2).

Melchizedek was king of Salem at the time Abraham defeated the forces of Kedorlaomer. Upon Abraham's return from the northern part of Canaan, Melchizedek met him and offered him bread and wine. We are told that Melchizedek was a priest of God Most High, that he blessed Abraham, and that he received a tenth of the spoils Abraham had gathered (Gen. 14:18–20).

Both the Genesis account and the Epistle to the Hebrews portray Melchizedek as a historical figure who was a contemporary of Abraham.[2] Melchizedek was king of Salem, a city generally identified with Jerusalem (Ps. 76:2),[3] and he was priest of God Most High. In the Gentile world of Abraham's day, traces of true worship of God the "Creator of heaven and earth" remained (Gen. 14:19). Melchizedek served Abraham's God and "had carried on the tradition from the time of Paradise when mankind recognized only one true God."[4]

Abraham gave Melchizedek a tenth of the spoils. Although Genesis 14:20 ("Then Abram gave him a tenth of everything") is very brief, the author of Hebrews reasons from the silence of Scripture and constructs his argument on the significance of the king-priest Melchizedek. The Genesis account teaches that Abraham had sworn an oath to God that he would not keep any of the spoils for himself (Gen. 14:22–23). Abraham recognized Melchizedek as God's representative and therefore by giving Melchizedek a tenth he brought the tithe to God.

Melchizedek as king-priest was God's representative, for he was king of righteousness as his name implies. He was a king who established and promoted righteousness in his kingdom. Also, he was king of Salem, and the

---

2. Jewish writers, the Dead Sea Scrolls, and early Christian authors interpret Melchizedek's person in various ways, from an angel (i.e., an eschatological deliverer) to a historical figure. See "Excursus I: The Significance of Melchizedek," in Philip Edgcumbe Hughes's *Commentary on the Epistle to the Hebrews* (Grand Rapids: Eerdmans, 1977), pp. 237–45. For a detailed bibliography see Bruce A. Demarest's "Melchizedek, Salem," in *NIDNTT,* vol. 2, pp. 590–93. Also see his *History of Interpretation of Hebrews 7:1–10 from the Reformation to the Present* (Tübingen: Mohr Siebeck, 1976).

3. The name *Salem* is identified by some writers with Salim near Aenon (John 3:23), where John the Baptist stayed. However, Josephus associated Salem with the city of Jerusalem (see his *Jewish Wars* 6.438 and his *Antiquities of the Jews* 1.180, LCL).

4. Gerhard Charles Aalders, *Bible Student's Commentary: Genesis,* 2 vols. (Grand Rapids: Zondervan, 1981), vol. 1, p. 289.

word *Salem* means "peace." Of course, the two characteristics, righteousness and peace, are messianic (see Isa. 9:6–7). They describe Jesus, who according to Psalm 110:1 and 4 fills the roles of priest and king.

3. Without father or mother, without genealogy, without beginning of days or end of life, like the Son of God he remains a priest forever.

We ought not take this verse literally, for the author, reasoning from silence (Gen. 14:18–20), is comparing Melchizedek with the priests who descended from Aaron. The writer expected a priest to establish and prove his priestly descent. During the time of Ezra and Nehemiah, the priests determined on the basis of the law of Moses that only the descendants of Aaron were to serve as priests in the sacrificial system (Exod. 28 and 29; Lev. 8, 9, and 10; Num. 16, 17, and 18; Ezra 2:61–63; Neh. 7:63–65).

We can understand that belonging to this close-knit community of priests was a unique privilege; a priest presented sacrifices from the people to God and served as an intermediary between man and God. "Thus a priest is one who brings men near to God, who leads them into the presence of God."[5] A prerequisite for holding the office of priest, therefore, was a proven genealogy. This genealogy was of the greatest importance. For example, the Jewish historian Josephus assures his readers that he was born into a priestly family, that he can prove his descent, and that he has found his genealogy recorded in "public registers."[6]

Melchizedek, by contrast, does not have a genealogy; the names of his father and mother are lacking. Yet this man is priest of God Most High. Melchizedek's age is not mentioned either. Yet for all the other persons prominent in the history of salvation genealogical information is supplied (for example, Adam lived 930 years [Gen. 5:5]; Noah, 950 years [Gen. 9:29]; and Abraham, 175 years [Gen. 25:7]). Melchizedek, therefore, is unique. He does not fit into the genealogies recorded in Genesis. He seems to belong to a different class.

What the author of Hebrews has written about Melchizedek applies directly to the Son of God. In comparing Melchizedek with Jesus, the author uses the word *like* (7:3, 15) because he sees a similarity. He does not say that these two are identical; he only compares and discerns resemblance. Melchizedek was a historical figure, in the writer's opinion; but because genealogical references that would classify him as a member of the Levitical priesthood are not available, he states that Melchizedek "remains a priest forever."

---

5. Geerhardus Vos, *The Teaching of the Epistle to the Hebrews* (Grand Rapids: Eerdmans, 1956), p. 94.

6. Josephus, *Life* 1.6 (LCL). Emil Schürer, in *A History of the Jewish People in the Time of Jesus Christ,* 5 vols. (Edinburgh: Clark, 1885), vol. 1, div. 2, p. 210, writes: "*The primary requisite in a priest was evidence of his pedigree.*" Italics his.

Greek Words, Phrases, and Constructions in 7:1–3

Verse 1

τοῦ ὑψίστου—this form is an adjective in the superlative, but is understood to indicate rank: in the highest degree. The adjective serves the purpose of describing the only true God whom both Abraham and Melchizedek worship (Gen. 14:19–20, 22). It occurs thirteen times in the New Testament, nine times in the Gospel of Luke and Acts, and once in Hebrews (7:1).

κοπῆς—although the word occurs once in the New Testament, from its usage in the Septuagint (Gen. 14:17; Deut. 28:25; Josh. 10:20; Jth. 15:7) the meaning is clear. Derived from the verb κόπτω (I cut), it refers to a slaughter, or figuratively to a defeat.

Verse 3

ἀπάτωρ ἀμήτωρ—these two nouns appear only in Hebrews 7:3, in classical Greek literature, and in Philo. The nouns refer to orphans, foundlings, illegitimate children, and disowned sons or to gods who came into being without father or mother. Philo uses these words in his allegorical interpretation on the origin of the high priest.[7] In Hebrews 7:3, we note the additional word ἀγενεαλόγητος (without genealogy) used climactically by the author of Hebrews to show that in the early chapters of Genesis, where genealogies are frequent, a priestly genealogy for Melchizedek is missing. The three Greek words, therefore, must be understood in the historical setting of Genesis.

ἀφωμοιωμένος—the perfect passive participle of the verb ἀφομοιόω (I make similar) expresses duration; the compound form makes the participle emphatic. Note that Melchizedek is compared with the Son of God, not the Son of God with Melchizedek.[8] That is, the focus is on the eternal Son of God. Also note that the author of Hebrews writes not "Jesus" or "Christ" but "Son of God." The appellation stresses his eternal rather than temporal existence.

διηνεκές—this neuter adjective is derived from the verb διαφέρω (I carry through) in its aorist form διήνεγκα; it means "continuous, uninterrupted." Only the writer of Hebrews employs the word (7:3; 10:1, 12, 14).

2. The Significance of Melchizedek
7:4–10

In chapter 7 the writer of Hebrews presents an exegesis of Psalm 110:4 ("You are a priest forever, in the order of Melchizedek"), which is quoted in 5:6 and referred to in 5:10 and 6:20. Stating the quotation in summary form, the author explains it in reverse order. He begins with the name *Melchizedek* and places it in a historical context (7:1–3); in the next section he discusses the words *priest* (7:4–10) and *priestly order* (7:11–12); he devotes

7. Gottlob Schrenk, *TDNT,* vol. 5, pp. 1019–21. Also see Otfried Hofius, "Father," *NIDNTT,* vol. 1, p. 616.

8. John Albert Bengel, *Gnomon of the New Testament,* edited by Andrew R. Fausset, 7th ed., 5 vols. (Edinburgh: Clark, 1877), vol. 4, p. 403.

two verses to the personal pronoun *you* (7:13–14); and he elaborates on the expression *forever* in the next ten verses (7:15–25).[9]

4. Just think how great he was: Even the patriarch Abraham gave him a tenth of the plunder! 5. Now the law requires the descendants of Levi who become priests to collect a tenth from the people—that is, their brothers—even though their brothers are descended from Abraham.

Having placed Melchizedek in historical perspective, the author wants the readers to pay particular attention to the greatness of this priest who received tithes from and blessed Abraham. In the minds of his Hebrew audience Abraham was considered a great man; he was called the friend of God (II Chron. 20:7; Isa. 41:8; James 2:23) and the father of the nation Israel, the patriarch (Isa. 51:2). The writer stresses the word *patriarch* to underscore the greatness of Abraham.

However, someone greater than Abraham appeared at the time when Abraham returned victoriously from defeating four kings in northern Canaan and from setting five kings free. Abraham had reached a pinnacle in his leadership career in the southern part of Canaan. But upon his return, Abraham paid tribute to Melchizedek by giving him a tenth of the plunder. Literally the text reads: "Abraham gave him a tenth of the top of the heap." Abraham gave him the best!

Even though customs and cultures differ with respect to tithing, we have no difficulty understanding that the one who receives the tithe (Melchizedek) is greater than the one who gives the tithe (Abraham). The readers of the Epistle to the Hebrews had to acknowledge the superiority of Melchizedek.[10] They were acquainted with the command on tithing specified in the law of Moses (Lev. 27:30–33; Num. 18:21, 24, 26–29; also see Deut. 12:17–19; 14:22–29; 26:12–15).

Perhaps we may parallel the tithing of the ancients and our paying taxes. All of us are familiar with taxes, although the tax laws vary from time to time and from area to area. Similarly the rules on tithing recorded in the Old Testament vary and may reflect changing circumstances in the development of the Israelite nation.[11] However, the writer of Hebrews is not interested in stressing differences in tithing; his intention is to stress the receiving of the tithe.

"The law requires," says the writer, that the priests gather the tithe. He mentions the name of Levi, not that of Aaron, in order to show that the work of collecting the tithe belonged to the entire tribe of Levi—the Levites

---

9. Kistemaker, *Psalm Citations,* p. 118.

10. Jewish writers identified Melchizedek with Shem the son of Noah, who may have been a contemporary of Abraham (Gen. 11:11). If Shem were living at the time of Abraham, he would be more venerable than the patriarch. Consult Nedarim 32b, Nashim, and Sanhedrin 108b, Nezikin, *Talmud,* vol. 3.

11. Gerald F. Hawthorne, "Tithe," *NIDNTT,* vol. 3, p. 852.

and the priests.[12] According to the law, the Levites were to gather the tithe and they in turn would give a tenth to the priests (Num. 18:28).

We make three observations.

a. In 7:4–10, the author of the epistle employs names representatively: Abraham is called the patriarch—the head of a nation and the father of believers; Levi, whose descendants become priests, is the tribal head.

b. Levi stands closer genealogically to Abraham than to Aaron, so the author is able to refer to the rest of the Israelites as "their brothers [who] are descended from Abraham."

c. Because of the writer's exegetical method of explaining the quotation from Psalm 110:4, the word *priest* assumes added importance in the present context. This particular term has great significance in the author's discourse on the priesthood of Christ.

In verses 4 and 5 the author presents a series of contrasts: the priests as descendants of Levi are more respected than the rest of the people; father Abraham is greater than his descendants; Melchizedek, because he received the tithe, is superior to the patriarch Abraham.

6. This man, however, did not trace his descent from Levi, yet he collected a tenth from Abraham and blessed him who had the promises. 7. And without doubt the lesser person is blessed by the greater.

Already before Abraham met Melchizedek, God had given the patriarch the promises (Gen. 12:2–3; 13:14–17) and had blessed him. Abraham became the great-grandfather of Levi, whose descendants became priests in Israel.

Melchizedek, by contrast, had no genealogy and had not received the promises. He stood alone in all his grandeur as king of Salem and priest of God Most High. Abraham, fully aware of Melchizedek's stature, offered him tithes and in return received blessing when Melchizedek said:

> Blessed be Abram by God Most High,
> Creator of heaven and earth.
> And blessed be God Most High,
> who delivered your enemies into your hand. [Gen. 14:19–20]

This priest of God Most High did not exact tithes from Abraham as Levitical priests imposed a tithe on their fellow Israelites in later years. Of his own accord Abraham gave Melchizedek a tenth of the spoils, because he recognized him as God's representative. And this representative imparted a divine blessing on Abraham.

Simple logic tells us, says the writer, that "the lesser person is blessed by the greater." This fact is evident in three instances: the blessing that Isaac pronounced on Jacob, that Jacob gave his sons, and that Moses bestowed upon the Israelites (Gen. 27:27–29; 48:15–16; 49; Deut. 33). Sons do not

12. F. W. Grosheide, *De Brief aan de Hebreeën en de Brief van Jakobus* (Kampen: Kok, 1955), p. 166.

bless their fathers, but dying fathers pronounce blessings on their sons. In the case of Melchizedek blessing Abraham, we see that the king-priest delivers the blessing of God Most High to the patriarch. Abraham had given Melchizedek a tithe of the plunder because Abraham saw he was God's representative.[13] In return this representative invoked God's blessing upon Abraham. Melchizedek functioned as God's mouthpiece and, therefore, was greater than Abraham. He acted in the capacity of priest, and that made him superior to Abraham.

8. In the one case, the tenth is collected by men who die; but in the other case, by him who is declared to be living. 9. One might even say that Levi, who collects the tenth, paid the tenth through Abraham, 10. because when Melchizedek met Abraham, Levi was still in the body of his ancestor.

In our age and culture we are somewhat puzzled when we read 7:8–10. If the author of Hebrews presents an explanation of Genesis 14:18–20, and if on the basis of the silence of Scripture he reads matters pertaining to Melchizedek, Abraham, and Levi into the text, we have difficulty understanding him.

The author, however, is a trained theologian who applies logic in a manner differing from ours. He reasons like a rabbi of the first century. He uses a methodology in explaining the Scriptures that is strictly rabbinical. He is a typical Jewish-Christian author who, filled with the Holy Spirit, writes the inspired Word of God.

Two points stand out in the author's presentation.

a. The permanent priesthood of Melchizedek. The exact wording is that Melchizedek "is declared to be living." Does this mean that Melchizedek never died? If he were a supernatural being, he would be the Son of God. But the writer says that Melchizedek was "like the Son of God" (7:3). Although Scripture is silent about the death of Melchizedek, we nonetheless conclude that he died. Yet in the two places (Gen. 14:18–20; Ps. 110:4) in which his name is mentioned Melchizedek (in relation to his priesthood) is described as "living." This means that the priesthood of Melchizedek is permanent.

b. By contrast, there was a succession of Levitical priests. A priest might assume his priestly duties "as soon as the first signs of manhood made their appearance," but according to rabbinical tradition "he was not actually installed till he was twenty years of age."[14] The period of service for a priest might cover twenty to thirty years, but the end would come. The writer of

---

13. John Calvin, *Epistle to the Hebrews* (Grand Rapids: Eerdmans, 1949), p. 161. Also see Hans-Georg Link's article "Blessing" in *NIDNTT*, vol. 1, pp. 206–15.

14. Schürer, *History of the Jewish People*, vol. 1, div. 2, p. 215. Note also that the following passages imply that a priest was installed at age thirty and served until he reached the age of fifty: Num. 4:3, 23, 30, 35, 39, 43, 47; also see I Chron. 23:3. Num. 8:23–26 speaks of Levites twenty-five years of age. And I Chron. 23:24, 27; II Chron. 31:17; and Ezra 3:8 mention the twenty-year-old priest.

the epistle describes the priests as "men who die." Their term of office is limited.

"One might even say" is an expression that occurs only once in the New Testament. What is being said is rather unusual, because Levi, the great-grandchild of Abraham, is said to have paid Melchizedek a tithe. The use of the name *Levi* must be understood figuratively, for Levi himself did not collect tithes—his descendants did. Also Abraham, who paid the tenth to Melchizedek, functions as a representative; he represents the tribe of Levi that was appointed to collect the tenth.

From our perspective, the author's reasoning may be somewhat difficult to accept. And yet the Bible is replete with examples of representatives whose actions affected the lives of their descendants. For example, Joshua made a peace treaty with the Gibeonites that bound the Israelites for centuries (Josh. 9:15). In the same way, Abraham represented the Levitical priesthood, which was entrusted with the task of gathering the tithes of the people, and in this capacity Abraham offered the tithe to Melchizedek. The Levitical priesthood paid homage to the priesthood of Melchizedek.

Consider also the time when Melchizedek met Abraham. The meeting took place years before the birth of Isaac and more than a century before Levi was born. Abraham, then, represented Levi and his descendants. The author of Hebrews modestly writes, "Because when Melchizedek met Abraham, Levi was still in the body of his ancestor." The point is that Melchizedek's priesthood is to be preferred to that of Levi.

Doctrinal Considerations in 7:1–10

In this section (7:1–10) the author stresses the principle of life with reference to Melchizedek and to Levi. Melchizedek is portrayed as a person "without beginning of days or end of life" (7:3) and as one "who is declared to be living" (7:8). Because of his likeness to the Son of God and because he thus is a type of Christ, Melchizedek lives on scripturally although not historically. The author of Hebrews bases his theological observations on the scriptural references to Melchizedek.

The principle of life the author applies to Levi as well, but in a different way. The descendants of Levi entrusted with the task of collecting the tithe are subject to death; they are "men who die" (7:8). But Levi, as the tribal head, existed "in the body of his ancestor" (7:10) at the time Melchizedek met Abraham.

In Hebrews 7:1–10 the writer purposely avoids speaking about Christ. He places the greatness of Melchizedek in historical perspective in order to compare Christ with the king-priest in succeeding verses. The superiority of the Son of God, however, the author demonstrates by saying that Melchizedek is "like the Son of God" (7:3).

The focus, then, is on the greatness of Melchizedek, who surpassed the patriarch Abraham. To underscore the position of Abraham the author notes that the patriarch "had the promises" (7:6). Abraham represents the line of believers. For example, Abraham is listed first in the genealogy of Jesus recorded in Matthew 1. Abraham is the father of believers. Yet Melchizedek, says the writer of Hebrews, transcends him because Melchizedek received Abraham's tithe.

Paying the tithe to the priest of God Most High was Abraham's acknowledgment that God himself had given him the victory in the conflict and the plunder of the battlefield (Gen. 14). Thus he paid the tithe to God's representative.

The principle of tithing God instituted by law (for example, Num. 18:21) and enjoined the Israelites to comply. The tithe represents a tenth part of that which God gives the tither. In Old Testament times, the tithe sustained the priest, the Levite, and the services at the sanctuary. In the New Testament, Jesus teaches that "the worker deserves his wages" (Luke 10:7); Paul repeats this rule both indirectly and directly when he writes concerning the financial support of those who proclaim the gospel (I Cor. 9:14; I Tim. 5:17–18).[15] The New Testament, however, lacks specific injunctions about tithing.

Greek Words, Phrases, and Constructions in 7:4–10

Verse 4

θεωρεῖτε—this verb can be either the present indicative or the present imperative. In view of the verb's position in the sentence—it stands first and thus receives emphasis—the present imperative is preferred. The verb θεωρέω conveys the meaning of looking intently at someone or something for the purpose of intellectual study.

ἀκροθινίων—the genitive neuter plural is a compound from ἄκρος (the highest) and θίς, θινός (heap). For example, the flour at the top of the heap was considered the best part. The noun ἀκροθίνια means "first fruits."

πατριάρχης—this is a compound noun derived from πατριά (nation) and ἄρχω (I rule). The word appears four times in the New Testament and describes David (Acts 2:29), the twelve sons of Jacob (Acts 7:8, 9), and Abraham (Heb. 7:4). The author of Hebrews places the noun, preceded by the definite article, at the end of 7:4 for emphasis.

Verse 5

τὴν ἱερατείαν—this noun, translated "priestly office," occurs twice in the New Testament, here and in Luke 1:9. (Its synonym ἱερωσύνη appears four times in Hebrews [7:11, 12, 14 (variant reading), 24]). The word "expresses the actual service of the priest and not the office of priesthood."[16]

λαόν—in the Epistle to the Hebrews this noun generally refers to the church (see 2:17; 4:9; 10:30; 11:25; 13:12) and is qualified by the phrase *of God.* In 7:5, the author explains the word *people* by adding the note *that is, their brothers.*

Verse 6

δεδεκάτωκεν—the perfect active indicative from the verb δεκατόω (I collect tithes) reflects the permanence of the action—the lasting effect of the tribute to Melchizedek. The tense of this verb stresses the significance of the deed.

---

15. John Owen, *An Exposition of Hebrews,* 7 vols. in 4 (Evansville, Ind.: Sovereign Grace, 1960), vol. 3, p. 354.

16. B. F. Westcott, *Commentary on the Epistle to the Hebrews* (Grand Rapids: Eerdmans, 1950), p. 176.

εὐλόγηκεν—the perfect active indicative from the verb εὐλογέω (I bless) is translated as a simple past tense *he blessed.* The perfect tense, however, expresses the permanence of Melchizedek's blessing. Hebrews 7 features numerous verbs in the perfect tense (see vv. 6, 9, 11, 16, 20, 23, 26, 28).

Verse 8

ὧδε μὲν . . . ἐκεῖ δέ—unfortunately this precise balance in grammatical structure with *here* and *there* has been omitted for stylistic reasons in numerous translations.

ἀποθνῄσκοντες—the present tense of this active participle from the verb ἀποθνῄσκω (I die) has been chosen and placed deliberately before the noun ἄνθρωποι (men). The word order in the Greek is unique. Literally translated, 7:8 reads: "And here on the one hand tithes dying men receive, there on the other hand it is declared that he lives."

---

11 If perfection could have been attained through the Levitical priesthood (for on the basis of it the law was given to the people), why was there still need for another priest to come—one in the order of Melchizedek, not in the order of Aaron? 12 For when there is a change of the priesthood, there must also be a change of the law. 13 He of whom these things are said belonged to a different tribe, and no one from that tribe has ever served at the altar. 14 For it is clear that our Lord descended from Judah, and in regard to that tribe Moses said nothing about priests. 15 And what we have said is even more clear if another priest like Melchizedek appears, 16 one who has become a priest not on the basis of a regulation as to his ancestry but on the basis of the power of an indestructible life. 17 For it is declared:

"You are a priest forever,
in the order of Melchizedek."

18 The former regulation is set aside because it was weak and useless 19 (for the law made nothing perfect), and a better hope is introduced, by which we draw near to God.

B. Melchizedek's Superior Priesthood 7:11–19

1. Imperfection of the Levitical Priesthood 7:11–12

One of the recurring motifs in the Epistle to the Hebrews is that of God introducing a new order and thereby bringing the old order to an end. In 4:8 Joshua's concept of rest is completely overshadowed by God's rest. In 8:13 the first covenant is declared obsolete because the new covenant has taken its place. And in 7:11–12 the Levitical priesthood (which was established by divine law) has been superseded by the priesthood of Melchizedek; this necessitates a change in that law.

11. If perfection could have been attained through the Levitical priesthood (for on the basis of it the law was given to the people), why was there still need for another priest to come—one in the order of Melchizedek, not in the order of Aaron?

The old order changeth,
yielding place to new.

Thus wrote Alfred Tennyson about the death of King Arthur. These two lines, although from a different setting, capture the thought of Hebrews 7:11. The termination of the Levitical priesthood did not take place when Jesus died on the cross. The Aaronic order came to an end with the destruction of the temple in A.D. 70. The new order, however, was inaugurated with Jesus' death and existed simultaneously with the Levitical priesthood until Jerusalem was destroyed.

The Aaronic priesthood that had served the nation Israel since the exodus proved to be a failure in procuring salvation for God's people. That is, says the writer of the epistle, because "the blood of goats and bulls and the ashes of a heifer sprinkled on those who are ceremonially unclean sanctify" the people and cleanse them only on the outside (9:13). The priests could not cleanse the soul from sin. Inwardly the burden of guilt and the stain of sin remained. Only the blood of Christ, says the author, will "cleanse our consciences from acts that lead to death, so that we may serve the living God" (9:14).

The Levitical priesthood was established centuries after that of Melchizedek (Gen. 14:18–20). God had not forgotten the priestly order of Melchizedek, for through David he spoke of this order again in Psalm 110:4.

No one therefore could ever say that the order of Melchizedek was replaced by the Levitical priesthood. The fact that God himself in David's psalm declares that his Son (see Ps. 110:1 and Matt. 22:41–45) is priest forever in the order of Melchizedek is irrefutable evidence of the superiority of this priesthood (Ps. 110:4). By implication, contends the author, the Levitical priesthood did not attain perfection. It was meant to be provisional, for it was superseded by an entirely different order—that of Melchizedek.

Even though the author of Hebrews bases his argument on Scripture and puts it to his readers in the form of a question, the matter itself was a sensitive one for the Jewish religious structure of his day. Under the administration of the Levitical priesthood the law was given to the people. The law was then inseparably linked to the religious hierarchy of Israel. Anyone who dared to change the Aaronic priesthood was accused of tampering with the law of Moses. And anyone who was accused of speaking contrary to the law could be killed. In fact, Stephen was put to death because, so his accusers said, he spoke against the law (Acts 6:13). Paul was beaten by an angry mob that shouted, "This is the man who teaches all men everywhere against our people and our law and this place" (i.e., the temple; Acts 21:28).

God, however, did not give the people his law in order to displace the Aaronic priesthood; the priesthood itself was linked to the law. Without the priesthood there was no law! That is basic. The priests taught God's law and his promises. These men with all their imperfections were the mainstay of Israel's faith, for the very words of God were entrusted to them (Rom. 3:2).

12. For when there is a change of the priesthood, there must also be a change of the law.

In this sentence the first word *for* is significant because it tells us how the change will take place. In the preceding verse we are told that the Aaronic priesthood was unable to reach perfection. In 7:12 we learn that a change in the law must accompany the change in the priesthood.

We ought to look at the verse, however, through the eyes of a person of Jewish descent in the first century of the Christian era. The law of God was valid eternally and could not be terminated. The apocryphal literature of that era, as well as the rabbinical books of somewhat later date, speak of the lasting validity of the law.[17] Jesus, in a certain sense, reflected that sentiment when he said: "I tell you the truth, until heaven and earth disappear, not the smallest letter, not the least stroke of a pen, will by any means disappear from the Law until everything is accomplished" (Matt. 5:18). But Jesus fulfilled the law (Matt. 5:17), not to set it aside but to effect a change.

If then a change of the law had to occur, God himself would have to accomplish the change. And this is exactly what God did when, centuries after the law was given, he said through David, "The LORD has sworn and will not change his mind: 'You are a priest forever, in the order of Melchizedek' " (Ps. 110:4). God changed the law by appointing his Son high priest in another order and confirming the change with an oath (Heb. 7:28). With the coming of Christ the priestly order was transformed and transferred.[18] With his once-for-all sacrifice, Christ fulfilled the law and made the Levitical priesthood obsolete.

2. Inappropriate Service for Judah's Descendant
7:13–14

No one could ever object to Jesus' high priesthood in the order of Melchizedek by saying that the Levitical order had superseded the priesthood of Melchizedek. Psalm 110:4 is ample proof that God himself centuries later appointed his Son, by oath, in the priestly order of Melchizedek.

13. He of whom these things are said belonged to a different tribe, and no one from that tribe has ever served at the altar. 14. For it is clear that our Lord descended from Judah, and in regard to that tribe Moses said nothing about priests.

The Hebrews would have no difficulty accepting the messianic teaching of Psalm 110, with its distinct reference to the royal office of the Messiah. Also the Scriptures clearly taught them that the Christ was to come from David's family (II Sam. 7:12; Ps. 89:3–4; Jer. 23:5) and from the town of Bethlehem (Mic. 5:2; Matt. 2:6; and see John 7:42). And when the Gospels in written form began to circulate, the genealogies of Jesus recorded in Matthew 1:1–17 and Luke 3:23–38 showed his royal descent from the line of David.

To make Jesus, who belongs to the tribe of Judah, serve at the altar is contrary to the law. Remember that Uzziah king of Judah "entered the temple of the LORD to burn incense on the altar of incense" and was stricken

---

17. SB, vol. 1, pp. 244–46.

18. Ceslaus Spicq, *L'Épître aux Hébreux,* 3d ed., 2 vols. (Paris: Gabalda, 1953), vol. 2, p. 190.

with leprosy (II Chron. 26:16–21).[19] God had appointed the descendants of Levi to minister first at the tabernacle and later at the temple (Num. 1:50–53; 3:10, 38; 4:15, 19–20). Anyone from another tribe who approached the sanctuary would be put to death.

Psalm 110:4, in the context of the Epistle to the Hebrews, teaches two points. First, God overruled the law concerning the Levitical priesthood, because he as the maker of the law had the authority to change it. Second, belonging to the priestly order of Melchizedek is entirely different from being a descendant of any of the tribes of Israel.

Jesus descended from the tribe of Judah (Ps. 132:11; Isa. 11:1, 10; Luke 1:32; Rom. 1:3; Rev. 5:5). But his descent could attest only to his royalty. Moses said nothing about priests from the tribe of Judah, and therefore Jesus would trangress the Mosaic law if he assumed the priestly functions given to the descendants of Aaron.[20]

As a descendant of David, Jesus established not an earthly kingdom, but a spiritual kingdom. Similarly, Jesus did not inaugurate another priestly order to replace the Aaronic priesthood here on earth. Jesus is the "great high priest who has gone through the heavens" (Heb. 4:14). His priesthood is spiritual, heavenly, eternal.

3. Indestructible Life
7:15–19

Jesus' priesthood finds its origin not in the Levitical order but in the order of Melchizedek. The writer of the Epistle to the Hebrews purposely states that Jesus was confirmed as priest not by proving his descent from Levi but by demonstrating the indestructibility of his life.

15. And what we have said is even more clear if another priest like Melchizedek appears, 16. one who has become a priest not on the basis of a regulation as to his ancestry but on the basis of the power of an indestructible life. 17. For it is declared:

> **"You are a priest forever,**
> **in the order of Melchizedek."**

We who live in a different era and in another culture are unable to fathom the turmoil that must have taken place when Jew and Christian realized the Levitical priesthood had definitely ended in A.D. 70. After Jesus' ascension, Christians continued to attend the prayer services and festivals at the temple in Jerusalem (Acts 3:1; 20:16; 21:26). The end of an era, however, had come

---

19. Both David and Solomon, belonging to the tribe of Judah, offered sacrifices on several occasions (see II Sam. 6:13, 17–18; 24:25; I Kings 3:4; 8:62–64). But the sacrifices apparently were performed by the priests at the request of David or Solomon.

20. In an interesting study Philip Edgcumbe Hughes traces the descent of the Messiah from Levi and Judah from the teaching of the Dead Sea Sect; *The Testaments of the Twelve Patriarchs*; and the writings of Irenaeus, Origen, and Cyprian. See his *Hebrews*, pp. 260–63. Also consult R. H. Charles, *The Apocrypha and Pseudepigrapha of the Old Testament in English*, 2 vols. (Oxford: Clarendon, 1913), vol. 2, pp. 282–367. And see M. deJonge's article "Christian Influence in the Testaments of the Twelve Patriarchs" in *Studies on the Testaments of the Twelve Patriarchs*, ed. M. deJonge (Leiden: Brill, 1975), p. 222.

because Jesus by his death on the cross had fulfilled the law. Jesus had become the great high priest, but not in the Aaronic order; he appeared as a priest like Melchizedek.

The Christian community had to realize the significance of Jesus' sacrifice in relation to the Levitical priestly order. When the author told the Hebrews that he had much to say about Jesus' priesthood in the order of Melchizedek, he mentioned that his teaching was *hard* to explain (5:11). The time had come for believers of Jewish descent to understand the implications of Jesus' sacrifice on the cross: by his once-for-all sacrifice, Jesus had fulfilled the demands of the law and thus ended the need for sacrifices. The Levitical priesthood then was obsolete. Because the author's contemporaries were conditioned to think of the priesthood only in terms of the Levitical order, his emphasis on the priesthood of Christ was indeed "hard to explain" and no doubt hard to accept.

The Aaronic priestly order terminated because of Christ's sacrificial death; the priesthood of Christ, however, continues. We should note that the writer calls Jesus a "priest like Melchizedek"; he uses the term *priest,* not *high priest.* Concludes Geerhardus Vos: "Where a comparison with Aaron is expressed or implied, Christ is called *High Priest* (2:17; 4:14; 5:1; 7:26, 28; 8:13; 9:11–12). When the comparison is between Christ and the Levitical order, He is called priest."[21]

Christ's priesthood is different for two reasons.

a. Jesus did not have to base his priesthood on a genealogy that proved his descent from Aaron. He was like Melchizedek in that no ancestry is mentioned.

b. A priest in the Levitical order served on a temporary basis because he eventually died. By contrast, Jesus is a priest forever. That is, as an only priest—no other priests are serving with him—he lays claim to "the power of an indestructible life." A Levitical priest served because an external law gave him the privilege of service; Jesus serves because of an inward power that characterizes an endless life.[22]

The expression *indestructible life* is unique in the New Testament. Although Jesus offered himself as a sacrifice on the cross, his life did not end. He conquered death and lives forever, presently seated at God's right hand in heaven (Heb. 1:3). Through his unique sacrifice he fulfilled the responsibilities of the Aaronic priesthood, and through his endless life he assumes the priesthood in the order of Melchizedek.

Lest someone object to the priesthood of Christ, the writer once again quotes Psalm 110:4 and introduces the psalm citation with the words *for it is declared.* The implied agent is God himself. God has appointed Jesus high priest forever, in the order of Melchizedek. The author purposely repeats himself, for he has quoted and alluded to Psalm 110:4 a number of times

---

21. Vos, *Teaching,* p. 94.

22. "The 'law' is an outward restraint: the 'power' is an inward force," observes Westcott in *Hebrews,* p. 184.

(5:6, 10; 6:20; 7:11; also see 7:21, where he stresses the permanence of Jesus' priestly office by referring to the oath God swore).

18. The former regulation is set aside because it was weak and useless 19. (for the law made nothing perfect), and a better hope is introduced, by which we draw near to God.

This rather lengthy sentence falls into three parts that show balance and contrast. The first part has an explanatory clause that is placed within parentheses.

a. the former regulation—a better hope
b. is set aside—is introduced
c. because—by which
it was weak and useless—we draw near
(for the law made
nothing perfect)

a. The first part of the contrast consists of the adjective *former* and the noun *regulation.* The word *former* actually means "introductory" or "that which precedes." The implication is that the introductory regulation is temporary and will be succeeded by that which is permanent. The author of Hebrews continues to explain the significance of a tentative regulation that must yield to something that is abiding. The regulation was intended for the members of the priesthood; the hope (anchored in Jesus Christ, 6:19–20) is for every believer.

In the second part of this sentence, the adjective *better* emphasizes the quality of the hope. Although hope was present during the era of the Levitical priesthood, after the sacrifice of Christ hope has taken on a new dimension.[23] The author speaks of better hope in the sense of a true, living, new, and perfect hope. It is the hope that the believer has in Jesus Christ through his gospel. And that good news for the believer—forgiveness of sins, eternal life, and entrance to heaven—constitutes the better hope that surpasses "the former regulation."

b. The second part of the contrast concerns the action of both regulation and hope: the one is set aside, the other is introduced. For the writer to state categorically that the divine command about the Levitical priesthood was discarded and to add that "the law made nothing perfect" called for courage. A believer trained in Old Testament law considered the command about the priesthood in particular and the law in general sacrosanct.

But the author is able to write these words in full confidence. He indicates that the "former regulation" was introductory to something much better. In fact, the "better hope" has arrived and the time has come to put the substitute away. In his providence God instituted the Levitical priesthood. The priests offered animal sacrifices so the people might obtain remission of sin. These

23. The adjective *better* occurs eighteen times in the original Greek of the New Testament (twelve of which occur in the Epistle to the Hebrews—1:4, 6:9; 7:7, 19, 22; 8:6; 9:23; 10:34; 11:16, 35, 40; 12:24).

sacrifices by themselves could not cleanse the consciences of the believers (9:14) and were inadequate to atone for sin; they pointed to Christ. After Jesus as the Lamb of God brought the supreme sacrifice that "takes away the sin of the world" (John 1:29), the need for animal sacrifices offered by the priests was eliminated.

"A better hope is introduced." The author does not say to whom or to what we are introduced, but the context reveals that we are brought into the presence of Jesus our high priest. The believer no longer needs to approach God through the services of a mortal priest. He can go directly to Jesus Christ, for through him he has direct access to the throne of grace (4:14–16). His hope, then, is centered in Jesus Christ, his Savior and Lord.

c. The third element in the contrast gives the cause and the means. The Levitical priesthood was discarded *because* the regulation "was weak and useless"; and *by* a better hope we have access to God.

We nowhere read that the Levitical priesthood and the accompanying regulation were of no value. They had their rightful place in the era prior to the coming of Christ. However, the command with its bearing on the priesthood was "weak and useless." It was incapable of removing the curse God had pronounced upon the human race; it could not effect eternal salvation for the believer. David testified to the inadequacy of animal sacrifices when he confessed his sin to God: "You do not delight in sacrifice, or I would bring it; you do not take pleasure in burnt offerings" (Ps. 51:16). The command was external and pertained to the duties performed by the priests; it was unable, however, to lead the believer into the presence of God.

What the law could not do, for it made nothing perfect (Rom. 8:3), Jesus did by his perfect sacrifice on the cross: he opened the way to God. In the capacity of high priest Jesus, by entering the Most Holy Place, reconciled God and man. Therefore the believer has full communion with God.

Doctrinal Considerations in 7:11–19

In the desert of Sinai God delivered the Ten Commandments to the Israelites to make them into "a kingdom of priests and a holy nation" (Exod. 19:6; also see I Peter 2:9). Although the people affirmed the objective to live obediently before God ("We will do everything the LORD has said," Exod. 19:8; 24:3), they never attained perfection. The Israelites were sinners whose transgression had to be removed.

"Israel, in its sinful life, could not exist before God; it needed atonement provided by another life. Yet the lives of the sacrificial animals could not accomplish this atonement."[24] Also the priesthood, instituted to lead the Israelites in a life of consecration and perfection, failed. That God later declared on oath the inauguration of a priest in the order of Melchizedek (Ps. 110:4) proved the weakness of the Aaronic priesthood.

---

24. S. G. DeGraaf, *Promise and Deliverance,* trans. H. Evan Runner and Elisabeth Wichers Runner, 3 vols. (Saint Catharines: Paideia, 1977), vol. 1, p. 301.

God himself imposed his law on the Israelites. As lawgiver he stood above the commandments and ordinances he had enacted. Thus at the proper time he could supplant a particular law—the one pertaining to the Levitical priesthood—and institute a new order. The priesthood in the order of Melchizedek differed radically from that of Aaron. It was not based on law, although it was confirmed by oath (Ps. 110:4). Rather it is a *spiritual* priesthood, fulfilled in Jesus Christ and settled in heaven (Heb. 4:14; 6:20; 7:26; 8:1; 9:11; 10:21).

Jesus' priesthood is distinct from the priestly order of Levi's descendants. His priesthood coincides with his kingship (Ps. 110:1–2) and therefore is *royal.* Jesus is king and priest at the same time. Aaron and his heirs could be only priests.

The brevity of life of the priests in the order of Aaron testified to the passing character of the Levitical office. The priestly genealogies were silent witnesses to the transitory nature of the priesthood. By contrast, the priesthood of Jesus is eternal.[25]

Greek Words, Phrases, and Constructions in 7:11–19

Verse 11

τελείωσις—the ending -σις reveals a process of the act of reaching perfection. The noun stems from the verb τελειόω (I accomplish, make perfect).

ὁ λαός—the definite article with the noun conveys the idea that the law was given, via the priesthood, to *all* the people of God.

νενομοθέτηται—the perfect passive, third person singular, of the verb νομοθετέω (I enact laws) marks the time when the law was given and expresses the lasting significance of the event.

ἕτερον—of the five times the author uses this adjective, three refer to Jesus' priesthood (7:11, 13, 15). The author stresses the dissimilarity of Christ's priestly office and the Levitical priesthood.

Verse 12

νόμου—a change in the priesthood necessitated a change in the law. Jesus became high priest not in the Levitical order (on the basis of law), but in the τάξις (order) of Melchizedek.

μετάθεσις—together with the present passive participle μετατιθεμένης (genitive absolute) this noun with its ending -σις denotes a process of change.

Verse 13

μετέσχηκεν—the perfect active, third person singular of the verb μετέχω (I partake) directs attention to a point in time in which Jesus became a descendant of Judah. The perfect signifies continuous validity; the active voice shows that Jesus voluntarily became man.

προσέσχηκεν—the author has a penchant for choosing cognate expressions. This verb, from προσέχω (I apply myself to), demands a supplied ἑαυτόν (himself) and a dative for the object (altar).

---

25. Westcott, *Hebrews,* p. 183.

Verse 14

πρόδηλον—this adjective from πρό (openly) and δῆλος (evident) is closely related to κατάδηλος (thoroughly evident) in verse 15.

ἀνατέταλκεν—the perfect active, third person singular, of ἀνατέλλω (I rise, descend from) is related to ἀνατολή in Luke 1:78, where the reference to the rising of the sun is a metaphor of the Messiah's coming.

Verse 16

ἐντολῆς σαρκίνης—the adjective σαρκίνης modifying the noun *commandment* points to the lineage that a priest had to prove before he could assume office.

γέγονεν—from the verb γίνομαι (I become), the perfect active demonstrates the endless duration of Christ's priesthood.

Verse 18

ἀθέτησις—this noun appears also in 9:26. It derives from the privative ἀ (not) and the verb τίθημι (I place). With the ending -σις it denotes a process of annulling a commandment. Also, it is a juridical term.

Verse 19

ἐπεισαγωγή—this compound noun consists of ἐπί (toward), εἰς (into), and ἀγωγή (leading). It means "an introduction." The word occurs only in this verse in the entire New Testament.

---

20 And it was not without an oath! Others became priests without any oath, 21 but he
became a priest with an oath when God said to him:

"The Lord has sworn
 and will not change his mind:
'You are a priest forever.' "

22 Because of this oath, Jesus has become the guarantee of a better covenant.
23 Now there have been many of those priests, since death prevented them from continuing
in office; 24 but because Jesus lives forever, he has a permanent priesthood. 25 Therefore
he is able to save completely those who come to God through him, because he always lives to
intercede for them.
26 Such a high priest meets our need—one who is holy, blameless, pure, set apart from
sinners, exalted above the heavens. 27 Unlike the other high priests, he does not need to
offer sacrifices day after day, first for his own sins, and then for the sins of the people. He
sacrificed for their sins once for all when he offered himself. 28 For the law appoints as
high priests men who are weak; but the oath, which came after the law, appointed the Son,
who has been made perfect forever.

C. Christ's Superior Priesthood 7:20–28

1. By Oath 7:20–22

The Aaronic priesthood was instituted by divine law; Christ's priesthood, by divine oath. A law can be annulled; an oath lasts forever.

True to form, the author first introduces a new concept with a simple word or phrase, then returns to it later to give a complete explanation. In 7:22 he mentions the word *covenant*; in the next two chapters he explains the doctrine of the covenant to the fullest extent.

20. And it was not without an oath! Others become priests without any oath, 21. but he became priest with an oath when God said to him:

> **"The Lord has sworn**
> **and will not change his mind:**
> **'You are a priest forever.' "**

22. Because of this oath, Jesus has become the guarantee of a better covenant.

The first word *and* is significant. It provides additional proof of the superiority of Christ's priesthood. The proof comes from the first part of Psalm 110:4. The author of the epistle quotes and alludes to this psalm citation a number of times (5:6, 10; 6:20; 7:11, 17) to call attention to the priesthood of Christ in the order of Melchizedek.

How did Christ become a priest? Psalm 110:4 unequivocally states that God swore an oath when he appointed Christ. This is unique. God told Moses to consecrate Aaron and his sons to the priesthood and stipulated, "The priesthood is theirs by a lasting ordinance" (Exod. 29:9). But God did not swear an oath; he only administered an ordinance. No law was enacted when God appointed Christ to the priesthood of Melchizedek. Instead God swore an oath.

By human standards Christ, not God, should have sworn the oath of office. For example, when a government official is about to assume his task, he is sworn in. The appointee declares on oath that he will execute his duties to the best of his ability in accordance with the laws of the land.

In this instance, however, God purposely takes the initiative and swears an oath. He confirms his promise to Abraham by swearing an oath to guarantee that his purpose does not change (Gen. 22:16; Heb. 6:13). A second time, when God installs his Son as priest in Melchizedek's order, he swears an oath to vouch for the unalterable nature of the appointment. When God's people confess sin, God changes his mind (see for example Exod. 32:14). But when God swears an oath, his purpose is unchangeable. Because he swore an oath when he instituted Christ's priesthood, that priesthood is eternal.

What is the purpose of confirming Christ's priesthood with an oath? "Because of this oath," says the writer, "Jesus has become the guarantee of a better covenant." Two concepts the author introduces. One is embodied in the word *guarantee* (which appears once in the entire New Testament) and the other in the word *covenant* (an expression that recurs seventeen times in the epistle).

Even though the term *guarantee* is unique, its synonym *mediate* is not (Gal. 3:19–20; I Tim. 2:5; Heb. 8:6; 9:15; 12:24). These two words in the epistle are interchangeable, and the writer uses them to stress God's absolute reliability in fulfilling the covenant he has made with his people. God has appointed his Son not merely to be the guarantor who represents man to God. In addition, Jesus is the believer's guarantee that all God's promises will be fulfilled. That is, no promise God has made to us can ever be broken, for Jesus gives the assurance that his perfection will be our perfection,[26] our bodies "will be like his glorious body" (Phil. 3:21), and his ascension guarantees our entrance into heaven (John 14:3).

Note that the author uses the name *Jesus* purposely. This name summarizes the work of our Savior—he saves "his people from their sins" (Matt. 1:21). The writer places the name last in the sentence (in the Greek) to give it full emphasis.

The second concept that the author introduces is contained in the noun *covenant,* qualified by the adjective *better.* In context the adjective actually means "eternal." The covenant God makes with his people is an agreement that has two parties, promises, and a condition. The parties are God and his people. The promises are: "I will put my laws in their minds and write them on their hearts," says God, "I will be their God, and they will be my people" (Jer. 31:33; Heb. 8:10). And the condition is faith.

Why is this covenant called "better"? In the old covenant that God made with the Israelites at Mount Sinai, Moses acted as mediator between God and his people. But Moses could never guarantee the covenant. In the new covenant Jesus is both mediator and guarantor because of his atoning work. Jesus guarantees the fullness of God's covenant with us.

> To Thee, O Lord, alone is due
> All glory and renown;
> Aught to ourselves we dare not take,
> Or rob Thee of Thy crown.
> Thou wast Thyself our Surety
> In God's redemption plan
> In Thee His grace was given us,
> Long ere the world began.
> —Augustus M. Toplady
> (Revision by Dewey Westra)

---

2. For Eternity
7:23–25

In this passage, the author states an additional reason that Jesus' priesthood differs from that of Aaron: the Levitical priesthood attests to its transitoriness by the deaths of those who held the priestly office; Jesus, who is eternal, fills an everlasting office as intercessor for "those who come to God."

23. Now there have been many of those priests, since death prevented them from continuing in office; 24. but because Jesus lives forever, he

---

26. Oswald Becker, *NIDNTT,* vol. 1, p. 372. Also see Herbert Preisker, *TDNT,* vol. 2, p. 329.

has a permanent priesthood. 25. Therefore he is able to save completely those who come to God through him, because he always lives to intercede for them.

These verses form one lengthy sentence in the Greek text. They convey three basic ideas that can be described in the terms *problem* (v. 23), *person* (v. 24), and *purpose* (v. 25).

a. The problem relates to the length of the priest's term in office. By law, the Aaronic priesthood would "continue for all generations to come" (Exod. 40:15), but in reality the priestly office was temporal. Every priest was subject to death, and therefore a seemingly endless succession of priests emerged. Death determined the extent of the high priest's service, for death is no respecter of persons. The high priest was powerless in the face of death.

A somewhat literal translation of the first part of this verse reads, "and they that have become priests are many."[27] The list of names of high priests who served for long or short periods of time is extensive,[28] but the concluding comment for every one of them is this: "and he died."

b. Next, the author contrasts the Levitical priesthood with the person of Jesus. What a contrast when we look at Jesus! The priests were many; Jesus is the only priest. Their term of office was limited by death; "Jesus lives forever." The Aaronic high priest was overcome by death; Jesus conquered death.

The writer of Hebrews has chosen the name *Jesus* to illuminate the earthly life of our Lord. This name describes his birth, ministry, suffering, death, resurrection, and ascension. However, Jesus is no longer a citizen of this earth; his residence is in heaven, where he abides forever. Because of his eternity, Jesus' high priesthood is unchangeable. That is, no one can terminate his priestly office. Death is conquered. And God has sworn an oath that his Son will serve as priest forever in the order of Melchizedek. No one can take Jesus' place, for he is the one and only high priest.

c. What purpose does Jesus' permanent priesthood serve? In fact, it serves many purposes. First, "he is able to save completely those who come to God through him." Jesus is a Savior who does his work completely, fully, and to perfection.[29] He sets man free from the curse of sin and accomplishes restoration between God and man; through Jesus man is united with his God (John 17:21).

Second, Jesus as eternal high priest lives not for himself, but for the people who look to him for help (2:17–18; 4:14–16). He is their Mediator, truly God and truly man. Without ceasing he pleads for us; standing between

---

27. The context of 7:23 calls for a translation in the past tense. This is exactly what most translators have used. The exception is the NEB: "Those other priests are appointed in numerous succession, because they are prevented by death from continuing in office."

28. See Josephus, *Antiquities* 20.10 (LCL).

29. Numerous translators understand the first clause of 7:25 to refer to time rather than to extent or degree. Thus GNB, NASB, NAB, RSV, and *Moffatt* have the reading "he is able to save *forever*" (with individual variations; italics added).

God and man, he constantly intercedes for those who come to God in prayer (Rom. 8:34; Heb. 9:24). God grants us everything we need for the furtherance of his name, his kingdom, and his will. He answers our prayers for daily sustenance, remission of sin, and protection from the evil one.

Third, Jesus taught: "No one comes to the Father except through me" (John 14:6). The writer of Hebrews repeats this very thought and reminds his readers that prayers to God must be offered in the name of Jesus.

Fourth, knowing that Jesus is always praying for us in heaven, we long to be with him. We have the assurance that as he lives eternally before God so shall we live forever with him. Presently we come to God in prayer, but at the end of our earthly stay he will take us home to be with him eternally.

Doctrinal Considerations in 7:20–25

When God swears an oath he establishes the absolute dependability and trustworthiness of his word. His oath is somewhat different from that of man. Man swears by God to testify of his innocence, to declare his intention to keep a vow, and to speak the truth before a court of law. God swears by himself—because there is no one greater by whom he can swear—to give further substance to his promise (with Abraham, Gen. 22:16), to his covenant (with Israel's forefathers, Deut. 4:31), and to his confirmation of his Son's priesthood (Ps. 110:4). When God adds an oath to what he has said, his word is unalterable.

Christ's priesthood is unchangeable because it is not bound to a law. The Levitical priesthood instituted by law was open to transgression and violation. Christ's priesthood in the order of Melchizedek was confirmed by oath and therefore is inviolable.[30]

When the author of the Epistle to the Hebrews mentions the concept *salvation,* he always links it directly to the atoning work of Jesus. Thus the salvation Christ offers the believers is eternal (5:9); it is described as great (2:3); and its author has been made "perfect through suffering" (2:10).

Greek Words, Phrases, and Constructions in 7:20–25

Verse 20

ὁρκωμοσίας—this combination of ὅρκος (oath) and ὄμνυμι (I swear) occurs four times in the New Testament (Heb. 7:20 [twice], 21, 28). In Hebrews 6:16 the author writes the noun and the verb separately (see Luke 1:73; Acts 2:30; James 5:12). The preposition (adverb) χωρίς governs the genitive case.

οἱ μέν—this construction balanced by ὁ δέ in the next verse expresses contrast: priests over against Jesus. The author employs this device three times (7:18–19; 7:20–21; and 7:23–24).

εἰσὶν . . . γεγονότες—the perfect middle participle of γίνομαι (I become) combined with a form of the verb *to be*, εἰσὶν (present active), constitutes a periphrastic construction. See also 7:23.

---

30. Walther Günther, *NIDNTT,* vol. 3, p. 585.

Verse 22

διαθήκης—this noun derived from the verb διατίθημι (I decree) appears seventeen times in Hebrews out of a total of thirty-three times in the New Testament. The author of Hebrews develops the doctrine of the covenant chiefly in chapters 8 and 9.

ἔγγυος—only in this verse does ἔγγυος occur in the New Testament. See also the Septuagint, where it appears three times (Sir. 29:15, 16; II Macc. 10:28). It conveys the idea of guarantor and is a synonym of μεσίτης (mediator).

Verse 23

διά—this preposition followed by the neuter article τό and the present passive infinitive κωλύεσθαι (to be hindered) expresses the reason that the number of priests increased: they were prevented from continual service by death (θανάτῳ).

παραμένειν—the complementary infinitive, present active, of παραμένω (I continue in office). This compound verb referring to priests on earth is set in opposition to the simple present active verb μένειν (to remain) referring to Jesus (v. 24).

Verse 24

ἀπαράβατον—as a verbal adjective the word expresses a passive idea: "it cannot be transgressed." This compound finds its origin in ἀ (not), παρά (beyond), and βαίνω (I go, walk, step).

Verse 25

ζῶν—the present active participle from ζάω (I live) may denote cause: because he lives.

ἐντυγχάνειν—Jesus lives for the purpose of making intercession. The word occurs only five times in the New Testament (Acts 25:24; Rom. 8:27, 34; 11:2; Heb. 7:25) but frequently in other sources. The basic meaning of the verb is "to approach someone with a petition." In this verse the present active infinitive is introduced by εἰς τό.

---

3. In Sacrifice
7:26–27

After explaining the quotation from Psalm 110:4, the author of Hebrews presents a comprehensive summary. He gives a full description of our only high priest Jesus Christ and compares his perfect sacrifice with the daily sacrifices offered by the Levitical priests. Jesus' death on the cross was a once-for-all event.

26. Such a high priest meets our need—one who is holy, blameless, pure, set apart from sinners, exalted above the heavens.

The writer has arrived at a peak in his discussion of Christ's priesthood. He looks back at the magnificence of Jesus' position and describes his greatness in the one word *such.* He stands in awe of the magnitude of the work of salvation performed by our heavenly high priest. And he looks forward.

The author diverts his attention to the needs of the believers on earth and includes himself in the expression *our need.* He realizes that Jesus is not a distant high priest, enthroned in heaven, far removed from the daily needs of his people. Jesus is eminently suited to be our high priest.

Why is Jesus qualified to meet our needs? He is sinless. With respect to his character, he is holy, blameless, and pure. And regarding his status, he is separated from sinners and exalted above the heavens.

The author lists five characteristics.

a. *Holy.* Jesus is holy. That means he is like God and in every aspect without sin.[31] He is incomparably pure and as God's high priest he fulfills the will of God flawlessly. His chief desire is to glorify God's name and to extend God's rule.

b. *Blameless.* The adjective *holy* concerns the inner disposition of Jesus; the word *blameless* relates to his external life. Note the implied contrast between Jesus, who is blameless, and the Aaronic high priests, tainted by sins, who were blameworthy. Aaron had to bring a "sin offering to make atonement for himself and his household" (Lev. 16:11) before he could function as a high priest for the people of Israel. Jesus, however, is completely sinless and therefore free from guilt and blame.

c. *Pure.* The environment of sin has a way of touching everyone entering that environment. Sin defiles the person it touches. Although Jesus lived on earth and ministered to sinful people, he himself remained undefiled. He may be compared with a physician who works among the sick at the time of an epidemic, but who is immune. Jesus is unstained by sin.

d. *Set apart.* The reason that Jesus remains untouched by sin lies in the act of separation. Jesus has been separated from sinners by God. Although he fully shares our humanity, he does not participate in our sin. He is therefore different. Although he was called a friend of sinners (Matt. 11:19), he himself remained without sin. I think that interpreting the phrase *set apart from sinners* to refer only to the ascension of Jesus is one-sided.[32] As our heavenly high priest Jesus sympathizes with us in our weaknesses, because he has been tempted just as we are tempted. He knows our problems, because he is one of us—except that he is sinless (2:14; 4:14–15).

e. *Exalted.* Already in Hebrews 1:3, the author referred to Jesus' exaltation by depicting him seated "at the right hand of the Majesty in heaven." In 7:26 the writer describes the position of Christ in comparable terms. He says that Jesus has been "raised to greater heights than the heavens."[33] Paul also speaks of Christ's exaltation: "He who descended is the very one who

---

31. Horst Seebass, *NIDNTT,* vol. 2, p. 238. Also see Friedrich Hauck, *TDNT,* vol. 5, p. 492.

32. For example, Bengel in his *Gnomon,* vol. 4, p. 409, explains the phrase in one short sentence: "He was separated when he left the world." From the Babylonian Talmud we learn that the high priest would separate himself from his house for seven days before the Day of Atonement and take up residence in one of the rooms of the temple. See Yoma 1:1, Seder Moed, *Talmud,* vol. 3. And see SB, vol. 3, p. 696.

33. Bauer, p. 850.

ascended higher than all the heavens" (Eph. 4:10). The meaning is clear: Jesus occupies the highest position imaginable.

27. Unlike the other high priests, he does not need to offer sacrifices day after day, first for his own sins, and then for the sins of the people. He sacrificed for their sins once for all when he offered himself.

Sometimes we have to make a trite remark to convey a fundamental truth. Thus we say that verse 27 follows verse 26 in order to point out that 7:26 is introductory to the next verse. This simple fact is frequently overlooked, and explanations of 7:27a are varied.

For example, one explanation is that the phrase *day after day* means "year after year." That is, once a year on the Day of Atonement the high priest enters the Most Holy Place. Therefore the phrase refers to the annual sacrifices on that particular day. However, the writer is fully acquainted with the Mosaic stipulations, for he indirectly mentions the Day of Atonement in 9:7, 25 and 10:1, 3. Why would he write "day after day" when in fact he meant once a year?

Another explanation relates the phrase *day after day* to the daily grain offering and burnt sacrifice offered by Aaron and his sons (Lev. 6:14–16; Exod. 29:38–42; Num. 28:3–8). Although the explanation has merit, difficulties surround this interpretation.[34]

A third possibility is to interpret the phrase as a reference to the daily offerings in general and to the Day of Atonement in particular.[35] This explanation is all-inclusive and, in a sense, moves from the lesser sacrifices to the greater sacrifice on the Day of Atonement.

The contrast in 7:27 is between Jesus and the Aaronic high priest, and because of the introductory verse (26) the emphasis falls on the negative: Jesus "does not need to offer sacrifices day after day." Our heavenly high priest is completely different; he is sinless, blameless, spotless. He has no need to offer a sacrifice for himself either on a daily or an annual basis. He is set apart from sinners. He is holy.

High priests appointed to represent sinful people were themselves defiled by sin. Coming before God, they were fully conscious of their own sins which in effect nullified their efforts to serve God. To become efficient, they had to offer animal sacrifices that removed their own sins. Then they brought sacrifices to God for the sins of the people. God told them that the blood of an animal atoned for sin. They had to admit that the constant repetition of these offerings was a clear indication that these sacrifices could not cope with the enormity of sin. The Aaronic priesthood displayed the marks of temporality and basic ineffectiveness. It had to be replaced by a priest who is eternal and by an offering that is effective.

---

34. The writers of SB, vol. 3, p. 698, point out that the order of presenting the offerings was first for the sins of the high priest and then for the sins of the people of Israel (Lev. 16:6–19; Heb. 7:27). According to the practice that prevailed in later years, the burnt offering for the sins of the people came first and the grain offering for the high priest last.

35. Hughes, *Hebrews,* p. 277.

Jesus, the Savior of his people, "sacrificed for their sins once for all when he offered himself." He offered himself because God asked him to make this supreme sacrifice and thus atone for the sins of his people. God told the Israelites to sacrifice animals as substitutes; he gave his Son as *the* substitute. God forbade the people of Israel the practice of offering human beings to idols (Lev. 18:21; 20:2–5; II Kings 17:17, 19; Ezek. 20:31); he himself offered his only Son (John 3:16).

Jesus voluntarily died on the cross and by his death presented himself as the once-for-all sacrifice. The expression *once for all* reveals that the Levitical system has come to an end. The author of Hebrews introduces this thought and explains the details in a subsequent chapter.

4. To Perfection
7:28

The time has come for a concluding statement. The writer summarizes his teaching on the eternal priesthood of Jesus before he begins a new topic: the covenant.

28. For the law appoints as high priests men who are weak; but the oath, which came after the law, appointed the Son, who has been made perfect forever.

The Epistle to the Hebrews is an epistle of contrasts. And this verse is no exception. Note the structure:

For—but
the law appoints—the oath appointed
as high priests men—the Son
who are weak—who has been made perfect forever

The law given by God to Moses has been compared with the oath God swore centuries later. In both instances—the giving of the law and the swearing of the oath—God appoints. First he appoints a high priest; then he appoints the Son. The institution of the priesthood took place in the early part of the forty-year period in the wilderness. The oath was given in a subsequent century (Ps. 110:4).

The law appoints "as high priests men who are weak." The term *weak* does not refer to physical ailments, for Jesus shared our weaknesses when he was on earth (4:15). Rather, it relates to our sinful condition and is therefore synonymous with sin. God appoints high priests who are weak because of their sinful state. He knew that these men would succumb to sin and reveal their moral weakness.

The writer has chosen the term *weak* perhaps purposely to make a distinction between sin committed in weakness and sin perpetuated deliberately. A high priest who sinned intentionally could not remain in office. For premeditated and willful sin, God does not provide atonement (Heb. 9:7).

God placed sinful high priests in office by law; he appointed his Son as high priest by oath. The superiority of the Son to the Aaronic high priests the writer of Hebrews succinctly demonstrates, for the swearing of the oath was of greater importance than the giving of the law. A law can be repealed; an oath stays forever. The Son is not subject to weakness or change, because he "has been made perfect forever."

The expression *Son* reminds us of chapter 1, where the author teaches the Son's superiority to creation, including the angels (1:2, 3, 5, 8; also see 3:6; 4:14; 7:3). The Son is eternal; high priests are mortal and therefore temporal. The Son is sinless and consequently perfect; high priests are sinners and in need of redemption. The Son because of his suffering on the cross has been made perfect (2:10). Because of this perfection "he is able to save completely those who come to God through him" (7:25).

Doctrinal Considerations in 7:26–28

Jesus our high priest is holy. This adjective *holy* in the original Greek appears only eight times in the New Testament (Acts 2:27; 13:34–35; I Tim. 2:8; Titus 1:8; Heb. 7:26; Rev. 15:4; 16:5); five are quotations from and allusions to the Old Testament. The word is unique, and for this reason the author of Hebrews uses it to portray the holiness of Jesus. When it is applied to men—for example, in Titus 1:8 Paul writes that among other requirements an elder must be holy—the term implies a participation in Jesus' holiness.[36]

Jesus has taken a place that is higher than the heavens. Before coming to earth, Christ was in heaven. But after his atoning work was completed and he ascended to heaven, he was "exalted above the heavens." The idea expressed by the author is set forth in a comparative way: Christ is not in heaven but in a place that is even higher than the heavens.

The author of Hebrews teaches that Jesus is priest and at the same time became sacrifice. Christ in his once-for-all offering of himself on the cross fulfilled the responsibility of the priesthood of Aaron (9:25–26). By his death he put an end to the offerings for the sins of the people (7:27; 9:12; 10:10, 18). By oath appointed, Jesus serves as high priest forever in the order of Melchizedek.

The Aaronic high priest could never present a genuine sacrifice as requested by God. A genuine sacrifice could be brought only by Jesus, who had the power to defeat death (2:15; 9:27–28) and the ability to show perfect obedience (5:8–10).

Greek Words, Phrases, and Constructions in 7:26–28

Verse 26

ὅσιος—this adjective, related to the noun ὁσιότης (devoutness) and the adverb ὁσίως (in a holy manner), conveys the idea of partaking of God's holiness.

ἀμίαντος—derived from the privative ἀ (not) and the verb μιαίνω (I stain; defile), this verbal adjective has a passive connotation in the sense of "he cannot be defiled." The word denotes moral purity, especially with reference to the high priest (see

36. Westcott understands the concept *holy* as "a particular moral position." See his *Hebrews*, p. 194.

also Heb. 13:4, where the word is used in the context of marriage). Undefiled, according to John Albert Bengel, means to derive "*no stain* from other *men*."[37]

κεχωρισμένος . . . γενόμενος—the first participle is the perfect passive from χωρίζω (I separate); the second is the aorist middle from γίνομαι (I become). The perfect tense denotes the lasting state which delineates a difference between Christ and man. The use of the aorist tense implies that there was a time in which Jesus was not exalted above the heavens.

Verse 27

ἀναφέρειν—the present active infinitive is a compound of ἀνά (up; again) and φέρω (I bring). The verb is paralleled by προσφέρω (I offer), which occurs nineteen times in Hebrews; ἀναφέρω appears four times. In 9:28 both verbs are used. Westcott makes the following distinction: "From these usages [in the Septuagint] it appears that in ἀναφέρειν (*to offer up*) we have mainly the notion of an offering made to God and placed upon His altar, in προσφέρειν (*to offer*) that of an offering brought to God. In the former the thought of the destination of the offering prevails: in the latter that of the offerer in his relation to God."[38]

Verse 28

τῆς μετὰ τὸν νόμον—the definite article τῆς specifies the oath God swore: after the law was given. The author of Hebrews places the word of the oathswearing (ὁ λόγος) over against the law (ὁ νόμος). God gave the Israelites his law in the days of Moses; he swore an oath in the time of David (Ps. 110:4).

τετελειωμένον—this perfect passive participle from the verb τελειόω (I complete) communicates the idea of permanence. The passive voice intimates that God is the agent. The Son has been made "perfect through suffering" (2:10). The writer of Hebrews purposely uses the term υἱόν (son) without the definite article to express the absolute significance of Jesus' sonship. Only Jesus is the Son of God, "made perfect forever."

Summary of Chapter 7

Melchizedek, mentioned only twice in the entire Old Testament (Gen. 14:18; Ps. 110:4), is the focus of attention in the first part of Hebrews 7. The author of the epistle demonstrates his theological skills as he explains the priesthood of Christ in the order of Melchizedek.

From a modern point of view the writer's arguments appear to be somewhat labored. He seems to be reading more into the Old Testament passages that mention Melchizedek than the passages actually say. But the original readers were Hebrews. They believed that the divinely instituted Levitical priesthood was inviolable. They knew that the priesthood of Aaron had to be perpetual, because God himself had ordained the priesthood by law.

The author of Hebrews counters the objections of readers of the Old

---

37. Bengel, *Gnomon,* vol. 4, p. 409. Italics his.

38. Westcott, *Hebrews,* p. 197. Also consult Konrad Weiss, *TNDT,* vol. 9, pp. 61, 66.

Testament Scriptures by discussing the differences between the Aaronic priesthood and the superior order of Melchizedek. These differences consist of the absence of a genealogy for Melchizedek; the homage and tithe Abraham paid Melchizedek; and the confirmation of Melchizedek's priesthood by divine oath centuries after the Levitical priesthood was established by law.

The evidence that shows God's design in terminating the temporal priesthood of Aaron and inaugurating the eternal priesthood of Melchizedek is irrefutable. Jesus, to whom the author indirectly referred and who at last is mentioned by name, has become high priest in Melchizedek's order and is a "guarantee of a better covenant" (7:22).

Already in earlier passages the author describes the characteristics of the high priest (2:17–18; 4:14–15; 5:1–5). In 7:26–28 the writer centers his explanation of the heavenly high priest on holiness, sinlessness, sacrifice, and perfection. The theme of Jesus' perfection, introduced in 2:10 and implied in 7:11, culminates in the words: "the Son . . . has been made perfect forever."

8

Jesus: High Priest and Sacrifice, *part 1*

8:1–13

Outline

8:1–2	A. The Heavenly Sanctuary
	B. Jesus the Mediator
8:3	1. High Priest
8:4–6	2. Service
8:7–13	C. God's New Covenant

8 1 The point of what we are saying is this: We do have such a high priest, who sat down at the right hand of the throne of the Majesty in heaven, 2 and who serves in the sanctuary, the true tabernacle set up by the Lord, not by man.

A. The Heavenly Sanctuary
8:1–2

The claims to Jesus' priesthood the author expounded in chapter 7. In Hebrews 8, he explains the task of the high priest, Jesus Christ, and alludes to Psalm 110:1.

1. The point of what we are saying is this: We do have such a high priest, who sat down at the right hand of the throne of the Majesty in heaven, 2. and who serves in the sanctuary, the true tabernacle set up by the Lord, not by man.

The preceding chapter delineates the surpassing excellence of Christ's priesthood in the order of Melchizedek. The author of Hebrews provides the readers with a lucid exposition of Psalm 110:4. However, he does not want them to lose sight of the first verse of that psalm. That verse portrays Jesus as king. Jesus, therefore, is the king-priest, as Psalm 110 clearly teaches. Although the writer has stressed the importance of Jesus' priesthood in the Melchizedekian order, he desires his readers to recognize Jesus' kingship, too. Hence, he writes the introductory clause, "the point of what we are saying is this," and asserts that our high priest sat down at the right hand of God and serves in the true tabernacle.[1]

In the introduction of the Epistle to the Hebrews the author implicitly mentions the priesthood and the kingship of the Son (1:3; also see 1:13). After completing his priestly duties, Jesus "sat down at the right hand of the Majesty in heaven." In Hebrews 10:12 and 12:2 the writer returns to this same theme: Jesus is priest and king.

In typical Hebraic form, the writer's choice of the phrase *of the Majesty in*

---

1. Most translations use the word *point* (with variations) in Heb. 8:1. Thus RV and ASV have "chief point"; the NAB, NASB, NEB, NKJV, MLB, and R. C. H. Lenski have "main point"; JB has "great point"; GNB, "whole point"; and NIV, *Moffatt*, and RSV simply "point." However, the KJV features the term *the sum*; and *Phillips*, "to sum up."

heaven is a substitute for the word *God.* Jesus sat down in the place of honor: at the right hand of God.

The verb *to sit down* is significant. "Sitting was often a mark of honour or authority in the ancient world: a king sat to receive his subjects, a court to give judgment, and a teacher to teach."[2] The Book of Revelation in particular describes God, who sits on the throne (4:2, 10; 5:1, 7, 13; 6:16; 7:10, 15; 19:4; 21:5), and Jesus, who shares that throne (1:4–5; 3:21; 7:15–17; 12:5).

The throne of God and the sanctuary (the true tabernacle) bring king and high priest together into one place. This is not at all surprising if we think of the tabernacle in the desert, where God placed his throne in the Most Holy Place (Lev. 16:2). God took up residence behind the veil in the Tent of Meeting. In Revelation 16:17, temple and throne are mentioned together: ". . . out of the temple came a loud voice from the throne, saying, 'It is done!' " Justice and mercy flow forth from the throne and the sanctuary, from the king and the high priest.

By his sacrificial death, Jesus finished his atoning work on earth. Upon his ascension, he entered the presence of God (the sanctuary) and sat down at God's right hand. Says the writer of Hebrews, Jesus "serves in the sanctuary, the true tabernacle set up by the Lord, not by man."

Three matters come to mind when we consider Hebrews 8:2.

a. Jesus is serving in the sanctuary. His ministry in the heavenly sanctuary is superior to the priestly service on earth (8:5–6) because he is the only high priest who has ascended to heaven. God did not need to descend to earth to accept a sacrifice offered by priests. God had appointed the heavenly high priest by oath to serve eternally in God's sanctuary. Jesus brought his once-for-all offering and, entering the true sanctuary, began his priestly ministry in the presence of God.[3]

b. Jesus serves in the sanctuary that is the true tabernacle. The writer of Hebrews does not leave the reader in doubt regarding the identity of tabernacle and sanctuary and their place. In the next chapter he explains the term *tabernacle*: Christ "went through the greater and more perfect tabernacle that is not man-made, that is to say, not a part of this creation" (9:11). And he adds: "For Christ did not enter a man-made sanctuary that was only a copy of the true one; he entered heaven itself, now to appear for us in God's presence" (9:24).[4] Tabernacle and sanctuary are the same.

c. Jesus serves as high priest in the true tabernacle. This true tabernacle

---

2. Richard Thomas France, *NIDNTT,* vol. 3, p. 588. Also see Carl Schneider, *TDNT,* vol. 3, p. 442.

3. Leopold Sabourin, "Liturge du sanctuaire et de la tente véritable (Héb. VIII 2)," *NTS* 18 (1971): 87–90.

4. For a systematic presentation of the various interpretations of the expression *the true tabernacle,* see Philip Edgcumbe Hughes, *Commentary on the Epistle to the Hebrews* (Grand Rapids: Eerdmans, 1977), pp. 283–90. See also the same material published under the title "The Blood of Jesus and His Heavenly Priesthood in Hebrews. Part III: The Meaning of 'The True Tent' and 'The Greater and More Perfect Tent,' " *BS* 130 (1973): 305–14.

has been set up by the Lord, as the writer reminds us. What he means is that God gave Moses a copy of the tabernacle which the Lord God showed him (Exod. 25:9, 40). The copy was on earth; the true tabernacle is in heaven. Does Scripture mention a tabernacle in heaven? Yes, Isaiah says that he saw "the Lord seated on a throne, high and exalted, and the train of his robe filled the temple" (Isa. 6:1; see also Mic. 1:2). That sanctuary has not been erected by man, but by God. God would never have set it up if he had not appointed Christ to serve in that tabernacle. After his atoning work was accomplished, Jesus entered God's sanctuary and there represents the interests of all his people. From God's tabernacle flow blessings that surpass any blessings from the Levitical sacrificial system.

---

3 Every high priest is appointed to offer both gifts and sacrifices, and so it was necessary for this one also to have something to offer. 4 If he were on earth, he would not be a priest, for there are already men who offer the gifts prescribed by the law. 5 They serve at a sanctuary that is a copy and shadow of what is in heaven. This is why Moses was warned when he was about to build the tabernacle: "See to it that you make everything according to the pattern shown you on the mountain." 6 But the ministry Jesus has received is as superior to theirs as the covenant of which he is mediator is superior to the old one, and it is founded on better promises.

B. Jesus the Mediator
8:3–6

3. Every high priest is appointed to offer both gifts and sacrifices, and so it was necessary for this one also to have something to offer. 4. If he were on earth, he would not be a priest, for there are already men who offer the gifts prescribed by the law.

An effective teacher repeats his lesson often in the same words. The writer of Hebrews is no exception, for 8:3 is a virtual repetition of 5:1. Besides, the author continues his descriptive method of teaching by presenting contrast. Note the contrast in 8:3.

1. High Priest
8:3

for—and so
every high priest—for this one also
is appointed—it was necessary
to offer—to have to offer
both gifts and sacrifices—something

The New International Version omits the first word *for* that has its counterpart in *and so.* Although the term *high priest* is qualified by the adjective *every,* the text conveys the implication that there had been a long succession of high priests. Over against the numerous high priests stands Jesus. The author of Hebrews does not refer to him by name; he says "this one" in order to remind the reader of the priest-king serving in the heavenly sanctuary.

The contrast between the continual offerings of the high priest in the form of "both gifts and sacrifices" and the single offering, simply mentioned as "something," is significant. What this "something" consists of the author does not specify in 8:3, but in 9:14 he elaborates. Also, in the original Greek the two verbs *to offer* delineate the difference, in that the first one, pertaining to every high priest, indicates continuous occurrence. The second *to offer* verb, used with reference to Jesus, shows a single event.

2. Service
8:4–6

In 8:4 the author continues his use of contrasts with a conditional sentence that is contrary to fact. That is, the two parts of the sentence demand counterparts which are implied.

"If he were on earth"—but he is in heaven
"he would not be a priest"—but he is our priest

The sanctuary in which Christ serves as high priest is in heaven, not on earth. During his ministry on earth he could not be priest at all because he belonged to the tribe of Judah, rather than the tribe of Levi. However, the writer of the epistle does not state or imply that Christ could not bring his once-for-all offering on Calvary's cross.[5] He only notes that those who are part of the Levitical priesthood offer gifts that are "prescribed by the law." Jesus did not belong to the priestly clan of Levi and therefore could not serve at the altar. Instead, he serves in the true tabernacle, in the presence of God.

5. They serve at a sanctuary that is a copy and shadow of what is in heaven. This is why Moses was warned when he was about to build the tabernacle: "See to it that you make everything according to the pattern shown you on the mountain."

The contrast continues. This verse explains the service, the building, and the pattern of the tabernacle on earth; the next verse portrays Jesus as the mediator of a better covenant. Hebrews 8:5 describes the construction of the earthly sanctuary. Three main points stand out.

a. "Copy and shadow." Jesus entered the heavenly sanctuary in God's presence, but the priests served God in the tabernacle that the Israelites constructed in the time of Moses.[6]

The two words *copy* and *shadow,* although different in meaning, complement each other; one provides what the other lacks. The term *copy* denotes substance, and the noun *shadow* may be understood as a "reflection . . . of

5. Geerhardus Vos, *The Teaching of the Epistle to the Hebrews* (Grand Rapids: Eerdmans, 1956), p. 113.
6. Throughout his epistle the writer directs the reader's attention to the period that the nation Israel spent in the desert. The temple he never mentions; rather, the tabernacle is for him the place of worship (Heb. 8:2, 5; 9:2, 3, 6, 8, 11, 21; 13:10).

the heavenly original."[7] We receive the mental picture of the heavenly original casting a shadow on the earth. But this shadow has form and substance.

The writer of Hebrews intends to say that the priests who served in the sanctuary had to realize the limitations: the tabernacle structure was but a copy and the sacrifices were only a shadow. In the following chapter, where he elucidates the significance of sacrifices, the author explains the meaning of 8:5. Says he: "It was necessary, then, for the copies of the heavenly things to be purified with these sacrifices, but the heavenly things themselves with better sacrifices than these. For Christ did not enter a man-made sanctuary that was only a copy of the true one; he entered heaven itself, now to appear for us in God's presence" (9:23–24; also see 10:1).

b. "Build the tabernacle." If Moses built a tabernacle according to a copy of a heavenly original, what then is the appearance and the function of the heavenly sanctuary? Speculation about a heavenly sanctuary originated with, and at the same time fascinated, Jewish teachers in the time of the apostles and afterward.[8] They speculated on what Moses was permitted to observe when God instructed him. Did Moses see more than what is recorded in Exodus 33:18–23 (when God showed him the glory of the Lord)?[9]

No tabernacle of the same proportions as Moses built exists in heaven. Scripture fails to give any dimensions of the celestial tabernacle. Nor do we have the liberty to say that the heavenly tabernacle exists only in the mind of God. Avoiding either extreme, we ought to take note of the following Scripture passages where God instructed Moses to build the tabernacle:

1. "See that you make them according to the pattern shown you on the mountain" (Exod. 25:40).
2. "Set up the tabernacle according to the plan shown you on the mountain" (Exod. 26:30).
3. "Make the altar hollow, out of boards. It is to be made just as you were shown on the mountain" (Exod. 27:8).
4. "The lampstand was made exactly like the pattern the Lord had shown Moses" (Num. 8:4).[10]

Because the Bible is a book about man's redemption and not a revelation about heaven, we ought to let the Scripture speak. Where the Scriptures are

7. Heinrich Schlier, *TDNT,* vol. 2, p. 33. Also see Ralph P. Martin, *NIDNTT,* vol. 2, p. 291.

8. For instance, see the writings of Philo, *Life of Moses* 2.76; *Allegorical Interpretation* 3.102. And the *Talmud,* Kodashim, vol. 1, relates a saying from Rabbi Jose ben Judah: "An ark of fire and a table of fire and a candlestick of fire came down from heaven; and these Moses saw and reproduced, as it is written, 'And see that thou make them after their pattern, which is being shown thee in the mount' " (Menachoth 29a). Also see SB, vol. 3, pp. 702–4.

9. John Owen, in his *Exposition of Hebrews,* 7 vols. in 4 (Evansville, Ind.: Sovereign Grace, 1960), vol. 6, pp. 44–45, remarks: "Whether this representation were made to Moses by the way of internal vision, as the temple was represented unto Ezekiel, or whether there were an ethereal fabric proposed unto his bodily senses, is hard to determine."

10. The construction of the temple of Solomon followed a plan David gave Solomon in writing. " 'All this,' David said, 'I have in writing from the hand of the Lord upon me, and he gave me understanding in all the details of the plan' " (I Chron. 28:19; also see v. 12).

silent, we must be reticent. All we know is that Christ entered the heavenly sanctuary that is not manmade (Heb. 9:24). Its earthly counterpart was the ancient tabernacle that Moses erected according to the pattern God showed him.

c. "The pattern." Moses received from God the blueprints for the construction of the tabernacle and was repeatedly told to follow the instructions carefully (Exod. 25:40; also see Acts 7:44).

What precisely did Moses see when God gave him the pattern? To put it differently: Did Moses receive only the pattern, or did he see the original? If he were given the blueprint of the tabernacle, then he received, in effect, a plan from which he had to build a model—the tabernacle in the desert.[11]

We do not know what Moses saw when God gave him the pattern for the earthly tabernacle. Scripture tells us that our high priest Jesus Christ has gone "through the greater and more perfect tabernacle that is not manmade, that is to say, not a part of this creation" (Heb. 9:11). This information is a source of comfort for us because we know that as our heavenly high priest, Jesus intercedes for us. He is our mediator.

6. But the ministry Jesus has received is as superior to theirs as the covenant of which he is mediator is superior to the old one, and it is founded on better promises.

This verse is actually a continuation of 8:4, with the pronoun *he* (i.e., Jesus) as the subject of the sentence. Although the author of Hebrews contrasts Jesus with the Levitical priests, in 8:6 the primary emphasis is upon the difference in covenants rather than the difference in ministry. The author somewhat abruptly introduces the concept of covenant that he mentioned in 7:22. He is ready now to explain the implications of the new covenant that is superior to the old covenant. And he shows that the Christ is the mediator of this new covenant.

Twice in this verse the word *superior* occurs: the ministry Jesus has obtained is superior to that of the priests, and the new covenant is superior to the old one.

What is the ministry Christ has received?[12] The word *ministry* relates to the work in the tabernacle or sanctuary. If Jesus had merely fulfilled the responsibilities of the Aaronic priesthood with his personal sacrifice, his work would be incomplete. Jesus fulfilled the obligations of the Levitical priesthood and ushered in the era of the high priest in the order of Melchizedek. The old system has yielded its place to the new, and in that new covenant Jesus has become the mediator.

In Old Testament times, high priests served as mediators between God

---

11. F. W. Grosheide, *De Brief aan de Hebreeën en de Brief van Jakobus* (Kampen: Kok, 1955), p. 189. See also Leonhard Goppelt, *TDNT*, vol. 9, p. 258.

12. The term *ministry* belongs to a word group that includes, in the original Greek, the verb *to serve* (10:11), the noun *ministry* (8:6; 9:21), the noun *servant* (1:7; 8:2), and the adjective *serving* (1:14).

and man. They were mediators on the basis of the old covenant God had made with his people, but this covenant has become obsolete (8:13) because the new one has taken its place. In succeeding verses the author explains why the new covenant is superior to the old one.

However, the author gives a preliminary reason as to why the new covenant is better than the old. Says he, "It is founded on better promises." By implication, the promises given by God to his people in earlier days were inadequate. The promises of the old covenant went together with the law of Moses; new covenant promises include God's law put in the minds and written on the hearts of his people, the teaching of knowledge of the Lord, and the forgiving of sin (8:10–12).

Doctrinal Considerations in 8:1–6

When Jesus told the disciples in the upper room on the eve of his death, "And if I go and prepare a place for you, I will come back and take you to be with me that you also may be where I am" (John 14:3), his promise included sitting with Christ on his throne (Rev. 3:21). Christ "has made us to be a kingdom and priests to serve his God and Father" (Rev. 1:6). Believers are kings and priests with Christ. What a glorious promise!

Christ's divine kingship differs from that of earthly kings. His kingship is one of service: he intercedes for his people; that is, he presents the prayers and praises of his people before the throne of God.[13] He guarantees a place for his people in his Father's house. Christ is the king-priest who rules and serves his people.

The Levitical priests served God in the sanctuary erected by man. Incidentally, the writer of the epistle consistently quotes from and alludes to passages of the Old Testament that mention the tabernacle. Never does he mention the temple in Jerusalem. Even in Hebrews 13, where he continually exhorts the readers and addresses his contemporaries, he refers to the tabernacle (13:10), the high priest who takes animal blood into the Most Holy Place ("but the bodies are burned outside the camp" [13:11]), and to Jesus, who "suffered outside the city gate" (13:12). The context for the author's teaching is the experience of the Israelites in the wilderness. That means the writer refers to the beginning of the nation Israel when God made a covenant with the Israelites at Mount Sinai, gave his people the law, and instituted the Levitical priesthood.

Jesus, having fulfilled the responsibilities of the Aaronic priesthood, serves God eternally in "the true tabernacle" as high priest in the order of Melchizedek. Thus his priesthood is superior to that of the sons of Levi. Jesus by his sacrificial death fulfilled the demands of the Old Testament law and therefore made the old covenant obsolete. The new covenant, sealed with the blood of Christ, is superior to the old one (Matt. 26:28; Mark 14:24; Luke 22:20; I Cor. 11:25).

---

13. B. F. Westcott, *Commentary on the Epistle to the Hebrews* (Grand Rapids: Eerdmans, 1950), p. 229.

Greek Words, Phrases, and Constructions in 8:1–6

Verse 1

κεφάλαιον—this neuter substantivized adjective, without the definite article, means "the main point" or "the summary." The first meaning is preferred.

ἐπὶ τοῖς λεγομένοις—the preposition ἐπί followed by the dative case may be translated "about"[14] or "in addition to."[15] The definite article τοῖς and the present passive participle λεγομένοις are in the neuter dative plural case. The author uses the present tense to stress the significance of his discussion—"the things that are being said."

Verse 2

τῶν ἁγίων—the neuter genitive plural adjective with the definite article is substantivized and refers to the sanctuary. The author does not distinguish between tabernacle and Most Holy Place (but see 9:3).

λειτουργός—the difference between the two word groups represented by the verbs λειτουργέω (I serve in a public office or religious ministry) and λατρεύω (I serve) is not very pronounced in the Epistle to the Hebrews, because both word groups relate to the worship of God.[16]

Verse 3

δῶρά τε καὶ θυσίας—the phrase is a repetition of Hebrews 5:1.

προσενέγκῃ—the aorist tense signifies single occurrence. The verb is the aorist subjunctive active of προσφέρω (I offer). The use of the subjunctive is futuristic.[17]

Verse 5

κεχρημάτισται—the perfect passive indicative of the verb χρηματίζω (I admonish, instruct) denotes instruction given by God to man in the form of revelation. This divine revelation often was conveyed as a warning. The perfect tense implies lasting validity.

ὅρα ποιήσεις—the present active imperative ὅρα and the future active indicative are placed next to each other without the use of καί. The words, as a quotation, are from Exodus 25:40, with minor variation.

Verse 6

τέτυχεν—the verb τυγχάνω means "I hit the mark" and, more generally, "I attain." The use of the perfect indicates duration.

---

14. A. T. Robertson, *A Grammar of the Greek New Testament in the Light of Historical Research* (Nashville: Broadman, 1934), p. 605.

15. Bauer, p. 287. Also see Harvey E. Dana and Julius R. Mantey, *A Manual Grammar of the Greek New Testament* (New York: Macmillan, 1957), p. 107.

16. R. C. Trench, *Synonyms of the Greek New Testament* (Grand Rapids: Eerdmans, 1953), p. 126. See also Klaus Hess, *NIDNTT,* vol. 3, pp. 549–53; and Hermann Strathmann, *TDNT,* vol. 4, pp. 58–65 and 215–22.

17. Robertson, *Grammar,* p. 928.

ὅσῳ—this relative adjective lacks the corresponding adjective τοσούτῳ. Compare Hebrews 1:4.

ἥτις—the indefinite relative pronoun takes the place of the simple relative pronoun. It denotes cause and thus gives the reason why the new covenant is superior to the old one.

νενομοθέτηται—see Hebrews 7:11.

---

7 For if there had been nothing wrong with that first covenant, no place would have been sought for another. 8 But God found fault with the people and said:

"The time is coming, declares the Lord,
when I will make a new covenant
with the house of Israel
and with the house of Judah.
9 It will not be like the covenant I made with
their forefathers
when I took them by the hand
to lead them out of Egypt,
because they did not remain faithful to my covenant,
and I turned away from them,
declares the Lord.
10 This is the covenant I will make with the
house of Israel
after that time, declares the Lord.
I will put my laws in their minds
and write them on their hearts.
I will be their God,
and they will be my people.
11 No longer will a man teach his neighbor,
or a man his brother, saying, 'Know the Lord,'
because they will all know me,
from the least of them to the greatest.
12 For I will forgive their wickedness
and will remember their sins no more."

13 By calling this covenant "new," he has made the first one obsolete; and what is obsolete and aging will soon disappear.

C. God's New Covenant 8:7–13

One of the author's characteristics is to quote lengthy passages from the Old Testament (for example, in 2:6–8 [Ps. 8:4–6]; 3:7–11 [Ps. 95:7–11]; and 10:5–7 [Ps. 40:6–8]). Usually he explains and applies these passages in the succeeding context. However, when he quotes Jeremiah 31:31–34 in 8:8–12, he refrains from giving an explanation in the following chapter—instead, he quotes the passage again, in 10:16–17. The author puts the quotation in the present context to prove his point that God has revealed the replacement of the old covenant by the new.

7. For if there had been nothing wrong with that first covenant, no

place would have been sought for another. 8a. But God found fault with the people and said . . .

Unfulfilled conditional sentences appear repeatedly in the Epistle to the Hebrews (see among others 4:8, 7:11, and 8:4). Also in 8:7 the sentence is conditional. The argument demands an implied response: "if there had been nothing wrong with that first covenant" (but there was, for it was inadequate), then "no place would have been sought for another" (but God indeed confirmed the new covenant in Jeremiah 31:31–34).

For the author of the epistle, the Old Testament had not lost its validity when New Testament revelation overshadowed it. Not at all. For him, the Old Testament remained the living Word of God (1:1). But the coming of Christ and his ministry brought fulfillment to promise and prophecy. Therefore the writer explains the passage from Jeremiah 31 in the light of Jesus' coming. When Christ came into the world, he abolished the old and established the new. The author employs the terms *first* and *second* ("another" in the NIV).[18]

Speaking through David, in Psalm 110:4 God revealed the superiority of Melchizedek's priesthood; this superiority is also revealed through Jeremiah's prophecy. In this prophecy God also revealed the superiority of a new covenant. God himself instructed his people in the Old Testament Scriptures, but these truths remained hidden until the author of Hebrews employed them in his teachings.

Did God make a mistake when he established a covenant that had to be replaced in later years? No, God's word is true and without error. The fault in the first covenant did not lie with God but with the people who were God's covenant partners. They did not keep the conditions stipulated in the covenant, and therefore "God found fault with the people."[19] However, if the people were to blame for not keeping the covenant stipulations, the covenant itself could still be faultless. But in quoting Jeremiah 31:31–34, the author of the epistle shows the weakness of the first covenant: it was not put in the minds or written on the hearts of the people (8:10).[20] Therefore, the old covenant had to be replaced by the new.

8b. "The time is coming, declares the Lord,
when I will make a new covenant
with the house of Israel
and with the house of Judah.
9. It will not be like the covenant
I made with their forefathers
when I took them by the hand

---

18. The author has a penchant for the use of the adjective *first.* See 8:7, 13; 9:1, 2, 8, 15, 18; 10:9.

19. "The context does not seem to indicate that the intrinsic nature of the commandments was changed, but rather the mode of reception of the covenant," says Thomas McComiskey in *NIDNTT,* vol. 2, p. 145.

20. John Calvin, *Epistle to the Hebrews* (Grand Rapids: Eerdmans, 1949), p. 187.

to lead them out of Egypt,
because they did not remain faithful to my covenant,
and I turned away from them,
declares the Lord."

A covenant is drawn up when two parties agree on a contract. The contract spells out stipulations that the parties must honor and a condition that, in case either party fails to meet the requirements of the contract, the contract loses its binding force.

In 8:8b–9, a description of the old covenant is given: the two parties are mentioned; the stipulations of the covenant are implied; and the condition is applied.

a. *Two parties.* Twice in the first part of the quotation the prophet Jeremiah uses the phrase *declares the Lord.* The Lord God of Israel made a covenant with his people when he led them out of Egypt and had them stand at the foot of Mount Sinai to receive his law (Exod. 20:1–17). The first party in the covenant is God. He initiated it; he addressed the people of Israel at the beginning of their nationhood; and he turned away from them when they failed to remain faithful to the Sinaitic covenant.

God declared that he would "make a new covenant with the house of Israel and the house of Judah," but he did not disclose when the new contract would be signed. The reference *the time is coming* is decidedly indefinite. In historical perspective, the prophecy of Jeremiah could not have been directed to Israel's restoration after the exile, because the Old Testament indicates that the old covenant was in force after the exile.[21] The prophecy, therefore, heralds the coming of the Messiah and the establishing of the new covenant in his blood (see Matt. 26:28 and parallels).

The phrases *house of Israel* and *house of Judah* call attention to the reunification of the nation Israel; however, because the ten tribes of Israel failed to return after the exile, the phrases ought to be understood in a more universalistic sense to include both Jews and Gentiles.

b. *Implied stipulations.* The old covenant God made with the people of Israel was God's promise that he would be their king. As king, God demanded obedience from his people. For this reason he gave them the law at Sinai and told them that they would be "a kingdom of priests and a holy nation" (Exod. 19:6).

The Israelites were asked to obey God's law with heart, soul, and strength (Deut. 6:5) and thus to demonstrate their constant love for God. They listened to God's commandments but neglected to obey him. The law remained something external, for it was not written on their hearts. Consequently, they refused to remain faithful to God's covenant.

c. *Applied condition.* God's response to the rebellious Israelites was to turn away from them. The relation between God and his people at first had been

21. Gerhard Charles Aalders, *De Profeet Jeremia,* Korte Verklaring, 2 vols. (Kampen: Kok, 1954), vol. 2, p. 88.

intimate. God said, "I took them by the hand to lead them out of Egypt." God wanted his people to walk with him hand in hand, in full assurance and confidence. But when the Israelites decided to walk alone, to disobey God's law, and to ignore his voice calling them to himself, he "turned away from them."[22] That is, God neglected them by leaving them to their own willful ways. Instead of demonstrating tender loving care for his covenant people, God assumed an attitude of unconcern for obstinate covenant breakers. By turning away from them God made it known that the time for a new covenant would come. He remains a covenant God.

10. "This is the covenant I will make with the
house of Israel
after that time, declares the Lord.
I will put my laws in their minds
and write them on their hearts.
I will be their God,
and they will be my people.
11. No longer will a man teach his neighbor,
or a man his brother, saying, 'Know the Lord,'
because they will all know me,
from the least of them to the greatest.
12. For I will forgive their wickedness
and will remember their sins no more."

The description of the new covenant is positive; the stipulations are not implied but clearly stated in the form of four promises (8:6).

a. *Written law.* For the third time in this lengthy quotation Jeremiah writes "declares the Lord." God himself makes the new covenant with the people who belong to the messianic age. That is, Jew and Gentile as believers make up "the house of Israel." The era of the old covenant, characterized by the exclusiveness of the nation Israel, has made way for a new age in which all nations are included (Matt. 28:19).

Who belongs to the house of Israel? All those people, says God, in whose minds I will put my laws and upon whose hearts I will write them. The expressions *minds* and *hearts* (parallel terms) represent man's inner being. God's people experience the permeating power of God's Word, so that his law becomes a part of their conscience. That conscience is directed to the law of God, much the same as a compass needle invariably points north.

b. *Covenant God.* Throughout Scripture God's recurring message to his people is the promise: "I will be their God, and they will be my people" (see, for example, Exod. 6:7; Lev. 26:12; Jer. 7:23; 11:4; II Cor. 6:16; Rev. 21:3). God wanted to make the Israelite nation his special people; they were his "treasured possession." However, Israel could lose this favored status if the

---

22. The translation of Jer. 31:32b in the Hebrew text ("because they broke my covenant, though I was a husband to them, declares the LORD") differs from the reading in Heb. 8:9b, which is based on the Septuagint.

people refused to keep the law of God. The covenant stipulated that God's people would live a life of obedience.

In New Testament times, too, God addresses the believers in Jesus Christ and gives them the covenant promise: "I will be [your] God, and [you] will be my people." In this new covenant, God is inseparably united with his people because God's law has been inscribed on their hearts. He communicates with his people through his revelation, and they communicate with him through prayer. He encourages them to approach the throne of grace with confidence (Heb. 4:16), and he makes it known that his name has been written on their foreheads (Rev. 14:1; 22:4). He wants to have them address him as Father, for they are his children.

> Ye children of God's covenant,
> Who of His grace have heard,
> Forget not all His wondrous deeds
> And judgments of His word.
> The Lord our God is God alone,
> All lands His judgments know;
> His promise He remembers still,
> While generations go.
> —*Psalter Hymnal*

c. *Universal knowledge.* The next promise flows from the preceding promises. The knowledge of the Lord shall be universal. In the history of Israel, God's revelation came piecemeal "through the prophets at many times and in various ways" (Heb. 1:1), and in one instance the Book of the Law was discovered in the temple of the Lord. While the Book of the Law gathered dust, the people lived in ignorance (II Kings 22; II Chron. 34:14–28). Ignorance of God's revelation was appalling, and God's prophets repeatedly registered their complaints (see Isa. 1:3; Jer. 4:22; Hos. 4:6).

What a difference in New Testament times! Knowledge of the Lord will be universal, covering the earth "as the waters cover the sea" (Isa. 11:9; Hab. 2:14). The need for individual teaching—"a man teach his neighbor, or a man his brother," "from the least of them to the greatest"—will disappear because all people will know the Lord. Filled with the knowledge of the Lord, even novices in the faith are able and equipped to witness for him. All those who have the law of God in their hearts and minds acknowledge God's grace and mercy. They know that their sins have been forgiven and that their record has been wiped clean.

d. *Complete remission.* When God forgives sin, he does so by never remembering man's sin again. That means that when forgiven, man is like Adam and Eve in Paradise: without sin. Man, forgiven by God, is accepted as if he had never sinned at all. God says, "I will remember [his] sins no more." In the new covenant, grace and mercy are freely given to all God's children. God gives these blessings in the name of his Son, who is the mediator of a new covenant. This new covenant established through the death of Jesus on the cross is the believer's guarantee that his sins are forgiven and forgotten.

13. By calling this covenant "new," he has made the first one obsolete; and what is obsolete and aging will soon disappear.

God himself introduced the word *new* when he said, "I will make a new covenant with the house of Israel and with the house of Judah" (8:8). In Christ the new covenant has become reality; consequently, the old covenant has become obsolete. God himself told his people, at first through the prophecy of Jeremiah and then in New Testament times through the writer of Hebrews. The Jew of the first century, therefore, had to realize that the era of the covenant God made with his people at Sinai had ended.

Already in the days of Jeremiah, approximately six hundred years before the birth of Christ, God spoke of a new covenant. By implication, the existing covenant was then already "obsolete and aging."[23]

What then is the difference between the old and the new? For one thing, in the days of the old covenant the sinner repeatedly had to present animal offerings to the Lord God to obtain remission of sin. In the new covenant sinners are forgiven through the one-time sacrifice of Jesus. Their offerings consist of dedicated lives that express gratitude to God and joyfully keep his commands.

The old covenant was rather restrictive; it was made with Israel, God's special people. The new covenant embraces all nations; all those who believe in Jesus Christ are his "treasured possession." Therefore, with the coming of Pentecost, the new covenant made its presence felt. The old covenant had to be put away.

The writer of Hebrews, however, does not specify a time or describe circumstances when the old covenant will disappear. His conclusion to chapter 8 is rather general: "and what is obsolete and aging will soon disappear."

Doctrinal Considerations in 8:7–13

The old covenant was based on the law of God given to the Israelites during the first part of their wilderness journey. Although the law which was basic to the covenant was perfect, it could not make man perfect (Heb. 7:11, 19). Because of the inherent weakness—not in the covenant, as such, but in man—God inaugurated a new covenant. The new came forth out of the old and for a while both covenants existed side by side: the new took over when the old began to disappear (8:13).

The inadequacy of the old covenant was completely overshadowed by the adequacy of Christ. Christ became the mediator of this new covenant that was superior to the old covenant. The writer of Hebrews employs comparative adjectives to indicate the difference between old and new: Christ's *superior* ministry, the *superior* covenant, and the *better* promises (8:6). Jesus is "the guarantee of a *better* covenant" (7:22; italics added).

---

23. Hughes ventures the idea that 8:13 is an oblique reference to the temple services prior to the destruction of Jerusalem. He sees this reference, then, as a silent witness to the time when the epistle was written—before A.D. 70.

Whereas the old covenant was an external manifestation of God's grace, the new covenant involves the individual believer. God made the old covenant with the nation Israel and gave the people his laws written on tablets of stone. He establishes the new covenant with the believer in Christ and writes God's law on the believer's heart. With this law written on his inmost being, the believer has an intimate relationship with God through Christ.

The new covenant has two parties: God and his people. To be precise, the people of God are the true believers who have experienced genuine repentance and who demonstrate saving faith in Christ. God gives his people the promise: "I will be [your] God, and [you] will be my people" (8:10). God assumes that his people will keep the demands of his law written on their hearts, that they will always show their love and obedience to him, and that they will grow in their knowledge of salvation. God will not forget his promise. In fact, "He cannot and may not break His covenant; He has committed Himself to maintaining it with a freely given and precious oath: His name, His honor, His reputation depends on it."[24]

Greek Words, Phrases, and Constructions in 8:7–13

Verse 7

εἰ—this conditional particle, followed by the imperfect indicative ἦν in the protasis and οὐκ ἄν in the apodosis, introduces the contrary-to-fact condition.

τόπος—the word *place* refers to the history of redemption.

Verse 8

μεμφόμενος—together with ἄμεμπτος (blameless) in 8:7, the present middle participle derives from μέμφομαι (I find fault). The participle can take either αὐτούς as direct object or αὐτοῖς. The external manuscript evidence for either reading is about equally divided. The reading αὐτοῖς can also be connected with the verb λέγει (he said to them).

συντελέσω—the future active indicative from συντελέω (I fulfill) differs from the Septuagint text (Jer. 38:31), which reads διαθήσομαι (from διατίθημι, I decree, ordain). In this rather lengthy citation—the longest in the entire New Testament—numerous variations from the Septuagint text appear. Whether these variations originated during the process of copying the text or because of liturgical usage in the church is difficult to determine.[25]

καινήν—the adjective is used with διαθήκη in I Corinthians 11:25 and II Corinthians 3:6, in addition to Hebrews 8:8. The adjective conveys the idea of newness that comes forth out of the old and may even exist alongside the old: the Old Testament and the New Testament.

Verse 9

ἐπιλαβομένου μου τῆς χειρὸς αὐτῶν—the genitive absolute construction consists of the aorist middle participle from ἐπιλαμβάνομαι (I take hold of) and the personal

24. Herman Bavinck, *Our Reasonable Faith* (Grand Rapids: Eerdmans, 1956), pp. 274–75.

25. Simon J. Kistemaker, *The Psalm Citations in the Epistle to the Hebrews* (Amsterdam: Van Soest, 1961), pp. 41–42.

pronoun μου from ἐγώ (I). The participle governs the genitive case of τῆς χειρός (the hand); the pronoun αὐτῶν is possessive. The construction of this phrase is somewhat unusual.[26]

ἠμέλησα—the aorist active indicative of ἀμελέω (I neglect, disregard), derived from ἀ (not) and μέλω (I care for). The verb is expressive. See also Matthew 22:5, I Timothy 4:14, and Hebrews 2:3.

Verse 11

γνῶθι τὸν κύριον—the second aorist active imperative of γινώσκω (I know) expresses the concept of learning the commandments of God. The verb is followed by εἰδήσουσιν, the future perfect of οἶδα (I know), understood as a simple future indicative. The contrast between γινώσκω and οἶδα is significant in this verse. The first means acquiring knowledge, the second possessing knowledge.

Verse 13

ἐν τῷ λέγειν—the articular present infinitive with the preposition ἐν is in the dative case. The dative expresses time; that is, "while he is saying."

πεπαλαίωκεν—from the verb παλαιόω (I make old), the perfect active suggests action with lasting result. The active, not the passive, is used to indicate that God has declared the covenant old.

ἀφανισμοῦ—this noun, translated as "disappearance," derives from the verb ἀφανίζω (I make invisible), which is a compound of ἀ (not) and φαίνω (I appear). The genitive case is dependent on the adverb ἐγγύς (near), which is pressed into service as a preposition.

Summary of Chapter 8

In some ways chapter 8 is an extended commentary on 7:22, where the author introduces the concept *covenant.* He explains the word by quoting at length from a prophetic passage in the Book of Jeremiah. Yet he fails to interpret the term *covenant.* He does that in the following chapter (9:15–22). The quotation from Jeremiah 31:31–34, however, serves the purpose of showing the readers that God himself in the days of Jeremiah had already declared the covenant made with Israel to be obsolete.

The author, as a careful teacher of theology, utilizes the Old Testament Scriptures to show that God revealed the appearance of the new covenant centuries before the birth of Christ. Just as God himself appointed Christ as high priest in the order of Melchizedek, so he established a new covenant of which Christ would be the high priest.

The old order of the Levitical priesthood eventually had to come to an end. The sanctuary at which the priests served was "a copy and shadow of what is in heaven." By contrast, the sanctuary at which Jesus serves as high

---

26. Robertson, *Grammar,* p. 514.

priest is the true tabernacle in the presence of God himself. The earthly sanctuary was temporal; the heavenly sanctuary is eternal.

As the heavenly tabernacle is superior to the earthly sanctuary, so the new covenant, of which Jesus is the mediator, is superior to the old covenant. The new covenant is better because of the promises God gives to his people. And Jesus, who is the mediator of this new covenant, guarantees these promises: to know God, to treasure his revelation, and to experience complete forgiveness of sin.

9

Jesus: High Priest and Sacrifice, *part 2*

(9:1–28)

Outline

	D.	The Earthly Sanctuary
9:1–5		1. The First Covenant and the Tabernacle
9:6–10		2. The High Priest and the Most Holy Place
	E.	Jesus' Sacrificial Blood
9:11–14		1. Christ's Blood Cleanses Our Consciences
9:15		2. Christ's Death and the First Covenant
9:16–22		3. Christ's Blood Procures Forgiveness
9:23–28		4. Christ's Perfect Sacrifice

9 1 Now the first covenant had regulations for worship and also an earthly sanctuary. 2 A tabernacle was set up. In its first room were the lampstand, the table and
the consecrated bread; this was called the Holy Place. 3 Behind the second curtain
was a room called the Most Holy Place, 4 which had the golden altar of incense
and the gold-covered ark of the covenant. This ark contained the gold jar of manna, Aaron's
staff that had budded, and the stone tablets of the covenant. 5 Above the ark were the
cherubim of the Glory, overshadowing the atonement cover. But we cannot discuss these
things in detail now.
6 When everything had been arranged like this, the priests entered regularly into the outer
room to carry on their ministry. 7 But only the high priest entered the inner room, and that
only once a year, and never without blood, which he offered for himself and for the sins the
people had committed in ignorance. 8 The Holy Spirit was showing by this that the way into
the Most Holy Place had not yet been disclosed as long as the first tabernacle was still
standing. 9 This is an illustration for the present time, indicating that the gifts and sacrifices
being offered were not able to clear the conscience of the worshiper. 10 They are only a
matter of food and drink and various ceremonial washings—external regulations applying
until the time of the new order.

D. The Earthly Sanctuary
9:1–10

1. The First Covenant and the Tabernacle
9:1–5

Every chapter in the Epistle to the Hebrews has its own central message. For example: chapter 5, Christ is superior to Aaron the high priest; chapter 7, Christ is high priest in the order of Melchizedek; and chapter 9, Christ offers himself as a sacrifice once for all.

Although the topic of the covenant has become an integral part of the epistle at this point, the author nevertheless has to link the topic to the continuing discussion of the priesthood of Christ. In chapter 9 the author of Hebrews brings together these two strands and weaves them into a grand design. He portrays the construction of the tabernacle of the desert period, enumerates the various furnishings inside the sanctuary, and mentions the Most High Place with the ark and the cherubim.

1. Now the first covenant had regulations for worship and also an earthly sanctuary.

The writer of Hebrews contrasts the old and new covenants in the last verse of the preceding chapter. Consistently he calls the old covenant the first (8:7, 13; 9:1, 15, 18). Because he has already spoken of the tabernacle Moses was told to build (8:5), he now has to show a connection between covenant and tabernacle.

As a trained theologian the writer has the Old Testament Scriptures at hand. The first covenant was confirmed by the people of Israel just before Moses received the design for the construction of the tabernacle (Exod. 24). The design for the tabernacle and its contents, the regulations for worship, and the construction of the "earthly sanctuary" are recorded in succeeding chapters. Incidentally, the descriptive adjective *earthly* must be understood as the counterpart of the description *greater and more perfect* that is applied to the "tabernacle that is not man-made" (9:11; also see 8:2).

The covenant, says the writer, includes two matters.

a. "Regulations for worship." God did not leave the practice of worship to the invention of the Israelites. With the design for the tabernacle, God also gave Moses the detailed ordinances for divine worship (see, for instance, Exod. 29, 30). In other words, Moses passed on to the Israelites God-ordained regulations for worship.

b. "Earthly sanctuary." Rules for worship and the mandate for the erection of the sanctuary are closely connected in Exodus 25–30. And even in Hebrews 9:1, the phrases *regulations for worship* and *earthly sanctuary* are joined by a connective particle that is translated "and also."

The word *sanctuary* may have been chosen for stylistic reasons. The writer uses the term *tabernacle* in the next verse, but throughout his epistle he refrains from employing the expression *temple*. Some commentators see this choice of words as a clear indication that when the author wrote Hebrews, the Jerusalem temple already had been destroyed. Other commentators say that the choice is a matter of basics: the tabernacle is basic to the temple. Although this comment is commendable, I think that the determinative factor in the writer's choice of words, at least for chapters 8 and 9, is the close link between the confirmation of the covenant (Exod. 24) and the mandate to construct the tabernacle (Exod. 25–27).

2. A tabernacle was set up. In its first room were the lampstand, the table and the consecrated bread; this was called the Holy Place. 3. Behind the second curtain was a room called the Most Holy Place, 4. which had the golden altar of incense and the gold-covered ark of the covenant. This ark contained the gold jar of manna, Aaron's staff that had budded, and the stone tablets of the covenant.

Mainly from passages in Exodus 16, 25, 26, and 30, as well as in Numbers 17, the author gleaned the information for his description of the interior and furniture of the tabernacle. Note that he describes the tabernacle as a structure with two rooms: the first room is called the Holy Place, and the second room is known as the Most Holy Place.

a. *The first room.* In the Holy Place, the larger of the two rooms, were the lampstand, the table, and the consecrated bread. The lampstand, according to Exodus 25:31–39, was a most beautifully crafted piece of furniture. It was made of seventy-five pounds (thirty-four kilograms) of gold, consisting of a base and shaft from which six branches extended—three to one side of the shaft and three to the other. At the top of these six branches and shaft were cups decorated "like almond flowers with buds and blossoms" (Exod. 25:34). The lampstand was placed on the south side of the Holy Place (Exod. 40:24).

The table, made of acacia wood, was about 3¾ feet (about 1.1 meters) long and 2¼ feet (about 0.7 meter) wide. It was covered with pure gold (Exod. 25:23, 24), and the "bread of the Presence" (Exod. 25:30) was placed on it. The table was located on the north side of the Holy Place (Exod. 40:22).

Twelve loaves of bread, representing the twelve tribes of Israel, were placed on this table (Lev. 24:5–9). The bread was known as "the bread of presentation" or "consecrated bread" (see Matt. 12:4; Mark 2:26; Luke 6:4). The author of the epistle mentions table and bread in the same breath to indicate that they belong together.

b. *The second room.* Inside the tabernacle was another curtain that separated the Most Holy Place from the Holy Place. This room contained, according to the writer of Hebrews, "the golden altar of incense and the gold-covered ark of the covenant." Questions about these two items have caused much debate. We shall consider them in sequence.

1. "The golden altar of incense." The altar for burning incense was made of acacia wood and covered with pure gold. It was square, about 1½ feet (about 0.5 meter) in length and width and about 3 feet (about 0.9 meter) high (Exod. 30:1–6). God instructed Moses to "put the altar in front of the curtain that is before the ark of the Testimony" (Exod. 30:6), and this is exactly what Moses did (Exod. 40:26). The writer of the Epistle to the Hebrews, however, states that the altar was with the ark in the Most Holy Place, but this is contrary to the divine instructions Moses received and followed. See the diagram of the tabernacle (Fig. 1).

Obviously, we face a problem that is not easy to solve. Some commentators are rather quick in saying that the author must have made a mistake or was

Figure 1

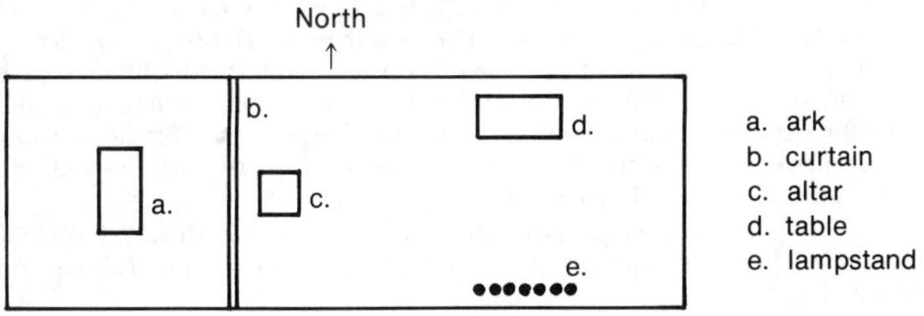

unacquainted with the description of the interior of the tabernacle.[1] But that is hardly plausible in view of the detailed knowledge of the Old Testament Scriptures he exhibits in his epistle. Admittedly, the author could have been influenced by the description of Solomon's temple in which the altar "belonged to the inner sanctuary" (I Kings 6:22). However, the author of Hebrews makes no mention of Solomon's temple. In the postexilic temple the altar of incense was located in the Holy Place, not in the Most Holy Place (Luke 1:11). Zechariah was a priest (not a high priest) who "was chosen by lot . . . to go into the temple of the Lord and burn incense" (Luke 1:9). He could serve only in the Holy Place.[2]

Other commentators take the expression *the altar of incense* to mean "censer," that is, a container for burning incense. This interpretation, which was common in the Middle Ages and the time of the Reformation (see the Bible translations of that day), is based on the translation of the Greek word for "altar of incense."[3] In II Chronicles 26:19 and Ezekiel 8:11, the translation is "censer." The interpretation, then, is that the high priest used the container for burning incense once a year and that he left it permanently in the Most Holy Place. Thus the censer was always with the ark in the inner sanctuary. This view does not seem to remove the difficulties we face. The passages in Exodus 30 and 40 speak of an altar, not of a censer. Also, the altar of incense filled an important function in the Holy Place. Every morning and every evening Aaron or one of his male descendants had to burn incense on the altar (Exod. 30:7–8). The altar of incense was much more significant than a censer.

However, on the Day of Atonement the high priest had "to take a censer full of burning coals from the altar before the LORD and two handfuls of finely ground fragrant incense and take them behind the curtain" (Lev. 16:12). On that special day, once a year, the censer became the extension of the altar of incense. The smoke of the incense had to conceal the atonement cover of the ark, so that the high priest would not die (v. 13). The function of the altar could not be obstructed by a curtain separating the Most Holy Place from the Holy Place. Thus, the censer momentarily entered behind the curtain as an extension of the altar of incense.

We should also note that on the Day of Atonement the high priest cleansed

---

1. Hugh Montefiore, *The Epistle to the Hebrews* (New York and Evanston: Harper and Row, 1964), p. 145, writes: "Possibly our author has made a slight slip and placed the altar in the wrong part of the Tent." Myles M. Bourke in "The Epistle to the Hebrews," *The Jerome Biblical Commentary,* vol. 2, *The New Testament and Topical Articles* (Englewood Cliffs, N.J.: Prentice-Hall, 1968), p. 396, states: "It seems that the author has made a mistake here, caused probably by the fact that he was not speaking from personal knowledge of the Temple, which replaced the Mosaic Tabernacle, but was merely repeating, and in this case misinterpreting, the description of the Tabernacle found in Exodus."

2. For comments of Jewish contemporaries see Philo in *The Life of Moses* 2.101 (LCL); Josephus, *Jewish Wars* 5.21 and *Antiquities of the Jews* 3.147, 198 (LCL); and *Talmud*, Yoma 47a; Moed 3. SB, vol. 3, p. 737.

3. The KJV and RV read "golden censer."

the altar of incense by sprinkling animal blood on the horns of the altar (Exod. 30:10). Once a year the altar was "most holy to the LORD" (v. 10) and could be mentioned with the ark of the covenant.

In Hebrews 9 the author stresses the prominence of the Day of Atonement (v. 7). For him, the altar of incense and the ark were the most important objects.

2. "The gold-covered ark of the covenant." A chest made of acacia wood, the ark was 3¾ feet (about 1.1 meters) long, 2¼ feet (about 0.7 meter) wide, and 2¼ feet (about 0.7 meter) high. It was completely covered with pure gold. It was permanently located in the Most Holy Place except when the Lord God told the Israelites to continue their wilderness journey. Then the priests were to carry the ark. Later, except when the ark was in Philistine cities and in the houses of Abinadab (I Sam. 4 and 6) and Obed-Edom (II Sam. 6:10–12), the ark remained in the tabernacle and subsequently the temple.[4]

The ark "contained the gold jar of manna, Aaron's staff that had budded, and the stone tablets of the covenant." These objects came from Israel's history. First, the jar filled with manna was placed "before the LORD to be kept for the generations to come" (Exod. 16:33). The author of Hebrews used the Septuagint translation of the Hebrew text, for that translation has the reading *gold jar*. Only the author conveys the information that the gold jar had a place inside the ark.

The second item was Aaron's staff that "had not only sprouted but had budded, blossomed and produced almonds" (Num. 17:8). This staff was put "in front of the Testimony" (v. 10). The Old Testament provides no information about depositing the staff inside the ark. If the ark indeed contained this rod, it would have had to conform to the size of the ark. When the ark was placed in the temple of Solomon, it contained nothing "except the two stone tablets that Moses had placed in it at Horeb" (I Kings 8:9; II Chron. 5:10). Because of Scripture's silence, we are unable to draw any conclusions on these matters.

The two stone tablets inscribed with the Ten Commandments were to be placed in the ark. And this was exactly what Moses did (Deut. 10:1–5). The author of Hebrews calls the ark and the tablets covenant objects. That is, both the ark and the Ten Commandments testified to the covenant relationship God had with the Israelites. The ark symbolized God's sacred presence in the midst of his people and gave visual meaning to God's promise, "I will be your God." The two stone tablets were a constant reminder to the people of Israel to keep the law of God, so that in obedience they could be his people.

5a. Above the ark were the cherubim of the Glory, overshadowing the atonement cover.

The writer returns to his description of the lid of the sacred chest. It was

---

4. After the exile, the rebuilt temple seemed to have had nothing at all in the Most Holy Place. Josephus, *Jewish Wars* 1.152–53; *Antiquities* 14.71, 72 (LCL).

made of pure gold and measured 3¾ feet (about 1.1 meters) by 2¼ feet (about 0.7 meter). On top of the cover were two angels, called cherubim, made of hammered gold. These two faced each other, with wings outspread covering the ark, and looked down toward the ark (Exod 25:17–22; 37:6–9).

God placed cherubim at the east side of the Garden of Eden "to guard the way to the tree of life" (Gen. 3:24). The posture of the cherubim on the cover of the ark projects the idea of guarding the way to God. Between the two cherubim God dwells, for from that place Moses heard God speak (Num. 7:89). God is "enthroned between the cherubim" (I Sam. 4:4; II Sam. 6:2; II Kings 19:15; Ps. 80:1; 99:1; Isa. 37:16).

The expression *cherubim of the Glory,* an obvious reference to God's glory, represents a glimpse of the heavenly glory. As Paul puts it in his First Epistle to Timothy: "God . . . alone is immortal and . . . lives in unapproachable light, whom no one has seen or can see" (6:15–16).

With their outspread wings the cherubim were "overshadowing the place of atonement." Another translation for "atonement cover" is "mercy seat." God appeared "in the cloud over the atonement cover" (Lev. 16:2), and no one, not even the high priest, was permitted to approach God. Who then might come before God? Only on the Day of Atonement might the high priest come sprinkling the blood of a bull seven times on the atonement cover (Lev. 16:14). The lasting ordinance was: "Atonement is to be made once a year for all the sins of the Israelites" (v. 34). God showed mercy once a year.

5b. But we cannot discuss these things in detail now.

The author is vitally interested in showing the insufficiency of gifts and sacrifices brought to God, for they could not "clear the conscience of the worshiper" (9:9). He is eager to discuss the sufficiency of Christ's sacrifice (9:11–14). Therefore, he somewhat abruptly discontinues the consideration of the tabernacle furniture. An extended discussion on this topic would not suit the author's purpose.

Greek Words, Phrases, and Constructions in 9:1–5

Verse 1

εἶχε—the descriptive imperfect active indicative of ἔχω (I have, hold) relates to the entire span of history in which the old covenant functioned.

ἡ πρώτη—the noun must be supplied. The context seems to suggest the word διαθήκη (see 8:13). Some manuscripts have the reading σκηνή (tabernacle).

δικαιώματα—this noun belongs to the family that has the basic root δικ (show, point).[5] The noun translated "regulations" lacks the definite article (see 9:10). The -μα ending of the singular expresses the result of an action; that is, God spoke to the Israelites and laid down divine regulations.

---

5. Bruce M. Metzger, *Lexical Aids for Students of New Testament Greek* (Princeton, N.J.: published by the author, 1969), p. 54.

λατρείας—this noun can be either a genitive singular as an objective genitive (for worship) or an accusative plural (see 9:6, which has the definite article). The genitive singular is preferred.

Verse 2

σκηνή—the position of this noun is unique: without the definite article it stands first in the sentence and thus receives all the emphasis it needs. The noun, however, is defined by the definite article and adjective ἡ πρώτη. The adjective conveys the idea of two rooms in one tabernacle, not two tabernacles.

ἅγια—the accent mark indicates that this substantivized adjective is the neuter plural, not the feminine singular, which is ἁγία. The adjective lacks the definite article (see also 9:24). The writer of Hebrews builds a sequence of τὸ ἅγιον (9:1), ἅγια (9:2), and ἅγια ἁγίων (9:3). Says Norman H. Young, "It is best to take verse 2 as a neuter plural and allow the use of this form for a description of the outer tent (as in verse 2) as exceptional."[6]

Verse 3

μετά—this preposition controls the accusative case of τὸ καταπέτασμα as an accusative of place. For the use of καταπέτασμα, see Hebrews 6:19. This noun is modified by the adjective δεύτερον, which implies a first curtain of less importance than the second.

ἅγια ἁγίων—the definite articles are lacking. See the Septuagint reading of Exodus 26:33; I Kings 6:16; 7:50; 8:6; II Chronicles 4:22; 5:7.

Verse 4

ἔχουσα—as a feminine present participle of ἔχω (I have, hold), it takes θυμιατήριον (altar) and κιβωτόν (ark) as direct objects. The participle does not differentiate and treats both objects alike.

περικεκαλυμμένην—a perfect passive participle derived from the compound περί (around) and καλύπτω (I cover). In 9:4, the author emphasizes the beauty of the Most Holy Place by using the noun *gold* once and the adjective *golden* twice.

Verse 5

αὐτῆς—the antecedent of this pronoun is τὴν κιβωτόν (9:4). It is in the genitive case because of the adverb ὑπεράνω (above) used as a preposition.

κατασκιάζοντα—this present active participle from κατασκιάζω (I overshadow) has a single occurrence in the New Testament. It is an intensive compound with the meaning "covering the lid of the ark completely with shade." And last, the participle is plural, because its subject χερουβίν is a transliterated plural.

---

6. Norman H. Young, "The Gospel According to Hebrews 9," *NTS* 27 (1981): 198. James Swetnam, in "Hebrews 9:2," *CBQ* 32 (1970): 205–21, gives the interpretation that "what the author has in mind when he uses the word *hagia* is the elements of the eucharistic bread" (p. 208).

2. The High Priest and the Most Holy Place 9:6–10

The author of Hebrews in 9:6–10 places in sharper focus the contrast alluded to in 9:1. He shows that the "regulations for worship" were external and consequently temporal. And he notes that the high priest entered the Most Holy Place only once a year; priests had no access to the inner sanctuary. As representatives of the people, priests and high priests faced limitations.

6. When everything had been arranged like this, the priests entered regularly into the outer room to carry on their ministry. 7. But only the high priest entered the inner room, and that only once a year, and never without blood, which he offered for himself and for the sins the people had committed in ignorance.

From a description of tabernacle and sanctuary furniture, the author moves to an explanation of the duties of priests and high priest. He notes that "the priests entered regularly into the outer room to carry on their ministry." The Old Testament teaches what these duties were: to burn incense every morning and evening (Exod. 30:7–8), to tend to the lamps of the lampstand "from evening till morning" (Exod. 27:21), and to replace the twelve loaves on the table each Sabbath (Lev. 24:8–9). The New Testament teaches that according to a custom of that day, priests were chosen by lot to enter the temple and burn incense (Luke 1:9).

However, because priests were not allowed to go beyond the Holy Place, they did not have access to God. That privilege was given to the high priest. But even he was restricted in approaching God. First, of all the people in Israel, he alone was appointed to enter the presence of God. Next, he was permitted to come before God only once a year, that is, on the Day of Atonement (the tenth day of the seventh month—about the end of September to the beginning of October [Lev. 23:26; Num. 29:7]). On this particular day, the high priest entered the Most Holy Place. A third restriction was that he might never enter without the sacrificial blood of an animal: the blood of a bull at first and then the blood of a goat (Lev. 16:14–15). The high priest, therefore, went into the inner sanctuary twice. The last stipulation concerned sin. The high priest sprinkled the blood of the bull on and in front of the cover of the ark (called the atonement cover) as a sin offering for himself and his household (Lev. 16:11, 14). He offered this blood to God for the purpose of covering his sin and the sin of his family. After that, he entered the Most Holy Place again, but now with the blood of a goat. This he sprinkled on and before the atonement cover. This offering covered the sins of the people (vv. 15–16).

Whereas the Old Testament teaches that the high priest made "atonement for the Most Holy Place because of the uncleanness and rebellion of the Israelites, *whatever their sins [had] been*" (Lev. 16:16, italics added), the author of Hebrews writes that the high priest offered sacrifices "for the sins the people had *committed in ignorance*" (Heb. 9:7, italics added). The Old Testament makes a clear distinction between sins committed unintentionally (that is, in ignorance) and those sins man commits defiantly. Unintentional sins will be forgiven; intentional sins cannot be forgiven, for the man who commits them "blasphemes the LORD" (Num. 15:22–31, especially v. 30). The writer of Hebrews underscores the consequences of intentional sin (see 3:16–19; 6:4–6; and 10:26–27). He also mentions the duties of the high priest, who "is able to deal gently with those who are ignorant and are going astray" (5:2). The good news is that God forgives sin. Nevertheless, access to God was restricted when the old covenant was in force.

8. The Holy Spirit was showing by this that the way into the Most Holy Place had not yet been disclosed as long as the first tabernacle was still standing.

The author's high view of Scripture is expressed once more. In Hebrews 3:7 he introduced the Holy Spirit as speaker of a psalm citation (see also 10:15). The Spirit speaks and interprets the Word of God. He discloses the meaning of the Word (John 14:26; 15:26) and guides the believer in the truth.[7] The Holy Spirit makes it plain that he is involved in the work of redemption.

We note two things.

a. The way to God's presence was not yet opened during the time of the old covenant. That means the people were not allowed to enter the tabernacle; only the priests went into the outer sanctuary to perform their duties. The priests, however, were forbidden to appear before God in the inner sanctuary; only the high priest, as the representative of the people and the priests, might enter the Most Holy Place once a year. Apart from this single exception, God had effectively separated himself from man. A curtain veiled the way to God.

b. The Holy Spirit indicated that "the way into the Most Holy Place had not . . . been disclosed" until the coming of Jesus. By his death, the Son of God opened the way to God. When Jesus died on Calvary's cross, "the curtain of the temple was torn in two from top to bottom" (Matt. 27:51; Mark 15:38). Although the Most Holy Place was empty at the time of Jesus' death, the tearing of the curtain signified that the separation between God and man had ended.

This separation would not end "as long as the first tabernacle was still standing." The word *first* may mean first in rank. If this is the interpretation of "first," the word refers to the inner sanctuary. But because of the tearing of the curtain, the first room had ceased to exist separately. The first and second rooms became one, and man gained access to God without priestly mediation.

We can also understand the expression *first* to mean the earthly sanctuary made by Moses in the desert. The implied second sanctuary, then, is the heavenly "tabernacle set up by the Lord" (Heb. 8:2; see also 9:11).

---

7. The tense of the participle *showing* in Heb. 9:8 can be translated either in the past tense (NAB, NIV) or in the present tense (JB, GNB, MLB, RSV, NEB, *Phillips*, NASB).

Of the two interpretations, the second seems to be more in line with the author's train of thought. He exhorts the believers to approach God, for "we have confidence to enter the Most Holy Place by the blood of Jesus" (10:19).

9. This is an illustration for the present time, indicating that the gifts and sacrifices being offered were not able to clear the conscience of the worshiper.

Some translations take the words "this is an illustration for the present time" parenthetically.[8] But this is not necessary if we understand the antecedent of the word *this* to be "the first tabernacle." This structure and all that is represented served as an illustration—the original Greek has the word *parable.* What does the illustration prove? It shows that the sacrificial system of the first tabernacle period failed to bring perfection because "the gifts and sacrifices being offered were not able to clear the conscience of the worshiper."

The writer sees the first tabernacle as an illustration of that which is real. The illustration itself, then, is not identical to reality. To make this clear to the reader, the author introduces the word *conscience.* That is a significant word, for man's conscience is the barometer of his moral sensitivity to deeds performed. Before the death of Christ, believers driven by a guilty conscience brought gifts and sacrifices to God. But these offerings, given to the priest who served as intermediary, did not quiet the awakened conscience of the worshiper. Gifts and sacrifices failed to remove guilt that continued to bother the believer's conscience. They could not clear the conscience of the sinner who came to God with offerings. They were unable to make the worshiper whole, perfect, and complete with respect to his conscience.

Therefore, the illustration points to reality. Gifts and sacrifices made the believer outwardly clean, ceremonially, but the blood of Christ removes sin, cleanses the conscience, and makes man whole. That is reality (see Heb. 9:13–14).

10. They are only a matter of food and drink and various ceremonial washings—external regulations applying until the time of the new order.

What do these gifts and sacrifices accomplish? The first thing we must keep in mind is that they were on the same level as divine injunctions that regulated the life of the Old Testament believer. These commandments pertained to the daily practices of eating, drinking, and staying clean outwardly. Next, these regulations were imposed on the believer by God when he spoke through Moses. God gave the Israelites rules concerning clean and unclean foods (Lev. 11; see also Heb. 13:9), grain offerings and drink offerings (Num. 6:15, 17; 28:7–8), and matters of cleanliness (Num. 19:13). These rules and regulations are only external. The writer stresses the word *only* to mean "that and nothing more." We see that the author has returned to the subject of external regulations that he introduced in 9:1.

To return to the question: "What do these external rules accomplish?" We

---

8. See the RSV, NEB, and *Moffatt.*

must say they were not unprofitable. God gave them to his people for their own benefit and well-being; also he gave them the assurance that they were his special people who lived in harmony with his laws and rules. But apart from these objectives the external regulations did not advance the believer in his search for the cleansing of his soul. External rules achieve external objectives. A God-fearing Israelite could abstain from unclean food, cleanse himself from defilement, offer acceptable gifts and sacrifices to God; yet he remained within the structure of the old covenant. Keeping the commandments actually became a preventive action on the part of the Israelite; this enabled him to stay within the nation Israel and to continue as a member of God's people. But the external ceremonial rules and regulations were not meant to cleanse the believer's conscience and to renew him spiritually.

In both verses 9 and 10, the author employs the word *time*—"for the present time" and "until the time of the new order." Both verses convey the idea of a limited period: the first use refers to the time in which we see the first tabernacle as an illustration of reality; the second relates to the coming of the messianic age in which the new order prevails.

Practical Considerations in 9:1–10

We know that the Jewish people of Jesus' day were burdened by the numerous manmade laws they had to observe (Matt. 23:3–4). For instance, on one particular Sabbath, Jesus' disciples picked ears of grain, rubbed them in their hands, and ate the kernels of grain (Luke 6:1 and parallels). In the eyes of the Pharisees, the disciples had transgressed the commandment "Remember the Sabbath day by keeping it holy" (Exod. 20:8). They were guilty on two counts: first, they had violated the manmade law "you shall not harvest on the Sabbath" when they picked the ears of grain; and second, they had rubbed the ears of grain in their hands in violation of the manmade law "you shall not thresh on the Sabbath."

Although we may smile at practices current in first-century Palestine, we ought to be careful not to elevate our traditions to the level of law and enforce them rigidly. Especially with traditions relating to worship services, we have a tendency to be unbending. Although many of our traditions have become sacred, we should be careful not to stress external observances of certain practices at the expense of internal attitudes and needs. "The sacrifices of God are a broken spirit; a broken and contrite heart, O God, you will not despise" (Ps. 51:17).

Through the faithful preaching of God's Word, man's conscience must become increasingly sensitive. As a compass needle constantly points north, so our consciences always must turn to Scripture first. Our spiritual forefathers, discussing matters pertaining to life or conduct, used to ask, "What does the Bible say?" That question is still valid today.

Greek Words, Phrases, and Constructions in 9:6–10

Verse 6

κατεσκευασμένων—the perfect passive participle in the genitive absolute construction derives from the intensive compound verb κατασκευάζω (I prepare thoroughly). The perfect tense denotes the resultant state of those things that had been arranged.

διὰ παντός—the noun χρόνου (in the genitive case) should be supplied to make the phrase complete, but it was never used. The expression means "always, continually, regularly."

εἰσίασιν—this present active indicative form is from the compound verb εἰς (into) and εἶμι (I go).

Verse 7

ἅπαξ τοῦ ἐνιαυτοῦ—the genitive of time is introduced by the adverb ἅπαξ (once). This adverb appears fifteen times in the New Testament, eight of which are in Hebrews.

ἀγνοημάτων—apart from three occurrences in the Septuagint, this noun appears only once in the New Testament. The -μα ending indicates the result of an action; the privative ἀ (not) combines with the verb γνοέω (from γινώσκω, I know). The genitive case depends on the preposition ὑπέρ.

Verse 8

δηλοῦντος—the present active participle in the genitive absolute construction from δηλόω (I make known) is followed by the indirect discourse clause with the accusative subject τὴν ὁδόν (the way) and the perfect passive infinitive πεφανερῶσθαι (from φανερόω, I reveal).

τῶν ἁγίων—because the adjective can be either masculine or neuter, it can be interpreted to mean "saints" (masculine) or "holy things" (neuter). The context favors the use of the neuter with the translation *Most Holy Place.* The genitive is objective.

ἐχούσης—with the noun σκηνῆς (tabernacle) it forms the genitive absolute construction.

Verse 9

ἐνεστηκότα—the perfect active participle derives from ἐνίστημι (I am present, have come).

τελειῶσαι—the aorist active infinitive from τελειόω (I complete, perfect) governs the accusative present participle τὸν λατρεύοντα (the worshiper). The aorist is ingressive.

Verse 10

μόνον—an adverb. The meaning is "only that and nothing more." As a first word in the sentence, it is rather emphatic.

διορθώσεως—derived from διά (through) and ὀρθός (straight), this noun in the genitive case conveys the idea of making something thoroughly straight, of bringing about a reformation.

---

11 When Christ came as high priest of the good things that are already here, he went through the greater and more perfect tabernacle that is not man-made, that is to say, not a part of this creation. 12 He did not enter by means of the blood of goats and calves; but he

entered the Most Holy Place once for all by his own blood, having obtained eternal redemption. 13 The blood of goats and bulls and the ashes of a heifer sprinkled on those who are
ceremonially unclean sanctify them so that they are outwardly clean. 14 How much more,
then, will the blood of Christ, who through the eternal Spirit offered himself unblemished
to God, cleanse our consciences from acts that lead to death, so that we may serve the living
God!

15 For this reason Christ is the mediator of a new covenant, that those who are called may
receive the promised eternal inheritance—now that he has died as a ransom to set them free
from the sins committed under the first covenant.

16 In the case of a will, it is necessary to prove the death of the one who made it, 17 because
a will is in force only when somebody has died; it never takes effect while the one who made
it is living. 18 This is why even the first covenant was not put into effect without blood.
19 When Moses had proclaimed every commandment of the law to all the people, he took
the blood of calves, together with water, scarlet wool and branches of hyssop, and sprinkled
the scroll and all the people. 20 He said, "This is the blood of the covenant, which God has
commanded you to keep." 21 In the same way, he sprinkled with the blood both the tabernacle and everything used in its ceremonies. 22 In fact, the law requires that nearly everything be cleansed with blood, and without the shedding of blood there is no forgiveness.

23 It was necessary, then, for the copies of the heavenly things to be purified with these
sacrifices, but the heavenly things themselves with better sacrifices than these. 24 For Christ
did not enter a man-made sanctuary that was only a copy of the true one; he entered heaven
itself, now to appear for us in God's presence. 25 Nor did he enter heaven to offer himself
again and again, the way the high priest enters the Most Holy Place every year with blood
that is not his own. 26 Then Christ would have had to suffer many times since the creation
of the world. But now he has appeared once for all at the end of the ages to do away with sin
by the sacrifice of himself. 27 Just as man is destined to die once, and after that to face
judgment, 28 so Christ was sacrificed once to take away the sins of many people; and he will
appear a second time, not to bear sin, but to bring salvation to those who are waiting for
him.

E. Jesus' Sacrificial Blood
9:11–28

1. Christ's Blood Cleanses Our Consciences
9:11–14

Repetition is the mother of learning. This is a basic rule that the author of Hebrews applies consistently. He introduced the theme of the high priest's entering the Most Holy Place in 9:7; he expands it in 9:11–12; and he summarizes it in 9:25.[9] Christ offered his own blood to obtain redemption for his people.

11. When Christ came as high priest of the good things that are already here, he went through the greater and more perfect tabernacle that is not man-made, that is to say, not a part of this creation. 12. He did not enter by means of the blood of goats and calves; but he entered the Most Holy Place once for all by his own blood, having obtained eternal redemption.

---

9. Young, "The Gospel According to Hebrews 9," p. 199.

These two verses form one beautifully constructed, balanced sentence.[10] The basic thought is that Christ went through the tabernacle (v. 11) and entered the Most Holy Place (v. 12). Commentators have been puzzled by the identity of the tabernacle: what does the author of Hebrews mean by the phrase *greater and more perfect tabernacle?*

Let us note the following points as we seek an answer.

a. *Arrival.* The author returns to his theme that Jesus is high priest (2:17; 3:1; 4:14; 5:5, 10; 6:20; 7:26–28; 8:1–2). He purposely introduces Jesus as Christ (not as Jesus or Son) to show that he is the Messiah, the One whom Israel expected to come. And he states that Christ's arrival has indeed occurred, for Christ has appeared as high priest.

The text can be translated in two ways. Some translations read, "Christ came as high priest of the good things that are already here." Other translations have the reading "of the good things to come." The one translation relates to the present; the other, to the future.

How do we resolve the difficulty? That is, which of the two translations is to be preferred? The reading *good things to come* is similar to the wording of Hebrews 10:1. Possibly a scribe copying 9:11 may have been influenced by the reading of 10:1. The more difficult reading is the one that lacks an immediate parallel and therefore is preferred—in this case "the good things that are already here."

What are these good things that Christ has provided? The author of Hebrews does not say. But we assume that he intimates the close fellowship that God has with his people, the knowledge of God and his law in the hearts and minds of his people, and the remission of sin that God has given his people (8:10–12). The blessings Christ has brought since his coming are innumerable; for this reason the author speaks in general terms and writes "the good things that are already here."

b. *Destiny.* Christ "went through the greater and more perfect tabernacle that is not man-made." We ought to note that the writer has chosen the official title *Christ* and not the personal name *Jesus.* He places the emphasis, then, on the official function of Christ as high priest.

Also we note that 9:11 has a parallel in 8:1–2, "We do have such a high priest, who sat down at the right hand of the throne of the Majesty in heaven, and who serves in the sanctuary, the true tabernacle set up by the Lord, not by man." And 9:11 has another parallel in 9:24, "For Christ did not enter a man-made sanctuary that was only a copy of the true one; he entered heaven itself, now to appear for us in God's presence." These passages reveal that "the greater and more perfect tabernacle" is in heaven, that is, in the presence of God. We ought not take the words *went through* literally in the sense that Christ passed through the tabernacle to another place. In 4:14 the author of Hebrews writes that "we have a great high priest who has gone

---

10. In the original Greek, verses 11 and 12 form one lengthy sentence that has been carefully constructed. See the article by Albert Vanhoye, "Par la tente plus grande et plus parfaite . . ." in *Bib* 46 (1965): 1–28. Also see James Swetnam's article, "The Greater and More Perfect Tent. A Contribution to the Discussion of Hebrews 9:11," in *Bib* 47 (1966): 91–106.

through the heavens." He wishes to convey the thought that Jesus has gone into heaven.

The writer expresses himself rather pointedly by saying that the greater and more perfect tabernacle is not manmade, "that is to say, not a part of this creation." In the early centuries of the Christian era, Bible interpreters understood the word *tabernacle* in 9:11 to mean Christ's body, but the author of Hebrews rules this out by his explanatory comment that the tabernacle is "not a part of this creation." Anything belonging to God's creation, even the visible sky, is ruled out by the author's pointed comment. God's dwelling in heaven, where angels surround his throne and the numberless multitudes of saints sing his praises, is uncreated; it does not belong to creation revealed to us by God's Word and work. The tabernacle that Moses built and God filled with his glory (Exod. 40:35) differs from "the greater and more perfect tabernacle" in heaven. The heavenly tabernacle gives the saints free access to God because no veil separates God and man. Christ opened the way to God on the basis of his mediatorial work on earth.

c. *Means.* How did Christ enter heaven? By means of his death on the cross! The writer puts it this way: "He did not enter by means of the blood of goats and calves; but he entered the Most Holy Place once for all by his own blood."

The expression *goats and calves* is a reminder of the Day of Atonement. On that day, once a year, the high priest entered the Most Holy Place with the blood of a bull and of a goat. The high priest had to sprinkle the blood of the bull as an atonement for his own sins and the blood of the goat as an atonement for the sins of the people (Lev. 16:11–17). The implication is that the blood of animals effected forgiveness and reconciliation.

How different with the great high priest Jesus Christ! Christ "entered the Most Holy Place once for all by his own blood, having obtained eternal redemption." He is high priest and sacrifice at the same time. He is the people's representative before God. He sheds his blood in behalf of his people.

Obviously, the writer depicts the atoning work of Christ figuratively. That is, when Jesus died on the cross, he did not enter the Most Holy Place of the temple. And when he cried, "It is finished" (John 19:30), he did not need to take his blood into the heavenly tabernacle.[11] Christ completed his atoning work on Calvary's cross. When he suffered and died on the cross, in a sense he entered the Most Holy Place of the temple. God affirmed this by tearing the curtain of the temple in two from top to bottom (Mark 15:38).

d. *Purpose.* The purpose for Christ's sacrificial death is summarized in the clause *having obtained eternal redemption.* After his figurative entrance into the Most Holy Place of the temple in Jerusalem, he once for all, on the strength of his own sacrificial blood shed on the cross, procured redemption of ever-

---

11. Leon Morris, *The Expositor's Bible Commentary,* vol. 12, *Hebrews* (Grand Rapids: Zondervan, 1981), p. 86.

lasting validity for all his people. Christ obtained this redemption for himself, that is, for the benefit of his people.[12] He bought his people with the price of his blood; he redeemed them with his death. Their redemption became eternally valid when Christ figuratively entered the Most Holy Place. "In bringing many sons to glory," writes the author of Hebrews, "it was fitting that God . . . should make the author of their salvation perfect through suffering" (2:10).

13. The blood of goats and bulls and the ashes of a heifer sprinkled on those who are ceremonially unclean sanctify them so that they are outwardly clean. 14. How much more, then, will the blood of Christ, who through the eternal Spirit offered himself unblemished to God, cleanse our consciences from acts that lead to death, so that we may serve the living God!

These two verses show contrast—characteristic of the Epistle to the Hebrews. The author states a fact that relates to the animal sacrifices of the Old Testament era. God had stipulated by law how sinners might be cleansed and restored to holiness. He had ordained these laws to sanctify those who were ceremonially unclean. But merely observing these laws affected the sinner only externally, not internally. Those who were sprinkled, as the text says, were cleansed with respect to their bodies. Their consciences, however, remained unaffected.

In the preceding verse (v. 12) the writer already mentioned "the blood of goats and calves." The reference, of course, is to the stipulations the high priest had to observe on the Day of Atonement (Lev. 16). In addition, the author now describes the practice of sprinkling the unclean person with water of cleansing (Num. 19). A red heifer in perfect condition and that had never been harnessed had to be slain and burned. As it was being burned, the priest had to throw cedar wood, hyssop, and scarlet wool onto the heifer. The ashes then were gathered and kept for use in the ceremony of sprinkling the water of cleansing.

Anyone who had touched a dead body was considered unclean for seven days. Ashes from the burned heifer were put into a jar; fresh water was poured over them; and with hyssop dipped into the water, an unclean person was sprinkled on the third and seventh days.

Allegorical interpretations of this passage (Num. 19) are numerous. For example, the heifer symbolizes the propagation of life; ashes are an antidote to pollution; the colors of the red heifer and of the scarlet wool portray vitality; cedar wood stands for durability; and hyssop is the emblem of cleansing. However, fanciful elucidations are highly subjective and ultimately of little value. We do well to look at the author's purpose for introducing the matter of "the blood of goats and bulls and the ashes of a heifer."

The author contrasts two incidents: the ceremonial acts performed by the believer to secure cleansing and the shedding of the blood of Christ. The

---

12. Burkhard Gärtner, *NIDNTT*, vol. 3, p. 529.

religious observance of the Day of Atonement, although significant in itself, nevertheless fostered an external perception of the sacrifices. This became especially evident in the act of sprinkling the water of cleansing on the person who was declared unclean because of defilement. A person who had touched a dead body was considered unclean, but water of cleansing sanctified him. The thought that uncleanness was something external and not internal prevailed. Jesus rebuked the Pharisees on one occasion when he said, "Now then, you Pharisees clean the outside of the cup and dish, but inside you are full of greed and wickedness" (Luke 11:39).

The argument that the author develops proceeds from the lesser to the greater. The *lesser* part is the ceremonial act of using the blood of goats and bulls and the ashes of a heifer to sanctify a sinner externally. The *greater* part is that the blood of Christ cleanses the sinner's conscience to make him an obedient servant of God. Unquestionably, sin is an internal matter that issues from the heart of man. The writer of Proverbs calls the heart "the wellspring of life" (4:23). And Jesus describes the heart as the source of evils: "For from within, out of men's hearts, come evil thoughts, sexual immorality, theft, murder, adultery, greed, malice, deceit, lewdness, envy, slander, arrogance and folly" (Mark 7:21–22). The act of cleansing man from sin must begin with his inner being; as the author of Hebrews writes, "our consciences." How are our consciences cleansed? I call attention to the following phrases.

a. "The blood of Christ." Although the blood of animals in a sense served the same function as did the blood of Christ, the contrast introduced by "how much more" is so immense that we cannot speak of a comparison. The blood of Christ is the agent that cleanses the conscience of man, that breaks him from "acts that lead to death," and that makes man willing and ready to serve God. Christ's blood cleanses man from sin. Robert Lowry sang:

> For my cleansing this I see—
> Nothing but the blood of Jesus;
> For my pardon this my plea—
> Nothing but the blood of Jesus.

b. "Through the eternal Spirit." Some translations render the word *spirit* with a capital letter, and others use a lower-case letter. In the original Greek all the letters were written uniformly, so that we cannot determine whether the author of Hebrews meant one or the other.

What can we learn from the theological context of this passage? What do the Scriptures say? Again, we cannot be certain as to the exact intention of the author as we view the rest of Scripture. The four Gospels say nothing about the Holy Spirit's role in the suffering of Christ. On the other hand, when Jesus preached in his hometown synagogue at Nazareth, he read from the prophecy of Isaiah, "The Spirit of the Lord is on me" (Luke 4:18; Isa. 61:1; and see Isa. 42:1). Says Donald Guthrie, "The statement in Hebrews is a logical deduction from the gospel portrait of Jesus."[13] Even though we would have been more certain if the author had written "Holy Spirit" instead of "eternal Spirit," we know that Jesus was indeed led by the Holy Spirit. For example, Luke writes: "Jesus, full of the Holy Spirit, returned from the Jordan and was led by the Spirit in the desert, where for forty days he was tempted by the devil" (Luke 4:1–2).

c. Christ "offered himself unblemished." As high priest, Christ presented himself as a sacrifice. He offered himself to God spontaneously and blamelessly. But unlike the Aaronic high priest who had to sacrifice an animal to remove his own sin, the sinless Christ offered his body for the sins of his people. He laid down his life for his sheep. As John, describing the death of Jesus on the cross, testifies, Jesus "bowed his head and gave up his spirit" (19:30). Jesus willingly, purposefully, and conscientiously faced death and offered himself to God.

Why did Christ offer himself to God? To "cleanse our consciences from acts that lead to death." In 6:1 the author introduced the phrase "from acts that lead to death." The wording implies the destructive effects of sin in the life of the believer. That is, the blood of Christ effectively cleanses man's conscience by turning him from a life that leads to spiritual death to a life spent in love and obedient service for God. The believer keeps God's commandments not because of obligation but out of a sense of gratitude for what Christ in God has done for him. The believer, saved from a life of sin that leads to death, now lives a life of service for his living God.

Doctrinal Considerations in 9:11–14

The biblical doctrine of atonement encounters opposition voiced by those advocates who portray God as a God of love. They contend that God could not have demanded that Christ shed his blood in order to appease an angry God.[14] They object to a "blood theology" because, they say, it runs contrary to the love of God. However, the love of God does not annul his justice. Man is a sinner who because of sin stands condemned before God. Of his own free will, Christ took the place of sinful man and paid the penalty for him. By shedding his own blood, Christ endeavored to obtain eternal redemption, that is, "to bring salvation to those who are waiting for him" (9:28). The writer of Hebrews unequivocally teaches the doctrine of atonement. Says he, Christ "entered the Most Holy Place once for all by his own blood" (9:12).

In this section and in other parts of his epistle, the author of Hebrews teaches the unique doctrine that Christ became priest and sacrifice. Christ became subject and object at the same time: he served at the altar as priest and was laid on the altar as sacrifice. Christ shed his blood as sacrifice on Calvary's cross and figuratively

---

13. Donald Guthrie, *New Testament Theology* (Downers Grove, Ill.: Inter-Varsity, 1981), p. 568. Also see F. F. Bruce, *The Epistle to the Hebrews,* New International Commentary on the New Testament series (Grand Rapids: Eerdmans, 1964), p. 205.

14. Louis Berkhof, *Systematic Theology* (Grand Rapids: Eerdmans, 1953), p. 382.

as high priest entered the Most Holy Place of the temple. Scripture teaches that the offering of his sacrifice was completed on earth; in the capacity of high priest, Christ entered "the greater and more perfect tabernacle" in heaven, that is, the presence of God.

The writer of Hebrews deletes numerous details from the laws concerning the Day of Atonement and the ceremonial cleansings for persons declared unclean. He purposely omits these details to put in stark relief the contrast between the external observance of religious ceremonies and the inner transformation of a man cleansed by the blood of Christ. That, for him, is the difference between life in the days of the old covenant and that in the era of the new covenant.

Greek Words, Phrases, and Constructions in 9:11–14

Verse 11

παραγενόμενος—this aorist middle (deponent) participle of the verb παραγίνομαι (I arrive, appear) shows that Christ served as high priest before his ascension to heaven. The participle, expressing a temporal connotation, points to the entire ministry of Christ. The preposition παρά (alongside of) strengthens the main verb γίνομαι and gives it direction.

γενομένων—the aorist middle participle from γίνομαι (I am, become) has a variant in a number of leading manuscripts. The variant is μελλόντων—present active participle of μέλλω (I am about to). The first reading, however, seems to have a better geographical representation of manuscripts and is therefore preferred. See also 10:1 for similar wording of the second reading.

χειροποιήτου—a compound adjective consisting of the noun χείρ (hand) and the noun ποιητής (a maker). The adjective occurs six times in the New Testament and generally is used with reference to buildings; that is, temples (Mark 14:58; Acts 7:48; 17:24; Eph. 2:11; Heb. 9:11, 24).

Verse 12

τὰ ἅγια—the substantivized adjective in the neuter plural preceded by the definite article stands for the sanctuary and even the Most Holy Place in tabernacle and temple.

λύτρωσιν—this noun conveys the meaning *ransom, deliverance, redemption* and appears three times in the New Testament (Luke 1:68; 2:38; Heb. 9:12). In the context of Hebrews 9 the word connotes as much ransom as redemption. See also 9:15.

Verse 13

εἰ—the particle introduces a simple fact conditional clause that expresses certainty. The apodosis to this lengthy sentence is given in 9:14.

ῥαντίζουσα—the feminine present active participle from the verb ῥαντίζω (I sprinkle) modifies the noun σποδός (ashes), which is feminine. Perhaps it is best to link the participle only to the noun *ashes* and not to the preceding noun τὸ αἷμα (blood).

Verse 14

πόσῳ μᾶλλον—the combination of these two words always introduces a so-called dative of degree of difference. The difference lies in the comparison stated in the two parts of the conditional sentence, beginning with εἰ γάρ (for if).

αἰωνίου—some manuscripts have the variant reading ἁγίου (holy) that removes the ambiguity created by the reading *eternal.* However, the manuscript evidence lacks the strength to give the reading *holy* authenticity.

καθαριεῖ—the future tense from the verb καθαρίζω (I cleanse) expresses certainty because its fulfillment is expected.

ἡμῶν—to determine whether the reading should be ἡμῶν (our) or ὑμῶν (your) is not easy, because the manuscript evidence is equally divided. Perhaps the author's use of exhortations in the broader context favors the translation *our.*[15] On the whole, although the difference itself is insignificant, the author seems to include himself whenever he addresses the recipients of his epistle.

---

2. Christ's Death and the First Covenant
9:15

Weaving his artistic verbal cloth, the author of Hebrews is ready to bring in the concepts of mediator and covenant. In chapter 8, especially verse 6, he introduced the role of mediator that Jesus has been given. Having explained Christ's death and its effect in chapter 9, he now develops the significance of this mediatorial role in relation to the covenant that God has made with his people.

15. For this reason Christ is the mediator of a new covenant, that those who are called may receive the promised eternal inheritance—now that he has died as a ransom to set them free from the sins committed under the first covenant.

When the author writes "for this reason," he wants us to look at verses 13 and 14 specifically and the preceding context generally. In these two verses, the writer contrasts the sacrifices of the first covenant with the sacrifice of Christ that introduces a new relationship. In verse 15, the author summarizes and says, "Christ is the mediator of a new covenant."

Before we proceed any further, we ought to take note of the institution of the first covenant, recorded in Exodus 24. Moses read the Law of God to the Israelites, who responded, "Everything the Lord has said we will do" (v. 3). Then burnt offerings and fellowship offerings were presented to God, and blood was sprinkled on the altar. Moses then read the Book of the Covenant to the people, who said, "We will do everything the Lord has said; we will obey" (v. 7). Thereupon Moses, sprinkling blood on the people, said, "This is the blood of the covenant that the Lord has made with you in accordance with all these words" (v. 8).

---

15. Bruce M. Metzger, *A Textual Commentary on the Greek New Testament* (London and New York: United Bible Societies, 1975), p. 668.

Here are the characteristics of this covenant:

1. The covenant God made with his people had two parties: God and the Israelites entered into a solemn commitment on the basis of the content of the Book of the Covenant.
2. The covenant was sealed by the death of animals that were offered to God. The blood of those animals was sprinkled on altar and people.
3. The covenant was ratified by the people who promised obedience to God.

Why did this covenant become obsolete? The author quotes a lengthy passage from Jeremiah 31 in chapter 8, and in the first part of the next chapter he explains that the regulations of the first covenant were external (9:1, 10). "The gifts and sacrifices being offered were not able to clear the conscience of the worshiper" (9:9). Sins committed against God, as a violation of the covenant promise, could not be erased from man's conscience by presenting gifts and offerings to God. The blood of animals sacrificed to atone for man's transgressions sanctified him outwardly, but inwardly man struggled with a guilty conscience.[16] The first covenant, then, needed to be replaced.

By his sacrifice on the cross, Christ validated the new covenant that he instituted at the time he celebrated the Passover with his disciples. He said: "This cup is the new covenant in my blood, which is poured out for you" (Luke 22:20; also see the parallel passages in Matt. 26:28; Mark 14:24; and I Cor. 11:25).

Christ has become the mediator of this new covenant (12:24). He stands between God and man. By his death he removes sin and guilt, and thus all "those who are called may receive the promised eternal inheritance." Through the mediatorial work of Christ, they who are effectively called inherit salvation. And that inheritance is eternal.

What is the meaning of "new" in the expression *new covenant*? First, the new comes forth out of the old. That is, the new covenant has the same basis and characteristics as the old covenant. Next, in both covenants, sacrifices were presented to God; but whereas the sacrifices offered to atone for the transgressions of the people in the time of the first covenant could not set the sinner free, the supreme sacrifice of Christ's death redeemed God's people and paid for their sins. Moreover, in the structure of the first covenant, the mediator (i.e., the high priest) was imperfect. In the new covenant Christ is the mediator who guarantees the promise of salvation. God puts his laws in the minds and writes them on the hearts of his redeemed people, so that as a result they know God, experience remission of sin, and enjoy covenantal fellowship with him.

---

16. "The implication is that these transgressions were the reason for the lack of efficacious reception of the heritage connected with the first diatheke." See James Swetnam, "A Suggested Interpretation of Hebrews 9:15–18," in *CBQ* 27 (1965): 380.

Greek Words, Phrases, and Constructions in 9:15

Verse 15

γενομένου—the aorist middle (deponent) participle of the verb γίνομαι (I am, become) in the genitive singular is part of the genitive absolute construction with the noun θανάτου (death). The aorist denotes single occurrence.

ἐπί—as a preposition with the dative it expresses time or occasion and is translated "under." The GNB translation is, "while the first covenant was in effect."

παραβάσεων—this articular noun in the genitive plural of παράβασις (transgression) is used figuratively: it refers to the sinner who committed the transgression.

κεκλημένοι—of all the New Testament epistles, only Hebrews has the perfect passive participle of καλέω (I call). The use of the perfect expresses the all-inclusive extent of the call.

---

3. Christ's Blood Procures Forgiveness
9:16–22

The word *covenant* implies sin. Sin necessitates the making of a new covenant and the shedding of blood. The shedding of blood leads to death and remission of sin.

16. In the case of a will, it is necessary to prove the death of the one who made it, 17. because a will is in force only when somebody has died; it never takes effect while the one who made it is living.

At times a word can have two entirely different meanings that can be distinguished only by the context in which they are used. For example, the word *letter* may mean either "one of the letters of the alphabet" or "an epistle." In English this one word serves two meanings; in other languages two different words express these meanings.

In the original Greek one word (*diathēkē*) serves the purpose of conveying the concepts *covenant* and *will* or *testament.* In 9:15 the context is a religious setting, and the word means "covenant"; the author speaks of the new covenant of which Christ is the mediator and of the first covenant which, by implication, has been superseded. In the next two verses (16 and 17), the writer switches from the religious setting to a legal framework.[17] Now he introduces the concept of a last will. A lawyer draws up a will for a client who apportions his belongings to various people and agencies. But this last will becomes valid only upon the death of the person who made it. While the person is living, the will is nothing but a document, even though a lawyer testifies to its legality. Also this will may be changed and rewritten, but the moment the maker of the will dies, the words in the will are unalterable.

How do verses 16 and 17 relate to 9:15? What is the connection between the word *covenant* and the word *will*? In verse 15 the author teaches that Christ, the mediator of a new covenant, died a sacrificial death to redeem

17. Johannes Behm, *TDNT,* vol. 2, p. 131.

those who will receive their promised inheritance. In the following two verses, he states that the death of the maker of a will validates this document. The implication is that the maker of the covenant is God, who has also made a will. Christ, the Son of God, is not the maker of a covenant or a will. Functioning as a mediator and as a guarantor, he sees that the conditions of the covenant are met and that its promises are honored. Christ died to fulfill these conditions. But at the same time, Christ's death validates the last will and testament, so that believers indeed "may receive the promised eternal inheritance" (9:15). Christ is their guarantor.

In a sense, verses 16 and 17 serve as an analogy. But analogies have their limitations, and so does this one. Upon his death, a person leaves his possessions to his heirs; these heirs themselves face death and in time die. Christ, however, died but rose from the dead; the heirs receive an eternal inheritance and live with him forever.[18]

18. This is why even the first covenant was not put into effect without blood. 19. When Moses had proclaimed every commandment of the law to all the people, he took the blood of calves, together with water, scarlet wool and branches of hyssop, and sprinkled the scroll and all the people. 20. He said, "This is the blood of the covenant, which God has commanded you to keep." 21. In the same way, he sprinkled with the blood both the tabernacle and everything used in its ceremonies. 22. In fact, the law requires that nearly everything be cleansed with blood, and without the shedding of blood there is no forgiveness.

Two matters stand out: first, the expression *first covenant* relates to the same phrase in 9:15. Therefore the two intervening verses, given in the form of an analogy, may be placed within parentheses.[19] Second, in verses 18–22 the word *blood* appears six times. Because of this repetition it receives emphasis in this section. We shall examine the term *blood* in the context of each verse in which it occurs.

a. "Not put into effect without blood." The institution of the first covenant is recorded in Exodus 24. Moses read the law of God to the people, presented burnt offerings and fellowship offerings to God, sprinkled the blood of young bulls (sacrificed in these offerings) on the altar and on the people, read the Book of the Covenant to the people, and said, "This is the blood of the covenant that the LORD has made with you in accordance with all these words" (Exod. 24:8). The writer of Hebrews observes that this first covenant was sealed with blood.[20] And he notes the connection between the first and the second covenants: Christ shed his blood and thus sealed this

18. R. C. H. Lenski in *The Interpretation of the Epistle to the Hebrews and of the Epistle of James* (Columbus: Wartburg, 1946), p. 307, cautions not to press the analogy too far. Also see Bruce, *Hebrews,* p. 213.

19. Geerhardus Vos, *The Teaching of the Epistle to the Hebrews* (Grand Rapids: Eerdmans, 1956), p. 40.

20. John Murray, *The Covenant of Grace* (London: Tyndale, 1953), p. 27.

new covenant with his blood. His death made the new covenant valid and effective.

b. "The blood of calves." If we compare the biblical account of the institution of the first covenant, recorded in Exodus 24, with the description in Hebrews 9:19, we must conclude that the writer of Hebrews relied on oral tradition, extrabiblical material, or the five books of Moses. Perhaps he gained his material from various passages of these books. The differences are pronounced:

Exodus 24:5–6, 8	*Hebrews 9:19*
Then [Moses] sent young Israelite men, and they offered burnt offerings and sacrificed young bulls as fellowship offerings to the LORD. Moses took half of the blood and put it in bowls, and the other half he sprinkled on the altar...[and] on the people.	[Moses] took the blood of calves [and goats],[21] together with water, scarlet wool and branches of hyssop, and sprinkled the scroll and all the people.

On the Day of Atonement the priests offered a young bull and a goat (Lev. 16:3–28). The author of Hebrews, therefore, could have combined the account of the sacrificial ceremony of the Day of Atonement with that of the institution of the first covenant. Also, he may have gleaned the phrase "scarlet wool and branches of hyssop" from the description of the ceremony of the cleansing of a person with an infectious skin disease (Lev. 14:4, 6). In these verses the expression *scarlet yarn and hyssop* occurs. Then, in the passage that describes the water of cleansing, hyssop, scarlet wool, and water are mentioned (Num. 19:6, 9, 18).

According to the Exodus account, Moses sprinkled the blood of young bulls on the altar and on the people. He read to the people from the Book of the Covenant. We may assume that he sprinkled blood on this book, too. Philip Edgcumbe Hughes surmises that "on the day of solemn ratification of the former covenant, Moses would have sprinkled not only the altar he had built and the people but also the book he had written."[22]

c. "The blood of the covenant." From a New Testament perspective we immediately see a resemblance between the words of Moses cited by the author of Hebrews and the words spoken by Jesus when he instituted the Lord's Supper.

Moses said to the Israelites, "This is the blood of the covenant that the LORD has made with you in accordance with all these words" (Exod. 24:8).

---

21. Most translations include the words *and goats*. The NIV omits them, no doubt on the basis of the principle that "in general the shorter reading is to be preferred." Editions of the Greek New Testament support the inclusion of the disputed words, although they are put in brackets to indicate a measure of uncertainty.

22. Philip Edgcumbe Hughes, *Commentary on the Epistle to the Hebrews* (Grand Rapids: Eerdmans, 1977), p. 376.

The writer of Hebrews has Moses say, "This is the blood of the covenant, which God has commanded you to keep" (Heb. 9:20). The variation of "the LORD has made with you" and "God has commanded you" is one of form, not of content.

We would have expected the author of Hebrews to refer directly to the well-known words spoken by Jesus at the institution of the Lord's Supper and repeated whenever this supper is celebrated. Jesus said, "This is my blood of the covenant, which is poured out for many" (Mark 14:24). The purpose for Christ's shed blood is given more explicitly in Matthew's Gospel: "for the forgiveness of sins" (Matt. 26:28). The connection between the words that Moses spoke when the first covenant was instituted and the words that Jesus uttered when he brought into practice the celebration of the Lord's Supper is plain. Perhaps because of the self-evident link, the writer of Hebrews has left the missing details for the readers of his epistle to supply.

d. "Sprinkled with the blood." Once again we note a difference between the Old Testament account (Exod. 40:9–11) and the words of the author of Hebrews (9:21). When Moses set up the tabernacle, God told him to "take the anointing oil and anoint the tabernacle and everything in it; consecrate it and all its furnishings, and it will be holy" (Exod. 40:9). The writer of Hebrews, however, asserts that Moses "sprinkled with the blood both the tabernacle and everything used in its ceremonies" (9:21). In the account of the ordination of Aaron and his sons, we read that Moses killed a bull and with the blood purified the altar. Already he had consecrated the tabernacle and everything in it, including the altar, with oil; he even anointed Aaron with oil (Lev. 8:10–15). Because of this parallel account in the Book of Leviticus, we can safely assume that the writer with his intimate knowledge of the Old Testament Scriptures relied on the account of Leviticus more than that of Exodus.

Josephus comments on the inaugural ceremonies of the tabernacle and the ordination of Aaron and his sons. He, too, speaks of purifying Aaron and his sons and their garments "as also the tabernacle and its vessels, both with oil that had been previously fumigated . . . and with the blood of bulls and goats."[23] Josephus, like the author of Hebrews, is fully acquainted with the biblical record in Leviticus 8. Yet both writers contend that Moses purified with the sprinkled blood the tabernacle and its vessels. That information is not found in Leviticus; most likely it had come to them by oral tradition.

e. "Cleansed with blood." The writer of Hebrews testifies that his constant emphasis on purification with blood is not his own idea. He bases it on the law of God. Says he, "In fact, the law requires that nearly everything be cleansed with blood" (9:22). That law is recorded in Leviticus 17:11 where God through Moses says to the Israelites: "For the life of a creature is in the blood, and I have given it to you to make atonement for yourselves on the altar; it is the blood that makes atonement for one's life."

---

23. Josephus, *Antiquities* 3.206 (LCL).

Note that the author writes, "The law requires that *nearly* everything be cleansed with blood" (italics added). The term *nearly* leaves room for exceptions, because some items might be cleansed by water or by fire (see Lev. 15:10 and Num. 31:22–24).

f. "Shedding of blood." The second part of Hebrews 9:22 is even more direct: "and without the shedding of blood there is no forgiveness." These two—the pouring out of blood and the forgiveness of sin—go hand in hand. The one does not exist without the other. The first part of the verse implies that exceptions were permitted, for the author says that "nearly everything" needs to be cleansed with blood. But in the second half of the verse, the writer does not allow exceptions. He posits negatives: *without* the shedding of blood there is *no* forgiveness.

The absolute demand for blood to secure remission of sin responds to the terms of the covenant. Transgression of the laws of the covenant that were agreed upon and ratified by the Israelites constitutes a serious offense. This sin can be removed only by death, that is, the substitutionary death of an animal whose blood is shed for the sinner.

The new covenant, instituted by Christ on the eve of his death, is sealed in his blood that has been shed on Calvary's cross for remission of sin. Jesus' words, "This is my blood of the covenant, which is poured out for many for the forgiveness of sins" (Matt. 26:28), are clearly echoed in the second part of Hebrews 9:22.

Doctrinal Considerations in 9:16–22

When God promised Abraham that he would bless him and give him numerous descendants, he confirmed his promise with an oath. The oath that God swore made his promise unalterable (Gen. 22:16–17; Heb. 6:16–17). When God made a covenant with his people, he gave it to them as a last will and testament. To make this will valid for his people, God's Son died. Upon Christ's death, the will became effective, and its wording, unalterable.

God made a covenant with sinful people. He instructed them to sacrifice animals whose shed blood would cleanse them from sin. But because the people of Israel did not remain faithful to the covenant God had made with them, through the prophet Jeremiah he announced that he would make a new covenant with people upon whose minds and hearts his law was written (Jer. 31:31–34; Heb. 8:8–12).

Christ became the mediator of this new covenant, and through his faithfulness, he fulfilled its demands. For the sins of his people he shed not the blood of animals but his own. The writer of Hebrews posits God's demand for restitution of a broken covenant agreement by saying, "Without the shedding of blood there is no forgiveness" (9:22). The counterpart of this statement is the Christian's jubilation, "Because Christ shed his blood, I have been forgiven!"

Greek Words, Phrases, and Constructions in 9:16–22

Verse 16

φέρεσθαι—the present passive infinitive of φέρω (I carry) means "to bring news by announcing it." The translation *to announce* is therefore acceptable: "The death of a testator must be announced" (*Moffatt*).

Verse 17

ἐπὶ νεκροῖς—the Greek is rather descriptive by saying that a will is made valid on the basis of corpses; that is, when death has occurred.

μήποτε—the use of the negative participle μή instead of οὐ is noteworthy, for it shows that the author expects debate on the validity of a will.

Verse 18

ἐγκεκαίνισται—this compound verb in the perfect passive indicative (from ἐγκαινίζω, I renew, initiate) portrays the lasting effect of the first covenant from the day God initiated it in the Sinai desert to the time Christ instituted the new covenant on the eve of his death.

Verse 19

λαληθείσης—the genitive absolute construction governs this aorist passive participle of λαλέω (I speak) and the adjective πάσης (every) and noun ἐντολῆς (commandment). The words ἐντολή and ὁ νόμος (the law) are virtually synonymous in this context. Moses read them to the people from the scroll.

Verse 22

σχεδόν—an adverb derived from the verb ἔχω (I have, hold), that is, "to be held near," and thus "nearly, almost." The word appears three times in the New Testament (Acts 13:44; 19:26; Heb. 9:22).

αἱματεκχυσίας—the author coins a noun from the noun αἷμα (blood) and the verb ἐκχύνω (I pour out). These two words also occur in Jesus' declaration, "This is my *blood* of the covenant, which is *poured out* for many for the forgiveness of sins" (Matt. 26:28, italics added; see also Mark 14:24 and Luke 22:20).

ἄφεσις—this noun includes the concept *sins.* It refers to the forgiveness of sins, and as such it is an echo of Matthew 26:28.

---

4. Christ's Perfect Sacrifice
9:23–28

Characteristic of the author's style is his frequent repetition of a certain theme. For example, in chapter 8 he wrote that as high priest Christ entered the heavenly sanctuary (8:2). He repeats this theme in the next chapter.

Christ came as high priest, he says, and "went through the greater and more perfect tabernacle that is not man-made" (9:11). Once more he returns to this theme in the following verses (9:23–28).

23. It was necessary, then, for the copies of the heavenly things to be purified with these sacrifices, but the heavenly things themselves with better sacrifices than these.

In this text two matters stand out: the copies of heavenly things and the heavenly things themselves. The copies, of course, are the earthly sanctuary and everything pertaining to it; the heavenly sanctuary is in the presence of God. We shall consider these two successively.

a. "Copies of the heavenly things." The author says that the purification of the tabernacle, altar, utensils, and scroll was necessary. The word *necessary* indicates that the law requires that these items be purified. And that is exactly what the author states in the preceding verse (9:22). He concludes that "without the shedding of blood there is no forgiveness." God himself instructed the people of Israel, through Moses, to cleanse themselves from sin by shedding the blood of animals at the altar of the sanctuary. This blood was adequate to allow the high priest to enter the Most Holy Place of the tabernacle, but a better sacrifice was needed before a mediator could appear in God's presence in heaven.

b. "The heavenly things themselves." The tabernacle built by Moses was "a copy and shadow of what is in heaven" (8:5). The heavenly sanctuary is "the greater and more perfect tabernacle that is not man-made" (9:11). Christ entered this sanctuary after he had shed his blood on Calvary's cross.

The author of Hebrews now refers to the blood of Christ as "better sacrifices." The plural term *sacrifices* stands for the singular "blood of Christ." The adjective *better* marks the difference between earthly things and heavenly things; that is, the blood of animals cleansed the tabernacle and everything pertaining to it, so that the high priest might enter the Most Holy Place. The blood of Christ cleanses the heavenly things, so that he might enter heaven in God's presence (9:24).

Was it necessary to cleanse heavenly things? The heavenly sanctuary is not manmade and therefore is untainted by sin. It does not need to be cleansed. Before we are able to answer the question, we must understand the expression *heavenly things* in a spiritual sense. The true sanctuary, says the author of Hebrews, is heaven itself (9:24), and heaven is the place where God and his people dwell together. It is the place where the people of God serve him by offering themselves as living sacrifices. Then why does the author write that the heavenly things had to be cleansed? Heaven became a sanctuary for God's people only when the blood of Christ was shed for them. Christ's blood, then, became the basis for their entrance into heaven.

Without Christ's blood God does not open heaven for us and does not accept our living sacrifices. We stand condemned before God in our sins, and heaven remains closed to us. However, the blood of Christ has made heaven into a sanctuary for us, so that we may live there. At the same time, it remains God's dwelling place.

The blood of Christ provides remission of our sins but also sanctifies our presence in heaven. It makes us more delightful than angels and our service of praise more acceptable than that of the angels. We are God's adopted sons and daughters who are "heirs of God and co-heirs with Christ" (Rom. 8:17).

Moreover, Christ's shed blood gives heaven itself added significance. Not only is heaven the sanctuary for God's people, but it is also the place where its inhabitants testify of Christ's redeeming love, his marvelous grace, and his sanctifying power. To Christ they sing a new song, recorded in Revelation 5:9–10:

> With your blood you purchased men for God
> from every tribe and language and people and nation.
> You have made them to be a kingdom and priests to serve our God.

24. For Christ did not enter a man-made sanctuary that was only a copy of the true one; he entered heaven itself, now to appear for us in God's presence.

Even though God caused the veil in the temple to split from top to bottom at the time of Jesus' death (Matt. 27:51), Jesus himself never entered "a man-made sanctuary." When the author of Hebrews spoke of "better sacrifices" (9:23), he made a comparison between the animal sacrifices and the blood of Christ. Although we readily see that Christ's sacrifice is better, we see that in essence the comparison is inadequate.

Animal sacrifices were temporary measures; the high priests, mortal; and the sanctuary, a manmade copy. By contrast, Christ's once-for-all sacrifice is permanent; our high priest, eternal; and the heavenly sanctuary, the true one.

The writer of the epistle first notes which sanctuary Christ did not enter, namely, a manmade copy of the original. The high priest once a year entered the Most Holy Place of this earthly sanctuary to enter the presence of God on behalf of the people. Second, the author notes that Christ "entered heaven itself" and, by implication, the true sanctuary. He entered heaven as high priest to represent us in the presence of God. Only once a year the Levitical high priest spent a few moments in the Most Holy Place as man's representation before God; however, Christ, always in God's presence, constantly represents us as our attorney-at-law (Rom. 8:34; Heb. 7:25; I John 2:1).

25. Nor did he enter heaven to offer himself again and again, the way the high priest enters the Most Holy Place every year with blood that is not his own. 26a. Then Christ would have had to suffer many times since the creation of the world.

By drawing a parallel with the Levitical high priest, the author of Hebrews underscores the profound differences between Christ's priesthood and the

Levitical priesthood. The writer is questioned, as it were, by a Jewish reader who poses a number of arguments.

a. As high priest Christ could never have entered the Most Holy Place of an earthly sanctuary. He belonged to the tribe of Judah, not to the tribe of Levi.

True, that is why he entered heaven.

b. A Levitical high priest annually offered sacrificial blood before God in the Most Holy Place. If Christ is high priest, he will have to do the same in heaven.[24]

Correct, but Christ offered himself on the cross. He shed his blood at Calvary, not in the heavenly sanctuary.

c. The high priest offered the sacrifices of a bull and a goat on the Day of Atonement, but Christ offered himself only once.

Yes, but apart from those people who were raised from the dead, man cannot die twice.

d. On the Day of Atonement the high priest presented animal blood to God, but Christ offered his own blood.

True; if Christ had offered blood other than his own, he would have been identical to the Levitical high priest. Note that the high priest could not present his own blood as a sacrifice, because he himself was a sinner. Christ, the sinless One, could and did offer his own blood for sinners.

e. Once a year the high priest went in and out of the Most Holy Place, but Christ entered the heavenly sanctuary only once.

Exactly. If Christ had to leave heaven and come to earth to die once more—which is absurd—his atoning work would be worthless. Christ's sacrifice is unique.

The writer of Hebrews sums up the matter in one telling statement: If Christ had to offer himself again and again, he "would have had to suffer many times since the creation of the world." And that, of course, cannot be. Rather, Christ's sacrifice on the cross is so effective that it removes the sins of all the Old Testament believers. His sacrifice is retroactive and goes back to the creation of the world, that is, to the time that Adam fell into sin. Thus, Christ's sacrifice is valid for all believers, whether they lived before or after the coming of Christ. His sacrifice is for all times.

26b. But now he has appeared once for all at the end of the ages to do away with sin by the sacrifice of himself.

After making a statement that obviously could not be true, the author now describes conclusively the reason for Christ's coming into the world: "to do away with sin." The adverb *now* refers not to time but to reality. The writer in effect is saying: "This is how it is."

Why did Christ appear on this earth? In simple terms: to cancel sin. He

---

24. The NIV correctly inserts the phrase *did he enter heaven.* The sentence in the Greek is incomplete and needs to be supplemented with the inserted phrase to achieve balance and to complete the meaning.

removed the debt of sin that was written on the believer's account. Christ's coming brought an end to that debt. And the account now shows the word *paid.*

How did Christ remove sin? He himself became the sacrifice that was required to pay for the sins of the whole world (I John 2:2). As Christ's forerunner, John the Baptist, put it: "Look, the Lamb of God, who takes away the sin of the world!" (John 1:29). Christ had no substitute. He sacrificed himself as a substitute for sinners. By his death he paid the debt "to take away the sins of many people" (9:28).

What is the significance of Christ's appearance? The Levitical high priest year after year entered the inner sanctuary. His entrance into God's presence had only a temporal effect. By contrast, Christ's appearance is a single occurrence—it happened once for all. He entered heaven once, that is, at the time of his ascension. The effect of his single appearance lasts forever.

When did Christ come? The author of Hebrews writes, "at the end of the ages." This does not have to refer to the end of time, because in the same context the writer says that Christ will appear a second time (v. 28). The expression apparently points to the total impact of Christ's coming and the effect of his atoning work. And because of his triumph over sin, we live in the last age.

27. Just as man is destined to die once, and after that to face judgment, 28. so Christ was sacrificed once to take away the sins of many people; and he will appear a second time, not to bear sin, but to bring salvation to those who are waiting for him.

The writer of the epistle has a fondness for the word *once*; he uses it eight times (6:4; 9:7, 26, 27, 28; 10:2; 12:26, 27).

In the contrast expressed in these two verses, the term *once* takes a prominent place: "man is destined to die once" and "Christ was sacrificed once." Because of Adam's sin God pronounced the sentence of death upon the human race (Gen. 3:19). Every person faces death once, with the exception of those people who were raised from the dead. No one can escape death. By becoming human, Christ was placed under the same death sentence. He, too, died once.

By implication, man receives the death penalty because of sin. The author of Hebrews indicates as much by adding the clause "and after that to face judgment." Death and judgment follow each other in logical sequence, for man must appear in court to account for sin. "For God will bring every deed into judgment, including every hidden thing, whether it is good or evil" (Eccl. 12:14).

The exact time of the judgment the writer of the epistle purposely omits. He calls attention not to judgment as such but to Christ who "will appear a second time." His concluding remark is that Christ brings "salvation to those who are waiting for him." And that is most important. The writer does not minimize the significance of the judgment. He introduces the topic here; in the next chapter he applies it.[25] He says that if we "deliberately keep on sinning," then all that is left is "a fearful expectation of judgment and of raging fire that will consume the enemies of God" (10:26, 27).

In the comparison that characterizes verses 27 and 28, the emphasis falls on Christ. The Messiah was sacrificed once; and he will appear again.

At the conclusion of his teaching about the atoning work of Christ, the author writes that Christ was sacrificed. In the context of this chapter, the writer has made it clear that Christ offered himself as a sacrifice for sin. Therefore, the words *was sacrificed* must be understood within the context in which they are used: Christ offered himself for the purpose of removing the sins of many people.

Already Isaiah prophesied about the redemptive work of Christ. In the well-known chapter on the suffering Messiah, Isaiah writes: "My righteous servant will justify many, and he will bear their iniquities. . . . For he bore the sin of many, and made intercession for the transgressors" (53:11–12).

Not only has Christ completed his atoning work as high priest; he has also given us the promise that he will return. The Scriptures are very explicit about the return of Christ; it is a promise that is mentioned again and again. When Christ returns, says the author of Hebrews, he comes not to remove sin. That task he finished when he came the first time. When he comes again, he brings salvation to those who are awaiting him.

The last part of verse 28 expresses a note of joy and happiness: Christ is coming! They who are eagerly expecting his return constantly pray the petition found at the conclusion of the New Testament and uttered in response to Jesus' promise, "Yes, I am coming soon." They pray, "Amen. Come, Lord Jesus" (Rev. 22:20).

Joyfully the believers look forward to the day of Jesus' return, for then the Lord will dwell forever with his people, as he has promised. Upon his return he will bring full restoration to all who eagerly await him. When Christ dwells forever with his people, they experience salvation full and free.

Doctrinal Considerations in 9:23–28

The Epistle to the Hebrews is an epistle that features contrasts; in every chapter and in numerous verses, the author compares Christ with angels, Moses, Aaron, or the Levitical priesthood. In this particular section, he shows the unsurpassable excellence of the high-priestly work of Christ. A high priest was appointed to represent the people before God, but the actual time he spent in God's presence was minimal; it occurred only once a year on the Day of Atonement. Our great high priest entered heaven once and stays forever in the presence of God as our mediator, advocate, intercessor, and guarantor.

Moreover, the high priest had to present animal blood before God in the Most Holy Place. His own blood would have been unworthy because he himself was a

25. Guthrie, *New Testament Theology*, p. 863.

sinner. But even animal blood had only a limited effect, for the high priest had to appear before God every year again with additional blood. The writer of Hebrews somewhat later observes, "It is impossible for the blood of bulls and goats to take away sins" (10:4). The sacrifice of Christ's blood, however, has lasting effect. It terminates the ruling power of sin in the mind of man (Rom. 8:2).[26] Christ's blood cleanses the church, so that he is able to present it "without stain or wrinkle or any other blemish . . . holy and blameless" (Eph. 5:27). And the blood of Christ wipes the record clean: a sinner forgiven by God stands before him as if he had never sinned at all.

Last, the Levitical high priest, after performing his duties in the inner sanctuary, reappeared to the people he had represented before God. But when Jesus returns from the heavenly sanctuary, he comes to restore his people by granting them the gift of salvation. When Christ comes again, "he will appear as the perfecter of salvation" for all those who put their trust in him and await his return.[27]

Greek Words, Phrases, and Constructions in 9:23–28

Verse 23

ἀνάγκη—this noun appears four times in Hebrews (7:12, 27; 9:16, 23) and expresses a condition imposed by a law or binding obligation. It is stronger than the verb πρέπει (it is fitting) and similar to δεῖ (it is necessary). The noun stands first in the sentence to receive emphasis.

Verse 24

ἐμφανισθῆναι—the aorist passive infinitive of ἐμφανίζω (I make visible) expresses the culminative idea. Christ's appearance is once for all and has lasting significance.

Verse 26

ἔδει—the use of the imperfect active indicative in this clause is the same as in a conditional sentence that expresses unreality. The first part (*protasis*) of the conditional sentence is lacking. The writer gives only the last part (*apodosis*).[28]

πεφανέρωται—the perfect passive indicative of φανερόω (I reveal, appear) refers to "Christ previously hidden from view in heaven but after his incarnation made visible on earth as a man among men."[29]

---

26. John Owen, *An Exposition of Hebrews,* 7 vols. in 4 (Evansville, Ind.: Sovereign Grace, 1960), vol. 6, p. 403.

27. Johannes Schneider and Colin Brown, *NIDNTT,* vol. 3, p. 215.

28. "When a condition is assumed as unreal and refers to present time, the imperfect tense is used both in the protasis and apodosis in normal constructions. . . . [In] Heb. 9:26 . . . we only have apodosis." A. T. Robertson, *A Grammar of the Greek New Testament in the Light of Historical Research* (Nashville: Broadman, 1934), p. 887.

29. Joseph H. Thayer, *A Greek-English Lexicon of the New Testament* (New York, Cincinnati, and Chicago: American Book Company, 1889), p. 648.

Verse 27

κρίσις—the author has chosen a word that reveals action, that is, the process of judging. By contrast, the noun κρίμα shows the result of this judicial activity; it is the verdict, the sentence of condemnation.

Verse 28

ὁ Χριστός—note the use of the definite article. Although the noun occurs without the article in 9:24, here the emphasis on Christ's designation, the Messiah, is pronounced.

προσενεχθείς . . . ἀνενεγκεῖν—the author has a play on words with two verb forms that find their roots in φέρω (I bear), πρός (toward), and ἀνά (up).

Summary of Chapter 9

To point out the supremacy of Christ's priesthood, the author of Hebrews presents a description of the earthly tabernacle, its contents, and the priestly ministry in and around this sanctuary. The sacrifices, however, were external observances, for they were unable to cleanse the guilty conscience of the sinner.

With the blood of animals man could not obtain redemption, for he remained unclean. How different the sacrifice of Christ! By his one offering, Christ cleansed the sinner's conscience, led him from death to life, and became the mediator of the new covenant.

In this chapter the author presents an exposition on the meaning of the covenant. Because sin affected the stipulations of the first covenant, God told Moses to sacrifice animals and to sprinkle their blood on the tabernacle, its contents, and on the people. "Without the shedding of blood there is no forgiveness."

When Christ came in the official capacity of high priest and mediator of the new covenant, he offered himself once for all and entered the heavenly sanctuary to appear in behalf of the believers in the presence of God. By his death on the cross, Christ removed "the sins of many people."

The chapter ends with the promise that Christ will return, not to remove sin as a high priest, but to bring salvation to those who wait for him in faith. Jesus is coming again.

10

Jesus: High Priest and Sacrifice, *part 3*

(10:1–18)

and More Exhortations

(10:19–39)

Outline

Jesus: High Priest and Sacrifice (continued)

F. Jesus' Effective Sacrifice

10:1–4 1. Shadows of Reality

10:5–10 2. Jesus Christ Set Aside the Shadows to Establish Reality

10:11–14 3. Jesus Offered One Sacrifice

10:15–18 4. Covenant, Law, and Forgiveness

More Exhortations

A. An Exhortation to Persevere

10:19–22 1. In Full Assurance of Faith

10:23 2. By Professing Hope

10:24 3. Toward Expressing Love

10:25 4. In Attending the Worship Services

B. A Warning to Pay Attention

10:26–27 1. To the Knowledge of the Truth

10:28–31 2. To God's Judgment

C. A Reminder to Continue

10:32–34 1. As in the Past

10:35–39 2. So in the Present

10 1 The law is only a shadow of the good things that are coming—not the realities
themselves. For this reason it can never, by the same sacrifices repeated endlessly
year after year, make perfect those who draw near to worship. 2 If it could, would
they not have stopped being offered? For the worshipers would have been cleansed
once for all, and would no longer have felt guilty for their sins. 3 But those sacrifices are
an annual reminder of sins, 4 because it is impossible for the blood of bulls and goats to
take away sins.

5 Therefore, when Christ came into the world, he said:

"Sacrifice and offering you did not desire,
but a body you prepared for me;
6 with burnt offerings and sin offerings
you were not pleased.
7 Then I said, 'Here I am—it is written
about me in the scroll—
I have come to do your will, O God.' "

8 First he said, "Sacrifices and offerings, burnt offerings and sin offerings you did not desire,
nor were you pleased with them" (although the law required them to be made). 9 Then he
said, "Here I am, I have come to do your will." He sets aside the first to establish the second. 10 And by that will, we have been made holy through the sacrifice of the body of Jesus
Christ once for all.

11 Day after day every priest stands and performs his religious duties; again and again he
offers the same sacrifices, which can never take away sins. 12 But when this priest had
offered for all time one sacrifice for sins, he sat down at the right hand of God. 13 Since
that time he waits for his enemies to be made his footstool, 14 because by one sacrifice he
has made perfect forever those who are being made holy.

15 The Holy Spirit also testifies to us about this. First he says:

16 "This is the covenant I will make with them
after that time, says the Lord.
I will put my laws in their hearts,
and I will write them on their minds."

17 Then he adds:

"Their sins and lawless acts
I will remember no more."

18 And where these have been forgiven, there is no longer any sacrifice for sin.

Jesus: High Priest and Sacrifice

F. Jesus' Effective Sacrifice
10:1–18

1. Shadows of Reality
10:1–4

The author of Hebrews is about ready to furnish additional proof from Scripture that Jesus had come to set aside the numerous offerings for sin.

God had prepared a body for Jesus, who appeared to do God's will. And by his sacrifice Christ effectively removed sin. The difference between the sacrifices offered during the Levitical era and the one and only sacrifice of Christ is profound.

1. The law is only a shadow of the good things that are coming—not the realities themselves. For this reason it can never, by the same sacrifices repeated endlessly year after year, make perfect those who draw near to worship.

As is characteristic of the epistle, contrast is a predominant feature in this verse. Here the law, presumably the entire Old Testament, is depicted as a shadow of the real things. That is, the author of Hebrews contrasts earthly institutions with heavenly realities. He already introduced this contrast when he mentioned the sanctuary in the desert. He called it "a copy and shadow of what is in heaven" (8:5).

The word *shadow* has numerous connotations. Here are a few familiar ones: the shadow of the umbrella protected them from the hot sun; fleeting shadows dart across the field; this man cannot stand in the shadow of his predecessor; the shadow of the sundial indicates the time of day.

The author of Hebrews employs the term *shadow* in the sense of an indicator of "the good things that are coming." The wording is similar to that of 9:11, "the good things that are already here." The writer fails to explain what he means by the words *good things that are coming.* We assume that he means the blessings of salvation (see Isa. 52:7; Rom. 10:15).

The noun *shadow,* however, stands for the dim representation of the real things; the writer calls them "the realities themselves." What he actually means is this: these realities bask in the heavenly light and cast a shadow (as an indicator) upon practices stipulated by Old Testament law. We know that these practices pertained to the sacrifices offered to God year after year. The law prescribes the ritual, for example, for the sacrifices on the Day of Atonement. But this legislated worship failed to make the worshiper holy. "The law is only a shadow," writes the author.

What then are the realities themselves? Simply put, they are the atoning work of Christ and its consequences. Later the writer says, "Because by one sacrifice [Christ] has made perfect forever those who are being made holy" (10:14). In Christ, then, we inherit the good things to come.

> How vast the benefits divine
> which we in Christ possess!
> We are redeemed from guilt and shame
> and called to holiness.
>
> —Augustus M. Toplady

The sacrifices of the Levitical system were unable to perfect the worshiper. That observation minimizes not the Old Testament law, which God himself enacted, but the effectiveness of the sacrifices.

2. If it could, would they not have stopped being offered? For the worshipers would have been cleansed once for all, and would no longer have felt guilty for their sins. 3. But those sacrifices are an annual reminder of sins, 4. because it is impossible for the blood of bulls and goats to take away sins.

The author's rhetorical question demands a positive answer: yes, they would have stopped. But among the people of Israel who lived before and after the exile, the art of offering sacrifices to God had become a mechanical deed. It was no longer a matter of a personal relationship with God. A mechanical conception of the act of sacrificing animals to God controlled the mind of the worshipers. The act of shedding blood seemed to them to secure forgiveness of sins.

The Jews should have known, however, that these animal sacrifices were totally inadequate. Animal sacrifices were mere substitutions, nothing more. Although God had instituted these practices so that man would not have to offer his own life, they were only substitutes. The writers of the Old Testament Scriptures voice God's dissatisfaction with the sacrificial system. They write that the significance of a sacrifice to God ought to be found not in the animal that was offered but in the worshiper's heart that was broken and contrite (I Sam. 15:22; Ps. 40:6; 50:8–10; 51:16–17; Isa. 1:10–12; Jer. 7:21–23; Hos. 6:6; Amos 5:21–23).

God takes sin seriously. He is not satisfied with a sacrifice that is presented to him without a broken and a contrite heart. He desires a life of obedience and dedication to doing his will.[1]

Believers in Old Testament times knew that an animal sacrifice would not be able to cleanse them from sin. Every year on the Day of Atonement the high priest would enter the Most Holy Place with blood of a slain animal. But the high priest could never say to the worshipers: "This blood has removed your sins once for all, and therefore this sacrifice has been the last." No, the annual return of the high priest from the inner sanctuary on the Day of Atonement proved that the sacrifices were inadequate and ineffective. The worshipers continued to feel guilty for their sins.

The covenant that God had made with the people of Israel had one serious deficiency: it was unable to take away the consciousness of sin. "The main deficiency in the old covenant was that it could not accomplish forgiveness."[2] The blood of sacrificial animals cannot take away sin. Only the blood of Christ, shed once for all, removes sin and cleanses man's consciousness of guilt. The sacrifice of Christ put an end to the sacrifices stipulated by Old Testament law. "Christ is the end of the law," says Paul (Rom. 10:4). The writer of Hebrews intimates a variant: "Christ is the end of old-covenant sacrifices." By offering himself as sacrifice, Christ marked the end of the

---

1. Simon J. Kistemaker, *The Psalm Citations in the Epistle to the Hebrews* (Amsterdam: Van Soest, 1961), p. 126.
2. Julius Schniewind and Gerhard Friedrich, *TDNT,* vol. 2, p. 284.

Levitical priesthood with its sacrifices and offerings, and terminated the validity of the first covenant.

2. Jesus Christ Set Aside the Shadows to Establish Reality 10:5–10

5. Therefore, when Christ came into the world, he said:
"Sacrifice and offering you did not desire,
but a body you prepared for me;
6. with burnt offerings and sin offerings
you were not pleased.
7. Then I said, 'Here I am—it is written about me
in the scroll—
I have come to do your will, O God.' "

The contrast between the Levitical sacrificial system and Christ's sacrifice is summarized in the expression *therefore.* "When Christ came into the world" is actually a Semitic way of saying "when Christ was born."[3] Especially in the Gospel of John, the phrase refers to Christ's coming in human form to his people (1:9; 6:14; 12:46; 16:28; 18:37).

The author of Hebrews introduces a psalm quotation that comes from David. However, the author makes the quotation messianic by putting it on the lips of Christ. Note the emphasis the writer places on the fact that Christ speaks: "he said" (10:5), "then I said" (10:7), "first he said" (10:8), and "then he said" (10:9). With this quotation the author bases his teaching on the Scriptures of the Old Testament. In this quotation, Christ says that he offers himself to do the will of God. And that is the essential meaning of true sacrifice.

Before we come to the purpose of the quotation in the context of this chapter, we should note these points.

a. *Parallelism.* The words of Psalm 40:6–8 display typical Hebraic parallels common in the wisdom literature of the Old Testament. The author of Hebrews is fully aware of this literary device, because in his explanation of the quoted words he changes the poetical lines to prose (10:8–9).

In parallel columns, here is the quotation in somewhat abbreviated form:

Sacrifice	—	with burnt offerings
and offering		and sin offerings
you did not desire	—	you were not pleased
but a body you prepared	—	here I am, I have come to
for me		do your will

3. German scholars aptly refer to this linguistic similarity. See SB, vol. 2, p. 358; Edward Riggenbach, *Der Brief an die Hebräer* (Leipzig and Erlangen: Deichert, 1922), p. 300; Gustaf Dalman, *The Words of Jesus* (Edinburgh: Clark, 1909), p. 172; and Otto Michel, *Der Brief an die Hebräer,* 10th ed. (Göttingen: Vandenhoeck and Ruprecht, 1957), p. 223.

These three parallel expressions constitute the message Christ brings. The last lines, of course, are completely dissimilar in wording; the meaning about doing the will of God, in the body God prepared for Christ, is clear.

b. *Difference.* The difference in wording between Hebrews 10:5 ("but a body you prepared for me") and Psalm 40:6 ("but my ears you have pierced") appears formidable. It stems from the Greek translation, the Septuagint, which the writer of Hebrews used exclusively in quoting from the Old Testament. For him and for his readers, the Septuagint version was Scripture. We have no knowledge how the difference arose. Attempts to explain this difference by referring to Exodus 21:6 and Deuteronomy 15:17 are not at all convincing. In these passages a law is prescribed concerning a servant who voluntarily decides to stay with his master for life and as a sign of servanthood has his ear lobe pierced. Not the outer ear but the inner ear is important. Therefore, Isaiah 50:5 is more helpful. The prophet writes, "The Sovereign LORD has opened my ears, and I have not been rebellious." The prophet listens obediently to God's voice to do his will. And that is the meaning of the words "but my ears you have pierced."

c. *Meaning.* The two lines "sacrifice and offering" and "with burnt offering and sin offerings" are not merely eloquent poetry but also indicate the totality of Jewish sacrifices. Although God told the people of Israel to offer sacrifices, he took no pleasure in these offerings. Telling are the words of Samuel to Saul recorded in I Samuel 15:22:

> Does the LORD delight in burnt offerings and sacrifices
>   as much as in obeying the voice of the LORD?
> To obey is better than sacrifice,
>   and to heed is better than the fat of rams.

God is not satisfied only with sacrifices. Sacrifices are but substitutes. Instead he wants genuine, devoted service. He delights in perfect obedience to his will.

God prepared a body for Christ, and Christ showed complete submission to his Father's will. The psalmist says that God pierced—that is, opened—the ears. The author of Hebrews adopts the reading "a body you prepared for me."[4] Both readings signify the same thing: ears have been opened so one may hear and obey God's will. Whereas the one word—ears—is more specific, the other—body—is more general. But both convey the same meaning.

Why did the writer of Hebrews quote Psalm 40:6–8? He found in this quotation the best proof to show the reality that puts aside the shadow of the Levitical sacrifices. The sacrifices, only shadows, are not important; obe-

---

4. The writer of Hebrews quotes from the Septuagint because this translation was familiar to him. In his epistle he provides no indication that he was familiar with the Hebrew text. The Septuagint reading, however, presents the basic meaning of the Hebrew original, even though the words differ.

dience to God's will counts. God delights in obedience (Rom. 12:1–2). Moreover, the words "Here I am, I have come to do your will, O God" have been recorded "in the scroll."[5] That is, the psalmist already testifies to scriptural warrant for the coming of Christ in human form. Although no references are provided, we assume that the psalmist had in mind the books of Moses. And last, in this quotation Christ speaks directly in the first person singular—"Here I am . . . I have come to do your will, O God"—about his work of redemption.

8. First he said, "Sacrifices and offerings, burnt offerings and sin offerings you did not desire, nor were you pleased with them" (although the law required them to be made). 9. Then he said, "Here I am, I have come to do your will." He sets aside the first to establish the second. 10. And by that will, we have been made holy through the sacrifice of the body of Jesus Christ once for all.

As he has shown in other places, the author is an expert in understanding the meaning of the Old Testament Scriptures (see, for example, 2:8–9; 3:16–19; 7:2–3). After quoting Psalm 40:6–8, he presents a brief commentary on these verses. He turns the poetry of the psalm citation into prose and comes to the heart of the matter. He divides the quotation into two parts.

First, Christ said, "Sacrifices and offerings, burnt offerings and sin offerings you did not desire, nor were you pleased with them." The first part, then, expresses the thought that God found no pleasure in the offerings his people presented to him. The author immediately adds the concessive statement, "although the law required them to be made."

But let us go back to the beginning of human history recorded in Genesis. God looked with favor on the offering that Abel brought him, but with disfavor on Cain's offering. Why was Abel's offering—"fat portions from some of the firstborn of his flock"—acceptable, and the offering of Cain—"some of the fruits of the soil"—unacceptable (Gen. 4:3–5)? The writer of Hebrews answers by saying, "By faith Abel offered God a better sacrifice than Cain did. By faith he was commended as a righteous man, when God spoke well of his offerings" (11:4).

The author of Hebrews asserts not that God has an aversion to offerings presented to him, but that sacrifices offered without faith and obedience are an abomination (Isa. 1:11–14; Amos 5:21–22). Through Hosea God says to Israel, "For I desire mercy, not sacrifice, and acknowledgment of God rather than burnt offerings" (6:6).

Second, Christ said, "Here I am, I have come to do your will." The term *will* appears four times in the context of this chapter (10:7, 9, 10, 36). It occurs only once more in Hebrews, in the benediction (13:21). The will of

5. Representative translations of this phrase are "in the scroll of the book" (JB), "roll of the book" (RSV), "volume of the book" (KJV), and "the book of the Law" (GNB).

God is central in the life of Christ, and the author of Hebrews exhorts his readers to persevere and do the will of God.

God takes no delight in sacrifices. He is pleased with the unfaltering trust and obedience of his children. Christ, the Son of God, came into this world for the purpose of showing submission and learning "obedience from what he suffered and, once made perfect, he became the source of eternal salvation for all who obey him" (Heb. 5:8–9).

The author summarizes the two statements of Christ in one pithy sentence, "He sets aside the first to establish the second." Christ offered himself as a sacrifice for sin on Calvary's cross. By this act he terminated the Levitical sacrificial system—he set it aside. Next he showed his faithfulness to God by doing his will, and thus he established the second. Doing the will of God caused Jesus to pray in the agony he experienced in the Garden of Gethsemane, "Father, if you are willing, take this cup from me; yet not my will, but yours be done" (Luke 22:42). Christ fully submitted to God's will in perfect obedience.

And what is the effect of that will? The author succinctly includes all believers by saying, "And by that will, we have been made holy." Salvation originates not in man, but in God. By his will we are separated from the world and called to holiness. The implication is that we were alienated from God and lived in a world of sin. Because of God's will, this has changed: "we have been made holy." The verb indicates that at a given moment, someone acted in our behalf to sanctify us, and we have become pure. The writer of Hebrews already referred to this act when he wrote of God's will to make the author of salvation perfect through suffering. "Both the one who makes man holy and those who are made holy are of the same family" (2:11). The one who makes men holy is Jesus Christ.

Rather pointedly the author writes, "Through the sacrifice of the body of Jesus Christ once for all." Apart from the last chapter of Hebrews, where the combination *Jesus Christ* appears twice (13:8, 21), the double name occurs only once in the instructional part of the epistle—in the present context. The writer wants to stress that both the human (Jesus) and the divine (Christ) natures were involved in making us holy. Moreover, Jesus Christ performed the act of sanctification in our behalf by sacrificing his body. This is the only place in the epistle where the author mentions the *bodily* sacrifice of Jesus. The purpose for the stress on the "sacrifice of the body of Jesus Christ" is to demonstrate the reality of his physical death. It is also a reflection of the Septuagint wording of the psalm citation, "but a body you prepared for me" (Heb. 10:5).

And last, the sacrifice of Christ's body is the counterpart of the animal sacrifices of the Levitical system. The difference, however, between the bodily sacrifice of Christ and the sacrifices of animals is profound: Christ's sacrifice was *once for all*; animal sacrifices were countless. Next, Christ offered his own body as a sacrifice; the worshiper in the era of the first covenant offered substitutes. Then also, Christ presented his body voluntarily; animals were sacrificed forcibly against their will.[6] Christ's obedience to his Father's will effected our liberation from the power of sin and conformed us to a life dedicated to God's service. Thus we reflect God's holiness and perfection as we respond to Jesus' exhortation, "Be perfect, therefore, as your heavenly Father is perfect" (Matt. 5:48; see also Lev. 11:44–45; 19:2; 20:7; I Peter 1:16).

Doctrinal Considerations in 10:1–10

For readers of Jewish origin who considered the law of God their most precious possession, the author's assertion—"the law is only a shadow of the good things that are coming"—must have been astounding. If the law was their treasured possession, it would be difficult to imagine that far more desirable things were in store for them. The writer of Hebrews calls these things "the realities themselves," and he explains that they consist of Christ and his redemptive work. Writing to Jewish readers in Colosse about religious observances, Paul says almost the same thing. He writes, "These [regulations] are a shadow of the things that were to come; the reality, however, is found in Christ" (Col. 2:17).

By quoting and applying the verses from Psalm 40, the author of Hebrews shows that Christ has come to do God's will. In doing that will, Christ offered his body as a sacrifice, fulfilled the requirements of the Aaronic priesthood, and terminated the Levitical sacrifices. If Christ had fulfilled only the demands of the Aaronic priesthood, however, there would not have been a new covenant. The writer of Hebrews teaches that after Christ had offered himself without blemish to God, he became the mediator of a new covenant. He cleansed the consciences of the members of this covenant, "so that we may serve the living God!" (9:14). This refers to a higher priesthood that is eternal; it is called the priesthood in the order of Melchizedek. Christ fulfilled the requirements of this priesthood in his dedication to do God's will.

When Christ came into the world, "he [set] aside the first to establish the second" (Heb. 10:9). The author of Hebrews uses the terms *first* and *another, new,* or *second* when he discusses the covenant (8:7, 13; 9:1, 15, 18). Explaining the psalm quotation in 10:8–9, the writer first quotes the words about the sacrificial system of the Aaronic priesthood and then cites the words pertaining to Christ's perfect obedience to God's will. These two verses, in effect, describe the two covenants and the two phases of Christ's priesthood. To atone for the sins of his people (2:17), Christ had to sacrifice his body once for all (10:10). He fulfilled the demands of the first covenant and terminated the first phase of his priesthood; that is, the Aaronic priesthood. Christ established the second covenant when he came to do God's will. Then he also established the second phase of his priesthood, the one of Melchizedek. The Aaronic priesthood typifies Christ's passive obedience; the priesthood of Melchizedek, Christ's active obedience.

---

6. James Denney, *The Death of Christ* (London: Tyndale, 1960), pp. 122, 131. Also see F. F. Bruce, *The Epistle to the Hebrews,* New International Commentary on the New Testament series (Grand Rapids: Eerdmans, 1964), p. 234; and Leon Morris, *The Expositor's Bible Commentary,* vol. 12, *Hebrews* (Grand Rapids: Zondervan, 1981), p. 100.

Greek Words, Phrases, and Constructions in 10:1–10

Verse 1

κατ' ἐνιαυτόν—the noun ἐνιαυτός (year) is preceded by the preposition κατά, which gives it a distributive meaning *annually*.

εἰς τὸ διηνεκές—the compound adjective derives from διά (through) and ἠνεκής (from ἤνεγκα, the aorist of φέρω, I carry, bear); it means "carrying through" or "continually." In the New Testament the phrase appears only in Hebrews (7:3; 10:1, 12, 14).

Verse 2

ἐπεὶ οὐκ ἂν ἐπαύσαντο—this is the second part (apodosis) of a second class (contrary-to-fact) conditional sentence.[7] The first part (protasis) is lacking and has been supplied as "otherwise" (JB, RSV), "were matters otherwise" (NAB), and "if it could" (NEB, NIV).

Verse 3

ἀνάμνησις—a noun with a -σις ending to denote a process. It derives from the verb ἀναμιμνήσκω (I remind), occurs four times in the New Testament (Luke 22:19; I Cor. 11:24, 25; Heb. 10:3), and "denotes an unassisted recalling."[8]

Verse 7

ἐν κεφαλίδι βιβλίου —the noun κεφαλίς is a diminutive of the noun κεφαλή (head). It referred to the knob of a rod that held a scroll (βιβλίον); eventually the noun κεφαλίς was used to designate the scroll itself.

γέγραπται—the perfect passive from the verb γράφω (I write) signifies resultant state with lasting effect.

Verse 8

ἀνώτερον—an adverb in the comparative degree from ἄνω (above); thus a higher place in the written column.

αἵτινες—this indefinite relative pronoun has a concessive connotation and may be translated "although."

Verse 9

εἴρηκεν—the perfect active of the deficient verb λέγω (I say) is the main verb of the sentence. The perfect tense indicates completed action with continuing result.

---

7. A. T. Robertson, *A Grammar of the Greek New Testament in the Light of Historical Research* (Nashville: Broadman, 1934), p. 963.

8. Joseph H. Thayer, *A Greek-English Lexicon of the New Testament* (New York, Cincinnati, and Chicago: American Book Company, 1889), p. 40.

Verse 10

ἡγιασμένοι ἐσμέν—the perfect periphrastic construction of the perfect passive participle of ἁγιάζω (I make holy) and the present tense of εἰμί (I am) express action with lasting effect. The participle is descriptive.

---

3. Jesus Offered One Sacrifice 10:11–14

11. Day after day every priest stands and performs his religious duties; again and again he offers the same sacrifices, which can never take away sins. 12. But when this priest had offered for all time one sacrifice for sins, he sat down at the right hand of God.

The quotation from Psalm 40:6–8 included the work of the high priest on the Day of Atonement and the daily duties of every priest. "Sacrifices and offerings, burnt offerings and sin offerings" comprise the entire sacrificial system carried out by the high priest and priests. The author of Hebrews, therefore, highlights the work of the priest and contrasts it with the redemptive accomplishment of Christ. The contrast is complete:

Verse 11	*Verse 12*
Day after day	But[9]
every priest	this priest
stands	sat down
he offers	when [he] had offered
again and again	for all time[10]
the same sacrifices	one sacrifice
which can never	for sins
take away sins	

Day after day the rituals at the sanctuary continued, for when the one priest offered the last sacrifice at the conclusion of a day, the next priest made preparations for the first sacrifice the next morning. Literally rivers of animal blood flowed because of these continual sacrifices; and the succession of the priests, who served by division and were chosen by lot (Luke 1:8–9), seemed to be unending. Innumerable priests had served in times before Jesus' appearance and many served during his ministry. The work of the priest was essentially futile; he had to do the same thing over and over again, and thus his work was never finished. He could never sit down to take

---

9. In the original Greek the two particles *men* and *de* express contrast in verses 11 and 12. They could be translated as "on the one hand" and "on the other hand," but the NIV has omitted a translation for *men* (v. 11) and gives *de* as "but" (v. 12).

10. The phrase *for all time* can be taken with the clause *when he had offered* or with the main verb *sat down*. The majority of translations take the phrase with the clause (NIV, NEB, MLB, RSV, ASV, RV, NKJV, KJV, and *Phillips*); others translate it with the main verb (JB, NAB, *Moffatt*).

a rest from his labors. As the writer of Hebrews puts it, "Every priest *stands*" (italics added). In the sanctuary the furniture included table, lamp, altar of incense, and the ark, but no chair. Furthermore, the sacrifices offered by the Levitical priest were powerless to free man from sin. The words *take away* actually mean to take away sins that completely envelop man and from which only Christ can free him.

By contrast, after offering his one sacrifice for all time Christ *sat down* because he had finished his redemptive task and terminated the Levitical priesthood. His sacrifice effectively removes sin and breaks the power of sin. He entered a period of rest after accomplishing his work, much the same as God rested from his labors upon concluding his work of creation.[11]

Christ entered heaven and took his seat of honor at the right hand of God. He was fully entitled to that place as the priest who has fulfilled his task of removing sin and as the king who has conquered sin and death. What a difference between the priest who performed his religious duties at the sanctuary and Christ, who sat down next to God.

> The priest of the Old Testament stands timid and uneasy in the holy place, anxiously performing his awful service there, and hastening to depart when service is done, as from a place where he has no free access, and can never feel at home; whereas Christ sits down in everlasting rest and blessedness at the right hand of Majesty in the holy of holies, His work accomplished, and He awaiting its reward.[12]

13. Since that time he waits for his enemies to be made his footstool, 14. because by one sacrifice he has made perfect forever those who are being made holy.

> The Lord unto His Christ has said,
> Sit Thou at My right hand
> Until I make Thine enemies
> Submit to Thy command.
> —*Psalter Hymnal*

Psalm 110:1 appears frequently in the Epistle to the Hebrews as a direct quotation or an allusion (1:3, 13; 8:1; 10:12; 12:2). Because of Jesus' interpretation and application of this verse in answer to the question of the Pharisees, "What do you think about the Christ? Whose son is he?" (Matt. 22:42 and parallels) and frequent allusions to this quotation in Paul's epistles (Rom. 8:34; I Cor. 15:25; Eph. 1:20; Col. 3:1), I assume that Psalm 110:1 was a basic tenet of faith in the early church. The author of Hebrews employs this verse almost verbatim; he modifies the wording to fit the context of his writing.

---

11. Michel, *Hebräer,* p. 266. Luke's description of "the Son of Man standing at the right hand of God" (Acts 7:56) ought not be forced, because of the symbolism involved.

12. Franz Delitzsch, *Commentary on the Epistle to the Hebrews,* 2 vols. (Edinburgh: Clark, 1877), vol. 2, p. 161.

Since the time of his ascension, Christ has been "waiting for the moment when his enemies will be made his footstool."[13] He waits for the appropriate time, much the same as a farmer waits for the land to yield its produce in harvest season (James 5:7; also see Heb. 11:10). His enemies are all those who oppose Christ's dominion, authority, and power. "The last enemy to be destroyed is death" (I Cor. 15:26). Christ waits for the final destruction of his enemies.

The conquering of Christ's enemies is not as important as the one offering by which he perfected for all times "those who are being made holy." The author of Hebrews teaches the same truth repeatedly. In 2:11 he writes, "Both the one who makes men holy and those who are made holy are of the same family." In 10:10 he refers to the will of God and says, "And by that will, we have been made holy through the sacrifice of the body of Jesus Christ once for all." And last, he speaks of "the blood of the covenant that sanctified" the sinner (10:29).

When does sanctification take place? The use of the present tense of 2:11 and 10:14 seems to indicate that making someone holy is a process, not a once-for-all act. "We have been made holy" (10:10) but are exhorted to "make every effort . . . to be holy" (12:14). We see that sanctification is something received but not yet achieved.[14]

The sacrifice of Christ, unique in itself, brought about holiness for the believer. That is, every believer receives these benefits of Christ's sacrifice on the cross: his sins are forgiven; his conscience is cleansed; he has peace with God, assurance of salvation, and the gift of life eternal. Christ has perfected the believer forever.[15] But even though the author writes that Christ "has made perfect forever those who are being made holy," he shows in other passages the work of perfection is not yet complete in the recipients of his epistle. They are encouraged to resist sin, endure hardship, and submit to discipline (12:4, 7, 9). Perfection, in a sense, is here already and is also not yet here. We have this certainty, however, that we are perfected in Christ, who removed our sin by his sacrifice.

4. Covenant, Law, and Forgiveness 10:15–18

In a few verses the writer of Hebrews brings the teaching part of his epistle to a close. He summarizes the scriptural teachings of Jeremiah 31:33–34, quoted in chapter 8, and draws the conclusion that forgiven sin is forgotten.

---

13. Ernst Hoffmann, *NIDNTT,* vol. 2, p. 245.

14. Donald Guthrie, *New Testament Theology* (Downers Grove, Ill.: Inter-Varsity, 1981), p. 661, asserts, "The N[ew] T[estament] is more concerned with the process of sanctifying or of becoming sanctified than with debating the nature of sanctification."

15. John Owen, *An Exposition of Hebrews,* 7 vols. in 4 (Evansville, Ind.: Sovereign Grace, 1960), vol. 6, p. 493. Owen writes that the purpose of Christ in offering himself was to sanctify the believer first and afterward to perfect him.

15. The Holy Spirit also testifies to us about this. First he says:
16. "This is the covenant I will make with them
after that time, says the Lord.
I will put my laws in their hearts,
and I will write them on their minds."

Once again the author demonstrates his high view of Scripture. He quotes two verses from the prophecy of Jeremiah and ascribes them to the Holy Spirit. In chapter 8, he introduces God as the speaker for this particular passage, but that is nothing new for the author of Hebrews. He introduces either God, Jesus, or the Holy Spirit as speaker. For him the Old Testament Scriptures are divine and are ascribed to the Triune God. God through the Spirit is the author of Scripture (see II Peter 1:19–21).

The writer repeats two verses from the passage quoted from Jeremiah 31:31–34 in chapter 8. The wording is not entirely the same, but the meaning is identical. The first verse (Jer. 31:33) gives the heart of the quotation: God's promise to establish a new covenant with his people. The author has chosen this text to illustrate that with the coming of Christ and the completion of his sacrificial work, the era of the new covenant has commenced. God makes a new covenant with his people, puts his laws in their hearts and writes them on their minds. Believers redeemed by Christ live a life of gratitude by keeping God's commandments. These laws are an integral part of their covenant relationship to God.

17. Then he adds:
"Their sins and lawless acts
I will remember no more."

This second verse (Jer. 31:34) differs considerably from the Old Testament wording. However, we ought not judge the author by modern standards, but we should understand that the author, guided by the Holy Spirit, had the freedom to vary the wording. The meaning remains the same.

These two selected verses from the prophecy of Jeremiah accentuate the accomplishment of Christ's atonement. The Old Testament believers experienced God's forgiving grace, for David writes, "I acknowledged my sin to you . . . and you forgave the guilt of my sin" (Ps. 32:5). And he says elsewhere, "As far as the east is from the west, so far has he removed our transgressions from us" (Ps. 103:12). What is new in the prophecy of Jeremiah, quoted in Hebrews, is that God remembers sins no more in the time of the new covenant. God has forgiven the believer's sins through the one sacrifice of Christ and therefore will never recall them. Sins are forgiven and forgotten.

18. And where these have been forgiven, there is no longer any sacrifice for sin.

For the Christian, because he has never known the ritual of animal sacrifices, the words "there is no longer any sacrifice for sin" are somewhat matter-of-fact. But for the person of Jewish descent in the second half of the first century, these words must have struck with thunderous finality. The age-old Levitical system of presenting sacrifices to God was rendered pointless with the death of Christ. To be sure, the termination took place in A.D. 70 when the Roman army destroyed the sanctuary in Jerusalem.

Christ's sacrifice was final, for it brought an end to all sacrifices for sin. What man was unable to do because of his sin, the curse of death, and his inability to keep the law of God, Christ did. He paid the penalty, removed the curse, and lived a life of perfect obedience. With characteristic brevity B. F. Westcott lists three consequences of sin:

> debt which requires forgiveness,
> bondage which requires redemption,
> alienation which requires reconciliation.[16]

Forgiveness of sins consists of God's pardoning sinners on the basis of Christ's sacrifice and accepting sinners as sons or daughters who have never sinned at all.[17] Set free from the slavery of sin, they have received the gift of life eternal (John 17:3) because they belong to the new covenant of which Christ is the mediator. And the terms of his new covenant call for only one sacrifice offered by Jesus Christ.

Doctrinal Considerations in 10:11–18

In these last few verses, the didactic part of his letter, the writer summarizes his thoughts and concludes that the daily sacrifices are inconsistent with the priesthood of Christ.[18] He reintroduces selected verses from Jeremiah 31:31–34 to stress the significance of the new covenant and the complete remission of sin.

More implicitly than explicitly, the author teaches that all three persons of the Trinity are involved in the work of atonement. At the right hand of God the Father, the Son takes his seat upon completion of his sacrificial work on earth. The Holy Spirit testifies to the establishing of the new covenant that God has made with people whose sins have been forgiven through the bodily sacrifice of Jesus Christ.

Jesus teaches his disciples the Lord's Prayer, to which he adds the comment: "For if you forgive men when they sin against you, your heavenly Father will also forgive you. But if you do not forgive men their sins, your Father will not forgive your sins" (Matt. 6:14–15). The author of Hebrews, guided by the words of Jeremiah's prophecy, teaches that God forgives and forgets man's "sins and lawless acts." The counterpart of this doctrine is that we must not only forgive our fellow man who sins against us. After we have forgiven him we must forget the wrong he has committed. We, too, must live by the principle that forgiven sin is forgotten sin.

---

16. B. F. Westcott, *Commentary on the Epistle to the Hebrews* (Grand Rapids: Eerdmans, 1950), p. 316.

17. R. C. Trench in his *Synonyms of the New Testament* (Grand Rapids: Eerdmans, 1953), p. 119, comments on man's forgiveness: "He, then, that is partaker of the [forgiveness], has his sins forgiven, so that, unless he brings them back upon himself by new and further disobedience (Matt. 18:32, 34; II Peter 1:9; 2:20), they shall not be imputed to him, or mentioned against him any more."

18. John Calvin, *Epistle to the Hebrews* (Grand Rapids: Eerdmans, 1949), p. 230.

Greek Words, Phrases, and Constructions in 10:11–18

Verse 11

ἕστηκεν—the perfect active indicative of the verb ἵστημι (I set, place; stand) has the force of a present tense.

λειτουργῶν—a present participle used circumstantially from the verb λειτουργέω (I perform a religious duty) can best be translated as a finite verb preceded by "and."

αἵτινες—the indefinite relative pronoun is concessive, "although."

περιελεῖν—this compound second aorist infinitive from αἱρέω (I take away, remove) has a perfective idea in the sense of "to take away altogether."[19]

Verse 13

τὸ λοιπόν—the neuter singular used adverbially from λείπω (I leave) has the meaning *the future, from now on.*

τεθῶσιν—because of the temporal conjunction ἕως (until) this verb has been placed in the subjunctive. It is an aorist passive from the verb τίθημι (I place).

Verse 14

τετελείωκεν—the perfect active indicative from τελειόω (I finish, bring to an end) depicts the completed state of the action.

ἁγιαζομένους—this same participle also appears in 2:11. It is a present passive participle with an implied agent.

Verse 18

ὅπου—an adverb of place which lacks the corresponding adverb ἐκεῖ (there) to complete the balance of the sentence.

περί—this preposition is followed by the genitive case of the noun ἁμαρτία (sin) and means "concerning."

---

19 Therefore, brothers, since we have confidence to enter the Most Holy Place by the blood of Jesus, 20 by a new and living way opened for us through the curtain, that is, his body, 21 and since we have a great priest over the house of God, 22 let us draw near to God with a sincere heart in full assurance of faith, having our hearts sprinkled to cleanse us from a guilty conscience and having our bodies washed with pure water. 23 Let us hold unswervingly to the hope we profess, for he who promised is faithful. 24 And let us consider how we may spur one another on toward love and good deeds. 25 Let us not give up meeting together, as some are in the habit of doing, but let us encourage one another—and all the more as you see the Day approaching.

---

19. Robertson, *Grammar,* p. 617.

More Exhortations

A. An Exhortation to Persevere
10:19–25

1. In Full Assurance of Faith
10:19–22

The epistle basically consists of two parts: a dogmatic section (1:1–10:18) and a practical section (10:19–13:25). In the first segment exhorting is the exception; teaching the rule. In the last segment the emphasis is on exhorting and admonishing, with some teaching in chapter 11.

The triad faith, hope, and love stands out clearly in verses 22, 23, and 24. The author discusses the meaning of faith in chapter 11. With numerous admonitions he counsels his readers to hope—that is, to persevere and endure (chap. 12). Love is expressed in helping one another; chapter 13 features many instructions about putting love to work. In a sense, the three verses that include the triad present a brief summary of the next three chapters.

19. Therefore, brothers, since we have confidence to enter the Most Holy Place by the blood of Jesus.

The word *therefore* looks back to the preceding section with its lengthy discussion of the once-for-all sacrifice of Christ and the forgiveness of sin. The author invites the readers to approach God because, he says, "we have confidence to enter the Most Holy Place." These words echo an earlier exhortation, "Let us then approach the throne of grace with confidence" (4:16).

The designation *Most Holy Place* is deliberately chosen. In Old Testament times only the high priest was permitted to enter the inner sanctuary once a year as representative of the people. He entered into God's presence to sprinkle blood on the ark to atone for sin. In New Testament times we have access to God because Jesus shed his blood for our sins and because at his death "the curtain of the temple was torn in two from top to bottom" (Matt. 27:51). We are even encouraged to come into God's presence with confidence.

Note that the author of Hebrews writes, "by the blood of Jesus." He uses the name *Jesus* as a reminder that Jesus saves his people from sin (Matt. 1:21) and that Jesus "is not ashamed to call them brothers" (Heb. 2:11). The writer, too, belongs to the family of Jesus and for that reason addresses his readers as "brothers" (see 3:1, 12; 13:22).

20. By a new and living way opened for us through the curtain, that is, his body.

Translators of the original text of the New Testament are usually guided by a simple rule of thumb: "Translate Greek as it comes." That is, the sequence of the Greek text is carried over more or less into the translation. The translation of Hebrews 10:20 conveys the meaning that the expression *body* clarifies the noun *curtain.* However, other translators and commentators do not follow the above-mentioned rule. Understanding the text differently, they want to interpret it as follows: "By the new, living way which he has opened for us through the curtain, the way of his flesh."[20] In other words, the word *flesh* has become an explanation of "way," not of "curtain." Jesus, then, inaugurated "a new and living way" that consists of his humanity.

To achieve a smooth translation, however, the translators have had to supply the expression *way* in the phrase *the way of his flesh.* The original does not say this. The remark perhaps could be made that if the author of Hebrews had wanted to give an explanation of "a new and living way," he would have done so. Now the evidence appears to favor an explanation for the term *curtain.*[21]

The term *way* is described as "new and living." Unfortunately the translation of "new" is incomplete, for the Greek word actually means "just slaughtered." It is a term relating to religious sacrifices. The adjective *living* signifies that the way Christ has opened up for us is not a road without an exit: a dead-end street. Rather, this road leads us to salvation, into the very presence of God.

Christ has dedicated the way by opening the curtain, "that is, his body." At his death the curtain to the Most Holy Place had to be torn from top to bottom. Likewise the body of Jesus had to be broken, and his blood had to be shed to open for us the way to God. By his sacrifice on the cross, Christ has removed the veil between God and his people.

21. And since we have a great priest over the house of God, 22. let us draw near to God with a sincere heart in full assurance of faith, having our hearts sprinkled to cleanse us from a guilty conscience and having our bodies washed with pure water.

The believer has been given double assurance that he may approach God, first, because he has confidence through the shed blood of Christ and, second, because Jesus is the "great priest over the house of God." Should there be any hesitation at all in the mind of the believer, the writer of Hebrews is saying, let him look to the one and only great priest, Jesus Christ (4:14).

We are exhorted to come to God; in this earthly life we do so in prayer. The great priest takes our prayers and as intercessor presents them for us to God. This priest has been given the responsibility of caring for the church, that is, the house of God (3:6). Christ's priestly task continues even after his atoning work on earth is finished (John 19:30). He has been appointed as the mediator of the new covenant (8:6), and "he is able to save completely those who come to God through him, because he always lives to intercede for them" (7:25).

---

20. NEB. See also Westcott, *Hebrews,* p. 320; Ceslaus Spicq, *L'Épître aux Hébreux,* 3d ed., 2 vols. (Paris: Gabalda, 1953), vol. 2, p. 316: Hugh Montefiore, *The Epistle to the Hebrews* (New York and Evanston: Harper and Row, 1964), p. 173.

21. Numerous short studies on this verse have been published, including those by Joachim Jeremias, "Hebräer 10, 20: tout' estin tes sarkos autou, (Heb. 10, 20): Apposition, Dependent or Explicative?" *NTS* 20 (1974): 100–104; and G. M. M. Pelser, "A Translation Problem. Heb. 10:19–25," *Linguistics and Bible Translating. Neotestamentica* 9 (1974): 53–54.

Believers are absolutely secure because they have a great priest representing them. This great priest never loses sight of those who belong to the house of God, for he and they belong to the same family (2:11).

Even though the author is not explicit, we are exhorted to approach God. In the parallel passage (4:16) he tells us to come to the throne of grace in prayer. The writer now takes this parallel a step further and describes how we are to draw near to God in prayer. Besides having confidence we must come with "a sincere heart in full assurance of faith."

The author stresses that the heart must be sincere if faith is to be genuine. The word *sincere* describes the heart of a person who is honest, genuine, committed, dependable, and without deceit. When the believer's heart is sincere, faith is evident in full assurance. The believer has complete confidence in God, because he fully accepts the truth of the gospel. By contrast, doubt keeps the believer from approaching God. Doubt insults whereas faith exalts.

When the author of Hebrews writes that we draw near to God with "hearts sprinkled to cleanse us from a guilty conscience" and with "bodies washed with pure water," he refers to the internal (hearts) and the external (bodies). The phrase *washed with pure water* reminds us of baptism. But baptism by itself is only an external act objectively experienced. Its counterpart is the sprinkling of our hearts with the blood of Christ (Heb. 9:14). This sprinkling is an internal act that is subjectively appropriated.[22] We are exhorted to approach God with body and soul cleansed from sin.

The heart is the center of our moral life. Says the writer of Hebrews, "Our hearts [are] sprinkled [with the blood of Christ] to cleanse us from a guilty conscience." That blood sets the believer free. He now may freely approach the throne of grace because his conscience is clear. In faith he has claimed for himself forgiveness of sin through Christ. He knows that Christ has removed forever the guilt that hindered him from coming to God.

Baptism was not unknown to the Jew. The law of Moses stipulated that the high priest on the Day of Atonement should bathe himself before putting on his garments to enter the sanctuary (Lev. 16:4; see also Exod. 29:4; Lev. 8:6). And Ezekiel prophesies that God will sprinkle clean water on his people to cleanse them from spiritual impurities (Ezek. 36:25). In his epistle the writer of Hebrews mentions "pure water" used to wash our bodies. That water symbolically cleanses the believer from sin. "Christ loved the church [the house of God] and gave himself up for her to make her holy, cleansing her by the washing with water through the word" (Eph. 5:25–26).

2. By Professing Hope
10:23

23. Let us hold unswervingly to the hope we profess, for he who promised is faithful.

---

22. F. W. Grosheide, *De Brief aan de Hebreeën en de Brief van Jakobus* (Kampen: Kok, 1955), p. 240. Also see Bruce, *Hebrews*, p. 250.

Here is the second exhortation. In the preceding verse the writer tells the readers to draw near to God. Now he exhorts them to "hold unswervingly to the hope we profess." In the preceding passage he introduces the concepts of baptism and remission of sin. Now he speaks of confession of hope as a natural consequence of baptism.

We assume that in the early church a basic confession existed either in the form of "Jesus is Lord" (I Cor. 12:3) or as a trustworthy saying (I Tim. 3:16; II Tim. 2:11–13). Whether the writer of Hebrews has a particular confession in mind is not certain, but he makes it clear that his readers hold to a confession (3:1; 4:14; 10:23; 13:15). The content of this confession is the expectation that Christ will fulfill all the promises he has made and that all those who profess the name of Christ possess these promises. The author states that we profess hope, a virtue he has emphasized throughout his epistle (3:6; 6:11, 19; 7:19; 10:23). Hope relies on faith and looks to the future.

Faith is therefore placed in God alone who is able to fulfill the promises he has made, for God is faithful. We are told to keep on voicing our hope and to do so unfalteringly. God himself unfailingly has honored his promises. In fact, to make his promises unbreakable, God added an oath (Heb. 6:17). "He can as soon cease to exist as cease to be faithful to His promise."[23] The God who saved the believer through the sacrificial death of Christ has promised never to leave "the soul that on Jesus has leaned for repose." And God is faithful, for he promises the believer,

> Never will I leave you;
> never will I forsake you. [Heb. 13:5]

3. Toward Expressing Love
10:24

24. And let us consider how we may spur one another on toward love and good deeds.

This is the third exhortation and the third virtue of the triad faith (v. 22), hope (v. 23), and love (v. 24). Earlier in the epistle the author elaborated on this triad (6:10–12). In harmony with the conclusion of Paul's letter of love (I Cor. 13:13) and other passages where he mentions the triad (Rom. 5:1–5; Gal. 5:5–6; Col. 1:4–5; I Thess. 1:3; 5:8; and see I Peter 1:21–22), the writer of Hebrews shows that love is the greatest because it reaches out to others. Love is communal. For man, love extends to God and one's neighbor. Moreover, "God demonstrates his own love for us in this: While we were still sinners, Christ died for us" (Rom. 5:8).

Carefully consider how we may ardently incite one another to love and to do good works, says the writer. Put your mind to work to find ways to provoke—in the good sense of the word—each other to increase your expres-

23. John Brown, *An Exposition of Hebrews* (Edinburgh: Banner of Truth Trust, 1961), p. 464.

sions of love that result in doing noble works.[24] Jesus' summary of the law, that is, the royal law (James 2:8), "Love your neighbor as yourself," often is abbreviated to "Love yourself." But this royal law extends beyond the neighbor to God himself. Deeds done in love for the neighbor honor God the Father. Therefore, keeping and fulfilling the second part of the summary, "Love your neighbor as yourself" (Matt. 22:39), actually constitute keeping and fulfilling the first part of the summary, "Love the Lord your God with all your heart and with all your soul and with all your mind" (Matt. 22:37). And Paul calls the commandment to love one another a "continuing debt" (Rom. 13:8). "Therefore love is the fulfillment of the law," he concludes (v. 10).

4. In Attending the Worship Services
10:25

25. Let us not give up meeting together, as some are in the habit of doing, but let us encourage one another—and all the more as you see the Day approaching.

One of the first indications of a lack of love toward God and the neighbor is for a Christian to stay away from the worship services. He forsakes the communal obligations of attending these meetings and displays the symptoms of selfishness and self-centeredness.

Apparently some members of the Hebrew congregation to whom the epistle originally was addressed showed a disregard for attending the religious services. They did so willfully by deserting the "communion of the saints." From sources dating from the first century of the Christian era, we learn that a lack of interest in the worship services was rather common. The *Didache,* a church manual of religious instruction from the latter part of the first century, gives this exhortation: "But be frequently gathered together seeking the things which are profitable for your souls."[25]

In an earlier chapter the author of Hebrews warns the readers not to follow the example of the disobedient Israelites in the desert, and not to turn away from the living God (3:12). The author exhorts the readers to "encourage one another daily . . . so that none of you may be hardened by sin's deceitfulness" (3:13). He realizes that among some of the members spiritual zeal has declined. Therefore once more he says, "But let us encourage one another" (10:25). Not only the writer of this epistle but also all the members of the church have the communal task of encouraging one another daily. Together we bear the responsibility, for we are the body of Christ.

---

24. Westcott, *Hebrews,* p. 325, expresses his disappointment in our inability to translate the Greek adequately. We translate "good deeds," but the original emphasizes that the deeds themselves are noble.

25. *The Didache (The Apostolic Fathers,* vol. 1), 16.2, p. 333 (LCL). Also see the Epistle of Barnabas (*The Apostolic Fathers,* vol. 1), 4.10, p. 353 (LCL). Even in Jewish sources the same concern is expressed. Rabbi Hillel said, "Separate not thyself from the community" (Aboth 2.4, p. 14, *Talmud*). And Josephus writes in a similar vein; see his *Antiquities of the Jews* 4.203–4 (LCL).

As Christians we must look to the future, that is, to the day when Jesus returns. The closer we come to that day, the more active we should be in spurring one another on in showing love and doing deeds acceptable to God. We would have appreciated more information about "the Day," but the author is as brief as other writers of the New Testament who mention it (see, for example, Matt. 25:13; I Cor. 3:13; I Thess. 5:4). Says Philip Edgcumbe Hughes: "When spoken of in this absolute manner, 'the Day' can mean only the last day, that ultimate eschatological day, which is the day of reckoning and judgment, known as the Day of the Lord."[26]

Practical Considerations in 10:19–25

Of the well-known triad faith, hope, and love, hope seems to be neglected. Writers of the New Testament, however, do not neglect it, for they mention it as many times as faith and love. The Christian in his spiritual life appears to stress the virtues of faith and love, but he says little about hope.

Yet hope guides the believer, for it provides him freedom from the fear of death. He keeps his eyes on Jesus, who has conquered the power of death. He knows that in Jesus he has salvation, righteousness, eternal life, and the assurance of resurrection from the dead. That hope will be realized when Jesus returns.

Christianity is a religion of love that reaches out and brings people together. Sports, performances on the stage or screen, and politics draw large crowds. But Christianity holds people together because it emphasizes participation in worship, praise, and work. Christians need each other to strengthen the wonderful bond of love they share in Jesus Christ.

The author's exhortation to "spur one another on toward love" precedes his remarks about church attendance. When the believer attends the worship service, he expresses his love for Jesus. He realizes that Jesus, the head of the church, is present at the service and desires his presence. To say it somewhat differently, the head of the church cannot function without the body. The believer is part of the body of Christ, which Christ presents "to himself as a radiant church, without stain or wrinkle or any other blemish, but holy and blameless" (Eph. 5:27).

Greek Words, Phrases, and Constructions in 10:19–25

Verse 19

ἔχοντες—this present active participle from ἔχω (I have) denotes cause. It indicates why the believer may draw near to God.

εἴσοδον—from the combination of εἰς (into) and ἡ ὁδός (the way); this noun can mean either the act of entering or entrance. The context favors the first meaning. τῶν ἁγίων is an abbreviated form of τά ἅγια τῶν ἁγίων and refers to the Most Holy Place (see Heb. 9:2, 12).

---

26. Philip Edgcumbe Hughes, *Commentary on the Epistle to the Hebrews* (Grand Rapids: Eerdmans, 1977), p. 416.

Verse 20

πρόσφατον—a compound adjective from πρό (before) and σφάζω (I slay). This term in time signified something new or recent.

σαρκός—this genitive singular noun stands in apposition to the antecedent καταπετάσματος (curtain). To link the genitive σαρκός to the accusative ὁδόν is difficult and grammatically unsound.

Verse 22

προσερχώμεθα—the present middle subjunctive has a variant reading in the form of the present middle indicative. The external evidence (manuscripts) and the internal evidence (context) favor the present subjunctive. This is the first of three hortatory subjunctives; the other two are κατέχωμεν (v. 23) and κατανοῶμεν (v. 24).

ῥεραντισμένοι—together with λελουσμένοι the participle features the perfect tense and the passive voice.[27] The action of the verbs (ῥαντίζω, I sprinkle; and λούω, I wash) occurred in the past but has lasting effect in the present.

Verse 24

ἀλλήλους—this reciprocal pronoun appears only here in the entire epistle. It seems to relate much more to the noun παροξυσμόν (provoking, encouraging) than to the verb κατανοῶμεν (let us consider), even though the verb governs the pronoun as a direct object.

Verse 25

ἐγκαταλείποντες—the present active participle shows that the staying away from the meetings happened. The compound form of the verb indicates a forsaking, that is, an abandoning of the congregation.

ἐπισυναγωγήν—according to Walter Bauer, this noun does not differ from the noun συναγωγή.[28]

ἑαυτῶν—this is the abbreviated *koine* Greek form for ἡμῶν αὐτῶν and is simply translated "our."

---

26 If we deliberately keep on sinning after we have received the knowledge of the truth, no sacrifice for sins is left, 27 but only a fearful expectation of judgment and of raging fire that will consume the enemies of God. 28 Anyone who rejected the law of Moses died without mercy on the testimony of two or three witnesses. 29 How much more severely do you think a man deserves to be punished who has trampled the Son of God under foot, who has treated as an unholy thing the blood of the covenant that sanctified him, and who has insulted the Spirit of grace? 30 For we know him who said, "It is mine to avenge; I will repay," and again, "The Lord will judge his people." 31 It is a dreadful thing to fall into the hands of the living God.

---

27. Robertson, *Grammar,* p. 486, calls them passive verbs with rather remote accusative.
28. Bauer, p. 301.

B. A Warning to Pay Attention
10:26–31

1. To the Knowledge of the Truth
10:26–27

Forsaking the congregation at worship leads to serious consequences. The author warns the believers that the sequel to sinning deliberately is falling "into the hands of the living God" (10:31).

26. If we deliberately keep on sinning after we have received the knowledge of the truth, no sacrifice for sins is left, 27. but only a fearful expectation of judgment and of raging fire that will consume the enemies of God.

The word *deliberately* stands first in the original Greek, and as the opening word of the sentence it receives all the emphasis. The term occurs only twice in the New Testament, here and in I Peter 5:2. It refers to something done intentionally.

In the Old Testament the distinction is made between sins committed unintentionally and sins committed intentionally. The first can be forgiven; the second cannot. Moses writes, "But anyone who sins defiantly, whether native-born or alien, blasphemes the Lord, and that person must be cut off from his people" (Num. 15:30; see also Lev. 4:2, 22, 27; 5:15, 18; Num. 15:24 for unintentional sins).

The author of Hebrews is rather specific. He writes concerning a person who sins intentionally and who keeps on doing this in open rebellion against God and his Word. To reach his readers in a pastoral manner, he even includes himself in the warning not to sin defiantly. He is not talking about a believer who falls into sin unintentionally and finds forgiveness in God's grace and mercy. Rather, he points to the same sin that Jesus calls the sin against the Holy Spirit (Matt. 12:32; Mark 3:29) and that John describes as "a sin that leads to death" (I John 5:16). Although he employs different terms, the writer virtually repeats the same thought he expressed in 3:12 and 6:4–6, where he speaks of falling away from the living God.

Those who turn away from God and "have received the knowledge of the truth" can never say that they sinned in ignorance. The phrase *knowledge of the truth* relates to God's revelation in general and the gospel in particular (see I Tim. 2:4; II Tim. 2:25; 3:7; Titus 1:1). They who at one time received this truth, but now have turned against God and his revelation, are without excuse. Nothing can save them. They know that Christ's sacrifice is the only sacrifice that removes sin. If they deliberately reject Christ and his atoning work, they reject salvation. For them, says the writer, "no sacrifice for sins is left."

What then is left? "Only a fearful expectation of judgment and of raging fire that will consume the enemies of God." A decision against Christ taken deliberately can only result in judgment. And judgment is not merely something that happens at the end of time. Evidence already is being gathered and presented to the jury in preparation for the judgment day. And that is a fearful expectation!

The emphasis falls on the adjective *fearful.* The word occurs three times in the New Testament, all in this epistle (10:27, 31: 12:21). This adjective is translated "fearful," "dreadful," and "terrifying." In all three instances its use pertains to meeting God. The sinner cannot escape God's judgment and, unless he has been forgiven in Christ, faces an angry God on that dreadful day.

Not only the judgment awaits the sinner who will receive the verdict, but also the execution of that verdict. The author vividly portrays the execution as a raging fire that will consume all those who have chosen to be enemies of God. Actually he echoes the words of Isaiah's prophecy, "Let the fire reserved for your enemies consume them" (Isa. 26:11).

2. To God's Judgment
10:28–31

28. Anyone who rejected the law of Moses died without mercy on the testimony of two or three witnesses.

Let no one think that God deals lightly with his enemies and shows them mercy. If anyone deliberately rejected the law of Moses in Old Testament times, that person was put to death without mercy. God instructed the Israelites to banish the sin of apostasy by killing the person who willfully despised God's commandments and turned to idols instead. "Then all Israel will hear and be afraid, and no one among you will do such an evil thing again" (Deut. 13:11; see also vv. 1–10 and 17:2–7). This was a warning to Israel to keep God's law and to serve him wholeheartedly.

Should someone break the commandments, he would not be killed. Only when two or three witnesses verified that he had intentionally despised God and rejected the law of Moses would this offender be put to death. The stipulation that a person be tried on the testimony of two or three witnesses was a rule observed and applied in biblical times (Num. 35:30; Deut. 17:6; 19:15; Matt. 18:16; John 8:17; II Cor. 13:1). Appeal of the sentence would not be granted. The writer of Hebrews summarizes the essence of the verdict in the words *without mercy.* According to God's instructions, the guilty person had to be killed, and the example was to serve as a deterrent.

29. How much more severely do you think a man deserves to be punished who has trampled the Son of God under foot, who has treated as an unholy thing the blood of the covenant that sanctified him, and who has insulted the Spirit of grace?

Once again the author of Hebrews employs the device of contrast. He sets the times of the old covenant over against those of the new covenant. He compares the penalty of physical death with the much more severe sentence of spiritual death. And he differentiates between rejecting the law of Moses and despising the Son of God and the Spirit of God. He asks the reader to reflect on this difference.

The sinner who rebels against God in the times of the new covenant rejects the person of Christ, the work of Christ, and the person of the Holy Spirit. And thus he has committed the unpardonable sin. The writer delineates this sin in three parts.

a. Person of the Son of God. Note that the author again employs the title of Christ, which he used extensively at the beginning of the Epistle to the Hebrews. The title is the highest accorded to Christ. No one can be compared to this Son, for he excels all: angels, Moses, Aaron, and Melchizedek.

What does the sinner do? He tramples under foot this Son of God. To trample something under foot is what we do when we get rid of a bothersome insect.[29] Thus the sinner figuratively takes the exalted Son of God and grinds him into the dirt.

b. Work of the Son of God. The second part is even more significant because it relates to the meaning and purpose of the new covenant. Jesus inaugurated this covenant by his blood to cleanse his people and sanctify them (Matt. 26:28 and parallels).

Jesus shed his precious blood and paid the supreme sacrifice. But this shed blood means nothing to the rebellious sinner. He regards Jesus' blood as the blood of any other human being and Jesus' death as that of any other mortal. He considers Jesus to be a mere man whose death has no significance and whose redemptive work has no value.

The author contrasts the defiant sinner within the Israelite community with the Christian who has abandoned the church; his point is that ignorance cannot be used as an excuse. The sinner knows the Christian faith, for he was sanctified by the blood of the covenant. That is, at one time he professed his faith in Christ, listened to the preaching of the Word of God, and partook of the holy elements when he celebrated the Lord's Supper. But his faith was not an internal fulfillment. In word and deed he now repudiates his relationship to Christ's work. He breaks with his past.

c. Person of the Holy Spirit. The third clause in the description of the unpardonable sin relates to insulting the Spirit of grace (Matt. 12:32; Mark 3:29). The sinner intentionally insults the person of the Holy Spirit. In his conduct, the sinner points out the stark contrast between insults hurled at the Holy Spirit and grace granted by the Holy Spirit. The Spirit is the source of grace (Zech. 12:10). Insulting the third person of the Trinity is the height of sin that cannot be forgiven. Says John Calvin, "To treat him with scorn, by whom we are endowed with so many benefits, is an impiety extremely wicked."[30] God himself confronts the sinner and metes out punishment.

30. For we know him who said, "It is mine to avenge; I will repay,"

---

29. The expression *trample under foot* (or variants) is common in the Old Testament (see, for example, II Kings 9:33; Isa. 26:6; Dan. 8:10; Mic. 7:10; Mal. 4:3). In the New Testament it occurs five times (Matt. 5:13; 7:6; Luke 8:5; 12:1; Heb. 10:29).

30. Calvin, *Hebrews,* p. 248.

and again, "The Lord will judge his people." 31. It is a dreadful thing to fall into the hands of the living God.

Understandably believers are grieved when they hear about and see the conduct of a person who leaves the Christian community by scornfully rejecting the Son of God and insulting the Holy Spirit. They know that vengeance belongs to God, for this is the teaching of his Word.

The author of Hebrews takes the words "It is mine to avenge; I will repay" from the Song of Moses (Deut. 32:35).[31] This song was well known to the readers because they sang it in their worship services. The wording differs somewhat in the original Hebrew and its Greek translation; therefore, scholars have made the suggestion that "the citation in this form may have been stereotyped by apostolic example in the language of the primitive church."[32] The citation occurs in the selfsame wording in Romans 12:19. We may assume that it circulated in the early church as a proverbial saying.

The second quotation comes from both the Song of Moses (Deut. 32:36) and the Book of Psalms (Ps. 135:14). "The Lord will judge his people," writes the author of Hebrews. The intent is to emphasize that judgment is unavoidable. In an earlier setting the writer speaks of the coming judgment (9:27; and see 10:27) and presents it in the form of an accepted truth.

God will judge his people; no one escapes his judgment. Those whose faith is rooted in Jesus Christ find a God of grace and mercy. Their sins have been forgiven because of the Son's sacrifice on the cross. And they will hear the verdict *acquitted.* But they who have spurned the person and work of Christ and have arrogantly despised the Holy Spirit face the infinite wrath of God, the judge of heaven and earth.

When a sinner repents of his sin, approaches the throne of God, and pleads for mercy, God hears and answers. David experienced this when he sinned against God by counting the number of fighting men in Israel and Judah. Said David, "Let us fall into the hands of the LORD, for his mercy is great" (II Sam. 24:14; see also I Chron. 21:13). The sinner who breaks God's law purposely to grieve God has passed the stage of repentance (Heb. 6:4–6). He falls "into the hands of the living God" (also see Heb. 3:12), and that confrontation is indescribable. The writer of Hebrews says it is dreadful.

Practical Considerations in 10:26–31

Preaching sermons on hellfire appears to be something that happened in the past but not today. This type of preaching is considered an oddity of the eighteenth century; it should not be heard from a twentieth-century pulpit.

---

31. The writer of Hebrews usually quotes the Septuagint translation, but not here. The Septuagint has, "In the day of vengeance, I will repay."

32. Delitzsch, *Hebrews,* vol. 2, p. 190. Also see K. J. Thomas, "The Use of the Septuagint in the Epistle to the Hebrews" (Ph.D. diss., University of Manchester, 1959), p. 122. Perhaps the phraseology of the citation prevailed in an oral tradition on which the writers of the Targums and the writers of the New Testament relied.

True. Sermons ought to proclaim the gospel of salvation, the call to repentance, the assurance of pardon, and the message of reconciliation between God and man. Proportionally, Scripture says little about God's burning wrath that consumes his enemies. If Scripture sets the example, we should follow its practice.

Nevertheless, no preacher may fail to warn the people of the dire consequences of turning away from the living God. The recurring theme of the Epistle of Hebrews is one of warning God's people. Note these three texts:

3:12 "See to it, brothers, that none of you has a sinful, unbelieving heart that turns away from the living God."

4:1 "Therefore, since the promise of entering [God's] rest still stands, let us be careful that none of you be found to have fallen short of it."

4:11 "Let us, therefore, make every effort to enter that rest, so that no one will fall by following their example of disobedience."

The terrifying consequences of living a life of intentional sin ought to be mentioned in sermons. In Hebrews we read that every believer has the responsibility to seek the spiritual welfare of his fellow Christians. We may call this corporate responsibility because it is our mutual task. And pastors may refer to hellfire in their sermons, for such a warning also belongs to the full message of God's revelation.

As the pastor warns the wayward, so he encourages the faint-hearted. A believer may lack the assurance of salvation, fearing that he has committed the sin against the Holy Spirit. But the unpardonable sin cannot be attributed to a person who doubts his or her salvation. Only the person who demonstrates an open and deliberate hatred toward God, divine revelation, and Christ's accomplished work of salvation has committed that sin. The doubter, then, needs words of encouragement. He should be invited to repeat the reassuring words of Paul, "Yet I am not ashamed, because I know whom I have believed, and am convinced that he is able to guard what I have entrusted to him for that day" (II Tim. 1:12).

Greek Words, Phrases, and Constructions in 10:26–31

Verse 26

ἑκουσίως—an adverb derived from the adjective ἑκών (voluntary, willing, of one's own free will).

ἁμαρτανόντων—the genitive absolute construction with a present active participle denoting a condition. The first person plural pronoun ἡμῶν completes the construction. Note that the present participle (indicating duration) and not the aorist participle (depicting a single occurrence) is used.

τὴν ἐπίγνωσιν—the compound noun is preceded by the definite article and has a perfective connotation; that is, the compound noun is more precise than the noun γνῶσις (knowledge). ἐπίγνωσιν has the meaning *recognition, acknowledgment.*

Verse 27

τις—this indefinite pronoun, usually translated "someone" or "something," should be taken with the adjective φοβερά. It strengthens the adjective and means "a *very* fearful expectation."[33]

---

33. Robertson, *Grammar,* p. 743. Italics his.

ἐκδοχή—the noun has its origin in the verb ἐκδέχομαι (I expect, await). It appears only here in the New Testament. The noun controls two objects in the genitive case: judgment and fire.

ζῆλος—although translations treat this word as an adjective (raging; NIV, JB), it is a noun that means "jealousy"; that is, the fierceness of fire.

Verse 28

ἀθετήσας—the aorist active participle from ἀθετέω (I nullify, reject) conveys the idea of annulling the law of Moses, resulting in a complete break with the old covenant.

ἐπί—this preposition may be translated "in the presence of."

Verse 29

ποσῷ—the dative case points out the degree of difference between physical death and eternal punishment. It introduces the hermeneutical rule of contrast "from the lesser to the greater."

ἀξιωθήσεται—the future passive of ἀξιόω (I consider worthy) controls the genitive case τιμωρίας (punishment). The verb usually has the positive connotation of receiving rewards; here it means deserving punishment.

ἡγησάμενος—the aorist middle participle of ἡγέομαι (I think, regard) and ἡγιάσθη (the aorist passive of ἁγιάζω, I make holy) are a play on words in the Greek text.

Verse 31

τὸ ἐμπεσεῖν—an aorist infinitive of the directive compound ἐμπίπτω (I fall into). The aorist shows single occurrence. It is succeeded by the preposition εἰς (into).

ζῶντος—the present active participle from the verb ζάω (I live) describes God as distinct from manmade idols that are dead.

---

32 Remember those earlier days after you had received the light, when you stood your
ground in a great contest in the face of suffering. 33 Sometimes you were publicly exposed
to insult and persecution; at other times you stood side by side with those who were so
treated. 34 You sympathized with those in prison and joyfully accepted the confiscation of
your property, because you knew that you yourselves had better and lasting possessions.
35 So do not throw away your confidence; it will be richly rewarded. 36 You need to
persevere so that when you have done the will of God, you will receive what he has promised. 37 For in just a very little while,

"He who is coming will come and not delay.
38 But my righteous one will live by faith.
And if he shrinks back,
I will not be pleased with him."

39 But we are not of those who shrink back and are destroyed, but of those who believe and are saved.

C. A Reminder to Continue
10:32–39

1. As in the Past
10:32–34

As a pastor sensitive to the needs to his people, the author changes his remarks from admonition to praise, from reproof to commendation. He heartily approves of the works of love and mercy they showed to those who were persecuted and those who lost their possessions. The writer draws a parallel to his warning against falling away (6:4–6) and to his tribute to the readers for their demonstration of love and their willingness to help (6:9–11).

32. Remember those earlier days after you had received the light, when you stood your ground in a great contest in the face of suffering.

Times of hardship, persecution, and suffering remain indelibly fixed in man's memory. Memories come to mind with the simple question, "Do you recall?" Yes, the readers vividly remembered those early days when at first they had professed their faith and received the sacrament of baptism. In those days they received the light (6:4). But as soon as they had become Christians, they faced hostility.

Especially in Jewish circles the sign of Christian baptism indicates the breaking point, and Jewish converts to the Christian religion are excommunicated and subject to abuse and insult, if not persecution. The recipients of the Epistle to the Hebrews had experienced first hand suffering for their faith in Jesus. And they had not forgotten this "great contest," even though the present was calm and peaceful. They recalled the intensity and the duration of this difficult period in their lives.[34] Their faith was tested, and they emerged victoriously in spite of and because of the suffering they endured. Not only had they personally endured hardship, but also they had reached out in love to others who experienced similar treatment.

33. Sometimes you were publicly exposed to insult and persecution; at other times you stood side by side with those who were so treated.

The readers of this epistle knew what it meant to be objects of public ridicule and persecution. The text indicates that these conditions persisted for an extended period. Wherever the church begins to develop and grow, opposition can be expected. The "Hebrews," who were known as traitors to the Jewish faith, had become the target of abuse. In effect, they were treated as outlaws. As aliens in a foreign land, they were deprived of legal protection. Persecution was their lot. To them the Beatitudes of Jesus were especially meaningful. "Blessed are those who are persecuted because of righteousness, for theirs is the kingdom of heaven. Blessed are you when people insult you, persecute you and falsely say all kinds of evil against you because of me" (Matt. 5:10–11).

They stood side by side with those who endured the same hostility. They demonstrated the love of Christ to fellow church members who faced harassment, maltreatment, and deprivation. The members of the congregation stood together in aiding one another in the hour of need.

34. You sympathized with those in prison and joyfully accepted the confiscation of your property, because you knew that you yourselves had better and lasting possessions.

Christians are expected to visit the prisoners. Jesus commends the righteous for having visited the captives: "I was in prison and you came to visit

34. Michel, *Hebräer,* p. 239.

me" (Matt. 25:36; also see vv. 39, 43, 44). Prisoners depended on relatives, friends, and acquaintances for food, clothing, and other needs (see, for example, Acts 23:16; 24:23; 27:3; II Tim. 4:13). The writer of Hebrews exhorts his readers to "remember those in prison as if you were their fellow prisoners" (13:3).

Moreover, the readers of the epistle were obedient to the words of Jesus, "Do not store up for yourselves treasures on earth. . . . But store up for yourselves treasures in heaven" (Matt. 6:19, 20). Cheerfully they gave up their property when, presumably, governmental authorities confiscated their goods. Their lasting possession was stored up for them in heaven, and in that knowledge they rejoiced. These readers lived in harmony with the precepts that Jesus taught in the gospel (Matt. 5:12; Luke 6:23; James 1:2).

The author of Hebrews seems to develop a sequence of the events that had occurred in the lives of his readers. First, they had endured a period of suffering when they "had received the light" (v. 32). Then they were exposed to public insult and persecution (v. 33). Also, they supported fellow believers who suffered similar abuse. And last, they had lost their property, perhaps in a time of political or religious turmoil (v. 34).

We would appreciate seeing a chronicle of events with exact dates and places. But the writer of Hebrews provides no historical information on when and where events took place. Therefore, we can work only with hypotheses that by nature are quite subjective.

The author's remark that the readers were in the category of second-generation Christians (2:3) makes an early date for persecution somewhat difficult to accept. For example, the persecution following the death of Stephen (Acts 8:1) may have occurred in A.D. 32. And the persecution that resulted in the death of James, brother of John, and the imprisonment of Peter (Acts 12:1–3) can be dated rather accurately for April A.D. 44. Both Stephen and James died in Jerusalem.

Rome witnessed the expulsion of the Jews in A.D. 49 during the reign of Emperor Claudius.[35] We can be reasonably sure that Jewish Christians were involved in this persecution—Luke mentions Aquila and Priscilla (Acts 18:1–2).[36] How severe the terms of this edict may have been is not known. Eventually those who were expelled returned to Rome (Rom. 16:3).

Then, following the burning of Rome in A.D. 64, Nero instigated severe persecutions directed primarily against the Christians.[37] Christians were

---

35. Suetonius, *Claudius,* 25.4 (LCL). "Since the Jews constantly made disturbances at the instigation of Chrestus [another form of Christus], he expelled them from Rome."

36. F. F. Bruce, *New Testament History* (Garden City, N.Y.: Doubleday, 1980), p. 297.

37. Tacitus, *Annals* 15.44 (LCL). Bruce, *Hebrews,* p. 267, rules out identifying the persecution of the Hebrews with the Neronian persecution. Says he, "It could never have been said to Roman Christians after A.D. 64 that they had 'not yet resisted unto blood, striving against sin'; that is precisely what they had done, and right nobly." Bruce, then, links the Hebrew persecution to the decree of Claudius. However, the clause "you have not yet resisted to the point of shedding your blood" (Heb. 12:4) must be seen in the context of the imagery used in verses 1–3. The clause should not be taken out of context and applied to historical references of an earlier chapter.

publicly oppressed when they faced wild animals in the arena or were burned at the stake. Because the author of Hebrews fails to provide any hints when the recipients of his letter endured persecution and loss of property, we assume that the events resulting from Claudius's decree and from Nero's cruel tactics mark the background of 10:32–34. As I already noted, the writer appears to develop somewhat of a sequence in these verses. The one event follows the other. Now he looks back into history and asks his readers to recall the hardships they had experienced.

2. So in the Present
10:35–39

35. So do not throw away your confidence; it will be richly rewarded.
If the readers suffered for their Christian faith in earlier days, will they at present throw away the confidence they showed in the face of persecution? Apparently time has elapsed, and the believers are living in a period of peace and safety. Their boldness in confessing their faith in Christ has fallen into disuse. And because they have not exercised their gift of confidence, they are ready to discard it.

Faith must be confessed boldly and confidently. In difficult circumstances the believer puts his faith in God and readily confesses the name of his Lord and Savior. But in a time of ease the Christian faces no necessity of taking a stand. His faith wavers and declines. Writes the author of Hebrews, "And without faith it is impossible to please God, because anyone who comes to him must believe that he exists and that he rewards those who earnestly seek him" (11:6). The confidence he expresses does not relate to the freedom we have in coming to God in prayer (4:16) or with a sincere heart (10:19, 22). Rather, the author wants the readers to exhibit their confidence or courage toward man (see also 3:6).

God will richly reward the believer who courageously confesses his faith. He rewards the Christian not because he has deserved the reward in the sense of having merited or earned it. God dispenses his gifts to those who earnestly seek him, not in terms of counting "human values and achievements, but [in terms of] a joyful hopefulness" that God has promised.[38]

36. You need to persevere so that when you have done the will of God, you will receive what he has promised.

The writer shows tact and pastoral concern. He exhorts the readers to persevere; as in the past they stood their ground in the face of suffering (10:32), so now they ought to persevere in doing the will of God. When he writes the phrase *the will of God,* he immediately reminds the recipients of the obedience of Christ, who came to do the will of God (10:7, 9–10). The exhortation, then, is to follow Christ in obediently keeping the commandments. And when they persevere in faithfulness to God's will, they will "receive what he has promised."

38. Paul Christoph Böttger, *NIDNTT,* vol. 3, p. 143.

The expression *promise* is a key word in the Epistle to the Hebrews.[39] It stands for forgiveness of sins, in terms of the new covenant, but especially for complete salvation in Jesus Christ.[40] God's promise to man is unbreakable. What God has promised, the believer will receive.

37. For in just a very little while,
"He who is coming will come and not delay.
38. But my righteous one will live by faith.
And if he shrinks back,
I will not be pleased with him."

Steeped in the Old Testament Scriptures, the author cites prophecy to support his exhortation to persevere. Whether the introduction to the quotation, that is, the words "in just a very little while," was purposely taken from Isaiah 26:20 is debatable. Isaiah 26 is a song of praise that was chanted or read in the worship services of the ancient synagogue and of the early Christian church.[41] However, the phrase "in just a very little while" also appears in nonbiblical Greek literature and may simply be a colloquial expression. The meaning of the phrase expresses the thought that the period of waiting will not be long. In fact, the adverb *very* makes the phrase all the more pointed.

The author of Hebrews has taken a quotation from the prophecy of Habakkuk and has given it a decidedly messianic interpretation. He follows not the Hebrew text but the Septuagint translation, and for his own purposes introduces some changes. A comparison of the passage in parallel columns is helpful:

Habakkuk 2:3b, 4	*Hebrews 10:37b, 38*
3b. Though it [the revelation] linger, wait for it; it will certainly come and will not delay.	37b. He who is coming will come and will not delay.
4. "See, he is puffed up; his desires are not upright—[Septuagint: And if he shrinks back I will not be pleased with him.] but the righteous will live by his faith."	38. But my righteous one will live by faith. And if he shrinks back, I will not be pleased with him.

Although the text of Habakkuk relates to the revelation, the writer of Hebrews makes the wording personal and applies it to the Messiah. The phrase *he who is coming* is a descriptive title of Christ (see Matt. 11:3; Luke

39. The noun *promise* occurs fifty-three times in the New Testament, fourteen of which are in Hebrews (4:1; 6:12, 15, 17; 7:6; 8:6; 9:15; 10:36; 11:9 [twice], 13, 17, 33, 39). The verb appears fifteen times, four of which are in Hebrews (6:13; 10:23; 11:11; 12:26).

40. Ernst Hoffmann, *NIDNTT,* vol. 3, p. 73.

41. Ernst Werner, *The Sacred Bridge* (London: D. Dobson, 1959), p. 140. The early church used nine songs taken from the Old Testament and five from the New Testament. See Kistemaker, *Psalm Citations,* p. 47.

7:20; Rev. 1:4, 8; 4:8). Christ comes quickly and will not delay. When the time arrives for his return, God's revelation will be fulfilled.

Habakkuk prophesies against the Babylonians and portrays them as haughty people who are ruthless and a law unto themselves (Hab. 1:6–7). He refers to them collectively and says, "See, he is puffed up; his desires are not upright." In the Septuagint the reading is, "And if he shrinks back I will not be pleased with him." The contrast is between the godless Babylonian and the righteous Israelite who put his faith in God.

The writer of Hebrews turns the two sentences around. He inserts the personal pronoun *my* and writes, "But my righteous one shall live by faith." Because Paul also uses this line, although without the pronoun (Rom. 1:17; Gal. 3:11), we assume that these words were familiar to the early Christians. The author adds the second part—"and if he shrinks back, I will not be pleased with him." The order, therefore, is reversed.

The difference between Habakkuk's prophecy and the wording of Hebrews is that in the prophecy the Babylonian is contrasted with the Israelites: the one is godless; the other, a devout believer. In Hebrews, "my righteous one" is the same person who shrinks back. In rearranged form the quotation addresses the recipient of the epistle.

The righteous person who perseveres does not receive God's promise on the basis of keeping the law and doing the will of God. He receives the promise by faith.[42] The object of faith, of course, is understood. The believer places his faith in Jesus Christ. Out of a relationship of trust and confidence, the believer lives.[43]

In the face of opposition, persecution, and temptation, the believer ought to stand firm in his faith. Should he shrink back in fear, should he abandon his faith, and should he eventually turn away, God "will not be pleased with him." Instead God's displeasure will rest upon him because he has forsaken the author of his salvation.

The quotation from Habakkuk, then, contains a warning to remain true to God. That does not mean that the recipients of Hebrews are forsaking their Lord. On the contrary, the author encourages them by writing reassuring words.

39. But we are not of those who shrink back and are destroyed, but of those who believe and are saved.

As in many other passages, the author identifies himself with the readers. He places himself on their level when he uses the personal pronoun *we.* He points out two classes: "those who shrink back" and "those who believe." The first group perishes; the second is saved.

The pastor-writer encourages his people. He gives them words of comfort

---

42. Grosheide, *Hebreeën,* p. 253. The writer of Hebrews avoids advocating works righteousness whereby man earns his salvation. Man is declared righteous on the basis of faith in Christ.

43. A few manuscripts have transposed the personal pronoun and have the reading, "But the righteous will live by faith in me."

and assurance. He says, "We belong to those people who believe and are saved." He knows the readers of his epistle and is confident that they will continue to believe. And the people realize that the person who shrinks back faces eternal condemnation, whereas he who believes obtains salvation. The contrast is clearly delineated. No one can plead ignorance, for the one road leads to destruction; the other, to life.

In the concluding verses of chapter 10, the author introduces the concept *faith*. He sets the tone for a lengthy discussion about the heroes of faith by tracing sacred history from Abel to the prophets.

Practical Considerations in 10:32–39

"You . . . joyfully accepted the confiscation of your property." This statement seems incongruous, unreal. All of us have a natural inclination to cherish and protect our own belongings. We are not unwilling to help people in need. Indeed we give cheerfully. But we certainly do not shout for joy when our possessions are taken from us.

When Jesus asks us to love our enemies, to do good to those who hate us, to bless those who curse us, and to pray for those who mistreat us (Luke 6:27–28), we readily consent. And when he continues and asks us to turn the other cheek when someone strikes us (Luke 6:29), we nod our heads and are willing to endure physical abuse. But when Jesus says, "Give to everyone who asks you, and if anyone takes what belongs to you, do not demand it back" (Luke 6:30), we object. Our belongings are valuable to us, and we certainly make our unhappiness known when someone takes them from us. Jesus, however, wants us to cling not to earthly but to heavenly possessions. Treasures laid up in heaven are lasting; those on earth are fleeting.

The recipients of Hebrews understood and applied the words of Jesus. When their possessions were taken away and when their property was confiscated, they realized they "had better and lasting possessions" in heaven.

When a member of the Jewish community converts to Christianity, a period of conflict begins in his family, household, and locale. The Hebrew or Jew who becomes a Christian faces alienation, especially when he receives the sacrament of baptism. The temptation to renounce Christ and return to the fold of Judaism is real, for being surrounded once more by relatives and friends signifies an end to persecution and hardship. The Epistle to the Hebrews is a letter of encouragement and admonition to all those who have confessed Christ as their Savior. Let no one shrink back and renounce Christ. Turning one's back on him leads to condemnation and destruction. Do true believers fall away? No. By his Word and Spirit, God enables them to remain faithful to the end.

Greek Words, Phrases, and Constructions in 10:32–39

Verse 32

τὰς πρότερον ἡμέρας—the use of the definite article and the position of the adverb πρότερον (earlier) reveal that much time has elapsed since the occurrence of events to which the author alludes.

φωτισθέντες—the aorist passive from φωτίζω (I bring light to) may be understood spiritually to refer to accepting the truth of the gospel and being baptized (see John 1:9; Eph. 1:18; Heb. 6:4).

Verse 34

δεσμίοις—this noun has been subject to change. Writes Bruce M. Metzger: "The reading that best explains the origin of the others is δεσμίοις [prisoners], which is supported by good representatives of both the Alexandrian and the Western types of text, as well as several Eastern witnesses. Through transcriptional oversight the first iota was omitted, resulting in the reading δεσμοῖς [bonds]. Then, in order to improve the sense, copyists added a personal pronoun, either αὐτῶν [their], referring to those mentioned in ver[se] 33b, or μου [my], in imitation of the statements of Php 1:7, 13, 14, 17; Col 4:18."[44]

ὕπαρξιν—the collective noun is actually the equivalent of the more common ὑπάρχοντα (property).

Verse 35

μὴ ἀποβάλητε—the aorist subjunctive preceded by the negative particle conveys the idea that the readers of the epistle were not throwing away their confidence. The writer only warns them never to think about doing this. The aorist subjunctive as imperative is balanced by the present imperative ἀναμιμνήσκεσθε (v. 32).

ἥτις—as an indefinite relative pronoun it has a causal connotation.

Verse 36

ὑπομονῆς—the noun derived from the verb ὑπομένω (I remain, endure) is introduced by ὑπεμείνατε (v. 32).

κομίσησθε—in 6:15 the synonym ἐπέτυχεν appears (also see 11:33). The verb κομίζω (in the middle: I receive, obtain) has the meaning of personally appropriating the promise. Its synonym ἐπιτυγχάνω (I attain, obtain) is a more general term.

Verse 39

ἡμεῖς—this personal pronoun stands first in the sentence, receives all the emphasis, and supports the verb ἐσμέν that is understood in the second part of the verse. The sentence is perfectly balanced to feature the opposites in the contrast.

ὑποστολῆς—a noun derived from ὑποστέλλω (in the middle: I shrink) has its counterpart in πίστεως. And the noun ἀπώλειαν (destruction) from ἀπόλλυμι (I destroy) is balanced by περιποίησιν ψυχῆς (saving of the soul).

Summary of Chapter 10

The first section of chapter 10 is actually a continuation of the theme and content of the preceding chapter. In chapter 9 the author writes of the

---

44. Bruce M. Metzger, *A Textual Commentary on the Greek New Testament* (London and New York: United Bible Societies, 1975), p. 670.

unique sacrifice of Christ, and in the first eighteen verses of chapter 10 he summarizes the teachings concerning this unique sacrifice. That is, Christ came to set aside the shadows of the Levitical priestly service. By his death he established the era of the new covenant.

Quoting Psalm 40:6–7, the writer of Hebrews underlines the significance of Christ's sacrifice over against animal sacrifices. Christ came to do the will of God. That is important, for God takes no pleasure in sacrifices and offerings of animals that were devoted to God as substitutes to atone for man's disobedience.

The difference between the sacrificial system of the old covenant and that of the new covenant is the repetitive nature of presenting sacrifices in the one, and the once-for-all offering in the other. The sacrifice of Christ is sufficient to sanctify his people. They have God's law written on their hearts and minds. And they know that because of Christ's perfect sacrifice, their sins have been forgiven.

The second part of chapter 10 is also the beginning of the second part of the epistle. This segment features exhortations and admonitions. The readers are exhorted to enter the presence of God because Christ has opened the way by shedding his blood.

The writer encourages the believers to remain true to their confession; he challenges them to demonstrate their love in word and deed; and he admonishes them to seek the fellowship of the saints at worship.

He calls their attention once more (see 3:16–19; 6:4–6) to the sin of falling away from God. He describes the horrible consequences of deliberately sinning against God. The warning against unbelief, "See to it, brothers, that none of you has a sinful, unbelieving heart that turns away from the living God" (3:12), is a recurring refrain in the epistle. In the present section the same warning, although in different wording, is given twice.

But besides warning the people, the author also encourages them. As a loving pastor, he tells them that God will richly reward their faith. They ought to persevere in doing the will of God and live by faith. Because of their faith in God, they are saved.

The chapter ends with the introduction of the concept *faith*. And faith is the subject of the next chapter.

11

The Heroes of Faith

11:1–40

Outline

11:1–3	A.	A Definition of Faith
11:4–7	B.	Three Examples of Faith: Abel, Enoch, and Noah
	C.	The Faith of Abraham
11:8–10		1. The Promised Land
11:11–12		2. The Promised Son
11:13–16		3. The Promise
11:17–19		4. The Test of Faith
11:20–22	D.	The Faith of Isaac, Jacob, and Joseph
	E.	The Faith of Moses
11:23–26		1. Moses' Childhood and Position
11:27–29		2. Moses' Leadership
11:30–31	F.	Faith at Jericho
	G.	Known and Unknown Heroes of Faith
11:32–35a		1. Those Who Triumphed
11:35b–38		2. Those Who Suffered
11:39–40		3. Commendation

11 1 Now faith is being sure of what we hope for and certain of what we do not see. 2 This is what the ancients were commended for.
3 By faith we understand that the universe was formed at God's command, so that what is seen was not made out of what was visible.

A. A Definition of Faith
11:1–3

The writer delights in recounting the history of the heroes of faith recorded in Scripture. Before he cites examples, however, he composes a brief definition of faith. He does not write a dogmatic exposition. Instead he formulates a few clear, straightforward sentences.

1. Now faith is being sure of what we hope for and certain of what we do not see.

As we study this verse, let us note the following points:

a. *Faith.* The word *faith* in the New Testament has many aspects. For example, when the Judean Christians, whom Paul had sought to destroy, spoke of their belief in Christ, they said, "The man who formerly persecuted us is now preaching the faith he once tried to destroy" (Gal. 1:23). Faith, then, is a confession, much the same as we call the Apostles' Creed the articles of our Christian faith. However, this is not the meaning of faith that the writer of Hebrews conveys.

For the evangelists who wrote the Gospels, Jesus Christ is the object of faith. John summarizes this emphasis when he states the purpose of his Gospel, namely, "that you may believe that Jesus is the Christ, the Son of God, and that by believing you may have life in his name" (John 20:31). Also, the Acts show that in the first century, "a personal faith in Jesus was a hallmark of the early Christians."[1]

Still another aspect of faith is Paul's emphasis on appropriating, that is, claiming salvation in Jesus Christ. Paul contends that God puts the sinner right with him through faith: "This righteousness from God comes through faith in Jesus Christ to all who believe" (Rom. 3:22). And Paul explains that faith comes from hearing the Word proclaimed (Rom. 10:17).

---

1. Donald Guthrie, *New Testament Theology* (Downers Grove, Ill.: Inter-Varsity, 1981), p. 588.

The author of Hebrews recognizes these same aspects of faith featured by other writers of the New Testament. However, his use of the concept *faith* must be understood primarily in the context of the eleventh chapter of his epistle. The heroes of faith have one thing in common: they put their undivided confidence in God. In spite of all their trials and difficult circumstances, they triumphed because of their trust in God. For the author, faith is adhering to the promises of God, depending on the Word of God, and remaining faithful to the Son of God.

When we see chapter 11 in the context of Hebrews, the author's design to contrast faith with the sin of unbelief (3:12, 19; 4:2; 10:38–39) becomes clear. Over against the sin of falling away from the living God, the writer squarely places the virtue of faith.[2] Those people who shrink from putting their trust in God are destroyed, but those who believe are saved (10:39).

b. *Assurance.* What is true faith? In 1563 a German theology professor, Zacharias Ursinus, formulated his personal faith:

> True faith—
>   created in me by the Holy Spirit through the gospel—
> is not only a knowledge and conviction
>   that everything that God reveals in his Word is true,
> but also a deep-rooted assurance
>   that not only others, but I too,
>   have had my sins forgiven,
>   have been made forever right with God,
>   and have been granted salvation.
>   These are gifts of sheer grace
>   earned for us by Christ.[3]

The author of Hebrews expresses that same assurance in much more concise wording: "Faith is being sure of what we hope for." The expression *being sure of* is given as "substance" in other translations.[4] The difference between these translations arises from understanding the original Greek word *hypostasis* subjectively or objectively. If I am sure of something, I have certainty in my heart. This is a subjective knowledge because it is within me. Assurance, then, is a subjective quality. By contrast, the word *substance* is objective because it refers to something that is not part of me. Rather, sub-

---

2. F. W. Grosheide, *De Brief aan de Hebreeën en de Brief van Jakobus* (Kampen: Kok, 1955), p. 255.

3. Heidelberg Catechism, answer 21.

4. See, for example, the KJV, NKJV, and NEB. Other translations have "confidence" (*Phillips,* Lenski), "we are confident" *(Moffatt),* or "guarantee" (JB). The RV, ASV, RSV, NASB, NAB, and MLB have "assurance." Helmut Köster, in *TDNT,* vol. 8, pp. 586–87, argues that the term *hypostasis* (substance) refers to "the reality of the goods hoped for, which have by nature a transcendent quality." Or, "among the meanings that can be authenticated the one that seems to fit best here is *realization . . . in faith things hoped for become realized,* or *things hoped for become reality.*" See Bauer, p. 847. Both Köster and Bauer favor understanding *hypostasis* subjectively.

stance is something on which I can rely. As one translation has it, "Faith is the title-deed of things hoped for."[5] That, in fact, is objective.

To come to a clear-cut choice in the matter is not easy, for the one translation does not rule out the other. The translation *confidence* or *assurance* has gained prominence, perhaps because 3:14 also has the same word: "We have come to share in Christ if we hold firmly till the end the confidence we had at first." In the case of 11:1, even though the objective sense has validity, the subjective meaning is commended.

The author teaches the virtue of hope wherever he is able to introduce the topic (3:6; 6:11, 18; 7:19; 10:23). Hope is not an inactive hidden quality. Hope is active and progressive. It relates to all the things God has promised to believers: "all things of present grace and future glory."[6]

c. *Certainty.* Although the brief statement on faith consists of only two phrases, they are perfectly balanced. Note the structure:

Faith	
is	
being sure of	certain of
what we hope for	what we do not see

In short, assurance is balanced by certainty. These two nouns are in this text synonymous. Certainty, then, means "inner conviction."[7] The believer is convinced that the things he is unable to see are real. Not every conviction, however, is equal to faith. Conviction is the equivalent of faith when certainty prevails, even though the evidence is lacking. The things we do not see are those that pertain to the future, that in time will become the present. Even things of the present, and certainly those of the past, that are beyond our reach belong to the category of "what we do not see." Comments B. F. Westcott, "Hope includes that which is internal as well as that which is external."[8] Hope centers in the mind and spirit of man; sight relates to one of his senses (Rom. 8:24–25).

Faith, therefore, radiates from man's inner being where hope resides to riches that are beyond his purview. Faith demonstrates itself in confident assurance and convincing certainty.

2. This is what the ancients were commended for.

A somewhat literal translation of this verse reads, "It is for their faith that

---

5. James Hope Moulton and George Milligan, *The Vocabulary of the Greek Testament Illustrated from the Papyri and Other Non-Literary Sources* (London: Hodder and Stoughton, 1930), pp. 659–60.

6. John Owen, *An Exposition of Hebrews,* 7 vols. in 4 (Evansville, Ind.: Sovereign Grace, 1960), vol. 7, p. 7.

7. Bauer, p. 249.

8. B. F. Westcott, *Commentary on the Epistle to the Hebrews* (Grand Rapids: Eerdmans, 1950), p. 350.

the men of old [the elders] stand on record" (NEB).[9] The faith demonstrated by the ancients gained them God's approval. The term *ancients,* more literally "elders," refers to the same group of people listed as "forefathers" in 1:1. All of them have one thing in common: their faith. For that faith they are commended by God.

The writer of Hebrews begins his list of the heroes of faith with Abel and Enoch. For both of these illustrations, he uses the verb *to commend.* In verse 4 we read, "By faith [Abel] was commended as a righteous man," and in verse 5, "For before [Enoch] was taken, he was commended as one who pleased God." It would not be necessary for the author to say that everyone mentioned in the list was commended. All the ancients whose names are recorded in sacred history experienced God's favor because of their faith. For their faith they were recognized by God and by his people.

3. By faith we understand that the universe was formed at God's command, so that what is seen was not made out of what was visible.

At first sight we are inclined to read verse 3 with verse 1 and consider verse 2 the logical heading of the list of the men of faith. But we have no justification for rearranging the author's design. He begins his illustrations of demonstrating faith with a comment about creation. No one was present at creation to observe the formation of the world. "Where were you when I laid the earth's foundation?" God asks Job (38:4). By using the plural *we understand,* the author includes himself and all his readers in the confession that God created the world.

The first declaration in the long list of the verses beginning with "by faith" is so rich in meaning that we do well to discuss this verse phrase by phrase. Before we enter upon a full discussion, however, we should note that verse 3b is translated in two ways. That is, the negative adverb *not* is placed either before the verb *to make* or before the word *appear*—apart from variations in translating this verse. The verse can be translated either "so that what is seen was not made out of what was visible"[10] or "so that what is seen was made out of things which do not appear."[11] Translators are about equally divided on this particular issue. We shall discuss the matter as it presents itself in the sequence of the verse.

a. "By faith." This is the first occurrence in a series of twenty-one uses of the phrase *by faith.* After these the author tells the readers that he lacks the time to write about additional Old Testament saints who also showed their faith (11:32–38). "These were all commended for their faith" (11:39).

b. "We understand." The author and his readers are able to understand

---

9. The expression *elder* describes a person who is both aged and dignified. Spanish-speaking people honor a gentleman by calling him "don." Not every gentleman, however, receives this title; it is given to him who has gained the respect of the community.

10. Among the translations that negate the verb *to make* are the KJV, NKJV, RV, ASV, NASB, NIV, and JB.

11. The translations that negate "to appear" include the RSV, NEB, NAB, GNB, MLB, *Phillips,* and *Moffatt.*

God's creation by faith. Although we are unable to observe that which is invisible, in our minds we recognize the power of God. Understanding creation—even in a limited sense—means that we reflect in faith on the relationship of Creator to creation.[12] In Romans 1:20 Paul provides a striking parallel that even in translation is close.

Romans 1:20	*Hebrews 11:3*
For since	By faith we understand
the Creation of the world	that the universe was formed
God's invisible qualities...	at God's command,
have been clearly seen, being understood from what has been made	so that what is seen, was not made out of what was visible

c. "The universe was formed." Translations vary from "world" or "worlds" to "universe" (see Heb. 1:2). The concept includes "the whole scheme of time and space" *(Phillips).* Moreover, God gave form, shape, and order to the universe. According to the creation account in Genesis, "God created the heavens and the earth" (1:1) and then proceeded to give structure and variety to a formless and empty earth.

d. "At God's command." We are immediately reminded of the six commands God spoke at the time of creation (Gen. 1:3, 6, 9, 14, 20, 24). "By the word of the LORD were the heavens made," says the psalmist (Ps. 33:6). Purposely God created the world in such a manner that man can understand its origin only by faith. God made the world by his command. "For he spoke, and it came to be; he commanded, and it stood firm" (Ps. 33:9).

e. "So that what is seen." The author of Hebrews refers to that which visibly exists in God's creation—that is, light, sky, stars, earth, and countless other things.[13] Man is able to see all these entities with his physical eyes. These things, however, have not been made of what can be observed.

f. "Was not made out of what was visible." Because no one was present at the time of creation, eyewitness reports do not exist. Man must rely on what God has revealed to him about the creation of the universe and the formation of the world. And by faith man ascertains that creation originates with God.

How should verse 3 be translated? I have adopted the translation that negates the verb *to make,* for this translation appears to favor the flow of the argument. The word *visible* implies that at one time this creation did not exist and therefore is not eternal. Creation has a beginning. Moreover, prior to creation, the invisible prevailed.[14] We would have been happy to receive more revelation concerning this point, but the author of Hebrews

---

12. Günther Harder, *NIDNTT,* vol. 3, p. 128.

13. John Albert Bengel, *Gnomon of the New Testament,* ed. Andrew R. Fausset, 7th ed., 5 vols. (Edinburgh: Clark, 1877), vol. 4, p. 445.

14. Grosheide, *Hebreeën,* p. 260.

provides no further information where God's revelation is silent. We do well not to speculate (Deut. 29:29).

Practical Considerations in 11:1–3

Chapter 11 is the chapter about faith in the Epistle to the Hebrews. Earlier in the letter the author introduces the concept *faith* when he speaks of the disobedient Israelites. These people heard the message of the gospel, but they "did not combine it with faith" (4:2). They persevered not; instead they followed their own willful way. The writer stresses the aspect of perseverance of faith (10:36) and places faith conspicuously over against unbelief. Faith, then, is the confidence the believer expresses when he faces blatant unbelief.

This unbelief surrounds the believer especially when the origin of the world becomes the topic of discussion. Modern man refuses to accept the creation account recorded in Genesis. For him the teaching of evolution solves problems and answers questions. Because this doctrine is a substitute for the biblical account of creation, man rejects God and his Word. Countering unbelief, the Christian unwaveringly maintains his faith. He confidently teaches the creation account that God has revealed in Scripture.

Greek Words, Phrases, and Constructions in 11:1–3

Verse 1

ἐλπιζομένων—this present passive participle in the plural lacks the definite article to give the participle a broader range. The case is genitive—not subjective but objective. The present tense implies continued activity.

ὑπόστασις—a compound noun, derived from ὑπό (under) and ἵστημι (I stand), it has been translated as "substance," "being" (Heb. 1:3), or "confidence" (Heb. 3:14).

οὐ βλεπομένων—the present passive participle is preceded by the negative particle οὐ, not μή. The use "of οὐ with the participle means that the negative is clear-cut and decisive."[15] The present tense is descriptive. The genitive case is objective.

Verse 3

νοοῦμεν—closely linked to πίστις, the verb νοέω (I perceive with my mind) discloses that faith is not blind assent but engages man's intellect and mind.

ῥήματι θεοῦ—both nouns appear without a definite article. In the following passages the definite article occurs: Luke 22:61; John 3:34; 8:47; Acts 11:16. The absence of the article, the use of ῥῆμα instead of λόγος, and the reference to the creation account make the translation *at God's command* unique.

εἰς τὸ μὴ . . . γεγονέναι—"we have a clear example of result,"[16] not of purpose. The use of the perfect infinitive shows permanence. That which has been created has lasting validity and stability. The definite article need not precede the infinitive without any intervening words (see, for example, Mark 5:4; Acts 8:11; I Peter 4:2).

---

15. A. T. Robertson, *A Grammar of the Greek New Testament in the Light of Historical Research* (Nashville: Broadman, 1934), pp. 1137–38.

16. Ibid., p. 1003.

For this reason, the negative particle μή fits in better with the infinitive construction than with the preposition and participle ἐκ φαινομένων.

---

4 By faith Abel offered God a better sacrifice than Cain did. By faith he was commended as a righteous man, when God spoke well of his offerings. And by faith he still speaks, even though he is dead.

5 By faith Enoch was taken from this life, so that he did not experience death; he could not be found, because God had taken him away. For before he was taken, he was commended as one who pleased God. 6 And without faith it is impossible to please God, because anyone who comes to him must believe that he exists and that he rewards those who earnestly seek him.

7 By faith Noah, when warned about things not yet seen, in holy fear built an ark to save his family. By his faith he condemned the world and became heir of the righteousness that comes by faith.

B. Three Examples of Faith: Abel, Enoch, and Noah 11:4–7

The contrast between faith and unbelief is exemplified in the lives of the forefathers. The writer presents the positive element *faith;* nevertheless, by mentioning the name *Cain,* he introduces an example of disobedience and unbelief.

4. By faith Abel offered God a better sacrifice than Cain did. By faith he was commended as a righteous man, when God spoke well of his offerings. And by faith he still speaks, even though he is dead.

The author places the name of Abel, and by implication that of Adam, at the beginning of his list of Old Testament saints. Adam's son Abel occupies a special place in sacred history, for even Jesus calls him righteous (Matt. 23:35; Luke 11:51).

With reference to Abel, note the following points:

a. Abel presented a "better sacrifice" than did his brother Cain. As a tiller of the soil, Cain brought some of its fruits. Abel, the shepherd, sacrificed the fat of "some of the firstborn of his flock" (Gen. 4:4). Is the word *better* (literally, "greater") an indication that animal sacrifices were more acceptable to God than were the fruits of the field? No. We should look not at the gifts but at the giver. The historical context is quite explicit. In Genesis 4:6–7 we read: "Then the LORD said to Cain, 'Why are you angry? Why is your face downcast? If you do what is right, will you not be accepted? But if you do not do what is right, sin is crouching at your door; it desires to have you, but you must master it.' "

The Septuagint version of verse 7 reads, "Did you not sin when you offered [your sacrifice] correctly, but did not divide it correctly?"[17] Throughout his epistle the author of Hebrews shows that he depends on this Greek

---

17. Clement of Rome says the same thing: "If thou offeredst rightly, but didst not divide rightly, didst thou not sin?" *The Apostolic Fathers,* vol. 1, I Clem. 4:4 (LCL).

translation of the Old Testament. But the author's choice of version is not at issue. The fact remains that Cain's attitude toward God was sinful. In effect, God pleaded with him to repent, to change his way of life, and to conquer sin. However, the writer introduces Cain's name only for contrast; he is interested in Abel's faith. Notice, for example, that the expression *by faith* occurs three times in this verse (NIV).

b. Abel was a "righteous man." He lived in harmony with God and man and therefore became known as a righteous man. How God communicated with Abel is not known. One assumes that as God spoke directly with Cain, so he addressed Abel. There is no reason to resort to interpretations that hold that God communicated through symbols, such as fire that came down from heaven to consume Abel's sacrifice or smoke that ascended from this sacrifice.[18] The Genesis account provides no further information on how God "looked with favor on Abel and his offering" (4:4). God looked on Abel's heart and was pleased with the motives of the giver. As Paul puts it, "God loves a cheerful giver" (II Cor. 9:7).

c. Even after his death, Abel is a constant witness. The text ("he still speaks, even though he is dead") can be interpreted to refer to Abel's blood. God says to Cain, "Your brother's blood cries out to me from the ground" (Gen. 4:10; see also Matt. 23:35; Luke 11:51; Heb. 12:24). But the writer of Hebrews stresses the concept *faith,* not the avenging of Abel's blood. The difficulty of relating faith to blood that has been shed ought not be bolstered by a quick reference to Revelation 6:10, where the souls under the altar cry out, "How long, Sovereign Lord, holy and true, until you judge the inhabitants of the earth and avenge our blood?" Not the blood of Abel, but the faith of Abel is important; therefore, the reference to the souls under the altar is of little consequence. The author places Abel before the readers as a righteous man who lived by faith (Heb. 10:38). Abel is at the top of the list of the Old Testament heroes of faith. Even after his death, his example encourages people to seek the Lord, because he rewards those who earnestly seek him. Abel, then, is the father of believers of the time before Abraham. His faith in God still speaks as a constant witness.

5. By faith Enoch was taken from this life, so that he did not experience death; he could not be found, because God had taken him away. For before he was taken, he was commended as one who pleased God.

As Abel showed his love toward God, so Enoch, a member of the seventh generation in the family of Adam (Gen. 5:1–24; Jude 14), served the Lord. The writer of Hebrews chooses Enoch as the next person who exemplified a life of true dedication to God. The Genesis account is rather brief:

---

18. Speculation about why Abel's sacrifice was better than Cain's has occupied numerous commentators from ancient times to the present. One of Rembrandt's paintings portrays the two brothers as they present their offerings to God. The smoke of Abel's sacrifice spirals heavenward; that of Cain's fails to ascend.

> When Enoch had lived 65 years, he became the father of Methuselah. And after he became the father of Methuselah, Enoch walked with God 300 years and had other sons and daughters. Altogether, Enoch lived 365 years. Enoch walked with God; then he was no more, because God took him away. [5:21–24]

Whereas the information about Abel comes to us in the form of a historical account, the details concerning Enoch are recorded in a genealogy. Yet the facts are sufficiently clear. All the other people mentioned in the genealogy are described by the same refrain, "and then he died." But "Enoch was taken from this life, so that he did not experience death." And the writer introduces this sentence with the expression *by faith.* Because of his faith, Enoch did not face death but was translated to glory.

When the author says, "Enoch was taken from this life," he actually repeats the conclusion of the Genesis account. The conclusion rests on the clause *Enoch walked with God,* which appears twice in his genealogy.[19] What does the phrase *walk with God* mean? It means that a person lives a spiritual life in which he tells God everything (see Gen. 6:9). Enoch lived a normal life of rearing sons and daughters, but his entire life was characterized by his love for God. For this reason God took him to heaven.

Note that the author writes the phrase *was* (or: *had) taken* three times. Enoch's faith was so strong and his relationship to God so close that he was kept from dying. The curse of death pronounced upon Adam and his descendants did not prevail against Enoch, for God transformed him. Enoch "was commended as one who pleased God."[20]

6. And without faith it is impossible to please God, because anyone who comes to him must believe that he exists and that he rewards those who earnestly seek him.

This text teaches a spiritual truth that touches the spiritual life of every believer. It is one of the most eloquent expressions of faith and prayer in the Epistle to the Hebrews. By comparison, Paul's declaration that "everything that does not come from faith is sin" (Rom. 14:23) is short. In one beautifully constructed verse, the writer of Hebrews communicates the method of pleasing God, the necessity of believing his existence, and the certainty of answered prayer.

a. How do we please God? By walking with him in faith! We must fully trust God and confide in him as our closest friend. "Without faith it is impossible to please God." The word *impossible* is a reminder of Hebrews 6:4. It conveys the idea that faith is the indispensable ingredient for pleasing God.

---

19. In the intertestamental period, several writers mentioned Enoch. For example, in Sir. 44:16 we read, "Enoch pleased the Lord, and was taken up; he was an example of repentance to all generations" (RSV). See the extracanonical books Wis. 4:10; Jub. 4:17–21; 10:17; I En.

20. The author of Hebrews takes the Old Testament quotation of Gen. 5:24 not from the Hebrew text but from the Greek translation.

b. Why do we pray to God? When the believer prays to God, he must believe that God exists. Although God's existence is an established truth for the believer, repeatedly he will ignore God by failing to pray to him. God, however, desires that the believer pray continually.

c. How do we seek God in prayer? Earnestly, in full confidence! The sinner receives pardon; the suppliant, mercy; and the righteous, peace. God invites us to come to him in full assurance that he will hear and answer prayers. "So," says the writer, "do not throw away your confidence; it will be richly rewarded" (10:35).

Rewards can never be earned. In his sovereign goodness, God grants rewards not in terms of payments, but as blessings on his people. God grants us the gift of life eternal. "No human action can in any way counterbalance this in value."[21] God's rewards to us are free, for he is sovereign.

7. By faith Noah, when warned about things not yet seen, in holy fear built an ark to save his family. By his faith he condemned the world and became heir of the righteousness that comes by faith.

One person demonstrated his faith in God in a world of unbelief, and that person was Noah. In the historical account of the flood, we read that God told Noah about an impending flood that would destroy life because of man's great wickedness. God warned Noah that he would wipe out men, animals, and birds when a period of 120 years had ended (Gen. 6:1–7). Noah found favor in God's eyes, for "he walked with God" (Gen. 6:8–9). Like his ancestors, Abel and Enoch, he put his full trust in God.

God instructed Noah to build an ark of specific and adequate size to hold his family and all the animals and birds that God wanted to keep alive. God informed Noah "about things not yet seen" (see Heb. 11:1).

Although the Scripture bears no record of the ridicule, the harassment, and the delays Noah had to endure while he built a huge ship, presumably on dry land, we can be sure that he felt the rough edge of unbelief. Jeers, taunts, and scorn constituted his daily diet of opposition.

Noah stood alone in the midst of a hostile world. Apart from the immediate members of his family, he could not find any support. To believe in God amid fellow believers is relatively easy. But to have no one to lean on except God is the true test of faith. Noah believed and "in holy fear built an ark to save his family." On the one hand he expressed deep reverence to God, and on the other hand he was terrified because of the coming destruction. He was filled with holy fear at the prospect of God's judgment on the sinful world. For if he had not believed God's warning, he would not have been afraid. His faith drove him to fear and to build. Obediently he followed the instructions God gave him. He constructed the ark and by doing so demonstrated his firm confidence in God. His faith became his testimony

---

21. Paul Christoph Böttger, *NIDNTT,* vol. 3, p. 143. Also see John Calvin, *Epistle to the Hebrews* (Grand Rapids: Eerdmans, 1949), p. 272.

that condemned the unbelieving world around him. Noah's faith stood diametrically opposed to the unbelief of the world.

Scripture describes Noah as a righteous man (Gen. 6:9). Ezekiel writes of the possibility that God would send a famine to a country that sins against him; should Noah, Daniel, and Job be in that country, "they could save only themselves by their righteousness" (Ezek. 14:14, 20). And Peter calls Noah "a preacher of righteousness" (II Peter 2:5). The writer of Hebrews says that Noah "became heir of the righteousness that comes by faith." No prophet ever preached such a message of doom as Noah did for such an extended time—120 years. Moreover, Noah preached to the entire world of that day.

By his faith Noah inherited the gift of righteousness. His ancestor Abel "was commended as a righteous man" (Heb. 11:4). Noah, however, became the possessor of righteousness; that is, his way of life was a pattern of righteousness always in opposition to unbelief. His life was a constant example of obedience to God's will. Throughout his righteous life, Noah found God's favor. By faith he pleased God.

Practical Considerations in 11:4–7

The heroes of faith who preceded Abraham were true pioneers: Abel, Enoch, and Noah. These men stood virtually alone in their contest of faith; unbelief and disobedience surrounded them and a believing community to support them did not exist.

Consider Abel, for instance. His father and mother had fallen into disobedience and were driven out of Paradise. His brother refused to listen to the voice of God and became a servant of sin (Gen. 4:7). Abel, by contrast, desired to serve God and to do God's will. He put his trust in the Lord. He was a solitary figure, a true pioneer, a child of God.

We know very little about the world in which Enoch lived. The writer places Enoch's name in a genealogy and refrains from writing historical details. Nevertheless, he singles out Enoch's characteristic: Enoch walked with God. All the other persons mentioned in the genealogy (Gen. 5:3–32) lack this description. Only Enoch is known as a man of faith.

And last, Noah walked with God (Gen. 6:9). He, too, stood (with his own family) as a pioneer of faith. The world forsook him, yet he remained faithful.

Note the following:

For his faith Abel paid the price of his life.

Because of his faith Enoch was taken from this life.

By faith Noah saved his own family's life.

Greek Words, Phrases, and Constructions in 11:4–7

Verse 4

πλείονα—the accusative singular, masculine and feminine, comparative adjective of πολύς (much, many) signifies not quantity but rather quality. The translation *better* is therefore preferred.

αὐτοῦ τοῦ θεοῦ—a variant of this reading (αὐτοῦ τῷ θεῷ), in spite of its manuscript support, "provides no satisfactory sense."[22] The genitive τοῦ θεοῦ and the present active participle μαρτυροῦντος form the genitive absolute construction.

δι' αὐτῆς—this feminine singular pronoun can refer to either the antecedent πίστις (faith) or θυσία (sacrifice). Because of the writer's emphasis on faith, the New International Version and the New English Bible relate both δι' ἧς and δι' αὐτῆς to πίστις.

Verse 5

ηὑρίσκετο—the imperfect passive of εὑρίσκω (I find) expresses repeated action in the past. That is, the people kept on looking for Enoch.

μεμαρτύρηται—the use of the perfect tense reveals continued action from the past to the present.

Verse 7

βλεπομένων—artistically the author of Hebrews links this verse to the introductory statement (v. 1). Note, however, that in verse 1 the negative particle precedes the participle, whereas here it is μηδέπω (not yet).

δι' ἧς—three antecedents in the feminine precede the relative pronoun ἧς. They are πίστις, κιβωτός, and σωτηρία. As in verse 4, the context favors the word *faith.*

---

8 By faith Abraham, when called to go to a place he would later receive as his inheritance, obeyed and went, even though he did not know where he was going. 9 By faith he made his home in the promised land like a stranger in a foreign country; he lived in tents, as did Isaac and Jacob, who were heirs with him of the same promise. 10 For he was looking forward to the city with foundations, whose architect and builder is God.

11 By faith Abraham, even though he was past age—and Sarah herself was barren—was enabled to become a father because he considered him faithful who had made the promise. 12 And so from this one man, and he as good as dead, came descendants as numerous as the stars in the sky and as countless as the sand on the seashore.

13 All these people were still living by faith when they died. They did not receive the things promised; they only saw them and welcomed them from a distance. And they admitted that they were aliens and strangers on earth. 14 People who say such things show that they are looking for a country of their own. 15 If they had been thinking of the country they had left, they would have had opportunity to return. 16 Instead, they were longing for a better country—a heavenly one. Therefore God is not ashamed to be called their God, for he has prepared a city for them.

17 By faith Abraham, when God tested him, offered Isaac as a sacrifice. He who had received the promises was about to sacrifice his one and only son, 18 even though God had said to him, "It is through Isaac that your offspring will be reckoned." 19 Abraham reasoned that God could raise the dead, and figuratively speaking, he did receive Isaac back from death.

---

22. Bruce M. Metzger, *A Textual Commentary on the Greek New Testament* (London and New York: United Bible Societies, 1975), pp. 671–72.

C. The Faith of Abraham
11:8–19

1. The Promised Land
11:8–10

Abraham is known as the father of believers, and thus the writer of Hebrews devotes much time and space to this patriarch. Abraham lived with promises God had given him, and in faith he accepted their reality.

8. By faith Abraham, when called to go to a place he would later receive as his inheritance, obeyed and went, even though he did not know where he was going. 9. By faith he made his home in the promised land like a stranger in a foreign country; he lived in tents, as did Isaac and Jacob, who were heirs with him of the same promise. 10. For he was looking forward to the city with foundations, whose architect and builder is God.

Abraham's faith triumphed in at least three different instances. First, God asked him to go to a land that he would show Abraham and give to him as an inheritance. Yet of that land, which proved to be Canaan, Abraham never owned a foot of ground except the burial plot he bought for Sarah, his wife (Gen. 23:3–20; Acts 7:5). Second, God promised that he would make of Abraham a great nation. When he reached his one hundredth birthday, his son Isaac was born; and fifteen years before Abraham's death, his grandsons Jacob and Esau entered the world. But Abraham never saw "descendants as numerous as the stars in the sky and as countless as the sand on the seashore" (Heb. 11:12). Also, God called Abraham to sacrifice his son Isaac, for God wanted to test Abraham's faith. And that faith triumphed.

One other observation. Noah received instructions to build an ark to save his family from impending doom. Although he had to wait for 120 years before the flood came, he nevertheless saw the fulfillment of God's warning and the result of his own faith. Abraham, however, received two promises—the inheritance of the Promised Land and the formation of a mighty people as his descendants. But he never saw these promises fulfilled in his lifetime, even though he lived for 175 years. Abraham, to be sure, lived by faith.

As we consider Abraham's faith in respect to the Promised Land, we note:

a. *A place.* A more literal translation of the first part of verse 8 is, "By faith, while he was being called, Abraham obeyed to go out to a place which he was about to receive as an inheritance." As soon as God called, Abraham responded obediently and was ready to do the Lord's bidding. "Leave your country, your people and your father's household and go to the land I will show you" (Gen. 12:1). In faith Abraham left, not knowing where the Lord would lead. What a break with his kinsfolk! Abraham could not even inform his relatives where he was going, because he did not know.

What were the reasons for Abraham's departure? God wished to fulfill his promise to Abraham to make him into a great nation, to bless him, and to make Abraham's name great (Gen. 12:2–3). God also called Abraham to make his own name great. Through the patriarch, God revealed himself as the faithful covenant God who keeps his promises.

b. *A land.* Abraham received God's promise that he would become heir of a place God would give him. That place was the land of Canaan, the land of the promise. Abraham traveled from Haran to Canaan, leaving his relatives behind in Paddan Aram. He lived in the southern part of Canaan in tents. He remained an alien and in a sense an outsider who had little in common with the local population.[23] That Abraham lived in a tent indicated that he was a wandering herdsman who possessed countless animals, but no land.

Yet God had promised the land to Abraham, and he repeated the promise to Isaac and to Jacob. For three generations the heirs of the land lived in faith with a promise. Not until the twelve tribes of Israel entered the land under the leadership of Joshua were they able to claim the promise and make the land their own.

c. *A city.* Abraham's stay in Canaan was as temporary as the pegs he drove into the ground to keep his tents pitched. He constantly moved from place to place, and so did his son and his grandson. His stay may have been temporary, but his faith was enduring.

Abraham's faith in God reached beyond the promise of a place or a land, even though God had promised the land to him and his descendants. Abraham knew that earthly possessions are temporary; he always kept his eye of faith on "the city with foundations, whose architect and builder is God."

> In the land of fadeless day
> Lies the city foursquare;
> It shall never pass away,
> And there is no night there.
> —John R. Clements

The father of believers walked with God; "he was called God's friend" (James 2:23). In faith he knew that the city God had designed and built has everlasting foundations (Rev. 21:14, 19). He looked forward to the new Jerusalem, "the city of the living God" (Heb. 12:22), to which all believers come to find accommodation.

Abraham knew that his earthly dwelling could not be compared with the heavenly city of which God himself was architect and builder. In faith he envisioned the eventual gathering of all believers for the feast of redemption. He anticipated the coming and the work of the Christ, for in him all believers are one with the Son and the Father.

By faith Abraham, although living in tents, looked to the permanent city. For him this city marked the fulfillment of the promises God had made.

---

23. Hans Bietenhard, *NIDNTT,* vol. 1, p. 690, defines an alien as "one who lives among resident citizens without having citizen rights yet enjoying the protection of the community."

Therefore Abraham looked not at the process of salvation, but at its conclusion.

2. The Promised Son 11:11–12

The author of Hebrews follows the historical sequence of the Genesis account. He moves from the promise of the land to the promise of the son.

11. By faith Abraham, even though he was past age—and Sarah herself was barren—was enabled to become a father because he considered him faithful who had made the promise. 12. And so from this one man, and he as good as dead, came descendants as numerous as the stars in the sky and as countless as the sand on the seashore.

The translation of the New International Version differs sharply from others. At first sight the reader may regard the translation of verse 11 as a radical departure from the well-known wording of that text. The Revised Standard Version provides a representative reading of verse 11: "By faith Sarah herself received power to conceive, even when she was past the age, since she considered him faithful who had promised." The New American Standard Bible has "ability to conceive" instead of "power to conceive," but adds this informative marginal note, "Literally, *power for the laying down of seed*" (italics in original). That literal translation is the essence of the problem because the italicized phrase "is used of the sexual function of the male."[24] In other words, the subject of verse 11 is Abraham, not Sarah.

Explanations for this curious problem are numerous, and the translations themselves reflect them. Here are a few explanations:

a. The writer of Hebrews places the expression *and Sarah herself* near the beginning of the original Greek sentence, immediately after the phrase *by faith.* He seems to indicate, by the nominative case, that Sarah is the subject of the sentence. The translators of the New International Version and the Good News Bible have inserted the name *Abraham* to show that the patriarch is the logical subject and that the name *Abraham* suits the broader context.

b. The Greek idiom, translated literally and modestly as "power for the laying down of seed," always refers to the male and not to the female. Therefore, to translate the idiom as "power to conceive" is contrary to linguistic usage. It fails to do justice to the original text and appears to be an accommodation to the presence of the name *Sarah.*

c. Many commentators take the approach that as husband and wife are one so Abraham and Sarah should be mentioned together. They contend that the original Greek for the words *Sarah herself* may be read as a dative. The reading then is, "By faith he [Abraham] also, together with Sarah,

---

24. Friedrich Hauck, *TDNT,* vol. 3, p. 621. Also see Joseph H. Thayer, *A Greek-English Lexicon of the New Testament* (New York, Cincinnati, and Chicago: American Book Company, 1889), p. 330.

received power to beget a child."[25] Plausible as this explanation may be, the fact remains that manuscript evidence cannot provide definite proof for this reading.

d. Still others suggest that the subject of verse 11 is Sarah and that the idiom "power for the laying down of seed" actually means "she received power to establish a posterity."[26] The difficulty this suggestion meets is that Abraham, not Sarah, is the father and founder of the nation Israel.

e. Perhaps we should understand the words "and Sarah herself was barren" to be a parenthetical thought of the author. If the words referring to Sarah had not been in the text, no one would have difficulty translating and interpreting the text. Verse 11 expresses the thought that Abraham "was enabled to become a father" and is a natural introduction to verse 12. To delete the clause about Sarah is unthinkable because of manuscript support for these words. But to understand it as a parenthetical comment is feasible and sensible.[27]

Also Paul comments on Abraham's faith in God, who would make him "the father of many nations." Says Paul, "Without weakening in his faith, he faced the fact that his body was as good as dead—since he was about a hundred years old—and that Sarah's womb was also dead" (Rom. 4:19). Abraham trusted that God would honor his promise. God is faithful.

The result of Abraham's faith is that from one man numerous descendants were born. The author of Hebrews knows that his readers are fully acquainted with the history of the patriarch. Therefore, he minimizes his allusions to that history. He says that Abraham was "as good as dead" and that his offspring were "as numerous as the stars in the sky and as countless as the sand on the seashore" (Gen. 15:5; 22:17; 32:12; Exod. 32:13; Deut. 1:10; 10:22).

Both Abraham and Sarah were well advanced in age—Sarah considered herself "worn out" and her husband "old" (Gen. 18:12). That Abraham married after Sarah's death and had six children (Gen. 25:1–2) has no bearing on this matter. The author of Hebrews is interested in the fulfillment of the promise of God: Isaac, the son of the promise (Gen. 21:12; Rom. 9:7; Heb. 11:18).

---

25. F. F. Bruce, *The Epistle to the Hebrews,* New International Commentary on the New Testament series (Grand Rapids: Eerdmans, 1964), p. 302. Also see R. C. H. Lenski, *The Interpretation of the Epistle of the Hebrews and of the Epistle of James* (Columbus: Wartburg, 1946), p. 393; Otto Michel, *Der Brief an die Hebräer,* 10th ed. (Göttingen: Vandenhoeck and Ruprecht, 1957), p. 262; and Leon Morris, *The Expositor's Bible Commentary,* vol. 12, *Hebrews* (Grand Rapids: Zondervan, 1981), p. 119.

26. Thomas Hewitt, *The Epistle to the Hebrews* (Grand Rapids: Eerdmans, 1960), p. 175. Also see Philip Edgcumbe Hughes, *Commentary on the Epistle to the Hebrews* (Grand Rapids: Eerdmans, 1977), p. 473; and Bauer, p. 409.

27. Metzger, *Textual Commentary,* p. 672, reports on the deliberations of the Editorial Committee: "Appreciating the lexical difficulty, but unwilling to emend the text, a majority of the Committee understood the words [and Sarah herself was barren] to be a Hebraic circumstantial clause, thus allowing [Abraham] (ver. 8) to serve as subject of [he received] ('by faith, even though Sarah was barren, he [Abraham] received power to beget. . . .')."

Countless descendants of Abraham formed the nation Israel. And through Abraham all nations on earth were blessed (Gen. 12:3; Gal. 3:8). But more significantly, Abraham's descendants ultimately are all believers (Rom. 9:6–8; Gal. 3:7–9, 16, 29; 4:28). All believers in Christ call Abraham their father, for in effect, the promised Son is the Christ, not Isaac.

3. The Promise
11:13–16

In Old Testament times believers looked for the coming of Christ. These believers lived by faith, not by sight, for they were the recipients of the promise.

13. All these people were still living by faith when they died. They did not receive the things promised; they only saw them and welcomed them from a distance. And they admitted that they were aliens and strangers on earth.

When the author says "all these people," he means the people who were recipients of the promise, namely, Abraham, Sarah, Isaac, and Jacob. God gave Abraham the promise about the land and repeated it to Isaac and to Jacob. Yet the patriarchs remained tent-dwellers who lived in the land as "aliens and strangers." They received the promise of innumerable offspring; yet when they died, the patriarchs had only sons and grandsons. In short, "they did not receive the things promised." Their faith, however, sustained them, for they believed that God would honor his word and eventually fulfill the promises he had made.

The patriarchs discerned the fulfillment of God's promises in the future. In faith they welcomed this fulfillment, although from a distance. That is, with their eyes of faith, they saw God's goodness in fulfilling promises in his time. But with their physical eyes they saw "that they were aliens and strangers on earth." The list of those believers who considered themselves "aliens and strangers on earth" is extensive. For example, Moses received the promise that the nation Israel would possess Canaan, but he himself never entered the land; he was permitted to see it from one of the mountaintops of Moab (Num. 27:12; Deut. 3:27; 32:49; 34:1–4). Throughout his life Moses was a wanderer who moved from Egypt to Midian and eventually to the border of Canaan. Moses "persevered because he saw him who is invisible" (Heb. 11:27). To the day of his death, he remained an alien and a stranger.

14. People who say such things show that they are looking for a country of their own.

Believers know that this earthly scene is transitory and their heavenly home abiding. Therefore, they fully recognize their temporary stay on earth and long for their eternal dwelling in heaven. Believers do not flee this world (John 17:11, 14). This world, redeemed by Christ, is the Christian's workshop. And whatever honest and honorable occupation the believer pursues, God will bless. Nevertheless, this present earth shall pass away, but according to God's promise, "we are looking forward to a new heaven and a new earth, the home of righteousness" (II Peter 3:13).

15. If they had been thinking of the country they had left, they would have had opportunity to return. 16. Instead, they were longing for a better country—a heavenly one. Therefore God is not ashamed to be called their God, for he has prepared a city for them.

The author of Hebrews intimates that the patriarchs would have had many opportunities to return to their country of origin; to be sure, Abraham had left Ur of the Chaldeans, "the land of his birth" (Gen. 11:28). They could have retraced their steps and moved from Canaan via Haran to Mesopotamia.

Had the patriarchs indeed contemplated returning to their native country, they would have broken faith with God and would have lost the promise God had given them. Abraham had been called away from the land of his father and forefathers, who "worshiped other gods" (Josh. 24:2). He could not return because he had responded in faith to God. Therefore, for Abraham and his son and grandson to retrace their steps to the land of Abraham's origin was unthinkable. In obedience to God's call, the patriarch had entered Canaan, and in full reliance upon his God, he stayed in the Promised Land. Isaac and Jacob showed the same obedience, for Jacob, after spending a number of years in Paddan Aram, returned to the southern part of Canaan. Also, Abraham, Sarah, Isaac, Jacob, and Joseph were buried in the land of the promise.

The other side of the proverbial coin is that the patriarchs sought not an earthly heritage but a heavenly one. Says the writer of Hebrews, "They were longing for a better country." They had their sight set, in faith, on a heavenly country. They looked for life eternal with God who had given them the promises. And their faith was rewarded, for Jesus himself, in answering the Sadducees' question about the resurrection, said, "But about the resurrection of the dead—have you not read what God said to you, 'I am the God of Abraham, the God of Isaac, and the God of Jacob'? He is not the God of the dead but of the living" (Matt. 22:31–32; and see Mark 12:26–27; Luke 20:37–38; Exod. 3:6; 4:5).

God is God of the living. Everyone who puts his faith in God enters that heavenly country mentioned by the author of the epistle. And God is not ashamed to be his God. What an honor to be called children of God! God permits us to bear his name, for he already has prepared a place for us. We are privileged above all others because "our citizenship," as Paul puts it, "is in heaven" (Phil. 3:20). All who in faith long for the heavenly city that God has prepared receive celestial citizenship (John 14:2; Rev. 21:2). "We are hence to conclude, that there is no place for us among God's children, except we renounce the world, and that there will be for us no inheritance in heaven, except we become pilgrims on earth."[28]

---

28. Calvin, *Hebrews,* p. 285.

4. The Test of Faith
11:17–19

After departing somewhat from his theme of Abraham's faith with the introduction of a few verses as a parenthetical thought (vv. 13–16), the writer of Hebrews returns to this theme. He summarizes and concludes his remarks on Abraham's faith on the basis of a vividly historical incident: Abraham's willingness to sacrifice his son Isaac.

17. By faith Abraham, when God tested him, offered Isaac as a sacrifice. He who had received the promises was about to sacrifice his one and only son, 18. even though God had said to him, "It is through Isaac that your offspring will be reckoned." 19. Abraham reasoned that God could raise the dead, and figuratively speaking, he did receive Isaac back from death.

Genesis 22 contains the story of Abraham's greatest test of faith. This story reveals Abraham's readiness to obey God at the expense of Isaac, to cling to God's promises even though obedience to God's command would nullify it, and to believe that God would raise Isaac from the dead. We note three points.

a. *Obedience.* Abraham's faith had triumphed when God directed him to the land of the promise and when God gave him Isaac, the son of the promise. But had Abraham reached a plateau of faith? Was his faith dormant and inactive?[29] Would Abraham be able to submit to a much greater test of faith? Would he be willing to offer his son Isaac as a sacrifice to God?

The writer of Hebrews says that God tested Abraham and implies that the test lasted from the moment God called him to sacrifice Isaac on one of the mountains of Moriah until the angel of the Lord stopped him from slaying Isaac. God tested Abraham to see whether the patriarch's love for God was stronger than his fatherly love for his son Isaac. Therefore, God asked Abraham to sacrifice his son at a place far removed from where they lived. Presumably Sarah may not have been informed about God's command to sacrifice Isaac.

If God had taken Isaac's life by natural or even accidental death, Abraham's faith would have been severely tested. But God asked Abraham to take Isaac and with his own hands kill his son for a sacrifice to God. Job could say, "The LORD gave and the LORD has taken away" (1:21); but Abraham would have to say, "The Lord has given me a son and wants me to give him back as a sacrifice."

Abraham obeyed. He fully complied with God's request. In fact, if God had not intervened, Isaac would have been killed. Abraham showed his unwavering faith in God in humble obedience to God's word. He demonstrated his love for God above anyone else, even his son Isaac.

b. *Promise.* That Abraham responded not in blind faith and slavish obe-

---

29. Ceslaus Spicq, *L'Épître aux Hébreux,* 3d ed., 2 vol. (Paris: Gabalda, 1953), vol. 2, p. 352.

dience is clear from the second part of verse 17 and verse 18. Abraham had received God's promises, especially this word: "It is through Isaac that your offspring will be reckoned" (Gen. 21:12; also see Rom. 9:7). Abraham knew that in Isaac the promise of the multitude of descendants would be fulfilled. Descendants of Isaac would include all the spiritual offspring of Abraham.[30] Thus, with the death of Isaac, the line of believers would be terminated.

The author of Hebrews writes that Abraham "was about to sacrifice his one and only son" (v. 17). Certainly Abraham had Ishmael, but this son belonged to the Egyptian servant Hagar. Isaac, not Ishmael, was the heir, the son of the promise.[31] If Isaac's life were to end, the salvation of the world would not take place. For through Isaac, God's promise of salvation would come to realization. Actually, the promise remained in effect, for God prevented Abraham from terminating Isaac's life and from nullifying the promise. Abraham was about to kill his son, but God said, "Do not lay a hand on the boy. Do not do anything to him. Now I know that you fear God, because you have not withheld from me your son, your only son" (Gen. 22:12).

c. *Power.* In genuine faith Abraham believed that God would raise Isaac from the dead. He knew that God's power is unlimited and that God can make that which is dead come back to life. Abraham himself had experienced that: he who was "as good as dead" (Heb. 11:12) was able to procreate a son through God's power. Abraham's faith reached a mountaintop of trust in God when he said to his servants, "Stay here with the donkey while I and the boy go over there. We will worship and then we will come back to you" (Gen. 22:5). He knew that Isaac would return with him. He believed that God would give life to the dead (Rom. 4:17), even though no one as yet had been raised from death.

Of course, Isaac did not die, someone may say, and therefore a resurrection from the dead did not take place. The author of Hebrews anticipates this observation, and to avoid any misunderstanding he adds the phrase that is translated as "and figuratively speaking." Because Abraham's obedience was complete, Isaac had no way of escape. Only God's direct intervention saved his life, and thus "figuratively speaking" he was brought back to life.

What is the meaning of the expression *figuratively speaking?* Is Isaac a figure of Jesus Christ? Both have the designation *one and only son.* Both were appointed to be a sacrifice, except that for Isaac a ram served as substitute. Commentators in the early church and the Middle Ages were apt to see a parallel between Isaac and Christ and to say that Isaac prefigured Christ.[32]

However, a word of caution is in order. The writer of the Epistle to the Hebrews nowhere regards "the sacrifice and salvation of Isaac as a type of

---

30. James Swetnam, *Jesus and Isaac: A Study of the Epistle to the Hebrews in the Light of the Aqedah* (Rome: Biblical Institute Press, 1981), pp. 95–96, 128. Says Swetnam, "The spiritual 'seed' is composed of all those who believe that God can give eternal life" (p. 129).

31. James M. Bulman, "The Only Begotten Son," *CTJ* 16 (1981): 64.

32. Hughes in *Hebrews,* pp. 484–85, tabulates the christological interpretations from the first century through the sixteenth.

Christ's death and resurrection," and "the idea is nowhere found in the New Testament."[33] No one disputes the well-known truth that the New Testament is the fulfillment of the Old Testament. But we ought to avoid making a writer say more than he intends to convey.

The conclusion of this matter is that the author of Hebrews stresses the unique faith of Abraham. By faith Abraham offered his son Isaac and received him back from the dead. The writer implies that Isaac actually never died, and therefore the incident must be understood figuratively and not literally. In this sense Abraham received Isaac back from death.

Practical Considerations in 11:8–19

God called Abraham "to go to a place he would later receive as his inheritance" (v. 8). That was not easy for Abraham, for he had to leave his relatives and go to an unknown land. The patriarch believed God and obeyed his Word. God still calls men and women to leave their loved ones and their familiar surroundings to bring the gospel to people living in other lands. These men and women serve "in the army of the Lord." Obediently they respond to God's call and give their time and talent in complete dedication to God. These "soldiers of the cross" are indeed aliens and strangers in foreign lands.

In a sense, all Christians are strangers on this earth. The Bible warns us not to attach ourselves too firmly to this earthly scene. Scripture tells us that this earth really is not our home. The Christian looks and longs for his eternal home. He sings,

> I am a stranger here,
> within a foreign land;
> My home is far away,
> upon a golden strand;
> Ambassador to be
> of realms beyond the sea,
> I'm here on business
> for my King.
>
> —E. T. Cassel

Faith has its counterpart in obedience. Faith and obedience are two sides of the same coin. Abraham learned that faith and obedience go together, especially at the time when God called him to sacrifice his son Isaac.

Note this sequence: Abraham believed and loved God, who promised him a son. After many years of waiting, Abraham received this promised son and loved him. Then God called Abraham to sacrifice Isaac. If Abraham sacrificed Isaac, he would keep God but lose his son. If he disobeyed God, Abraham would keep his son but

---

33. Hugh Montefiore, *The Epistle to the Hebrews* (New York and Evanston: Harper and Row, 1964), p. 200. Swetnam in *Jesus and Isaac* speaks of a foreshadowing (p. 123). He adds, however, that "Abraham was not aware of the Christological aspects of his actions" (p. 127). And Bauer explains the offering of Isaac "as a type (of the violent death and of the resurrection of Christ)," p. 612.

lose God. Abraham chose to obey God, and thus he placed the problem of losing his son of the promise in the hands of God. He believed that God could raise Isaac from death. In short, Abraham's life with God bore the motto *Trust and Obey.*

Greek Words, Phrases, and Constructions in 11:8–19

Verse 8

καλούμενος—this present passive participle of καλέω (I call) depends on the main verb ὑπήκουσεν, which is the aorist active of ὑπακούω (I obey). The present tense shows duration; the aorist, single occurrence. At the time God was calling, Abraham obeyed.

Verse 9

παρῴκησεν—both this verb in the aorist active and the aorist active participle κατοικήσας derive from the verb οἰκέω (I dwell, inhabit). The prepositions παρά and κατά modify the meaning of the verb. The first one expresses a temporary idea; the second one denotes permanence.

Verse 10

ἐξεδέχετο—the preposition ἐκ in this compound verb indicates direction. The verb in the imperfect middle (deponent) exhibits continued action in the past. Abraham was constantly "looking forward" to the heavenly city God had prepared for him.

δημιουργός—derived from δήμιος (public) and ἔργον (work), this compound rises above the interpretation *public worker;* it means "builder, designer, architect." It is synonymous with κτίστης (creator). Writers of both the Old Testament and the New Testament prefer to use the verb *to create* and derivatives rather than the term employed in this verse, a fact that is evident from the single occurrence of this compound noun in the entire New Testament.

Verse 11

στεῖρα—numerous Greek texts and translations omit this adjective (barren). The Editorial Committee of the United Bible Societies' Greek New Testament, however, by majority vote regarded the deletion as an omission caused by a scribe who was copying an earlier manuscript that had the adjective.[34] Therefore, the text of the United Bible Society and Nestle-Aland include this adjective.

Verse 12

νενεκρωμένου—from the verb νεκρόω (I put to death), the participle in the genitive case is appositive to ἑνός (one) and in the perfect tense shows duration of time.

34. Metzger, *Textual Commentary,* p. 673.

Verse 13

κατὰ πίστιν—only twice (11:7, 13) in the entire epistle does this construction occur. The author of Hebrews used these two instances as synonyms of the expression πίστει.

λαβόντες—the aorist active participle is one of four aorist participles in verse 13. They are "receiving," "seeing," "greeting," and "admitting." The main verb ἀπέθανον (they died) attains significance.

Verse 15

εἰ μέν—the contrary to fact conditional sentence with the imperfect conveys the meaning "of an unreal hypothesis in the past of a continuous nature."[35] That is, if the patriarchs had kept on thinking of their fatherland, they would have had ample opportunity to return. Verse 15 shows contrast with verse 16 in the use of μέν . . . δέ. These two verses comprise one unit. The adverb νῦν (now) "serves to contrast the real state of affairs with an unreal conditional clause."[36] The translation *instead* serves verse 16 well.

Verse 17

προσενήνοχεν—this perfect active verb from προσφέρω (I offer) is followed by the imperfect active προσέφερεν. The perfect tense reveals that the sacrifice actually took place in the demonstration of Abraham's willingness and obedience. The imperfect, by contrast, points to Abraham's attempt to sacrifice Isaac.

πειραζόμενος—the present passive participle of the verb πειράζω (I try) has the meaning of being put to the test to prove a person's faith (see John 6:6).

Verse 19

ὅθεν—an adverb from the relative pronoun ὅ and the enclitic θεν indicating motion away from a place or a deduction on the basis of reality. The adverb occurs six times in Hebrews (2:17; 3:1; 7:25; 8:3; 9:18; 11:19) and conveys the meaning *therefore.*

ἐκομίσατο—the aorist middle of κομίζω (I carry away) is much more precise than a form of the verb λαμβάνω (I receive), for it signifies recovering something that is one's possession. In a sense, Isaac belonged to Abraham.

---

20 By faith Isaac blessed Jacob and Esau in regard to their future.

21 By faith Jacob, when he was dying, blessed each of Joseph's sons, and worshiped as he leaned on the top of his staff.

22 By faith Joseph, when his end was near, spoke about the exodus of the Israelites from Egypt and gave instructions about his bones.

---

35. Robertson, *Grammar,* pp. 921, 1015. Robertson calls the construction "a classical idiom, though uncommon."

36. Bauer, p. 546.

D. The Faith of Isaac, Jacob, and Joseph
11:20–22

The son, grandson, and great-grandson of Abraham span the generations and centuries by faith. In their old age, with death approaching, the patriarchs Jacob and Joseph passed on blessings and instructions concerning the Promised Land.

20. By faith Isaac blessed Jacob and Esau in regard to their future.

In this verse and the next two verses, the author unfolds an interesting description of the patriarchal blessings. Note that in the case of Abraham's sons, not Ishmael but Isaac received the blessing. Isaac was the son of the promise. In the next generation, not Esau, the first-born, but Jacob received the covenant blessing that God had given to Abraham and his descendants. Next, not Reuben, Jacob's first-born, but Joseph received the blessings in his sons Manasseh and Ephraim. And last, not Manasseh, Joseph's first-born, but Ephraim received the choice blessing. God's electing love is independent of the rules and regulations concerning the right of the first-born (Deut. 21:15–17). The reason that the names of the patriarchs Isaac, Jacob, and Joseph appear in the list of the heroes of faith is that they exhibited their faith in God.

Isaac knew that he was the recipient of God's favor. God appeared to him and repeated the promise he had made to Abraham: "I will make your descendants as numerous as the stars in the sky and will give them all these lands, and through your offspring all nations on earth will be blessed" (Gen. 26:4). And when Isaac sent Jacob on his way to Paddan Aram, he blessed his son with a similar blessing. Said he, "May God Almighty bless you and make you fruitful and increase your numbers until you become a community of peoples. May he give you and your descendants the blessing given to Abraham, so that you may take possession of the land where you now live as an alien, the land God gave to Abraham" (Gen. 28:3–4). Isaac virtually repeated the words of the ancient promise first given to Abraham. For this reason the author of Hebrews lists Isaac among the men of faith. Isaac blessed Jacob and Esau in faith (Gen. 27:27–28, 39–40). Jacob, not Esau, however, continued in the line of faith, as the writer notes afterward (Heb. 12:16–17).

Even though Isaac was an old man when he blessed his sons, his hour of death came more than forty years later (Gen. 27:2; 35:28–29). He lived to be 180 years old. His son Jacob pronounced the patriarchal blessing on the sons of Joseph when he was ill and expected the end of his life (Gen. 48:1, 21).

21. By faith Jacob, when he was dying, blessed each of Joseph's sons, and worshiped as he leaned on the top of his staff.

The writer of Hebrews omits any reference to the blessings that Jacob pronounced on his sons as the patriarch predicted the future (Gen. 49). Instead he selects the incident when Jacob blessed Joseph's sons as a demonstration of Jacob's faith. That historic moment was indeed significant. Note these points:

a. In his first act of blessing, Jacob addressed Joseph and repeated the words of the promise God had given to Abraham, Isaac, and Jacob. God had told Jacob, "I am going to make you fruitful and will increase your numbers. I will make you a community of peoples, and I will give this land [of Canaan] as an everlasting possession to your descendants after you" (Gen. 48:4). This was the patriarchal blessing passed on from one generation to the next.

b. When Joseph with his two sons came to Jacob, he received the blessing of the first-born. He received a double portion not of Jacob's herds and flocks, but of the promised land of Canaan. Not Joseph himself, but each of his two sons Manasseh and Ephraim received this blessing. They became two tribes in Israel because Jacob accepted Manasseh and Ephraim as his own sons (Gen. 48:5).

c. Blessing the two sons of Joseph, Jacob functioned as king of the Promised Land. The patriarch crossed his arms and granted the blessing of the first-born not to Manasseh but to Ephraim (Gen. 48:12–20). In the course of time, the tribe of Ephraim indeed became a leader in Israel. In faith, Jacob looked into the future and was given prophetic insight. He knew that God would fulfill the patriarchal blessing in the sons of Joseph.

d. Convinced that God would fulfill his promise, Jacob gave Joseph instructions to bury him in the cave of Machpelah in the land of Canaan (Gen. 47:29–31; 50:12–14). Jacob's grave in the Promised Land would serve as a testimony and an encouragement to his descendants that they, too, would enter their inheritance.

e. Jacob worshiped his God as he leaned on his staff.[37] He fully acknowledged God's power and presence in the development of the patriarchal blessing. He worshiped in faith.

22. By faith Joseph, when his end was near, spoke about the exodus of the Israelites from Egypt and gave instructions about his bones.

Of all Joseph's earlier trials and experiences in which his faith had been tested, the writer of Hebrews selects none. He is interested in the promise of God that Abraham's descendants would inherit the land of Canaan. Therefore, the words Joseph spoke to his brothers at the end of his life are important. He said, "I am about to die. But God will surely come to your aid and take you up out of this land to the land he promised on oath to Abraham, Isaac and Jacob" (Gen. 50:24). The golden thread of the promise binds the patriarchs in faith that transcends the generations.

At the age of seventeen (Gen. 37:2), Joseph was sold to Midianite mer-

---

37. The sentence "and [he] worshiped as he leaned on the top of his staff" is a quotation from Gen. 47:31. The NIV at this verse has the word *staff* in the text with the footnote, "Israel bowed down at the head of his bed." The difference in wording centers on one Hebrew noun which, with the same consonants but with varying vowels, can mean either "staff" or "bed." The Septuagint features the term *staff*. As he does elsewhere, the writer of Hebrews follows this translation.

chants who took him from his native land to Egypt. Joseph returned briefly to Canaan for the burial of his father Jacob (Gen. 50:4–14). He had lived at the court of Pharaoh, had married an Egyptian, and had the Egyptian name *Zaphenath-Paneah.* Nevertheless, Joseph remained true to the God of his fathers, and when he knew that the end of his life was near, he prophesied concerning the patriarchal blessing. He predicted the exodus of Jacob's descendants from Egypt. And in faith he told these descendants to carry his bones from Egypt to Canaan (Gen. 50:25). When the exodus occurred, "Moses took the bones of Joseph with him" (Exod. 13:19). "And Joseph's bones, which the Israelites had brought up from Egypt, were buried at Shechem" (Josh. 24:32) within the land allotted to the tribe of Ephraim.

Joseph's command to bury his bones in Canaan was not an act of nostalgia or superstition, but an act of faith. Prophetically he spoke of the exodus and in faith saw that his remains would be carried to the Promised Land. He believed that God would fulfill his word.

Practical Considerations in 11:20–22

What a joy to see the "faith of our fathers" spanning the generations! The author of Hebrews lists the names of Isaac, Jacob, and Joseph. Each belonged to the covenant that God had made with Abraham when God said, "I will establish my covenant as an everlasting covenant between me and you and your descendants after you for the generations to come, to be your God and the God of your descendants after you" (Gen. 17:7). God keeps his word throughout the generations.

When parents see the love of the Lord in their children, who express a desire to do his will, their hearts are filled with gratitude to God. To see the next generation take up the torch of faith is an evident sign of God's faithfulness.

But when parents see their sons and daughters turn away from God and his Word, in spite of the training in home, church, and perhaps school, their parental hearts grieve. Isaac and Rebekah endured constant grief when Esau lived a life of disobedience (Gen. 26:34–35). And on his deathbed Jacob pronounced a curse on Simeon and Levi (Gen. 49:7). Salvation cannot be inherited; it is a gift of God. Parents of spiritually wayward sons and daughters need to pray that God in his grace will give them this gift. By exercising their faith, they trust in God's unlimited power to save their prodigal son or daughter.

Greek Words, Phrases, and Constructions in 11:20–22

Verse 20

καί—although some leading manuscripts omit this conjunction, external textual evidence for its inclusion is strong. The translators of the New International Version have omitted it. Other translations include it and take it either as a connective or as an emphatic: "By faith Isaac blessed Jacob and Esau, even regarding things to come" (NASB).

Verse 22

τῆς ἐξόδου—the writer of Hebrews employs this noun with the definite article as a technical term for the exodus of the Israelites. The term occurs frequently in the Septuagint as a designation for Israel's departure from Egypt. In the New Testament it appears in three places: in Luke 9:31 and II Peter 1:15, it refers to death; and in Hebrews 11:22, to the exodus.

---

23 By faith Moses' parents hid him for three months after he was born, because they saw he was no ordinary child, and they were not afraid of the king's edict.

24 By faith Moses, when he had grown up, refused to be known as the son of Pharaoh's daughter. 25 He chose to be mistreated along with the people of God rather than to enjoy the pleasures of sin for a short time. 26 He regarded disgrace for the sake of Christ as of greater value than the treasures of Egypt, because he was looking ahead to his reward. 27 By faith he left Egypt, not fearing the king's anger; he persevered because he saw him who is invisible. 28 By faith he kept the Passover and the sprinkling of blood, so that the destroyer of the firstborn would not touch the firstborn of Israel.

29 By faith the people passed through the Red Sea as on dry land; but when the Egyptians tried to do so, they were drowned.

E. The Faith of Moses
11:23–29

1. Moses' Childhood and Position
11:23–26

Abraham is the father of believers, but Moses is the father of the nation of Israel. The author of Hebrews devotes five sections that begin with the formula *by faith* to Moses (vv. 23, 24, 27, 28, 29). The first of these instances relates to Moses' parents; the last, the people of Israel.

23. By faith Moses' parents hid him for three months after he was born, because they saw he was no ordinary child, and they were not afraid of the king's edict.

The writer of Hebrews opens the Book of Exodus and reads about the cruel command of Pharaoh to kill all the Hebrew male children at birth. A Levite and his fianceé, Amram and Jochebed, decide to get married. Subsequently they are blessed with the birth of a son. Now they face the possibility of losing their child. They act boldly in faith. Seeing that their son is a most attractive child, they defy the king's command. What gives Amram and Jochebed the courage to disobey? Most likely, they see in their strikingly handsome son a sign of God's approval (see Exod. 2:2; Acts 7:20).[38] And because of God's favor they continue to exercise their faith. They hide Moses

---

38. Josephus in his *Antiquities of the Jews* 2.201–16 (LCL) relates that Moses' father had a vision. God exhorted him not to despair, because Moses would deliver the Hebrew race from Egyptian bondage. John Brown in *An Exposition of Hebrews* (Edinburgh: Banner of Truth Trust, 1961), p. 539, asserts that the writer of Hebrews concurs with the Jewish belief of a special revelation to which Josephus refers.

for three months until necessity dictates that they devise new ways to protect him. Unafraid of the king and his men, they decide to hide Moses among the reeds of the Nile River.[39] God protects Moses royally when the daughter of Pharaoh tells Jochebed to nurse the child and pays her for the service. When Moses is old enough to leave his parental home, he enters the royal palace of Pharaoh. God honors the faith of Moses' parents, because he protects Moses by having him live in the palace of Pharaoh who had given orders to destroy the male babies of the Hebrews.

24. By faith Moses, when he had grown up, refused to be known as the son of Pharaoh's daughter.

Stephen relates that Pharaoh's daughter took Moses "and brought him up as her own son." He concludes, "Moses was educated in all the wisdom of the Egyptians and was powerful in speech and action" (Acts 7:21–22). Apparently Stephen had access to a source of oral tradition, for he states that Moses was forty years old when he decided to throw in his lot with the Hebrew slaves. In spite of his training at Pharaoh's court, Moses put his faith in Israel's God and severed his ties with Pharaoh's daughter. He refused to be recognized as an Egyptian prince, for he knew himself to be a descendant of Abraham, a son of the covenant that God had made with the patriarch, and a Hebrew who longed to be free. He identified with the oppressed Hebrew slaves.

The author of Hebrews writes that Moses *by faith* "refused to be known as the son of Pharaoh's daughter." The title *son of Pharaoh's daughter* was prestigious in Egypt and entailed power and privileges. To break the tie with the daughter of Pharaoh and to choose to be identified with the mistreated Hebrew slaves called for faith and courage. Moses acted not rashly in youthful fervor but maturely as a man who at the age of forty was fully educated. Deliberately he associated with "the people of God," the Hebrews.

25. He chose to be mistreated along with the people of God rather than to enjoy the pleasures of sin for a short time.

In God's providence, Moses received training that enabled him to become a leader of a nation. He was uniquely qualified to lead the nation Israel out of Egypt to the Promised Land. Thus he regarded himself as God's appointed deliverer of Israel. Says Stephen, "Moses thought that his own people would realize that God was using him to rescue them, but they did not" (Acts 7:25). Although Moses had been trained, he was not yet ready to govern the nation Israel. His own people were not yet ready to accept him.

Moses, however, had cast his lot with the Israelites. His people, not the Egyptians, were the recipients of God's promises to Abraham, Isaac, and Jacob. Should he have sided with the Egyptians and turned his back on the

---

39. In his commentary on the faith of Moses' parents, Calvin writes, "We must, however, remark, that the faith here praised was very weak; for after having disregarded the fear of death, they ought to have brought up Moses; instead of doing so, they exposed him" (*Hebrews*, p. 293). I cannot agree with this observation, for it appears to militate against the concluding part of Heb. 11:23, "they were not afraid of the king's edict." Faith banishes fear.

people of God, he would have committed the sin of apostasy. In the words of the writer of Hebrews, he would have turned "away from the living God" (3:12). The choice Moses faced, then, was not so much between either being mistreated or enjoying the pleasures of Egypt as between either associating with the people of God or falling into the sin of apostasy.[40] Moses chose mistreatment and identified himself with God's people.

Moses could have taken a halfway position. As the son of Pharaoh's daughter, he might have said that his influence would be incalculable in setting the Israelites free. In earlier times Joseph had wielded his power and authority in the interest of Jacob and his descendants. No one would have chided Moses if he had stayed in Egypt. But Joseph by faith predicted the exodus and made his brothers promise to take his bones with them for burial in Canaan. Likewise Moses sided with the Hebrew slaves and renounced his royal title *son of Pharaoh's daughter.*

26. He regarded disgrace for the sake of Christ as of greater value than the treasures of Egypt, because he was looking ahead to his reward.

This verse relates three main thoughts.

a. *Christ.* The writer is rather explicit in his wording, for he refers to *the* Christ, in the original Greek. Elsewhere in his epistle he says, "Jesus Christ is the same yesterday and today and forever" (13:8). Because Christ transcends the centuries, the author of Hebrews confidently asserts that Moses endured disgrace for the sake of Christ. Moses considered disgrace for Christ of greater significance than all the glittering riches of Egypt. The writer, therefore, implies that even though Moses never used the name *Messiah,* he was fully aware of his presence and his coming.

Nevertheless, the reader of this passage faces some problems in interpreting it. For instance, Moses had no idea of the person and work of Christ as we know Jesus from the pages of the New Testament. Moses had the promises God had given to his ancestors, Abraham, Isaac, and Jacob. These promises related to the growth of the nation Israel, the inheritance of Canaan, and the coming of the Christ. Moses saw the fulfillment of the promise that Abraham's descendants would be "as numerous as the stars in the sky and as countless as the sand on the seashore" (Heb. 11:12; see also Gen. 15:5; 22:17; 32:12). And he realized that the time for the exodus and the return to Canaan was imminent. That he believed in the coming Deliverer is not in question. The problem of understanding the meaning of the word *Christ* centers on Christ's place in the context of the Old Testament.

Some commentators seek an explanation in symbolism. They point to the fulfillment of the prophecy in which God says, "out of Egypt I called my son" (Hos. 11:1) and see an identification of Christ with the nation Israel. Both of them came forth out of Egypt. Others understand the expression *the Anointed* (the Messiah) to refer in a collective sense to Israel (Ps. 89:50–51). Still others think that Christ accompanied the Israelites during the time of

---

40. Spicq, *Hébreux,* vol. 2, p. 357.

the exodus and the journey to the Promised Land (I Cor. 10:4). Based on Scripture, all these comments are helpful in understanding the text at hand. However, we ought not expect more from a text than the author intends to convey.[41]

b. *Comparison.* The emphasis falls on this comparison: "disgrace for the sake of Christ as of greater value than the treasures of Egypt." This is a comparison of spiritual riches and earthly treasures. The words of the Beatitudes readily come to mind: "Blessed are you when people insult you, persecute you and falsely say all kinds of evil against you because of me. Rejoice and be glad, because great is your reward in heaven" (Matt. 5:11–12).

To insult is a passion that originates in man's sinful heart. Man directs this passion against his fellow man, especially the person who is righteous. And insult directed against man is ultimately directed against God. We know that the Israelites endured daily abuse from their ruthless Egyptian taskmasters (Exod. 1:11–14). God saw the misery of the Israelites, heard their cries, and was concerned about their suffering (Exod. 3:7). Moses deliberately sought identity with these Hebrew slaves because he believed that God would set his people free and fulfill his promises. Moses knew that gaining spiritual objectives for the cause of God's people was incomparably better than becoming heir to the riches of Egypt. He pursued his spiritual objectives, even though that pursuit resulted in scorn, derision, abuse, and disgrace. Moses, however, "was looking ahead to his reward."

c. *Compensation.* Although Scripture clearly teaches that no man is able to earn salvation, the term *reward* (for example, see Heb. 10:35; 11:6) appears repeatedly. That is, God rewards man on the basis of divine sovereignty and not because of merit. "Every claim to one's deserts must fall silent in the face of the demand for total obedience."[42] But Jesus' word is reassuring to every believer who seeks to do God's will. Jesus said, "And if anyone gives even a cup of cold water to one of these little ones because he is my disciple, I tell you the truth, he will certainly not lose his reward" (Matt. 10:42). In his sovereign grace God rewards anyone who diligently seeks him in faith. And that is exactly what Moses did in Egypt. He looked to God for his reward.

2. Moses' Leadership
11:27–29

27. By faith he left Egypt, not fearing the king's anger; he persevered because he saw him who is invisible.

What does the writer mean when he writes "he left Egypt"? Moses left Egypt twice. The first time he fled because he feared for his life after he

---

41. Hewitt, *Hebrews,* p. 181. Johannes Eichler and Colin Brown suggest that Moses identified himself with Israel's lot and considered Israel God's anointed. "This interpretation has the further advantage of being compatible with all the other instances of faith in Heb. 11 drawn from OT history." *NIDNTT,* vol. 2, p. 835.

42. Böttger, *NIDNTT,* vol. 3, p. 141.

had killed an Egyptian (Exod. 2:14–15). Between the first and the second time lies a forty-year period (Acts 7:30).

Considering the flow of the author's thought in respect to the flight of Moses in chapter 11, we note that he selects significant incidents that underscore Moses' faith. He begins with the act of faith exercised by Moses' parents (v. 23). In the next section he presents Moses as a man of faith at Pharaoh's court. The summary of this period of Moses' life begins with the formula *by faith.* Then, describing Moses' faith in three sentences, the author mentions Moses' refusal to be called son of Pharaoh's daughter, his choice to identify with the people of God, and his decision to endure disgrace rather than enjoy royal treasures (vv. 24–26). Next the writer selects Moses' departure from Egypt as an example of an act of faith (v. 27). Also, the account of the institution of the Passover, whereby the first-born of Israel were saved, depicts Moses as a man of faith (v. 28). And last, the crossing of the Red Sea represents the faith of Moses and the Israelites (v. 29). The writer of Hebrews, then, enumerates specific events from the life of Moses in which his faith triumphed.

Was Moses' flight from Egypt after he killed an Egyptian an act of faith? The Exodus account relates that Moses was afraid and that Pharaoh tried to kill him (Exod. 2:14–15). If Moses left Egypt in fear, we have difficulty believing that his flight was an act of faith. Why would the author of Hebrews select this incident as an example of Moses' trust in God? Moreover, the writer adds that Moses did not fear the anger of the king. This observation makes the interpretation of Moses' flight to Midian rather complicated.

By contrast, after Moses had waited forty years in Midian, God called him and spoke to him from the burning bush. He instructed Moses to go to Pharaoh and to bring the people of Israel out of Egypt (Exod. 3:10). This was an assignment that demanded faith. Moses repeatedly objected until God reassured him that the elders of Israel would listen to him (v. 18), that God would "make the Egyptians favorably disposed" to the Israelites (v. 21), that Moses would perform miracles (Exod. 4:1–9), and that Moses' brother Aaron would accompany him (vv. 14–16). After receiving these divine instructions, Moses became a man of faith who was unafraid of Pharaoh. The responsibility of leading the people of Israel out of Egypt was assigned to Moses in his capacity of Israel's leader. Furthermore, the entire verse—"By faith he left Egypt, not fearing the king's anger; he persevered because he saw him who is invisible"—refers to all the confrontations Moses had with Pharaoh in his effort to gain freedom for God's people.[43] That "he left Egypt" is then the culmination of a series of events. One of these events is the institution of the Passover, to which the author of Hebrews pays par-

43. Spicq, *Hébreux,* vol. 2, p. 359. Lenski in *Hebrews,* p. 411, notes that Moses' fearlessness toward Pharaoh is described in Exod. 10:28–29.

ticular attention in the next verse.[44] And the clause "not fearing the king's anger" covers the period of the ten plagues and Pharaoh's pursuit of the Israelites to the waters of the Red Sea (Exod. 14:5–28).[45] Moses is the man of faith, who tells the people not to be afraid, to stand firm, and to see the Lord fight for them (vv. 13–14). By faith Moses was unafraid, for he knew that God was on his side.

The words "he persevered because he saw him who is invisible" take on added meaning against the setting of Moses' experience of seeing the burning bush in Midian. Also, God spoke to Moses repeatedly in Egypt. During the wilderness journey, "the LORD would speak to Moses . . . , as a man speaks with his friend" (Exod. 33:11; also see Num. 12:7–8). Although Moses was not permitted to see the face of God, he did see his back (Exod. 33:23). The abiding presence of God, especially during Moses' trying days in Egypt, strengthened Moses' faith. Because of God's instructions, Moses was able to persevere in faith and accomplish his task to lead the people of Israel out of Egypt.

From the general context of the account in Exodus, the author of Hebrews moves to a specific incident: the institution of the Passover celebration.

28. By faith he kept the Passover and the sprinkling of blood, so that the destroyer of the firstborn would not touch the firstborn of Israel.

"By faith," writes the author of Hebrews. In selecting the mountaintop experiences of Moses' life of faith, the author takes the incident of the institution of the Passover feast. This experience was different from the preceding instances. For the first time the Israelites themselves were involved, for they with Moses had to exercise their faith in God. Second, this experience was essentially spiritual. In the days of Abraham, God instituted the sacrament of circumcision. When the Israelites were about to leave Egypt, God inaugurated the Old Testament sacrament of the Passover. And he appointed Moses to instruct the people of Israel to implement this sacrament. Moses' task of instructing a nation of slaves in the meaningful celebration of the Passover was an act of faith. To understand the meaning of the phrase *by faith,* we must note the following points:

a. *Institution of Passover.* God told Moses to keep the Passover and to sprinkle the blood of the lamb that was slain. The word *Passover* is a popular translation of the Hebrew original which may mean "to pass over by sparing" someone.[46] Obviously, the word relates to the Exodus account, where Moses

---

44. Some commentators find the order of events in Heb. 11:27–28 difficult to explain because the Passover observance (v. 28) took place before the actual departure from Egypt (v. 27). Grosheide in *Hebreeën,* p. 274, remarks that the writer of Hebrews departs from a strict chronological order more often (see 11:21).

45. The NEB translation is, "By faith he left Egypt, and not because he feared the king's anger." In their respective commentaries on this verse, Bruce and Hughes favor the NEB translation and apply it to Moses' flight from Egypt into Midian.

46. Thayer, *Lexicon,* p. 493. However, Ludwig Koehler points out that the meaning of the Hebrew original is "not yet etymologically explained at all satisfaction [sic]." *Lexicon in Veteris Testamenti Libros* (Leiden: Brill, 1953), p. 769.

instructs the elders of Israel to slaughter the Passover lamb. They had to put some of the blood of the lamb on the top and sides of the doorframe of the houses of the Israelites. "When the LORD goes through the land to strike down the Egyptians," said Moses, "he will see the blood on the top and sides of the doorframe and will pass over that doorway, and he will not permit the destroyer to enter your houses and strike you down" (Exod. 12:23).

Moses instituted the festival of Passover as an annual event. On the fourteenth day of the month Nisan (approximately March-April), each family had to select and kill a year-old male lamb, without blemish, at sundown (Exod. 12:5; Lev. 23:5; Deut. 16:6). The blood of the lamb had to be smeared on the doorposts and lintel of the house. The lamb was roasted and eaten with unleavened bread and bitter herbs. Everything had to be eaten that evening. If food was left, it had to be burned (Exod. 12:10; 34:25). The meal had to be eaten in haste. And the festival had to be observed as "a lasting ordinance" (Exod. 12:14).[47]

b. *Sprinkling of blood.* Before the Israelites were to leave Egypt, they had to sacrifice a lamb and put some of its blood on the doorposts and lintel of their house. God would go throughout the land of Egypt and strike down every first-born of man and animal. But if a house had the blood of a lamb on its doorpost and lintel, God would spare its inhabitants. Moses listened obediently to God's instructions and in faith passed them on to the Israelites. Could he expect the Israelites to obey the command of God? If they failed to listen, they would suffer the death of their first-born. And Moses himself put full confidence in God. If the blood of the lamb proved to be ineffective in protecting the first-born from the destructive power of the angel of death, his role as leader of the people would end abruptly. To establish Moses' authority in spiritual matters, the people of Israel would have to see that not one first-born died in those houses where the blood of a lamb had been sprinkled. How many first-born among the Israelites were spared? We know that the nation numbered 603,550 men who were twenty years or older (Num. 1:45). Moses' faith stood the test when numberless first-born of man and animal were saved.

c. *Salvation of first-born.* Why would God strike down the first-born of the Egyptians and protect those of the Israelites? Certainly not because of any merit in the nation Israel. Within a relatively short time, all the Israelites of twenty years and older would hear the verdict: all of them would perish in the wilderness, except Joshua and Caleb (Num. 14:29–30). God spared the first-born because the Israelites believed God and obeyed his word. Their first-born were spared because the atoning blood of the Passover lamb was

---

47. Literature on the subject of Passover is extensive. A few representative studies are Judah Benzion Segal, *The Hebrew Passover from the Earliest Times to A.D. 70* (London: Oxford University Press, 1963); Jakob Jocz, "Passover," *ZPEB,* vol. 4, pp. 605–11; Joachim Jeremias, "Pascha," *TDNT,* vol. 5, pp. 896–904; and Bernd Schaller, "Passover," *NIDNTT,* vol. 1, pp. 632–34.

sprinkled on the entrance of their homes. The Israelites had to see physically and spiritually that salvation comes from the Lord.

The festival of Passover became the sacrament of the Lord's Supper. The Passover lamb in the New Testament times was Jesus Christ, who gave his life as the Lamb of God to take away the sin of the world (John 1:29, 36; I Peter 1:19). Christ Jesus "gave himself as a ransom for all men" (I Tim. 2:6).

The author of Hebrews says nothing about the work of Christ at this point. He depicts the life of faith of Moses and the Israelites. Their keeping of the Passover feast was the beginning of an observance that would lead to and end in the sacrifice of the Lamb of God. Covered by his blood, countless believers are saved.

29. By faith the people passed through the Red Sea as on dry land; but when the Egyptians tried to do so, they were drowned.

In the eighth century John of Damascus composed a hymn in which he gave expression to the joy the Israelites experienced after crossing the Red Sea.

> Come, ye faithful, raise the strain
> Of triumphant gladness;
> God hath brought his Israel
> Into joy from sadness;
> Loosed from Pharaoh's bitter yoke
> Jacob's sons and daughters;
> Led them with unmoistened foot
> Through the Red Sea waters.
> —translated by John Mason Neale

Israel expressed joy and gladness in the so-called Song of Moses (Exod. 15:1–18), and no wonder—faith had triumphed. The Israelites looked back upon the waters of the Red Sea and saw that the Lord had fought for them and had given them the victory (Exod. 14:14).

But what of Israel's faith in crossing the Red Sea? Instead of acting in faith they cowered in fear. No faith is evident in their complaint against Moses: "Was it because there were no graves in Egypt that you brought us to the desert to die? What have you done to us by bringing us out of Egypt? Didn't we say to you in Egypt, 'Leave us alone; let us serve the Egyptians'? It would have been better for us to serve the Egyptians than to die in the desert!" (Exod. 14:11–12). And the fact that the Israelites, except Joshua and Caleb, died in the desert because of their lack of faith in God makes the phrase *by faith* rather general.

The writer of Hebrews has already spoken about the lack of faith of the Israelites. Candidly he asks, "Who were they who heard and rebelled? Were they not all those Moses led out of Egypt?" (3:16). But because of the faith of those who genuinely believed in the promise that God would save the nation Israel from the imminent attack of the Egyptian military forces, God led his people safely to the other side of the Red Sea. From the Exodus account we learn that Moses' faith was undaunted. By faith he knew that the Lord would deliver the Israelites and the Egyptians would meet defeat (14:13–14).[48]

The contrast with respect to faith and unbelief is not between the faithful minority and the complaining, terrified Israelites. Rather, the contrast is between the nation Israel that expressed faith in God and thus was victorious and the unbelieving king and army of Egypt who perished in the waters of the Red Sea. The Israelites listened to Moses' instructions; they saw the Red Sea divided and the path through the sea as dry land; they noticed that the pillar of cloud had shifted from being in front of them to being behind them; and in the light of that cloud they reached the other shore. The Egyptians tried to do exactly the same thing. But it was not the same.[49] The Egyptian army spent the night in darkness; they followed the Israelites into the sea; they experienced difficulties in driving their chariots; and they suddenly saw the waters of the Red Sea rising. All of them drowned; "not one of them survived" (Exod. 14:28). They had entered the Red Sea without faith in Israel's God. When they realized that the Lord was fighting for the Israelites, it was too late.

The Israelites were victorious because they had listened to the instructions God had given to Moses. They had acted in faith. But this act of faith is indeed the only one recorded. The writer of Hebrews chooses this act in view of Moses' trust in God. The next act relates to the fall of Jericho's walls, but that happened forty years later when the next generation had taken the places of their parents. This generation differed from the one that left Egypt. Whereas the people leaving Egypt failed to trust the Lord, the new generation faithfully executed divine instructions.

Practical Considerations in 11:23–29

Among the heroes of faith stand Amram and Jochebed, the father and mother of Moses. They put their full confidence in God when they married, when children were born, and when hiding the infant Moses became an impossible task. Moses' resourceful parents exercised their faith, used their imagination, and demonstrated their courage when they constructed a simple basket made of papyrus reeds, tar, and pitch. They placed the three-month-old Moses in the basket, had Moses' sister watch him, and put the basket among the reeds of the Nile. Undoubtedly they knew that Pharaoh's daughter would bathe along the riverbank. When Pharaoh's daughter found the infant, Moses' sister offered to find a nurse for the child. Thus Jochebed was asked to nurse the child, was paid for her services, and was assured of Moses' safety.

---

48. In his commentary on Hebrews, Brown queries whether the faith of the Israelites when they crossed the Red Sea was saving faith. He writes "that the faith of the revelation made to Moses respecting the Israelites obtaining a safe passage through the Red Sea, was not what we ordinarily term saving faith" (p. 566).

49. Bengel, *Gnomon,* vol. 4, p. 454; "when two do the same thing, it is not the same thing."

By faith parents are able to protect their children from the constant attack of evil in our society. They realize that Satan "prowls around like a roaring lion" seeking to destroy their children (I Peter 5:8). Parents resist the devil by standing firm in their faith. They build spiritual homes in which they train their children to fear and love the Lord. With their children, they faithfully attend the worship services of a church true to Scripture. And with ingenuity, wherever God gives opportunity and occasion, they provide Christian day school education for their children. And, of course, they spend much time in prayer in behalf of their sons and daughters.

The first few years of his life Moses spent in the slave hut of his godly parents. Amram and Jochebed taught him to fear God. But when the day came to take Moses to the royal palace, they knew that he would be educated in the culture of the Egyptians and in a pagan religion. Humanly speaking, they had lost a son to the secular world of that day. But the amazing fact is that Moses loved God and "chose to be mistreated along with the people of God" (Heb. 11:25). Instead of being called "son of Pharaoh's daughter," he was called "friend of God."

What happened? Joseph had been the second-in-command in Egypt (Gen. 41:43). In a similar fashion, Moses faced the prospect of ascending the Egyptian throne. Instead Moses associated with God's people and turned his back upon the "treasures of Egypt." Why? Because Moses believed God! In faith he accepted God's promises. In every situation he sought God, trusted him, and knew that God "rewards those who earnestly seek him" (Heb. 11:6). As a child of God, Moses talked to and trusted in his heavenly Father. And God blessed him.

Although times, customs, and circumstances today differ from those of Moses' day, spiritual choices are the same. Young people today must make the same choice Moses made in ancient Egypt. Earnestly and sincerely they ought to seek God in prayer, strive to do his will, ask for wisdom, and cling to his promises.

After the exodus, the people of Israel knew God not only as the God of Abraham, Isaac, and Jacob, but as the Lord God, who had brought them out of Egypt, the land of slavery (see Exod. 20:2). Today God's people know him as the Father of the Lord Jesus Christ (Rom. 15:6; II Cor. 1:3; 11:31; Eph. 1:3; I Peter 1:3). That is, because of his Son Jesus Christ, God is the Father of everyone who believes in Jesus.[50] Moses "regarded disgrace for the sake of Christ as of greater value than the treasures of Egypt, because he was looking ahead to his reward" (Heb. 11:26). In the New Testament we have received God's complete revelation and know that "Jesus Christ is the same yesterday and today and forever" (Heb. 13:8).

Greek Words, Phrases, and Constructions in 11:23–29

Verse 23

ἀστεῖον—this two-ending adjective is a derivative of the noun ἄστυ (city) and is the opposite of the adjective ἄγροικος (rustic).[51] It occurs in the Septuagint text of Exodus 2:2; Judges 3:17; Judith 11:23; and Susanna 7; and in the New Testament text of Acts 7:20 and Hebrews 11:23. The adjective has perplexed translators, as

---

50. Herman Veldkamp, *Zondagskinderen,* 2 vols. (Franeker: Wever, n.d.), vol. 1, p. 113.
51. Thayer, *Lexicon,* p. 81.

is evident from the many translations: "proper child" (KJV), "goodly child" (RV, ASV), "fine child" (JB, NEB), "beautiful child" (RSV, NAB, GNB, MLB, NASB, *Moffat,* NKJV), and "no ordinary child" (NIV). The word may designate someone who is "fair to look on and comely."[52]

Verse 24

υἱὸς θυγατρὸς Φαραώ—the phrase is devoid of definite articles to emphasize the dignity of Moses' status. He bore the title *son of Pharaoh's daughter.*

Verse 25

ἑλόμενος—as a second aorist middle participle from αἱρέω (I take; in the middle: I choose, prefer), this form is modified by the adverb μᾶλλον (rather). The adverb is somewhat redundant with the participle in the middle voice, not in the active voice. The aorist tense of the participle coincides with that of the main verb ἠρνήσατο (he refused) in the preceding verse. The contrast with the aid of μᾶλλον . . . ἤ features the durative present infinitives συγκακουχεῖσθαι (to suffer with) and ἔχειν (to have).

The durative idea is expressed in the adverb πρόσκαιρον (for a while) and the noun ἀπόλαυσις (enjoyment), which shows progression in the -σις ending. The noun ἁμαρτίας is an objective genitive; it is descriptive of the noun *enjoyment* and is the equivalent of "*sinful* enjoyment."

Verse 26

ἡγησάμενος—from the verb ἡγέομαι (I consider), this aorist middle participle expresses action that is simultaneous with that of the main verb ἠρνήσατο in verse 24.

The Greek word order is significant because it shows emphasis. The words *of greater value* stand first, and the phrase in opposition, "disgrace for the sake of Christ," appears last in this part of the sentence. The genitive of τοῦ Χριστοῦ is objective.

μισθαποδοσίαν—the noun occurs three times in Hebrews (2:2; 10:35; 11:26). Only in this verse does it have the definite article which takes the place of a possessive pronoun: *his* reward.

Verse 27

κατέλιπεν—the compound in the second aorist active is directive. The verb is often used to indicate abandoning a heritage, giving up riches, and leaving one's native land.[53]

μὴ φοβηθείς—the aorist passive participle denotes cause. The New English Bible even inserts the conjunction *and,* an addition which has no manuscript support: "By faith he left Egypt, and not because he feared the king's anger."

ὁρῶν—although the main verb ἐκαρτέρησεν (he persevered) is in the aorist, the participle from ὁράω (I see) is in the present tense.

---

52. R. C. Trench, *Synonyms of the New Testament* (Grand Rapids: Eerdmans, 1953), p. 388.
53. Spicq, *Hébreux,* vol. 2, p. 359.

Verse 28

πεποίηκεν—this verb from ποιέω (I make, do), in combination with the word πάσχα, means "to keep the Passover" (see Exod. 12:48, LXX; Matt. 26:18; and the expression τοῦτο ποιεῖτε in Luke 22:19; I Cor. 11:24, 25). The verb, however, in the perfect active indicative, has two objects ("Passover" and "the sprinkling of blood"). Admittedly, the verb suits the first object better than the second.[54] The perfect tense, to be sure, relates to the institution of the Passover feast that was celebrated annually afterward and became the sacrament of the Lord's Supper in New Testament times.

τὰ πρωτότοκα—by using the neuter plural, the author indicates that he wants the noun, preceded by the definite article, understood in the widest possible sense to include male and female, man and animal.

θίγῃ—the verb θιγγάνω (I touch) appears three times in the New Testament (Col. 2:21; Heb. 11:28; 12:20). In these passages it occurs as the aorist active subjunctive. The verb governs the genitive case.

Verse 29

διέβησαν—the subject of the verb must be supplied; it is intimated by the use of αὐτῶν in the preceding verse. The verb derives from διαβαίνω (I go through), is a directive compound, and is culminative aorist.

ἧς πεῖραν λαβόντες—although the feminine relative pronoun in the genitive case follows the noun γῆς (land), it finds its antecedent in θάλασσαν (sea). The noun πεῖραν (attempt) and the aorist participle of λαμβάνω (I take) are an idiomatic expression for "experiencing."

---

30 By faith the walls of Jericho fell, after the people had marched around them for seven days.

31 By faith the prostitute Rahab, because she welcomed the spies, was not killed with those who were disobedient.

F. Faith at Jericho
11:30–31

The writer of Hebrews deliberately by-passes the forty-year journey from Egypt to Canaan. He wants to indicate that the people of Israel refused to exercise faith and that, devoid of faith, they perished in their disobedience. Except for Joshua and Caleb, all the Israelites who were twenty years or older died in the desert. Their sons and daughters demonstrated faith in Israel's God when they conquered the fortress city of Jericho.

30. By faith the walls of Jericho fell, after the people had marched around them for seven days.

The story of Jericho's fall is well known (Josh. 6:1–24). Joshua, the successor of Moses, received God's promise: he and all the Israelites would take possession of the land from Lebanon to the Negev desert, and from the river

54. Lenski, *Hebrews,* p. 412.

Euphrates to the Mediterranean Sea. Repeatedly God instructed Joshua to be strong and courageous (see Josh. 1:6–7, 9).

Joshua and the Israelites put their faith in God, and because of their faith they were prosperous and successful. Whereas their fathers had refused to follow the pillar of cloud into the Promised Land (Deut. 1:32–36), they, by contrast, trusted the Lord God, crossed the Jordan, and conquered Jericho.

Jericho was strategically located on the eastern flank of Canaan. Nomadic tribes from the desert to the east would cross the Jordan and invade the land. The heavily-walled city of Jericho filled with mighty warriors prevented the invaders from entering the main valleys that provided access to the central part of Canaan.[55] The city itself was comparatively small; it had a circumference of 600 meters and measured approximately 225 by 80 meters.[56]

Because of their access to fresh water and storehouses of food, the people of Jericho could bide their time behind the massive city walls. However, the people of Israel received God's promise to Joshua: "See, I have delivered Jericho into your hands, along with its king and its fighting men" (Josh. 6:2). God told the Israelites to march around the city once every day for six days and on the seventh day seven times. And on that last day, when the priests sounded their trumpets on the seventh time around, Joshua commanded the people to shout, "for the LORD has given you the city!" (6:16). They had to devote the city to God as a first-fruit offering of their conquest. God brought down the walls of Jericho, which was situated on a volcanic rift prone to earthquakes.[57] Regardless of the means by which God destroyed Jericho, the fact remains that Joshua and the people of Israel put their faith in him. That is the point the writer of Hebrews makes: "By faith the walls of Jericho fell." Faith in God can move mountains.

The writer of Hebrews could have chosen to recount the incident in which the sun stood still in the middle of the sky for a full day (Josh. 10:13) at the request of Joshua. That feat was an act of faith. Says the writer of Joshua, "There has never been a day like it before or since, a day when the LORD listened to a man" (10:14). But the author of Hebrews excludes this incident and mentions the destruction of Jericho instead. By implication he cites the faith of the people of Israel. Purposely, however, he places the faith of the

---

55. Howard M. Jamieson highlights the commercial interests of Jericho's citizenry. Because of their proximity to the Dead Sea, the citizens traded salt, bitumen, and sulphur. Also, agricultural products abounded because of the fresh water available in the area. See his article "Jericho" in *ZPEB,* vol. 3, pp. 451–55.

56. Marten H. Woudstra, *The Book of Joshua,* New International Commentary on the Old Testament series (Grand Rapids: Eerdmans, 1981), p. 109. Also see Martin Noth, *The Old Testament World,* trans. Victor I. Gruhn (Philadelphia: Fortress, 1966), p. 147.

57. John J. Bimson, *Redating the Exodus and Conquest* (Sheffield: Journal for the Study of the Old Testament, 1978), p. 129. Archaeologists have discovered debris of walls that resemble those of medieval castles and of brown, black, and red-colored ashes of burnt material (see Josh. 6:24). Bimson concludes that the excavated city "would fit excellently as the large walled city which the biblical narrative says Joshua faced on crossing the Jordan" (p. 128).

immoral and pagan prostitute Rahab next as a contrast to the faith of the Israelites.

31. By faith the prostitute Rahab, because she welcomed the spies, was not killed with those who were disobedient.

Both James and the author of Hebrews refer to Rahab and call her forthrightly "the prostitute" (James 2:25). Matthew lists her name as the mother of Boaz in Jesus' genealogy (Matt. 1:5). She was one of Jesus' forebears because she believed in Israel's God.[58]

Faith knows no barriers. Consider the evidence against Rahab, for she was

a pagan Canaanite,
a prostitute, and
a woman.

Rahab's faith triumphed. Her fellow citizens were destroyed, but she and her extended family lived because of her faith in Israel's God (Josh. 2:8–13; 6:25). God did not condone her sinful practice of prostitution; instead he granted her grace and salvation. And although in Israel the man, not the woman, was heir of God's promises, in matters of faith distinctions disappear (Gal. 8:28).

Rahab believed Israel's God. She received no promise of salvation, no gospel of faith and repentance, and no assurance of acceptance. She had heard the reports about the exodus from Egypt, the conquest of the land east of the Jordan, and the destruction of the Amorites. Her confession of faith was based on the works of God. She said, "The LORD your God is God in heaven above and on the earth below" (Josh. 2:11). Hers was a simple but basic confession. She believed in God and trusted in him to deliver her from the impending destruction of her people and her city.

The author of Hebrews writes, "By faith the prostitute Rahab . . . was not killed with those who were disobedient." By using the expression *disobedient,* the writer places the inhabitants of Jericho on the same level as the rebellious Israelites who perished in the desert. He asks, "And to whom did God swear that they would never enter his rest if not to those who disobeyed?" (3:18). Unbelief results in disobedience; faith in obedience. Rahab believed and welcomed the spies into her home. At great personal risk she protected them from the king's soldiers, who knew that the spies were in Rahab's house. Rahab not only believed; she also put her faith to work in the interest of God's people (James 2:25). And last, she trusted God that at the time of the siege of Jericho her life and those of the members of her family would

58. Donald J. Wiseman, "Rahab of Jericho," *Tyn H Bul* 15 (1964): 8–10. Woudstra, in *The Book of Joshua,* mentions that the Targums call Rahab an innkeeper. This expression "in the Targums always receives an unfavorable sense" (p. 69, n. 7). Also see Josephus, *Antiquities* 5.7–9 (LCL).

be spared (Josh. 2:14–21).[59] We see somewhat of a parallel in the case of the Philippian jailer who asked Paul and Silas, "Men, what must I do to be saved?" They replied, "Believe in the Lord Jesus, and you will be saved—you and your household" (Acts 16:30–31).

Joshua spared the life of Rahab's family and placed them "outside the camp of Israel" (Josh. 6:23). Nevertheless, because of her faith, Rahab was welcomed by the Israelites, married Salmon, and became the mother of Boaz, who was the great-grandfather of David (Ruth 4:21; Matt. 1:5–6).

---

32 And what more shall I say? I do not have time to tell about Gideon, Barak, Samson,
Jephthah, David, Samuel and the prophets, 33 who through faith conquered kingdoms,
administered justice, and gained what was promised; who shut the mouths of lions,
34 quenched the fury of the flames, and escaped the edge of the sword; whose weakness
was turned to strength; and who became powerful in battle and routed foreign armies.
35 Women received back their dead, raised to life again. Others were tortured and refused
to be released, so that they might gain a better resurrection. 36 Some faced jeers and flogging, while still others were chained and put in prison. 37 They were stoned; they were
sawed in two; they were put to death by the sword. They went about in sheepskins and
goatskins, destitute, persecuted and mistreated— 38 the world was not worthy of them.
They wandered in deserts and mountains, and in caves and holes in the ground.

39 These were all commended for their faith, yet none of them received what had been
promised. 40 God had planned something better for us so that only together with us would
they be made perfect.

G. Known and Unknown Heroes of Faith
11:32–40

1. Those Who Triumphed
11:32–35a

The list of individuals mentioned as heroes of faith is coming to a close, but not because the author has depleted his sources. He simply lacks the time to enumerate additional heroes. Instead of describing their deeds of faith, the writer merely records the names of those stalwarts known from Scripture.

32. And what more shall I say? I do not have time to tell about Gideon, Barak, Samson, Jephthah, David, Samuel and the prophets.

Ever since the beginning of the epistle, the author modestly refrained from mentioning himself. Here, however, for the first time he uses the first person singular pronoun *I.* In the concluding part of his epistle, he refers to himself again in the first person singular (13:19, 22, 23).

---

59. Clement of Rome refers at length to Rahab and the spies. However, when he comments on the scarlet cord (Josh. 2:21), he gives it New Testament fulfillment. He writes, "And [the spies] proceeded to give her a sign, that she should hang out a scarlet thread from her house, foreshowing that all who believe and hope on God shall have redemption through the blood of the Lord. You see, beloved, that the woman is an instance not only of faith but also of prophecy" (*The Apostolic Fathers,* vol. 1, I Clem. 12:7–8, LCL).

"What more shall I say?" He hesitates in view of the numberless examples of men and women who lived by faith. He takes a sample of names: some of them belong to the period of the judges; others, to that of the kings. To be sure, the author fails to present the names in chronological order. He should have said Barak (Judges 4–5), Gideon (Judges 6–8), Jephthah (Judges 11–12), Samson (Judges 13–16), Samuel (I Sam. 1–16), and David (I Sam. 16–31; II Sam.; I Kings 1–2:12). But the writer of Hebrews has no intention of listing the names chronologically. In effect, he follows the order Samuel gave in his farewell speech to the people of Israel: "Then the LORD sent Jerub-Baal [also called Gideon], Barak, Jephthah and Samuel, and he delivered you from the hands of your enemies on every side, so that you lived securely" (I Sam. 12:11). We have no indication why Samuel and the author of Hebrews follow a sequence differing from the chronological one.

The names appear in the sequence of three pairs: Gideon before Barak, Samson before Jephthah, and David before Samuel. The first one named in each set seems to be the more popular.[60]

a. Gideon fought with only three hundred men against the multitude of Midianite soldiers. By following faithfully the instruction from God, Gideon became a hero of faith. With his God Gideon was always in the majority (Judges 7:7).

b. Barak refused to do battle with Sisera and Jabin's army unless the prophetess Deborah went with him (Judges 4:8). With the prophetess to guide him, Barak fought the Canaanites and defeated them (Judges 4:16; and see 5:1).

c. Samson captures the imagination of everyone relishing physical prowess. But his love affair with Delilah not only deprived him of his strength; it also placed a permanent blot on his name. Yet Samson displayed unshakable faith in Israel's God when he prayed for strength to mete out justice to his enemies. God heard his prayer. "Thus [Samson] killed many more when he died than while he lived" (Judges 16:30).[61]

d. Jephthah's name is indissolubly tied to his rash vow that compelled him to sacrifice his only daughter (Judges 11:39–40). Nevertheless, Jephthah was filled with the Spirit of God. God used him to defeat the Ammonites and to punish the tribe of Ephraim. He was a man of faith.

e. David stands at the head of the kings of Israel. Because he trusted God, David was enabled to conquer his enemies, build his kingdom, and strengthen the people of Israel. He was Israel's statesman and spiritual leader.

f. Samuel was a prophet, who was called a seer (I Sam. 9:9). He stands

---

60. Henry Alford, *Alford's Greek Testament: An Exegetical and Critical Commentary,* 4 vols. (Grand Rapids: Guardian, 1976), vol. 4, pt. 1, p. 228.

61. James C. Moyer evaluates Samson: "His life is a negative example of a charismatic leader who came to a tragic, yet heroic, end. Nevertheless, his partial victory over the enemy was reason to be named with the heroes of the faith (Heb. 11:32)." *ZPEB,* vol. 5, p. 252.

first among the prophets and was an outstanding leader in Israel. The people turned to him, for they knew that God's favor rested on him.[62] God answered his prayers offered in faith. Said Samuel, "As for me, far be it from me that I should sin against the LORD by failing to pray for you" (I Sam. 12:23).

The author no longer provides a commentary on the lives of the heroes of faith. Instead he summarizes categories of deeds of faith.

33. Who through faith conquered kingdoms,
administered justice, and
gained what was promised.[63]

Although the author omits details, the common denominator he supplies is the expression *through faith.* This expression is a slight variant of the constantly recurring term *by faith.* The writer seems to intimate that the readers themselves ought to furnish details from their own knowledge of the Bible.

a. Who "conquered kingdoms"? Certainly Joshua did when he took possession of the Promised Land. The description is even more apt for David. He conquered the nations surrounding Israel and thus extended the borders of the Promised Land in fulfillment of God's sacred oath. God had sworn that he would give the land to the descendants of Abraham, Isaac, and Jacob. He had promised Moses that this land would extend from Lebanon in the north to the Negev in the south, and from the river Euphrates in the east to the Mediterranean Sea as the western border (Deut. 1:7–8). David fulfilled that promise through faith.

b. Who "administered justice"? The names of the judges in Israel come to mind, especially the name of Samuel. The people of Israel said that Samuel had not cheated or oppressed anyone (I Sam. 12:4). Kings of Israel and Judah administered justice in behalf of the people, as Scripture attests:

> David reigned over all Israel, doing what was just and right for all his people. [II Sam. 8:15]

> When all Israel heard the verdict [Solomon] had given, they held the king in awe, because they saw that he had wisdom from God to administer justice. [I Kings 3:28]

> Jehoshaphat, king of Judah, appointed judges in the land and told them, "Consider carefully what you do, because you are not judging for man but for the LORD, who is with you whenever you give a verdict. Now let the fear of the LORD be upon you. Judge carefully, for with

62. Samuel J. Schultz, *The Old Testament Speaks* (New York: Harper and Row, 1960), p. 122.

63. Westcott in *Hebrews,* p. 377, neatly categorizes verses 33–34 into the literary symmetry of three triplets. The first triplet includes "material victory, moral success in government, spiritual reward." The second triplet describes personal escape from "wild beasts, physical forces, human tyranny." The last triplet describes the characteristics of "strength, the exercise of strength, the triumph of strength."

the LORD our God there is no injustice or partiality or bribery." [II Chron. 19:6–7]

c. Who "gained what was promised"? Because the expression *promises* is in the plural, I think that the author intends to call to mind numerous promises God had made to his people. Already the writer spoke of Abraham, who after waiting for the son of the promise received Isaac (Gen. 21:1–2; Heb. 6:15). At the end of his life, Joshua said to the elders, leaders, judges, and officials of Israel, "You know with all your heart and soul that not one of all the good promises the LORD your God gave you has failed. Every promise has been fulfilled; not one has failed" (Josh. 23:14). Indeed, God's promises to his people are innumerable, as the Scriptures themselves testify.

The author continues to enumerate the deeds of faith performed by his people. They are the heroes of faith,

who shut the mouths of lions,
34. quenched the fury of the flames,
and escaped the edge of the sword.

a. Among the biblical examples of people who fought lions is Samson, who tore a lion to pieces with his bare hands because "the Spirit of the LORD came upon him in power" (Judges 14:6). Also, David told Saul that while David was keeping the sheep of his father Jesse, he would rescue a sheep from the mouth of a lion or a bear and kill the wild beast (I Sam. 17:34–37). David testified that God delivered him from the paw of the lion. And from the lions' den, Daniel answered King Darius: "O king, live forever! My God sent his angel, and he shut the mouths of the lions" (Dan. 6:21–22). Centuries later Paul wrote, "But the Lord stood at my side . . . and I was delivered from the lion's mouth" (II Tim. 4:17).

b. The three friends of Daniel withstood the heat of the fiery furnace. Shadrach, Meshach, and Abednego, accompanied by someone who looked "like a son of the gods" (Dan. 3:25), walked around in the fire.[64] Nebuchadnezzar confessed that God "sent his angel and rescued his servants! They trusted in him" (v. 28).[65]

c. Who escaped the edge of the sword? On numerous occasions David fled to safety when he was pursued by Saul. Elijah fled the murderous Jezebel and went to Mount Horeb in the Sinai Peninsula (I Kings 19:8–10). Elisha heard that the king of Israel wanted to kill him during the famine in besieged Samaria (II Kings 6:31–32).

---

64. Edward J. Young, *The Prophecy of Daniel: A Commentary* (Grand Rapids: Eerdmans, 1949), p. 94. Also see John F. Walvoord, *Daniel: The Key to Prophetic Revelation* (Chicago: Moody, 1971), p. 191.

65. Mattathias, the father of Judas Maccabeus, addressed his sons when he was about to die. He enumerated the heroic deeds of many persons who are also mentioned by the author of Hebrews; for example, he referred to Abraham, Joseph, Joshua, and David. Says Mattathias, "Hananiah, Azariah, and Mishael [the Hebrew names for Shadrach, Meshach, and Abednego] believed and were saved from the flame" (I Macc. 2:59, RSV).

Still other heroes of faith received divine aid in overcoming weaknesses. They were the people

whose weakness was turned to strength;
and who became powerful in battle
and routed foreign armies.

a. Who was weak and became strong? Of course, Samson. Just before he died, God strengthened him to execute the superhuman feat of pushing the pillars of the temple of Dagon from their places (Judges 16:29–30). Hezekiah prayed to God when Isaiah told him that he would die. God answered his prayer and granted Hezekiah fifteen additional years (Isa. 38:1–8; II Kings 20:1–6; II Chron. 32:24). And when the weak remnant of the exiles returned from Babylonian captivity, God gave the leaders Nehemiah and Ezra and the people strength to rebuild the city of Jerusalem and the temple.

b. Who were the mighty in battle? And who put foreign armies to flight? Here are a few names and examples:

> So David triumphed over the Philistine with a sling and a stone; without a sword in his hand he struck down the Philistine and killed him. [I Sam. 17:50]
>
> Jehoshaphat, king of Judah, faced a vast army from Edom. The king defeated the enemy because God fought for his people (II Chron. 20:1–30).
>
> Hezekiah, king of Judah, knew that a mighty Assyrian army had taken all the fortified cities of Judah and was marching toward Jerusalem. Because of Hezekiah's faith in God, an angel of the Lord struck down 185,000 Assyrian soldiers in one night (II Kings 19:35; II Chron. 32:21). Sennacherib, king of Assyria, withdrew his army and returned to Nineveh.

35a. Women received back their dead, raised to life again.

In the Old Testament we read that both Elijah and Elisha raised boys from the dead and gave them back to their mothers. The widow of Zarephath, who was not of Israel, believed. When she received her son from Elijah, she said, "Now I know that you are a man of God and that the word of the LORD from your mouth is the truth" (I Kings 17:24). The Shunammite woman came to Elisha because she knew that this "man of God" would be instrumental in raising her son from the dead (II Kings 4:8–37).

The New Testament provides the example of the widow of Nain who received her son when Jesus raised him from the dead (Luke 7:11–15). Mary and Martha received their brother Lazarus when Jesus called him forth from the grave (John 11:1–44). And the widows in Joppa welcomed Dorcas back when Peter raised her to life (Acts 9:36–41).

2. Those Who Suffered
11:35b–38

In the next few verses the author summarizes the physical suffering that the heroes of faith endured. They were martyrs for God's cause. By faith they conquered even though they lost their lives.

35b. Others were tortured and refused to be released, so that they might gain a better resurrection.

The instrument on which people were tortured in ancient times was called the *tympanum.* Presumably it consisted of a large wheel on which victims were stretched out. Then they were beaten to death.[66] In the Maccabean period during the first part of the second century before Christ, an almost ninety-year-old scribe named Eleazar was put on the rack and endured blows that led to his death. Said Eleazar, "It is clear to the Lord in his holy knowledge that, though I might have been saved from death, I am enduring terrible sufferings in my body under this beating, but in my soul I am glad to suffer these things because I fear him" (II Macc. 6:30, RSV). In this same period seven brothers and their mother were tortured by King Antiochus Epiphanes. They were put to death one after the other. One theme of this gruesome tale is that the martyrs believed in the "everlasting renewal of life" (II Macc. 7:9; also see vv. 14, 23, 29, 36).[67]

Accounts from the dark days of persecution that led to the Maccabean revolt were well known to the Jewish people whom the author of Hebrews addressed. These martyrs suffered and died because of their faith. They looked for a better resurrection. That is, they did not expect to return to this earthly life. A better resurrection, however, is an everlasting renewal of life in the presence of God.

Saints of the Old Testament era had a vague idea about the doctrine of the resurrection. But during the immediate centuries before Christ's coming to earth, the teaching of a resurrection after this life developed. And later when Jesus was about to raise Lazarus, Martha expressed this doctrine when she said, "I know he will rise again in the resurrection at the last day" (John 11:24). By faith believers endured suffering and hoped for a better resurrection in the life hereafter.

36. Some faced jeers and flogging, while still others were chained and put in prison.

The author of Hebrews moves from specific incidents to the more general occurrences of jeering, flogging, and being chained and imprisoned. From the New Testament we learn that jeering, flogging, and imprisonment were rather common. Jesus had to endure the sneers of Jews and soldiers. He suffered flogging during his trial at the court of Pontius Pilate. The apostles repeatedly spent time in prison. For example, Paul writes to the Corinthians, "I have worked much harder, been in prison more frequently, been flogged more severely, and been exposed to death again and again" (II Cor. 11:23).

The recipients of the Epistle to the Hebrews had experienced public insult and persecution. They themselves had seen the inside walls of a prison (10:33–34). They knew that their trust in God would be richly rewarded.

---

66. Thayer, *Lexicon,* p. 632.

67. Bruce M. Metzger, *An Introduction to the Apocrypha* (New York: Oxford University Press, 1957), p. 147.

Old Testament examples of people who were mocked, scourged, or imprisoned include the prophet Michaiah, who was slapped in the face and sent to prison for predicting the future (I Kings 22:24–28). Jeremiah was beaten by the officials of King Zedekiah and placed in prison for a long time (Jer. 37:14–21; also see 20:1–3; 38:1–13). And at the time of the Maccabean revolt, King Antiochus Epiphanes had the seven brothers and their mother tortured "with whips and cords" (II Macc. 7:1, RSV).

Once again the writer of Hebrews becomes specific in listing the types of suffering that believers had to bear. He puts three of them in brief succession.

37a. They were stoned;
they were sawed in two;
they were put to death by the sword.

a. Because stones are plentiful in Israel, the practice of throwing stones to kill someone was common. The law of Moses specified that a blasphemer had to be stoned by the community (Lev. 24:14–23). Naboth the Jezreelite, although he was innocent, was put to death by the scheming Jezebel (I Kings 21:10–15). Also, prophets of the Lord God met a similar fate. Zechariah, son of Jehoiada the priest, died in the courtyard of the Lord's temple during the reign of Joash, king of Judah (II Chron. 24:21–22; Matt. 23:35; Luke 11:51). That the practice of stoning the prophets had been quite prevalent in ancient Israel is evident from Jesus' remark in his discourse of the seven woes. "O Jerusalem, Jerusalem, you who kill the prophets and stone those sent to you, how often I have longed to gather your children together" (Matt. 23:37).[68]

b. Nowhere in Scripture is there a parallel to the clause "they were sawed in two." Tradition is strong that the prophet Isaiah was cut in half with a wooden saw.[69] This happened during the reign of King Manasseh. The Old Testament has no record of this incident.

c. Prophets who were killed by the sword are the contemporaries of Elijah. Complains the prophet to God, "The Israelites have rejected your covenant, broken down your altars, and put your prophets to death with the sword" (I Kings 19:10). King Jehoiakim in the days of Jeremiah struck down with the sword the prophet Uriah. This prophet prophesied in the name of the Lord and predicted the destruction of Jerusalem (Jer. 26:20–23). And John the Baptist died at the hand of Herod's executioner because he had told Herod, "It is not lawful for you to have your brother's wife" (Mark 6:14–29).

Many of the unknown heroes of faith were living in miserable conditions

---

68. Jews in Egypt, objecting to Jeremiah's admonitions, stoned him to death. Consult Tertullian, *Scorpion Antidote 8;* and Jerome, *Against Jovinian* 2.37.

69. Captives were put to work and cut wood and stone (II Sam. 12:31; I Chron. 20:3). But the cruelty of cutting a person in two seems to have been inflicted only on Isaiah. For Jewish sources see Yebamoth 49b and Sanhedrin 103b, *Talmud.* Early Christian references are Justin Martyr, *Dial.* 120; Tertullian, *Of Patience* 14; also see the apocryphal book the Ascension of Isaiah.

and sordid circumstances. **37b. They went about in sheepskins and goatskins, destitute, persecuted and mistreated— 38a. The world was not worthy of them.** The prophet Elijah is an example of those servants of God who lived in abject poverty. His lifestyle became a message of God's impending judgment on Israel. Elijah's appearance suited his prophetic calling. He was depicted as "a man with a garment of hair and with a leather belt around his waist" (II Kings 1:8). His successor Elisha inherited his coat, and in successive generations a garment of hair was the distinctive attire of a prophet (Zech. 13:4). With this apparel the prophet proclaimed a message of repentance and faith in God. John the Baptist, dressed in "clothing made of camel's hair, with a leather belt around his waist" (Mark 1:6), preached "a baptism of repentance" (v. 4). The darker hair of a camel or of a goatskin gave the prophet's garment more of a mournful appearance than did the lighter colored sheepskins.[70]

These prophets of old, persecuted and mistreated, were the world's refugees. Their adversaries denied them bread to eat and water to drink. Consider the plight of Elijah. He depended on the ravens to supply him with bread and meat, and he obtained drinking water from the brook Kerith (I Kings 17:2–6). King Ahab sent search parties to every nation and kingdom to find Elijah, so that he might put the prophet to death (I Kings 18:9–10). In the eyes of Ahab, Elijah was not worthy to live on the face of the earth.

The text, however, says the exact opposite: "the world was not worthy of them." That is, God's enemies cannot be compared with God's servants. These servants are great in honor and stature. King Ahab cannot be measured against Elijah, and King Herod is no match for John the Baptist. By their faith, believers tower above an unbelieving world in which God has placed them for man's benefit.

Referring to the prophets of the Old Testament era, the writer of Hebrews says, **38b. They wandered in deserts and mountains, and in caves and holes in the ground.** Obadiah, in charge of King Ahab's palace, "hid a hundred of the LORD's prophets in two caves, fifty in each, and supplied them with food and water" (I Kings 18:13; and see v. 4). Elijah fled into the Negev desert (I Kings 19:4). For him the land of Israel was no longer safe.

Caves were rather numerous in Israel (I Sam. 13:6). As fugitives, David and his men had no difficulty finding shelter from their pursuers or from the elements of nature (I Sam. 24:1–13). Constantly they endured the hostilities of Saul and his soldiers.

The believer is always surrounded by an unbelieving world. He is often lonely but never alone, for Jesus is his faithful companion in life. Confesses Henry F. Lyte,

---

70. Franz Delitzsch, *Commentary on the Epistle to the Hebrews,* 2 vols. (Edinburgh: Clark, 1877), vol. 2, p. 289.

Man may trouble and distress me,
'Twill but drive me to Thy breast;
Life with trials hard may press me,
Heaven will bring me sweeter rest.

3. Commendation 11:39–40

The author has come to the end of his discourse on the heroes of faith. Throughout the chapter the expression *by faith* is the golden thread that characterizes the life and deeds of God's people. He concludes this chapter by commending these heroes of faith and by including the readers of his epistle in God's blessing.

39. These were all commended for their faith, yet none of them received what had been promised.

In this text the writer stresses a positive element and a negative. We consider them in sequence.

a. *Positive.* The word choice in the first part of this verse reminds us of the beginning of the chapter. After the brief definition of faith, the author writes, "This is what the ancients were commended for" (11:2). Then he provides examples of those who have been commended: Abel (v. 4) and Enoch (v. 5). He seems to imply that all the other people he mentions are commended for their faith—all the known and unknown believers. And who commends these saints? God, of course.[71] God forgets none of his children. He recognizes everyone who acts in faith, because he has promised to be the God of his people (see, for instance, 8:10). As Father of his children, he expects them to put their trust in him. Instinctively a child puts full confidence in his parents and sometimes expects a parent to perform impossible feats. So God wants the believer to come in faith and ask for seemingly impossible things. Why? Because God takes pleasure in commending the believer for his faith.

b. *Negative.* Although believers in Old Testament times received words of praise for exercising their faith, and although many promises that God had given them were fulfilled in their lifetime, they failed to obtain that which had been promised. They saw some promises come true, but not the one promise of the coming of Christ. The writer of Hebrews already stated that the Old Testament believers saw and welcomed the promises in Christ from a distance (11:13). These believers looked forward to a heavenly country where God himself had prepared a place for them. At the conclusion of this chapter, the author once more testifies that although the saints received divine approval for their faith, they did not obtain that which had been promised.[72]

---

71. Lothar Coenen, *NIDNTT,* vol. 3, p. 1047.

72. The RSV expresses the concessive idea in verse 39 more directly: "And all these, *though* well attested by their faith, did not receive what was promised" (italics added).

What, precisely, did these Old Testament believers not receive? They had the promise of the coming of the Messiah and salvation in him. They were the heirs of the messianic prophecies (Gen. 3:15; 49:10; Num. 24:17; II Sam. 7:13; Job 19:25; Ps. 2:6–12; 16:10; 22:1; 45:6–8; 110:1; and numerous passages in the books of the prophets). But all these believers died before Jesus appeared on earth. To be sure, they died in faith and entered heaven. Nevertheless, they entered the presence of God with the promise that they had received and in expectation of its fulfillment. Their understanding of the plan of salvation was vague and incomplete. With the revelation God had given them, they tried to understand the mystery of redemption.[73] Peter testifies to this when he writes, "Concerning this salvation, the prophets, who spoke of the grace that was to come to you, searched intently and with the greatest care, trying to find out the time and circumstances to which the spirit of Christ in them was pointing when he predicted the sufferings of Christ and the glories that would follow" (I Peter 1:10–11).

The author of Hebrews ends the chapter by including the readers of his epistle in the discussion of faith and the promise of salvation in Christ. Before he began this discussion, he already had exhorted his readers to persevere in faith, "so that when you have done the will of God, you will receive what he has promised" (10:36). He brings the Old Testament saints and New Testament believers together in Jesus Christ. He considers them one family, and "a family is not complete unless all its members are present."[74]

40. God had planned something better for us so that only together with us would they be made perfect.

Here the pastor speaks not with words of exhortation or admonition. Rather, he teaches his readers the unity and continuity of the believers of both the Old Testament and New Testament eras.[75] He is saying that they (the heroes of faith) and we (believers in Jesus Christ) are one. In the next chapter the writer brings the "great cloud of witnesses" and the readers of his epistle together in Jesus (12:1–2). Jesus is the originator, the author, and the captain of faith. He leads the believer to perfection.

Says the writer, "God had planned something better for us." In view of its repeated use in Hebrews, we know that the word *better* relates to the era of fulfillment in Jesus Christ.[76] That is, believers who belong to the Christian era have become recipients of the promised salvation in Christ. The Old Testament believers look forward to this fulfillment. Because we look back

---

73. Owen, *Hebrews,* vol. 7, p. 215. Also consult Brown, *Hebrews,* p. 593.

74. Montefiore, *Hebrews,* p. 212.

75. Consult Hughes, *Hebrews,* p. 517. He quotes Moffatt, who writes, "The conclusion of the whole matter rather is (vv. 39, 40) that the reward of their faith had to be deferred till Christ arrived in our day. The [perfection] is entirely wrought out through Christ, and wrought out for all. It covers all God's People (compare 12:23), for now the Promise has been fulfilled to these earlier saints."

76. In the original Greek, the comparative adjective *better* appears nineteen times in the New Testament, thirteen of which are in the Epistle to the Hebrews (1:4; 6:9; 7:7, 19, 22; 8:6 [twice]; 9:23; 10:34; 11:16, 35, 40; 12:24).

upon the accomplished work of Christ, by faith we are able to appropriate the fullness of salvation. In other words, we are privileged above the saints who had only the promise.

What is the significance of Christ's coming for the Old Testament believers? The author puts it this way: "Only together with us would they be made perfect." During the time of the old covenant (Heb. 8:6–7), believers were unable to reach perfection. With his coming, Christ brought "many sons to glory" (2:10) and made them perfect (10:14). Through his atoning work, Christ caused Old Testament and New Testament believers to share in his perfection (12:23).[77]

Christ, then, perfects believers, for he is the perfecter of their faith (12:2). No believer can ever make himself perfect, because this work belongs to Christ. However, this does not mean that man should remain idle. Not at all. The author of Hebrews spurs his readers on to perseverance in the faith. Both Old and New Testament believers not only share the perfection Christ provides; they also have a common faith. And as the heroes of faith diligently exercised their faith, so the readers of the Epistle to the Hebrews must persevere. The saints of the Old Testament era serve the New Testament believers as incentives to persevere in faith. In the unity we have with them, we know that through faith we inherit the promise of salvation (6:12; 13:7).

Practical Considerations in 11:32–40

The word *saint* makes us think of a person who walks around with hands folded, with eyes turned heavenward, and with a halo around his head. Somehow we get the impression that he is not one of us. But when the author of Hebrews takes us to the art gallery of the Old Testament and shows us the portraits of Gideon, Barak, Samson, Jephthah, David, Samuel, and numerous other people, he confronts us with paintings of people in action. These saints are our brothers and sisters in faith. The paintings are scenes of battles, feats of courage, and instances of suffering. The dominant people in these portraits are ordinary men and women. They have one thing in common, and that is faith.

These people are saints, and because of this common faith, we are intimately related. We belong to the same family, for their trials and triumphs are ours, too. And just as they depended on divine help, we also trust in the Lord for aid. They spent their time in prayer; so do we. We pray and work for the coming of Christ's kingdom; as the second petition of the Lord's prayer has it, "your kingdom come" (Matt. 6:10). And thus as prayer partners and coworkers for God (I Cor. 3:9), we ourselves are saints who put faith into practice.

Ever since childhood we have been told not to boast about ourselves. Solomon said it well: "Let another praise you, and not your own mouth; someone else, and not your own lips" (Prov. 27:2). But we must not only listen to what the author of Hebrews tells about our spiritual possessions; we must also tell everyone about

---

77. Reinier Schippers, *NIDNTT*, vol. 2, p. 64. Also see Guthrie, *New Testament Theology*, p. 597.

them. In fact, we have to brag about them because they are so much better than the possessions of the Old Testament believers. We have a better salvation (6:9), a better hope (7:19), a better covenant (7:22), better promises (8:6), and better and lasting possessions (10:34). We are privileged sons and daughters of God, heirs and coheirs with Christ (Rom. 8:17). We may not keep silent. God wants us to talk about our riches in Christ, so that others, too, may share our spiritual wealth.

By contrast, the Old Testament believers, mentioned in Hebrews 11, had only fragments of God's revelation. With these bits and pieces, they persevered in faith. We, who have God's full revelation in Jesus Christ, ought to strive more earnestly to do the will of God (Heb. 10:35). "A small spark of light led them to heaven; when the sun of righteousness shines over us, with what pretence can we excuse ourselves if we still cleave to the earth?"[78]

Greek Words, Phrases, and Constructions in 11:32–40

Verse 32

λέγω—an instance of the deliberative subjunctive in a rhetorical question.

διηγούμενον—the present middle participle (from διηγέομαι, I relate) modifies the accusative singular personal pronoun με. The gender of the participle is masculine.

Verse 33

διὰ πίστεως—this construction is a variant of πίστει, much the same as κατὰ πίστιν (v. 13). Compare also δι' ἧς (vv. 4, 7) and δι' αὐτῆς (v. 4).

κατηγωνίσαντο—derived from καταγωνίζομαι (I overcome), this verb in the aorist middle is a compound with perfective force.[79] The compound consists of κατὰ (down) and ἀγωνίζομαι (I fight).

ἐπέτυχον—a verb in the aorist active from ἐπιτυγχάνω (I obtain) governs a genitive case.

Verse 34

παρεμβολάς—the accusative plural of the compound noun παρεμβολή derives from παρά (along), ἐν (in), and βάλλω (I throw). Here it refers to an army that is placed in line of battle.

ἀλλοτρίων—from ἄλλος (another), with the meaning *belonging to another.* The secondary meaning is "foreign," that is, "enemy."

Verse 36

ἕτεροι—in verse 35 the term ἄλλοι occurs. Although the two words are quite often differentiated, here they are synonymous.

πεῖραν ἔλαβον—see verse 29.

---

78. Calvin, *Hebrews,* p. 308.

79. Robertson, *Grammar,* p. 606.

Verse 37

ἐπρίσθησαν—from πρίζω (I cut in two with a saw), the aorist passive form perhaps has led to dittography in the word ἐπειράσθησαν (they were tempted). But the expression *they were tempted,* sometimes appearing before the verb *they were sawed in two* and sometimes after it, breaks the sequence of those verbs used for describing the administration of the death penalty. In short, ἐπειράσθησαν does not fit the context. Conjectural emendations of this form are numerous.[80]

Verse 39

μαρτυρηθέντες—the aorist passive participle of μαρτυρέω (I testify) has a concessive denotation.

διὰ τῆς πίστεως—see verse 33. The definite article takes the place of the possessive pronoun *their.*

τὴν ἐπαγγελίαν—some manuscripts, perhaps because of verse 13, have the plural. The singular also appears in 9:15 and 10:36.

Verse 40

προβλεψαμένου—the aorist middle participle from the compound πρό (before) and βλέπω (I see) is with τοῦ θεοῦ a genitive absolute construction and has a causal meaning. In the middle voice the verb means "to provide."

ἵνα—the conjunction seems to introduce a result clause instead of a purpose clause.

τελειωθῶσιν—from τελειόω (I complete), this form is the aorist passive subjunctive. The verb occurs nine times in Hebrews out of a total of twenty-three times in the New Testament. The negative μή appears to negate χωρὶς ἡμῶν more than the verb itself.

Summary of Chapter 11

What is faith? The author answers this question by giving the readers first a brief definition and then the application of faith in the lives of many believers. The definition is not designed to be comprehensive; rather, it is introductory in nature. Using examples taken from life, the writer demonstrates the characteristics and qualities of faith.

After an initial reference to the origin of the world, the author chooses his illustrations from specific periods of history. First, from the period between creation and the flood he selects the names of Abel, Enoch, and Noah. These people lived by faith and experienced intimate fellowship with God. With these examples, the writer depicts a gradual progression: Abel's faith

---

80. Metzger, *Textual Commentary,* p. 674. The editions of the United Bible Society and Nes-Al delete the word; many translations (RSV, GNB, JB, NAB, NEB, NIV, and *Moffatt*) do the same. Editions that retain the word are TR, Bover, Merk, BF, and Nes-Al (25th ed.); so do the KJV, NKJV, RV, ASV, NASB, and MLB. J. B. Phillips expands the verb into a clause: "they were tempted by specious promises of release."

eventually resulted in physical death; Enoch's faith brought translation to glory; and Noah's faith provided salvation for him, his family, and the animals.

Then, from the period of the patriarchs, the author selects incidents from the life of Abraham. He shows Abraham's obedience relative to traveling to the land of Canaan, the birth of a son, and the sacrifice of Isaac. The patriarchs died without seeing the promises of God fulfilled: they longed for life eternal in a heavenly city. Also, Isaac, Jacob, and Joseph looked to the future.

From the time of the exodus from Egypt to the conquest of Canaan, the writer gleans events from the life of Moses: his birth, childhood, education, and departure from Egypt. He also relates the faith of the Israelites in crossing the Red Sea and in marching around Jericho's walls. A brief remark on Rahab's faith concludes his comments about that era.

When the author comes to the period of the judges, kings, and prophets, he lists only some representative names. He summarizes the types of trials and triumphs that believers endured and enjoyed. Although he refrains from providing details, he intimates a relation between these persons and deeds of faith.

In his conclusion, the writer discloses that the Old Testament saints and the readers of his epistle share a common faith and together reap the benefits of a fulfilled promise. Believers are made perfect through the work of Christ.

12

Admonitions and Exhortations, *part 1*

12:1–29

Outline

	A. Divine Discipline
12:1–3	1. Look to Jesus
12:4–6	2. Accept Correction
12:7–11	3. Endure Hardship
12:12–13	4. Be Strong
	B. A Divine Warning
12:14–17	1. Live in Peace
12:18–21	2. Consider Mount Sinai
12:22–24	3. Look at Mount Zion
12:25–27	4. Apply the Prophecy
12:28–29	5. Worship God

12 1 Therefore, since we are surrounded by such a great cloud of witnesses, let us
throw off everything that hinders and the sin that so easily entangles, and let us
run with perseverance the race marked out for us. 2 Let us fix our eyes on Jesus,
the author and perfecter of our faith, who for the joy set before him endured the
cross, scorning its shame, and sat down at the right hand of the throne of God. 3 Consider
him who endured such opposition from sinful men, so that you will not grow weary and lose
heart.

4 In your struggle against sin, you have not yet resisted to the point of shedding your
blood. 5 And you have forgotten that word of encouragement that addresses you as sons:

"My son, do not make light of the Lord's discipline,
and do not lose heart when he rebukes you,
6 because the Lord disciplines those he loves,
and he punishes everyone he accepts as a son."

7 Endure hardship as discipline; God is treating you as sons. For what son is not disciplined
by his father? 8 If you are not disciplined (and everyone undergoes discipline), then you
are illegitimate children and not true sons. 9 Moreover, we have all had human fathers who
disciplined us and we respected them for it. How much more should we submit to the Father
of our spirits and live! 10 Our fathers disciplined us for a while as they thought best; but
God disciplines us for our good, that we may share in his holiness. 11 No discipline seems
pleasant at the time, but painful. Later on, however, it produces a harvest of righteousness
and peace for those who have been trained by it.

12 Therefore, strengthen your feeble arms and weak knees. 13 "Make level paths for
your feet," so that the lame may not be disabled, but rather healed.

A. Divine Discipline
12:1–13

1. Look to Jesus
12:1–3

Using a series of examples taken from the history of God's people, the author continues to exhort his readers. Earlier he exhorted them to persevere in doing the will of God (10:36); now he tells them to run the race with perseverance and to look to Jesus. Believers in the Old Testament era had only the promise. In New Testament times believers have the fulfillment of the promise and therefore see Jesus.

1. Therefore, since we are surrounded by such a great cloud of witnesses, let us throw off everything that hinders and the sin that so easily entangles, and let us run with perseverance the race marked out for us.

The contemporaries of the first readers of Hebrews had developed an interest in sports. Athletes contended in a local stadium, while spectators sat on the tiered seats around the arena. Although Christians perhaps were not fully involved (because the games provided an excuse for pagan excesses), they were thoroughly familiar with the sports of their day. From the world of sports, the author borrows the imagery of spectators, apparel and condition of contestants, and the contest itself.

Note these points:

a. *Cloud.* The author places himself on the same level as that of the readers. He is one with them, for he is a contestant, too. With his fellow contestants, he looks up at the stands and sees a multitude of spectators. The writer of Hebrews calls them "a great cloud of witnesses." This may be an idiomatic expression that means the same as our term *a host of people.* The word *witness,* however, has two meanings. First, it refers to a person who watches the scene before him; his eyes and his ears tell him what is happening. Next, the word means that a person is able to talk about what he has seen and heard.

The witnesses are not silent. In fact, the writer of Hebrews says of Abel, "And by faith he still speaks, even though he is dead" (11:4). The heroes of faith mentioned in chapter 11 speak, but they do so through the pages of Scripture.[1] They cheer us on, so to speak, for the race we run concerns the cause of Christ. Through their biblical voices they encourage us in our contest of faith.[2] The witnesses surround us, for they have an interest in our achievement (11:40).

b. *Hindrance.* "Let us throw off everything that hinders," writes the author. He looks at the clothes we wear and the physical condition we are in. When we run a race, we dress in suitable sportswear designed to provide minimum weight and maximum comfort. And to qualify as runners, we strive to lose extra body fat by strengthening our muscles. That which is bulky in our bodies must disappear, for it hinders us in the race that we run.

What are the impediments that hinder us? Jesus says, "Be careful, or your hearts will be weighed down with dissipation, drunkenness and the anxieties of life" (Luke 21:34). Paul instructs, "But now you must rid yourselves of all such things as these: anger, rage, malice, slander, and filthy language from your lips" (Col. 3:8; also see James 1:21; I Peter 2:1).[3]

---

1. R. C. H. Lenski, *The Interpretation of the Epistle to the Hebrews and of the Epistle of James* (Columbus: Wartburg, 1946), p. 424.

2. Scripture teaches elsewhere (Rev. 7:9, for example) that the saints in heaven surround the throne of the Lamb. From the term *witness,* however, we cannot exclude the idea *spectator,* although the emphasis may be more on testifying than on viewing. Says B. F. Westcott, "They are spectators who interpret to us the meaning of our struggle, and who bear testimony to the certainty of our success if we strive lawfully (II Tim. 2:5)." *Commentary on the Epistle to the Hebrews* (Grand Rapids: Eerdmans, 1950), p. 391. Also consult F. W. Grosheide, *De Brief aan de Hebreeën en de Brief van Jakobus* (Kampen: Kok, 1955), p. 283. And see Hermann Strathmann, *TDNT,* vol. 4, p. 491.

3. That the impediment hindering the athlete has general significance is evident from the wording "*everything* that hinders" (italics added).

c. *Sin.* A hindrance in itself is not a sin, but because it impedes a contestant a hindrance can become sin. Sin entangles, much as a flowing robe that reaches down to the ground would entangle a runner in ancient times. Put this impediment aside, says the author of Hebrews. "Let us strip off anything that slows us down or holds us back, and especially those sins that wrap themselves so tightly around our feet and trip us up."[4]

The writer is rather specific. He calls sin *the* sin. What does he mean? He refrains from answering this question, but other passages of Scripture suggest that the sin of covetousness ranks chief among man's transgressions. Remember that Eve fell into sin because she *desired* to gain wisdom (Gen. 3:6). The last commandment in the Decalogue forbids covetousness (Exod. 20:17; Deut. 5:21). And this commandment actually serves as a summary to point out that the preceding commandments implicitly are directed against man's covetousness. In his letter to the Colossians, Paul calls evil desires and greed idolatry (3:5; also see Eph. 4:22). Even though the author of Hebrews refers to *the* sin, he himself leaves the precise meaning an open question. The intent of his exhortation is that we ought to avoid sin, for it impedes our movement in the race that we must run.

d. *Race.* When the writer exhorts us to "run with perseverance the race marked out for us," he echoes the words of Paul: "I have fought the good fight, I have finished the race, I have kept the faith" (II Tim. 4:7). Paul spoke these words at the end of his life when he knew he was approaching the finish line and the "crown of righteousness" waiting for him.[5]

We, the contestants, must run the race with perseverance. Our objective is to come to the finish line. But as we keep on running the course that God laid out before us, we keep our eye of faith fixed on Jesus. He encourages us to persevere in the contest, for he himself has run the same race. Jesus is the one who strengthens the runner and enables him to endure.

2. Let us fix our eyes on Jesus, the author and perfecter of our faith, who for the joy set before him endured the cross, scorning its shame, and sat down at the right hand of the throne of God.

The main emphasis in this verse lies in the opening clause. All the other clauses describe Jesus in respect to his work, endurance, and position.[6] Notice that the author introduces the name *Jesus* so the readers will concentrate on his earthly life.

a. "Fix our eyes on Jesus." Immediately the refrain of the invitational hymn composed by Helen H. Lemmel comes to mind:

---

4. The paraphrase of Kenneth Taylor (LB) is quite descriptive at this point.

5. In his epistles Paul frequently employs the imagery of a race (I Cor. 9:24–26; Gal. 2:2; Phil. 2:16).

6. In his article "Chiasmus, Creedal Structure, and Christology in Hebrews 12:1–2" (*Biblical Research* 23 [1978]: 37–48), E. B. Horning examines the structure of verses 1 and 2 and concludes that the passage shows an inverse parallelism with nine clauses, of which the center line is "keeping our eyes on Jesus the pioneer and perfecter of the faith."

> Turn your eyes upon Jesus,
> Look full in his wonderful face;
> And the things of earth will grow strangely dim
> In the light of his glory and grace.

As contestants engaged in running the race, we have no time to look around. We must keep our eyes focused on Jesus and must do so without distraction. The writer of Hebrews does not place the name *Jesus* among those of the heroes of faith; he gives him special recognition, for he calls him "the author and perfecter of our faith." Jesus is "the author of [our] salvation" (2:10), who as forerunner has entered the heavenly sanctuary (6:19–20) and has opened "a new and living way" for us that leads to this sanctuary (10:20).[7] He is the Beginning and the End, the Alpha and the Omega (Rev. 1:17; 21:6; 22:13). And he whom God perfected through suffering (Heb. 2:10) perfects his brothers and sisters who have placed their trust in him. As originator and perfecter of our faith, Jesus has laid its foundation in our hearts and in time brings faith to completion. He can do this because he is able, and he will do this because he is our brother (Heb. 2:11–12). In a similar vein, Paul encourages the Philippians when he says that God "who began a good work in you will carry it on to completion until the day of Christ Jesus" (1:6). Therefore, "turn your eyes upon Jesus."

b. "Joy set before him." How do we interpret the word *joy*? Does the writer mean that Jesus exchanges heavenly joy for earthly sorrow? Or does he mean that because of the joy awaiting Jesus after his death, Christ willingly "endured the cross"? Some scholars think that Jesus chose death on the cross in place of the joy of heavenly bliss he enjoyed in the presence of God (II Cor. 8:9; Phil. 2:6–7). They are of the opinion that this is what the author means to say.[8] Other scholars disagree. They believe that the intent is to convey this message: To obtain the joy God had planned for him, Jesus obediently suffered the agony of death.[9]

The evidence appears to favor the second interpretation. The context in general and the phrase *set before him* in particular support this approach. That is, God destined the path of suffering for Jesus (Isa. 53:4–6) and afterward filled him with joy (Ps. 16:11; Acts 2:28). The clause "for the joy set before him" seems to point to the future. It relates to Jesus' exaltation when he was glorified after his death on the cross.

c. "Endured the cross." In his epistle the author seldom speaks directly

---

7. Otto Michel, *Der Brief an die Hebräer,* 10th ed. (Göttingen: Vandenhoeck and Ruprecht, 1957), p. 291.

8. Consult, for example, Westcott, *Hebrews,* p. 397; Grosheide, *Hebreeën,* p. 286; John Calvin, *Epistle to the Hebrews* (Grand Rapids: Eerdmans, 1949), p. 313; Murray J. Harris, *NIDNTT,* vol. 3, p. 1180; and P. Andriessen and A. Lenglet, "Quelques passages difficiles de l'Épître aux Hébreux (5:7, 11; 10:20; 12:2)," *Bib* 51 (1970): 215–20.

9. For instance, refer to Ceslaus Spicq, *L'Épître aux Hébreux,* 3d ed., 2 vols. (Paris: Gabalda, 1953), vol. 1, p. 387; Lenski, *Hebrews,* p. 428; and Philip Edgcumbe Hughes, *Commentary on the Epistle to the Hebrews* (Grand Rapids: Eerdmans, 1977), pp. 523–24.

about the earthly life of Jesus. In fact, this is the only time he mentions the word *cross.* That term, together with the verb *endured,* mirrors the entire passion narrative of Jesus' trial and death. Jesus stood alone during his trial before the high priest and before Pontius Pilate. Jesus endured the agony of Gethsemane alone. And he alone bore the wrath of God at Calvary. In his suffering Jesus visibly demonstrated his faith in God. In obedience he sustained the anguish of death on the cross.

d. "Scorning its shame." The Jews who demanded Jesus' crucifixion wanted to place him under the curse of God. They knew that God had said, "Anyone who is hung on a tree is under [my] curse" (Deut. 21:23; see also Gal. 3:13). They wanted Jesus to experience the utmost shame. He took the curse upon himself to set his people free and to experience with them the joy God had set before him. Indeed, the author and perfecter of our faith triumphed when he sat down at God's right hand.

e. "And sat down." With a few strokes of his pen, the writer provides an account of Jesus' life, death, resurrection, and ascension. The crowning point, of course, is Jesus' enthronement at the right hand of God. That place of honor belongs to him and will be his for all eternity. The author repeatedly quotes and alludes to Psalm 110:1: "Sit at my right hand until I make your enemies a footstool for your feet" (1:13). He develops a definite progression of thought.[10] Note these verses:

1:3 "he sat down at the right hand of the Majesty in heaven"
8:1 "who sat down at the right hand of the throne of the Majesty in heaven"
10:12 "he sat down at the right hand of God"
12:2 "sat down at the right hand of the throne of God"

Jesus accomplished his task on earth, assumed his place in heaven, and now assures the believer of divine assistance in the race marked out for him.

3. Consider him who endured such opposition from sinful men, so that you will not grow weary and lose heart.

Look carefully at the entire life of Jesus, says the author of Hebrews to his readers, and consider what he had to encounter. He literally tells them to compare their lives with that of Jesus and to take careful note of all that Jesus had to endure. Jesus came to fulfill the messianic prophecies, and therefore he came to his own people; "but his own did not receive him" (John 1:11). Instead, Jesus met willful unbelief and unmitigated opposition. He endured the hatred of a sinful world set against the truth of God. If, then, Jesus experienced such opposition, would not his followers share the same lot (John 17:14)?

The writer reveals himself to be an excellent pastor. He knows the tendency to look at the Christian and not at the Christ. Introspection causes spiritual weariness and discouragement, but looking at Jesus renews the

10. Westcott, *Hebrews,* p. 396.

Christian's strength and boosts his courage. Therefore, directing attention to Jesus, the author exhorts the Christian to consider the suffering Christ sustained not only on the cross but throughout his ministry. When the Christian realizes that Jesus withstood the hatred of sinful men for the sake of the believer, the Christian ought to take courage. Then his own problems become easier to bear, and he, too, will be able to continue and eventually complete the race marked out for him.[11]

Practical Considerations in 12:1–3

We are individualists who take pride in our achievements. But sometimes this attitude, commendable as it is, can develop into a complex. That is, we think that we are alone in this world, for we are the only Christians who have kept the faith. We feel somewhat like the prophet Elijah, who complained that he was the only one left (I Kings 19:10). As a consequence, discouragement sets in.

We are not alone, however. First, consider the countless multitudes that have kept the faith and have been translated into glory. The writer of Hebrews describes them as "a great cloud of witnesses." Next, we must look to Jesus, the author and perfecter of our faith. He is always near us and ready to help. And last, we are part of the body of Christ, the church. We have numberless brothers and sisters who are fighting the good fight of faith.

Yet, as runners engaged in a race, we are individuals. Every believer must run the race that God has set out for him. And everyone has his own set of obstacles, his own track, and his own capabilities. To run the race God has given us, we must put aside everything that hinders us. The clothing of a long-distance runner consists of shirt, shorts, and shoes, and weighs less than a pound. On the track of faith, we are told to travel far. Therefore we must travel light.

The Christian's life of faith is more than one outstanding feat, a single accomplishment, and a sudden burst of spiritual energy. The believer looks to Jesus without distraction, for then he perseveres and lives a life of holiness. Then he progresses as he travels the road of sanctification.

We bear our cross, but we do not carry the cross Jesus bore. He carried the cross alone. We carry ours by unwaveringly looking at him. From his exalted position in heaven at God's right hand, Jesus enables us to persist, to endure, and to be faithful to God and his Word.

Greek Words, Phrases, and Constructions in 12:1–3

Verse 1

τοιγαροῦν—a combination of τοί (or τῷ), γάρ, and οὖν that functions as "a particle introducing a conclusion with some special emphasis or formality, and gen-

---

11. Apparently the words *grow weary* and *lose heart* were current in the world of sports. Writes James Moffatt, "Aristotle uses both to describe runners relaxing and collapsing, once the goal has been passed." See his *Epistle to the Hebrews,* International Critical Commentary series (Edinburgh: Clark, 1963), p. 199.

erally occupying the first place in the sentence."[12] It means "therefore," "consequently," "then."

καὶ ἡμεῖς—although translations fail to render the exact equivalent of the Greek, the combination of these words is emphatic: we ourselves, too.

τοσοῦτον—this correlative adjective denotes quantity. By contrast, the adjective τοιαύτην (v. 3) denotes quality.

ἔχοντες—denoting cause, this is a present active participle.

νέφος—literally the word means "cloud," but as an idiom we may translate it as "throng" or "host."

μαρτύρων—besides the double meaning the expression μάρτυς has (witnessing by eye or ear; and testifying God's truth), in the New Testament it conveys the idea *martyr* (Acts 22:20; Rev. 2:13; 17:6).

ὄγκον—apparently derived from φέρω (I carry) in the aorist ἐνεγκεῖν.[13]

ἀποθέμενοι—the aorist middle participle from the compound verb ἀπό (away) and τίθημι (I place) means "laying aside from yourselves every weight."[14]

εὐπερίστατον—because this verbal adjective appears once in the New Testament, a modification (εὐπερίσπαστον, easily distracting) occurs in two major manuscripts. The compound derives from εὖ (well), περί (around), and ἵστημι (I stand).

τὴν ἁμαρτίαν—even though the author uses the definite article, places a verbal adjective between the definite article and the noun, and gives the noun in the singular, he fails to communicate the nature of ἁμαρτία; instead, he points to sin itself.

τρέχωμεν—the hortatory subjunctive, because of the present active first person plural, reveals that the readers already are engaged in the race.

Verse 2

ἀφορῶντες—the compound present active participle from ἀπό (away) and ὁράω (I see) signifies that we ought to look to Jesus without distraction; that is, everything else takes second place. The present tense is durative.

ἀρχηγόν—in the New Testament the noun occurs four times (Acts 3:15; 5:31; Heb. 2:10; 12:2) and in each passage refers to Jesus. He is the ruler, leader, author, prince. The genitive τῆς πίστεως is objective.

κεκάθικεν—although manuscript P^{46} has the aorist active indicative ἐκάθισεν, the perfect active indicative appears to be the original reading. The perfect tense relates the action that happened in the past and is effective for the present and future.

Verse 3

τοιαύτην—it denotes quality (cf. v. 1).

τὸν ὑπομεμενηκότα—the use of the definite article directs attention to Ἰησοῦν (v. 2). The participle, from ὑπομένω (I remain), is the perfect active; it reveals that

---

12. Joseph H. Thayer, *A Greek-English Lexicon of the New Testament* (New York, Cincinnati, and Chicago: American Book Company, 1889), p. 627.

13. Ibid., p. 437. Also refer to Philo, *Allegorical Interpretation* 3.45 (LCL); and Josephus, *Jewish Wars* 4.319; 7.443 (LCL).

14. A. T. Robertson, *A Grammar of the Greek New Testament in the Light of Historical Research* (Nashville: Broadman, 1934), p. 810. Also see Robert Hanna, *A Grammatical Aid to the Greek New Testament* (Grand Rapids: Baker, 1983), p. 412.

Jesus endured opposition in the past, but that even in the present the effects are evident.

ἑαυτόν—the manuscript evidence favors the reading αὐτόν or even αὐτούς. However, the reading of the reflexive pronoun in the singular, although poorly supported by manuscripts, fits the context of the passage.[15]

ἐκλυόμενοι—the present passive participle, denoting manner, depends on the aorist active subjunctive κάμητε (from κάμνω, I am weary). The expression ταῖς ψυχαῖς (your souls), as a dative of respect, must be construed with the participle, not the verb.

---

2. Accept Correction
12:4–6

Sin is a power that is universal in its opposition to God and his revelation. The writer of Hebrews portrays it as a personified force that man confronts and fights. Sin affects everyone and everything. Jesus is the only one who was not influenced by sin, for he conquered sin. The author exhorts his readers to look at Jesus (v. 2) and to strive against sin.

4. In your struggle against sin, you have not yet resisted to the point of shedding your blood.

The metaphor in this verse—"resisted to the point of shedding your blood"—comes from the sports arena. The author goes from one sport to the other, from the imagery of the race to that of boxing.[16] In boxing, blood flows from the faces of the contestants when they withstand vicious blows. At times serious injuries result in death.

The imagery of withstanding the opponent to the point of shedding blood serves as a parallel to the readers' struggle against sin. No specific sin is mentioned. Sin, however, with its mysterious power is a formidable opponent that must be resisted unto death. Martin Luther, who frequently encountered the power of Satan and sin, exhorts the Christian in his well-known hymn:

> Let goods and kindred go,
> This mortal life also;
> The body they may kill,
> God's truth abideth still,
> His kingdom is forever.

The text itself reveals nothing about the political world in which the readers lived. In earlier days they had stood their ground when they had been

---

15. Bruce M. Metzger, *A Textual Commentary on the Greek New Testament* (London and New York: United Bible Societies, 1975), p. 675.

16. John Albert Bengel, *Gnomon of the New Testament,* ed. Andrew R. Fausset, 7th ed., 5 vols. (Edinburgh: Clark, 1877), vol. 4, p. 462. The paragraph division differs in Bible translations; for example, JB places verse 4 with the preceding verses to show continuation of the imagery from sports. The GNB, NKJV, RSV, NEB, and TR include verse 3 with the following section on discipline. The NIV, Nes-Al, and the United Bible Societies editions begin a new paragraph at verse 4.

publicly insulted, had been persecuted, and had seen their property confiscated (Heb. 10:32–34). But those days belonged to the past, and the writer repeatedly indicates that the recipients of the epistle were enjoying a period of rest and ease that had caused spiritual relaxation.

The writer admonishes rather than exhorts the readers that they should resist sin to the point of shedding blood. The possibility of persecution on account of their faith in Jesus was real. If Jesus endured the persecution and shed his blood, his followers ought not entertain illusions of being exempt.

> Our fathers, chained in prisons dark,
> Were still in heart and conscience free;
> How sure will be their children's peace
> If they, like them, contend for thee!
> —Frederick W. Faber

5. And you have forgotten that word of encouragement that addresses you as sons:

> **"My son, do not make light of the Lord's discipline,**
> **and do not lose heart when he rebukes you,**
> **6. Because the Lord disciplines those he loves,**
> **and he punishes everyone he accepts as a son."**

Believers in the first century had access to the Scriptures when they attended the worship services. There they memorized passages from the Old Testament, especially those from the Psalter, Proverbs, and Prophets. The New Testament reveals that Proverbs 3 was well known; writers quote from and allude to it more than any other chapter of this book.[17] When the author of Hebrews calls to mind Proverbs 3:11–12, he refers to a text that was basic to training believers in the church. But the readers were slow to learn (Heb. 5:11) and had forgotten the passage from Proverbs 3. The writer, then, spells it out for them.

We note the following points:

a. *Jesus.* The readers ought to recall the word of encouragement from Proverbs 3 that addresses them as sons. They are sons because of Jesus, the Son of God. Throughout his epistle the writer of Hebrews has indicated the importance of the Son and its implications for the sons (see especially 2:10–11). The one exists for the others. As Son of God, Jesus had to suffer, learn obedience, and become "the source of eternal salvation for all who obey him" (5:8–9). To be sure, the suffering of Christ is unique; it cannot and need not be repeated by his followers. However, the principle of discipline remains the same. Scripture addresses the followers of Jesus as sons, and thus they can expect correction and rebuke.

b. *Sons.* The writer says that the Word of God addresses God's children

---

17. Simon J. Kistemaker, *The Psalm Citations in the Epistle to the Hebrews* (Amsterdam: Van Soest, 1961), p. 51. Also refer to Nes-Al, Appendix 3; Philo, *Preliminary Studies* 175 (LCL); I Clem. 56:2 (*The Apostolic Fathers,* vol. 1, LCL); and SB, vol. 3, p. 747.

and encourages them. God speaks to his sons and daughters through his Word. He says, "My son, do not make light of the Lord's discipline, and do not lose heart when he rebukes you." That is, believers should see and feel the hand of God in their difficulties. The use of the expression *not make light of* suggests that they ought to view discipline as coming directly from God. If the readers of the epistle take discipline lightly, they will also think lightly of the suffering Jesus had to endure. However, they have to take God's corrective measures most seriously and understand that God gives his children adversities for their spiritual well-being. When they accept good as well as trouble from God (Job 2:10), they will not become discouraged and lose heart. Then they know that God is their Father.

c. *Father.* God, as our heavenly Father, "disciplines those he loves, and he punishes everyone he accepts as a son." The last part of this quotation comes from the Septuagint. The Old Testament reads, "Because the LORD disciplines those he loves, as a father the son he delights in" (Prov. 3:12). The variation affects the wording but not the intent of the verse.

Discipline, then, is a privilege that God extends to those he loves. This almost sounds contradictory until we see that discipline is not extended to the ungodly. They receive his judgment. God disciplined his people Israel as a consequence of their transgressions, but he displays patience and forebearance with his enemies until the measure of their iniquity is full (Gen. 15:16; Matt. 23:32; I Thess. 2:16). Discipline is a sign that God accepts us as his children.

Does God punish his children? He does send us trials and hardships designed to strengthen our faith in him. Adversities are aids to bring us into a closer fellowship with God. But God does not punish us. He punished the Son of God, especially on Calvary's cross, where he poured out his wrath on Jesus by forsaking him (Ps. 22:1; Matt. 27:46; Mark 15:34). As sin-bearer, Jesus bore God's wrath for us, so that we who believe in him will never be forsaken by God. God does not punish us, because Jesus received our punishment. We are disciplined, not punished.

Moreover, we should accept God's rebuke, discipline, and castigation as evidence of his love to us. If we do this, we demonstrate that we indeed are his children and as a result grow in faith and trust.

Practical Considerations in 12:4–6

Jesus employs a metaphor about tending a vineyard when he says that he is the true vine and his Father the gardener (John 15:1). What is the work of this gardener? "He cuts off every branch in me that bears no fruit, while every branch that does bear fruit he prunes so that it will be even more fruitful" (v. 2). When a gardener has finished pruning, a vine has only its essential branches left. At the end of the next growing season, the gardener reaps an abundant harvest.

God plunged Job into grief when he allowed Satan to take the lives of Job's ten children. Job lost all his earthly possessons. His wife told him to curse God and die, and his friends proved to be the world's most wretched comforters. Yet Job's faith triumphed; he knew that his Redeemer lived; and he received from God "twice as much as he had before" (Job 42:10).

In a time of permissiveness, Solomon's proverb points out a basic flaw: "He who spares the rod hates his son" (Prov. 13:24). The reverse is that "he who loves him is careful to discipline him." God loves us and therefore disciplines us. He removes hindrances to our spiritual development to make us partakers of his holiness and sharers in his rewards.

Greek Words, Phrases, and Constructions in 12:4–6

Verse 4

ἀντικατέστητε—the second aorist indicative, second person plural, is composed of two prepositions, ἀντί (against) and κατά (down), and the verb ἵστημι (I stand). Followed by the prepositional phrase πρὸς τὴν ἁμαρτίαν the verb is directive as well as intensive. The aorist is ingressive. Note the assonance in this verse: four words begin with the vowel ἀ.

ἀνταγωνιζόμενοι—in the main verb (ἀντικατέστητε) and in this participle the preposition ἀντί appears. The author has chosen these two forms to express the seriousness of fighting sin. The participle in the present middle (deponent) signifies continuity.

Verse 5

ἐκλέλησθε—from the verb ἐκλανθάνομαι (I forget), the perfect tense reveals that not a temporary loss of memory but an inability to recall is meant. The perfect expresses that an act accomplished in the past has lasting results. Verbs of forgetting (and remembering) have a direct object in the genitive case.[18]

ἥτις—an indefinite relative pronoun, although used as a relative pronoun, has its antecedent in παρακλήσεως.

ὀλιγώρει—the verb in the present active imperative has the participle μή. This combination means that the action is in progress but must be discontinued.

Verse 6

παιδεύει—the present active indicative form exhibits progress in the activity of training a child (παῖς).

μαστιγοῖ—derived from the verb μαστιγόω (I scourge), the present active indicative implies that God indeed strikes with a whip.

3. Endure Hardship
12:7–11

How does the writer of Hebrews apply the quotation from Proverbs 3:11–12? He knows that every son and daughter of God endures periods

18. Robertson, *Grammar,* p. 508.

of hardship. Whether God's children experience the pain of accident, misfortune, or loss, they need encouragement.

7a. Endure hardship as discipline; God is treating you as sons.

In times of affliction, says the author, keep in mind that all your setbacks come from God; he is training you in godliness and has accepted you as sons. The adversities you encounter are blessings in disguise, for behind your difficulties stands a loving Father who is giving you what is best. God's children, then, must always look beyond their trials and realize that God himself is at work in their lives.

Translators differ in their reading and understanding of the Greek text of this verse. Here are the three representative translations:

KJV "If ye endure chastening, God dealeth with you as with sons."
RSV "It is for discipline that you have to endure. God is treating you as sons."
NIV "Endure hardship as discipline; God is treating you as sons."

The King James Version, based on a variant Greek reading, translates this verse as a conditional sentence. The evidence for the reading is rather weak.

A common translation is that given by the Revised Standard Version. The verse is a statement of fact and informs the reader that the recipients of Hebrews endured suffering as discipline.

The New International Version renders the verse as a command. The author-pastor tells his readers what they must do. The choice is difficult, but the general context of the first part of this chapter features many sentences as commands (imperatives).

7b. For what son is not disciplined by his father?

The question is rhetorical. Of course a son submits to his father's rule; otherwise he would not be a true son.

The concept *discipline* in ancient Israel was not limited to describing physical punishment but included the concept *education.*[19] That is, the father as head of the household taught his children the law of God, the tradition of the elders, and the skills of a trade. Education was meant to inculcate obedience to God's law, respect for authority, and a love for their national heritage.

The point of verse 7 is that God himself is educating his children. The writer employs the illustration of a human father teaching his son. In a similar way God himself is giving his children moral and spiritual training. In the case of the recipients of Hebrews, the writer relates that they made light of the training God gave them. Therefore, the readers needed a pastoral admonition to submit to discipline. God trains them as sons, so that they may take their place next to the Son of God.

8. If you are not disciplined (and everyone undergoes discipline), then you are illegitimate children and not true sons.

---

19. Georg Bertram, *TDNT,* vol. 5, p. 604; and Dieter Fürst, *NIDNTT,* vol. 3, pp. 776–77. Also consult Günther Bornkamm, "Sohnschaft und Leiden," *Judentum, Urchristentum, Kirche* (1960): 188–98.

This verse can be interpreted to mean that the readers were illegitimate children, spiritually. But that is not the case, because the writer has already stated that they are sons of God (vv. 5–7). He presents his argument in the form of a simple conditional sentence that expresses reality. He rebukes the people on account of their carelessness in accepting divine discipline. Certainly God gave them spiritual training, but they had failed to pay attention to what God was teaching them. This careless attitude toward discipline placed them in the same category as illegitimate children. These children had no claim to inheritance; they were a source of shame and embarrassment to their father; and they were denied the discipline, coaching, and grooming that true sons received.

Careful training within a family setting has always been an accepted norm, and people are expected to receive training as part of their development in social graces. Not to accept discipline is a mark of rebellion against authority. The readers of the epistle, however, had shown disregard for this norm and had slighted God who disciplined them. They had to be told to observe the norm, accept discipline, and behave like sons. Should they continue to neglect God's teaching, they would be regarded as illegitimate children. These children have no claim to spiritual sonship and to a spiritual inheritance—that is, salvation—to which the writer of Hebrews repeatedly refers (1:14; 6:12; 9:15; 12:17). In short, sons need instruction.

9. Moreover, we have all had human fathers who disciplined us and we respected them for it. How much more should we submit to the Father of our spirits and live!

In the preceding verse the author addresses the readers directly by using the second person plural pronoun *you.* In verse 9 the wise counselor includes himself and says "we." Again he introduces an illustration from family life. He does so by comparing human fathers with God, the heavenly Father. Thus we note two parts:

a. "We have all had human fathers." The writer speaks in general terms and refrains from mentioning exceptions, for example, orphans. In family circles the head of the household is the father; he trains the children to behave and to conduct themselves properly.

Reflecting on his own youth, the author declares that children accept discipline without question. Did we resist our fathers when they corrected us? Of course not! We respected them in harmony with the commandment, "Honor your father and your mother" (Exod. 20:12; Deut. 5:16). As the time-worn saying has it, "A father is someone you look up to—no matter how tall you grow."

b. "We submit to the Father of our spirits and live." As he has done many times in his epistle, the writer employs the expression *how much more* to illustrate the extent of his comparison (2:2–3; 9:14; 10:29; 12:25). He follows the teachings of Jesus, who compared human fathers' giving good gifts with the heavenly Father's giving good gifts (Matt. 7:11; Luke 11:13).

The contrast is explicit and implicit in the last part of the verse:

human fathers—Father
bodies—spirits
death—life

We ought to avoid reading too much into verse 9, for the author wishes only to convey that he is comparing the human with the divine, and mortality with immortality. He intimates that obedience to God results in eternal life, for he is our heavenly Father. Comments F. F. Bruce, "As 'the fathers of our flesh' are our physical (or earthly) fathers, so 'the Father of (our) spirits' is our spiritual (or heavenly) Father."[20]

10. Our fathers disciplined us for a little while as they thought best; but God disciplines us for our good, that we may share in his holiness.

The comparison continues. Children are in their parental home for the time of childhood and adolescence. The years in which they receive parental discipline are relatively few; they end when the child becomes an adult. Fathers (and mothers) seek that which is best for their children, but often make mistakes. Their skills in rearing sons and daughters are limited, for they have to learn by doing. With the best of intentions, they sometimes fail in either method or purpose. In disciplining their children, parents frequently lack wisdom; corrective measures are at times too severe, and at other times are abandoned. Punishment is administered in many instances not in love but in anger. Parents who are honest with themselves and with their children admit their shortcomings.

What a difference when we consider God's discipline! He never makes a mistake, always chastens in love, scourges us, and at the same time comforts us. His discipline does not end when we have reached adulthood. Throughout our earthly life he trains us; although we often disappoint him, he never forsakes us. His patience toward us seems unlimited in spite of our lack of progress.

God has a definite purpose in mind for disciplining us. He wants us to "share in his holiness." Whereas human fathers train their children to conduct themselves appropriately, God disciplines us for holiness. That is, he wants us to become like him, perfect and holy (Matt. 5:48; Lev. 11:44–45; 19:2; 20:7; I Peter 1:15–16). God prepares us for life eternal. Therefore, we cheerfully accept God's discipline, for we know that the adversities we experience are for our spiritual welfare. As Paul says to the Corinthian believers, "For our light and momentary troubles are achieving for us an eternal glory that far outweighs them all" (II Cor. 4:17).

11. No discipline seems pleasant at the time, but painful. Later on, however, it produces a harvest of righteousness and peace for those who have been trained by it.

---

20. F. F. Bruce, *The Epistle to the Hebrews,* International Commentary on the New Testament series (Grand Rapids: Eerdmans, 1964), pp. 359–60. For the expression *Father of our spirits,* compare Num. 16:22; 27:16; Rev. 22:6.

Once more the author uses the device of contrast. This time he contrasts discipline of the present with results garnered in the future. Whatever discipline you experience at the moment, he tells his readers, whether it is physical, psychological, or spiritual discipline administered by God or man, it does not seem to be pleasant.

We do not relish correction, even though we readily acknowledge that discipline is a necessary part of our development. Discipline that is painful comes in many forms: spankings, suspension of privileges, loss of possession, departure of a loved one, serious injury, illness, unemployment, and persecution. When these adversities strike, we experience pain; our first reaction to affliction is not one of joy. We know that James writes, "Consider it *pure joy,* my brothers, whenever you face trials of many kinds" (1:2, italics added). But joy arrives later when we are able to look back and see the benefits we have received from these trials.

The message of Hebrews is the same. The suffering you encounter is painful, says the writer, but when the period of distress has ended, you will be able to see results: "a harvest of righteousness and peace." Your reward will be a right relationship with God and man in which peace reigns supreme. You are the peacemakers. Says James, "Peacemakers who sow in peace raise a harvest of righteousness" (3:18).

Who receives these blessings? They are "for those who have been trained by" discipline. Those who willingly have endured hardship as discipline and who have submitted themselves to the will of God in their lives are the recipients of righteousness and peace. They have been trained, writes the author. At the conclusion of this section he employs the expression *train.* He borrowed the word from the world of sports to remind the readers that they are engaged in a contest that demands perpetual training.

Practical Considerations in 12:7–11

To be sure, the addressees are sons, for this is the term the author uses. His intention, however, is not to give the impression that daughters are excluded from discipline. Rather, he employs the terminology of his day and expresses himself according to the norms of his culture. By addressing the men, he includes the women. They, too, are the recipients of God's discipline.

When God sends sorrow or sickness, we often hear those afflicted ask, "Why me?" They search their hearts and minds and try to find out why God is displeased with them, why he sends them adversity. Scripture speaks directly to these questions and gives this answer: "Because the Lord disciplines those he loves."

Guido de Brès, author of the Belgic Confession of Faith, was executed on the last day of May 1567, in Belgium. Just before he was brought to the gallows, he wrote a letter to his wife in which he said, "O my God, now the time has come that I must leave this life and be with you. Your will be done. I cannot escape from your hands. Even if I could, I would not do it, for it is my joy to conform to your will." This martyr had learned to endure hardship as discipline by submitting joyfully to God's will.

"Spare the rod, and spoil the child." Some fathers may have the mistaken notion that they need not discipline their offspring. In their view discipline is the opposite of love and thus should never be applied. When a lack of discipline leads to licentiousness, the results can be tragic for the child, for his parents, and for society. God, however, disciplines his sons and daughters because he loves them. He trains them in this earthly life and prepares them for eternity. Already in this life they harvest the fruits of righteousness and peace, and in the life to come they share God's holiness.

Greek Words, Phrases, and Constructions in 12:7–11

Verse 7

εἰς—with the accusative this preposition denotes cause.

παιδεύει—this verb (third person singular, present active indicative) has the synonym διδάσκω (I teach). The verb παιδεύειν "suggests moral training, disciplining the powers of man, while διδάσκειν expresses the communication of a particular lesson."[21]

Verse 8

εἰ—the force of the conditional sentence with the present indicatives ἐστε (in the protasis and apodosis clauses) is strong. The simple fact condition states reality that is tempered by the phrase ἧς μέτοχοι γεγόνασιν πάντες. The perfect tense of γεγόνασιν (from γίνομαι, I become) expresses the general truth of the statement.

ἄρα—introducing a conclusion, this conjunction is emphatic.

Verse 9

μὲν . . . δέ—in verses 9, 10, and 11 the author uses this literary device to show contrast.

εἴχομεν—the imperfect tense from ἔχω (I have) is best translated in the perfect: "have had."

πολὺ μᾶλλον—the combination of the accusative singular πολύ with the adverb μᾶλλον is akin to the expression πολλῷ μᾶλλον—the dative of degree of difference.

Verse 10

ὀλίγας ἡμέρας—the accusative of time answers the question, "How long?"

εἰς τὸ μεταλαβεῖν—with the preposition εἰς and the definite article, the aorist infinitive connotes purpose. The infinitive has a synonym in μέτοχοι (v. 8).

Verse 11

εἰρηνικόν—adjectives with the suffix -ικος convey the idea *"belonging to, pertaining to, with the characteristics of."*[22] The adjective εἰρηνικός therefore pertains to peace, but also means "bringing peace."

---

21. Westcott, *Hebrews,* p. 400.

22. Bruce M. Metzger, *Lexical Aids for Students of New Testament Greek* (Princeton, N.J.: published by the author, 1969), p. 43. His italics.

γεγυμνασμένοις—the perfect middle participle in the dative plural derives from γυμνάζω (I exercise). The perfect tense indicates progress that was initiated in the past and continues to the present. The dative is the indirect object.

---

4. Be Strong
12:12–13

This section about discipline is now coming to an end. With a pastoral exhortation and additional imagery about athletics, the author concludes his remarks. As in many other passages, he supports his teaching by alluding to the Scriptures.

12. Therefore, strengthen your feeble arms and weak knees. 13. "Make level paths for your feet," so that the lame may not be disabled, but rather healed.

On the basis of what he wrote in the preceding verses, the writer says conclusively, "Therefore." This is what you must do, he exhorts: "Strengthen your feeble arms [literally, hands] and weak knees." Apparently he employs a proverbial saying, because the expression *feeble hands and weak knees* occurs elsewhere. First, in the messianic passage that describes the joy of the redeemed, Isaiah jubilantly encourages the believers: "Strengthen the feeble hands, steady the knees that give way; say to those with fearful hearts, 'Be strong, do not fear; your God will come, he will come with vengeance; with divine retribution he will come to save you' " (35:3–4). I assume that this messianic chapter of Isaiah's prophecy was well known to the people who worshiped in the synagogues or churches of the first century.[23]

Second, Eliphaz the Temanite reminds Job of his influence. "Think how . . . you have strengthened feeble hands. Your words have supported those who stumbled; you have strengthened faltering knees" (Job 4:3–4). And third, the writer of Ecclesiasticus describes the life of an unhappy husband: "Drooping hands and weak knees are caused by the wife who does not make her husband happy" (Sir. 25:23, RSV).

The author of Hebrews speaks as a coach to the members of a sports team, and he uses sayings that are familiar to them. Although the race is not yet finished, the runners are tired. They need an encouraging word from their coach, who utters the proverbial saying, "Strengthen your feeble arms and weak knees."

The coach continues and says, "Make level paths for your feet." This is a quotation from Proverbs 4:26 that is completed with the parallel statement "and take only ways that are firm." However, the writer of Hebrews adds his own rejoinder to the line from Proverbs. Says he, the reason for making the track level for the footrace is "that the lame may not be disabled, but rather healed." Before a runner sets himself to a footrace, he examines the track

---

23. Isa. 35 was understood as a messianic prophecy (see Matt. 11:5; Mark 7:37; Luke 7:22).

carefully. He realizes that unevenness can make him vulnerable to a fall. He is in danger of spraining his ankle and consequently of being disqualified from the race. Especially when fatigue sets in, the possibility of sustaining injury is real. For that reason, the paths should be leveled.

Not all the runners are in perfect physical condition. Some are handicapped—that is, lame. Yet in spite of their condition—whether this condition arose before or during the race is of no account—they must persist, continue, and eventually complete the race.[24] By encouraging these handicapped runners and by removing dips and bumps in the road, the able-bodied athletes perform a distinct service. The result will be that the weak also reach the finish line.[25] If the paths are not leveled, the lame will be disqualified.

What idea is the author conveying with these illustrations from the world of sports? He stresses the necessity and obligation of corporate responsibility that the believers have. In earlier passages he instructed the readers to take this responsibility seriously:

3:13 "But encourage one another daily, as long as it is called Today, so that none of you may be hardened by sin's deceitfulness."
4:1 "Therefore, since the promise of entering his rest still stands, let us be careful that none of you be found to have fallen short of it."
4:11 "Let us, therefore, make every effort to enter that rest, so that no one will fall by following their example of disobedience."
6:11 "We want each of you to show this same diligence to the very end, in order to make your hope sure."

The body of Christ consists of many parts, as Paul reminds us (I Cor. 12:12–27). All the parts of the body form a unit, and no part exists for itself. As a result, each part is accountable to the whole, and the whole takes care of the individual parts. The "strong ought to bear with the failings of the weak" (Rom. 15:1).

Greek Words, Phrases, and Constructions in 12:12–13

Verse 12

διό—this inferential conjunction contracted from διά (because of) and ὅ (which) occurs nine times in Hebrews (3:7, 10; 6:1; 10:5; 11:12, 16; 12:12, 28; 13:12).

τὰς παρειμένας χεῖρας—the perfect passive participle in the feminine plural (from παρίημι, I relax, loosen) is used as a descriptive adjective and modifies the

---

24. Donald A. Hagner suggests, "Where there is weakness and drooping limbs there may also be lameness." See his *Hebrews,* Good News Commentary series (New York: Harper and Row, 1983), p. 205.

25. Hughes chooses the translation of the KJV, "lest that which is lame be turned out of the way." He interprets the clause by applying it to Hebrew Christians who might turn from the true path and thus commit "themselves to the irremediable sin of apostasy" (*Hebrews,* p. 535).

noun χείρ (hand). In this instance, the part stands for the whole—that is, the word *hand* may mean "arm."[26]

παραλελυμένα—this perfect passive participle derived from the compound παρά (on the side of) and λύω (I loose) as a descriptive adjective qualifies the noun γόνυ (knee). Both this participle and the one preceding are in the perfect tense, signifying a completed action with lasting effect.

ἀνορθώσατε—a first aorist active imperative, second person plural (from the compound verb ἀνορθόω, I erect, restore strength) strictly speaking applies better to γόνατα than χεῖρας.

Verse 13

τροχιάς—from the verb τρέχω (I run), this noun in the accusative plural signifies wheel tracks or paths. A related noun is τροχός (wheel).

ποιεῖτε—the external and internal evidence favors the present active imperative, not the aorist active imperative ποιήσατε.

ἐκτραπῇ—in the aorist passive subjunctive, third person singular, this verb derived from ἐκτρέπω (I turn away) "is often taken here, because of the context, as a medical technical term *be dislocated.*"[27] The combination ἵνα μή with the subjunctive expresses negative purpose.

ἰαθῇ—the aorist passive subjunctive, third person singular (from ἰάομαι, I heal, cure) is indeed passive in spite of the deponent.

---

14 Make every effort to live in peace with all men and to be holy; without holiness no one
will see the Lord. 15 See to it that no one misses the grace of God and that no bitter root
grows up to cause trouble and defile many. 16 See that no one is sexually immoral, or is
godless like Esau, who for a single meal sold his inheritance rights as the oldest
son. 17 Afterward, as you know, when he wanted to inherit this blessing, he was rejected.
He could bring about no change of mind, though he sought the blessing with tears.

18 You have not come to a mountain that can be touched and that is burning with fire; to
darkness, gloom and storm; 19 to a trumpet blast or to such a voice speaking words that
those who heard it begged that no further word be spoken to them, 20 because they could
not bear what was commanded: "If even an animal touches the mountain, it must be
stoned." 21 The sight was so terrifying that Moses said, "I am trembling with fear."

22 But you have come to Mount Zion, to the heavenly Jerusalem, the city of the living God.
You have come to thousands upon thousands of angels in joyful assembly, 23 to the church
of the firstborn, whose names are written in heaven. You have come to God, the judge of all
men, to the spirits of righteous men made perfect, 24 to Jesus the mediator of a new covenant, and to the sprinkled blood that speaks a better word than the blood of Abel.

25 See to it that you do not refuse him who speaks. If they did not escape when they
refused him who warned them on earth, how much less will we, if we turn away from him
who warns us from heaven? 26 At that time his voice shook the earth, but now he has
promised, "Once more I will shake not only the earth but also the heavens." 27 The words
"once more" indicate the removing of what can be shaken—that is, created things—so that
what cannot be shaken may remain.

---

26. Bauer, p. 880.
27. Ibid., p. 246.

28 Therefore, since we are receiving a kingdom that cannot be shaken, let us be thankful, and so worship God acceptably with reverence and awe, 29 for our God is a consuming fire.

B. A Divine Warning
12:14–29

1. Live in Peace
12:14–17

In clear speech and in direct commands, the pastor-author tells the readers how to live holy lives before God. In fact, he tells them what to do, what to avoid, and what to learn from history. Besides, his remarks are echoing teachings from many parts of Scripture.

14. Make every effort to live in peace with all men and to be holy; without holiness no one will see the Lord.

This verse sets a positive tone and is introductory to the rest of the passage. Let us look at this passage point by point.

a. *What to do.* The first command is: pursue peace! Keep on pursuing one goal—that is, peace; do not rest until you have attained it. When spiritual life flourishes in the family circle and in the congregation, peace holds the members together. But when disharmony stunts the spiritual life of family or congregation, peace has left, just as a fleeting shadow skips across the fields. Pursuing peace implies banning quarrels. "Live in peace with all men," says the writer. What do the words *all men* mean? Do they include enemies? According to Jesus' teaching, the answer is yes. Jesus said, "Love your enemies and pray for those who persecute you, that you may be sons of your Father in heaven" (Matt. 5:44–45). And they who are called sons of God are the peacemakers (Matt. 5:9). "The peace makers are the true Israel and acknowledged by God as His children."[28]

A recurring refrain in the Old Testament as in the New is the command to live at peace with one another. David exhorts the Israelites, "Turn from evil and do good; seek peace and pursue it" (Ps. 34:14; see also I Peter 3:11). In his Epistle to the Romans, Paul stresses the pursuit of peace twice: "If it is possible, as far as it depends on you, live at peace with everyone" (12:18) and "Let us therefore make every effort to do what leads to peace" (14:19).[29] Peace is attained through close communion with Jesus Christ, the Prince of Peace (Isa. 9:6; Col. 3:15).

The second command is: pursue holiness. Peace and holiness are two sides of the same coin. Holiness is not the state of perfection already attained. Rather, the word in the original Greek refers to the sanctifying process that occurs in the life of the believer. To put it differently, the believer reflects

---

28. T. W. Manson, *The Sayings of Jesus* (London: SCM, 1950), p. 151.

29. Additional passages that refer to pursuing peace are Mark 9:50; II Cor. 13:11; I Thess. 5:13; II Tim. 2:22. Also consult Hartmut Beck and Colin Brown, *NIDNTT,* vol. 2, pp. 780–83; and Werner Foerster, *TDNT,* vol. 2, pp. 411–17.

God's virtues. In so doing, he becomes more and more like Christ who through the Holy Spirit continues to work in the believer's heart. As the writer of Hebrews says, Jesus is the one who makes the believer holy (2:11). Therefore, we as believers must do everything in our power to obtain holiness.

The conclusion to these two commands is this: without peace and holiness no one will see the Lord. Only the pure in heart, says Jesus, will see God (Matt. 5:8; compare I John 3:2). A holy God can have communion only with those who are at peace with him (Rom. 5:1) and those who have been made holy through the work of Christ (Heb. 2:10; 10:10, 14; 13:12). God's holy wrath is directed against those who are unholy (Heb. 10:29). The unrighteous person cannot stand the sight of Christ's appearance, for his wrath is terrible (Rev. 6:15–17). Isaiah says that angels cover their faces in the presence of God (6:2); how then could an unholy person see God?

15. See to it that no one misses the grace of God and that no bitter root grows up to cause trouble and defile many.

Now comes the warning; the author instructs us what not to do.

b. *What to avoid.* First, the writer reasserts the corporate responsibility of the believers. "See to it that no one misses the grace of God" (compare 3:12; 4:1, 11). As members of the body of Christ we are responsible for each other. We have the task of overseeing one another in spiritual matters, so that we may grow and flourish in the grace of God and not come short of it. That is, no one should be allowed to straggle, for if this happens he becomes Satan's prey and will miss God's grace (II Cor. 6:1; Gal. 5:4). Mutual supervision within the entire body stimulates the spiritual health of the individual members. Avoid, therefore, the indifference to one another manifested by Cain, who asked, "Am I my brother's keeper?" (Gen. 4:9). Instead we should ask each other about our spiritual well-being, although perhaps not in the quaint wording of the Methodist preacher who inquired, "How is it with thy soul, brother?" But certainly as members of Christ's body we must put similar questions to our brothers and sisters in the Lord.

Second, if mutual oversight is neglected, other problems arise. Missing the grace of God becomes falling into apostasy. And falling into apostasy is equivalent to serving other gods. The author of Hebrews more or less quotes from the Septuagint version of Deuteronomy 29:18 (v. 17, LXX), where Moses tells the Israelites: "Make sure there is no man or woman, clan or tribe among you today whose heart turns away from the LORD our God to go and worship the gods of those nations; make sure there is no root among you that produces such bitter poison."

The roots of many weed plants spread rapidly and produce plants in all the places where the roots grow. These roots develop undetected; the resultant rapid multiplication of plants is quite unsettling. Roots and plants spell trouble for crop-producing plants that are then deprived of necessary nutrients and as a result yield a reduced harvest.

With this picture borrowed from the world of agriculture, the author of Hebrews looks at the church and compares a person who has missed the grace of God (and has fallen away) with a bitter root. Such a person causes trouble among God's people by disturbing the peace. With his bitter words, he deprives the believers of holiness. Says the writer, he defiles many. The verb *defile* actually conveys the idea of giving something color by painting or staining it.[30] Avoid such bitterness, for it will defile you. "To the pure, all things are pure, but to those who are corrupted and do not believe, nothing is pure" (Titus 1:15).

16. See that no one is sexually immoral, or is godless like Esau, who for a single meal sold his inheritance rights as the oldest son.

Third, the author tells the readers to avoid immorality. He uses the example of Esau and calls him a godless person. Esau was trained in the godly home of Isaac and Rebekah, but he deliberately chose to live a life that grieved his parents. He married two Canaanite women who were a source of grief to his parents (Gen. 26:35). Scripture does not condemn Esau for marrying these women and does not call him a fornicator. Instead the Bible reports that when Esau noticed his father's grief, he married a daughter of Ishmael son of Abraham (Gen. 28:9).

How do we interpret the term *immoral*? Some commentators understand it literally and argue that Esau's married life was tantamount to fornication.[31] But Scripture fails to provide the evidence. Others understand the word *immoral* spiritually and say that Esau committed spiritual adultery. But Scripture teaches that spiritual adultery is committed by the nation Israel, not by individuals. And still others hold that Jewish tradition and legend affirm that Esau was a fornicator.[32] However, we do well to rely on the information in Scripture, even though tradition has a value all its own.

The New International Version solves the problem by separating the two adjectives *immoral* and *godless*. The first adjective applies to the readers, for in the next chapter the writer repeats his admonition. Says he, "Marriage should be honored by all, and the marriage bed kept pure, for God will judge the adulterer and all the sexually immoral" (Heb. 13:4). The author describes Esau not as an immoral but as a godless person. The second adjective, then, applies to Esau who had no regard for God's blessing and promise which he, as the first-born, would receive. He despised his birthright and displayed utter indifference to the spiritual promises God had given to his grandfather Abraham and his father Isaac.[33] He refused to follow in the footsteps of his forefathers, and thus his name is omitted from the list of

---

30. R. C. Trench, *Synonyms of the New Testament* (Grand Rapids: Eerdmans, 1953), p. 110; J. I. Packer, *NIDNTT*, vol. 1, p. 447; and Friedrich Hauck, *TDNT*, vol. 4, pp. 644–46.

31. Hughes, *Hebrews*, p. 540. Also consult Franz Delitzsch, *Commentary on the Epistle to the Hebrews*, 2 vols. (Edinburgh: Clark, 1877), vol. 2, pp. 333–34; and Spicq, *Hébreux*, vol. 2, p. 401.

32. SB, vol. 3, pp. 748–49.

33. Esau's indifference to God's promise can be seen in his remark to Jacob, "Look, I am about to die. What good is the birthright to me?" (Gen. 25:32). His only concern was for temporal matters. See Gerhard Charles Aalders, *Bible Student's Commentary: Genesis*, 2 vols. (Grand Rapids: Zondervan, 1981), vol. 2, p. 82.

the heroes of faith. His brother Jacob, however, is mentioned because he blessed Joseph's sons and transmitted God's promises to them.

What does the writer of Hebrews teach? Simply this: abstain from immorality and avoid godlessness.

17. Afterward, as you know, when he wanted to inherit this blessing, he was rejected. He could bring about no change of mind, though he sought the blessing with tears.

In the conclusion of the passage the author reminds the readers of what they should learn from history.

c. *What to know.* Throughout his epistle, the writer has warned the readers not to turn away from the living God (3:12), for the result of such a deed is disastrous. He used two examples, one from Old Testament history and one from his own time. First he took the illustration of the rebellious Israelites who because of their unbelief died in the desert (3:16–19). Next he pointed to some of his own contemporaries who had heard the Word preached and had received the sacraments of baptism and the Lord's Supper, but had fallen away of their own accord. For these people, said the author, repentance is impossible (6:4–6; compare 10:26–31).

Now once more the writer returns to this subject. Taking the example of Esau, he shows that Esau deliberately rejected the faith of his father and his grandfather by despising his birthright; therefore, he himself was rejected. God rejected him. Moreover, that rejection was final and irrevocable. Years after he had sold his birthright, his father Isaac wanted to give him the blessing, but was unable to do so (Gen. 27:30–40). Suddenly Esau realized that God had by-passed him, but his heart had hardened so much that "he could bring about no change of mind." Repentance was impossible for him. The author adds that Esau "sought the blessing with tears." According to the Genesis account, Esau showed no sign of penitence, only anger toward his brother Jacob. Hence with his tears he sought not repentance, but only the blessing.[34]

The lesson is obvious. We must know that unbelief leads to hardening of the heart and to apostasy. He who has fallen away from the living God finds that God has rejected him. Therefore, we must strive for peace and holiness, avoid immorality and godlessness, and know that falling into the hands of the living God is most dreadful (Heb. 10:31).

Practical Considerations in 12:14–17

Society today fosters individualism, and this trait, unfortunately, has also taken hold in the church. Even though we lustily sing, "We are not divided, all one body we," each one goes his own way.

Scripture teaches that the church members need spiritual care and oversight.

---

34. The KJV has this reading: "though he sought *it* carefully with tears" (italics added). The term *it* can refer to repentance or to the blessing. The historical context favors the latter.

The pastor is called overseer and shepherd of God's flock (Acts 20:28; I Peter 5:2–3). He needs to know us personally and somewhat closely. I favor the practice of the pastor who, accompanied by an elder or a deacon, visits every family and every individual once a year. The pastoral visit, then, is strictly for the purpose of helping one another spiritually. The intent is not to embarrass anyone or to meddle in someone's private business, but to inquire tactfully about spiritual needs, to speak a word of encouragement, to help and support. These annual visits strengthen the bond of unity in the church.

As every farmer knows, neglect causes weeds to grow and multiply. Similarly, neglect of pastoral duties in a congregation causes church members to drift away. And a member who is drifting eventually separates himself from the church. The truth of the matter is that separation from the church inevitably leads to separation from God.

The message of the Epistle to the Hebrews is relevant today. As members of the body of Christ, we must do everything in our power to prevent fellow members from drifting away from God and his Word. We have the solemn responsibility to guard against signs of unbelief and disobedience, to promote peace and holiness, and to further the cause of unity and harmony in the church. Peter puts it succinctly: "But grow in the grace and knowledge of our Lord and Savior Jesus Christ" (II Peter 3:18).

Greek Words, Phrases, and Constructions in 12:14–17

Verse 14

διώκετε—the second person plural, present active imperative exhorts the readers to actively continue their pursuit of peace.

τὸν ἁγιασμόν—preceded by the definite article, this noun as direct object of the main verb expresses the process of sanctification, not the state or the fact of sanctification. Nouns ending in -μος describe action.[35]

Verse 15

ἐπισκοποῦντες—derived from ἐπισκοπέω (I oversee), the present active participle functions in an imperatival construction. The word itself has derivatives in English: "episcopal" and "bishop."

ἐνοχλῇ—the present active subjunctive from ἐνοχλέω (I cause trouble) is part of a negative purpose clause. The compound consists of ἐν (in) and ὄχλος (crowd). The form ἐν χολῇ as an alternative reading is a conjecture.

μιανθῶσιν—the aorist passive subjunctive, third person plural (from μιαίνω, I stain, paint; pollute) suggests finality because of the aorist tense.

Verse 17

ἴστε—although this form may be either imperative or indicative, the context favors the indicative. The form itself is a literary term from οἶδα (I know) in the second person plural. It occurs three times in the New Testament (Eph. 5:5; Heb. 12:17; James 1:19).

---

35. Metzger, *Lexical Aids,* pp. 42–43.

ἀπεδοκιμάσθη—the author seems to take pleasure in word play: in verse 16 Esau sold (ἀπέδετο) his inheritance; in verse 17 he was rejected (ἀπεδοκιμάσθη) by God. The form is the aorist passive, third person singular, from ἀποδοκιμάζω (I reject).

ἐκζητήσας—the participle in the aorist active from ἐκζητέω (I seek out, search for) is intensive because of the compound form.

---

2. Consider Mount Sinai
12:18–21

At first appearance, it seems the author introduces an entirely new topic: the contrast between Mount Sinai and Mount Zion. But this is not quite the case, for the topic is already introduced in elementary form in the brief clause "without holiness no one will see the Lord" (12:14). As the readers strive for peace and holiness, they ought to know the difference between the time of the old covenant and that of the new covenant. They are different from the Israelites who received the Ten Commandments at Mount Sinai. Therefore, the writer says, **18. you have not come to a mountain that can be touched and that is burning with fire; to darkness, gloom and storm.**

The context of the word choice and the contrast with verse 22 demand that the concept *Mount Sinai* be understood. In the better Greek manuscripts, the term *mountain* is omitted, and many translations show this omission.[36] However, similarity with Deuteronomy 4:11 is telling. Moses reflects on the experience at Sinai and recalls for the benefit of the Israelites, "You came near and stood at the foot of the mountain while it blazed with fire to the very heavens, with black clouds and deep darkness" (see also Exod. 19:18; Deut. 5:22–23).

The focus is not so much on the place itself as on the appearance of God who revealed his majesty and power. The Israelites had consecrated themselves outwardly by washing their clothes (Exod. 19:10–11). Inwardly they trembled with fear when they looked at the mountain, for they had come to "darkness, gloom and storm." In these awesome aspects of nature, God appears to his people and expects them to increase their reverence for him.[37] The author of Hebrews confirms this point when at the conclusion of this passage he writes, "Let us be thankful, and so worship God acceptably with reverence and awe, for our God is a consuming fire" (12:28–29).

The Israelites saw the spectacle of fire, smoke, clouds, and an electrical storm; they also were witnesses **19a. to a trumpet blast or to such a voice**

---

36. Despite the weak manuscript attestation, TR includes the word *mountain*. Translations vary: the RSV, JB, *Moffatt*, and *Phillips* omit it; the RV, ASV, and NASB print the word *mount* or *mountain* in italics to indicate that the Greek text provides no (or insufficient) support; the MLB, NAB, NKJV, and NIV have the word *mountain* ("mount," KJV) without notation; the NEB is rather expansive and approaches a paraphrase: "Remember where you stand: not before the palpable, blazing fire of Sinai." And the GNB has, "You have not come, as the people of Israel came, to what you can feel, to Mount Sinai."

37. John Owen, *An Exposition of Hebrews*, 7 vols. in 4 (Evansville, Ind.: Sovereign Grace, 1960), vol. 7, p. 311.

speaking words. They fully understood that the fiery storm raging at the top of Mount Sinai was much more than a display of natural forces. God himself was present and made himself heard by the sound of the trumpet (Exod. 19:16; 20:18).[38] Then God spoke to the people and gave them the Decalogue—that is, the covenant (Deut. 4:13). God came to the Israelites with this covenant so that the fear of God himself might reside in his people to keep them from sinning (Exod. 20:20). The overwhelming sight and the thunderous voice of God struck mortal fear into the hearts of the people, so **that those who heard it begged no further word be spoken to them** (see also Exod. 20:19; Deut. 5:25–26).

Scripture reveals that the people at Mount Sinai heard the voice of God, but the words he spoke failed to penetrate the hearts and minds of the Israelites. They asked Moses to listen to all that God would tell him and then relay the commandments to them. They were willing to listen and obey, but the spectacle was too much for them (Deut. 5:27–28).

The Israelites were awestruck, **20. because they could not bear what was commanded: "If even an animal touches the mountain, it must be stoned."** The author of Hebrews chose this particular passage from Exodus 19:13, that renders the general meaning but not the exact wording, to demonstrate the majesty of God's holiness. No one might touch God's holy mountain, not even an animal that strayed near it. Should man or animal touch the mountain, God said, "he shall not be permitted to live"(Exod. 19:13). The Israelites had to execute the person or animal by stoning him to death or by shooting him with arrows. They were not allowed to touch him.

The stress, then, is on God's holiness. God wanted the people to be aware of his sacred majesty. The Israelites were filled with fear and terror. Even Moses, to whom God would speak as to a friend, was afraid (Exod. 33:11). **21. The sight was so terrifying that Moses said, "I am trembling with fear."** Moses was the intermediary between God and man, for he was God's spokesman. Nevertheless, at the sight of God's majesty and on hearing God's voice utter the Ten Commandments, Moses was one with the people and shook with fear.

The accounts recorded in Exodus 19–20 and Deuteronomy 4–5 are silent about the fear of Moses. And Moses' statement on being afraid ("I feared," Deut. 9:19) occurs partially in the context of God's anger expressed against the Israelites when they had worshiped the golden calf. Possibly the author of Hebrews had access to an oral tradition, much the same as Stephen had received the information that "Moses trembled with fear" at the sight of the burning bush (Acts 7:32). And Paul, in mentioning Jannes and Jambres, may have used the same tradition (II Tim. 3:8).[39] When God reveals his

---

38. At the time of Christ's return, the trumpet will sound from the heavens (see Matt. 24:31; I Cor. 15:52; I Thess. 4:16).

39. According to Shabbath 88b, *Talmud,* Moses ascended Mount Sinai and feared the consuming breath of the angels. Michel, *Hebräer,* p. 315, refers to rabbinic traditions. Haggadic formulations similar to Heb. 12:21 appear in I En. 89:30 and I Macc. 13:2. Consult Kistemaker, *Psalm Citations,* p. 53.

holiness to man, fear and trembling result. Isaiah saw the Lord God "seated on a throne, high and exalted," and cried out, "Woe to me! I am ruined! For I am a man of unclean lips, and I live among a people of unclean lips, and my eyes have seen the King, the LORD Almighty" (6:1, 5). So Moses trembled with fear at Mount Sinai when he saw God's majesty and glory in awesome display.

Greek Words, Phrases, and Constructions in 12:18–21

Verse 18

οὐ—as the first word in the sentence, this negative particle receives emphasis, especially with the contrast of ἀλλά (v. 22).

προσεληλύθατε—derived from the compound προσέρχομαι (I approach), the perfect active indicative, second person plural is repeated in verse 22. The perfect shows lasting results. The word *proselyte* derives from this verb form.

γνόφῳ καὶ ζόφῳ καὶ θυέλλῃ—the lack of definite articles in this verse emphasizes the characteristics of the nouns. Note the use of rhyme in the first two nouns γνόφος (darkness) and ζόφος (gloom). A θύελλα is a whirlwind.

Verse 19

σάλπιγγος ἤχῳ καὶ φωνῇ ῥημάτων—the absence of definite articles for these four nouns is designed to stress their characteristics. The nouns are placed in chiastic order. Also note that the term ῥῆμα "usually relates to individual words and utterances" and λόγος "can often designate the Christian proclamation as a whole in the N[ew] T[estament]."[40]

ἧς—this feminine singular relative pronoun in the genitive has its antecedent in φωνή and is construed with οἱ ἀκούσαντες. The use of the genitive with the verb ἀκούω depicts the *hearing,* not the *understanding* of the voice that spoke.

Verse 20

ἔφερον—the imperfect active tense of φέρω (I bear) is descriptive.

κἄν—as a contraction of καὶ ἐάν, the word introduces the future more vivid condition that has the aorist active subjunctive θίγῃ (from θιγγάνω, I touch) in the first clause and the future passive indicative λιθοβοληθήσεται (from λιθοβολέω, I stone) in the second.

τοῦ ὄρους—the genitive case depends upon the preceding verb.

---

3. Look at Mount Zion 12:22–24

The author is a literary artist who develops his argument with contrast and balanced clauses. Although the two sections (vv. 18–21 and 22–24) of the argument fail to correspond at every point, the second portion itself consists of seven parts (two in verse 22, three in verse 23, and two in verse 24).

---

40. Otto Betz, *NIDNTT,* vol. 3, p. 1121.

22. But you have come to Mount Zion, to the heavenly Jerusalem, the city of the living God. You have come to thousands upon thousands of angels in joyful assembly, 23. to the church of the firstborn, whose names are written in heaven. You have come to God, the judge of all men, to the spirits of righteous men made perfect, 24. to Jesus the mediator of a new covenant, and to the sprinkled blood that speaks a better word than the blood of Abel.

a. "Mount Zion, . . . the heavenly Jerusalem." What a difference between the description of Mount Sinai and that of Mount Zion! What a contrast! The first scene is one of doom and dread; the second scene portrays life and joy. In the first portion of the argument Mount Sinai is not even mentioned, for the Israelites were not to stay there. In the second part, Mount Zion is described as "the heavenly Jerusalem" and as "the city of the living God."

The verb *have come* intimates that the readers of Hebrews have arrived at a permanent place. That is, the temporary conditions of the old covenant have ended, and the everlasting terms of the new covenant now prevail. That the expression *Mount Zion* ought to be understood spiritually and not literally is evident from the explanation "the heavenly Jerusalem, the city of the living God." The new Jerusalem is the place where Jesus, the mediator of the new covenant, dwells.[41]

> Zion, founded on the mountains,
> God, thy Maker, loves thee well;
> He has chosen thee, most precious,
> He delights in thee to dwell;
> God's own city,
> Who can all thy glory tell?
> —*Psalter Hymnal*

Mount Zion is the highest elevation in the city of Jerusalem. As a fortress it was fiercely defended by the Jebusites, who were defeated at last by David. In time, the fortress, including the surrounding area, was called the city of David, but poets and prophets used the name *Zion* and designated it God's dwelling place (see, for instance, Ps. 2:6; 20:2; 99:2; 135:21; Isa. 4:3–5; Jer. 8:19).

The writer of Hebrews employs the adjective *heavenly* to signify that the place he mentions is not the southeast corner of Jerusalem, but the heavenly Zion where God dwells with all the saints (Rev. 14:1; 21:2). The citizens of the heavenly Jerusalem are known as sons and daughters of Zion. It is the place where "God himself will be with them and be their God" (Rev. 21:3). The heavenly Jerusalem excels its earthly counterpart, for sin and death are banished eternally in heaven; the city has no need of sun or moon, "for the glory of God gives it light, and the Lamb is its lamp" (Rev. 21:23). The living God lives among his people forever.

---

41. Eduard Lohse, *TDNT*, vol. 7, p. 337. Also consult Helmut Schultz, *NIDNTT*, vol. 2, p. 329.

What an honor to live in that city! Consider this: Moses was given the honor of climbing Mount Sinai and being with God for forty days and forty nights (Exod. 34:28). We shall be with him in heaven always. Mount Sinai is a windswept, uninhabited mountain; the new Jerusalem is a city populated by the saints who dwell permanently in Zion with their living God (Gal. 4:26; Phil. 3:20).

b. "Thousands upon thousands of angels." Already Abraham looked "forward to the city with foundations, whose architect and builder is God" (Heb. 11:10; cf. 13:14). That city is the habitation of countless angels as well. Certainly the New International Version has the translation "thousands upon thousands of angels," but this is an expression that appears in Revelation 5:11 and stands for countless thousands.[42] "Then I looked and heard the voice of many angels," says John, "numbering thousands upon thousands, and ten thousand times ten thousand." This "joyful assembly" of angels sings a song of glory, honor, and praise to the Lamb (see also Dan. 7:10).

Translations differ on the exact position of the Greek word translated as "assembly." Depending on the placing of a comma, the word *assembly* or its equivalent is taken either with angels or with "the church of the firstborn" in the next verse (v. 23).[43] Commentators are divided on this matter. However, it appears that the translation "thousands upon thousands of angels in joyful assembly" is preferred because the author of Hebrews "perhaps intended to offset any thought that angels were angels of judgment."[44] Angels were commissioned to deliver the law at Mount Sinai (Acts 7:53; Gal. 3:19; cf. Deut. 33:2; Ps. 68:17); by contrast, they constitute a joyful assembly at Mount Zion, the heavenly Jerusalem (see Rev. 5:11–13). In heaven angels rejoice when they see that one sinner repents (Luke 15:10). They are sent out to serve all those who inherit salvation (Heb. 1:14).

c. "Church of the firstborn." When the writer of Hebrews says to the readers, "You have come to Mount Zion, to the heavenly Jerusalem, the city of the living God," and then mentions the festive gathering of an immense number of angels, he could be misunderstood. Because he places the scene in heaven, the readers might say that they as yet have not come to the heavenly Jerusalem. But when he says, "[You have come] to the church of the firstborn, whose names are written in heaven," he definitely addresses the readers. They are the ones who belong to the new covenant, and their names already have been recorded in the Book of Life (see also Luke 10:20; Phil. 4:3; Rev. 3:5; 13:8; 20:12).

---

42. Bauer, p. 529.

43. Editors of Greek New Testament editions put a comma after the word *angels* and therefore show that the expression *assembly* ought to be part of the following verse. These translations have adopted the punctuation of the Greek editions of the New Testament: KJV, NKJV, RV, ASV, NASB, GNB, NEB, and *Phillips*. Translators of the RSV, NAB, JB, MLB, NIV, and *Moffatt*, however, take the term *assembly* or *festal gathering* (or a variant) with the phrase *thousands upon thousands of angels*.

44. Donald Guthrie, *Hebrews*, Tyndale New Testament Commentary series (Grand Rapids: Eerdmans, 1983), p. 261. Also consult Lenski, *Hebrews*, p. 456.

That the believers belong to the church on earth is evident from the clause "the spirits of righteous man made perfect." They are still sinners, and their spirits have not yet been glorified to join the church in heaven. They are on earth; their names, however, are written in heaven.

What is meant by the expression *first-born*? The New Testament shows repeatedly that Jesus is the first-born. Of the nine occurrences of this word (Matt. 1:25; Luke 2:7; Rom. 8:29; Col. 1:15, 18; Heb. 1:6; 11:28; 12:23; Rev. 1:5), seven refer to Jesus. One passage (Heb. 11:28) relates to Egypt's first-born slain by the angel of death, and the other passage (Heb. 12:23) concerns believers. The privilege of the first-born is that he is able to lay claim to the inheritance. Christ is therefore the heir, and we are coheirs with him (Rom. 8:17). We value our birthright, whereas Esau despised it (Heb. 12:16). We are first-born because of Christ who makes us holy, and we who are made holy belong to the same family (Heb. 2:11).[45]

Recording the names of the first-born males in Israel was done at God's command. Moses counted all their names and made a list (Num. 3:40). In heaven all the names of those believers included in the new covenant are written in the Book of Life.[46]

d. "God, the judge." God is judge of all men, and no one is higher than God. At Mount Sinai he came to Israel to give the people his law and to make a covenant with them. There he did not appear as judge, only as lawgiver.

Here the readers of Hebrews learn that God is judge of all men, and (by implication) that everyone must appear before him. Seated at Mount Zion, the heavenly Jerusalem, God summons his people to the judgment seat, not to condemn them, but to justify them. God declares them righteous because of his Son who paid their debt (II Tim. 4:8). God's right hand is filled with righteousness, says the psalmist (Ps. 48:10). God rewards his people by renewing them after his image of true righteousness, holiness, and knowledge (Eph. 4:24; Col. 3:10).

e. "Spirits of righteous men." Who are these "spirits of righteous men made perfect"? Some commentators are of the opinion that these spirits belong to Old Testament believers; others think that the writer refers to New Testament saints who have died.[47] But all believers of both Old Testament and New Testament times, who have been translated to glory, are declared righteous. They have been made perfect on the basis of Jesus' work; he is "the author and perfecter of our faith" (Heb. 12:2).

---

45. Karl Heinz Bartels, *NIDNTT,* vol. 1, p. 669. Also see Wilhelm Michaelis, *TDNT,* vol. 6, p. 881.

46. Although the writer has the readers of his epistle in mind, he has not excluded those saints who died before the coming of Christ (see Heb. 11:39–40).

47. Bruce, *Hebrews,* p. 378, for example, argues that "they are surely believers of pre-Christian days." By contrast, Bengel in *Gnomon,* vol. 4, p. 473, asserts that they "are New Testament believers."

What then is the relation between the saints on earth and the saints in heaven? The saints in glory have been perfected, for they are set free from sin. Their souls are perfect; their bodies wait for the day of resurrection. In principle, the believers on earth share in the perfection Christ gives his people. They enjoy the prospect of joining the assembly of the saints in heaven. Only death separates the church below from the church above. When death occurs the believer obtains the fulfillment of Christ's atoning work (Heb. 2:10).

f. "Jesus the mediator." In earlier chapters the writer explained the covenant (7:22; 8:6, 8–12; 9:4, 15–17, 20; 10:16, 29); once more he reminds the readers that Jesus is the mediator of a new covenant. He purposely uses the name *Jesus* to bring into focus the suffering, death, resurrection, and ascension of Jesus.

At Mount Sinai Moses served as mediator between God and man; and with respect to the covenant God made with his people, Moses was the intermediary. But Mount Sinai represents that which is temporary: Moses died, and the first covenant eventually came to an end. To be sure, God replaced it with a new covenant (Jer. 31:31–34; Heb. 8:8–12), and Jesus became the mediator of it. The readers of the epistle observed that the establishing of a new covenant was relatively recent. It occurred when Jesus died on Calvary's cross (also see Matt. 26:28). Moreover, the readers ought to look not to Moses, who mediated the old covenant, but to Jesus. As mediator of the new covenant, he calls the believer to joyful and thankful obedience; he removes the burden of guilt and cleanses the sinner's conscience; he grants him the gift of eternal life; and he functions as intercessor in behalf of his people.

g. "Sprinkled blood." When Moses formally confirmed the first covenant at Sinai, he sprinkled blood on the altar, the scroll, the people, and even the tabernacle (Exod. 24:6–8; Heb. 9:17–22). Sprinkled blood signified forgiveness of sin, for "without the shedding of blood there is no forgiveness" (Heb. 9:22). Jesus inaugurated the new covenant by shedding his blood once for all at Golgotha. Because of that sprinkled blood, believers enter the presence of God as forgiven sinners (Heb. 10:22; I Peter 1:2).

You have come, says the author, "to the sprinkled blood that speaks a better word than the blood of Abel." The comparison is somewhat unequal. The blood of Abel called for revenge, and God placed a curse upon Cain for killing his brother Abel (Gen. 4:10–11). The blood of Christ removed the curse placed upon fallen man and effected reconciliation and peace between God and man. Abel's blood is the blood of a martyr that evokes revenge. The blood of Jesus is the blood of the Lamb of God who "takes away the sin of the world" (John 1:29).

The deliberate contrast accentuates the significance of Jesus' blood that proclaims the gospel of redemption. The blood of Jesus sets the sinner free. And that is the better word the author wishes to convey.

Practical Considerations in 12:22–24

"Why do you go to church on Sunday?" Your answer may be: "Because I want to worship the Lord my God together with his people." You may also say: "I attend the worship services because the blood of Jesus shed for me has cleansed me from all my sins. I enter the very presence of God as a forgiven sinner cleansed by the blood of the Lamb."

Sermons about the blood of Jesus are few. Certainly on Good Friday pastors describe the suffering and death of Christ, and the people sing "Alas! and did my Savior bleed." But neither preacher nor parishioner dwells on the concept *Jesus' blood.* The thought of blood is too gruesome. The repulsiveness of blood causes us to turn to pleasantries instead, and thus we miss the message of Jesus' "blood that *speaks* a better word than the blood of Abel" (italics added).

What is the message of the blood? It tells me that Jesus removed the curse, lifted the burden of guilt, and forgave my sins. It assures me that I have peace with God and that I have been set free to live a life of obedience. It tells me that God loved me so much that he had his Son die for me.

I go to church not to hear a theological lecture or to receive some pastoral advice on how to avoid conflict, but to learn that the blood of Jesus daily speaks to me and brings me the message of salvation. I have been delivered from the bondage of sin because of Jesus' blood. Throughout the week, but especially on Sundays, I am reminded of the words of an Italian hymn, translated by Edward Caswall,

> Grace and life eternal
> In that blood I find;
> Blest be his compassion,
> Infinitely kind!

Greek Words, Phrases, and Constructions in 12:22–24

Verse 22

ὄρει καὶ πόλει—in this passage (vv. 22–24) the author omits the definite articles before the nouns to stress their characteristics and qualities instead of categorical designations. The noun πόλει stands in apposition to ὄρει and describes permanence. The datives are the dative of place.

Verse 23

ἀπογεγραμμένων ἐν οὐρανοῖς—the noun ἀπογραφή appears in Luke 2:2 and Acts 5:37, where it means "census." Derived from the compound verb ἀπογράφω (I register), the perfect passive participle shows that the registration has taken place and that its effect continues to remain valid. Note the use of the plural οὐρανοῖς (see also 1:10; 4:14; 7:26; 8:1; 9:23; 12:25).

καὶ κριτῇ θεῷ πάντων—word order rules that the translation should be "and to a judge who is God of all" (RSV) instead of "to God, the judge of all" (NIV). Arguments for one or the other translation divide commentators and translators. For the phrase *judge of all,* see Genesis 18:25.

τετελειωμένων—the perfect tense in the passive participle from τελειόω (I complete) discloses lasting effect. This is the last time the writer uses a form (noun, verb, or adjective) from this verb family. The perfect tense appears in three verses (7:28; 10:14; 12:23).

Verse 24

νέας—in preceding passages (8:8, 13; 9:15), the writer described the covenant as καινή. Here it is νέα. Writes R. C. Trench, "νέος refers to time, καινός to the thing."[48] The covenant that is καινή originates in the old covenant, whereas the covenant that is νέα can be described as recent.

ῥαντισμοῦ—literally translated, the expression is "to the blood of sprinkling." The noun occurs twice in the New Testament (Heb. 12:24; I Peter 1:2). Of the six instances the verb ῥαντίζω (I sprinkle) appears in the New Testament, four are in Hebrews (9:13, 19, 21; 10:22).

---

4. Apply the Prophecy 12:25–27

The Epistle to the Hebrews displays one overriding characteristic: contrast. At times the author employs the comparison "how much more" or "how much less" (see, for instance, 9:14; 12:9). In this particular passage he contrasts earth with heaven, the old revelation with the new revelation, and "they" and "them" with "we" and "us."

25. See to it that you do not refuse him who speaks. If they did not escape when they refused him who warned them on earth, how much less will we, if we turn away from him who warns us from heaven?

Note that the writer addresses three groups of people: you (the readers), they (the Israelites), and we (the author and the readers).

a. Throughout this epistle, the warning against turning a deaf ear to God has sounded clearly in the ears of the addressees. Think, for example, of the direct warning: "See to it, brothers, that none of you has a sinful, unbelieving heart that turns away from the living God" (3:12). This admonition has been repeated in various forms in the letter, and every time it calls the readers to pay close attention.

The writer does not accuse the readers of rebellion. He does not say that they are guilty of refusing to listen to God's voice. Rather, he addresses them pastorally and exhorts them to heed the Word of God when they hear it. He reminds them of how the Israelites died in the desert.

b. Avoiding details, the author selects a few key words to describe the plight of the Israelites. They received their just punishment when they rebelled against God (2:2; 3:16–19; 4:2; 10:28). They could not escape when they refused to heed God's warnings. The time came when God pronounced the verdict that every person who was twenty years old and older would die

---

48. Trench, *Synonyms of the New Testament,* p. 225. The French language makes the distinction between novelty and new: "une invention est *nouvelle,* une expression *neuve*" (Trench's italics).

in the desert (Num. 14:29). Escape was impossible. As God's representative, Moses had warned the Israelites repeatedly, but they had repudiated the spoken word. They failed to realize that rejecting God's Word is tantamount to rejecting God.[49] If then history reveals the dire consequences of Israel's rebellion in the desert, how much less will we escape?

c. The author includes himself in the comparison. He conveys the thought in the form of a condition, "if we turn away from him who warns us from heaven" (see 10:26 for a similar inclusion). If we do not listen to the voice of Jesus who warns us from heaven, escape is even less possible than it was for the Israelites. The contrast is between the piecemeal revelation of God, communicated to the people by Moses on earth, and the full revelation in Jesus Christ that "was first announced by the Lord" (Heb. 2:3). Indeed, "how shall we escape if we ignore such a great salvation?" Jesus continues to speak to his people through his servants, the ministers of the gospel, for "in these last days [God] has spoken [and continues to speak] to us by his Son" (1:2).

26. At that time his voice shook the earth, but now he has promised, "Once more I will shake not only the earth but also the heavens."

Again the writer reminds the readers of the experience at Mount Sinai. From numerous places throughout the Old Testament Scriptures, they learned that the shaking of the mountains when God gave his people the Decalogue was an extraordinary event.[50] The speaker obviously is God, whose voice shook the mountain and made the people tremble with fear. But the same voice also utters a promise that has recurring and lasting significance. Through the prophet Haggai, God spoke to the Israelites concerning the rebuilt temple and said, "In a little while I will once more shake the heavens and the earth, the sea and the dry land. I will shake all nations, and the desired of all nations will come, and I will fill this house with glory" (2:6–7). From the literature of the Jewish rabbis, we learn that this particular passage was considered to be messianic.[51]

The prophet predicted a shaking of the heavens and the earth. The writer transposes the terms *heaven* and *earth* to show the sequence of the effect of Christ's work. The earth shook when Jesus died and when he arose (Matt. 27:51; 28:2), but more importantly the preaching of the gospel and the outpouring of the Holy Spirit shook the entire world. The heavens also experienced change: the angelic hosts sing Christ's praises (Rev. 5:12); angels rejoice when one sinner repents (Luke 15:10); angels are sent out to minister to the needs of the believers on earth (Heb. 1:14); and angels long to look

49. Hagner, *Hebrews,* p. 216. Because the writer of Hebrews uses the expression *on earth,* he seems to say that it was Moses who warned the Israelites. This is the view, for instance, of Moffatt, *Hebrews,* p. 220, and Hugh Montefiore, *The Epistle to the Hebrews* (New York and Evanston: Harper and Row, 1964), p. 234. Some commentators, including Bruce, *Hebrews,* p. 381, assert that God is the speaker. Apart from the divine appearance at Mount Sinai, God speaks to the people through Moses.

50. Consult Exod. 19:18; Judges 5:4–5; Ps. 68:7–8; 77:18; 114:4, 7.

51. See the *Talmud,* Sanhedrin 97b, p. 659; SB, vol. 3, p. 749; Kistemaker, *Psalm Citations,* p. 54.

into the mystery of salvation (Eph. 3:10; I Peter 1:12). It is Christ, therefore, who is at the center of this upheaval on earth and in heaven. He will cause heaven and earth to shake when he appears a second time (Matt. 24:29; II Peter 3:10).

27. The words "once more" indicate the removing of what can be shaken—that is, created things—so that what cannot be shaken may remain.

Every now and then, the writer provides somewhat of a commentary on Old Testament quotations he cites. Here he lifts out the expression *once more* and explains it by saying that created things can be shaken and thus are temporary. They will be removed. Permanent things are those that cannot be shaken.

What kind of a commentary is this? In fact, the reader needs a commentary on the author's explanation before he is able to understand the intent. First, the writer comments on the entire quotation from Haggai 2:6, not just the expression *once more.* Next, in the original Greek he reminds the reader that he used the term *removing* earlier (7:12), where it is translated as "change." "For when there is a change of the priesthood, there must also be a change of the law." An example, then, of temporary things is the Levitical priesthood that came to an end when it was replaced by the eternal priesthood of Christ. Also, the prophet Isaiah foresees the end of this present world when he transmits what the Sovereign Lord says: "Behold, I will create new heavens and a new earth. The former things will not be remembered, nor will they come to mind" (65:17; also see 66:22). And last, the only things that survive this world are those that are unshakable and eternal. The kingdom of Jesus Christ cannot be shaken.

Greek Words, Phrases, and Constructions in 12:25–27

Verse 25

βλέπετε—the present active imperative, second person plural of βλέπω (I see) introduces a negative command.

παραιτήσησθε—the negative particle μή with the aorist passive subjunctive from παραιτέομαι (I reject, refuse) denotes a command not to begin to reject God. By contrast, μή with a present imperative implies that an action that must be stopped is already in progress.

τὸν λαλοῦντα—the present active participle preceded by the definite article in the masculine accusative singular refers to God (see Heb. 1:1–2). The present tense signifies repeated and continued speech. Attention is drawn to the fact that God speaks (λαλεῖν), not to the content of his words, for then the verb λέγειν is used.[52]

εἰ—this particle introduces a simple fact condition that expresses reality. To make the reality even more certain and vivid, the author writes the negative particle οὐκ (not). Normal usage demands the word μή.

---

52. Trench, *Synonyms of the New Testament,* p. 287.

ἐξέφυγον—the compound form intensifies the meaning of the verb φεύγω (I flee). The aorist tense reveals single occurrence.

ἐπὶ γῆς—this prepositional phrase has its counterpart in ἀπ' οὐρανῶν and relates to the present active participle χρηματίζοντα. The participle is understood in the second part of the verse.

ἀποστρεφόμενοι—from ἀποστρέφω (I turn away), the participle is in the present middle and denotes condition: "if we turn away."

Verse 26

τότε, νῦν δέ—contrast is the author's penchant. Here it is the *then* over against the *now*.

ἐπήγγελται—the perfect middle from ἐπαγγέλλομαι (I promise) connotes that the promise, although made in the past, is valid for the present. Therefore, the writer introduces the verb with the phrase νῦν δέ.

Verse 27

τὸ δέ—the neuter nominative singular article takes the quotation ἔτι ἅπαξ as its noun (see also Eph. 4:9). The writer has commented on quotations in numerous places (see 2:8–9; 3:15; 4:3–7; 10:8–10).

μετάθεσιν—derived from the verb μετατίθημι (I change), the word has a -σις ending that signifies process.

ὡς πεποιημένων—this phrase is actually an explanatory note. The particle ὡς means "that is," and the perfect passive participle is in apposition to σαλευομένων, which is the present passive participle.

---

5. Worship God
12:28–29

The last two verses of the chapter flow forth from the immediately preceding paragraph. At the same time, however, they form the conclusion.

28. Therefore, since we are receiving a kingdom that cannot be shaken, let us be thankful, and so worship God acceptably with reverence and awe.

What a statement! "We are receiving a kingdom." If there is a kingdom, there is also a king. And a king makes his rule known to his subjects, for they are part of the kingdom. We are receiving the governing rule, the administration, so to speak, of Jesus Christ. The writer of Hebrews already mentioned that we have come "to Jesus the mediator of a new covenant" (12:24). That covenant relation becomes reality when we receive the kingdom, the rule of Christ. As a trustworthy saying has it, "If we endure, we will also reign" with Christ (II Tim. 2:12). That is not at all surprising, for both the Old Testament and the New reveal that "the saints of the Most High will receive the kingdom and will possess it forever" (Dan. 7:18; see also Rev. 1:6; 5:10). Jesus confers a kingdom on us and grants us the honor of sitting on thrones (Luke 22:29–30; Rev. 20:4–6).

The kingdom we receive is unshakable; it remains forever; it is eternal (Dan. 7:14). Those in the kingdom, then, cannot be shaken, remain forever, and partake of eternity. The privileges Christ grants his people are unbelievably rich. God told the Israelites at Mount Sinai that if they kept his covenant, they would be for him "a kingdom of priests and a holy nation" (Exod. 19:5–6). That kingdom, however, came to an end because it was temporary. How different for us, the New Testament believers, who are in the new covenant! We receive "a kingdom that cannot be shaken."

Moreover, we are in the process of receiving an unshakable kingdom. Jesus taught us to pray for the coming of his kingdom (Matt. 6:10; Luke 11:2). His kingdom is here; at the same time we admit that it has not yet come. Hence we pray the well-known petition of the Lord's Prayer, "your kingdom come."

Because of the royal recognition we receive, we are exhorted to give thanks—"let us be thankful." The literal translation of this clause is, "let us have grace."[53] However, usage indicates that the words *have grace* form an idiomatic expression that means "give thanks."[54] Luke uses this idiom in relating the parable of the farmer and his servant (Luke 17:9), and Paul employs it in his pastoral Epistles (I Tim. 1:12; II Tim. 1:3).

Let us live a life of thankfulness, says the author of Hebrews, and by doing so let us worship God. Giving thanks in word and deed and worshiping God are two sides of the same coin. Worship is not limited to a formal worship service on Sunday. Horatius Bonar understood this when he wrote,

So shall no part of day or night
From sacredness be free,
But all my life, in every step,
Be fellowship with Thee.

How do we worship God acceptably? The writer reminds us of Enoch who walked with God, pleased him, and was commended for his faith (11:5; also see 13:21). Our worship must be pleasing to God on the one hand, and on the other we must approach him with reverence and awe (5:7). And the reason for serving God with reverence and fear is expressed in the concluding verse of this chapter.

29. For our God is a consuming fire.

These words were spoken by Moses when he exhorted the Israelites not to serve idols. "For the LORD your God is a consuming fire, a jealous God" (Deut. 4:14; see also 9:3). Even though Christ has granted us unusual privileges, we must be aware of God's awesomeness and holiness. Therefore we worship him with reverence and awe.

---

53. This is the translation in the KJV, NKJV, RV, and ASV. The JB has "let us therefore hold on to the grace"; and the NAB, "we . . . should hold fast to God's grace."

54. With variations, numerous translations have this reading. Consult John Brown, *An Exposition of Hebrews* (Edinburgh: Banner of Truth Trust, 1961), p. 668. Also see Bauer, p. 878.

Practical Considerations in 12:28–29

The author of Hebrews tells us to worship God acceptably with reverence and awe. But if we take note of worship conducted throughout the world, we conclude that God cannot be averse to variety because he is worshiped in numerous ways. This observation is correct only inasmuch as we worship God in harmony with his Word.

The Word of God ought to take the central place in a worship service, for through the reading and the preaching of his Word God makes his will known to his people. The sermon, then, is the main part of worship. God speaks, and we listen. Preaching must be the proclamation of God's Word and should never be replaced by discourses on unrelated topics. The preacher as Christ's ambassador delivers the message his sender has entrusted to his care. When preaching takes place, God's people worship.

Greek Words, Phrases, and Constructions in 12:28–29

Verse 28

βασιλείαν—without the definite article the noun expresses the qualities and characteristics of the kingdom.

ἀσάλευτον—as a verbal adjective the word modifies the noun βασιλείαν, expresses inability, and serves as a passive.

παραλαμβάνοντες—this present active participle must be understood in the causal sense. The present indicates continued action.

ἔχωμεν . . . λατρεύωμεν—although textual evidence supports either the indicative or the subjunctive reading, the context favors the subjunctive which then is translated as a hortatory subjunctive.

Verse 29

καὶ γάρ—five times the author uses this combination to show emphasis (4:2; 5:12; 10:34; 12:29; 13:22).

καταναλίσκον—a present active participle from the compound verb κατά (down) and ἀναλίσκω (I consume, destroy). The compound exhibits intensity.

Summary of Chapter 12

This is a chapter of exhortations, commands, and applications. It is a rather practical chapter in which the pastor exhorts us, the believers, to live a Christian life. In his own direct manner, the writer exhorts us to stimulate our Christian hope by enduring hardship and affliction. He begins by encouraging us to exercise perseverance, to look to Jesus, to struggle against sin, to submit to discipline, and to overcome weakness.

He encourages us to pursue peace and holiness and warns us against apostasy, immorality, and godlessness. Esau serves as an example, for as Isaac's first-born he should have received the birthright with its spiritual implications. Instead he despised this right and consequently rejected God.

Before he continues to write about the subject of apostasy, the author contrasts the fear and dread of the Israelites who received the law at Mount Sinai with the joy and perfection of believers who come to the city of God at Mount Zion.

Once again he exhorts us to listen to the voice of God. Failure to heed his Word results in punishment. As the Israelites who rejected God did not escape, so we who have God's revelation through Jesus will not escape if we fall away.

Therefore, the writer says, we ought to live thankful lives because we are part of the everlasting kingdom of Jesus Christ. By living thankfully, we serve God in acceptable worship with deep respect and veneration.

13

Admonitions and Exhortations, *part 2*

13:1–25

Outline

13:1–6	C.	Communal Obligations
	D.	Ecclesiastical Duties
13:7–8		1. Remember Your Leaders
13:9–11		2. Avoid Strange Teaching
13:12–16		3. Strive for Holiness
13:17		4. Obey Your Leaders
13:18–21	E.	Prayers and Benedictions
13:22–25	F.	Final Greetings

13 1 Keep on loving each other as brothers. 2 Do not forget to entertain strangers,
for by so doing some people have entertained angels without knowing it.
3 Remember those in prison as if you were their fellow prisoners, and those who
are mistreated as if you yourselves were suffering.
4 Marriage should be honored by all, and the marriage bed kept pure, for God will judge
the adulterer and all the sexually immoral. 5 Keep your lives free from the love of money
and be content with what you have, because God has said,

"Never will I leave you;
never will I forsake you."

6 So we say with confidence,

"The Lord is my helper; I will not be afraid.
What can man do to me?"

C. Communal Obligations 13:1–6

The sequence of exhortations which the author began in the preceding chapter continues. Some commentators are of the opinion that the exhortations in this section are unrelated.[1] Others see the hand of a literary artist at work in the construction of this passage.[2] The writer mentions the topic *love* in its expression in society: among the brothers, for strangers, for prisoners, and for the underprivileged. The second topic concerns the home, in which marriage and morality are upheld; and the third subject is contentment based on confidence in God.

1. Keep on loving each other as brothers. 2. Do not forget to entertain strangers, for by so doing some people have entertained angels with-

---

1. James Moffatt refers to them as "a handful of moral counsels." See his *Epistle to the Hebrews*, International Critical Commentary series (Edinburgh: Clark, 1963), p. 224. Looking at the entire chapter, Donald Guthrie labels its content "a series of apparently disconnected exhortations and other incidental teaching." See his commentary on *The Letter to the Hebrews*, Tyndale New Testament Commentary series (Grand Rapids: Eerdmans, 1983), p. 266.

2. Otto Michel, *Der Brief an die Hebräer*, 10th ed. (Göttingen: Vandenhoeck and Ruprecht, 1957), pp. 328–29. Michel detects four sets of admonitions: showing brotherly love and hospitality (vv. 1–2), visiting prisoners and those who are mistreated (v. 3), honoring marriage and wedding vows (v. 4), avoiding greed and fostering contentment (vv. 5–6). Albert Vanhoye, in "La question littéraire de Hébreux 13:1–6" (*NTS* 23 [1977]: 121–39), sees a much more elaborate threefold structure in the first six verses (vv. 1–3, 4, 5–6).

out knowing it. 3. Remember those in prison as if you were their fellow prisoners, and those who are mistreated as if you yourselves were suffering.

The practical application of Christian love in the context of the society in which the readers lived is fourfold.

a. In the Christian community brothers and sisters care for one another, and a spirit of brotherly love and affection prevails. In a world rife with hostility against the Christian church, love for each other within the community needs constant encouragement. B. F. Westcott makes this telling observation: "The love of the Jew for his fellow Jew, his 'brother,' was national: the Christian's love for his fellow-Christian is catholic. The tie of the common faith is universal."[3] Christians recognize each other as brothers and sisters in the Lord, for together they form the worldwide community of believers. The writers of the New Testament repeatedly admonish the Christians to cultivate brotherly love (Rom. 12:10; I Thess. 4:9; Heb. 13:1; I Peter 1:22; II Peter 1:7). To express the concept *brotherly love,* they use the word *philadelphia.* The members of the church in Philadelphia in effect demonstrated this love (Rev. 3:7–13).

b. The writer of Hebrews counsels the readers to extend their love from their own circle to all men. They are to entertain strangers; that is, by opening their homes to travelers, they show the love of Christ. In ancient times, hotels as we know them today were nonexistent, and the inns had the reputation of being unsafe.[4] Travelers were dependent on local residents to provide lodging and offer hospitality.

The readers of Hebrews have apparently become indifferent to the needs of the traveler; however, the writer exhorts them to be mindful of their fellow man who needs a roof over his head. He reminds them of Abraham, Lot, Gideon, and the parents of Samson, who entertained angels (Gen. 18:1–15; 19:1–22; Judges 6:11–23; 13:3–21). Providing food and accommodation for a stranger is an act of kindness. Furthermore, Christians who entertain a stranger in their own home have an opportunity to introduce him to the gospel of Christ. If the traveler accepts Christ in faith, he will spread the good news along the way.

Providing hospitality was considered a virtue in the first-century Christian church. In his letter to the Romans, Paul writes, "Practice hospitality" (12:13). And in his pastoral Epistles Paul stipulates that an overseer in the church must be hospitable (I Tim. 3:2; Titus 1:8; also see I Peter 4:9) and that among their good deeds widows must be able to list hospitality (I Tim. 5:10).[5]

c. "Remember those in prison as if you were their fellow prisoners." Earlier in his epistle, the writer commends the readers for their loving care of

3. B. F. Westcott, *Commentary on the Epistle to the Hebrews* (Grand Rapids: Eerdmans, 1950), p. 429.

4. "It is common knowledge that inns existed in Greek times and throughout the period of the Roman empire. Generally they were considered bad, the traveler being subject not only to discomfort, but also robbery and even death." Robert C. Stone, "Inn," *ZPEB,* vol. 3, p. 280.

5. Hans Bietenhard, *NIDNTT,* vol. 1, p. 690.

prisoners (10:34). Visiting prisoners was a common practice in ancient times. Jesus refers to it in his discourse on the sheep and the goats: "I was in prison and you came to visit me" (Matt. 25:39, 43). And Luke writes about Paul's imprisonment in Caesarea and in Rome (Acts 24:23; 28:16). Paul was given much freedom, was allowed to have his own rented house in Rome, "and welcomed all who came to see him" (Acts 28:30).

Prisoners depended on relatives and friends to provide food, clothing, and other necessities. The numerous references to Paul's experiences as a prisoner reveal that his friends came to take care of his needs (Acts 24:23; 27:3; 28:10, 16, 30; Phil. 4:12; II Tim. 1:16; 4:13, 21). Prisoners, then, had to be remembered; otherwise they suffered hunger, thirst, cold, and loneliness.

Travelers came to the homes of the recipients of Hebrews and received hospitality. By contrast, the author now admonishes his readers to leave their homes, go to the prisoners, and empathize with them. The writer tells them to take care of these prisoners "as if you were their fellow prisoners." Show them the love of Christ by ministering to their needs!

d. The last exhortation is to remember the people who are mistreated. The words remind us of another passage: "Sometimes you were publicly exposed to insult and persecution; at other times you stood side by side with those who were so treated" (10:33). The admonition need not refer only to what the readers of Hebrews had done in the past. The suffering of the underprivileged is universal. Does the author leave the impression that the unity of the Christians is all-important? A more literal translation of the text—remember "those who are ill-treated, since you yourselves also are in the body" (NASB)—perhaps supports this interpretation. And a cross-reference to Paul's discourse on the unity of the body of Christ points in that direction (I Cor. 12:26). However, it is better to think especially of the physical body, because mistreatment pertains to physical suffering. Therefore, the translation "as if you yourselves were suffering" is appropriate.

The admonitions to extend a helping hand to the stranger, the traveler, the prisoner, and the sufferer actually are exhortations to fulfill the command to "love your neighbor as yourself" (Lev. 19:18; Matt. 22:39; Mark 12:33; Luke 10:27; Rom. 13:9; Gal. 5:14; James 2:8).

4. Marriage should be honored by all, and the marriage bed kept pure, for God will judge the adulterer and all the sexually immoral.

From the second part of the summary of the law ("Love your neighbor as yourself"), the writer proceeds to the commandment "You shall not commit adultery" (Exod. 20:14; Deut. 5:18). Moreover, he moves from the social sphere to the private circle of husband and wife. Love for the neighbor, whoever he may be, most effectively flows forth from a home in which husband and wife work together in mutual love. When marriage is honored in the home, love emanates to society in numerous ways. For this reason the author stresses the necessity of maintaining the sanctity of married life.

In the New Testament nearly every writer discusses marriage, because a stable marriage is a building block in the structure of society. Also, in this chapter of exhortations, the author of Hebrews instructs the readers concerning holy living within the bonds of marriage.[6] He is actually saying, "Let marriage be precious to all of you." Marriage is a treasure we receive from God who has instituted it. Therefore, marriage must be honored by all.

The clause "and the marriage bed kept pure" is a euphemism. The author warns the people not to break the marriage vow by committing adultery. Marriage is sacred, and defilement of it is sin. Why is having sexual relations outside the bonds of matrimony sin? Here is the answer: "God will judge the adulterer and all the sexually immoral."

The world in which we live considers loose living inconsequential: sex is fun, not sin. But in God's eyes illicit sex is sin that deserves punishment.[7] The writer of Hebrews clearly speaks to offenders and warns them of God's judgment (10:30–31). What kind of punishment does God administer? Scripture says that "neither the sexually immoral nor idolaters nor adulterers nor male prostitutes nor homosexual offenders . . . will inherit the kingdom of God" (I Cor. 6:9–10; Eph. 5:5; Rev. 21:8; 22:15). They perish in their sin. Christians, then, must set the example of living sexually pure lives (I Thess. 4:7) and keep the commandment "You shall not commit adultery."

5a. Keep your lives free from the love of money and be content with what you have.

The next commandments in the Decalogue are "You shall not steal" and "You shall not covet" (Exod. 20:15, 17; Deut. 5:19, 21). In a sense the commandments to which the author alludes are closely related; they uncover man's desire for someone's wife, possessions, and property.[8] The Christian must uproot "the love of money," because it leads to all kinds of evil (I Tim. 6:10). Paul counsels Timothy in these pithy words, "But godliness with contentment is great gain" (I Tim. 6:6). And he himself confesses: "I have learned to be content whatever the circumstances. I know what it is to be in need, and I know what it is to have plenty. I have learned the secret of being content" (Phil. 4:11–12). Certainly Scripture does not teach that the Christian ought to seek a life of poverty. God told Adam to fill the earth and subdue it (Gen. 1:28), but he warns man against the *love* of money, for that attitude leads to greed, and greed is idolatry (Col. 3:5).

5b. Because God has said,

> **"Never will I leave you;**
> **never will I forsake you."**

---

6. In the original Greek the verb *to be* is to be supplied in the first part of verse 4. Some translations supply the indicative verb *is* ("Marriage is honorable," KJV, NKJV, NEB); others have the translation "Let marriage be held in honor" or a variant (RSV, ASV, NASB, NAB, JB, MLB, GNB, NIV). The latter is preferred because the general context has many verbs in the imperative mood.

7. John Albert Bengel, *Gnomon of the New Testament,* ed. Andrew R. Fausset, 7th ed., 5 vols. (Edinburgh: Clark, 1877), vol. 4, p. 494. Says Bengel, "He most of all punishes them, whom man does not punish."

8. Paul discloses that immoral people commit sexual sins, as well as sins of theft and greed (Rom. 1:26–29; I Cor. 5:10–11; 6:9–10; Eph. 5:3–5; Col. 3:5–6).

The choice is simple: either love the Lord your God or love money. "You cannot serve both God and Money" (Matt. 6:24; Luke 16:13). Instead of worshiping that which is created (money), Christians are exhorted to worship the Creator and to put their trust in him.

Introducing an Old Testament quotation with the words *God has said,* the author is true to form. For him God is the author of Scripture, and the voice that speaks is the voice of God. To find the exact wording of the quotation in the Old Testament, however, is not easy. Rather, the text itself appears in varying form in many places, and always signals God's faithfulness and assurance. Jacob fled from his brother Esau and in a dream heard God say to him, "I am with you . . . I will not leave you" (Gen. 28:15). Near the end of his life, Moses encouraged the Israelites and said, "For the LORD your God goes with you; he will never leave you nor forsake you" (Deut. 31:6, 8). When Joshua began his work as leader of the Israelites, God said, "I will never leave you nor forsake you" (Josh. 1:5). And last, when David instructed Solomon to build the temple, he encouraged him with these words, "Do not be afraid or discouraged, for the LORD God, my God, is with you. He will not fail you or forsake you" (I Chron. 28:20).[9]

I conclude that because of its frequent usage the quotation had become proverbial. In all probability, the words were part of the liturgy in the ancient synagogue and early church. The people, then, were quite familiar with this text.[10]

6. So we say with confidence,

> **"The Lord is my helper; I will not be afraid.**
> **What can man do to me?"**

Once again the author places himself on the same level with his readers, for together they confess their confidence and trust in God. They recite the words from Psalm 118:6 and do so courageously. For them the quotation is a confession of faith. If we look at the passages liturgically, we notice that in the Old Testament text in the preceding verse, God is the speaker. The testimony of faith in the lines from Psalm 118:6 is the response of the people. Apparently this psalm citation belonged to the liturgy of synagogue and church.[11] The New Testament writers frequently quote from this psalm,

---

9. The quotation coincides to a degree with the Septuagint (Deut. 31:6). The text of Heb. 13:5b, however, appears verbatim in Philo, *Confusion of Tongues* 166 (LCL). To say that the author of Hebrews borrowed the wording from Philo does not explain why Philo's version differs from the Septuagint. Interestingly, both Philo and the author of the epistle introduce the quotation with the information that God is the speaker.

10. In his *Commentary on the Epistle to the Hebrews,* 2 vols. (Edinburgh: Clark, 1877), vol. 2, p. 374, Franz Delitzsch writes, "We may rather conclude that, in the liturgical or homiletical usage of the Hellenistic synagogues, the passage Deut. 31:6 assumed this shape." Also see Simon J. Kistemaker, *The Psalm Citations in the Epistle to the Hebrews* (Amsterdam: Van Soest, 1961), p. 56; and Gerhard Kittel, *TDNT,* vol. 1, p. 465.

11. Ernst Werner, *The Sacred Bridge* (London: D. Dobson, 1959), p. 57. Compare Michel, *Hebräer,* p. 333.

interpret it christologically, and indicate that it served as a source of joy and happiness for God's people.

"What can man do to me?" Nothing, because the Lord is my helper. The forces of unbelief cannot do anything unless the Lord gives them permission. The believer, however, need not be afraid when God is on his side. The Scottish reformer John Knox fearlessly stood his ground against formidable opposition and said, "A man with God is always in the majority."

Practical Considerations in 13:1–6

Pastors living next door to the church building often receive visits from idle wanderers who look for a quick handout of money, food, or clothing. Should the pastor supply the necessities of life and show hospitality to the outcasts of society? Scripture teaches that the apostles did not think that it was right "to neglect the ministry of the Word of God" to take care of the needy (Acts 6:2). They appointed seven men and turned the responsibility of caring for the poor over to them.

Society today differs remarkably from that of the first century when prisoners could freely receive visitors. These prisoners depended on visitors to supply them with their daily needs. Today this is no longer the case. Certainly we should still visit prisoners. However, we ought to extend and expand the concept *prisoner* to include the shut-ins and the elderly who are confined to a bed, a hospital room, or a private home. These people welcome visits, treasure moments of fellowship, and are thankful for the attention they receive.

And last, in a world saturated with sex, the Christian who lives by the commandment "You shall not commit adultery" appears to be out of touch with reality. Not so. When God created man and woman, he set the rules for marital relations. And these rules have not been invalidated. God wants his people to make his commandment known in the society in which he has placed them. The apostles faced a sexually perverted world when they began to preach the gospel of salvation. They faithfully preached and taught the rules for wholesome living. That is one of the reasons that we read so much about marriage in the New Testament, for God's Word transformed society in the first century. It will do so again in our age. Keep the commandment, and live a pure and wholesome life!

Greek Words, Phrases, and Constructions in 13:1–6

Verse 2

φιλοξενίας—this noun and the preceding φιλαδελφία are related, for both have the same base as φίλος. Hospitality is the practical result of brotherly love. The genitive case depends on the main verb.

μὴ ἐπιλανθάνεσθε—the present middle imperative preceded by the negative particle μή discloses that the readers of the epistle had become lax in showing hospitality. They no longer provided shelter for the traveler.

ἔλαθόν τινες ξενίσαντες—a Greek idiom that reveals a transposition of words in

---

12. Bengel, *Gnomon*, vol. 5, p. 412. Also consult A. T. Robertson, *A Grammar of the Greek New Testament in the Light of Historical Research* (Nashville: Broadman, 1934), p. 551.

which the main idea is conveyed in the participle and the secondary thought in the verb. The phrase stands for λαθόντες ἐξένισαν.[12]

Verse 3

μιμνῄσκεσθε—the present middle imperative governs the genitive case of τῶν δεσμίων (the prisoners). Verbs of forgetting and remembering take a genitive case as direct object.

ἐν σώματι—because of the absence of the definite article, the author does not intimate that he refers to the members of the body of Christ. Rather he is thinking of the physical bodies of believers.

Verse 4

ἐν πᾶσιν—this adjective can be either masculine or neuter in the dative plural. Even though the neuter fits the context ("in all respects"),[13] translators prefer the masculine ("by all").

ὁ θεός—these words appear last in the sentence to receive emphasis.

Verse 5

ἀφιλάργυρος—a compound verbal adjective derived from ἀ (not), φίλος (friendly), and ἄργυρος (silver).

οὐ μή σε ἀνῶ—in this particular line five negatives appear. The Greek cannot express the idea any more forcefully. In English the lines from the well-known hymn "How Firm a Foundation" come close: "That soul, though all hell should endeavor to shake, I'll never, no never, no never forsake!"

Verse 6

ὥστε—with the accusative ἡμᾶς as subject of the present infinitive λέγειν, this is a result clause.

οὐ φοβηθήσομαι—in the future passive indicative from φοβέω (I fear), this form means "I shall not be afraid" in the durative sense.

---

7 Remember your leaders, who spoke the word of God to you. Consider the outcome of their way of life and imitate their faith. 8 Jesus Christ is the same yesterday and today and forever.

9 Do not be carried away by all kinds of strange teachings. It is good for our hearts to be strengthened by grace, not by ceremonial foods, which are of no value to those who eat them. 10 We have an altar from which those who minister at the tabernacle have no right to eat.

11 The high priest carries the blood of animals into the Most Holy Place as a sin offering, but the bodies are burned outside the camp. 12 And so Jesus also suffered outside the city gate to make the people holy through his own blood. 13 Let us, then, go to him outside the camp, bearing the disgrace he bore. 14 For here we do not have an enduring city, but we are looking for the city that is to come.

15 Through Jesus, therefore, let us continually offer to God a sacrifice of praise—the fruit of lips that confess his name. 16 And do not forget to do good and to share with others, for with such sacrifices God is pleased.

17 Obey your leaders and submit to their authority. They keep watch over you as men who

---

13. R. C. H. Lenski, *The Interpretation of the Epistle to the Hebrews and of the Epistle of James* (Columbus: Wartburg, 1946), p. 471.

must give an account. Obey them so that their work will be a joy, not a burden, for that would be of no advantage to you.

D. Ecclesiastical Duties 13:7–17

1. Remember Your Leaders 13:7–8

Three times in this chapter the author stresses the word *leaders*: "remember your leaders" (v. 7), "obey your leaders" (v. 17), and "greet all your leaders" (v. 24). In the first instance, the concept *leadership* is related to Jesus Christ himself.

7. Remember your leaders, who spoke the word of God to you. Consider the outcome of their way of life and imitate their faith. 8. Jesus Christ is the same yesterday and today and forever.

The author of Hebrews employs the verb Paul uses when he writes, "Remember Jesus Christ, raised from the dead, descended from David" (II Tim. 2:8). The verb means "call back to mind that which you know about a person." The writer exhorts his people to think of those leaders whom death has taken away. The expression *leader* is rather broad and somewhat vague, so that it fails to contribute anything to our understanding of the historical background of the Epistle to the Hebrews.[14] The word itself gives no assurance that the author had apostles in mind. That probability, however, is not excluded. Whether the author referred to Paul and Peter is speculation. What we do know is that the leaders "spoke the word of God" to the people. They were, then, preachers of the gospel of Jesus Christ and had been instrumental in building the church, that is, the body of Christ. These founding fathers had passed away, but the readers still remembered their labors.

The next command is to "consider the outcome of their way of life." The verb *consider* actually means to "look at again and again," to "observe carefully."[15] The author urges the people to look attentively at the lives these leaders lived and at the totality, that is, the result, of their lives. "Observe how they closed a well-spent life" (MLB). Look at their lives from beginning to end!

And the third command follows: "Imitate their faith." The writer wishes to leave the impression that these leaders were to be considered heroes of faith, similar to those listed in chapter 11. Follow in their footsteps; perform deeds of faith, and speak words of faith. We are not told whether these leaders suffered martyrdom. That is not the point. The readers of the epistle must imitate their faith. Faith is all-important. "We more easily contemplate

---

14. Clement of Rome and the writer of Hermas feature the expression (with a slight variation) in their writings. Consult I Clem. 1:3; 21:6; 44:5, *Apostolic Fathers,* vol. 1 (LCL); and Hermas, Visions, 2.2.6; 3.5.1; 3.9.7, *Apostolic Fathers,* vol. 2 (LCL).

15. Bauer, p. 54.

and admire the happy death of godly men than imitate the faith by which they have attained to it."[16]

In this fast-changing world, nothing seems dependable and permanent. Leaders come, and leaders go. One leader, however, is unchangeable: Jesus Christ. Says the author, "Jesus Christ is the same yesterday and today and forever." More sermons have been preached on this text than on any other verse from Hebrews, so that this verse almost has attained confessional status in the church.

First, note that the writer uses both names, "Jesus" and "Christ." The name *Jesus* embraces the work and word of God's Son on earth. He has come to save his people from their sin. The name *Christ* is the official title that expresses the divinity of the Son. The double name occurs only three times in Hebrews (10:10; 13:8, 21).

Next, not only Christ's divinity but also his changelessness the author explains in the first chapter of his epistle. For instance, quoting Psalm 102:27, he says, "But you remain the same, and your years will never end" (1:12; and see 7:24).

Furthermore, note the sequence of time: past, present, and future. The term *yesterday* relates to the mediatorial work of Jesus on earth, proclaimed and confirmed to the readers by those who heard him (2:3). The expression *today* refers to the intercessory work Jesus performs in heaven, where he represents the believer in God's presence (Rom. 8:34; Heb. 7:25; 9:24). And the word *forever* pertains to the priesthood of Christ. He is priest forever (5:6; 6:20; 7:17, 21, 24, 28).

For the readers of the epistle, Jesus is the same. That implies faith on the part of the believers, for they can depend on him because he remains true to himself. He is the first and the last, the one "who is, and who was, and who is to come, the Almighty" (Rev. 1:8).

Greek Words, Phrases, and Constructions in 13:7–8

Verse 7

τῶν ἡγουμένων—the definite article designates the group of leaders. The present tense of the middle participle (from ἡγέομαι, I lead) expresses the function of the leader. The noun ἡγόυμενος refers to a ruler (Sir. 17:17), prince (Sir. 41:17), governor (Acts 7:10), military leader (I Macc. 9:30), and spiritual leader (Acts 15:22).

οἵτινες—as an indefinite relative pronoun, the word connotes cause and description.

ἐλάλησαν—the aorist tense indicates action accomplished in the past. The verb λαλέω (I speak) depicts the mode of speech; the verb λέγω (I speak), its content.

ἀναθεωροῦντες—dependent on the main verb μιμεῖσθε (present middle imperative), this present active participle assumes the imperative mood. The compound

---

16. Bengel, *Gnomon,* vol. 4, p. 495.

can be either directive (to look up) or intensive (to look at again). The intensive is preferred.

Verse 8

ὁ αὐτός—with the definite article the intensive personal pronoun in the attributive position means "the same." The verb *to be* is understood in this short sentence.

---

2. Avoid Strange Teaching
13:9–11

At first glance, the exhortations and admonitions in this segment seem rather unrelated. However, the author reveals a definite sequence. Leaders proclaimed the word of God; they taught the gospel. And that word is as abiding as Jesus Christ is changeless. Therefore, do not depart from the doctrine of Christ.

9. Do not be carried away by all kinds of strange teachings. It is good for our hearts to be strengthened by grace, not by ceremonial foods, which are of no value to those who eat them.

Some of the readers were susceptible to teaching that was different from and contrary to the Word of God. Influenced by that teaching, they were "carried away," as the author says. We assume that this development had not yet become a great concern, for this is the only reference to it in the entire epistle. But because of the danger of drifting away from the moorings of the Christian faith, the writer warns the people against "all kinds of strange teachings." He does not say what these teachings are. However, from other parts of the New Testament, we learn that in the second half of the first century, traveling philosophers were influencing the people with teachings opposed to the apostolic doctrine. Paul warns the Ephesian elders to be on guard against savage wolves. Says he, "Even from your own number men will arise and distort the truth in order to draw away disciples after them" (Acts 20:30). And he rebukes the Galatians for "turning to a different gospel—which is really no gospel at all" (1:6–7). Then, he admonishes the Colossians to avoid being taken "captive through hollow and deceptive philosophy, which depends on human tradition and the basic principles of this world rather than on Christ" (2:8; compare Eph. 4:14). Moreover, these Colossians were told by some philosophers to observe self-imposed rules on food, drink, festivals, celebrations, worship, and discipline. Paul concludes, "These [rules] are all destined to perish with use, because they are based on human commands and teachings" (2:22).[17] These teachings, therefore, were varied and of foreign origin. To interpret the verse as a reference only to

---

17. For additional references to false teachings, consult Eph. 5:6; I Tim. 1:3–7; 4:1–3; 6:3–5; II Tim. 2:18; 4:3–4; Titus 3:9; II Peter 2:1–3, 9–22; II John 7–10; Jude 5–16; Rev. 2:2, 6, 14–16, 20–24.

Jewish law is unwarranted and contrary to the remainder of the verse that mentions "ceremonial foods."[18]

The contrast in the last half of the verse is between the spiritual and the material. "It is good for our hearts to be strengthened by grace, not by ceremonial foods, which are of no value to those who eat them." Grace is placed over against foods. Even though the term *grace* is not defined, we are not amiss in understanding it as the grace of God. Throughout his epistle the writer has spoken of this divine grace (2:9; 4:16; 10:29). He has even explained the term in the context of living peaceful and holy lives (12:14–15). The grace of God provides inner strength for the believer and benefits him spiritually.

But teachers of a strange philosophy think that by adhering to strict dietary regulations they are able to advance spiritually. The New International Version has rendered the last part of the verse somewhat freely, "by ceremonial foods, which are of no value to those who eat them." The original has only the noun *foods.*[19] Nevertheless, the general context allows for the explanatory adjective *ceremonial.* Also, the original has the reading "which are of no value to those who walk." That is, those who adhere to food regulations receive no benefit from them. And no wonder. Paul tells the Romans who are passing judgment on one another regarding eating habits, "Do not allow what you consider good to be spoken of as evil. For the kingdom of God is not a matter of eating and drinking, but of righteousness, peace and joy in the Holy Spirit" (14:16–17). To the Corinthians he writes, "But food does not bring us near to God; we are no worse if we do not eat, and no better if we do" (I Cor. 8:8). Philip Edgcumbe Hughes summarizes the matter cogently: "Food goes into the stomach for the strengthening of the body; but only *grace* strengthens *the heart,* that is, the vital center of man's being and personality and the source of his conduct and character."[20]

10. We have an altar from which those who minister at the tabernacle have no right to eat.

If in verse 9 the emphasis is on that which is spiritual, so much more is this the case in verse 10. The author of Hebrews speaks figuratively when he uses the word *altar.* It has a connotation that is different from the ordinary meaning of a structure made out of stones. In a sense, we do exactly the same thing when we say that at a meeting held in a stadium the evangelist extended the altar call. Now the term *altar call* in that setting has nothing to do with the altar. Rather it describes people who at the invitation of the evangelist come forward and make a decision to commit their lives to Christ.

---

18. F. F. Bruce writes, "The strange teaching which laid such insistence on food was probably some form of syncretistic gnosis, perhaps with Essene or quasi-Essene affinities." See his *Epistle to the Hebrews,* New International Commentary on the New Testament series (Grand Rapids: Eerdmans, 1964), p. 398.

19. Johannes Behm, *TDNT,* vol. 1, p. 643; Hans Kropatschek, *NIDNTT,* vol. 2, p. 268.

20. Philip Edgcumbe Hughes, *Commentary on the Epistle to the Hebrews* (Grand Rapids: Eerdmans, 1977), p. 574. His italics.

For the writer, the altar is the cross on which Jesus offered himself as a sacrifice to God.[21] And to the Christian the cross is a symbol that represents the completed work of redemption. As the author of Hebrews repeatedly confirms, Christ offered his sacrifice once for all (9:25, 26, 28; 10:9, 12, 14). The clause *we have an altar,* then, stands for the cross, which symbolizes the redemption Christ offers his people.

The second part of the verse—"from which those who minister at the tabernacles have no right to eat"—is open to interpretation. First, the reference is to the Levitical priests who were told to take the "hides, flesh and offal" of a bull and a goat and burn them outside the camp (Lev. 16:27). But this reference is too restrictive, for the phrase "those who minister at the tabernacle" seems to include all Jewish worshipers who came to the tabernacle. Note that the writer says *at,* not *in,* the tabernacle. Next, Christians could be accused of having no altar and hence no real religion.[22] But after the destruction, the Jews no longer had an altar either. Nevertheless, the writer of Hebrews can say, "We have an altar, that is, spiritually speaking, the cross of Jesus Christ." Then, does the author intimate that only Christians can partake of the holy elements at the celebration of Communion, from which Jews are excluded? If this is true, we in effect make the Christian communion table the equivalent of the altar. Certainly the believer partakes spiritually of the Lord's body and blood when he eats and drinks the holy elements. And the identification of the celebration of the Lord's Supper with the altar is most attractive. By doing so, however, we affirm that we have a visible and tangible altar. This is not what the author of Hebrews means. He places the sacrificial work of Christ over against the animal sacrifices of Old Testament times. In 13:10, when we consider it in the light of the entire epistle, the writer's intent is to show the superiority of Christ's work to that of the Aaronic priesthood.[23]

11. The high priest carries the blood of animals into the Most Holy Place as a sin offering, but the bodies are burned outside the camp.

Repetition is one of the trademarks of Hebrews. In earlier chapters the author writes about the Day of Atonement when the high priest sacrifices a bull and a goat and takes their blood into the inner sanctuary of the tabernacle (5:3; 7:27; 9:7). In his description of the duties performed on the Day of Atonement, the writer explains the purpose of these sacrifices. These

---

21. A. Snell, "We Have an Altar," *Reformed Theological Review* 23 (1964): 16–23. John Owen asserts, "The altar which we now have is *Christ alone,* and his sacrifice. For he was both priest, altar, and sacrifice, all in himself" (his italics). See his *Exposition of Hebrews,* 7 vols. in 4 (Evansville, Ind.: Sovereign Grace, 1960), vol. 7, p. 438.

22. Irenaeus, *Heresies* 4.17–18. Also consult Bruce, *Hebrews,* p. 400.

23. Donald Guthrie, *New Testament Theology* (Downers Grove, Ill.: Inter-Varsity, 1981), p. 781. Roman Catholic scholars identify the altar with the celebration of the Eucharist. Also, Michel advocates that the words *eat, body,* and *altar* can best be understood within the context of the Eucharistic liturgy. See his *Hebräer,* p. 343.

animals were slaughtered as a sin offering for the people. The removal of sin is the dominant feature of the religious duties the high priest and his helpers carried out on that special day.

The high priest offered a "bull for his own sin offering to make atonement for himself and his household" (Lev. 16:6). Then he sacrificed one goat as a sin offering for the people, and the other goat he sent away "into the desert as a scapegoat" (vv. 10, 22). He sprinkled the blood of the bull on the ark inside the Most Holy Place for his own sin and the blood of the goat for the sin of the people.

Sent into the desert, the live goat carried all the sins of the people (v. 22). The man who released the goat had to wash his clothes and take a bath before entering the camp (v. 26). The bodies of the bull and the goat had to be taken outside the camp and burned (v. 27). The person who burned the hides, flesh, and offal of these animals had to wash his clothes and take a bath before he could return to camp (v. 28). All this was done to point out that sin pollutes. The sacrifices themselves were considered polluted, even though the blood of these animals was sprinkled on the ark in the Most Holy Place. Hence, the priests were not allowed to eat the flesh of these sacrifices because these animals represented sin.

The implied contrast is that the sacrifice of Christ on the cross has removed sin once for all for all his people. By his death he ended the ceremonial rituals of the Day of Atonement, because he entered the heavenly sanctuary to represent the believer in the presence of God.

Practical Considerations in 13:9–11

Any gardener knows that after he has prepared his garden and has sown vegetable or flower seeds, the weed seeds germinate, grow, and develop much faster. Weeds flourish while the garden plants cope with setbacks of weather and disease.

This simple illustration aptly portrays the religious scene today. Evangelical churches are growing, but their growth seems insignificant compared with that of sects and cults. Sects have often been called "the unpaid bills of the Christian church." They prosper and develop; nothing seems to hinder them: they have their origin in Christianity, but they refuse to have anything to do with the church. Their message is no longer the direct teaching of the Old and New Testaments. Additional teaching or "revelation" is not only central; it also serves to reinterpret the Bible and is even called Scripture in some instances. Cults, of course, have their roots in movements other than the Christian faith. Adherents teach philosophies and modes of life that are unrelated and foreign to the Christian. Therefore, the admonition of the author of Hebrews is as relevant today as when he wrote it: "Do not be carried away by all kinds of strange teachings."

What then is basic? God's revealed Word stands forever. As Peter says, it is "the living and enduring word of God" (I Peter 1:23) that is preached. Furthermore, throughout the centuries the Holy Spirit has led the church in understanding God's truth revealed in Scripture. Differences do exist and doctrinal emphases vary, but those believers who hold to the historic Christian faith confess that their faith is rooted in God's abiding and changeless Word. Christians form the body of the Lord Jesus Christ and find their common unity in him. Anticipating differences of opinion in the church, Paul writes to the Philippians and to us, "All of us who are mature should take such a view of things. And if on some point you think differently, that too God will make clear to you" (3:15).

Greek Words, Phrases, and Constructions in 13:9–11

Verse 9

ξέναις—as an adjective in the dative plural modifying the noun διδαχαῖς (teachings), it relates to something that is new, in the sense of foreign (see Acts 17:18). The dative case is the dative of means.

μὴ παραφέρεσθε—the present passive imperative preceded by the negative particle μή shows that some people were indeed being carried away by strange teachings. The present tense is iterative; that is, the phenomenon occurred more often.

οἱ περιπατοῦντες—from the verb περιπατέω (I walk), the present active participle with the definite article represents a group of people other than the readers of the epistle. In context the term is idiomatic and can best be paraphrased in translation.

Verse 11

ζῴων—this noun in the genitive plural (from ζῷον, animal) is preceded by the relative pronoun ὧν. The word itself is unique in referring to the animals (bull and goat) that were sacrificed on the Day of Atonement.

περί—the sequence of the prepositions is noteworthy in this verse: περί (for; almost in the sense of "for the sake"), εἰς (into), and διά (by, through [agency]).

κατακαίεται—the use of the compound verb is to stress the intensive idea (to consume, burn up). The present tense in this verb with the preceding εἰσφερέται is a literary device of the author (compare 9:6–7).

---

3. Strive for Holiness
13:12–16

Paragraph divisions are somewhat difficult to determine, as a cursory comparison of translations reveals. Whatever the division, the flow of thought from verses 9–16 is continuous. I have separated verses 9–11 from 12–16 to emphasize the theme of holiness.

12. And so Jesus also suffered outside the city gate to make the people holy through his own blood.

On the basis of the preceding verse the author of Hebrews makes a comparison. He compares the implied purpose of the sacrifices made on the Day of Atonement to the suffering Jesus experienced on the cross. As he explains in earlier parts of his epistle, Jesus' sacrifice is once for all and incomparably superior. To speak, then, of a parallel in these verses is only partly accurate; only the phrase *outside the city gate* is equivalent to "outside the camp." The comparison in general points to Jesus' work to make his people holy.

The writer assumes that the readers are fully acquainted with the gospel. In his epistle he seldom alludes to Jesus' life on earth (5:7–8; 10:12; 12:2). Here he describes the place where Jesus suffered—outside the city of Jerusalem. He writes that Jesus suffered; he implies the agony Jesus endured on Calvary's cross.

The high priest annually entered the Most Holy Place, sprinkled animal blood, and atoned for the sin of the people. Jesus became sin for us (II Cor. 5:21), bore the curse that rested upon us (Gal. 3:13), and according to the law was condemned to die outside the city gate (John 19:17–18).[24] For instance, the son of the Israelite woman who blasphemed the name of the Lord had to be taken outside the camp, and the people were to stone him to death (Lev. 24:11–16, 23; also see Num. 15:35). Achan was taken outside the camp to the valley of Achor where the Israelites stoned him (Josh. 7:24–26; cf. Acts 7:58).[25] Because of man's sin, Jesus had to suffer outside the city gate where he endured God's wrath.

Outside the city gate of Jerusalem, Jesus paid for our sins by suffering the agony of hell on the cross when he cried, "My God, my God, why have you forsaken me?" (Matt. 27:46; Mark 15:34). Through the shedding of his blood, Jesus removed the sin of his people and made them holy. That is, by fulfilling the stipulations concerning the removal of sin on the Day of Atonement (Lev. 16:26–28), Jesus cleansed his people and sanctified them. The author of Hebrews briefly summarizes the purpose of Jesus' suffering: "to make the people holy through his own blood." In many places he has explained this point and therefore has no need to elaborate on it now (see 2:11; 10:10, 14; 12:14).

13. Let us, then, go to him outside the camp, bearing the disgrace he bore. 14. For here we do not have an enduring city, but we are looking for the city that is to come.

Statement after statement in this particular section is conclusive ("and so," v. 12; "then," v. 13; "for," v. 14; "therefore," v. 15). On the basis of this teach-

---

24. If Golgotha is located at the present-day cemetery where, according to tradition, Jesus was crucified, we can see an interesting confirmation of the parallel "outside the city gate" and "outside the camp." Michel, *Hebräer,* p. 345. However, we cannot be absolutely certain about the location of Golgotha.

25. Bruce, in his commentary on Hebrews (p. 403), makes the interesting observation that because the people worshiped the golden calf, sin had defiled the camp of the Israelites. Moses, therefore, would pitch a tent outside the camp where God would meet him and speak to him face to face (Exod. 33:7–11). Hughes also mentions this incident. See his *Hebrews,* p. 581. And consult Helmut Koester, "Outside the Camp: Hebrews 13:9–14," *HTR* 55 (1962): 299–315.

ing in general and the message of the preceding verses in particular, the author exhorts the readers to go to Jesus "outside the camp."

First, we look at the exhortation from a Jewish point of view. The Jewish Christian must leave the family structure in which he learned the precepts and commandments, the ceremonies and traditions, the prejudice and pride of the Jew. He is asked to go to Jesus upon whom the Jewish people invoked God's curse by hanging him on a cross (Deut. 21:23). To go to one who bears the curse of God is to share "the disgrace he bore."[26] By choosing for Christ, the Jew rejects Judaism and thus faces expulsion, alienation, and at times persecution. The author of Hebrews reminds the readers of the suffering, public insult, and persecution they had endured in earlier days when they became Christians (10:33).

Next, every reader is exhorted to go to Jesus who was cursed by God, because through Jesus we have access to God.[27] We identify with him, for through him we are made holy (Isa. 52:11; Ezek. 20:41; II Cor. 6:17). He bore disgrace to set us free from the guilt of sin and to remove the curse from us. That means that the world of sin vents its hatred against us for going to Jesus (John 17:14). Christians are not taken out of the context of a sinful world but are placed in it to be witnesses for Christ. In his list of the heroes of faith, the writer notes that Moses "regarded disgrace for the sake of Christ as of greater value than the treasures of Egypt, because he was looking ahead to his reward" (11:26). Christians bear the name of Christ and are commanded by him to deny themselves, take up their cross, and follow him (Matt. 10:38; 16:24). The Christian keeps his eye of faith fixed on Jesus (12:2). He knows that this present world will not remain unchanged, but will pass away.

"For here we do not have an enduring city." The words echo an earlier statement of the author when he discussed those people who lived by faith but who did not see the promises fulfilled in their lifetime. "And they admitted that they were aliens and strangers on earth" (11:13). They longed for a better country, a heavenly country, much the same as Abraham looked forward to a heavenly city (11:10; and see 12:22). Thus, the writer repeats his former remarks, by saying conclusively, "We are looking for the city that is to come." Do Christians live in an ethereal world detached from the pressing realities of everyday life? Certainly not! Christians are to be "the salt of the earth" and "the light of the world" (Matt. 5:13, 14). Wherever God in his providence has placed them, they are to be Christ's ambassadors (II Cor. 5:20). They are to represent Christ by boldly speaking the Word he has given them. Yet they know the brevity of life and the fleeting nature of this

---

26. Colin Brown says that the author "sees a heightened symbolism in the crucifixion of Jesus outside Jerusalem." See *NIDNTT,* vol. 3, p. 965. Also consult David Hill, *NIDNTT,* vol. 2, p. 29; and Joachim Jeremias, *TDNT,* vol. 6, p. 922.

27. F. W. Grosheide, *De Brief aan de Hebreeën en de Brief van Jakobus* (Kampen: Kok, 1955), p. 314.

world. Therefore, they look and long for their eternal dwelling: "a city that is to come."

15. Through Jesus, therefore, let us continually offer to God a sacrifice of praise—the fruit of lips that confess his name.

First in the sentence stands the phrase *through Jesus*. That is significant. Because of the once-for-all sacrifice of Jesus, the need for offering sacrifices to God had ended. Are Christians, then, without sacrifices and without a priest to present these offerings to God? No.

We are exhorted to go to Jesus outside the camp. He is our eternal, faithful, and merciful high priest. He represents us in the presence of God, and he prays for us. To come to God the Father we must go through the Son (John 14:6). Set free from the burden of guilt and sin, we want to express our thanks to God. This we do through Jesus. We offer to God not the material sacrifices that Christ made superfluous but the continual confession of praise and thanks. Whereas Jesus offered himself once, we present our praises continually. Our entire life ought to be a song of adulation expressed in words and deeds.

The Israelites expressed their thankfulness by offering cakes of bread to the Lord as a sacrifice of thanksgiving (Lev. 7:12). But Christians show by a dedicated life of obedience their thankfulness to God. The Ten Commandments are not a set of dos and don'ts; rather, for the Christian, they are rules for thankful living.

How then do we live before God? Paul and Peter have something to say on this subject:

> Therefore, I urge you, brothers, in view of God's mercy, to offer your bodies as living sacrifices, holy and pleasing to God. [Rom. 12:1]
>
> Give thanks in all circumstances, for this is God's will for you in Christ Jesus. [I Thess. 5:18]
>
> You also, like living stones, are built into a spiritual house to be a holy priesthood, offering spiritual sacrifices acceptable to God through Jesus Christ. [I Peter 2:5]

The author of Hebrews specifies what the sacrifice of praise should be: "the fruit of lips that confess his name." The expression *fruit of lips* comes from Hosea 14:2, where the prophet urges the people of Israel to return to the Lord and pray, "Forgive all our sins and receive us graciously, that we may offer the fruit of our lips." And the phrase *confess his name* may be taken from the Septuagint translation of Psalm 54:6, "I will praise [confess] your name, O Lord." God reveals himself in his name, and therefore his name is revelation. The psalmist makes God's revelation known to the people. Similarly the author of Hebrews intimates that a life of praise should be a continual confession of God's name.

16. And do not forget to do good and to share with others, for with such sacrifices God is pleased.

Living a holy life consists of loving the Lord with heart, soul, and mind, and of loving one's neighbor as oneself. The early Christians illustrated their love for the Lord by devoting themselves to the teaching of the gospel, the worship services, communion, and prayer (Acts 2:42). But they also showed their love for their fellow man by sharing everything they had (Acts 4:32). In fact, they took care of the poor so that "there were no needy persons among them" (v. 34). Love for the Lord has its counterpart in love for the neighbor. These two go hand in hand. When we say that we love the Lord, we must be ready to help our neighbors in need. This is what the Macedonian believers did. Says Paul, "Entirely on their own, they urgently pleaded with us for the privilege of sharing in this service [showing generosity] to the saints" (II Cor. 8:3–4).

The readers of the Epistle to the Hebrews had neglected their ministry to the needy (see also 13:2). Praising God in the local worship service they observed, even though some people stayed away (10:25). But praise and love were not always put to practice in relieving the needs of the poor (6:10; 10:33–34). The writer tells the readers "to do good and to share with others." He sees these deeds of love and mercy as sacrifices of praise. And with these sacrifices God is pleased.

When the author says that God is pleased with good deeds, he reminds us of his description of Enoch's life. Enoch was commended for his intimate fellowship with God (11:5). Also we are reminded of our duties to care for the needy, for if we keep the royal law—"Love your neighbor as yourself" (James 2:8)—we do well and please God.

Practical Considerations in 13:12–16

"Do good," says the writer of Hebrews. Do we have to be reminded to do good? Doing good ought to be the Christian's way of life. But, sad to say, at times we forget, and our worship becomes lip service and not life commitment. If our Christian religion is nothing more than talk, it is dead. Words and deeds are two sides of the same coin. God wants us to praise him with both lips and life.

In a word game, arranging the letters *g o o d* is relatively simple. The same set of letters, however, can also be divided into two words that read, "Go do!" That means translating the word into deed. I must go and do to be good in the sight of God.

When I attended elementary school, the teacher used to mark my papers with the comment *good.* Of course, that meant I had learned my lesson well but not well enough to receive the comment *excellent.* Scripture does not use that remark.[28] When the servants appeared before the master with ten and four talents respectively, they heard him say, "Well done, you *good* and faithful servant!" (Matt. 25:21, 23, italics added). Being good Christians means that we look for opportunities to do the things that please God and that bring joy to our fellow man.

---

28. Herman Veldkamp, *Zondagskinderen,* 2 vols. (Franeker: Wever, n.d.), vol. 1, p. 32.

Greek Words, Phrases, and Constructions in 13:12–16

Verse 12

ἁγιάσῃ—the aorist active subjunctive from the verb ἁγιάζω (I make holy) has been occasioned by τὰ ἅγια (the Most Holy Place) in the preceding verse. The subjunctive stands in a purpose clause. The aorist is constative.

τὸν λαόν—this is the last time in the epistle that the author uses the expression *the people.* In the thirteen times it occurs, it refers to God's people.

Verse 15

οὖν—this inferential conjunction is "absent from several early and important witnesses. It is difficult to decide whether copyists added the word, which seems to be needed at this point, or whether it was accidentally omitted in transcription."[29]

αἰνέσεως—the noun derived from the verb αἰνέω (I praise) shows by its nominative singular ending αἴνεσις that this is an action noun that denotes progress. This feature is amplified by the prepositional phrase διὰ παντός (continually).

ὁμολογούντων—as a present active participle, the word stands in apposition to χειλέων (lips), from which it takes the genitive case. It is followed by the dative case τῷ ὀνόματι (his name), which is the direct object of the participle. The difference between the simple verb ὁμολογέω and the compound verb ἐξομολογέω is insignificant.

Verse 16

τῆς δὲ εὐποιΐας καὶ κοινωνίας—although a few manuscripts have a definite article before κοινωνίας, the preferred reading omits it. Because the article is not repeated, the second noun is descriptive of the first.[30]

τοιαύταις—an adjective in the dative plural feminine, describing quality. The dative expresses cause.[31]

ὁ θεός—note the position of the noun. It stands last for emphasis.

---

4. Obey Your Leaders
13:17

This verse has no connection with the preceding verses. We need to go back to verse 7 where the same expression *your leaders* occurs. And in verse 24 the writer once more employs that expression.

17. Obey your leaders and submit to their authority. They keep watch over you as men who must give an account. Obey them so that their work will be a joy, not a burden, for that would be of no advantage to you.

---

29. Bruce M. Metzger, *A Textual Commentary on the Greek New Testament* (London and New York: United Bible Societies, 1975), p. 676.

30. Henry E. Dana and Julius R. Mantey, *A Manual Grammar of the Greek New Testament* (New York: Macmillan, 1957), p. 147.

31. Robertson, *Grammar,* p. 532.

In this particular verse, the author emphasizes three points.

a. *Obedience demanded.* Those leaders who had spoken the Word of God in earlier days were no longer present. They must be remembered for their conduct and faith, says the author of Hebrews (13:7). Successive leaders have taken their place. The writer is not interested in the status of these leaders—he gives no hint whether they were elders, overseers, preachers, or teachers. Rather, he asks the reader to obey them.

A lack of obedience prevailed among some of the readers. Note, for example, the author's admonition not to "be carried away by all kinds of strange teachings" (13:9). The leaders needed help and encouragement. Thus the appeal to obey them and to submit to their authority is timely. Of course, the readers could question whether this authority was self-imposed by the leaders or delegated to them by Christ. If a leader is a dedicated minister of the Word of God, he proves thereby that Christ has given him authority. And if Christ has entrusted him with the task of assuming leadership, the people need not question his authority (Acts 20:28; Eph. 4:11; I Peter 5:1–3).

b. *Care provided.* The leaders have taken their God-given task seriously. "They keep watch over you." They literally lost sleep over the spiritual welfare of the believers. They know the word God spoke to the prophet Ezekiel: "Son of man, I have made you a watchman for the house of Israel; so hear the word I speak and give them warning from me. When I say to a wicked man, 'You will surely die,' and you do not warn him or speak out to dissuade him from his evil ways in order to save his life, that wicked man will die for his sin, and I will hold you accountable for his blood" (3:17–18).

The leaders stay with the congregation, are vigilant in caring for the members, nurture them spiritually, ward off deceitful attacks, and administer discipline when necessary. Writes John Calvin, "The heavier the burden they bear, the more honour they deserve; for the more labour any one undertakes for our sake, and the more difficulty and danger he incurs for us, the greater are our obligations to him."[32] These leaders are accountable to God, for he is their overseer. That is not to say that the members are not held accountable. Certainly they are. They, too, are told to work together harmoniously so that the task of the leaders is a joy and not a burden.

c. *Joy experienced.* Throughout his epistle the author has stressed the corporate responsibility of the believers. To mention one example, he exhorts the readers to encourage one another, "so that none of you may be hardened by sin's deceitfulness" (3:13). In a similar fashion, as a body they are to respond to their leaders, for then there is joy in the interpersonal relationships in the church. They receive the Lord's blessings by obeying the leaders God has given them. If they all respond favorably the work of their leaders becomes increasingly joyful.

When the members refuse to obey and fail to respect their leaders, the work in the church becomes burdensome. The members ought to realize

---

32. John Calvin, *Epistle to the Hebrews* (Grand Rapids: Eerdmans, 1949), p. 353.

that neither they nor the leaders own the church. The church belongs to Jesus Christ, to whom the readers are responsible. Should they make the work and life of the leaders difficult, they would be the losers. The leaders can testify before the Lord that they warned the wayward person who chose not to turn from his sin. That person will die in his sin, but the leaders are free from blame (Ezek. 3:19). Ultimately, then, the Lord avenges and judges his people (Heb. 10:30; Deut. 32:35–36; Ps. 135:14). Pastorally and prudently the writer of Hebrews observes that a sad instead of a glad report on the spiritual conduct of the readers will not be advantageous to them.

Greek Words, Phrases, and Constructions in 13:17

Verse 17

ὑπείκετε—with πείθεσθε this form is a present imperative. It derives from the verb ὑπείκω (I submit to authority) that appears only here in the entire New Testament. The verb is classical Greek.

ἀγρυπνοῦσιν—this verb from ἀγρυπνέω (I keep awake, keep watch) occurs in the Gospels (Mark 13:33; Luke 21:36) and Paul's epistles (Eph. 6:18; as a noun in II Cor. 6:5; 11:27). The verb describes an absence of sleep due to an alert mind.

ἀποδώσοντες—preceded by the participle ὡς and the noun λόγον (account), this future active participle of ἀποδίδωμι (I render) denotes purpose.[33]

ἵνα ποιῶσιν—here is an instance of result instead of purpose.

---

18 Pray for us. We are sure that we have a clear conscience and desire to live honorably in every way. 19 I particularly urge you to pray so that I may be restored to you soon.

20 May the God of peace, who through the blood of the eternal covenant brought back from the dead our Lord Jesus, that great Shepherd of the sheep, 21 equip you with everything good for doing his will, and may he work in us what is pleasing to him, through Jesus Christ, to whom be glory for ever and ever. Amen.

E. Prayers and Benedictions 13:18–21

The conclusion to the epistle is rather personal. Earlier, in two succeeding sentences, the author refers to himself in the first person singular—"And what more shall I say? I do not have time" (11:32). Now he uses the first person plural, as well as the singular, and requests prayer.

18. Pray for us. We are sure that we have a clear conscience and desire to live honorably in every way. 19. I particularly urge you to pray so that I may be restored to you soon.

Apparently the writer was one of the leaders in the church that receives

---

33. Robertson feels that the participle "is as much cause as purpose." See his *Grammar,* p. 1128. And Robert Hanna asserts that the participle "expresses a subjective motive, meaning 'with the thought that they must.' " See his *Grammatical Aid to the Greek New Testament* (Grand Rapids: Baker, 1983), p. 414.

his epistle. Tension between him and the readers developed, perhaps because of his teachings about the priesthood of Christ. These doctrines were hard for Jewish believers to accept, for they were accustomed to thinking of the priesthood in terms of the duties of the Levitical priests only. Probably the author's direct warnings against apostasy were not readily heeded by some members of the church. The author has put his teachings and admonitions in an epistle addressed to the readers. He realizes that the letter itself will not remove tension. However, he reduces it by putting himself in debt to them.

a. *Prayer.* The request for prayer is similar to those in Paul's epistles and fits into the spiritual climate of the first century (Rom. 15:30; II Cor. 1:11–12; Eph. 6:19; Col. 4:3–4; I Thess. 5:25; II Thess. 3:1). The writer places himself in the position of one who asks a favor. He knows that if the readers pray for him, the bond of unity between himself and the recipients of his letter is strengthened. And if they pray, they indicate that the message he conveys has been well received.

The first person plural in this verse can be understood literally. However, its close connection with the next verse, where the first person singular is used, seems to favor the interpretation that *we* and *us* should be understood editorially. That is, the author speaks about himself. Also, in the broader context, he does not mention other leaders (but see 13:23).

b. *Clear conscience.* The original text has the word *for,* which links the request for prayer to the reason that prompted the request. The sentence, then, is as follows: "Pray for us, for we are sure that we have a clear conscience." The writer is trying to say to the readers that he is aware of their uneasiness about his instruction and exhortations, but he himself bears no ill will. He can understand that some of the readers are not pleased with abolishing Levitical precepts because of the tradition of the fathers. But in his own heart the writer is persuaded that his conscience is clear. He has dedicated himself to the service of the Lord and therefore he desires to live honorably in every respect. He wants to help the readers and be of service to them as a faithful pastor. In short he is saying, "Trust me." The readers can be assured that their pastor is not leading them in the wrong direction with his teachings about priesthood and covenant.

Nowhere in the New Testament is the break with the traditions of the Old Testament era spelled out so clearly as in the Epistle to the Hebrews. Whether the writer is too progressive in his teachings may have been a relevant point of discussion among the readers whose religious and cultural roots are in Jewish tradition. Certainly the letter writer is no traditionalist who upholds the practices of the past. His task is to explain God's progressive revelation to the readers. He knows that his pastoral work has been and is performed honorably. He expresses the desire that he may be permitted in the near future to continue his pastoral duties among the readers. As he sees his relationship to the readers, his conduct has been above reproach.

c. *Special request.* Once more the author asks the readers to pray for him.

But now he makes a specific request: "Pray that I may be restored to you soon." The New International Version gives the reading "I particularly urge you to pray." But this translation is open to misunderstanding. For it could be interpreted to mean that all people, particularly the writer, urge the readers to pray. The original, however, expresses a repetitive idea in the sense of *more*: "I urge you all the more" (NASB) to pray in my behalf. The writer intimates that he wishes more and more to urge communal prayer for their eventual reunion. His desire is to be with the members of the church as soon as possible.

Where is the writer? What keeps him from visiting the readers? To these and similar questions we have no answer; and we do well not to speculate. To put it differently, at one time the readers knew exactly what the writer meant. With the passing of time the explanatory comments that were needed to understand these personal remarks were lost. What is important, however, is that we realize the significance of the author's special request: he desires that the church ask God for a speedy reunion of pastor and people. When this happens, the writer knows that the bond of peace and harmony is strong. He prays for unity in the Lord. Hence he utters the pastoral benediction that is unique, for it is a summary of many elements in his epistle (see 7:14, 16, 22; 9:12, 15; 11:5–6; 12:28; 13:16).

20. May the God of peace, who through the blood of the eternal covenant brought back from the dead our Lord Jesus, that great Shepherd of the sheep, 21. equip you with everything good for doing his will, and may he work in us what is pleasing to him, through Jesus Christ, to whom be glory for ever and ever. Amen.

In the immediately preceding verses (vv. 18–19), the author requests prayer for himself. Now he offers a prayer for the people he addresses. What a moving prayer! The wealth of theology and language in this benediction that virtually concludes his epistle compares favorably with the beauty and fullness of the first few verses of the introduction with which the author begins his epistle. The author is a literary artist and a masterful theologian.

In the first part (v. 20) of the benediction, note the following points:

a. "God of peace." The writer puts the subject *God* first. He describes God as "the God of peace." That is meaningful, for he is the one who creates peace in the hearts and lives of people. Peace comes from God. Note the author does not pray, "May the peace of God," but "May the God of peace." God, then, is the peacemaker who is able to dispel distrust and dissent. And God grants the gift of peace to his people, so that they in turn are able to effect peace among their fellow men. Paul prays these words—"the God of peace"—rather frequently in benedictions at the conclusion of his epistles (see Rom. 15:33; 16:20; II Cor. 13:11; Phil. 4:9; I Thess. 5:23; II Thess. 3:16). The formula, therefore, seems to have been quite common in the early church.

b. "Brought back from the dead." God brought Jesus back from the dead, says the author of Hebrews. The doctrine of Jesus' resurrection is fundamental to the Christian faith, for one of the requirements for holding the office of apostle was to be a witness of the resurrection (Acts 1:22). In their preaching, testifying, and writing, the apostles proclaimed the resurrection of Jesus. Even though Paul was not a disciple of Jesus, as were the other apostles, he encountered the resurrected Jesus on the Damascus road. Therefore, in his writings Paul teaches the resurrection and at the same time affirms his apostleship (see Gal. 1:1).

The writer of the Epistle to the Hebrews mentions the resurrection of Jesus once, in the benediction. Indirectly he includes this doctrine when he introduces the topic of Christ's exaltation at the right hand of the Majesty in heaven (1:3). He writes about the "great high priest who has gone through the heavens" (4:14) and he supposes that the readers will understand that Jesus rose from the dead and ascended to heaven. And in his summation of fundamental Christian doctrines, he lists the resurrection of the dead (6:2). Last, he alludes to the possibility of God's raising Isaac from the dead (11:19) and the actuality of women receiving the dead who were raised to life (11:35). He cannot claim to be a witness of Jesus' resurrection. As a second-generation believer, he heard the gospel from the immediate followers of Jesus (2:3). The author, then, briefly states that God raised Jesus from the dead and links this reference to Jesus' office.

c. "Shepherd of the sheep." The words "the great Shepherd of the sheep" remind us of Jesus' teaching that he is the good shepherd who lays down his life for the sheep (John 10:11; also see Isa. 63:11). In effect, the metaphor of the shepherd who dies for his sheep is equivalent to that of the high priest who offers himself as a sacrifice for his people. Especially the adjective *great* is telling, for the writer of Hebrews calls Jesus the great high priest (4:14). The two concepts, then, complement each other, although as Guthrie observes, "There is a tender aspect to the shepherd figure which is not as vivid in the high priest."[34] Peter depicts Jesus as the Chief Shepherd (I Peter 5:4). This great shepherd shed his blood and laid down his life for his sheep—in other words, his people—to obtain for them eternal redemption and to establish with them the eternal covenant that God had promised.

d. "Blood of the eternal covenant." Through the prophets Isaiah, Jeremiah, and Ezekiel, God announces his intention to establish an everlasting covenant with his people (Isa. 55:3; 61:8; Jer. 32:40; 50:5; Ezek. 16:60; 37:26). This covenant is everlasting because it is sealed in blood—to be precise, the blood of the Messiah. In the messianic prophecy of Zion's king who enters Jerusalem on a donkey (Zech. 9:9; also see Matt. 21:5 and parallels), God promises his people deliverance "because of the blood of my covenant" (Zech. 9:11).

Two major themes dominate the epistle: the high-priestly work of Christ, summarized in the expression *blood,* and the covenant that is eternal. In this verse, once again and for the last time these themes are highlighted. God's

---

34. Guthrie, *New Testament Theology,* p. 388.

covenant with his people will remain forever. That covenant has been sealed with Christ's blood which was shed once for all (9:26; 10:10).

e. "Our Lord Jesus." These three words—four words in the original—appear last to receive all the emphasis in the verse. A literal translation of the verse is, "Now the God of peace, who brought up from the dead the great Shepherd of the sheep through the blood of the eternal covenant, even Jesus our Lord" (NASB).

In addition to using the given name *Jesus,* which calls to mind the earthly ministry and humanity of Christ, the author of Hebrews designates him "Lord" (2:3; 7:14). Although the title *Lord* occurs infrequently in Hebrews, its use in the Christian world was common, for it served as a brief confession of faith (for example, see I Cor. 12:3). In the benediction at the end of his epistle, the author wants to emphasize the sovereignty of Jesus. As in the introduction where he briefly points to the priestly and kingly offices of Christ (1:3), so in his benediction he combines in one sentence a reference to the priesthood and kingship of Jesus.

In the second part of the benediction (v. 21), we note these considerations:

a. "May God . . . equip you." The first part of the benediction consists of a summary of what God has done in Christ; the second reveals what God is doing in Christ's people. In this section the author utters a prayer in behalf of the readers and asks God to equip them to do his will. The verb *to equip* actually means to make someone complete. It connotes the act of restoring—that is, perfecting—something. Some translations have the reading "may the God of peace . . . make you perfect" (NEB; also consult KJV; RV; ASV). God strengthens man so that shortcomings may be overcome.[35] He supplies us with every good thing so that we may be able to do his will.

A plaque with simple wording adorns a wall in our family room. Every member of the family can testify to the truthfulness of the wording. Here is the text:

> The will of God
> can never lead you
> where the grace of God
> cannot keep you.

b. "May [God] work in us." In preceding verses the writer encourages the reader to live a life that is pleasing to God (11:5–6; 12:28; 13:16). A person who lives such a life is commended by God himself and is rewarded (II Cor. 5:9–10). But man looks to God for help, direction, and wisdom. And because of the eternal covenant he has made with us through Jesus Christ, he grants us assistance. The writer of Hebrews prays that God may work in us to do that which pleases him. And Paul, writing to the church in Philippi, formulates the human and the divine in salvation. Says he, "Work out your

35. Reinier Schippers in *NIDNTT,* vol. 3, p. 350, states that in the New Testament the meaning of the verb in question is "to prepare, establish, form, and equip."

salvation with fear and trembling, for it is God who works in you to will and to act according to his good purpose" (Phil. 2:12–13).

Why is God willing to work in us? The author is almost repetitious in the wording of this benediction. He spells out that through Jesus Christ—note the combination of the two names (also see 10:10; 13:8)—God himself works in us and equips us to do his will. Through Jesus Christ, therefore, we are in God, and God works in us (John 17:21).

c. "To whom be glory." Translations vary, because in the original Greek it is not clear whether glory ought to be attributed to God or to Jesus Christ. Some commentators think that because God is the subject in the benediction, the author means to say that God should receive the glory. Moreover, in greetings and benedictions glory is given to God (Rom. 11:36; 16:27; Gal. 1:5; Eph. 3:21; Phil. 4:20; I Tim. 1:17; Jude 25). But some of them ascribe glory to Jesus Christ (II Tim. 4:18; II Peter 3:18; Rev. 1:6; 4:11). In the benediction in Hebrews, the flow of the sentence seems to indicate that Jesus Christ should receive the glory. Obviously the formula itself is the stock phrase "glory for ever and ever. Amen." And, therefore, the writer may not have intended a clear choice. For him they are the familiar words at the conclusion of a benediction. Amen, so let it be!

Practical Considerations in 13:18–21

The psalmists teach us that prayer is praise. God is to be praised for his work in creation and redemption. But prayer also concerns the practical matters of life, as Jesus teaches us in the Lord's Prayer. After three petitions about the name, the kingdom, and the will of God, he teaches us to pray for daily bread, forgiveness of sin, victory in temptation, and deliverance from evil. God is interested in everything we do. We have the privilege of praying not only for ourselves, but also for our fellow man. We may bring all our needs to God in prayer.

> What a friend we have in Jesus,
> All our sins and griefs to bear!
> What a privilege to carry
> Everything to God in prayer!
> O what peace we often forfeit,
> O what needless pain we bear,
> All because we do not carry
> Everything to God in prayer!
> —Joseph Scriven

When someone is making a decision, we often advise him, "Let your conscience be your guide." But if a conscience is seared by sin, it is of little help in making the right choices. Jonathan Edwards compared man's conscience with a sundial: "As the sundial cannot make the hour known when the sun does not shine upon it, so conscience is not a plain or safe guide to duty unless it is enlightened by God's Word." Man's conscience should be directed to the Scriptures, much the same as the needle of a compass invariably points north.

Greek Words, Phrases, and Constructions in 13:18–21

Verse 18

προσεύχεσθε—first in the sentence, this verb is an imperative in the present tense, middle as a deponent. The present tense expresses continued action: keep on praying.

πειθόμεθα—the same verb, although in the second person plural, appeared in 13:17. There the meaning is "obey;" here it is "persuaded." Some translators (including those of the NIV) omit the postpositive conjunction γάρ in their versions. The word should be maintained, for the conjunction makes the author's intent clear.

ἔχομεν—the repeated use of the first person plural in pronoun and verb appears to be the editorial "we."[36]

ἀναστρέφεσθαι—as a present passive infinitive from ἀναστρέφω (I turn back), the verb means "to conduct oneself in life" (see Heb. 10:33).

Verse 19

τάχιον—this comparative adverb, like περισσοτέρως (all the more), "appears to have a true comparative sense in this verse, 'more quickly,' or 'sooner.' "[37]

ἀποκατασταθῶ—from the compound ἀποκαθίστημι (I restore), this verb is the aorist passive subjunctive. The subjunctive is used because of the indirect command structure of παρακαλῶ and ἵνα.

Verse 20

ὁ ἀναγαγών—the articular aorist active participle, derived from ἀνάγω (I bring up), may connote either bringing someone *up* from the dead or bringing him *back* from the dead.

τὸν μέγαν—the position of the adjective together with the definite article is rather emphatic.

ἐν αἵματι—the instrumental use of the preposition reflects Semitic form in this instance current in the Septuagint. The noun αἷμα lacks the definite article.

Verse 21

καταρτίσαι—this is one of the few occurrences of the optative mood—one of the sixty-seven instances in the New Testament. The form is the first aorist active optative of καταρτίζω (I restore). The subject of the verb is ὁ θεός. The sentence conveys a wish.

εἰς τὸ ποιῆσαι—the preposition εἰς with the articular infinitive expresses purpose. The aorist tense of the infinitive is constative.

ποιῶν—in a few major manuscripts this participle is preceded by αὐτῷ. However,

36. Robertson, *Grammar,* pp. 677–78.

37. Hanna, *Grammatical Aid,* p. 415. Also see Friedrich W. Blass and Albert Debrunner, *A Greek Grammar of the New Testament and Other Early Christian Literature,* rev. and trans. Robert W. Funk (Chicago: University of Chicago Press, 1961), sec. 244 (1).

the pronoun is unintelligible and "may be a homiletic expansion."[38] Therefore, we do well to delete it.

ἡμῖν—because of the preceding form ὑμᾶς, a number of Greek manuscripts have the reading ὑμῖν. By applying the rule that the more difficult reading is the more original, we are able to explain the presence of the second person plural pronoun better than that of the first person plural pronoun. Thus we favor the reading ὑμῖν.

ᾧ—the relative pronoun in the dative singular, as indirect object, has its nearest antecedent in the immediately preceding Ἰησοῦ Χριστοῦ. For this reason, we apply the words to Jesus and not to ὁ θεός, the subject of the sentence.

---

22 Brothers, I urge you to bear with my word of exhortation, for I have written you only a short letter.
23 I want you to know that our brother Timothy has been released. If he arrives soon, I will come with him to see you.
24 Greet all your leaders and all God's people. Those from Italy send you their greetings.
25 Grace be with you all.

F. Final Greetings
13:22–25

The last few verses of this epistle are too brief to tell us something about the time and circumstances in which the letter was written. The names of Timothy and of Italy, although interesting, are of very little help in this respect. The author is not giving us newsworthy items. Rather, he is writing a "word of exhortation." That is the purpose of his "short letter."

22. Brothers, I urge you to bear with my word of exhortation, for I have written you only a short letter.

In this somewhat personal section of the epistle, the author addresses the readers as brothers (3:1, 12; 10:19). He follows the custom of his day and therefore ought not be faulted for failing to mention the feminine gender.

A second time he says "I urge" (see 13:19), but now almost apologetically as he explains what he wants the readers to do. Says he, "Bear with my word of exhortation." Actually, he tells the readers to put up with his word of exhortation; or, in less colloquial terms, he is asking them to listen carefully to what he has to say.

What does the expression *word of exhortation* mean? Throughout his epistle the writer has been a faithful pastor to his people by exhorting them to listen attentively and obediently to the Word of God. Although at first glance his letter may seem to be a doctrinal treatise, the epistle consists of pastoral admonitions that are supported by teachings derived from a sound knowledge of the Old Testament. The conclusion that we draw therefore is that the Epistle to the Hebrews indeed is a word of exhortation written by a dedicated pastor who watches over the spiritual well-being of his people.

---

38. Metzger, *Textual Commentary,* p. 676.

Besides admonishing them, the pastor also teaches them new truths concerning Jesus Christ. They may have objected to these teachings and perhaps to his exhortations. Therefore he urges them to listen to him as he addresses them in this word of exhortation (compare Acts 13:15).

"For I have written you only a short letter." The tone is apologetic. A few times in the body of his letter the author shortened his remarks (5:11; 9:5; 11:32) and stated that he lacked time even though he had much to say. The letter itself can easily be read in one sitting; let us say, during a worship service. Moreover, the adjective *short* need not be taken literally.

Last, the word *letter* is significant. The writer speaks of a letter, not a theological treatise. He wants to communicate the truth and chooses the form of a letter. The exhortations, the personal remarks (especially those in the last part of chapter 13), and the greetings make this writing a letter.

23. I want you to know that our brother Timothy has been released. If he arrives soon, I will come with him to see you.

Actually this verse has the appearance of a postscript at the end of the letter. As the New English Bible has it, "I have news for you."

"Our brother Timothy has been released." Is this person Paul's faithful fellow worker? Perhaps. Certainly we do not have proof. But because the writer calls Timothy "our brother," indications are that he is Paul's companion. In early Christian literature, only the coworker of Paul bears the name *Timothy.* A few times Paul calls Timothy "our brother" (II Cor. 1:1; Col. 1:1; I Thess. 3:2; Philem. 1). He invites Timothy, a native of Lystra, to accompany him on his second missionary journey (Acts 16:1–3). Timothy traveled widely, helped Paul in writing letters (for example, II Corinthians), served as Paul's good will ambassador to Corinth, and was the pastor of the church at Ephesus. In short, Timothy was well known.

Timothy had been in Rome during Paul's first imprisonment (Phil. 1:1; Col. 1:1; Philem. 1). From Rome Paul wrote the so-called prison Epistles (Ephesians, Philemon, Colossians, and Philippians). During Paul's second imprisonment at Rome, he urged Timothy to come to him quickly (II Tim. 4:9).

We have no information about Timothy's imprisonment. The writer of Hebrews only states, "Our brother Timothy has been released." Presumably he had been imprisoned for his Christian testimony and was released. The author is not sure what plans Timothy may have, but one thing is certain: "If he arrives soon, I will come with him to see you." Where Timothy will arrive and at what place the writer resides is not known. Whether the author needed Timothy's moral support in respect to the Jewish Christians who received his letter remains an open question.

24. Greet all your leaders and all God's people. Those from Italy send you their greetings.

Three times the leaders attract attention. First, they are to be remembered and imitated (v. 7). Then they are to be obeyed because they have authority (v. 17). And now they receive greetings. At the conclusions of letters, writers generally add salutations. Paul, Peter, and John in their respective epistles convey greetings.

The author of Hebrews, however, makes a distinction between leaders and God's people by repeating the adjective *all*. If he had said, "Greet all your leaders and people," he would have given the impression that the letter was addressed to one particular church. Apparently the writer sends greetings to all the church leaders, and he greets all God's people who formed a segment of the church. This segment, then, consists of a group of Jewish Christians called Hebrews.[39]

Where did the readers live? A hasty answer would be Rome. The writer says, "Those from Italy send you their greetings." If the expression *those from Italy* had only one meaning, we would be able to decide whether the readers lived in Rome or not. The expression can mean, first, that the author writes from Rome to a group of Christians living outside of Italy. He includes his Italian friends in Rome in the greetings he sends to the group. This view was commonly held by the church fathers. And numerous Greek manuscripts had a subscription at the end of the epistle that said, "Written to the Hebrews from Italy [Rome] by Timothy" (KJV).[40] Needless to say, subscriptions were added by scribes at a later date.

The second interpretation is that the author addressed his epistle to Christians at Rome from a place outside Italy. His friends who hail from Italy send greetings to their relatives and acquaintances in Rome. This seems to be an acceptable interpretation, and scholars generally advance this theory.

Whether we accept the first or the second interpretation, the fact remains that we have to work with hypotheses because the text itself is not clear.

25. Grace be with you all.

The final greeting is customary. Paul writes either "the grace of the Lord Jesus [Christ] be with you [all]" (Rom. 16:24; I Cor. 16:23; II Cor. 13:14; I Thess. 5:28; II Thess. 3:18) or "the grace of our Lord Jesus Christ be with your spirit" (Gal. 6:18; Phil. 4:23; Philem. 25), or "grace be with you [all]" (Col. 4:18; I Tim. 6:21; II Tim. 4:22; Titus 3:15). Some manuscripts add the word *Amen*; others delete it. The addition of the word is easier to explain than its deletion. Therefore, the New International Version ends the Epistle to the Hebrews with "Grace be with you all."

Greek Words, Phrases, and Constructions in 13:22–25

Verse 22

ἀνέχεσθε—instead of the infinitive ἀνέχεσθαι featured in a few manuscripts, the better reading is the present middle imperative (compare 13:19, where the infini-

39. Grosheide, *Hebreeën*, pp. 27–28. Westcott notes that "the letter was not addressed officially to the Church, but to some section of it." See his *Hebrews*, p. 451.

40. In his *Textual Commentary*, p. 678, Metzger lists the variant readings of the subscriptions. Some are rather lengthy. For example, here is the reading of Manuscript 431: "This Epistle to the Hebrews was written from Italy by the apostle Timothy who was sent to them by the blessed Paul in order that he might set them on a straight path."

tive occurs with παρακαλῶ). The compound verb ἀνά (up) and ἔχω (I have, hold) corresponds to the idiom *to put up with.* The verb governs the genitive case in τοῦ λόγου.

καὶ γάρ—this emphatic combination appears only five times in the entire epistle (4:2; 5:12; 10:34; 12:29; 13:22). It means "for indeed."

διὰ βραχέων—the preposition διά is followed by the plural adjective in the genitive case. The adjective actually modifies the understood noun λόγων (words). The literal translation of the idiomatic expression "in few words" is better understood adverbially—that is, "briefly."

ἐπέστειλα—from ἐπιστέλλω (I write a letter), this aorist active indicative is the so-called epistolary aorist. The writer places himself in the time of the recipient of the letter and thus views the act of writing as having taken place in the past.

Verse 23

γινώσκετε—because the word stands first in the sentence, this verb is the present active imperative, not the present active indicative. It can best be translated as "I want you to know" (NIV).

ἐὰν τάχιον ἔρχηται—the particle ἐάν introduces a conditional sentence with a subjunctive verb ἔρχηται in the protasis and a future middle indicative ὄψομαι in the apodosis. The first part of the sentence expresses uncertainty. For the comparative adverb τάχιον, see verse 19.

Verse 24

ἀσπάσασθε—the aorist middle imperative from the verb ἀσπάζομαι (I greet) derives from σπάω that is preceded by the intensive ἀ and means "I draw to myself," in the middle voice. Generally a greeting was expressed by embracing and kissing. Here the greeting is conveyed by a letter.

Summary of Chapter 13

The last chapter of the Epistle to the Hebrews gives the letter a personal touch. The writer reveals his pastoral concerns for the believers and makes his desire known to be in their midst again.

The content of this chapter does not consist of some loosely connected exhortations. The writer encourages the readers to express their Christian love in the social context of their day: love for the brothers and sisters in the Lord, love toward the traveler in need of a roof over his head at night, and loving compassion and empathy for prisoners and people who are mistreated. From the love for the neighbor in the narrow and broad senses, the writer moves to the love in the home; that is, the bond of marriage, the husband's relationship to his wife and vice versa. He includes the admonition not to love money, but to be content and trust God. The first section of this last chapter, then, delineates the requirements of the summary of the law, in reverse order: love your neighbor as yourself, and love the Lord your God.

In the second part of the chapter the author enumerates some ecclesiastical duties and concerns. He begins with an exhortation to remember those leaders whose service on earth has ended. Imitate their faith, he says, and look at the lives they lived. From the topic of church leaders the author goes to that of doctrine. Stay away from doctrines that deviate from the truth. Rather, consider the work of Jesus, who suffered and died in disgrace outside the city gate. Thankfulness for salvation comes to expression by confessing God's name, doing good deeds, and sharing with others. Church leaders and church members ought to work together harmoniously so that the obedience of the members is a source of joy to the leaders.

The last section of the chapter includes a personal request for prayer, a beautifully worded benediction, an announcement of the writer's intended visit accompanied by Timothy, greetings to leaders and people of the church, and greetings from Italian friends. The letter ends with the final greeting, "Grace be with you all."

Select Bibliography

Commentaries

Alford, Henry. *Alford's Greek Testament: An Exegetical and Critical Commentary.* 4 vols. Vol. 4, pt. 1, *Prolegomena and Hebrews.* 1875. Grand Rapids: Guardian, 1976.

Bengel, John Albert. *Gnomon of the New Testament.* Edited by Andrew R. Fausset. 7th ed. 4 vols. Vol. 4. Edinburgh: T. and T. Clark, 1877.

Bleek, F. *Der Brief an die Hebräer.* 2 vols. Berlin: F. Dummler, 1828–40.

Bristol, Lyle O. *Hebrews: A Commentary.* Valley Forge: Judson, 1967.

Brown, John. *An Exposition of Hebrews.* Edinburgh: The Banner of Truth Trust, 1961.

Bruce, F. F. *The Epistle to the Hebrews.* New International Commentary on the New Testament series. Grand Rapids: Eerdmans, 1964.

Buchanan, George W. *To the Hebrews.* Anchor Bible. New York: Doubleday, 1972.

Calvin, John. *Commentaries on the Epistle to the Hebrews.* Grand Rapids: Eerdmans, 1949.

Davidson, A. B. *The Epistle to the Hebrews.* Edinburgh: T. and T. Clark, 1882.

Davies, J. H. *A Letter to the Hebrews.* London: Cambridge University Press, 1967.

Delitzsch, Franz. *Commentary on the Epistle to the Hebrews.* 2 vols. Edinburgh: T. and T. Clark, 1877.

Gouge, William. *Commentary on Hebrews.* 1655. Grand Rapids: Kregel, 1980.

Grosheide, F. W. *De Brief aan de Hebreeën en de Brief van Jakobus.* Kampen: Kok, 1955.

Guthrie, Donald. *Hebrews.* Tyndale New Testament Commentaries series. Grand Rapids: Eerdmans, 1983.

Hagner, Donald. *Hebrews.* Good News Commentary series. San Francisco: Harper and Row, 1983.

Héring, J. *The Epistle to the Hebrews.* Translated by A. W. Heathcoat and P. J. Allock from French original of 1955. London: Epworth, 1970.

Hewitt, Thomas. *The Epistle to the Hebrews.* Tyndale New Testament Commentaries series. Grand Rapids: Eerdmans, 1960.

Hughes, Philip Edgcumbe. *A Commentary on the Epistle to the Hebrews.* Grand Rapids: Eerdmans, 1977.

Jewett, Robert. *Letter to Pilgrims: A Commentary on the Epistle to the Hebrews.* International Critical Commentary series. 1924. New York: Pilgrim, 1981.

Lang, G. H. *The Epistle to the Hebrews.* London: Paternoster, 1951.

Lenski, R. C. H. *The Interpretation of the Epistle to the Hebrews and of the Epistle of James.* Columbus: Wartburg, 1946.

Michel, Otto. *Der Brief an die Hebräer.* 10th ed. Göttingen: Vandenhoeck and Ruprecht, 1957.

Moffatt, James. *Epistle to the Hebrews.* International Critical Commentary series. Edinburgh: T. and T. Clark, 1963.

Montefiore, Hugh. *The Epistle to the Hebrews.* New York and Evanston: Harper and Row, 1964.
Neil, W. *The Epistle to the Hebrews.* Torah Commentaries. London: SCM, 1955.
Owen, John. *An Exposition of Hebrews.* 7 vols. in 4. Evansville, Ind.: Sovereign Grace, 1960.
Peake, A. S. *Hebrews.* Century Bible. New York: Henry Frowde; Edinburgh: T. C. and E. C. Jack, 1914.
Pink, Arthur W. *An Exposition of Hebrews.* 2 vols. Grand Rapids: Baker, 1954.
Riggenbach, Edward. *Der Brief an die Hebräer.* Leipzig and Erlangen: Deichert, 1922.
Schneider, Johannes. *The Letter to the Hebrews.* Grand Rapids: Eerdmans, 1957.
Snell, A. *New and Living Way.* London: Faith Press, 1959.
Strathmann, Hermann. *Der Brief an die Hebräer.* Das Neue Testament Deutsch. Göttingen: Vandenhoeck and Ruprecht, 1937.
Spicq, Ceslaus. *L'Épître aux Hébreux.* 3d ed. 2 vols. Paris: Gabalda, 1952–53.
Westcott, B. F. *Commentary on the Epistle to the Hebrews.* Grand Rapids: Eerdmans, 1950.
Windisch, J. *Der Hebräerbrief.* Tübingen: Mohr, 1931.

Studies

Berkhof, Louis. *Systematic Theology.* Grand Rapids: Eerdmans, 1953.
Bruce, F. F. "The Kerygma of Hebrews." *Interpretation* 23 (1969): 3–19.
———. "Recent Literature on the Epistle to the Hebrews." *Themelios* 3 (1966): 31–36.
Buchanan, George W. "The Present State of Scholarship on Hebrews." In *Christianity, Judaism and Other Greco-Roman Cults: Studies for Morton Smith at Sixty,* edited by J. Neusner, vol. 1, pp. 299–330. Leiden: Brill, 1975.
Deissmann, Adolf. *Bible Studies.* Winona Lake, Ind.: Alpha Publications, 1979.
Elbogen, Ismar. *Der Jüdische Gottesdienst.* Frankfurt: Kaufmann, 1931.
Guthrie, Donald. *New Testament Introduction.* Downers Grove, Ill.: Inter-Varsity Press, 1970.
———. *New Testament Theology.* Downers Grove, Ill.: Inter-Varsity, 1981.
Harrison, E. F. "The Theology of the Epistle to the Hebrews." *BS* 12 (1964): 333–40.
Hoekema, A. A. "The Perfection of Christ in Hebrews." *CTJ* 9 (1974): 31–37.
Kistemaker, Simon J. *The Psalm Citations in the Epistle to the Hebrews.* Amsterdam: Van Soest, 1961.
Ladd, George E. *A Theology of the New Testament.* Grand Rapids: Eerdmans, 1974.
Morris, Leon. *The Gospel of John.* New International Commentary on the New Testament series. Grand Rapids: Eerdmans, 1970.
Ridderbos, Herman N. *Mattheüs.* Korte Verklaring. 2 vols. Kampen: Kok, 1952.
Ridderbos, Jan. *De Psalmen.* 2 vols. Kampen: Kok, 1955.
Schürer, Emil. *A History of the Jewish People in the Time of Jesus Christ.* 5 vols. Edinburgh: T. and T. Clark, 1885.
Smalley, S. S. "Atonement in Hebrews." *Evangelical Quarterly* 33 (1961): 126–35.
Vos, Geerhardus. *Biblical Theology.* Grand Rapids: Eerdmans, 1954.
———. *The Teaching of the Epistle to the Hebrews.* Grand Rapids: Eerdmans, 1956.
Werner, Ernst. *The Sacred Bridge.* London: D. Dobson, 1959.

Select Bibliography

Tools

Aland, Kurt, et al. *The Greek New Testament.* 3d ed. United Bible Societies, 1975.

Bauer, W., W. F. Arndt, F. W. Gingrich, and F. W. Danker. *A Greek-English Lexicon of the New Testament.* 2d ed. Chicago: University of Chicago Press, 1978.

Berkhof, Louis. *Principles of Biblical Interpretation.* Grand Rapids: Baker, 1950.

Brown, Colin, ed. *New International Dictionary of New Testament Theology.* 3 vols. Grand Rapids: Zondervan, 1975–78.

Danby, H., ed. *Mishna,* Moed Yoma. London: Oxford University Press, 1967.

Epstein, I., ed. *The Babylonian Talmud.* 18 vols. London: The Soncino Press, 1948–52.

Hanna, Robert. *A Grammatical Aid to the Greek New Testament.* Grand Rapids: Baker, 1983.

Hodges, Zane C., and Arthur L. Farstad. *The Greek New Testament According to the Majority Text.* Nashville and New York: Nelson, 1982.

Josephus, Flavius. Loeb Classical Library Series. London: Heinemann; New York: Putnam, 1966–76.

Kittel, Gerhard, and Gerhard Friedrich, eds. *Theological Dictionary of the New Testament.* Translated by G. W. Bromiley. 10 vols. Vols. 1–9. Grand Rapids: Eerdmans, 1964–76.

Merk, Augustinus. *Novum Testamentum.* 9th ed. Rome: Pontifical Biblical Institute, 1964.

Metzger, Bruce M. *A Textual Commentary on the Greek New Testament.* London and New York: United Bible Societies, 1975.

Nestle, E., and Kurt Aland. *Novum Testamentum Graece.* 26th ed. Stuttgart: Deutsche Bibelstiftung, 1981.

Phillips, J. B. *The New Testament in Modern English.* New York: Macmillan, 1958.

Philo. Loeb Classical Library Series. Vol. 1–6. Cambridge, Mass.: Harvard University Press; London: Heinemann, 1966–71.

Robertson, A. T. *A Grammar of the Greek New Testament in the Light of Historical Research.* Nashville: Broadman, 1934.

Strack, H. L., and P. Billerbeck. *Kommentar zum Neuen Testament aus Talmud und Midrasch.* 5 vols. München: Beck, 1922–28.

Thayer, Joseph H. *A Greek-English Lexicon of the New Testament.* New York, Cincinnati, and Chicago: American Book Company, 1889.

Zuntz, Gunther. *The Text of the Epistles.* London: Oxford University Press, 1953.

Index of Authors

Index of Scripture

Leviticus

Numbers

Deuteronomy

Joshua

Mark

Luke

Romans

I Corinthians

Extrabiblical References

Apocrypha

Judith

I Maccabees

II Maccabees